COST CONTAINMENT
IN HOSPITALS

Efraim Turban, Ph.D.
Editor

in collaboration with
John Tanner, M.D.

AN ASPEN PUBLICATION®
Aspen Systems Corporation
Germantown, Maryland
London, England
1980

Library of Congress Cataloging in Publication Data
Main entry under title:

Cost containment in hospitals.

Includes bibliographies and index.

1. Hospitals—Cost control. 2. Hospitals—
Administration. I. Turban, Efraim. [DNLM:
1. Cost control. 2. Economics, Hospital—
United States. WX157 C8366]
RA971.3.C583   362.1'1'0681   80-13272
ISBN: 0-89443-279-6

Library of Congress Catalog Card Number: 80-13272
ISBN: 0-89443-279-6

Printed in the United States of America

1 2 3 4 5

Dedicated to
the Memory of
My Father

CONTENTS

CONTRIBUTORS

M. Wayne Alexander

Mark L. Andersen

Bruce P. Arneill

Charles J. Austin

Darrell L. Bankes

A.C. Bennett

Ben I. Boldt, Jr.

Frank M. Braden

Montague Brown

D.M. Cain

Robert W. Carithers

Thomas F. Cawsey

Romeo Cercone

H. Mac Clymont

K.R. Curry

Walter Danco

J. Durham

Ron Durrwachter

James O. Elliott

Barbara Ellis

Terrill F. Ellis

D. Faltin

Charles J. Ferderber

Paula J. Ford

Leonard B. Fox

Bruce Frerer

J.M. Ganong

W.L. Ganong

R. Neal Gilbert

Ted Gillespie

Phyllis Giovannetti

Paul Gray

Lawrence W. Green

John R. Griffith

David H. Gustafson

James B. Henry

Stephen L. Holmes

Charles E. Housley

Nancy J. Howes

M. Hundert

Norman Jaspan

John Jeffreies

William Kast

John D. Kauffman

THOMAS F. KELLY
JOHN G. KING
MERIAN KIRCHNER
JAMIE KOWALSKI
CARL G. KRETSCHMAR
D.H. LEE
HOWARD L. LEWIS
KENNETH LILLE
CARL R. LINDENMEYER
J. S. LO
H. MACCLYMONT
JAN MARGOLIS
GWEN MARRAM
D. PATRICK MAZZOLLA
STEPHEN MELESKO
HOWARD MINTZ
JAMES A. MORGAN
M. MORIUCHI
S. MYERS
S. NAGY
B. NOYES
D. PATTERSON
JOSEPH O. PECENKA
GEORGE N. PETRIE
S. PETTIT
JAMES PIPER
H.D. PLUNKETT
M. PRIMAVESI
P.F. PRINGLE

AHMED RIFAI
RODNEY L. ROENFELDT
GLENWOOD L. ROWSE
S. RUSSELL
G.O. SAXTON
ARTHUR SCHMIDT
DAVID H. SCHROEDER
ROBERT E. SCOTT
CAROLYN S. SHANOFF
DONALD G. SHROPSHIRE
RAMESH K. SHUKLA
WILLIAM E. SMITH
HELLENA SMEJDA
SONYA M. SNYDER
B.W. STEVENSON
J.B. STOLTE
KELLY TESTOLIN
G. EDWARD TUCKER, JR.
EFRAIM TURBAN
STEPHEN VEAZIE
ROBERT A. VRACIU
WILLIAM C. WEDLEY
ALAN C. WHITTAKER
K.F. WIGZELL
ARTHUR V. WOLFE
KENT J. WOLFE
PAUL R. WOZNIAK
M. ZAKOS
LEON ZUCKER

Acknowledgments

I extend warm appreciation to the authors whose papers comprise this book. These individuals made this book possible. To each, I say thank you.

Most of the papers in this text were previously published in periodicals. I should like to thank all of them for giving me permission to reprint these articles.

Several persons contributed to the development of this collection. Of great value were the comments made by Mrs. Sylvia Urlich and Mr. Lenny Fox. The manuscript was reviewed by Mr. Leon Zucker, the chief inflation fighter at Jackson Memorial Hospital, who also composed the last paper in the book. I also acknowledge the encouragement given by Dr. Karl Magnusen, Associate Dean of the School of Business at Florida International University.

Last, but not least, thanks goes to Ms. Amy Conhagen, who not only helped to find the appropriate papers, but also assisted in the editing of the original parts of the text.

Introduction

Inflation has been formally declared the nation's number one economic problem. Unfortunately, it is the services most essential to human survival—food, housing, transportation, and health care—that are the major contributors to inflation. Many recent discussions and analyses of the causes of health care inflation have suggested ways to limit the spiraling costs of health care.[1,2] The major obstacle to containing these health care costs is the system's vast complexity, composed as it is of powerful political associations, sophisticated technologies, complex reimbursement mechanisms, a high degree of specialization, and a rampantly inelastic consumer demand. Furthermore, in the health care field the consumer does not order the service provided, and in most cases the payment for services is made by a third party (e.g., Blue Cross). In such a system, there is little incentive for either the health care consumer or provider to contain costs. As a result, health care costs have been rising about twice as fast as the general cost of living. Government attempts to change the situation by introducing national health insurance or by encouraging the development of health maintenance organizations (HMOs) have so far had little or no success.

There are some signs, however, that this situation may be changing. A sharp reduction in hospital expenses was achieved in Seattle in a plan that involved a special account set up by an insurance company for each patient. The family doctor managed the account, paying that patient's medical bills.[3]

The deliverers of health care, especially the hospitals, are talking about voluntary cost containment. ("Let's regulate ourselves before the government does it for us!") *Health Resources News* reports that members of the American Hospital Association were warned by government officials that "if the health sector doesn't put its own house in order, there may well be a groundswell of sentiment to have someone else do it for them."[4] Several states are currently controlling hospital rates, and North Dakota voters recently attempted (1979) to pass an initiative to make that state the first in the nation to regulate all health charges. Under a new state regulation the New Jersey rate-setting commission would establish rates for 383 illnesses. Patients will then be billed by illness rather than by their length of stay. This program will be fully implemented by 1983. All these efforts showed some success. Hospital costs in 1978 climbed at a slower rate, compared to the general rate of inflation, than in any previous year.

Developing cost containment incentives or programs that significantly change the demand pattern for health care services may take years. Other possible cost-controlling changes, such as turning the nature of the industry from labor-intensive to computer-automated, may take even longer. In the meantime, the health care administrator or consultant who is truly interested in containing costs needs to know what can be done today about today's costs. This book attempts an answer; it is dedicated to those individuals and their efforts.

THE NATURE OF COST CONTAINMENT

Note that the term *cost containment* is widely used rather than cost reduction. The reason is that, while cost reduction is possible in some areas of a health facility, it is generally unlikely that costs can be reduced for the entire facility. Even in a health care facility where cost reduction for the entire institution is possible, it is probably only a one-time opportunity. Once the "fat" has been trimmed, more reduction is virtually impossible. Some of the reasons mentioned for this impossibility are the increased use of sophisticated equipment, the rapid technological obsolescence in the industry, the high degree of specialization, and the consumer's tendency to buy the best possible service. In addition, the ever-climbing rate of general inflation contributes to the problem.

Because the best that can be expected is control of costs at a reasonable level, the term cost containment may be somewhat misleading. The basic idea of a cost containment attempt is to increase productivity, namely, to get the most out of any given resources. Increased productivity sometimes requires additional expenses (e.g., in case of expanding services). Therefore, a term such as cost effectiveness could be used to describe the subject of this book.

Cost effectiveness programs have been used in several industries for many years. Competition and the desire to maximize profits were the major incentives for attempts to make the best out of the available resources. There are numerous cost effectiveness and reduction texts that describe or prescribe cost reduction programs.[5,6] In some cases, cost reduction ideas can be transplanted from manufacturing and other services to health care settings. In other cases, special tools and approaches are required for the health care facility.

A STRATEGY FOR COST CONTAINMENT—OVERVIEW

Any administrator who seriously considers cost containment should view it as a large scale program that will require considerable resources in its initial stages. Furthermore, it should be viewed as a permanent effort to keep tight control over spiraling costs. Establishment of a cost containment committee, and creation of a suggestion plan may be necessary components of an overall plan, but alone they are not sufficient. For a cost containment program to be successful, it must be comprehensive and must involve as many employees as possible.

NOTES

1. M. Zubkoff et al., eds., *Hospital Cost Containment* (New York: Milbank Memorial Fund, 1978).
2. J. R. Griffith et al., eds., *Cost Control in Hospitals* (Ann Arbor, Mich.: Health Administration Press, 1976).
3. *Wall Street Journal,* June 14, 1979.
4. U.S. Department of Health, Education and Welfare, Health Resources Administration, Public Health Service, *Health Resources News,* October, 1978.
5. L. R. Higgins, *Cost Reduction from A to Z* (New York: McGraw-Hill, 1976).
6. A. Raymond, *Controlling Production and Inventory Costs* (Englewood Cliffs, N.J.: Prentice-Hall, 1978).

BIBLIOGRAPHY

"Health Costs: What Limit?" *Time,* 28 May 1979.
Maxmen, J. *The Post Physician Era.* New York: John Wiley, 1976.

ORGANIZATION FOR COST CONTAINMENT

Efforts to contain costs are being made in one form or another in many health care facilities. Most of these efforts, however, are sporadic; at best, they can be considered only one building block in the entire cost-limiting program. For a cost containment program to be successful, it must be well managed, and all the participants in the system must cooperate.

Chapter 1 of this book deals mostly with these issues. Bennett's article (Reading 1) opens this collection by concentrating on cost reduction efforts. (This article was written in the early 1970s when the inflation rate was low enough to make cost reduction feasible in many areas.) The framework set by this article can fit not only cost reduction but any cost containment or cost effectiveness program. It views an effective cost containment program as a logical system involving people and their attitudes, methods, and managerial support.

THE MANAGEMENT OF A COST CONTAINMENT PROGRAM

A cost containment program must be properly planned, implemented, and monitored. There are several techniques and methods for organizing and executing the cost containment program.

A general framework for organizing a cost containment program is proposed in the article by Fox and Mintz (Reading 2). The paper presents a four-stage strategy: (1) cost *awareness,* (2) cost *monitoring,* (3) cost *management,* and (4) cost *incentives.* Fox and Mintz advocate the use of an employee suggestion program. As the "most effective cost awareness strategy" of the various existing programs, the Buck-A-Day (BAD) program is recommended. The paper reports the experience of Mercy General Hospital in Miami, Florida, with the implementation of the program. The 12 steps of the BAD program are appended to the article.

Another interesting formal program is known as the Maritz Hospital plan.[1] Tatter also presents a methodology for planning and operating a suggestion system.[2] Effective suggestion programs can yield as much as $6 for each dollar spent.

THE COST CONTAINMENT COMMITTEE

In the core of any cost containment program is the cost containment committee. Lille and Danco (Reading 3) present the essential procedures for establishing a cost containment committee. More detailed information can be found in the American Hospital Association's publication, *Organizing a Cost Containment Committee in the Hospital.*[3]

THE PARTICIPANTS IN A COST CONTAINMENT PROGRAM

While the administration of the health care facility is responsible for the management of the program, the participants in the health care system really make it work. Specifically, the physicians, the employees, and the patients can and should make a contribution. It is extremely important that participants possess cost awareness or, as it is called in Stolte's article (Reading 4), cost consciousness. Although the article deals mainly with European health care systems, the differences from the U.S. system with respect to cost containment are not significant. Doctors play a major role in cost determination, and facility employees, nurses in particular, can eliminate waste. An interesting issue raised in Stolte's article is the social cost of illness to the patient, the patient's family, and to society.

Physician Participation

Physicians have a profound effect on facility costs. They are responsible for admitting patients, for ordering tests and treatment, for determining length of stay, for requesting costly equipment, and for making unique and inconvenient demands on personnel. Kirchner (Reading 5) presents an overview of what doctors are doing and can do to contain hospital costs. Some additional ideas can be found in an article by Liswood et al. in which they analyze an equipment request process and propose a special committee.[4] Alternatives to hospitalization, such as home care, day surgical centers, the use of paramedics, and the use of prepayment plans (HMOs), may be used to control costs,[5] but cost containment ideas that are not controlled by the facility administrator have not been included in this book.

Finally, the issue of cost awareness by physicians was studied by Dresnick et al.[6] They report that, in general, physicians are unaware of the economic impact of the care they provide.

The Nurse's Role in Cost Containment

In hospitals and in some other health care facilities nurses comprise a large portion (sometimes one-half) of the total employees. Furthermore, they are the ones that see and treat the patients for a longer time than anybody else. The Ganongs' article (Reading 6) presents an overview of nurses' effect on cost containment, mainly through control over the budget. The article discusses two types of organizational structure as they relate to the degree of control that nurses have over expenditures.

The Role of the Patient and the Public in Cost Containment

Proper public and patient education can contribute significantly to the containment of health care costs. An overview of this topic is given in Green's article (Reading 7). Some other interesting references for this topic are Turner's discussion of the physician's role in patient education and Roccella's survey.[7,8]

COST CONTAINMENT STRATEGIES

The last paper in this chapter, by Vraciu and Griffith (Reading 8), outlines possible strategies for cost containment at the health care facility. Four major strategies are discussed: (1) amenities reduction and purchase delays, (2) improved market efficiency, (3) input price reductions, and (4) improved production efficiency.

NOTES

1. W. Warren, "Hospitals Are Saving More Than Lives—The Texas Voluntary Effort," *Texas Hospitals* 34, No. 1 (June 1978): 18–21.

2. M.A. Tatter, "Turning Ideas into Gold," *Management Review* 64 (March 1975): 4–10.

3. American Hospital Association, *Organizing a Cost Containment Committee in the Hospital* (Chicago: AHA, 1976).

4. S. Liswood et al., "A Doctor's Role in Controlling Hospital Costs," *Canadian Hospital* 49 (February 1972): 62.

5. R.L. Johnson, "Cutting Costs by Controlling Physicians," *Hospital Progress* 58 (November 1977): 70.

6. S. J. Dresnick et al., "The Physician's Role in the Cost-Containment Problem," *Journal of the American Medical Association* 241 (13 April 1979): 1606–1609.

7. J. Turner, "Our Patient Education Literally Pays for Itself," *Medical Economics* 55 (6 March 1978): 150–162.

8. E.J. Roccella, "Potential for Reducing Health Care Costs by Public and Patient Education," *Public Health Reports* 91 (May-June 1976): 223.

BIBLIOGRAPHY

Aden, G. "Cost Containment is the Principal Purpose of Rate Review." *Hospitals, JAHA,* 16 July 1976.

Aland, K.M., and Walter, B.A. "Hospitals in Utah Reduce Costs, Improve Use of Facilities." *Hospitals, JAHA,* 16 March 1978.

Bays, K.D. "Cost Containment: Some Private Solutions to a Public Problem." *Medical Products Salesman,* August 1977.

Bennett, A.C. *An Employee Idea Program.* New York: Metromedia Publishing Co., 1969.

Bennington, J.L., et al. *Management and Cost Control Techniques for the Clinical Laboratory.* Baltimore: University Park Press, 1977.

Branson, R.M. "Informed, Involved Employees Aid Hospital's Cost Control Program." *Hospitals, JAHA,* 1 July 1978.

Buldak, R. "The Department Manager's Role in Cost Containment." *Hospitals, JAHA,* 1 November 1974.

Chassin, M.R. "The Cost Containment of Hospital Costs: A Strategic Assessment." Supplement to *Medical Care,* Chapter II (cost-sharing), October 1978.

Cleverly, W.D., ed. "Cost Containment Parts I and II." *Topics in Health Care Financing,* Spring 1977 and Summer 1977.

Control of Health Care Cost—An Annotated Bibliography. NTIS/PS-78/0317, 1978.

Controlling the Cost of Health Care. U.S. Department of Health, Education and Welfare, National Center for Health Services Research. DHEW Pub. No. (HRA) 77-3182, May 1977.

Corklin, M.S. "Hospital Cost: The Reason Is People." *Trustee,* April 1972.

Cost Containment Digest of Hospital Projects. Chicago: American Hospital Association, 1977.

Cost Containment: Selected Bibliography. Chicago: American Hospital Association, 1977 and 1978.

Dowling, W.L. "Prospective Rate Setting: Concept and Practice." *Topics in Health Care Financing,* Special Issue, Winter 1976.

Fenton, F.T., and Walters, R.W. "Organization, Policy Affect Hospital's Cost." *Hospital Financial Management,* February 1977.

Glass, A.L., and Warshaw, L.J. "Minimal Care Units: Mechanisms for Hospital Cost Containment." *Health Care Management Review,* Spring 1978.

Greenwald, D., and Henrikson, K. "Hospital Care Shows Biggest Spending Gains." *Modern Healthcare,* June 1976.

Griffith, J.R., et al., (eds). *Cost Control in Hospitals.* Ann Arbor: Health Administration Press, 1976.

Griffith, J.R., et al. "Practical Ways to Contain Hospital Costs." *Harvard Business Review,* November-December 1973, Reprinted in *Hospital Financial Management,* January 1975.

Guthrie, V.D. "How a Small Hospital Benefitted from Its Cost Containment Committee." *Hospital Financial Management,* December 1978.

Hughes, E.F.X., et al. *Hospital Cost Containment Programs: A Policy Analysis.* Cambridge, Mass.: Ballinger Publishing Co., 1978.

Karr, D.D. "Cost Containment—Synonym for Good Management." *Osteopathic Hospitals,* July-August 1978.

Koncel, J.A. "Ambulatory Surgical Center Lowers Costs, Not Services." *Hospitals, JAHA,* 10 October 1978.

Lachner, B.J. "Cost Accountability of the CEO and Board." *Hospital Program* 58 (1977): 60.

Lamont, G.X. "Creativity and Hospital Costs: It's All in the Approach." *Hospitals, JAHA,* 1 October 1978.

Lindner, J., Jr. "Point of View: Better Management, Not Just More Money: Physician Involvement." *Health Care Management Review,* Summer 1977.

Ludwig, P.E. *Dollars and Sense.* Battle Creek, Mich.: Kellogg Foundation, 1971.

Michela, W.A. "Physician Remuneration Has Impact on Hospital Costs." *Hospitals, JAHA,* 1 August 1977.

Perry, M.C. "Controlling Costs—The Patient's Role." *Internist,* August 1978.

"Physicians' Role in Cost Containment." Special report. *Review*-Federation of American Hospitals, April 1979.

Raphaelson, A.H., and Hall, C.P., Jr. "Politics and Economics of Hospital Cost Containment." *Journal of Health Policies, Politics, Policy and Law,* Spring 1978.

Robinette, T.K. "Effective Middle Management in the Era of Cost Controls." *Hospitals, JAHA,* 1 May 1977.

Schaffer, D.H. "Cost Containment: Everybody's Bandwagon." *Hospitals, JAHA,* 1 April 1978.

Schweitzer, S.O., ed. *Proceedings of the International Conference on Policies for the Containment of Health Care Costs and Expenditures.* Fogarty International Center, HEW, 1978.

Scroggins, R.E. "Hospitals' Costs: A Joint Trustee-Administrator-Physician Responsibility." *Trustee,* August 1972.

Seubel, Jr. "Hospitals Must Establish Cost Containment Programs." *Hospitals, JAHA,* 1 May 1976.

Simpson, W.G. "Eleven Steps to a More Efficient Hospital System." *Trustee,* February 1978.

Solomon, S. "How One Hospital Broke Its Inflation Fever." *Fortune,* 18 June 1979.

Stevens, C.M. "Hospital Costs: On Rationalizing the Physician-Hospital Relationship." *Inquiry,* September 1977.

Swearington, L.L. "Staff's All-Out Ongoing Efforts Help Hospital Fight Inflation." *Hospitals, JAHA,* 16 September 1978.

"Unhealthy Costs of Health Care." Special report. *Business Week,* 4 September 1978.

Warner, K.E. "Effects of Hospital Cost Containment on the Development and Use of Medical Technology." *Milbank Memorial Fund Quarterly,* Spring 1978.

Weltmann, A.J. "Maybe You Can't Afford a Short-stay Surgical Center." *Hospital Financial Management,* October 1976.

Whelan, Sister Mary James. "Team Effects Cost Control." *Hospitals, JAHA,* 1 November 1972.

Zubkoff, M., ed. *Health: A Victim or Cause of Inflation?* New York: Milbank Memorial Fund, 1976.

Zubkoff, M., et al. *Hospital Cost Containment.* New York: Milbank Memorial Fund, 1978.

1. Cost Reduction Is the Whole Idea for the Whole Staff

A.C. BENNETT

Reprinted with permission from *Hospital Topics*, March 1974, pp. 12-16.

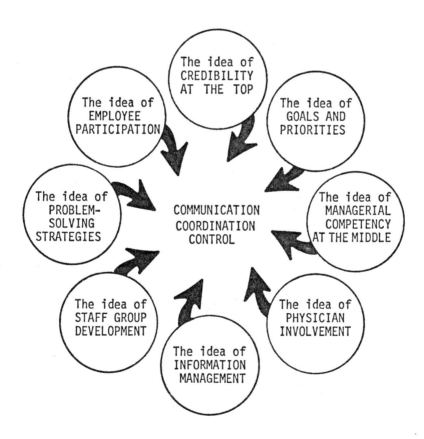

"New answers are needed," is the cry heard when the problem of cost reduction is the focus of discussion. What is frequently disregarded is that *new answers* are sometimes obtainable from *old ideas* whose time had already come, but their arrival has been ignored, and they still stand alone and unused.

"Every idea is an incitement," said Oliver Wendell Holmes, and "the only difference between the expression of an opinion and an incitement in the narrower sense is the speaker's enthusiasm for the result."

With much enthusiasm I place before you eight substantial ideas which you will recognize but perhaps have not accepted or implemented as a productive source for assisting you in your efforts to contain or reduce costs. They are vital ideas that won't keep. Something must be done about them. Certainly, something more than what some hospital administrations are doing about them right now.

The two terms or ideas of *cost reduction* and *cost containment* are frequently expressed as having an equivalence of meaning. The *cost reduction* idea, to me, applies to a single unit-system like a hospital; *cost containment* comes from a wider society which provides the money, and which has problems of resource-allocation.

One implies that there is something you can do locally to hold things in line; the other hopes that you can do something about things like inflation. In this day and age, we are actually faced with rising costs as much from inflation—in its many forms and levels of manifestation—as we are from local excesses or extras.

Cost reduction and cost containment aren't the same thing. True cost reduction is painful and difficult; cost containment usually means holding the line.

The simple fact is that true cost reduction is more than a purely economic problem. It involves people and their attitudes and behavior as much as it does the basic monetary unit of operation. It is a socio-economic problem which, if to be effected, requires administration's conceptions about the nature of cost reduction to be re-examined and viewed in its human context. It is this underlying thesis that runs through this entire article.

The eight ideas looking for administrative sponsorship and action bring clear evidence that we must re-examine our thinking about the nature of cost reduction. In so doing, managers can bring about changes in their own personal state of mind requisite to introducing new and more effective approaches to reducing hospital costs. Traditional remedies based on stubbornly-held-to-perspectives will continue to lead the search for improvements to the same conceptual dead end where many of us find ourselves today.

The need for renewal of a "human resource" view of the cost reduction problem leads to the first of my proposed eight ideas.

1. THE IDEA OF CREDIBILITY AT THE TOP

A successful cost reduction program is difficult to launch and even more difficult to sustain. This is so because the program is all too often one in which we play the old numbers game of dollars and cents alone, void of a concentration and emphasis on people and the contribution they can make to the cost reduction process of the hospital.

Saul Gellerman holds that "the way most people act at any given time depends more on the 'culture' in which they find themselves than on their personal characteristics." "Thus," Gellerman continues, "our behavior is determined to a large extent by what we learn to assume about other people's expectations."

If we accept Gellerman's postulate, we conclude that the "culture" of the organization—that is, the unwritten code that governs conduct of people within the organization—becomes, in effect, the upper limits of its achievements, whether it be in cost reduction or in any other management program.

People tend to live up to the expectations placed in them, but most people will do only that which they think is expected of them. The impetus for this expectation must come from the top. The chief executive officer in his desire to get an effective cost reduction effort underway needs to close the credibility gap between the theory he believes and the behavior he displays. What is required on his part is a leadership style that creates a climate or "culture" built on confidence, believability, efficiency, effectiveness and results.

And in the eyes of his people, the administrator's leadership style and behavior will be judged on the value of his ability and capacity to use the human resources available to him wisely, extensively and profitably.

If failures have been experienced in cost reduction programming, certainly they have not come from a lack of dedication, nor a lack of energies on the part of administrations. Rather, they have come, from the lack of striking a suitable balance between the economic and human resource aspects of the problem.

Surely, it is not enough, even if we try our very best, to make superficial controls work in terms of dollars only at the expense of failing to tap the energies of people at all organizational levels which can be sparked by the motivations and incentives set by those at the top.

In spite of the constructive promises of an increasing orientation of administration to people, we will continue to discern a damaging degree of disillusionment and disinterest on the part of people regarding cost reduction, unless administration initiates action on a second essential idea—

2. THE IDEA OF GOALS AND PRIORITIES

There is evidence that too many administrations have not as yet learned that more can be accomplished at less cost and with less damage to institutional spirit and development if periodic agendas of goals and priorities are established. Goals and priorities give purpose to administrative action taken regarding cost reduction.

- Without a clearly defined purpose, it is difficult to communicate to those outside the hospital what the organization is doing to meet the cost reduction obligation.
- Without a purpose, there is no single thought to communicate to those within the organization.
- Without a purpose, there is no benchmark for measuring progress in reducing costs.

The same query asked in a different way is: "What kind of future are you looking at?" In other words, are you making the mistake of being short-term defensive, reacting to a local holler, and just trying to save dollars? (just "saving dollars" is a very weak objective; it's never worked very well.) Or is there a purpose to your efforts for the future? The quality to be sought here is a realistic tie-in between short-term improvement and long-term purposes.

A *second* property of effective goals and priorities is that they should lead us to a "targeted" approach to reducing costs.

Here the underlying question for management at all levels to ask is: "What concentration of efforts will produce the best possible economic results and performance from the resources available to the organization?"

There is a quality of selectivity which needs to surface as a result of answering this question. It requires of the administrator and his management staff not only some serious thinking about what is possible and desirable, but a focusing on things to accomplish rather than on those things which should not be done.

Are we willing to be selective in the cost reduction process or do we find ourselves going for everyone—that is—everyone with the "10% approach" which is defective. Such across-the-board cuts are defective in that management isn't even trying to find out whether it's cutting the wrong costs—the very costs that are producing the greatest income or a meaningful service for the future.

It is quite possible that some units may need *more* dollars. How many times we have witnessed situations where an increase for that one last piece of equipment resulted in a department or work unit breaking through to a new level of productivity. The important point is if we are being selective in "targeting" our efforts, do we have an objective basis for whom we go after and whom we leave alone?

A *third* attribute of effective goals and priorities is that they need to be flexible, and at the same time, governable.

Continuing evaluation to determine the need for modifying goals and priorities is an important task in order to keep options open and to avoid rigidity in programs and policies.

As important is the task of monitoring cost reduction efforts. This suggests that the administrator should have some clear ideas what he wants to accomplish in the first place, and has some good information in a feedback system so he knows whether or not he's getting to where he wants to go.

Finally, the fashioning of cost reduction goals and priorities must evolve as a consequence of shared values, shared beliefs, shared attitudes determined through close consultation with key managers at all levels.

The administrator cannot achieve meaningful cost reduction alone, since it is a process which cannot exist independently of the actions of managers at all levels of organization. The administrator must ask himself every time: If I try this route or suggestion for cost reduction, who will I have to work with and through?

Since it is well within the control of managers at any level of the organization to influence the integrity and substance of cost reduction efforts, it is important that attention be given to—

3. THE IDEA OF MANAGERIAL COMPETENCY AT THE MIDDLE

This is perhaps the most central idea of the entire cost reduction process. When the continuity of competent management is not ensured in a hospital, the anticipated effort may be a serious deterioration in such vital areas as individual performance and productivity, and employee morale—essential factors for achieving more efficient health care services.

Far too many health care organizations still fail to understand the cause-and-effect relationships between their failure to act in this area and the cost problems which plague them.

In all too many cases, rising costs of operation give birth to the attitude that manager-development is a costly "luxury" which administration cannot afford on an ever-tighter budget and that it can be postponed "until things get better." Since poor managers invariably increase costs, this is almost the classic illustration of "false economy."

I emphasize one main point: an organizational atmosphere that permits and encourages its department heads and supervisors to experience the act of managing is what management development is all about. Classroom instruction and traditional training methods are no substitute for the real knowledge of how to manage that comes only from the experience of performing the "people problem" and decision-making responsibilities of a manager.

This needs to go far beyond the familiar principle of "delegation of responsibility"—Rightly so, the delegation concept is generally recognized by social scientists and professional managers as having serious vulnerability if not accompanied by:

- an attitude and approach on the part of the "boss" that permits and encourages subordinate managers to experience increasing responsibility and autonomy.
- suitable job design that allows supervisory personnel to devote sufficient time to the exercise of managerial responsibilities.
- finally, the presence of an adequate and equitable performance evaluation and reward system.

A recent United Hospital Fund report on management says:

> The manager should be knowledgeable about the *financial aspects* of operations, particularly budget development, in order effectively to plan and administer the expenditure of funds for current and future operations.

A knowledge of financial administration was seen by most administrators interviewed as one of the most significant requirements for an effective manager, yet as many as 40% of the department heads interviewed reported they had no involvement whatever in planning and preparing budgets for their departments. Instead the controller—or in some instances the administrator of the hospital—prepares and presents the budget to the managers as a "fait accompli." As many as 40% have not experienced the actual managerial task of budget preparation!

Commitment at the middle-manager level to cost reduction is fundamental to program success, and commitment on the part of middle-managers must be built on competency and their involvement in the decision-making process relating to the organization's cost reduction goals and priorities.

4. THE IDEA OF PHYSICIAN INVOLVEMENT

Cost reduction as an outcome of greater efficiency in the use of resources is a function of management. And "management" in this sense involves medical personnel as well as administrative personnel.

In dealing with the idea of Physician Involvement, again it is the administrator who is the principal change-agent within the hospital. And what is called for is the search for ways of improving the interactions and interrelationships between the administrative and professional staff.

Evidence continues to come in showing that the idea of involving the physician in participative management within the organization needs a great deal more work.

The Fund's management development study provides a good case in point. It revealed a persistent reluctance on the part of top administration to encourage the participation of physicians in management training situations based on the belief that they would not have an interest in doing so.

Interestingly enough, however, a good number of physicians indicated they share the sentiments of other middle-management personnel who feel they need help in meeting managerial requirements, and also feel that *more and better training* conducted within the hospital setting is needed to give this help.

Several directors of professional service departments confessed to be at a considerable loss in understanding, for example, the financial aspects of department management.

Since the professional department manager is very likely to be preoccupied with the professional and technical aspects of his work, his concept of evaluation might be expected to remain professional rather than managerial. On the other hand, the administrator's interests in the economic aspects of the situation might cause his concept to remain dollar-oriented. Under these circumstances, he too might lose sight of the broader managerial perspectives.

Neither of these positions is appropriate. Both orientations miss the point that *unless a collaborative, managerial evaluation of performance is undertaken,* the true level of departmental effectiveness and efficiency cannot be ascertained, and meaningful cost reduction cannot be effected.

Defensive budgeting and professional harassment are not the effective tools in developing this collaborative, managerial evaluation of performance of which I speak. Rather, the tools to be used are those which can generate the kind of information that will allow a professional unit director and the administrator to describe and evaluate the effectiveness and efficiency of the unit in a mutually-acceptable set of terms.

5. THE IDEA OF INFORMATION MANAGEMENT

Probably the simplest approach of all to cost reduction is to get some hard information about what is going on, whether it has to do with the evaluation of a professional service department or any other functional component of the hospital. Getting a good detailed picture of what's happening—(What's being done in the unit? How much is being done? Of what type? Arriving when? From what services? With what predictability and smoothness? etc.) cuts through a lot of private empire-protecting and self-survival.

Every manager has his own particular vision of the world around him and his own special information resources and every administration has its own outlook on the communication process. The task required is:

- with regard to the external world, to increase the flow of information that communicates to people within the organization the changing conditions and forces that originate beyond the walls of the hospital.
- with regard to the internal world, to develop, at three different levels, a communication network system that provides at the highest level sufficient information so that people in the organization agree on a common purpose. At a second level, provides to "need to know" managers information which indicates "how things are going" from which they learn whether or not some action should be taken. And at still another level provides some form of an early warning network or "sensing device" to ensure that critical and costly centers of activity are not ignored until they blossom into full-scale problems.

6. IDEA OF STAFF GROUP DEVELOPMENT

Personnel administration, management engineering, and computer systems constitute three main sources of assistance which can offer the technical capabilities needed to acquire sufficient information to generate effective change in the hospital's cost picture.

Interestingly enough, in those hospitals that have all three of these staff groups, under-development of their potential stems as much from a breakdown in communication, coordination and cooperation among the three staff groups as it does from the management of each independently.

Competent staff specialists can also assist hospital management in another important way—

7. THE IDEA OF PROBLEM-SOLVING STRATEGIES

If we are to find new answers to the kinds of corporate problems, which if solved could advance our cost reduction efforts, we will need to discover new ways of pursuing these problems in a more coordinated way than has been demonstrated to date.

If any successes in maintaining effective coordination do appear on the hospital scene, they are often the result of the initiative and ingenuity of *individual managers,* and not part of any organizational plan or strategy to overcome the obstructions inherent in traditional organizational theory and design such as the one-man one-boss principle and the divisionalization of functions.

However, even if we do accept these organizational forms and practices, it does not necessarily follow that our actions toward change for improvement; toward cost reduction need to be fragmented. Here is where the idea of *problem-solving strategies* offers some new answers to an old problem.

The idea calls for introducing the kinds of strategies that will cause our management functionaries to be concerned about goals—"cost reduction" goals—rather than functional purposes. The most devastating consequence of the competition, jealousies and infighting caused by the artificial departmental boundaries is its inconsistency with the common commitment. The rich diversity of experience and viewpoints could, instead, be our greatest resource in achieving meaningful cost reduction.

The kinds of strategies that are available to management relate to both individuals and groups. For example, statistics on turnover or absenteeism alone often falls short of experiencing needed action. But studies show that when the personnel staff specialist works on a one-to-one basis with a supervisor in whose area these happenings are proving to be out of line, significant improvements in the personnel cost picture can be facilitated.

Another strategy is the assignment of special problem-solving projects to individual managers or supervisors.

In the use of *groups,* setting up of task forces to deal with projects with cost reduction goals is a strategy to consider. The big difference here is that membership in these ad hoc groups are based on the professional skills each individual can bring to bear on the problem with little regard for formal organizational lines. It's a strategy that tends to result in having structure and status give way to accomplishment.

There are a number of strategies and mechanisms available to a management which is seeking to transform organizational members from being part of the "cost" problem into taking part in its solution.

8. FINALLY THERE IS THE IDEA OF EMPLOYEE PARTICIPATION

The investment required of management in fostering the concept of employee participation in cost reduction is the development of a problem-solving climate within the hospital and a set of specific participative methods that suitably fit within the environment it has created.

The outcome of this kind of investment is a planned system of upward communication that can help management improve its achievements in cost reduction through employee participation.

There are many promising single techniques that can be introduced within this framework. I devoted an entire writing to one such approach. *An Employee Idea Program,* a text published by Metromedia in 1969. It prescribes in detail, guidelines for implementing a structured program designed to encourage and assist employees to contribute to work improvement. Interestingly enough, the "Idea Program" concept has found increasing acceptance within the past two years. Other techniques available to hospital managements include:

- department or unit meetings specifically devoted to the subject of improvement
- direct communication between top management and non-management personnel. One that's been used successfully by industry is to invite selected employees to monthly president luncheons to discuss problems at work
- inservice training in the area of cost effectiveness for supervisory and non-supervisory employees
- brainstorming sessions centering on cost reduction problems—have been very successfully used by nursing personnel
- the establishment of special employee councils
- non-management task forces or possible membership on management task forces.

2. A Strategy for Cost Containment—The Use of a Suggestion Plan

LEONARD B. FOX III AND HOWARD MINTZ

Reprinted with permission of the authors.

INTRODUCTION

This paper presents an approach to cost containment. In the first sections it describes the purpose and scope of cost containment as an organizational outcome along with a methodology for developing an overall cost containment strategy. It emphasizes the need for developing such a strategy before deciding on and choosing any specific techniques for containing costs, and then focuses on a specific strategy component, cost awareness, and develops the rationale for choosing one particular approach.

The latter sections of this paper go into depth in describing a predesigned employee suggestion program which was chosen as the vehicle for developing cost awareness throughout the organization.

FORMULATION OF A COST CONTAINMENT STRATEGY

For discussion purposes it helps to take a system's model view of the cost containment strategy formulation process which is presented in Figure 1. The input variables are defined as those elements which get us in the cost containment business in the first place; a commitment to put forth some effort to achieve some desired results in containing costs. Consequently, the

Figure 1 System Model for Cost Containment Strategy Formulation

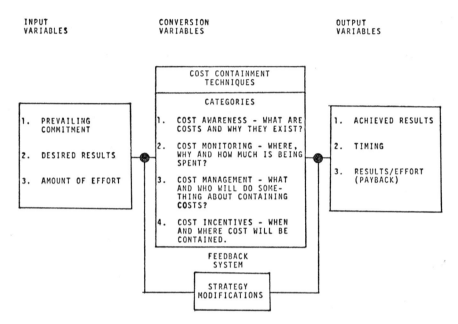

output variables parallel these input elements but with a focus on results. Will the commitment and effort put forth achieve the results in a timely manner and with a reasonable payback? Thus formulating a balance between inputs and outputs will define the choice of conversion variables— cost containment techniques—appropriate to the situation. Strategy formulation then becomes a balancing act, specifying the most appropriate technique(s) for a given level of commitment to achieve some result within a given time and within a given amount of effort.

For example, it may be a commitment by the Board of Directors to reduce the historical annual increase in operating cost from 14% per year to an average of less than 7% over the next three years. The only limitations are *that the quality of existing services does not decrease and that proposals for capital expenditures have a maximum of two years to payback.* Such a commitment to cost containment opens strategy formulation to a variety of alternative techniques. The level of results required cannot be handled by a simple memorandum. A conscious strategy encompassing a significant depth and breadth of activities will be necessary with each cost containment technique chosen integrated logically with the entire process. To achieve this level of sophistication it becomes necessary to specify organizational stages consistent with the cost containment strategy. These stages are:

1. *Cost Awareness*—Intensifying organizational awareness of what costs are, how they can be managed and the processes that are available to contain them. The focus is on all costs and by all individuals—from the person that sweeps the floor to the chairperson of the board.
2. *Cost Monitoring*—Providing a mechanism and the media for identifying, reporting and monitoring all costs. Analyzing the relationship between these costs and the costs of individual, functional as well as the overall organizational performance. The focus is on where, how much and why dollars are spent.
3. *Cost Management*—Establishing a responsibility and accountability system for communicating and controlling the attainment of plans, strategies, programs and objectives involving cost containment. The focus is on what can be done and will be done to contain costs, and by whom.
4. *Cost Incentives*—Maintaining incentives and compensation mechanisms that motivate continuing cost containment efforts and reward performance in proportion to cost containment contribution, individually and collectively. The focus is on when and where the effort is most appropriate.

Each one of these development stages individually can result in significant short-run cost containment results. But for continuing long-term results, the presence of all stages and their sequence of development is critical. Cost incentives can be very costly without a good cost monitoring mechanism or an effective cost management program. And what good is it to be aware of cost if the system for managing and controlling cost is not present?

COST AWARENESS TECHNIQUE RATIONALE

Viewing the overall hospital strategy for cost containment, one of the first steps was to seek a program that had high cost awareness impact. At the same time it had to be easily integrated with an existing but slothful employee suggestion program which management envisioned revitalizing in the near future. Another requirement was that it complement, and where possible further the development of an emerging program of problem oriented task forces. A major limitation was that the chosen program must not rely too heavily on incentive compensation techniques because such programs are difficult to manage (one of the reasons the existing employee suggestion program was so sluggish), and because the strategy specified that such techniques be implemented much later in the stages of program development.

Four basic alternatives were identified as having a potential to fit within the above described situation. A list of criteria was developed to compare these alternatives as to their cost awareness potential and aid in the decision of which to choose. This list appears in Table 1.

1. *A hospital wide training and education program dealing with cost containment.* The AHA's "Cost Containment Through Operations Management" falls into this category of program. It was pilot tested and found to have below average potential of achieving criteria objectives. It would require a long time to implement on a hospital wide basis. The focus was on classroom techniques and case studies which did not offer sufficient assurance that they would be implemented on the job. The biggest weakness was acceptability. A significant proportion of non-supervisory personnel found the material difficult to understand and to relate to day-to-day activities.

2. *A cost containment committee with a network of sub-committees or task forces charged with identifying cost containment opportunities, proposed action and follow-up implementation.* This approach was also pilot tested and found lacking in two critical areas. First, *not everybody was involved* which created acceptance problems. The committee activities were viewed as being "Gestapoish" and received a lot of criticism for *jumping to conclusions without adequate facts.* Secondly, the committee had difficulty in keeping focused to the problems at hand, resulting in either a lot of circular activity, or worse yet, defining problems in such broad terms that practical solutions could not be identified. This made this approach difficult to manage.

3. *Employee suggestion program with a lot of publicity and incentive rewards.* This particular approach had been going on for several years with some minor success. Participation was found to be mostly proportional to the amount of publicity being given to the program as well as the nature and amount of cash awards issued. Ideas came in spurts with over 90% being either gripes or suggesting improvements in employee benefits. It was very difficult to manage especially when a cash compensation had to be determined, and a significant amount of public relations effort was needed to keep a focus on cost savings ideas. Although this approach offered the highest cost awareness potential relative to the other approaches and the established criteria, it would require significant modifications to be the accepted alternative.

Table 1 Criteria for Cost Awareness Potential

Rating Scale Low High Potential Potential Potential 1 . . . 3 . . . 5 Cost Awareness Program Selection Criteria	Training and education oriented programs (e.g., AHA)	Cost containment committee approach	Standard employee suggestion program with intensified P.R.	Modified employee suggestion program Buck-a-Day
1. Involves all hospital personnel.	2	2	4	4
2. High focus on cost and potential $ savings.	3	4	3	5
3. Short implementation span (Less than six months)	2	3	4	5
4. Short payback span (Less than one year)	2	2	4	4
5. At least 5 to 1 payback in three years.	2	4	3	4
6. Minimal reliance on dollar incentives.	4	5	1	5
7. Easy to manage.	3	2	1	4
8. Effective in identifying current and potential problems.	4	3	3	3
9. High acceptability.	1	1	5	4
10. High visibility.	2	2	4	5
Total Points	25	28	32	43

4. *Modified employee suggestion plan: Buck-A-Day (BAD).* What was needed was a program that would be easy to manage and at the same time maintain a high focus on cost and potential dollar saving ideas without too much reliance on cash incentives. The Buck-A-Day program fit these requirements most adequately. The Buck-A-Day program is an employee suggestion program developed by Industrial Motivation, Inc. The program was implemented successfully in industry and most recently was transformed to the health care area. Dozens of hospitals in Pennsylvania and New York attempted the program which is designed as a four week self-administered process, consisting of 12 steps.

IMPLEMENTATION OF BAD

The most rewarding experience with the Buck-A-Day program was that it was fun. The designed levity and high visibility made cost awareness and even cost cutting a real and practical activity for a large number of employees. A significant by-product was an increase in morale that was very perceptible. In fact, during the three week period when BAD idea cards were collected, over 1,000 cards were processed which is three times more than the number of suggestions received in one year with the standard employee suggestion program. But to be fair, we must admit that everything was not "wine and roses." The management of the program was not as easy as anticipated and required extensive amount of follow-up to correct for this misconception. Further, the decision to not involve the medical staff resulted in some negative publicity that could have been avoided.

Overall, the program was a big success. Over $700,000 of cost saving ideas were identified. Some of them had been previously anticipated by management, but because those who would be affected made the suggestion, implementation was much smoother than what could be anticipated by management edict. In some cases it expedited pending decisions on projects that had been bouncing around in limbo for a long time.

Hindsight suggests that future application of this program include the following modifications:

1. Some of the propaganda material should be changed to be more palatable to a broader public.
2. Everyone in the hospital should be involved. This suggests that doctors, patients and even visitors should have the opportunity to participate. For these groups maybe an emphasis on quality or improving services would be more appropriate.
3. A substantial amount of front end work is needed, much more than

what is suggested by the program designers, to educate and train department managers on the importance and need for effective idea review at their level. This is suggested to speed up implementation as well as to avoid burdening the coordinator with a lot of follow-up work.

As a final note on the program's impact and acceptance by the organization, it must be emphasized that the primary intent was not to be the ultimate in cost containment techniques. Its main purpose was to fit within the overall strategy of cost containment as a vehicle to develop cost awareness throughout the organization. For it to be a key in cost containment as an organizational outcome it needs to be followed, and followed soon by the other conversion variables of the overall strategy; cost monitoring, cost management and cost incentives.

PROGRAM RESPONSE

To access the hospital's response to the program there are a number of dimensions that must be considered. The first clearly relates to quantity and quality of submitted ideas. Another dimension relates to other cost containment activities that were subsequently established; activities that would not have been otherwise undertaken. Finally, and perhaps the most intangible dimension, the modification of employee behavior due to a heightened awareness of cost containment.

The quantity of ideas submitted were overwhelming, with more than 500 different ideas submitted on well over 1000 idea cards. Quality varied greatly with many ideas having no associated savings and others with tremendous savings. Submitted ideas fell into a number of categories covering most aspects of hospital operations. All the ideas generated fell into one of the following general descriptions:

- New ideas
- Existing ideas never brought to resolution
- Existing ideas that upon closer examination were found to be feasible.
- Ideas already implemented that were not being followed and required reinforcement.

As a result of the program other cost containment activities were subsequently established. In the case of forms control a Forms Control Committee was established. Though the idea was not new in the hospital, the large number of submitted ideas relating to forms highlighted the need to improve control of this situation. This same concern related to supplies, hence a major revamping of the inventory control and purchasing system to improve control and achieve a reduction in supply costs. The concern with copier costs resulted in an evaluation by Planning & Management Services which isolated a potential forty percent reduction in current copier costs.

Employee behavior changes were not readily measured, and hence the assessment must be subjective at this point. There does seem to be a much greater awareness of costs on the part of the employees, which may or may not result in a reduction in operating costs. Costs are now being discussed in circles previously relatively immune to cost considerations and seem to be affecting decisions at all levels.

IDEAS' PROCESSING AND IMPLEMENTATION

Perhaps the most critical phase of any suggestion program involves the dispositioning and implementation of the submitted ideas. As designed, the idea cards submitted were to be evaluated by the employees' supervisors who were to recommend implementation and estimate the annual savings. Unfortunately, this occurred only in isolated cases and the Planning & Management Services Department found itself with a basket full of idea cards that needed to be reviewed and evaluated. Simultaneously within the hospital, there was great interest in what the ideas were and what savings were associated with them.

The first step in dealing with these ideas was their division into subject categories for which summary lists were generated. These lists were to be used by coordinators who would assist in assessing the merits and feasibility of the submitted ideas. Development of these lists was time consuming and involved eliminating duplicate ideas, clarifying and consolidating. The final lists consisted of the consolidation of the reviewed ideas along with the estimated annual savings to the hospital. In many instances the cost savings estimates were not submitted with the ideas, hence a brief outline on how to measure their impact was provided.

The next step in the implementation was the distribution of these lists to key administrative personnel along with the selection of department heads to serve as coordinators. Selected department heads were invited to serve as "GOOD" (Getting Our Opportunities Developed) guys. They were selected for their management expertise and were charged with the responsibility of reviewing a select number of the submitted "BAD" ideas and weighing their merits. At the initial "GOOD" guys meeting the coordinators were informed of their responsibilities and selected the category they wished to work on. In order to provide a fresh look at the ideas, department heads were encouraged to select categories other than those coming directly under their control. This also enabled better communications and understanding between departments. Along with the summary list of ideas for their category, the idea cards and evaluation sheets were provided. A sample of the evaluation sheet developed to assist the coordinators appears in Figure 2. Subsequent meetings were then periodically held to discuss progress of their review and interim findings. At the final meeting all coordinators were to have dispositioned their assigned ideas as follows:

- Immediate implementation
- Elimination
- Implementation pending further investigation
- Already implemented

One year after the BAD idea month, ideas with cost savings amounting to approximately $130,000 per year have been implemented. Implementation of most of these ideas occurred independently of the coordinator's activities. Of all the 505 ideas submitted approximately 70% of the ideas have been dispositioned by the coordinators within one year. Those ideas that have been dispositioned for implementation have cost savings of approximately $790,000 per year. The cost savings of the remaining 30% of the ideas do not seem to have as large cost savings associated with them.

COST BENEFIT ANALYSIS

To determine the cost-benefit of the BAD program all the associated program costs and savings were isolated. These costs are:

- The BAD program had a one time purchase price of $13,000.
- No additional manpower expenditures were required to run or evaluate the program.
- There were approximately 1,500 manhours of existing hospital personnel's time involved with the program. Since this was done with available staff and no overtime costs were incurred, there was no additional expense to the hospital.
- The direct program savings in the first year amounted to $130,000. These savings are recurring and will be realized in subsequent years (as measured by the base year) as long as they remain in effect and external factors do not change their impact.
- The potential net savings in the second year could amount to $790,000 with cost avoidance in this amount in subsequent years anticipated.

Figure 2 Sample Idea Evaluation Sheet

Bad Idea Evaluation Sheet

Category: _PERSONNEL_   Idea Number: _3_

Use Volunteers as Clerks in Telescom.

Implementation costs (enter estimated amount)

Initial: _0_

Recurring: _0_

Types of savings (enter estimated annual amount)

Manpower – Expense Reduction :	$25,584
Workload reduction :	0
Supplies expense reduction :	0
Equipment expense reduction :	0
Increased source of revenue :	0
Energy expense reduction :	0
Other :	0

Estimated annual net savings: _$25,584_

Comments: _Telescom operates 24 hours per day, seven days per week and requires bilingual staff. Volunteers could not insure this coverage._

Disposition (check one):

Immediate implementation: _____

Elimination: _X_

Implementation pending further investigation: _____

Already implemented: _____   O.R.

Reviewed by: _____

Side 1

Data

Type	Value	Source
Full time responsibility cannot be given to volunteers, currently they provide coverage during breaks.		Director of Nursing
Average hourly salary	$3/hour	Director of Volunteers
Average number of FTEs per year.	4.1 FTEs	Director of Personnel

Computation

Write Equations, Assumptions and Data Values Used

$$\text{Average number of FTEs per year} \times \frac{\text{Hours worked per year}}{} \times \frac{\text{Average hourly salary}}{} = \text{Annual* manpower expense}$$

$$4.1\ \text{FTEs} \times \frac{2080\ \text{hours}}{\text{FTE}} \times \frac{\$3.00}{\text{hour}} = \$25,584/\text{year*}$$

*Excluding fringe benefits.

Side 2

The Steps of Buck-A-Day-Program*

1. CHECK THE BOTTOM LINE—Take a cold, hard objective look at your balance sheet. Is your cost of operation higher than it should be? Is waste, rework and inefficient procedures devouring too many of those pressure profit dollars? If so,

2. TAKE A STAND—Inflationary price increases can't be passed along forever. There are big rewards for managers who can hold the line in an expanding economy. Those who enforce self-discipline continue to be successful. Those who don't, never get to cash their stock options.

3. SET A TARGET—How about save a Buck-A-Day. It is something everyone can relate to and the numbers add up. Say you have 1,000 people and each one reduces costs by $1 a day. The result is $250,000 a year in savings and lots of it goes right to the bottom line.

4. MAKE IT INTERESTING—Let's face it, cost reduction is usually rather dull. Jazz it up. Give it some pizazz. Create some excitement. If you want to inspire people to take action you have to first get their attention. Call the program BAD Month. Join the BAD Guys!

5. GET EVERYONE INVOLVED—An effective program must involve everybody. It's got to start off with some flare, move quickly and finish before everyone tires of the effort. Check Buck-A-Day's track record. Its helped hundreds of companies produce big savings, fast.

6. LOOSEN UP THE CONTROLS—People bring more than just their skills to their jobs. They also have a wealth of practical knowledge and experience that's too valuable to be wasted. Seek out their ideas. It could be the best BAD move you'll ever make.

7. DON'T BE BUREAUCRATIC—Lots of companies have programs that are supposed to encourage employee ideas. But many of them get so burdened down with procedures and restrictions that nobody takes them seriously. Relax the rules for one month. Open up the communication channels, and the results will surprise you.

8. THINK ABOUT YOUR JOB—Everyone is always ready to tell the other guy or management how to do their jobs. But real progress comes when a climate for self-improvement is created. Buck-A-Day asks people to look for economies in their own work area. After all, who knows the job better than the person doing it?

9. BE REALISTIC—Don't expect people to change well-established performance patterns and no one will come up with an idea to eliminate his own job. But Buck-A-Day will give everyone a new sense of cost awareness, and people will respond with cost saving ideas. Many of them will be tangible and significant.

10. ENCOURAGE NEW APPROACHES—Many of us fail to recognize the value of a new idea when it is first introduced. Once the employee is convinced that management really wants to improve performance the good ideas will come forth. And, by focusing on a seemingly modest goal, major cost reductions are given added significance.

11. GIVE RECOGNITION—You don't need big cash awards or expensive prizes to get your employees to participate. People will concentrate on the things they think are important to their leaders. In return they need and expect recognition. BAD Month gives everyone a chance to be a hero.

12. COMMUNICATE RESULTS—The big additional benefit of Buck-A-Day is the renewed spirit and improved morale that comes from people working together toward a common objective. Everyone wants the security that comes from being part of a profitable, successful organization. Your employees will help. Ask them.

---

*Developed by Industrial Motivation of New York, N.Y.

3. AHA Recommends Cost Containment Committees

KENNETH LILLE AND WALTER DANCO

Reprinted, with permission, from *Hospitals, Journal of the American Hospital Association,* vol. 50, no. 10, May 16, 1976, pp. 69-72.

Cost containment is not a new concept. Hospitals have for some time struggled to identify areas in which meaningful and useful cost reductions could be achieved. In these efforts, they have been largely successful. However, the extraordinary cost pressures that hospitals now face require a new approach to cost control. If hospitals' efforts are to have maximum success, they must be carefully coordinated so that no area is left uninvestigated and no area is unintentionally omitted from a cost containment program.

A useful method for achieving these goals, the AHA believes, is through a cost containment committee. In November 1975, the Board of Trustees of the American Hospital Association passed a resolution urging all hospitals to establish such committees. Further, it instructed AHA staff to develop recommendations for the planning, implementation, and operation of these committees so that hospitals could move rapidly to their establishment. The following article is based on the first draft of the guidelines that have been prepared by staff. For the completed document, see AHA, *Organizing a Cost Containment Committee in the Hospital,* Chicago: 1976.

SETTING GOALS

The single purpose of the cost containment committee is to assist management in containing costs. Its tasks may range from investigating through advising to participating in the implementation of cost containment measures.

Its tasks reflect its goals, which depend on the administration and the needs of the hospital.

Setting goals for the cost containment committee is a vital step in ensuring an effective work group. Administration, board members, medical staff, department managers, and other leaders within the institution should be identified and included in this goal-setting process.

Committee goals should be clearly stated, attainable, and measurable. They must fit into the larger organization goals, must complement them, and must become shaped by the needs of line and staff goals, policies, and procedures. The goals also must be realistic and attainable. Goals perceived as being unrealistically high or low will not be considered seriously. The goals must be high enough to challenge, yet attainable, if there is to be concerted effort and support from all involved.

Finally, the goal-setting process must include some tool for measuring the extent of goal accomplishment. Specific goals developed in this manner will focus on high priority issues and those with the greatest return for the time, manpower, and money invested in them. Decisions and review points need to be made by management throughout the goal-setting process.

COMMITTEE STRUCTURE

The form for the committee should suit the function set forth in the committee goals. The structure of an investigative committee will differ from that of an advising committee. Also, the structure of the committee will be effected by the management style of the administrator.

Considerations for the formal shape of the cost containment committee should include group size, reporting relationships, membership skills, and committee goals. How many persons are needed to conduct the work of the committee? Is there a chairperson? Who reports to the chairperson? Are there subcommittees? Is the administrator a member of the committee? What knowledge and skills should be present in the committee? What departments, service areas, and work shifts should be represented? What tasks do the overall goals require?

An organization chart showing how the cost containment committee fits into the existing structure should be designed. The chart should show relationships to other hospital committees, reporting lines, rank within the committee, and the number of members anticipated.

AUTHORITY AND MEMBERSHIP

Before the committee members begin to function in their new capacity, ground rules may be extensions or modifications of existing procedures, bylaws, rules, and policies or additions to them to cover the unique activities of the committee.

The following checklist may be useful in establishing the ground rules for the committee:

- Procedures for committee work established.
- Mechanics of reporting established.
- Limits of authority and responsibility stated.
- Confidential information identified, and procedures for handling it stated.
- Committee meeting schedule prepared.
- Linkage between cost containment committee and other committees established.
- Linkage between committee and administration established.
- Linkage between committee and board of trustees established.
- Access to financial data determined.
- Access to departmental data determined.
- Policies on investigative reports established.
- Policies and procedures for the creation, expansion, or disbandment of the committee established.
- Policies and procedures on reports and other communications from the committee established.

The most likely candidates for committee members include both formal and informal leaders in hospital, such as department heads, supervisors, and technical experts. Criteria for selecting committee members include knowledge of the hospital and its personnel, knowledge of financial or management systems, leadership abilities, ability to solve problems, ability to communicate clearly, and ability to work in a group.

The committee should be composed so that there is homogeneity with regard to tasks and heterogeneity of working patterns and experiences. This opens the group to a variety of behaviors that in turn opens the members to options, choices, and alternatives. The committee membership should be balanced and, at the same time, weighted toward the positive. Healthy skepticism needs to be balanced so that positive actions result from the committee's work.

Various mechanisms may be used to select members. A search group may recommend candidates for membership. Members of the staff may volunteer. Whatever the mechanism for generating candidates, however, the final selection decision is the responsibility of the administrator.

COMMITTEE COMMUNICATIONS

The types of communications to, within, and from the cost containment committee must be identified, and an adequate structure to support communications may be built. The checklist in the table that follows may be helpful in identifying the types of ongoing communications needed and the support available to committee members. Each hospital should develop its own originator/recipient/assistance relationships. The information on this checklist will be useful during the indoctrination and orientation of new committee members.

COMMITTEE WORK

To assist a committee in identifying specific tasks, a grid of the type shown in Figure 1 may be useful. A worksheet grid of this kind can be useful in identifying not only the ongoing tasks of the cost containment committee, but also the tasks for organizing this committee. Additional tasks and additional committee members will likely be included in the grid by individual hospitals.

A primary committee task is to become conscious of its hospital's costs and of how these costs compare with its past performance and with those of other hospitals of similar size with similar services in order to evaluate the reasonableness and effectiveness for these costs.

The committee must enter the work of cost containment with a questioning attitude and with assurances that its work will contribute to the managerial decisions that will help the hospital meet its goals.

Communications checklist*			
Communication device	*Originator*	*Recipient*	*Assistance*
Memos			
Reports/recommendations			
Status/progress reports			
Meeting minutes			
Charts and tables			
Computerized data			
Telephone calls			
Financial/operations reports			
Policy/procedure changes			

*This table only suggests a checklist model. The individual hospital will need to adapt it to its specific needs and capabilities.

EDUCATION AND ORIENTATION

A key factor in organizing an effective committee is preparing its members for committee work and maintaining support through continuing technical education. An orientation for committee members includes an awareness and understanding of costs; of the objectives, structure, and operating procedures for the committee; and of the committee's mission. Orientation instructors should be selected with great care and should include the administrator and any board members who will work closely with the committee and will ultimately be in the position of evaluating the committee's work.

Not all committee members need to begin as experts in analyzing operating statements, systems reports, inventory procedures, and a host of related technical items, but the committee should begin with some member expertise in these areas to counsel, educate, and assist other members.

COST CONTAINMENT STUDIES

The process for conducting a cost containment study involves the following steps:

1. Clearly define the topic of study.
2. Define terms. If a study is repeated for historical purposes, it is essential that data collected tomorrow carry the same meaning as data collected today and yesterday.
3. Collect relevant data. Paying attention to detail in searching activities ensures collecting and recording the proper information.
4. Organize data for meaningful analysis. Study reports need to be concise, accurate, and direct. Often graphs, tables, and charts help to organize and communicate cost containment data in a useful and meaningful fashion. An example of such a report is shown in Figure 2.
5. Analyze findings and summarize.

The study illustrated in Figure 2 is a preliminary study, because it attempts to illustrate potential areas for more detailed study. By itself, information that average occupancy is low or that the average cost per inpatient day is high is interesting but hardly sufficient for cost containment recommendations. A more detailed study design would be concerned with:

- A particular controllable cost.
- Data related to factors that affect the cost.
- Baseline or historical data that serve as a basis for comparison.

- Data-gathering methods that do not interfere with day-to-day operations.
- Methods that use existing sources of data to minimize costs, time, and manpower.
- Techniques for organizing and presenting the data.
- Manpower knowledgeable in the topic area and skilled in gathering the necessary data.

Figure 1 Cost Containment Task Assignment*

	Hospitals in region	National	Our hospital
Average occupancy			
Average length of stay			
Average cost per inpatient day			
Average hourly rate (salary)			
Average annual salary			
Average ratio of personnel to patient load			

- Time required to conduct and complete the study.
- Resources available, such as periodicals, books, and previous studies on this study topic.
- Support services available for technical review and analysis of the data.

Figure 2 Preliminary Comparative Cost Containment Study*

Tasks	Committee members					
	Administration	Medical staff	Public Relations	Nursing	Housekeeping	Maintenance
Orienting new committee members						
Containment project						
Obtaining and summarizing project data						
Suggesting alternative courses of action						
Assisting staff in implementing change						
Monitoring the success of cost containment projects						
Assisting staff to recognize the need for cost containment						
Demonstrating the achievements of the cost containment efforts						
Providing management with requested support in communication with external organization						

*Obviously, the listed tasks and committee members are only suggestions.
A more detailed grid will need to be developed by individual cost containment committees.

Figure 3 Cost Containment Worksheet

Department/service:
Central services

Persons most directly affected:
Central services manager, nursing service supervisor, and laboratory manager.

Persons who can contribute:
Medical staff—O.R. service, utilization review committee, accounting/purchasing manager, and public relations supervisor

Purpose/scope of cost containment study:
To evaluate costs and volume of work in preparing surgical packs.

Procedure:
1. Contact persons most directly affected for a meeting with the administrator. Discuss purpose/scope of the study. Focus on variable costs, enlisting support.
2. Meet with persons who can contribute information to the project. Discuss scope/purpose of cost containment study, again enlisting support.
3. Meet with cost containment committee to assign task force and department liaison for study. Discuss agreements/understandings with others.

Often the work of the cost containment committee will involve studies of cost behavior within a department or service. At the start of these studies, the manager of the department or service, if not already a member of the committee, should meet with the administrator and the committee to discuss the cost study, to plan the study strategy, and to be advised if not involved in the conduct of the study.

Prior to a study, a listing of the persons directly affected by it and of those who can contribute to its successful completion should be developed. The worksheet in Figure 3 shows one approach to a cost containment study within a department or service. A worksheet of this kind is a useful tool to prepare for an investigation of cost behavior in which staff may feel possessive or sensitive about cost and operations data.

EXTERNAL RELATIONSHIPS

Because the cost containment committee assists the administrator, he may decide to use the work of the committee to demonstrate to community groups, intermediaries, and government agencies that conscientious work on cost containment is being done within the hospital. Judicious use of information from the cost containment committee is important. At no time should the committee or its members directly contact outside groups. However, the administrator may choose to have members of the committee present to discuss committee work with the board of trustees, with the public relations representative, or with outside groups. Hospital policies on communications and on the use of sensitive or privileged information should be reviewed and modified if necessary to cover this aspect of the cost containment committee's work.

4. Cost Consciousness as a Condition of Cost Containment in Hospital

J.B. STOLTE

Reprinted with permission from *Hospital and Health Services Review*, February 1979, pp. 52-54.

An unexpected phenomenon may be frightening and lead to panicky, irrational behaviour. This seems to apply to the rising cost of health care. In virtually all developed countries it seems to have taken almost everyone by surprise. Reactions are manifold. Scapegoats are looked for. The hunt for available villains is on. Accusations of egoistic abuse of opportunities, of negligence and even of culpable stupidity fly about. One of the more polite reactions is the suggestion that at least part of the explanation of the rising cost of health care is to be found in a loss of perspective. Some or all parties involved do not fully realise any more that in this field, as everywhere else, things and services have to be paid for one way or another, at least in many cases. Because of this loss of perspective, it is assumed, health care services are claimed for and rendered indiscriminately. Comprehensive health care insurance and national health care services allegedly bring this loss of perspective about. Cost consciousness is lost. As a consequence pleas are made to regenerate cost consciousness as a means of cost containment. As is often the case, however, with catchphrases of this kind it is a rather imprecise expression of a complex phenomenon. Cost consciousness is mentioned mostly when in fact the lack of it is meant. Several elements seem to be involved:

1. information and understanding the information, leading to awareness

2. readiness to react upon the information
3. ability to react.

As lack of cost consciousness is considered to lead to rising costs through indiscriminate use, cost consciousness is expected to lead to cost containment, mostly in the sense that rise of costs is diminished. In reality, of course, cost consciousness may even lead to higher costs, as the relations between cost and output are realised.

Cost containment is also an ambiguous term. What is meant by it seems to be either putting a ceiling to costs or preventing wastage. In the last case there is not much difference from efficiency.

WHO CARES?

From what is put forward, it seems that citizens, health care workers and politicians are all lacking cost consciousness. The citizens ask for too many services of too costly a kind, and the politicians succumb to the pressure for more and better services all the time. The insurance companies and sick funds lack the knowledge and insight to put their bargaining power at work to the best advantage. Doctors do not have to take into consideration the pocketbook of their patients in their prescriptions any more. Because of that they give rein to their tendency to maximise and to innovate. Hospital management too may be insufficiently cost conscious in furthering prestigious investments. This is the more easy to do when tariffs are set in such a way that they cover all costs in a not-for-profit setting.

In all these instances the decision maker has not to face the financial consequences of his decisions directly himself. With citizens this is considered to induce almost unlimited demand for health care services by many writers, economists in particular. This is very doubtful, however, as costs are not to be equated with payments or financial costs. Health care services are not sought after for their own sake. They are often accompanied by unpleasantness. Opportunity costs of the time involved in getting and giving health care have always to be faced. Therefore demand for health care services is inherently limited. It is the effectiveness of this constraint that makes health care insurable. An unlimited risk cannot be insured.

Many people seem to find that there is at least some and perhaps even rather much unjustified demand for health care services in general, but also for hospital services. This is partly due to faulty behaviour of citizens, partly to questionable decision making by their doctors. Both the behaviour of citizens as would-be patients and of doctors in this respect may be characterised by lack of cost consciousness.

DOCTORS' ATTITUDES

Hospital managers do not have many instruments at their disposal to promote cost consciousness in citizens or patients. Perhaps their position is somewhat stronger with doctors, hospital doctors in particular. Few will dispute that doctors are quite cost conscious in respect of the remunerative consequences of their dealing with patients. On the whole, however, they do not really often go too far in this respect. The fact is that decency, social pressure and the opportunity costs of leisure time do countervail undesirable tendencies to a large degree. What seems the case when a plea is made for inducing more consciousness of cost in doctors is that they should be made aware of the fact that their medical decisions have cost consequences far beyond their personal gain. Many if not most of these decisions are virtually autonomous ones, and rightly so.

It is the individual patient whom the doctor regards as his real principal. To him his loyalty belongs in the first place. It is clear, however, that with their decisions in respect of diagnosis and treatment doctors very often allocate resources over which they have no property rights and the use of labour of people who are not in their employment. They have not to bear the financial consequences themselves. As this removes a constraint it is considered to raise costs. The issue is somewhat more complicated, however, than may appear at first glance.

The essence of medical decision making is involved. Formerly the doctor saw himself as a fiduciary with at least some responsibility for the patient's pocketbook as well as for his health. In quite a few cases this put him up against a painful dilemma. It was just this that brought about comprehensive health insurance and national health care services. They took away an alien element from medical decision making. As a consequence, the doctor nowadays very often does not know and is not aware of the cost involved in his medical decisions. His lack of consciousness in this respect can be construed as having taken away an inducement to cost containment. This does not mean that the alien element should be reintroduced in medical decision making, however. The consequences thereof may be seen in those cases in western Europe where doctors still have their own expensive apparatus like x-ray machines and their own personnel or where they exploit a hospital. Then the medical decision making may be influenced to an important degree by factors like productivity and profit.

INCENTIVES?

It has been suggested that the system of budget in one of its various forms may be the answer, particularly when the use of money eventually saved is put at the discretion of the doctor or of the entire personnel involved. When the savings are used to increase the income of the workers, the quality of their work is at stake. This seems to have been the reason to discard the method after a trial of some 2-3 years in the USSR around 1970. When the savings are to be invested in the hospital the objections are less important, but the setting of priorities in respect of the investments may become a source of difficulties. The white elephant syndrome—unbearable running costs through unwise investment—is all too well known.

In Holland the separation of the secondary cost consequences from medical decision making in the hospital is almost complete now. The last step was made when the sick funds agreed to be billed directly by the hospital for out-patient services, separated from the doctor's fee. The influence of the way the doctor is paid upon medical decision making is a separate problem. Some people advocate the salaried position of the hospital doctor, others are of the opinion that he should remain an entrepreneur. The consequences of either system are very difficult to assess and compare. The opportunity costs of leisure time are of importance here.

There is always the problem of assuring quality (of medical services) when resources shrink. It has induced many people in many countries to look for possibilities of balancing quality and constraints. Some of the more publicised are the medical audit and PSRO (Professional Standards Review Organisation). These reflect the American scene and culture and the way the American hospitals work. They are not really transplantable to the European scene. PSRO seems to become a failure and it is, of course, of significance that it was designed to somehow replace medical audit. Methods like these, instead of leading to cost containment, have induced with some and possibly quite a few doctors a kind of defensive medicine, characterised by superfluous diagnostic and even therapeutic procedures without real use and perhaps even doing harm to the patient. One may observe similar behaviour with trainees in response to too demanding chiefs of departments.

CHOICE OF TREATMENT

As quite often several forms of treatment are available for treating a specific illness it has been advocated to try to make doctors choose the cheapest one by putting them up to a strict budget under their own control. The philosophy behind it seems to be that in these circumstances doctors will take the best solution for the money available. In some cases this has worked. One has to be careful, however, not to attribute the choice to the financial constraints too easily. It may be that the alleviation of social costs to the patient or the pressure to help as many patients as possible has been the real inducement. There is also the problem of the risk to the patient involved in changing routine acquired during training and developed over years of practice. Quite often it is very difficult, again, to judge which method is best or equivalent. Standardisation of an activity like medicine, half science and half art, is not possible as yet and attempts in that direction may prove dangerous. Then also there is the pressure from the patient and his family for newfangled diagnostic procedures and therapeutics, fanned by the mass media, and sometimes even bolstered up by litigation. It certainly causes wastage from time to time, but it is not easy to combat.

Perhaps even more important, the hospital doctor is not really in touch with the patient in his own environment. He therefore cannot take the social consequences (costs) to the patient and his family into consideration effectively. This is then more of a difficulty in countries where the general practitioner has faded out of the scene and therefore cannot perform the role of agent in respect of their interest.

WASTE

As I see it, the main thing with cost consciousness and cost containment is looking for wastage and weeding it out as it endangers value for money. Most people are reasonable enough to reject wastefulness as wrong when they recognise it. It must, however, be pointed out to them the right way. With doctors and nurses this means that the facts have to be presented to them in their own "language", and taking into consideration their system of values. Otherwise they will get confused and irritated. Facts of life like opportunity costs and social costs must be explained to them clearly and consistently. It must be shown to them what they and their patients have to forgo when certain of their demands would be satisfied. Doctors—specialists in particular—should apprehend that aside from financial consequences their decisions bring with them many social costs to the patient and his family. It is a pity that little attention is paid to this side of medicine in the curriculum. Much useful and paying research could and should be done—in spite of inherent difficulties—to compare methods of treatment, taking into consideration outcome and total costs (financial consequences and social costs). Interestingly enough quite often wasteful behaviour in medical matters is just bad medicine. Unnecessary medical intervention, be it diagnostic or therapeutic, is not only waste but in most cases it is detrimental to health. Every day spent in hospital that could just as well have been spent at home is wrong. The hospital is a dangerous place to be in both from the physical as from the psychosocial point of view. Many kinds of costly screening are deplorable because they lead to thrusting the sick role upon people who will not benefit from it and will certainly not become happier by it. There are many more examples.

Providing doctors (and patients) with concrete information about the financial consequences of medical treatment is not of much avail. It is thought to reinstitute awareness of costs and thereby to induce more reasonable behaviour. In countries like France and Belgium, however, where patients have to pay the doctor directly, to be refunded (in part) afterwards by the insurance company, the behaviour of doctors and patients does not appear to differ very much from that in countries where no payment of patient to doctor is involved at the moment of use or slightly later. Sometimes doctors are provided with information concerning the financial consequences of their decisions in such a way that they may compare their own performance with that of others in the same field. It may induce more cost-consciousness and lead to cost containment, but it also may make the more thrifty spend more, perhaps providing better service. Either way the onus of proof may be difficult to meet.

INVESTMENT

Cost consciousness and cost containment are not only of importance with running costs. With investments they are perhaps even more important as these determine capacity and thereby fixed costs in the hospital to a very large extent. Fixed costs are 80 per cent of all hospital costs at least. Doctors and nurses tend to maximise in respect of investments. This tendency is very much related to their loyalty to the patient. Anything that may benefit the patient is asked for without much consideration of costs. This maximising has to be curbed one way or another, however, as it puts the continuity of operation of the institute at stake. On the other hand one has to be careful not to go too far with curbing as one has to keep the conditional loyalty of doctors and nurses to the institute intact too. A balance has to be struck, which will never be easy. It can be pointed out, however, that doctors and nurses on the one hand and hospitals on the other are mutually dependent and therefore it is in the interest of the workers too that continuity of operation of the institute is assured. Of course, the board and the managers should set an example, refraining from investments that have mainly a status seeking character.

Doctors and nurses should be asked to substantiate their proposals for investments by providing detailed information about expected performance and about costs in terms of personnel, maintenance, extra space to be provided, etc. The accounting department and the purchase department will give them every help to gather the information needed, of course. The exercise proves itself salutary time and again and has put a timely end to many an ill considered demand.

I do not regard letting the medical and/or nursing staff divide amongst themselves the money available for investments of a medical or nursing nature a good solution. It may favour the vociferous members and vested interests.

Of course there is abuse in health care and hospitals as in every other sphere of human activity and social life, as there is also indifference and negligence. The main instruments to combat them are adequate socialising of the people involved into their roles by education and training and social pressure. The main source of effective social pressure upon doctors is the medical staff itself. One should not expect too much of medical audit and similar methods in this respect, however. They may even be used as a smokescreen.There is no reason to be pessimistic although there are not many means at the disposal of the manager to intervene directly. One has to take into consideration that the modern hospital is a very young institution and that as an organisation it is still steadily learning how to cope with its mission and how to behave rationally. This is where the task of hospital management lies. It asks for much specific knowledge and skills, for perseverance and patience and above all for courage.

CONCLUSIONS

1. In the concepts of cost consciousness and cost containment all costs have to be taken into consideration, not just the financial consequences of decisions. The social costs are at least as important.
2. One should beware of reintroducing the alien element of secondary financial consequences to be weighed in medical decision-making as such. It goes against the real interests of the patient.
3. The hospital manager should set an example himself by showing awareness of cost consequences with every pertinent decision. He must look for instruments to enhance cost consciousness with doctors and nurses, pointing out that through their autonomous decisions a substantial part of the scarce means at the disposal of the hospital are allocated. He must show them that continuity of operation of the organisation is at stake and that they have a tremendous vested interest in this.
4. Some of the instruments are (a) showing that unnecessary diagnostic and therapeutic procedures are not only wasteful but quite often just bad medicine; (b) giving information about costs in such a way that the relation with good patient care is made clear; (c) pointing out the

importance of the social costs to the patient and his family; (d) putting the onus of justification of proposals for investment upon the proposers.

5. The fact that the modern hospital is a very young and rather special organisation that is steadily learning should be appreciated. Rough treatment is counterproductive here. This should dominate the idea of cost consciousness being a condition of cost containment in this environment.

5. Can Doctors Truly Do Much about Hospital Costs?

MERIAN KIRCHNER

Who's to blame for the hospital cost crisis?

As a large segment of the public sees it, *you* are. In a recent Roper poll, 65 per cent of the respondents cited doctors' actions as the cause of hospital cost inflation. Since it's doctors who admit the patients and order the services, they're obviously the key to the whole problem—or so goes the conventional wisdom.

What's more, it's argued, hospitals are forced into extravagant spending—on the latest in medical technology and on frills such as parking lots and plush offices for the medical staff—by the demands of their attending physicians. "Hospitals don't have patients," the saying goes. "Hospitals have doctors, and *doctors* have patients."

Well, there's no getting around it—you do admit patients and order services, and you do exert a powerful influence on your hospital's spending. You don't, of course, have as much power as your critics suppose. Often you're under pressure from patients who may bad-mouth you for running up costs when they talk to pollsters but want you to go all out when they're sick themselves. What's more, patients have health insurance that may cover all the costs you incur on their behalf if they're hospitalized but leave them to foot the bill for diagnostic tests or minor surgery done on an outpatient basis.

Nevertheless, from now on you'll be pushed harder than ever to hospitalize your patients less, monitor the cost of their hospital care more closely, and help your hospital save money instead of dreaming up ways in which to spend it.

There's really nothing very new about many of the money-saving practices you're being urged to adopt, from preadmission testing to early discharge. What *is* new is the apparent determination of a lot of doctors to start acting upon them and spreading the word to colleagues.

Over the past year, at least half a dozen state medical societies have formed cost containment committees, and so have two specialty societies—the American Urological Association and the American Academy of Orthopaedic Surgeons. A small bandwagon had begun to roll even before the Voluntary Cost Containment Program was launched in 1977 by the American Hospital Association, the Federation of American Hospitals, and the American Medical Association.

The Voluntary Effort, as it's called for short, is a response to Congressman Dan Rostenkowski's "challenge" to the health-care industry to contain hospital costs on its own if it wants to avoid mandatory Federal controls. The program has enlisted the participation of all 50 state medical societies, along with hospital associations, hospital suppliers, insurance carriers, and representatives of business, labor, and consumer groups. Statewide screening committees aim to reduce the rate of increase in hospital spending to no more than two percentage points this year and next. The Voluntary Effort also is seeking the cooperation of every hospital medical staff in the U.S.

Until quite recently, it's fair to say, most doctors—like most hospital trustees, hospital administrators, and, for that matter, patients—were not particularly cost conscious. There were few incentives to save money, and many incentives toward free spending.

So why do the leaders of the current cost containment drive believe things will be different now? "I think the climate has changed completely," says family physician F.W. Van Duyne, who heads the Michigan State Medical Society's cost containment committee. "Doctors realize that if hospital costs don't come down, the Federal Government will move in—with regulations that bear no relation to quality of care."

The Voluntary Effort wants to make sure that doctors everywhere get the message. "And I hope and pray they act upon it," says Robert B. Hunter, a G.P. from the state of Washington who's chairman of the A.M.A. board of trustees and represents the A.M.A. on the Voluntary Effort's steering committee.

THE BROAD PICTURE: SMALL SAVINGS ADD UP

How much of a difference can individual doctors' efforts make? The answer is, plenty. What *you* might do to reduce the cost of your patients' hospital care will vary with your specialty and your own practice habits—but small changes can add up to a lot of money.

Paul M. Ellwood Jr., a physician turned health planner, has estimated that doctors could cut hospital costs by as much as 10 to 15 per cent. Some simple calculations based on figures from Blue Shield show that this isn't as unlikely as it might sound.

If in 1975 each of the nation's patient-care physicians had reduced the length of stay by one day for just one patient every week, the savings would have amounted to more than $2 billion. If, in addition, each doctor had avoided overnight stays for two more patients each week—by use of preadmission testing or ambulatory surgery facilities, for instance—$4 billion more would have been saved. If each doctor had reduced the number of X-rays he ordered each week by one and the number of lab tests by five, savings would have totaled $670,000,000. All this adds up to more than $6.6 billion—and that represents 13.6 per cent of total hospital expenditures for 1975, which reached $48.7 billion.

Savings on a scale like this would wipe out the double-digit inflation that has plagued our hospitals for the past decade. If hospital spending in 1975 had been $6.6 billion less than it was, the increase over the previous year would have been only about 2 per cent instead of 17.6 per cent.

WHAT MEDICAL STAFFS ARE DOING IN HOSPITALS

Already there are examples of the kind of medical staff involvement in cost control that the Voluntary Effort seeks to promote.

At Massachusetts General Hospital, for instance, the utilization review committee has for the past two years been zeroing in on the problem of excessive use of X-rays and lab tests. Data from the radiology department and lab are fed into a computer that produces statistical reports on the tests performed—so many c.b.c.s, so many chest X-rays. The U.R. committee passes the findings along to the general executive committee, which consists of all department chiefs, and from there they go to the doctors on each section. The object is not to crack down on individual doctors—the computer doesn't turn out physician profiles. It simply shows the kind and number of tests being ordered throughout the hospital.

"It's an educational mechanism," says Lawrence Martin, assistant general director of Mass General, "and it seems to work." The number of X-rays taken at this 1,084-bed university hospital in Boston was down 5,000 in 1977 from 1976, and there was no increase in the number of lab tests.

Mass General also has a resource allocation board, made up of five physicians and four members of the administrative staff. This panel reviews all requests for expanded services and the addition of new services. In its two years of life, the board has turned down about half the requests it has received.

In Martin's opinion, the performance of the physician-members of the board has effectively refuted the charge that doctors are spendthrifts. "What really impresses me," he says, "is the responsible way the doctors behave—they're more responsible than the lay members of the board."

Doctors at 443-bed Winchester Memorial Hospital in Winchester, Va., are launching a cost committee that will operate independently of the U.R. committee. It will sample charts, challenging expenditures that appear to be unnecessary or redundant, and suggesting ways that staff members might cut the cost of their patients' care.

The cost-conscious physicians at Winchester Memorial were in the forefront of a campaign to persuade the Joint Commission on Accreditation of Hospitals to modify its stand on tissue review. Until recently, the J.C.A.H. required that all tissues—and even foreign objects—removed in the course of any surgical procedures be sent to the pathologist. Winchester Memorial surgeons had developed a lengthy list of tissues that, in their opinion, yield no useful information under pathological examination and should be exempted from this rule. They had, in fact, stopped sending these tissues for review last summer—but then they were threatened with loss of accreditation if they didn't conform. In the 1978 edition of the J.C.A.H. Accreditation Manual for Hospitals, however, the standard is revised to such an extent that Winchester Memorial will be able to return to its former procedure.

Still another medical staff has sought to cut spending through a graduated bed system. Like so many of the ideas that are being advanced today, this concept has been around for some years without gaining wide acceptance. But now perhaps its time has come.

Moses H. Cone Memorial Hospital in Greensboro, N.C., has had a small "progressive care" unit for the past 10 years. Patients who are almost ready to leave the hospital but still require close supervision—newly diagnosed diabetics who are learning to adjust their insulin, for instance—can live in motel-like comfort for $25 a day in semiprivate rooms or $30 in private ones. Meals are extra—the patients can eat in the hospital cafeteria or, with their doctors' approval, dine out. The wing is staffed by one L.P.N. and "just about breaks even," according to Gregg Watters, associate director of the hospital.

In the fall of 1977, at the instigation of the medical staff, the 427-bed institution opened an "intermediate care" unit in an under-utilized medical-surgical wing. It's for patients who still need some nursing attention—for shots or glucose injections, perhaps—but can take care of most of their own needs. Because the unit is so new, its charges haven't been set, but Watters anticipates that the daily rate will be about $20 below the $68 to $76 range for conventional beds.

As family practitioner George Wolff sees it, his hospital's three-stage progressive system combines economy with better quality of care: "It involves the patient in his own care, and you feel more comfortable when you send him home."

LOCAL MEDICAL SOCIETY INITIATIVES

In at least one locality—Genesee County in upstate New York—doctors went all out to stop a multimillion-dollar hospital expansion plan they viewed as unnecessary.

Early last year, two hospitals in Batavia, N.Y.—Genesee Memorial and St. Jerome—each announced plans for expansion of ancillary facilities that would have totaled about $12,000,000. The county medical society took a strong stand against the duplication of facilities this spending would have created. It enlisted the aid of the local newspaper in the campaign and bombarded state legislators and health planning officials with mail opposing the project. "It wasn't easy," says medical society president David Harrington. "We found out that you've got to go in with your sleeves rolled up. People feel more strongly about their hospitals than they do about their own mothers."

After heated community debate that spilled over into a series of regional H.S.A. meetings, the hospitals agreed to scale down their spending plans to less than $6,000,000. They haven't merged, even though the medical society hoped they would. But they have set up a Joint Hospital Coordinating Commission, made up of board members, administrators, and chiefs of staff from both institutions. The commission is charged with seeking ways to cut operating costs through sharing of facilities and economies of scale in purchasing.

STATE SOCIETY PROGRAMS

The state medical societies that have gotten into cost containment in recent months are concerned both with showing doctors how to reduce the hospital costs generated by their own practices and with involving other interested parties in the effort.

In Minnesota, the Commission on Health Care Costs organized by the medical association includes representatives of the insurance industry, business, labor, and government along with doctors and hospital people. Says Chairman Richard J. Frey: "We've got to get *everybody* to make changes—doctors, institutions, third parties, and patients."

The medical society's cost containment committee—chaired by two St. Paul otolaryngologists, Richard B. Carley and Jerome A. Hilger—is studying areas of potential savings in which doctors can play a key role if the insurance companies make realistic changes in their coverage—preadmission testing, for one. The Blues in particular have made considerable progress in this respect, but the commercial carriers still lag.

"The way we look at it," says Carley, "the insurance companies can't do anything but win if they liberalize coverage for preadmission testing." To prove this point, the committee has launched a pilot study in which one hospital will absorb the costs for which patients are not reimbursed.

There'll also be pressure on the carriers to provide better reimbursement for in-office surgery, including a modest service charge to cover the physician's overhead—cost of supplies and depreciation of surgical equipment—as well as his fee. Carley estimates that he and his partners could save Blue Shield $40,000 a year doing in-office myringotomies if they were reimbursed in this fashion, as hospitals already are.

In an effort to analyze exactly how hospitalization can be minimized and its cost reduced, the Minnesota task force has enlisted the cooperation of the state specialty societies. Every specialty is preparing a list of its members' 10 most common reasons for hospitalizing patients or 10 most frequently performed surgical procedures and examining how to cut the cost of each one.

In Michigan, the medical society is examining such areas as the cost of lab work, preadmission testing, in-and-out surgery, discharge planning, curtailing weekend admissions, and reducing nonemergency use of the E.R. The lab committee is preparing criteria for the use of diagnostic procedures.

The state society's journal, *Michigan Medicine,* is running regular features and symposia on cost containment. Material on the subject is included in the information packages that go out every month to county medical societies. In addition, the task force is preparing a series of "Practical Guides" on such subjects as preadmission testing for distribution to county societies and hospital staffs throughout the state.

In Illinois, the medical society has formed a Cost Effectiveness Task Force in cooperation with the state hospital association and clinic managers' association, the Blues, and the Chicago medical society and hospital council.

"Like everybody else, we're searching," says general surgeon Jerry Ingalls, who heads the task force. "We're trying to determine, in the most honest way we know, what can be done." With this end in view, the task force is holding a series of meetings throughout the state with representatives of labor and management, legislators, and consumer groups.

A SPECIALTY SOCIETY CAMPAIGN

The American Urological Association launched its cost containment drive a year ago. "It's easier for us than for some specialties, perhaps," says Chicago urologist Herbert Sohn, "because we're such a small group and we do so much hospital work. We've only got about 6,000 members, but our patients account for at least 15 per cent of all hospital admissions." Nevertheless, the urologists' program might easily serve as a model for other specialty societies.

The committee is working on minimum appropriate standards of care for each urological disorder—standards that doctors could use, at their own discretion, as guidelines for controlling the cost of their patients' care. "A lot of doctors are afraid of this kind of thing," committee chairman William Kiser concedes. "They're concerned that the Government will latch onto the guidelines and say nobody can *exceed* those standards." But he also hopes that doctors will see them as a potentially helpful line of defense in malpractice suits and feel a little less pressure to "order the book" in every case for purely defensive reasons.

The A.U.A. has begun presenting lectures and exhibits on cost containment at national and sectional society meetings. It plans to make an *economic* "Clinical-Pathological Conference," analyzing a typical patient's bill, a regular feature in the *Journal of Urology*.

INDOCTRINATION IN COST CONTAINMENT

Another aspect of the A.U.A. program is cost containment education of doctors in training—an area that has been virtually ignored until now. Of the 90 medical schools that responded to an A.U.A. questionnaire, only 23 had any kind of program in the socio-economic aspects of medical practice. Of the 23, only nine offered more than a single hour on the subject. Now the society is preparing a curriculum for use in medical schools and urology residency programs.

At the residency level, of course, a lot of the training is done by the attending physicians. It's a well-known fact of hospital life that residents want to please their attendings. If you make it clear that you're *not* pleased by the ordering of daily electrolytes for a patient who's making an uncomplicated recovery from an appendectomy, or an 18-channel chemistry panel and serology for a healthy 18-year-old who's scheduled for repair of a football knee, residents will soon learn to be more selective.

At Denver General Hospital, attendings, residents, and students participate in a weekly teaching session based on the traditional surgical mortality and morbidity conference that they call the "Economic M.&M." It's the same idea as the urologists' "Economic C.P.C."—instead of reviewing the patient's case history, they review his hospital bill.

"There for all to see is the $30 cost of blood gas level determination, repeated three times in a morning," says Ben Eiseman, who's a professor of surgery at the University of Colorado. "So is the pointless culture request that was done on gallbladder contents just because it's 'routine,' and probably never reviewed. And the chest X-ray repeated on admission, even though a similar film had been taken a week earlier on an outpatient basis."

The Economic M.&M. is popular, Eiseman reports. "Surgeons of all ages vie to get a patient on the list. It's almost a catharsis of conscience."

There's no reason, of course, why a physician in private practice can't institute his own "Economic M.&M.," routinely reviewing all his patients' hospital bills—and leaders of the cost containment efforts are urging you to do just that.

THE BOTTOM LINE: COSTS VS. BENEFITS

As the A.M.A.'s Hunter sees it, "The most important thing doctors can do is to keep cost uppermost in their minds. Consider the cost-benefit ratio every time you order anything."

For doctors whose training was based on the very different principle that it's the physician's job to do everything he can for every patient with no consideration of cost, this idea will take some getting used to—particularly when it comes to cutting back on diagnostic procedures that have come to be considered routine. And the continuing malpractice crisis doesn't make it any easier.

There's no denying that there's an element of risk in *not* ordering the book on every occasion. Dr. Richard J. Jones, director of the A.M.A.'s Division of Scientific Activities, has stated that the routine ordering of X-rays and ECGs for all patients admitted to the hospital isn't necessary. But, he adds, "As soon as you start criticizing redundancy, you run into cases where it was a good thing. Once in a thousand times, an ECG *can* change significantly in a week."

So the key question is: How much can costs be cut without sacrificing quality of care?

A lot of thoughtful physicians who are deeply committed to cost containment are worrying about this question. But the answer they're coming up with is that as doctors rely somewhat less on costly diagnostic procedures, they'll have to sharpen and place more reliance upon their own clinical skills. Says Michigan family physician Robert E. Paxton: "The art of physical diagnosis has been overshadowed by the practice of defensive medicine. We should be able to rely on our ability as clinical diagnosticians without unnecessary multiple screening tests and X-rays, and be ready to defend it in court if necessary, too."

Jerry Ingalls of the Illinois task force looks at it this way: "We're asking doctors to look hard at time-honored practice habits. Then it will be up to them to decide to make changes—or to decide that change will compromise quality. If that point comes, they'll have to put it up to the other parties, the insurance carriers and the purchasers of health insurance, and ask them what they really want."

6. The Nurse Manager's Role in Cost Containment

J.M. GANONG AND W.L. GANONG

Reprinted with permission from *Nursing Management*. Copyright ®
1976 Aspen Systems Corporation.

THE NURSE MANAGER'S ROLE IN COST CONTAINMENT

Nurse managers, given the information and tools to use, quickly learn to recognize the validity of this viewpoint [cost containment] and to discharge their budgetary responsibilities with expertise. This [article] is devoted to budgeting as related to operating expenses because this is the portion of the total budget over which nurse managers have major influence. They can do something about operating expenses. They have little or no control over the capital budget—the planned expenditures for major projects, items of equipment or facilities that will be amortized rather than being paid for as part of the current year's expenses. Yet nurse managers need to be sufficiently familiar with the budgeting procedure for capital items so that they can submit budgetary requests for equipment or facilities when they believe they can be justified on a cost/benefit basis or for their expected contribution to patient care programs. Thus the major part of this [article] is devoted to annual budgetary planning and control from the point of view of nurse managers who have—or should have—this responsibility for their own patient care units, sections or departments.

The significance of the nurse manager's fiscal responsibility is dramatized through a Financial Organization Chart for the nursing service operating expense budget in a department of nursing. The first example, Figure 6:1, is a university hospital of approximately 350 beds. The total annual operating

Figure 6:1   A Financial Organization Chart for Nursing Service Operating Expense Budget, 1975–1976

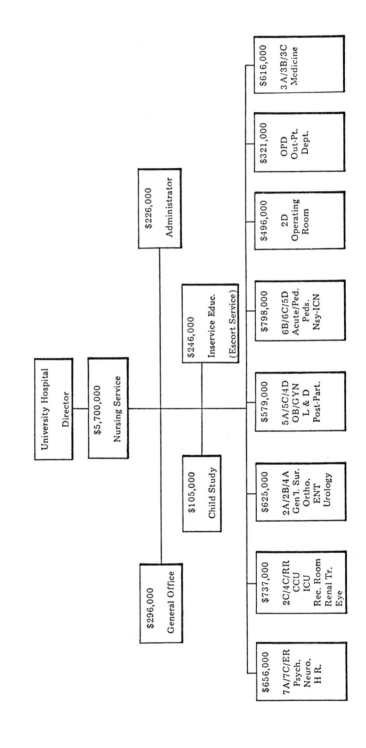

budget of 5.7 million dollars, for which the director of nursing has responsibility, is approximately 40% of the total operating budget for the entire hospital—a percentage quite typical for general hospitals in the 300- to 500-bed size category. Variations of a few percent from this figure are usually due to the inclusion or exclusion of certain departments (OR or Central Supply, for example) in the nursing service budget.

Note in the example that the patient care units are grouped in eight clusters, each group having its own nurse manager reporting to the director of nursing. These eight nurse managers have individual responsibility for operating budgets ranging from $321,000 to $798,000, depending upon the number, size and nature of the patient services offered in each group of units. Payroll expenses alone make up over 90% of the operating expenses for this department of nursing. Here again, the percentage is typical for comparable hospitals. No wonder, then, that escalating wages over the past decade have had such an impact on the costs of hospitalization. And no wonder that nurse managers have been exhorted to operate with the minimum size of staff, use the lowest salary classification of personnel who can do the work, avoid scheduling staff for overtime work and take advantage of every other means possible to contain payroll expenses. Many nurse managers feel with considerable justification that they have been fighting a losing battle because of the wage/price spiral, the state of the economy, and the difficulty (in many areas) of recruiting the kind and quantity of personnel to build stable, competent patient care teams.

In the second organization chart example, Figure 6:2, the arrangement of the unit clusters and the reporting relationships as shown were developed by the nurse managers to meet existing needs and opportunities and to serve as the basis for a longer-range developmental plan. The chart indicates that responsibility for day-to-day operations is shared by two associate directors reporting to the director of nursing service. The head nurses report either to a supervisor or directly to one of the two associate directors. The clinical specialists also report to one of the two associate directors and serve in a staff capacity for their respective unit clusters. As clinical specialists, they are available also to the entire department when their individual clinical skills are required. The projected operating expenses for the fiscal year have been added to the chart. The recommendation and rationale for adopting the organizational plan as shown was as follows:

Recommendation: Adopt the organizational structure depicted on the attached chart effective July 1.

Rationale: This organizational plan—

1. Provides maximum capability to support cost containment goals of administration;

2. Continues our hospital's tradition of providing the best in patient care;
3. Builds upon the assets and demonstrated potential of nursing personnel;
4. Provides for flexibility and rapid response to changing demands and conditions;
5. Has the built-in mechanism for effective budgetary control;
6. Vests authority and accountability in those key nursing personnel who have responsibility for day-to-day operations and patient care;
7. Provides adequate and competent staff support to the nurse managers; and
8. Strengthens the department's ability to achieve interdepartmental, hospital-wide communications and cooperation.

Budgeting and cost containment will continue to be vital areas of concern for nurse managers. To cope with these matters, nurse managers deserve the best practical staff support and service that can be made available. Some nursing departments are providing such help within the department of nursing by establishing a position of Coordinator of Systems and Planning, or comparable title. Persons in such a position, suitably qualified, earn their salaries many times over each year through savings and improvements in staffing, methods and procedures, work simplification, new product analysis and so on. They are nursing management engineers, with or without portfolio. They provide vital supporting services on demand to the nurse managers who have the direct fiscal responsibility on each unit, unit cluster, section and division of the nursing department. Working together, they can demonstrate laudable results in operational management.

Nurse managers can set up simple graphs and charts (e.g., man hours/patient day, operating expenses/month) to help control expenses on a day-to-day basis and contribute to real cost containment results. *In our experience an organizational approach works better than a more limited systems, technically-oriented approach.* The organizational approach is one which places responsibility for fiscal management in the nurse managers at every level and provides them with what they need to carry out that responsibility. Under such circumstances the nurse manager delivers often unforeseen, commendable results in money management and patient care.

Figure 6:2 Budgetary Control Responsibility within the Department of Nursing

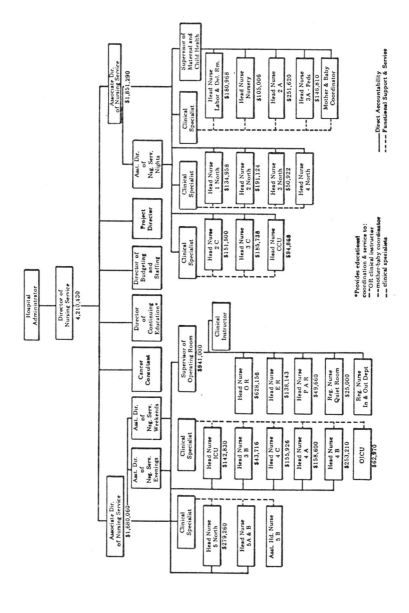

7. The Potential of Health Education Includes Cost Effectiveness

Reprinted, with permission, from *Hospitals, Journal of the American Hospital Association,* vol. 50, no. 9, May 1, 1976, pp. 57-61.

Whether health education should be an institutionalized part of medical care already has been decided. Operational questions now are increasing, because health education programs in medical care settings are increasing in number and variety.[1,2] The operational questions are essentially administrative and educational. In focusing on these questions, one must draw on rather meager data. Moreover, in the final analysis, all estimations of health education's cost benefits based on the current organization of health services could be rendered invalid by the enactment of one of the several national health insurance bills now before Congress. For these reasons, this article will discuss operational questions that will be relevant in the future rather than discuss rehashed answers to questions posed in the past. This article also will discuss the benefits of health education from the perspective of hospital and health services administration.

REDUCE BROKEN APPOINTMENTS

One of the most difficult problems in clinic management is the vicious cycle of patient dissatisfaction leading to broken appointments, then to overscheduling of appointments, then to increased waiting time, and then to further patient dissatisfaction. The only promising point of intervention in the cycle is to ensure patient satisfaction. Health education can contribute to patient satisfaction through helping patients understand the reasons for waiting time, the procedures of the clinic, and what the physicians are doing while the patients are waiting.

A study in Ohio evaluated the effects of a film designed to explain clinic procedures and waiting time to patients while they were in the waiting room. Such films, slides, or videotapes may effect patient satisfaction and interest by reducing boredom, by entertaining the patients, and by making the wait more tolerable. Of course, an investment in videotape has other applications in hospital education and training.[3]

More direct health education approaches have had demonstrated effects in reducing the problem of broken appointments. Fletcher documented reduction of broken appointments and improvement of follow-up through carefully structured exit interviews conducted by a follow-up clerk for patients leaving the Johns Hopkins Hospital emergency department.[4] In another instance, a slight but not significant improvement in regularity of attendance by lower socioeconomic black clinic patients was achieved through teaching centered mainly on their conditions and treatment.[5] The attendance rate of patients at another medical clinic, in comparison with a rate of 72 percent of a control group, was influenced most by postal card reminders (86 percent) and by phone calls from nurses and physicians (82 percent).[6]

Patient dissatisfaction can be reduced by means other than strictly educational methods. Health education strategies must be supported by or accompanied by certain administrative adjustments. For example, it has been repeatedly demonstrated that having an appointment with a specific physician increases the likelihood that the appointment will be kept.[7,8]

Among the objectives and the benefits of health education, high priority should be placed on reducing broken appointments, because most other benefits—administrative and medical—depend on it. It is crucial to continuity of care, to the monitoring of compliance with medical regimens, to detection of side effects and other problems related to the management of disease among ambulatory patients, and to the success of health education efforts designed to provide reinforcement on return visits.

Furthermore, the patients who most often break appointments generally are those who most need continuity of medical and educational treatment. They usually are less educated,[9] lower socioeconomic, non-white, and young.[6]

Most important, a high rate of broken appointments not only is a cause but also a symptom of poor staff-patient relationships.[9-11] Williams and others have found that practice settings in which patients were most satisfied achieved the best compliance. [12-14] Attempts to blame the weather[15] and the personalities of the patients[9] have yielded little or no correlation with breaking appointments or with dropping out of treatment. Unless the cycle of broken appointments can be ended, quality of care will continue to suffer.

REDUCE UNPAID BILLS

By increasing patient satisfaction, health education also can reduce unpaid bills. Unpaid bills represent a substantial loss to private physicians, to group practices, and to hospitals. Health education might increase patient satisfaction and payment of bills, because it tends to be prevention-oriented. According to Albright, "Anything attached to preventive medicine holds an attraction to the patient, even the bill."[16] For example, pediatricians have one of the lowest rates of unpaid bills, probably because much of their practice is essentially preventive care and health education.

Perhaps health education could be included in the invoice. The computer that prints out the service code and the charge also could print out an explanation of the procedures for which the patient is being charged. Research and evaluation on the relationships among patients' knowledge; satisfaction; and paying of bills, premiums, or fees are needed, unless national health insurance obviates the need.

REDUCE MALPRACTICE SUITS

Unsatisfactory staff-patient relationships also contribute to malpractice suits. Several studies have shown that, in general, "patients tend to be more dissatisfied about the information they receive from their physicians than about any other aspects of medical care."[17] Yet, in a survey, physicians reported that health education is their third most frequent clinical activity in office practice.[18] Thus, there is a discrepancy between the perceptions by patients of what they receive and those by physicians of what they give. Evidence from a variety of sources clearly indicates that patients tend to underreport the amount of information they receive and that physicians tend to overreport the amount they give. More formal patient education, then, can improve patients' learning and satisfaction and can help medical staff members improve their effectiveness as communicators.

GAIN COMMUNITY SUPPORT

A secondary benefit of health education should be increased community support for hospital programs. Patients and their families should respond more positively to the appeals of a hospital for community support, if they understand the functions and the needs of the hospital and are satisfied with their own experiences there. This expectation applies as much to municipal decision makers as to private citizens.

IMPROVE, SPEED DIAGNOSIS

It would seem difficult to argue (although some physicians still do) that a more knowledgeable patient cannot provide a better medical history on which to base a diagnosis than an unknowledgeable patient can. For example, an informed patient is more likely to have used a thermometer at home before reporting a recent history of fever, so that he could be more specific about temperature variations. He also should be better able to recount previous episodes of illness and medical treatment. Thus, his cooperation should help to improve the accuracy of diagnosis.[17,19]

Health education should benefit the patient by increasing the earliness with which he seeks diagnosis and treatment. The evidence affirming the importance of patient knowledge in reducing delay is compelling, even though reporting of some symptoms is complicated by numerous emotional and social variables. [20,21]

IMPROVE PATIENT COMPLIANCE

Health education can contribute to increased patient compliance with medical regimen through ensuring that the patient understands the instructions and the rationale, has developed the skills to implement the regimen, and believes strongly in the importance and the efficacy of the regimen for improving or maintaining his health.

Reviews of the literature on compliance have concluded that the two variables having the most consistent association with compliance are the physician-patient relationship and continuity of care,[22,23] both of which can be modified through health education. Becker and his coauthors confirmed these associations and identified the specific kinds of knowledge and beliefs held by mothers who comply with prescribed regimens for their children. Their knowledge and beliefs include their perception that the illnesses are potentially serious threats to their children, their confidence in the ability of physicians and medication to reduce the threats, and their satisfaction with their interactions with clinic staff members.[24]

The effectiveness of health education in modifying such beliefs and attitudes has been widely documented. The problem for further research in health education concerns the relative cost effectiveness of different combinations of educational inputs (patient, family, provider, community) in achieving changes in behavior for different patient groups.[25-29]

One of the more frustrating aspects of practicing medicine is the "revolving door" by which the patient leaves treatment only to return because of the same health practices and conditions that originally made him sick or injured. Health education traditionally has been directed more to this problem than to others, with mixed success and failure. Encouragingly, the successes have been distributed over the full range of health problems, suggesting that no problem is entirely impervious to health education. However, the failures have been similarly distributed, reminding us that success cannot be guaranteed for any problem. The failures tend to be concentrated on health practices for which there are family economic barriers to adoption.[30]

ACHIEVE BEST COST BENEFITS

Cost-benefit analyses of alternative health services clearly favor preventive health programs and self-care programs with a major health education component. For example, when the choice is between investing marginal capital in expanded pulmonary surgical facilities and investing in smoking cessation clinics, the cost benefits are compelling. Even if the success rate in smoking cessation clinics is "only" 20 percent, it compares very favorably with lung surgery success rates of less than 10 percent; the costs are lower per case, and the long-term economic benefits are far greater for the younger smoker who quits than for the older lung cancer victim whose lung is successfully removed.

As financing mechanisms keep changing, patients are becoming increasingly confused about their rights,[31] the health benefits available to them under their insurance of medical assistance plans,[32] the resources open to them, and even the expectations of health providers concerning what they should do when faced with symptoms of health problems.[33] Under one, uniform financing mechanism for medical care, these utilization problems would be partially eliminated. Without health education, however, patients would continue to behave according to their old habits. Garfield warns that this behavior would swamp the medical care system if the fee were zero.[34]

Health education can help prepare the patient and his family for self-care,[35,36] can inform them which symptoms to ignore and which symptoms to report to the physician,[5] and can impress on them the importance of the follow-up visit schedule.[4,6-8,37] These procedures should help reduce unnecessary use of emergency services for symptoms that could be managed at home, unnecessary readmissions for complications that could have been prevented, unnecessary appointments and telephone inquiries about trivial symptoms, and broken appointments for follow-up care.

Health education can reduce utilization in other ways, as demonstrated in Egbert's study of physician influence with patients in a preoperative session on postoperative experience. The patients in the experimental group were not informed about postoperative pain by the anesthetist. The amount of postoperative narcotics required by the informed patients was reduced by one-half. These patients were discharged by their surgeons (who were unaware of the educational treatment the patients had received) an average of 2.7 days sooner than the patients in the control group were discharged.[38,39]

Some of the functions of a hospital-based health education program are the identification and the coordination of educational resources and services in the community and the referral of patients accordingly. Training programs and workshops for the staffs of various institutions contribute to coordination and sharing of resources and referrals. These efforts also can be conducted among departments within a large hospital. The problems and the benefits of developing such cooperative efforts in health education are described in various case studies.[40,41]

ENCOURAGE CONSUMER ROLE

Health education and consumer participation are inseparable. The same motives that lead hospital administrators to an interest in health education lead them—independently or consequently—to an interest in consumer participation.[31,42] It is a fundamental principle of planning health education programs and materials that consumers be involved in their formulation. In addition, their participation is a natural and feasible way to start the process by which they might become involved in other aspects of hospital planning and management.

Moreover, there also is a growing convergence of mutual interests between persons who have been concerned exclusively with health education and those who have been concerned with volunteer services other than health education.[43]

REDUCE MORBIDITY, MORTALITY

The few data available on long-range effects of hospital-based health education on morbidity and mortality are impressive. For example, in the Kaiser-Permanente Health Plan in Oakland, CA, a minimal health education effort urged middle-aged men to have multiphasic health checkups that cost only $4 per man per year and that resulted in a net saving of more than $800 per man over seven years. This cost benefit was the result primarily of the lower disability and mortality rates of the men who were urged to have the checkups.[44]

A study in the Health Insurance Plan of New York demonstrated the benefits of educational efforts to recruit women for multiphasic screening to reduce breast cancer mortality.[45] The greatest cost benefits were derived from the follow-up efforts to urge the women to return for periodic screening,[46] because detection increases and mortality was reduced with successive rounds of screening. The basic recruitment costs involved two mailings and one telephone call; the five-year benefits involved a one-third reduction in mortality from breast cancer.[47]

CONCLUSION

In balance, a very favorable economic forecast for health education emerges, assuming that allocation decisions will be based on rational and objective considerations. The potential benefits of health education far outweigh the costs, and the ratio of benefits to costs will almost certainly be greater than the corresponding ratios for most medical and surgical procedures directed at the same problem.

REFERENCES

1. Schechter, D.S. Hospital trainers tell problems, needs. *Hospitals.* 48:65, May 16, 1974.

2. Peters, S.J. Health education in a hospital setting: report of a status study. *Rx: Education for the Patient—Proceedings.* Carbondale: Southern Illinois University, 1975.

3. Sigafoos, T., and Jordan, J. Staff development via videotape. *Hospitals.* 46:40, Dec. 1, 1972.

4. Fletcher, S.R. A study of the effectiveness of a follow-up clerk in an emergency room. Master's thesis, Johns Hopkins University, School of Hygiene and Public Health, Baltimore, 1973.

5. Tagliacozzo, D.M., and others. Nurse intervention and patient behavior: an experimental study. *Amer. J. Public Health.* 64:596, June 1974.

6. Shroeder, S.A. Lowering broken appointment rates at a medical clinic. *Med. Care.* 11:75, Jan.-Feb. 1973.

7. Alpert, J.J. Broken appointments. *Pediat.* 34:127, July 1964.

8. Rockart, J.F., and Hofmann, P.B. Physician and patient behavior under different scheduling systems in a hospital outpatient department. *Med. Care.* 7:463, Nov.-Dec. 1969.

9. Rosenzweig, S.P., and Folman, R. Patient and therapist variables affecting premature termination in group psychotherapy. *Psychotherapy: Theory, Research, and Practice.* 11:76, Spring 1974.

10. Freemon, B., and others. Gaps in doctor-patient communication: doctor-patient interaction analysis. *Pediat. Res.* 5:298, May 1971.

11. Charney, E., and others. How well do patients take oral penicillin? A collaborative study in private practice. *Pediat.* 40:188, Aug. 1967.

12. Williams, T.F., and others. The clinical picture of diabetic control, studies in four settings. *Amer. J. Public Health.* 57:441, Mar. 1967.

13. Wagner, S., and others. Patient outcome in a comprehensive medical clinic: its retrospective assessment and related variables. *Med. Care.* 6:144, Mar.-Apr. 1968.

14. Caplan, E.K., and Sussman, M.B. Rank order of important variables for patient and staff satisfaction with outpatient service. *J. Health and Soc. Behavior.* 7:133, Summer 1966.

15. Jonas, S. Influence of the weather on appointment-breaking in a general medical clinic. *Med. Care.* 11:72, Jan.-Feb. 1973.

16. Albright, R. Economics of doctor-patient relations. In: Jaco, E.G., editor. *Patients, Physicians and Illness.* Glencoe, IL: The Free Press, 1958, p. 511.

17. Waitzkin, H., and Stoeckle, J.D. The communication of information about illness. *Adv. Psychosomatic Med.* 8:180, 1972.

18. Senezaro, P., and Williamson, J. A classification of physician performance in internal medicine. *J. Med. Educ.* 43:389, 1968.

19. Bernstein, L., and Dana, R.H. *Interviewing and the Health Professions.* 2nd ed. New York: Appleton-Century-Crofts, 1973.

20. Antonovsky. A., and Hartman, H. Delay in the detection of cancer: a review of the literature. *Health Educ. Monographs.* 2:98, Summer 1974.

21. Green, L.W., and Roberts, B.J. The research literature on why women delay in seeking care for breast symptoms. *Health Educ. Monographs.* 2:129, Summer 1974.

22. Marston, M. Compliance with medical regimens: a review of the literature. *Nurs. Res.* 19:312, July-Aug. 1970.

23. Mitchell, J.H. Compliance with medical regimens: an annotated bibliography. *Health Educ. Monographs.* 2:75, Spring 1974.

24. Becker, M.H., and others. A new approach to explaining sick-role behavior in low-income populations. *Amer. J. Public Health.* 64:205, Mar. 1974.

25. Simonds, S.K. Current issues in patient education. Address, Health Counselor's Workshop, Association of Medical Clinics, Minneapolis, Feb. 17, 1974.

26. Green, L.W. Toward cost-benefit evaluations of health education: some concepts, methods, and examples. *Health Educ. Monographs.* 2:34, Suppl. 1, 1974.

27. ——Evaluation of patient education programs: criteria and measurement techniques. In: *Rx: Education for the Patient. Proceedings.* Carbondale, IL: Southern Illinois University, 1975.

28. ——Should health education abandon attitude-change strategies? Perspectives from recent research. *Health Educ. Monographs.* 1:25, no. 30, 1970.

29. Simonds, S.K. Motivation and health insurance. *Proceedings of Second National Convention on Health Education.* Chicago: American Medical Association, 1966.

30. Green, L.W. Diffusion and adoption of innovations related to cardiovascular risk behavior in the public. In: Enelow, A.J., and Henderson, J., editors. *Proceedings: Applying Behavioral Science to Cardiovascular Risk.* New York: American Heart Association, 1975, p. 84-108.

31. Annas, G.J., and Healey, J.M. The patient rights advocate: redefining the doctor-patient relationship in the hospital context. *Vanderbilt Law Rev.* 27:243, Mar. 1974.

32. Green, L.W., and Wang, V.L. Observations on national health plans from the perspective

of public health education. Background document for a CBS television documentary, prepared for Holt, Rinehart and Winston, 1970.

33. Kalmer, H. Patient-professional congruence related to anticipated care seeking behavior in a prepaid ambulatory setting. Doctoral dissertation, Johns Hopkins University, School of Hygiene and Public Health, Apr. 1976.

34. Garfield, S.R. The delivery of medical care. *Sci. Amer.* 222:15, Apr. 1970.

35. Green, L.W., and others. *Research issues in self-care: Measuring the decline of medicocentrism.* Rockville, MD: National Center for Health Services Research, Conference on Self-Care, Mar. 1976.

36. Rosenberg, S.G. Patient education leads to better care for heart patients. *HSMHA Health Rep.* 86:793, Sept. 1971.

37. Jonas, S. Appointment-breaking in a general medical clinic. *Med. Care.* 9:82, Jan.-Feb. 1971.

38. Egbert, L.D., and others. The value of the postoperative visit by an anesthetist. *J. Amer. Med. Assn.* 185:553, Apr. 17, 1964.

39. ———Reduction of postoperative pain by encouragement and instruction of patients: a study of doctor-patient rapport. *New Engl. J. Med.* 270:825, Apr. 16, 1964.

40. Shapiro, I.S. The teaching role of health professionals in a formal organization. *Health Educ. Monographs.* 1:40, no. 36, 1973.

41. Fiori, F.B., and others. Health education in a hospital setting: report from a Public Health Service project in Newark, New Jersey. *Health Educ. Monographs.* 2:11, Spring 1974.

42. Metsch, J.M., and Veney, J.E. A model of the adaptive behavior of hospital administrators to the mandate to implement consumer participation. *Med. Care.* 12:338, Apr. 1974.

43. Bartow, J.C. Volunteer services. *Hospitals.* 48:181, Apr. 1, 1974.

44. Collen, M.F., and others. Multiphasic checkup evaluation study: preliminary cost benefit analysis for middle-aged men. *Preventive Med.* 2:236, June 1973.

45. Shapiro, S., and others. Periodic breast cancer screening in reducing mortality from breast cancer. *J. Amer. Med. Assn.* 215:1777, Mar. 15, 1971.

46. Fink, R., and others. Impact of efforts to increase participation in repetitive screenings for early breast cancer detection. *Amer. J. Public Health.* 62:328, Mar. 1972.

47. Shapiro, S., and others. Lead time in breast cancer detection and implications for periodicity of screening. Paper presented at American Public Health Association annual meeting, San Francisco, Nov. 5, 1973.

8. Cost Control Challenge for Hospitals

ROBERT A. VRACIU AND JOHN R. GRIFFITH

Reprinted with permission from *Health Care Management Review,* Spring 1979, pp. 63-69.

American health care is emerging from an era in which it held a highly favored position in the American economy. The old era was characterized by a rapid increase in health insurance, first private and later federal programs, that has stimulated the use of health services; subsidies for capital growth (Hill-Burton program and tax-exempt bonds) which allowed for rapid growth in health facilities; and government-funded research which led to new technologies whose dissemination was rapid and rarely based upon careful analysis of the costs and the benefits. The result has been a 15 percent or greater increase in health care expenditures in most of the last decade.

In an environment as rapidly changing as ours, no sector of the economy will keep such a favored position indefinitely. Sectors of the economy such as the space industry and education are recent examples of favored industries that are losing their generous fiscal support. It is being made increasingly clear to the health industry that its "fat" years are over.

If the guidelines for the 1950s, 1960s and early 1970s were for virtually unlimited and subsidized expansion, the guidelines for the 1980s will be clearly more restrictive. We have already witnessed actions by the federal and state governments and business to restrain the rate of cost increases in those facets of the health industry which are under their control. These actions reflect a change in attitude toward health spending; there is every indication that this attitude will continue and intensify.

Proposals abound for ways to contain costs in the health services industry. Debate will continue not only on the form of future regulations but also on the amount of reduction desired. Nevertheless there is a strong indication that the underlying goal of the final program will be to restrict the growth of expenses on a long-term basis to some level related to either the consumer price index (CPI) or growth in the economy.

For example, reference to these targets can be found in President Carter's legislative proposal,[1] in the National Health Planning Goals,[2] the Joint Steering Committee of the American Hospital Association (AHA), American Medical Association (AMA) and FAH[3] and in public statements by corporate leaders such as Zink of General Motors. In assuming such a goal, it is noteworthy that neither a current dollar nor a real dollar reduction in health care expenditures has been suggested. Rather the consensus is that it is sufficient to reduce the rate of increases until it equals a "national economy-wide average," even though there are obvious disagreements over what this average is as well as how to reach it.

The cost-containment proposals currently under consideration share this goal of reducing the rate of increase of national expenditures for hospital care. Although the proposals differ in how the maximum allowable increase (MAI) will be translated into individual hospital expenditures, it is likely that, at some point, each hospital will have a target expenditure level which is derived from the national target. In fact, one has been accepted by the Voluntary Effort of AHA, AMA and FAH. The existence of such a hospital-specific target level, referred to as MAI, and its recognition by the hospital industry represent a significant change from the current modus operandi in most states.

To operate successfully under this new scenario, hospital managers must change their attitudes. The chief executive and chief financial officers of hospitals, and at least the finance committee of the board, must understand the form of the constraint and the ultimate level of severity as it affects the hospital's budgeting and planning decisions.

CHARACTERIZING THE TARGET

The ultimate form of the national ceiling will have a major impact on management autonomy, the possible reactions and the ultimate success of any cost-containment program. Four definitional concerns are associated with specifying that "form": total costs versus total charges, total versus unit costs, GNP versus CPI indices and general versus hospital-industry-specific CPI.

Total Costs versus Total Charges

A cost-containment constraint based on restricting total costs would be different from one based on total charges (net of allowances). In absolute amounts, the difference between the two is the hospital's surplus or generation of capital from operations. If the target is defined in terms of total costs, then no constraint is applied to the generation of capital per se. A hospital could theoretically raise charges at a greater rate than the MAI and increase its planned surplus, i.e., its generation of capital. If, however, the target were defined in terms of total charges, capital generation would be available only if the hospital could successfully contain total costs at a level less than the increase in revenues. Under cost-based reimbursement, of course, the difference between the two bases disappears.

Total versus Unit Costs

Approaches to control such as unit cost, e.g., per diem cost or per admission cost, are not necessarily consistent with the assumed goal of constraining total hospital costs. In the absence of effective utilization controls, a hospital could, for example, increase services to a fixed population, shift patient mix to lower intensity of services, etc., and lower the unit costs. The evidence shows that the total costs of providing health care to the service population will rise, even though the unit costs are controlled.[4] The individual hospital will, in effect, translate its increased volumes into a larger percentage increase in total costs than the one imposed on the unit cost.

GNP versus CPI Indices

While increases in both GNP and CPI have been suggested as targets for allowable increases, they will have different impacts on the "tightness" of cost constraints. This is because the increase in GNP is equal to the sum of an increase in expenditures attributable to inflation plus real growth in GNP. The inflation component is measured by the GNP implicit price deflator, a number which is analogous to the CPI. Allowing total hospital costs to increase only at a rate equal to the CPI excludes "real growth" of GNP. The differences for 1976 and 1977 were 6.0 and 4.9 percent respectively.[5]

The hospital industry's percentage of total GNP would decrease over time under a MAI set equal to the CPI. It would remain constant if the MAI were equal to the total growth in GNP.

General versus Hospital-Industry-Specific CPI

A price index is constructed by weighting the price increases of some set of commodities. The specific component rates (price increases) and weighting vector will influence the final weighted amount, and thus the MAI faced by hospitals. Two alternatives for defining the component rates are: (1) the actual rates of increase for the inputs of hospital services; and (2) the component and subcomponent rates of surrogate commodities in the CPI and WPI.

The first method is susceptible to charges that hospitals will not aggressively try to minimize the prices of purchased goods. To the extent that prices paid by hospitals for labor, supplies, utilities, etc., exceed economy-wide averages, the increases would be allowed by the first method, regardless of the appropriateness. The second approach is more normative in that it restricts allowable increases to an economy-wide average, and is likely to be more restrictive.

The final index reflects a weighting of these component rates. Its accuracy depends upon the vector of weights used. Not only do hospitals use inputs in different proportions from other industries or purchasers, but regional and interhospital differences do exist, and for defensible reasons. These problems can be addressed by using weights which are region or hospital specific.

Variations in MAI

Individual hospitals' MAIs will not be equal, and certainly they will not be constant every year. For example:

- Year-to-year fluctuations in the general economy are likely, and correspondingly, economic indicators such as growth in GNP or CPI are likely to vary.
- There are likely to be both regional and temporal variations in inflation rates for input factors.
- There are likely to be differences between institutions to reflect shifts in service populations.
- There may be ranges established which reflect different levels of hospital performance.

COST CONTAINMENT STRATEGIES

Faced with a MAI in total operating costs, the challenge for many hospital administrators will be to reduce the rate of increase without reducing the quality of care. The exact amount of required reduction, if any, will depend upon the level of the target ceiling and the budget decisions of each hospital. Some hospitals will find that their "natural" rate of increase is below the ceiling and will not require additional reductions. The target ceilings associated with current proposals—e.g., 13 percent with the Voluntary Effort and nine percent plus significant pass-through amounts from the Carter administration's cost-containment proposal—are well above the current national inflation rate for hospital input prices (approximately eight to nine percent). (These estimates are based on actual price incereases for the hospital industry. Aggregrate inflation estimates derived from component price increases in more generic industries can be two to three percentage points lower.) The GNP increased 11 percent (current dollars) from 1976 to 1977; and, because of such factors as decreasing lengths of stay, regional differences in wage rates and increased access to ambulatory care in nonhospital settings, would be a comfortable ceiling for many hospitals.

However, many hospitals will be faced with a need to develop strategies for reducing their "normal" rate of increase. This will be particularly true if the target ceiling is set at a rate lower than currently contemplated, as hospitals are forced to live under a MAI for several successful years, and if a hospital experiences significant increases in demand without adequate volume adjustments built into the ceiling.

Four general categories of cost-containment strategies are available to hospital administrators. Since administrators need a framework for examining cost-containment options with a three- to five-year planning horizon, this article focuses on likely effectiveness and time lags rather than providing a laundry list of options. Although some strategies appear to have adequate potential to meet even a CPI-level MAI for many years, time lags of several years can delay the realization of savings. Thus advance planning will be a vital administrative response.

Short-Term Amenities' Reductions and Purchase Delays

There are a number of short-term strategies to pursue for an immediate expense reduction: minor benefits to employees might be reduced, educational programs cut back, planning activities curtailed, community relations reduced, plant and equipment replacement deferred and implementation of new services and equipment purchases delayed. These short-term strategies reduce existing operating expenses, defer capital costs and may defer increases in operating expenses associated with new programs.

Potential savings from these strategies clearly would vary substantially among hospitals. Expenditures for such items are not likely to disappear either completely or permanently, since they make a long-term contribution to patient satisfaction, recruitment and community support. Moreover, these types of activities do not represent a major part of a typical hospital's budget, and it is unlikely that for any group of hospitals savings are likely to exceed two to five percent.

Regardless of the amount, the savings will accrue immediately. The savings will, however, benefit the hospital only once since in subsequent years they reduce the costs used as the "base" in the percentage increase calculation.

Input Price Reductions

At some point where goods and services are purchased, management has some ability to affect the negotiated price. This is illustrated in the negotiation of wages and salaries where the administrator can bargain harder and perhaps hold down the total settlement. Ironically, this particular strategy is denied by many administrators, but the 1977 Carter proposal specifically forestalled it by making non-supervisory labor costs a "pass through." It appears that some administrators feel they cannot, and others feel they should not, bargain hard to control wage increases. Since the so-called gap between health care workers' earnings and earnings in other industries has been closing,[6] it is reasonable to expect future increases in hospital labor rates to be close to the general level of wage increases if hospitals bargain as hard as other employers. If the number of employees per unit of output remains constant, changes in the rate of increase in labor costs will be reflected in the total. Similar savings might be expected through group purchasing (both of supplies and capital equipment) and substitution of less expensive inputs, e.g., revision of insurance programs. Substitution of less expensive capital for labor, as in the case of computerizing labor-based activities, is a more complex way to reduce expenditures. Projects of this kind may be very attractive because they can fix the cost of some inputs, e.g., through long-term leases, however they can cause adverse labor and reimbursement consequences.

In general, this second strategy has only limited opportunities. Better management, harder bargaining and good luck might yield a savings of one or two percentage points per year compared to present practices. While the savings associated with more effective negotiations may be incurred more than once, possible hidden costs include the likelihood that the other side will respond in turn. The savings associated with group purchasing and substitution of less expensive inputs will generally benefit the hospital only in the year of implementation.

Savings may be realized from these strategies in a reasonably short period of time or may lag one to two years. Negotiations with employee groups and unions generally occur once a year. The hospital's "toughened" negotiating position might require prior work and delaying activities, e.g., developing a good system to resolve grievances and implementation of a system to measure productivity. Shared purchasing arrangements and implementation of computerized systems often take one to three years before savings are realized.

Improved Production Efficiency

The typical hospital faces a wide range of opportunities to improve its internal efficiency (output divided by input) given a constant volume of services. These opportunities range from the simple—employee suggestion programs for improved methods, optimum inventory purchasing policies, etc.—to more complicated changes in the technology—setting capacity to correspond to demand via admissions scheduling, variable staffing, operating room scheduling and contracting with outside organizations to provide services which take advantage of economies of scale. The simple methods still have potential since few hospitals have done everything that can be done. The payouts, however, are equally modest—often in the tens of thousands of dollars per year, sometimes less. A one-percent savings in a medium-sized hospital corresponds to more than $100,000.

The more complex approaches are rapidly becoming more popular. Their payment is quite promising in many settings, but installation cost time lags are correspondingly high.

These strategies are likely to require advance expenditures for increased management capabilities such as the use of industrial engineers and well-trained assistant administrators. Some require new capital, and most require time to plan and negotiate. A prerequisite to implementing the more fruitful of these strategies is a strong commitment on the part of department supervisors and sometimes physicians to improve efficiency by undertaking changes in procedures. Relatively serious retraining is sometimes involved.[7] Even with well-intentioned, well-trained supervisory staff, effectively designed manpower budgeting and reporting systems must be in place in order to recover a real savings. As a result, strategies in this category are often implemented piecemeal and time lags of one to ten years might be expected before savings are realized.

How much these general efficiency strategies will save, net of investment, is unclear. Although engineers are fond of citing figures in the ten- to 15-percent range for potential improvements,[8] it is not clear that all of this potential is real and it is even less clear whether the savings could be realized in the near term. While the cost savings associated with each improvement is by itself a one-time savings, the process of searching for more efficient technologies is likely to yield additional ideas and subsequent savings. Thus, important savings from this area are likely over a continuing period, but immediate returns are limited.

Improved Market Efficiency (Volume Reduction)

Evidence abounds that shows a wide variation in physicians' approaches to the basic hospitalization decisions, e.g., when to admit, when to operate and when to discharge.[9,10] These decisions are reflected in population measures of the admissions rate, the discharge rate and the rate of various types of surgery. When carefully compiled data are assembled, it appears that these statistics vary by as much as 100 percent in populations where there is no recognizable difference in terms of risk of illness or where the differences in risk explain a small part of the observed variations in utilization. Further evidence is found in the performance of HMOs where the rates of admission are slightly lower, length of stay much lower and rates of surgery generally lower than those of comparable US populations under conventional delivery systems.[11,12] Communities have been identified that have maintained low levels of use for many years without apparent ill health or dissatisfaction.[13]

Taken as a whole, this evidence suggests strongly that potential exists for reducing the use rate of hospital services without adversely affecting the quality of care. Further, the responsibility for achieving these lower use rates lies jointly with the physician, hospital representative and community. Analysis of the HMO and the low-use communities suggests that important decisions about organization of services that influence utilization are made by all parties, but that the hospital's commitment to making available adequate ambulatory care services and creating a milieu that encourages cost-effective clinical decisions is not only a prerequisite but an important catalyst.

This fourth category of cost control includes programs that reduce the volume of inpatient services. Such programs either shift services to a lower cost setting or reduce the total number by eliminating unnecessary services. Such programs include preadmission testing and ambulatory surgery (substitute outpatient for inpatient services), utilization review (reduce number of admissions and length of stay) and discharge planning (substitute lower-cost chronic care services). The net effect of many of these programs will be to decrease the volume of patient days. Others will eliminate unnecessary ancillary services.

However, evidence suggests that hospital administrators turn first to other cost-control strategies[14] since the complexities of involving the medical staff slow progress.[15] Consequently, significant changes in volume are likely to occur only after several years in a cost-control environment, reflecting long lead times before strategies are implemented and further lags before they become effective. The magnitude of the dollar savings will vary according to the hospital's willingness to curtail services and the hospital's operating conditions. An approximation can be obtained by using a simple linear cost function: Total Costs = Fixed Costs + (Unit Variable Costs × Number of Patient Days). Using this definition, it can be shown that the percentage change in patient days (×) necessary to change total costs by (a) percentage points is: × = b/a, where (b) is the percent of total costs which are variable with patient days. Thus, if 50 percent of a hospital's costs are considered variable over a three- to five-year period, then a two-percent decrease in patient days is necessary to decrease total costs by one percent.

HOSPITAL RESPONSES

The estimates of the potential savings associated with these four strategies are tenuous at best. There is such variance in hospital operations and capabilities that speaking in general terms has little meaning; individual hospitals might be able to pursue a single strategy for years, achieving any amount of required reduction in costs.

However, as the MAI becomes more binding for hospitals, administrators will be forced to think in terms of three- to five-year planning horizons for implementing cost containment strategies. Such a time frame is necessary because of the lead times associated with different categories of cost-containment strategies. An individual hospital should recognize these lead times and develop a package of strategies which matches the cost savings with the expected MAI.

For the purpose of discussing hospital behavior, hospitals can generally be judged by two criteria. The first is the hospital's production efficiency, i.e., the relation between inputs and outputs. Common measures include cost per patient day (stratified by size, location and type of institution) or position in hospital administrative services (HAS) distribution. The second criterion is that of market efficiency, i.e., the relative amount of care used by the hospital's service population. Data on these use rates are only crudely estimated, but an increasing number of regions are attempting measurement.[16] Methodological problems interfere with measuring and interpreting a specific hospital's position on either criterion, but it is generally possible to identify gross differences.

An administrator facing a specific MAI has a number of areas in which cost-containment activities can be directed. For planning purposes, a useful way of displaying the possible trade-offs is to view the MAI as the sum of

Figure 1 Percentage Increases Associated with Cost-Containment Strategies Relative to MAI

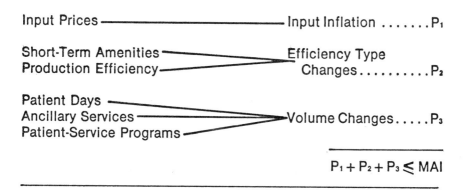

Input Prices ———————————— Input Inflation . . . . P_1

Short-Term Amenities ——————— Efficiency Type
Production Efficiency ———————— Changes . . . . P_2

Patient Days ——
Ancillary Services ———————————→ Volume Changes . . . . . P_3
Patient-Service Programs ——

$$P_1 + P_2 + P_3 \leq MAI$$

three-percentage increases or decreases. (See Figure 1.) Thus a hospital facing an input price inflation rate of nine percent and a MAI of 13 percent can increase total cost up to four percent for reasons other than increased input prices. On the other hand, if the MAI is seven percent and the input inflation rate is nine percent, a two-percent decrease in total costs due to improvements in efficiency and/or a decrease in volume must occur.

Since the input inflation rate was approximately nine percent in 1977,[17] if the MAI is linked to increases in GNP—10.8 percent in 1977—the hospital could increase amenities, decrease efficiency and/or increase volume to the point of increasing costs by approximately two percent. The figure used for the Voluntary Effort, 13 percent, is not particularly demanding. On the other hand, if the MAI were linked to CPI—6.8 percent in 1977—then hospitals would have to decrease amenities, improve efficiency and/or decrease volume to generate approximately two percent in savings.

While individual hospitals will react differently to a binding MAI, a set of general responses can be speculated (not necessarily proposed) for the industry as a whole.

General Responses

1. Hospitals will tend to view the MAI as a target.
2. Hospitals will tend to implement strategies for cost containment in the order listed above. Decreases in volume will be the last resort.
3. There will be an incentive for hospitals to delay cutback until necessary and in some sense to "save" potential cutbacks.

4. Some hospitals will fail to initiate the latter strategies (volume reductions and production efficiency) until the associated lag times exceed the time in which savings can be realized from other opportunities. These hospitals will deplete capital, and be forced into austerity budgets, mergers and/or bankruptcy.
5. The required decrease in volume which corresponds to a required reduction in expenses is a function of the variable costs of operation. Over a three- to five-year planning horizon, hospitals can expect the proportion of variable costs to be reasonably high, e.g., if 70 percent of total costs are variable, a one-percent increase or decrease in total costs corresponds to a 1.4 percent increase or decrease in volume. This high percentage of variable costs will be achieved in well-run hospitals by coordinating capital purchases/replacements and staffing decisions with volume reductions.

Comparative Behavior

1. Less efficient hospitals are in a better position to delay reductions in volume in order to live within a specific MAI. Stated in another way, the more efficient hospitals will be relatively harder hit by any MAI. The benefits of retaining large amounts of slack within the hospital are somewhat of an illusion, however. Less efficient hospitals typically lack systems for strategic planning or cost control and are unable to manage the liquidation of the slack as needed.
2. Hospitals in a high-use-rate area will have a greater ability to reduce volume. Hospitals in a low-use-rate area will have more difficulty reducing volume, and any highly efficient hospital in such an area will have more difficulty living within the MAI. This is because these hospitals have "used up" potential cost-saving activities.
3. The successful hospitals under the new environment will be characterized by good information, decision and control systems. That is, they will be able to develop specific applications of all four strategies, integrate them smoothly into a long-range plan and operate according to the plan. Given the number of cost containment opportunities, the quality of management will determine success or failure far more than the current financial position.

REFERENCES

1. "Hospital Cost Containment Act of 1977." H.R. 6575 introduced in the U.S. House of Representatives (April 25, 1977).

2. "National Health Planning Goals." HEW National Health Planning Council (January 6, 1978).

3. See announcement in *Health Care Week* 1:26 (January 9, 1978) p. 1.

4. Dowling, W.L. et al. "The Impact of the Blue Cross and Medicaid Prospective Reimbursement Systems in Downstate New York." Report submitted to HEW Office of Research and Statistics, Social Security Administration (June 1976).

5. *Economic Report of the President, 1978* (Washington, D.C.: Government Printing Office 1978) Table B-2, p. 259.

6. Yett, D.E. *An Economic Analysis of the Nurse Shortage* (Lexington, Mass.: Lexington Books 1975).

7. Munson, F. and Hancock, W. "Implementation of Hospital Control Systems," in Griffith et al., eds. *Cost Control in Hospitals,* (Ann Arbor: Health Administration Press 1976) p. 297-316.

8. Bartscht, K. and Coffey, R. "Management Engineering—A method to Improve Productivity." *Topics in Health Care Financing* 3:3 (Spring 1977) p. 39-62.

9. Wennberg, J. et al. "Health care delivery in Maine: I—Patterns of Use of Common Surgical Procedures, II—Conditions Explaining Hospital Admissions." *Journal of Maine Medical Association* 66 (1975) p. 123-130, 255-261.

10. Lewis, C.E. "Variation in the Incidence of Surgery." *New England Journal of Medicine* 281 (October 16, 1969) p. 880-884.

11. Roemer, M. and Schonick, W. "HMO Performance: The Recent Evidence." *Health and Society* (Milbank Memorial Fund Quarterly)(Summer 1973) p. 271-318.

12. Gaus, C.R., Cooper, B.S. and Hirschman, C.G. "Contrast in HMO and Fee-For-Service Performance." *Social Security Bulletin* (May 1976) p. 3-14.

13. Griffith, J.R. and Chernow, R. "Cost-Effective Acute Care Facilities Planning in Michigan." *Inquiry* 14:3 (September 1977).

14. Allison, R.F. "Administrative Responses to Prospective Reimbursement." *Topics in Health Care Financing* 3:2 (Winter 1976) p. 97-111.

15. Munson and Hancock. "Implementation of Hospital Control Systems."

16. Griffith, J.R. "A Proposal for New Hospital Performance Measures." *Hospital and Health Services Administration* (Spring 1978) p. 60-84.

17. *Rate Controls* 2:5 (Published by Arnold P. Silver, C.P.A., Phoenix, Arizona, May 1978) p. 8.

CHAPTER 2

HUMAN RESOURCE MANAGEMENT SYSTEMS

The most important component of the health care industry is its human resources. Personnel expense is the single largest health care expense item, ranging from 50 to 70 percent of facility budgets. It is only logical, then, to concentrate containment efforts in this area. There is another important reason why the manpower area provides the greatest potential for cost containment: it is an area that is almost wholly within the administrator's authority.

Manpower systems are difficult to control in health facilities, especially acute care facilities, because of the fluctuating demand for services, the need for 24-hour services, and the rapid technological developments that create demands for specialized skills. Thus, manpower shortages limit the administrator's control over salaries, and competition for qualified personnel makes it necessary to keep less than fully utilized employees on during slack periods, as a reserve against periods of increased demand. Despite the difficulties, human resource management should be the prime target for cost containment efforts.

Attempts to improve manpower utilization and productivity concentrate around the following areas:

- building a manpower management system
- methods of scheduling and staffing
- personnel administration

- personnel development and motivation
- productivity monitoring and control

The 11 articles and papers in this chapter cover the major points of these topics.

BUILDING A MANPOWER MANAGEMENT SYSTEM

A manpower management system should be an internal control device that provides management with a continuous overview of the needs for, availability, development, and productivity of human resources. In order to develop such a manpower system, it is necessary to:

- develop staffing standards
- establish a manpower budget system
- introduce a performance reporting system
- build up a position control mechanism
- select appropriate staffing and scheduling models
- develop motivation schemes
- implement an effective personnel department
- develop human resources

The first article in this chapter (Reading 9) deals with a computerized nursing personnel system that includes scheduling, staffing, quality monitoring, and performance reporting.

SCHEDULING AND STAFFING

Proper scheduling and staffing can produce significant savings for the health care facility. For example, substitution of a less skilled employee for a more skilled employee can result in a new savings. Replacing overtime by regular time is another savings possibility. Organizational structure (e.g., team vs. primary nursing), impact staffing, and scheduling may also result in savings. Of the various scheduling and staffing models we elected to include two in this chapter.

Other scheduling models which may result in savings and which are not discussed in this book are:

- flexible scheduling (see Katz and McNally)
- four-day work week (see Welsh)

- 12-hour shifts (see Ganong)
- unit managers (see Gupta, Reese, and Rosenkrantz)

(See Bibliography for additional information about these authors.)

Patient Classification System

Nursing personnel account for almost one-half of a hospital's staff. Shortages of registered nurses are evident in many parts of the country, especially for the night shift. The basic idea of a patient classification system is that the nursing staff should be a function of patient care needs. Such a system can help management to predict the number of registered nurses, licensed practical nurses, and nurse's aides that the facility will need, based on projection of admissions and census. An overview of this topic with an extended bibliography is provided by Giovannetti (Reading 10). Patient classification and mix is used to establish appropriate staffing levels and to predict staffing needs.

Team vs. Primary Nursing Units

One of the most debated issues in nursing administration is the team vs. primary organizational structure. An actual comparison is reported in Marram's article (Reading 11). It was concluded that primary care is about 7 percent less expensive, yet provides better care and satisfaction than team nursing does.

PERSONNEL ADMINISTRATION

Proper personnel administration is an essential component of any manpower management system. The personnel department is responsible for recruitment, testing, evaluation, fringe benefits, wage and salary administration, education, and turnover analysis and control. Three areas of personnel administration are covered in this book: labor turnover, absenteeism, and fringe benefits. For these and other areas of personnel administration see Metzger. (See Bibliography.)

Labor Turnover

Employee turnover in health care facilities, specifically in hospitals, is very high, sometimes 100 percent a year. The cost associated with replacing one employee—recruiting, orientation, etc.—is estimated to average about $1000 in 1979. A proper analysis of the reasons for turnover, coupled with appropriate preventive measures, may result in substantial savings. The paper by Cawsey and Wedley (Reading 12) deals with both the cost and control over turnover. Although written for other industries, the article covers methods that are applicable to the health care facility.

Absenteeism

Several health care institutions are plagued with excessive absenteeism which may result in poor care and/or excessive cost. Snyder (Reading 13) suggests a management approach to minimize absenteeism through recording and evaluating employees' attendance patterns, counseling and disciplining employees when necessary, and applying attendance policies with consistency. One innovative idea proposed to fight absenteeism is a monthly lottery in which prizes are awarded to those employees with perfect attendance.[1]

Fringe Benefits

The primary objective of a fringe benefit program is to attract, retain, and motivate competent employees. Benefits are used as incentives toward greater productivity and low employee turnover. If this is accomplished at a reasonable cost, then a benefit program is profitable. Benefits costs have risen in recent years at the rate of about 19 percent per year, a higher rate than any other component of compensation. It is predicted that by 1985 the fringe benefit bill could be as high as the straight salary bill. Turban (Reading 14) reviews the many fringe benefits and suggests measures for curbing their costs.

PERSONNEL DEVELOPMENT AND MOTIVATION

Behavioral scientists have long maintained that savings can result from the application of behavioral theories to manpower management. Theories of leadership, motivation, and communication have been practiced for decades in industry. Terms such as *organizational development, management by objectives, theory of needs,* and *behavior modification* can be found in many health care journals. Three topics were selected for this book: human resource development, behavior modification, and participatory management.

Human Resource Development Program

An overall program involving several behavioral and managerial techniques to develop and maintain human resources is presented in Margolis' paper (Reading 15). Significant progress is reported in reducing turnover and absenteeism, in improving quality of care, in reducing loss, and in reducing grievances. In addition, morale and productivity increased as a result of the introduction of such a program.

Behavior Modification

An application of the theory of behavior modification may result in increased productivity and may reduce accidents, turnover, and absenteeism. This is the assessment of Alexander's paper (Reading 16).

Participatory Management

Involvement of employees in management as a means of improving productivity is another controversial topic. Braden's paper (Reading 17), however, presents participatory management as extremely beneficial in implementing a hospital pharmacy cost containment program.

PRODUCTIVITY MONITORING AND CONTROL

All the methods and measures suggested so far are extremely helpful in the planning and development of a human resource system. However, for such a system to be efficient it must have an appropriate control mechanism. The two remaining articles of this chapter deal with this aspect.

Wittaker and Holmes (Reading 18) describe a case study in which manpower is controlled through a budgetary mechanism that involves manhours rather than money. Such a system provides the basis for position control.

The last article in this chapter is by Andersen (Reading 19) and provides a detailed review of a productivity monitoring system for human resources. Such a system involves setting up standards, establishing a reporting scheme, devising statistical analysis and productivity reports, and analyzing alternative staffing and scheduling modes. The system provides a tool for effective manpower allocation and utilization as a medium for cost containment.

Labor performance monitoring systems are increasing in popularity. Several states' hospital association management engineering teams are active in this area. A comparative analysis of such systems can be found in an article by Row.[2]

NOTES

1. J. Wallin and R.D. Johnson, "The Positive Reinforcement Approach to Controlling Employee Absenteeism," *Personnel Journal* 55 (August 1976): 390-392.

2. C.F. Row, "Labor Performance Monitoring Systems: A Comparative Analysis in Hospital Applications," *Hospital and Health Services Administration* 21 (Summer 1976): 60-70.

BIBLIOGRAPHY

Able, R.L., and Breeden, J.L. "Model for the Cost of Labor Turnover." *Hospital Forum,* March 1972.

Bahr, J., et al. "Innovative Methodology Enhances Nurse Deployment, Cuts Costs." *Hospitals, JAHA,* 16 April 1978.

Branden, F.M. "Achievement Through Participatory Management: The Key to Survival." *Hospital Pharmacy* 13 (1978): 403-404.

Cochran, J. "Refining a Patient-Acuity System Over Four Years." *Hospital Progress,* February 1979.

Diggs, W.W. "New Methodology Affords 'Grasps' on Minimum Nursing Staff." *Southern Hospital,* January-February 1979.

Duffey, R. "How to Reduce the 'No Show' Rate." *Dimensions in Health Service,* February 1976.

Duffus, A.J., and Smith, N. "Temporary Staffing Service: An Answer to Fluctuating Needs in Hospital Staffing." *Hospital Topics,* November-December 1976.

Ganong, W.L., et al. "The 12-Hour Shift: Better Quality, Lower Cost." *Journal of Nursing Administration,* February 1976.

Godfrey, M. "Your Fringe Benefits: How Much Are They Really Worth?" *Nursing,* January 1975.

Gupta, I., et al. "How the Revised Unit Management Program at Cook County Hospital Eliminated 87 Jobs and Saved $400,000." *Hospital Topics,* September-October 1975.

Hohman, J. "Nurse Mentor System Cuts Costs, Boosts Quality of Patient Care." *Hospitals, JAHA,* 1 January 1979.

Howell, D.L., and Stewart, G.T. "Labor Turnover in Hospitals." *Personnel Journal,* December 1975.

Katz, E. "Flexible Scheduling Using Part-Time Nurses." *Dimensions in Health Service,* March 1978.

Kearney, W.J. "Improving Work Performance Through Appraisal." *Human Resource Management* 17 (1978): 15-23.

Kirkup, V. "Absenteeism: Who Indulges?" *Hospital Topics,* March-April 1977.

Lehman, M.W., and Friesen, O.J. "Centralized Control System Cuts Costs, Boosts Morale." *Hospitals, JAHA,* 16 May 1978.

McNally, J.K. "Flexible Staffing: The Key to Better Utilization of Nursing Personnel." *Hospital Financial Management,* February 1970.

Metzger, N. *The Health Care Supervisor's Handbook* (Germantown, Md.: Aspen Systems Corp., 1978).

Odell, H. "Curb Excessive Absenteeism: Bolster Self-Confidence." *Health Services Manager,* March 1977.

Overton, P., et al. "Patient Classification by Type of Care." *Dimensions in Health Service,* August 1977.

Park, J.W. "Job Enrichment—How to Get Your Employees to Work for You." *Hospital Financial Management,* November 1978.

Raajtes, R.B. "Control Personnel Costs Through Man-Hour Budgeting." *Hospital Financial Management,* March 1972.

Reece, D.A., et al. "Division Management System Replaces Unit Management." *Hospital Topics,* January-February 1979.

Rosenkrantz, J.A. "Unit Manager: Front Line Administrator." *Modern Hospital,* February 1974.

Small, J.E. "Monitoring Staffing and Productivity." *Hospital Progress,* February 1975.

Stephens, T.A., et al. "An Application of Operant Conditioning to Absenteeism in a Hospital Setting." *Journal of Applied Psychology* 63 (1978): 518–521.

Strilaeff, F. "How Work Organization Affects Nursing Turnover." *Dimensions in Health Service,* May 1978.

Tabaka, A.V. "Are Your Fringe Benefits a 'Good Buy'?" *Hospital Purchasing Management,* July 1977.

Tsui, A. "Diagnosis of Turnover Can Convert Causes to Assets." *Hospitals, JAHA,* 16 July 1977.

Welsh, J.N. "Four-Day Work Week Implemented, Productivity Factors Improved." *Hospitals, JAHA,* 16 April 1975.

Wolfe, A.V., and Wolfe, J. "Results-Oriented Compensation-Benefit to Hospitals and Employees." *Hospital Topics,* May-June 1978.

9. Juggling Staff To Reduce Costs

M. MORIUCHI, J. DURHAM, B. NOYES, M. ZAKOS,
AND M. HUNDERT

Reprinted from *Dimensions in Health Service,* April 1978, pp. 13–14, by
permission of Canadian Hospital Association.

Computer systems have been developed for personnel staffing, scheduling, allocation and reporting for patient care services with the prime objective of improving the utilization of the hospital nursing personnel. The systems accomplish this objective by providing management with a clear understanding of the relationship between workload, staffing levels and quality of patient care. The systems also provide mechanisms for monitoring and controlling these relationships in the hospital.

One such system was developed in California at Mount Zion Hospital and Medical Centre to reduce costs and increase the quality of patient care. Mount Zion is a voluntary, non-profit teaching hospital and medical center in San Francisco. The hospital is licensed for 499 beds, plus 36 bassinets with an average occupancy of 85 percent. Nursing service at Mount Zion has approximately 500 positions assigned to direct patient care and the average nursing hours per patient day on medical surgical floors falls between 4.0 and 5.0 (excluding unit clerks).

A FOUR-PART SYSTEM

The nursing management system developed at Mount Zion consists of four interrelated elements which support the hospital's staffing process:

- Personnel scheduling: a computerized system for scheduling days on and off for all nursing personnel subject to hospital and nursing service policies.

- Variable staffing: includes workload monitoring and personnel allocation:
  - Workload monitoring: quantifies the need for nursing care based upon established standards of care. This component is used daily to measure workload and to determine required staffing levels for each shift.
  - Personnel allocation: provides information to adjust and augment the scheduled staff to meet daily workload demands of each unit. This component is concerned with balancing staff and workload through personnel allocation and selective patient placement.
- Quality monitoring: provides 'process' measures of the quality of nursing care by evaluating the actual delivery of nursing care to individual patients.
- Management reporting: provides various levels of management with appropriate performance measures regarding quantities and qualities of nursing care.

The most novel element of this system is the variable staffing methodology by which shift-to-shift adjustments to staffing are made with the assistance of an on-line computer assisted allocation system (OLAS). The variable staffing methodology has effected substantial cost savings resulting from the implementation of the total nursing management system.

Variable staffing looks at the daily allocation of nurses among and to units in order to match available staff with patient needs. The need for variable staffing arises because of the day-to-day changes in both the workload on a patient unit and the number of staff available. Workloads vary because of fluctuations in census and in the day-to-day needs of each patient. Absenteeism, illness, resignations, new hirees, and training programs change the number of staff available to the unit. Since allocation is a dynamic staffing problem, access to accurate information and the timely use of data is of critical importance.

The primary goal of a variable staffing program is to reduce or contain nursing costs by minimizing variations in the staff-size-to-workload ratio from day-to-day on individual units and among nursing units. Using concepts such as "float staff," "pulling," and "call-ins," staff are allocated to units in such a way as to optimize the matching of staff to workload and to minimize discrepancies between required and paid hours.

Under a variable staffing system, the timeliness of allocation decisions is of extreme importance. People calling in absent usually notify the nursing office immediately prior to their normal time to report for work, thus causing a need to adjust assignments or augment scheduled staff immediately preceding and sometimes into the beginning of a shift. The development of an on-line system at Mount Zion facilitates more informed allocation decisions by providing immediate access to information about workload and staff availability in each unit in the hospital.

The first step of the shift-to-shift variable staffing system, determines workload and staffing requirements using the Workload Monitoring System. This technique utilizing the on-line computer system, automatically computes the workload and related staffing requirements for each unit. In the second step of the process the system compares required and scheduled staff for each unit and lists available float and casual personnel. The system assists the staffing coordinator to allocate available staff and call in additional staff based upon each unit's relative needs as well as individual employee preferences and capabilities which are preprogrammed into the system.

The on-line computer support assists in ensuring a better match between workload and staff size, minimizes day-to-day changes in personnel assignments and minimizes personnel dissatisfaction by recognizing personal skills and preferences. The system ensures that the ultimate decision on who goes where is made by the decision-maker and not the computer program. The on-line computer programs simply provide timely information to aid in the decision process.

The workload monitoring system developed for Mount Zion uses a patient classification system which indicates the amount of nursing time required by a typical patient in each category. The time requirements and the number of patients in each category are called down to the nursing office at approximate times during each shift.

When the counts are received in the nursing office, they are entered into the OLAS. The OLAS automatically calculates the workload for the unit and determines the suggested staffing levels for that unit.

The scheduled staffing for each unit is updated daily to account for schedule changes, sick calls and unauthorized absences. Changes in schedules are entered through a terminal in the nursing office.

Once staffing requirements have been determined and scheduled staffing has been updated, the difference between required and actual staffing is calculated automatically and displayed on the terminal. If patient classification changes or if further sick-calls are received and are entered into the system, the files for all screens will reflect the most current information.

ALLOCATING THE STAFF

The system searches through all the nursing units to determine which are the most critically understaffed. (This is based on a set of priorities which ensures that specialty areas are considered before Med/surg units). A description of the workload and scheduled staffing of the most critically understaffed unit appears on the screen first, along with a list of float, casual, and personnel available from other units who are *qualified* to work on the unit being considered.

To select and allocate a staff member, the staffing coordinator enters the ID number of the staff member. This will remove the staff member's name from the available resource list and assign him or her to the unit being staffed.

The user has the capability of calling up the unit's roster of scheduled staff during the allocation process. This feature was added so that the user has the ability to look at the currently assigned staff before allocating float or part-time personnel.

The staff are allocated, the next most critically understaffed unit is displayed on the terminal. The allocation process continues until all available resources are used.

After the allocation process is completed, the *roster program,* which displays staffing for each unit, will include the assignments of float, casual and pulled personnel. Adjustments can be made for late call-ins and no-shows. A copy of the final roster is printed each night to serve as a supplementary record to staff schedules in the nursing office.

Just before the start of the shift, all float, casual and registry personnel arrive in the nursing office to get their assignment for the shift. Prior to the implementation of OLAS, the only record of the assignment was on a worksheet which was often in use by the staffing coordinator or supervisor making final scheduling adjustments. Thus, their work was constantly being interrupted. With OLAS, the Float Program is called and the list of all personnel pulled from their home unit, float, casual, and registry personnel appears on the screen. Therefore, as the personnel arrive, they can look at the screen and get their assignments.

With the completion of this step, the allocation process is complete for the shift. The steps are then repeated for each shift.

The major objective during the design of this function was to supply decision makers with appropriate information on a timely basis from established files whenever possible. The most obvious source of such files was OLAS. OLAS' files contained the most up-to-date listing of staff by unit, by shift and by category of personnel.

Thus, two major manpower reports were designed to access and utilize OLAS' files. The manpower reporting programs were also designed to interface with the hospital's payroll systems so that the data from both files could be compared.

With the implementation of the Nursing Systems Program Mount Zion Hospital achieved:

- Personnel satisfaction (reduction in turnover, sick call-ins, overtime, shift rotation, and an effort to satisfy scheduling preferences)
- Cost savings through staffing adjustments (reduction in nursing hours per patient day and cost avoidance through alteration of full time/part time mix)

One item currently being considered is to integrate OLAS with a time and attendance system. In this way consistent reporting can be ensured and much of the manual effort required to maintain the present time card system could be eliminated.

The second major enhancement to the system that is being considered is expansion to the admitting office. Clearly, the system contains information that would be of use in assigning patients to beds. Selective admitting strategies are expected to add substantially to the improved matching of staff to workload.

10. Understanding Patient Classification Systems

PHYLLIS GIOVANNETTI

Reprinted with permission from *Journal of Nursing Administration,* February 1979, pp. 4-6, 8-9.

Over the past 15 years hospital inpatient classification systems have received attention for the primary purpose of nurse staffing. Attention has ranged from basic research to the development, refinement and implementation of staffing methods utilizing various patient classification systems. In numerous reports and articles on the use of patient classification systems the real or potential successes outweigh the failures. The demand for patient classification as a means for nurse staffing has been specifically documented in the negotiated contracts of several state nurses' associations,[1] and in a recent survey of priorities in clinical nursing research the need for valid and reliable methods for establishing nursing staffing patterns ranked high.[2]

While the present demand for patient classification systems suggests their importance and value, there is still a long way to go in making the systems generally available. It is time to redefine and reflect, to explore what patient classification systems mean in nursing and to discuss some of the major methodological issues crucial to their development, understanding, and usefulness.

DEVELOPMENT IN NURSING

Patient classification may be generally defined as the grouping of patients according to some observable or inferred properties or characteristics. There are, obviously, any number of possibilities for classification. Many systems use such characteristics as blood type, medical specialty, diagnosis, and insurance coverage, with each classification serving some unique function. In nursing, the term *patient classification* means the categorization of patients according to some assessment of their nursing care requirements over a specified period of time. The most common purpose has been for determination and assignment of nursing care personnel. To encompass both the definition and the purpose, the term *patient classification system* is commonly used. It refers to the identification and classification of patients into care groups or categories, and to the quantification of these categories as a measure of the nursing effort required.

The development of patient classification systems in nursing has been in response to the variable nature of nursing care demands. In hospitals there may be wide swings in the demand for nursing care from day to day and from shift to shift, and these fluctuations are independent of the number of patients in the unit.[3-6] In patient care units where nursing care requirements are largely homogeneous, such as in self care units, this is less likely to be true. Because the number of patients in a unit may not be an adequate indicator of the demand for care, grouping patients into categories that reflect the magnitude of nursing care time provides a more rational and sensitive approach to determining the need for nursing care resources.

The exact number of patient classification systems presently in existence is not known. Aydelotte reported some 40 pieces of patient classification literature in 1973, and it is likely that the number has since tripled.[7] An unofficial count reveals some 1,000 hospitals presently using some form of patient classification system. The majority of these systems are based on a relatively small number of approaches such as those proposed by Conner,[3] CASH,[10] CSF Ltd.,[9] MEDICUS,[8] and the University of Saskatchewan.[11]

Although these systems do not solve all staffing problems, they do provide useful means for establishing an appropriate base line staff, and for allocating personnel to meet daily fluctuations. In the face of a paucity of rational means of determining a staffing policy, the question is less "Should I use a patient classification system?" but more "How do I select a workable patient classification system?"

Two common types of classification systems have been identified by Abdellah and Levine as "prototype evaluation" and "factor evaluation."[12] The difference between the two relates to the actual design of the classification instrument. The first generally describes the characteristics of patients typical to each category. In the second (and more common) type a number of critical indicators or descriptors of direct care requirements are separately rated and then combined to designate a patient's category. The two types are also respectively referred to as "subjective" (prototype evaluation) and "objective" (factor evaluation) instruments. This terminology is misleading, however, because some measure of subjectivity is inevitably involved in any assessment of patients' nursing care requirements.

CRITICAL INDICATORS OF CARE

The descriptors of patients' nursing care requirements are frequently referred to as the *critical indicators of care.* Critical is not used in the medical sense; it means those components that are most crucial to correctly identifying the appropriate category of care. Since the primary purpose of patient classification is to determine the need for nursing care resources, the critical indicators represent those activities that have the greatest impact on nursing care time. Observational studies of nursing care have helped identify the critical indicators; typically they include nursing activities associated with feeding, bathing, and ambulation. Other major activities include those associated with preoperative preparation, observations, special treatments, and incontinence care.

The number and scope of critical indicators used for patient classification systems have received a great deal of criticism, primarily aimed at their seeming lack of comprehensiveness and limited attention to the psychosocial and teaching components of nursing care. Some of this criticism is perhaps warranted, but much is not. Several observations are important.

First, although patient classification requires patient assessment, it does not constitute a comprehensive assessment, nor does it intend to replace the more detailed assessment necessary for patient care planning. Second, patients' psychological, social, and teaching requirements are largely met by nurses while providing care related to feeding, bathing, ambulation, and other physical or technical functions. Thus the inclusion of critical indicators specific to emotional support and teaching is often redundant (but may be added to enhance acceptability of a patient classification system). Third, the subjective nature of classification systems permits consideration of patients' psychosocial and teaching requirements in the selection of critical indicators. For example, although a patient may be physically capable of bathing himself, because of his emotional state or level of anxiety he may be unable to do so without encouragement and support from his nurse. In this instance, the critical indicator most appropriate to this care would be "bath with assistance." This consideration is not likely to be revealed by a cursory view of the classification instrument itself but is frequently mentioned in the accompanying guidelines and instructions. Therefore, in critiquing patient classification instruments, attention must be given to the guidelines and instructions for selecting determiners. Finally, the number of critical indicators need not restrict the possibilities for categorization; for example, it is quite possible to classify patients into four categories of care using fewer than four critical indicators. Although such systems may be valid, they are uncommon because they are not generally acceptable to the nursing profession; they do not appear to consider the magnitude of nursing care or the uniqueness of each patient.

QUANTIFICATION OF PATIENT CARE

As previously noted, almost all patient classification systems are used in conjunction with some quantification—an estimation of the nursing care resources associated with each category of care. Although many approaches are used, two methods for quantification are common; one based on average care times for each patient category, and the other based on standard care times for specific nursing procedures. Using the first method, the average amount of direct nursing care provided within each care category is determined from observational studies. The number of patients in each care category multiplied by the corresponding average care time provides an estimate of the total average direct care time required. This figure, coupled with an estimate of the total average indirect care time (also determined from observational studies), gives the total average nursing care time required for a specified group of patients.

In the second approach, a standard time is calculated for each nursing care activity. Total direct care time is determined by multiplying the number of times each activity occurs by the appropriate standard time. Total care time is then determined by the addition of a coefficient representing indirect care time. In addition to original sources of information, literature reviews are available for more extensive descriptions of the various methods and procedures used for quantification.[7,12,13,14]

Whether the system uses average care times, standard times for procedures, or a combination of both is of less importance than the data collection techniques used and the manner in which the observational studies are conducted. While a particular classification instrument may be applicable to a variety of settings, the quantification coefficients are not transferrable. Average care times or standard times are not necessarily the same from institution to institution or even from one nursing unit to another. A multitude of factors affect the determination of care times, such as type of nursing organization, physical facilities design, treatment modalities, physician practices, availability of nursing skills, and attitudes of treatment personnel.

Thus, institutions interested in using a patient classification system need to determine their own quantification or index of workload. Two options are open. The first involves selecting the quantification figures developed by a similar institution and then, on a trial-and-error basis, adjusting them to the setting.[11] The second involves the institution conducting its own observational studies. This approach, although more costly, can provide much worthwhile information on the practice of nursing care. Conducting observational studies, however, requires knowledge and experience in the use of the necessary methods and techniques.[15,16]

The data obtained through these quantification techniques relate directly to the practices, procedures, and behaviors existing at the time of the observations. For this reason, inefficiencies and outmoded practices should be identified and corrected and the quantification coefficients appropriately adjusted. In this way, the average care times or standard times will not reflect and perpetuate inefficient practices. Regardless of the approach taken, the quantification of patient care to estimate workload must not replace input based on professional nursing judgment or experience....

RELATIONSHIP TO QUALITY OF CARE

The issues relating to effectiveness and quality must not become confused. Patient classification systems can be extremely effective in matching workload generated by patients to numbers of nursing personnel. There is no evidence, however, that the effective utilization of nursing personnel hours has any direct relationship to the quality of care. The number of nursing personnel is only one input of the total patient care system, while the quality of care as measured by patient outcomes is one output. Although we remain hopeful that the structure and process of care have some bearing on the outcome of care, there is little evidence to define the nature of this relationship. Attempts to draw a direct relationship between the two ignore the existence of other important factors and mask the impact of the interaction effects which are a part of the complex model.

Patient classification systems should thus be considered as tools to aid in the effective allocation and utilization of nursing personnel resources. Until we have evidence to support, for instance, the notion that an understaffed unit does not provide "quality" care, we must not place the systems on a pedestal by suggesting that they improve the quality of care. At this time, they offer us a productivity formula for a predetermined standard of care. It is hoped, as we strive to develop outcome measures, that we will have a productivity formula that considers the level of quality as well as the volume of nursing output, and is sensitive to changes in both.

CONCLUSIONS

Patient classification systems, when developed and used appropriately, can be an important aid in the effective determination and allocation of nursing resources. Benefits have been demonstrated from their use in the short term daily allocation of staff and in long-term budget planning. Patient classification systems have also proved useful in developing facilities in which to provide care more effectively.[18,19] Their heuristic nature has been beneficial to many research investigations, particularly as a guide for recent studies relating to criteria for quality of care measures.[20] In addition, several hospitals are using patient classification systems as a basis for determining patient charges.[21,22]

Perhaps one of the least credited advantages of a well-developed and operational patient classification system is its ability to lessen the monumental problems associated with the determination and allocation of nursing personnel. Freed from some of the daily struggles associated with staffing, nurses may transfer their energies to other current and critical problems such as implementing standards of care and developing outcome measures.

Many other uses of classification systems have been cited but their capabilities are highly contingent upon the degree of understanding and acceptance within a facility. Understanding involves awareness and knowledge of classification systems capabilities with recognition that: 1) they are based on a unidimensional and partial assessment of patient requirements for care; 2) quantification is primarily based on the existing practice of nursing; and 3) their value is enhanced by adequate measures of reliability and validity. Acceptance must extend beyond the nursing department to include hospital administration and physicians. The lack of attention and effort directed to this crucial step has been the major reason for the failures experienced by some in the implementation and application of the systems.

Imperfect as patient classification systems may be in determining the true needs of patients, they do, when used appropriately, provide a rational approach to the problem of nurse staffing. While we wait for a more perfect system, a well-developed patient classification system is better than no system at all.

REFERENCES AND NOTES

1. Washington State Nurses Association. *Why RN's strike.* In *The Seattle Times,* July 26, 1976, and personal communication regarding contracts in California and Montana.

2. Lindeman, Carol A. *Delphi Survey of Clinical Nursing Research Priorities.* Boulder, Colorado: WICHE, August, 1974.

3. Connor, R.J. A Hospital Inpatient Classification System. Doctoral dissertation, The Johns Hopkins University, Industrial Engineering Department, 1960.

4. Jelinek, Richard C. A structural model for the patient care operation. *Health Services Research,* 2:3, Fall-Winter 1967, pp. 226-242.

5. Giovannetti, P. Measurements of patients' requirements for nursing services. In Research on Nurse Staffing—Report of the Conference, DHEW Publication No. (NIH) 73-434. U.S. Department of Health, Education and Welfare, May 1972, pp. 41-56.

6. Wolfe, Harvey, and Young, John P. Staffing the nursing unit, part I. Controlled variable staffing. *Nurs. Res.,* 14:3, Summer 1965, pp. 236-243.

7. Aydelotte, Myrtle K. Nurse Staffing Methodology—A Review and Critique of Selected Literature. DHEW Publication No. (NIH) 73-433. U.S. Department of Health, Education, and Welfare, January 1973.

8. Jelinek, Richard C., Linn, Tim K., and Brya, James R. Tell the computer how sick the patients are and it will tell how many nurses they need. *Modern Hospital,* 121:6, December 1973, pp. 81-85.

9. Community Systems Foundation. *Nursing Systems Service Application Description.* Ann Arbor: University of Michigan, 1967.

10. Commission for Administrative Services in Hospitals. *Staff Utilization and Control Program.* Nursing Service Orientation Report, Medical/Surgical, 1967.

11. Giovannetti, P., and McKague, L. *Patient Classification System and Staffing by Workload Index—A Working Manual.* Saskatoon, Saskatchewan: Hospital Systems Study Group, University of Saskatchewan, 1973.

12. Abdellah, F. and Levine, E. *Better Patient Care Through Nursing Research.* New York: The Macmillan Company, 1965.

13. Jelinek, Richard C., and Dennis, Lyman C. A Review and Evaluation of Nursing Productivity. DHEW Publication No. (HRA) 77-15. U.S. Department of Health, Education and Welfare, 1976.

14. Giovannetti, P. Patient Classification in Nursing: A Description and Analysis. DHEW Publication No. (HRA) 78-22, HRP 0500501. U.S. Department of Health, Education and Welfare, July 1978.

15. U.S. Public Health Service. How to Study Nursing Activities in a Patient Unit. Public Health Service Publication No. 370, Revised 1964. Government Printing Office, 1964, 142 pages. Note: A new revised edition is expected to be completed in 1978.

16. Giovannetti, P., McKague, L., and Bicknell, P. *The Development, Implementation, and Evaluation of a Workload Index for Holy Family Hospital.* Saskatoon, Saskatchewan: Hospital Systems Study Group, University of Saskatchewan, 1973.

...

18. Sjoberg, K., Heiren, E., and Jackson, M.R. Unit assignment—a patient centered system. *Nurs. Clin. North Am.,* 6:2, June 1971, pp. 333-342.

19. Haldeman, J.C., and Abdellah, F.G. Concepts of progressive patient care. *Hospitals,* 33:10, May 16, 1959, pp. 38-42, and 33:11, June 1, 1959, pp. 41-46.

20. Jelinek, Richard C., et al. A Methodology for Monitoring Quality of Nursing Care. DHEW Publication No. (HRA) 76-25. U.S. Department of Health, Education, and Welfare, January 1974.

21. Holbrook, F.K. Charging by level of nursing care. *Hospitals,* 46:16, August 16, 1972, pp. 80–88.

22. St. Luke's Hospital Medical Center. Unpublished correspondence, June 20, 1974.

11. The Comparative Costs of Operating a Team and Primary Nursing Unit

GWEN MARRAM

Reprinted from *The Journal of Nursing Administration,* May, 1976 by permission of The Journal of Nursing Administration, Inc., and Nursing Resources, Inc., formerly Contemporary Publishing, © 1978.

The concept of cost-effectiveness, when applied to the delivery of nursing services, may be measured by two different criteria: 1) a nursing service agency may deliver the same quality care at lower cost than another agency, 2) an agency may deliver higher quality care than another, while maintaining similar costs and similar task performance efficiency. In either case, it can be concluded that one agency, or even one unit, is more cost-effective than another.

The growing concern over costs has led many nursing directors to be wary of implementing primary nursing because it may require enlarging the RN staff. Since salary costs are the chief operating expense of any unit, the concern is well-founded. No health care program will be effective unless we can control its costs and make the most efficient use of personnel.[1]

To get some evidence of the cost of primary nursing, Marram, Schlegel, and Bevis conducted a survey of nine hospitals across the country in 1971 that had reported they were employing primary nursing.[2] None of the hospitals surveyed reported increased operating costs for a primary nursing unit vis-a-vis their team or case method units. Three of the hospitals indicated that the primary units were less costly to operate than the team units. Administrators from one hospital attributed the reduced cost to the use of 10,000 fewer nursing hours per year with primary nursing. Although the primary units had a higher proportion of RN staff, the units were operating more effectively and with less cost than other units as measured by cost per patient per day.

Other administrators indicated greater productivity on their primary units and a reduction in "extra" nursing hours. Many primary nurses were reported to put in overtime without requesting reimbursement. This overtime was staff nurse-initiated; primary nurses were more likely to come in early, stay late, or come in when they were off-duty to complete care plans or special projects. This behavior was attributed to the high morale and greater sense of accountability to the patient among nurses on the primary units.

To investigate further the comparative cost of primary nursing, Marram collected data in two additional hospitals that had primary units—one with a unit staffed entirely by RNs, and another staffed with a combination of RNs, LPNs and aides.[3] Data on salary costs and extra nursing hours costs compiled over 1½ years revealed that, on the total RN unit, neither salary costs nor total number of staff differed from those in other units in the hospital. Marram explained this outcome on the basis of staff experience levels. The total RN unit was staffed by new graduates at the first level in the pay scale. In the same hospital, the team unit auxiliary staff had more experience and, therefore, higher salaries than might be expected. Marram also found that the primary unit had approximately one-half the number of sick hours and absences as the team unit. The second hospital also revealed no essential differences in staffing and salaries. Both the team and primary units had the same proportion of RNs, aides, and LPNs.

Other than these preliminary studies, there are essentially no substantial data on the over-all costs of primary nursing compared to team nursing. A complete and open revelation of costs would help hospitals assess the feasibility of each modality.

THE STUDY

It was the purpose of this study to identify the nursing care costs of operating a team unit and a primary unit and to determine if there were significant cost differences between them.

The present study was conducted at a 500-bed acute-care hospital in the Boston metropolitan area. The two units chosen for the research were matched on several criteria:

1. Both units were medical-surgical units.
2. The average length of hospital stay for patients did not differ greatly.
3. Both units had approximately the same patient capacity; the primary unit 27 beds and the team unit 24 beds.

The primary nursing unit had converted from team nursing more than three years prior to the study. Both units were regarded as efficient and effective.

A questionnaire was prepared to ascertain the costs of operating each unit for the period April 1974 to April 1975. The questionnaire asked about sick, vacation, and overtime taken by staff, the number of positions budgeted, the number of positions filled, and any differential costs in inservice education and extrahospital reimbursed education.

The questionnaire was completed jointly by the director, assistant director and the hospital's administrative assistant to nursing, using figures from computer summary sheets and payroll cards.

FINDINGS

Master-staffing Plans

At the time the research was conducted, the primary unit had ten RNs, three LPNs, and six aides. The team unit had nine RNs, four LPNs, and six aides. One RN on both units and one aide and one LPN on the team unit put in 32 instead of 40 hours.

The master-staffing pattern was identical for both units: ten full-time RNs, four full-time LPNs and six full-time aides. The primary unit lacked one LPN and the team unit lacked an RN.

Although the master plan called for identical staffing for each unit, the plan was based on the expectation that the team unit would have three fewer patients than the primary unit (24 compared to 27 on the primary unit).

Salary Budget Projections

The 1974–1975 salary budget projections for each unit were:

- Primary Unit = $239,162
- Team Unit = $248,066

The team unit budget was $8,904 higher than that of the primary unit. In March 1975, the estimate for actual salaries projected that the team unit would spend $11,193 more than the primary unit for the year 1974–1975 ($251,166 versus $239,973).

The 1975–1976 salary budget for the primary was set at $255,503, $406 less than the $255,909 budgeted for team unit.

In sum, the projected salaries for 1974–1975 were greater for the team unit. The projected salary budget for 1975–1976, while showing a decreased differential, revealed that the team unit would still require more funds for salaries.

Usually, unit salary budgets vary in relation to the experience of staff members. However, in the two units studied (excluding the head nurse and assistant head nurse on each unit), the primary unit had more RNs with more than 1½ years experience than did the team unit. However, the HN, AHN and LPN aide salaries on the team unit are a factor causing the team unit's salary budget to be higher since the longevity of these staff was greater on the team unit.

At the time of the study, the primary unit was operating without an LPN, and the team unit without an RN. Because it generally takes less money to support an LPN position than an RN position, full staffing would further widen the gap in salaries, making the team unit even more expensive to operate.

Actual Operating and Salary Costs

Because the team unit was closed for 2½ months, from July 1, 1974 to September 16, 1974, and the intermediate period of the next three months was viewed as atypical, the six-month period from April 13, 1974 to July 18, 1974 and January 19, 1975 to April 12, 1975 was used to calculate differences in actual operating and salary costs.

Operating costs include such items as routine dressing packets, general supplies, and repairs. The primary unit's six-month operating costs were $10,537, while the team unit's were $9,085. The primary unit spent $1,452 more than the team unit.

The outcome is reversed for salary expenditures. The primary unit's actual salary costs were $103,044 compared to $112,276 for the team unit. The primary unit spent $9,232 less on salaries than did the team unit during the six-month period.

Had the team unit stayed open and staffing remained constant, its salaries would probably have been at least $18,464 more than for the primary unit from April 1974 to April 1975, even though the team unit was staffed for three fewer patients.

When we group operating and salary costs together, we find that the primary unit functioned at less cost to the hospital during the six-month period, at $113,581, compared to $121,361 for the team unit.

Another way to look at the costs of staffing a unit is to examine the number of nursing hours expended.

Regular nursing hours are the number of hours actually put in, at the designated pay level of staff, to service a unit for some period. Regular nursing hours do not include overtime, holiday, vacation or sick time utilized on a unit. These costs are categorized as extra nursing hours since they do not refer to actual time spent in delivering nursing care on the unit but do account for added expense to the hospital's budget.

Time Spent in Nursing Hours

The primary unit invested 17,882 regular nursing hours and the team unit (with fewer patients) invested 18,351 hours to deliver nursing care during the six-month period. The cost for the primary unit (17,882 hours) was $83,358, while the cost for the team unit (18,531 hours) was $89,282.

The primary unit not only operated less expensively in terms of regular nursing hours, but it also proved more economical in terms of "extra hours" charged to the hospital budget. "Extra hours" is the time spent for overtime, sickness, vacation, or holidays.

Table 1 presents the hours expended by each unit on holidays, sickness, vacation, and overtime. In everything but overtime hours, the team unit cost the hospital more time.

While the primary unit put in 87 more overtime hours, costing the hospital $598 more than the team unit, the team unit consistently put in for more sick time (181 more hours at a cost of $925). The team unit used both more holiday time (estimated at 120 hours and costing $615) and, in five out of the six months, more vacation time (288 hours at $1,639).

Overtime included, the primary unit required 502 fewer "extra" nursing hours and cost the hospital $2,558 less for "extra" hours during the six-month period.

It is important to note here that the six-month period selected for analysis did not include the usual holiday period from November to January when one can expect irregular accumulations of holiday time but did include the months of May and June when vacations are taken. Also, the team unit knew three months in advance that it was closing. The months before the unit was closed could have been used by selected staff to take extra time off.

Table 1 Number and Percentage of Extra Nursing Hours on Each Unit Over a Six-Month Period

	Primary Unit (Total Regular Hours: 17,882)		Team Unit (Total Regular Hours: 18,531)	
	No. Hrs.	(Percent)	No. Hrs.	(Percent)
Sick Hours	528	(2.9)	709	(3.8)
Holiday Hours	488	(2.7)	608	(3.3)
Vacation Hours	747	(4.2)	1035	(5.6)
Overtime Hours	285	(1.6)	198	(1.1)
Total Extra Hours	2048	(11.4)	2550	(13.8)

However, in Table 2, an analysis of the first three months of 1975 indicates that the established pattern continues, the only difference being that the percentage of holiday and vacation hours is lower. This is to be expected after the Christmas season. The fact remains that, except on overtime, the team unit used relatively more hours.

Table 2 Number and Percentage of Extra Nursing Hours on Each Unit Over the Period January 19, 1975 – April 12, 1975

	Team Unit (Total Regular Hours: 10,299)		Primary Unit (Total Regular Hours: 10,108)	
	No. Hrs.	(Percent)	No. Hrs.	(Percent)
Sick Hours	409	(3.9)	304	(3.0)
Holiday Hours	296	(2.9)	224	(2.2)
Vacation Hours	499	(4.8)	343	(3.4)
Overtime Hours	101	(.9)	173	(1.7)
Total Extra Hours	1305	(12.5)	1044	(10.3)

Inservice and Educational Costs

Another hidden cost to hospitals is the cost for inservice programs and reimbursed education outside the hospital (for example, workshops or courses). The hospital indicated there was no difference in the time spent conducting inservice programs on the two units.

The costs for reimbursed education outside the hospital indicated some minor differences for the two units. During the period April 1974 to April 1975, the primary unit and team unit each sent one person to take a course, costing $64 and $66, respectively. The primary unit sent six people to attend a workshop, costing $277. The team unit requested no funds for reimbursed workshop participation.

Cost Per Bed

For the six-month period, the total operating costs were $113,581 for the primary unit and $121,361 for the team unit. These costs included the money expended for salaries as well as general operating expenses. If we divide these costs by the number of beds (27 for the primary unit and 24 for the team unit), we arrive at a per bed cost of $4,206.70 for the primary unit, and $5,056.71 for the team unit. The primary unit was $850.01 per bed cheaper for the six-month period. The cost per bed per month on each unit was $701.12 for the primary unit, and $842.79 for the team unit. The primary unit was $141.67 per bed per month cheaper to operate than the team unit. This is a significant difference and cannot be overlooked in establishing the cost-effectiveness of the two units.

SUMMARY

It was the premise of this study that nursing services can be categorized as more cost-effective if they deliver the same quality care for less cost, or produce higher quality care at the same cost.

The results of this study of the costs of primary and team nursing as they operate in one large metropolitan hospital are important. While the criteria of cost-effectiveness and/or task accomplishment efficiency are not, and should not be, the sole criteria by which a nursing care modality is judged, they are important criteria in this era of skyrocketing health care costs.

If one of the key concerns of nursing directors about primary nursing is the fear of higher costs, this study indicated that primary nursing can be implemented without greater expense and, under certain conditions, at less expense than team nursing.

One important variable in measuring cost-effectiveness seems to be the longevity of staff. On the two units studied, staff nurses on the primary unit had longer work experience than staff nurses on the team unit, yet the longevity of auxiliary workers and/or assistant head nurse and head nurse on the team unit affected the salary expenditures. The exact proportion of longevity among staff members should be a concern of any director interested in cost-effectiveness. When and with what personnel, does longevity become a burden instead of an asset to a unit?

It is important to note that even if the longevity of staff were equalized on the two units, the primary unit would still have proved more cost-effective. The primary unit was staffed almost identically to that of the team unit and had exactly the same master plan, yet accommodated three more patients than the team unit. Likewise, the primary unit proved more efficient in regular nursing hours expended.

This study is part of a larger comparative study of these two units, the results of which will be reported elsewhere. The data suggest that the primary unit not only costs less to operate but also that higher quality care outcomes were more likely to be associated with the unit. The research indicates that, although both units were regarded as very good units, on the primary unit:

1. Nursing staff and patients were more highly satisfied
2. Nursing staff revealed higher degrees of professionalism and reported that they more often got highly involved with their patients
3. Patients perceived the nursing care to be more individualized and personalized
4. Nurses performed more tasks more frequently for all or most of their patients and spent more time on professional tasks
5. Nursing assessments more often incorporated the patient's perception of his illness, nursing needs were more often recorded and included a wider variety of needs, and nursing care plans were more frequently completed.

The primary unit not only appears to be providing more individualized, patient-centered care, but it is also cost-effective, providing both higher quality care and reduced expense.

The study's finding that primary nursing can be practiced at less expense and provide better patient and nurse outcomes should stimulate further cost-effectiveness research in other institutions.

REFERENCES

1. RN Notes and Quotes, *RN Magazine,* Vol. 37, No. 6, 1974, p. 27.
2. Marram, G., et al. *Primary Nursing: A Model for Individualized Care.* St. Louis, Mo.: C.V. Mosby, 1974, pp. 155–156.
3. Marram, G., et al. 1974.

12. Labor Turnover Costs: Measurement and Control

THOMAS F. CAWSEY AND WILLIAM C. WEDLEY

Many practitioners and writers on labor turnover start their analysis by stating that turnover is expensive. While the high costs are usually self-evident, very few of these proponents for action actually calculate the expense. Most writers, for example, either describe the causes or variables associated with departures, or they explain actions which are supposed to help lower labor turnover. Yet, these same proponents frequently find that executives resist "logical" suggestions which will ameliorate the problem, unconvinced by the exhortations of personnel managers and others that something should be done.

In some respects, the inability of personnel managers to implement new procedures is their own fault. Their refusal to quantify the costs not only deemphasizes the magnitude of the problem, but also eliminates the method of communication which the corporate executive understands best—that is, dollars, the bottom line of the income statement. By couching their arguments in subjective terms, personnel managers fail to communicate with the ultimate decision makers in credible terms. Financial, production and marketing managers justify their proposals with return-on-investment calculations and, as a consequence, tend to be more successful with their project proposals. If personnel managers expect to increase or maintain their stature, then they will have to justify their proposals with more objective data.

Labor turnover costs *can* be measured and used as justification for programs to reduce turnover. These cost measurements provide a benchmark for monitoring and measuring the success of a project and proving whether or not the intervention has been beneficial.

THE COST OF TURNOVER

Firms which calculate their turnover costs generally find that the expense is much larger than anticipated. Table 1 illustrates this. The annual expense can amount to millions of dollars,* and the cost each time a turnover occurs is generally greater than $1,000. The only exception shown in Table 1 is the shoe industry. Its low figure ($400 to $500) can be explained by the minimal training performed in that industry. Nevertheless, the shoe industry has a high turnover rate, and its total cost is large. It is significant that only quantifiable measures of costs are generally included in these figures.

More important to the firm, however, is the turnover cost per employment position. Each time a job position has a change of personnel, that position incurs a chargeable cost which is equivalent to increasing its total annual wage cost. If turnover in a position is high and if several people occupy it during the year, then the total wage and turnover costs for that position can be extremely large. The last column in Table 1 indicates that the surveyed firms had an *average* turnover cost per employment position which varied between $400 and $3,769. Assuming that the typical worker earns $12,000, then the average turnover costs per position represent from 3.3 percent to 31.4 percent of the wage bill. For some firms, therefore, turnover costs represent a very large proportion of total labor costs.

Another important factor to notice in Table 1 is that firms measure turnover costs in different ways. They usually include hiring and training expenses in their cost components and, to a lesser extent, in the cost of separations. Other relevant and frequently larger expenses are the cost of lost productivity, overtime and extra employment, increased maintenance and the general disruption associated with the socialization of a new employee. If anything, the turnover costs in Table 1 tend to underestimate the magnitude of the problem.

The cost components which should be included in calculating turnover costs depend upon the requirements of the analysis and the difficulty of collection. Whichever components are considered important, a standardized and simple format is needed.

THE MEASUREMENT OF TURNOVER COSTS

Presumably, it should be easy to measure turnover costs in companies.

---

*The Canadian dollar is worth approximately 88% of the American dollar.

Table 1 Recent Data on Labor Turnover Costs in Canadian Companies

Study	Source	Number of Workers	Total Annual Turnover Cost	Components of Turnover Costs	Cost per Turnover	Turnover Cost per Employment Position
67 Canadian mining companies	MacMillan et al. 1974	29,533 salaried and hourly paid	$11.9 million	Separation, hiring, training & breaking-in costs	$1,012	$402
Canadian mining industry	Mining Association of Canada, 1974	120,000 salaried and hourly paid	$48 million	Hiring and training	$1,100	$400
International Nickel Co., Thompson, Manitoba	Boydell, 1975	1,300 hourly paid workers	$4.9 million	Hiring, training, lost productivity, extra employment, increased maintenance	$3,732	$3,769
Cominco Ltd., Trail, B.C.	Fricker, 1975	2,700 hourly paid workers	$2,133,781	Hiring and training costs	$1,963	$790
Galand Ore Co., Atikokan, Ontario	McIntosh, 1975	—	$391,035	Separation, hiring & training costs	$2,384	n.a.
Lumber Manufacturers, Pemberton, B.C.	Wedley, 1975	145 hourly paid workers	$341,000	Estimate	$1,000	$2,350
Two lumber manufacturing plants, Vancouver area	Wedley & Fulton, 1975	1,232 hourly paid	$983,000	Estimate	$1,000	$798
National consumer finance firm	Cawsey, Lord & Kudar, 1976	839 account representatives and managers	$1.3 million	Selection, training & severance	$1,491 to $4,707	$1,549
2 Canadian shoe manufacturers	Portis, 1976	Piece-rate workers	$400,000	Training costs	$400 to $500	n.a.

The definition of it would be simply the number of turnovers times the cost per turnover.

While the measurement of turnover is not difficult, it does require the systematic collection of data in a form that management frequently does not have. Turnover statistics that are in the hands of first-line supervisors or in the files of personnel departments cannot always be used by top management in their decision processes. To evaluate and control turnover requires the development of procedures which collect the data and put it in aggregate form that can be understood and interpreted.

To do this, a company must first calculate the costs of turnover. There are five steps to this:

1) The definition of turnover for the company
2) The identification of relevant cost components
3) The determination of measurable and unmeasurable turnover costs
4) The determination of controllable vs. uncontrollable turnover
5) The calculation of total turnover costs.

The Definition of Turnover for the Company

The first step in calculating turnover costs is to obtain accurate and reliable turnover statistics or data. Generally, all companies have the basic raw data necessary to systematically compile turnover statistics. However, many fail to collect and put it in a meaningful form.

One of the problems in doing this is that there is no agreed-upon definition of turnover. Several definitions are frequently used. For example, turnover could be defined as:

• Number of quits divided by the labor force times 100
• Number of hires divided by the labor force times 100
• Number of quits plus the number of hires divided by twice the labor force times 100
• Number of quits minus the departures of temporary employees divided by the labor force times 100.

The definition chosen will affect the results shown. For example, if the labor force is increasing, then the number of hires divided by the labor force times 100 does not present an accurate representation of the true turnover, but would overstate the problem. Conversely, if the labor force is decreasing, then the number of quits divided by the labor force times 100 would also overstate the turnover. At times, fluctuations in the apparent turnover rate are nothing more than the addition or deletion of temporary labor from the work force: for example, students who join the company for summer work programs will affect the turnover rate unless they are deleted from the calculation. While the company incurs recruiting costs for temporary employees, the overall costs are not as significant as those for full-time employees.

A company may decide on any one of these definitions, but it is important that the one definition chosen is kept to. A consistent definition of turnover and accurate data over a period of time allows longitudinal examination of turnover trends. If the definitions of turnover are common across companies with an industry, intercompany comparisons can also be made.

The Identification of Relevant Cost Components

Zimmerman (1971) grouped turnover costs into six categories:

- Costs incurred when an individual leaves the organization
- Costs of advertising the position and recruiting and selecting someone for it
- Costs of new employee orientation and training, if necessary
- Costs of equipment underutilization due to employee absence
- Cost of lost production because of personnel changing jobs
- Cost of lost productivity due to lack of training.

As mentioned earlier, some of these costs are difficult or even impossible to measure. In particular, the costs of underutilization of equipment, lost production and lost productivity are hard to get a handle on.

A more detailed look at Zimmerman's first three costs is given in Table 2. Here the costs are divided into four different categories: recruitment, selection and placement, on-the-job activities and separation or exit. For the firm attempting to identify the relevant cost components, each of these individual costs needs to be examined. Some are reasonably easy to identify on an aggregate basis, such as interviewing cost per turnover when a full-time interviewer is used.

In most cases, if firms follow Table 2 and calculate only the costs which are clearly identifiable and measurable, the total cost per turnover is still significant. These costs provide a valuable argument for personnel managers in turnover-reduction programs. (It would be likely that any costs considered would still understate the actual costs.)

Table 2 Relevant Turnover Cost Components

RECRUITMENT	SELECTION AND PLACEMENT	ON-THE-JOB ACTIVITIES	SEPARATION
1) Advertising	1) Letter of application	1) Putting person on the job	1) Exit interview
2) College recruiting	2) Application blanks	2) Safety or working equipment	2) Severance pay
3) Employment agency fees	3) Interviewing ■ Personnel department ■ Line managers	3) Indoctrination and on-the-job training	3) Extra Social Security
4) Literature ■ Brochures ■ Pamphlets	4) Medical examinations	4) Formal training programs ■ Waste of materials	4) Extra U.I.C. (unemployment)
5) Employee prizes and awards	5) Reference checking	5) Break-in ■ Increased production ■ Increased supervision ■ Increased maintenance ■ Increased accidents	5) Reduced productivity ■ Increased waste of materials ■ Increased maintenance ■ Loss in productivity of exiting employee ■ Loss in productivity of colleagues ■ Increased accidents
6) Public relations activities	6) Psychological testing		
	7) Applicant's travel expenses ■ Actual travel ■ Reservations ■ Conducted tours		
	8) Personnel department overhead		

The Determination of Measurable and Unmeasurable Turnover Costs

As mentioned previously, some costs are extremely clear-cut and easy to measure, such as costs for advertising specific management positions and for administration of psychological or skill tests. Other costs are not so obvious (e.g., the cost of management time used in interviewing prospective candidates). The cost of things such as the level of productivity of the individual is even more difficult to measure. Is it acceptable to simply assume the salary as the cost, or should attempts be made to measure the cost of lost production during the learning period? Are both "real" costs, or would it be double-counting to include both? Some effects of turnover are very subtle, and the resulting costs are thus difficult to determine. For example, it can be argued that turnover rates affect morale and that there is a real and significant cost to low morale. If the topic of conversation is not, "How are things going?" but "When are you going to leave?" then turnover begins generating further turnover. This in turn leads to more recruitment costs, which add to the problem. In one firm where turnover rates were over 200% per year, it was evident that turnover did breed more turnover with significant further costs (Boydell, 1975).

The Determination of Controllable vs. Uncontrollable Turnover

In calculating turnover costs and making related decisions, it is important to consider only the turnover that results from controllable factors. Table 3 outlines some of the reasons for turnover and classifies them as controllable or uncontrollable.

Clearly, management cannot and would not want to eliminate all turnover within the firm. Like it or not, many turnovers are unavoidable: people retire, people become ill, people leave for family and personal reasons which are beyond the control of those in the firm. However, some categories of turnover are more controllable than others. For example, management has some control over the nature of the work, the working conditions, supervision and wages. Turnover for these reasons is at least partially controllable.

The Calculation of Total Turnover Costs

Once the turnover rate is established, the cost per turnover is specified in measurable terms, and the component of avoidable turnover is identified, then the total turnover costs can be calculated simply. (The total cost of

Table 3 Controllable* and Uncontrollable Turnover Categories**

Controllable Categories
Secured other job
Returned to school
Nature of work
Working conditions
Wages

Uncontrollable Categories
Pension
Health
Deceased
Family reasons

Not Classified
Discharge
Personal reasons
Housing conditions

* Controllable here means that the company could
have a major influence over whether the individual
leaves. Thus, "returned to school" is controllable in
that the company might entice the employee to stay.
"Pension" is uncontrollable in that once the company
has an established plan, people will leave the
company according to that schedule.

** These classifications have been derived from exit
interviews.

---

avoidable turnover, incidentally, is the number of avoidable turnovers times the cost per turnover.)

In many cases, it is possible and valuable to calculate "standard costs" of turnover. This figure, if accepted by management, provides an average figure of the normal cost per turnover, as well as a quick and easy way of estimating possible savings that might result from reductions in the turnover rate. These standard cost figures can be updated periodically and are also valuable information for the control system described below.

CONTROLLING LABOR TURNOVER COSTS

Once labor turnover costs are measured, how can they be used for control purposes? The basic idea is to prepare projections of labor turnover for various positions, work groups or divisions. These figures are then used to impute projected costs. Labor turnover budgets are prepared (using the standard costs of a turnover), and later the actual figures are compared to the projected and budgeted figures.

The sample form demonstrates how monthly control information can be summarized. The information in this format serves several functions. Its first is to impress upon the responsible person the costs associated with labor turnover and the need to lower these costs. The direct association of the costs to a department or division induces further pressure to do something about them. Of course, the responsible managers do not have complete control over the variables which affect labor turnover, but they frequently have more influence than they, and others, realize.

The second function of the control form is to specify and document an agreed-upon budget. The budget is established through a process of negotiation with the responsible person. The current projections are then used as a framework for establishing some kind of target, which must be reasonable and attainable for the budget to have true meaning. Care must be taken to assure that the responsible manager does not overestimate his or her ability to lower costs. Next, the total budget is broken down into monthly expectations. This breakdown, along with the current monthly projections, provides a benchmark for monitoring the effect of any subsequent changes which are designed to influence turnover.

The final function is the actual monitoring. Each month, the number of departures is recorded according to the reason for termination, and the associated actual costs are calculated. The actual costs can then be compared to the budget. The responsible manager can easily record this information, thereby monitoring his or her own progress. This monitoring can subsequently lead to actions to reduce turnover levels to some optimum. This optimal level is a delicate balance at which turnover costs are minimized while still allowing a sufficient flow of new employees with fresh skills, talents and creativity. In other words, total cost minimization is not the desired objective—some level of labor turnover is both necessary and desirable.

THE RESPONSIBLE MANAGER

In decentralized organizations with established profit centers, the turnover budget should be assigned directly to the line manager as part of his or her overall budget. By including turnover costs as part of this budget, the line manager is more likely to work toward the best possible system.

Example of a Monthly Labor Turnover Control Form

LABOR TURNOVER CONTROL

Responsibility: T.P. Bettison
Average Work Force — 310
Current T.O. Rate — 6.3/mos.; 75.6/yr.
Current T.O. Cost — $44,372/mos.; $532,465/yr.

Job Classification — Plant Operators

Cost Components:		
(1) Separation	$	80
(2) Hiring		427
(3) Training		438
(4) Adjustment		123
(5) Lost Production		432
(6) Lost Productivity		272
Total		$2,272

Month	Current Projection		Budget		Actual Number					Actual Cost		Comments
	No.	Cost	No.	Cost	Quits	Dismissal	Layoff	Other	Total	Amount	% of Budget	
Jan.	23	52,256	18	40,896	14	2			16	36,352	88.8	
Feb.	14	31,808	10	22,720	7	1			8	18,176	80.0	
March	18	40,896	16	36,352	13			2	15	34,080	93.7	
April	15	34,080	11	24,992	11	1		1	13	29,536	118.2	
May	20	45,440	16	36,352	13	1	20		34	33,408	91.9	Only separation costs occur for the 20 layoffs.
June	15	34,080	11	24,992	5	2			7	15,904	63.6	
July	13	29,536	10	22,720	5				5	11,360	50.0	
Aug.	29	65,888	24	54,528	13	2		2	17	38,624	70.8	
Sept.	26	59,072	21	47,712								
Oct.	22	49,984	18	40,896								
Nov.	20	45,440	17	38,624								
Dec.	18	40,896	15	34,080								
TOTAL	233	529,376	187	424,864								

From the perspective of the personnel manager, making the line manager responsible has some additional benefits. Personnel managers are usually well aware of the costs and problems of labor turnover, but they are seldom in a position to directly influence or introduce corrective action. Most frequently, the personnel manager is placed in an advocacy position of having to urge line managers to try to reduce turnover. All too frequently, such actions lead to accusations that the personnel department is meddling in the affairs of others and overstepping its advisory role. But if line managers were made responsible for turnover costs, then the need to advocate would reverse. They would then seek out the personnel manager for help, particularly if they have gone over budget, thus giving him or her a much more significant role.

Finally, whether turnover responsibility is decentralized or centralized, the personnel department should still maintain labor turnover control forms similar to the one above. Aggregations of control forms for separate departments or divisions will provide progress information on turnover control for the entire organization. The personnel department can then give feedback to each department, comparing its turnover to the firm's overall record. In addition, the detailed cases of particularly successful departments can be presented as examples for others. Corporate managers understand and are influenced by such figures. If human relations managers want to increase their credibility, then they will have to start incorporating such statistics in their project proposals, an objective means of communication that will help earn them the respect of corporate management.

BIBLIOGRAPHY

Algar, R.D. Personal communications.

Boydell, Gary. "International Nickel Company of Canada." Case study, University of Western Ontario, London, Canada, 1975.

Cawsey, T.F., Lord,R.J., and Kudar, R. "Turnover: Symptom or Disease?" Working paper *Response to the A.I.B.* The University of Western Ontario, 1976.

Cawsey, T.F., Lord, R.J., and Kudar, R. "Turnover: Symptom or Disease?" Working paper No. 162, The University of Western Ontario, May 1976.

Cawsey, T.F. and Richardson, P. "Turnover Can Be Managed." *The Business Quarterly* 40 (Winter 1975): 57-63.

Cawsey, T.F. and Richardson, P. *Labour Turnover in the Mining Industries: A Summary of Course Practices.* Working paper No. 153, University of Western Ontario, 1975a.

Dominion Bureau of Statistics, Labour Division. *Hiring and Separation Rates in Certain Industries,* 72-006. March–August 1966, June 1968.

Economic Council of Canada. *People and Jobs—a Study of the Canadian Labour Market.* Ottawa: Information Canada, 1976.

Financial Post, April 10, 1976.

Fricker, R. "Cominico Limited (Trail)." Case study, University of Western Ontario, 1976.

Globe and Mail, July 7, 1976.

Grubel, H.G., Maki, D., and Sax, S. "Real and Insurance Induced Unemployment in Canada." *Canadian Journal of Economics,* May 1975, pp. 174-191.

Mackasey, B. "No Proof that UIC Abused." *The Financial Post,* March 16, 1974, p. 6.

MacMillian, J.A., Tulloch, J.R., O'Brien, D., and Ahmad, M.A. *Determinants of Labour Turnover in Canadian Mining Communities.* University of Manitoba, 1974.

McIntosh, G.M. *A Conference on Getting and Holding Manpower in Northwestern Ontario.* Atikokan, Ontario: Quetico Centre, May 1975.

Mining Association of Canada. *Labour Turnover and Shortages in the Canadian Mining Industry: Principal Statistics of the Problem.* Ottawa, Canada: Mining Association of Canada, August 1974.

Muir, J.D. "Unemployment Insurance Proposals—Insurance or More Welfarism?" *The Canadian Personnel and Industrial Relations Journal,* 18 (March 1971): 24-29.

Nickson, M. *Geographic Mobility in Canada, October 1964-October 1964,* [sic] Special Labour Force Studies No. 4. Ottawa: Dominion Bureau of Statistics, April 1967.

Pinfield, L.T. and Hoyt, G.C. *A Systems Analysis of the Impact of Increases in Labour Turnover.* Discussion paper 74-6-3, Simon Fraser University, 1974.

Portis, Bernard. *Reducing Labour Turnover in the Canadian Show Industry.* London, Canada: University of Western Ontario, 1976.

Ross, P.S. and Partner. *A Study of Manpower in the Logging and Sawmilling Industry of British Columbia.* Vancouver, B.C., 1973.

Vanderkamp, J. *Mobility Behavior in Canadian Labour Force,* Special Study No. 16. Economic Council of Canada, February 1973.

Wedley, William C. *Community and Corporate Development in the Pemberton Valley,* a report prepared for the Pemberton Valley Labour Force Development Committee, October 1975.

Wedley, William C. and Fulton, Sandy M. *Turnover Reduction Through Foreman Involvement in the Selection Process.* Working paper no. 151, The University of Western Ontario, 1975.

Woodward, Robert S. "The Capital Bias of DREE Incentives." *The Canadian Journal of Economics,* August 1974b pp. 501-510.

Woodward, Robert S. "Effective Location Subsidies: An Evaluation of DREE Industrial Incentives." *The Canadian Journal of Economics,* August 1974b, pp. 501-510.

Zimmerman, T. "The True Cost of Turnover." *Management of Personnel Quarterly,* Summer 1971.

13. Controlling Absenteeism Can Help Curb Hospitals' Costs

SONYA M. SNYDER

Reprinted, with permission, from *Hospitals, Journal of the American Hospital Association,* vol. 52, no. 17, September 1, 1978, pp. 102-103.

Because of the high and increasing cost of health care, hospitals need to explore all avenues for reducing costs. Reducing absenteeism is one practical means of reducing expenses. Most supervisors realize that absenteeism is a troublesome problem, but they rarely realize how costly it is. Absenteeism is costly because it involves excessive payment of overtime rates, decline in employee morale, and decreased productivity. Morale suffers and accuracy declines when employees have to double their work loads; the quality of patient care may decline; and the hospital may have to pay two and one-half salaries when it schedules an employee for overtime to cover the paid absence of another employee.

In order to reduce absenteeism costs, pertinent terms must be defined, accurate records must be kept, and costs and results must be measured.

Absence is any time away from scheduled work time, including tardiness and leaving early, but not including scheduled vacation time, holidays, jury duty, and so forth. This article will deal only with absences of at least one-half of a working day. The absenteeism rate is determined as follows:

$$\frac{\text{Number of days absent}}{\text{Number of days worked}} \times 100.$$

In computing the absenteeism rate, it is suggested that only the first five days of an extended absence be counted.

Absence frequency is the number of periods of absence. An employee who has 10 one-day absences presents a different problem than does an employee who has one absence of 10 days.

Paid sick time refers to absences for which employees are compensated by sick leave benefits. The cost of paid sick time is not the total cost of absenteeism; however, it is the one cost that can be substantiated and measured easily.

MANAGEMENT ROLE IN CONTROL

To effectively control absenteeism, it is necessary that management support a hospitalwide program that is applied in the same manner in each department. Supervisors should be held accountable for controlling absenteeism. They must know the hospital's policy on attendance and must ensure that their employees know the policy.

Attendance problems can be determined only by maintaining an accurate, separate record for each employee. The record should indicate for each absence the date, the day of the week, whether it occurs before or after a day off, and the specific reason. An employee's absence should be recorded immediately, and, if a problem pattern of absences appears, the employee should be counseled immediately. Supervisors should watch for frequent, short absences; absences on days before or after regular days off; absences after paydays; absences on the same day of the week or month; and other patterns.

When necessary, a supervisor must counsel and discipline an employee who has a problem pattern of absences. Discussion of the employee's problems that may be affecting his attendance may help to pinpoint solutions to these problems and enable the employee to correct the situation. For example, it may be necessary for the supervisor to insist that the employee obtain medical care. Counseling often will help an employee improve his attendance record; however, if chronic absenteeism continues, firm discipline is required. Suspension or discharge may be necessary.

For example, at Copley Memorial Hospital, Aurora, IL, a nurse assistant had a bad attendance record for about seven years. In February and in June 1976, she finally received written warnings about her excessive absenteeism and tardiness. A period of good attendance followed each warning before absences and tardiness recurred. In September, this employee received a five-day suspension. Her attendance has been excellent since the suspension. She probably will need periodic reminders about her attendance, but she now is a better employee in that she can be depended on to carry her work load as scheduled.

A paid sick leave program sometimes offers employees incentive to take extra days off with pay. It is important that employees be informed that such misuse of sick leave is cause for discipline.

Some hospitals have eliminated that incentive by implementing sick leave programs that do not pay employees for the first one or two days of absences. This type of program helps to curb one-day or two-day absences that are abuses. However, it can have a negative effect on conscientious employees. This problem could be alleviated by converting the unpaid days to paid days only for employees who have accumulated at least 15 sick leave days or whatever other limit seems appropriate.

Copley Memorial Hospital established a paid personal time (PPT) incentive. The sick leave plan allows accrual of up to 75 days. If an employee has accrued at least 24 days, he may use three days per calendar year as PPT. If an employee has accrued at least 50 days, he may use six days per year as PPT. PPT is subtracted from sick leave accrual, but it is not considered to be an absence unless it is unscheduled. It is provided to be used for family illnesses, medical appointments, and other personal business; however, it may be used for any reason as long as it is scheduled with supervisors' approvals.

HOSPITAL'S CONTROL PROGRAM

According to the hospital's records for all employees in 1975 and 1976, the hospital had an absenteeism rate of 3.9 percent, or 10 days per year per full-time equivalent employee. In 1976, sick pay was $221,631.20, or more than $250 per full-time equivalent employee. According to various sources, including the Bureau of National Affairs, which has surveyed more than 300 companies and which publishes quarterly reports, the median absenteeism rate for American industry was 3.0 percent for both 1975 and 1976.[1] All of this information indicated that the hospital could make some substantial reductions in its absenteeism rate and its sick pay. Consequently, it began an absence control program.

At a seminar, all supervisors discussed the absenteeism problem, their expectations regarding reducing absences, and the revised sick leave program, including PPT. They also held meetings with all employees. In addition, supervisors held private conferences with each employee to discuss the employee's attendance record. The discussion was documented. Any employee who had five or more absences in the past year was scheduled for a follow-up conference to be held four months later. Each employee's absence record also is reviewed during the employee's annual evaluation for a merit increase, and the record affects the amount of the increase. A poor record could cause the employee to be placed on probation and could delay any increase.

Two months after these meetings, the hospital began to keep detailed statistics on each department's absenteeism rate. A monthly attendance honor roll bulletin that listed all departments with absenteeism rates of 2.6 percent or less was distributed, an honor roll poster was displayed near the cafeteria, and departments received recognition for each month that they were listed on the honor roll. The absence control program rapidly achieved improvement. The absenteeism rate dropped from 3.9 percent in 1975 and 1976 to 2.1 percent or less for the last seven months of 1977. Had the 1977 sick pay continued at the 1976 rate, the hospital would have paid an additional $64,000 in 1977. Instead, allowing for $30,000 of PPT to offset this $64,000, a savings of $34,000 in sick pay was achieved.

SUMMARY

A program to reduce absenteeism can achieve considerable savings in payroll expenses, can improve employee morale, and can improve patient care. The key to success is management's concern and the first-line supervisors' efforts to keep employees informed about management's expectations regarding attendance. Moreover, the policies must be fair and must be administered with consistency from department to department.

NOTES

1. Bureau of National Affairs. *Bulletin to Management.* Washington, DC: BNA, Mar. 11, 1976, and Feb. 24, 1977.

14. Health Care Cost Containment Through Fringe Benefit Management*

EFRAIM TURBAN

INTRODUCTION

Fringe benefits play an important role in the health facility personnel system. Their primary objective is to attract and motivate competent employees. They are used as incentives for greater productivity and for employee loyalty. Despite their importance many health care institutions do not always manage them properly, resulting in much waste. The purpose of this paper is to briefly survey what these benefits are and then to suggest a framework for their efficient management.

THE MAGNITUDE AND IMPORTANCE OF FRINGE BENEFITS

The value of fringe benefits in health care facilities ranges from 20 to 50 percent of a total compensation package. For example, in Tabaka's article[14] it is shown that for an annual base salary of $9,000 there is additional $3,594 in benefits (39.8%). Based on the experience of the last 20 years, benefits are increasing at a much faster rate than either salaries or the consumer price index. It is conceivable that by 1985 benefits could cost an employer as much as 68 percent of the total compensation package. As the health care industry is highly labor-intensive, labor cost (and consequently fringe benefits cost) amounts to a major portion of the facility operating expense.

---

*This article is based in part on a paper written by Sandra Sparber at Florida International University.

In any cost containment program one should look at fringe benefits not only because of their magnitude and increasing rate, but also because they are usually mismanaged. There are 25 to 50 different benefits which may be managed by several individuals in several different departments.

One important reason for proper management of fringe benefits is the fact that a large portion of their expense is fixed in nature. That is, while savings in hours worked reduce the base wages, the fringe benefits are not reduced proportionally, but much less than that.

Finally, in addition to the cost of the benefits themselves, there is the additional cost of managing them. Record keeping, computer time, publications and legal fees are some of the functions that are necessary for managing benefits.

Fringe benefits are treated here in five major categories: legal requirements, insurances, pension plans, payments for time not worked and service-oriented benefits.

LEGALLY REQUIRED BENEFITS

There are three major benefits that are required by law: social security (FICA), unemployment benefits and workmen's compensation. The FICA rates are determined by the government and cannot be economized upon. With respect to unemployment benefits there are several available options. The cost here is greatly dependent on the turnover rate, a topic discussed in an earlier paper.

Considering unemployment benefits, the hospitals have the option of being a directly reimbursable employer, i.e., paying claims only, or of being insured (paying a percentage of the payroll). In the former case, the hospital may insure itself (using an insurance company) against claims or use a self-insurance option. (See Chapter 5 for an analysis.) The cost to the employer may range from less than one percent up to five percent of the base salary.

Workmen's compensation can be administered in several ways. Self-insurance is one of them. A good risk management program (see Chapter 5) can contribute significantly to savings in this area.

INSURANCE

The following items are included in this category:

- Health (sickness) insurance
- Accident insurance
- Life insurance

- Disability insurance
- Dental insurance
- Major medical insurance
- Prepaid optical benefit
- Prepaid legal services

The benefits in this section may cost four to eight percent of the base salary. As far as the various types of insurance are concerned, the health care facility has the option of being self-insured, joining a group insurance plan, or joining an HMO (available now in some areas even for dental work). The best way to contain costs here is to do a proper insurance analysis and to make the deductible amount as large as possible. Employee health education may contribute to cost containment efforts in this area. Shopping around and negotiating may result in substantial savings.

For major considerations of insurance options see Tabaka's article.[14]

PENSION PLANS

Various types of pension plans exist in health institutions. While retirement plans are relatively new to the industry, they are spreading quickly.

Pension plans may be arranged through an insurance company, may be self-managed, or may be managed by some pension group. Costs can be contained through a careful analysis of the plans' management (using competitive bidding if not self-managed). A pension plan can be used to reduce turnover by having the plan vested in the employee only after a certain period of employment (e.g., 5 years).

Considerations such as an early retirement option, the possibility of a lump sum benefit payment and eligibility for inclusion in the plan (e.g., the employee must be with the institution at least one year), can lead to additional savings.

PAYMENTS FOR TIME NOT WORKED

Payments for time not worked can easily amount to 20 percent of the base wages. They include holidays, sick leave, vacations, severance pay, coffee and lunch breaks, jury or military duty pay, paying for time used for education (training, school, attendance at professional meetings) and leave of absence without pay.

Cost can be contained in several of these areas: for example, making sure that employees do not extend their breaks, checking upon the real importance of professional meetings, limiting the time off that can be taken for school.

Sick leave is one of the most abused areas. It is strongly related to absenteeism. Some of the methods that are used to curb absenteeism will reduce the abuse of sick leave, too. For example, a lottery system can be used in which any employee who did not miss a work day in a given month is eligible to participate in that month's lottery. Then, those who did not take sick leave in one year participate in that year's large prize lottery (such as a trip for two to Europe). Some hospitals allow accrued sick leave (or a portion of it) to be used towards early retirement. Others will allow a portion of the unused sick leave to be paid at retirement time as a lump sum.

SERVICE-ORIENTED BENEFITS

The last category of benefits is the longest one. It includes items such as: free parking, uniform allowance, drug discounts, longevity pay, free annual physical examinations, day care centers, discounted meals, tuition reimbursement, employee parties, holiday gifts or bonuses, birthday gifts, mileage reimbursement, credit union membership, food items sold at discount in the facility, discounts for goods in various stores in the community.

Some of these benefits cost very little or even nothing. However, when you add them all together, they can total 10 percent or more of the base salary, plus the cost of their management. In general, costs may be contained here by shopping around for the least expensive suppliers, by giving such benefits only to employees who have served in the health facility longer than a year and by controlling the use of these benefits.

CONCLUSION

Fringe benefits are necessary components of a compensation package. Because of income tax considerations there is a tendency to increase fringe benefits faster than salary and wages. The monetary value of the benefits is rapidly increasing, amounting to anywhere between 20 to 50 percent of the base wage and salary.

Proper management of fringe benefits may result in a substantial contribution to cost containment. For benefits to be cost effective, the following steps are recommended:

    a. Centralize all benefits under a benefit manager.
    b. Put a dollar value on the benefits, and constantly compare it to benefits offered by area facilities.

c. Conduct an annual detailed community fringe benefit survey, similar to a salary survey.

d. Consider the option of self-insurance as well as other insurance options.

e. Be very careful in determining eligibility. Since most benefits are not directly related to output or productivity, longevity of service, loyalty and productivity (whenever possible) should be considered in eligibility decisions.

f. Stop abuse of certain fringes.

g. Attach a clear dollar value to all negotiated benefits during labor negotiations.

Every benefit program must be properly managed. Too much concern for containing costs may hurt the facility's competitive ability to attract competent employees. Spending more than necessary means cash flow problems, high costs, possible benefits abuse, and it is just a waste of money.

REFERENCES AND BIBLIOGRAPHY

1. Bakker, A.J., et. al., "Employee Benefits: A National Survey," *Medical Group Management* 22, p. 8, Jan. 1975.

2. Batemen, J.M., "Nursing Staff, Annual Leave and Public Holidays," *Health Soc. Service*, J 3, 1976.

3. Birky, K.R., "Self-insuring Workers' Compensation: Does It Really Save?" *Topics in Health Care Financing*, Summer 1977.

4. Boffa, J. and Burek, M., "Financial Projection in Prepaid Dental Care Plans," *Health Care Management Review* 2:59, Winter 1977.

5. Farrell, Richard, "Compensation Benefits," *Personnel Journal*, November 1976.

6. Finefort, F.C., "A New Look at Occupational Safety," *The Personnel Administrator*, November 77, Vol. 23.

7. Hanna, J.B., "Can the Challenge of Evaluating Benefit Costs Be Met?" *The Personnel Administrator*, November 1977.

8. Hauge, J., "Employees' Wages and Benefits," *Hospitals*, June 16, 1977.

9. Pilenzo, Ron, "Compensation Going Beyond the Dollar Sign," *The Personnel Administrator*, Sept. 1977.

10. "Reduction in Health Care Employee Benefit Fund—Ordered," (N.Y. Health Employee Union Package) *Hospitals*, May 16, 1977.

11. Steinforth, A.W., "Factors and Forces Influencing Pension Plan Costs," *Topics in Health Care Financing*, Summer 1977.

12. Schultz, Richard, "Benefit Trends," *The Personnel Administrator*, Sept. 1977.

13. Sutton, H.L., Jr., "HMO—Can It Help Employers Control Exploding Health Care Benefits Costs?" *Employee Relation Law*, Spring 1977.

14. Tabaka, A.V., "Are Your Fringe Benefits a Good Buy?" *Hospital Purchasing Management,* July 1977.

15. Cost Effective Human Resource Development in Health Care

JAN MARGOLIS

The term human resource development (HRD) was coined as recently as 1971 or '72 and many managers today still use terms like "human productivity" or "employee motivation" to describe its activities. It is not a theory and it's not a scientific concept. It is a catchall term, like mental health or community medicine, encompassing a wide range of organizational processes, structure and functions which contribute to organizational productivity and employee satisfaction.

Our hospital's management sees HRD as focused on the managing and developing of human resources at work. Its activities deal with planned change in the work itself and with the realignment of task-decision structures. It involves a wide range of subfields from the organizational and behavioral sciences such as manpower planning, career development, professional and technical training, and organizational development.

Effective human resource development should not be seen as something that can be merely delegated to an HRD department and forgotten. Rather, human resources development is a continuous process which starts with and is led by the chief executive officer (CEO). The CEO is the central link in bringing about organizational improvement. For example, because the CEO is a model, the top model, for the rest of the organization, a negative chaotic leadership climate in the top team will spread to the rest of the organization. He or she is shaping the way in which power and authority are used in the organization. When the CEO develops a positive and productive work culture within his or her own team, subordinates will do the same within their work units, and the subordinates' subordinates will do the same. It links down through the organization.

For example, four years ago we had a total top-management change in our hospital. The climate of the hospital was negative; top-management leadership had been weak and negative; employees had little pride in their work and the hospital was developing a reputation as an institution that really didn't provide quality patient care.

- Attrition in the nursing staff was 32 per cent. Considering that it costs $1,018 to recruit one registered nurse and $850 for orientation, the high attrition was extremely expensive.
- Absenteeism was very high.
- Grievances were averaging 15 a year.
- Patient complaints were averaging 65 per cent.
- Loss from our inventory and distribution systems for linen alone was averaging $40,000 a month.
- Morale was poor.

Clearly, productivity was at a very low ebb. What to do? Three years ago, our CEO began to build a human resource management system which has resulted in significant cost savings to the hospital and there is every indication that it has contributed greatly to the improved quality of patient care. This resulted in...

- Attrition among RNs dropping from 32 per cent to 12 per cent in two years and the YTD is averaging six per cent.
- Absenteeism (or call-ins) averaging about four or five a day.
- Grievances dropping from 12–15 yearly to two during 1976.
- Recent diagnostic studies indicate morale is high and that the majority of employees at all levels now feel they are a contributing part of a growing, innovative, dynamic institution. This pride is reflected in a variety of ways—from the employees' freedom to suggest improvements to the intangible expression of professionalism in the behavior and dress of the employees and their concern for the appearance of the physical plant.

WHAT HAPPENED?

What happened? The CEO had a dream and made his dream a reality. He assembled a competent, high-powered top-management team and introduced the concept of "human resource management." An interdisciplinary group of 12 professionals was formed into an HRD unit for the purpose of supporting the CEO and all other levels of management in their efforts to meet organizational goals and objectives through the effective management of its people, its technology, and the organizational processes that help workers communicate and apply their knowledge and skills to their jobs.

To support the concept of role modeling, six well-respected line managers were brought into the department to work with six OD trainer, clinical, consultative types. And we set about our job of supporting the CEO in his renewal of the hospital.

My intention is to present three concepts central to the development of a cost effective human resource management system; to briefly outline our model and lastly to cite our evaluation procedures to measure our impact on quality care and cost savings to the hospital. In considering human resource development in a hospital, for example, we must be aware that we are dealing with a system which is in dynamic interaction with the community it serves.

Indeed, we are dealing not with an organization in isolation, but a complex social system.

ENVIRONMENTAL PRESSURES

Significantly impacting on the hospital system are a variety of environmental factors. For our purposes here, I will focus on those factors specifically relating to the developing and managing of human resources.

1. The complexity and specialization of medical technology necessitates a labor-intensive industry. Ongoing advancements in medical technology require larger and larger numbers of trained health-care personnel to operate the sophisticated facilities required to support this technology. As a result, 57.5 per cent of all hospital expense is personnel.
2. The *obsolescence rate* of all employee classifications is accelerating (professional, technical, service and maintenance).
3. Increased social pressures and federal pressures for Civil Rights and Affirmative Action compliance have mandated the fuller utilization of minorities and women in the work force. Consequently, many health-care institutions are investing heavily into upward mobility programs and training of minorities for jobs at all levels of the occupational ladder.
4. The national trend toward boredom or alienation among workers is often reflected in increases in absenteeism, turnover, alcoholism and

drug abuse. The Ford Foundation reports that there are now more people in the adult labor force with at least one year of college than there are higher-level jobs to absorb them.

"Dead-End Careers"

Many hospital workers are bumping into dead-end careers. They enter technical jobs typically that have only two levels—technician or chief technician. Unfortunately, most institutions do not aggressively develop people from within to assume larger or more diversified areas of responsibility. Health institutions tend to hire for specialized or supervisory and managerial positions predominately (sic) from the outside.

5. The consumer demand for cost containment is increasing. It is significant to note that national expenditures for health care quadrupled from $25.9 billion in 1960 to $104.2 billion in 1974.
6. Quality assurance and mandatory continuing education: Because of the need to continually update clinical knowledge as well as the procedural changes that typically accompany new technologies, many accrediting and licensing bodies require mandatory continuing education units for accreditations and for licensure.

For example, the Joint Commission on Hospital Accreditation requires that hospitals have certain education programs such as for the anesthesia services, nursing, nuclear medicine, medical records and various special-care units.

The issue of mandatory continuing education is made even more complex because of pressures from our third-party payors. For example, Medicare will not reimburse for laboratory costs if our pathology department is not accredited by the College of American Pathologists and/or the Center for Disease Control in Atlanta. These regulators require a certain amount of training, continuing education, licensure, certification and experience for the technologists.

Consequently, financial reimbursement to the hospital from one party (in this example it's Medicare) is dependent upon accreditation from two other parties (College of American Pathologists and CDC) which is dependent upon mandatory continuing education for professional staff in order for them to maintain their licenses!

FOCUS OF HRD

What HRD specifically focuses on in a hospital (or any other system are the core processes by and through which resources (money, facilities, people) are developed and managed.

The *goals* of a system usually emanate from the organization's mission statement. The interrelationship of various levels of goals and objectives is typically an area of considerable tension in organizations. The application of HRD technology can help managers manage these conflicts creatively and constructively.

The *technology* and the tasks of an organization are direct results of the organization's goals. For example, the actual tasks required to care for a surgical patient are highly dependent upon the technological systems that are available.

Organizational structure is influenced by the technology as well and concepts of task groupings such as units, departments and divisions. How these task groupings relate to one another constitutes the design of the work flow.

The *human social system,* the employees, are influenced by four things: their own skills and abilities as workers; the management style and philosophy of their superiors and the superior's superiors; the formal personnel system (such as staffing, rewards, performance reviews, and collective bargaining) and the informal norms of their work group.

These four core processes or subsystems are in a dynamic balance with one another. Change in one system will likely impact on another. For example, a technological improvement such as switching from a manual to a computerized on-line admitting system in our hospital significantly impacted on the design of jobs and work flow of people in three separate departments—not to mention the change in skills required to do the job.

HUMAN RESOURCES MANAGEMENT MODEL

We believe we have pioneered in the development of a human resource management model which effectively helps to manage these core processes. Our model deals with three critical properties of human resource management: development, utilization and engineering:

1. Human Resource Development: (Focuses on the human-social system of the organization.) Activities include:

- *Career development* (counseling; career planning; educational and occupational referral services; tuition assistance)
- *Staff development* or continuing education (clinical skill training to either maintain, advance or refresh current skill levels; new product usage; interpersonal skill development; in-house Bachelor and Associate Degree Programs in Nursing)

- *Upward Mobility programs* (GED; secretarial training; medical secretarial training)
- *Orientation processes* (new employee training; new graduate internship; RN refresher training)
- *Pre-Supervisory assessment programs* (assuring an internal supply of competent managerial candidates for promotion whenever vacancies occur)

2. Human Resource Utilization (Traditional Personnel Function): (Focuses on the human-social system and the structural system. In large hospitals like ours where so many of our administrative procedures are computerized, this aspect of human resource management is very affected by the sophistication of the technological system.) Activities include:

- Staffing (assignment, transfer, promotion, separation)
- Rewards (incentive programs, financial rewards, etc.)
- Appraisal (performance review)
- Labor relations
- Grievance systems
- Benefits program
- Wage and salary administration
- Recruitment of new employees
- Payroll administration

3. Human Resource Engineering: (Focuses on all the systems, especially goals, structure and tasks): Activities include:

- Industrial Engineering: (staffing patterns, inventory systems, supply systems, materials management)
- Organizational Development: (a planned process of applying a set of concepts and values, utilizing a definable technology, in order to optimize the attainment of organizational and individual objectives)

  OD technology includes interventions such as team-building, process consultation, role clarification, training, management by objectives, etc., and is applied after a period of diagnosis and linkage to organizational resources available to help solve problems. Most OD technology deals with improving the "processes" by which people relate to one another and work together such as the design of jobs, structure of reporting relationships, communication patterns (formal or informal) and clarity of roles. Its purposes are growth of people; to foster an open problem-solving work climate; to improve methods of conflict resolution and to develop more effective collaboration among functional groups.

- *Manpower Planning* (a sophisticated technology for facilitating the effective placement of people within the organization): Manpower planning provides management with the criteria for determining whether particular training or development needs exist; with a way of identifying available manpower supplies and projected shortages; and provides direction for outside recruitment programs. For example, at our hospital we are developing computerized educational and skill inventories for all employee classifications. We are developing many of our training activities from needs identified by the plan.

Whether the three functions of human resource management development, utilization and engineering should be housed within a single corporate entity or spread into strategic parts of the organization (i.e., separate training department, personnel department, industrial engineering department, OD department, etc.) is a decision best determined by the size and management style of the organization. However, if they are separated, some "linking-pin" mechanism must be in place to assure overall manpower coordination.

In considering the management of human resources, let's not forget that we are not many years ahead of the time when business economics was centered on capital to the neglect of the human factor in production. Over the last decade, we have seen the importance of the human resource factor increasingly stressed. In proposing the ideas I've stressed here we know that an enormous gap still exists between what is and what we still must do to manage our human resources effectively. The building blocks must be shaped and assembled, one at a time.

We seek to create organizational environments where people won't have to stand up and be counted. They will count—and that will make all the difference.

16. Using B Mod to Motivate and Train Hospital Employees

M. WAYNE ALEXANDER

Reprinted with permission from the November 1977 issue of TRAINING, The Magazine of Human Resources Development. Copyright Lakewood Publications, Minneapolis, MN (612) 333-0471. All rights reserved.

Hospital administrators and supervisors face the same employee-related "human" problems as their counterparts in other industries. Such problems as accidents, low productivity, absenteeism, turnover, and inefficiency plague us also.

Take the example of Nurse Jones, an otherwise competent night shift RN, who often fails to measure and record the blood pressure of pre-operative patients before she goes home in the mornings. Her supervisor has instructed her to do so, but she "forgets," or "doesn't have time." To the supervisor this behavior, or rather the absence of it, is undesirable. It means the patient is not ready for surgery at the appropriate hour, the surgeons are inconvenienced, and the routine is broken. How can the supervisor motivate Nurse Jones to regularly monitor and record the blood pressure of all preoperative patients before she completes her shift? Should Nurse Jones be punished for forgetting? Should she be sent to a memory course?

Using the behavior modification approach, the supervisor can reinforce appropriate blood pressure-taking behavior. By reinforcing the desired activity, the frequency with which it is performed will increase. If Jones' supervisor comments favorably and pays attention to her when she correctly monitors and records blood pressure, the tendency for this activity to occur will increase. If the consequence of the behavior is no reinforcer, or punishment, the behavior will diminish in frequency. In other words, if monitoring blood pressure results in making Nurse Jones late for her carpool—if it is punishing to her—she will not do it.

141

REINFORCE IMMEDIATELY

Administering a reinforcer at the proper time is crucial to the effectiveness of behavior modification. Reinforcement must *immediately* follow a behavioral response if it is to be effective. The timing is extremely important because delay in presenting the reinforcer can cause the wrong behavior to be reinforced. Praising Nurse Jones for her correct vital-signs monitoring behavior will be effective if she has just completed that behavior. However, if she has finished that and is now drinking a cup of coffee, the coffee-drinking response could be reinforced instead. A reinforcer given immediately following a correct response is most likely to increase the frequency of that behavior.

MOTIVATING WITH PUNISHMENT

A punisher is anything which follows a response and decreases the frequency of that response. Why not punish Nurse Jones when her behavior deviates from the standard?

Punishing a response often causes the employee to avoid the punisher rather than to change behavior. The result can be absenteeism, tardiness, turnover, and accidents rather than an increase in the desired behavior.

Many of the motivational practices supervisors traditionally use—such as suspensions, forced layoffs, ridicule, and reduced pay—are punishers. Suppose an employee who is late to work three days in a row is threatened with a disciplinary layoff for one day if late again. To avoid the punisher, he or she eventually quits, and the organization is forced to find a replacement. It is much more desirable from everyone's standpoint to use positive reinforcement to modify behavior.

SCHEDULES OF REINFORCEMENT

A supervisor can't possibly trail an employee around administering positive reinforcement each time a correct behavior is exhibited. Fortunately, a response need not be continuously reinforced in order for it to be learned and maintained. Behavior can be reinforced on a random basis, much as a slot machine pays off, and still produce the desired response. This intermittent scheduling of reinforcement can be quite effective.

Supervisor Smith can reinforce Nurse Jones' behavior whenever it is observed. A "Good job, Jones" given at various times during the day will be sufficient to maintain a high frequency of the behavior it follows. A continuous schedule, where every correct response is reinforced, works best when the behavior is first being learned. Once learned, an intermittent schedule can be more effective than a continuous schedule in maintaining high levels of desired behavior.

17. Achievement Through Participatory Management: The Key to Survival

FRANK M. BRADEN

Reprinted with permission from *Hospital Pharmacy*, volume 13, July 1978, pp. 403-406.

One aspect of a pharmacy director's job is spending time to evaluate his or her functions as a manager. The pharmacy director must make an effort to periodically clear out the busy office of both projects and people. Do not feel guilty because you are doing "nothing." The individual must sit alone, and ask two basic questions: Why was I hired for this job? and even more important: Why does the hospital administration retain my services? A quip answer might be "because I am good at running a pharmacy," but before the feeling of security sets in, let's discuss what a pharmacy director's activities really entail.

Under the pharmacy director's leadership are areas such as interactions with physicians and nurses, ordering, stocking and dispensing of drugs, hiring, disciplining and discharging of staff and a multitude of other daily routine tasks. This would adequately describe a director's role, according to most job descriptions, but does it describe the role of a manager? Although the individual may be doing a reasonable job in the aforementioned functions, a manager should be hired and remain in his position primarily because of his or her ability to produce and achieve.

As an administrator, I look for the ability to accomplish in the people I hire. Hospitals need leaders who believe that "A manager's role is to improve on what exists and to create that which needs to be." The difference which sets a true manager apart from a person just filling a manager's position is his ability to be a creative thinker who can and does achieve.

One of the great modern day corporate leaders, Crawford Greenewalt, a chemist, worked his way up from the bottom to the corporation president of the DuPont Company. He states in his book, *The Uncommon Man* that: "A manager should be an uncommon man, a common everyday person who achieves, who does things and by so doing becomes uncommon."[1] Greenewalt's thesis is too simple for most job descriptions or management theoreticians to agree with, but it is the basis for that which makes a true manager. Management, by definition, must be the art and science of achieving innovative things. If it is not, we will never be able to withstand the devastating standards, criteria, and cost control demands set for implementation in the near future. Not only are we regulated on one side by the federal government and required to cut costs, but also on the other side by groups such as The Joint Commission on Accreditation of Hospitals who demand of us implementation of concepts that will exert tremendous cost pressures for years to come.

EXPANDING FUNCTIONS AND COST CONTAINMENT?

The field of pharmacy itself is in a state of flux and will remain so. A reading of the latest JCAH standards clearly indicates that sophisticated drug distribution systems (i.e., unit dose and IV admixture) must be implemented. Clinical pharmacy is also here, although many physicians may argue the point. The government has mandated that pharmacists play a major role in decision-making promoting rational drug therapy throughout the health care delivery system.

Hospital administrators need true managers—not simply people who fill out time cards and schedules—but people who are creative, and can cultivate innovative ideas that meet the needs of the institution more efficiently and effectively. In other words, hospitals need the "uncommon man."

According to a recent survey,[2] well over one-half of the American public demands a lowering of the spiraling costs of health care as well as increased service. The health care executive must, therefore, have managers who can be innovative and yet still be cost effective. Pharmacists must begin to use modern management practices. Doing so offers an aid in helping the department and the hospital survive these difficult times.

For those of you who feel there is no way you can increase your efficiency or effectiveness because you just don't know how, look again. There are always ways to improve. There are many techniques available, for instance, to increase management skills, and to make your department truly creative and innovative in terms of cost control.

PARTICIPATORY MANAGEMENT (PM)

The most rewarding and potentially the easiest technique to generate creative ideas is through the realization that people in your department may themselves have innovative thoughts. Certainly a true manager can't rely on himself alone to be all things to all people. One way to reach the goal of a creative department then is to get the staff involved. You must find ways to encourage them to use their creative powers to the betterment of your department. Involvement is not accomplished or felt by simply asking as you walk through the pharmacy, "How are things going today, Mary?", but by involving your personnel in the department's operation.

One method to obtain staff involvement is called Participatory Management (PM). PM can be defined as a management process that allows joint decision making by manager and employee, with concentration on where the department needs to be in the future, and how it plans to get there. Let me stress that Participatory Management does not mean that you allow your staff to dictate what they are going to do. It doesn't mean that you are soft on them or a "buddy" to them. In fact, management thought now asserts that a firm but fair manager is more effective than the "good friend" type. PM is a form of management that allows, under your leadership, and with your knowledge of the institution's overall goals, the setting of departmental standards and joint creation of achievement objectives.

Why then should your staff be involved in the department operation? The first reason, as stated, is that all people have ideas and many times the ideas are good and innovative. Second, even though you may be creative yourself, to achieve your creative ideas, you must be able to count on the support of the people affected by or involved in any new ideas or programs.

In starting a unit dose program, for example, if your staff, especially the supervisors, are involved in the inception, they will be committed to the program because of this involvement. A program will never be uncommon unless the people who are doing the actual work are totally committed to it. In fact, if employees are not dedicated to a program, their ego state does not rise or fall according to the program's success or failure. If their attitude is negative, no matter how good a program is, it is not going to work or be uncommon, because it is your program and not theirs.

How do you get people involved? How do you start participatory management in your department? First of all, by not being an inhibitor to your staff's ideas. When employees perceive you only as a person who says no, or a manager who always replies, "We better not do that this year, maybe later when we are not so busy," or "Let's not do that, it's too much work," they will stop suggesting creative ideas. As circumstances allow, these frustrated achievers are the people who will simply leave the organization.

Begin PM by asking your employees their opinions. Give them projects related to a new program and set realistic goals and objectives together. Put them on committees. If you have been an inhibitor in the past, change may take time, but it is the only way to make your department "uncommon."

PM IN UNIT DOSE IMPLEMENTATION

Let's look for a moment at how you might initiate a unit dose program using the participatory management approach. What should your first steps be? First, make sure your boss agrees to an evaluation of unit dose. Secondly, you must totally educate yourself and your entire staff concerning all aspects of the unit dose concept. Start discussing the advantages of unit dose with physicians, nurses, hospital administration, and all professional staff members. Third, set up meetings with your staff to define what has to be done. Also, at this point you must redouble your efforts to convince any staff members that remain hesitant regarding the advantages of implementing the concept. This can be accomplished by giving each person, including your reluctant staff, some aspect of the program to work on. You must set the final objectives to be reached within specific time frames. Constantly review their efforts and apply direction as needed. Above all, keep meeting as a group to allow for interaction of opinion and to allow a sounding board for program dissatisfaction.

Next, formulate the unit dose proposal. Prepare a report for both administration and nursing. Once the proposal is accepted, again set up groups within your staff to work on the implementation aspects. By all means include nursing staff in all your meetings. This is important especially at this point. Nursing personnel may have to be constantly reminded of the advantages, not only to the patient, but to themselves as well.

Once you begin implementation, keep your lines of communication open. Do this by having joint meetings of pharmacy, nursing, physicians and administration. At first glance, it may appear that implementing unit dose amounts mainly to having meetings. In actuality, meetings serve the purpose of allowing people to voice their opinions and concerns. Meetings bring criticism and complaints out into the open where they are discussed and acted upon, a better method than having the program sabotaged by people who are negative.

Implementing unit dose can be a traumatic event, but the use of PM can make it easier. Let me emphasize that participatory management does not demand, as is illustrated in this unit dose example, that you give up your rights as a manager. There are rights that you must maintain to keep the department moving in the direction in which your institution wishes. PM asks only that you involve your staff and that you realize that everybody can be uncommon and capable of creative thoughts. PM demands that you maintain the unsaid understanding that you are the final authority.

There are several systems that involve the use of PM. One of these is Management by Objectives. I will not go into a detailed description of how to implement an MBO program since many books and articles have been written covering the subject. Again, it is simply a management technique that is based on the participatory management approach that everybody can be an achiever if properly motivated.

IT IS GOING TO GET ROUGH

If I have not convinced you that being an achiever will set you apart and above pharmacy directors who are being replaced each year, let me re-emphasize that hospitals are receiving less and less reimbursement for their services. President Carter's proposed hospital cost containment act will dictate to hospital administrators what they can charge for services. It will limit the rate of increase for all charges to a maximum of 9% per year. While this may seem a reasonable figure when compared to the national cost of living increase which is estimated to be between six and eight per cent per year, it is actually five to seven per cent less than the hospital's actual cost increases. For example, the cost of pharmacy supplies this year has risen an average of 10%. The cost of some individual drugs has increased as much as 25%.

I could go further and mention many new expensive services offered by hospitals or the cost of malpractice insurance which has gone up, for many hospitals, over 500% in the past four years. Most of us, however, already know these figures. Stated bluntly, a nine per cent increase in hospital charges per year, without cost control of other segments of the industry, will not allow for the present level of hospital activity to continue. It is just not large enough.

What does this mean to the hospital pharmacy? If a nine per cent ceiling is placed on hospitals, it will demand the shrinking of services. Your administrator will not have a choice. He will have to begin to cut out—not the luxuries which were eliminated years ago, but the real backbone operations of the hospital. Pharmacy service is a high expense area which will most certainly come under scrutiny. Cost control by the government could, for example, lead to use of only generic equivalents in hospitals or drug discretion could be limited to the point that some drugs would be considered too expensive for general use. To help stop this encroachment, the pharmacy director must be cost effective and efficiency conscious.

In the future then, institutional administrators will have to look critically at individual departments such as pharmacy. The difficult decisions that administrators must make are related to cessation of programs and services. This, many times, includes replacing present managers with people who are willing to make "tough" decisions. Managers who can find ways to do the same work better, with less manpower or to implement new programs like unit dose or clinical pharmacy with a minimum of additional staff. These are the type of individuals that administrators require.

Your administrator does not have a choice. For his sake and for that of the patient he has to find techniques that are creative. His end results must be higher efficiency. If you want to be or remain part of the hospital management team, you must cultivate a creative department. It matters little if you make out schedules correctly or that you can fill prescriptions as fast or as well as your staff members. An administrator needs more. As Greenewalt states, he needs the "Uncommon Man."

REFERENCES

1. Greenewalt, C.: The Uncommon Man. New York, McGraw Hill, 1959.
2. Harris, L.: Poll published by Sentry Insurance Co., 1977.

RELATED READING

1. Carrol, S. J. and Tos, H. L.: Management By Objectives. New York, MacMillan, 1973.
2. Drucker, P. F.: Beyond the stick and carrot: hysteria over the work ethic. *Psychology Today*, 15:87–93 (Nov) 1973.
3. Drucker, P. F.: The Practice of Management. New York, Harper and Row, 1954.
4. Ford, R.: Motivation Through the Work Itself. New York, American Management Association, 1969.
5. Herzberg, F.: One more time: how do you motivate employees? *Harvard Business Review*, 46:53–62 (Jan–Feb) 1968.
6. Likert, R.: New Patterns of Management. New York, McGraw-Hill, 1961.
7. Locke, E. A.: Toward a Theory of Task and Motivational Incentives. *Organizational Behavior and Human Performance*, 42:157–189 (April) 1974.
8. McGregor, D.: The Human Side of Enterprise. New York, McGraw-Hill, 1960.
9. Sherwin, D. S.: Management of Objectives. *Harvard Business Review*, 54:149–160 (May–June) 1976.
10. Skinner, B. F.: Science and Human Behavior. New York, MacMillan, 1953.
11. Vroom, V.H.: Work and Motivation, New York, Wiley, 1964.

18. Man Hour Budgeting: A Refinement of Managerial Control

ALAN C. WHITTAKER AND STEPHEN L. HOLMES

Reprinted with permission from *Hospital Topics,* January/February 1976, pp. 14-16.

THE QUESTION OF ACCOUNTABILITY

These days, the word "accountability" is used abundantly to include, among other things, a multitude of sins allegedly being committed within the health care industry. In the hospital, more specifically, the term is directed toward innumerable situations. However, most of these so-called iniquities relate basically to the cost and quality of care as viewed by the patient and the general public.

This article describes a management tool which can be utilized to achieve a more efficient and effective operation and serve to enhance the accountability of the hospital for cost and quality of patient care.

THE LIMITS OF DOLLAR BUDGETING

Budgeting for revenue, expense and capital items is a requirement of every facility which participates in Medicare, Medicaid and with other third party payors, and which exercises any degree of what can be labeled good management.

"Dollar budgeting" does not provide for the type of control which is needed; inflationary factors, various regulations and technological changes eliminate it as a fixed standard. Dollar budgeting at this point in time can be described as a floating platform, adjusting to the tides, with the flood tide being most prevalent.

HUMAN RESOURCE ACCOUNTING

Commonwealth Doctors Hospital in Fairfax, Va. instituted a system of "human resource accounting." The aim—if greater control could be established over personnel resources, historically constituting from sixty to seventy percent of the service-intensive hospital budget, then substantial progress would necessarily be realized overall.

The essence of this system is man-hour budgeting. It is predicated on predetermined base hours which, according to the census are adjusted upward to reflect variable staffing needs associated with increasing workloads. After an initial twelve months of experience (but with no historical data to rely on), the outcome has been an overall 98% "effective" rate and a realistic measure of accountability.

THE BUDGETING PROCESS; NURSING SERVICES
AN EXAMPLE

Like dollar budgeting, participation of department heads is a prerequisite to the initial phase of projection. In the case of Nursing the task involved not merely a determination of patient days, but also a categorization of patients by type, severity of illness, etc.

This done, the philosophical question of intensity of service had to be answered and translated into specific numbers and types of personnel based on engineered standards of productivity, quality, etc.

The base finally established corresponded to a census level projected to represent a reasonable expectation on an average patient day. If the census—averaged over a two-week pay period—dropped below this base, no decrease in staffing was effected.

Where it rose above, however, an upward adjustment in man-hours was provided. (Being in the enviable position of increasing patient volumes, adjustments downward were generally discounted via the budget but accomplished by a decrease in on-call and overtime.)

VARIABLE ADJUSTMENT

The adjustment made was equal to 40% of the average census over the base level, the 40% being a variable factor used by the Cost of Living Council during the Phase IV of the Economic Stabilization Program to compensate a hospital for changes in volume—that is, with respect to the Government's assumption about the relationship of fixed and variable costs.

As an example, if the base level were 100 and the average daily census for a two week period were 110, then budgeted hours of, for instance, 7200 (or 90 full-time equivalents FTE's), would be adjusted upward by 4.0 percent to 7488—or an increase in staff of 3.6 FTE's.

$$
\begin{array}{rl}
.10 & \text{percentage increase in average census over base} \\
\times\ .40 & \text{variable factor} \\
\hline
.04 &
\end{array}
$$

$$
\begin{array}{rl}
.04 & \\
\times\ 7200 & \text{budgeted hours} \\
\hline
288 & \text{adjusted hours}
\end{array}
$$

$$
\begin{array}{rl}
7200 & \\
+\ 288 & \text{adjusted hours} \\
\hline
7488 & \text{adjusted budgeted hours}
\end{array}
$$

As another example, if there is a working base level census of 250 and an average daily census of 270 experienced during the particular accounting period, then budgeted hours of 7200 (or 90 FTE's) would be adjusted upward by 3.2 percent to 7430.4—or an increase of 2.88 FTE's.

$$
\begin{array}{rl}
.08 & \text{percentage increase in average census over base} \\
\times\ .40 & \text{variable factor} \\
\hline
.032 &
\end{array}
$$

$$
\begin{array}{rl}
.032 & \\
\times\ 7200 & \text{budgeted hours} \\
\hline
230.4 & \text{adjusted hours}
\end{array}
$$

$$
\begin{array}{rl}
7200 & \text{budgeted hours} \\
+\ 230.4 & \text{adjusted hours} \\
\hline
7430.4 & \text{adjusted budgeted hours}
\end{array}
$$

PERFORMANCE EVALUATION

The variance between the resulting "adjusted budgeted hours" and actual hours, stated for the specific two-week period and also year-to-date, thus represented a measure of the effectiveness and efficiency of managerial control over the individual department or service, whether it was Nursing in general, or a particular sub-department such as a medical unit, central supply or the operating room.

By dividing (adjusted) budgeted hours by actual hours and multiplying by 100, a numerical effective rate could be obtained. Therefore, if a nursing unit was budgeted for 1200 hours per pay period and had actual hours of 1400, the effective rate was 86%. Nursing Service at this hospital performed with a 99% effective rate during 1974.

Effective and efficient use of hours, though, was not just a matter of an optimal ratio of personnel to patients. Budgeted hours were established to include both productive and non-productive hours so that holiday, vacation and sick leave were reflected. In addition, overtime was computed in actual hours as time and a half so that the full effect of the cost would be realized.

PEER PRESSURE

What developed was an incentive to avoid excessive variances due to these reasons and to minimize their occurrence. On the nursing unit, peer pressure was more likely to be exerted by those who would have to bear the workload of the ones who always called in sick. Likewise, more balanced scheduling of holidays and vacations was encouraged, and overtime was limited to occasions of true need.

EXERCISING CONTROL

In a department such as Nursing with over half of the total personnel in the hospital, exercising control over so many variables can be a formidable task. Obviously as with any budgeting process, feedback is essential and the same holds true with man-hours. Performance reports were prepared every two weeks in accordance with the payroll period, and reflected the previous fourteen patient days. (See chart on next page.)

While this analysis was in effect retrospective, it still offered the benefit of learning from recent experience.

A significant factor in adjusting to staffing needs was anticipation of the cyclical nature of hospital admissions. For example, not filling until September 15 a staff nurse position left vacant by a June 15 resignation, represented a reasonably safe assumption about the census dropping during summer (although not all such predictions proved true).

More specific indication of staffing needs was achieved by close attention to postings to the surgery schedule. The numbers and types of cases were

Dept. Code	14 Day Budgeted	14 Day Actual	Variance + Over – Under	YTD* Budgeted	YTD Actual	Variance YTD + Over – Under
640 (ICU)	760 (9.5)	705	– 55	12318	12276	– 42
641 (CCU)	760 (9.5)	696.50	– 63.50	12318	12179	– 139
660 (OR)	2000(25)	1835.25	– 164.75	32416	32929	+ 513

*Reflects adjustments due to changing census over 16 pay periods.

very informative in this regard. Emphasis placed on the man-hour budget encouraged this type of planning.

Whatever the inadequacies for anticipating exact fluctuations in census level, the mere fact that management personnel were tuning themselves in to the daily workload and relating it to their staffs, served to raise their consciousness of the importance of man-hours in controlling costs and being accountable.

THE RESULTS

Overall, the hospital performed well with respect to staying within budgeted—or adjusted budgeted—hours. In fact, using the formula noted previously, year-to-date hospital figures yielded a 98% effective rate. More specifically, it was determined that for the whole of 1974, the hospital was only six FTE's over the budget.

This is not to say that greater deviations, either for the entire facility or for individual departments, were not experienced—they were. What it says—and this is the significant point regarding man-hour budgeting—is that over the course of the year the level of staffing as directly related to patient days, was within six FTE's of being that which was initially budgeted according to established standards for high quality care and efficient utilization of resources.

For a starter, this is not a bad record. Obviously, criticism can be leveled at the variance of six FTE's which at average annual salaries of $8,500 total slightly over $50,000. But with an operating budget of over $5.8 million, more than $3 million of which is for salaries, the figure by comparison becomes insignificant. At least knowledge of a specific variance exists and attention can be directed to its correction, whether that be elimination of excess staff where the reasons for the variance are unjustified or even addition of staff where more personnel are needed.

The man-hour budget is a refinement of existing methods to exercise control over the end product, dollars. True, there are problems and shortcomings; already noted were those associated with the retrospective nature of feedback on performance. Also of possible concern is the fact that the workload of some departments is not necessarily directly related to patient census. Experience at this hospital, however, has shown that over the long-run, adjustments balance out.

The point remains that control—formerly nonexistent—of that portion of the hospital budget which constitutes nearly sixty percent of costs, is now very much in evidence as department heads along with other management and supervisory people attempt to meet the needs of their respective services.

CONCLUSION

Human resource accounting as practiced through the man-hour budget offers the potential of exercising specific control over utilization of hospital personnel, the largest single expense and most important component in this service-intensive industry.

Through adjustment of this budget according to variable patient workloads, the hospital can continue to maintain its desired level of quality care and better meet the standards of accountability set by the community and others interested in quality patient care at economical cost.

19. Productivity Monitoring: A Key Element of Productivity Improvement

MARK L. ANDERSEN

By far the most important and costliest resources a hospital has are its personnel and their productivity. And, almost invariably, they offer the greatest opportunities for cost containment. However, whenever personnel cuts are recommended, the possibility of reduced quality of care is frequently cited as a barrier to increased efficiency. The challenge for hospital management, of course, is to provide the same quality of service—or better—at lower cost, or at least less rapidly rising cost. Successful implementation of a productivity improvement program requires that management have a thorough understanding of what productivity levels mean in various hospital departments and how productivity measures can be derived.

Analyzing productivity levels is only one step in an overall productivity improvement and monitoring process that should include:

- Assessing current productivity levels to determine the potential for improvement. This encompasses forecasting productivity levels and their financial impact, at least to the end of the current fiscal year, if not through the next year.
- Developing productivity objectives and standards for each department, using a weighting system to measure work force requirements accurately. This may involve using more than one unit of output for a department or cost center.

- Developing management action plans to improve productivity to the desired levels.
- Monitoring the action plans and providing feedback to management and department personnel to track changes and adjust action plans as necessary.

Management must express interest in and commitment to improving productivity throughout this process to develop department head support for such a program. Working with department heads throughout the implementation and operation of the process, management should seek advice and recommendations from them and other personnel (including physicians) about the program and ways in which productivity could be improved. Care must be taken to overcome the typical response to productivity improvement—resistance, fear of job loss, loss by a department head of part of a "domain."

Productivity monitoring, a key element of any productivity improvement process, should be initiated only if the hospital is willing to dedicate adequate resources to the effort. The overall goals of this process are to identify out-of-line departments for immediate action, and initiate periodic monitoring for long-term control and improvement. Using a two-step approach to productivity monitoring, such as that used by the Ernst & Whinney Productivity Monitoring System, a hospital can save money and reduce employee resistance to this kind of program.

PRODUCTIVITY IMPROVEMENT PROCESS

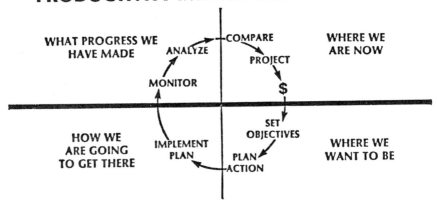

PRODUCTIVITY ASSESSMENT

The first phase of a productivity monitoring program is an assessment of the hospital's productivity, department by department, against appropriate operating indicators. Initially, the hospital should develop indicators based on historical data to determine whether staffing changes—warranted or not—have occurred compared to the time period used to develop the operating indicators. After this is done, the hospital may also wish to use operating indicators based on a survey of a peer group of hospitals to develop a gross indicator for comparative purposes. It must be remembered that such comparisons provide "gross" comparisons as no two hospitals are alike and the comparisons are useful only as a means of identifying wide variations in productivity. Nonetheless, the comparisons serve as a starting point for identifying areas for potential productivity improvement programs. Further, the hospital may also wish to compare itself to regional, state or national industry averages. Again, the objective of this phase is to identify departments that may be operating at inappropriate productivity levels or appearing to be staffed inappropriately, offering potential savings through productivity improvement.

```
                       ERNST & WHINNEY HEALTH CARE PRODUCTIVITY MONITOR
             COMPARATIVE OPERATING INDICATORS USING SURVEY COMPARISON WITH GROSS IMPACT
                                 COMMUNITY MEMORIAL HOSPITAL
                                     AS OF OCT 31, 1979

        DEPARTMENT           HOURS/UOS  ------- --FTE-- --------- AVG COST  --GROSS   IMPACT--
            COST CENTER       WORK  COMP   WORK   COMP  VARIANCE PER  FTE      $         RANK

70 SPECIAL SERVICE SUMMARY

   9973 LABOR/DELIVERY           - DELIVERY

      YEAR-TO-DATE        : 14.72 10.40   8.8    6.2      2.6    4,094
      FISCAL YR PROJECTION: 14.42 10.40   8.5    6.1      2.4   16,379     39,312      5

   9972 INTENSIVE CARE           - ICU PT. DAYS

      YEAR-TO-DATE        : 16.14 16.50  37.7   38.5     (0.8)   3,802
      FISCAL YR PROJECTION: 17.89 16.50  40.9   37.7      3.2   15,209     48,672      2

   9970 SPECIAL SERVICES         - TOTAL PT. DAYS

      YEAR-TO-DATE        :  0.07  0.06   1.4    1.3      0.1    4,312
      FISCAL YR PROJECTION:  0.06  0.06   1.2    1.2      0.0   17,249                10

   70 SPECIAL SERVICE SUMMARY    - TOTAL PT. DAYS

      YEAR-TO-DATE        :             47.9   46.0      1.9
      FISCAL YR PROJECTION:             50.6   45.0      5.6              87,984
```

The findings of this assessment should report year-to-date figures as well as projected results to the end of the current year, incorporating trends and seasonal fluctuations in utilization. Personnel cost variances accounting for the variations in departmental wages should be reported to management. Knowing only that a department is overstaffed or understaffed does not provide sufficient information upon which to make a management decision regarding the importance of potential changes in staffing; the cost impact of the overstaffing should also be identified. An example of such a report is found on page 159.

Hospitals using this approach should repeat the comparative process at regular intervals, e.g., quarterly or semi-annually, for adequate management control and decision-making. Departments reporting improvement should receive appropriate recognition; those reporting no improvement should be reviewed, and new approaches to improve their productivity should be discussed. This first step—productivity assessment—helps management to identify areas with the greatest potential for productivity improvement, and allows management to measure the impact of productivity improvement action plans.

PRODUCTIVITY PERFORMANCE MONITORING

Performance monitoring, the second phase of a productivity monitoring program, focuses on departments identified in the first phase in which monthly monitoring based on detailed standards is cost-justified. Departments not requiring detailed performance monitoring because they are relatively efficient or are too small should continue using as a measure of productivity performance the comparative indicators developed in the first step. These departments should be monitored monthly as well, allowing action to be taken as soon as it is deemed necessary.

Detailed time standards should be developed for each major departmental procedure or activity. Productivity measurement should not be attempted using a single measure and a weighted standard. For example, as a measure of output, nursing units should use patient days by acuity level, not merely total patient days. This allows management to document the volumes of individual procedures produced, apply to those volumes a time standard tailored for each procedure, and thereby pinpoint changes in service intensity and staffing requirements.

To make allowances for hospital policies or operating constraints which require the provision of services that may reduce productivity—such as 24 hour coverage in the emergency room or specific turn-around times in the laboratory—the hospital should also establish target productivity levels. Use of these administrative "allowances" enables the hospital to track actual productivity levels. It also equips the hospital to monitor performance based on targeted productivity levels, and to document changes in service intensity (hence, required costs). An example of this type of report follows:

```
                    ERNST & WHINNEY HEALTH CARE PRODUCTIVITY MONITOR
             PRODUCTIVITY & IMPACT USING PSU STANDARD WITH GROSS IMPACT
                            ·COMMUNITY MEMORIAL HOSPITAL
                               AS OF  OCT 31, 1979
```

DEPARTMENT COST CENTER		WORK	TARGET	VARIANCE	PCT PROD	PCT TGT	AVG COST PER FTE	GROSS IMPACT	GI RANK	PROD RANK
70 SPECIAL SERVICE SUMMARY										
9973 LABOR/DELIVERY										
CURRENT MONTH	:	8.7	6.7	2.0	57.7	77.0	1,365	2,730		
YEAR-TO-DATE	:	8.8	6.2	2.6	52.9	70.5	4,095	10,647		
FISCAL YR PROJECTION:		8.5	5.6	2.9	49.4	65.9	16,380	47,502	8	16
9972 INTENSIVE CARE										
CURRENT MONTH	:	38.0	36.2	1.8	81.0	95.3	1,267	2,281		
YEAR-TO-DATE	:	37.7	34.3	3.4	77.3	91.0	3,802	12,927		
FISCAL YR PROJECTION:		40.9	35.5	5.4	73.8	86.8	15,210	82,134	5	3
9970 SPECIAL SERVICES										
CURRENT MONTH	:	1.5	1.3	0.2	82.4	86.7	1,437	287		
YEAR-TO-DATE	:	1.4	1.3	0.1	88.3	92.9	4,312	431		
FISCAL YR PROJECTION:		1.2	1.2	0.0	95.0	100.0	17,250		17	1
70 SPECIAL SERVICE SUMMARY										
CURRENT MONTH	:	48.2	44.2	4.0	76.9	91.7		5,298		
YEAR-TO-DATE	:	47.9	41.8	6.1	73.3	87.3		24,005		
FISCAL YR PROJECTION:		50.6	42.3	8.3	70.3	83.6		129,636		

Because this process should be performed at least monthly, forecasts of staffing requirements for coming periods should be presented for use by department heads in determining the most appropriate times to make staffing changes. These forecasts should be based on expected volume and must incorporate seasonal variations to be of use to the hospital.

STANDARDS DEVELOPMENT

A key element of productivity monitoring is the development of meaningful comparative indicators in Phase 1, and accurate, detailed standards in Phase 2. Each phase requires a different type of productivity measure, developed through different methods. The first phase provides the hospital a measure of productivity against relatively fixed standards without knowing whether or not the standards are really comparable or productivity can be improved. The second phase provides management a tool to monitor internal productivity.

Standards, more appropriately called operating indicators, used in the first phase can be developed from a number of sources. Most easily, historical data may be used to produce indicators which will provide information describing current performance compared to that of the last year or a combination of several previous years without accounting for changes in service intensity. Also, budget data may be used to compare year-to-date performance to budgeted performance. Another source of operating indicators is the industry norm, an average based on the performance of other institutions in the hospital service area or throughout the country. As mentioned earlier, truly comparable interhospital data is not available because of the inherent differences among hospitals. Any figures developed in this manner should only be used as guides for further investigation, not as definitions of staffing requirements. This data is available through such sources as local or state hospital associations, or independent survey of hospitals selected according to specific operating characteristics. If the latter approach is taken, it is suggested that department heads be involved in selecting comparable hospitals, because they are likely to be aware of specific similarities or differences among them.

Several work measurement techniques may be used to develop performance standards for the second phase, productivity performance monitoring. The applicability of these techniques depends on the nature of the work being measured and the availability of trained personnel to do the measuring. The techniques discussed here are stopwatch timing and self-logging.

Stopwatch timing is particularly suited to short-cycle activities or repetitive work. In this process, the operation under consideration is divided into elements about thirty seconds long, each of which is timed. Stopwatch timing provides a very accurate measure of time requirements but is not well suited to many hospital activities beyond routine housekeeping and service functions. Because of the wide variances among patients, stopwatch techniques do not lend themselves to use with direct patient care activities. Stopwatch timing has been used in developing nursing time standards to devise detailed standards for each nursing activity (e.g., application of bandage) but the record-keeping required can be extremely burdensome—even if nursing personnel accept this approach to staffing.

Self-logging is a work measurement technique in which employees record their own activities. Each employee maintains an activity log or series of activity log-in/log-outs. Each activity to be measured must be determined and described in advance. The table of activities to be analyzed should include the major activities of the department or personnel involved, and may include both clinical and non-clinical tasks. After the logs have been maintained for a specified period (anywhere from one week to several months), the data must be summarized and average time requirements calculated to determine the time requirements for each activity. Self-logging is easy to install and understand but requires close attention, particularly in the early stages, to ensure accurate data collection.

REPORTING

Ideally, any productivity monitoring system will have the ability to produce reports using several different sets of comparative indicators or standards, allowing management to examine performance relative to each set of performance measures. With this type of information available, management can analyze staffing variances according to the different standards and discuss the reasons for the variances with department heads to understand and improve operations.

As with any other management information system, reports must be timely, readable, and understandable. To facilitate timeliness, the system should be able to use data as it becomes available. For example, the labor input (hours worked and/or paid) should be accrued by the system, rather than by hospital personnel, saving time and improving data accuracy.

Additionally, the reports should be presented in a manner consistent with the reporting hierarchy of the hospital, allowing various levels of summarization. For example, each nursing unit should be able to monitor the utilization of nursing personnel by job category (e.g., R.N., L.P.N., etc.) as well as report accumulative results to the Director of Nursing.

The reports should include this information:

- number of FTEs that actually worked
- number of FTEs that should have worked (i.e., a target figure based on performance standards, output and administrative allowances)
- actual productivity
- productivity incorporating administrative allowances

- average cost per FTE
- staffing and cost variances highlighting both excess staffing and excess costs

SUMMARY

A properly installed and maintained productivity monitoring system as part of an overall productivity improvement process can help management control manpower utilization. Defining target levels of staffing based upon actual operating practices and levels of output provides the information necessary for labor control utilization.

A productivity monitoring system can also provide a number of valuable by-product benefits such as:

- improving the balancing of work load/work force relationships
- identifying areas in which excess capacity exists (although staffing reductions may not be feasible)
- developing and maintaining meaningful staffing standards related to the provision of quality patient care
- justifying cost increases based on documented increases in the service intensity
- developing the data base necessary for future planning and control of resources through budgeting and rate setting.

CHAPTER 3

PRODUCTIVITY IMPROVEMENT TECHNIQUES

There are numerous productivity improvement techniques, some of which are used in labor productivity and some of which are used in the management of other resources. The following topics are presented in this chapter:

- the concept of productivity
- operations management
- management engineering
- work simplification and method improvement
- work measurement and standards
- work sampling
- wage incentive systems
- value analysis
- activity measurement programs

THE CONCEPT OF PRODUCTIVITY

Productivity, the ability to produce, is essential to the survival of any health care facility. Productivity per employee or per dollar invested must be improved in order to contain costs. Wolfe and Wolfe (Reading 20) define the concepts of effectiveness (doing the right things) and efficiency (doing things right) as the basis for measuring productivity. Productivity is broken

165

down into three factors: management, process, and product. Improved productivity can be achieved by the so-called good manager, who is characterized by 20 factors ranging from "being fair to employees" to "having guts."

A systematic approach to improved productivity is presented in the article by Kelly and Ellis (Reading 21). The paper outlines a three-phase process for productivity improvement in hospitals.

OPERATIONS MANAGEMENT

Frerer's paper (Reading 22) presents the methodology of hospital cost containment through operations management as it was developed by the American Hospital Association. This approach was disseminated to hundreds of users who participated in the self-administered training programs.

MANAGEMENT ENGINEERING

Management engineering is the term commonly used to describe the process of improving productivity in health care facilities. Because management engineering, which is based on the principles of industrial engineering, has shown significant success with the increased use of computers, the traditional management engineering function is increasing its scope to include computer systems. As a result, its name has been changed to *health systems engineering*. Gustafson et al. (Reading 23) give an overview of this function, reviewing the areas in which health systems engineering can be used to improve productivity.

The remaining papers in this chapter describe specific management engineering tools.

WORK SIMPLIFICATION AND METHODS IMPROVEMENT

One of the traditional approaches to increased productivity was methods improvement, also known as work simplification. As developed in industry, the basic idea of methods improvement is to improve the manner in which work is performed by using a systematic analysis to arrive at an efficient and economical use of motions, time, and efforts. Ferderber (Reading 24) presents an overview of the most commonly used tools and instruments of work simplification, such as process and time flow charts, and gives examples showing applications in various hospital departments. A complete presentation of this topic can be found in Bennett's text on methods improvement in hospitals.[1]

WORK MEASUREMENT AND WORK STANDARDS

Work measurement is done in order to set work standards, determine appropriate staffing, appraise performance, and prepare budgets. Melesko (Reading 25) describes the various techniques of work measurement and discusses the process of using data collected in work measurement to develop work standards for hospitals.

WORK SAMPLING

Of all existing work measurement methods, work sampling is the one most suitable for the health care industry. Cercone et al. (Reading 26) describe the essentials of work sampling as well as its application.

WAGE INCENTIVE SYSTEM

Employee productivity can be increased by various motivation methods (see Chapter 2, Human Resource Management Systems). While the effectiveness of some of the behavioral methods is still debatable, there is very little doubt that monetary incentives are extremely effective in almost any setting.

Standard incentive systems such as those used in industry are difficult to implement in health care institutions, mainly because of the quality of care issue. The most sophisticated wage incentive plan is the one that has been operating since 1965 at Baptist Hospital, Pensacola, Florida. The program measures productivity in terms of labor, supply utilization, and quality assurance.[2] Austin's paper (Reading 27) provides a survey of all the major incentive plans that were in operation in 1970. Although some of these plans have been improved since then, they still represent a true picture of incentive systems in the U.S. health care industry.

VALUE ANALYSIS

Most of the productivity improvement techniques described earlier deal with labor, while value analysis deals with all aspects of productivity. Rifai, Pecenka, and Ford's article (Reading 28) introduces this tool and its application to hospital management.

ACTIVITY MEASUREMENT PROGRAM

Productivity is defined as the ratio of output to input, or the ratio of things done to resources used. Activity measurement programs are attempts to measure the productivity of various departments by measuring their output and relating it to the input (resources) used. For example, dividing the number of tests performed in a day by the number of man hours expended indicates the number of tests performed in an hour. The labor cost per unit of output can be determined in a similar manner. Such measurements can be used for comparative analysis. Mazzolla and Kauffman (Reading 29) present a case study of an activity measurement program in which an electrocardiogram (EKG) department is used as an example.

The final paper in this chapter, by Lindenmeyer and Kast (Reading 30), describes the activities of Western Michigan University in helping hospitals apply management engineering tools in their cost containment efforts. The paper presents a methodology of the approach developed (termed *design for function*), describes its benefits, and gives several examples of projects performed.

Several of the methods described in this chapter are presented in Johannides' text.[3]

NOTES

1. A.C. Bennett, *Methods Improvement in Hospitals* (New York: Preston Publishing Co., 1975).

2. P.N. Groner, *Cost Containment Through Employee Incentive Programs* (Germantown, Md.: Aspen Systems Corp., 1977).

3. D.F. Johannides, *Cost Containment Through Systems Engineering* (Germantown, Md.: Aspen Systems Corp., 1979).

BIBLIOGRAPHY

American Hospital Association. *The Management of Hospital Employee Productivity—An Introductory Handbook.* Chicago: American Hospital Association, 1973.

Balkonis, B.J. "The CAP Time Study: Source of Workload Unit Values." *Medical Laboratory Observer,* September 1978.

Bartscht, K.G., and Coffey, R.L. "Management Engineering—A Method to Improve Productivity." *Topics in Health Care Financing,* Spring 1977.

Bennett, A.C. "Controlling Hospital Costs Methods Measurement." *Hospital Topics,* August 1972.

Bennett, J.E., and Krasny, J. "Functional Value Analysis: A Technique for Reducing Hospital Overhead Costs." *Topics in Health Care Financing,* Summer 1977.

Brown, J. "Cost Containment Through Increased Productivity." *Tennessee Hospital Times* 18 (1977): 8-9.

Carpenter, W.W. "Developing a Unit of Service to Measure Productivity." *Hospital Financial Management,* July 1978.

Carvana, R.A., and Aspinall, C. "Change Vacation to Accrual Basis and Improve Cash Flow." *Hospital Financial Management,* December 1977.

Clark, S. "Work Sampling—Can It Help You?" *Hospital Administration in Canada,* November 1976.

Davidson, M.P. "Work Measurement Standards." *Building Operating Management,* August 1977.

Davis, R.N. "Productivity Improvement Can Cut Costs." *Hospitals, JAHA,* 16 February 1975.

Duckett, S.J., and Kristofferson, S.M. "An Index of Hospital Performance." *Medical Care,* May 1978.

Elliott, V.F. "Word Processing—An Offshoot of Work Simplification." *Hospital Progress,* September 1977.

Employee Incentive System for Hospitals. U.S. Department of Health, Education and Welfare, Pub. No. (HSM) 72-6705, 1972.

Evers, J.H., and Wallace, E.T. "Controlling Hospital Costs by Methods Measurement." *Hospital Topics,* August 1972.

Ferderber, C.J. "Work Simplification: Working Smarter, Not Harder." *Hospital Financial Management,* April 1972.

Flagg, W.G. "Management Engineering: Still Much to Be Done." *Hospitals, JAHA,* 1 April 1978.

Frerer, B. "Hospital Cost Containment Through Operations Management." *Hospital Financial Management,* December 1974.

Greenfield, H.I. *Hospital Efficiency and Public Policy.* New York: Praeger Pub., 1973.

Griffith, J.R. *Measuring Hospital Performance.* Glenview, Ill.: Inquiry Pub., 1978.

Groner, P.N. "Employee Incentives." *Topics in Health Care Financing,* Spring 1977.

Guidelines to Greater Hospital Productivity. Washington, D.C.: National Commission of Productivity and Work Quality, 1976.

Klarman, H.E. "Application of Cost-Benefit Analysis to Health System Technology." *International Journal of Health Service* 4 (1974): 325-352.

Krieg, A.F., and Yapit, M.K. "A Streamlined Work Flow Can Boost Productivity and Morale." *Medical Laboratory Observer,* December 1978.

Larson, R. "Central Service: Work Measurement." *Hospitals, JAHA,* 16 February 1970.

Lenore, Sister Mary. "Work Measurement." *Hospital Progress,* March 1972.

McProud, L.M., and David, B.D. "Applying Value Analysis to Food Purchasing." *Hospitals, JAHA,* 16 September 1976.

Meyer, D. "Work Load Management System Assures Stable Nurse-Patient Ratio." *Hospitals, JAHA,* 1 March 1978.

Myers, K.G. "Operations Management Can Contain Costs." *Hospital Financial Management,* January 1973.

"The PMR—Measuring Productivity." *Texas Hospitals,* February 1977.

Small, J.E. "Monitoring Staffing and Productivity." *Hospital Progress,* February 1975.

Somers, J. "Purpose and Performance: A System Analysis of Nurse Staffing." *Journal of Nursing Administration,* February 1977.

Thielman, C.F. "Four Departments, One Aim: Find a Better Way." *Hospitals, JAHA,* 1 June 1961.

Van der Wall, C.A. "The Team Approach to Productivity Improvement and Cost Containment." *Purchasing Administration,* April 1978.

Weinstein, M.C., et al. "Foundations of Cost Effectiveness Analysis for Health and Medical Practices." *The New England Journal of Medicine*, 31 March 1977.

20. Improving Department Productivity

ARTHUR V. WOLFE AND KENT J. WOLFE

Reprinted with permission from *Southern Hospitals,* September/October 1978, pp. 14-15.

What hospital administrator and his managers do not stand for an efficient, effective organization? Specifically, what do "efficiency" and "self-effectiveness" mean to administrators and managers?

Various administrators and managers undoubtedly would word their answers differently; but, generally, most would consider "efficiency" and "effectiveness" to mean essentially the same thing. They would equate these two words with trying hard and usually accomplishing what the person is trying to accomplish. This misunderstanding of the meaning of these two words is a major limitation in current efforts to improve productivity.

Confusion between these two terms comes naturally from the job title of the old "efficiency expert." Confusion also comes from the lack of precision in management terminology, among many practicing administrators.

If effort and success with one's effort are what a manager understands these two words to mean, his organization has only the two choices to reduce services or increase charges.

A dictionary definition of "efficiency" gives a different answer: "Efficiency is the ratio of output to input; the ratio of what is produced to what it costs to produce it," with costs measured in dollars, time, change in relationship of one hospital department to another, change in reaction of patients and the public, etc.

"Efficiency" does not necessarily mean "effectiveness." If a lot of work is put in and almost as much results are gotten out, that is high efficiency.

But, also, if very little work is put in [, and] a high proportion of results is obtained, that is both high efficiency and effectiveness.

FIRST QUESTION: WHAT WORK SHOULD BE DONE?

The first question always should be: What work should be done? Almost every organization of any size has some employee or section doing some work with high efficiency but the need for that particular work has long since disappeared. Yet, no one has asked the all-important management question: Does this work still need to be done?

Benjamin Franklin is frequently quoted on this point. "Tis far better," he said, "to do the right thing middling well than to do the wrong thing with great dispatch." Specialists in the productivity movement believe that Franklin's wisdom is the heart and essence of productivity improvement.

Sometimes the decisions as to what work a department should be doing are best reached by the head of the department, often with the help of his immediate assistants. Often, it is desirable to get the ideas of employees, or at least the senior employees in the department. And sometimes it is best, even necessary, to coordinate the decision with other hospital departments, the medical staff, and/or other hospitals.

If the work is especially costly or there is an expansion of services or beds, it would need not only Board approval, but also Planning Agency approval. In all cases, significant changes in type of work to be performed would need the approval of the department head's superior.

SECOND QUESTION: TO WHAT STANDARD?

Almost every department in a hospital has certain types of work that must be performed to high, Grade A standards. Frequently, these standards are set for hospitals and individual departments by accrediting and/or regulatory agencies.

But, most of the work in the world, including some hospital work, is not worth the cost of doing it perfectly and immediately. The high cost of buying the latest equipment and/or facilities; of hiring the highest quality employees; of spending great amounts of money training, paying, motivating and supervising employees; and of giving every patient Grade A service in every area is not worth the great extra cost.

Non-medical tasks in a hospital—such as clerical, maintenance, dietary—can be performed to a good Grade B level rather than to Grade A level. Even the per patient level of R.N. staffing is a variable that can be managed to a considerable degree, yet still maintain the level needed to meet both internal and external constraints.

Effectiveness, then, is doing work that should be done and doing it to the appropriate quality for the type of work being performed.

THREE PRODUCTIVITY FACTORS

Technically speaking, all variables affecting productivity can be classified into three broad categories: management, process and product factors.

Practically speaking from an individual manager's point of view, all productivity variables can be divided into two broad categories: variables he can be [sic] something about and those he cannot do something about. Obviously, a manager can do something about a productivity variable if his department has both the knowledge and the authority to make a change.

Although productivity improvement often is initiated in formal programs by an internal or external productivity improvement consultant, most of a hospital's level of productivity is produced in two ways: (1) by top management making improvements in all three productivity categories, and (2) by department management making improvements in one category: the management factor category.

Management is a unique process. The individual manager needs to be intensely aware that management has nothing to do with being busy. Some of the hardest working, most faithful department heads in hospitals are busy all day long doing clerical or other technical tasks, "setting an example" it is sometimes called. Meanwhile, the department goes unmanaged. These busy non-managers tend to give themselves away with their stock answer to almost every problem: Hire more people.

Management researchers, and hospital administrators, have discovered that there is no one best management style that needs to be followed by each manager as he and his people perform their work in accordance with required standard practices. Yet, few managers accomplish desired results unless they follow recognized professional practices.

After the tough decisions have been made on what work is to be done and to what quality level this work will be performed, and after any organization redundancies have been eliminated and clear lines of accountability have been established, the professionalism of each manager can be judged against the following standards:

A GOOD MANAGER—

1. Knows that a department needs leadership, that it will not plan and run itself without good management.

2. Sees himself or herself primarily as a professional manager rather than as the head nurse, head maintenance man or some other most-skilled technician in his department.
3. With his administrator, identifies general work objectives for his whole department and specific work objectives for each section of his department. Identifies and designates key result areas for his department, even if they are hard to quantify, such as "friendliness to patients and visitors."
4. Organizes people and jobs into sensible work units, training and changing routines and assignments as needed.
5. Hires and promotes people on the basis of probable capability to perform well on the job involved.
6. Estimates the probable performance level of each subordinate on each of his specific tasks; then delegates appropriate responsibility and authority in each task area to each subordinate.
7. Within his hospital's constraints, pays his employees fairly, according to: (a) level of complexity of the employee's job, (b) quality and quantity of work the employee is producing, and (c) employee's length of service.
8. Trains (or has an appropriate person train) each employee by modern, formal methods, one task at a time in planned sequence.
9. Decides which leadership approach is best with each employee and changes his leadership behavior to meet different management situations and the specific needs of each employee.
10. Motivates employees. Removes barriers to getting a good job done.
11. Generally, supervises in an in-between manner, rather than in a too-tight or too-loose manner.
12. In accordance with his administrator's general standards of quality, quantity, cost and time, sets patient-oriented standards, responsive to the problems of the average patient.
13. Measures work produced by comparing actual work produced with the standards expected from that employee. Uses productivity data to identify problem areas and to evaluate alternative improvement strategies, as well as to monitor employee performance standards.
14. Within his hospital's constraints, rewards or does not reward employees for how well they meet the standards set for their job. Tries to correct any employee not doing his fair share of usable work.
15. Is cost conscious. Puts the interests of the hospital (and patients) ahead of the interests of any incompetent employee. At all times clearly distinguishes between a productive hospital department and a welfare agency.

16. Generally (at least at first), attempts to use mistakes of an employee as a learning opportunity, not as a reason for discipline.
17. After informing employees of work rules, administers discipline fairly and firmly, with no-nonsense, results-oriented approach according to: the severity and frequency of the offense committed, the apparent intent and attitude of the employee, the circumstances under which the offense took place and the work record of the employee.
18. Has the analytical skill to decide what changes are needed in his department. Defines the problem. Asks whether the problem is worth the probable cost of solving it. Evaluates the present situation. Sets objectives. Develops alternatives. Establishes decision-making criteria.
19. Has guts, often the most needed management quality, to carry out his carefully thought-out decisions and to make the changes needed, to discipline himself to spend his time and emotional energy on what his department most needs from him.
20. Has the will to manage.

CONCLUSION

The general decline in productivity nationwide and the problems of business recovery and inflation are having their impact on the hospital industry as on every other industry. Of particular importance to hospitals and other service industries is the fact that pay costs nationwide have been outstripping productivity increases over the last ten years.

The 1973 AHA productivity handbook pointed out that "many hospital administrative personnel have been reluctant to attack the task of managing their employees' productivity." Two years later, the 1975 Annual Report of the National Commission of Productivity and Work Quality stated, "only 15 percent of the Nation's 7,000 hospitals offer in-service training programs for management personnel and few, if any, specifically address the issue of productivity."

Therefore, if a hospital is to meet its local and national obligations, each manager will join his hospital administrator in regularly doing three things:

1. With or without the assistance of a productivity improvement specialists (sic), re-think what work needs to be done by his department and determine to what standards this work will be done and how it will be done.
2. Inventory his own management practices by comparing them with the 20 management practices listed above. Make any adjustments needed in his management practices.

3. Inform his administrator of any productivity variable outside of his department's capability and/or authority which appears to have high probability of gain from the work of a productivity improvement specialist.

Hospital productivity will increase significantly as each manager fits good management practices to his own managerial style.

21. Toward More Effective Management of Hospital Productivity

THOMAS F. KELLY AND TERRILL F. ELLIS

Reprinted with permission from *Health Care Horizons,* 1976, pp. 9-12.

As hospital administrators continue to seek ways to deal with rising hospital costs and with consumer pressures to lower or stabilize rates—problems which have been squeezing virtually every institution during the past three to four years—they have begun to focus on improving productivity levels within hospitals through more efficient delivery of patient services as a possible solution. By 1975, many of the individual hospital efforts to improve productivity had begun to be coordinated on both a regional and national basis, providing a foundation for more widespread implementation of proven techniques. Many of these efforts have been initiated at the federal level.

Most institutions, lacking an effective measurement system that would routinely monitor productivity levels, have been unable to maintain the necessary feedback mechanism to assure that productivity goals are met over the long term. Some institutions are now implementing such monitoring and reporting systems.

ELEMENTS OF PRODUCTIVITY IMPROVEMENT

Productivity improvements occur when the amount or quality of output from a given process is increased without a corresponding increase in the amount or quality of input resources; similarly, productivity is improved if a given output and quality is achieved with reduced input resources.

Although this traditional definition is particularly applicable to a production process, it can also be applied to patient service and other functions performed within a health care institution, either on an overall basis (entire hospital) or at a detail level of work activity (e.g., inhalation therapy department). Output, however, is generally more difficult to quantify and measure in this environment than in industry. Nonetheless, this concept should be examined further; there are current trends in hospital practice which affect levels of productivity both favorably and adversely.

TRENDS AFFECTING PRODUCTIVITY LEVELS

Health care productivity levels in recent years have increased for a variety of reasons, including:

- Rapidly increasing technological improvements, particularly in the areas of diagnostic and treatment equipment and procedures. In most cases, service output level and quality are increased significantly with less than a corresponding increase in output costs.
- Replacement of outdated structures with modern facilities designed to provide for more efficient delivery of patient care services. Such changes often improve the quality of patient service, making the productivity increase difficult to measure objectively.
- Upgrading of management and supervisory capabilities of hospital administrative personnel through more intensive in-service programs. This is an excellent example of improving input quality (e.g., supervisory ability of department head) and thereby increasing output level and/or quality.
- Implementation on a local or regional basis of shared and contract services programs in areas such as purchasing, patient billing, laundry, laboratory and other support and ancillary services. Productivity improvements usually occur through a shift in the mix of the input resources from hospital personnel to purchased services. Output quality may also improve.

Despite these trends, the reality of day-to-day operations indicates that there are often as many factors tending to decrease productivity levels as there are steps being taken to increase them. For example:

- Inflation in salary, supply and other operating costs that are not fixed obligations continues to raise input costs. Annual cost increases in excess of 12 percent are being experienced in many of these hospital cost components.

Exhibit A. Productivity Management and Reporting System/
Conceptual Illustration of Development Process

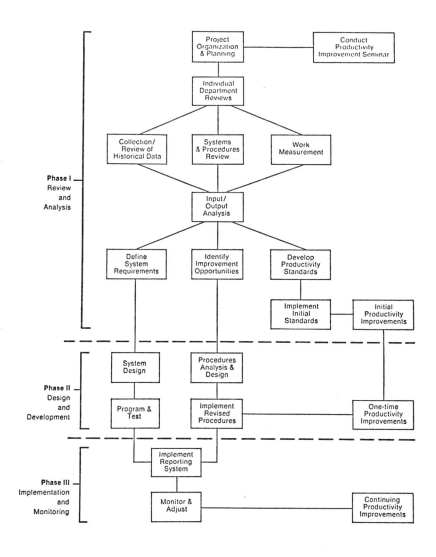

- More sophisticated and complex medical practices have resulted in greater intensity of services being required for a given diagnosis or patient stay. Also, the number of diagnostic procedures required per case has been increased to minimize the potential for malpractice claims. Because these increases generally work to the hospital's economic benefit (revenues increase in proportion to the additional services provided) they are not generally considered unfavorable trends from an overall viewpoint.
- Fringe benefit levels are increasing dramatically in response to outside pressures, new government regulations and other factors, boosting inputs with no proportionate rise in outputs.
- Patients themselves are demanding more services, resulting in increased input resources relative to the output levels achieved. Again, because the quality of the output is affected, objective measurement becomes more difficult.

A PRODUCTIVITY MANAGEMENT SYSTEMS CONCEPT

The concept of monitoring and controlling input and output levels to improve hospital productivity implies the use of effective resource and workload measurement and reporting procedures. Although most hospitals have not yet developed such a system, it is vital to the successful tracking and systematic improvement of productivity levels within an institution. In this context, the focus should be on the *process* rather than the specific techniques, as shown in the flow chart. The process of developing and implementing a productivity management and reporting system can be broken into three distinct phases: Phase I, detailed review and analysis, Phase II, system design and development, and Phase III, implementation and monitoring.

ORGANIZING THE SYSTEMS DEVELOPMENT PROJECT

Before the productivity management and control system can be implemented, however, project plans should be established. One of the first considerations is the organization of the project team. At a minimum, this team should consist of the project director, staff and steering committee.

The project director should be an individual with broad management responsibility in the hospital. The degree of leadership he displays will, in many cases, influence the entire outcome of the project.

The project staff should consist of a group of analysts experienced in implementing management engineering techniques in a hospital environment.

In many cases, internal resources can be effectively supplemented through the use of outside consultants. The project team should also include personnel with data processing, accounting and management information systems expertise, and, if possible, personnel with experience in implementing productivity improvement systems in other environments.

The steering committee should consist of key hospital personnel with an interest and involvement in the outcome of the project, including representatives from the major areas of hospital operations. The committee should also include representatives from the board of trustees and the medical staff.

In addition to organizing the project team, preliminary activities should include establishing a detailed work plan to develop and implement the system, preparing a time schedule for each activity, and assigning specific responsibilities.

As a final step, the project director should consider conducting a productivity improvement seminar for hospital personnel to increase the project awareness and commitment of the staff.

PHASE I—REVIEW AND ANALYSIS

After the project planning process has been completed, the project team conducts individual department productivity reviews. These reviews should include in-depth analyses of historical data, systems and procedures, and may include the application of work measurement techniques and other management engineering tools to obtain data not available within the current reporting system.

The analysts should, as a part of the review, conduct interviews with all department heads and section chiefs to gain a clear understanding of departmental service demands and resources employed. Through these discussions, the analysts should obtain additional information on department objectives and operations, including:

- department goals and service objectives
- organization and supervisory staff assignments
- routine functions performed
- staffing levels and work schedules
- workload volumes and fluctuations
- procedural flows
- internal and external operating constraints.

A key activity in this phase of development is the input/output analysis, which is performed after all the necessary data is collected and reviewed.

The input/output analysis is designed to identify existing volume/cost relationships and to establish patterns of correlation between the resources required to perform a process and the output of that process. This data will ultimately provide the means to measure productivity changes within the unit.

Based on the input/output analysis, three separate activities (which can be conducted simultaneously) should be initiated. The first activity is defining the preliminary system requirements for the productivity management and reporting system. (Note that the preliminary design will not address the detailed procedures but should instead provide a conceptual overview of the system to be developed.)

The second activity is establishing initial productivity objectives for each department within the hospital, possibly broken down into sub-objectives for each unit for function within the department. This objective can be expressed in terms of the expected level of output per unit of input—for example, the relative values of tests performed per man-hour of laboratory technician time, or the number of nursing hours per patient day in a nursing unit. The use of relative value systems in certain ancillary departments, such as laboratory, assists in relating input and output measures more realistically. The initial productivity standards should be consistent with historical data or other input data collected through work measurement and other techniques to gain management and staff acceptance.

The third activity is identifying operations improvements which can only be achieved through modifications to the operating systems and procedures. These improvement opportunities will be prioritized and assigned to project team members in later phases of the project.

PHASE II—DETAIL SYSTEM DESIGN AND DEVELOPMENT

Once the preliminary system design and initial productivity objectives have been reviewed and approved by the project steering committee, the project moves into the detail design and development phase. Depending on the requirements established in the first phase for the reporting system, this phase could result in orientation toward automated system development or might require only a manual reporting system. Most of the effort in this phase of the project is in developing the detail system documentation, which should include:

- input data requirements and forms
- output report formats
- files to be maintained

- general and detailed systems flow charts
- data control concepts
- manual procedures and paper flow.

As a parallel activity to the system design, the project team can implement the operations improvement opportunities identified early in the project. This involves working with the appropriate department heads to revise existing processes and schedules and to make the necessary procedural changes to effect the desired productivity improvements.

PHASE III—IMPLEMENTATION AND MONITORING

Once the detailed productivity management and reporting system has been designed and tested, the project team should develop an implementation plan. At this point, the role of the project team should be to train hospital personnel in the use of this system, to monitor the implementation of the system and to work on unforeseen problems which will invariably arise.

The implementation process should include reviews by the project team after the system has functioned for a period of time. These reviews assure that the original objectives are being maintained and that unauthorized modifications are not being developed within the user departments. It may also become evident during such subsequent review that adjustments to the initial productivity standards should be made to more accurately reflect current operating conditions in a given department. These adjustments are often necessitated by the addition of new programs or other changes in the operation, and should be expected on a routine basis.

USING THE SYSTEM EFFECTIVELY

The purpose of the productivity management and reporting system is to tell hospital administration the status of productivity trends in the hospital. If the overall attitude of administration toward productivity improvement is positive and participatory, the results will likely be substantially better than if the system is used as a tool for identifying and highlighting "problem" departments. Thus, it may be as important to emphasize department achievements above established productivity levels as it is to identify areas which fall below productivity objectives.

Achieving and maintaining higher levels of productivity throughout the hospital should be considered an ongoing responsibility of supervisory and management personnel within the hospital. The productivity management and reporting system will provide the management team with a chart of these efforts, but the attitudes and spirit with which the objectives are pursued will, in the final analysis, determine the hospital's success in achieving more efficient delivery of patient services.

22. Hospital Cost Containment Through Operations Management*

BRUCE FRERER

Reprinted with permission from *Review of Hospital Operations*, August 1974, pp. 23–24.

A NEW APPROACH

Operations Management is a workable and integrated approach to the cost containment problem. It is an analytical process, designed to work effectively within the existing management structure of a health care institution. Basically, it involves the definition of operating service levels required for each institutional function, the identification of alternative ways of providing the required service levels and the selection and implementation of the most cost-effective alternatives. As with any management process, Operations Management is only as effective as the thought and effort devoted to its application. It does represent, however, a methodology which, if diligently followed, will result in successful cost containment.

The Operations Management approach (see Diagram A) consists of several action steps. After defining the problem, appropriate data must be gathered. Documentation such as organization charts, statements of objectives, budgets and forecasts should be gathered and analyzed. Operating parameters must be defined and such resources as personnel, money, services, buildings, supplies and equipment (as currently utilized by function) should be identified. Service levels should be challenged to make certain that they are necessary or vital to the objectives of the institution. Oppor-

---

*This article is an abridged version of the original.

Diagram A*

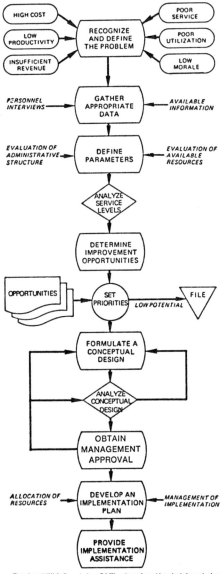

tunities for improvement should be assigned priorities depending upon their ultimate benefits. Alternative approaches or recommendations should be developed and analyzed. For each alternative, a conceptual design should be developed which identifies changes in organization structure, systems, operating procedures and resource allocation.

When these steps have been taken, specific management approval must be obtained and an implementation plan must be developed.

The implementation plan should specify assignments, responsibilities, target dates, milestones and measurable end products. And it should include the modification of the existing budget once the improvements are achieved. Using this plan, management can measure and monitor implementation performance.

The implementation team should be assisted on a day-to-day basis by management to resolve problems and to modify the implementation plan where necessary.

CRITERIA FOR SUCCESS

Operations Management is a relatively straightforward and logical approach to cost containment, and its application should be successful in every institution. There are, however, conditions which typically limit the success of the traditional techniques of cost containment and could also impair the successful application of Operations Management. These conditions can be grouped under a single generic heading—managerial bias.

Managerial bias is typified by such attitudes as a feeling that the problems will solve themselves; a feeling that the problems are beyond solution; an unwillingness to admit past errors; emotional involvement; avoidance of detailed and quantitative analysis; a disregard for the human element of the institution; and conflicts between departmental and overall hospital objectives. Managerial bias may result in deferral of action, avoidance of the issue, poorly conceived ideas, preconceived solutions, inadequate analysis and a failure to fully implement.

To be effective and to overcome managerial bias, an Operations Management project must be a joint effort between management, supervisory and operating personnel, and it must be responsive to the needs of the personnel it will impact. The limitations of the institution, and its ability to assimilate change, must be understood by the project staff.

The Operations Management approach calls for a "top down" identification of problems and opportunities for improvement together with a "bottom up" implementation of rational, objective and defensive solutions. There must also be a consensus of opinion concerning the definition of current problems, institutional objectives and the means for getting from one to the other (see Diagram B).

A PRACTICAL APPROACH

To provide health care institutions with an effective approach to cost containment, the American Hospital Association, with the assistance of Touche Ross, has formalized the Operations Management approach, and has developed a self-administered training program directed at department heads and first-line supervisors.

The program is designed to enable a health care institution to effectively train its own personnel in the techniques of Operations Management. The program is designed for five, weekly, two-hour sessions. It consists of an instructor's manual, participants' manuals, a slide presentation, and a variety of case studies to enable the participants to develop the necessary analytical skills for effective cost containment. The program is available through the American Hospital Association and is a must for every health care institution that wants to learn more about Operations Management and wishes to control its costs.

Diagram B* The Operations Management Approach

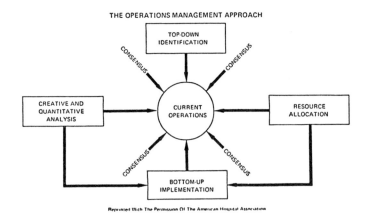

THE OPERATIONS MANAGEMENT APPROACH

Reprinted With The Permission Of The American Hospital Association

23. Opportunities for Improvement in Health Systems Engineering

DAVID H. GUSTAFSON, GLENWOOD L. ROWSE,
NANCY J. HOWES, AND RAMESH K. SHUKLA

Reprinted, with permission of the Blue Cross Association, from *Inquiry,*
Vol. XIV, No. 1 (March 1977), pp. 87–95. Copyright © 1977 by the
Blue Cross Association. All rights reserved.

Health systems engineers (frequently referred to as industrial or management engineers) are employed by hospitals and other health care institutions to study facility design and utilization, information flow, personnel utilization, and the degree to which performance objectives are being met, in the expectation that they will be of aid in reducing costs and improving the quality of and access to care. Initial reports on the work of health systems engineers (HSEs) in meeting these objectives were very encouraging;[1] and articles citing their successes continue to appear in the literature.[2] However, there now appears to be an undercurrent of pessimism regarding the ability of HSEs to have significant impact on the cost, quality and access problems of health care institutions.

CURRENT ASSESSMENTS OF HEALTH SYSTEMS ENGINEERS

Pessimism regarding HSEs seems to arise from two conditions: the constriction in the environment in which HSEs operate, and the weakness or unsuitability of the skills they bring to the job. Some writers believe that HSEs did, in the past, have an impact on cost, but that opportunities for cost reduction in the areas they are currently focusing on have diminished greatly.[3] Part of the reason for this belief is a perceived restriction on innovation in the health field resulting from such factors as wage and price controls in the past, and the possibility of national health insurance in the future.

189

Other writers consider HSEs deficient in the skills that are needed to attack cost, quality and access problems that are ripe for a systems engineering approach.[4] For example, a study by Gustafson, Doyle and May[5] on hospital employee incentive systems (an area of purported strength for HSEs) found that numerous attempts to install such systems had been unsuccessful, with only a few notable exceptions. One of the major reasons for this lack of success was seen to be the inability of HSEs to measure productivity and tie it to individual employees or employee groups.

On the other hand, problem areas that HSEs have the skills to address are often seen as peripheral. The authors found in site visits related to another aspect of this study that health systems engineering methods were seldom considered an important arm of the hospital's decision-making apparatus.[6] In this vein, a study by Hardwick and Wolfe[7] in which hospitals participated in an incentive reimbursement program supported by intensive HSE studies indicated that the rate of return from the program was very low, far less than 1 percent of the hospital budget. Wolfe has since concluded that problems of the type attacked in that study, essentially methods improvement, layout, and workflow, hold little potential for materially reducing hospital costs.

This mixed prognosis on the ability of health systems engineering to substantially affect basic health issues extends to the more mathematical arms of HSE. Stimson and Stimson[8] reviewed the literature on the application of operations research to hospitals, as well as conducting their own site visits. They found that "most operations research studies in hospitals have shortcomings that have precluded their being implemented."[9] Stimson and Stimson also report that Young, in his review, "was hard pressed to name a single instance where application of operations research had initiated or led to a major decision in the health sciences."[10] Participants at a conference on the role of operation research in the health field reached similar conclusions;[11] while in the closely-related field of information systems, Freeman and Gue[12] discovered a corresponding lack of success.

These very mixed predictions of the likelihood that systems engineering will have a favorable impact on the pressing problems in the health field are due in part to the difficulty of demonstrating the effectiveness of systems engineering programs. This suggests the need for better evaluative techniques for measuring effectiveness, so that a thorough and accurate assessment of the impact of HSEs in the health arena can be undertaken. It is also necessary to examine the role being played by health systems engineers today vis-a-vis the major problems facing health care institutions. If HSEs are to help devise ways to reduce costs and improve access to and quality of care, it is first essential to identify the present barriers to achieving these goals, and then to ascertain the appropriate systems analysis skills to address them. This paper seeks to provide an overview of the factors that seem to influence the success or failure of health systems engineering programs.

METHODOLOGY

The research for this study was done by means of site visits and survey questionnaires sent to health systems engineering users and to active HSEs.

Site Visits

Prominent health systems professionals were asked to nominate various HSE programs and to indicate their opinions of where these programs fit along a scale of success to failure. Nominated institutions were sent a questionnaire requesting information about program objectives, staffing, budgets, length of program existence, experience and educational background of staff, subjective factors of success, and present and expected areas of difficulty in meeting program objectives.

The researchers selected various types of health care organizations to visit from this sample, including engineering programs in public health, planning, and financing agencies, and consulting firms. These visits were supplemented by information from nine other site visits of HSE programs conducted earlier for the American Hospital Association.[13]

Site visit teams included health systems researchers, administrators, engineers and HSE educators. One day was spent at each site, where from six to 15 staff members were interviewed, including representatives from top and middle management, staff specialists, physicians, and nurses.

The protocol for each interview included questions from the following categories:

- History and background of the program or project: how and why was this project developed, who financed it, and how were HSEs involved?
- Environmental factors: what environmental factors (social, political, economic, and others) contributed to the success or failure of the project? (To be assessed by questioning or observation.)
- Organizational structure: who undertook the major responsibilities and decision-making, and who had authority in different areas and phases of the project? What were the organizational relationships of the project with other subunits of the total organization?
- Design of the study: by whom, when and how was the study designed?
- Design phase, implementation phase and evaluation phase: who was or is in charge, what tools and techniques were/are used, and how explicit was/is the overall methodology for the project?

Table 1 Composite List of Important Barriers to Improving the Quality, Cost and Accessibility of Health Care Services

Barriers	Problem Impact		
	Access	Cost	Quality
Consumers lack understanding of preventive measures.	*	*	*
Consumers lack understanding of when services are needed.		*	*
Third-party payment policies do not adequately discriminate between poor and good quality care.			*
Incentives for quality care provided by competitors, governing boards, third-party payers, and consumers are minimal.	*	*	*
Lack of quality care standards.			*
Consumers and providers view service as a reactive rather than a preventive function.	*		*
Organization and coordination of all health services is (sic) inadequate.		*	*
Inability to agree on health goals.	*		*
Consumers lack means of providing incentives to improve quality.		*	*
Services are not accessible when needed.			*
Consumers hesitate to take issue with the physician.		*	*
Information and measures causally relating treatment interventions to outcomes are largely absent.	*	*	*
Fee for service system encourages an increase in the volume of services provided but not in the quality of services.	*	*	*
Consumers lack understanding of availability of services.	*		*
Providers lack skills to evaluate proposed innovations.	*	*	
Needed cost benefit information does not exist.		*	
The increasing and changing nature of demand for health services.		*	
Inflation.		*	
Implementation skills for cost reduction projects are lacking.		*	
Cost reduction projects have had the wrong forms.		*	
Providers lack management skills.		*	
Consumer problems in financing their health care.	*		
Incentives do not exist for physicians to locate in rural or ghetto areas.	*		
Services not reimbursed by third-party payers are not sought.	*		
Legal and educational barriers to use of paramedical personnel.	*		
Design skills needed to improve accessibility are not present.	*		
Economic barriers prohibit wide distribution of high cost/low demand services.		*	

- Knowledge, attitudes and skills of the HSEs on the project: what were the HSE's perceptions of the knowledge, attitudes and skills required or expected of them? What knowledge, attitudes and skills did the administrators and others expect the HSEs to have?
- Knowledge, attitudes and skills possessed by other project members.
- Attitudes of key people in the organization toward the project or program.
- Strengths and weaknesses of the program or project.

Surveys

Early in the project, over 240 health systems experts responded to a survey designed to establish normative standards regarding the types of problems that HSEs should be addressing (see Table 1) and the kinds of knowledge, attitudes and skills necessary to handle such problems.[14]

A random sample of 80 HSE users and 80 HSEs was asked to rank the knowledge, attitude and skill categories developed from the preliminary survey, using their own experiences as HSEs or their contract with HSEs as guidelines. Rankings were obtained for both the importance of the items to job success, and the need for improvement on the part of HSEs. In addition, the HSE users were asked to describe the major weaknesses of HSEs and the projects they would like to see them address.

Interpretation

The findings from the site visits by the research team were compared to the set of normative standards developed from the surveys. The remainder of this paper discusses the differences found between the reality discovered in the site visits and the ideal projected by the rankings of users and HSEs through questionnaire surveys. This treatment does not focus on the effectiveness of health systems engineering, but rather on those experiences of HSEs and users that could contribute to a better understanding of ways of making better use of the skills and talents of HSEs in the health field.

FINDINGS: BARRIERS TO SUCCESS

The success of the systems engineer in a health setting appears to be related to three factors: 1) the problems attacked by the HSEs; 2) organizational structure of HSE services; and 3) the attitudes, knowledge, and skills possessed by the HSEs.

Problems Attacked

It is assumed that HSEs, if they are to be effective, must address problems that are important to their institution; that is, HSEs will have the greatest impact if they solve basic and major problems.[15] This section analyzes the degree to which HSEs have applied themselves to various types of problems, and discusses the implications of discrepancies between the problems that were classified as most significant by HSEs and HSE users, and the areas where most HSE efforts have been expended. Table 2 shows the four major problem areas and the frequency that these problems act as barriers to the attainment of health system goals.

It is significant that although only 25 percent of the barriers to success in achievement of goals are seen to be operational problems, our research shows that more than 75 percent of the HSE's time is spent in that area. It can easily be seen that the effectiveness of HSEs is seriously diminished by expending large amounts of time on problems that have only minimal importance for improving cost, quality and access features of the health system.

There are two basic aspects of the inappropriateness of the tasks HSEs have hitherto addressed. First, the impact that HSEs attain by dealing with operational problems appears to be marginal when compared with the potential impact they could have by attacking planning and policy problems. Research has shown, for example, that the more powerful HSE skills are better suited to the solution of planning and policy problems than they are to operational problems.[16] Furthermore, the researchers found in their site visits that systems engineering programs that focused on operational problems were predicting returns of four or five to one on the salaries of the systems engineers,[17] whereas the few projects visited in which HSEs were dealing with planning and policy problems were expecting much larger returns relative to effort and cost.

Some of these projects dealing with planning and policy issues and their results were:

- A project for determining the number of inpatient beds needed in a community was responsible for reducing hospital construction costs by more than $200-million.
- A third-party financing organization has implemented an HSE-designed system of prospective reimbursement, developed with statistical forecasting and control techniques at a cost of $150,000. In a pilot test in five institutions, the first-year reduction in the rate of cost increases was significant. The saving is currently $120,000 per year for each institution, and there are now 17 institutions in the program.

Table 2 Problem Types and Extent of Prevalence

Problem Type	Percent Prevalence
Operational Problems	25

Those that require the refinement of existing procedures to improve productivity or satisfaction in health systems. Projects of this type occur primarily in delivery settings and focus on techniques for establishing standards, improving work methods and personnel utilization, accomplishing facilities layout, developing simple communication and monitoring procedures, and locating and providing needed information for decision-makers.

Planning and Policy Problems	70

These involve the need for identifying appropriate policies and procedures that alter the health system at an organization-wide or interorganizational level. Projects dealing with these problems are currently being undertaken primarily in planning agencies, but should in the future also be undertaken at the upper management levels of delivery systems. Usually these projects are of a complexity that would benefit from considerable data collection, analysis, and the interaction and agreement of many diverse types of professionals. Outcomes of these projects include identification and redistribution of inequitable services across delivery areas, increased emphasis on the provision of preventive services to consumers, better definition of and agreement on health goals, new consumer financing mechanisms, innovative reward and incentive systems for health professionals, improved types of delivery units, provision of new computer and other management service mechanisms, and better coordinative links among various health organizations.

Educational Problems	50

These involve the need to improve the knowledge and skills of consumers or providers involved with the health system.

Research and Development Problems	20

Those for which considerable data need to be collected under rigidly controlled conditions in order to develop effective and optimal solutions.

- A public health unit is installing a completely new system for detecting and treating infectious disease. A systems engineer used simulation and modeling to compare the estimated performance of the new system to other strategies for detecting and treating infectious disease; the analysis served as the basis for altering the approach of the new system.

From these examples, it can be seen that HSEs have consumed most of their energies on operational problems, despite the fact that HSE users and HSEs themselves feel that planning and policy issues are three times more important in the improvement of the health system, that operational projects show a far lower rate of return in economic terms than do policy and planning ones, and that research suggests the HSE skills are better suited to the solution of planning and policy problems than to operational pursuits.

A second way to demonstrate the inappropriateness of the tasks currently addressed by HSEs is to compare the situation in health systems engineering with that in other industries. Successful staff specialists in other fields usually address the key agenda items of the governing elites and provide information that would help to shape and inform their decisions.[18] Our site visits, on the other hand, suggested that the primary concern of staff specialists in the health field were operational problems that were quite divorced from the interests of the governing elites. The research literature suggests that staff specialists in general, and systems engineers in particular, can improve their effectiveness by "penetrating the agendas of the elites" and discovering the policy issues that are of critical concern to decision-makers. Systems engineers could utilize their unique skills and perspectives to provide these elites with information that would improve their decision-making in the major area of concern, policy and planning.

In this organizational vein, it was found in site visits that HSEs are generally quite concerned with their position in the organizational hierarchy. Studies have shown their concern to be counter-productive, since organizational position has a very low correlation with staff effectiveness.[19]

Why, then, have HSEs so often been assigned operational tasks, when there are higher priority problems where their skills would be more beneficial? Four possible explanations come to mind:

1. Health systems may have little motivation to make broad organizational changes to improve the cost, quality and access aspects of health care. Smaller problems of an operational nature are less threatening and still have marginally acceptable payoffs. However, with the increasing pressure on the health system to control costs and improve quality and access, the need for staff assistance to planners and policy-makers is becoming more apparent and the barriers against the use of

HSE skills in these areas may be breaking down.

2. HSEs have not been able to prove that they can deal with policy-level problems. As Stimson and Stimson suggest, the isolated instances of success are easily outweighed by failures.[20] Controlled studies of the degree of success in the application of HSE tools at planning and policy levels are imperative at this point to demonstrate effectiveness and to increase the legitimacy of HSEs.

3. The use of HSEs has been largely limited to hospitals, where opportunities for far-ranging impact are fewer and where there is more resistance to using HSEs in top-level ways. With the development of Health Systems Agencies, both financial and organizational opportunities should exist for HSEs to have an impact at the multi-institutional policy level. The authors feel that HSEs could be utilized in similar influential ways at the corporate planning levels of hospitals and clinics. These settings would also allow the HSEs the best showcase for their talents. However, opportunities in these areas will be limited until a number of impressive HSE successes can be demonstrated and documented.

4. HSEs appear to be overly concerned with whom they report to in the organizational structure, while earlier discussion of studies of successful staff organizations indicated that position in the organizational hierarchy is not a good predictor of success. Rather, as Hage and Dewar[21] suggest, a staff person's ability to identify critical issues that concern decision-makers and his or her willingness to address those issues is far more important. HSEs could be far more effective if they were to concentrate on determining powerful issues rather than powerful persons within the organizational structure.

Organizational Structure of HSE Services

Another problem that inhibits the success of the HSE in a health setting is the internal organization of HSE services. It is essential that a staff specialist has the opportunity to reinforce his or her expertise through communication with other specialists, and to draw upon complementary skills when necessary. The HSEs interviewed in this study were not able to do this effectively, since they still practiced in large part either alone or with one other HSE in individual hospitals. Although there do exist HSE organizations that offer their services to several hospitals, which permits professional interaction, the HSE is generally isolated professionally.

In all but a few cases, the HSEs interviewed were the only staff person working on a problem, with minimal guidance from decision-making elites. This places a severe restriction on the ability of the HSE to address more complicated issues of policy and planning, since one or two HSEs cannot possess all the skills and knowledge needed in complex problem-solving efforts. Policy-level problems usually require access to modeling, operations research, and other quantitative systems engineering skills and methods, as well as knowledge of organization theory, finance, law, medicine, and nursing. Our study revealed that practicing HSEs were very limited even in the HSE skills they had been trained in, which makes their access to other HSE specialists even more vital. Supportive expertise in non-HSE areas can be provided by the institution to some extent, but the availability and commitment of the institution's resources to this type of problem-solving effort has been severely limited.

Support from other knowledge and skill resources has also been restricted by the HSE's lack of understanding of the issues that are critical to administrators, and his own inability to communicate. HSEs must be able to tap the knowledge of administrators and other users of HSE services as to the full configuration of the policy and planning issues they wish to address. This goes both ways, of course; administrators must more clearly define the types of information and assistance they expect from HSEs in solution efforts. In many cases, administrators, health providers and the HSEs themselves have not agreed on what the precise HSE goals and authority are. This ambiguity can only hinder cooperation among groups. For a time at least, HSEs must take the responsibility for dealing with these ambiguities and constraints.

One mechanism that has been shown to be effective in staff groups in other settings is the boundary spanner.[22] This person bridges the gap between elites in the organization and the technical staff, since his possession of a value system common to both groups allows him to understand and articulate the views of both sides. In a health organization, the boundary spanner could be a member of the administrative staff in frequent communication with staff specialists and organizational elites, who is cognizant of the types of information and support that decision-makers need. This boundary spanner could draw the expertise of many fields into the complex decision-making process.

The development of multidisciplinary staff organizations that would have a broad, multi-institutional impact may be more difficult, but the benefits that would accrue could be enormous. The development of such organizational structures could be facilitated by investigating alternate methods of regionalizing services, and by utilizing more staff specialists in planning and policy agencies.

In short, the organizational structures within which most HSEs currently practice appear to be ineffective, inefficient, and outmoded. Major changes must be made if the special skills of HSEs are to be used to best advantage in addressing critical health issues, and if experts from other fields of knowledge are to be drawn into a synergistic solution effort that would produce optimal answers.

Knowledge, Attitudes, and Skills of HSEs

Previous sections of this article have touched briefly on the strengths of HSEs in regard to knowledge, attitudes and skills; in this section we will focus on their weaknesses in these areas as seen by the HSEs and HSE users interviewed in this study.

The attitudes of the systems engineer were felt by HSEs and users to be more important to engineering success than either knowledge or skills. In terms of relative contribution to success, attitudes were rated by the 160 respondents at 40 percent, knowledge at 30 percent, and skills at 30 percent. The most common attitude weaknesses of practicing HSEs were identified as: 1) inflexibility; 2) not accepting political processes as an important part of social change; 3) failing to recognize the significant limitations of many analytical and organizational techniques; 4) minimizing the importance of the values, ideas and feelings of others; and 5) inadequate concern for the agendas of decision-making elites. Similar findings were suggested by Hoos[23] in her analysis of systems engineers in public policy positions.

These attitudes are difficult but not impossible to influence. Better student selection processes, field experiences, and other formal educational techniques during training could help to alleviate these problems.

Systems engineers in the health field seem to be fairly competent with respect to those traditional industrial engineering tools that work well with operational-level problems. The situation is different, however, in policy-level problems, which require a higher degree of sophistication in the use of complex quantitative tools for measuring benefits, forecasting trends, and modeling systems. Most practicing HSEs have not attained this level of knowledge or skill.

The greatest weakness of HSEs found by this study lay in the skills and knowledge that support the use of systems tools: 1) communication or interaction skills; 2) factual knowledge about the health services system; 3) understanding of change processes and skills for implementing change; 4) knowledge of sources of specialized information and assistance in the HSE field and in related areas; and 5) sensitivity to the political and social influences that bear on decision-making. Other important HSE weaknesses that were mentioned less frequently were lack of awareness of group process techniques for information collection, and unfamiliarity with future role models for HSEs.

To illustrate the way in which HSE weaknesses in knowledge, skills and attitudes handicap their effectiveness in helping to bring about change in a particular health organization, a brief foray into change theory will be useful. Basically, the change process has three distinct phases: unfreezing, changing, and refreezing.[24] During the unfreezing phase of the change process, people begin to recognize a need for change. In successful change efforts, the unfreezing phase is characterized by these factors: 1) the costs and benefits of existing delivery systems is known; 2) comparisons can be made of performance within the organization, or across organizations; 3) predictions of future benefits and costs are accurate; 4) the goals of the organization are agreed upon and well-defined; and 5) the values of decision-makers are understood by staff people. Systems engineering tools could be very helpful in gathering the information necessary for the first three of these preconditions for success, but our site visits revealed that HSE skills are very seldom used during this phase of the change process.

The changing phase involves the design and implementation of change. During this stage in successful programs, the following occur: 1) problem-solving is divided into workable phases; 2) causes of problems are ascertained; 3) premature closure on solutions is prevented; 4) each phase of problem-solving draws upon the most qualified people available (which means that different people will be involved in different phases, rather than having a static change group); and 5) objectives become more specific as problem-solving progresses.

Many HSEs have been trained in the systems approach, which is a problem-solving strategy. This strategy has recently been modified to be more useful in health or other social systems, and coupling this modified systems approach with skills in group process techniques could produce a systems engineer well prepared to contribute to this stage of the change process. However, many changes will have to occur in the training and use of HSEs before this vision becomes a reality.

The refreezing phase of the change process consists of the evaluation and institutionalization of the innovation. In this stage, successful change programs seem to be characterized by: 1) careful planning and conduct of initial implementation efforts; 2) a thorough evaluation of the success of new programs; 3) involvement of other potential program users during its test phase; and 4) sensitivity toward the socio-political, behavioral, and psychological problems that can interfere with change.

The health system has not been successful in providing these conditions. For the most part, our study found that implementation efforts were haphazard, program evaluation was given only lip service, users were not generally involved in demonstration projects, and little consideration was given to the side effects of new programs. Systems engineering skills such as scheduling, resource allocation and program evaluation techniques could be beneficially utilized during this phase, but at this time the health system does not recognize the contribution HSEs could make in this area.

Our discussion of the weaknesses of HSEs in both knowledge and skills and in attitudes highlights our finding that deficiencies in technical skills were less important than in the interpersonal sphere. As we have noted, three of the five top weaknesses in the knowledge and skills area, according to both users and HSEs themselves, dealt with interpersonal relations. Further, analysis of the tasks involved in the change process reinforces the importance of interpersonal skills, since HSEs must frequently interact with a broad range of health professional specialists and consumers in a very political environment to obtain their understanding, support and expertise in order to initiate and complete every stage of the change process.

Educational programs for HSEs have traditionally focused on technical skills at the expense of important adjuncts to that technical training. It is felt that attention to improving these supportive attitudes and skills in both practitioners and HSE students would have the greatest immediate impact on enhancing engineering effectiveness for any given project.

CONCLUSION

The weaknesses of health systems engineers presented in this article should not be viewed as a testimonial against the potential effectiveness of systems engineering, for an equally extensive list could be developed for any profession. Instead, for the ultimate benefit of health service systems and consumers, we need to recognize that the potential of HSEs has not been met. Efforts need to be directed toward understanding and correcting these weaknesses to assist HSEs in developing their potential. To summarize, we suggest that the HSE can play an important role in efforts to control costs and improve access to and quality of care in the health system. But in order for this to happen, the role of the HSE needs further definition, and significant changes are needed before the HSE can play this role effectively.

REFERENCES AND NOTES

1. Smalley, H. E. and Freeman, J. R. *Hospital Industrial Engineering* (New York: Reinholdt, 1966).

2. Salvekar, A. "Management Engineering Reduces Costs/Improves Care." *Hospital Progress* 56:28–36 (January 1975).

3. Ludwig, P. E. *Dollars and Sense: An Approach Towards Hospital Cost Containment and Quality Improvement Through Management Engineering Programs* (Battle Creek, Michigan: Kellogg Foundation, 1971).

4. *Ibid.*

5. Gustafson, D.; Doyle, J.; and May, J. *Incentives for Hospital Employees* (Washington, D.C.: GPO, 1972).

6. Gustafson, D.; Rowse, G.; and Howes, N. "Roles and Training of Future Health Systems Engineers," in: *Education for Health Administration,* Vol. II (Ann Arbor: Health Administration Press, 1975) pp. 76-104.

7. Hardwick, P. C. and Wolfe, H. *An Incentive Reimbursement, Industrial Engineering Experiment* (Washington, D.C.: Department of Health, Education and Welfare Publication No. (HSM) 72-3003, December 1971).

8. Stimson, D. and Stimson, R. *Operations Research in Hospitals: Diagnosis and Prognosis* (Chicago: Hospital Research and Educational Trust, 1972).

9. *Ibid.,* p. 39.

10. Young, J. P. "No Easy Solutions," in: Chacko, G. K. (ed.) *The Recognition of Systems in Health Services* (Arlington, Va.: Operations Research Society of America, 1975) pp. 395-398.

11. Shuman, L. R.; Speas, R. D.; and Young, J. P. *Operations Research in Health Care—A Critical Analysis* (Baltimore: Johns Hopkins University Press, 1975).

12. Freeman, J. and Gue, R. "Information Systems and Operations Research in Health Care," paper presented to Second Operations Research Society of America Health Applications Symposium, "Health Operations Research: A Critical Analysis," Atlantic City, New Jersey, November 1972.

13. Gustafson, Doyle and May, *op. cit.*

14. Gustafson, D. H.; Rowse, G. L.; and Howes, N. J. *Roles and Training for Future Health Systems Engineers* (Madison: University of Wisconsin, Engineering Experiment Station, 1974) 400 pages.

15. Hage, G. and Aiken, M. *Social Change in Complex Organizations* (New York: Random House, 1970).

16. Gustafson, Rowse and Howes, *Roles and Training, op. cit.*

17. *Ibid.;* and Gustafson, Doyle and May, *op. cit.*

18. Pelz, D. and Andrews, F. *Scientists in Organizations* (New York: Wiley and Sons, 1966).

19. Hage, G. and Dewar, R. "Elite Value vs. Organization Structure in Predicting Innovation," *Administrative Science Quarterly* 18:1-8 (September 1973).

20. Stimson and Stimson, *op. cit.*

21. Hage and Dewar, *op. cit.*

22. Filley, A. and Delbecq, A. *Program and Project Management in a Matrix Organization: A Case Study* (Madison: University of Wisconsin Press, Bureau of Business Research and Seminars, 1974).

23. Hoos, I. *Systems Analysis in Public Policy* (Berkeley: University of California Press, 1972).

24. Howes, N. J. *Change Factors Related to the Institutionalization of the Multiunit Elementary School,* unpublished doctoral dissertation, University of Wisconsin, 1974.

24. Work Simplification: "Working Smarter, Not Harder"

CHARLES J. FERDERBER
Reprinted from the April 1972 issue of *Hospital Financial Management*.
Copyright 1972 Hospital Financial Management Association.

Accelerated spending in the health care industry has created a tremendous rise in the cost of medical care. The public has been reluctant to accept that this is due to the nature and complexity of hospitals—particularly since three-fourths of the total health care cost today is borne by insurance carriers.

In 1970, over $63 billion was spent in the health care industry and by 1973 the projection is $80 to $100 billion. The cost staggers the imagination. Interestingly enough, approximately $54 billion was spent for taking care of the sick while less than $10 billion a year was spent on preventing diseases.

Hospital administrators are deeply concerned with the high cost of health care, particularly hospital costs. The media are too quick to criticize hospital management by applying their "instant expertise" to isolated instances of high cost. The greatest single expenditure for hospital expenses lies in labor costs which account for 70% of the total budget. Progress in hospitals has somewhat a reverse effect that it has in industry: it creates a greater labor requirement, since the health industry is service oriented. No real way has been found to automate patient care. While it's true that some hospital activities do lend themselves to automation, no one has proven savings on automated TLC (Tender Loving Care).

There has been more progress in the health care industry in the last 30 years than the last 30 centuries. Over half of the drugs used today were merely a researcher's dream 10 to 15 years ago. Hospital care equals services, and no amount of criticism or legislation is going to change this. We can, however, institute cost containment programs—and that brings us to at least one proven method called "Work Simplification."

Work simplification was the product of many great management engineers, among them Frank and Lillian Gilbreth, Alan Mogenson, Frederick Taylor and Ralph Barnes, as well as others. Initially, work simplification tools and techniques were aimed primarily at industry, but it has a great potential use in hospitals today. Work simplification simply defined is "working smarter, not harder." Or it is "an organized application of common sense." It's not something to be feared, but merely a means of applying certain proven industrial engineering techniques to problem situations in a hospital. Anyone in middle management or above can readily assimilate these techniques and apply them to problem-solving.

In any hospital there is an untapped wealth of talent among the employees mainly because they are not encouraged to come up with new ideas. Most employees have ideas about what to improve but do not have the wherewithal to incorporate them into documented recommendations. The objective of any work simplification program is to:

A. develop an openminded friendly atmosphere.
B. develop a breeding ground for ideas.
C. encourage activity.
D. stimulate thinking.
E. foster success.

How does one create an atmosphere conducive to change and creativity? Simply by accepting employees' ideas with enthusiasm. This does not necessarily mean accepting and implementing all ideas. One can, however, provide a fair hearing. Creativity is contagious and will be self-rewarding. Consider the emotional blocks that frequently undermine creativity.

The creativity pattern consists of six points:

Orientation—This is merely pinpointing the problem.
Preparation—Gathering pertinent data—fact finding.
Analysis—This is breaking down relevant material.
Developing a hypothesis—This phase is developing the idea to a logical conclusion.
Synthesis—This is putting the facts together to form an idea for consideration and perhaps lead to improvement of the problem.
Verification—Judging the resultant ideas and improvements that have been implemented—the follow thru phase.

Do you recognize these remarks frequently heard by industrial engineers or those trying to improve a situation?

"I just don't have time to fool with this gadgetry." What this really means is "I'm too busy to be efficient."

"It's all right for the other fellow but leave my department alone." This statement indicates that the individual is insecure in his position, and does not welcome any other ideas.

"Why should I change—it's been a good practice for 25 years." This is probably the expression most commonly used by many who cannot accept change, while implementation of more modern concepts was the very thing that provided his salary increase.

"I don't approve of change for change's sake." In other words, stay out of my department.

"I'm too busy." Perhaps too busy to be efficient.

To the industrial engineer these remarks are understandable. He has learned that new ideas do not come easily and that implementation is even more difficult. One must recognize their existence. One must also recognize human behavior and job insecurity, especially when the employees come up with ideas that the manager should have thought of himself. The best computers we have today are not the electronic monsters but the human brain, and if given half a chance or perhaps a voice, they can pleasantly surprise us.

There are seven separate steps of problem solving, all totally related to each other. Each step is in itself extremely important, and if one step is left out the problem-solving process will break down.

STEP 1—SELECT A JOB SITUATION

This sounds fairly easy. To find a good problem area, look for problem indicators. These indicators can be piled up work loads; taking work home; backlogs; excessive time required to do the job; filled in-baskets; simple jobs that require too much time; poor morale; or just plain nonproductivity. When deciding on what to improve, I recommend using "funnel vision," which is what it implies, a very narrow field of vision. By taking too broad a subject one can get mired down in too much detail and getting back to the original problem can be elusive. It is better to be selective, taking a single idea and following it through to its conclusion. For every job or procedure there are three parts; *getting ready, doing,* and *putting it away.*

Figure A

ORGANIZATIONAL UNIT CHARTED: PLANT OPERATIONS				WORK DISTRIBUTION CHART						
☑ EXISTING ORGANIZATION ☐ RECOMMENDED ORGANIZATION			NAME: J. R. ALLEN		NAME: O. R. CULHANE			NAME: JOHN JOSEPH		
CHARTED BY: J. R. ALLEN			POSITION: Director, Plant Operations		POSITION: Foreman, Electrical Shop			POSITION: Foreman, Carpenter Shop		
ACTIVITY NUMBER	ACTIVITY	HOURS PER WEEK	WORK COUNT	TASKS	HOURS PER WEEK	WORK COUNT	TASKS	HOURS PER WEEK	WORK COUNT	TASKS	HOURS PER WEEK	WORK COUNT
1	Repairs and Maintenance of Plant Equipment	47	8	Supervise Plant Operations	9		Supervise Subordinates	7		Assign Work to Subordinates	2	
				Answers Plant Inquiries	5		Assign Work	3		Inspect Jobs	4	
				Inspects Shops	7		Repair Electrical Equipment	7	8	Demonstrates Repairs	3	
2	Process Work Orders	8	110				Work Orders Repairs	4	35	Work Orders Repairs Records Incoming Supplies	4	75
3	Prepare Weekly & Monthly Reports	27		Audits Budget Reports	6		Prepares Drafts and Types	9		Prepares Drafts and Types	10	
				Signs Reports	2							
4	Inventory & Supply Requisitions	20		Signs Requisitions	2		Orders and Issues Supplies	4		Orders and Issues Supplies	8	
							Inventory	1		Inventory	5	
5	Preventive Maintenance	5		Preventive Maintenance	3		Cleanup & Preventive Maintenance	1		Cleanup & Preventive Maintenance	1	
6	Miscellaneous	13		Attends Conferences	6		Attends Conferences	4		Attends Conferences	3	
	TOTALS (Manhours)	120			40			40			40	

By concentrating on eliminating the doing, one automatically eliminates the other two parts.

STEP 2—BE SURE TO CONSULT ALL CONCERNED

Embarking upon a study without consulting all individuals directly concerned is a sure way to be defeated before beginning. It is impossible to get total cooperation in the fact-finding or problem-solving phase without having consulted all concerned. Avoid any criticism, or better still, involve the area of action in the planning process. This creates a favorable climate for change. A note of caution—don't get caught in an organizational crossfire. One of the best ways to consult all concerned, other than personal contact, is to publish a letter of intent, approved by the administrator or chief of the department. State what you plan to do and the method you plan to employ.

STEP 3—GET ALL THE FACTS

Bernard Baruch is credited with saying that "every man is entitled to his opinion, but no man has the right to be wrong in his facts." Work simplification techniques provide the tools for getting the facts simpler and quicker than otherwise. When getting the facts, consider existing policies and procedures; layouts; personnel involved; job descriptions; engineered standards; time standards; schedules and work-load statistics. After collecting the facts and exhibits that might possibly be needed, i.e., forms, reports, etc., then tie in the narrative, making reference to the appropriate exhibits. The simple techniques of flow process charting, time flow charting, horizontal flow charting, work distribution, layout, time and motion, and other problem solving tools are invaluable for the fact finding phase. Getting the facts can be very challenging. Don't make the mistake of checking out a procedure with but one person—try to corroborate this with others. You'll generally find a point or two was missed when checking with one person. When getting the facts, do not consider only the first problem that develops because there will surely be many more to follow. Stick to the basic idea and follow it through in its entirety, making sure that no detail is left out, that the system as it exists now has been rechecked. Once the problem is fully recognized, the solution becomes relatively simple.

Figures A through E are examples of measuring work distribution flows. Work distribution charting shows the distribution of work on one form by recording in one place all the activities of the department or specific area within the department, and the contributions each individual makes toward the accomplishment of each activity. Initially you prepare an activity list (See Figure B) which is nothing more than a very short summary of the functions of that particular department. The example used is Plant Operations. If work units or volume of work performed are important to the activity, this is inserted in the right column, Figure B. Following the activity list, you then ask each employee to prepare a task list as shown in Figures C, D, and E. The tasks should be in order of importance. You always work on the base of a 40-hour week. Keep it simple and descriptive. After listing all the tasks of each employee, indicate in the column marked "Activity Number" the activity that that particular task fits. In other words, "Supervises Plant Operations," (Figure C) would correspond to the activity, Number 1, "Repair and Maintenance of Plant Equipment." You then insert "1" under Activity, and so on. This is a judgment, but be consistent throughout.

After the Activity List and the Task List have been prepared, project the same information in the manner shown on Figure A, the "Work Distribution Chart." This is a word picture of what each individual in that par-

Figure B

ACTIVITY LIST FOR WORK DISTRIBUTION CHART		
DEPARTMENT OR SERVICE PLANT OPERATION	**SUPERVISOR:** J. R. ALLEN Director, Plant Operation	**DATE:** February 5th, 1970
ACTIVITY NR	**ACTIVITY**	**ACTIVITY UNITS AND OR VOLUME (OPTIONAL)**
1	Repair and Maintenance of Plant Equipment	13
2	Process Work Orders	135
3	Prepare Weekly and Monthly Reports	
4	Inventory and Supply Requisitions	
5	Preventive Maintenance	
6	Miscellaneous	

ticular department, service or section is doing, and how much time is spent doing each task within that particular department. As we stated earlier, challenge every detail. This can be done by asking these questions:

- What activities take the most time, and should these activities take the most time?
- Is there misdirected effort?
- Are the skills used properly?
- Are employees doing too many unrelated tasks?
- Are the tasks spread too thinly?
- Is the work distributed evenly?

You will note on Figure A, under Activity 3, that supervisors are preparing drafts and typing. Considering the high cost of a foreman of the electrical shop or of a carpenter shop, you are paying too high a price for typing and preparing drafts, as well as for ordering and issuing supplies and inventory. Notice also that foremen are involved in clean-up and preventive maintenance. Preventive maintenance would properly apply to a foreman, but not clean-up. Delegate this responsibility to a less skilled employee.

Another example of a work simplification tool is the flow process chart procedure, Exhibit F. This is an excellent tool and probably the most popular with students. It's a simple device that you use to chronologically follow a person, or a single object, such as a form or requisition, or a procedure such as preparing medication, a prescription showing in detail what happens in a flow process. Notice the symbols which are self-explanatory and interconnected with lines to show how an item or man proceeds through a single procedure. The important things to remember in charting flow process are: (a) to state the job to be studied; (b) to be specific as to what is being studied (Figure F shows dispensing medicines with medicine cards); (c) to choose a subject to be followed, a person or materiel, a part of an article, a paper form; (d) to always pick a beginning and ending point; (e) to decide on the ground to cover, no more, no less, but to put down every step, no matter how slight; (f) to then write a brief description of each detail, every operation: transportation, storage, delay and inspection.

Figure C

TASK NO.	DESCRIPTION	HOURS PER WEEK	WORK COUNT	ACTIVITY NO.
1	Supervises Plant Operations	9		1
2	Answers Plant Inquiries	5		1
3	Inspects Shops	7		1
4	Audits Budget Reports	6		3
5	Signs Reports	2		3
6	Signs Requisitions	2		4
7	Preventive Maintenance Programs	3		5
8	Attends Conferences	6		6

TASK LIST
FOR WORK DISTRIBUTION CHART

NAME: J. R. ALLEN
WORKING TITLE: DIRECTOR, PLANT OPERATION
DEPARTMENT OR SERVICE: Plant Operation
SUPERVISOR: R. J. SAMPSON Administrator
DATE: February 5th, 1970

FORM NO. 600-B-109 (8-68)   TOTAL ⟶ 40

Figure D

TASK NO.	DESCRIPTION	HOURS PER WEEK	WORK COUNT	ACTIVITY NO.
	TASK LIST FOR WORK DISTRIBUTION CHART			
	NAME: O. R. CULHANE	**WORKING TITLE:** FOREMAN, ELECTRICAL SHOP		
	DEPARTMENT OR SERVICE Plant Operation	**SUPERVISOR:** J. R. ALLEN Director, Plant Operation	**DATE:** February 5th, 1970	
1	Supervises Subordinates	7		1
2	Assign Work	3		1
3	Repair Electrical Equipment	7	8	1
4	Work Orders Repairs	4	35	2
5	Prepares Drafts and Types	9		3
6	Orders & Issues Supplies	4		4
7	Inventory	1		4
8	Cleanup and Preventive Maintenance	1		5
9	Attends Conferences	4		6
	FORM NO. 600-B-109 (8-68) TOTAL ➤	40		

Apply the symbols: "O" for an operation, or in other words, an action taking place. Transportation is any movement over two feet. Inspection is any visually scanning or checking. A "D," again self-explanatory, is a delay; and an inverted triangle represents filing. Always enter the time, quantity and distance. Distance is always in feet and time always in minutes.

You will notice, in the upper right hand corner of the form, the summary of all operations, all transportations, inspections, delays, storages, etc. Again we challenge every detail. What is done? Where is it done? When is it done? Who is doing it? How is it done? And in each case you apply the big question *"why?"* *Why* is it done at all? *Why* is it done in this particular place and why it is done then? *Why* does this person do it? *Why* is it done this way? Generally after questioning what is being done, some entire procedures can be eliminated. Again consider that every job consists of three parts: the make-ready, the doing, and the put-away. Of course, if you eliminate the do, you automatically eliminate the make-ready and put-away. So when charting flow process, always concentrate on the blacked in "do"

Figure E

TASK NO.	DESCRIPTION	HOURS PER WEEK	WORK COUNT	ACTIVITY NO.
1	Assigns Work to Subordinates	2		1
2	Inspects Jobs	4		1
3	Demonstrates Repairs	3		1
4	~~Records Incoming Supplies~~ Work Orders Repairs	4	75	2
5	Prepares Drafts and Types	10		3
6	Orders & Issues Supplies	8		4
7	Inventory	5		4
8	Cleanup and Preventive Maintenance	1		5
9	Attend Conferences	3		6

T A S K L I S T
FOR WORK DISTRIBUTION CHART

NAME: JOHN JOSEPH

WORKING TITLE: FOREMAN, CARPENTER SHOP

DEPARTMENT OR SERVICE: PLANT OPERATION

SUPERVISOR: J. R. ALLEN, Director, Plant Operation

DATE: February 5th, 1970

FORM NO. 600-B-109 (8-68)　　　TOTAL ⟶ 40

operation. Do not make the mistake of sitting at your desk trying to figure out exactly what goes on in the sequence of a flow process charting. One must follow it, step by step, through an entire process by visually going through each action that takes place.

There is another tool that we find convenient for those who feel that they are involved in unnecessary activities but yet cannot pinpoint what the unnecessary activities are. This can be done simply by utilizing the time flow charts shown in Figure G. Again one should rely on the use of codes. Devise any type you wish. At the end of each day, or of the time period that is used, total up the times and apply the percentages. Time flow charting can be done by the individual himself or by some other observer.

STEP 4—CHALLENGING EVERY DETAIL

When we say challenge every detail, we mean the entire activity should be questioned. Don't assume because an activity has been in existence several

Figure F Flow Process Chart Present Procedure

FLOW PROCESS CHART					SUMMARY					
			ACTIONS		PRESENT		PROPOSED		DIFFERENCE	
					No.	Time	No.	Time	No	Time
PROCESS Dispensing Medicines with Medicine Cards			OPERATIONS		8	395				
			TRANSPORTATIONS		2	110				
☐ MAN OR ☒ MATERIEL			INSPECTIONS		5	230				
CHART BEGINS March 17, 1969	CHART ENDS March 21, 1969		DELAYS		0	---				
CREATED BY Miss Jones, R.N.			STORAGES		3	32				
			TOTAL		18	767				
DEPARTMENT Nursing Service			TOTAL FEET		300 ft.					

Details of [X] PRESENT METHOD ☐ PROPOSED METHOD	Symbols	Distance in Feet	Quantity	Time	Analysis Why? What? Where? When? Who? How?	NOTES	Analysis Change Eliminate Combine Sequence Place Person Improve
1. Trans. Med. Order to card	●⇨☐D▽		20	10	X	Eliminate card	X
2. Trans. Med. Order to Kardex	●⇨☐D▽		20	10			
3. Put card in card box	O⇨☐D▽		20	10	X	No cards	X
4. Remove all cards	O⇨☐D▽		80	3	X	No cards	X
5. Sort as to patient	O⇨☐D▽		80	12	X	No cards	X
6. Check cards with Kardex	O⇨☐D▽		80	30	X	Improve	X X
7. Place card in by time	O⇨☐D▽		80	12	X	No cards	X
8. Pull cards for hour & sort	O⇨☐D▽		20	10	X	No cards	X
9. Check card with Med.	O⇨☐D▽		200	50			X
10. Dispense medicine	O⇨☐D▽		200	50			
11. Check med. with card	O⇨☐D▽		200	50	•		X
12. Take to patient	O⇨☐D▽	150	200	100			
13. Identify patient (Wristband)	O⇨☐D▽		200	50			
14. Check med. with card	O⇨☐D▽		200	50	X	No cards	X
15. Administer Medication	O⇨☐D▽		200	200			
16. Return to nurses station	O⇨☐D▽	150	20	10			
17. Chart med. from card	O⇨☐D▽		200	100			X
18. Sort cards for next dose due	O⇨☐D▽		20	10	X	No cards	X
19.	O⇨☐D▽						
20.	O⇨☐D▽						
21.							

Figure G Time Flow Chart

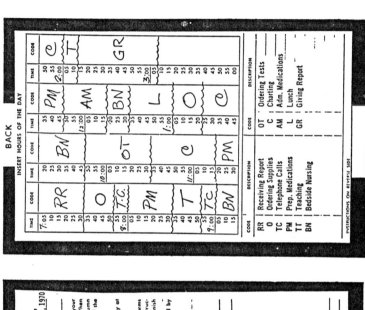

years that it is the best way to do the job or even that it is still necessary. Always ask these questions: "What is being done?", "Where is it being done?", "When is it being done?", "Who is doing it?", and "How is it being done?" By asking the question, "What is being done?", you may decide to eliminate the procedure. The next three, "where," "when," and "who," lead to combining sequences or changing parts, and, of course, the "how" always leads to simplification. By following the questioning attitude you will generally find that you can eliminate useless work. Hospital forms and statistics are frequently instituted by new supervisors and continued long after the supervisor has left. By tradition, we continue to process the statistics and fill out the necessary forms whether they are presently used or not. Frequently much of this statistical data ends up in a wastebasket. Always ask the question "WHY?"

STEP 5—DEVELOPING THE PREFERRED SOLUTION

This is considered the evaluation step, where we scrutinize all the facts, the exhibits, the data collected and then ask these questions:

- Will this new idea save time?
- Will it save effort?
- Will it save material?
- Will it save equipment?
- Will it save space?
- Will it result in better services for the patient?
- Can we justify the cost?

Then, write up a detailed solution, or perhaps several solutions.

STEP 6—SELL AND IMPLEMENT THE IDEA

Selling the idea is probably the toughest part of any designed improvement. The best way to sell an idea is through a well documented study showing the benefits, the changes and the improvement expected. Care must be given to the implementation of an idea, unless you perhaps plan a test to determine its feasibility. In our hospital, Deaconess, a Nursing Unit has been established for the purpose of testing ideas prior to full implementation. This gives us an opportunity to shake down the idea totally, to make any changes and corrections, or in some instances to abandon the idea. The nursing personnel in this test unit give their full cooperation in the evaluation of any new system or idea.

There are many human problems involved in the business of change. There will be resentment and criticism, but this can be overcome by establishing a rapport with the persons involved in the change. A sincere regard for the other fellow's problems and ideas is necessary. Personnel do not like to be told that they are wrong. Encourage individuals to participate in the improvement, making it a joint interest. The rewards will come back twicefold.

Another note of caution: do not design a $10,000 a year system to correct a $500 a year loss. In this day of increased costs, consideration must be given to the increased use of labor. A five dollar labor cost to process a $1.00 requisition is economically unsound.

If the improvement is quite involved, consideration should be given to teaching the system to all employees on all shifts. Also issue printed instructions for all concerned. Always use the "we," not the "I" approach to improvement. Remember that no improvement will be successful unless the person using it accepts it, and is enthusiastic about it.

STEP 7—FOLLOW THRU AND GIVE RECOGNITION

It is essential to see for yourself the outcome of your project and to make any necessary adjustments. And finally, acknowledge those that assisted you in the project—be it verbal or written. You'll find real friends and helpers for future projects.

In summary, Work Simplification is a must in hospitals. There are some good references available on work simplification:

Argyle Analearn Associates, *Idea Program.*

Bennett, Addison C., *Methods Improvements in Hospitals.* Philadelphia: J. B. Lippincott Co., 1964.

———, *An Employee Idea Program and Method Improvements in Hospitals.* Philadelphia: J. B. Lippincott Co., 1961.

Lehrer, Robert N., *Work Simplification.* New Jersey: Prentice Hall, 1957.

Smalley, Harold E. and Freeman, John R., *Hospital Industrial Engineering.* New York: Reinhold Publishing Corp., 1966.

At Deaconess Hospital we have published Hospital Work Simplification pamphlet specifically for our students. Courses are held two or three times a year, with no more than 12 students per 12 hours course. Hospitals contemplating such a program should ensure that the person selected to teach this subject is qualified and fully understands the principles of Work Simplification.

One of the most important by-products of Work Simplification is that it promotes better communications and a better understanding of the work to be accomplished.

25. Developing Work Standards for Hospitals

STEPHEN MELESKO

Reprinted from *Management Controls,* November 1974, pp. 239-245, copyrighted by Peat, Marwick, Mitchell & Co.

Labor standards have been used in hospitals for many years, but they have been confined primarily to the service departments such as laundry, housekeeping, maintenance, dietary, central supply and clerical. Several approaches to the use of unit value, weighted unit or similar systems in physician-controlled departments have been tried, but a universally accepted system for developing labor standards for the operating rooms, recovery rooms and anesthesiology, radiology and pathology departments has not been established. This article sets forth an approach that can be useful in these areas. But first, however, an elucidation of what is meant by standards in this context would be helpful.

The word *standard* has many definitions, and similarly many meanings have been attached to such phrases as *standard time, labor standards* and *production standards.* For the purposes of this article, the following meanings are assigned: A *standard* is a criterion or bench mark with which actual performance can be compared. By *labor standard,* we mean the time which is determined to be necessary for a qualified worker, working at a normal pace under capable supervision and experiencing normal fatigue and delays, to do a specified amount of work of acceptable quality when following the prescribed method.

Some of the common uses of standards, regardless of industry, are in connection with: labor budgets; staffing levels; incentives—individual, group, hospital (incentive reimbursement rewards); scheduling of work;

evaluation of cost improvement of equipment, material and systems; standard cost—for tasks, sections or departments; and management evaluation—performance and utilization indices.

FACTORS AFFECTING STANDARDS

In considering the use of standards for physician-controlled departments, we should analyze all the factors that would affect the standards or their use. Activity mixes—such as patient age, type of patient, type of test, examination, operation or procedure—will vary among hospitals and departments.

Activity will fluctuate by day, week, month, season or year. Each department within a hospital could realistically have different levels of quality for patient care. Methods and procedures change as administration, management and technology change, and require different tests, selected profiles or special exams. Equipment varies from fast to slow or automatic to manual with different schedules for utilization because of qualified personnel and unscheduled downtime. The layout of a given department varies from hospital to hospital, with resulting differences in travel time and expenditure of effort.

Personnel skills are usually highly diversified because of different training, job knowledge or the classification of employees being utilized. Some departments may use students or volunteers who perform productive tasks but also require teaching time. Schedules vary for nights, weekends and call time.

When we consider the use of labor standards, we must also decide whether we want to use broad or detailed units of measure because these units will affect the type of data and control desired. These factors are variables that could have an effect on work performed in physician-controlled departments, thereby increasing the complexity of developing standards.

TECHNIQUES AVAILABLE

The techniques available for developing standards are varied, ranging from the simple utilization of historical data to highly refined, predetermined time systems. These will now be briefly discussed.

Historical data utilizes any available labor and time statistics to establish broad standards. These standards identify the impact of variables but, in most cases, adequate data are not available in a form that will produce meaningful standards.

Time studies use actual stopwatch observations to develop standards. These studies produce accurate standards but they are time-consuming, and the leveling and maintenance of data require technical competence and judgment. Furthermore, employees often react negatively to being timed. (Leveling is the adjustment of observed time values to correspond more closely to the time which is deemed to be fair for doing the work or task in question.)

Standard data is based on the compilation of data from time studies or a predetermined time system into common elements that are used for performing a given class of work. Once the data are established, this method is consistent, economical and easy to apply but technically trained personnel are necessary to develop it. Also, it must be kept current to be effective.

Ratio delay (work sampling) is a statistical sampling technique to determine what proportion of classifications of activity is present in the overall work cycle. This approach is quick, economical and reliable but has limited application for specific task standards.

Predetermined time systems are procedures in which all work elements are divided into the basic motions required for their performance. Assigned predetermined time values are used for division of the work elements. These systems are very accurate and consistent and they do not require leveling. However, they do require highly trained technical personnel and are time-consuming to use.

Self-logging uses a statistical analysis of the task time data logged by each employee. This approach is easily understood and analysts are easily trained. However, it can only be used for group standards, and accuracy is based on the sample size used.

The method selected depends upon individual goals or objectives, available skills, and the intended use of the standards.

The self-logging technique is a practical approach for general use in areas with highly variable conditions such as physician-controlled departments. It is an effective method of securing data on activities that are otherwise difficult to measure. Let us assume then that the technique is to be adopted. What basic principles and what precautions should be borne in mind? The standard should be:

- Meaningful to all hospital management, adaptable to future plans, and applicable to existing conditions and mix of procedures.
- Simple and understandable by all personnel, and it must be relevant (i.e., based on units of work as now organized and activity data presently in existence).
- Reproducible in other departments or possibly other hospitals.
- Achievable with the skills available to the hospital.

- Acceptable, lead to action, and encourage and facilitate cost reduction and control.
- Implemented and used.
- Maintainable economically and practically.
- Viewed favorably throughout the hospital.

BASIC METHODOLOGY

The standards are developed from the actual times recorded on the individual work activity records (self-logging forms) of each employee. Department heads should be totally involved in order to become completely knowledgeable regarding the concepts. This makes them better able to utilize and update the system. In order to obtain meaningful time and activity data for the entire department, it is most important with this type of approach that all personnel, including supervisors, actively participate. As in any program, the hospital administration should provide full support.

Group meetings are ideal for explaining the detailed methodology to all participants. This is the time to determine what is to be done, how it is to be done, who will be involved, and when it will be done. There are three major procedures that should be developed prior to starting: defining the units of measure (tasks); the logging techniques; and the statistical data to be collected during the logging period.

- *Units of measure (tasks).* We should first determine the breakdown among classifications of employees to be used for the work being performed within a department (i.e., technician, orderly, clerk, etc.). Once the classifications are established, we identify the tasks that will normally be performed by each group and decide which will be used for logging time. The tasks should be easily definable, and there should be logical breaks between tasks. The times for these individual tasks will be used to develop standard times and then labor standards for specified department reporting units. These reporting units selected should be based on current available activity statistics so that the application of the standards will be meaningful and updating will be easy. Reporting units could be patients, exams, minutes, tests, weeks, etc. Exhibit 1 is an example of tasks and employee classifications that could be used for the operating room. The illustrated tasks include productive time (both fixed and variable), delay, personal and standby time.
- *Logging techniques.* When designing the forms for self-logging, we should keep in mind the time that will be required to record the data so that the form will be simple to use. Once the data are recorded, review

Exhibit 1 Operating Room Task List

Task no.	Task	Task unit
1	<u>Personal</u>	
	A. Dress in OR attire	Occ.
	B. Rest periods	Occ.
	C. Meals	Occ.
	D. Miscellaneous	Occ.
2	<u>Preparation</u>	
	A. Scrubbing — gown and glove	Patient
	B. Set up — major) scrub or	Patient
	C. Set up — minor) circulate	Patient
	D. Prepare patient (wash, paint, drape)	Patient
	E. Prepare instruments, packs & supplies (specify)	Patient
	F. Restocking and rotating, room set up	Occ.
	G. Getting patients	Patient
	H. Miscellaneous (specify)	Occ.
3	<u>Surgical procedure (list procedure)</u>	
	A. Scrub	Patient
	B. Circulate	Patient
	C. Assist (1st or 2nd)	Patient
	D. Other departments (specify)	Occ.
	E. Miscellaneous (specify)	Occ.
4	<u>Clean-up</u>	
	A. OR room after case — infected	Occ.
	B. OR room after case — non-infected	Occ.
	C. OR room end of day	Occ.
	D. Other areas	Occ.
	E. Cleaning and/or sterilizing instruments	Occ.
	F. Miscellaneous (specify)	Occ.
5	<u>Delays</u>	
	A. Equipment	Occ.
	B. Patient	Occ.
	C. Doctor	Occ.
	D. Miscellaneous (specify)	Occ.
6	<u>Clerical</u>	
	A. Phone	Occ.
	B. Log — statistics	Occ.
	C. Scheduling	Occ.
	D. Secretary and clerical duties	Occ.
	E. Requisitions (ordering)	Occ.
	F. Billing	Occ.
	G. Messengers	Occ.
	H. Miscellaneous (specify)	Occ.
7	<u>Orderly or aide</u>	
	A. Transport patient (specify dept.)	Patient
	B. Lab, x-ray, etc. (specify)	Occ.
	C. Miscellaneous (specify)	Occ.
	D. Preps (shave)	Patient
	E. Assisting nurses	Occ.

Exhibit 1 (continued)

8	Education — supervision		
	A.	Assigns, directs, coordinates	Occ.
	B.	Reviews statistics	Occ.
	C.	Orientation and in-service (students)	Occ.
	D.	Evaluates and counsels	Occ.
	E.	Scheduling and staffing	Occ.
	F.	Planning (specify)	Occ.
	G.	Helps when necessary	Occ.
	H.	Attends classes or meetings	Occ.
	I.	Miscellaneous (specify)	Occ.
9	Stand-by		
	A.	Call (from hospital)	Occ.
	B.	Call (from home)	Occ.
	C.	Call in	Occ.
	D.	Stand-by	Occ.
	E.	Miscellaneous (specify)	Occ.

and summary should be easy. Exhibits 2 and 3 are examples of two types of forms. Exhibit 2 would be most applicable for personnel performing successive (nonrepetitive) tasks, and Exhibit 3 for personnel performing repetitive tasks.

• *Statistical profile.* Exhibit 4 is an example of the type of statistical data that would be recorded by the department head during the logging period. The data would indicate the mixture of patients, types of tests or exams, and case load, and would serve as the basic department profile.

The foregoing procedures should be completely understood by all participants prior to commencement of the actual time logging. The logging period should be long enough to include normal fluctuations in activity volume, type and mix, but not too long or employees will lose interest and generate inaccurate data.

DEVELOPMENT OF STANDARDS

During the self-logging period, a qualified observer should monitor and sample the employee forms to ensure that the data are being recorded correctly. Corrections should be made quickly to avoid collecting unusable information.

After the time logging has been completed, the raw task times should be summarized by employee classification and separated into productive, per-

Exhibit 2 Daily Task Sheets

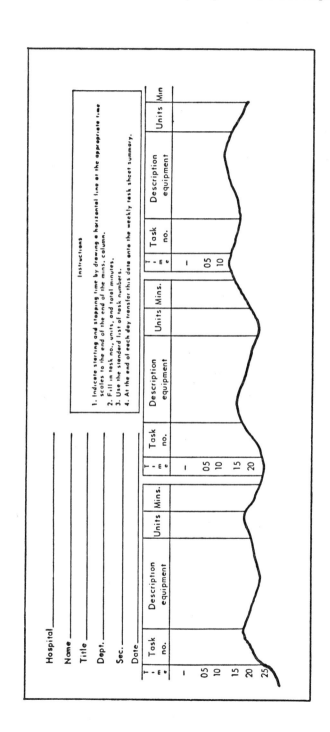

Exhibit 3

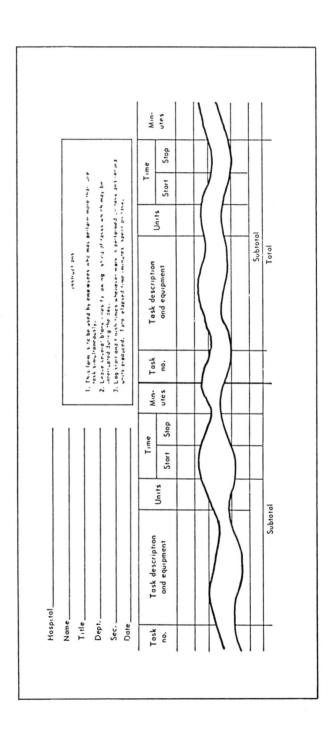

Exhibit 4 Sample Department Weekly Summary Sheet

Sample department weekly summary sheet

Hospital _____ Operating room _____ Operating room no. _____

For Week ending Sunday, _____, 1974

Day	No. of operations¹				O.R. minutes²				O.R. mins. available³				Percent utilization⁴			
	7 am to 12 noon	12 noon to 3:30pm	3:30 pm to 7am	Daily total	7 am to 12 noon	12 noon to 3:30pm	3:30 pm to 7am	Daily total	7 am to 12 noon	12 noon to 3:30pm	3:30pm to 7am	Daily total	7 am to 12 noon	12 noon to 3:30pm	3:30pm to 7am	Daily total
					A	B	C	D	E	F	G	H	A - E	B - F	C - G	D ÷ H
Monday									300	210	930	1,440				
Tuesday									300	210	930	1,440				
Wednesday									300	210	930	1,440				
Thursday									300	210	930	1,440				
Friday									300	210	920	1,440				
Mon-Fri subtot.									1,500	1,050	4,650	7,200				
Saturday									300	210	930	1,440				
Sunday									300	210	930	¹,440				
Sat-Sun subtot.									600	420	1,860	2,880				
Weekly total									2,100	1,470	6,510	10,080				

1 – If operation starts in one time period and runs into next period, indicate number only in time period in which it starts.

2 – Time from patient's entry into O.R. to exit. If operation starts in one time period and runs into next period, break total O.R. minutes into respective time periods.

3 – Indicates maximum availability of room. Do not enter anything in these columns.

4 – Indicates ratio of O.R. minutes to O.R. time available for each time category.

sonal and delay times. At this point, the task times should be purged of any non-representative times caused by training, student activities, problems or abnormal values. After purging, the normal time should be calculated for each task, using the gross mean or another selected method.

As stated previously, these task times will be used to develop a standard time for a departmental reporting unit, so a frequency (occurrence ratio of each task within the total reporting unit) must be calculated that will indicate the number of times a task is performed per reporting unit. When we apply this factor to each normal task time, we obtain the normal task time per reporting unit, and the sum of the task times is the normal reporting unit time. We can also calculate a personal allowance for each classification of employee, using the actual time logged for the personal time tasks. The personal allowance, expressed as a percentage, is applied to the normal reporting unit time to obtain the standard time per reporting unit. This procedure is then repeated for each reporting unit and each classification of employee.

It is seldom possible to keep the employees busy 100 percent of the available time in these departments because of delays inherent in the type of work, standby time, waiting time and unavoidable interruptions. Also, no employee performs at the level of 100 percent. In order to develop accurate budgets and staffing levels, this must be taken into consideration and the standards adjusted accordingly. We can either calculate the actual performance level of the department employees from the logged time and apply this to our standard time, or we can select a higher performance level to allow for future improvement.

The standard reporting unit time multiplied by the actual or forecast volume of the reporting unit is the standard hours produced or required. If these standard hours are adjusted for the projected performance level and the hours required for evening, night and weekend shifts and call-time added, the result will be the expectancy level hours required for each classification of employee in each department. This is the number of hours that a department should require (or did require) to perform a given volume of work over a specified period of time. Exhibit 5 is a flow chart that shows the logic steps for computing the expectancy level. This is the basic tool for developing labor budgets and manning levels. Exhibit 6 is an illustration of a budget calculation worksheet.

An example of the computation required for an OR nursing budget follows:

Total normal task times = 1.38 hrs/surgical case
Personal allowance = 8%
Standard hours per case = 1.50

Exhibit 5 Logic for Computation of Expectancy Levels

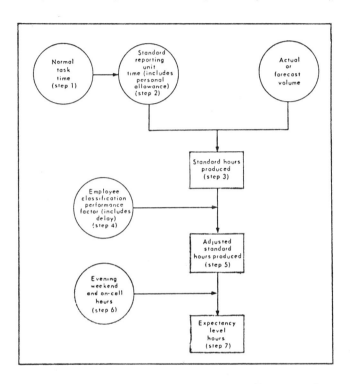

Forecast Volume = 5,200 cases

5,200 cases × 1.50 std. hrs./case = 7,800 standard hours required

Projected Productivity = 90%

Adjusted standard hours required = $\dfrac{7,800}{.90}$ = 8,677 hours

Adjusted standard hours required:

Normal shift (8 a.m.–4 p.m.)	8,677
Evening shift (4 p.m.–12 p.m.)	2,080
Weekends (8 a.m.–12 p.m.)	1,664
On-call hours (12 p.m.–8 a.m.)	2,920
Expectancy level hours	15,341

Exhibit 6   Staffing Budget Calculation Worksheet

Staffing budget calculation worksheet

Hospital _____ Department _____ Section _____

Employee classification _____ Period from _____ to _____

Item	Reporting unit (specify) (1)	Standard hours per reporting unit (2)	Forecast performance factor (3)	Adjusted standard hours per reporting unit (4) = (2) ÷ (3)	Forecast volume (5)	Forecast hours (6) = (4) × (5)	Average hourly rate (7)	Salary budget (8) = (6) × (7)
Measured work								
Sub-total							$	$
Unmeasured paid work								
On-call - not worked								
On-call - worked								
Special shifts (specify)								
Sub-total							$	$
Fringe benefits								
Vacation								
Holiday								
Illness, absence								
Others (specify)								
Sub-total							$	$
Total budget hours and salaries							-	$

CONCLUSION

Even after standards have been developed, they may never be used because of internal politics, poor salesmanship or other reasons. If the standards are too technical and not easily understood by the personnel responsible for their implementation, they will not be used. They should be simple and easy to understand.

Another problem that may be encountered is reluctance to use standards because of the feeling that all costs are fixed anyway. This statement, however, is not accurate. Both schedules and workloads are variable, and the so-called fixed costs vary accordingly, but they can be controlled by sharing services and by careful utilization of personnel.

But the key to the successful use of standards is the full involvement of all participants. This involvement creates an atmosphere of cooperation and interest through understanding. The physicians and technicians involved will have participated in developing the standards themselves, thus making them eager for the success of the program.

26. Measuring Activity by "Work Sampling"

ROMEO CERCONF, M. PRIMAVESI, D. FALTIN,
H. MacCLYMONT, S. NAGY, AND S. PETTIT

Reprinted from *Dimensions in Health Service,* Journal of the Canadian Hospital Association, November 1978, pp. 20–22, 34, 36, © 1978.

During the Spring of 1977, St. Thomas Psychiatric Hospital decided to develop a quality assurance control program within the Nursing Department. It was hoped that the development of such a program, similar to that instituted at Misericordia Hospital, Edmonton, Alberta, would eventually result in a staffing system based upon workload. This would differ from the current staffing system which tended to be based upon just numbers of patients.

A search was made of the available literature, only to find that little of the information pertained to psychiatric facilities. It was then felt that before developing the quality assurance program, a survey should be made to determine what nursing activities were occurring and the time involved. If any changes had to be made, they could be identified and implemented before commencing the quality assurance program. Work sampling was the method chosen and is described in more detail later in the article. Over a period of five months, all 17 wards of the hospital were sampled.

OBJECTIVES OF THE STUDY

The long term objectives of the entire quality assurance control program were to provide:

(a) a system to monitor the quality of nursing care

(b) a means of comparing the amount of work to the amount of staff available on a daily basis
(c) a means by which ward workloads and staffing ratios could be compared

The specific objectives of the work sampling study were:

(a) to determine how nursing personnel divide their time between direct care, indirect care, non-nursing activities, non-productive time and off ward activities
(b) to determine the time spent on minor activities within the major categories by labor class in minutes
(c) to determine the average amount of nursing care each patient received daily
(d) to determine the need for a redistribution of work load and/or staffing throughout the three shifts.

Throughout the hospital, the average percentage of direct care given by all staff was 23.3 percent on the day shift and 35.2 percent on the evening shift. This resulted in each patient receiving an average of 33.3 minutes of direct care on days and 32.4 minutes on evenings. (Refer to Table 3)

On the whole, the Psychiatric Nursing Assistants provided most of the direct care throughout the hospital and the ward supervisors the least.

One unexpected finding was that the amount of direct care did not increase as a result of an increase in staff. Too many staff tended to allow each person to do less.

On the whole, the majority of the staff's time was spent in indirect care activities. The amount fluctuated from 44.2 percent on the day shift to 34 percent on the evening shift.

A further breakdown of this category showed that approximately 29 percent (about 77 mins/staff) of the time was spent in paperwork related activities, and approximately 42 percent (about 110 mins/staff) in staff-staff interactions including both individual and group situations.

Prior to the study commencing, it was thought that the non-nursing category might be relatively high, however this was not true. The study revealed an average of 9 percent of the staff's time was spent performing non-nursing duties. It was thus felt that the hospital's support services were adequate. It was also found that these activities were being appropriately delegated according to labor class.

The standard set for the hospital was 11.8 percent. The study results showed that the staff spent an average of 13.5 percent in non-productive activities on days and 15.4 percent on evenings. It was also felt that some non-productive time was buried within some of the direct and indirect patient care activities. On the whole, the non-productive time increased on the evening shift, particularly after the patients had gone to bed.

Absent time varied from 9.5 percent on days to 7 percent on evenings. Based upon the results of the first four wards, it was felt that a portering service might be of value. This service was instituted on a trial basis. The result was a reduction in ward absent time and an increase in the direct care time. However, the porters were not well utilized throughout the day. The service was not continued.

WORK SAMPLING

Work sampling is a work measurement tool. In many cases this tool can provide valuable, accurate information about staff, or machines, in less time and at a lower cost than by other means. Work sampling provides a simple effective way of measuring indirect or non-repetitive activities.

This method of work measurement gathers information by making random observations of workers without using a timing device.

The theory of work sampling is based on the law of probability, and includes the techniques of statistical quality control. A study can be made for a short period of time or for long periods.

STEPS TO PERFORM A WORK STUDY

There are more advantages and disadvantages to work sampling. However, we did choose this method and did find it successful. The following is an outline of the steps that are taken to perform this type of study.

1. Establish Objectives. Objectives must be clearly defined and made known to everyone involved. There could be several objectives established.

2. Select Area of Study. A specific area to be studied should be established. The area to be studied could be one, or many wards depending on the number of staff on each. Usually no more than 20 staff can be observed per cycle.

Some criteria for choosing which ward is to be studied could be that a ward has complained about

- excessive paper work
- insufficient staff
- ineffective support services

You may just wish to establish a general data base on all wards for future quality assurance programs.

3. Select Observers. The study group consisted of a nursing educator, a nursing supervisor and two registered nurses. These people acted as the observers and analyzed the data. Also on the team was the Executive Housekeeper who had had experience as a systems analyst. The sixth person had hospital administration qualifications. Some of our reasons for selecting specific observers were:

- knowledge about nursing (procedures)
- objectivity in viewing other staff
- willing to participate in group discussion
- supervisory personnel
- an aptitude for math

It is best if the observers do not observe staff who they normally work with.

4. Train Observers. Once the observers have been selected they should have some training in how work sampling works. It is advisable to have the observers participate in establishing the categories of work to be studied.

At this point we ensured that all observers viewed each category in exactly the same way. In our case the observers did more than just observe. They also compiled data, and most important they analyzed the data and presented the findings.

5. Inform the Staff. We now have established objectives, selected the area of study, selected and trained the observers. Before the observations began the staff were informed about the study. They were told the objectives of the study, and basically how the study would be done. Good staff relations is very important. Everyone should be informed of exactly what will happen during the study. Another point presented was that nothing would be kept confidential during the observations. Staff observed were allowed to view the observation sheets at any time.

6. Make Observations. It is advisable to simulate observation trips so individuals become more familiar wth the observers and less conscious of their presence. The basic rules in making observations were:

1. observations must be made at random times
2. the order in observing the people should be random
3. observations must be instantaneous

7. Compile and Analyze Data. The data was then compiled to determine the amount of time staff spend in each of the categories. Data was compiled for all staff on days and evenings, by labor class, by hour of the day, and by ward.

A great deal of time could be spent on this section. It is up to the coordinator of the study to determine what information is essential and limit the time spent on analysis.

8. Check Accuracy of Data. To determine the accuracy involved, in any given percent figure for any activity, the following formula can be used.

$$E = 2\sqrt{\frac{P(1 - P)}{N}}$$

E = a limit of error
P = percent occurrence as a decimal
N = number of observations made

In our case we wanted to be able to say, that for the major categories of work, 95 percent of the time the true value of the percent of time spent would be X percent ± Y percent.

We had to keep in mind that we were not trying to set standards, but only provide data for analysis. Therefore we required only broad limits of accuracy for analysis purposes.

9. Present Findings. Once the data had been compiled and summarized we presented our findings to the staff. In many cases we could not say what was acceptable and what was not, as we did not have any other data to compare to.

We did however make some comparisons between similar wards. The data was presented to both the supervisors and eventually to the staff. Reaction to the data ranged from very hostile to very apathetic.

Overall, the data was felt to be useful and of benefit. It answered many questions about what was happening on each of the wards.

Some examples of our findings included:

1. that a portering service was found to be uneconomical,
2. that the unit dose system for medications was proven to be cost effective,
3. that staff scheduling was identified as a problem in some areas,
4. quantitative data about nursing activities,
5. average quantity of direct nursing care received by each patient,
6. a reallocation of staff resources in some areas.

Table 1 Entire Hospital—All Staff—Major Categories

Based on 510 Minutes/Day

DAYS		EVENINGS	
Direct %	23.3	Direct %	35.2
	min. 118.8		min. 179.5
Indirect %	44.2	Indirect %	34.
	min. 225.4		min. 173.4
Non-Nursing %	9.5	Non-Nursing %	8.5
	min. 48.5		min. 43.4
Non-Productive %	13.5	Non-Productive %	15.4
	min. 68.9		min. 78.5
Absent %	9.0	Absent %	7.0
	min. 48.5		min. 35.7

Table 2 Major Category Comparison by Labor Class—Days and Evenings

Based on 510 Minutes/Day

		DAYS			EVENINGS	
		SUPERVISOR	RN	PNA	RN	PNA
DIRECT CARE	%	12.8	24.1	32.3	34.5	36.0
	mins.	65.3	122.9	164.7	176.0	183.6
INDIRECT CARE	%	67.4	49.9	32.9	43.8	30.8
	mins.	343.7	254.5	167.8	223.4	157.1
NON-NURSING	%	3.3	6.8	12.4	4.9	9.4
	mins.	16.8	34.7	63.2	25.0	47.9
NON-PRODUCTIVE	%	12.3	10.9	12.6	13.4	15.5
	mins.	62.7	55.6	64.3	68.3	79.1
ABSENT	%	4.2	8.3	9.8	3.4	8.3
	mins.	21.4	42.3	50.0	17.3	42.3

Table 3 Average Direct Care Received by Each Patient

SHIFT	Days and Evenings				
	DIRECT CARE PERCENT	STAFF OBSERVED WARD	TOTAL DIRECT MINUTES	AVE. NO. OF PATIENTS ON WARD	AVE. MINS. RECEIVED BY EACH PATIENT
DAYS	23.3	5.4	641.7	19.3	33.3
EVENINGS	35.2	4.2	754.0	23.3	32.4

REFERENCES

1. Designing, Monitoring and Managing Nursing Care Systems; Misericordia Hospital, Edmonton, Alberta 1977.
2. Motion and Time Study; G. Nadler, McGraw-Hill, Toronto, 1955 pp. 158-170.

27. Wage Incentive Systems: A Review

CHARLES J. AUSTIN

Reprinted from *Hospital Progress,* April 1970, pp. 37–41, by permission of Edward J. Pollock, Publisher, © 1970.

Wage incentives are systems of remuneration under which the earnings of a worker or group of workers are related directly to the output (or cost reductions) of the individual or group. Wage incentives have a long history in American industrial life. The scientific management movement and the World War II industrial production crisis focused considerable attention upon their use. However, despite widespread application in American industry, incentive systems have been used only rarely in hospitals. This article reviews the various types and characteristics of wage incentive systems and discusses their actual and potential application in hospitals.

GENERAL CHARACTERISTICS OF WAGE INCENTIVE SYSTEMS

Wage incentive systems contain two essential elements: 1. The establishment of performance standards for jobs and tasks carried out in an organization; and 2. variation of employe earnings based upon individual or group performance measured against pre-established standards. *Individual incentive* systems measure the productivity of each worker and vary his earnings accordingly. *Group incentive* plans measure the output of operating units within the organization (or the entire organization itself), and all employes in the group share equally in the savings or additional profits that result from their efforts. Compensation from incentive systems may be paid immediately, as a supplement to employes' regular earnings, or

239

may be placed in trust for subsequent bonus payments or savings plans (deferred incentive systems).

The theory of wage incentives is quite simple. Monetary reward is considered a basic and important motivating force, and it is assumed that workers will improve productivity and/or help to reduce costs in order to achieve added remuneration. It should be noted, however, that money is not the only human motivator. Any effective wage incentive system must be integrated with other types of motivation that fulfill equally important human needs. Douglas McGregor,[1] in commenting upon a group wage incentive plan, states that, in addition to bonus earnings, the plan must provide "... a formal method providing an opportunity for every member of the organization to contribute his brains and ingenuity as well as his physical effort to the improvement of organizational effectiveness."

There are two main justifications for the use of wage incentives in an organization: worker motivation and improved management efficiency.[2] The worker motivation theory seems to be most applicable in situations in which the work is routine; standards are easier to establish and workers have good control over their output. On the other hand, the management efficiency theory appears to have more general applicability, since the establishment of performance standards serves as an effective stimulus for reviewing organizational objectives and operating methods and procedures. Improved management efficiency may well be more important to hospitals than worker motivation, since the objective of efficiency requires hospitals to completely review existing management systems and practices.

For the successful application of wage incentives, the following steps must be taken:

1. Management must be convinced of the value of the incentive plan and support it vigorously.
2. The details of the plan must be established in close reference to organizational goals. If goals are not clearly defined, their establishment becomes the single, most important step in the entire process.
3. Once the plan has been developed, it must be carefully explained and "sold" to employes.
4. Sound standards must be determined, established, and maintained. Undoubtedly, this step is the most difficult task. Some of the problems connected with the establishment of performance and/or cost reduction standards are discussed below.
5. After all the preliminary work has been completed, the system must be initiated and tested. Since the initial standards for measurement and determination of incentive pay are based upon a considerable amount of intuition, it should be made clear to all concerned that the initial

period of operation will be a test period for evaluation and subsequent adjustment of standards and procedures.

Many different plans and formulae for computing incentive pay have been developed. These various plans range from piecework pay to profit-sharing. The details of these various plans are beyond the scope of this article, but the various types of wage incentive formulae are discussed in detail in Wolf's, *Wage Incentives as a Management Tool.*[3] No magic formula is applicable to all situations. The details of any plan must be tailored to fit the goals and institutional character of the organization that is establishing the incentive system.

PROBLEMS

Despite the apparently desirable characteristics of incentive pay, these plans have not been overwhelmingly successful. Lincoln[4] describes one study which revealed that over 60 per cent of a group of profit-sharing plans had failed. Many problems are associated with the use of incentive plans. Review of individual incentive systems indicates that the problems experienced in this type of incentive system fall into two categories: problems associated with establishing output standards, and problems concerned with maintaining an acceptable wage structure. Wolf[5] identified many aspects of these problems in his study of 26 companies using individual incentive plans:

> The negative aspects of wage incentives...include tendencies toward deception of time study men, slowdowns, strikes, pressure for rapid rating of incentive jobs, pressure to apply the incentive idea to work that is neither standardized nor measurable in meaningful units, grievances over standards, ceiling on output, fraudulent practices, and friction among workers.

Lincoln[6] attributes most failures of incentive systems to ineffective management—failure of management to do its part.

Group incentive systems have been developed to overcome the problem of bickering over standards and to promote teamwork in the organization. One such system is the Scanlon Plan.[7]

The Scanlon Plan is a group incentive system developed in the mid-1930's by Joseph Scanlon, who worked for a small steel company that was experiencing severe financial difficulties. The success of Scanlon's plan caused it to be championed by students of employe motivation, most prominent of whom were Douglas McGregor and Frederick G. Lesieur.

The philosophy of the Scanlon Plan is that of management by integration and self-control.[8] It stresses the concept of teamwork with a minimum number of administrative controls. The elements of the plan include: A suggestion system, a group incentive scheme, and a profit-sharing plan. The profit-sharing plan differs from other such plans in that cost-reduction (not increased profits) is the basis for determining group bonus. The typical Scanlon formula measures the ratio of labor cost to total production value. As the percentage of labor cost decreases, workers are rewarded even though profits do not necessarily increase because of other factors beyond the control of workers. Such a formula seems to be potentially applicable in the non-profit hospital.

Group incentive plans are not without problems. A study[9] of six companies using the Scanlon Plan, conducted by Industrial Relations Counselors, Inc., revealed that two employers abandoned the plan after a brief experience with it. Some of the problems included: Limitation of company flexibility (the plan is difficult to operate in organizations whose products and services are constantly changing); unwieldy administration required in large operations; and the need for management reorientation, since the plan emphasizes the role of the individual worker in improving efficiency (frequently considered management's prerogative). The plan also tends to be idealistic and minimizes the extent of conflict in organizations.

Despite these many problems, studies of individual and group incentive systems demonstrate many successful applications of the theory, both in improved worker motivation and in management efficiency.

WAGE INCENTIVE PLANS IN HOSPITALS

The hospital literature contains very few descriptions of wage incentive systems actually in operation in U.S. hospitals. This is not to imply that hospitals have not used incentives, but it certainly indicates that wage incentives have not been extensively used in the hospital field. Five hospital systems that have established incentive systems are discussed below.

1. Baptist Hospital, Pensacola, Fla.[10,11,12] Baptist Hospital has had a group incentive plan since January, 1965. The plan is operated on a departmental basis, with each productivity-share-plan tailored to the department in which it is used. Departmental productivity-share-plans and formulae are developed jointly by management, department heads, and key employes. Once the plan is developed, a meeting is held with all employes of the department to initiate the plan, and periodic follow-up meetings are held to review progress. Following publication of a monthly report, each department head computes the incentive amount for the month and forwards it to the payroll department. A supplemental but separate paycheck is prepared for each employe and distributed at a special monthly departmental meeting for this purpose.

The plan at Baptist Hospital has been implemented in phases. A brief discussion of some of the departmental implementations follows.

Laundry. Productivity is measured in terms of pounds of quality linen produced. All production over a threshold value contributes to the bonus amount, after overtime hours and value of supplies used in excess of a defined maximum are subtracted. Quality control is provided through inspections by the hospital laboratory, the American Institute of Laundry, and the department supervisor. Productivity is reported to have increased from 42 pounds of linen per man-hour to 50 pounds, with supply costs reduced from 84¢ to 56¢ per pound.

Surgery. This was the first professional department to use the incentive plan. Output is measured in terms of cost per operation. Stated results indicate that, under the incentive plan, the cost per operation increases at a rate of one dollar per year, while before the plan was implemented, costs had increased at a greater rate. Cost of supplies has steadily decreased under the incentive plan.

Housekeeping. Man-hours have been reduced for three consecutive fiscal years and standards of supply costs are now being established.

Nursing. The productivity-incentive plan was introduced in the nursing department in May, 1966. Productivity is measured by relating man-hours of nursing service and supply costs to average census. For fiscal years 1966 and 1967, the average census remained constant while both man-hours and supply costs decreases.

Several other departments participate in the plan, including radiology (cost per procedure); laboratory (cost per procedure); dietary (cost per meal); coffee shop (gross profit, net income); electrodiagnostics (cost per procedure); and medical records (reduction in man-hours and supply costs). The over-all results show the same pattern—reduced costs and increased salary per man-hour for employes.

2. Memorial Hospital, Long Beach, Calif.[13,14,15] The Long Beach plan, called MERIT (Memorial Employes Retirement Incentive Trust), is a group incentive plan applied on an over-all basis to all employes in the hospital. The plan is designed to combine financial incentive with work simplification and is similar in some respects to the Scanlon Plan. The basic measurement of productivity is a formula which relates expense to income. Donald Carner[16] outlined the basic characteristics of the system as follows:

The MERIT program places a minimum of one per cent and a maximum of five per cent of payroll in a trust account for the employe to be invested and held until his retirement. All regular full-time employes with six months of service are eligible on application, provided they agree to save and deposit in the trust account not less than two per cent of their salary. The hospital's obligation is determined by a formula which relates expense to income. The better the job we do as hospital employes, the greater the hospital's deposit in the trust account.

The MERIT system is an example of a deferred incentive plan, since the incentive pay is placed in trust and invested. Employes become vested in the plan on a straight line percentage basis over a 10-year time span. After 10 years in the plan, an employe is fully vested and would receive both his contribution and the full hospital contribution plus interest and dividends accumulated should he retire or leave the hospital.

During the initial year of operation, the ratio of expenses to operating revenue was reduced from 94.77 per cent to 89.80 per cent, resulting in a hospital contribution of $168,794 to the trust fund or 8.6 per cent of the annual salary of each participant in the plan.

3. University of Michigan Hospital, Ann Arbor.[17] The medical records department of the University of Michigan Hospital operates an individual incentive program. The program is applied only to typists in the department who transcribe dictation for medical records.

A stroke counter is placed on each typewriter. A threshold value is established, and bonus points are awarded for production exceeding this value. Credit is given according to the various degrees of extra skill and effort required for different types of jobs. Jobs vary according to the dictator, clerical corrections, and assistance given other operators.

The reported results indicate: "...1. decidedly increased output; 2. standards of performance established and maintained with ease; 3. maximum utilization of equipment; 4. submarginal producers easily detected." The primary disadvantage of the system seems to be that the urge for production tends to lower the standards of accuracy—a difficult problem, since 100 per cent checking of the transcribed work is not practical.

4. East End Memorial Hospital, Birmingham, Ala.[18] This proprietary hospital operates a group incentive system on a departmental basis, similar to the one operated by Baptist Hospital in Pensacola. Monthly bonus pay is awarded on the basis of cost reductions obtained through increased productivity and lower usage of supplies and materials.

Productivity incentives have been applied to personnel in nursing service, operating room, recovery room, emergency room, dietary, and housekeeping. Nursing service incentives are computed on the basis of two factors: reduced man-hours per patient-day and reduced supply costs per patient-day.

Hospital management personnel maintain that the system helped contribute to a 5.4 per cent return on investment for stockholders during 1967 while maintaining a per-diem cost well below the American Hospital Association's Hospital Administrative Services' median for hospitals in this size category.

5. Montana Deaconess Hospital, Great Falls, Mont.[19] Montana Deaconess Hospital established a departmental group incentive system in 1966. Average cost per productivity unit (patient-day, surgical operation, laboratory procedure, etc.) was computed for a three-month period for each department participating in the plan. Subsequent monthly savings in reduced unit costs are divided two ways: one-half reverting to the operating budget and one-half distributed as additional pay to departmental employes. Base-line unit costs are recomputed for the same three-month period each year.

SOME GENERAL OBSERVATIONS

In reflecting on the small number of reports of wage incentive plans in actual use in hospitals, several thoughts occur. It is possible that many hospitals are using wage incentive systems but have not reported them in the literature. This explanation appears doubtful, however, when one examines the amount of publishing on other topics in the hospital field. A second possible explanation might be that hospital administrators do not believe that financial incentive plans are applicable to the non-profit environment, where patient care supersedes all other organizational objectives. A "cultural barrier" may exist which discourages the use of techniques borrowed from the free enterprise sector. A third possible explanation is that the general level of administrative expertise in hospitals should be raised through professional training and continuing education programs for hospital administrators. In this way, management techniques, such as incentive systems, might become better known and be given wider utilization.

It is interesting to note that hospitals appear to be reluctant about experimenting with individual incentive systems. Group plans are much more popular.

Two major defects in the reports describing incentive systems in actual use in hospitals should be mentioned. Although these reports include evaluation of the financial results of each plan, the evaluations are incomplete. Increased productivity and/or decreased costs are reported, but there is no discussion of factors, other than improved employe productivity, which might contribute to improved performance, particularly the possible contribution of new technology (e.g., new and better equipment in the laundry). Although these factors are probably considered in computing incentives, some further discussion of them would be helpful.

A second reporting defect is the lack of discussion of the impact that employe incentive plans have on the quality of patient care. Although this question of quality control is difficult to answer, it is of sufficient importance to be included in the evaluation of any incentive plan.

DISCUSSION

Based upon a study of the industrial experience with wage incentives and their limited application in hospitals, the following points are suggested for further discussion:

1. Hospitals present a potentially fruitful area of application for wage incentive plans. The fact that hospital costs are rising rapidly cannot be disputed. Need for improved efficiency and productivity does not, of course, guarantee the success of an incentive plan. However, if one considers the fact that hospital services do not change rapidly, that hospital outputs (e.g., patient-days, lab procedures, meals served) are definable and capable of measurement, and that hospital cost centers are fairly well-defined through the formal organizational structure, the case for incentives seems to be well-established.

2. Individual incentives could be used more widely in hospitals. Although hospitals will probably be more inclined to develop group incentive plans, there are departments in which individual incentive systems could be tested. Most larger hospitals, for example, now have data processing departments where the individual productivity of keypunch and machine operators could be measured. Dietary, housekeeping, medical records, and patient accounting are other departments in which individual incentive systems might be feasible.

3. The literature seems to ignore the question of incentive pay for hospital executive management personnel. There is no good way to reward top management with extra incentive pay, other than by measuring the total performance of the organization. Although total performance is difficult to measure, the potential payoff in improved administration bears investigation.

4. Agencies outside the hospital must stimulate the development of incentive systems. Some government agencies are now providing such stimuli in their contracting practices by authorizing the cost of incentive payments to employes of their contractors. Third party insurers'

interest in improved productivity promises the development of similar plans on the medical horizon.

5. Many obstacles must be overcome before wage incentives can be widely used in hospitals. Specifically:

   a. Productivity and cost standards must be established. Few hospitals now have such standards. However, efforts toward establishing standards are beginning to be made as a result of the stimulus given by organizations such as the Commission for Administrative Services to Hospitals, the University of Michigan Program in Hospital Administration, and other groups that have developed systems for determining proper staffing for different hospital functions.

   b. Management training and developing programs are needed to demonstrate how incentives can be used in hospitals. Baptist Hospital, Pensacola, Fla., has initiated a series of workshops on Hospital Productivity-Incentive Management. In addition the University of Wisconsin Center for the Study of Productivity Motivation has sponsored similar conferences. However, more such efforts are needed, particularly in university-based programs.

   c. Many existing hospital accounting systems are inadequate to support an incentive system. To establish standards and measure performance, a good cost accounting system is essential. Some hospitals still do not have data on expenses incurred at the various cost centers in the hospital. Such accounting systems must be developed before any major improvements in administrative efficiency can be expected.

   d. Wage incentive plans must be tied to other improvements in hospital personnel administration, particularly programs of recruiting, training, and professional development.

In summary, Andrew Pattullo[20] of the Kellogg Foundation states the case for incentives quite well:

> I do not believe that there is either any overt or covert move to "capture" this country's hospital system. But I do believe that there is a general restlessness regarding the public's investment in medical care, and a growing sentiment that full value is not being received. The field can move in several directions to explore ways not only to contain costs but to improve care. Examine in good conscience how your hospital can gain greater productivity and cost control and also achieve better patient care. It will inevitably lead you into paths that appear unmarked and hazardous. But they may well be paths that will preserve the voluntary hospital system.

REFERENCES

1. D. McGregor, *The Human Side of Enterprise,* New York, McGraw-Hill, 1960, p. 113.

2. W.B. Wolf, *Wage Incentives as a Management Tool,* New York, Columbia University Press, 1957, p. 8.

3. *Ibid.,* pp. 10-16.

4. J.F. Lincoln, *Incentive Management,* Cleveland, Ohio, Lincoln Electric Co., 1951, p. 146.

5. Wolf, *op. cit.,* p. 70.

6. Lincoln, *op. cit.,* p. 148.

7. Industrial Relations Counselors, Inc., *Group Wage Incentives—Experience with the Scanlon Plan,* New York, IRC Memo #141, 1962.

8. McGregor, *op. cit.,* p. 110.

9. Industrial Relations Counselors, Inc., *op. cit.,* p. 5.

10. P.N. Groner, *Department Productivity—Incentive Programs,* unpublished report from Baptist Hospital, Pensacola, Fla., August, 1968.

11. J.H. Schill, "Productivity Sharing—A Boon for Patients, Employees, Morale," *Hospital Topics,* August, 1966, p. 63.

12. J.J. Jehring, *The Use of Subsystem Incentives in Hospitals: A Case Study of the Incentive Programs at Baptist Hospital, Pensacola, Florida,* Center for the Study of Productivity Motivation, Madison, University of Wisconsin, January, 1968.

13. D.C. Carner, "Employes Profit by Sharing the Savings," *Modern Hospital,* October, 1961, p. 87.

14. D.C. Carner, *A Program for Hospital Incentives,* Center for the Study of Productivity Motivation, Madison, University of Wisconsin, June, 1962.

15. J.J. Jehring, *Increasing Productivity in Hospitals: A Case Study of the Incentive Program at Memorial Hospital of Long Beach,* Center for the Study of Productivity Motivation, Madison, University of Wisconsin, 1966.

16. Carner *(Modern Hospital), op. cit.*

17. R.J. Hinds and K. Sheetz, "Incentive Plans Improve Medical Records Skills," *Modern Hospital,* April, 1964, p. 10.

18. V. Boyer and A.M. Smith, "This Incentive Plan Improves the Care and Lowers the Cost," *Modern Hospital,* September, 1968, p. 103.

19. G.V. Bailey, "Hospital Pays Employees Who Improve Their Productivity," *Modern Hospital,* September, 1968, p. 109.

20. A. Pattullo, "The Voluntary Hospital System," in *Reducing Costs in Hospitals,* Center for the Study of Productivity Motivation, University of Wisconsin, Madison, 1966, p. 6.

28. Value Analysis Pinpoints Costs

AHMED RIFAI, JOSEPH O. PECENKA, AND
PAULA J. FORD

Reprinted from the July 1978 issue of *Hospital Financial Management*, pp.
26–29. Copyright 1978 Hospital Financial Management Association.

Passing on the costs of inefficiency in the form of patient charges is fast
coming to an end. President Carter's recent request to Congress to limit
hospitals' investments for construction and equipment—as well as increases in charges—has put that issue prominently in the public eye. This
has been added to an already widespread public belief that hospitals are in-
efficiently operated. That belief in large part stems from the continuous increase in the rate of hospital charges, which has been greater than the rate of
increase in the general costs of goods and services.

Hospital cost-saving problems are similar to those of a business firm. If a
hospital does not constantly monitor costs and attempt to control them,
they tend to quickly exceed break-even points. The incentive to keep costs
within limits is obvious. However, keeping costs within limits requires efficient managers who can maximize the utilization of inputs to achieve maximum output with high quality.

To continue the analogy between hospitals and manufacturing firms, one
may think of a hospital as an organization whose primary goal is service.
The inputs of a hospital consist of: 1) labor of various grades (doctors,
nurses, technicians, etc.), 2) fixed assets (building, beds, equipment), and
3) cash, converted to tangible variable assets (food, drugs, bedding, supplies, etc.).

The output of a hospital can be viewed from two different angles: quantity and quality. Quantity can be measured in terms of admissions,
discharges, duration of stay, number of outpatients, etc. Quality is more

difficult to measure because of many subjective elements. However, the quality component of a hospital is comparable to the quality component of a product: a function of its input quality. In other words, if a hospital has highly qualified doctors, highly skilled nurses, technologically advanced equipment and skilled management, the quality of services received by its patients is likely to be high.

There is another factor which should not be overlooked in the input-output relationship of hospitals, that is, economies and diseconomies of scale. As Greenfield explains it:

> In an archetypical firm with fixed and variable costs, the cost per unit of output will be a function of that output. At low levels of output "overhead" or fixed costs are concentrated in a relatively few output units, resulting in relatively high costs. At very high levels of output the ratio of variable to fixed costs is similarly highly unbalanced with resulting high costs. Applying these factors to hospital activity we would expect that the hospitals' cost per patient day would be high at low levels of output (say 10 percent bed occupancy or capacity) and would be high, too, at high levels of output (say 95 percent to 100 percent of capacity) and that they would be lower for some range of capacity between the extremes.[1]

Undoubtedly, in order to decrease hospital costs and to increase their technical efficiency, efficient managers are required to coordinate hospital inputs in such a way as to: 1) increase the professional contributions of their labor force (doctors, nurses, technicians, etc.), 2) maintain their equipment in optimum condition for a long period of time, and 3) reduce unnecessary costs and idle time for all hospital personnel, equipment and facilities.

"Value analysis" (or "value engineering" as it is sometimes known) enters the picture as one technique for increasing hospital efficiency and reducing costs.

THE VALUE ANALYSIS CONCEPT

Starr points out that "...the fundamental notion of value analysis is that the quality of the production output must be maintained while at the same time the cost of output should be decreased."[2] He further explains that although this technique is applicable to "...all phases of the production process, in practice, it emphasizes the selection of the input materials."

Thus, the primary goal of value analysis is to provide/produce a given service product at less cost without affecting its quality, durability or appearance. To effectively achieve this goal certain analytical steps have been developed for systematic evaluation.

1. Information Gathering

Basic facts need to be gathered on the work performed, its related components and the costs related to performing the service. The information is recorded from direct observation and direct measurement of the quantity of work in the service. At this stage, the value analyst seeks answers to questions such as:

1. What is the function of the service?
2. What are the technical procedures required to provide the service?
3. What kinds of input are required?
4. How many days are required to provide the service?
5. What are the costs of providing the service?
6. Where is the service performed?
7. Who should perform the service?
8. Is there any duplication or overlapping of activities in performing the service?
9. What are the consequences of not providing the service?
10. Are there cost-free ways of providing the service?

These data may then be subjected to analysis.

2. Analysis of Facts

This is perhaps the most important step in value analysis, since it is here that the recorded facts are subjected to detailed examination and the status quo is critically questioned and challenged. This step reconsiders the purpose and function of the service, the place where it is performed, its sequences, its specific components and the means by which it is done. Essentially, this step leads to an integrated understanding of the totality, the system—an understanding on the basis of which the next step of creative search may then proceed.

3. Creative Search

In this step the value analyst seeks answers from such diverse specialists as physicians, pharmacists, nurses, purchasers, quality control engineers, suppliers, etc., to questions such as the following:

1. Can alternative materials or other inputs be used?
2. Can the service be simplified?
3. Can alternate methods be used?
4. Can costs be reduced by turning to alternate methods or equipment?
5. Can any step be eliminated?
6. Can the duration of the service be reduced?

Changes found as the result of creative search may then be adopted if they lead to cost reductions without materially affecting the quality or nature of the service. The following are a few examples of the benefits of value analysis for a hospital; they are by no means exhaustive.

Materials. The value analyst can examine each item of material used to check the possibility of replacing it with another that will provide the same function at reduced cost. For example, needles, syringes, hand towels, bed linens, medical gowns, diapers, etc., can be replaced by disposable items. Such a move eliminates the costs of laundering, sterilization and the costs of equipment and space needed for those services. Even if no direct cost reduction occurs, financial and physical sources of possible infection are eliminated, enhancing the quality of patient care.

It is true that in some situations it is cheaper to use sterilized non-disposables, but it should not be overlooked that sterilized materials are occasionally sources of infections. For example, recent research by Kowalski and Peck revealed that 60 percent of hospital-acquired infections can be traced to the use of sterilized instruments.[3]

Resource conservation. Water shortages in many parts of the country have highlighted this as an area in which value analysis can be useful to prevent waste and reduce cost. Specifically with regard to water conservation, the value analyst would study water requirements in order to determine whether recirculated water can be reused in other functions. The value analyst would also inspect water distribution systems to detect loss or waste. Similar investigation would also be applied to similar resources such as electricity, oxygen, gas and oil.

Value analysis can be used effectively to reduce communication costs. The value analyst would collect information with regard to the telephone expenses of each hospital department. Investigations would attempt to answer such questions as: Who is authorized to make long distance calls? Should more controls be established? Do any policies exist regarding to whom long distance calls should be placed and when? What is the duration of these calls?

In the area of office supplies, the value analyst would begin by reviewing all items, taking into consideration the following factors: Can many unnecessary items be eliminated or combined? For example, there may be too many different types of pencils, ball point pens, erasers, staplers, etc. Miles identified that the cost of ordering lab forms was reduced by eliminating the excessive number of different colored forms and getting all hospitals to use standard forms.[4] In this case, standardization can reduce both ordering and inventory costs.

Personnel. Since labor costs in hospitals constitute about 60 percent of total cost, value analysis here becomes imperative. The nontechnical work performed by nurses and technicians might be examined by a value analyst. Miles cites a project relating value analysis to the excessive amount of nontechnical work to be done in the lab. The improvements in this case included listing duties, reassigning the nontechnical aspects of lab work to nontechnical personnel and obtaining voluntary help.[5] Accordingly, nonprofessional personnel and volunteers can be trained to carry out such functions as reception, mail delivery, transportation of patients and supplies, instrument washing and some routine work in the emergency room. Using volunteers and nontechnical personnel can free more costly nurses and technicians to provide and supervise direct care—the higher cost, specialized aspects of their job descriptions.

Space utilization. In the previously mentioned project there was need for service improvement, such as reducing delays and overcrowding in certain areas. Value analysis can determine the extent to which examining or operating rooms are utilized by analyzing the length of time that each room is utilized, who uses it, the purpose for which it is used and the amount of time the room remains empty. Analysis and an integrated understanding of these factors can lead to better scheduling, increased efficiency, reduction of overcrowding and delays in acquiring critically needed space. Proper space utilization is essential not only for maximum use of available space but also to avoid delays, such as in scheduling tests for outpatients and in scheduling surgery. These two factors are especially crucial in the following area, medical procedures.

Medical procedures. It is appropriate to perform certain surgical procedures on an outpatient basis. Value analysis can be used to determine those which can be effectively performed without subjecting the patient to costly overnight stays in the hospital. Phalem observed:

> ...that up to 45 minor, elective surgical procedures can be performed on an outpatient basis and that more than 90 percent of these procedures can be accomplished while the patient is under general anesthesia. Moreover, outpatient surgery programs have

proved to be not only cost effective but invariably less expensive than inpatient stays for the same service.[6]

Doctors and technical staff may also find cost-reducing ways to conduct surgical procedures in the areas of pre-op, preparation of equipment and post-surgical procedures. For example, in one case study there was a need to avoid costly delays caused by not ordering tests sufficiently in advance of surgery. Serveral factors were found to be useful in avoiding such delays: having an anesthesiologist check all patients, using pre-op flags, and providing early notification to the operating room when a patient was placed on the operating room schedule, or of any changes in the schedule.[7]

THE VALUE ANALYST

The value analyst should be an individual with inventive and creative talents, being capable of developing simple mechanisms and methods that can save effort and costs. He/she should also be capable of gaining the cooperation of the people who offer the service. In a sense the value analyst should be a human relations specialist, tactful in questioning people regarding their work efficiency, mollifying the doubts or fears such questions may create.

Value analysis frequently requires uninterrupted and prolonged investigation to determine unnecessary costs. This kind of work cannot be simply assumed as an additional responsibility by a line manager, who should not have time to devote to such work. For this reason value analysis should be viewed as a staff function.

Generally such a staff role is mainly advisory, thus the value analyst should occupy a position high enough in the organization hierarchy to insure that the recommendations will be taken seriously and acted upon. It is also argued that the value analyst should report directly to some administrative officer high in the organizational hierarchy.

CONCLUSION

Value analysis as applied to the hospital setting is a systematic and dynamic appraisal of its inputs and processes aimed at improving or maintaining efficient utilization. While the goal is to reduce costs without reducing hospital services, in the present era of escalating costs simply maintaining present cost levels is commendable. Coupled with increasing costs is the issue of increasing pressures to conserve scarce resources. Thus, methods of conserving or substituting for such resources also becomes an important aspect of value analysis.

While many of the services rendered by the hospital occur as isolated events, just as others are obviously team efforts, the patient's total stay in the hospital ought to be conceived of as a single coordinated effort to terminate that stay. Value analysis also speaks to that "coordinated effort" issue—the process opens communication channels between medical and auxiliary personnel. Thus it provides the incidental benefits of increased communication flows across many hospital areas, lending to greater integration of effort and reduction of inefficiency.

While its benefits have been proven in business and manufacturing firms, value analysis applied to the hospital setting can thus far only be described as sketchy or piecemeal. It is worthy of deliberate application to the total hospital with potential value in both the financial and medical aspects.

REFERENCES

1. Harry I. Greenfield, *Hospital Efficiency and Public Policy* (New York: Praeger Publishers, 1973) p. 16.

2. Martin K. Starr, *Production Management* (Englewood Cliffs, NJ: Prentice Hall, Inc., 1972) p. 292.

3. Jamie Kowalski and Patricia Peck, "Standards Needed for Sterilization Monitoring," *Hospital Progress,* April 1976, p. 52.

4. Lawrence P. Miles, *Techniques of Value Analysis and Engineering* (New York: McGraw Hill, 1972) pp. 78-81.

5. Ibid.

6. James F. Phalem, "Planning a Hospital-based Outpatient Surgery Program," *Hospital Progress,* June 1976, p. 64.

7. Miles, op. cit., pp. 78-81.

29. Activity Measurement Program System Promotes Productivity

D. PATRICK MAZZOLLA AND JOHN D. KAUFFMAN

Reprinted with permission from *Hospital Topics*, November/December 1978, pp. 26–31.

Hospitals have been faced continually with the challenge of improving productivity and the management of human resources. However, a major obstacle has always been the availability of an appropriate management reporting and control system, which could accurately measure and track productivity and resource management performance. York Hospital, a 570 bed teaching, community, general hospital in southeastern Pennsylvania, has developed an internal computerized system, which has been effective in improving productivity and resource management capabilities and performance.

In 1973, York Hospital administration requested a series of management reports to aid department heads in relating department activity to labor costs and productivity. Several established outside manpower reporting programs were reviewed by Administration and the department of Management Services. However, it was felt that none of the existing programs seemed to be appropriate in both design and philosophy for York Hospital. Management Services was requested to investigate the feasibility of developing an inhouse program.

Management Services returned with a proposed system called AMP (Activity Management Program), which was presented as a detailed and comprehensive resource management and productivity program which could be effective and acceptable for measuring and reporting activity and performance at York Hospital.

The AMP system had multiple indicators of performance such as weighted units per direct manhour, labor cost per weighted unit, and revenue per weighted unit. Specifically, the weighted units per direct manhour figure was used as an overall indicator of department productivity.

OBJECTIVES

The AMP system was designed to meet the following objectives, in order to facilitate department director and administration discussions relating to activity and productivity:

- To provide a department productivity indicator for evaluation.
- To provide a staffing basis for control purposes.
- To provide a staffing basis for budgeting purposes.
- To provide a department activity monitor.
- To provide indicators relating department activity and resources.

The tentative AMP system was given administrative approval for implementation. The program implementation was divided into three phases. Phase one was composed of twenty-five "production-oriented" departments, phase two was to consist of twenty-five nursing stations, and phase three was to consist of ten administrative and medical departments.

The measures of activity and corresponding weighted unit values were developed specifically for York Hospital based on actual work measurement studies, discussions with department personnel, historical hospital trends and department performance. In addition, they drew from five years of compiled data from management engineering studies conducted by Management Services at York Hospital.

Furthermore, the program utilized the hospital's own data processing resources making more detailed and less expensive feedback and reporting available. Data input requirements were minimized by loading the procedures, weighted units, and job code classifications into computer master files.

Each AMP department reported the number of every type of their procedures to Management Services. In some cases, the procedures were accumulated automatically as patient charges from computerized billing system reports. When the AMP system was processed on the computer, the manhours and labor costs were collected automatically from the hospital payroll system, while the revenue figures were collected automatically from the income system.

The system received considerable inhouse support since the development, design, control, monitoring, and personnel participation evolved internally. Department heads felt strongly that tracking their activity and performance over time was more appropriate and "sensitive" than comparing it with a mean or median from a state, regional, or national group. Thus, the intent and acceptability of the AMP system was based upon identifying and tracking changes in activity/resource ratios and productivity departmentally, in order to promote management improvements.

METHODOLOGY

A methodology was developed for working with departments on the AMP system. A single measure of activity for the department was defined jointly between Management Services and department personnel. The decision was made on what appeared to be the one best overall measure of activity for the department. In some cases, this measure was simply a gross number of procedures.

A work measurement analysis was conducted to determine normal time values for each procedure as well as the basis for development of a weighted unit value.

From results of the work measurement analysis, a configuration of weighted units per each procedure was developed and approved by both Management Services and the department. Then department job codes and their corresponding manhours were differentiated into direct and indirect categories. Direct manhours were defined as the hours worked by line personnel, who actually performed the procedures. The manhours worked by supervisory and support personnel, as well as all department holiday, vacation, and sick time hours paid were reported as indirect.

Relationships were defined between weighted units and corresponding operating variables such as manhours, labor cost, and revenue. Finally, an appropriate data collection reporting procedure for the department was developed and integrated into the overall AMP input reporting system.

The AMP system is concerned with accurate, up-to-date information and the capability to make changes over time. It provides an effective yet simple method of updating both activity measures and job code classifications.

The basis of the AMP system updating is the initial detailed documentation of procedures and identification of equipment, which permits required changes to be easily identified and quickly made.

REPORT AND CONTROL GRAPH

To provide for timely reporting, AMP reports are processed monthly. All departments report their monthly activity by the tenth of the following month, so that reports may be processed and returned to the departments by the twentieth of that month.

Detailed information is provided in the AMP report showing relationships among activity, manhours, labor costs, and revenue (see Exhibit A for an example of a report for the EKG department).

The information shown under activity measurement is the gross number of procedures, broken down by inpatient and outpatient, which had been reported by the department. The total weighted unit figure reflects the mix of procedures in the department workload. It is the summation of the weighted unit value for each procedure multiplied by the number of each procedure performed that month.

The manhours figures display the direct and indirect manhours for the department for each month. The revenue information shows the average inpatient and outpatient revenue per weighted unit processed for each month.

The bottom line, weighted units per direct manhour, is the indicator of productivity achieved by the department for each month and is the basis of the AMP control graph.

Exhibit A York Hospital Activity Measurement Program 1976–77

YORK HOSPITAL
ACTIVITY MEASUREMENT PROGRAM
1976-77

RUN-DATE 07/22/77   DEPT. NO.   712   PAGE 12
                                                            EKG

	JULY	AUG-UST	SEPT.	OCTO-BER	NO-VEM-BER	DE-CEM-BER	JAN-UARY	FEB-RU-ARY	MARCH	APRIL	MAY	JUNE	Y-T-D
ACTIVITY MEASUREMENT													
IN-PATIENT	1097	1375	1499	1440	1657	1351	1566	1391	1787	1450	1602	1305	17520
OUT-PATIENT	408	387	448	376	427	406	442	438	369	340	473	398	4912
TOTAL	1505	1762	1947	1816	2084	1757	2008	1829	2156	1790	2075	1703	22432
WEIGHTED UNITS													
IN-PATIENT	1028	1310	1423	1352	1540	1300	1459	1286	1658	1313	1425	1201	16295
OUT-PATIENT	332	303	319	316	324	393	328	353	346	297	382	361	4054
TOTAL	1360	1613	1742	1668	1864	1693	1787	1639	2004	1610	1807	1562	20349
MANHOURS													
DIRECT	563	682	580	642	641	599	564	539	643	566	630	553	7207
INDIRECT	152	8	45	37	90	45	64	0	38	96	82	32	690
TOTAL (D&I)	715	690	625	679	732	645	628	539	682	662	712	585	7898
LABOR COST PER WEIGHTED UNIT $													
DIRECT	1.405	1.499	1.159	1.363	1.200	1.325	1.175	1.255	1.182	1.296	1.273	1.338	1.283
INDIRECT	.400	.025	.091	.076	.181	.093	.129	.000	.068	.217	.164	.076	.123
TOTAL	1.806	1.524	1.251	1.440	1.381	1.419	1.305	1.255	1.250	1.514	1.437	1.414	1.406
REVENUE PER WEIGHTED UNIT $													
IN-PATIENT	28.593	26.066	23.226	23.640	20.255	24.705	21.677	22.635	22.390	25.304	22.291	26.793	23.743
OUT-PATIENT	29.789	31.980	26.630	29.667	27.762	25.190	29.298	29.062	30.245	32.525	26.714	29.238	28.623
TOTAL	28.885	27.177	23.850	24.782	21.560	24.818	23.076	23.373	23.746	26.636	23.226	27.358	24.715
WEIGHTED UNITS/DIRECT MANHOUR	2.410	2.360	3.000	2.590	2.900	2.820	3.160	3.040	3.110	2.830	2.860	2.820	2.820

The AMP report is distributed with an accompanying control graph (see Exhibit B for an example of the control graph for the EKG department). The control graph depicts monthly values of weighted units per direct manhour for the department. It is a graphic representation of how this indicator of productivity changes with time.

Included on the control graph is the average weighted units per direct manhour for the prior fiscal year as a base line for comparison of variations. In addition, the monthly values for the previous fiscal year are shown as a broken line to aid in identifying seasonal and monthly variations and trends.

The left vertical axis shows weighted units per direct manhour values, which are uniquely defined for each department. The right vertical axis shows a percent variation in the indicator of productivity, both positive or negative (sic), which can be used for cross-department comparisons of productivity improvement or decline.

Each department head and his appropriate administrator receives a copy of the department's report and control graph. Administrators receive reports and graphs for all departments which report directly to them.

Exhibit B

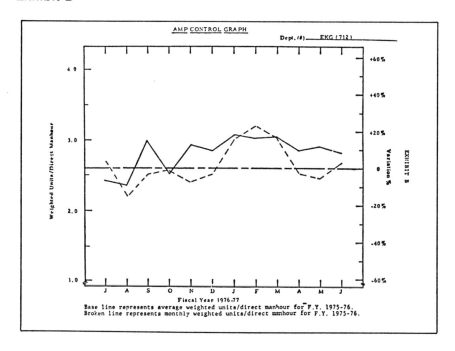

Proper interpretation of the report and control graph is critical. Attention by department heads and administration should be focused initially upon the indicator of productivity, i.e. weighted units per direct manhour and its movement and magnitude over time as shown on the control graph.

Any trends should be examined in the movement of the indicator of productivity and investigated for cause and effect. Causes for changes in the indicator of productivity can be identified by reviewing the report and the factors causing them determined and discussed by department heads and the administration (sic).

This includes changes in direct manhours as well as changes in weighted units themselves. Reasons for changes could be any of the following: abnormal vacation, holiday, or sick time, personnel additions; increased or decreased activity; change in activity mix; or use of new equipment or procedures.

EKG DEPARTMENT EXAMPLE

A more detailed look at how the AMP system was developed and how it operates can be provided by using the EKG department as an example. EKG was one of the first departments on the AMP system with initial work having been done in 1973.

The measure of activity of a revenue producing department is usually the revenue producing procedures performed by the department personnel. The first step in the AMP installation of EKG was to identify and document all procedures being done with special attention being paid to the equipment used. This attention to detail during installation has facilitated the maintenance and updating of the AMP system throughout the years. The detailed EKG procedure documentation is shown in Exhibit C.

Through the use of time study techniques, normal time values were established for each EKG procedure. The key factor in determining the normal values was the time required for a trained technician to complete each procedure. EKG's performed by other than department personnel were reported separately.

As mentioned previously, a unique basis unit of measure is defined for each department to become the weighted unit used in the AMP reports. In this case, the most common procedure, inpatient EKG's performed by an EKG Technician, was selected.

The weighted unit values for each procedure were determined by dividing the normal time for each procedure by the normal time of an inpatient EKG performed by a technician. The present EKG procedures and their weighted unit values are shown in Exhibit D.

Exhibit C

EKG PROCEDURE DOCUMENTATION Inpatient EKG's Done by Technician Procedure	Average Time (Decimal Minutes)
Place paste and leads on patient's chest	0.93
EKG machine (Marquette-Series 3000) time	0.86
Remove leads and paste from patient's chest	0.48
Type mounting card, EKG file envelope, and patient file card	1.14
Mount EKG tracing	0.69
File EKG tracing in file	0.25
Take dictation	1.47
Type physician's interpretation on mounting card	0.63
Type physician's interpretation on patient's file card	0.56
Transportation time	8.00
TOTAL TIME	15.01

Exhibit D Weighted Unit Values

WEIGHTED UNIT VALUES		
PROCEDURE	INPATIENT	OUTPATIENT
EKG's done by technician	1.0	0.5
EKG's done by others	0.3	0.3
Treadmill	4.4	4.4
Master 2-Step	2.1	2.1
Holter System	3.2	3.2

Difference between inpatient and outpatient weighted unit values reflect the transportation time required for the technician to reach the patient and return.
The weighted unit values for EKG's done by others does not include the time required to produce the tracing, since this work was done by personnel outside of the EKG department.
Holter System procedures were added in 1976.

The final installation step in EKG was to classify the job codes into either a direct or an indirect category. The job categories in the EKG department consisted of Senior EKG Technician, EKG Technician, and EKG Trainee.

A review of the job descriptions and analysis of daily activity revealed that all personnel were involved directly with patient care activities, i.e. EKG procedures. Therefore, all EKG job codes were classified as 100% direct.

Review of the monthly EKG activity starts with the control graph, which displays changes in weighted units per direct manhour, i.e., the indicator of EKG department productivity. The EKG control graph, shown in Exhibit B, illustrates an increase in the level of productivity which started in November and continued to the end of the fiscal year in June.

Cursory interpretation of the graphs shows that productivity has increased during the fiscal year, and the level of productivity is above that of the previous fiscal year.

The causes for changes in the productivity indicators illustrated by the control graph can be determined by examining the detailed information in the report and comparing it with the previous year's report.

Review of the EKG report, shown in Exhibit A, points out that weighted units per direct manhour increased 17% from the first to the twelfth month of the fiscal year. Comparison of the end of the year totals with those of the previous year reveal a 6% increase in productivity, which had been illustrated on the control graph.

Additional evaluation reveals that the 6% increase in productivity was caused by an 11% increase in weighted activity partially offset by a 5% increase in direct manhours.

The AMP system has been operating successfully for four years at York Hospital. Department heads and the administration have found it to be a viable management tool for reporting, tracking and controlling productivity and resource management performance.

AMP reports are being utilized widely as a basis for staffing, workload balancing, budgeting, position control, and working with the HAS reports. Presently, the implementation of phase two is under way.

Activity Measurement Program
Section Headings Description

Activity Measurement

This is the best single indicator of overall department activity. Both inpatient and outpatient activity are reported.

Weighted Units

Weighted units are used when activity measurement consists of different procedures varying in time. Weighted units reflect the relative variation in time required for the different procedures. Weighted units are individually defined for each department.

Manhours

These are manhours actually paid for the month reported, and they are divided into direct and indirect categories.

Direct Manhours is the time or portion of time actually worked by those people directly involved with the measured department activity.

Indirect Manhours is the time or portion of time of those people involved in supervision or other activities not directly related to measured department activity. This category also includes manhours paid for vacation, sickness, and holidays for all department personnel.

Labor Cost per Weighted Unit

This shows the average labor cost for producing a weighted unit of activity. Both the direct and indirect components of cost are shown.

Revenue per Weighted Unit

This shows the average revenue produced by the department for each inpatient and outpatient weighted unit.

Weighted Units/Direct Manhour

This ratio is an indicator of departmental productivity. It is uniquely defined for every department and is the value plotted on the AMP Control Graph.

30. Designing for Function: An Approach to Health Care Systems Cost Containment

CARL R. LINDENMEYER AND WILLIAM KAST

Reprinted with permission from *Industrial Management*, September–October 1977, pp. 13–18.

Western Michigan University Department of Industrial Engineering provides assistance to hospitals in their cost containment efforts. The Health Care Systems Design (HCSD) program was initially supported by the Kellogg Foundation through the University of Michigan's Hospital System Improvement Program. Since HCSD's inception in 1971, it has grown from a single participating hospital to seven participating institutions; acute care hospitals ranging from under 100 beds to over 400 beds, a state mental health facility and a university health center. The program has grown because the "Design for Function" concept works—producing results; results that the participating institutions incorporate into their cost containment/system improvement programs. Two of the hospitals in the program have hired former students to operate their management engineering.

DESIGNING FOR FUNCTION

The approach that the program has successfully applied is based on the "IDEALS CONCEPT" (Nadler, 1967) and the Value Engineering approach (Miles, 1961). Perhaps the best approach to illustrating the "Design for Function" strategy is to contrast it with the more typical conventional problem solving approach. A conventional approach to the solution of a hospital system problem would be to:

1. Define the problem.
2. Analyze the present system. Take it apart—separate out each system detail. Make flow process charts and diagrams graphically portraying the existing system and collect large amounts of data surrounding the present operation.
3. Scrutinize and question each detail as provided in the previous step.
4. Consider possibilities for improvement on each of the system details and evaluate alternatives.
5. Recommend changes in the present system and implement.

The "Design for Function" approach differs significantly from the conventional strategy in both philosophy and action. The following sequence of steps has been effectively used in both new system design and cost containment projects in hospitals:

1. Define the function of the system. What is the system's mission, aim, or purpose? Incorporate into the study those allied systems that have a significant impact upon the originating system's function.
2. Collect only those data which are required to design the best system to achieve the stated function. Present system data need only be collected where necessary for cost/benefit comparison.
3. Design alternative "ideal" systems that will fulfill the intended function at the lowest possible cost. Minor constraints and restrictions should not influence the system design specifications at this point. Research, creativity techniques including brainstorming, and the use of the checklists (idea prompters) should be used.
4. Evaluate the alternatives and select the most promising as a target for final design and recommendation. Restrictions and constraints are considered at this point in the project.
5. Make recommendations and implement the new system design.

Advantages of Designing for Function

There are many significant advantages of the "Design for Function" approach in our Health Care Systems Design projects. Probably the most important of these is that we are not just "patching up the old dog" but often developing an entirely new approach to achieving necessary function. A very real danger in the approach that emphasizes present system analysis is that you "put on blinders" that make it quite difficult to generate truly innovative and cost saving solutions.

Employees often perceive the questioning approach used in the conventional design strategy as a personal critical attack. The "Design for Function'' approach enlists their support and contributions of all in the creative process of developing ideal systems.

Data collection is minimized. Only those data required for ideal system development or for cost/benefit analysis are gathered.

It is our thesis that a hospital's new systems design and cost containment efforts are best served through a strategy that encourages a high level of creative thought. ''Designing for Function'' has been proven a successful approach. The design and improvement of health care systems through our student projects has demonstrated this effectiveness.

A COOPERATIVE APPROACH

The HCSD Program has many educational and research facts; one of the most result-oriented is management engineering project work conducted by teams of industrial engineering students. The cooperating health care institutions offer a variety of systems design and cost containment projects. The HCSD Program administrator and technical consultant meet with a hospital representative to establish a project description and set of study objectives, estimate the resource requirements and agree upon a manpower assignment.

Teams of students select educationally appropriate projects on the basis of interest and background. Although project strategies will differ, an approach that has proven successful in many instances will be discussed.

Project Definition and Work Plan

After an initial conference with the hospital representative, the team prepares a statement defining the project and outlining a plan of action to achieve the project objectives. The ''WH'' or questioning approach is useful here:

1. *What?* What system is to be designed? For what function (mission, aim, or purpose) are we designing this system to accomplish? What are the problems that initiated the project? What are some of the intended results or benefits of a successful project?
2. *How?* How do we proceed? Here, the team will specify the study steps including data collection, research, new or improved system design activities, and report preparation.
3. *When?* When will each of the study steps be completed? Deadlines are added to the sequence of project tasks.
4. *Where?* Where do we get the data required? Where (including other hospitals) would research be helpful?

5. *Who?* Who are the key personnel involved in the system under study? Who will be our best sources for required information?

RESULTS

Over fifty projects have been conducted and have provided cost savings, systems improvements, management information and educational benefits to the institutions and people involved with the program.

- Cost savings total $248,855 or $4879 per project average.
- Systems improvements:
    Enhanced quality of service activities.
    Improved facilities layout.
    Activity scheduling systems (manual and computerized).
    Reduced or eliminated materials handling.
    Improved work procedures.
    Traffic flow improvements.
- Management information:
    Utilization reporting or activity monitoring.
    Feasibility studies for new services and for alternative courses of action.
    Surveys.
- Educational:
    Function determination to assist those involved to understand the activity under study.
    Research and publications.
    Intra-institution exchange of information.

APPLICATIONS

Physical Examination Procedure

A systematic approach to a routine patient physical examination requires the patient to make several position changes. The function of this procedure makes certain clinical observations concerning the patient's condition. A restructuring of the basic physical examination allows all observations of the patient in the supine position to be accomplished at one time, those in a sitting position are done together and those in standing position are done together. The new method requires patients to change position only twice, saves an average of fifteen minutes per examination, causes less patient discomfort and allows more patients to be seen. This procedure is not valuable for non-ambulatory patients where movement is often painful and slow.

Food Service

The function of a kitchen in a Food Service system is to provide good food on an economical basis. The hospital is composed of several buildings which are not connected. Two kitchens serve this complex, with covered transportation vehicles. By consolidating the kitchens and shortening the transportation lines, the kitchen can more fully respond to its function in the food system, with a $63,000 cost savings each year for a one time investment in remodeling of $45,000.

Central Transport Service

A patient transportation system's basic function is to move patients in a safe manner among and between the nursing units and ancillary departments. The old system provided transport personnel to each department who, in addition to the basic function, were double scheduling patients for services, not providing second shift and weekend coverage, allowing slack time for some transporters while others were overloaded. Each department felt that their transport function was secondary to the function of the department. A feasibility study indicated that the basic patient transport function was necessary, it should be an independent function, and could be better achieved through a centralized and improved system. Annual savings through staff reduction totaled $43,860.

Physical Therapy

The patient care aspects of the Physical Therapy make it difficult for management to determine the utilization of its resources. By developing activity descriptions and standard times for each activity, management was able, after allowing time for indirect activities, to completely assess the use of their Physical Therapy resource. The students, by performing a function determination, can provide a basis upon which to assess the need of the various indirect activities as they relate to the main purpose of Physical Therapy.

EDUCATION AND RESEARCH

One of the primary functions of the HCSD Program is to provide "real world" learning experiences for our Industrial Engineering students.

Beyond this obvious purpose however, we have found that significant educational benefits accrue to the cooperating institution's administration and employees. By exposing hospital personnel to the "Design for Function" concept more creativity and openness to change can result. Administrators can better see the inter-relationships of the various hospital sub-systems and are encouraged to evaluate those systems under their leadership against system function statements. Department managers can change their problem-solving style from the "put out the fire" method to total systems development and long-range planning.

Several of our studies have employed a research strategy to develop the most appropriate system to accomplish the intended function. One, a graduate student project, addressed the question of the need for and use of productivity indicators both on a departmental and entire hospital basis. A second study involved the design of a new Emergency Department and employed a research strategy to determine the function of the new facility. Industrial engineering techniques were then used to convert these concepts into a functional layout.

CONCLUSION

Hospital administrators and other health care professionals will more effectively achieve their cost containment goals by applying the "Design for Function" concept. Educators in the hospital administration and management engineering fields will find this problem-solving philosophy an important facet in the preparation of degreed practitioners. At Western Michigan University we have found "Designing for Function" particularly effective in our field project oriented courses.

Health care institutions and higher education will both benefit from cooperative ventures such as we have described. It would seem quite appropriate for the hospital administrator to contact a nearby college or university and initiate a program that can be an educational and results-producing experience for all those concerned.

REFERENCES

1. Miles, Lawrence D., *Techniques of Value Analysis and Engineering*. New York: McGraw-Hill Book Company, Inc. 1961.

2. Nadler, Gerald, *Work Systems Design: The IDEALS Concept*. Homewood, Illinois: Richard D. Irwin, Inc. 1967.

3. HCSD Projects:
   Simplification of the Physical Examination—1974.
   Study of Physical Therapy—1971.
   Central Transportation System—1971.
   Emergency Room Component Design—1972.
   Kitchen Consolidation—1974.
   Hospital Productivity—1974.

CHAPTER 4

BUILDINGS, EQUIPMENT, ENERGY, AND MATERIAL MANAGEMENT

People are the most important resource in health care delivery, but quality care cannot be delivered without equipment, energy, and supplies. Cost containment opportunities are available in all these areas. In this chapter the following topics are reviewed:

- material management systems
- buildings
- maintenance management
- energy management
- waste disposal
- inventory control
- equipment leasing vs. buying
- group purchasing

MATERIAL MANAGEMENT SYSTEM

The material management system in health institutions involves many functions and employees. The expenditures controlled by this system amount to 46 percent of the total hospital expenses. This 46 percent is divided between supplies and equipment (27 percent), and related labor (19 percent).[1] In addition, the material management system has an impact on the value of the assets of the health institution, since it controls some or all of the maintenance activities. Obviously, there are many cost containment opportunities in such a system.

The structure, functions, organization, and control of the hospital's material management system are discussed in Kowalski's paper (Reading 31). The article contains recommendations on procedures, such as an exchange cart system and proper hospital design.

BUILDINGS

Substantial cost savings can be realized during the initial construction of health facilities (e.g., by appropriate planning) and during expansion and modification (e.g., by proper control of contractors). Also, proper maintenance of the buildings, grounds, and equipment may contribute to cost containment.

The operating expenses of a properly designed health facility, a new wing, or even a new unit, are much lower than those of an improperly designed facility. Details of proper planning are given by Arneill (Reading 32).

MAINTENANCE MANAGEMENT

Maintenance of buildings, grounds, and equipment can become rather expensive if not properly executed. Advanced health care institutions use computers in their preventive maintenance system, but not all facilities can afford this degree of sophistication. A good maintenance management program can be rather simple to organize, however, as shown by Plunkett's paper (Reading 33).

ENERGY MANAGEMENT

Two factors make energy management increasingly important in health care facilities. First, the cost of energy is rising; second, the demand for energy is rising as the use of automation increases.

Hospital energy costs run between two and six percent of the total budgets. The greatest energy use is concentrated in the following systems:

- environmental control: heating, ventilation, and air conditioning (40-60% of all energy)
- lighting: (10-20%)
- laundry: (8-15%)
- food service: (5-10%)

- medical equipment: (3-5%)
- sterilization and incineration: (2-3%)

We elected to include two energy-related papers in this text. The first one, by Jeffries and Testolin (Reading 34), is a case study that illustrates ways to cut energy use significantly in a medical center. Piper's paper (Reading 35) introduces the concept of an energy audit as a systematic way to conserve energy by identifying and analyzing those measures whose investment cost is justifiable.

WASTE DISPOSAL

Trash disposal is a problem and expense in any health care institution. Incineration of solid waste can solve this problem for facilities that are medium to large in size, with the added benefit of energy creation through a heat recovery system. A case study (Reading 36) illustrates the application of such a system.

INVENTORY CONTROL

A major area of concern in materials management is proper inventory control. The cost of keeping inventory is steadily increasing, largely as a result of the increased costs of capital evident in higher interest rates. One of the best approaches to inventory control, especially in large institutions, is to use a computerized system that is based on operations research/management science models. Bankes' selection (Reading 37) explains the use of such a system in a hospital. Another way to cut inventory costs is to keep no inventory; this is a possibility in places where daily deliveries are feasible, as shown in Shanoff's paper (Reading 38).

LEASING VS. BUYING

One of the most controversial issues in materials management is the question of leasing as opposed to buying equipment. One reason for the disagreement is the lack of standardization of the costs that should be considered in such an analysis. Henry and Rosenfeldt (Reading 39) show an appropriate cost analysis procedure. After reviewing the advantages of leasing, they conclude that leasing may turn out to be extremely expensive.

GROUP PURCHASING

A classical and frequently mentioned cost containment tool is group purchasing of supplies, materials, and sometimes equipment. The advantages and the potential savings, as well as the limitations are presented in King's article (Reading 40). A group purchasing plan frequently involves a product selection committee that is either a part of a group purchasing organization or a subcommittee of the facility's cost containment committee.[2,3]

OVERVIEW

The last article of this chapter (Reading 41) includes a list of 49 cost containment ideas in the material management system.

NOTES

1. AMSCO Fact Summary, SC-2533. In C.E. Housley, *Hospital Materiel Management* (Germantown, Md.: Aspen Systems Corp., 1978).

2. C.E. Housley, *Hospital Materiel Management* (Germantown, Md.: Aspen Systems Corp., 1978).

3. L.C. Boergadine, "Committees Ensure Cost Efficiency in Purchasing," *Hospitals, JAHA* 51 (June 16, 1977): 133–135.

BIBLIOGRAPHY

Arneill, B.P. "Design Master Plan Cut Hospital Costs, Increased Efficiency." *Modern Healthcare,* March 1977.

Ballentine, R., et al. "ABC Inventory Analysis and Economic Order Quantity Concept in Hospital Pharmacy Purchasing." *American Journal of Hospital Pharmacy,* June 1976.

Blan, G.J., and Browne, K.H. "Energy Management: Total Program Considers All Buildings' Systems." *Hospitals, JAHA,* 16 September 1978.

Bradley, J.A., and Janco, J.W. "Professional Energy Audit Points Way to $100,000 Annual Savings." *Hospital Progress,* June 1978.

Carpenter, W.W. "Negotiate the Best Price: Getting Tough with Vendors." *Hospital Financial Management,* June 1979.

Colling, W.C. "Practical Approach to Low Cost Maintenance Management." *Hospitals, JAHA,* 1 October 1977.

"Connecticut Hospitals Will Save $363,000 on Fuel." *Modern Healthcare,* April 1977.

Cooper, R.J. "The Energy Crisis Challenge." *Hospital Progress,* May 1975.

Dessler, F.R.S., and Speiger, W.F. *Practical Energy Management in Health Care Institutions.* Philadelphia, Pa.: Blue Cross of Greater Philadelphia, 1977.

Downey, G.W. "Hospitals Will Get Fuel They Need, and a Bigger Bill." *Modern Hospital,* January 1974.

Drue, R. "Five Steps to Lower Costs and Improve Equipment Maintenance." *Hospitals, JAHA,* 16 August 1977.

Ellis, B. "Energy Management and Its Dollar and Sense." *Hospitals, JAHA,* 16 March 1977.

Energy Management in Health Care Institutions, HEW Pub. No. 76-619; U.S. Department of Commerce and U.S. Department of Health, Education and Welfare, 1976.

Fundingsland, D.W., and Mall, P.L. "Telephone Services, Reduce Costs." *Hospital Topics,* September 1969.

Gent, D.I. "Energy Crunch Hits Hospitals." *Hospital Financial Management,* January 1977.

Greenbert, F.E. "Health Facility Preventive Maintenance, Increased Need in a Fiscal Crisis." *Hospital Topics,* July-August 1978.

Hardy, O.B., and Lammers, L. "Build Less Total Space But Achieve More Usable Space." *Hospitals, JAHA,* 16 March 1976.

Heckler, T.M., and Sweetland, J. "Minimizing Costs Through Facilities Planning." *Topics in Health Care Financing,* Summer 1977.

Henning, T. "How to Put Waste to Work." *Modern Healthcare,* December 1974.

Henning, W.K. "Managing Materials in Today's Hospital." *Hospitals, JAHA,* 16 June 1977.

Johnson, T.R. "Zeroing in on Potential Energy Savings." *Building Operating Management,* October 1977.

Kowalski, J. "Comprehensive Materials Management: St. Mary's Medical Center, Racine, WI." *Hospital Progress,* March 1977.

Lanier, J.C. "Materials Management Cut Costs with Internal, External Controls." *Hospitals, JAHA,* 16 December 1978.

Mitchell, R.C. "Hospital-wide Inventory Turnover Provides Positive Results." *Hospitals, JAHA,* 1 July 1978.

Moran, A.D., and Moore, W.R. "Energy Conservation Program Saves $89,000: De Paul Hospital, Norfolk, VA." *Hospital Progress,* May 1977.

Olstein, M., and Shriley, J.M. "Management Energy." *Hospital Financial Management,* November 1977.

Rohr, R. "Hospital Waste Converted into Energy Source." *Hospitals, JAHA,* 16 February 1978.

Satterfield, T.F. "Financial Managers Play Important Role in Control of Energy Cost Use." *Hospital Financial Management,* October 1976.

Shaul, R.L., Jr., and McLaughlin, C.P. "A Second Look at Leasing." *Health Care Management Review,* Spring 1977.

Smejda, J. "What You Know About Materials Management Can Save You Plenty." *Hospital Financial Management,* April 1976.

Smith, M. "A Rational Approach for Making Major Equipment Purchases." *Hospitals, JAHA,* 16 December 1977.

Smith, S.W. "Leasing, an Effective Source of Capital Asset Financing." *Hospital Financial Management,* September 1974.

Stadnik, J.K. "How to Measure Materials Management Effectiveness." *Hospital Purchasing Manager,* February 1977.

Stafford, D. "Monitoring Materials Flow Through Inventory Control." *Hospitals, JAHA,* 16 June 1977.

Taylor, W.J. "Careful Planning Can Reduce Cost Problems in Hospital Construction." *Hospitals, JAHA,* 16 February 1978.

Traska, M.S. "Hospital Corporation of America Pioneers Program in Gradual Trend Toward Energy Controls." *Modern Healthcare,* March 1977.

Watch, R. "Capital Budget Decision-Making for Hospitals." *Hospital Administration,* Fall 1970.

Williams, J.D. "How Do You Evaluate Capital Investment?" *Hospital Financial Management,* February 1974.

Wulfinghoff, D.R. "Economics of Energy Conservation in Health Care Facilities." *Hospital Topics,* May-June 1979.

31. Comprehensive Materials Management

JAMIE KOWALSKI

Reprinted from *Hospital Progress,* March 1977, pp. 76–83, by permission of Edward J. Pollock, Publisher, © 1977.

Much has been written about the concept of comprehensive materials management, a system in which all supply functions are consolidated under one department and director. While this concept has gained acceptance in many hospitals over the last 10 to 15 years, most of what has been written to date concerns only a small part of materials management—purchasing and inventory control. These are important and popular topics, but they are just a small part of a comprehensive materials management system.

Hospitals which can provide the necessary administrative and financial support, plus the commitment, coordination, and cooperation among hospital departments required to develop a comprehensive system, can expect results in terms of economy—thousands of dollars saved annually—accountability, and quality of service. Based on these expectations, St. Mary's Medical Center, Racine, WI, has developed a materials management program that is concerned with all supply functions and the important role each of these plays in supporting patient care. The major supply functions handled through this department and delineated in this article are: purchasing; printing; material distribution, with particular emphasis on receiving and storage; elements of financial control, including control of inventory and patient supply charges; and centralized processing.

Because the relationship between administrative and physical control of material is critical, any extra layer of red tape or any extra persons between the purchasing department and the distribution department will reduce the coordination, responsiveness, and accountability essential to a successful supply system. Thus, a director of materials management can help solve problems regarding supplies and their distribution. Such a person can provide the expertise and consistency that hospital departments need. The materials management director can unify and coordinate a number of inter-related and interdependent functions (see Figure). Rather than letting control of the system fall by chance to the individuals who are a part of its operation, a director can see that system, policy, and procedure are developed by management. These functions can maintain consistency, even though specific personalities are apt to change.

SERVICE-ORIENTED, CENTRALIZED PURCHASING

The purchasing department, as an integral part of the materials management system, is service-oriented. In addition to its basic responsibilities of prudent and competitive buying, a good purchasing department also provides product information to interested parties. Professional and aggressive product research, evaluation, and ultimate negotiation, accomplished by the individual hospital or by group purchasing, are imperative if the purchasing department is to be responsive to the needs of the user departments. Without such responsiveness, the hospital will certainly fall victim to the perils of "back door" buying, the too well known practice of department heads and supervisors contacting vendors on their own. An extremely costly practice because the departments may be buying items at higher cost than the purchasing department is generally able to negotiate, "back door" buying can be avoided by allowing, inviting, or soliciting input from the departments and by producing results consistently on a timely basis.

While being responsive to departmental needs, purchasing must retain the right of prudent substitution in order to save money and to circumvent frequent product shortages or transportation delays. Without substitution strategy, the hospital may well face problems with stock-outs, which are critical because of the nature of the hospital's product, patient care.

All purchasing can and should be done by the purchasing department under the purchasing agent because centralizing the purchasing function allows for expertise and consistency in evaluation, substitution, and negotiation, which the chiefs of pharmacy, dietary, or lab may not be able to provide. The centralized purchasing department can set up and coordinate all necessary documentation, from request and justification, to the purchase order/contract, to the receiving ticket.

ANALYZING THE HOSPITAL'S PRINTING NEEDS

The print shop should be considered part of a comprehensive materials management system because its responsibility for the hospital's copying and duplicating operations provides a service and source of supply to the hospital departments and staff.

The materials management department analyzes, with the help of various vendors, utilization of copying/duplicating equipment, types of alternative equipment available to meet the needs of the hospital and individual departments, and the advantages of inhouse versus outside vendor printing of forms. Purchasing negotiates for maintenance, supply, and paper prices and the purchase or rental of equipment. These coordinated efforts can achieve considerable savings.

The materials management department should analyze the capabilities of duplicating equipment to print forms in view of other priorities such as public relations pamphlets, brochures, and training manuals. In many instances, proper form design will permit inhousing printing, which is generally more economical when time, materials, and production-run size (less may be needed in storage, since the source is inhouse) are all considered in the "cost."

Careful analysis of form design can save money. Duplication can be eliminated when analysis of the objectives of forms shows how two that are similar can be revised somewhat and combined into one. When multicopy forms are found to contain more copies than are really necessary, a needless expense can be eliminated. On the other hand, forms lacking sufficient copies can cause needless use of a copier and much wasted time.

INVENTORY INVESTMENT CAN BE REDUCED

Using an Economic Order Quantity or an ABC (correlating control effort with item or transaction value) system, materials management can substantially reduce investment in inventory, improve the cash flow position, and reduce administrative costs. This can be accomplished effectively with either a manual or a computer system. A computerized system, however, is preferable because of the speed with which the computer can provide data necessary for evaluating inventory conditions and trends, revising reorder points, analyzing vendor performance, adjusting balance-on-hand requirements, and identifying obsolete or stagnant items for use and/or removal from inventory.

Computer inventory systems do not necessarily cost less or require fewer personnel to operate, but they can provide the management tools to make an inventory control system much more effective. The purchasing department can share in the capabilities of a computerized inventory system by using information quickly obtained to take advantage of discounts or sales.

The receiving function has long been neglected as an area that can provide service and/or cost savings. As part of the materials management

Figure: Materials Management Functional Relationships

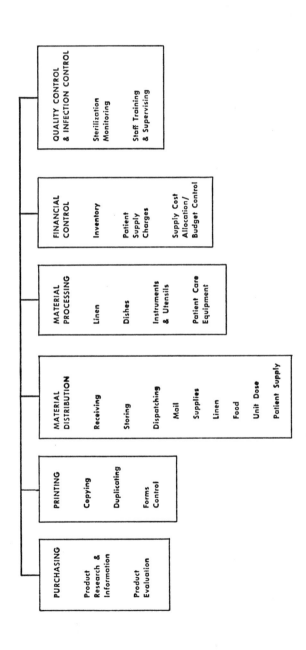

system, a centralized receiving system can provide a number of benefits.

A centralized receiving system can help control a number of administrative costs. Through consolidating in a single area the paperwork required for processing supplies, through standardizing forms used and procedures followed, the receiving function can be coordinated with the purchasing department, which ordered the item; with the accounting department, which will pay for the item (after receipt has been verified/documented); and with the user department, which originally wanted/needed the item.

Centralized receiving makes good use of staff. Receiving personnel, who have handling and processing of supplies and equipment as their sole responsibility, can concentrate on that function. Procedures are more likely to be applied consistently when a single department is responsible for the receiving function, rather than its being fragmented. The receiving personnel can expedite problem solving, too, by handling any questions regarding proof of receiving.

Supplies or equipment that need to be returned can be better coordinated by a receiving crew, which has actual contact with the shippers on a daily basis and which is familiar with proper packaging techniques, shipping rates, and schedules. The purchasing department, working closely with the receiving staff, can expedite returns by correct and timely processing of the necessary paperwork.

STORAGE, UNDERPINNING OF OTHER SYSTEMS

Because economical and effective storage is crucial to inventory control and to the purchasing and distribution functions, it should be considered an integral part of comprehensive materials management. In many management seminars and articles, storage costs are estimated to add up to 35 percent of the value of the inventory to yearly inventory costs. Since a 300-bed hospital may carry up to $200,000 in inventory, storage becomes a substantial cost, which must be controlled.

Well-designed storage space facilitates effective management of the storage function. Planners of new hospitals have a particularly good opportunity to arrange for adequate storage space and/or room for expansion. Whether a hospital is still in the planning stage or is long established, its administrators may select from several formulas used to determine how much storage area the institution needs. One hospital used a factor of 30 square feet per bed—an adequate amount for that hospital. Too much space is not an answer to the problem of how much. Too much space is costly and can lead to needless items filling in the empty spaces and a gradual expansion of the inventory. It is better to make a careful decision about how much space is needed and then to lay out and utilize this amount effectively.

An effective purchasing department may even be able to negotiate the storage of items by the vendor until a very short time before the hospital actually needs them. This concept is sometimes known as stockless inventory and is associated with the prime vendor concept, in which the hospital contracts for the majority of its purchases with a single supplier.

As hospital administrations increase their efforts to better utilize staff, dollars, and facilities, they are allocating less and less storage space to ancillary departments and more to a central stores area for two reasons. First, this storage method provides a better control mechanism for total inventory because it permits more direct access to what is actually on hand at a given time. Second, since many department supervisors are neither concerned with nor knowledgeable about inventory control, providing just enough storage space in the user department for what the department needs for a given (generally short) period of time (sic).

EFFECTIVELY MANAGING SUPPLY DISTRIBUTION

The next step toward achieving a comprehensive materials management program in the hospital is to establish an effective supply distribution system in order to provide control of supplies and charges and, at the same time, to provide continuity of supply for good patient care.

As part of this distribution system, supply quotas should be established for all user departments. These quotas (supply quantities needed for a given period of time) are best established by analyzing a combination of historical data regarding each department's supply usage and projected needs identified by the department's supervisor or department head.

Distribution personnel can make bulk deliveries of supplies to user departments on a scheduled basis. The user departments order stock from inventory on a particular day each week and receive it that day or the next. A weekly schedule, requiring approximately the same number of work hours daily to fill orders from stock, can be set up to meet peak demands for user departments by staggering their regular order days. Alternatively, the materials management department may wish to design sophisticated systems for automatically sending supply quotas to the departments unless notified otherwise.

The principle behind scheduling bulk weekly orders from inventory can be applied just as effectively in scheduling an exchange cart system for supplies and linen. Many hospitals have already implemented such a system for linen, but it is only recently becoming a popular, though relatively expensive, mechanism for distributing supplies.

BENEFITS OF EXCHANGE CART SYSTEM

The exchange cart system is superior to a conventional system in several ways. In a conventional system, the department makes out an order and sends it to stores or central service; the storeroom or central service personnel must gather the supplies, load them onto a cart or truck, take them to the floor, take them off the cart, and place them in the cabinet or closet—a total of five steps. Utilization of an exchange cart system cuts the number of steps to two—restocking the cart and sending it to its destination. A study conducted by the author showed that implementing a cart system could reduce inventory stored on the patient care floors as much as 200 percent.

The cart itself is better utilized when it serves as both the transport and the storage module. The cart takes the place of closed cabinets and drawers that many times "hide" items that are needed quickly; thus, in emergency situations it is generally more helpful than these storage places. Its standardization is a benefit to "float" personnel, who do not have to remember that a special item is stored in a different location on each floor. On any floor, the item can be found on the cart. The carts are set up in basically the same way for all areas, though the quantity and variety of supplies may differ depending on the type of patients served on each floor.

One of the major benefits of this system is that the cart, with all its supplies comes to the user automatically at the same time every day. Consequently nurses need not take time from patient care to make out a long list of supplies for the entire floor. The predetermined quotas of supplies can be revised as the needs in any given area change—generally at least semiannually.

Items on the cart are in their "broken down" state, i.e., they have been removed from their shipping cartons and are ready for use. This eliminates nursing time to unpackage the items and keeps possibly contaminated (by insects, vermin, bacteria) boxes and packages from ever reaching the patient care area. Carts with wire shelves collect much less dust and debris than those with conventional solid wood or metal shelves or cabinets.

Regular inventory turnover is another benefit of the cart system. The 24-hour quota of supplies will be depleted and the sterile supplies will be used or resterilized daily. Older items, which in a conventional system could sit for months in the back of a cabinet or the bottom of a drawer, are used first; and hoarding is virtually eliminated.

HOSPITAL DESIGN WILL DETERMINE CART DISTRIBUTION

The method by which carts are physically distributed throughout the hospital should be determined by an analysis of the hospital's needs, which, in turn, are very much dependent upon the facility's design. For example, a sprawling, horizontal building, with long distances to elevators and/or from user areas, may justify an automated cart transportation system. A generally less expensive semiautomated operation may be more appropriate for hospitals that are more vertical in design. Carts are manually pushed to an automated elevator or "carlift system."

Utilizing a "dedicated" elevator system—for carts and equipment only—will greatly benefit whatever cart distribution system is selected because such elevators will speed delivery, cut down on traffic jams in crowded "people" elevators, and ultimately give the materials management department a chance to responsively serve hospital departments. Better still, separate clean/dirty elevators facilitate the overall infection control program.

Up-to-date pneumatic tube systems can provide relatively low-cost movement of small or paper items that in the past required transporting by people. The improved design of today's systems makes them a much more reliable source of materials movement than the older systems.

Large pneumatic tubes (16″) can also be used to transport soiled linen and trash to a central location where it is further processed, handled, or disposed of. This type of system can be expensive to install but may save thousands of dollars in work hours over a period of three to five years or more.

Consistent with the objectives of the infection control program, hospitals may find these larger pneumatic tube systems a more "secure" means of handling soiled linen and trash, since they are not transported through corridors and in "people" or clean supply elevators. Their path is controlled and segregated from point of use to point of disposal or of reprocessing. Dedicated "soiled" elevators for handling such items can also be used effectively, and generally at a lower installation cost than a tube system. Any comparison of systems for handling soiled material must include a comparison of installation and operational costs of tubes to costs of elevators, manpower, and carts.

PATIENT SUPPLY CABINET FINAL DISTRIBUTION STEP

Many hospitals implementing a comprehensive materials management system incorporate the patient supply cabinet as the final step in the supply distribution system. This cabinet, located in each patient's room or the adjacent alcove or corridor, contains the basic patient care supplies that may be required for a 24-hour period (i.e., linen, toilet tissue, paper towels, med cups, tissues, needles and syringes). The cabinet may also have a section for the patient's chart, a locked area for medications (compatible with a unit-dose system), and a separate area for holding soiled items until a pickup occurs.

This system, which eliminates needless running by both materials management and patient care personnel, is based on setting up adequate quotas of supplies to be stocked in the cabinet on a 24-hour basis and on the input of the patient care personnel, who must anticipate the extra items needed for each particular patient for the next 24-hour period. These extras can be made available in the cabinet, where they are at the nurse's fingertips. To be effective this advanced planning must be supported by all patient care personnel. When this system is operating well, it avoids the anxieties of waiting for necessary supplies and saves time, energy and money.[1] If the nurse should forget to order an item, it still would be available on the exchange cart held in a clean utility/hold room on each floor or in the materials management area, which can be contacted by a telephone call.

Soiled, reprocessable supplies are picked up from the supply cabinet on a scheduled basis and sent to the decontamination area for reprocessing. A "soiled" utility room is generally provided to store these items temporarily until they can be accumulated in a batch and sent.

CONTROL OF PATIENT SUPPLY CHARGES

A charge ticket attached to each chargeable item distributed to supply carts and patient supply cabinets and the subsequent, daily reconciliation of the supplies missing and the charge tickets available for processing provides a useful control on patient charges for expendable supplies and equipment. Reconciliation can be handled by materials management personnel at the patient supply cabinet on restocking rounds or when the carts are exchanged. If charge tickets are missing, the nursing staff is notified and initiates the investigation to find the missing charges. Most hospitals that implement this control procedure find substantial reductions in lost charges as personnel become acclimated to the system. One hospital in which the author worked lowered losses from $500 a month to approximately $100.

Through purchasing's records and price lists, the materials management department has access to information directly involved with costs, labor, and the purchase price of supplies. With this information available, the department can adjust patient supply and equipment charges when costs change. Prompt attention to these changes is highly important to the financial situation of the hospital because failure to adjust the selling price of much-used items can speedily create thousands of dollars of lost revenue.

ADVANTAGES OF CENTRALIZED PROCESSING

Important to comprehensive materials management is a centralized material processing (or reprocessing) system—a system that brings together the entire function of processing reusables in the hospital, including patient utensils, surgical instruments, dishware, patient care equipment, linen, and trash.

Such a system removes the responsibility and facilities (space and equipment) for doing the reprocessing from the departments that have done their own in the past (surgery, respiratory therapy, obstetrics, emergency) and consolidates in one central area the reprocessing equipment and staff.

Handling reprocessing in this manner has many advantages. Productivity and utilization of equipment is greatly improved when the function is centralized. In addition, economies of assembly-line-type production can be achieved by well-planned department layout and equipment purchases. For example, two high-speed volume sterilizers usually will cost less than several smaller ones and will afford greater utilization because they are used 16 to 24 hours a day, as opposed to just a few hours in a decentralized situation.

The actual costs of reprocessing are reduced when nurses and other patient care personnel are not involved with this task. These generally more highly paid people are best utilized for direct care of patients, leaving the support functions to the support personnel. These processing personnel become quite "professional" in their expertise and development of techniques that improve both quality and productivity.

Where reprocessing is a less than fully centralized operation, duplication is created because there must be more than one "soiled" receiving area. Another disadvantage is that the traffic patterns that must be developed in a decentralized system may hinder infection control and traffic programs. Decentralized operations may also require staff increases.

EVALUATING ALTERNATIVE LAUNDRY ARRANGEMENTS

The pros and cons of alternative laundry arrangements should be evaluated in full as part of comprehensive materials management. Many hospitals are planning new construction and are not including a hospital laundry, arguing that inhouse facilities are too expensive. While commercial laundries may offer a lower price per pound, additional factors should be considered in evaluating bottom-line costs. When a commercial laundry processes the linen, there still must be space provided and staff available at the hospital to sort, count, inspect, and assemble the linen for distribution; and the cost of this space and staff labor must be added to the total cost. Furthermore, the commercial laundry is usually concerned with more than one customer and may not give the hospital's linen the top priority in quality or speed of service provided by an inhouse laundry. Most hospitals will experience an increase in linen inventory when processing at a commercial laundry, due to increased turnaround time and, in many cases, increased loss of linen because one hospital's laundry gets mixed up with another's. St. Mary's increased linen in inventory by $1,100 to have enough to handle the extra turnaround time.

Another alternative available to hospitals is the cooperative laundry—facilities shared by several hospitals. This concept has not been put into practice as often as the others; but if community hospitals can work together, they may experience the benefits of a system similar to a commercial operation but over which they have more control.

The processing of dishware is also a materials management function that requires evaluation. Dishes, considered patient "utensils," are reprocessable and should be handled on a soiled-to-clean basis so that they are properly contained and processed before being used again by patients, visitors, or employees.

Materials management distribution systems, utilizing carts to send food trays to patient floors, can use the same carts after the meal is served to collect and return trays and utensils for reprocessing. Upon arrival in the decontamination area, the dishes are processed and the carts are sanitized in a cart washer or by hand.

The centralized material-processing function, from decontamination through terminal sterilization, enhances the probability of improved aseptic technique and infection control. The flow from separate "soiled" to clean areas and the utilization of processing equipment such as washer/sterilizers and sonic washers protect the personnel who handle these items, the rest of the hospital personnel, and ultimately the patients. The machines clean better and faster than most manual methods.

Many conventional surgery departments sterilize instruments with the "flash" (unwrapped, high-speed, high-temperature) method. This can be very difficult to do while maintaining aseptic technique in the operating room. In this age of consumer protection, it is prudent for the hospital to employ every technique at its disposal to assure sterility of the items it provides in patient care and to extend their sterile state for a maximum time.[2] Terminal sterilization will aid this effort. Studies have shown that wrapped sterile items remain sterile for a definite period of time and are generally easier to handle without contamination. The surgery department may still require a flash sterilizer, but only as an emergency back-up.

CENTRALIZED DEPARTMENT CAN MAINTAIN HIGH QUALITY

A department that has as its main function the correct and timely processing of all reusables is more likely to keep up to date on innovations in the reprocessing field. Quality control is much easier to set up, implement, and monitor in a centralized system. While some persons may argue that other departments have equally responsible and qualified personnel, the objective of the centralized system is to allow patient care personnel all the time needed for this primary task by removing as many other responsibilities from them as possible.

The user departments help materials management establish the procedures used in the processing of their instruments and/or equipment, and they help train the personnel who will assume processing responsibilities for them. The user departments also provide specifications for new or replacement instruments and equipment. This method has proven successful from both an operational and a human relations point of view.

SURGICAL CASE CART SYSTEM

One more element of the comprehensive materials management concept is a surgical case cart system. The surgical case cart contains 95 percent of the supplies and instruments needed for a given surgical procedure. The surgery department identifies what is required for the case and notifies the materials management technician responsible for the assembly of case carts; then the cycle begins. The technician assembles all the items on a case cart and sends the cart to surgery as scheduled.

When the surgery is completed, the materials management technician sorts the trash, linen, and reprocessables and places them on the same cart on which they came to surgery. Clean, unused items are separated so that they may be returned clean and reused. In making a choice between closed carts (solid stainless steel on all sides) and open carts for this purpose, a point against closed carts is that they may be difficult to clean and dry thoroughly, especially in modern cart washers. If an open cart is chosen, a reprocessable cart cover should be used when the cart is moved to the "soiled" cart lift in order to contain the soiled items and to ensure consistent application of the soiled/clean separation concept. This utilizes the cart fully and minimizes handling of soiled items.

Emergency back-up supplies and instruments are available in back-up carts in the sterile operating room corridor. These are necessary for supplies and instruments that are limited in number and/or critical in terms of quick availability. The surgery staff establishes what back-up supplies it needs, and materials management provides those items.

The reprocessing cycle described in this article takes more time than does a conventional system; however, it produces better results. If the hospital administration chooses to use the system, it must provide an ample supply of instruments, reprocessable utensils, and equipment to support the cycle's turnaround.

Each hospital in its efforts to analyze the concepts of a comprehensive materials management program and what such a program is supposed to provide—the right items in the right quantity at the right place at the right time for the right cost to the hospital—must realize that the development of the concepts into a workable system will require commitment, innovation, coordination, and cooperation among hospital departments, which might see materials management as "empire building" rather than as a service from which they can benefit. Also required for a working materials management program is investment in a competent director, who is not just a retitled purchasing agent; the necessary equipment; and enough time to fully realize the objectives established for the program. With this type of support, the hospital can expect the economy, accountability, and quality of service that comprehensive materials management can provide through elimination of duplication; through improved utilization and productivity of staff and equipment; and through control of quality, cost, and revenue.

NOTES

1. See "Evaluating the Material Supply Cabinet," by Mohan V. Kirtane, *Hospital Progress,* January 1976, pp. 76–78.

2. See "Standards Needed for Sterilization Monitoring," by Jamie Kowalski and Patricia Peck in *Hospital Progress,* April 1976, pp. 52–54.

32. Design Master Plan Cuts Hospital Costs, Increases Efficiency

BRUCE P. ARNEILL

Reprinted with permission from *Modern Healthcare*, March 1977, pp. 68–69.

Today we have the tools to "master plan" good hospitals out of the topsy-turvy expansions of old infirmary buildings that go back as far as the stage coach. With the pressures of a bad economy, high inflation, minimal federal spending, high fuel rates and tougher regulatory agencies, hospital boards should initiate imaginative master planning for their total facilities.

The bandaid method must come to an end unless it's part of a carefully developed and phased-in master plan. Clearly conceived goals must be set. So often, it seems no matter what size the hospital, communities and hospitals do not want to spend money or time on difficult, front-end planning that could save considerable money over the years and produce greater efficiency and safety.

Producing a good master plan requires the expertise of many specialists. It takes time not only to gather all the necessary data and relate it to the needs of a community and its economics but also to make trial-and-error experiments on how to re-juggle the existing physical plant into a truly effective hospital. Considering the operational costs over 10 years and the alternatives, the relative costs of such planning are minimal.

Ideally, the hospital should designate a full-time administrator who would report to the executive administrator and the building committee. In a smaller hospital, the facility engineer or administrator could be the coordinator.

Experience can be brought into the planning committee through the inclusion of lawyers, architects, bankers, contractors and developers. But remember, hospital development is different, more intricate, much slower and more costly than any other type of building because of input and controls by hundreds of people. Also remember that, although the cost of renovating old space or building new facilities seems extremely expensive, the operational costs per year can equal half of the building cost.

The greatest trick is how to make the best use of what you have and how to keep it operational while you sculpt out of the existing facility a modern physical plant over a four-year period or longer. Project costs in 1977 can run well over $125 per square foot. Construction costs can easily run over $100 per square foot and rise rapidly depending on the geographical location as well as the type of facility.

With strong involvement and support from the community, board, planning committee, medical and administrative staff, selection of the planning team is the next priority. An outside hospital consultant and an experienced hospital architectural firm are a must. Sometimes these two distinct professions, along with engineers and other specialists, are part of one firm, but in most cases, people see the advantage of hospitals employing the hospital consultant separately from the architect so that there are no conflicts of interest. Tragically, politics or local friendships quite often affect the process.

When interviewing architects, it is important that large and small firms, package dealers, or the combined hospital consultant-architectural firm be considered. This provides the building committee with a broad and knowledgeable basis for selection. All conflicts of interest between these professionals and their consultants should be reviewed. That also applies to the building committee, board and staff. The fact is that the hospital consultant, architect and staff, structural engineer, mechanical engineers, and other myriad consultants will be working with the hospital for many years just on the initial programs. Ideally, these same consultants will continue to be the facility advisors for years to come. Outside consultants can also be devil's advocates in many situations. If they are not local citizens, there are some advantages because they are not tied to local business, politics or activities in a self-serving or personal way.

Quite often a master plan program and budget are developed for the hospital by a hospital consultant and some staff or a committee. Then the architect is hired and asked to meet the suggested requirements of the proposed program. I personally feel there are problems in this method because the input of the architect and engineers can, and usually does, affect the original proposal dramatically. Also, because years always seem to slip by, the estimated costs have increased substantially and the funds available have decreased.

So, synchronizing the hospital planning team, hospital consultant and architect are most important. Obviously, the first major tasks fall in the domain of the hospital consultant. But it seems that the hospital could bring its architectural team on board early in the process when the existing physical plant is under scrutiny.

Scheduling and clear, tough goals should be established with all parties. Often, people do not face the realities and complexities of producing good planning. It takes time and numerous open meetings among dozens of people. Therefore, continual workshop meetings should be scheduled regularly with deadlines established. These can change later as a true picture of the master plan and of dollars required evolves.

In round numbers, one will find it takes a good year or more to have a hospital consultant and architect produce material for application for a certificate of need, because the involvement of the hospital, its medical staff and building committee must be part of the open process. It can take easily another year to break ground and then at least another year (and often two) to complete the first phase. With strict scheduling and good administration, it's minimally a three- or four-year process and often strings out to five, six and even seven years.

Time is of the essence; thus, methods for construction must be established early. It makes good sense to have a respected, experienced contractor and/or architect on the building committee to provide guidance and understanding. The majority of work should be put out to bid on the hospital, whether under construction management or to open bids by general contractors. No architect, contractor or other business head on the board or building committee should be hired in any way for the project.

The money and time that has appeared to be saved by fast-tracking does not always pay off in the long run because of obvious complexities and length of hospital projects. The few months saved at the beginning potentially can produce bad decisions and errors that may not show up until months or years later and may affect the hospital forever. If a facility can break ground in time to be closed in before winter, and if a realistic schedule can be developed where drawing and construction can go on parallel with bidding and pricing procedures, the fast-track method is certainly worth considering.

All of these relatively new crash programs and budget systems must be thoroughly scrutinized and carefully administered by the hospital and architect. Because of today's fantastic pressure on administrators to push for speed and low costs, doors have been flung open to a new breed of salesmen who claim that they can produce miracles and also have the best systems. Because of various definitions of building costs and construction process and time, even honest sales pitches can be extremely misleading. Be careful. Investigate all firms and their track records. If one of the speed-up, design-construct methods is used, the parties involved must have a great trust and confidence in each other and must be strongly motivated to cooperate and produce at the same speed to achieve a clear-cut goal.

Figure 1

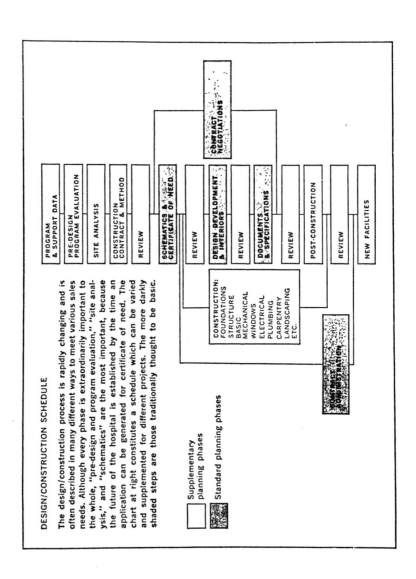

DESIGN/CONSTRUCTION SCHEDULE

The design/construction process is rapidly changing and is often described in many different ways to meet various sales needs. Although every phase is extraordinarily important to the whole, "pre-design and program evaluation," "site analysis," and "schematics" are the most important, because the future of the hospital is established by the time an application can be generated for certificate of need. The chart at right constitutes a schedule which can be varied and supplemented for different projects. The more darkly shaded steps are those traditionally thought to be basic.

☐ Supplementary planning phases

▓ Standard planning phases

PROGRAM & SUPPORT DATA

PRE-DESIGN PROGRAM EVALUATION

SITE ANALYSIS

CONSTRUCTION CONTRACT & METHOD

REVIEW

SCHEMATICS & CERTIFICATE OF NEED

REVIEW

DESIGN DEVELOPMENT & INTERIORS

REVIEW

DOCUMENTS & SPECIFICATIONS

REVIEW

POST-CONSTRUCTION

REVIEW

NEW FACILITIES

CONTRACT NEGOTIATIONS

CONSTRUCTION: FOUNDATIONS STRUCTURE BASIC MECHANICAL WINDOWS ELECTRICAL PLUMBING CARPENTRY LANDSCAPING ETC.

CONTRACT ADMINISTRATION

33. Good Maintenance Management Means Big Savings

H. D. PLUNKETT

Reprinted from "Dimensions in Health Service" Journal of the Canadian Hospital Association, pp. 32–34, © 1977.

Many problems arise due to so-called building age or obsolescence. Much of this trouble can be avoided in the initial programming by management to prevent the premature death of the plant.

Buildings are like people; they are built and used by people and the original design and intended use often is overshadowed by the passage of time and the habits of all the building users. Management and maintenance can team up to save money and labor, provide a comfortable safe environment for patients and staff, extend building and equipment life, increase depreciation benefits by getting extended life out of buildings and equipment, decrease plant operating costs, plan for future plant, equipment and alteration to permit an organized attack on these programs to maintain the above, review past errors, eliminate future mistakes, and refine the whole process in general.

At a plant maintenance and engineering show in Philadelphia some years ago, an industrially oriented speaker suggested a 28 per cent saving in maintenance costs will increase company profits by four per cent. In the financial picture of Canada's health care system this means anything we can do to reduce maintenance costs will give that many more dollars to direct patient care. By savings, the Philadelphia speaker did not mean cut off the maintenance department but make it more efficient. This is not hard to do; the hardest part is to get common sense into user, management and maintenance to work together as a team to expand the idea that teamwork promotes efficiency.

To start with, the common denominator is mutual communication and respect. Even under the most unfortunate circumstances of bad communication, obligatory record keeping can direct groups into a mutual stream of exchange which in time breaks down barriers and develops the team concept of maintenance cost reduction which can be an excellent management tool.

SAVINGS TIPS

Users and management can eliminate a tremendous amount of maintenance cost by:

1. Buying equipment that is not unreliable, expensive to repair or that will create internal building damage.
2. Limiting and controlling use of the building by staff, patients and others to prevent physical damage (will nurses ever learn adhesive tape was not meant for the hanging of pictures?).
3. Setting sensible standards for color, signs, door exits, private, public areas, etc.
4. Using the technical expertise of maintenance people or allowing them to acquire it themselves.
5. Ensuring that purchased materials and equipment are not obsolete. (In a large public new building in Toronto, the day after it was occupied the control valves on the "new" heating system were unavailable as they had become obsolete.)
6. Having clear-cut policies as to responsibilities in who pays for what and why. The Rideau Regional Centre is pestered by electric wheelchair repairs which is really an owner-user responsibility as with such things as the stores, gasoline pumps, gardener's mowers etc.
7. Hiring qualified, experienced and mature maintenance staff. Aunt Minnie's nephew may be "a good young lad," but the lost time and damage cost of a non-productive worker can go a long way to reduce that 28 per cent saving mentioned before.
8. There is no point in having good help in maintenance without adequate equipment to work with. One may lose here on savings temporarily, but make it up later in reduced labor costs. Do not buy if you can contract more cheaply.
9. Ensure that adequate and complete records are kept of materials used and time taken by whom and for what, a process that will involve the help and co-operation of accounting, stores, purchasing etc.

10. Encourage upgrading, training, education and field visits by the maintenance staff to keep them abreast of modern methods, materials and equipment. An example where this was not done is a plasterer who because he was not trained or was not aware of it, was unwilling to use epoxy grout and materials that could solve a myriad of problems in almost 15 acres of terrazzo floors.

GROUND RULES

As the hockey stick is bent to suit the player and the favorite club is picked for the location of the golf ball, maintenance and management should become one to be effective. However, experience has shown that so often due to lack of understanding proprietory feelings build up. To be successful certain ground rules should be laid out:

- Department heads, unit heads and directors, should countersign all maintenance requests going to the maintenance department.
- Have a maintenance request form in duplicate showing location, date, requester, approval of department head and the requested action.
- The maintenance department should have a repair order (in duplicate) to redefine the job in trade jargon, stating worker to do the repair, time, materials used (or material requisition number) special instructions etc. The original goes to the trade, the other is an office control copy.
- Institute a hospital-wide order that workmen report to maintenance supervisory staff only. How many "ten minute jobs while you are here" have blossomed into economic monstrosities and derailed the regular maintenance schedule?
- Enforce hours of work, break times and regulate holiday times.
- Establish a strong emergency repair system to permit fast efficient emergency repairs. Sometimes in the heat of an emergency an unknowing person can create greater havoc by not acting in a sensible way. This can increase costs, damage, down time etc.
- Off-hour coverage by maintenance is a questionable matter. Is it more economical to call in trades for evening, night and week-end repairs or is it better to set up a work schedule and rotate staff? Each individual hospital or facility would have to analyse this situation for itself.
- Record areas worked in, the number of jobs done, by whom, and develop a cost per repair ratio.
- Set up a preventive maintenance program (not only for equipment but the building as well). This is very important. Many buildings are so busy catching up on 25 years of unplanned catch-as-catch-can

maintenance that preventive maintenance suffers. Extra funds and personnel beyond regular staff and budget will expedite this. However since the goal is to save money for direct patient care, unless funding is available patience is required because none of it is achieved overnight but only by dogged determination. Every action causes an effect that can be experienced now or in the future and this applies to maintenance of your plant.

A new board and administrator do not want really to hear or think about buildings anymore. They want their hospital to do what it was built for to care for the patient. The attitude is spend no more money but heal the unhealthy. This is the first in a long line of causes that scares board and administration into early and expensive retirement of buildings and equipment. A new plant needs three to five years to "bed" down.

SENSIBLE SERVICING

Things will work but not effectively due to set up requirements which are the first step in decay. Who will drive a new automobile without taking it in for servicing to ensure one enjoys the maximum life from it? Buildings and the plant are the same. Therefore, it does not suffice to send Aunt Minnie's little Joe out with a screwdriver to fix a ventilation system worth 25 per cent of the hospital's capital cost. Although extensive repairs are not needed, the old adage of "tender loving care" is.

Apart from the careful set up of building equipment, user instruction is important. The Rideau Regional Centre has a very rare and strange temperature control system and some of the maintenance incumbents from 25 years back, still do not know how it is supposed to work. Fortunately, there are a few open-minded recently hired employees, whose background and trades education has allowed them to pick up the process quickly. With modern technology advancing at the rate it is qualified interested maintenance help is a must and management must make room in planning to save in the future by allowing scope for this difficult time in a building and plant's life.

Each area, building and administration is different, therefore broad principles need to be adapted to the situation. Still the principle of merging maintenance and management to provide savings to the hospital can be successful and rewarding, environmentally as well as monetarily.

34. Reduce Energy Cost up to 35% by Following These Simple Steps!

JOHN JEFFRIES AND KELLY TESTOLIN

Reprinted with permission from *Hospital Topics,* May/June 1979, pp. 45, 47, 48.

One of the boldest challenges to face Engineering Services in the 1970's is energy management. In the next 20 years, the enterprises of the U.S. will consume more energy than in all the years since the Boston Tea Party.

The cost of that energy will be astounding. Electricity costs are expected to rise from 15 to 20% a year; natural gas and oil, 10 to 15%. Water costs will increase, although not quite as much.

The only abundant and technologically available energy source, coal, faces stiff environmental concerns. You can begin to meet this challenge and reduce energy costs at your facility up to 35% by following the simple steps put into practice at Memorial Hospital Medical Center of Long Beach, California.

The 850 bed medical center encompasses 28 acres, its buildings total 750,000 square feet. Employing 2,600 people, it is one of the largest non-profit hospitals on the West Coast.

Memorial's Engineering staff realized that, as in most hospitals, much of the physical plant and many engineering practices were developed in an earlier era of inexpensive and abundant energy.

By examining equipment and re-thinking old practices, Memorial was able to significantly reduce utilities consumption without the need for large capital investment. The medical center's program suggests a utility-by-utility approach.

ELECTRICITY

The Engineering staff discovered early in their program that a great deal of energy waste resulted from the fact that the operation of electrically powered devices was not closely correlated to demand. The following steps were taken:

- Photo cells were installed on parking lot lighting, turning them off at dawn and on at dusk. Savings: 4,500 KWH per month.
- Clock timers on air handling units in the business office reduced loads during off hours. Savings: 9,000 KWH per month. Similar timers on the Family Practice building save 7,500 KWH per month.
- A de-lamping program removed or reduced number of lights throughout the building for significant savings. Hospital staff found the lowered lighting levels more pleasant.

  The removal of unnecessary flood lamps from one service area alone saves 290 KWH per month. This was followed up with a re-lamping program which replaced 40 watt fluorescent tubes with 35 watt Wattmizer tubes. These tubes provide the same amount of light but at a savings of 5,000 KWH per month.

- Shutting down air handling motors in the receiving area during the cooler seasons saves 5,000 KWH per month.
- Standby controls on X-Ray film processors reduced the electrical heating load for a savings of 5,000 KWH per month.

The Central Plant provided some of the most significant savings opportunities.

- Two hot water pumps were shut down completely without affecting the output or quality of the heating system. Savings: 15,000 KWH per month.
- Better scheduling for the use of three chillers units allowed reduced operation of the least efficient saving 286,000 KWH per month.

The above measures led to reduced electrical consumption at the medical center of 339,820 KWH per month. At today's costs this represents a yearly savings of $12,335.00.

WATER

Water conservation took on even greater importance in the face of drought conditions existing in California during 1977. As with electricity, wasteful equipment and practices had been conceived and installed when energy was cheap. Once discovered, the Engineering staff found ways to change them.

- Flow restrictors installed on 1,200 sinks saves 1,300,000 gallons per year.
- Tip-Tap faucets (push button devices producing a timed water flow) on sinks saves an additional 1,100,000 per year.
- Flow restrictors on toilet flush valves save 1,500,000 gallons per year.
- Flow valves on 335 shower heads save 2,000,000 gallons per year.
- Installation of a circulation pump and heat exchanger on a gas sterilizer saves 1,500,000 gallons per year of water previously heated and dumped down a sewer drain.

Through the combination of all these efforts, Memorial's water consumption was reduced by 7,400,000 gallons per year, valued today at $3,500.00 annually.

GAS

Although difficult to quantify, as gas usage is dependent on climatic conditions, Memorial estimates gas savings at $6,000 per year. The hospital's primary use of natural gas is for firing steam boilers in the Central Plant, and these savings were achieved by fine tuning boiler burners and chemically treating the feedwater to prevent buildup and corrosion that can rob a boiler of efficiency.

OTHER SAVINGS

Several other ideas were presented and implemented which do not fit neatly into any one utility category. These include the following:

- Chemical treatment of cooling tower condensor water increased the efficiency of heat transfer in the chiller units.
- The installation of automatic blowdown valves on boilers helped keep the chemical balance of blowdown water in effect, thereby maintaining the efficiency of the systems operation.
- Air handling equipment controls were recalibrated for greater efficiency.

THE ENERGY MANAGEMENT SYSTEM

Evolving out of their studies of electricity usage, the Engineering staff's interest in the installation of an ENERGY MANAGEMENT COMPUTER (to control electrically powered apparatus throughout the medical center and minimum (sic) electrical demand) resulted in a cross country tour by the Director to evaluate existing installations.

After thorough analysis and cost justification, Memorial's system was purchased and placed into service in January 1978.

Presently the unit is programmed for 125 pieces of air handling equipment. When it receives a signal pulse from the power company's electric meter, the computer predicts the hospital's kilowatt demand for the day.

A maximum demand figure has been established in conjunction with power company rate schedules. Whenever that demand level is approached, the computer searches its memory banks for units it can temporarily shut off so as not to exceed that demand.

During normal demand hours, "shedding programs" have been established to cycle equipment on and off at various time intervals during the day without disturbing patient or employee comfort.

Other programs have been established for areas occupied only during daylight hours, and for early mornings and weekends.

PAYBACK IN ELEVEN MONTHS

At its present operational stage, the system is load shedding 7,000 KWH per hour, or a surprising 2,250,000 KWH per year. This represents $81,675.00 per year in reduced electrical consumption.

Applied against the unit's purchase price of $50,000.00 the hospital expects to achieve a minimum payback of 11 months. The computer is now being programmed to handle the Central Plant, air chillers, lighting systems and elevators in the future.

OVERALL RESULTS

The overall results of Memorial's energy management and conservation program have been most gratifying....

FUTURE PLANS

Spurred by their early success, the Engineering department plans to continue to develop its energy management expertise. Further investigations are in order for the Central Plant and the areas of lighting and computerized controls.

In addition, energy audits are planned to scrutinize energy waste associated with ventilation, infiltration (the passage of outside air through building structures), area occupancies, solar heat gain, electrical equipment rating and paper recycling.

SUMMARY

By following the steps of the Engineering department at Memorial, you can produce significant savings for your hospital and have real impact in energy conservation. Significant capital investment is not required—only the time needed to address and redesign energy wasting equipment and practices.

35. The Energy Audit: Back to the Basics

JAMES PIPER

Reprinted from *Hospital Progress*, April 1979, pp.66–69, by permission of Edward J. Pollock, Publisher, © 1979.

Most of the industrial buildings now in use were designed and constructed when fuels were readily available and inexpensive. Their mechanical and electrical systems were designed to minimize initial costs, but have little reference to energy use. Hospitals are no exception in this regard. It has been estimated that more than 90 percent of the nation's existing hospitals were designed before 1973 and are energy inefficient. As a result, the cost of energy has become one of the leading items in the hospital budget, and hospital administrators have sought to reduce energy use through the implementation of energy conservation measures.

When the price of energy nearly doubled following the 1973 embargo imposed by the OPEC nations, the federal government urged that building operators and managers reduce energy use through end-use modifications, such as resetting thermostats and reducing lighting levels. Even though these end-use modifications were energy conserving, they did not constitute an effective energy-management program. True energy management requires that every energy-using system or piece of equipment within the building be made to operate as efficiently as possible, thus using the smallest amount of energy to function. An energy audit that examines all the energy-using elements yields many more energy-saving measures than can be identified by an end-use approach. The audit goes far beyond just telling administrators the how, when, and where of energy use in their facilities. The audit also tells them how much a specific energy conservation

307

measure will save them, thus providing a basis for choosing the most cost-effective measures for implementation.

WHY THE AUDIT APPROACH?

When administrators have been pressured to reduce energy costs in the past, most have responded either by doing nothing and rationalizing that increased energy costs are passed on anyway or by investing in some of the energy conservation devices currently being marketed, without fully understanding the potential or consequences of those devices. Unfortunately, both responses are equally unrealistic. Administrators who do nothing but increase hospital charges to cover increased energy costs will soon find themselves under growing governmental pressure to keep health care costs under control. Administrators who invest in energy conservation equipment without understanding how that equipment fits into the overall energy plan for the facility may find that the equipment is not the best investment or that it is not compatible with future energy plans. What these administrators lack is an understanding of energy use within a hospital and the knowledge of what can be done to reduce it.

The energy audit takes an entirely different approach to conservation. The audit considers every building individually. To help the administrator understand how to conserve energy, the audit first discloses how energy is being used and how the use in one system or subsystem is interrelated with the use in another. It then discloses what measures will produce savings in particular buildings. Once this understanding is achieved, the administrator will be able to consult with technical personnel to determine what measures should be implemented to save energy.

By taking the energy audit approach to energy conservation, administrators will receive three primary benefits: suggestions for the elimination of energy waste; expansion of the area of investigation, which in turn expands the number of options for conservation; provision for flexibility so that administrators may decide when to implement what measure.

WHO CAN BENEFIT FROM THE AUDIT APPROACH?

The purpose of the energy audit is to identify and analyze measures that, once implemented, will result in a sufficient reduction in energy use to recover the implementation cost in a reasonable period of time. Every hospital that conducts a thorough energy audit is able to identify cost-effective conservation measures; however, it is impractical to study every hospital building, since in some cases the money saved may not cover the cost of conducting the audit. In addition, administrators may be faced with budget constraints that allow them to audit only a portion of their facilities. Therefore, a two-step approach should be used to select those buildings that offer the greatest potential for energy conservation and that will make the best use of available funds and manpower. The approach should include (1) data gathering and (2) establishment of selection criteria to choose the building for study.

In order to determine how efficiently a building is using energy and its potential for energy conservation, it is necessary to gather data on the building's energy use in the past and its physical and operational characteristics. To provide an accurate indication of energy use, data should be gathered for a one-year period and summed to determine the annual use of electricity, natural gas, fuel oil, coal, and purchased steam. Most of this information can be gotten from monthly utility bills, but care should be taken that those bills do not include areas not being studied.

Data about a building's physical and operational characteristics that are important to the selection of facilities include the function of the building, hours of operation, services provided (heating, cooling, lighting, etc.), gross floor area, age, and projected replacement or remodeling dates.

After data have been gathered, selection criteria may be established. The first of these is the energy budget, a measure of how much energy is being used during a one-year period, related to the facility's gross floor area. Expressed in BTU/square foot per year, the energy budget helps hospital administrators determine how energy efficient their facilities are in relation to others.

Figure 1 may be used to calculate a facility's energy budget. Annual energy-use data are entered by fuel type in the first column. To convert these fuels to their BTU equivalents, the values for each fuel are multiplied by its corresponding conversion factor and entered in the third column. The BTU equivalents are then summed and divided by the gross floor area (millions of square feet) to get the energy budget for the facility.

The General Services Administration (GSA) has established energy budget guidelines for new and existing facilities. For new buildings that are mostly office space, 55,000 BTU/square foot per year is the recommended target value. While it would be impractical to reduce energy use in existing facilities to this level, the GSA recommends that existing office buildings be targeted for 75,000 BTU/square foot per year.

Hospitals, due to their more intensive energy requirements, will have a somewhat higher energy budget. Most hospitals operate in the range of 100,000 to 500,000 BTU/square foot per year, with a few requiring as much as 1,000,000 BTU/square foot per year. By examining their own energy budgets, hospital administrators will be able to gauge how one facility com-

Figure 1 Energy Budget Worksheet

	Fuel Use	Conversion Factor	Millions of BTU/yr
Natural gas—cubic feet		0.001	
Fuel oil #2—gallons		0.140	
Fuel oil #6—gallons		0.150	
Anthracite coal—tons		27.8	
Bituminous coal—tons		28.0	
Sub-bituminous coal—tons		25.2	
Lignite coal—tons		22.0	
Steam—10^3 pounds		1.0	
Propane—pounds		0.022	
Electricity—kwh		0.003	
Total—10^6 BTU/yr			_____
Gross Building Floor Area—10^6 sq ft			_____
Energy Budget—BTU/sq ft-yr			_____

pares with another and what an individual hospital's potential for energy conservation is. If a particular energy budget is high, the energy audit is most likely worthwhile. If it is low, other criteria should be examined before ruling out the audit.

Another selection criterion that may be used is the ratio of monthly energy use to peak demand. Unless it can be accounted for by some special function, a low ratio indicates inefficient electrical energy use. A ratio of 720 kwh electrical energy use to 1 kw peak demand is the optimum condition, and a ratio of 400 kwh/kw or less indicates that the energy use may be inefficient.

While an examination of energy-use patterns will give an indication of the facility's energy efficiency, it is also important to examine any long- and short-range plans for each of the buildings. If a building is to be replaced or remodeled soon, it would not be worthwhile to conduct an energy audit unless the building has an unusually high energy budget or unless the major energy-using systems are not scheduled for replacement. Similarly, a building with a relatively low energy budget may be selected for study if it is to be used for a long period of time.

After the selection criteria have been examined, there may still be some question of the value of an audit for a particular hospital. Rather than committing the hospital to the full-scale audit, administrators may have an energy consultant help them with the first phase—the walk-through survey.

The walk-through survey is the most basic form of the energy audit. With it, those factors that affect energy use in hospitals can be identified. The survey is conducted by a team consisting of an architect, an engineer, and representatives from the hospital's management and maintenance groups. The survey team spends one or more days touring the facilities, examining the physical characteristics of the structure and the operational characteristics of the energy-using systems. Where questions arise, mechanical, electrical, and architectural drawings are examined.

Once the walk-through has been completed, the survey team compiles a report assessing the energy conservation potential for the hospital and the measures that would help save energy. Because of budget and time limits, the survey team cannot evaluate every possible energy conservation measure. Therefore, survey recommendations can include only those items that are easily identified. Many other items, while noted in the report, cannot be recommended until a more detailed investigation and analysis have been completed.

In spite of its limitations, the walk-through survey has several helpful applications. First, it can be used in buildings that do not have a large number of sophisticated energy-using systems or pieces of equipment. The survey can identify some energy-conserving opportunities that would be recommended following a detailed study without the expense of that study. Second, the walk-through survey can identify major energy-saving measures at a fraction of the cost of the full-scale audit. Third, the walk-through survey can be used to justify the expense of the full-scale audit if sufficient potential energy-conserving measures have been pointed out.

THE FULL-SCALE AUDIT

The full-scale audit is an extension of the basic walk-through survey. While the survey gives only generalized conservation impressions of the team and identifies only major conservation measures, the full-scale audit completely analyzes energy use within the facility and details what is required to minimize energy use in a master energy plan for the hospital.

The first phase of the full-scale audit is the modeling of the energy use of the existing facility. In order to model it accurately, the audit team must gather data on all the major energy-using systems and equipment and how they are being operated. If a walk-through survey has been conducted, some of the information will already be available. Due to the nature of the walk-through survey, however, additional data will have to be obtained from equipment manufacturers, building drawings, operating and maintenance personnel, and possibly a second tour of the facility. It is essential that the audit team gather sufficient information to obtain an understanding of how the facility and its systems are functioning so that data for the energy-analysis model can be adequate.

Once the data have been compiled, the audit team may select one of the numerous energy analysis models currently in use. There are two basic approaches that the models take in analyzing energy use within buildings: manual or computerized calculations. The manual approach makes use of algorithms to estimate energy use within a building system or an entire facility. The algorithms, consisting of a series of mathematical equations, charts, and graphs, have evolved from a number of complex studies on energy use where data were obtained from extensive metering of utilities or by simulating the building operation on a computer. By combining these algorithms, the audit team can model the annual energy use of the existing facility and determine how much energy is going where.

The computerized approach makes use of a program specifically designed to simulate the operation of a building system or an entire building for a one-year period using weather data. Although a number of different programs have been developed, the most commonly used technique is to determine the energy requirements hour by hour and then integrate the results to determine the annual energy use.

Both analysis approaches can generate an accurate estimate of the energy flow within the facility. Manual techniques are particularly suitable for buildings that lack a large number of sophisticated energy-using systems. Computerized techniques can be best applied in buildings having a large number of complex systems or where the number of energy conservation measures to be analyzed makes calculation by manual techniques impractical. Once the facilities have been examined, the audit team will be able to select the approach best suited for that particular application.

After the energy model has been selected, set up, and tested, it can be used to analyze all possible energy conservation measures identified during the survey portion of the audit. These measures must be analyzed for both their energy and economic impacts, including energy savings, implementation cost, and pay-back. Only after the total analysis has been completed can the audit team select those measures that should be implemented in the hospital.

A final report is submitted to the hospital administrator concerning the findings of the audit. But that report is much more than a list of what measures would save how much energy for what price. The report is the master energy plan for the hospital. In addition to the audit recommendations, the report gives all the background information used in reaching those recommendations, including survey data, cost estimates, energy pricing, and any assumptions made during the study. The report also details measures analyzed but rejected and measures not analyzed, with reasons for each action. Given this background, an administrator can take a second look at those rejected measures, should conditions under which the study was conducted change or some new constraint be placed on energy use.

THE AUDIT TEAM

The field of energy conservation is new and rapidly evolving; so it is no surprise that a great deal of confusion exists among hospital administrators and operating personnel about who should be selected to conduct the energy audit. Energy experts, engineers, architects, designers, contractors, equipment manufacturers, and utility companies all offer their services. But since each group represents a highly specialized area within the overall energy conservation field, no one group can adequately address all the necessary areas for a comprehensive energy audit. An effective audit requires that a team be formed from both inhouse and outside personnel, each contributing expertise. A typical audit team would include an energy consultant, a hospital administrator, an engineer, an architect, and representatives from the hospital's building operators.

The energy consultant, directing the audit procedure, works with each team member, coordinating efforts into a concise and well-documented energy management plan for the hospital. It is the consultant's responsibility to see that the measures recommended as feasible for that particular installation also represent the best possible solution.

The hospital administrator's primary responsibility is to see that the audit is initiated and carried out to meet the objectives established by the hospital. Selecting inhouse personnel to assist with the audit, the administrator makes their time available as required. To gain expertise not available inhouse, professional help from outside consulting firms may be used. The hospital administrator provides the audit team with operating costs, fuel and energy use data, and other information required in the analysis. Whenever it is necessary to gain access to the facility, the administrator makes the arrangements.

The engineer and architect are responsible for surveying the facilities, analyzing the existing conditions and methods of operation, and identifying and analyzing possible energy conservation measures. When necessary, they consult with utility companies on existing and anticipated rates and with equipment manufacturers on performance characteristics of specific pieces of equipment.

The hospital's building operators provide information on the equipment-operating schedules, on the operating parameters of each space, on the building's maintenance, and on measures already implemented to save energy. Only through the combined efforts of these groups can the energy audit become an effective tool.

Energy management has two basic steps: identification of energy-conserving measures and implementation of those measures. The energy audit takes the administrator through the first step by identifying measures that will save energy and presenting them in a conservation program plan. It is then up to the administrator to take energy management through its second step, implementation.

How rapidly progress is made will be determined primarily by the budget limitations. Some measures can be implemented at little or no cost simply by changing the way the facility is operated. Some modifications may require operating funds to make a minor repair or adjustment. Other modifications may require extensive capital funding. But in any case, the energy audit will have given the hospital administrator an understanding of the how and why of energy use in a facility and what can be done to improve it.

36. Incineration of Solid Waste—A Case Study

EFRAIM TURBAN

In 1976, the U.S. Environmental Protection Agency ruled that all wastes coming off the hospital floor can be classified as contaminated materials. As a result of this determination, Palm Beach County (Florida) issued notification that no infectious wastes were to be accepted at landfill sites. Bethesda Memorial Hospital in Boynton Beach, Florida, which had been having its trash dumped at landfill sites, now had to have it trucked to A.G. Holley Hospital in Lantana, Florida, for disposal in its incinerator.

Analysis revealed that the expense for this trash disposal method was $19,110 per year; hence, it was decided to explore the possibility of installing an incinerator on the hospital grounds. Investigation revealed that an appropriate incinerator will cost $96,398, plus the expenditure of $45,000 for a building to house it properly.

The operating costs of $5,899 per year coupled with $7,069 annual depreciation expense (assuming a 20-year life) developed total annual costs of $12,968 versus the previous hauling costs of $19,110—hence, an annual savings of $6,142. However, there was an additional bonus to the system. It included an energy recovery system from the incinerating process that generated sufficient steam to develop an additional $11,606 in fuel savings. Thus, this cost containment idea produced threefold results: it saved energy, generated annual total savings of $17,748, plus $7,069 in depreciation, and protected our ecology by proper disposal of contaminated trash. Thus, the incinerator will pay for itself in less than four years. (For further discussion see Henning in the bibliography of Chapter 4.)

37. Practical Pointers: Computer Keeps Inventory at Optimum Stock Level

DARRELL L. BANKES

Reprinted from the July 1973 issue of *Hospital Financial Management*, pp. 40–41. Copyright 1973 Hospital Financial Management Association.

The decision to select a good computerized inventory system at Phoenix Baptist Hospital was made after extensive research into the following areas:

(a) time and cost of implementing the computer program.
(b) the program's value as to timely, accurate and necessary reporting.
(c) cost savings after implementation of the program.

To give readers a detailed step-by-step analysis of these areas would take considerable time; therefore, I will merely brief the reader on the highlights.

IMPLEMENTATION

The implementation of the program, which consisted of 1000 stock items from office supplies to medical and surgical supplies, was accomplished in approximately one week's time by our purchasing agent at no additional cost to the hospital.

REPORTING

A weekly inventory analysis report furnished on Monday morning of each week shows all activity of the previous week. This report furnishes the following information:

(a) Numeric listing of all stock items (hospital assigned numbers which correspond to location of items in the stock area).
(b) Manufacturer's identification (printed on the purchase orders for the vendor's information).
(c) Vendor's identification number (hospital assigned numbers to enable computer to identify vendor for purchase order printing).
(d) Cost of each stock item.
(e) Purchase quantity (determined by the computer on the min-max basis).
(f) Item's category code (for special print-outs of items by category such as a listing of all Medical and Surgical items in stock).
(g) Accounting code (assigned by the accounting department and used for month-end distribution of expenses to the departments and identifying the items between Office Supplies, X-Ray Supplies, IV Solutions, etc.).
(h) Units issued last year, current year-to-date and last three months usage by month (used in determining min-max amounts).
(i) Reorder point (determined by the program).
(j) Maximum order quantity (determined by the hospital purchasing agent).
(k) Number of months the item has had no usage (calculated by computer).
(l) Out-of-stock items (determined by the computer).
(m) Lead time (established by the purchasing agent).
(n) Whether the item is purchased through cooperative purchasing contract (coded by the purchasing agent).
(o) Standard package unit.
(p) Back orders (calculated by the computer).
(q) Purchase order number of the back order.
(r) On-hand quantity.
(s) Value of inventory on hand.

Along with the weekly inventory analysis report, the necessary purchase orders (which are printed on the computer) are furnished for any items below the reorder point.

At month-end, a departmental distribution report is furnished showing each department's monthly stock items withdrawn from inventory and priced on the first-in first-out method (FIFO).

COST SAVINGS

The cost savings after implementation have been reflected in the elimination of one purchasing clerk, whose duties were to post all transactions to the 1000 inventory stock-record cards. This is now accomplished in approximately two hours per week by the data processing clerk on an Addo-X keypunch machine. Also approximately two hours per day have been saved in the pricing and extending of the old inventory stock requisition forms, not to mention the month-end calculations necessary for departmental distribution of costs. The cost of the computer program runs approximately 30¢ per line-item per month. The dollar savings to the hospital is $130 per month, but the value of improved inventory control levels, adequate reporting and departmental efficiency cannot be measured in dollars.

SUMMARY AND CONCLUSION

The computerized inventory system has worked wonders at keeping the inventory at a realistic level to insure adequate patient care as well as eliminating surplus stock where unnecessary and where valuable capital was invested. It has also kept backorders at a minimum and improved the purchasing cycle of ordering and receiving merchandise.

38. "No-Inventory" System Nets $200,000 Savings

CAROLYN S. SHANOFF

Reprinted with permission from *Purchasing Administration,* Volume 2(7), August 1978, pp. 1, 3.

Larry York, vice president, general services at Emanuel Hospital, Portland, Ore., says there is "absolutely no inventory whatsoever" for 92% of all the items that are used at the hospital's 26 nursing stations.

That's a heck of a way to run a hospital, right?

Right, at least for York. He gets daily deliveries from an American Hospital Supply Corporation (AHSC) warehouse several blocks from the hospital, and his system has saved the hospital almost $200,000 since 1976.

"The concept behind the system is total life cycle materials management," York said, "from acquisition to disposition. We want to know not just what things cost, but what they cost to use.

"Materials management can have a significant impact on the cash flow of an organization," York added. "It's been estimated that a typical hospital storeroom contains an average inventory of $630 per bed. A 300-bed hospital would carry an average inventory of $189,000. With a 30% holding cost, the conservative, on-going, non-direct carrying cost would be $56,700.

"I can't think of one financial administrator who wouldn't love to return this $56,700 back to the cash flow of his operation."

As York explained it, the system demands organization and cooperation.

"Each day, we tell AHSC what we've used and what we need," York said. "Most important, we know every day, 24 hours a day, what has been used and what to charge for.

"We pay once a month for what we've used, after it's been used," he added. "We maintain a fairly stable situation that way, too. Our monthly invoices range from $20,000 to $24,000."

York says the zero-inventory system was a major cost containment effort at Emanuel.

"It became obvious that the key to a good materials handling system is the absence of handling materials," York said. "Repeated handling adds no intrinsic value—it only adds cost. Eliminate handling, and you eliminate costs, including people costs, inventory shrinkage and investment in inventory."

But he's happiest when he's more specific about the actual dollar savings the system has brought about.

"In the last two years, we have reduced our capital investment in inventory in the storeroom by $161,000, our inventory in central supply by $12,000, and our inventory at the nursing stations by $26,000," he said.

"What's more," he added, "we have increased the revenue for patient charge items by $80,000, and we're seeing an on-going savings of almost $114,000 a year."

York said he introduced the daily delivery system four-and-one-half years ago, and he says it has been in constant development ever since.

"We began in one nursing station so that we could work out the bugs," he said. "The changeover has been gradual. We didn't want to push this system on anybody. We've waited for the others to ask for it, and sure enough, they all have."

According to York, while 92% of the supplies used at the nursing stations are delivered daily by AHSC in a station wagon, an additional 2% comes from central processing. The remaining 6% are purchased in the traditional way.

York believes that the 554-bed Emanuel Hospital is the only one in the country with a low-inventory, daily delivery system. But he doesn't think they'll be in the spotlight for long.

"I suspect this method of doing business is catching on," he said. "I've had observers here from all parts of the U.S., as well as from Europe. It can work if the warehouse is anywhere from around the corner to 40 or so miles away from the hospital."

Despite York's years of experience as a materials manager and his expertise in the low/no inventory area, he told PA that two acronyms help him carry out his responsibilities—OCS and KISS.

Said York, "OCS is 'organized common sense'. KISS means 'keep it simple, stupid'. If you follow those words, you can't go too far off base."

39. Cost Analysis of Leasing Hospital Equipment

JAMES B. HENRY AND RODNEY L. ROENFELDT

Reprinted, with permission of the Blue Cross Association, from *Inquiry*, Vol. XV, No. 1 (March 1978) pp. 33–37. Copyright © 1978 by the Blue Cross Association. All rights reserved.

For many years, hospitals throughout the United States have used funds from grants, donations and other free money sources to underwrite capital expenditures for equipment. Unfortunately, these free funds have not kept pace with the rapid increase in demand for capital expenditures. As an alternative to the outright purchasing of equipment, some hospitals have turned to leasing. Although no exact figures are available, it is estimated that over $300 million worth of assets are leased to hospitals in the United States each year.[1]

In an attempt to determine why hospitals choose to lease, administrators and controllers of 25 non-profit hospitals in South Carolina were interviewed. Several reasons were offered for their choosing leasing as a financing vehicle. Six of the reasons most frequently suggested are listed below:

1 The asset is viewed to have a high degree of technological obsolescence, therefore the ability to trade in equipment is desired.
2 Service is better on leased equipment than on purchased equipment. The ability to stop making lease payments seems to influence performance on maintenance contracts.
3 The asset is only available under a lease agreement.
4 The hospital can be reimbursed faster under a lease than under a purchase agreement.
5 Leasing provides capital funds when other sources are scarce.
6 Leasing rates are lower than borrowing rates.

Each of the hospital officials interviewed indicated a strong interest in the cost of leasing, but all had little insight as to how one might determine financial charges. Most of those sampled who felt that leasing rates were less than borrowing rates did not compare the financial cost of leasing with debt financing using present value analysis. The objective of this paper is to provide some information concerning the financial cost of leasing for hospitals by examining 58 noncancellable contracts obtained from 17 of the 25 hospitals interviewed. The hospitals ranged in size from 52 to 603 beds, and the contracts varied from $3,990 to $424,500 in asset cost, totaling $3,067,498 in assets. The contracts were initiated in the years 1971–1976 and varied in length from 36 to 84 months.

The following sections describe the guidelines used to determine whether a financing arrangement is a true lease or lease-purchase, outline the cost measurement procedure used to evaluate the sample of leases and lease-purchase financing alternatives for non-taxpaying facilities, and present the financial costs which are currently being incurred by the hospitals with these financing arrangements. It should be pointed out that this analysis is concerned only with determining the effective interest rates for the financing alternatives; it does not consider the impact of third-party reimbursement. Many hospital officials are not aware of the effective rate of interest on their lease contracts, and the following analysis is intended to explicitly indicate the range of these rates.[2]

TRUE LEASE VERSUS CONDITIONAL SALE

Although several types of arrangements are frequently referred to as lease financing by lessors and lessees, hospitals should be aware of the differences in financing arrangements, since some lease contracts are actually conditional sales. With a true lease, rental payments are expensed for reimbursement during the year in which they occur; on the other hand, with a lease-purchase (conditional sale financed by a leasing company), the asset cost is depreciated and reimbursed over its useful life. The guidelines for reimbursement of a true lease are basically the rules outlined by the Internal Revenue Service for corporate taxpaying entities.[3] Non-profit hospitals and taxpaying facilities, therefore, face similar rules.

In summary, these rules state that a lease will be construed as a sale if any equity interest in the property is built up by the lessee during the life of the contract; or secondly, if rental payments are not considered to be fair rent; or thirdly, if an asset is purchased at termination of the contract for a price less than fair market value. Furthermore, interest payments should not be stated as a separate cost in addition to principal.

The feature in a contract that most often causes a lease to be construed as a conditional sale is when the predetermined salvage value indicated in the contract is not equal to fair market value. Contracts allowing for transfer of title for an amount less than fair market value—such as a nominal fee, dollar option, 10% of original cost, or call for abandonment—would not likely qualify for true lease status, but instead be construed as a lease-purchase. In addition, side letters that are separate from the contract which state a specific purchase price less than fair market value do not change the nature of the contract; if honored, they will likely result in the financial arrangement being considered a conditional sale.

COST OF LEASING

Cost Measurement for Non-profit Facilities

Many lessees in the sample were of the opinion that the only relevant data to include when measuring an interest rate on a lease contract is the cost of the equipment and the rental payments during the period of the lease. Leasing companies typically compare this so-called "running rate," represented by r_L^* in equation (1), to the hospital's estimated cost of borrowing money in the debt market.

$$C_o = \sum_{t=0}^{N} \frac{L_t}{(1 + r_L^*)^t} \tag{1}$$

Where:

C_o = Capitalized value or cost of the asset.
L_t = Lease payment in period t.
r_L^* = Effective before-tax interest rate on lease contract with a zero salvage value.
N = Length of lease contract.

An obvious flaw in this type of analysis is ignoring the value of the asset at the end of the lease. A true lease requires the lessee to pay fair market value for the asset at contract termination if the lessee desires to own the asset. If a debt financing arrangement is used and the asset is purchased under a conditional sale, the hospital has title to the asset at termination of contract with no additional payment necessary. To be consistent in measurement when comparing these alternatives, one must either assume the hospital sells the asset under the purchase agreement and will not exercise a purchase option under the lease, or assume that one keeps the asset if purchased and will exercise a purchase option under the lease. A running rate that ignores a fair market value purchase option cannot be compared with a debt financing rate unless the salvage value is zero. Inclusion of salvage value when calculating a measurement rate for a lease contract can be accomplished by adding a term to equation (1) as follows:

$$C_o = \sum_{t=0}^{N} \frac{L_t}{(1 + r_L{}^*)^t} + \frac{S}{(1 + r_L)^N} \tag{2}$$

Where:

S = Estimated fair market value of asset at termination of lease contract.

r_L = Effective before-tax rate on lease contract assuming a salvage value of S.

In the event an asset has a salvage value greater than zero, it is evident that the true effective before-tax rate on the lease contract is greater than the running rate.[4] Since it is difficult to estimate the salvage value with great precision, a useful approach is to use more than one estimate.[5] This will result in a range of rates which may be compared to the debt rate. With this approach, the hospital analyst can be made aware of the sensitivity of effective lease cost to salvage value, as well as being provided with an indication of his margin for error in estimation before making a decision.

Effective Before-Tax Lease Rates for Sample Data

Effective before-tax rates for salvage values of 0%, 10%, 25%, 40%, and 50% of original cost are calculated for the true lease contracts in the sample. Before-tax rates are also calculated for lease-purchase contracts. It is assumed that the assets are purchased at termination of the lease-purchase contracts for the stated option price.

To identify changes in rates caused by changes in general interest rates, three periods—May 1971 to July 1973; August 1973 to February 1975; and March 1975 to June 1976—are established based on prime rates existing during the period. Prime rates ranged from 4⅜ to 8¾%, 8½ to 12%, and 6½ to 8½% for each period, respectively. A contract is assigned to each period based on its origination date and further categorized by its initial cost. Tables 1 through 3 present before-tax measurement rates computed for 53 contracts with maturities of 60 and 84 months.

Table 1 Before-tax Lease Rates for Hospital Equipment,*
March 1975–June 1976, Prime Rate: 6½–8½%

Equipment cost	Estimated salvage value (Percentage of cost)					Lease-purchase
	0%	10%	25%	40%	50%	
$0–$49,999	8.8%	11.9%	15.8%	19.1%	21.0%	
	11.4	14.3	17.9	21.1	23.0	
	11.5	14.4	18.1	21.2	23.1	
	12.6	15.3	18.6	21.6	23.3	
	13.8	16.3	19.6	22.5	24.3	
						18.5%
						19.6
						26.1
$50,000–$99,999	12.6	15.3	18.7	21.6	23.3	
	83.7	84.6	85.6	86.7	87.3	
						10.7
$100,000 & over	10.2	13.1	16.8	19.9	21.8	
	11.9	14.6	18.1	21.0	22.8	

*All 60-month contracts.

Table 1 contains data for the third and most recent period, with contracts originating between March 1975 and June 1976 when the prime rate ranged from 6½–8½% (three contracts were proposals submitted by leasing companies but not yet accepted by the hospital). Running rates ranged from 8.8 to 13.8% with the exception of one extremely high rate of 83.7% for a proposed contract. Although some hospital equipment may not be considered as a prime investment for commercial banks, not all assets should be considered as high risk; yet all but a few of the contracts had running rates which far exceeded the prime rates. If one assumes a 25% purchase option, the majority of the sample lease cases appear to be very expensive.

Importance of salvage value in determining effective lease rates is evident by the sensitivity of rates to varied salvage estimates. For example, the 13.8% running rate increases to 19.6% with an estimated salvage value of 25% of equipment cost. It is impossible to generalize about the size of salvage value which is appropriate for every piece of equipment, but estimates obtained from hospital administrators and leasing companies tended to range between 10% and 40% of original cost. Effective rates ranged from 11.9 to 16.3% and 19.1 to 22.5% for salvage values of 10 and 40% respectively (excluding the extreme case with a rate exceeding 80%).

Although no discernible relationship exists between equipment cost and true leasing rates, the rate (10.7%) for the one lease-purchase contract for equipment costing over $50,000 is considerably less than rates for three lease-purchase contracts with costs under $50,000 (18.5 to 26.1%). Including estimated salvage value in the lease analysis is a crucial factor when determining whether the lease is more or less expensive than a lease-purchase or alternative debt financing arrangement. It was clear in the sample interviews that restrictions on some hospitals, preventing them from borrowing directly from banks, undoubtedly increased their financing cost

Table 2 Before-tax Lease Rates for Hospital Equipment,* August 1973–February 1975, Prime Rate: 8½–12%

Equipment cost	Estimated salvage value (Percentage of cost)					Lease-purchase
	0%	10%	25%	40%	50%	
$0–$49,999	11.3%	14.1%	17.7%	20.8%	22.6%	
	11.9	14.7	18.2	21.3	23.1	
	16.8	19.2	22.4	25.2	26.9	
	67.1	68.0	69.3	70.5	71.3	
						9.1%
						14.5
						21.5
						26.1
$50,000–$99,999	8.8	11.6	15.2	18.3	20.1	
	10.0	12.9	16.6	19.7	21.6	
	16.9	19.3	22.5	25.3	27.0	
	17.2	19.6	22.7	25.4	27.0	
	23.2	25.4	28.2	30.7	32.2	
						12.0
$100,000 & over	20.5	22.7	25.7	28.3	29.9	

*All 60-month contracts.

by forcing them to use true lease and lease-purchase financing agreements. The restrictions apparently put hospitals at a decided cost disadvantage for raising capital—without accomplishing the attempted objective of limiting debt financing—since both the true lease and lease-purchase are in essence noncancellable debt-type agreements.

Tables 2 and 3 contain effective before-tax lease rates for the second and

Table 3 Before-tax Lease Rates for Hospital Equipment, May 1971–July 1973, Prime Rate: 4⅜–8¾%

Equipment cost	Estimated salvage value (Percentage of cost)					Lease-purchase*
	0%	10%	25%	40%	50%	
$0–$49,999	6.2%	9.7%	14.1%	17.6%	19.7%	
	11.0	13.9	17.6	20.7	22.6	
	11.2	14.1	17.8	20.9	22.8	
	11.2	14.4	18.4	21.8	23.8	
	11.5	14.2	17.7	20.6	22.4	
	11.5	14.2	17.6	20.6	22.4	
	11.5	14.2	17.7	20.6	22.4	
	11.9	14.6	18.0	21.0	22.8	
	11.9	14.6	18.0	21.0	22.8	
	15.2	17.6	20.9	23.7	25.4	
	9.2*	11.0	13.3	15.2	16.4	
	9.2*	11.0	13.3	15.2	16.4	
	9.2*	11.0	13.3	15.2	16.4	
	9.2*	11.0	13.3	15.2	16.4	
	9.2*	11.0	13.3	15.2	16.4	
	9.2*	11.0	13.3	15.2	16.4	
	9.2*	11.0	13.3	15.2	16.4	
	9.2*	11.0	13.3	15.2	16.4	
$50,000–$99,999	20.3	22.5	25.5	28.2	29.8	
	9.2*	11.0	13.3	15.2	16.4	
	13.0*	14.5	16.5	18.3	19.3	
	13.0*	14.5	16.5	18.3	19.3	
$100,000 & over	9.2*	11.0	13.3	15.2	16.4	
	9.2*	11.0	13.3	15.2	16.4	
	9.2*	11.0	13.3	15.2	16.4	

*All rates with asterisk indicate 84-month contracts and are from the same hospital. All other contracts are 60-month duration. There were no lease-purchase contracts available during this time period.

first periods respectively. These data also indicate a wide variation in rates among contracts. These two periods have extremely different prime rates— 8½ to 12% for August 1973 to February 1975, and 4¾ to 8¾% for May 1971 to July 1973—with lease rates for the first (earliest) period generally lower than for the second period.

The misleading nature of considering only running rates is illustrated by additional information obtained for two true lease contracts initiated during the first period. Each contract was about to expire and the hospital was currently negotiating with the leasing company to determine the fair market value of the equipment. The leasing company has established a fair market value for one piece of equipment equal to almost 25% of original cost. The running rate for the contract was 11%, but the effective rate including the required salvage value was 17.5%. Similarly, the effective rate on a second contract which had a running rate of 11.2% was increased to over 20% due to a salvage value equal to 33% of original cost being established at the end of the contract.

Three of five shorter term contracts not included in the tables illustrate even more dramatically the importance of including salvage value estimates in cost evaluation. The contracts were terminated and fair market value purchase-options were exercised. The two 48-month contracts with running rates of 6.9% and 4.3% terminated with a hospital paying salvage values of 36 and 37½% of cost, respectively. These actual salvage values increased the effective lease rates to 19.3 and 18.5%. Also, a purchase option on a 36-month contract, with a running rate of 1.8%, was exercised at 52% of cost, resulting in an effective rate of 26.7%.

SUMMARY

This paper provides information concerning interest rates on true leases and lease-purchase agreements for hospital equipment. Since the salvage value estimate is extremely important for determining the effective rate of a true lease contract, various estimates are used. This procedure provides the analyst with a range of rates comparable with the debt rate and also indicates the sensitivity of the lease rate to changes in salvage values.

The effective rates on the lease and lease-purchase contracts were quite high. Most rates ranged from 12% to 25%, depending upon the salvage value estimate. But some rates were considerably higher, with one contract having a rate of 87%.

REFERENCES AND NOTES

1. Henry, J. B., "Finding the Cost of a True Lease," *Hospital Financial Management,* December 1976, pp. 19-25.

2. Cagnon, J. A., "Leasing: Is It Really the Answer To Your Needs?" *Medical Instrumentation,* Vol. 11, No. 1, January-February 1977, pp. 48-50.

3. See Internal Revenue Service, Rev. Rul. 55-540.

4. For additional discussion see: Henry, J. B., and Roenfeldt, R. L., "Hospital Equipment Financing," Contract 600-75-0115 with the Social Security Administration, Department of Health, Education and Welfare.

5. Although risk associated with the salvage value is not explicitly considered in equation (2), it is indirectly considered by examining the effect of different salvage values upon the effective interest rate. For a detailed comparison of alternative lease-cost measurement techniques and alternative adjustments for risk, see Bower, Richard S., "Issues in Lease Financing," *Financial Management,* Winter 1973, pp. 25-34.

40. Group Purchasing: A Cost Containment Tool

JOHN G. KING

Reprinted with permission from *Topics in Health Care Financing*,
Vol. 3, No. 3, Spring 1977, pp. 19–24, 36–38.

In this chapter is examined how group purchasing may be applied as a tool for improving the cost effectiveness of an institution, and reviews research conducted on the factors influencing effective purchasing programs and describes several different types of group purchasing programs operating in one state.

Hospitals account for nearly 40 percent of the $119 billion annual health care expenditures.[1] The nonlabor expenditures have recently moved to the forefront in the administrator's priorities of cost control. It is estimated hospitals spend an average of $7,000 per bed for purchased materials, equipment and services or in excess of $10 billion annually. Nonlabor expenditures have increased at a rate one and one-half times faster than have labor costs in hospitals in recent years.[2]

A second reason for recent attention to the cost of materials is the so-called "Prudent Buyer Principle." Section 2103 of the *Medicare Provider Reimbursement Manual* was revised in March, 1975 to more clearly delineate the Prudent Buyer Principle and to include some examples of its application.[3]

The principle is quite clear, but its application is not. The principle states:

All payments of providers of services must be based on the 'reasonable cost' of services covered under Title 18 of the Act and related to the care of beneficiaries. Reasonable cost includes all necessary and proper costs incurred in rendering the services, subject to principles relating to specific items of revenue and cost.[4]

In its explanation of the above statement and in its examples, the Social Security Administration encourages group buying. They state:

Where a group of institutions has a joint purchasing agreement which seems to result in participating members getting lower prices because of the advantages gained from bulk purchasing, any potential subscribers in the area which do not participate in the group may be called upon to justify any higher prices paid.[5]

Speculation continues as to the implications and implementation of the Prudent Buyer Principle by the Social Security Administration. *Hospital Progress* recently reported in its November, 1975 issue the opinions of four professionals in the field.[6] So far, implementation has occurred in only a few institutions. But there is a growing feeling among the experts that hospitals may some day be required to justify their purchasing practices and results in the absence of participation in group purchasing.

TRENDS IN GROUP PURCHASING CONCEPTS

Group purchasing has been a common management practice in some hospitals for many years. Most of the older established group purchasing programs conduct centralized contract negotiation on behalf of a group of hospitals. Often cooperatives are formed or the activity is conducted by hospital associations. Participating hospitals purchase directly from suppliers or manufacturers taking advantage of the group contract.

Other forms of group purchasing have emerged and are characterized by centralizing the buying function. Hospitals do not operate individual purchasing departments but depend upon the central organization to combine volumes of supplies and/or equipment and conduct the buying function. These programs may or may not operate centralized warehousing.

Ammer describes such programs as Materials Management Centers when broad based materials management activities are performed.[7] Purchasing, inventory control and warehousing, supply standardization and common materials handling systems are coordinated by the Center for benefit of a group of hospitals. The hospitals obtain virtually all of their supplies through the Materials Management Center. Purchasing of non-inventory and capital items are usually included.

Group purchasing or the operation of a Materials Management Center can both be reinforced by internal materials management programs within the participating hospitals. Policies and procedures should establish an integrated program on the selection, storage, distribution, use and salvage or disposal of supplies.

The most important trend in the entire materials field is two-fold emphasis of more hospitals taking advantage of group purchasing and development of broader programs of materials management inside the hospital for optimal use of the materials dollar.

GROUP PURCHASING EXPANSION

The American Hospital Association conducted a shared services survey in September 1975 and in 1970. The surveys show that the number of hospitals participating in all forms of group purchasing increased from 11.4 percent to 22.6 percent of those responding to the questionnaire from 1970 to 1975. Only 22.6 percent of the 6,223 hospitals responding take advantage of group purchasing, indicating significant barriers to participation still exist. Perhaps the benefits derived from participation in group purchasing are perceived not to be worthwhile, or options for group purchasing are not readily available in all parts of the country.

Table 2-1 indicates that the participation in group purchasing by the nation's hospitals does depend upon bed size, but in a surprising way.[8]

Table 2-1 U.S. Hospitals Participating in Group Purchasing Programs—1970 and 1975 by Size

Hospital Bed Size	Hospitals Responding 1970	Per Cent Participating 1975	Per Cent Participating 1970
6–24	295	15.6	7.5
25–49	1087	19.2	5.9
50–99	1493	25.0	6.1
100–199	1370	24.9	12.0
200–299	691	25.0	16.2
300–399	426	27.0	20.7
400–499	275	21.8	26.2
500+	586	14.8	16.0
Total	6223	22.6	11.4

Small hospitals of under 100 beds that responded to the survey have lower percentage participation than have hospitals over 100 beds. This was particularly true in 1970, but still evident in 1975. The percentage increase in participation from 1970 to 1975 of the hospitals under 100 beds was greater than hospitals over 100 beds. The group purchasing concept did make inroads more rapidly in small hospitals from 1970 to 1975, yet 80 percent of these hospitals still do not participate in group purchasing.

The growth of investor-owned hospital systems has been one of the reasons for the increased participation in group purchasing by hospitals. These hospitals benefit from nationwide purchasing contracts arranged by the hospital management company. Proprietary hospital beds increased in the United States from 37,000 beds in 1960 to 73,400 beds in 1974. Almost 50,000 of these beds are owned or managed by the nine largest investor-owned companies.[9] The average size of the hospitals of these nine management companies is approximately 140 beds, so their impact is reaching smaller sized institutions.

Group purchasing has also spread to hospitals from multiple hospital systems in the nonprofit sector which are also growing. Development of these multiple hospital arrangements has occurred largely in the last ten to 15 years. In most cases, group purchasing is a part of their mode of operation.

The AHA survey does not provide information about the geographic distribution of hospitals in group purchasing or their ownership patterns. Hopefully, future surveys will provide analysis of these characteristics.

COST CONTAINMENT AND PURCHASING: A REVIEW OF SELECTED STUDIES

Few indepth studies have been made to measure comparative effectiveness of purchasing performance by individual hospitals or by group purchasing programs. Buyers and sellers are generally reluctant to share detailed information. A few studies of rather narrow scope do shed some light on the dynamics of the buyer-seller relationship of purchasing when conducted by hospitals not in group purchasing. The data from these studies provides interesting documentation that many hospitals are not performing the purchasing function effectively and opportunities for improvement are available through group purchasing and other management programs.

Phoenix Supply Study

Harold Fearon, Ph.D., conducted a study of 15 hospitals in the Phoenix area in 1967.[10] The hospitals ranged in size from 60 to 481 beds, ten hospitals ranging from 100 to 216 beds. Some hospitals had centralized purchasing functions within the hospital and some did not. None were part of a group buying program.

The study compared prices paid for 14 commonly used items. The prices were related to the hospitals according to organization of the purchasing department and quantities purchased. A wide range of prices was found on almost all 14 items. Nearly all buyers felt they were obtaining the lowest possible price, and price variations were small between hospitals. Those hospitals with centralized purchasing within the hospital obtained the lowest prices on 11 of the 14 items. In general, hospitals buying the largest quantities obtained the lower prices, but not always.[11]

Of particular significance in this and similar studies is the misconception and lack of knowledge on the part of the buyer as to what the low prices for a given product are in a given community at any given time. Two of the 14 products studied had a price range of 100 percent—one hospital paying twice the price of the other. Yet all the buyers believed that prices did not vary much and that they were getting a "good price."

Ohio Supply Studies

A study in 1972 by L.W. Margolis compared the prices paid by 19 Ohio hospitals on 25 common supplies.[12] Findings from the 19 hospitals were: 1) significant range in prices paid existed for every item studied, 2) the greatest variability in price occurred in drug items, 3) some hospitals paid both the highest and lowest prices depending upon the item, 4) larger hospitals did not consistently pay lowest prices, 5) prices for items purchased via group purchasing programs were in the lower range of prices paid for the item, and 6) most of those interviewed believed their prices to be "competitive" or "better." Yet most didn't know how their prices compared. Major conclusions of the study were: 1) the purchasing manager represents a significant influence upon the effectiveness of the purchasing department and upon prices paid for supplies and, 2) the evidence indicates many hospitals in the study might benefit from group purchasing—further study is needed.

A second study of Ohio hospitals in 1976 by Edward Webster, Jr., sought to study the prices for supplies in 12 hospitals.[13] The major purpose of the study was to determine the relationship of prices paid to size of hospital, religious affiliation, and group purchasing. Results of the study showed price was in no way statistically related to either size or religious affiliation. Group purchasing did not make a significant difference in the prices paid in this study group.

Minneapolis Drug Purchasing Study

A study by Kralewski on drug purchasing in 1965 showed significant variations in drug prices paid by Minneapolis hospitals.[14] He found that hospitals with greater volume had reduced prices. Significant price reductions also occurred when bids were taken. A study by Garwin further emphasized the role of the pharmacist in determining price.[15] The Kralewski study led to the formation of a group purchasing program in Minneapolis for drugs, which is described later in this paper.

An unpublished HEW study of nine nongovernmental hospitals in three states revealed substantial price variation in prices paid for the same item.[16] They concluded that purchasing practices, not size or other factors, largely determined price for a given drug.

Further Studies Needed

These studies indicate a need for further empirical studies in the effectiveness of purchasing for hospitals on a group or individual basis. Several studies indicate that the potential for savings through well-operated group purchasing programs could be substantial. Yet, no conclusive evidence exists and some studies show larger volumes do not automatically produce price savings. The literature available does not provide much information about the effectiveness or method of operation of the wide variety of group purchasing programs that have been developed. The pressures of cost containment, the formation and expansion of multiple hospital systems, and growth of all forms of shared services have contributed to several new forms of organizing group purchasing that differ from the more established cooperative. or hospital association based programs....

Program Acceptance

Group purchasing coupled with sound internal hospital materials management programs offers significant opportunities for hospitals and the industry at large to reduce costs. Yet these opportunities are often lost! Why? Several answers can be offered.

Cost containment efforts by administrators have tended to be directed most heavily in labor areas. The rate of cost escalation in recent years for nonlabor costs is exceeding labor costs. Administrators have not shifted or directed their attention fully to nonlabor costs. The formulation of policy for and supervision of materials management is often given second priority and delegated "out of sight, out of mind."

A study of hospitals in the western Pennsylvania area revealed some interesting factors affecting acceptance of hospital group purchasing.[26] The study found that the hospital purchasing manager's own perception of his role was a significant factor in his participation in group purchasing. The purchasing manager who saw his position broader than obtaining the lowest price and saw the group purchasing programs as a vehicle to enhance his professionalism was more likely than others to be involved heavily in group purchasing. The authors concluded the participants in group purchasing were the "front runners." Similar experience has been found in Minnesota. Group purchasing managers expressed feelings during interviews that the more progressive hospitals and administrators were more likely to participate in group purchasing; many hospitals who could benefit the most still were not participating.

Limitations

Group purchasing in itself has limitations unless coupled with a hospitalwide materials management effort. It is possible to achieve savings on high volume items through group buying, but maximum cost containment cannot be achieved unless attention is paid to good product selection, efficient inventory management and distribution of supplies.

Another caution is urged. Group purchasing may not always produce the lowest price. Research studies show great variations in price. Price is not always related to volume. The skill of the purchasing manager is often the key factor to the price obtained. Hospitals participating in group purchasing programs cannot assume they are getting the lowest possible price; group purchasing programs should not become complacent. Constant reevaluation of purchasing techniques must be routinely conducted by group purchasing managers.

Some geographic sections of the country do not have group purchasing programs available to hospitals or in the form hospitals desire.... Most of these programs began in small ways, with only 2 or 3 hospitals or with a limited number of products. Hospitals are urged to initiate, to experiment and to find ways of pooling their expertise and buying power.

Potential

The opportunities for improved materials management do exist. Prices can be lowered in many cases. Purchasing time can be saved and knowledge and experience pooled. Inventories can be reduced freeing up cash. Purchasing managers can devote more of their time to improved materials management. Better management reporting can be developed by sharing data.

These potential benefits exist in thousands of hospitals. Only those who seize the opportunity, who strike out to find the best system for their institution will derive the benefits.

REFERENCES

1. "The Problem of Rising Health Care Costs," Council on Wage and Price Stability, Washington, D.C.: April 1976.

2. Ammer, D.S. *Hospital Materials Management: Neglect and Inefficiency Promote High Health Care Costs.* (Boston: Northeastern University, Bureau of Business and Economic Research 1974).

3. "Commentaries on the SSA's 'Prudent Buyer Principle. " Editor's note. *Hospital Progress* 56:11 (November 1975) p. 44–50.

4. *Ibid.*

5. *Ibid.*

6. *Ibid.*

7. Ammer, *op. cit.*

8. American Hospital Association. Survey on Shared Services (September, 1975).

9. Brown, M. and Lewis, H.L. *Hospital Management Systems* (Germantown, MD.: Aspen Systems Corporation 1976).

10. Fearon, H., Ph.D. "Centralized Purchasing Can Cut Hospital Costs," *Hospital Progress* 49:1 (January 1968) p. 60–65, 86.

11. *Ibid.*

12. Margolis, L.W. "A Study on the Prices Paid by Hospitals on Selected Items." Thesis. (Columbus, Ohio: Ohio State University Graduate Program in Hospital and Health Care Administration 1972).

13. Webster, E.W. Jr. "A Model for Achieving Lower Prices for Routine Supplies in Hospitals." Thesis. (Columbus, Ohio: Ohio State University Graduate Program in Hospital and Health Care Administration 1976).

14. Kralewski, J.E. "Lower Drug Costs Through Group Purchasing." *Hospitals* 42 (October 1, 1968).

15. Garwin, A.W. "Hidden Benefits of Group Purchasing." *The Canadian Journal of Hospital Pharmacy* 23 (November-December 1970).

16. Margolis, *op. cit.*

***

26. Hahn, C.K. and Hardy, S.T. "Factors Affecting Acceptance of a Hospital Group Purchasing Program." *Journal of Purchasing* (August 1972).

41. The Many Ways to Contain Costs Through Effective Materiel Management

CHARLES E. HOUSLEY

Condensed from: Housley, C.E., *Hospital Materiel Management,* Aspen Systems Corporation, 1978; with permission from *Dimensions in Health Service,* Journal of the Canadian Hospital Association.

REDUCING OFFICIAL INVENTORY

Reduction of official inventories is a very potent area of cost containment for all hospitals. A recent survey of 500 hospitals of all sizes revealed that even the smaller institutions could reduce their official inventory by at least $100,000, while some of the larger ones could free over $1 million through inventory reduction. Such a buildup of supplies for which the hospital has already paid represents a sizeable investment that pays no dividends. When this stockpile has been reduced, the real money gained can be invested or be put to better use.

Another method that can be used by hospitals to cut inventory is to reduce automatically the amount of supplies by the annual cost increase for those supplies.

Being aware of the costs and disadvantages of inventory is one of the first steps in dealing with it. The second is to take an immediate physical count of all official inventory (central stores, pharmacy, and dietary) and devise an immediate plan of action to reduce it to approximately $300 per bed.

REDUCING UNOFFICIAL INVENTORY

Many hospital departments are "fat" with unofficial inventory. Their administrations have, however, generally ignored these supply stockpiles when attempting to contain costs because once this inventory is dispensed, it is officially out of sight.

It is safe to assume that unofficial inventory will be approximately three to five times the amount of the official inventory. Many hospitals can free from $100,000 to $500,000 of capital just in these areas alone.

To start, it is recommended that the materiel manager confer with top management and gain their support for unofficial inventory reduction programs. Next, he should organize inventory teams to perform an actual count of all supplies. Finally, the materiel manager should establish realistic maximum levels for all unofficial inventories and then take a physical inventory quarterly to ensure that the departments are following the guidelines.

AMALGAMATING SUPPLY, PROCESS, AND DISTRIBUTION FUNCTIONS AND AREAS

Hospital architects are still specifying that the central stores be in the basement, central sterile supply on the second or third floor, and the pharmacy on the first floor. Also, most still recommend that there be a separate central sterile supply department. It is high time we relate to them and to ourselves that these functions are similar and should be located together. As separate areas, they all have their own personnel, supervision, distribution, supplies, and inventories. If the functions are combined or located in close proximity, many of the tasks and duties can be shared.

In most cases, central stores and central sterile supply can be combined and the staff reduced. Pharmacy should be a part of this system, too, so that it can become a part of this one storage and distribution center. Unit dose carts from the pharmacy should be programed to be distributed at the same time by the same personnel as are the medical-surgical and linen carts.

ELIMINATING EXCESS PERSONNEL IN THE MATERIEL AREAS

The combination of the supply, process, and distribution functions can always be counted on to reduce the number of personnel by at least one or two in the smaller hospitals and by as many as twenty-five in the larger ones. Also, the purchase of disposables should result in reduction of personnel or their use cannot be justified.

USING CONSIGNMENT AS AN ALTERNATIVE TO PURCHASING

Consignment, the principle of having the manufacturer stock a commodity at the hospital but not charge for it until it is used, seems to be a promising option. This plan benefits the hospital greatly, but recently manufacturers have been reluctant to continue it because of their interpretation of the health devices legislation. Most manufacturers seemed to feel that under its provisions, if they let an item out on consignment, they had no control of the supply but still had the ultimate responsibility. Fortunately, there has been a recent clarification of the principle, and many manufacturers are once again favorably inclined to the use of consignment.

Hospitals and materiel managers should literally insist upon the use of consignment by the manufacturers for expensive supplies, even to the point of assuming responsibility for the proper storage of the supplies in writing.

STOCKLESS PURCHASING

Stockless purchasing can help to reduce both official and unofficial inventories at the same time. In fact, through stockless purchasing hospitals can cut enormous unofficial inventories to a workable level of $300 per bed.

PRODUCT STANDARDIZATION

Product standardization can bring about a materiel discipline that has never before been paralleled. To be the most effective as a means of cost containment, it must be a five-point program: standardization review, patient charge determination, procedural documentation, inservice delineation, and followup.

BUYING SPECIAL ITEMS LOCALLY

From time to time, most hospitals are in need of unique items of supply that may only be used once or twice every ten years. The cost conscious materiel manager should never think of stocking this type of supply. These kinds of items can best be purchased locally from such suppliers as hardware stores and pharmacies.

INDIRECT OR WHOLESALE DRUG PURCHASING

Pharmaceuticals are an expensive supply category and should be purchased with care and concern. For years, hospital purchasing agents have felt that they get the best possible prices by buying directly from the manufacturer. Most manufacturers do give a discount on direct purchases, but usually there is a certain minimum that must be bought; moreover, some drug manufacturers do not give hospital discounts. The prudent materiel manager should be alert to all direct purchase policies and compare them to an indirect drug prime supplier where no dollar minimums are required. In fact, in many cases, it will be to the hospital's benefit to purchase from the wholesaler, especially if the company will give prime supplier volume discounts regardless of quantities purchased. It will always be advantageous to purchase the slow moving or exotic drugs in the smallest quantities possible from the wholesaler. Hospitals should follow the example of the retail pharmacy, which keeps a low inventory worth about $20,000 and greatly utilizes the service of the wholesaler.

NEGOTIATING TERM INSTEAD OF FULL SERVICE CONTRACTS

Many equipment service companies decide without negotiation what preventive maintenance should be performed and the frequency of the service. Hospitals should take a hard look at all such contracts and demand that their input be considered in setting the service specifications. There is ample room for modifying most service contracts, and the prudent materiel manager will see to it that the hospital is getting adequate service for a justifiable cost.

CONTROLLING FORMS

In the modern hospital the panacea for all problems seems to be the creation of another printed form. For the most part, forms can be initiated, changed, and redeveloped without the permission or knowledge of anyone in authority. One of the most devastating characteristics of forms is that they are so easy to reproduce, especially since copy machines are located in almost all departments. It is estimated that the average-sized hospital of 350 beds will have some 600-700 different forms in its inventory.

Most hospital materiel managers agree that controlling forms is a definite problem. To deal with this issue, it is recommended that a survey referencing each form by initiating department, quantities used, description, and annual costs be completed. It should also indicate whether or not the form is an inventory item. The forms survey should bring out any duplication by departments and be the basis for the forms control program.

After this task has been completed, the materiel manager should refer the matter to the Product Standardization Committee, which should attempt to reduce the number of forms to around 250.

The Product Standardization Committee then should set certain policies such as the following:

1. Any new form regardless of its use must be submitted to the Product Standardization Committee for review and approval before being used in the hospital.
2. If a new form is approved, all quantities of the old form must be used before the new one is used. This policy can save the hospital money and reduce the number of unnecessary new forms.
3. A control numbering system should be initiated to identify the forms for usage and reordering.
4. Many medical staff forms are reviewed by the Medical Records Committee. When a proposed form has been approved, it should be submitted to the Product Standardization Committee for review and recommendations.
5. When a proposed form is submitted for review, it must be accompanied by printing and storage costs.
6. When a standard form is being considered for repurchase, it should be submitted to the Product Standardization Committee for review in case any changes are contemplated on a hospital-wide basis.

PURCHASING COPYING MACHINES

In the past, hospitals have had to lease or rent copying machines. However, things have changed and companies now sell their machines along with reasonable service contracts. First, it must be stated that the hospital should exert some kind of reasonable control over forms reproduction. The convenience and accessibility of copying machines have led to a proliferation of forms, often in senseless quantities. By purchasing the machines, at least the hospital is not burdened by a per copy charge. Second, the hospital should review its copying policies and experience in order to decide whether it is in the hospital's best interest to lease or buy.

SHARING INFREQUENTLY USED SUPPLIES WITH OTHER HOSPITALS

Hospitals that are located in the same locale should assist each other by stocking infrequently used supplies and equipment at only one hospital. This sharing would contain costs for each one in the group. At the end of a certain period, each would bill the others for services rendered. In this manner, even infrequently used supplies would be available at all times, duplication of supplies reduced, and much paperwork eliminated.

LIMITING THE NUMBER OF SUPPLIES IN THE CENTRAL STORES AREA

The materiel manager should review the number of items in central stores and decide whether they are absolutely necessary. Most hospitals can manage very well with 350 to 400 standard items, whereas they now have around 3,000. Reducing this number negates the need for computerization, frees up more space, and cuts out costly duplication.

DEVELOPING A DRUG FORMULARY

Another supply category that needs immediate attention is the standardization of drugs. In many hospitals, drug inventory represents a larger dollar volume than does the total supply inventory, and materiel managers have been reluctant to tackle this area because of their lack of knowledge of drugs. All drug expenditures and quantities should be questioned. A formulary should be developed and the number of drugs kept in inventory reduced to a minimum. Exotic and infrequently used drugs should be purchased in the smallest quantities possible and be dispensed directly to the patient without an inventory buildup.

REDUCING THE FREQUENCY OF LINEN CHANGES

Cost per processed pound of linen has become an accepted indicator for measuring the effectiveness of the laundry production. In most hospitals in the U.S., the cost will be somewhere between 15¢ and 25¢ per pound, with the figure rising as labor and indirect expenses increase. In an attempt to reduce this figure, many hospitals have given up their laundries and contracted with commercial laundries or centralized hospital laundries.

The cost reduction methods should involve linen use, not linen production. It may not be in the patient's best interest to change his or her bed linen every day. Of course, if the patient's condition warrants more frequent changes, these are made on an as-needed basis. This recommendation has great cost-saving potential for hospitals. For example, a hospital that has two million pounds of processed linen per year at 20¢ per pound pays a $400,000 laundry bill. If that hospital cut its production pounds by one-third, it would reduce its laundry costs by approximately $133,000.

PRIME SUPPLIER CONCEPT

The prime supplier technique can be effective as a cost containment measure. It can bring savings to the hospital through good prices regardless of quantities purchased, less paperwork, much less time spent interviewing vendors and less back orders. This technique is most effective when practiced on a group basis.

REQUESTING INSTANT CREDIT ON OVERCHARGES BY THE VENDORS

Any problem arising from overcharging or a supply shortage with an overcharge should be taken care of immediately by the sales representative through an instant credit. The hospital should take every opportunity possible to keep its cash moving or invested, never in use by someone else.

CENTRALIZING PURCHASING

The act of purchasing and negotiation can best be done by the professional materiel manager or purchasing director. Centralized purchasing can best achieve uniformity of quality, best prices, and procedural and policy standardization.

HAND WRITING PURCHASE ORDERS

It has been estimated that the processing of a purchase order can cost approximately $35, mostly because of labor costs. Much of the cost can be saved simply by writing the orders in a legible manner, instead of typing them.

USING FAX EQUIPMENT FOR PURCHASE DATA TRANSMISSION

The manner in which data are transferred to the supplier also can be a factor in cost reduction. FAX or facsimile equipment performs both data transmission and data receiving functions. To the user, the procedure is a matter of calling a telephone number at the receiving end, putting the telephone receiver on the FAX terminal, and then letting the two machines talk to each other. Transmission time for most purchase orders is about two minutes.

The machines can be leased for rates ranging from $29 to $60 each month; however, the responsive supplier will pay for the equipment. The advantages of using FAX equipment are as follows:

(a) Speed—There is no faster system available for the price.

(b) Efficiency—The documents are transmitted error free.
(c) Cost—The costs associated with the equipment can be included as a cost of doing business for the supplier.
(d) Convenience—Transmissions can be performed at any time as there is no need for a person to be at the receiving end.
(e) Flexibility—If necessary, the order can include a picture of the supply or equipment needed.

CONSOLIDATING REBATES, DISCOUNTS, AND ALLOWANCES INTO THE INVOICED PRICE

If you negotiate for rebates or discounts, be certain that these are figured into the invoiced prices. In some states if a separate rebate check is received monthly or yearly as is common practice, third parties consider the rebated amount as a reduction in revenue.

TOUGH BUT ETHICAL NEGOTIATION

The hospital purchasing agent or materiel manager should conduct tough negotiation sessions on an annual basis for all supply categories, and all major agreements on price and service should be effective for at least a year. It must, however, be remembered that concern about prices can overshadow the more important actions such as inventory reduction. Let's put the supply price negotiations into perspective. The maximum reduction obtainable from the toughest, most stringent type of negotiations is only about two percent if the hospital is getting good prices to begin with. At this rate the hospital could possibly pick up another $20,000 per each million dollars worth of purchases, so the money saved through purchasing is miniscule compared to that saved through internal materiel practices. In fact, hospitals practicing prudent purchasing should already be at a point beyond which the supplier cannot give.

INDUSTRIAL ENGINEERING APPLICATIONS

There are many situations in the materiel management function that the industrial engineer could assist. For instance, in many institutions there are intricate and confusing distribution patterns, including pack wrapping, tray makeup, soiled and clean material flow, and instrumentation set up, that could be greatly simplified by industrial engineering techniques.

REVIEWING AND STUDYING ALL PURCHASE ALTERNATIVES

Often there are many alternatives to purchasing a commodity or service. An important one is to make an item instead of to buy it. Presently, hospitals lean toward buying disposables, but this can be a very costly decision unless accompanied by a reduction in man-hours previously spent preparing that item. But, there are still some items, such as water for irrigation, that it would be more advantageous for the hospital to make than to buy.

Another decision is whether to buy or rent. One sees the need for this decision most when the hospital is running at a high occupancy and additional supplies and equipment are required for the period. It may not be necessary for the hospital to spend money for extra suction machines, for example, and the materiel manager must figure out at what usage level it would be better to buy or rent.

To buy or borrow is a third option that the materiel manager faces, and timing is of utmost importance with this decision. At midnight on a weekend, it may be easiest and quickest to borrow the needed equipment or supply from another hospital.

To buy or lease is a fourth question for the materiel manager. In most cases, leasing represents an expensive monthly payment. There are, however, a few applications for leasing that are justifiable. The foremost is the situation of obsolescence. If a piece of equipment is needed by the institution and has a short lifespan, it may be advantageous to lease it. Another is when the hospital needs a piece of equipment which it cannot afford outright. In most cases, however, the hospital will come out ahead if it buys supplies and equipment.

SUPPLY UTILIZATION STUDIES

Much emphasis is put on purchasing, processing, and distributing supplies, but hardly any attention is given to how that product is used in the institution. The materiel manager must set up standards and specifications for the efficient and effective use of all supplies and equipment.

ELIMINATING ALL BULK WAREHOUSING

In addition to central stores and central supply, many hospitals have added another duplicative effort by introducing warehousing into the supply picture. In addition to rent or the per square footage charge and indirect expenses, there is that ever present cost of inventory buildup. In other words, warehousing should be eliminated in today's hospital supply market, especially since no supply is more than a day away.

ESTABLISHING EFFECTIVE LIMITS FOR ALL SUPPLIES BASED ON AN ECONOMIC ORDER

Supply maximums and minimums actually represent good supply discipline since they indicate that the materiel manager has determined a limit above which he cannot go for economic reasons and below which he cannot go for supply service reasons. This maximum and minimum continuum should be reviewed on a periodic, seasonal basis to assure cost effectiveness and supply continuity of service. There has been much discussion about economic order quantities with complex mathematical ratios and complicated formulas, but in practice, these are more complicated than useful. If supply maximums and minimums are established realistically over a period of time, the economic order quantity is simply the difference between the maximum and the minimum.

BETTER UTILIZATION OF THE VENDORS

In the past, sales representatives have been noted for their hard sell and their marketing techniques. However, with the concept of materiel management evolving, the role of the salesman is changing. He should become a representative to a hospital from his company. In this role, the representative can be very beneficial to the hospital, performing the following functions for it.

(a) Advising the materiel manager or purchasing agent about quality products that may be less expensive than what the hospital is presently using.
(b) Assisting with annual physical inventory under the control and supervision of the materiel manager.
(c) Providing the hospital with information that can assist in establishing effective supply maximums and minimums.
(d) Informing the materiel manager or purchasing agent of price increases with enough notice that he does not feel pressure to take advantage of the offer.
(e) Providing the materiel manager with the monthly, quarterly, and annual reports on supply procurement and utilization.
(f) Obtaining supplies for the hospital from sources other than his own company when there is a definite need to do so. Such supply continuity is the responsibility of the prime supplier.

(g) Providing the materiel manager with future supply trends such as supply increases, supply stockouts, and product alterations.

EVALUATING NEW PRODUCTS AT THE VENDOR'S EXPENSE

If it is decided to evaluate a product, the supplier should provide the necessary material at his company's expense. This is merely a cost of doing business to the supplier, but is an unnecessary expense to the hospital. Also, it is advantageous for the hospital to request a reasonable evaluation period for most movable, capital equipment. This simple procedure can save the hospital thousands of dollars even in the short run.

CONTINUOUS PATIENT CHARGE REVIEW

In general, hospitals do not have the best record for establishing patient charge criteria. This entire area should be reviewed and made more effective by both the materiel and financial managers. Patient supply charges must be based upon many criteria, but one of the foremost is price. With the present trend of supply prices always in a state of flux, this fact alone should cause the patient supply charge to be reviewed and changed almost constantly.

INHOUSE BIOMEDICAL ENGINEERING EXPERTISE

Hospitals have large quantities of complicated, sophisticated, and very expensive patient care equipment, which must be tended to by trained biomedical engineers. The cost of such expertise on an as-needed basis is very expensive, so it makes sense for one or a group of hospitals to hire such a person on a full-time basis.

EFFECTIVE PREVENTIVE MAINTENANCE PROGRAMS

For the most part, supply rooms are filled with expensive equipment and supplies. It is the responsibility of the materiel manager to see that the appropriate preventive maintenance is given to all equipment and supplies under his jurisdiction. Remember, it can either be cared for now or totally replaced later.

AN ASSETS MANAGEMENT PROGRAM

Capital equipment is an important part of materiel management because generally it is through materiel management that the equipment is specified, ordered, received and distributed to the appropriate user. In addition, hospitals are reimbursed for capital equipment depreciation on a concise and factual schedule. The better this function is executed, the more justification the hospital has for receiving dollars through depreciation.

APPROPRIATE PRODUCT SUBSTITUTION

Hospitals are fortunate in that there often are several products which will provide about the same results. In many cases, the hospital materiel manager is hard pressed to prove one superior or inferior to the other. The establishment of an effective product standardization process involves the ability to choose product substitutes. Therefore, for every standard item, there should be an acceptable backup.

VALUE ANALYSIS

Value analysis is a technique that can be used very effectively by the Product Standardization Committee. The essence of value analysis is the questioning and challenging of the need for the function of each product or piece of equipment. Next, consideration should be given to alternate ways or methods to perform the product's function. Last, comparison studies must be performed. If acceptable methods are found to accomplish the same end more efficiently or inexpensively, then a change should be proposed.

RESULTS-ORIENTED PRODUCT INSERVICE PROGRAMS

No product or piece of equipment should ever gain entrance into the hospital without proper and thorough inservice programs. Both the hospital and supplier have major responsibilities in this area. The sales representative and hospital inservice coordinator should meet with all applicable personnel in small groups and provide practical instructions and then allow each employee to use the product or equipment under trained supervision.

PAY FOR CAPITAL EQUIPMENT PURCHASES ONLY AFTER INSTALLATION AND HOSPITAL APPROVAL

Most hospital equipment manufacturers and suppliers stipulate that the hospital make term payments on purchases, a policy heavily weighted in favor of the supplier. Hospital materiel managers should formulate a payment schedule that would give the hospital the upper hand. For example, all major capital purchases should be negotiated on the premise that no payment will be made until the installation has been approved by the necessary hospital authorities.

SIMPLIFYING THE PURCHASE PROCESS

Much time, effort, and expense can go into the purchase process. The tendency is omnipresent to complicate this function by much paper work, computerization keypunching, producing multiple copies, and holding time-consuming sales interviews. Take a hard look at your purchasing function and establish realistic purchase simplification objectives. For instance, try to decrease the number of vendors with whom the hospital is doing small amounts of business. Also make an effort to limit the purchase document to only one original piece of paper. Schedule all major negotiations on a two-year basis and monitor your prices on a periodic basis to determine the cost effectiveness of your prices.

QUESTIONING ALL COMPUTER APPLICATIONS IN THE MATERIEL AREAS FOR COST EFFECTIVENESS

Certainly there are possible applications for computerization in the purchase and inventory functions, but only after much thought and deliberation. The more reasonable approach lies in simplification not computerization, since computer time and computer operators' salaries are costly. To begin with, the materiel manager should reduce the number of supplies in inventory to a workable, manual level. Next, a time study should be performed to determine how much time and effort and expense are involved in the inventory process. Then request that a parallel study be performed using the computer.

SHARING SERVICES

Hospitals can certainly contain costs by shared programs. These programs do not always have to concern group purchasing or collections, but can involve simply sharing ideas, prices, and drug and product information systems. The whole idea behind sharing of services is that higher volumes mean lower costs for all institutions. Be careful, too, to guard against developing antagonisms with the management of hospitals with which you are sharing services.

QUESTIONING ALL AUTOMATED EFFORTS IN THE MATERIEL AREAS FOR COST EFFECTIVENESS

Most functions in the materiel areas must be people processed, and any time there is a disproportionate mix of automation and people, costs soar. Automation usually breeds high installation costs, system inflexibility, costly repair, and expensive operational costs. Vigorously question and contest all automated efforts in the name of cost containment and practicality.

NEGOTIATING FOR LONGER EQUIPMENT WARRANTIES

Never settle for less than a 12-month warranty on all parts and service on all major capital purchases, despite the trend for manufacturers to decrease the warranty to 6 months or even 90 days. In many cases, hospitals can get at least a two-year warranty if their negotiations are strong, and extended warranties at the manufacturer's expense can be at least as attractive as a very sizeable discount off the list price.

SUPPLY COST EMPHASIS AND AWARENESS PROGRAM

In most cases, the personnel who use the supplies and equipment, including the physicians, have no awareness of its costs. The materiel manager could address this by featuring a different supply display each week in a prominent place where all personnel would see it. In the display, the cost of the item should be made known with the percentage of cost increase over the past five years. It could also point up the cost of the item to the patient with a short summary of the factors which make up the cost, as well as the total number of the items used on an annual basis. Last, it should include some plea for containing costs by proper use of the item. The format of the cost awareness program could be flexible but continuous, because the number of items used and abused by the hospital is infinite.

RETURN FOR CREDIT POLICY

A hospital cannot afford to have its capital tied up in supplies that do not turn over at a constant rate and bring a fairly good rate of return. Therefore, the materiel manager should formulate a minimum turnover rate for all supplies kept in inventory, especially the more expensive ones. For instance, it could be the policy of the institution to return all supplies for credit after 90 or 120 days of inactivity. This policy will also prevent obsolescence and pilferage.

USING HOT AIR HAND DRYERS INSTEAD OF PAPER TOWELS

In some high use areas such as public toilets and rest rooms, there is much waste of paper towels. The materiel manager in coordination with the executive housekeeper should perform studies on these areas to determine the cost of paper towels on an annual basis, then compare these figures with the cost of installing hot air hand dryers.

USING ALL OF A PRODUCT BEFORE REPLACING IT

Many times new items are introduced into the hospital without considering the quantity of the old product in stock. As a result, the new product comes in and the old product is never used again. This is especially true of forms. The materiel manager should formulate a policy that a new product cannot be purchased unless all quantities of the old product are used first.

IN SOME CASES, LOWER THE STANDARDS OF QUALITY

There are some instances in which the product does not have to be of the best quality. For example, some nursing policies stipulate that underpads used for an incontinent patient be changed every two to four hours. The highest quality, most absorbent, larger underpad would be wasted in such cases, and the lesser quality, less expensive, smaller underpad would be quite acceptable. Try to match up the quality of the product with the situation.

QUESTION ALL PATIENT CONVENIENCE PRODUCTS

Since hospitals are put in the unenviable position of being the patients' keeper, decisions, are made that can raise the cost of their care in behalf of their best interests. For example, most hospitals use and charge for patient admission kits. The average cost to the patient for this item is between three and four dollars. Unfortunately, the patient has no say in this decision. The patient may already have a toothbrush, toothpaste, mouthwash, and everything else in the kit, but he gets it whether he needs it or not.

SUMMARY

In reference to cost containment and materiel management in hospitals, one is reminded of the following story:

A group of former hospital employees decided to go into business for themselves. They began a trucking company with a small fleet of heavy trucks. One of their feats was to take a three ton truck over a two ton load limit bridge to service a customer. They reasoned among themselves that rules were made to be broken, so they decided to take the three ton truck over the two ton load limit bridge. Well, of course, the inevitable happened; the bridge collapsed, and the truck went into the ravine. They rented a crane, got the truck out, fixed the truck and fixed the bridge. They again reasoned that since the new bridge was built of new material, they could run their truck over the bridge even though its load capacity was still two tons. The second time, the bridge collapsed, and the truck went into the ravine. They rented a crane, got the truck out, fixed the truck, and fixed the bridge. They went through this routine six times, until one of them stated that they must make a management decision since they weren't making any progress. Their decision, BUY THE CRANE.

CHAPTER 5

MANAGEMENT METHODS

Management is the planning and integration of effort, mobilization of resources, motivation of people, and provision of leadership to guide an institution toward its goal in an efficient manner. Management methods are the key to any successful cost containment program. In the previous chapters, specific management methods that are used in health care institutions to deal with organization for cost containment, manpower, productivity improvement, and efficient use of materials, supply, and equipment were reviewed. In this chapter more general management techniques that can be applied to any of the previous areas, to a combination of them, or to other areas in the health care institution are considered. Specifically, the following topics are presented:

- management audits
- time management
- computers and information systems
- shared and contract services
- management consulting services
- planning and forecasting
- control and performance analysis
- risk management

MANAGEMENT AUDITS

A management audit is a logical framework for evaluating administrative performance to ensure that:

1. Designated goals and objectives are met.
2. Policies and procedures are followed.
3. Inefficiencies and ineffectiveness are minimized.
4. Organization of positions, functions, and personnel are adequate for the optimal fulfillment of the mission of the health institution.

A proper management audit program can achieve these purposes by effectively evaluating results, by correctly perceiving problem areas, by initiating corrective actions, and by proposing appropriate management tools and procedures.

Management auditing is fairly well developed outside the health care industry. Perhaps the best known type of management audit is the one recommended by the American Institute of Management.[1]

In theory, a management audit is very similar to a quality of care audit; in many aspects the two are interrelated. The difference is that a quality audit is centered around factors that contribute directly to quality of care (cleanliness, proper professional skill, and availability of medical equipment), while a management audit is centered around factors that relate to an appropriate management system (planning activities, communication networks, performance evaluation procedures, motivation, reports, etc.).

The American Hospital Association developed a Program for Institutional Effectiveness Review (PIER) to help hospital managers assess and improve operational effectiveness. PIER is a self-administered executive audit program, designed to be used by a management team consisting of representatives from the hospital administration, its governing board, and its medical staff. PIER employs a systems analysis approach to examine key indicators of hospital operating performance and determine how each of the institution's components is contributing to overall institutional effectiveness.[2]

Gilbert (Reading 42) describes management audit under the name "operational auditing." Other names are sometimes used: executive audit, effectiveness review, and administrative control survey. The proposed plan outlines all major areas to be audited.

TIME MANAGEMENT

The article by Wolfe and Wolfe (see Chapter 3, Reading 20) lists 20 duties and characteristics of a good manager. A manager needs time to perform these duties, and lack of time is one of the major contributors to mismanagement. Therefore, any cost containment program should include the training of the facility administrators in the efficient and effective use of time. Time management is a topic for whole books, but Scott's article (Reading 43) calls attention to the major points in time management. It presents practical tips and suggestions on how to use time effectively.

COMPUTERS AND INFORMATION SYSTEMS

The application of computers to health care systems is increasing rapidly. Ten years ago only a very few, very large hospitals used computers, mainly in their accounting and payroll systems. Today, computers are being used by most American hospitals in a variety of applications: business offices, nursing services, and ancillary departments.

The potential of computers in reducing health care costs is discussed by Gray (Reading 44), who cites the literature of the early and mid-1970s. The benefits of computers in several areas are discussed. In the two years since Gray's article was published, it has been shown that computers can also be used to help contain the costs of labor. Of special interest are the studies conducted at Battelle Laboratory in Columbus, Ohio, and at El Camino Hospital in Mountain View, California.[3]

Veazie's paper (Reading 45) relates the use of computers to information systems. Health institution information handling expense has been estimated as 25–40 percent of the facility's total expense. Thus, the potential for automated data processing is significant. This paper constitutes an administrative review of the hospital computer "state of the art."

SHARED AND CONTRACT SERVICES

Integration of health services is one of the newest forms of cost containment. Such integration is done under several organizational forms, most notably under the forms of shared services, contract services, contract management, mergers, and affiliations. Brown and Lewis (Reading 46) provide an overview of this topic.

A more detailed analysis of shared services is given in Saxton's article (Reading 47), where the benefits of shared services are listed and the various types reviewed. Shared services, if properly managed, may result in a substantial savings.

CONSULTING SERVICES

Management consultants are used frequently by health care institutions. The major reasons for using them are: (1) the necessary expertise is not available internally; (2) the staff member with the necessary expertise is occupied with work of greater priority; and (3) an outsider, an unbiased observer, is needed. The results of using management consultants vary from highly successful to failure. Careful analysis prior to hiring a consultant is essential. Carithers' article (Reading 48) surveys the proper procedures for selecting an outside consultant.

PLANNING AND FORECASTING

Of management's major functions, planning is probably the most misused in the health care industry. The reasons for this are:

1. Rapid changes in the industry make it difficult to forecast and plan.
2. Increased government intervention puts more constraints on operations.
3. The nature of the industry lends itself to a crisis management or "fire-fighting" approach rather than to management through planning.

Yet, long-range planning is required for accreditation of hospitals, and the health systems agencies (HSAs) are pushing health institutions toward planning. Appropriate planning at the facility level may result in significant savings since it allows appropriate use of resources. A key element in any planning is demand forecasting. For further information on this topic see Clark and Lamont's article on census forecasting.[4]

CONTROL AND PERFORMANCE ASSESSMENT

It is possible to exercise some degree of control over any activity in the health care institution. Control involves measuring performance, comparing it to plans or goals, and taking necessary actions in the case of significant deviations.

Another phase of control is an attempt to compare performance in a health facility with the performance of similar facilities. Danco and Schmidt (Reading 49) present the Hospital Administrative Services (HAS) reports. The HAS provide subscribing hospitals with a monthly computerized report in which measures of each member hospital's performance are compared with (1) the national average, (2) the state average, and (3) the regional average. All comparisons are based on the member hospital's specific size. In addition, the hospital receives an "internal trend data" analysis, where current performance is compared to the "previous 3 months," "previous 12 months," and to the "same month in the previous year." The report covers about 200 measures of performance for the entire hospital and for every department in it.

RISK MANAGEMENT AND SELF-INSURANCE

Even though the pressure of malpractice suits has been reduced, appropriate risk management and evaluation of insurance alternatives are essential and constitute potential cost containment areas. These areas are presented here by two papers. Risk management is presented in the article by Morgan and Wozniak (Reading 50), describing a comprehensive hospital program. Schroeder (Reading 51) reviews and analyzes the various insurance options that are open to health institutions.

NOTES

1. For more information, contact the American Institute of Management, 607 Boylston Street, Boston, Massachusetts 02116.

2. For more information on PIER, contact the American Hospital Association, 840 North Lake Shore Drive, Chicago, Illinois 60611.

3. The National Center for Health Services Research (NCHSR) documented these studies. Information on them is available in Pub. #PB262106 from NTIS, U.S. Department of Commerce, 5285 Port Royal Road, Springfield, Virginia 22151.

4. B.B. Clark, and G.X. Lamont, "Accurate Census Forecasting Leads to Cost Containment," *Hospitals, JAHA* 50 June (1976): 43.

BIBLIOGRAPHY

Amber, R. "Automated System Upgrades Personnel and Payroll Records." *Hospitals, JAHA,* 1 November 1978.

American Hospital Association. *Guidelines: Selection of a Consultant for Health Care Institutions.* Chicago: American Hospital Association, 1975.

Anderson, J.F. "The Hospital Management Company: An Approach to Improved Efficiency." In *Health Care Horizons '77,* New York: Touche Ross & Co., 1977.

Barber, D.W. "Management Reports Can Help Control Costs." *Hospitals, JAHA,* 16 October 1977.

Berman, H. "Mergers and Consolidations: A Solution." *Hospital Administration,* Winter 1971.

Bex, M. "Minicomputers? Maxicomputers? For Hospitals, It's Not Which One But Both." *Hospital Financial Management,* July 1977.

Birky, K.R. "Self-Insuring Workers' Compensation: Does It Really Save?" *Topics in Health Care Financing,* Summer 1977.

Brown, B.L. Jr. *Risk Management for Hospitals: A Practical Approach.* Aspen Systems Corp., Germantown, Md., 1979.

Brown, M. "Multiple-Unit Hospital System Under Single Management." *Hospital and Health Services Administration,* Spring 1976.

Brown, M. "Contract Management." *Hospital and Health Services Administration,* Winter 1976.

"Contract Services." Special Report. *Modern Healthcare,* July 1977.

Cseszko, J.E., ed. *An Examination of Shared Services.* Chicago: American College of Hospital Administrators, 1974.

Danco, W. "Management Effectiveness: Annual Administration Review." *Hospitals, JAHA,* 1 April 1977.

Deignan, P.B. "Food Services Merge to Contain Cost and Enhance Menu." *Hospitals, JAHA,* 1 October 1978.

Dodson, B., Jr., and Latimer, B.W. *Strategies for Clinical Engineering Through Shared Services.* Battle Creek, Mich.: W.K. Kellogg Foundation, 1976.

Findly, M.C., and Jordan, R. "Hospital Leasing Decision Models." *Omega, The International Journal of Management Science,* May-June 1975.

Fischer, F.E. "The Advantages of Hospital Laboratory Consolidation." *College of American Pathologists,* August 1977.

Fitschen, F.A. "Shared Services: Two Viewpoints." *Hospital and Health Services Administration,* Spring 1978.

Gavin, M.P., and Kessler, P.R. "The Development of a Management Audit Program for Hospitals." *Hospital Administration,* Fall 1975.

Goodwin, P. "Bring Planning into the Management Function." *Hospital Financial Management,* June 1976.

Gregory, D.D. "A Hospital Self-Insurance Program: Employee Medical Benefits." *Health Care Management Review,* Spring 1979.

Guest, J., et al. "Computerized Appointment System Matches People, Places, Times." *Southern Hospital,* January-February 1979.

Guy, A.P. "Six Leasing Considerations." *Hospital Financial Management,* June 1976.

Halonen, R.J., and Becker, F. "Benefits of Self Insured Hospitalization Programs." *Hospital Progress,* May 1979.

Henry, J.B. "Finding the True Cost of a True Lease." *Hospital Financial Management,* December 1976.

Hepner, J.O. *Health Planning for Emerging Multihospital Systems.* St. Louis: C.V. Mosby Co., 1978.

Hoesing, S. "Computers and the Health Care Industry." *Dimensions in Health Service,* February 1979.

Johnson, E.A. "What Are the Elements of a Good Internal Management Audit?" *Medical Group Management,* January-February 1978.

Kantowitz, P. "Purchase, Repair, or Replace?" *Medical Electronics,* December 1977.

Kucera, W.R., and Ator, N. "Risk Management Alternatives to Commercial Insurance." *Hospital Financial Management,* October 1978.

Lawrence, J.F., and Hursaker, C. "Organizing for Systems Development." *Topics in Health Care Financing,* Summer 1978.

Lipman, A.G., and Madeux, B. "Computer-Based Formulary Service Reduces Costs, Eliminates Confusion." *Hospitals, JAHA,* 1 November 1977.

Makibbin, R.C. "Economics of Scale, Better Performance Often Exaggerated." *Modern Healthcare,* May 1977.

"Management: Combination of Shared and Contract Services Cuts Costs, Expands Options." *Modern Healthcare,* July 1977.

Maryland Hospital, Education Institute. *How to Choose and Use Management Consultants—A Hospital Buyer's Guide.* U.S. Department of Commerce, National Technology Information Service #HRP-0015716, 1976.

Mettrick, A. "Cost Savings by Computer." *Hospital Administration in Canada,* May 1978.

Morgan, J.A., and Wozniak, P.R. "Reducing Direct and Indirect Losses: The Hospital Safety Program." *Hospital Progress,* November 1977.

Newhouse, J.P. *Health Care Cost Sharing and Cost Containment.* Publ. No. P-5615. Santa Monica: Rand Corp., 1976.

O'Connor, T.J., and Efurd, N. "System Predicts Patient Census Forecasts Staffing Needs, Costs." *Hospitals, JAHA,* 16 March 1978.

Portnoy, S. "The Swelling Tide: Services and Management in Systems." *Hospitals, JAHA,* 1 April 1977.

Prowse, W.J. "Systems Planning for Hospitals." In *Health Care Horizons.* New York: Touche Ross & Co., 1978.

Purvis, G.P. "How Time Management Got Me Under Control." *Hospital Financial Management,* January 1979.

Risk Management Manual, A Guide to Safety, Loss Control, and Malpractice Prevention for Hospitals. Little Rock, Ark.: Federation of American Hospitals, Inc., 1977.

Rubin, H.W., and Staples, S.C. "Risk Management Is More Than Buying Insurance Policies." *Hospital Financial Management,* August 1978.

Sassone, P.G., and Schaffer, W.A. *Cost-Benefit Analysis—A Handbook.* New York: Academic Press, 1978.

Schilling, G. "Cost Containment Through Sharing." *Hospitals JAHA,* 1 January 1975.

Shaffert, T.K., ed. "Hospital Information System." *Topics in Health Care Financing,* Summer 1978.

Smith, H.L., and Besnette, F.H. "Effective Time Management." *Hospital Topics,* January-February 1978.

Smith, R.O. "How to Use Consulting Industrial Engineers." *Hospital Progress,* March 1972.

Starkweather, D.B., and Taylor, S.J. *Health Facility Combinations and Mergers.* Chicago: American College of Hospital Administrators, 1970.

Taylor, E. "Participation in Shared Programs Up Sharply, Survey Discloses." *Hospitals, JAHA,* 16 July 1977.

"Three Hospitals Join to Save $200,000 a Year." *Southern Hospital,* May-June 1977.

U.S. Department of HEW. *Services Shared by Health Organizations: An Annotated Bibliography.* DHEW Pub. No. (HRA) 77-14552 (624 references), March 1977.

Whitman, James T. "Service Firms—Remedy for Cost-Saving Problems?" *Hospital Financial Management,* May 1977.

Whitted, G.S. "Evaluating the Real Cost of EDP Proposals." *Hospital Financial Management,* January 1979.

Wood, J.C. "Risk Management." *Topics in Health Care Financing,* 1975.

Zimmerman, M.E. "Accounting for Leases." *Hospital Financial Management,* June 1979.

42. Operational Auditing Checks Effectiveness

R. NEAL GILBERT

Reprinted from the August 1977 issue of *Hospital Financial Management*, pp. 30-33. Copyright 1977 Hospital Financial Management Association.

Operational auditing today joins accounting control and internal check as a third function of internal control. The operational audit assures the effectiveness of the hospital's operations, and that these are carried out in accordance with management goals and objectives.

The internal auditor performing the operational audit function may be characterized as both a "trouble shooter" and a "fire fighter." The objective must be to deal both with routine performance and problems.

As a representative of administration, the internal auditor investigates and determines whether or not departments have a clear understanding of hospital and departmental objectives, whether they maintain proper records, whether they accurately record, protect and manage cash, inventories, equipment, supplies and personnel, and how they interact with other departments in the hospital. The auditor investigates all departments but concentrates on those that are particularly weak. Where assets are believed to be wasted or used unproductively the auditor suggests to administration how these assets (and perhaps personnel) can be put to better use. The auditor also investigates significant budget variances and works with department heads and physicians to improve departmental performance. The internal auditor's assignments are rotated randomly and is (sic) reviewed by external auditors.

APPROACH

The first step in an operational audit is an objective analysis. The objectives of the individual departments or functions must be defined and compared to see if they coincide with stated hospital policies and objectives. This step is designed to avoid goal displacement. Because of the complexities and diversification of hospital departments, both clinical, such as radiology or pathology, and nonclinical, such as pharmacy or physical therapy, it is not uncommon to find empire building. A department head or chairman may place the goals and objectives of the department above those of the hospital. For instance, a radiologist determined to make the department the most sophisticated and elaborate operation of its kind may undermine the overall institutional goals.

The next step in an operational audit is performance evaluation. The goal is to understand the role of the department. In evaluating operations, the auditor's purpose is not to evaluate the quality or delivery of medical care but rather to appraise and evaluate systems and subsystems within the hospital, and to develop measures of performance so that standards can be defined.

THE AUDIT PLAN

In appraising the operations of the hospital, the internal auditor prepares a detailed audit plan. The following elements should be considered in preparing operational audit plans for some of the more common functions of departments. These are intended as representative types of investigative procedures, and are not a complete listing of the steps the internal auditor takes in carrying out the operational audit function.

Planning and Budgeting

The objective of hospital planning and budgeting is to project, monitor and control the use of the financial resources of the hospital. The objectives of the auditor in reviewing this function are to ascertain that necessary, timely and accurate information is available about the amounts of resources required to fulfill hospital objectives, and that the information is being used properly to ensure that resources are available when needed.

1. Consider the need for planning beyond the immediate year (preferably three years into the future to comply with PL 92-603, Section 234) based on stated goals and assumptions.

2. Evaluate budget performance for previous years to determine if present budget plans are realistic.
3. Determine if the responsibility for budget preparation is properly assigned, and that the budget process allows time for review, adjustment, evaluation and approval.
4. Determine if estimates of revenues and expenditures take into account national and industry-wide economic trends, i.e., changes in the hospital's service area population, changes in medical staff, services offered by competing hospitals and other factors which might affect utilization.
5. Evaluate the manpower planning mechanism to see that projections are made of manpower needs for future years.
6. Evaluate the planning mechanism which projects departmental needs for additional facilities, renovation and modernization of existing facilities, installation of fixed equipment, and disposition of obsolete equipment, and their possible effect on the operating budget.
7. Review the accounting system to determine if timely and accurate cost and revenue data are being made available and utilized properly by administration.
8. Determine if there is periodic financial reporting which allows for the comparison of actual performance (cost, revenue, volume, etc.) with projected amounts.
9. Determine if the responsibility for maintaining budget control has been established on all appropriate levels and that amendments and revisions to the budget are held to a minimum.
10. Review the procedures for analyzing and projecting cash flows.
11. Ascertain that unallowable costs (nonreimbursable by third parties) are clearly identified and segregated in the accounting records and are excluded from revenue projections.

Management Information Systems

The objective of the operational auditor is to evaluate, and where necessary to develop recommendations for improving, the procedures which identify the informational needs of administration, and which provide timely and complete statistical, medical and financial information.

1. Ascertain if there is an organized method of identifying and updating informational needs of administration, the medical staff, the nursing staff, the board of trustees, and external planning and reimbursement agencies.

2. Determine if informational needs are coordinated with long-range planning activities.
3. Ascertain that periodic reviews of the management information system are made to ensure that it meets current needs and that means exist for modifications.
4. Determine if information gathered is necessary, complete, accurate, timely, and not duplicated elsewhere.
5. Evaluate the system which collects, catalogs, stores, retrieves, distributes and disposes of management information to determine if filing, storage and retrieval systems are adequate, economical, efficient and accessible.
6. Evaluate distribution to determine whether management information is distributed where it is needed and actively used where it is distributed. Furthermore, ascertain whether excess information is generated and distributed.

Personnel

The objective is to evaluate personnel needs and to ascertain if personnel are being used most advantageously. The internal auditor insures that each employee is provided with a job description, is properly classified, and is compensated according to that classification. The internal auditor also looks for potentially discriminatory practices.

1. Determine if the job within the hospital has been defined and classified.
2. Determine if a compensation plan exists which includes a scale of rates based upon the responsibilities which are defined in the job description.
3. Ascertain whether fringe benefits are reasonable when compared with other hospitals in the area.
4. Determine if there is a written policy on professional income earned outside the hospital and time spent on nonhospital activities which might impair productivity within the hospital.
5. Evaluate the policy regarding travel, business and educational expenses.
6. Determine if pertinent federal, state and local equal opportunity laws are being followed.
7. Evaluate recruitment, orientation and training procedures.
8. Review the procedures followed to evaluate applications for employment on the basis of merit and qualifications.
9. Evaluate the program for staff development.

Purchasing

To give direction and perspective on the purchasing function, the auditor should first obtain a rough estimate of the annual purchase volume of materials, supplies and services purchased by major category, as well as a summary of annual workload statistics for the purchasing department. This information shows the nature and size of the purchasing operation and can provide clues to opportunities for economies and other improvements.

1. Ascertain whether the purchasing organization has an operating manual which includes an organization chart, job descriptions, purchasing responsibilities, competitive buying, multiple buying sources, commitments and contracts, and conflict of interest.
2. Investigate whether an effective stocking program is used to avoid over- as well as understocking. Overstocking can tie up working capital and result in waste and obsolescence, while understocking can result in excessive requisitioning, purchasing, handling, and delays in patient care.
3. Make certain that the purchase requisitions give all the necessary information to enable the purchasing department to do its job, including adequate technical and performance specifications, sufficient lead time to shop the market, etc.
4. Determine that purchase orders represent complete negotiations with vendors, including prices, shipping, cash and quantity discounts, and delivery arrangements.
5. Investigate policy and practices for major purchase contracts and competitive bids.
6. Review the financial and statistical data available to the purchasing agent for the proper management of the department, such as, commodity buying volumes, vendor buying volumes, and vendor evaluation files.
7. Determine whether purchasing for pharmacy and dietary should be handled by the purchasing department.
8. Review the receiving function to determine if all ordered items are accounted for.

Equipment Procurement and Management

The objective is to determine if equipment and related services needed to carry out planned objectives are obtained on a timely basis and utilized properly.

1. Evaluate written procurement policies to determine if they are compatible with the hospital's capital budgeting system.
2. Review the procedures which enable the departments to evaluate alternative equipment and service suppliers and determine if there is a comparison of cost, quality, delivery, installation and maintenance.
3. Ascertain if there are written procedures for capital requests including requirements for adequate description and specifications, expected utilization, cost-benefit evaluation, and adequate review and approval.
4. Determine if capital requests consider the use of underutilized equipment already on hand elsewhere in the hospital.
5. Determine whether plant and equipment records are kept to provide a description of equipment, cost, location, and depreciation.
6. Determine whether there are procedures to minimize underutilization and explore the possible alternative use or disposition of underutilized equipment.
7. Determine whether there is a system for periodic evaluation of equipment to determine obsolescence, excessive wear, excessive cost of maintenance or lack of further need.
8. Develop a policy for disposal of used and obsolete equipment.

Facilities Management and Health and Safety

The objective is to ensure that hospital facilities are used appropriately and to maximum advantage. The operational audit should also make sure that employees, patients and hospital visitors are provided adequate health protection and freedom from hazards.

1. Ascertain whether there are written policies for the distribution and management of space.
2. Inquire whether definite responsibility for the assignment and utilization of space has been established.
3. Evaluate written policies on health and safety of personnel, patients and visitors.
4. Evaluate the informed-consent policy and determine whether it is being properly administered in diagnostic, treatment and therapy areas.
5. Review waste management policies with special emphasis on areas which produce or come in contact with contaminated or radioactive waste materials.
6. Evaluate the program of insurance coverage with the hospital's insurance agent for completeness and replacement value coverage.

7. Determine whether the hospital is operating in accordance with federal, state and local regulations concerning health, safety and pollution control.
8. Evaluate the security system to ensure that patients, personnel, facilities and other assets are protected against existing and potential hazards.

RECOMMENDATIONS

Upon completion of an operational audit, the auditor should prepare a detailed written report documenting existing and potential problems, together with recommendations to improve the operations.

In presenting recommendations to management, the internal auditor should wherever feasible estimate the dollar effect of savings, economies or increased revenues. These estimates should be made in conjunction with the department heads who should be interested in potential improvements and helpful in developing the necessary information to implement the recommended changes.

Recommendations should be presented to administrative personnel who will be responsible for implementing those changes deemed appropriate under existing constraints. The auditor may assist in the implementation phase if such participation is considered necessary by administration. The succeeding audit should include a follow-up report on the extent to which the recommendations have been implemented.

SUMMARY

Operational auditing is a comparatively new technique in which the internal auditor evaluates the effectiveness of operating procedures and controls. It permits administration to evaluate performance based on direct observations by an independent and impartial analyst. A well trained internal auditor can detect unnecessary activities, inefficiencies and deficiencies. Correcting these can result in either savings of time and resources or increased productivity and effectiveness. The internal audit function can also improve the quality of health care by reducing the possibility of breakdowns in the delivery system.

In performing operational audits, administration's objectives are analyzed, the means for their attainment are evaluated, and recommendations to improve the system are made. The operational audit is a continuing process with periodic review and feedback. As a "trouble shooter" and a "fire fighter'' the operational auditor can be a most effective arm of administration.

The health care industry should not only continue to follow the initiative of the for profit segment of the economy in operational auditing, but should also develop new ways to utilize this resource.

43. Principles and Techniques of Time Management

ROBERT E. SCOTT

Reprinted from *Hospital Progress,* May 1978, pp. 56–58, 90, by permission of Edward J. Pollock, Publisher. © 1978.

Time is a commodity that cannot be bought, sold, or borrowed. Time is a dominant factor in all relationships both in business and in private life.

The increase of cooperative efforts, as well as coordinated efforts or processes, depends upon temporal coordination, or timing. The order in which events are accomplished is of major importance. Ironically, the right things are usually done, but often in the wrong order.

Many factors can influence time management, both positively and negatively. Dissatisfaction with a job, boredom, or dissatisfaction with a superior can have such negative effects on time utilization as high rates of absenteeism, worker turnover, or tardiness. All of these effects could cause problems in the overall management of time.

Many interesting statements have been made about time and time management. Benjamin Franklin once said, "To love life is to love time, since time is the stuff of which life is made." Individuals' personal characteristics and values greatly influence how they use time. More important, efficient management of time is based on respect for it.

Demands are put on a manager's time from every level: from superiors, from the organization, from subordinates, and from self. In order to function effectively, managers should set aside a specific period each day for planning. It is essential that managers plan not only for the daily or weekly routine but also for the unpredictable, for the "periodic known" (that which one knows will happen but does not know when), and for emergencies.

According to R. Alec Mackenzie,[1] the problem is not so much how much time people have but, rather, how they use it. The key to effective time utilization is planning. The manager must first establish the objectives for the job or the task at hand. This can save both time and money.

When organizing time, the manager must develop a list of those goals which are most important. This should include both personal and professional objectives, including specific goals that concern family, salary, leisure, business achievement, and personal development. This list should be ranked in order of importance. Hence, a person should budget time in proportion to goal priority.

C.J. Hegarty suggests that the "glaring discrepancies between goal importance and the time invested are often the chief source of inefficiency. Work can be less often something you must do and more often something you want to do, if you...get organized."[2] Effective, results-oriented people manage their time with care. Those individuals whose time management is not goal-oriented may become quite good at getting either the wrong things done or the right things done in the wrong order.

Budgeting time combines time management with management by objectives. By setting aside specific blocks of time for each objective, one can accomplish both long-range and short-range goals. Since most short-term jobs present common time problems, proper sequencing of these activities is important to the success of long-term goals.

COMMUNICATIONS VITAL TO TIME MANAGEMENT

The manager should recognize that communications are essential for time to be managed effectively and for objectives to be met. Communications should promote understanding, which unifies efforts and reduces confusion and wasted time and motion. A manager should listen to problems at an early stage and handle them before a major crisis develops. Different communication methods are appropriate for different objectives. In planning and managing communications, the manager should consider the type of response required and also who needs the information. Whatever communication method an individual chooses, timing is important.

The following suggestions will ensure more efficient communications:

1. Using a dictating machine is more efficient than dictating to a secretary. Attend to incoming mail immediately. Equally important, handle mail only once and avoid a "pending" file.
2. Economy of words conserves time and improves understanding. A manager who cuts down on unnecessary written reports can save a

great deal of time. Memoranda or letters promote the organization of ideas. Also, the written word usually facilitates the attention of ideas. This saves time, avoiding recommunication. Another time-saver is communicating directly. "Beating around the bush" wastes time. People should also avoid wasting time making excuses or explaining failures. Rather, they should concentrate on avoiding past mistakes.

3. The telephone is an efficient communications tool if a rapid response is required or if the message is brief. The caller should select a time that is convenient for the listener. All telephone calls should be grouped into one time period so that the telephone will not become a time-interrupter. Before making telephone calls, a manager should have prewritten notes to aid in organizing the conversation and, thus, in achieving the best results.

4. Face-to-face communication is the most common and, without question, generally the best. Time can be saved if the conversation can be kept under control and if thoughts do not drift from one subject to another.[3]

5. Staff meetings can be either beneficial or detrimental to time management and efficiency. For maximum benefit, staff meetings should be held to a minimum, both in occurrence and in duration. To avoid confusion and additional time expenditure, the subjects to be discussed must be kept to a minimum, and each subject must be discussed as a separate and distinct entity. To maximize the time spent, attention must be directed to the identification of the problem, its causes, and possible solutions.

6. Charting problems or actions can help maximize the use of time by limiting the number of problems and visibly suggesting sequential steps for handling the situation. It also helps eliminate extraneous details.

7. Group meetings must be planned carefully so that time is not wasted. First, the manager must clearly state the purpose of the meeting. Planned attendance is important because nonessential people waste time. But, conversely, if the necessary persons are not present, communications will have to be duplicated, resulting in more wasted time. Small meetings are generally more efficient than large meetings, since better, more direct communications usually take place. The following guidelines for conducting meetings aid in efficient time utilization: (1) Begin the meeting on time and keep it on schedule. Otherwise, a chain of delays will be triggered. (2) Stick to the subject of the meeting and avoid unnecessary discussion. Minimize excessive talking. (3) Avoid controversy. Compromise facilitates action, while controversy impedes it. Friction, arguments, and hostility interfere with

thinking and good judgment, and they drain energy. Tension usually produces physical and mental fatigue. (4) Set a definite time limit for the meeting. Scheduling meetings right before lunch or late in the day usually encourages efficient use of time. For group meetings, time is better utilized if carefully written memos are sent out in advance. This provides important background information for discussion and informs subordinates about what kind of behavior, performance, and conclusions are desired as a result of the meeting.

Most professional people are under great time pressure, and their success is often measured by how much they can get done in a specified time period. While this is true, it has also been shown that very few supervisors and managers know how they really spend their time.[4] One of the major drawbacks to successful time management is the lack of concrete data about an individual's specific situation. Only when the manager has specific, reliable, and valid information about how time is actually being spent by individuals and groups can he or she direct appropriate actions for optimal productivity.

Solving time management problems involves the utilization of certain basic principles. Usually, successful managers use a combination of principles and techniques to develop the most effective strategy for their particular situations.

A number of tools are helpful in analyzing how time is used. The daily time log or diary is perhaps the most commonly used technique,[5] although it can be cumbersome and difficult to analyze unless specific activities can be categorized. That, however, is why the time log is an effective tool; it forces the user to identify habits and patterns and thus assess the necessity of changes. Simply recording what you are doing allows you to think about what you are doing. This act by itself can stimulate change.

After you collect the data, summarize it in categories for analysis: planning; controlling; problem solving; communicating. An alternate way of analyzing the data is categorizing the time spent in meetings, routine work, creative work, and emergencies. This technique yields objective, reliable data and can serve as a powerful catalyst for improving individual and group effectiveness.

In analyzing your log or diary, locate the sources and frequencies of interruptions. Management has been defined as "a series of interruptions, interrupted by other interruptions."[6] A manager must control interruptions. Through careful arrangement and control of activities the manager can minimize the number, impact, and duration of his or her interruptions. Although a manager should be accessible to subordinates, such access should be limited except in the case of emergencies because one hour of concentrated effort is worth more than two hours in 10 or 15 minute segments. Interruptions are often the result of poor communications. If interruptions cannot be avoided, the manager may find it necessary to leave the normal job environment during at least a period of the work day.

Managers should selectively ignore nonessential information. Only those things which are significant deviations from actual planned performance should be reported to the responsible executive. Research has shown that people are most productive when they work in blocks of uninterrupted time. In organizing time, the individual also needs a balance in activities.

In analyzing your daily time log, give special attention to two basic functions: managing and operating. Operating is doing things yourself, while managing is achieving objectives or results through others. Intelligent use of time requires that you use the time of others as effectively as you use your own. The allocation of time between these two functions varies with the level of management. As managers go up the management ladder, less time should be spent operating and more time should be devoted to managing. Chief executives should spend at least 75 percent managing. The firstline manager should be managing at least 40 percent of the time.

Planning is an essential tool in managing time. "Every hour spent in effective planning saves three to four hours in execution and gets better results."' More effective results occur through purposeful pursuit than by chance. Anticipatory action is usually more effective than remedial action.

After you list your objectives in priority sequence, you are ready to begin scheduling. The first step in scheduling is to make a realistic estimate of the time required for a particular task. Second, realistic deadlines must be set that allow both for the unexpected and for interruptions. When actually scheduling time segments, plan to spend time in significant amounts. In addition, schedule two or three projects concurrently so that you can work on one project while waiting for another.

MORE TIPS AND TOOLS

A person must guard against being distracted by trivia and by conflicting demands. The deadlines that are set must be met. This requires self-discipline. Adhering to them helps the manager overcome indecision and procrastination. Both priorities and established schedules must be reviewed periodically and revised when necessary.

It is a mistake to begin working on petty chores with the idea of working up to bigger projects. Begin with the most important task and work down. Also, check to determine whether you are spending time proportionately with various people in the organization. This time should be spent in productive activities, however, not meaningless interruptions in the form of "good relations" pleasantries.

Individuals have different rhythms that dictate at which times they are most efficient or effective. Effective persons organize time in order to handle the hardest tasks at their peak, or best, hour.

Management is constantly juggling the urgent and the important. One cannot ignore long-term consequences for the pressures of the moment. Managers must determine the difference between the urgent and the important. Urgency engulfs the supervisor, and yet the most urgent task is rarely the most important.

Supervisors or managers must not only be efficient, they must also be result-oriented. The manager should begin by completing the first task efficiently, on time, and with the intended consequences. This activity leads to effectiveness as well as efficiency.

Since the manager's day is mostly unstructured, wise judgment must be used in matching time with tasks. There is a difference between being busy and being productive. The effort expended should be merely a means and not an end in itself. The manager should focus on the desired results.

Individuals cannot control time; they can, however, control their behavior within time spans. Time management requires a change in habits and attitudes. There is often a discrepancy between what one does and what one should do. Time management is largely a matter of self-discipline.

The basis for an individual's value to a company is in productive time rather than total elapsed "working" time. Individuals should recognize the existence of a time management problem if they find themselves in any of the following situations: (1) wishing for more time; (2) constantly working long hours; (3) continually "fighting fires"; (4) wanting to make a larger contribution but unable to get started.

IMPORTANCE OF DELEGATING TASKS

Managers at every level not only have to manage their time in order to complete given tasks but also have to help others manage theirs through the assignment of specific tasks. Delegation of responsibility is essential to time management and to any organization. Delegation is the ability to achieve objectives through others. James T. McCay says that "if one cannot delegate, he cannot manage."[8] He also indicates that "authority for decision-making should be delegated to the lowest level possible, consistent with good judgment and available facts." While delegation is essential, it is one of the most difficult functions of management. Delegating minimizes routine and avoids delay. For maximum time management and efficiency, it is important that the manager delegate the right tasks. When delegating, the manager should explain to subordinates the scope of their authority so that they will not be inhibited or find it necessary to continually ask questions. Subordinates should be kept apprised of relevant developments so that they will not have to waste time by doing the job again. Delegation of responsibility promotes efficiency by avoiding overwork by managers and underutilization of subordinates.

Managers can also manage time better if they delegate more responsibility to secretaries or subordinates. One can conserve time by delegating such tasks as answering routine correspondence, controlling the telephone, and scheduling appointments. Managers should always let their secretaries know where they can be reached.

A manager's job is made up of routine work and creative work. The routine responsibilities must be performed to keep the hospital operating day to day, but the creative work determines a manager's contribution to the development of a unit or an enterprise. It is difficult for managers to find enough uninterrupted time to spend on creative work. For maximum utilization of time, an individual should work in pleasant, conducive surroundings, which will facilitate the accomplishment of objectives.

Time management experts have developed and tested many suggestions for various situations. One such suggestion deals with personal organization. Individuals should develop a habit of using "waiting" or idle time for reading and writing. Reading, especially, poses problems for the manager, since the quantity of reading materials can be overwhelming. The manager should continually try to improve reading speed, to read purposefully, and to decide what is important and what is irrelevant. Much of the manager's reading can be delegated to assistants who read the current literature, underline the important facts, and thus facilitate reading and skimming for the manager and others who read the same material.

Desk organization is a useful tool for time management. The desk top should only contain materials that are currently being used. Persons should keep all their files orderly and up to date and avoid using drawer space for "dead" storage. Anything that is not beneficial or usable should be thrown away. Keep a clean and neat desk. Documents and papers can get lost on a cluttered desk, and searching for misplaced items wastes time. Clutter will tend to create tension and frustration, a feeling of being disorganized and "snowed under."

Individuals should avoid incompletion, since it takes extra time to continually restart. Conversely, overcompletion should be avoided too. A job should not be stretched out beyond that which is necessary.

Individuals should work on tasks that have real potential. They should invest their time and effort in growing aspects of their organization or profession, and should guard against overemphasizing the parts of their job that they know best.

Time management is an essential tool used by every successful business person today. Improving the use of time is one of the best ways to improve managerial effectiveness. The return on invested time should be as valuable as the return on invested money. It is said that time is a valuable resource. Unless it is managed well, nothing else can be done well. After all, if you cannot manage your time, who can?

NOTES

1. See R. Alec Mackenzie, "Toward a Personalized Time Management Strategy," *Management Review,* February 1974, pp. 10–15.

2. Christopher J. Hegarty, "Get Yourself Organized," *Management Review,* September 1976, p. 56.

3. Alan Lakein, *How To Get Control of Your Time and Your Life,* New American Library, New York City, 1974.

4. John H. Jackson and Lawrence L. Steinmetz, "Time-Saving Techniques," *Supervisory Manager,* June 1972, pp. 31–34.

5. For an excellent example of a simple, workable time log, see Edwin C. Bliss, *Getting Things Done: The ABC's of Time Management,* Scribner, New York City, 1976, pp. 105–109.

6. Norman Hill, "Where Does Your Day Go?" *Supervisory Management,* May 1976, p. 25.

7. R. Alec Mackenzie, *New Time Management and Methods,* Dartwell Corporation, Chicago, 1975, p. 19.

8. James T. McCay, *The Management of Time,* Prentice Hall, Englewood Cliffs, NJ, 1959, p. 89.

44. The Computer and Hospital Productivity

PAUL GRAY

Reprinted with permission from *Topics in Health Care Financing,*
Winter 1977, pp. 41–46.

During the last decade, it has been a tenet of faith that the computer will improve hospital productivity. Hospital administrators, operations researchers, industrial engineers and computer scientists have all touted the computer as a source of productivity gains. Although there has been much talk about the success of computers, and numerous installations have been justified on the basis of anticipated productivity gains, little hard evidence exists proving or disproving their effectiveness. Hospitals are a labor-intensive service industry in which productivity is difficult to measure. The usual approach to increasing productivity is either to invest in equipment or to increase the efficiency of personnel.[1] To earn its keep, the computer must be able to displace cost and earn revenue which in total is larger than the computer investment.

USES OF THE COMPUTER

Computers are used in hospitals at three levels: administrative data processing, clinical data processing and medical information systems. At the first level, the role of the computer is the same in the hospital as in any business. It is used for billing, accounts receivable, payroll, accounts payable, general ledger and similar functions concerned with cash flow. It is also used for such hospital-specific counting functions as census, data collection and admission records. At this level, too, fall routine uses such as reporting laboratory data; maintaining inventory records on supplies, drugs and equipment; and staff scheduling. Some systems also provide menu planning, operating room scheduling and message services.

Clinical Data Processing

At the clinical data processing level, complete patient medical records are maintained during a patient's hospital stay. Such systems may also provide specialized services to the clinical laboratory, radiology, nursing stations and pharmacy. Typically, such systems provide immediate inquiry response by operating in "real time," and they provide "on-line" medical information which can be used in decision making in administering both the individual patient's hospital stay and the overall hospital. (*Real time* refers to computer operations which keep up with the current situation so as to provide immediate response. *On-line* implies the capability of obtaining such real-time information by interrogating the computer through a terminal that provides information in human-readable form.)

Medical Information Systems

The third level, a complete medical information system, although much talked about, does not really exist at present. Such systems would provide management information that can be used in decision making in administering both the individual patient's hospital stay and the overall hospital. (Hospitals are not unique in this respect; very few businesses have information systems which are really being used in ongoing decision making.)

The funds being allocated to information in hospitals are substantial. Ball estimates that United States hospitals spend between $7 and $10 billion annually (between one-quarter and one-third of total hospital budgets) to acquire and communicate information.[2] About one-half the amount is being spent on functions which could be automated through the use of computers.

An AHA study of 5,912 hospitals quoted by Ball indicates that more than 60 percent of the hospitals use computers in some form, either at Level 1 alone or at Levels 1 and 2 combined.[3]

COMPUTER SYSTEMS IN HOSPITALS

From the computer professional's point of view, hospital applications are a growth industry. Almost every conceivable arrangement for obtaining computer services is being used by hospitals. Only about one-quarter of the hospitals surveyed by AHA have their own computers. In some cases, these are completely programmed and operated by the hospitals. In other cases, either programming or the entire operation is contracted out. A number of firms provide facilities management for hospitals in which they provide a complete turnkey operation for a fee. The rest of the hospitals obtain their computer services on the outside through organizations specializing in providing data processing for hospitals through computer service bureaus, by sharing a computer with another hospital, or by using one of the time-sharing services that are commercially available.

Problems

They key problem in computer use is reliability. Particularly in those hospitals working at Level 2, the amount of time when the computer system is unavailable (due to breakdown or due to routine maintenance) must be minimal. In order to minimize problems, most computer systems either include a backup for the central computer, or they operate as a collection of minicomputers (small-scale computer systems that are lower in cost and in capability than full-scale machines) which share the load and can withstand failure of individual units.[4]

Costs

Determining the cost of computers is relatively straightforward. A typical balance sheet of computer costs, assuming that the computer (or computer time) is rented, is shown in Table 5-1. A typical balance sheet of benefits is presented in Table 5-2.

Table 5-1 Balance Sheet of Computer-Based Expenses

Annual Computer Expense:
    Equipment rental $_____
    Computer program   _____
    Program development   _____
    Operating (including space,
        power, keypunching, etc.)   _____
        Total Cost $_____

Table 5-2 Balance Sheet of Computer-Based Savings

Annual Cost Savings:

Net reduction in personnel	$_____
Increased employee productivity	_____
Recovery of lost charges	_____
Reduction of costs in special forms	_____
Long-term personnel savings (annualized)	_____
Total Savings	$_____

Benefits

Before discussing the nature of the savings, it is important to point out that unless the anticipated savings exceed the anticipated costs (and these figures have been estimated realistically, particularly on the savings side), a computer-based system should not be installed. Personnel savings are assessed in two ways: (1) immediate reductions in personnel because clerical positions are eliminated and (2) elimination of the need for hiring additional clerks in future years to cope with the increasing paperwork required for government, insurance companies and others.

Increases in employee productivity can come from several sources, among them: an increase in the number of revenue-producing services performed by the employee (e.g., in lab work), an increase in the number of patients cared for by an employee (e.g., in nursing), and a reduction in errors and consequent rework of errors such as in executing physicians' orders.

These increases have to be over and above those resulting from the consolidation of work among fewer employees, and they imply that the hospital will have to serve more patients.

Recovery of lost charges implies that the computer will provide more accurate recordkeeping which will result in improved billing and collection, as well as reduced cycle times on accounts receivable. Special forms for recordkeeping can be a major cost item in many operations.

WHAT LITERATURE SHOWS ON PRODUCTIVITY

The cost/benefit balance depends critically on the productivity gains that are achieved. To determine what is known about these gains in quantitative terms, articles from the following literature (from 1971 to mid-1977) were surveyed: hospital administrative and clinical literature, operations research and industrial engineering literature, and computer literature.

Reduction in Error, Nursing Requirements

The literature was quite disappointing. Although there are many articles that deal with hospital computer installations, and although some claim substantial savings, only one solid scientific study was found which attempted to evaluate productivity gains resulting from the introduction of computers. The paper described the changes that resulted from installing a ward information system on a medical floor at Johns Hopkins Hospital.[5] In this evaluation, where the focus was on the effects of the computer system on patient care by nurses, the costs, benefits and incremental expenditures of the system were measured. The results indicated that errors in carrying out physicians' orders were significantly reduced, that nurse time was being used more efficiently, that nursing requirements could be reduced, and that patient loads could be increased without increases in staff.

Productivity Gains

Many papers described the computer-based systems used and claimed benefits without substantiating them in detail. Here are some typical claims:

- Deaconess Hospital in Evansville, Indiana, reduced its personnel by 23, increased operating revenues by $180,000 and reduced its accounts receivable turnaround time by 16 days.[6,7,8]
- Canyon General Hospital in Anaheim, California, which has used a multiple minicomputer system since it opened, claims to use 40 fewer full-time people than other proprietary hospitals of similar size in Southern California.[9,10]
- Texas Institute of Rehabilitation and Research, a small 56-bed hospital, found that "both users and administration are satisfied that this hospital information system has resulted in more rapid patient recovery combined with a decrease in overall service costs." However, no data on magnitude of the savings were given.[11]

These articles gave ample description of how hospital computer systems are designed, very few indications of what the systems cost, and almost no quantitative discussions of the benefits achieved. (Our own search revealed a peak of publications on hospital computer systems between 1972 and

1974. Since that time, the number of related publications has diminished substantially.)

PAST, PRESENT AND FUTURE

The application of computers in hospitals has followed the classic path of technological innovation: replacement, systematic application and innovation. The automobile is a good analogy. The original cars were indeed horseless carriages, looking like the horse-drawn vehicle and performing only marginally better than them, if they worked at all. Then, over a period of decades new systems came into being involving not only the car but the roads on which they drove and the support systems available for them. Eventually, the car led to major changes in the way society lives, with suburbanization and other significant alterations in lifestyles.

The early years of computers in hospitals were, similarly, a period of using the computer to replace the recordkeeper. At present, we are reaching the stage where entire hospital systems (such as those at Canyon Hospital, mentioned earlier) are designed and installed at the same time the hospital is built. In the future, as physicians, nurses, administrators and others involved in hospitals become more able to work in a computer environment, we can anticipate that new, innovative uses will come about.

Innovative Systems

Some of these innovative systems are currently in development. For example, a team at George Washington University School of Medicine and Dentistry under Dr. Martin Rubin has been working on improving the patient/sample/physicians' orders linkages. Recognizing that a significant fraction of lab reports and physicians' orders for patients are incorrectly associated with patients, they have been working on a computer-based system that will be simple to operate and that will significantly reduce error rates. Their concept, based on the use of optically readable codes similar to the product codes being used on groceries, results in close integration between the patient and the information about the patient stored in the computer. Reduction in error rates is, of course, one of the classic ways of improving productivity.

Looking Forward to Greater Use of Computers

At present, for most hospitals, the computer is an integral part of their day-to-day operations. In many cases, its use has probably led to greater productivity than could be achieved without it. We say "probably" because the literature on scientific evaluation of computer productivity in hospitals is, to put it charitably, quite sparse. As both hospital people and computer people become more experienced (and more comfortable) with the use of computers in hospitals, we can look forward to innovations in which the long-touted potential of the computer for productivity improvement will become a reality.

Note: The author acknowledges Ronnie Chan for his invaluable help in gathering and organizing the literature on computers and health care productivity.

REFERENCES

1. Riggs, J.L. *Production Systems: Planning Analysis and Control* (2nd ed., New York, N.Y.: John Wiley & Sons, Inc. 1976).

2. Dall, M.J. "Computers: Prescription for Hospital Ills." *Datamation*, Vol. 21, No. 9 (September 1975) p. 50-51.

3. *Ibid.*

4. Carren, D.M. "Multiple Minis for Information Management." *Datamation*, Vol. 21, No. 9 (September 1975) p. 54-58.

5. Simborg, D.W., *et al.* "Ward Information-Management Systems—an Evaluation." *Computers and Biomedical Research*, Vol. 5 (1972) p. 484-497.

6. Ferberder, C.J. "A Standardized Solution for Hospital Systems." *Datamation*, Vol. 21, No. 9 (September 1975) p. 52-53.

7. Valentino, H.N. "Real Time HIS Has Medical Uses." *Hospitals, J.A.H.A.*, Vol. 48 (November 16, 1974) p. 54-58.

8. Fireworker, R.B. "Computerized Health Care Systems." *Journal of Systems Management*, Vol. 27, No.8 (August 1976) p. 28-33.

9. Carren. "Multiple Minis."

10. Fireworker. "Computerized Health."

11. *Ibid.*

SUGGESTED READINGS

Collen, M.F. (ed.) *Hospital Computer Systems* (New York, N.Y.: John Wiley & Sons, Inc. 1974).

Petters, J.R. *et al. Comprehensive Hospital Computer Applications Program* (National Technical Information Service Report PB-211 690, Rockledge, Fla.: Wuesthoff Memorial Hospital 1972).

45. Information Systems: In the Cost Containment Battle

STEPHEN VEAZIE

Reprinted, with permission, from *Hospitals, Journal of the American Hospital Association,* vol. 52, no. 7, April 1, 1978, pp. 105–112.

While the entertainment industry was depicting man's use of computer technology to create a multimillion dollar bionic family complete with dog, and pit robots and space ships in intergalactic battles, the health care industry was depicting the use of computer technology in an environment completely dominated by efforts to contain costs. These efforts have had a stifling effect on new developments in the health care field's use of computer science. This is an unfortunate situation when one considers the potential benefits that computer science could afford hospitals.

The expense of information handling in hospitals has been estimated as high as more than 40 percent of any hospital's total expenses. Typically, *the data processing budget has been approximately 2 percent of the total budget of most hospitals.* Because computer technology can improve the handling or processing of information, the potential for improvement in this area of hospital operations is significant.

Past efforts have shown that computer systems can be used for information processing in all hospital departments or functional areas. When a hospital has a high occupancy rate, the hospital can greatly benefit by keeping the housekeeping department automatically informed of admissions, discharges, and transfers (ADT). Likewise, the admitting department, nurses' stations, and other departments can benefit by having the housekeeping department enter into the system information on bed status. The relatively simple ADT application also can significantly reduce the number of wasted meals. The surgical suite can use computer systems for more complicated tasks (such as, scheduling, on-line monitoring of vital signs, and calculating blood and fluid mixture). In addition, this information can be made available to the attending physician by locating a computer terminal in the doctor's lounge.

Refinements of computer technology generated less expensive, more powerful hardware; more effective, easier to understand software; and improved computer operations management techniques. Hospitals can now acquire minicomputers that can be programmed in high-level languages that more closely resemble the spoken language, and management can now exert control over the previously mysterious, "black-box" computer operations. With increased emphasis on cost-justification, hospitals, however, must now be cautious of high expenditures that can be incurred with the acquisition of computer systems. The federal government has almost created a "Catch-22" situation by requiring more information from hospitals while decreasing support for development of computer systems in the health care industry. Nevertheless, many hospitals are either upgrading existing systems or implementing commercially available systems as confidence in the use of the systems increases.

The use of computer systems for cost containment were cited in a report published by the American Hospital Association in September 1977.[1] This report contained a list of cost containment projects undertaken by a sample of hospitals across the country. Sixteen specific examples of cost savings through the use of computer systems were listed. Twelve of these projects reported a total savings of approximately $1,224,600 per year. These savings were attributed to computer projects that ranged from computerized materials management to automated energy control systems. St. Thomas Hospital, Akron, OH, saved $70,000 and eliminated four clerical positions by updating its data processing capabilities in 1974, which included accounts receivable billings, direct-entry Medicaid billing, payroll, statistical data, and many other programs.[1] The Hospital Data Center of Virginia, a not-for-profit shared system center, has saved its 24 members a total of $8 million since 1966. The 16 projects in which data processing was used are indicative of hospital management's growing awareness that computer systems can play a vital role in the cost containment efforts of this nation's hospitals.

According to Hodge, "Nationwide, the cost reduction is estimated to be as much as $1.5 billion annually if cost-effective information systems were installed in every hospital with 200 or more beds. In fact, computer technology could be the single most important cost-cutting tool available to American hospitals today."[2] Hodge maintains that the *health care industry is labor-intensive and that major cost savings can result in the replacement of labor tied to information handling, with a capital equipment investment in hospital or medical information systems.* He also supports the idea that these systems are an example of cost-lowering technology as opposed to cost-increasing technology. Whereas technology (such as CT scanners) "raises the benefits of expensive care," cost-lowering technology "raises the benefits of inexpensive care." Inexpensive care is characterized by the more routine activities, such as admitting patients and ordering drugs, tests, and supplies. Hodge cites one source *that estimated that a 300-bed hospital might be able to obtain a net savings of $10 per patient day if it had a hospital or medical information system in operation.* Some preliminary studies have quoted net cost savings ranging from $3 to $9 per patient day. These findings have yet to be documented, but the possibility that they are true, at least partially, is resulting in the increasing acquisition of information systems.

INFORMATION SYSTEMS DEFINED

A hospital information system must be designed to facilitate the day-to-day operations of the hospital, and the systems must have, at a minimum, a financial module, an on-line ADT module, and terminals on the nurses' stations that are used to communicate to ancillary departments such as the laboratory and pharmacy, and provide automatic charge collection. On the other hand, a medical information system is one that does more than merely store and display medical data; it actually performs calculations with the data to produce medical interpretations, such as differential diagnoses or recommended therapeutic procedures. However, as these systems are redefined, the two types of systems will begin to merge.[3]

Even with this definition of hospital information systems, the levels or classifications of the systems differ, ranging from the relatively simple message switching and data collection systems to the relatively complex systems explained in detail by Hodge. Large mainframe computers frequently are the basis of the latter systems; many of the former systems are minicomputer-based. These message switching and data collection systems have been developed to communicate in various ways with financial systems. This communication feature represents a trend toward the combination of computer and communication technologies.

In the health care industry, efforts to contain costs and the rise in multi-institutional arrangements are contributing to resource sharing. In the computer industry, the development of mini- and micro-computers, teleprocessing, and networking are making the distribution of computer processing power quite attractive. In the past, terminals with almost no computing capability were connected to large, mainframe computers via various types of communication lines. According to Sahin, "The terminal is, however, increasingly acquiring processing capabilities, becoming more like a mini/microcomputer; time sharing is evolving into resource sharing, that is, into computer communication networks."[4] An example of this occurrence is the system that has been developed by the Fairview Community Hospitals in Minneapolis. At present, the participating hospitals are "linked to the other institutions...via a network of leased telephone lines and...intelligent terminals, which [are] minicomputer[s]..." with limited computing power. As the technology evolves, it is quite likely that these terminals will acquire more and more processing power. Even now, this system, "...through economies of scale, improves the quality of information services at a consistently low price to patients..."[5] Ultimately, computer technology might evolve to the point that, "if mini- and microcomputers rapidly diffuse into households as expected, connecting the household computer to the telemedicine nets may provide a greater electronic dispensation of medical care than is currently done over the telephones. As such, the widespread unavailability of house calls might be partly compensated for."[4]

CHANGING ATTITUDES

Applications of computer science in the art of medicine, such as the medical information systems as previously defined, still remain primarily within the research domain, but signs of changing attitudes among medical professionals are appearing. The medical profession has been somewhat slow in its acceptance of the use of automation to improve the practice of medicine. Increasing interest in automation, however, was highly visible at an international conference, MEDINFO 77, that was held during August 1977 in Toronto.[6]

This change in attitude also is apparent in the writings of a broad cross-section of the physician population. Fischer-Pap recognizes the problems as well as the benefits of computer technology, but believes that the benefits far outweigh the problems. "I am sure, for every human heartbeat in an American hospital, we will continue to hear a tic-tac, a click, a whirr, a clap or a schirr (of computers) in the decade to come."[7] Likewise, Fischer writes, "The most significant event in the Twentieth Century is the Computer Revolution.... By the greatest good luck, for medicine, the computer revolution is capable of solving the four major problems which now threaten the American Medical Systems.... Through all of these four problems run a common theme: The cost of medical care."[8]

The importance of this positive shift in attitude toward computer technology lies in the fact that the medical profession plays a key role in the successful use of computer science in health care delivery. In the past, the collaboration of the medical profession in the advancement of computer science either had not been sought or it had not been given. Failures in the design, development, and implementation of information systems were subsequently incurred because of the medical profession's disapprovement of the systems. According to Barnett, this will not continue to happen "...if there is a vigorous professional collaboration in the design and implementation of a hospital-wide information system, the system will provide probably the best means for effectively meeting the hospital's expanding needs for communications, storage, and retrieval of medical information."[9]

Just as the medical profession's interest in computer systems has been growing, hospital administrators also are becoming more active in the use of computer science. Hospital administrators have had considerable experience with computerized business office applications and are now looking seriously at more innovative applications. With the introduction of more imaginative applications, administrators' conception of what has been typically called data processing is changing to the broader concept of information systems.

MIS (Management Information Systems)

One of the most promising areas of investigation is the development of management information systems. These systems have been described as an enhancement of basic data processing systems "...by adding a simple data base, retrieval capabilities, and at least one or two planning or decision models."[9] Management information systems are much more instrumental in management decision support than the previous data processing systems. As Davis states, "Information and its use in the decision-making process is not only a prerequisite but is in general the prerequisite for good institutional management in the health care field."[10] Barker, who has effectively developed and used a management information system to contain cost, echoes this sentiment stating, "The success of any cost management program lies in its ability to identify costs, to analyze their potential for control, and to produce management information so that control may be exercised when possible."[11] To successfully develop and operate the types of systems that these two top managers described, it is necessary to move data processing from under the traditional control of the financial director to reporting more directly to the administrator. As Buck states, "Electronic data processing has much to offer hospitals when the chief executive officer (CEO) sees that it is properly managed."[12] Because these new systems cut across organizational boundaries, the CEO must assume responsibility for the development of information systems.

As information flow between departments or functional areas is heightened and improved, organizational changes occur. For example, the *medical records departments and the business offices of many hospitals have begun to work more closely together than ever before. Integration of financial information and medical record information is helpful for cost identification and is mandated by utilization review and PSRO regulations.* As Smith states, *"Computer department personnel must take the data that comes from the business office and medical records and produce information which is useable by both departments."*[13] *Tucker describes a utilization review (UR) system that requires close cooperation between the UR office and the admitting department that resulted in cost savings ranging from as high as $5,600 per month over manual review.*[14] Examples of organizational change among all departments in a hospital that has a comprehensive hospital information system could be listed, but possibly the most important or necessary change is the elevation of the information systems responsibility to a higher level in the hospital organizational structure.

However, computer professionals who specialize in hospital systems are at present a rare commodity.[15] As the health care field continues to become aware of the importance of information systems, efforts to attract computer professionals will increase. Also, new educational programs, such as the Medical Information Science program at the University of California (San Francisco), are being developed to train professionals in this area. In addition to this new breed of professionals, the role of management engineering in the successful development, implementation, and evaluation of hospital information systems (HIS) is becoming much clearer. As Freeman and Overton state, "Many hospitals have found that their management engineers' expertise can be of valuable assistance in the arduous task of evaluating and selecting an HIS... [and also] the implementation of an HIS."[16] They further describe the vital role of management engineers in improving the productivity of a hospital through use of an HIS. The prominence and subsequent effects of the growing introduction of these two disciplines into the organizational structure of hospitals will become more evident as the use of hospital information systems increases.

Although there have been few new dramatic developments of hospital information systems during 1977, there appears to be an increase in the use of existing systems. In an article on a survey conducted in 1975 and 1976, Larry Chervenak reports, "In the current survey, only 20 percent of the respondents reported that they do not use any type of data processing. In 1970, a total of 55 percent reported that they used no data processing."[17] This trend can be expected to continue and, as it does, new developments or applications should result.

Federal support of the development and evaluation of hospital information systems was severely lacking in 1977, but two reports published in 1977 should strengthen the emerging support of these systems. One report summarizes an evaluation project that has been in effect since 1971. The final summary of the report states, "It is the general conclusion of the Project to Demonstrate and Evaluate a Total Hospital Information System in a Community Hospital that operation of such a system in a community hospital is not only feasible, but also can be cost effective. Furthermore, it can bring about many improvements in the quality of health care delivery and play an instrumental role in the achievement of many more."[18]

The final economic analysis of this system by an independent research firm that was due in 1977 has been delayed to 1978. If this final analysis is favorable, as is expected, the development and implementation of hospital information systems should be stimulated.

The Office of Technology Assessment reported on three information systems: (1) the Technicon Medical Information System, (2) the Computer Stored Ambulatory Record (COSTAR) system, developed for an ambulatory care program, and (3) the Problem-Oriented Medical Information System (PROMIS), a system based on the problem-oriented medical record concept. Many factors, issues, and considerations of these systems were presented, but the dominant message was that there are significant, potential benefits to be gained from proper development and use of computer systems in health care delivery. Consequently, the report recommends that the federal government take a much larger role in the development and use of these systems than has been previously done.[19]

If the federal government decides to stimulate development and use of these systems, it will help to lessen the problems that have arisen between the regulator and the regulated. Although the federal government attempts to assist in the efforts to keep health care costs down, it also implements programs that continue to burden hospitals with high-cost reporting requirements. Information systems can help to reduce this problem if the systems are properly developed and used. According to Phillips, "The shape of hospital information systems in the near future will depend on alliances that form in response to government efforts in the health care field."[20] But more importantly, the government should direct its efforts to assist in the shaping of hospital information systems by providing incentives to hospitals to develop and use these systems.

Given the opportunity, hospitals will be the most effective force to win the cost containment battle. Hospital information systems could prove to be one of the best weapons to use in this effort. Thus, while 1977 was a period of time when hospitals began to sharpen their use of available systems in a cost-conscious manner, *1978 could begin a period of new developments and new benefits to the health care industry through advances in computer science.*

REFERENCES

1. American Hospital Association. Cost containment: digest of hospital projects, Sept. 1977.

2. Hodge, M.H. *Medical Information Systems: A Resource for Hospitals.* Aspen Systems Corporation. Germantown, MD, 1977.

3. Veazie, S.M., and Dankmyer, T. HISs, MISs, DBMs: sorting out the letters. *Hospitals.* 51:80, Oct. 16, 1977.

4. Sahin, K.E. Keeping up with...networking in computers. *Health Care Rev. Manage.* Vol. 2, Summer 1977.

5. Abrahamson, H.E. and Hatala, V.M. Urban-rural linkage brings advanced EDP capabilities within reach. *Hospitals.* 51:179, Oct. 16, 1977.

6. MEDINFO 77: Proceedings of the Second World Conference on Medical Informatics. eds. Shires, D.B., and Wolfe, H. North-Holland Publishing Company, 1977.

7. Fischer-Pap, L. Bless the *@Z! Things. *Hospital Physician.* Vol. 13, Aug. 1977.

8. Fischer, G.R. Computers and the regulation of medicine. *Delaware Medical Journal.* 49:2, Feb. 1977.

9. Barnett, G.O. and Zielstorff, R.D. Data systems can enhance or hinder medical nursing activities. *Hospitals.* 51:157, Oct. 16, 1977.

10. Davis, S. and Freeman, J.R., Ph.D. Management information systems: what hospital managers need. *Health Care Manage. Rev.* Harvard School of Public Health. July 1977.

11. Barker, W.D. Management reports can help control costs. *Hospitals.* 51:165, Oct. 16, 1977.

12. Buck, C.R. Assuring EDP effectiveness: the CEO's role. *Hospital Progress.* Vol. 58, April 1977.

13. Smith, L.H. Jr. Can medical records EDP and finance live happily together? *Hosp. Fin. Manage.* Vol. 31, Aug. 1977.

14. Tucker says computers offer hope for U.R. burden. *Hospital Peer Review,* Vol. 2, Feb. 1977.

15. Wall, J. The dearth of health computer specialists. *Dimensions in Health Services.* Vol. 54, Nov. 1977.

16. Freeman, J.R., and Overton, R.G. Data systems and management engineers work better together. *Hospitals.* 51:175, Oct. 16, 1977.

17. Chervenak, L. EDP is up. *Hosp. Fin. Manage.* Feb. 1977.

18. *Research Summary Series: Demonstration and Evaluation of a Total Hospital Information System,* DHEW Publication No. (HRA) 77-3188, July 1977.

19. *Policy Implications of Medical Information Systems,* Office of Technology Assessment, Congress of the United States, Washington, DC, November, 1977.

20. Phillips, D.F. Regulations and data systems: questions of demands versus needs. *Hospitals.* 51:85, Oct. 16, 1977.

46. Cooperation and Sharing

MONTAGUE BROWN AND HOWARD L. LEWIS

Reprinted with permission from *Hospital Management Systems*, 1976, pp. 19-26.

The rapid evolution of autonomous hospitals into systems is occurring in an environment long characterized by cooperation and sharing and competition for physicians, patients and financial support.

Health care literature is filled with reports of shared services, contract services, mergers, affiliations and contract management. These terms suggest that two or more entities have come together to produce goods, services, and engage in planning, as well as new trends toward integration of health services under various organizational and structural forms.[1]

SHARED SERVICES

The W. K. Kellogg Foundation, for example, has exerted considerable influence among hospitals to promote shared services. Robert A. DeVries, Program Director of the foundation, defines shared services as "those clinical or administrative functions that are common to two or more institutions, that are used jointly or cooperatively by them in some way for the purpose of improving service and/or effecting economies of scale, and that hold all participating parties at risk in the sharing venture."[2]

One of the most extensive national surveys of shared services was made in 1971 by Adrienne A. Astolfi and Leo B. Matti. According to their report: "Of the 5,727 short-term community hospitals contacted, 82.5 percent completed the survey questionnaire and of these, 66.6 percent reported that they share from 1 to 73 services with an average of 6.2 services shared per hospital. The five services most frequently shared by reporting hospitals are blood bank, purchasing of medical and surgical supplies, data processing, disaster plans, and professional staff in laboratories...." They found that most sharing was in purchasing—group buying of medical and surgical supplies, linens, drugs, housekeeping and laboratory supplies.

Considerable interest was also shown in increased use of group purchasing as a way to effect economies. Responding hospitals were interested in shared administrative services and joint programs in continuing education and in-service education. Astolfi and Matti concluded: "Clearly, both the extent of present involvement in sharing programs and the degree of interest (29,890 instances of interest in sharing reported) strongly suggest sharing's potential as a major method of delivery of health care services. Sharing indeed may serve as the foundation for the many recent concepts which have emerged regarding health care delivery through formal cooperative arrangements."[3]

CONTRACT SERVICES

Many hospitals have taken, however, a different approach to sharing and cost containment. They have opted for contract services—negotiation of arrangements with outside agencies to manage a specific function or service, such as data processing, electronic equipment, food service, laundry and linen, plant operations, and other services in the housekeeping and support category.

Kenneth T. Wessner, president of Servicemaster Hospital Corporation, said that benefits from contract services are:

> Greater control in the areas of personnel and finance; Experience that grows out of research, study, and firsthand acquaintance with a wide spectrum of proven methods and techniques; Flexibility to meet changing demands as hospitals grow in size and complexity; Continuity of day-to-day management; A supportive team to handle the details of work scheduling so as to eliminate critical disruptions due to illness, vacations, and emergency situations; Versatility to handle routine departmental needs and to meet emergencies as they arise; Resources to support the administrator in the areas of cost control, technology, personnel, and materials management; A philosophy of service on the part of the departmental head and his staff that should help to eliminate such comments as 'that's not my job,' 'we're short of help,' and 'if we had better people.'[4]

A study of the extent of contract services on the departmental level in 259 hospitals in five geographically diverse areas was made by Bernard L. Brown, Jr. He charted trends in contracting for 15 different services, including 9 clinical services, and found smaller hospitals (1 to 99 beds) contracted for the most services, followed by hospitals in the 100-199 and 200-299 bed categories. More than 40 percent of the smallest hospitals had outside contracts for pathology, radiology and laundry services.[5]

Computers and the electronic data processing equipment represent one of the newest areas of contract service. Some hospitals have gone to facility management agreements; many others, particularly small facilities which don't own any equipment, have turned to computer service centers for help. These hospitals buy the software system, send information—generally business office, financial, budgeting, and payroll information—to the service center for processing, where it is returned by courier as printouts, or received via Dataphone (telephone) hookup.

MERGER

Another current trend is merger—when two or more institutions join together as a single entity. One source charted this phenomena and found twelve mergers between United States hospitals from 1947 through 1961.[6] American Hospital Association data show another 135 mergers occurring in the nine-year period of 1962 through 1970.[7]

Most sources warn that these data are very likely incomplete, usually adding that many more mergers have probably taken place. It is believed, however, that many mergers have been concentrated in New York, New Jersey, and Pennsylvania. And there have been extensive studies of merger activity in Pennsylvania and New England.

James R. Neely, president of the Hospital Association of Pennsylvania (HAP) calls merger "the ultimate act of sharing costs and services." In October 1971, the HAP Board of Trustees approved a nine-point program for the association and included a statement to encourage hospitals to develop systems. The HAP goal was to "develop a program to create systems (health care corporations, health maintenance organizations, mergers, consortiums) of health care institutions throughout the state." The HAP said it would "provide encouragement, consultation, and assistance to institutions to achieve institutional consolidation," and would "encourage legal and economic sanctions to stimulate the development of systems."[8]

As part of this effort, John R. Clark, a project officer with HAP, was commissioned to study interinstitutional cooperation in the state. He found, by reviewing the available literature and interviewing administrators, planning agency officials and health planners, that there were

18 mergers (and one "demerger") among Pennsylvania hospitals from 1946 to 1969.

The usual reasons given to justify a merger, he said, include desires to improve educational programs, eliminate duplication, broaden the range of available services, increase community support, and improve planning; but the real reasons for the merger, according to him are operational and political. Hospitals lack money for modernization and replacement of facilities; they can't purchase the equipment they need, and they need money to operate their facilities. From 1920 to 1940, a number of specialty hospitals merged with general hospitals "because changing medical technology was creating the need for common equipment. However, economic forces are *primarily* responsible for the more recent merger trend which is occurring in an environment of increasing cost controls, higher standards for facilities and services, pressures to improve the utilization of personnel and services, and public concern for higher quality and more accessible services."[9]

The organizational aspects of mergers between hospitals in the New England states from 1960 to 1970 were extensively studied by Sally E. Knapp and Robert R. Lovejoy. Although unable to determine precisely the number of mergers in the area during the decade, they did provide valuable information on ten selected mergers and eight case studies in which hospitals decided to merge or not to merge. They concluded that "there appears to be an increasing likelihood that in the future external demands from state and regional authorities, coupled with national redirection of health policy, may furnish the most compelling rationale for hospital mergers."[10]

AFFILIATIONS

Affiliations represent another trend toward systems development. Richard Wittrup defined this trend "as an arrangement under which two or more institutions are engaged in a single program, with each responsible for separate parts.... The most common examples are found in education where students rotate from one institution to another, receiving some element of instruction in each. Other examples include formal arrangements between hospitals and nursing homes, between hospitals and neighborhood health centers, and between hospitals which refer patients to each other."[11]

Certainly the affiliation phenomena is widespread. There are 447 teaching hospitals in the United States,[12] most of which are affiliated with one or more of the 114 medical schools. And of the 175 VA hospitals in the United States, about 95 percent of these are affiliated with a medical school.

Wittrup believes these relationships tend to be more political than financial and that an element of dependency builds up between affiliated institutions. It is not difficult to see why: Medical schools need patient referrals and teaching patients; affiliated hospitals need house staff. "The dependency factor also causes affiliations to bind hospitals together more closely than do shared services," he says, "because a hospital using a shared laundry usually can get its linens washed elsewhere, but a teaching hospital usually has difficulty arranging another medical school affiliation. While each party to an affiliation retains its corporate autonomy, it can exercise its independence only at the expense of sacrificing programs." And he adds: "Hospitals commonly attach great importance to educational programs, particularly in medicine. For that reason, a medical school and its affiliated hospitals often are bound together, and that relationship can serve as the basis for a variety of other cooperative endeavors."[13]

CONTRACT MANAGEMENT

Still another trend toward systems development can be seen in the contract management of a hospital by an outside corporation. This rapidly growing phenomenon has important implications for systems development. In one report, over 150 management contracts in hospitals of 40 beds to more than 200 beds had been studied. The organization furnishing the management expertise included investor-owned chains, not-for-profit multiple-unit hospital systems, and a shared services organization.[14]

Under contract management, either the owners or a board of trustees contract with an outside organization that assumes responsibility for the general, day-to-day management of the institution. The managed hospital retains total legal responsibility and ownership of the facility, its assets and liabilities.

The individual brought in as administrator reports directly to the board of trustees, which must approve the appointment. The administrator serves as the chief executive officer. He prepares agendas for the board, usually in consultation with his contractor organization. The administrator and members of the contracting organization attend board meetings and participate fully. The administrator carries out policy, implements the budget, and works with medical staffs and community groups.

A top notch administrator is the key to a management contract. This individual must know hospital operations and have an extensive knowledge of reimbursement formulas, cash flow, and manpower cost control systems. But the administrator does not work in a vacuum. His contractor organization also brings specialized backup services to the contracting facility in key areas of management. A recent study shows that some managing companies can offer advisory services in 35 areas of need—ranging from patient admitting practice and labor relations to systems analysis and physician recruitment. Where the contractor organization is a medical school teaching center, the available backup medical, professional and management services may number over 100.[15]

Precontract feasibility studies indicate the services most needed by the managed hospital. Attempts are made to avoid overwhelming a hospital with all services simultaneously. Not all contracting organizations offer all services. Some but not all services would be provided without extra compensation above a basic agreement.

Contracts generally run for three years or longer. They provide that the hospital pay the contracting organization five to seven percent of either gross charges or gross revenues. Some not-for-profit contract management organizations charge only for direct costs incurred. The hospital may also pay the salary of the administrator. In a typical situation, say a 100-bed hospital, the gross revenue might be $2.7 million. The contracting company would receive $189,000 and a typical administrator's salary of $30,000 a year. All such expenses are legitimate expenses of the hospital and thus eligible for reimbursement by insurance agencies and government purchasers of care. In some cases, the hospital must also pay other administrative expenses and costs.

Investor-owned chains of hospitals, community hospitals, and church-owned facilities see many of the same advantages in selling management contracts. They increase revenue with little capital investment, spread overhead costs, gain new specialized personnel, serve new communities, cement important relationships with neighboring hospitals and possibly avoid the entry of new competition into their service areas.

Preliminary research shows that there are at least a dozen environmental forces that push a hospital toward contract management. Hospitals of small bed size, chronic low occupancy rate problems, deficit operations and old physical plants are prime candidates. In other instances, a hospital's clientele has increasing needs for medical care but a diminishing ability to pay for services. Some of the forces relate to geography: Inner city and rural areas, for example, can't always attract skilled and trained administrators and physicians. Still other forces relate to philosophy: Some trustees want their hospital run "like their own business." Other trustees no longer want to cope with increasing complexity without assured technical backup in every area of management. Finally, physicians as well as trustees seem more confident of an administrator who has a team of specialists to consult.[16]

Contract management seems easier than other options such as merger. It can be negotiated quickly with the only potential for immediate change in personnel limited to the administrator. Boards, physicians, and employees retain their positions. A management contract can be terminated to place the institution back in full control. There are also psychological reasons why a contract makes sense: Hospital personnel appear to develop few of the fears associated with mergers. Physicians express less opposition. Board members retain their autonomy and control without the threats to their existence implicit in other arrangements.

Possible disadvantages to contract management are: Backup advisors may be spread too thinly to give proper attention to the variety of institutions being managed. Standardized reporting systems may decrease the flexibility normally available to any individual unit even though they are often an improvement on existing information systems. Corporate personnel may lack sensitivity to local needs. The institution may find itself with a board which loses its capacity for probing investigation and an administrator whose loyalties are to a system outside the local institution. Potential conflicts may be resolved in favor of the contracting unit to the potential detriment of the hospital without full knowledge of the board.

Contract management provides, however, an easy method for boards of small hospitals to gain quickly an experienced administrator. This administrator (who might not take the job at all if he were isolated from needed management backup) has working access to specialists who can handle the complicated legal, regulatory, technological and financial problems facing all hospitals.

An early example of cooperation and sharing can be seen in the formation and growth of hospital associations and councils in cities, counties, states and regions. These are voluntary membership organizations that have been formed to deal with common problems. Associations represent forms of interinstitutional and intrainstitutional cooperation. They were originally established to raise standards, share educational programs, develop charitable resources and represent the collective interest of hospitals with federal and state governmental agencies and law-making bodies. Association staffs began to grow with the passage of the Hill-Burton Act in 1945. They have continued to expand in response to government regulation and the complexity of problems and issues that their constituents must deal with.

Shared services, mergers, contract service, contract management and associations all represent system trends. Not all of these trends lead to the development of hospital systems, but they represent steps in that direction...

NOTES

1. M. Brown, "Current Trends in Cooperative Ventures," *Hospitals* (June 1, 1974), pp. 40–44.

2. "Kellogg's Role in Fostering Shared Services," *Hospitals* (February 1, 1973), pp. 86–87.

3. A. A. Astolfi and L. B. Matti, "Survey Profiles Shared Services," *Hospitals* (September 16, 1972), pp. 61–65.

4. K. T. Wessner, "How to Purchase Contract Services," *Hospitals* (September 1, 1972), pp. 104, 108, 112.

5. B. L. Brown, Jr., "Contract Services: Outsiders on the Hospital Team," *Hospital Topics* (August 1965), pp. 62–64, 71.

6. "A Coordinated System for Institutionally Based Health Care Services," Hospital Educational and Research Foundation of Pennsylvania, report of one-year study by John R. Clark, August 1974.

7. Ibid.

8. Ibid.

9. Ibid.

10. S. E. Knapp and R. E. Lovejoy, *Hospital Mergers in New England: Organizational Perspectives* (Durham, New Hampshire: System Educators, Inc., 1972), p. 76.

11. R. Wittrup, "The Consortium Approach" in *A Decade of Implementation: The Multiple Hospital Management Concept Revisited, A Report of the 1975 National Forum on Hospital and Health Affairs,* Duke University, pp. 49–58.

12. 1975-76 AAMC Directory of Medical Education, pp. 305–326.

13. R. Wittrup, op. cit.

14. M. Brown and H.L. Lewis, "Ideas for Action," *Harvard Business Review* (May-June 1976), pp. 8, 13.

15. Ibid.

16. M. Brown and W. H. Money, "The Promise of Multihospital Management," *Hospital Progress* (August 1975), pp. 36–42.

47. The Value of Shared Service Organizations

G. O. SAXTON

Reprinted from *Dimensions in Health Service,* January 1979, pp. 28–29,
by permission of Canadian Hospital Association, © 1979.

With the introduction of the *Hospital Insurance and Diagnostic Services Act* of 1958, hospitals were required to make insured services uniformly available to all Canadian residents. The general attitude that pervaded the hospital field in the 1960s was to take care of more people in better ways.

In the 1970s the feeling that more and better services should be continued was tempered somewhat by the feeling that we should keep an eye on costs which by then had begun to escalate. One answer to escalating costs was to examine the inherent possibilities of shared services. The American Hospital Association and the Kellogg Foundation use the following definition to explain shared services.

"Shared services are those clinical or administrative functions which are common to two or more organizations, which are used jointly or cooperatively by them in some way for the purpose of improving service, containing costs and/or expecting economies of scale, and which hold all participating parties at risk in the sharing venture."

This definition is in sharp contrast to what has been called contracted or purchased services where essentially only one party is at risk and the secondary parties buy services or products without a stake in the survival or financial success of the venture.

The primary reason for initiating a shared service is cost containment and control.

Before establishing a shared service program one should fully appreciate that sharing is not a natural instinct and people will only share so much. There are a number of disadvantages in sharing. The principle one is loss of autonomy. This can manifest itself as a loss of image, for an institution must give up something in order to participate in a shared service arrangement, therefore, loses direct control when it participates in shared service arrangements. In order to conform with others, as is necessary in a shared service arrangement, an institution becomes standardized. Standardization tends to inhibit innovation and leads to mediocrity. All this is not to say that shared services are unsatisfactory but, that it is important to understand and assess as part of evaluating the disadvantages associated with shared services.

The advantages of shared services far outweigh the disadvantages. However, before embarking on such a program one cardinal fact must be established. The participating members must be truly committed to making the program succeed. Hidden agenda and lip service only will lead to disaster before the program is even inaugurated.

Some of the many benefits that can accrue to participants in a shared service program are the following:

- Save money
- Share expertise
- Save space
- Educate
- Maximize use of scarce resources
- Centralize data gathering
- Improve quality of patient care
- Conduct operational research
- Eliminate duplication
- Improve communications
- Improve maintenance
- Resolve transportation problems
- Afford new technology and make it accessible
- Coordinate planning & service capabilities

Obviously all of these goals and objectives cannot be attained by instituting a single program. Currently there are approximately 80 services in operation by the almost 200 shared services organizations operating in the United States and Canada. Some of the shared services organizations operate one or two programs whereas others may range from five to as many as 20 different programs.

Programs with the most immediate pay-back potential are group purchasing, health systems engineering and courier services. There are many other programs that have been identified to date that result in dollar savings and/or improved efficiency or effectiveness of services. Some programs are difficult to evaluate in terms of dollar return on investment. An example would be educational programs whereby personnel have a better grasp of the functions they are performing in relation to the total operation thus improving employee morale. This in turn will lead to increased productivity and decreased labor turnover. It is virtually impossible to quantify dollar savings to hospitals from programs such as education and safety.

The most common type of shared service organization presently in existence is a free standing type. This type is duly incorporated under either provincial or state laws as a not-for-profit organization. The raison d'être is to serve the needs of a group of hospitals or similar institutions to reduce costs of operation and where possible provide means to improve the quality of service rendered.

The founding or participating members generally appoint representatives from their respective institutions to membership on the board of directors. Frequently these members are the hospital executive directors and one or more lay Board members from the hospitals concerned.

The first major decisions to be made by a newly constituted board of directors are:

1. Size of constituency to be served
2. Types of institutions to be served
3. Types of programs to be instituted
4. Funding—both immediate and long term
5. Recruitment of chief executive officer

Depending on the geographical location of the proposed Shared Service Organization, the size and number of constituents to be served could be limited to a Metropolitan region, a County or some other geopolitical subdivision.

Initially this could be limited to any two or more of the following:

• Acute general hospitals
• Chronic care hospitals

- Long term hospitals
- Specialized hospital (pediatric, chest, etc.)
- Convalescent hospitals
- Nursing homes

As a program evolves, additional institutions could be invited to join.

TYPE OF PROGRAMS

There are basically two types. The first is administrative and is primarily concerned with what could generally be described as hotel type functions. The second type of programs is considered clinical. These would indicate sharing laboratory services, rehabilitation services and others.

FUNDING

The immediate or short term funding can probably be obtained from service clubs, foundations, participating hospitals or other philanthropic organizations within the community. Long term or operational funding should be generated from the participants as a direct result of the savings they will enjoy from the programs that are instituted. A fee structure for each service can be determined in advance and all services are payable on a fee for service basis. If some participants wish to opt out of specific programs, an administrative fee could be charged to defray the costs of maintaining such a program until this program is able to pay its own way.

CHIEF EXECUTIVE OFFICER

The criteria for selecting the chief executive officer should closely resemble that employed for hiring a hospital administrator. It is imperative that the individual chosen should have had some hospital experience and experience in dealing with a board of directors. Compatibility with all levels of hospital personnel is also a desired requisite. The chief executive director does have a peer relationship with the hospital administrators with whom he is in daily contact.

Shared service organizations have proven their worth since they were conceived about 20 years ago. It is surprising that only about seven groups exist in Canada and of this number only two, the Montreal Joint Hospital Institute begun in 1970 and the Children's Grace Shaughnessy Shared Service Organization in Vancouver begun late in 1977, offer more than two services. Shared laundry organizations number over 20 in Canada but most of these are single program entities and do not offer other services.

At the 1977 annual meeting of The American Hospital Association, shared service organizations were officially sanctioned and admitted as a type 6 membership within the association. A board of directors was elected and the A.H.A. provides full time staff specialists to assist in the development and maintenance of shared service organizations.

In the present climate of budgetary restrictions and scarcity of both human and financial resources shared service organizations are certainly one avenue that more hospitals should explore.

48. What to Expect from an Outside Consultant and How to Get It

ROBERT W. CARITHERS

Reprinted with permission from *Health Care Management Review*, Summer 1977, pp. 43-46.

In taking initial steps to engage an outside consultant, hospital trustees are making their important first move: They are admitting that the institution or some segment of it is not functioning satisfactorily or that special expertise is not internally available. Engaging a consultant, however, will not automatically solve their problems any more than retaining a lawyer will guarantee winning a case in court.

There are, of course, ways to optimize the value of a management consultant, but a hospital's trustees or directors must lay the groundwork at the beginning of the working relationship—in fact, before the beginning.

In preliminary discussions, for example, directors and administrators should define the problem as clearly as possible. This will provide a baseline for the consultant's task. The problem need not necessarily be a severe breakdown in any phase of the patient care programs or financial performance of the system. It may well be a perception that some operational area is doing less well than anticipated, that overall performance expectations aren't being met, or that an emerging situation could cause trouble.

SELECTING A CONSULTANT

No matter how large or small you determine your problem to be, select your consultant carefully. A good working relationship will hinge upon your conviction of the consultant's competency and integrity. Hindsights and afterthoughts can undermine the consultant's credibility, torpedo the implementation of his recommendations and create internal dissension.

Try to select the consultant who gives the impression of being more than just a repairman. The consultant should have a total grasp of the hospital system, as well as a state-of-the-art knowledge of the optimal performance of such a system and each of its components. His basic business is not only to provide solutions for recognized problem areas, but also to suggest improvements in areas that may be functioning adequately but might do better.

This means that you may have to interview several firms. And, as a further caution, do not use cost as a sole guideline. Consultants are not building contractors, and the lowest bid won't guarantee results. Good results are worth the cost; unsatisfactory results are a dead loss.

START-UP

A thorough definition of the project will generally be achieved only after a consultant is on board and has accumulated and analyzed enough information to isolate and think through the situation and its underlying causes. Once he has had sufficient time to present his overall project proposal to the board, the consultant should also be in a position to provide a fairly detailed estimate of his costs. They should parallel the project components in detail so that you can easily match costs to tasks and make any necessary cuts. Don't hesitate to ask for cost-benefit estimates for any aspect of the proposal.

It also pays to have a clear understanding of the consultant's fee system and schedule of interim billing to avoid misunderstandings. A consultant may ask for an initial retainer to cover the audit of the hospital (undertaken prior to presenting a full program). Take this as a good sign. It means he won't work on speculation in the hope of getting the larger contract.

The Consultant Comes in from the Cold

As the consultant begins working with hospital personnel, it is wise to remember he is an outsider and is perceived by some as an intruder. He is hired to tell people who take pride in their competence and skill how their jobs can be done more effectively, and he represents potential change. That some staff members will be disturbed, resentful or even obstructive is hardly surprising.

It's important, therefore, that he works with a clear mandate from the trustees and administration, and that his job and purpose are clearly understood by all hospital personnel. It is usually a mistake to communicate on a "need to know" basis. Rumors and gossip sprout readily from employees who supposedly don't need to know what's going on, and in fact don't know. A thorough briefing of all personnel at the outset is a sound investment in the success of the endeavor.

A consultant should, for his part, move at the very outset to confirm his own credibility with the Board, and to set a pattern of communication that allows for free and open exchange of ideas and criticism.

In overseeing the consultant's work, monitor progress and demand regular interim reports. This serves to keep directors and management informed and supports their commitment to the project. It also exposes areas where their own insights may be helpful. This is particularly true in the "human dimension": in questions involving hospital personnel and morale.

At the same time, you should check on whether a consultant is making reasonable demands on the administrator's time, and see to it that while seeking and expecting co-operative assistance from hospital personnel, he is not expecting staff members to do his job for him. And, you have every right to expect that the consultant's dealings with hospital staff will be carried out with tact and perception. He should have human sensitivity as well as analytic skills.

RECOMMENDATIONS TO EXPECT

One of the most frequent recommendations made by a consultant is to put into effect a comprehensive financial and operating reporting system. It's surprising how many hospitals lack one. This system, almost invariably computerized, is designed to provide not just monthly operating statements, but a complete readout of cash flow, accounts receivable and payable, inventory and critical operating ratios.

This recommendation is often interpreted by trustees as "change for the sake of change," but this is not so. Once such a reporting system is in effect, it can be expanded to provide month-to-month or year-to-year comparisons of the hospital's experiences and to furnish projections into the future. The resulting flow permits hospital management to see where changes or problems have emerged and to anticipate needed action by seeing problems develop.

A gradual buildup in accounts receivable, for example, is a warning. Is the problem in receipt of insurance or Medicare/Medicaid payments? Or is the admitting desk lax in verifying insurance benefits or other sources of payments? The default rate on uninsured patients can be as high as 35 percent, causing a severe drain that has to be controlled or compensated for.

An aging inner-city hospital was able to reverse a drastic financial crisis in a period of months by installing an effective reporting system at the recommendation of their consultant. This reversal showed immediately that cash inflow from third party payments was slow and haphazard, and that reimbursement rates needed to be renegotiated to reach the levels of costs. Similarly, charges in many instances were below hospital costs.

This was the first of a sequence of steps designed to enable the hospital to improve low salaries that were crippling staff morale, to buy some desperately needed equipment, and to redirect traffic flow to locate the busiest departments "up front." The hospital began to take on a new look, a new feel among staff that "something was happening," and ultimately, a new life. But the new life began in a probe of some rather haphazard financial statements.

Your consultant may also recommend setting up a staff reporting system by department, if one is lacking. This will measure the allocation of staff in relation to function and utilization. Observations and recommendations may also be expanded to embrace recruitment of new medical and paraprofessional staff. Often recruitment of doctors is fairly casual, and your consultant may recommend a systematic program in which doctors in the community are interviewed, a file on each maintained, and good prospects identified so that continuing contact can be initiated.

One large Northeastern hospital found itself in serious financial trouble within six months of opening its doors. Their consultant discovered that the primary problem was in a far too ambitious staffing plan in relation to census, and medical services were vastly underutilized. A massive marketing program was recommended and implemented, resulting in vastly improved occupancy and financial results.

Another project the consultant recommended and undertook was to gather data on other area hospitals of a similar size and environment. Their costs, methods, staffing procedures and operating systems provided a valuable frame of reference for comparison and stimulated ideas that helped the directors of the client hospital set a course for their institution's future.

"DO IT!"

Once you have recommendations, be prepared to act on them.

In any organization, there is a phenomenon that might be dubbed "organizational inertia." Things get filed. Enthusiasm runs down. New procedures make new demands of staff members who are already working hard at their jobs. Without consistent follow-through for up to a full year, the new procedures are likely to begin to bear a striking resemblance to the old procedures.

Be prepared as well for a "domino" effect; changes in one operational sphere will often imbalance another. The consultant knows this, and needs a reasonably broad mandate for change for his work to be most effective. And, it's often worthwhile to engage the consultant to follow up the implementation program by conducting a review of operations after three to six months.

This allows the consultant to make corrections or new recommendations, and safeguards the original investment in the project. An experienced management consultant deals not in "the solution," but in alternative solutions to a problem. Should the original recommendation hit hidden snags, such as union resistance, or if the hospital is for some reason not equipped to implement the plan, he can suggest other approaches. If the "first" solution is found to be unworkable, it is not the "best" solution.

WAS THE OPERATION A SUCCESS?

No consulting project is complete, of course, until the directors have evaluated its results and satisfied themselves that the project has been optimized.

Was the project a good investment? Have the problem-solving recommendations been implemented in large part, and with a minimum of organizational upheaval? Are the changes working?

Beyond these basics, has there been any "spin-off" from the consultant's work? A skilled consultant will often act as a catalyst to help draw out from trustees, administrators and staff many valuable ideas for change that lie dormant in a hospital organization. His presence focuses attention on changes in procedures and raises questions that in the pressure of day-to-day operations simply never get asked.

Your consultant can also be evaluated on what he did *not* do as well as what he did do. That is, confronting a problem realistically involves recognizing the boundaries of your hospital's resistance to change. Your consultant, then, must make a hard assessment of those flaws you are wiser to live with than attempt to change. No hospital runs on efficiency alone (thank heaven) and the best ones have a capacity for care that can't be quantified.

49. HAS: What It Does for a Hospital

WALTER DANCO AND ARTHUR SCHMIDT

Reprinted from the August 1974 issue of *Hospital Financial Management*, pp. 32–35. Copyright 1974 Hospital Financial Management Association.

In the 15 years since the inception of Hospital Administrative Services (HAS) we have witnessed an amazing growth of interest in improved methods for management of health care institutions. This is particularly evident in accounting, statistical and other quantitative approaches to management information systems.

HAS continues in the forefront of those providing management with meaningful, practical information. Wide acceptance of the HAS program by health institution administrators as well as the results achieved by its application, have confirmed its value to the field.

HISTORY

In 1959, under a grant from the W. K. Kellogg Foundation, a study determined that hospitals could be compared quantitatively; financial, man-hour, and other statistical data could be gathered and developed into operational indicators that would be useful to management. On the basis of this research HAS developed a comparative report which was made available on an experimental basis to about 150 hospitals. Interest in the program grew and by 1970 participation had increased to approximately 3,000 institutions.

The original HAS program was developed for general short-term hospitals, and these institutions still constitute the largest group. In addition, programs have been devised for the special needs of other health care facilities, including extended and nursing care institutions, public psychiatric hospitals, private psychiatric hospitals, and university and college health centers.

PURPOSE

Traditionally, health institution management has tended to look within the organization for evidence of its effectiveness. Accounting records and statistics were the primary source of data for planning evaluation and control. These were, and still are, extremely useful to management.

Today, however, there is widespread recognition that comparative data obtained externally provide a new dimension to management information for decision-making. They permit management to evaluate their institution against what the field as a whole is accomplishing. Comparative data do not provide a standard of performance, nor are they intended to do so. However, they do highlight differences due to services, policies or activities which may require management attention. The program provides a continuous monitor of total institution activity in a form which makes management by exception a reality.

HAS is designed for practical application to everyday management problems. The uses to which HAS is regularly put are manifold: evaluation of departmental productivity, allocation of financial and manpower resources, documentation of budgets, provision of information for public relations, communication with trustees concerning operational activities, evaluation of service contract costs, negotiations with third-party payers and many more.

BASIC SERVICE

HAS provides each participant with a monthly report consisting of two sections—Internal Trend Data and Group Median Data.

These reports are based on financial, man-hour and statistical data submitted each month by the institution and other participants in the program. The raw data are processed by computer and shown as meaningful management indicators. Indicators, such as "housekeeping man-hours per 1,000 square feet," reduce gross data to common bases giving management a reliable measure of activity and productivity. Indicators are presented in an easily understood form, making them excellent devices for communicating with lower management and others.

INTERNAL TREND DATA

The Internal Trend Data section summarizes data submitted by the individual institution, in both the unprocessed form and as management indicators. The data are presented for various time periods. This section is particularly useful for trend analysis and as a check on the accuracy of data submitted.

GROUP MEDIAN DATA

The Group Median Data section summarizes data submitted by the individual institution for the current month, and the average of the previous three months, using the same indicators that appeared in the Internal Trend Data section. In addition, comparative information is provided based on the data of other institutions in the same size group and according to various geographical breakdowns. By using median data from each grouping and a quarter ranking system, the Group Median Data section shows where the institution stands quantitatively in relation to similar institutions.

Comparative data are presented in the form of a median for each operational and departmental indicator. The median on each indicator is calculated for each group compared. For each size group, there are national and state size groups. Comparative groups may also be provided on a district or other special basis where the number of participants warrants setting them up.

Medians are selected by arranging all data for an indicator within a group by numerical value—from highest to lowest. The middle figure in the array is the median. The computer also divides the array of figures into quarters—from "1" (lowest) to "4" (highest). The individual institution's average of the previous three months' figure for the indicator is ranked with reference to each comparative group median, and the appropriate quarter

Internal Trend Data

Internal Trend Data	Same Month Previous Year	Average of Previous 12 Mos.	Average of Previous 3 Mos.	Current Month
Laundry + Linen-Expense Per Cent	2.8%	2.5%	2.1%	2.0%
—Laundry Cost Per 100 Pounds	15,291	14,870	12,889	12,300
	15.41	13.88	9.77	10.57
—Laundry Pounds Per Man-hour	23.91	24.61	34.96	34.85
—Pounds Per Patient Day	14.87	14.92	15.01	14.89
—Linen Cost Per Patient Day	.80	.96	1.23	1.23

Group Median Data

10 34 36 37 42 46 49 49 50 50 51 52 53 54 55 56 56 57 60 68 74 78 81 150

L   1   2   3   4   H

|←—— 25% ——|—— 25% ——|—— 25% ——|—— 25% ——→|

Median

Group Median Data

	Your Institution		Group Medians for Previous Three Months			
	Current Month	Avge. Previous 3 Mos.	District Group	State Group	National Group	Special Group
Laundry + Linen-Expense Per Cent	2.0	2.1	2.0 3	2.0 3	1.8 3	
—Laundry Cost Per 100 Pounds	10.57	9.77	9.44 3	9.56 3	9.05 3	
—Laundry Pounds Per Man-hour	34.85	34.96	37.44 1	35.33 1	35.48 1	
—Pounds Per Patient Day	14.89	15.01	15.25 2	14.58 3	15.00 3	
—Linen Cost Per Patient Day	1.23	1.23	.64 4	.40 H	.37 H	

ranking number is printed on the report. This method permits the institution to determine the amount of its variation from the median, and the approximate degree of the difference.

If the institution is at either extreme (consisting of about 5 percent of the total participants at both ends of the array), an L (lowest) or H (highest) is printed on the report instead of a quarter-ranking number. This permits management to quickly spot significant differences from the group.

PROGRAM IMPLEMENTATION

HAS is much more than just a data processing service. HAS helps the health care institution management team accomplish its goals in several ways:

- HAS field consultants help implement the use of HAS data by providing inhouse instruction to department managers. They provide guidance in reporting and analyzing data, conduct special surveys and encourage district meetings of health care managers for the purpose of analyzing HAS data and exchanging information.
- Special HAS publications promote the use of quantitative data in the management process. Among these are *Departmental Handbooks, Guide for Uniform Reporting, Progress Charts* and *Spotlights.*
- Seminars and workshops are conducted frequently at convenient locations to stimulate the imaginative and practical use of HAS data by all levels of health institution management.
- Comprehensive six-month reports are published to keep management abreast of current trends in the field, and to explore new ways of quantitatively assessing health care institutions.
- A Budget Analysis Program (BAP) is available, which permits an institution to submit its proposed budget data in the same format as its actual data. The budget data forms the basis of a report which is similar to the regular monthly HAS report. The BAP report permits management to review its budget in relation to its own previous six months actual plus the group medians for the average of the most current three months, and in terms of units of service rather than simply in gross dollars and man-hours. This means the hospital is working with an activity oriented budget and much of the activity can be derived from the statistics page of its regular monthly reports.

HAS has already proved its effectiveness as a management tool. But the health care field is a rapidly changing one. To meet this challenge, HAS continuously conducts dialogues with management and health specialty groups, and experiments with new ways of strengthening the program. The results of these efforts will continue to bear fruit for the betterment of health care institutional management.

50. Reducing Direct and Indirect Losses

JAMES A. MORGAN AND PAUL R. WOZNIAK

Reprinted from *Hospital Progress,* November 1977, pp. 88–89, 106, by permission of Edward J. Pollock, Publisher.©1977.

Safety programs, risk management programs, and loss control programs are becoming common terminology in the health care industry today. Hospital administrators need to have clear definitions of these terms, and, more important, they need to be aware of the steps necessary to instituting such programs.

At Little Company of Mary Hospital, Evergreen Park, IL, all the terms above are synonymous with the hospital's safety department and safety program. Since 1964 Little Company of Mary Hospital has employed a full-time hospital safety director, whose major areas of responsibility include: employee safety program, patient safety program, disaster planning, fire protection program, self-insurance program (worker's compensation, general and professional liability). At the present time the department personnel include an assistant safety director, fire marshal/safety instructor, safety intern, clerical secretary, and statistical secretary. Hospital administration founded the safety department primarily because the monthly safety committee did little more than meet, discuss safety problems and conditions, and return to work. Administration decided someone must follow up items uncovered at the safety committee meeting and take action to eliminate them.

A vital link in an effective loss control program is the safety department's relationship to the hospital board of directors. Through the chief executive officer, the safety department at Little Company of Mary Hospital submits a written annual report to the board listing all activities undertaken by the department during the calendar year. Included in this report are actual costs incurred, which assist in measuring the performance of the department and program. The safety director meets annually with the board to discuss departmental goals and current projects and to supply general information and answer questions. Also submitted is a quarterly litigation portfolio comprised of case summaries, which provides the board with the current status of all new, closed, or pending cases.

The safety program is functional; it pays for itself by keeping claims or potential claims at a minimum as well as by preventing reoccurrence of claims already made.

Three major reasons for loss control programs in the health care industry are (1) the desire to respond humanely to people, (2) the necessity of complying with the standards of regulatory and accrediting agencies, and (3) the desire to save the institution money.

The health care industry treats more than 10.7 million people each year involved in industrial, home, vehicle, and other types of accidents.[1] Its mission is to diagnose and treat these people and to bring them back to health. This goal raises the question, Why do unsafe actions and conditions exist that subject hospital patients, visitors, and employees to initial or to further injury? A loss control program should be initiated in an attempt to decrease these unsafe actions or conditions and to reduce incidents.

Hospitals must comply with the codes and standards set forth by a rising number of federal, state, and local regulatory agencies as well as by accrediting agencies. While codes and standards used by these agencies are nationally recognized as minimum compliance levels, each agency may use a different version of the same code. To compound this difficulty, accrediting agencies may, in addition to checking accepted minimum levels, go beyond these to create their own levels of performance. With the vast number of codes and standards used to review health care institutions, all facilities should initiate a loss control program to examine the institution's status prior to any actual survey, to correct violations, and to develop and maintain an ongoing program that ensures continued compliance.

The final reason for loss control is the money such a program can save. This is accomplished by preventing the occurrence or the reoccurrence of incidents that cause physical/mental injury, property damage, or other loss. Most incidents involving employee injuries have two cost factors—direct and indirect costs (see Figure)—and thus are often several times what they appear initially. Most institutions use only the direct cost—medical expense and lost-time wages—as the actual cost. As the Figure shows, several types of indirect costs may need to be considered in evaluating an incident and in

Figure   Costs of a Typical Employee Incident

	Direct (Insured)		Indirect (Uninsured)	
Medical	Emergency room visit	$25.00		
Time[1]	1 work day[2]	30.00	15-minute[2] interruption for 3 coworkers	$ 3.00
			40-minute lack of equipment for 2 coworkers	5.36
			4½-hour[3] supervisory investigation	27.00
			Overtime to complete job	75.00
Equipment[4]			Repair or replacement	175.00
Total		$55.00		

1. Possible additional costs: training a temporary replacement, hiring a new employee.
2. $4 hourly rate for 7½ hours.
3. $6 hourly rate.
4. Possible additional cost: equipment rental.

calculating its total cost. Indirect costs shown are only some possible costs; so no total is given.

An additional example of cost savings to the hospital, although not entirely attributable to the safety program, occurred in 1973. A quoted premium for professional liability insurance (malpractice) had escalated at the end of the third quarter by 190 percent. Most other health care providers' premiums had escalated 300 to 500 percent. The hospital discovered that a major reason for its "low" increase was that its effective loss control program resulted in good incident and claim experience and therefore kept costs down.

Another cost savings to the hospital under its present self-insurance program results from less frequent use of independent investigators. The safety department further investigates selected incidents when asked by the hospital's defense attorneys, thereby reducing the need for an outside investigator at a $20- to $35-per-hour fee plus expenses.

Instituting an effective loss control program can reduce the number of incidents and accidents, thus saving money. Insurance companies, for a multitude of reasons, are being forced to price themselves out of the market, and hospitals are faced with alternatives such as forming captive insurance companies or self-insuring. Under either alternative, loss control is still indicated to reduce costs of incidents, accidents, property damage, and claims.

Four basic processes involved in implementing a loss control program are investigating incidents, formulating recommendations for handling current incidents and avoiding future ones, regularly inspecting the institution for potential hazards, and implementing and maintaining an incident report system. While each of these areas could be described in great detail, looking at the elements of each process should suffice for the purposes of this article.

Investigating incidents. Incidents involving patients, visitors, and employees occur in most health care institutions, and most facilities use some type of report form. Unfortunately, this is usually the extent of the program. Each incident, no matter how slight, must be investigated to seek out the causal factors and to take corrective action to prevent a reoccurrence. The most practical approach to this element is instituting a training program (for example, as part of new employee orientation) to explain methods of reporting and investigating incidents and procedures for filling out incident report forms. Most incident report forms have three sections: description of incident, diagnosis and medical treatment rendered, and supervisor's investigation. The description of the incident should be written by the employee who discovers or is made aware of the incident. How is this accomplished? The employee should ask the following questions: What happened (factual information only)? When did it happen (exact time and date)? Where did it happen (exact location)? The employee's supervisor must investigate immediately, check the description for accuracy, and seek out causal factors. Most incidents result from unsafe actions (by an employee, patient, or visitor), unsafe conditions (equipment failure or physical barrier), or unsafe practices (a combination of unsafe action and condition). The questions the supervisor must ask are, Why did it happen? and How can it be prevented?

Formulating recommendations. Based upon the facts of the incident and the supervisor's investigation, a recommendation for preventing reoccurrence of the incident can be developed. The majority of incidents involving injury or property damage can be corrected by remedying behavior, engineering, or both. Behavioral remedies include education and training or disciplinary action; engineering remedies include replacing or finding alternatives for the equipment or condition at fault. The exact steps for correcting the problem depend upon the severity and complexity of the incident.

Conducting self-inspection. To survey the institution on a regular basis is a form of preventive maintenance through which hazardous conditions can be corrected before an incident occurs. The most effective way to carry out this function is to create a skilled inspection team that has access to applicable codes and standards for which the hospital is held accountable by regulatory and accrediting agencies.

Members of all departments should be held responsible for doing their own inspection on a predetermined basis. The inspection team should audit, on an unannounced schedule, different departments each month for a comparison study of hazards found. This would ensure the integrity of the inspection system. An excellent approach to the departmental inspection survey would be for the supervisor and a different employee each month to conduct the departmental inspection, thus enabling the department and all employees to be involved in the institution's safety activity.

Developing an effective incident-reporting system. This last element of a basic loss control program actually ties together the other three. The following system can be developed to ensure that the steps involved in incident investigation have been followed—including defining incidents, policy, and procedure; establishing recommendations; and conducting inspections.

A 24-hours-a-day, 7-days-a-week telephone reporting system should be instituted by which an incident involving injury or property damage must be reported to a designated office. Each business day, a log of reported incidents should be typed and sent to administration. Minimal information is needed for this sheet: name, classification (patient, visitor, or employee), room number (if patient), job status (if employee), date, time, location, description of incident, person reporting, and initials of person receiving the report. Administration is thus alerted so that if necessary, it can take immediate action.

Assuming that a safety director is on the staff, the next step is to see that all completed incident reports are sent to the safety department within 24 hours of the occurrence. The safety director can break down the incident report statistically to show where most incidents are occurring and what is causing them. These statistics are also indicators, showing where corrective action is needed. The safety director then sends the incident report to the appropriate administrative head for review and comment. After this, the reports are sent to the law firm or the insurance company for handling. It cannot be emphasized enough that the safety director must see all incident reports immediately in order to investigate further if the situation warrants. It is very hard to investigate an incident and to try to get accurate information two or three weeks after the occurrence.

The question is being asked constantly, How can safety attitudes be fostered? First, top administration and medical staff should issue a strong policy statement that the institution wants to provide a safe environment for everyone involved with it. This statement should also point out that every hospital employee—not just the safety committee or the safety department—is a member of the safety team.

Selling is the name of the game, as with any new product. Use of an employee suggestion program and awards, incentives, etc., are part of this game! A competitive format should also create awareness and proper attitudes.

What will the loss control program do for the institution? It will decrease operating costs by eliminating unsafe acts or conditions causing incidents that cost money. It will better prepare the institution for inspection and survey by regulatory and accrediting agencies. Showing that the institution "cares" about employees should improve their morale. In addition, by making patients and community aware of the hospital's loss control efforts, the program will provide a good public relations tool. Thus, a well-designed and effectively executed loss control program will benefit a hospital in many ways.

NOTE

1. *Accident Facts, 1976,* National Safety Council, Chicago, p. 3.

51. The Hospital's Insurance Options

DAVID H. SCHROEDER

Reprinted with permission from *Health Care Management Review,* Summer 1978, pp. 71-78.

Until recently hospitals have had few choices other than to commercially insure their professional and general liability coverage. Developing options to commercial insurance was hardly necessary because commercial insurance was readily available, reasonably priced and commonly used in the industry. However, with the advent of what may be properly termed an "insurance crisis" in which premiums soared, maximum limits were cut and availability was reduced to zero in some cases, new approaches needed to be developed. Revision Number 173 of the *Provider Reimbursement Manual,* published by the Bureau of Health Insurance with an effective date of April 1, 1977, made other alternatives to commercial insurance possible.

An intelligent insurance decision can be made only if the hospital is cognizant of the various methods of handling risk, is knowledgeable of funding choices available and has an appreciation of the advantages as well as disadvantage of each choice. The viability of each option and the perceived importance of the individual advantages and disadvantages for each option will differ with the hospital's individual set of circumstances. No single option is superior to that of another for all hospitals.

Risk may be managed in five ways. It may be (1) avoided, (2) reduced, (3) assumed, (4) transferred or (5) shared. These five ways of dealing with exposure are not mutually exclusive: an individual hospital in all probability will combine at least three of the above methods in its insurance program. With the exception of avoidance, all methods of dealing with risk require a form of funding. Methods of funding include (1) no insurance, (2) commercial insurance, (3) self-funding, (4) pooling, and (5) captive (single-owned, multi-owned).

The funding options, again, are not mutually exclusive, and in all probability some combination of the options is likely. Critical to each of the above options for the hospital's evaluation are availability, price, cost reimbursability, claims experience, etc. Equally critical and far more subjective in nature are the evaluation of risk assumptions, prospects for tort liability reform, trend of expanding judiciary interpretations of liability and other factors.

AVOIDING RISK

Assuming the hospital chooses to stay in the health care delivery business, a certain amount of exposure to risk is present. Risk avoidance may appear to be a senseless alternative and, as a result, may be prematurely dismissed. Avoidance has a direct immediate payback. Risk that is avoided does not have to be assumed, transferred or shared. Though total risk avoidance is impossible, partial avoidance needs to be evaluated. Partial avoidance may be considered in view of present activities as well as future activities.

To the extent the hospital is successful in avoiding risk, the necessity of funding for possible loss is reduced. With due regard for professional, social, geographic, demographic and financial considerations, high-risk procedures and services presently provided by the hospital may be accomplished equally well at another properly equipped and staffed facility. High-risk methods presently employed may have a safe alternative. Avoidance by shifting would appear to parallel national and local facilities planning objectives in reducing service duplication and cost.

High-risk services and methods are not limited to the exotic, esoteric and heroic. The hospital may avoid risk by initiation of such programs as self-care, through which the patient and family assume a larger part of the nursing care burden.

Consider risk exposure for new or expanded services offered in the future. If the hospital is self-funding, how does the new service affect previous actuarial projections?

An upward revision in the actuarial determination to accommodate the new service is risk exposure cost. If the risk exposure cost is such that the new service cannot be priced competitively, then at least one objective reason for not initiating the service is established. The individual hospital risk exposure cost is actuarially determined by examining such increments as patient days; admission; units of service by category; surgical procedures; number of employed physicians, surgeons and other professional medical personnel; and number of special care services. Incremental evaluation of risk cost as described above will sensitize the hospital to its risk exposure permitting risk considerations to become part of the new or expanded service decision. Important in the insurance decision is that exposure cannot be prevented, but it can be avoided.

REDUCING RISK

Formal risk reduction or risk management programs are receiving a greater amount of attention from hospitals today, but the concept is relatively new to them. The concept of risk management may best be conceptualized as the management of uncertainty. The use of the word *uncertainty* is preferred because it does not channel thinking solely to a preoccupation with the negative aspects of uncertainty—loss and damage. Providing high-quality patient care and maintaining high employee morale cannot be viewed as certain, but rather must be assured through management practices within the organization. A risk reduction program is a plan of assurance. To the extent assurance is successful, insurance is unnecessary.

The objective of risk reduction is a legitimate part of any insurance program without regard to the funding methods adopted. However, the financial benefits of a successful program will accrue more immediately and directly to the hospital that assumes a large self-retention (third option discussed below). Commercial insurers at this time do not have the historical data available to them to make an objective determination of a premium discount factor for application in the environment of an effective program.

Recent Interest

If risk reduction is a legitimate concept, why have hospitals only recently expressed interest in it? Hospitals have recently become interested in the organization, structure and elements of a *formal* risk reduction program. Risk reduction has been applied in hospitals, but unfortunately in an unspecified and fragmented manner. Committee charters did not clearly identify or give the risk control objective priority. The risk control function was delegated piecemeal to numerous in-house committees such as product evaluation, safety and patient care, and to outside agencies such as the hospital's insurance carrier. Little inter- or intra-hospital coordination of the risk control activity was effected.

Hospitals recognize the time has come for a formalized, goal-oriented program. The following reasons reinforce this conclusion.

- **Increased Liability Exposure.** Quoting a recent statement by the United Hospital Board of Trustees in Port Chester, New York, may best illustrate the point.

    > The ability to judge patient care is not within the sole province of physicians. If it were, the law would not place this burden on the trustees, nor would the courts hold the trustees responsible for actions of medical staff members.[1]

- **Expanding Judiciary Interpretations.** An example of expanding judiciary interpretation is illustrated in the Illinois Supreme Court decision *Renslow v. Mennonite Hospital.* The court's August 8, 1977 opinion held that a child has cause of action against a hospital for injuries resulting from alleged negligent conduct against his mother before he was conceived.
- **Regulation.** Bureau of Health Insurance Revision No. 173 requires capabilities of risk management and claims management as part of alternative funding programs.[2]
- **History.** Recent studies indicate that nearly 80 percent of patient injury incidents occur in hospitals and that 35 percent of all paid claims are assessed against hospitals.[3]

Necessary Principles

Principles necessary in the development of an effective risk reduction program include:

- Cooperation and Commitment. The development of the program should include the active participation of the hospital trustees, hospital management and hospital medical staff.
- Discriminatory Use of Outside Consultants. The consultant should be only an adjunct to management. Development of the hospital program should not be delegated to the outside consultant.
- Employing or Retaining Legal Counsel. Legal counsel must be well versed in malpractice issues, have a sense of proportion in what lawyers do well and what they do badly, be active in the review of the risk management program and, finally, have the confidence of the physicians.
- Developing a Data Collection Program. Data collection serves as both a detection means and an evaluation means. Data collection may be formal and informal. Formal data gathering may be by way of incident reports, medical care evaluation studies, complaints, suggestions, etc.

Informal data collection effort is accomplished by cultivating confidence and applying discretion.

- Recognizing that the Hospital's Exposure to Liability is Growing. Good historical claims experience may be deceptive in dealing with tomorrow's litigation environment.

ASSUMING RISK

Risk assumption by the hospital is a conscious decision to pay, from hospital assets, potential losses that may occur. Potential losses may be anticipated with appropriate funding provisions or left unfunded. Assumption of risk is often referred to as self-insuring. Because insurance implies spreading of risk, an attribute not common to most hospital self-funding programs, the term "self-retention" may be a more appropriate nomenclature.

Self-retention should be considered if one of the following four conditions is present.[4]

1. It is impossible to avoid the risk or to prevent the loss from occurring, and it is impossible to transfer the risk.
2. The maximum possible or probable loss is nominal. Should a loss occur, the hospital could absorb it out of current operations with no material adverse effect.
3. The probability of loss is so small that it can be ignored, or the probability of loss is so high that to transfer it would cost as much as the loss occurrence or loss occurrence limits.
4. The hospital can predict fairly well what its loss experience will be.

The hospital has three funding alternatives to consider if it chooses to assume the risk: "going bare," self-retention and single-owned captive insurance company.

Going Bare

"Going bare" may be characterized as a plan that makes no advance provision for loss. It does not fail to recognize the possibility of a loss; rather the plan is to assume the financial consequences of the loss in the period of occurrence. Proponents of this option believe defendants in litigation are selected based on their ability to meet settlement or award demands. As a result, the lack of visible insurance lessens the chances that the hospital will be selected if it is bare. The philosophy is, "You can't get blood out of a stone."

Going bare does not require administrative effort until such time as a claim is filed. Also, no cash demand is made on the organization until the loss is settled.

Principal disadvantages of going bare center largely on cost reimbursability and financial planning. Loss and related expense incurred *are not reimbursable* to the hospital under the principles of reimbursement if the hospital chooses not to maintain adequate protection against likely losses, either through the purchase of commercial insurance, self-funding or other alternatives available. (Note: Unfunded losses through a deductible are reimbursable if the aggregate deductible is no more than the greater of ten percent of the provider's net worth or $100,000: see Health Insurance Manual 15,2162.5.)

From an operating standpoint, the losses are unanticipated and, as a result, cannot be budgeted. Not being budgeted, they cannot be built into the product price. Operating statements may vary widely from year to year depending on the loss experience and, as a result, would be unduly influenced by chance results. Hospital equity is fully exposed to settlement demands and jury awards which may destroy the organization.

Self-Retention

The second funding alternative available to the hospital if the risk is to be assumed is self-retention. Self-retention differs from "going bare" in that the hospital adopts a plan to make an advance funding provision for a possible loss occurrence at some future time.

Self-retention may be advocated for one or more of the following reasons. First, by self-retention, the hospital can save part of the markup the insurer must make to cover expenses, contingency reserves and profit margin. The commercial insurer markup ranges between 20 and 45 percent of premium. Certain services such as claims administration, legal and loss control provided by the insurance company for the benefit of the insured would reduce the savings to the extent these services are secured and utilized from alternative sources.

Second, the hospital benefits from the timing difference between funding and loss. Earnings on funded dollars accrue to the benefit of the self-retention fund.

Third, by self-retention, the hospital has a greater incentive to control its losses. It is likely the hospital staff will be more acutely aware of loss prevention and loss reduction measures if the employer is directly and financially responsible and accountable for loss occurrences.

Fourth, by self-retention, the hospital can reduce its annual risk exposure expense. The hospital believes its expected losses will be less than that projected by the insurance company and reflected in the premium quote.

Subject to the extent actually realized, each of these possible advantages must be evaluated in the short-term financial perspective of a possible material loss. Actual loss experience in any single year may vary considerably with actuarially projected loss. In the event of a material loss early in the self-retention program, will the hospital be capable of withstanding the financial strain of the loss—or losses? Is the temperament of the governing board and management such that they can cope with a seriously adverse loss early in the self-retention program? Does the hospital have a bond indenture that permits self-retention, or is it required to insure (transfer the risk) for the comfort of its creditors?

Other immediate considerations include the welfare of hospital trustees and hospital employees. The hospital's directors' and officers' liability coverage may require the hospital to have professional liability insurance; and, in the absence of such insurance, the directors' and officers' policy is void. Hospital employees, including staff physicians, may be uncomfortable in their professional roles if the risk is assumed as opposed to transferred.

The confidence in actuarial projections is suspect. At the risk of oversimplification, trend projection from historical reflection is inadequate in the malpractice environment today. As previously stated, the hospital has increased liability exposure and is subject to expanding judiciary interpretation. An increasingly liberal jury is also a factor. The full reflection of these new and developing factors in the actuarial analysis is doubtful. The unfortunate result is the hospital improperly recognizes the risk and underestimates the magnitude of the potential loss.

No spread of risk is present in the individual hospital self-retention program. The laws of large numbers and probability analysis are of little comfort to the single hospital.

Single-Owned Captive

The third funding alternative available to the hospital if the risk is to be assumed is the formation of a single-owned captive insurance company. A captive is an incorporated, limited-purpose insurance company established to insure the hospital against malpractice and/or general liability losses that it may have. The single-owned captive serves to insure only the risks of its sole owner. The advantages and disadvantages applicable to self-retention funding also apply to the single-owned captive. The principal reason for forming a single-owned captive is to provide access to insurance markets not available to in-house funding.

Captive insurers may obtain certain covers from reinsurers that the hospital itself cannot obtain. By nature and tradition reinsurers are more flexible, permitting the captive to better tailor its insurance program. The reinsurer is not subject to as many legal restrictions as the insurer dealing with the individual hospital.[5]

Self-retention funding may be considered unsafe or risky for the hospital in the event of a material loss. Obtaining reinsurance transfers part of the risk previously assumed by the hospital to an insurer. (An in-house self-retention fund may accomplish in part the transfer of risk objective by obtaining excess coverage.)

The formation of a captive has some unique problems associated with it. First, the capitalization cost is not reimbursable to the hospital. Second, the Provider Reimbursement Manual requires the captive to meet six additional provisions before premiums are reimbursable. (The six unique provisions are identified under "Risk May Be Shared, Multi-Owned Captive," below.) Third, and currently the most serious problem is the unavailability of reinsurance in today's market; and this, ironically, is the principal reason for forming the captive.

TRANSFERRING RISK

Risk transfer is generally accomplished by two-party contract—one party assumes financial responsibility for the other party's risk in consideration of a premium. The hospital pays a certain cost (premium) to avoid responsibility for an uncertain financial loss (contingency insured against). Risk transfer has historically been the most common method of dealing with risk for hospitals. For this reason, the advantages and disadvantages of risk transfer are important.

Transfer of risk by way of insurance appeals to the hospital because it offers the following:

- spread of risk;
- premium reimbursement by third party cost reimbursers;
- fixed and known cost to the hospital;
- loss prevention and claims handling services;
- legal services;
- indemnification up to the insured limits for those who suffer loss; and
- flexible risk-funding tools—primary coverage, excess coverage, quota share.

Disadvantages of risk transfer by way of insurance include the following:

- little immediate reward for good loss experience;
- complex and esoteric pricing methods;
- nonavailability in some cases for primary coverage and an acute lack of excess insurers;
- premium in some cases approaches the insured limits;
- suspicion that present premium pricing may be to cover undercharges of previous years;
- sellers' market; and
- poor anticipatory planning on the part of insurers.

Commercial insurance may be contracted on an "occurrence" basis or a "claims-made" basis. The occurrence basis will cover losses reported at any time in the future that occurred during the specific policy year. The claims-made basis covers only those losses reported during the policy year. Premium cost to the hospital on a first-year claims-made contract will be lower than costs quoted on an occurrence basis because the insurer is not assuming liability for loss occurrences during the policy year that will be reported at some time in the future. The reduction in premium expense is only temporary; each succeeding year's premium expense increases to cover the tail.

Notwithstanding the recent problems associated with commercial insurance, transfer of risk should continue to be considered a viable option in the insurance program. Utilization of this option has desirable inherent characteristics for the program development to include flexibility and compatibility. Commercial insurance can be tailored to the adopted program either in the primary or the excess area. Commercial insurance may be first dollar, limited deductible, quota share participation, quota share with a stop loss, or self-insured retention. Additionally, commercial insurance premiums serve as a benchmark in determining reimbursability of other alternative programs. Other alternatives cannot exceed the commercial insurance cost.

SHARING RISK

Sharing of risk is the process by which uncertainty of loss is reduced. Sharing may or may not involve transfer of risk. Transfer of risk is not present in the shared program that assesses each individual hospital based on its own loss experience. Transfer of risk is present if the individual hospitals transfer their individual risks to the shared group. The uncertain financial loss of the individual hospital is exchanged for the more predictable loss experience of the sharing group.

Sharing of risk avails itself of selectivity and the law of larger numbers. The sharing group may make its service available to only those hospitals that meet the group's criteria, such as geographic location, size, claims experience, type of services provided, etc. The law of larger numbers holds that while uncertainty of the amount of loss to the individual hospital is very high, uncertainty of the total amount of loss to a large group is much lower, allowing a fairly accurate estimate of such total loss for the group. The foundation of insurance rests on this law.

Two funding alternatives are available to the hospital if it chooses to share the risk. The first alternative is the formation of a multi-owned captive, which is new to the hospital field though not new to industry in general. The second alternative is the establishment of a pooled trust, which is also new to the hospital field.

Multi-Owned Captive

As of March 1, 1977, twenty-one captives have been formed, 15 are operational, insuring 726 hospitals with an annualized premium exceeding $700 million. Of the 21 captives formed, eight were domiciled offshore.[6] More current estimates as of this writing indicate 40 captives have been formed.

Three primary reasons exist for the formation of a multi-owned captive. First, it allows the avoidance of existing state insurance commission regulations. Certain state insurance codes do not permit self-insurance (funding), or they force the hospital into a joint underwriting association. The state insurance commission may also have high capitalization and reserve requirements. Only two states, Nebraska and Colorado, have legislation specifically aimed at attracting captives. Second, a multi-owned captive allows the hospital to tailor an insurance plan not available in the market. The hospital may desire broader or more comprehensive coverage than that available in the conventional insurance market. Third, it allows access to the reinsurance market. Reinsurers deal only with insurers, and the captive is an insurer. Other considerations such as spread of risk, timing differences, etc. apply to the multi-owned captive but are not unique to this alternative.

Captives are a new concept to the hospital made possible by new regulations which are subject to novel interpretations. As recently as January 1978 the hospital would have been ill advised to adopt this alternative if the captive were interpreted to be related to the hospital either through ownership or control as defined in Chapter 10 of the *Provider Reimbursement Manual*. Reimbursement for premiums paid to the related hospital or association formed captive was doubtful since the requirements for an independent fiduciary relationship could not be established.[7,8]

Transmittal No. 190 updated the *Provider Reimbursement Manual* to specifically recognize the related captive and permit premium reimbursement to the hospital if the following six additional provisions are met.[9]

1. The captive insurance company must be established in and meet the appropriate insurance laws of one of the United States, District of Columbia, or foreign government, if it is formed offshore.

2. The excess of actuarially determined loss reserves and related operating expenses over actual losses and related operating expenses and gains and losses from investments must be taken into account in establishing reasonable premium levels, which shall not reflect a profit factor.

3. All rebates and distributions paid by a captive insurance company to providers must be offset against the providers' administrative and general expenses in the year received. However, if a captive insurance company is liquidated, no offset is required for the return of capitalization costs previously paid by providers receiving the rebate. If payments are made to other than providers, e.g., the home office of a chain organization, appropriate adjustment of providers' costs is still necessary. Proper allocation of distributions by the home office to the providers must be made, based on the appropriate facts in each situation.

4. If a provider terminates from the Medicare program, the provider must obtain a final determination of the adequacy of premium reserves as of the date of termination. This determination must be obtained from an independent actuary, commercial insurance company or broker as described in section 2162.7. If the reserves are deemed excessive at the date of termination, the excess amount must be offset against the provider's allowable costs in its final cost report. If reserves are deemed inadequate, additional premium payments subsequent to the date of termination are not allowable provider costs.

5. In the case of offshore captives, investments by a captive insurance company are limited to low-risk investments such as bonds and notes issued by the United States Government, or debt securities issued by United States corporations or governmental entities within the United States rated in the top two classifications by United States-recognized securities-rating organizations. (All such captives will be required to annually submit to a designated intermediary a certified statement from an independent certified public accountant or actuary attesting to compliance or noncompliance with this requirement for the

previous period.) These investments cannot be pledged or used as collateral for loans obtained by the captive or parties related to the captive either directly or indirectly, nor may investments be made in a related organization.

6. Loans or any transfer of funds by the insurance company to policyholders, owners of providers or parties related to them are prohibited.

These six provisions are unique to the captive alternative. Equity and administrative problems resulting from these additional provisions will undoubtedly be the subject of future debate between hospitals and the Medicare Bureau. The last sentence of provision 4 appears ripe for challenge from the standpoint of equity. Provision 5 raises Internal Revenue Service withholding questions which, if unresolved, may leave the offshore captive having access to only 70 percent of its investment income.[10]

Pooled Trust

The second alternative available to the hospital that chooses to share the risk is the establishment of a pooled trust. Unlike the captive, assets of the trust are supervised by a third party independent fiduciary.

The pooled trust has all of the advantages of self-retention funding, plus (if so structured) spread of risk. To the extent spread of risk is present, transfer of risk also exists. Transfer of risk may be partial or total depending on the funding structure alternative adopted. Funding alternatives include total risk sharing, risk apportionment by the amount of loss, risk apportionment by fixed percentage participation or risk apportionment on a regional basis.

The pooled trust shares the same problems as that of self-retention funding plus the problems associated with working with a group to establish the structure of the pooled trust. Additionally, some state insurance laws may not allow the establishment of a pooled trust. However, some states, such as Illinois, permit pooled trust for charitable, not-for-profit organizations only.

MAKING THE DECISION

The preceding five methods of dealing with risk and the funding alternatives for each method make up the basic building blocks available to the hospital in its insurance programming decision. Tailoring an individual hospital insurance program will include some combination of two or more of the five methods outlined. Because each method has unique advantages, the combination of as many of the five methods as possible may be desirable. Avoid the risk if possible without compromising the mission of the hospital. Reducing the risk assures high-quality patient care. Assuming the risk gives the hospital an immediate vested interest in a sound risk management program. Transferring the risk permits the hospital to substitute a fixed known premium cost for a larger unknown loss. Sharing the risk provides the hospital with selectivity of group participants and, to a limited extent, spread of risk.

Emphasis should be placed on the hospital's overall program for dealing with risk. The insurance program should be a medium- to long-range, goal-oriented plan the hospital is willing to live with and develop. The hospital should recognize in the program development both those factors over which it has control and those factors over which it has no control. To do otherwise would confuse an insurance program with a gambler's folly. Hospitals should also recognize that the first year of the adopted program may be imperfect. Program perfection is not so immediate as program initiation based on conservative conception.

REFERENCES

1. Hudson, E. "Trustees and Doctors of Hospital in Westchester in Fight for Control." *New York Times* (September 6, 1977).

2. Department of Health, Education, and Welfare, Social Security Administration. "Cost Related to Patient Care." *Medicare Provider Reimbursement Manual* HIM-15 Part I, Chapter 21 (Washington, D.C.: HEW).

3. Ashby, J. L., Stephens, S.K. and Pearson, S. B. "Elements in Successful Risk Reduction Programs." *Hospital Progress* (July 1977) p. 60.

4. Williams, C. A., Jr. and Heins, R. M. *Risk Management and Insurance* 3rd ed. (New York: McGraw-Hill Book Co. 1976) p. 190, 191.

5. Ibid. p. 195.

6. Friedman, E. "Hospital Insurance Captives: Their Time Has Come." *Hospitals, J.A.H.A.* 51 (March 16, 1977) p. 88.

7. American Hospital Association. Subject: Medicare Reimbursement of Limited Purpose Insurance Companies. (Correspondence to hospital-sponsored insurance organizations and allied hospital association executives from James L. Groves, Risk Manager, September 9, 1977).

8. Blue Cross Association. Administrative Bulletin No. 1177—Malpractice Protection Costs (Correspondence to directors of Federal Programs-List 35, and Reimbursement Managers-List 35C, from Merritt W. Jacoby, vice president, Medicare and CHAMPUS Administration, August 3, 1977); and update to Administrative Bulletin No. 1177, September 13, 1977.

9. HEW Social Security Administration. "Cost Related to Patient Care." *Medicare Provider Reimbursement Manual.*

10. Stoltz, M. K. "Hospital Insurance Deadline Postponed." *Health Care Week* (March 13, 1978) p. 1.

CHAPTER 6

COST CONTAINMENT THROUGH THE FINANCIAL MANAGEMENT SYSTEM

The financial complexity of health care organizations, whether run for profit or not, makes a quality financial management system necessary. Such a system has tremendous impact on expenditures and costs, as well as upon revenues; therefore, it must be carefully integrated into the cost containment program. Several of the topics discussed in the previous chapters involve financial management directly or indirectly, for example, work standards used as a basis for the budget. Planning of activities is usually supported by a budget. Also manpower position control systems tie into the budget, while comparative analyses, such as that of leasing vs. buying, involves cost analysis. The emphasis in this chapter is on budget and cost control as the most important responsibilities of financial managers in cost containment, but most other elements of financial management are also important in cost containment. It is, therefore, necessary to involve the institution's chief financial expert in any cost containment program.

In this chapter the following topics are included:

- financial modeling
- budgeting and cost control
- cost analysis
- collection and billing
- refinancing

FINANCIAL MODELING

Financial modeling of health care institutions is a new approach to the complexity of financial planning. Computerized simulation models are being used to make projections, evaluate proposals, and prepare financial statements or balance sheets. Various models have been developed by the large accounting firms, by management consultants, and by some medical centers. Boldt's paper (Reading 52) contains an overview of financial modeling followed by a discussion of specific financial models.

BUDGETS

Budget and budgetary control is an essential ingredient in any cost containment program. Furthermore, several experts in the area of cost containment, especially in nonprofit organizations, feel that budgetary control is not only the most important tool but sometimes the only effective one. For a budget to be used in a cost containment program it must possess the following characteristics:

- It must be based on actual needs as established by management engineering studies.
- It must be flexible enough to allow for rapid changes in the health care system.
- It must be supported by a timely reporting and information system (usually computerized).
- Budget analysis and budget adjustments must complement the budget.

An extensive review of the state of the art of hospital budgets can be found in the article by Holder.[1]

Russell's paper (Reading 53) deals with budget preparation from the point of view of planning and control. The concept of a multiyear plan, which is now required from hospitals, is related to budgets. The system described in this paper demonstrates cost savings and becomes a cost-effective management tool in progressive health facilities.

One of the most successful methods of budget control is to allocate the budget to "cost centers." In this system, department managers accept responsibility for a budget and are accountable for its use. Stevenson and Patterson (Reading 54) describe such a system that was successfully implemented at Vancouver General Hospital.

COST ANALYSIS

For savings to be correctly defined, the several types of costs that might occur in any given situation must be thoroughly understood. A cost savings measurement model is proposed by Kretschmar (Reading 55). Such a model makes it possible to compare alternative projects from a cost saving point of view.

Diagnostic costing is a management tool that is used to analyze systematically the variance between the budget, which is based on standard costs, and the actual expenditures. Gillespie's article (Reading 56) presents an application to the hospital control and reimbursement systems.

COLLECTION AND BILLING

Cost containment programs may pertain to improvements in revenues as well as reduction in costs. Better collection and faster billing are two examples of improved cash flow and increased revenue. Smejda's article (Reading 57) lists and describes the ten best collection techniques. These techniques include not only billing and follow-up of delinquent accounts but also improvements in the preadmissions, admissions, and business offices.

Computer-to-computer communication between the provider of health care services and the third party payer expedites payment of claims, eliminates errors, and improves cash flow and personnel efficiency. Such a pioneering Blue Cross and Blue Shield electronic billing project is described by Elliot and Tucker (Reading 58). Significant savings are projected for both providers and payers.

REFINANCING

Interest cost may be one of the major expenses of health care institutions. Restructuring of debts may save health care institutions considerable amounts of money.

The last article in this chapter (Reading 59), by Cain and Gilbert, presents an overview of the various options of refinancing and refunding. Specifically, liability management is described, and the reasons to consider refunding are presented with the mechanics of a bond refunding analysis and program.

NOTE

1. W.W. Holder, "Hospital Budgeting: State of the Art," *Hospital and Health Services Administration* 23 (1978): 51–59.

BIBLIOGRAPHY

Berman, H., and Weeks, L. *The Financial Management of Hospitals.* 3rd ed. Ann Arbor: Health Administration Press, 1976.

Boehmer, N. "Reducing Lost Charges: Daily Cart Exchange System." *Purchasing Administration,* May-June 1977.

Bowman, R.W. "Extend Use of Cost-Finding Techniques." *Modern Healthcare,* November 1977.

Brandow, R.H. "Explaining Hospital Costs with Graphs." *Hospital Financial Management,* May 1978.

Cain, M.D., and Gilbert, R.N., eds. "Capital Financing." *Topics in Health Care Financing,* Fall 1978.

Calamari, F.A., et al. "Zero-Base Budgeting—A Hospital Application." *Hospital Topics,* March–April 1979.

Caruana, R.Q., and Kudder, G. "Seeing Through the Figures with Ratios." *Hospital Financial Management,* June 1978.

Carr, A.V., and Parris, W.K. "Responsibility Accounting Measure of Management." *Hospital Financial Management,* January 1976.

Cleverley, W.O. *Essentials of Hospital Finance.* Germantown, Md.: Aspen Systems Corp., 1978.

Cleverley, W.O. *Financial Management of Health Care Facilities.* Germantown, Md.: Aspen Systems Corp., 1976.

Dahlfues, D.M. "Promissory Notes—Let Patient, Not Hospital, Assume Interest Cost." *Hospital Financial Management,* June 1978.

Dillon, R.D. *Zero-Base Budgeting for Health Care Institutions.* Germantown, Md.: Aspen Systems Corp., 1979.

Dillon, R.D. "Zero Base Budgeting: An Introduction." *Hospital Financial Management,* November 1977.

Dirksen, C.J. "Determining How and Why Your Costs Are Changing." *Hospital Financial Management,* December 1978.

Drebin, M.E. "Financial Information Systems: The Key to Hospitals' Survival." *Hospitals, JAHA,* 16 June 1978.

Frank, W.G. "Managerial Accounting Analysis of Hospital Costs." *Health Services Research,* Spring 1976.

Gilbert, R. Neal. "Four-Step Capital Budgeting." *Hospital Financial Management,* June 1976.

Griffith, J.R. "Budget Processes Integral to Effective Cost Control System." *Hospital Financial Management,* July 1977.

"Hard Times Forcing Tough Collection." *Modern Healthcare,* April 1975.

Haskett, J.A. "How to Make the Cash Flow Faster." *Modern Healthcare,* July 1975.

Herzlinger, R.E. "Fiscal Management in Health Organizations." *Health Care Management Review,* Summer 1977.

Holder, W.W., and Williams, T. "Better Cost Control with Flexible Budgets and Variance Analysis." *Hospital Financial Management,* January 1976.

Horwitz, R.M. "Flexible Budgeting: Tips for Switching." *Hospital Financial Management,* March 1977.

Ingram, J.C., "Uniform Accounting: How It Will Affect Hospitals." *Hospital Financial Management,* June 1977.

Johnson, R.A., and Priest, S.L. "How Switching to Tape Billing Improved Cash Flow." *Hospital Financial Management,* October 1977.

Lachner, B.J. "The ABC's of Cost Accountability." *Trustee,* December 1977.

Maber, M., and Metha, N. *Hospital Accounting Systems and Controls.* Englewood Cliffs, N.J.: Prentice-Hall, 1976.

MacStravic, R.E. "Containing Costs Through Regional Funding." *Hospital Financial Management,* June 1979.

Michela, W. "Defining and Analyzing Cost—A Statistical Approach." *Hospital Financial Management,* January 1975.

Milani, K., et al. "Hospital Budgeting Requires Planning, Organization and Cooperation." *Health Service Manager,* February 1978.

Mudarri, S.F., and DeNoble, R.A. "Better Methods to Determine True Cost of Hospital Care." *Management Controls,* September-October 1977.

Nestman, L.J. "Responsibility Accounting—A Tool for Better Planning and Cost Control in the Hospital." *Hospital Administration in Canada,* February 1974.

Pearson, D. "Payment Patterns." *Hospital Financial Management,* March 1978.

Phillip, J.P. "New AHA Indexes Provide Fairer View of Rising Costs." *Hospitals, JAHA,* 16 July 1977.

Raajtes, R.B. "Budget and Cost Control." *Hospital Financial Management,* March 1972.

Resinger, H.E. "Budgeting: Cost Control Through Planning." *College of American Pathologists,* August 1977.

Rowley, C.S. "Which Is Best to Find Cost Behavior." *Hospital Financial Management,* April 1976.

Saul, D.C. "Fiscal Management." *Hospitals, JAHA,* 1 April 1975.

Seawell, L., *Hospital Financial Accounting: Theory and Practice.* Chicago: Hospital Financial Management Association, 1976.

Singer, J.P. "Flexible Budgeting Techniques Provide Tool for Cost Control." *Hospitals, JAHA,* 1 July 1977.

Stevenson, B.W., and Patterson, D. "Vancouver General Hospital: Planning for Cost Control." *Dimensions in Health Service,* May 1976.

Suver, T.D., and Neuman, B.R. "Zero Base Budgeting." *Hospital and Health Services Administration,* Spring 1979.

Suver, T.D., and Newman, B.R. "Cost of Capital." *Hospital Financial Management,* February 1978.

Thompson, G.B., and Canron, W.G. "Hospitals, Like Industry, Must Apply Cost Accounting Techniques." *Hospitals, JAHA,* 16 June 1978.

Toomey, R.E., and Bruun, E.E. "Multihospital System Minimizes Management Costs Through Centralized Financial Operations." *Hospitals, JAHA,* 16 June 1978.

Tower, R.B., Jr. "Study Finds Definite Trend Toward Uniform Reporting." *Hospital Financial Management,* October 1978.

Wheeler, D.L. "Negotiating and Bidding for Good Results." *Hospitals, JAHA,* 16 June 1977.

Weaver, P.G. "Cost Analysis by Patient Diagnosis." *Dimensions in Health Service,* June 1977.

Whipple, D. "Controlling Hospital Costs: An Index Approach." *Inquiry,* March 1976.

Yorke, J.D. "Inventory Your Receivables—You May Increase Cash Flow." *Hospital Financial Management,* April 1977.

52. Financial Modeling: A Must for Today's Hospital Management

BEN I. BOLDT, JR.

Reprinted with permission from *Health Care Management Review,* Summer 1978, pp. 7-13.

As the administrator or financial manager of your hospital, have you ever considered the implications of your institution's capital project programs for the future financial success or survival of your institution? Do you understand how your hospital's cash flow requirements will be affected if the newly initiated renovation project incurred a 20-percent cost overrun? Have you taken time to analyze the financial implications of securing that new CAT scanner, but obtaining only 60 percent of the expected patient utilization?

If the answers to the above questions are "no" or "not recently," perhaps you are not providing the appropriate level of service to your institution. Capital projects bring about top major problems facing hospital management today: the planning for and utilization of cash. A one-time evaluation of a project may be adequate to reach a decision to proceed; but since most capital projects span a number of months or even years, a continuing analysis is also necessary to reflect the impact of program changes on hospital operations.

The analysis and evaluation of capital expenditure programs are not the only areas that require close and continuing attention. The requirement to provide sound financial planning for overall hospital operations is increasing almost daily as a result of new legislation and the continual change of reimbursement programs.

For example, the trend for hospitals and hospital groups to share services—both administrative and medical—encourages strong financial and operational planning. Shared services seem to be a good idea; but without careful planning and a program of continued analysis, today's cost-effective idea might result in unnecessarily high or unreimbursed costs tomorrow.

To meet the increasing demand for planning, the hospital administrator or financial manager will have to use financial planning techniques such as flexible budgeting (adjusting budgeted expenses and revenues to reflect actual versus planned volumes before determining actual to budget variances), preparation of quarterly or even monthly cost reports to estimate the year-end reimbursement situation, and multiyear financial projections to analyze the long-term impact of construction programs or changes in patient mix. However, even though the need is recognized and the desire to implement these planning techniques is sincere, one of the major stumbling blocks to the success of these techniques has been the amount of time which must be incurred to perform the required calculations either initially or when changes are made to the assumptions.

The financial model is an important tool which can relieve managers and their staff from the task of performing the repetitive mathematical calculations required for thorough financial planning. Simply stated, a financial model is a computer program that simulates, either in whole or in part, the financial operations of the hospital. It can perform predetermined calculations required by a flexible budget, a cost report or most other types of financial analyses. The financial model provides its user with two distinct groups of advantages:

1. Clerical Efficiency
   - It reduces the time necessary to initially prepare or revise the financial projections.
   - It reduces the cost of preparing and revising the financial projections.
   - It eliminates the arithmetical errors of manually prepared projections.

2. Planning Improvements
   - It improves the planning process since it allows more time to be directed at analyzing the problems encountered.
   - It provides insight into hospital operations by identifying (or forcing someone to identify) how factors within the hospital interact.
   - It provides an ability to quickly try numerous alternative strategies to find or identify those that provide optimum results.

Financial models can be classified into three major categories: general, industry or specific function, and custom.

THE GENERAL MODEL

General models include those models which provide pro forma financial statements and are not restricted to any one industry or purpose. The principal output of these models includes: an income statement, balance sheet, and statement of cash flow or change in working capital.

Within the general category, two types of financial models can be identified: unstructured and structured.

The *unstructured* model can be thought of as a matrix programmed on a computer in which the user has the ability to define the number of columns and rows to be used for calculations, and the mathematical relationships between these columns and rows. The level of detail and sophistication of the calculations can be as simple or complex as the user wishes to make it. The unstructured general financial model allows maximum flexibility in integrating modeling into the planning process; however, it also demands a substantial amount of technical know-how.

The *structured* model is similar in concept to the unstructured model except that the number of columns and rows that can be used within the matrix is fixed and many of the relationships between columns and rows are predefined and cannot be changed by the user. This type of financial model requires the user to input data in a specified format and identify the variable values to be used in the projections in a set manner. The model processes the input data and prepares output reports in a predetermined format.

The structured model provides an excellent tool for the less experienced user while providing most of the modeling capability found in the more sophisticated unstructured model.

An income statement comparing the beginning condition of an unstructured and structured model before data is entered for analysis appears in Table 1. As illustrated, the unstructured model requires the user to define the number of rows (revenue and cost elements) and columns (years or other time periods) to be used in the projections. The structured model has these items defined (in the illustration 10 rows and 4 years respectively), as well as defined type of data to be entered in the rows (Rows 1 and 2 are for revenue items, Row 8 is for general and administrative expenses, etc.).

The general category of financial models has many applications in the area of multiyear financial projections. For example, it can be used to answer types of planning questions such as: What is the expected impact on operating costs due to the planned renovation program? Can the hospital generate the necessary cash flow to undertake a $12 million construction program? What happens to the hospital's financial position if pediatric services are phased out and a 7-percent average occupancy is lost over the next five years?

Table 1 Comparison of Unstructured and Structured Financial Models

Unstructured

Time (Years)

Line No.	Title	Y_1	Y_2	Y_3	Y_4	Y_5	...	Y_n
1								
2	Must be							
3	defined							
4	by user							
5								
6								
7								
8								
9								
10								
...								
n								

Structured

Time (Years)

Line No.	Title	Y_1	Y_2	Y_3	Y_4
1	Revenue (1)				
2	Revenue (2)				
3	Total Revenue				
4	Variable Cost (1)				
5	Variable Cost (2)				
6	Fixed Expense (1)				
7	Fixed Expense (2)				
8	G & A Expense				
9	Other Expense				
10	Net Income				

These questions are answered by changing the projection variables affected by the criteria of the question. For example, when answering the first or second question above, users should ask themselves What items of my present plan are affected by the renovation or construction program? The "simplified" answer might be:

1. Income Statement
   - Interest expense will increase since monies are to be borrowed and repaid over a period of 20 years.
   - Salary expense will increase since more nursing staff will be required.
   - Fixed expenses will increase as a result of higher depreciation charges.
   - Heat, power and light will decrease because of the installation of more efficient systems.

2. Balance Sheet
   - Long-term debt will increase as a result of additional borrowing.
   - Short-term debt will be incurred to finance construction payments between long-term debt take-downs.
   - Fixed assets will increase to reflect the new facility being put into service.
   - Accumulated depreciation will increase as a result of the depreciation charges.

After identifying the known or estimated value of the variable changes, the user can input the data and run the model to reflect the effect of these changes on the income statement, balance sheet and cash flow statement.

The third question presents a situation where the principal variables affected are contained in the income statement. The number and type of changes will depend a great deal on the level of sophistication originally incorporated into the model. For example, a complex relationship might relate specific ancillary services (laboratory tests, x-ray procedures, etc.) within the hospital to the types of patients (general, medical, surgical, pediatric, obstetric, etc.) serviced. Alternatively, a simple case might relate only the overall average revenue or average cost per patient day to total patient days regardless of the type of patient. To illustrate, the income statement projection might change for the simplified case as follows:

- patient days will decrease because of the loss of pediatric patients;
- average revenue day will decrease since pediatrics has a higher average revenue/patient day which will be lost; and

- average cost/day will decrease since pediatrics has a higher average revenue/patient day which will be lost; and
- average cost/day will decrease as a result of the reduction in staff serving pediatrics.

These changes would be reflected in the input data and the model run to ascertain the effect on operating income, balance sheet and cash flow to answer the "what happens if" question.

THE INDUSTRY MODEL

The industry category of financial models is structured and has two principal applications within the health care industry: flexible budgeting and the preparation of cost reimbursement reports.

The Budget Model

The budget model provides a hospital with the ability to develop departmental budgets based on a desired level of service and expected occupancy rate. When all department-level assumptions are input, the model executes the calculations necessary to determine each department's budget as well as consolidating all departments to obtain the budget for the total hospital. Once the budget is established, the model provides the user with the ability to rapidly recalculate the budget to reflect varying conditions such as changes in occupancy and labor costs, increases in radiology service charges or other departmental revenue, or cost changes. Depending on the degree of sophistication used, this type of model offers to the hospital financial manager complete flexible budgeting capability.

The features that distinguish a forecasting model from a budget model are the length of time covered by the projections and the level of detail included. Typically, a budget model is designed to cover a one-year period by month and provides for totaling the months for each line item entered to obtain the budgeted amount for the year. Additionally, this type of model provides for not only revenue and expense data but operating statistics at the department level. The overall level of detail utilized in a budget model should correspond to the hospital's chart of accounts. This chart of accounts detail is desirable since it facilitates easy comparison of the actual results versus budgeted data throughout the year.

To illustrate the level of detail available, one operating budget model provides for:

- 19 routine service cost centers;

- 70 ancillary cost centers;
- 100 general and administrative cost centers;
- 80 expense classifications within each cost center; and
- nine methods for computing contractual allowance.

A major benefit of a budget model is the ability to develop meaningful departmental detail and be in a position to quickly analyze the impact of alternative courses of actions on the affected department(s) and the hospital in total. Examples of the types of options available within budget models for projecting financial and statistical data follow.

Predetermined Budgeted Amounts. With this simple option, predetermined budgeted amounts are entered for each budget period. This option may be used to enter constant value items such as depreciation, rental expense or other items which are relatively constant over the budget period. Research grants would also be entered using this option.

Constant or Varying Percentage of Another Budget Item. This type of option allows the user to interrelate budget line items. For instance, in many laboratories a professional fee is incurred as a percentage of the revenues derived from the department. If it is known that a change in the professional fee rate is to take place during the budget year the user can incorporate this option into the budget to reflect the specific percentage change and month in which the change will occur. Additionally, if the laboratory revenue is related to patient activity (patient days or admissions) the user can quickly see the professional fee expense to be incurred at the new rate for various levels of patient volume.

Constant or Varying Unit Increases. With this type of budget option, the user can prepare a budget reflecting dollar amount changes in patient revenue or other items budgeted on a dollar amount per unit of services or other items budgeted on a dollar amount per unit of services basis. For example, if patient days are budgeted by month, the effect of increasing the charge for a particular type of accommodation (semi-private, private, ward) by five dollars beginning in a specific month during the year can be quickly computed or analyzed.

By utilizing these types of budget options for either the revenue or expense for a unit of service, the user can "string" budget line items together to develop a detailed flexible budget. For example, the following types of calculations can be constructed:

- Patient days calculated by entering the occupancy percentage expected each year, the number of beds available and the days per year.
- Routine service revenues calculated by multiplying patient days by accommodation or by type of service (which could also be entered as a

percentage of total patient days) times the anticipated average daily charge for that accommodation or service. The daily charge may be budgeted using other projection options.

- Ancillary service revenues calculated using procedures and rate per procedure, or using average ancillary service charges per patient day or per outpatient visit for that department. Provisions are often available to accommodate general intensity of service factors applying to all ancillary departments or specific intensity factors applying only to specific departments.
- Operating expenses calculated based on cost per unit times number of units. Units may represent patient days, visits, procedures, meals served, employee hours or any other projection options. Professional fees (radiology, pathology, etc.) may be expressed as a percent of the revenues of a department. Employee fringe benefits may be expressed as a percent of wages and salaries.
- Contractual allowances calculated automatically based on a number of cost reimbursement and prospective reimbursement methods. The methods can include the standard Medicare, Medicaid and Blue Cross cost reimbursement formulas with cost ceilings, if applicable, or prospective reimbursement contracts which call for payment on an admission basis, per diem/visit basis or percentage of charge basis.

The Cost Reimbursement Model

The second type of application of the structured industry model is the cost reimbursement model. As the title implies, this model is specifically designed to prepare or recalculate a hospital's cost reimbursement report. The more advanced models allow for rapid recalculation and comparison of alternative allocation formula and reimbursement strategies. This capability allows the hospital financial executive to evaluate which of a number of allocation bases will provide the maximum reimbursement to the hospital or, alternatively, which is capable of answering the question, "What impact will that new Medicare regulation have on my expected reimbursement?"

Some of the capabilities provided by this type of model are:

- The model provides the user with the capability to experiment with various statistical bases, cost center composition and sequence of allocation alternatives. The effect of these alternatives on cost reimbursement can be quickly and economically determined.
- A user can quickly determine the effect of audit adjustments proposed by the Medicare intermediary. This information can assist the hospital.

in devising a strategy for discussing the adjustments with an intermediary.

- The model simplifies the preparation of cost reports by greatly reducing manual calculations and by automatically preparing worksheets for the cost report.
- Cost reimbursement and related contractual allowances can be estimated for interim periods.
- The model assists in developing realistic budgets and forecasts by providing the capability to determine cost reimbursement and related contractual allowances using budgeted and forecasted data.
- It allows analysis of reimbursement and preparation of special reports which assist in developing an appropriate reimbursement strategy.

Additionally, a few models have been designed with the user in mind. These provide for the following.

- Data being entered directly from the Medicare worksheets. This feature eliminates the need for information being entered on special input worksheets prior to entry to the system. The only requirement of the individual preparing the data for input is familiarity with the Medicare worksheets.
- Internal data exchange which enables the user to enter data once even though the data are used on several of the worksheets. These models automatically transfer the data to the appropriate worksheets.
- Preset standard cost centers and descriptions appearing on Form SSA-2552. Additionally, the user has the ability to modify the arrangement of cost centers and their descriptions as desired.

This provides almost complete freedom in choosing the appropriate number and composition of cost centers.

THE CUSTOM MODEL

The custom model is required when the simulation or analysis desired is so complicated or detailed that it cannot be performed by a model within the general or industry category. This category is best illustrated by a model used by a major midwest medical center.

The analysis to be undertaken was directed at assessing the cost impact of consolidating clinical services among the member institutions within the medical center. Figure 1 gives a conceptual illustration of the interactions required to implement the medical service transfers contemplated by the medical center.

Figure 1 Clinical Service Transfers Between Institutions within the Consortium: 1,000-Bed General Acute Care Hospital Specializing in Oncology

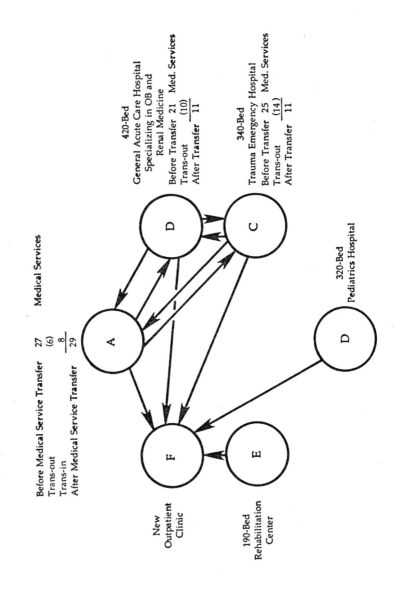

The model was designed to aid the planning process specifically in the area of projecting the cost changes resulting from a planned shared clinical service program, not only for the total medical center consortium, but at each institution within the consortium.

The model provides the planners with the capability to:

- project the cost impact of a specific shared clinical service program under consideration;
- project the cost impact of alternative programs; and
- update the financial projections related to an acceptable program with each year's current cost data and patient information.

The model is based on the concept that the patient utilization of an institution's ancillary services (laboratory, radiology, physical therapy, etc.) and therefore the ancillary service cost depend on the type of clinical service provided by the institution (pediatrics, oncology, renal medicine, etc.).

Accordingly, two types of data are used by the model: (1) data representing patient usage (patient profile) of ancillary services for each clinical service provided at each institution in the consortium, and (2) cost data for each institution segregated into fixed and variable elements.

The model integrates the patient profile data and cost data for each hospital to generate a cost matrix reflecting the operating costs of each ancillary service attributable to each clinical service "before" patient transfers and consolidations at each institution. Then each institution's "before" patient transfer cost matrix is operated on by the computer by relating the costs of each ancillary service used by each clinical service to the number of patients admitted to each respective clinical service.

After all changes are made to the cost matrix of each hospital, the computer prepares a report reflecting the costs, by ancillary service, for each clinical service within each institution and for the total medical center consortium, "after" the patient transfers associated with the proposed planned shared clinical service program. By comparing the change in costs between the "before" and "after" conditions, the planners are able to test the financial impact of the numerous clinical service transfer alternatives to identify those programs which will not only provide improved health care, but will provide that care at a lower cost.

As developed, the model does not address every potential financial evaluation problem associated with clinical service consolidation; however, it illustrates how the development of a custom computer model can assist health care planners or hospital financial executives to analyze some of the financial considerations encountered during the development of a hospital's or group of hospitals' long-range plan.

FINANCIAL MODELING—A VALUABLE TOOL

Experience gained in industry and more recently within the health care field at major for-profit hospital corporations and large nonprofit institutions indicates that almost any management problem or process, in which there is repetitiveness, some logic and numerous changes in the assumptions or decisions criteria, is a candidate for financial model application.

As hospital managers face this new era of financial and operational planning, they will be able to take a more aggressive position if they can quickly predict the outcome of their decisions or the impact of actions outside their span of control. Certainly financial modeling provides one of the answers to the increasing demand for more detailed and thorough planning and provides the ability to rapidly respond to the question, "What happens if..."

53. New Tools for Budgeting and Cost Analysis

S. RUSSELL

Reprinted from *Dimensions in Health Service, Journal of the Canadian Hospital Association,* November 1976, pp. 33–35, by permission of the Canadian Hospital Association, © 1976.

In January 1974, Systems Dimensions Limited (SDL) undertook a major research and development project to develop computer software and related administrative procedures to assist in health care planning, budgeting and cost analysis. The development process, including five pilot implementations, was completed in March 1976.

The primary pilot implementation site was York County Hospital (YCH) in Newmarket, Ontario, a typical community hospital offering a broad range of services. During the project, the hospital expanded its facilities from 258 to 307 beds to meet the needs of a growing population in the area, and introduced a mini-computer into the business office to automate the payroll general ledger and other financial applications to assist in the day-to-day management of the hospital. York County Hospital provided a good opportunity to develop and demonstrate some new concepts and systems to assist hospital management with planning, budgeting and cost analysis.

The various systems developed are identified by the term MEDIC, an acronym that stands for Method for Efficient Decision-making and Institutional Cost-Estimation. In general, the MEDIC systems have been designed to describe the activities of health care institutions and to operate on data available from patients, personnel and financial records.

The basic MEDIC concepts are provided in the analytical framework of cost centers, activities and resources that can be defined for each health care institution. A cost center is an organizational entity within the health care institution under the authority of a director or manager who assumes budgetary and planning responsibility for the unit. The function of a cost center is to provide service either directly in response to requirements generated by patients or to support the operation of the institution.

The term *activity* refers to services provided directly to patients. Each activity must be described in terms of an output measure of workload and the resources in terms of staff, space, supplies and expenses required to provide the service. The variable costs of activity-related resources fluctuate with changes in the activity workload which is affected by changes in the patient load. The overhead costs associated with cost center resources are usually fixed since they are not affected by normal changes in workload and patient load.

GENERAL FRAMEWORK

At this point, an example may be helpful. We can take the laboratory as the cost center and biochemistry as the activity with the workload measured in terms of the number of standard lab units. The resource requirements could be the technologist's time at the activity level and the lab manager's time at the cost center level as the overhead. There is a generalized analytical framework that can be applied to any area of hospital operation, for example, nursing, pharmacy, radiology, physiotherapy, etc., and to any level of detail from an individual hospital department to the institution as a whole.

Within this basic conceptual framework MEDIC provides the methodology and analytical systems for planning and budgeting at either the institu-

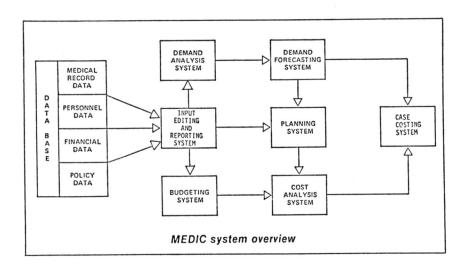

MEDIC system overview

tional or regional level. The preparation of next year's operating budget and the formulation of a long-term plan both require estimates of the demand for service and of the resources to meet that demand. MEDIC structures this process into four distinct phases:

- **Patient load.** Based on the current casemix, the number of cases and days by service is forecasted.
- **Workload.** Based on the expected patient load, the volume of work to each patient service is projected.
- **Resource requirements.** Based on the anticipated workload, total staff and dollar requirements are determined.
- **Unit costs.** Total dollar requirements are analyzed in terms of the direct and indirect costs of each patient service.

NEEDS ANALYSIS

This methodology provides a step-by-step approach to the analysis of needs before resources are committed. Performance can thus be reviewed by comparing unit costs of services on a historical as well as inter-hospital basis. The MEDIC methodology applies for both short-term budget decisions over the next twelve months and long-term planning decisions over the next five years.

There are seven MEDIC analytical systems described briefly, below; their inter-relationships are shown in the accompanying figure.

1. **Demand analysis:** measure of historical demand for patient services from medical record abstract files.
2. **Demand forecasting:** projection of future demand for patient services based on a population forecast and expected utilization rates.
3. **Planning:** estimation of future resource requirements based on patient demand and workload.
4. **Budget preparation:** annual iterative process of translating departmental objectives into resource requirements.
5. **Cost allocation:** distribution of overhead cost to patient services.
6. **Case (disease) costing:** analysis of cost of providing services to individual or groups of patients.
7. **Input editing and reporting:** checking for input errors and data reporting for all other systems.

All the MEDIC systems were tested on information provided by York County Hospital. In each pilot test, hospital management were interviewed, their informational needs determined, the source data collected and analyzed. Initially, budget and statistical information was combined manually to calculate unit costs, before computer programs were designed. Once the computer software was developed at SDL, YCH data was the first to be used to test and debug the systems. The result of each pilot test was documented in the form of a case study report and presented to the YCH management for comments. (There are nine case study reports available from SDL describing five MEDIC pilot implementations.) In this way, each of the MEDIC systems was tested once at YCH and at least once more at one of the other four pilot implementation sites.

DEMAND FORECAST

The first demand analysis was based on the 1973 HMRI (Hospital Medical Records Institute) patient medical record abstract file. The first demand forecast was based on the 1971 Canadian census data and a population forecast provided by the planning department of the regional municipality of York. Combining the service utilization rates by age and sex groups with the rapidly growing population base that has a younger age structure produces some dynamic results. For example, over the five-year forecast, the number of cases increased 46 per cent whereas the number of patient days only increased 44 per cent.

In the Ottawa Regional demand study for seven hospitals, the opposite phenomenon occurred because of an aging, slower growing population base, that is, the number of cases increased by 14 per cent and the number of patient days increased by 16 per cent. The assumption here is that medical and hospital technology, average length of stay and treatment mode, remain the same over the forecast period. However, the health care community is continuing to change by introducing new technology and procedures and by re-distributing facilities. These changes need to be planned into existence to meet the anticipated demand.

MULTI-YEAR PLAN

The first five-year plan for York County Hospital assumed no changes in policy. However, the bed capacity was increased from 258 to 343 to accommodate the 44 per cent increase in patient days. The planning exercise involved quantifying mathematical relationships of patient load to workload to resource requirements and dollar costs. Assuming constant dollars, it is interesting to note that the rate of increase in total costs is slightly less than the increase in patient days over the same time period. This indicates there is a potential to benefit from economies of scale. That is, the cost per patient or patient day is decreasing over time as the fixed costs are being spread over a greater patient load.

The multi-year plan can be used to answer a whole range of questions. For example, what is the impact of inflation, anti-inflation guidelines, union settlements, new technology, shorter length of stay, more out-patients, etc.?

The next stage in the MEDIC development process at York County Hospital was implementation of the budget preparation and cost allocation systems. Here, computer prepared worksheets, customized to the requirements of each unit in the hospital were used to collect workload and resource information directly from the department managers. This gave each manager the opportunity to think out and then record into the budgeting process the anticipated workload statistics and the number of full-time-equivalent (FTE) staff required to complete the job. For example, nursing workload could be measured in terms of days or hours of care and the staff in terms of the number of FTE RN's and RNA's.

BUDGET COMPARISONS

The real value of using the computer is to eliminate the many manual calculations required in compiling the budget requests and re-calculating a budget after a change, such as a budget cut. There are also many calculations in computing annual and monthly salary rates for each type of staff. According to Bob Breedon, comptroller at YCH, a real advantage on output for budget control purposes in the general ledger system that runs on the mini-computer is the distribution of anticipated monthly cash flow for each department.

From the hospital management point of view, the main benefit is the MEDIC system's ability to compare on the same page several different budget requests for different years. For example, it is possible to compare the budget request last year with last year actuals and this year's request. The department managers need budget comparisons to monitor their performance and to see where they are going.

The best basis for budget comparison according to CHAMS (Canadian Hospital Accounting Manual Supplement) is on unit costs, if the rules for allocating overheads are agreed to by the managers. Cost analysis in times of financial constraints is now in vogue. Using the computer to do the calculations for step down cost allocation makes sense, and can be repeated quite easily. Unit costs, with both the direct and indirect costs, can be compared on a quarterly or annual basis to see if there are any changes or improvements in productivity. For example, with radiology, the workload budget may change dramatically with the addition of a new service and new staff, but will the cost per X-ray go up or down?

There are some additional analyses that can be conducted on an as-required basis once unit cost information is available. For example, at York County Hospital a disease costing study was conducted in detail on 50 patients in five disease groups and in aggregate for all 12,000 patients in the 41 RSI (Relative stay index) categories. Once unit costs are available for a given time period for each service provided to patients, it is possible through additional abstracting from the patient medical record to determine the volume of service for each patient. All the MEDIC case costing system does is multiply the unit cost times the volume of service for each case and aggregate costs by service, or most responsible diagnosis.

It has been generally assumed in the field that a normal delivery of a baby is a reasonably inexpensive procedure. In the disease costing study, it appeared on the same cost curve as cholecystectomy and appendectomy. The average cost of a full-term newborn was twice the current per diem. In another study, disease costs were computed for their procedures that were being conducted on a day surgery basis to see if there were any cost savings.

In conclusion, the York County Hospital experience was invaluable in the development of MEDIC. The system offers a new tool in times of constraint that can demonstrate cost savings and become a cost effective management tool in the hospitals of tomorrow.

54. Planning for Cost Control

B.W. STEVENSON AND D. PATTERSON

Reprinted from *Dimensions in Health Service, Journal of the Canadian Hospital Association,* May 1976, pp. 11–13, by permission of Canadian Hospital Association, © 1976.

Recently, much discussion and action has taken place in the area of cost containment and hospital cutbacks. Ontario's hospitals have been among the hardest hit by government-imposed cutbacks in health care spending. Concerns about overspending in the various hospital service areas have brought about review of standards, especially where critical services are concerned. Particular attention has been given to the area of accountability and responsibility for meeting budget guidelines, since governments are unable or unwilling to pick up extra costs for maintaining normal services.

Many hospitals have attempted to deal with this issue of accountability. At Vancouver General Hospital, planning began approximately one year ago to develop a system of cost control and monitoring that would meet the anticipated concerns for health care spending. The following outline presents a brief review of the way in which this was done.

STEP I: OBJECTIVES OF THE PROGRAM

Discussions began informally with various members of the hospital administrative staff, with the purpose of establishing some method of allocating costs to various functional areas of the hospital, so that there could be accountability at the operational level. The next stage was to develop a program development task group composed of representatives of the major hospital divisions, including both line and staff departments.

471

One member of each major line division (hospital services and patient services) as well as two members of the finance department composed this development group. Specific objectives were defined for the task group members in regard to the establishment of a cost control and monitoring program, referred to as the cost centre program. The following points were discussed and agreed to:

- The two major hospital divisions (patient services and hospital services) will allocate cost centres to main accounts, so as to reflect as closely as possible the hospital's organizational and reporting structure.
- Both divisions should allocate and match to each cost centre the appropriate payroll and operational expenses, so as to reflect a centre of accountability.
- Both divisions should allocate budgets to cost centres for specific operational expenses (i.e., payroll, inventories, purchases, etc.).
- Upon implementation, all budget-expense amendments will be by cost centre as well as by main account number.
- The internal reporting budget system will be based on thirteen four-week periods instead of the present 12-week month calendar year. (This was done to bring other operational expenses (20 per cent of the total cost) in line with the present system of payroll expenditures (80 per cent of the cost).
- Consideration should be given to the methods and implementation of adjustments and accruals in certain expense categories (i.e., management salaries, direct purchases, etc.).
- External reporting concerns should be considered as a revision to the new thirteen-period budget reporting system.
- Each member of the task group should be given full authority to speak and make commitments on behalf of their respective divisions in regard to the implementation of the cost containment and monitoring program.

STEP II: PRE-IMPLEMENTATION PLANNING

Having defined specific objectives for the group, each member agreed to return to his respective division or area and begin the pre-implementation planning necessary to establish the program. The deadline date was some nine months later. The finance department had the added task of aligning the data system and internal accounting controls with the established Canadian Hospital Accounting Manual (C.H.A.M.) system.

The major divisional undertaking of the objectives listed in step one were considered as follows:

Objective 1

A review of the hospital's organizational structure, from top level administration to management operational levels, was performed in all major areas of accountability with regard to the budget. Having identified these areas, main account numbers were given to them. All sub-main account areas (minor areas of accountability included in main account areas) were then assigned cost centre numbers. An example of the format adopted is shown in Figure 1.

Objective 2

Having identified all major cost centres and main account numbers on the basis of functional accountability, the next objective was to describe each cost centre in terms of its type of resource allocation, such as personnel

---

Figure 1

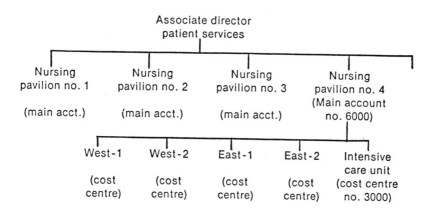

(including job classification), supplies, repairs and maintenance and so forth. The following is an illustration:

Main account no. 6000—Nursing-pavilion no. **4**
Cost centre no. 3000—Intensive care unit
  Sub-account
  090—Salaries general
      0396 Head nurse
      0398 Ass't head nurse
      0400 General duty nurse
      0405 Nursing aide I
      0402 Nursing unit clerk
  220—Instruments
  230—Sutures
  240—Gauze and cotton
  990—Miscellaneous

Objective 3

After each cost centre had been identified as having the resources to provide some defined function, the previous year's budget was used as a guide to establishing gross budget allocations for the various main accounts. More specific budgeting of operating costs such as personnel and supplies according to cost centres was not possible due to the lack of any reliable information. However, as the cost centres began to operate under the new system, a measure of their activities for the first few months would establish approximate budget guidelines upon which to allocate the total budget for the hospital. Continued monitoring of this activity was supported throughout the implementation phase.

Objective 4

Personnel in the functional areas assigned cost centre accountability reviewed methods of amending cost centres. This included adding new cost centres as new functions arose, and deleting out-of-date functional areas. These review sessions and discussions with personnel were beneficial and had the added effect of stimulating interest in new approaches to the delivery of services.

Objective 5

Because the personnel-payroll system is established on thirteen four-week periods and major changes would be required to switch this system to a 12-month accounting system, it was decided to leave the payroll as it was and to switch over all other accounting mechanisms to the thirteen-period method. This involved considerable work in managerial salaries and direct purchases. However, these concerns were lessened as the total system was reviewed and pulled together.

Objective 6

Several areas of accounting for anticipated costs had to be considered in view of the changeover in reporting time. A list of these concerns was made up, together with methods of accruing and adjusting for these special cases.

A SUB-SYSTEM

Objective 7

In British Columbia hospitals are required to report on a monthly basis. As well, there are specific requirements of reporting to other agencies, therefore, a sub-system had to be adopted. The requirements of this sub-system were a minor concern since the information base was computerized and costs recorded each day.

Objective 8

It was essential, during this pre-implementation planning phase, that those who had set the program objectives were responsible to see that such objectives were carried out. The time constraint on having the new system operative within a one-year period was dependent on having each member of the task group meet the objectives outlined. This authority for and commitment to the cost centre program was rewarded by having the initial planning document available by mid-summer of 1975, four months from the start.

ADMINISTRATIVE SUPPORT

When the agreed upon objectives were completed, the next phase was to receive general administrative approval to proceed with implementation of the program. Discussions were held with the various division heads and the executive director and the implementation plan revised. With approval, three other members were added to the new group, now referred to as the cost centre program implementation committee. These three new members included one more representative of each divisional area involved in major areas of accountability and line responsibility, as well as a representative of the data centre in charge of computer operations.

Implementation plans have continued since July, 1975, with the new system coming on line as of January 1, 1976. The major factor which accounted for the success of this program was commitment to meeting the objectives of the plan. The program is now running, but work and continued support is required to keep it going, as "bugs" are ironed out of the system and those responsible for cost control use it as a monitor to affect control.

It is hoped that the support which the divisions gave to the program in the planning stages will continue and thus accomplish the end result of cost control.

55. Know How to Analyze Costs in Evaluating Savings Projects

CARL. G. KRETSCHMAR

Reprinted with permission from *Hospitals, Journal of the American Hospital Association*, vol. 50, no. 18, September 16, 1976, pp. 69–72.

Most discussions of cost control in hospitals contain little documentation of expected or actual cost savings. However, in understanding cost savings measurement, it is necessary to understand the nature of costs and how the various types of costs are related to cost savings. The purposes of this article are to discuss some of the cost characteristics more relevant to cost savings and to suggest a model for cost savings measurement.*

TYPES OF COSTS

Each cost may exhibit characteristics that are not mutually exclusive. Therefore, in order to define cost savings, it is useful to elaborate on some of the more relevant characteristics that a cost may exhibit.

Costs may be direct or indirect costs. Direct costs are clearly identifiable with a good or a service. Indirect costs must be assigned or must be allocated to a good or a service.

Costs may be either real or opportunity costs. Real costs are reflected in actual flows of resources. Opportunity costs represent the potential benefits foregone or the costs avoided by the selection of a particular course of action. In some cases, opportunity costs can be quantified and can be included

*This article is based on work performed pursuant to Contract SSA-PMB-74-175 with the Social Security Administration, Department of Health, Education, and Welfare.

in the decision model. In other cases, opportunity costs must be identified and evaluated subjectively. The relevant opportunity costs always should be included in the final cost savings analysis.

Some costs can be shifted to other areas but do not reduce total system costs and, thus, do not represent cost savings.

Most costs can be described as fixed, variable, or semivariable. Fixed costs do not change with changes in volume, whereas variable costs vary directly and proportionately with changes in volume. Although all costs are variable in the long run, many costs incurred in hospitals are relatively fixed over short periods.

In differential cost analysis, alternative courses of action are judged by considering only the differences in costs among their alternatives rather than by evaluating each project's total costs. Any cost that does not vary among the alternatives is irrelevant to the decision-making process.

In measuring the cost of capital equipment, the problem is to assign a dollar value to the cost of capital. Direct real capital costs include historical cost depreciation and interest paid on the money borrowed to finance the capital acquisitions. The cost of capital also should include opportunity costs. When a hospital does not use debt financing, the interest that would have been earned had the money been invested should be calculated as an opportunity cost. In addition, the difference between historical cost and replacement cost depreciation should be calculated as an opportunity cost.

TYPES OF COST SAVINGS

There are at least four types of cost savings: (1) direct savings resulting from a net reduction of resource flows; (2) opportunity cost savings, such as those associated with avoiding costs or securing intangible benefits; (3) improvements in the quality of services without an increase in costs; (4) increased output of services without increases in costs.

Each of these types of cost savings can be divided into actual cost savings and potential cost savings. Actual cost savings have been experienced during a specified period; potential cost savings could be experienced when a plan is fully implemented. Potential cost savings should be estimated prior to implementing a cost containment program and, after the program has been put into operation, should be compared with actual cost savings in order to evaluate the success of the project.

The value of opportunity cost savings cannot always be measured accurately in monetary terms and, instead, must be described narratively. A positive opportunity cost represents a negative benefit and, therefore, can be described as a negative opportunity cost savings.

Hospitals have placed great emphasis on maintaining the quality of care through the influence of peer groups and federal legislation. Few monetary incentives currently exist to provide rewards for improving the quality of care. No agreement concerning how quality of care should be measured has been reached among authorities. Thus, the effects of cost savings programs on the quality of care could be considered opportunity cost savings and could be evaluated subjectively rather than as a part of a measurement model.

Reducing the average cost per unit by increasing output benefits payers of care but will not be reflected in most direct cost savings, because it may involve increased demands for services (sic)—a factor beyond the control of a hospital's administration.

MEASUREMENT MODEL

In order to evaluate cost savings projects, it is desirable to measure several of the types of cost savings. A proposed model for cost savings measurement is presented as a form that can be completed (Table 1).

Prior to the completion of a cost savings project, the potential and the opportunity cost savings can be estimated and should be entered in columns *d* and *f* of this form. Positive and negative opportunity cost savings should be entered in column *f*. The form provides space in column *g* to add opportunity cost savings to direct cost savings. However, it often is preferable to provide a narrative describing the characteristics of a particular opportunity cost savings rather than to estimate the dollar value of that cost savings; such characteristics could be considered subjectively.

When the project has been implemented, the form can be used to evaluate the success of the project by dividing all costs into the categories of labor, material, and capital. The annual direct costs that would have been incurred had the project not been implemented should be entered in column *a*; the annual direct costs that actually are experienced, in column *b*; and the annual direct costs that are expected when the plan is fully implemented, in column *c*. Subtracting column *c* from column *a* provides an estimate of potential direct cost savings. Subtracting column *b* from column *a* provides a measure of actual direct cost savings. Few cost savings programs achieve their entire potential in their first year, if at all.

The following discussion is intended to help clarify the process of implementing the cost savings measurement model.

Direct cost savings can be defined as the net decrease in cash flows throughout the hospital, caused by changes in programs or activities. The method of measuring these cost savings is best described as differential cost

Table 1 Cost Savings Measurement Model with Example Project Analysis

Effects of Cost Savings Plan
Year End _____

Hospital _____ Department _____ Prepared by _____
Date _____ Project _____ Approved by _____

Costs	a Prior costs	b New costs, actual	c New costs, annually expected	d Potential direct cost savings (a-c)	e Actual direct cost savings (a-b)	f Opportunity cost savings	g Total cost savings (d+f)
Direct labor							
Salaries	$48,730	$ 0	$ 0	$48,730	$48,730		
Engineering time		3,600			(3,600)		
Transfers to nonvacancies		6,820			(6,820)	$ 3,500	
Direct materials							
Supplies	-3,200	0	0	3,200	3,200		
Operating costs		15,500	10,500	(10,500)	(15,500)	120 sq. ft. floor space freed	
Equipment amortization	2,235	12,100	12,100	(9,865)	(9,865)	(11,040)	
Total	$54,165	$38,020	$22,600	$31,565	$16,145	($7,540)	

tracing—tracing the costs associated with a project, an activity, or a department and measuring the cost savings as the difference between what the costs actually were and what they would have been had no activities been changed. Differences in cost must be measured in terms of their impact on total hospital costs in order to eliminate the possibility of including shifted costs as cost savings. Differential cost tracing also should be used to measure actual and potential direct cost savings.

The cost of operating a hospital includes salaries, supplies and other expenses, and capital costs. The differential cost of salaries is measured as follows: (budgeted man-hours × budgeted wage rate) − (actual man-hours × actual wage rate). This measurement includes the effects on cost savings of changes in the mix of employees. The measurement also must be adjusted for the effects that reduced payroll has on fringe benefits and for the effects that employees who are transferred rather than discharged have. The value of the services performed by an employee who is transferred to a position that previously was not defined as vacant does not reduce resource flows within the hospital; it is an opportunity cost savings rather than a direct cost savings.

Direct actual supply costs savings are measured as follows: (actual cost of supplies) − (budgeted cost of supplies). Potential supply cost savings are measured as follows: (unit price prior to the cost savings project × quantity used per year) − (new unit price × new quantity used per year).

Capital costs can be measured using straight line depreciation plus the interest on borrowed capital. Depreciation is best measured by using replacement cost. When replacement cost is not readily available, price level depreciation can be used as an approximation. In addition, some administrators prefer to use historical cost depreciation in order to be consistent with the capital cost measure used for rate setting and for third-party reimbursement. Although historical cost depreciation is conceptually inferior to replacement cost depreciation, its use can be considered satisfactory. When the relevant depreciation charge for a cost savings project is based on the current cost of obtaining capital equipment, replacement cost, price level, and historical cost depreciation all are the same. Depreciation will increase as a result of implementing many individual projects and, thus, often will be a negative factor when measuring project cost savings.

When a hospital borrows the money necessary to finance a project, the interest paid is a direct cost. When a hospital finances a project using funds on hand, there is no actual interest expense. The interest that would have been earned had these funds been invested, however, is an opportunity cost.

It is necessary to consider the effects of opportunity cost savings in order to correctly evaluate a cost savings program. For example, reducing the average inventory level from $50,000 to $30,000 may not save a hospital any direct cost, but it does free $20,000 in working capital. If this $20,000 is invested, it will produce interest income, which is a direct cost savings; otherwise, freeing this capital is an opportunity cost savings. In this case, the effects of the opportunity cost savings can be measured by assuming some reasonable cost of capital.

Another type of opportunity cost savings occurs when the work load in a department is reduced but no employees are fired or transferred. No direct cost savings occur, but the hospital may be in the position to benefit by having these employees take on new tasks and assignments. In this case, the administrator may choose to make a monetary estimate of the value of the new activities. However, because such estimates are quite subjective, it may be preferable to provide a written description of such benefits.

An important factor in cost savings measurement is the cost of the engineering and other time necessary to initiate and to implement a cost savings project. Some of these costs, such as the time of an outside consultant, are direct. Other costs, such as a hospital employee's applying his time to the project rather than to his normal duties, are opportunity costs. However, any employee costs that would not have been incurred had the employee not participated in the project, such as overtime costs, should be included among direct costs rather than among opportunity costs.

EXAMPLE OF USE OF MODEL

An approach to cost savings that frequently is suggested in the literature—replacing personnel with equipment through automation—illustrates how the cost savings measurement model and form can be used.

The wage cost savings from reducing the staff will affect the annual cash flow. The costs of automation include an initial outlay and annual operating costs. The annual outlay in capital costs must be derived from a lump sum; it is suggested that straight line depreciation on estimated replacement cost be used to determine the annual effect on costs of capital expenditures. Replacement cost will equal historical cost during the year that capital equipment is acquired. When a previously acquired asset is retired, the cash value received for it is an immediate, one-time cash flow. To determine the annual effects of this cash flow, the cash received should be deducted from the cost of the new asset before depreciation is calculated. When an asset that is retired from use in one project is converted for use in another, the value of the asset to the department that will be using it should be deducted from the cost of the new equipment before depreciation is calculated. If the asset is diverted to a new use in a way that prevents an additional cash outlay, the cost savings is direct. If the asset is used in a way that may benefit the hospital but that does not prevent a cash outflow, the diversion of the asset represents an opportunity cost savings.

Assume that a project eliminates a department within a hospital and substitutes some automated equipment costing $150,000, with an estimated 10-year life and a $17,000 salvage value. Operating cost would be $15,500 for the first year but is expected to drop to $10,500 in future years.

Prior to automation, the departmental costs were as follows: salaries—$44,300; supplies—$3,200; movable equipment—$1,450; building space—$785; total—$49,735.

When the department was disbanded, one of its employees was transferred to another department but did not fill a position that previously was defined as vacant. The salary paid to that employee was $6,200 for the first year, and his actual value to the new department was estimated to be $3,500. The old equipment was sold for $12,000. The floor space previously used was converted to a storeroom that was useful but not necessary to the operation of the hospital. Fringe benefits for employees amounted to an average of 10 percent of wages and were not allocated in the ledger. The hospital paid $3,600 to an outside consulting firm to develop and implement the project.

Cost savings for this project are shown in Table 1. The department's total costs would have been $54,165 ($49,735 plus 10 percent of $44,300 for fringe benefits) if the department had not been eliminated. These figures are entered in column *a*.

New salaries and supply cost potentially could be reduced to zero; therefore, zero is entered in column *c*. Because one employee was transferred to an unnecessary position, the position, the actual salaries cost of $6,820 ($6,200 plus 10 percent for fringe benefits) must be entered in column *b*, and the value of this time ($3,500) must be entered in column *f* as an opportunity cost savings. The cost of the consulting engineer's time devoted to the project ($3,600) is a direct actual cost and is entered in column *b*. No actual supply costs were incurred during the first year, so zero is entered in columns *b* and *c*.

Equipment amortization of $12,100 ([$150,000 cost − $17,000 salvage value − $12,000 cash proceeds from equipment sales] ÷ 10 years) and operating costs of $15,500 were experienced in the first year that the department was automated and are entered in column *c*. Because the floor space that was converted to a storeroom did not prevent a cash outflow, it is an opportunity cost savings and is noted in narrative form in column *f*. The hospital used existing funds to purchase the automated equipment. Assuming an eight percent cost of capital, an opportunity cost of $11,040 ([$150,000 cost − $12,000 sale of existing equipment] × .08) is derived and is shown in column *f* as a negative opportunity cost savings.

Thus, the model shows direct actual cost savings to be $16,145; direct potential cost savings to be $31,565; and opportunity cost savings to be −$7,450 and the positive benefits of the use of additional storage space.

CONCLUSION

The model for measurement of cost savings that is recommended in this article is best described as differential cost tracing applied to direct actual cost savings. The model is intended to produce at least three cost savings measurements, each useful for different decision-making processes in evaluating proposed or existing cost savings plans.

56. Hospital Management by Diagnostic Costing

TED GILLESPIE

Reprinted from *Dimensions in Health Service, Journal of the Canadian Hospital Association,* August 1978, pp. 27–28, by permission of Canadian Hospital Association.

A great deal of attention has been focused on the spiralling cost of hospital care but there is an incomplete understanding of the nature of hospital costs and why they have risen at such an alarming rate. Hospital and government management do not have all the informational tools necessary to analyze hospital cost behavior in terms of the factors which determine changes in costs and productivity.

With the present information systems:

- The impact of changes in case mix on costs cannot be measured or evaluated,
- The impact of clinical management decisions on costs cannot be measured or evaluated,
- The impact of alternative treatment methods on costs cannot be measured or evaluated,
- The impact of treatment in different institutions on costs cannot be measured or evaluated.

If hospital managers, clinicians and government officials are to do an effective job containing health care costs, management tools must be developed which integrate the clinical, financial and productivity information systems.

THE CURRENT METHOD

Traditionally, hospitals have gathered and evaluated clinical and financial information independently without considering the interrelationships. The cost accounting methods currently utilized in most hospitals develop costs on a departmental or cost centre level. (sic) The costs of inputs (salaries, equipment and materials) with specific units of service. Consequently the costs of performing individual patient care services cannot be adequately analyzed or controlled.

Management engineering and cost accounting techniques can be used to develop standard costs for individual patient care services by identifying and costing the units of resource required to provide the service.

These standard costs identify both the amount and cost of resources consumed to perform a given service. Therefore this type of system can be used by hospital management:

- to monitor the utilization of the resource
- to monitor the ongoing departmental performance
- to monitor variations in spending patterns

If this type of system was used universally among institutions it would also be possible to monitor performance on an inter-hospital basis.

In the health care setting the consumption of resources is a function of a large set of complex and interrelated patient care processes. Standard costs, as described above, are useful in evaluating departmental performance, determining appropriate staffing levels and effectively analyzing the budget position. However, hospital management, in order to make informed decisions, must also be able to explain the variances between actual and budgeted expenditures, as a result of differences in patient mix and diagnosis. Standard costs are only one input to the management process.

DIAGNOSTIC COSTING

The impact of patient case mix, clinical management decisions, and alternative treatment methods must also be explained to adequately manage costs. Diagnosis and other clinical factors must be utilized to define a manageable number of diagnostic case types for which resource consumption profiles can be determined. By defining these consumption profiles by determining the resources normally used for each of these diagnostic case types a standard cost can be calculated by simply adding the costs of the individual resources consumed.

Table 1 Standard Cost for Lower G.I. Examination

Resources Input

A. Labor	Quantity	Unit Cost	Amount
Radiologist	0		0
Technician	9.4 Min.	$ .33	$3.10
B. Supplies			
8" × 10" film	1	$ .87	$ .87
10" × 12" film	1	$ .98	$ .98
C. Equipment	1	$ .30	$ .30
D. Facility	1	$1.12	$1.12
E. Overhead	1	$2.01	$2.01
			$8.38

Table 1 demonstrates the standard cost development for a lower G.I. examination. The costs of the individual resource components are added to develop the total cost for the examination.

APPLICATIONS TO INSTITUTIONAL MANAGEMENT

This approach to costing by diagnostic groupings has significant management implications. The development of specific treatment patterns for dealing with groups of patients provides a means of identifying the demands that will be placed on various hospital departments such as laboratory, pharmacy, dietary, etc. By forecasting patient volume according to the defined patient groupings, department managers will be able to anticipate demands that will be placed on their services.

In a similar fashion, budgets can be developed in direct relation to anticipated patient volume. The amounts of various resources for each patient grouping will be completely specified in the development of the costing by diagnosis system. Thus, a forecast of the number of admissions for all the patient groupings will completely specify the related workload that can be anticipated in each hospital department. Under the current methods, most hospitals and hospital departments develop budgets in relation to historical trends, with patient volumes being considered only in very gross terms.

The linking of resource consumption information to patient characteristics will provide managers with vastly improved means of monitoring and controlling the performance of hospital departments. Variances from budgetary projections would be directly explainable by:

- variances in projected patient volumes
- changes in treatment methods of the hospital patients
- inefficiencies in management techniques

In this way hospital managers will be able to exercise control not only over the operation of departments individually, but also over the integration of the services of all departments in the hospital.

In addition to helping managers control their operations, costing by diagnosis will provide clinicians with information which will help them understand the financial implications of alternative treatment plans. By integrating clinical and financial information in this way, the tension that commonly exists between clinicians and managers can be minimized.

APPLICATIONS TO HOSPITAL REIMBURSEMENT

Diagnosis related costing of hospital services can also be used to provide a much more equitable means of financing hospital care. Under diagnostic costing, each hospital's output is defined by the types of patients with which it deals and the services which it provides these patients.

The funding of hospitals should reflect the manner in which individual hospital services are combined to treat specific types of patient problems or diagnoses. Diagnosis related costing provides the basis for such a methodology. By evaluating the treatment patterns employed by all hospitals, guidelines can be established for the cost of treating a patient with each type or types of problems encountered by the health care system. Hospitals could then be funded in relation to the products of their operations—the number of patients of each type that were treated over a given period.

This approach would be equitable in that guidelines would be established not in relation to the cost of total hospital operation, which can be quite dissimilar among institutions as a result of differences in patient mix, but in relation to the cost of producing a unique product: the cost of treating a specific type of patient problem. Since treatments are related to patients and patient problems and not to institutions, treatment patterns and thus costs for dealing with a patient problem should be similar across all institutions.

In establishing a funding system there may be a need, however, to account for structural differences among institutions. Although the set of resources constituting a treatment package for a specific patient problem should not differ significantly among institutions. (sic) The cost of these inputs may. Structural differences such as age of physical plant, technological sophistication, wage rates, teaching requirements, etc., may have significant impact on the cost of individual elements of hospital care. Thus, in establishing guidelines for the cost of treating patient problems, it would be advisable to establish peer groups of institutions which are similar with respect to a definable set of structural characteristics. A set of cost guidelines would then be established for each peer group of hospitals.

A system of diagnosis related costing of hospital services will be able to identify the most efficient configurations of hospital services for dealing with individual and sets of patient problems. Together with projections of demands and related resource requirements, this type of information should facilitate the planning agencies' efforts to rationalize hospital services. The agencies will be better able to plan for the geographical distribution of hospital services and the allocation of service responsibilities among hospitals. This rationalization process, if current health care planning literature is to be believed, will result in significant savings in the total health care budget.

INTEGRATED INFORMATION

The system described in this article integrates the three key elements of hospital information:

- clinical
- financial
- productivity

This integration gives hospital management an understanding of the cost impact of clinical management decisions. The information produced will be acceptable and understandable by clinicians, administrators, government and other third party payors. Furthermore, the management tools necessary to understand, compare, monitor and control the cost consequences of management decisions are provided.

The two key features of the system's design are the standard costing of patient care services and the treatment profile for diagnostic groups. The diagnostic groups combine diagnosis and demographic information to form medically meaningful and statistically valid patient case types. The standard costing and treatment profiles are extremely useful management tools when used independently. However, by combining these tools an overall hospital performance model can be developed.

This system not only allows for better control of internal resources for hospital management but also provides a mechanism for more equitably distributing resources through the health care environment.

REFERENCES

1. Ernst & Ernst, *Diagnosis Related Costing & Financing of Hospital Services.* (A background paper prepared for the Strategic Planning & Research Branch of the Ministry of Health of the Province of Ontario), Ernst & Ernst, Toronto, 1977.

2. Ernst & Ernst and Puter Associates, Inc., *Diagnostic Related Patient Care Unit Systems,* (Proposal to U.S. D.H.E.W. Social Security Information), Ernst & Ernst, Chicago, 1976.

3. Thompson, J.D., Mross, D.C. and Fretter, R.B., *Case Mix and Resource Use,* Health Services Research Program, Institute for Social and Policy Studies, Yale University, 1975.

4. Griffith, J.R., *Quantitative Technique for Hospital Planning and Control,* Lexington, Massachusetts: Lexington Books, 1972.

57. CMPAs Reveal Their Ten Best Collection Techniques

HELLENA SMEJDA

Reprinted from the July 1976 issue of *Hospital Financial Management*, pp. 22–24, 26. Copyright 1976 Hospital Financial Management Association.

To find the ten best collection techniques for our readers, we sent out a brief letter to all Certified Managers of Patient Accounts. Solicited were "one or two techniques which have worked best," especially "new and unusual approaches."

The CMPAs who responded approached collections from four different angles. We chose three techniques in the management of patient accounts, two in preadmission, two in billing and three in follow-up of delinquent accounts.

We'd like to thank all who responded. Unfortunately we could not use everyone's ideas, usually because of similarity or duplication. But it was great to hear from so many who want to share their experience with other readers.

1. Mold the attitudes of *all* personnel in admitting, business office and collections so that they feel that collection is everyone's business. Carleton J. Smith, Jr., CMPA, makes sure that everyone in the business offices of St. Anthony's Hospital in St. Petersburg, Florida, realizes his or her important role in providing the best possible patient care at the lowest cost.

He attached a copy of an article in the chapter's newsletter *Sunspots* which reported that a recent survey of admitting, business office and credit employees revealed that:

- 12 percent felt that hospitals are charitable institutions and should expect to wait for their money

491

- 52 percent felt that hospital bills are unexpected and more time should be allowed for payment
- 40 percent felt that hospital costs are too high
- 27 percent felt that hospital room charges should be the same as, or lower than, hotel room charges
- 40 percent felt that the federal government could provide better health care at a lower cost.

The article presents several simple explanations on key issues, which can be used to educate employees. We excerpt a few here.

Hospitals are charitable institutions. True; dedication is important, but so are modern methods and costs.

Hospital bills are often unexpected. Again, true. But so are car repair and TV repair bills. All hospitals ask is the same consideration given to other suppliers.

Hospital costs are too high. Compared to what? Isn't everything else? Here's a simple chart that tells the story of rising costs:

	1958	1973
cost of living price index	100	125
number of services provided	20	60
number of employees per patient	2	3
minimum wage	$.64	$1.60
cost per patient day	$40	$100

The federal government can provide better health care at a lower cost. We have never heard one instance in which government, with its bureaucracy and resulting inefficiency, has been able to provide a service at a lower cost than private business.

Hospital employees are not overpaid. Because hospital costs are 70 percent labor and industry costs only 30 percent labor, the same wage increase costs a hospital much more than industry.

2. Audit the performance of the department, suggests Eleanor T. Dougherty, CMPA, from St. Thomas Hospital in Nashville, Tennessee. "Doing this twice a week unannounced takes little of my time," she writes, "but assures me that all personnel know I am interested and concerned with helping them reach their goals. It gives me an opportunity to see where they need 'brushing up' on any third party coverage, etc."

Dougherty audits:

- preadmission information for completeness
- admissions for any one day to determine whether insurance had actually been verified, giving special attention to questionable diagnoses, and to determine whether deposits have been requested
- previous day's discharges to see whether the patient's portion was collected per hospital policy; whether patients who were not able to pay were referred to credit personnel to make proper arrangements and whether courtesy discharges were given under the proper circumstances
- in-house accounts to see whether patients or their families were billed and further contacted as required.

3. Personally visit and establish rapport with third party representatives, such as Blue Cross, public assistance and major insurance carriers. "This personal touch pays handsome dividends," report Joseph Gagnon, FHFMA, CMPA, and Edwin Melhorn from Mount Auburn Hospital in Cambridge, Massachusetts.

4. Communicate that the hospital expects payment as soon as possible, is what Carol J. Altmann, CMPA, Northwestern University Hospitals, Chicago, sees as the best collection technique. Following is a rough draft of the letter she suggests sending out before, during or after admission:

Dear Patient:

Welcome to XYZ hospital. We hope your stay with us will be beneficial and that our service fulfills your expectations. We are dedicated to service and your full recovery is our goal.

In order for us to continue to be able to serve our patients it is necessary that we be paid for our services as promptly as possible. We therefore request that you check one of the following items so that we and you can agree to the manner of payment of your bill.

_____I will assign the payment of my hospitalization benefits to the XYZ hospital and will pay any amount not covered upon receipt of my weekly bill.

_____I will pay personally, each week, upon receipt of my bill.

_____I have Medicare and will pay the deductible amount and the noncovered charges weekly upon receiving my bill.

_____I am not sure that I will be able to pay in full each week either through my insurance coverage or personally. Therefore I request a financial counselor contact me about other arrangements that are available.

5. Maintain a preadmission office at the doctors' group practice with a full time clerk, suggests Terrance G. Brosseau, FHFMA, CMPA, from Bismarck Hospital, Bismarck, North Dakota. Most of the medical staff of this 200 bed hospital practice at a group clinic half a block from the hospital. By leasing an office in the group building, the hospital can have a clerk on the spot to accept and process referrals for all nonemergency situations.

Brosseau finds three advantages:

"1. We have a much better collection control of our self-pay patients...

2. Before this setup as many as 20-25 nonemergency patients would arrive for admission at the last minute. Because of the new system, many of these admissions are now done at the clinic, so when the patient arrives at the hospital, the service representative need only ask for the patient's signature, make up the name plate for the charge system, receive the room assignment and escort the patient to the appropriate floor.

3. This system has also helped us to do a better job of scheduling rooms."

6. The Nurse Discharge Diagnosis Form is another suggestion from Brosseau. "It definitely reduced by approximately 10 days of service the accounts receivable we are carrying on our books," he wrote. He explains the system:

It is our policy that all accounts will be billed to various insurance companies and agencies within five days of discharge. Three of the five days are used to keep the file on the computer so that all possible late charges may be fed into the computer. Two days are used to prepare and mail the bills.

The problem was that we were not getting the necessary doctor's diagnosis on the medical records for anywhere from 10 to 12 days after discharge (in some cases longer). Although the hospital's medical bylaws made provision for dealing with delinquent medical records, the amount of time that had to be allowed prior to considering the physicians delinquent was not in keeping with good business office policy.

We felt that the accounts should be billed in a much shorter period. As a result, we came up with the *nurse discharge diagnosis form*. Now, when the patient is admitted and taken to the appropriate floor for room assignment, one copy of this form is sent from the admission office directly to the nursing desk on the floor. It then becomes the nurses' responsibility to fill out the form prior to discharge, and to return the form directly to the business office.

The information on the form is:

a. date of admission
b. date of discharge
c. patient name and address
d. surgical procedures performed and when
e. discharge diagnosis from the nursing staff (either from own knowledge of case or by asking doctor)

"Through this system," writes Brosseau, "we are no longer dependent on the physician for a discharge diagnosis and are able to get our bills out much sooner, which results in a greater cash flow."

7. Use payment coupons for patients that cannot pay the balance upon discharge. Thomas E. Hill, CMPA, reports that the Grenada County Hospital in Grenada, Mississippi has been using coupons since 1974. He finds three advantages: the coupon serves as a reminder to the patient or guarantor that the payment is due, the remittance is properly identified when returned with the coupon and cash flow has increased. He describes the process:

> Upon discharge, the patient is asked to pay what his insurance will not cover, or the balance if he has no insurance. If the patient or guarantor is unable to pay or does not qualify for bank note financing, we ask him or her to sign a promissory note for the balance. The number of payments, the amount of the payments and the beginning payment date are shown on the note.
>
> Since we do not charge interest on balances outstanding, the blanks for finance charge and annual percentage rate on the disclosure statement are simply marked "0." After the terms of the payment agreement are explained, the patient is told that he will receive a coupon book in the mail within three days, and is told how to use the payment coupons. When the coupon book is mailed out, a form letter explaining the procedure is enclosed.

8. Send a warning letter that payment is past due. Robert H. Foster,

CMPA, reports that the Jefferson Memorial Hospital in Jefferson City, Tennessee, gets its best response from the following letter.

last payment due_____
balance $ _____

Dear

To date you have made no attempt to settle your account with us. We have tried by our various notices and letters to spare you the embarrassment of putting this account on our BAD DEBT LIST. Please don't force us into this unnecessary action.

If payment or suitable arrangements are not made within five days of the above date, we have no choice but to put this account in our BAD DEBT FILE.

Please prove to us your willingness to effect payment on this account by mailing to us your remittance today.

Thank you,

Collection Department
Jefferson Memorial Hospital

Writes Foster, "Our collection averages better than 95 percent, and this letter gets attention from the debtor."

9. Send an unidentified mailgram to the overdue account. Ed Golden and Ed Mullaney, CMPA, from Roosevelt Hospital in New York City contributed several ideas, of which this one was the most unusual. They write: "Sending a mailgram to the debtor without disclosing the nature or identity of the creditor is beneficial. The mailgram has the effect and impact of a telegram but costs considerably less. We ask the debtor to call a specific person at a specific telephone number, but do not list who we are or what we want."

10. Send a warning card from a separate internal "collection service" before turning accounts over to an outside collection agency. Robert B. Taylor, Jr., CMPA, writes that the best technique at Memorial Hospital in Hollywood, Florida, is the use of an internal collection service which is identified with the hospital. Before delinquent inpatient and outpatient accounts are turned over to an outside collection agency, the "Hospital Collection Service" sends out an official-looking *Notice of Impending Legal Action* card, with a return envelope addressed to a P.O. box.

"In our hospital," he reports, "the card was found to be superior to a letter with an attorney's signature. The psychological effect is tremendous, especially with a system that uses only computerized statements with messages before the card is mailed. The costs are relatively low, consisting only of renting a postal box and typing the card. The response in payment and phone calls for arrangements has justified use of this technique." The card is printed in green ink on a light green background; it is reproduced actual size (on the next page).

Notice of Impending Legal Action

IT IS OUR INTENTION TO HAVE OUR ATTORNEY PREPARE THE NECESSARY PAPERS IMMEDIATELY FOR FILING A SUMMONS AND COMPLAINT AGAINST YOU WITH THE REQUEST THAT HE HAVE THE SHERIFF OR CONSTABLE ATTACH SUCH PROPERTY AS NECESSARY TO SATISFY THE ABOVE CLAIM AFTER JUDGEMENT IS SECURED.

FILING OF THIS CASE WILL BE WITHHELD FOR TEN DAYS TO PERMIT YOU TO SETTLE WITHOUT COURT COSTS IF YOU SO DESIRE.

YOU WILL BE REQUIRED TO PAY ADDITIONAL AMOUNTS (INTEREST, COURT COSTS) IF A SUMMONS AND COMPLAINT ARE FILED.

Subject to the Laws of the

STATE OF FLORIDA

A Creditor may request an Attorney at-Law to attach after Judgment Property such as Automobiles, Jewelry, Boat, Live Stock, Crops, Machinery, House, Real Estate, Bank Account, Bank Vault, Stocks, Bonds, and Earnings, Commission of Salary.

You owe
MEMORIAL HOSPITAL

$

TO

Hospital Collection Service
P.O. Box 6909
Hollywood, Fla. 33021

58. Electronic Billing Saves Time, Money

JAMES O. ELLIOTT AND G. EDWARD TUCKER, JR.

Reprinted from the January 1979 issue of *Hospital Financial Management*, pp. 34–36. Copyright 1979 Hospital Financial Management Association.

Electronic submission of claims (ESC) makes more efficient use of manhours and increases cash flow. We expect to save $244,000 over the next five years. This is in addition to the savings in claims processing cost by Blue Cross.

On November 21, 1977, only 21 of the 125 claims processed through ESC had to be examined by Blue Cross clerks. The 104 routine claims, checked for clerical error by the computer at the hospital and then again at Blue Cross, went immediately to the professional review stage of processing and were then okayed for payment. No claims were lost and none wound up at the bottom of a stack.

ESC is a pilot program in Mississippi, with two other Mississippi hospitals presently on the system. The project is probably the first with such a wide scope of features in the nation, according to Blue Cross officials. More hospitals are expected to participate in the near future.

At University Hospital, all inpatient, outpatient clinic and emergency room claims for Blue Cross and Medicaid (better than half the hospital's total claim volume), are processed through ESC. If the Department of Health, Education and Welfare approves Medicare claims for inclusion, approximately two-thirds of the total claim volume will be handled by ESC.

BACKGROUND

Several years ago, University Hospital requested that Blue Cross-Blue Shield develop the capability to accept and process claims electronically,

ADVANTAGES OF ESC

Advantages of ESC and associated dollar benefits can be calculated as follows.

improved cash flow

1. Claims are processed without waiting for admit notices. At June 10, 1977, we had 135 claims waiting on admit notices (1704 days):

interest at 8 percent:

$$
\begin{array}{r}
\$267,528 \\
\times \qquad .08 \\
\hline
\$ \ 21,402
\end{array}
$$

2. We know about claims rejected due to missing or incomplete data and can resubmit the next day, rather than waiting the former 10-14 days. Assume outstanding rejected claims to be $100,000 at any time (about 75 claims), at 8 percent interest:

$$\$ \ 8,000$$

3. On manual claims, Blue Cross quits processing claims for payment four working days before payment date. Under ESC this time has been cut to a maximum of one day.

Number of claims over a five month period: 18,723

Number of working days in period (22/mo × 5):   ÷   110

$$\overline{}$$

Number of claims per day: 170   days

$$\times \qquad 4$$

$$\overline{}$$

Number of claims processed at a given time: 680

Average reimbursement per claim: × $ 244

$$\overline{}$$

$$\$165,920$$

Interest at 8 percent: ×   .08

$$\overline{}$$

$$\$ \ 13,273$$

improved personnel efficiency

Assume a 15 percent increase in claims production.

Current number of claims per hour:		2.1
Plus 15 percent:	✕	1.15
Revised production per manhour:		2.42
Number of claims per year:		59,227
Manhours required (59,229 − 2.42):		24,474
Divided by 2,000 hours:	÷	2,000
Number of clerks required (FTE)		12.24
Number of current clerks (FTE)		14.42
FTEs saved:		2.18
Average salary of clerk, including fringes:	✕	$ 6,578
Annual savings:		$ 14,340
Total annual benefits		$ 57,015

bypassing the creation of a paper claim. The purpose of this request was to reduce paper handling by both parties thereby reducing or containing claims processing costs. Blue Cross acts as Medicare intermediary and Medicaid fiscal agent for Mississippi in addition to its own regular business.

Blue Cross developed the system, as requested, and has asked five Mississippi hospitals to participate in a trial of the system. Presently, three hospitals totalling about 1,200 beds are on the system.

An analysis of University Hospital's claims volume for a five-month period showed that the volume handled by Blue Cross for its own plan as an intermediary/fiscal agent represented 76 percent of the claims volume and 56 percent of the dollar volume of claims filed. The reason for the large difference in claims volume and dollar volume is Medicaid outpatients. These claims, averaging $33 each, represented 42 per cent of claims volume, but only 4 per cent of the dollar volume. It was the hospital's high outpatient load, though, which made the computer system attractive, since the computer is ideally suited to handle high-volume, low-dollar items.

Cost/benefit comparison (University Hospital only)	annual	5-year life of application
annual benefits	$ 57,015	$285,075
development costs	-0-	$ 14,500
annual operating costs	5,280	26,400
TOTAL COST	5,280	40,900
EXCESS OF BENEFITS OVER COST	$ 51,735	$244,175

Payout period $\dfrac{(\$14,500 + 5,280)}{(\$57,015 \div 12\ )} = 4.2$ months

BASIC SYSTEM CONCEPT

The concept of ESC is really very simple.

1. From the accounts receivable files a "preliminary claim file" is created. This file is the basis for all future work.
2. The system prints a claim worksheet for review by a claims clerk with missing, incomplete or improperly formatted data flagged.

3. The clerk obtains missing data and inputs the data through a time-sharing terminal. The "release claim" code is also entered. If no data is missing, the claim can be coded immediately for release.
4. The "ready claim" file is then created.
5. At a given time daily, the "ready claim" file is transmitted over phone lines to Blue Cross.
6. Blue Cross's computer program screens the claims during transmission for incomplete or missing data. At the end of each transmission, Blue Cross provides a report of claims accepted and claims rejected because of incomplete or missing data.
7. After the claim is transmitted, the hospital computer prints a hard copy of the data transmitted to serve as a permanent claim record.

Other benefits not yet quantified, but probably achievable, include:

1. reduction of effort expended for Medicare/Medicaid logs
2. better public relations from more timely claims filing and payment
3. better collection effort on noncovered charges due to more timely payment by Blue Cross of covered charges
4. no lost claims by Blue Cross.

COST OF ESC

The University Hospital's cost for development by computer services was $14,500. Annual operating costs are estimated at $5,280. Compared to the savings, these are minimal.

SUMMARY

This cooperative venture between hospitals and third parties is one example of ways to achieve meaningful cost reductions. Such a program could not have been implemented if Blue Cross-Blue Shield of Mississippi and the hospitals involved had an adversary relationship. We recommend that other hospitals develop a good rapport with the Blue Cross plans and intermediaries so projects like this are possible. We find now that both organizations can legitimately say they are working together to contain costs through cooperative or shared service ventures.

59. Refinancing and Refunding Options

D. M. CAIN AND R. N. GILBERT

Reprinted with permission from *Topics in Health Care Financing*, Vol. 5, No. 1, Fall 1978, pp. 43–49.

Prior to the 1960s most hospitals viewed the use of debt capital as a necessary evil that should be repaid as soon as possible. Mortgages or bond issues were either close-ended to preclude the future incurrence of secured debt or structured with a balloon payment at the end of the designated loan term. Many hospitals ended up with several loan agreements outstanding concurrently, each secured by different assets or covenants. Loans to pledged collateral ratios would lose all meaningful relationship with the passage of time. Hospitals would scramble around addressing the central issue of whether the entire debt structure should or could be corrected.

The development of more appropriate financing vehicles such as the open-end mortgage and promissory note agreement permitted hospitals to finance as an ongoing business rather than through existing real estate values. Attention shifted to future cash flow and away from loan to plant-equipment ratios. The enactment of the Medicare and Medicaid programs as well as the proliferation of employee insurance plans helped to establish the credit-worthiness of the industry. Hospitals could confidently project that continued patient utilization would provide the necessary cash flow to repay borrowed capital. Many private lenders recognized the changing nature of health care finance and transferred outstanding hospital loans from the mortgage to the bond department. The security requirement of a mortgage on the property was often replaced by a set of operating and financial covenants (protective covenants) similar to those normally imposed on an industrial or utility borrower.

The changing structure of hospital finance also affected the responsibilities of the financial manager toward liability management. Hospital literature is replete with articles analyzing personnel management primarily because of the industry's labor intensive nature. Health care delivery, however, is also capital intensive. Few health care financial publications have addressed this critical subject from the perspective of the chief financial officer. For the foreseeable future, assuming a continued rate of inflation, current reimbursement policies and increasing plant and equipment obsolescence due to change in the delivery method of health care, debt will remain a permanent component of a hospital's capitalization. Not only will more time be spent in the future on liability management, but the techniques of the industry regarding the allocation of capital will also become a key ingredient in the capital expenditure process.

LIABILITY MANAGEMENT

Prudent financial management mandates matching the useful life of an acquired asset with a like maturity liability. A corollary principle is to establish the annual cost of that liability through a fixed rate of interest and planned amortization schedule (i.e., fixed debt service). Once these objectives are satisfied, prudent management seeks ways to reduce the schedule of annual payments associated with the new assets. How can the hospital finance its operations so that the total carrying cost of the physical plant is minimized?

Several options exist for accomplishing this management objective. Depending on money market conditions, hospitals can substitute one debt instrument for another, conduct open-market bond redemption programs or initiate a bond refunding program. Never have U.S. capital markets been so volatile and thus supportive of this form of liability management. For instance, hospitals can improve short-term liabilities cost by either renegotiating loan pricing to reflect true cost items or converting equipment ownership to appropriate lease contracts and vice versa. During periods of rising interest rates, hospitals can redeem outstanding bonds through secondary market purchases at discounts from book value while lower interest rate periods, in turn, permit total refunding programs.

The constraining factors to frequent refundings, however, are twofold. First, bond purchasers commit capital to long-term fixed interest rates investments only if protected against prepayment for a given time period. The specific requirement of buyers will determine their willingness to trade off higher yield for reduced refunding protection. Insurance companies may be the most demanding in terms of refunding protection while individuals tend to be more responsive to yield.

The second constraint is that refunding programs are expensive to implement. Besides fees paid to investment bankers, attorneys and various consultants, a hospital is usually required to pay some type of early prepayment penalty on the existing debt.

TYPICAL PREPAYMENT PROVISIONS

Typically, hospital bond issues are structured to provide investor prepayment protection (noncallable) for the first ten years with a slight premium declining thereafter to par. No distinction regarding source of repayment is specified in most public bond issues except for insurance proceeds paid for damage or condemnation. Private bond sales to institutional investors, however, usually distinguish the source of funds used in a bond redemption program. For instance, up to ten percent (five percent normal) of the issue can typically be redeemed at any time without penalty provided the source of prepayment is nonborrowed funds (i.e., earnings, gifts, grants or endowment). A special provision in many private loan transactions permits prepayment at any time at par should the hospital elect to issue debt in excess of "permitted debt convenants" and the existing lender cannot or will not consent to the necessary amendments. (Debt incurrence tests are generally more restrictive in private bond issues than public issues on the theory that waivers can be more easily negotiated due to the limited number of parties involved. Failure to reach an acceptable solution regarding additional funded indebtedness would permit redemption at par. This provision is commonly referred to as a "divorce clause.")

REASONS TO CONSIDER REFUNDING

Two benefits can be gained from an early redemption of long-term indebtedness—reduced annual interest expense and relief from burdensome indenture provisions. The opportunities to effect a refunding include:

- decline in prevailing interest rate levels below the interest rate on the outstanding debt;
- improvement in hospital's credit-worthiness;
- change in financing vehicle from taxable to tax-exempt bonds;
- concern over future money market conditions in light of an impending "balloon" loan payment; and
- incompatibility of existing loan provisions with the planned activities of the hospital.

MECHANICS OF BOND REFUNDING

The sale of new bonds where the proceeds are applied to the redemption of outstanding debt obligations is referred to as a refunding issue. The security description would then read "Revenue Refunding Bonds" or "Mortgage Refunding Bonds." Outstanding bond issues containing provisions against early redemption to a date not yet reached (including final maturity) can also be refunded through a technique referred to as advance bond refunding. The objective of refunding the outstanding bonds prior to the first call date is usually to exploit favorable current market conditions and thus "lock in" a guaranteed savings. An advance refunding also provides the opportunity to modify indenture constraints that now or with the passage of time may adversely affect hospital management.

To effect an advance refunding generally requires the defeasance (annulment) of the existing bond indenture so that the hospital assets or revenues become available as security for the investors in the refunding bonds issue. A straight refunding merely entails notification as required under the loan agreement and payment through refunding proceeds of the outstanding obligations.

Most bond indentures permit the release of bondholders' security at any time that sufficient consideration is paid. Existing pledges of property or revenues are terminated upon final payment of all principal and accrued interest or sooner if monies (including U.S. Government Obligations) deposited with a third party (bond trustee) will be sufficient to redeem all outstanding bond principal when redeemable, pay interest on such bonds as scheduled to the redemption date, and pay any premiums due the bondholders for early retirement. Most indentures will also permit a total defeasance when monies deposited, plus earned income, equal all future principal, interest and premium payments to the redemption date. This more liberal definition is referred to as the "net" or "net cash defeasance" whereas the former method is referred to as the "gross" or "full cash" defeasance. Recent IRS regulations preclude the advantages associated with a full cash defeasance if the indenture permits either method. Most bond issues can be defeased at any time, but the bondholder retains the investment as agreed until the first call date.

REFUNDING ANALYSIS

A financially successful refunding program is a function of the prepayment provisions and interest rates on the outstanding obligations and the cost of selling new bonds under current market conditions. Issuers or their advisors should have a working knowledge of prevailing interest rates of comparable bond issues as well as a sense for the direction of interest rates over the next few months. Small movements in the market can substantially affect the future cash savings of a refunding, thus making market timing a critical element to a successful refunding program. (See Figure 5-1.)

Once a reasonable estimate of the interest rate level available on the refunding bonds is established, the hospital and its underwriter can calculate the principal amount of new bonds necessary to refund the old issue. The need to issue more bonds than currently outstanding can negate the benefits of a lower interest rate. Much of the cost-benefit analysis in a hospital refunding program is a function of the cost reimbursement programs.

BOND REFUNDING PROGRAM

Uses of bond refunding program proceeds include outstanding bond principal, accrued bond interest expense, prepayment penalties and bond issuance expense. A straight bond refunding is relatively easy to implement and analyze. Key components to consider include:

* reimbursement treatment by third party payers for the call premium and unamortized bond discount on the original bond issue;
* reimbursement for costs associated with refunding program;
* accounting treatment for gain or loss from refunding; and
* accounting treatment for increased indebtedness (without increase in assets).

Depending on the treatment by payers such as cost-based Blue Cross plans and Medicaid (Medicare is uniform throughout the country), the benefits of lower annual interest expense may not justify the unreimbursed cost associated with retiring the outstanding debt. In many cases, cost-based reimbursement programs will recognize the increased liabilities, but a timing difference in payment will result. The hospital's auditors usually can provide classification on the accounting and reimbursement aspects of a debt extinguishment program.

ECONOMIC ANALYSIS OF ADVANCE REFUNDING

In addition to the reimbursement issues associated with a refunding and the accounting treatment which may affect fund balances and net income, an advance refunding also involves IRS codes that regulate the tax exemp-

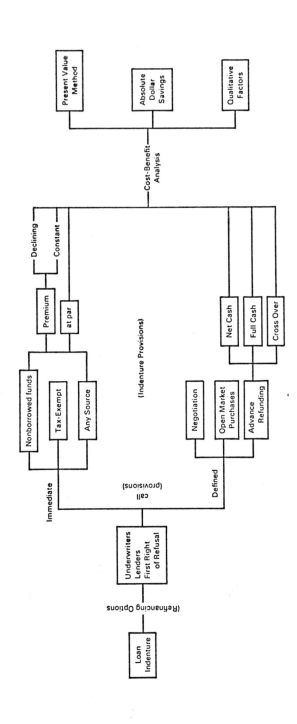

Figure 5-1. Bond Refunding Analysis

tion of the refunding bonds. The IRS has strict guidelines regulating the tax exemption of refunding issues and is currently concerned with the total costs associated with this financing technique to the municipal bond market.

In a proposed statement of position by the American Institute of Certified Public Accountants (AICPA) the following tentative conclusions were reached:

- The gain or loss from an advance refunding should be recognized when the old debt is defeased, generally on the date of the refunding.
- Since the old debt is legally satisfied, it is not a liability of the hospital and therefore should no longer be reflected on the balance sheet.
- The new debt should be reflected on the balance sheet at the date of refunding.
- When special obligation bonds are issued as part of a full cash refunding, they should not be included in the balance sheet because they will be serviced from the earnings of the proceeds of the advance refunding and, therefore, are an obligation of the escrow trustee, not the hospital.
- The call premium, unamortized premium or discounts, and initial issue costs should be recognized in the income statement over the remaining term of the old debt as an adjustment to the cost of borrowing the old debt.

***

CHAPTER 7

MISCELLANEOUS SAVINGS AND IMPLEMENTATION

The previous six chapters dealt with the methodology of cost containment and with general tools and techniques that can be applied in almost any department of the health care institution. For example, there are budgets in all departments, work standards and contract services can be applied in almost any area, and energy can be conserved in many departments. In this chapter, cost containment in specific areas is discussed.

FOOD SERVICES

Food service is one of the major expenses in the health care facility. Several of the cost containment methods previously discussed were successfully applied in food services (e.g., group purchasing, work measurement and standards, inventory control, and value analysis). Curry and Myers (Reading 60) analyze the various models that health care institutions use for preparing foods. In addition to the cost issue, the various alternatives are analyzed from a quality point of view.

PHARMACY AND DRUG MANAGEMENT

The pharmacy department is one of the major revenue-producing departments; probably as a result of this, it is not efficiently run in many institutions. Smith (Reading 61) maintains that pharmacy management expertise is crucial to cost control efforts. Many of the cost containment potentials are outlined.

LAUNDRY AND LINEN SERVICE

The control of linen consumption and replacement constitutes a major problem, whether the laundry is done in-house or not. Clean linen may be needed at almost any time, although most of the replacement is done at scheduled times. Linen theft and misuse comprise 20–40 percent of the total laundry and linen service cost. Ellis' paper (Reading 62) presents an overview of the many possibilities of cost containment in this area. Laundry costs can be significantly reduced if soft water is used, a fact documented in Durrwachter's paper (Reading 63).

LABORATORY MANAGEMENT

Like the pharmacy, the laboratory is a large income-producing department where productivity can be increased in many instances. Lo et al. (Reading 64) demonstrate a simple manual procedure for tabulating costs and production rates, then using this information to compute the monthly measures of performance (such as cost per specific type of test). Such a system can be used for planning purposes as well as for judging the laboratory workload and productivity.

CONTROLLING THEFT

Administrators dislike talking about it, but one expert claims that as much as 15 percent of hospital costs could be eliminated if employee theft were reduced to a minimum. Jaspan, a well-known authority on this subject, points out in his paper (Reading 65) the vulnerable areas in the health care institution and the types of thefts likely to occur. Some of the reasons for thefts are presented as well as prevention recommendations. The paper presents a complete security framework that should be taken into consideration when the architect draws up the plans for a new facility or a facility's expansion.

BUSINESS OFFICE

Several ideas can help in curbing business office costs. One such idea is to use microfiche. Reading 66 describes a case study involving microfiche in the Medical College of Virginia Hospitals. Petrie's paper (Reading 67) deals with a checkless payroll system and its savings.

REUSABLES VS. DISPOSABLES

Health care institutions use large quantities of various disposable items. With creeping inflation and the need to contain costs, the use of some disposables should be analyzed.

The special report of *Hospital Purchasing Management* (Reading 68) presents a method of using value analysis to compare disposables with reusables. In addition, the report gives the results of a survey that shows that the "battle" between reusables and disposables is continuing. This report does not deal specifically with such factors as infection rate.[1] Substantial savings in labor have been reported in the case of using disposables, however.[2]

TELEPHONE SYSTEMS

Significant savings may be made in almost any telephone system. One way to achieve a saving is to renegotiate rates and even consider replacing the telephone company, if necessary. Another way is to conduct a thorough analysis of needs and availability (some special consultants are available for this purpose) in order to reorganize the telephone system. The improvement made in the telephone system at Lakewood Hospital is discussed in Reading 69.

IMPLEMENTATION

The many ideas of cost containment proposed in the papers in this book, as well as dozens of other ideas that can be found in the literature, should provide a solid basis for organizing and implementing a cost containment program. Reading 70 is a case study in the form of a special report from Tucson Medical Center to the community it serves. This report describes the actual application of many of the ideas outlined in this book, and it covers some additional cost containment ideas, especially in the area of "Saving Through Technology and Innovation."

Last, but not least, is the case of Jackson Memorial Hospital, a large medical center in Miami, Florida. Zucker (Reading 71) summarizes the cost containment activities that led to dramatic savings over the last three years.

SUMMARY

The material in this book shows the reader hundreds of ways to contain the costs of health care. Most of the major sources of savings are presented. However, there are many more possibilities. For additional sources of cost containment ideas the reader is referred to the various bibliographies. There is no limit to man's ingenuity; with proper organization and inducements, it will be possible to contain health care costs so that quality care will be affordable for everyone.

NOTES

1. J. Romeo, "Reusable Surgical Packs Versus Disposable," *Southern Hospital* 44 (1976): 20–21.
2. I. Campbell, "Disposable: A Success Story," *Hospital Administration in Canada* 19 (1977): 40.

BIBLIOGRAPHY

Aland, K.M., and Walter, B.A. "Hospitals in Utah Reduce Costs, Improve Use of Facilities." *Hospitals, JAHA,* 16 March 1978.
Anthony, M.F., and Wilson, G. "Costly Materials Retrieved from Laundry Chutes." *Hospitals, JAHA,* 16 May 1978.
Basie, A., and Yeagley, W.E. "Word Processing Increases Capacity, Not Cost: How to Produce a $6.35 Letter for $1.36." *Hospital Progress,* September 1977.
Bendix, R., et al. "Computer Scheduling for the OR." *Modern Healthcare,* June 1976.
Bennett, A.C. "Reducing Hospital Costs" (Part 1). *Hospital Topics,* February 1973.
Bennett, A.C. "Reducing Hospital Costs" (Part 2). *Hospital Topics,* March 1973.
Berry, L. "Optimizing Custodial Efficiency." *Building Operating Management,* October 1977.
Bowling, J.C. "We Reduced Costs Through Centralization." *Medical Laboratory Observer,* February 1978.
Boyd, E.S., and Eaton, S.B. "Cost-Effective Radiology." *Applied Radiology,* July-August 1977.
Bush, V. "Hospital's Hidden Cost: Theft." *Modern Healthcare,* August 1975.
Cabor, E.E. "Modern Food Management: To Control Costs, Eliminate Some Foods, Review Purchasing Methods, Alter Recipes; Conserve Supplies." *Modern Hospital,* August 1973.
Carlson, D.J. "Cost Effectiveness of Laboratory Improvement Programs: The Viewpoint from the Private Sector." *Health Laboratory Science,* 14 (1977): 199.
Curry, W. "How Hospitals Are Controlling Costs." *Hospitals, JAHA,* 16 May 1976.
Doan, T.M. "Dollars and Sense of Custodial Training." *Cleaning Management,* July-August 1977.
Draper, S.D., Jr. "Investigating the Cost of Patient Transportation Centralization." *Hospitals, JAHA,* 16 April 1974.
Eisenberg, J.M., "Computer Based Audit to Detect and Correct Overutilization of Laboratory Tests." *Medical Care,* November 1977.

Elias, A. "Shared Clinical Laboratories." *Journal of the American Medical Association,* 6 September 1976.

Elliot, V.B. "Word Processing—An Offshoot of Work Simplification." *Hospital Progress,* September 1977.

Foster, J.T. "Here Are 66 Ways Hospitals Cut Expenses." *Modern Hospital,* September 1965.

Foster, J.T. "93 Ways Hospitals Are Cutting Costs." *Modern Hospital,* April 1964.

Flury, P.A., and Clark, M. "How to Cut the Cost of Lab Supplies." *Medical Laboratory Observer,* January 1977.

Gumbhir, A.K. "Cost Benefit Analysis of Unit Dose Drug Distribution System." *Hospitals, JAHA,* 1 May 1976.

Herz, L.M., and Souder, J.J., Jr. "Preparation Systems Have Significant Effect on Costs." *Hospitals, JAHA,* 1 January 1979.

Hogan, S.D. "Your Patient Mix Affects Costs." *Hospital Financial Management,* April 1978.

Jaspan, N., and Nagel, W., eds. "Theft in the Health Care Industry." *Topics in Health Care Financing,* Winter 1978.

Johnson, R.L. "Hospital Economics 19 Myths." *Hospital Financial Management,* 1975.

Kerr, M.I. "Increase Control of Operations to Reduce Linen Costs." *Hospitals, JAHA,* 1 December 1978.

Koncel, J.A. "The Four Cs of Food Service." *Hospitals, JAHA,* 16 August 1978.

Laverty, R.M. "Business Office Reorganizes to Give More Personalized Service." *Hospital Progress,* August 1974.

Lipman, A.G. "Computer Base Formular Services Reduce Costs, Eliminate Confusion." *Hospitals, JAHA,* 1 November 1977.

Magerlein, D.B., et al. "New Systems Can Mean Real Savings," Part 1. *Hospital Financial Management,* April 1978; Part 2, *Hospital Financial Management,* May 1978.

Marsh, W. "Cost Containment." *Southern Hospitals,* July-August 1978.

Marshall, E.A. "How to Cut Down Theft." *Hospital Administration in Canada,* January 1978.

Mueller, F. "Cost Containment: The Ever-Present Predicament." *Executive Housekeeper,* December 1977.

"New York Hospital Saves Money with Pillows, Printouts." *Hospital Financial Management,* October 1977.

"Order Central Concept: Unusual Approach to Paperwork Saves Nurses Time and the Hospital Money." *Hospital Topics,* July-August 1977.

Patrylak, J. "Counting X-Ray Retakes Reduces Cost." *Applied Radiology,* January-February 1978.

Peterson, R.R. "Cost Improvement Program Generates Major Savings." *Hospitals, JAHA,* 1 July 1978.

Petrie, G.N. "Checkless Payroll—Both Hospital and Employee Benefits." *Hospital Financial Management,* September 1978.

"Receiving Reports on Microfiche Saves Hospital Business Office Time, Money and Storage Space." *Hospital Financial Management,* January 1977.

Ryan, D.R. "One Hospital's Blueprint for Cost Containment." *Purchasing Administration,* January-February 1978.

St. Clair, N.L., et al. "Computer Provides Definite Linen Distribution and Control Mechanism." *Hospitals, JAHA,* 16 November 1977.

Saucier, S.J. "Computerized Food Buying Saves Money, Time." *Hospital Purchasing,* September-October 1977.

Schaeffer, D.H. "Cost Containment: Everybody's Bandwagon." *Hospitals, JAHA,* 1 April 1978.

"Self-sticking Labels Help Mt. Auburn (MA) Hospital Hold on to Charges." *Hospital Purchasing Management,* April 1977.

Slater, X. "A Cost Comparison-Unit Dose." *Hospitals, JAHA,* 16 April 1972.

Summers, J. "Beyond Dirty Linen: Linen Use Management As an Innovative Asset." *Health Care Management Review,* Spring 1979.

"The Safety and Security Officer: Trainer, Inspector and Psychologist." *Modern Healthcare,* July 1975.

Thueson, J. "Hospitals' Programs and Progress in Cost Containment Reported." *Hospitals, JAHA,* 16 September 1977.

Traska, M.R. "Hospitals See Silver Recovery Benefits." *Modern Healthcare,* February 1978.

Warren, W.R. "Hospitals Are Saving More Than Lives—the Texas Voluntary Effort." *Texas Hospitals,* June 1978.

Werner, M. "Strategy for Cost Effective Laboratory Testing." *Human Pathology,* March 1973.

Zellmer, W.A. "Hospital Cost Containment and the Pharmacist." *American Journal of Hospital Pharmacy,* January 1979.

Zink, M.M. "Alcoholism: The Disease That Drains Hospital Resources Away." *Hospital Financial Management,* August 1978.

60. Cost Containment in Dietary Service Systems in Hospitals

K. R. CURRY AND S. MYERS

Reprinted with permission from the authors.

1. INTRODUCTION

Essentially, there are two broad cost containment categories in the dietary services of a hospital. They are:

1. Selection of a food service system
2. Operating costs:
   a. labor
   b. food and supplies
   c. equipment
   d. utilizing the budget

This paper will examine these areas from the viewpoint of evaluating cost containment measures in relation to the goals of the institution and the department. The focus will be on questions which must be answered by the institution attempting to contain costs.

2. COST CONTAINMENT CONCEPTS

In studying cost containment concepts as they relate to the dietary department, it is necessary to keep in mind the unique role the hospital food service has to play in the care and treatment of patients. As a rule, the dietary department serves not only patients but also visitors, medical staff, volunteers, employees and special groups. Food, the product of a food production system, is a common denominator among people which reduces the complex production operation to the seemingly mundane and simple dimension of a "properly" baked potato, "delicious" custard or "good" tossed salad. Each person can define "properly," "delicious" and "good" for himself, whereas people in general cannot determine a "good" x-ray. This deprives the dietary department of the "mystique" attributed to other hospital services. It is the one department in which everyone considers himself an expert. The end product of the dietary department is a tangible product, more visible to the clientele it serves than most other types of hospital services. One consequence of this phenomenon is the instant feedback associated with acceptance or rejection of the product.

The above mentioned attributes are both a potential danger and a potential strength. The dietary department may serve as the scapegoat for troubles of an institution or it may provide the best public relations for the hospital.

The big question arising from the above concepts is: What kind of cost containment measures would keep the food service operating economically without sacrificing the quality of the service it renders? Several other questions arise from this major one—such as: What is the dividing line between continued initiation of cost control techniques and the reduction of quality in the service and food provided? Is there an "average cost per patient day" below which there could be an adverse effect upon the quality of service? Is it reasonable to expect a continued reduction in per patient costs or is it more realistic to seek ways of maintaining current costs as a reflection of current trends in escalated costs?

Cost containment may be implemented through control methods of existing practices or through the introduction of totally new programs. Reevaluation of current purchasing procedures including development of standards of quality, inventory control, delivery practices, preparation, portioning, menu planning, forecasting, pilferage and in-house food distribution may allow for flexibility to tighten controls.

3. DIETARY GOALS, OBJECTIVES AND EVALUATION

The first step in an effective cost containment program is the careful setting of its goals. Goals can be set in a number of ways, i.e., copied from a book or from last year's progress report, dictated by an administrator, submitted to the administrator by departments or in a variety of other ways. The key word in preparing goals is "careful." This means that thought and deliberation are necessary in the preparation of goal statements and that they be prepared as a realistic set of guidelines rather than as mere rhetoric.

Goals serve best as guidelines if those charged with meeting them agree with the goals. Obtaining consensus on the goals of a department is often time consuming. The temptation to hurry this process may appear to be saving time. Reaching agreement on goals sets a common direction for an organization and results in increased motivation to contain expenses.

The goals and objectives set by the department become the targets or the measures against which performance is measured. The comparison process shows either a positive or negative achievement of the goals and points out areas that need revisions.

The expectations for goals must be realistic in relationship to the resources which an institution is willing and/or is able to allocate to meet those goals. For instance, it is unrealistic to stipulate, as a goal of dietary, the provision of nutritional care and then furnish resources only for the supplying of food and not for the evaluation of whether the food was eaten by the patient, as nutritional care occurs only when food is consumed.

4. SELECTION OF FOOD SERVICE SYSTEMS

When a health institution is being developed or reorganized, a primary concern in cost containment is the selection of the food system itself. This system, historically, has been thought of as the Food Service System. However, in recent years, the increasing recognition of the importance of nutrition to the patient[1] and the advent of Standards of Practice for Patient Care[2] has broadened the concept to that of a Nutritional Care System. The food production portion of this system is more concrete and amenable to evaluation and correction than the nutritional care of patients. This paper will deal primarily with the food production system with reference, at times, to the need for applying cost-effectiveness measures to the direct patient care component of a nutritional care system.

In general, there are three types of systems (with multiple variations) which can be used for food production: contract food services, directed full production system, and directed convenience food system.

a. Contracted Food Services

Contracted Food Services are those allocated to business firms outside the hospitals or institutions. During the past few years there have been swings toward increased use of contract firms.[3] Subsequently, some facilities returned to institutional managed food services. The possible strengths of the contracted food services are as follows:

1. Transfer of time consuming administrative duties of staffing, scheduling and purchasing to contracting firm.
2. Increased purchasing power through the contracting firm (buying at discounts).
3. Enhanced ability to handle the complexity of food quality control and sanitation standards.

The possible weaknesses are as follows:
1. Orientation of the food service director toward the contracting firm rather than to the health facility.
2. Failure to meet pre-arranged standards set down in the contract.
3. Lack of loyalty on the part of employees to the health institution.
4. Failure of the contracting company to feel a sense of contribution to the facility's overall goals.

Food quality may be a problem, but this problem appears to occur with both in-house and contracted services. Food quality seems to be related more to the contractual agreement and/or willingness to commit resources than to the type of management.

b. Hospital Directed Full Production System

In this system the food is purchased with the expectation of a considerable amount of on-premise preparation. Specific convenience food items, such as bakery bread, may be included in this system. Food comes into the dietary department in various stages of preparation, from the raw form to ready-to-serve portions for items such as milk.

New trends in this area include cook-freeze and cook-chill. Both methods include advance preparation of food with freezing or chilling for later use.

The strengths of this system include:
1. In-house quality control
2. Lower cost than convenience systems
3. Flexibility in meeting special dietary needs of patients
4. Opportunity for employees' creativity

Weaknesses include:
1. High labor costs
2. Extensive equipment requirements
3. Variety of storage space required

c. Hospital Directed Convenience Food System

This system is one in which a large proportion of initial food preparation is done outside the health facility. Purchasing may be done either by contracting for the entire food needs to be delivered by a catering service, or by the purchase of specific items which are then organized, warmed and distributed by the health facility personnel.[3]

The possible advantages of this system are:
1. Low labor costs
2. Reduced need for preparation equipment

Disadvantages are:
1. Possible limitations to menu
2. High food cost[4]
3. Need for temperature controlled environment

d. Selection of a System

All of these systems require more than a cursory look at their strengths and weaknesses when determining which to use. A simplistic approach in the decision-making process (often used) may be to look at only the labor cost and then to jump to the conclusion that money may be saved by using a convenience system. Problems such as increased food costs and the relationship of the limited menu to goals for patient care may be ignored. Koogler and Nicholance[5] have listed the following major decision alternatives which must be evaluated in choosing a food system:

- Menu style—Hotel/restaurant type vs. cycle
- Make or buy—Ready foods vs. convenience foods
- Packaging—Preplates vs. bulk
- Inventory—Chilled vs. frozen
- Rethermalization—Centralized vs. decentralized[6]

In summary, cost may be contained in any of these systems if properly used. Shifting to another system may or may not reduce cost, depending on the various factors discussed.

5. EQUIPMENT

Many of the items of equipment for food production require a large outlay of capital and careful consideration must be given prior to purchase. Gage suggests a number of questions to be answered.[7] What is the equipment? For what will it be used? What are the alternatives for performing this function? Which three ways of doing the job in question show the greatest difference between "cost" and "value?" How much does it cost? How many parts does it have? Who will repair it? What ideas for further development do the answers to the above questions generate? What other functions and specifications should be incorporated? What is needed to sell the ideas to forestall roadblocks?

Does cost containment in the area of equipment mean utilizing old equipment more efficiently or purchasing new equipment as labor saving devices? When does the purchase of new equipment for a formerly performed function become economically feasible? The major question to be answered is when to stay with the old and when to acquire the new. When does spending money save money in the long run?

The type of service and the accompanying menu are prime considerations in the initial selection of equipment. Therefore, it is necessary to answer such questions as: Are there immediate or future plans for the reorganization of the dietary department? Will the equipment under consideration have a multiple purpose and be flexible in its use? Is the equipment utilized in the production of seasonal or fad foods (which may lose their appeal)? Is it time consuming and costly to maintain?

To determine the value of new equipment as a means of reducing labor costs, one method that can be used is to ascertain the cost of producing a specific number of units by using the old equipment (labor included) and compare the production of the same number of units with the new equipment. One may then determine if there is a positive relationship when utilizing the new equipment. It may be that positive results might also be shown by increasing the number of units produced at the same costs.

An important aspect to consider when selecting equipment, whether it be for a new facility or an established one (replacement), is the long term benefits or functionality of that equipment. One criterion that should be considered is the depreciation during the life of the merchandise. A simple method to determine this is straight line depreciation.[8] This method, calculated by dividing the life of the equipment in years into the cost of the equipment, allows the dietary director to keep a record of the current and projected worth of a piece of equipment.

One method of possible cost saving that has been suggested is the *leasing of equipment* for food service operations.... [See Article 33.]

6. RAW FOODS AND SUPPLIES

In a cost containment program of food and supplies, the major areas to be considered are purchasing, storage, utilization and the control measures initiated at each level. One of the newest trends in purchasing is group or cooperative buying, which has had a major impact by the reduction of costs through increasing the volume purchased.[9] Effective cost containment programs, utilizing group purchasing, have been implemented with results such as: reduction in total number of products purchased, reduction in total number of supplies needed, reduction in cash outlay, reduction in bookkeeping, better delivery, standardization and reduction in amount of dietitian's time needed for the purchasing functions.[10] These are all goals which are sought as methods of cost containment in any system utilized.

Whichever purchasing system is selected, the goal of all purchasing practices should be the purchase of food and supplies which reflect the standards of quality developed by the institution for the least cost. The type of food selected by an institution will be a reflection of these quality standards and will bear directly on the type of food service system utilized.

7. LABOR

Hospital wide, labor may comprise 50 to 65% of the total operating expense. The dietary department alone may comprise 6 to 10% of the number of employees on the payroll or 5½% of total facility expense.[11,12] Obviously, this is a significant proportion of the cost of hospital care.

To contain labor costs, labor staffing guidelines should be established which are compatible with the goals of the dietary department and the institution. Such guidelines should provide the capability of monitoring understaffing as well as overstaffing. Significant factors important in setting guidelines for labor needs are census level, menu complexity, facility objectives and philosophy, employee meal service and facility standards.[12]

Some strategies to save labor within a dietary department are not really labor saving but merely manipulations which move costs from one department to another without improving the overall performance of the entire institution. It behooves the dietary manager to look closely at the results of his/her labor saving strategy on other departments of the hospital.

It cannot be overlooked that the selection of the food service system has a direct bearing on the labor cost of the dietary department. It has been observed that in many instances, advance preparation systems, including cook-freeze and cook-chill operations, reduce both labor and food costs even with additions in equipment, energy and space requirements.[4]

8. BUDGETING

Analysis of the dietary department via the budgeting process can be useful in cost containment. The expense statements, revenue statements and statistical analysis of the operating budget provide vital information to the dietary department manager.

The purpose of using financial reports is to identify trends as they develop and to initiate prompt action in resolving potential problem areas.

A typical food service operating budget can be compiled from the following basic data gathered:

- number of patient days/patient meals served
- employee/cafeteria meals served
- special functions served
- salary and benefit expenses
- food costs
- supply expenses
- miscellaneous expenses
- cash receipts

These figures in turn can be used to compute the basic statistical indicators of:

- salary and benefit expenses costs per meal
- food costs per meal
- miscellaneous costs per meal
- net costs per meal

In addition, a food service operating budget can be used to provide productivity indicators such as meals served per hour, meals per patient day and net cost per patient day. Since no two health care institution food services are identical, there is a potential danger in comparing statistical indicators between them, especially when their reporting systems differ.[13]

SUMMARY

Cost containment is vital in the present day concern over the rising costs of health care. However, at the same time, quality of hospital services is expected. These opposing factors provide a challenging situation to directors of dietary departments.

Careful selection of a food service system and tight controls of operating costs are essential in meeting cost containment goals as they relate to the overall goals of a health care institution. The budget is the primary tool of gathering, analyzing, and planning for control of the resources of labor, food and supplies and equipment. Use of cost containment principles can result in delivering the best possible services to patients at the lowest possible cost.

REFERENCES

1. Butterworth, Chas. E. and George L. Blackburn, "Hospital Malnutrition" *Nutrition Today,* Mar.-Apr. 1975, pp. 8-18.

2. *American Dietetic Association - Professional Standards Review Procedures Manual,* April, 1976. PSRO Committee.

3. Cihlar, Carroll, "Experiments with Convenience Food System," *Hospitals, Journal of American Hospital Association,* Vol. 46, Aug. 1, 1971, pp. 81-83.

4. Herz, Matthew L. and James J. Souder Jr., "Preparation Systems Have Significant Effect on Costs," *Hospitals, Journal of American Hospital Association,* Jan. 1979, p. 89.

5. Bird, Randy C. and Thomas Morrow, "Convenience Versus Conventional Operation," *Hospitals, Journal of American Hospital Association,* Vol. 45, March, 1971, pp. 90-94,

6. Koogler, Glenn H. and Susan Nicholanio, "Analysis of a Decision for Prepared Food Systems," *Hospitals, Journal of American Hospital Association,* Vol. 51, Feb. 16, 1977, pp. 95-98.

7. Gage, W.L. *Value Analysis,* McGraw Hill, London, 1967.

8. Keiser and Kallio, *Controlling and Analyzing Costs in Food Service Operations,* Wiley, N.Y. 1974.

9. *Schweid, Paul, "Co-ops: They're Catching On," Hospitals, Journal of American Hospital Association,* Vol. 46, March 16, 1972, p. 106.

10. ———, "Adventist Hospitals Come Together," *Institutions,* Vol. Feeding, Feb. 15, 1976, p. 62.

11. ———, "Hospital Food Service Enters the New Age," *Food Management,* Nov. 1976, p. 34.

12. Henderson, Pat, "Labor Staffing Guidelines for Long Term Facilities," *Hospitals, Journal of American Hospital Association,* Jan. 1976. p. 79.

13. Kaud, Faisal A., "Operating Budgets are Valuable in Managing Finances," *Hospitals, Journal of American Hospital Association,* Nov. 16, 1977, p. 69.

61. Drug Cost Containment in the Hospital

WILLIAM E. SMITH

Reprinted with permission from *Hospital Formulary*, September 1978, pp. 695–698.

The whole is equal to the sum of its parts. That is a mathematical theorem we all learned in elementary school. This theorem is certainly true of national health insurance (NHI). The parts include at least the pharmaceutical industry, physicians, pharmacists, hospitals, government, the private health insurance industry, and patients; each has operational characteristics that contribute to the overall drug-related costs paid by government, third-party payers, and private patients.

Drug benefits for many inpatients in hospitals are provided by the existing Medicare and Medicaid programs. Private insurance also provides drug benefits for other inpatients. The cost of these drug benefits, and the level at which drug-related (i.e., pharmacy) services are received by inpatients has not yet been studied, discussed, or reviewed to any great extent, certainly not as much as drug benefits for outpatients.

I believe that third-party payers and private patients are paying too much for drugs, in comparison with the level of drug-related services they receive in our nation's hospitals. Pharmacy charges are too high when compared to the level of pharmacy expenses and to the drug-related problems experienced by hospital patients. Any discussion about drugs and NHI for inpatients will lead to a review of the essential drug-related services provided by hospital pharmacy personnel.

I practice in the hospital setting and have been involved in research for the past 12 years. My approach will be first to discuss specific terminology related to drug-related costs, the current status of hospital pharmacy services, and the expected changes in the future of hospital pharmacy services; and then to discuss briefly the topics of drug formularies, drug bidding, and drug utilization review. I intend to give some specific suggestions about the questions that I think need to be researched.

In the past decade, we have not been specific when talking about drug costs. Those two words, "drug costs," are meaningless to me because they are not specific enough. The result has been confusion and misunderstanding, a great contributor to our failure to resolve the issues. Let me illustrate my point by looking at specific terminology regarding drug costs as applied to the hospital situation:

1. Drug product cost is the purchase price charged by the manufacturer or the supplier.
2. Patient pharmacy charges are the total of drug product cost and pharmacy dispensing fees charged to the patient or the third-party payer.
3. Pharmacy costs are a total of the direct expenses of running the department and the indirect expenses for the hospital pharmacy operation assigned by the business office.
4. Direct pharmacy expenses are payroll, cost of goods, education, supplies, and services.
5. Indirect expenses are assigned to the department by the business office for building and maintenance, laundry and linen, administration, health, and welfare. This assignment is according to the Medicare allocation formula that has been given to hospitals.
6. Drug packaging costs include expenses for packaging unit dose medications.
7. Purchasing and inventory control includes the operational expenses for the purchasing, storage, processing of purchase orders, and the payment system for drug purchases.
8. Pharmacist costs are the expenses for the services provided directly by the pharmacist.
9. Pharmacy technician costs are the expenses for the activities performed by the pharmacy technicians.
10. Nursing medication system costs are the expenses for nursing personnel and supplies for medication-related activities.
11. Hospital medication system cost is the grand total of patient pharmacy charges plus the nursing medication system costs. Hospital medication system costs are about 10 to 12% of daily patient costs today.

Each of these elemental costs is a part of the total of drug-related costs to the patient or to the third-party payer, for the acquisition, receipt, and administration of drug products. I think any review of drug costs in a hospital must include an understanding of the relative impact of each one of these elemental costs.

I think a similar list could be derived for the community pharmacist, for government, and for the Medicaid programs. What I am suggesting is that we need to be much more specific when talking about the various elements of drug costs.

Most discussion so far has concentrated on outpatients. The inpatient situation is very different. These differences, which need to be recognized by the providers and by NHI, include the following:

1. Medication benefits are now provided by Medicare and Medicaid for many inpatients.
2. Reimbursement for medications by government is by a cost allocation formula based on costs, not by an individual dispensing fee.
3. Inpatients have a greater need for care than outpatients and require different levels of drug-related services from the pharmacy department.
4. Drug dispensing in the pharmacy is just one part of the total hospital medication system, which therefore requires different laws and regulations for dispensing, drug control, and accountability.
5. Many drug products are different and of greater drug product cost; IV solutions and injectable drugs are examples.
6. Drug administration to inpatients is done by nurses, anesthesiologists, respiratory therapists, and others; outpatients administer medications to themselves.

Obviously, therefore, the drug-related benefits for inpatients under NHI will be different from those for outpatients. It is important that we understand the current status of hospital pharmacy services to project what the future services and probable costs will be.

The pharmacy departments in most hospitals in this country have not made many changes in the last 20 to 25 years. They are centralized in the institution, remote from where the action is—the patient area. An increasing number of hospitals, however, have developed different medication systems, i.e., unit dose and IV admixture services. There has been some development of the pharmacist's clinical practice in the patient areas. There has been a development of organized drug information services. These changes, however, have been made largely in teaching hospitals and in the larger hospitals. It is important to understand that these changes have been a response from pharmacy personnel to the legitimate needs of patients, physicians, and nurses in the hospital setting, but the changes have come about slowly. Some reasons for the slow development are as follows:

1. There were inadequate pharmacy facilities to start with. One does not have to visit many hospital pharmacies in the United States to realize that too often they are very poor.
2. The pharmacy departments in most hospitals are minimally staffed. This becomes an important factor as attempts to change services are made.
3. There has been a substantial misconception that the newer services are too costly.
4. There has been a lack of interest and support from the medical profession, and in many hospitals, downright opposition to any change in the pharmacy operation.
5. Expertise in hospital pharmacy management is inadequate to cope with these problems.

The existing situation in hospitals, I think, needs to be explained for what it really is. The pharmacy department is a revenue-generating department. National figures will show that somewhere between 7 and 8% of the hospitals' patient revenue comes from the pharmacy department. Yet, at the same time, the pharmacy department's operating expense is in the neighborhood of 3 to 3½% of the total hospital expenses, with the cost of drugs representing probably half the pharmacy expenses.

Pharmacy charges are being affected more and more by the failure of hospitals to charge for their services on the basis of cost. The contractual relationships that exist between hospitals and physicians—notably those in radiology and pathology—are becoming an increasing factor in the hospitals' need to generate revenue in the nonphysician department. That is, pharmacy revenue is increasing, and yet at the same time, hospital management cannot afford to invest in adequate equipment, facilities, and personnel to improve drug safety. More than enough money is now being paid for pharmacy services and drugs to implement the changes needed to improve the safety of drug therapy.

Hospitals are trying to maximize the Medicare cost allocation formula, which includes drugs. Wherever a cost can be put into the indirect expenses of the pharmacy department to increase reimbursement from the government, that is what is happening. It is needed because the government reimbursement program does not generate the capital for institutions to do the things that they feel they need to do. This cost allocation formula is affected by the charges to patients, and by the direct and indirect expenses of the pharmacy operation, so that the larger the indirect expense allocation from business office for health and welfare, building maintenance and the like, assigned to the pharmacy, the greater the reimbursement to the hospital from Medicare.

When all put together, the overall net income—what remains after all expenses and indirect allocations are met—of many hospital pharmacy departments is in the neighborhood of 15 to 20% above expenses. A nonprofit hospital may achieve up to 10% above expenses. In many cases, the pharmacy department is now really the hospital department that is providing a lot of the revenue of the hospital. Pharmacy as a department and as a profession is faced with trying to increase the number of line items processed in the least amount of time. That is its measure of efficiency. Such an approach does not allow for time to be spent in professional activities relating to patient drug therapy.

With this kind of background, I think it is important to look at some of the forces that are acting on the pharmacy department. Since Medicare was instituted, most of the drug laws of this country have been rewritten. Thus, the pharmacy department finds itself with an increasing responsibility in the accountability for drugs throughout the institution, their security, and who has access to them.

The recent Joint Commission on Accreditation of Hospital Standards says that hospitals should develop unit dose systems; that there must be pharmacy-developed IV admixture programs; that where resources are available, there should be patient medication profiles; and that pharmacists are to be involved in drug utilization review (DUR), specifically for antibiotics. To meet these requirements will require an increase in the direct expenditures of the pharmacy department, and more time. And this, of course, will increase the amount of money that must come out of Medicare and other sources to pay for such services.

A couple of questions must be answered: First, what are the responsibilities and services of a pharmacist in a modern hospital? Second, how can these services best be provided—from a centralized or a decentralized location? I believe the answers will be different depending upon the type and size of the institution.

BIDDING AND FORMULARIES

Drug product cost certainly is not an insignificant cost item to a hospital. At my institution, I manage a $1.6 million drug budget in an 800-bed hospital. I am also involved in a drug bidding program with six other hospitals, and as the chairman of the drug committee, I represent those seven institutions. Drug formularies are now required by Medicare and Medicaid. The government will pay for drugs that are listed in the official compendium, the AMA's *Drug Evaluations,* or a hospital's own formulary. The formulary concept has been in operation for more than 20 years, and yet use of the concept, particularly in community hospitals, is probably low. The subject of formularies has not been adequately studied to date.

I think the findings would show that most hospitals do not have an effective formulary system. That is because the Pharmacy and Therapeutics Committee, which is a committee of the medical staff, often is not completely familiar with its roles and responsibilities, and the medical staff often views the responsibilities of the committee as an invasion of their privacy and interference with their prerogatives. But a formulary is one of the committee's responsibilities. Probably, many institutions that have formularies have adopted either the *Red Book* or the *Blue Book.* Others have adopted the American Hospital Formulary Service or some other book. Too many pharmacy directors do not have the knowledge nor the time to help develop their own formulary system. We have spent more than 300 man-hours putting together a formulary in our own institution. I just don't believe there are enough man-hours in the nation's hospitals for pharmacy personnel and the medical staff to come up with an effective formulary system, at least not the way things are structured now.

So what does a formulary system really do? It induces the dispensing of generic products, it allows participation in the drug bidding process, and it decreases the purchasing and inventory costs of the system by eliminating a lot of the infrequently needed drugs that are costly to buy, stock, and inventory.

The drug bidding process falls into three different categories. In a hospital, drugs can be purchased direct from the manufacturer or the wholesaler, and IV solutions as separate products. Each of these areas has different price lists and discounts, which give different prices for the same drug products. What this has led to, then, is inviting drug bids either by an individual hospital or by groups of hospitals. The bidding process does, in fact, reduce drug costs. Just recently we analyzed our drug purchasing program. Looking at the drug bid prices for 600 items as compared to the best catalog price of the manufacturer, we found a 25% reduction in the actual purchase price of these drugs.

I think that the increase in bidding activity that is going on in hospitals is leading to an increased cost to the manufacturer, and certainly will be an elemental cost in the determination of final list prices. The bidding activity needs to be looked at for all of the elemental costs involved. As one who prepares and operates a drug budget every year, I think there is no question that drug product costs are increasing, regardless of some of the statistics quoted. They have been increasing at our institution at the rate of 8 to 14% a year. Each month, I get a listing of from 200 to 350 price increases out of a base of 5,000 items, with a projection of $3,000 to $30,000 in increased cost per year for those items.

As a result, I think purchasing on bid will continue in an attempt to reduce drug product costs.

DRUG UTILIZATION REVIEW

DUR may be defined as an authorized, structured program that provides drug education for the medical staff. The expectations for DUR are improvement in the quality of drug use and reduction of drug product cost. By the very nature of DUR, it requires physicians and pharmacists to participate in this activity together. It requires their interest, their knowledge, and their time. I think we need to recognize that neither physicians nor pharmacists have been oriented to the DUR concept or methods, that DUR programs are still in their infancy, and that neither the benefits nor the costs of such programs have been documented. If DUR is needed and essential, then the "what's," the "why's," and the "how's" of conducting DUR programs need to be developed. The cost for these programs will, in fact, have to be paid for by government or others who, at the present time, are not willing to do so.

QUESTIONS THAT NEED ANSWERS

My overall theme is that rising drug costs and pressures on the hospital pharmacy department are going to increase operational costs at the same time that everyone wants to reduce costs. Somewhere in that process, there will have to be some understanding and definition of what drug-related services will be acceptable and what will not. One of the questions that I already have noted is that the scope of the drug-related services in the hospital needs to be defined. What is the pharmacist's role in seeing that all this is done? If we look ahead to the impact of the drugs of tomorrow, as the National Study Commission on Pharmacy did, and to those aspects that are being researched, there is no way that the existing relationship among the physician, the nurse, and the pharmacist, and the existing medication systems of control, can cope with the types of drugs that we will probably have in the next decade. There will have to be changes, and these changes will probably increase the operational expenses of drug activities in the hospital.

How can these services best be provided? From a centralized location, where most pharmacies are located? Or from a decentralized location, an approach with which I have had a great deal of experience? What kind of staffing levels are needed by patient type, by hospital type, and by size of hospital? If we consider using computerization to improve the operational aspects of a hospital, then we must obtain a certificate of need. There is not a pharmacy computer system around that will not have to go through the certificate-of-need process—a process that is very expensive. Somewhere along the line, we need to look at the computer systems regarding drugs, and decide which would be acceptable and could be approved without going through the certificate-of-need process.

What kind of reimbursement will be provided for the pharmacist's services that are not drug-product-related? Is there a better way to do it than the present cost allocation formula? Maybe we need to take a hard look at some kind of daily pharmacy service charge by levels of service and by types of patients, and also at reimbursement for the provision of special clinical pharmacy services.

In the drug formulary area, we need to define a formulary, its relationship to similar publications, and its cost transfer. How does it affect the dispensing process? How does it affect inventory control, purchase price, and the cost of running an inventory system? What are its costs of preparation? And what does it cost to administer and to keep under surveillance?

Drug utilization review needs to be defined, and its real cost of operation and benefits need to be determined.

Development of hospital pharmacy management is absolutely crucial and essential to any kind of efforts to control the cost of drugs in hospitals. This area of management has been a glaring deficiency in pharmacy education, and I am suggesting there must be some kind of traineeship program to develop the required personnel.

There is a great deal of money being paid to hospitals for what is now an inefficient and illogical drug processing system. There will be a great many changes occurring during the next decade. These all need to be looked at in putting together a national drug insurance program for inpatients.

A nationwide network of computer systems is probably technically feasible, but even if work started on it today, I doubt if it could be completed by 1985. Those who have been involved in trying to put together just one department's computer system know what the problems are, let alone trying to hook together 50,000 or 60,000 terminals. If the computer system is not going to work, then I think the question is: What kind of processing system will have to be put together?

It is a fact today that the community pharmacists of this country are subsidizing the existing Medicaid programs. I don't think you can find a group of pharmacists anywhere who are excited or enthusiastic about the Medicaid program, and who support it. They see themselves as being paid less than they should be paid. Community pharmacies are going out of business. Many people are getting out of community pharmacy. And if an even greater program of NHI is imposed on community pharmacists, better make sure that they will support it. Right now, unless it is very clear that they are going to be paid adequately for their services, I think it is very questionable what kind of support can be obtained.

There is therefore a need to look at what the pharmacists' roles and services are in the community pharmacy. How is that going to relate to the providing of services to whatever beneficiary group is included in an NHI program? And what are the costs of providing those services, and how are they going to be adequately paid? Without adequate compensation, it will never work. And then, of course, the alternative is to put together a completely different drug distribution system for patients, under national health insurance.

62. Cost Containment in Laundry and Linen Service

BARBARA ELLIS

Reprinted, with permission, from *Hospitals, Journal of the American Hospital Association,* vol. 52, no. 6, March 16, 1978, pp. 141-146.

As the voluntary effort toward cost containment takes hold, health care institutions everywhere will be looking for new ways to streamline their operations for maximum efficiency and effectiveness and to decrease their expenditure. The hospital laundry and linen service, which, too often in the past, has been relegated to a basement operation, is one area of hospital services that increasingly is and will be brought into the light for examination. Although hospital laundry and linen services generally constitute no more than two percent of a hospital's budget, this service offers significant opportunities for savings.

How to hold the line of costs while increasing the operational effectiveness of hospital laundry and linen services was the subject of an American Hospital Association seminar held January 18-20 in New Orleans.

Recently, the trend has been to move away from in-house operations to commercial or shared or central laundry services, said David Giancola, management consultant, Giancola Associates, Maryville, TN. Few hospitals are being constructed today with in-house laundries, and many now in existence are being closed, simply because they have become too expensive to build or operate, he said.

Although many hospitals have switched to alternative services, such as shared or central laundries or commercial services, some have found that these alternatives do not always solve their problems. Some hospitals say that after switching to alternative services, the quality of service and of the linen product is not comparable to that which they received in-house.

One problem looms distinct among all the others, however, no matter what type of service a hospital employs—shared, central, commercial, or in-house. The single biggest—and most costly—problem hospitals face in this area is the control of linen consumption and replacement costs, Giancola said. Linen replacement costs presently range from 20 to 40 percent of the total cost of a hospital laundry and linen service. An estimated 80 percent of the linen replaced is attributable to linen misuse, including theft, Giancola said, leaving only 20 percent to actually wear out.

It was with an eye to getting a handle on costs common to all, that speakers addressed meeting participants from various types of laundry and linen services at the seminar. "High-quality service" should be the goal for all, Giancola said, and high-quality service can be defined as "a clean, good-looking textile product in adequate supply, used when needed to perform a predetermined function."

All too often, however, laundry and linen services fall short of this goal. Speakers at the seminar addressed various reasons for this failing, among them the perpetuation of costly traditional linen use practices, the lack of managerial effectiveness and authority, the lack of administrative interest in and support of the linen service, and the lack of adequate factual information with which to pinpoint problems and make managerial decisions.

IS MORE BETTER?

Unnecessary and costly linen use practices must be changed, said Sam Berger, linen systems specialist, Whitehouse Manufacturing Company, New York City. Berger suggests taking a hard look at linen use practices to find what he terms "the truth behind the mythology of linen use." Does more linen really mean better patient care? Do many of the items in the linen mix really need to be there? Are those items of the most appropriate design and material for that function or are they merely an indulgence to a particular group or unit such as operating room personnel? Should the various specialities, (sic) such as operating room or obstetrical personnel, have complete autonomy in choosing speciality items, when these items create havoc in the laundry manager's system and unnecessary expenditures? Must linen always be delivered at 7 a.m., even when the laundry's operation could be enhanced by switching to another time?

Traditional practices must be reexamined, Berger said. For example, for many years, operating room personnel have been reluctant to switch to 50/50 blends, and laundry managers have been reluctant to suggest such a switch, because of fear of sparks being ignited in what has been traditionally regarded as a highly volatile and hazardous area. Some of these fears are unfounded today, Berger said, because safer equipment, procedures, and constructions are now being used. Hazards must be evaluated at each individual hospital and decisions must be based on facts, not mythology, Berger said, before suggestions such as switching to 50/50 blends are entirely disregarded.

There are other costly practices that bear examination, Berger said. One is the continued use of draw sheets. Often, these items can be easily eliminated from the inventory with no untoward consequences. Most nursing services have a written policy for changing beds—top sheet to bottom, bottom sheet to soil. However, not one hospital in 10 implements this policy, Berger said, and entire beds often are changed needlessly. Some hospitals are in the habit of keeping a blanket rolled up at the foot of every bed, regardless of whether the blanket is used or not. As is the case with other superfluous items, the blanket returns to the laundry unused when the bed is changed.

Often, linen packs are not used properly and thus contribute to needless waste, Berger said. Many packs contain a patient gown, even in institutions where patients are allowed to wear their own bed attire. Again, unused, the gowns return to the laundry after the pack has been opened.

Berger also questioned the practice of the daily bed change. Would patient care be adversely affected in your hospital, he asked, if beds were changed fewer than seven days a week? Of course, beds should be changed as often as required for the incontinent patient or simply for that patient who prefers a daily bed change, he said. However patient care generally is not adversely affected if the bed of an ambulatory patient is changed less often than daily, Berger said.

STREAMLINE THE MIX

Although standardization of the linen mix often is looked upon as a practice to be undertaken only if three or more hospitals are involved, that is not necessarily the case, Berger said. By streamlining the linen mix, processing techniques can be simplified in the in-house laundry as well as in the shared or central facility. Ideally, the linen mix should provide a good balance of tumble work and flat work, and adjustments should be made in the linen mix to accommodate equipment, he said.

Every linen item must have a predetermined function and that function should be written down as policy, Berger said. Every hospital should have a linen standardization committee that is immune to the demands of the various departments for speciality (sic) items that destroy the effectiveness of the system. Nonstandard items or items of a different color tend to return to the laundry unused, because if an alternative item is available, the less desirable item is rejected and returned, he said. Therefore, items such as colored gowns must all go to the same unit and not be in the general mix. Linen items that are visibly overrepaired also will be rejected and will return to the laundry unused.

Theft is another problem that too often is neglected, Berger said. Removing the opportunity for hoarding is one method for combatting theft, he said. Hospital personnel hoard when they feel that they may not have enough linen to last until the next delivery. The way to prevent hoarding is for the laundry manager to build up the credibility of his system, Berger said. If personnel have confidence in the system, they will not hoard. The way to build up credibility is to open the lines of communication to the various hospital departments through memos and meetings.

TWO HATS

Unfortunately, it is just such influence among hospital personnel that the typical laundry manager lacks, Berger said. Although given full authority as director of the laundry service, the laundry manager has little or no authority as director of the linen service. He is placed in the awkward position of being held responsible for what happens to the linen after it has been delivered without having full authority for controlling what happens. Nevertheless, he bears the burden for stains, tears, holes, theft, overuse, and misuse when it comes to budgeting time.

If costly linen use practices are going to be changed, the laundry manager must enlist the backing of top administration, Berger said. To do this, the laundry manager must be able to supply top administration with facts and figures specific to item and use-area; gross figures will not work, Berger said. By generating factual data on each linen item in a given use-area during a given period, the laundry manager will be able to pinpoint problems and win the support of administration for changing practices, Berger said.

Nelson L. St. Clair, executive vice-president, Riverside Hospital, Newport News, VA, related his experience with laundry and linen services from his vantage point as a hospital administrator. Recently, Riverside Hospital, together with other area hospitals, built a central laundry facility, the Peninsula Hospital Services Central Laundry, Newport News, VA. Although the in-house laundry at Riverside was an efficiently run operation, it was taking up valuable space needed to provide patient services.

In keeping with the voluntary effort to reduce operating expenses and capital expenditures, all hospitals should investigate the option of sharing laundry services, St. Clair said. Although not every institution has the funds to build a shared service facility, many in-house laundries presently have the capability of serving other hospitals in their area, he said.

Control of linen replacement and consumption requires a commitment from top administration on down, St. Clair said. If a hospital is doing a poor job with its laundry and linen service it should reexamine its linen use policies and procedures, he said. In this era of rising health care costs, there is no justifiable reason for a hospital to have 200–300 linen items in circulation, he said. Adequate service must be provided, but not ''blue sky'' service that is beyond the ability of the American public to pay for, he said.

Since entering the shared service arrangement, Riverside Hospital has for the first time been able to get a handle on its consumption and replacement problems, which were formidable, St. Clair said. (An article on this shared service laundry appears in the November 16, 1977, issue of *Hospitals.*) According to St. Clair, this was made possible because, for the first time, Riverside Hospital had the necessary data on linen use and replacement with which it could pinpoint problem areas. Also, Riverside Hospital's former in-house laundry manager was freed under the new arrangement to devote his full time to linen service management.

The shared service arrangement of which Riverside is a part uses a computer to generate these data. Delivery requirements are printed out at the beginning of each day based on the amount of soiled linen returned to the central laundry from each previously designated hospital linen use-area. If data show that a use-area needs additional linen, that use-area can be charged for that linen, and an equal amount of new linen can be added to the system in the central laundry. Not only do the linen replacement data allow the hospital to charge each use-area for the linen placed into use, they also provide the basis for new linen purchases. The data eliminate the need for periodic inventories, because the linen in use is updated daily. Data also allow linen replacement costs to be analyzed by use-area, so that problem areas of misuse or theft can be pinpointed and attended to.

The computer also prints a production report based on this data for use in the laundry. The report contains the number of wash loads of each wash category that must be produced and the exact number of pieces required to meet delivery requirements.

Using the new system, St. Clair says, he was able for the first time to identify a serious problem with theft. Data generated for 1977 indicated that $44,506 worth of linen had to be replaced. Of this figure, approximately 80 percent could be attributed to linen misuse and theft, the vast majority of which was believed to be patient theft. Thus, only 20 percent of the linen was left to wear out. The hospital is now using its closed-circuit television network to present patient education programs on how linen replacement costs affect the cost of health care. Spot checks of both patients and employees when leaving also are being made by security guards.

SUPPLY VS. CONTROL

Lack of adequate information with which to pinpoint problem areas and base management decisions is at the root of laundry and linen service problems, according to Giancola. Traditional laundry systems such as those in which nursing requisitions the amount of linen it believes is needed or cart systems based on even exchange fail because they are supply systems and not control systems. Traditional systems require the hospital to maintain a higher inventory of linen, they generate higher linen replacement costs, they create an uneven rate of linen issue, they provide no data that can be used for production scheduling in the laundry, and they provide no accountability for misuse of theft, he said.

All problems and complaints fall back on the laundry manager, who has no recourse for rectifying problems, Giancola said. Linen service then becomes an emotionally charged arena, in which the laundry manager finds that his pleas for efficient, effective laundry and linen practices fall by the wayside in competition with nursing and medical needs, whether real or fancied.

According to Giancola, soiled linen counting and delivery on a delayed even exchange basis according to the amount of soiled linen returned is the only answer to controlling hospital linen consumption and replacement problems. Hospital laundries must begin counting the soiled linen returned from each use-area and replace that linen with clean, he said.

Although computer assistance may be necessary for a laundry of the scope and size of the one previously described, the same principles can be applied to smaller operations without the use of a computer. Manual analysis of data specific to item and use-area will produce the same kind of savings and benefits experienced at Riverside Hospital even in the smallest hospital, Giancola said.

63. Documented Proof— Softened Water Cuts Laundry Costs

RON DURRWACHTER

Reprinted with permission from *Hospital Topics*, 1977, p. 6.

Most laundry operators know the value of softened water, but few have been able to document its benefits and savings as clearly as Ron Durrwachter, laundry manager at Washington County Hospital in Hagerstown, Maryland.

Durrwachter knew he had to present specific facts and figures to hospital management in order to justify purchase of a water softener. The 383 bed hospital is a non-profit institution and, like most, operates on a tight budget.

Through an unusual circumstance, Durrwachter was able to gather the figures he needed. The hospital used city water which came from two sources, one of them soft, the other hard. The soft water (2 grains hard) came from a reservoir supplied by rain. The hard water (about 12 grains) came from a river. When the reservoir ran dry, river water was used.

By keeping cost records during both reservoir and river use, Durrwachter was able to make a direct comparison of hard water and soft water operating costs. He then used these figures to project savings possible if water of near zero hardness were always available, as it would be with a softener.

Washington County Hospital laundry employs 26 people, operates six days a week, and handles more than 1,700,000 pounds of laundry per year.

Based on his studies, Durrwachter predicted the following if a softener were installed:

1. Reduced usage, and therefore cost, of washing supplies.
2. A reduction in linen replacement costs.
3. A savings in water costs.
4. A reduction in the cost of chemical softeners.
5. No increase in the number of laundry employees.

As a result of his documentation, the hospital approved acquisition of a softener. It was installed in February, 1976, and since that time all predictions made by Durrwachter have come true.

Reduced cost of washing supplies. In 1975, the hospital used 39,305 pounds of washing supplies. Washing supplies cost 87 cents per 100 pounds of linen processed. Since the softener was installed, monthly costs have averaged 43.5 cents per 100 pounds, or exactly half of that paid out in 1975.

In all of 1975, Durrwachter spent $15,000 for supplies. Cutting that cost in half means a saving of $7500.

"To be fair," Durrwachter said, "part of the savings is because I changed suppliers. However, the principal savings came from reduced usage occasioned by softening the water."

Reduced linen replacement costs. Every hospital faces the problem of linen replacement costs. At Washington County Hospital, the laundry handles sheets, pillow cases, nurses uniforms, towels, patient gowns, OB and surgical linens, the latter category making up about 25 per cent of the work load.

"Two laundry operations cause linens to wear out," said Durrwachter. "One is the mechanical action of washing and drying. The other is chemical action. We project a 40 per cent decrease in linen replacement per year with soft water, based on linen replacement figures of past years with hard and soft water. Translating this to dollar figures, we estimate that in the future we will spend only about $25,000 for new linens annually, compared to between $31,000 and $34,000 in previous years, an annual savings of $9,000."

Mechanical wear is being reduced because Durrwachter has eliminated one rinsing cycle in the washer. Soft water permits his clothes and linens to come clean with three rinse cycles instead of four formerly used. This also accounts for water savings.

Chemical wear is being reduced by reducing the use of bleaches and other special cleaning agents by roughly half. Soft water, providing a better cleaning action, does away with the need for heavy bleaching. The reduction in bleach costs—1600 pounds per year now versus about 2500 in past years—also accounts for some of the washing supply savings.

In 1975, the laundry used 5300 pounds of chemical softeners per year, to make up for the lack of softened water. Now they use 600 pounds per year, a reduction of almost 90 per cent.

It all adds up. Adding all savings together—supplies, linen replacement, water—Durrwachter finds that his total costs are reduced about one cent per pound of linen processed. Since he washes about 1,760,000 pounds per year, this amounts to a savings of $17,000 and more per year.

"In terms of capital equipment payback," he said, "these figures indicate that our savings in operating costs will permit us to pay for the softener in about 14 months time, and that includes the first year's operating costs."

64. A Simple Cost Control Format in Clinical Laboratories

J.S. LO, P.F. PRINGLE, K.F. WIGZELL, AND D.H. LEE

Reprinted from *Clinical Biochemistry*, August 1977, pp. 164–167, published by The Canadian Society of Clinical Chemists.

The laboratories in a hospital are constantly demanded by patients, physicians, hospital administrators and increasingly, governmental agencies to lower the costs of laboratory procedures and simultaneously to provide more ready and usable services. To meet these demands, priority must be established. The quality of services and individual attention must at times dictate over the expenses of economic consideration. With this priority clearly set out, the laboratory in its routine operation will be no different from any business organization that is interested in decreasing costs, increasing efficiency and promoting consumer satisfaction at all times. Consequently, the decision making process demands professional judgment as well as cost information. The DBS unit system—a Canadian Federal Government schedule of unit values for clinical laboratory procedures—is basically a time and motion unit for technologists' time in performing an analysis. This system is used primarily by the hospital administrations and government agencies as criteria in judging the laboratory workload and productivity.

If the laboratory management team relies only on the DBS unit system for purchases of capital equipment, personnel hiring or future planning, the following defects become obvious:

1. The DBS unit assigns no dollar value to the technologist's time. Therefore, it does not reflect actual economic conditions facing

549

laboratory personnel. This is a very serious shortcoming in view of the rampage of inflation in the last few years.

2. The DBS unit reflects no material and equipment costs.

3. In the last three years, the DBS units assigned to different test procedures have changed from year to year. More drastically the changes, largely decreases in value, have occurred in the chemistry section. In certain tests a 60% decrease from the previous year was noted. Furthermore, in the chemistry section the unit value has been changed from test procedure to the type of analytical instrument used. Such changes reflect the dynamic nature of clinical chemistry. On the other hand, one can no longer rely on the yearly DBS unit as a prediction for future growth or as a yearly indicator of workload.

4. The primary purpose of automation in clinical laboratories is to increase both accuracy and precision on the test procedures. Only when the above criteria are satisfied, should one consider the labour saving aspect of the instrument. If one accepts these premises then automated equipment will vary extensively from laboratory to laboratory. Small hospital laboratories with a very small workload therefore, will suffer greatly by having the DBS unit assigned to the instrument rather than the test procedure. However, by retaining manual procedures small hospitals would then have the advantage in claiming more units. This hinders the improvement of quality in clinical laboratories.

In order to have an objective picture of costing in the laboratory the following information must be available:

- Labour
- Raw Material
- Capital Equipment
- Overheads

Furthermore, without knowing the actual revenue in terms of dollars and cents the cost data will be useless in assessing one's productivity or efficiency.

We compensate for these defects by adopting the LMS unit system. The LMS unit, designated by the Ontario Medical Association, is the basis used by the Ontario Health Insurance Plan to pay independent laboratories. The unit includes all costs as well as profit margin. We chose to ignore overhead costs as these costs are infrequently allocated by hospitals to their various departments. Imitating Leontif's input output tables[1], we formulated two tables reflecting both the costs and revenue of the laboratories.

The procedures in compiling DBS and LMS data are as follows:

1. Technologists assigned to a specific workbench will record daily the number of tests, controls and standards.
2. At the end of the month the individual worksheets are then checked and totalled by the charge technologists in each laboratory section. The DBS units and LMS units (for actual patient tests only) are then converted and summarised according to various test procedures. The clerical section also independently tabulates the monthly number of actual patient tests done in the laboratory.
3. Monthly billing from various laboratory suppliers is divided and allocated to the various laboratory sections as indicated on the purchase requisitions.
4. Monthly payments to laboratory technologists and clerical staff are then calculated and formulated (Table 1). This table shows actual technologist time and cost in various sections. Any unusual increases or decreases can readily be detected leading to proper management action.
5. From the total of LMS and DBS units each laboratory section is then calculated according to the number of technologists at work during that particular month. Basic unit cost is then obtained. Table 2 shows the allocation of DBS and LMS per technologist. The income expenditure ratio accurately shows us how each laboratory section performs financially.

This simple system in our laboratory has proven helpful in allowing an instant overview of laboratory costs, without any complicated accounting system or computer printout. The revenue-expenditure ratio reflects the actual productivity of various sections in the laboratory. The compilation of these tables takes approximately six hours after all the monthly tabulations are in from different sections. We believe this information is important for decision making as well as justification to the hospital administration in either purchasing equipment or hiring of personnel. Adaptation of this system in the United States can easily be carried out by substituting CAP unit for the DBS unit. Revenues can be calculated according to individual laboratory charges rather than based on LMS units. In places where equipment is leased, a separate column can be added to Table 2 and allocated accordingly.

REFERENCE

1. Leontif, W.: Input-Output Economics, New York. Oxford University Press, 1966, pp. 223–251.

Table 1

FOR THE MONTH OF ....

Descriptions	Micro-Biology	Cytology	Histology	Blood Bank	Haema-tology	IV Team	Bio-Chemistry	Clerical	Class Wa...	Students	Totals
No of Persons on Staff	6.5	3	4	3	5	3	11	4	2	6	47.5
(hrs)	1067	495	671	495	825	495	1785(30)*	573.5	352	—	6758.5
Regular Salaries	$7710	$3220	$1194	$3462	$5389	$2967	$12517	$2739	$1475	—	$43673
Stand-By ($)	$195	—	$92.50	$75	$101.25	—	$285	—	—	—	$748.75
Call Back (hrs)	21.50	—	31	32.50	47.25	—	57.25	—	—	—	189.50
Overtime (hrs)	61.25	—	26.5	3.50	19.50	20.00	60.75	—	—	—	174.00
Evening Shift	—	—	3	—	4	—	26	—	—	—	33
Sick Leave (days)	—	—	—	2	1	2	4*	—	5	—	14
Vacation (days)	11	3	8	8	15	—	12	11.5 (LoA)	—	—	68.5
Travel & Education ($)	$20	—	$18	$86	$23	—	38	—	—	—	$185
Relief work ($)	—	—	$14.19	$288.80	$362.18	$448.72	—	—	$369	$147.25	$1630
(hrs)	—	—	3	44.50	45.50	$75	—	—	88	31	287
Total Labour Costs	$8613	$3220	$4892	$4301	$6569	$3569	$14106	$2739	$1844	$147	$50000

*2/3 pay

Table 2

FOR THE MONTH OF ....

Laboratory	No of Staff	No of Tests	DBS Units	LMS Units	DBS per Tech	LMS per Tech	% Total No of Tests	Material in Each Lab $	%	Regular Salaries	Cost per LMS Units	Cost per DBS Unit	Income/Expend
Serology	1	1474	9892	12569	9892	12569	3.8	22.65	0.18	1262	0.10	0.12	4651/1285
Microbiology	5.5	2091	65734	39228	11952	7132	5.4	1993.73	15.80	7351	0.24	0.14	14514/9345
Cytology	3	931	45811	12168	15270	4056	2.4	—	—	3220	0.26	0.07	4502/3220
Histology	4	1236	46347	21720	11587	5430	3.19	186.61	1.48	4892	0.23	0.11	8036/5079
Blood Bank	3	2934	41445	52734	13815	17578	7.53	1615.68	12.8	4301	0.11	0.14	19512/5917
Haematology	5	6244	55371	47880	11114	9576	16.12	1711.93	13.56	6569	0.17	0.15	17716/8281
I.V. Team	3	8074	95311	40370	31670	13457	20.85	1756.16	13.91	3569	0.13	0.06	14937/5325
Biochemistry	11	15742	191412	147967	17401	13452	40.65	5332.48	42.25	14106	0.13	0.10	54748/19438
Totals	35.5	38726	551223	374636	15527	10553	100%	12622.40	100%	45270	0.15	0.11	138615/57880

65. Structuring Security in a Hospital

NORMAN JASPAN

Reprinted with permission from Norman Jaspan, Norman Jaspan Associates, 60 East 42nd Street, New York, N.Y. 10017.

The principle that it is cheaper and more effective to treat a malady before it becomes inoperable is as true in the field of hospital administration as it is in patient care. Preventive management techniques scientifically applied to control internal dishonesty, exorbitant waste and to provide safety can slash hospital operating expenses and reduce patient care cost substantially.

The capital investment of all U.S. hospitals today is in excess of 30 billion dollars. It is the third largest industry, surpassing the investment in automobiles, railroads, and even telephone communications.

The responsibility of the hospital administrator is a formidable one, indeed. The operation of a hospital is not only big business, but a complex of many big businesses. The administration must contend with the problems of building maintenance; a pharmacy, hotel, laundry, restaurant, purchasing department, research and educational institution.

For these reasons, hospital complexes are one of the most challenging types of construction for which to design suitable security safeguards. From a cost and effectiveness viewpoint, there is no better time for developing a comprehensive program than at the blueprint stage. If management waits until after the building is erected, expanded or renovated additional and substantial expenses will be incurred in order to belatedly install safeguards which often are poor compromises.

There are five areas meriting attention:

1. Procedures governing the flow of food, drugs, supplies and equipment, from time of purchase until their receipt, as well as their storage and issuance.
2. Total hospital site. The problems of perimeter security, visitors, and pedestrian and vehicular traffic; the safety of patients, visitors, and employees.
3. Accountability of cash payments, accounts receivable and other valuables.
4. Protecting medical records and other confidential information.
5. Guard coverage and technology necessary for them to perform optimally.

HOSPITAL SECURITY DEFINED

An effective hospital security program will aim at achieving the highest attainable level of safety, protection of supplies and equipment, as well as the persons and belongings of patients and employees, without adversely affecting efficiency and control considerations. Of course, the practicality of all physical and procedural regulations has to be measured by their enforcibility. Any control measure and operating rules which require an enormous supervisory effort to enforce, or incur deep visitor and patient resentment, or high employee turnover are bound to be ineffective.

SCOPE OF PROGRAM

The security program has to aim at curtailment of fraudulent diversion. This includes two major categories of theft: (a) pilferage by employees, patients, visitors on the one hand, and (b) large scale diversion through collusive effort such as between drivers and receivers; maintenance men and outside contractors; laundry workers and outsiders; professional personnel and suppliers; to name but a few examples.

A security program must be based on an awareness of the relative risks and potential losses in both types of diversion.

THE UNIQUENESS OF HOSPITAL SECURITY

Pedestrian traffic through a hospital allows very little curtailment. It is possible to prevent unauthorized traffic through selective areas such as the pharmacy, laboratories, central supply, or medical records library. It is very difficult to curtail traffic through the corridors where patients, visitors, doctors, contractors and employees of all levels, are virtually indistinguishable. Consequently, the primary aim is to limit the exposure of supplies and equipment, whether in storage, transit or use.

The question of exposure of items is directly related to the problem of space utilization. The question of transit security is integral to vertical and horizontal transportation considerations, including material handling procedures, the type of conveyances used, and the required corridor dimensions and elevator facilities.

THE RECEIVING DOCK

The most vulnerable area for large scale diversion is the receiving dock. The best security is to provide a receiving dock exclusively for the use of receiving supplies and equipment.

Space and budgets permitting, there should be a separate dock for outgoing soiled and incoming fresh linen (unless the hospital has its own laundry within the complex.) A separate dock for trash removal should also be provided, both for security as well as hygienic considerations. There should also be a separate loading area for the morgue.

The receiving dock should be so located so as to require no pedestrian traffic across the dock nor in the immediate vicinity. The official employee exit ideally should be at the opposite end of the hospital so that the chance for exiting employees to come in contact with supplies and equipment in the process of being received is sharply curtailed.

Externally, it is most advisable to place the receiving dock in an area which can be fenced off from the nearest approach road. The basic security approach would be to have the gate and fence closed and locked whenever the receiving dock is unattended. Depending on traffic patterns in some hospitals this may call for a remote control gate; in others, a manually operated gate may suffice.

Internally, provision must be made to permit reliable dual accountability for those supplies which should be identified, verified, and perhaps weighed on the dock, and again verified and counted upon arrival in storage. Since space and flow considerations are of paramount importance here, it is inopportune to consider these matters after the architectural drawings are approved and construction begun.

At the linen dock, it is essential to prevent linen drivers from access to other areas of the hospital when they pick up soiled or deliver fresh linen. These pick ups are often performed in the very early morning when payroll considerations would make it inadvisable to staff the linen dock. Therefore, the linen dock must be sealed off through reliable lockup arrangements from the rest of the hospital, or approaches to the linen dock must be restricted by a gate controlled by a hospital employee who would supervise the linen loading and unloading operation. The importance of such measures is underscored by the fact that the stolen supplies and equipment are often concealed in soiled linen containers.

A separate trash removal dock should be also provided with similar precautions to prevent unsupervised access to hospital assets during the trash loading operation.

THE EMPLOYEE EXIT

The curtailment of employee pilferage can be ideally effected by requiring all employees to enter and depart from one exit. In hospitals which consist of one main building and only few auxiliary buildings this goal is attainable.

Channeling the flow of employee traffic through the designated exit, in spite of the availability of numerous fire exits and visitors lobbies, can be achieved by placing time clocks and locker rooms in strategic locations. Another consideration is the location of the employee parking lot to permit easy access during inclement weather.

LINEN SECURITY

In most urban communities linen is usually the most vulnerable supply item, it is easily disposable at a profit and it is a tempting target for pilferage for employees, patients, and visitors. Moreover, linen on the nursing floors is a supply item requiring the most frequent access by nurses and aides. Great care must therefore be taken in the relative location of nursing stations and other patient care areas to the location of linen closets or alcoves where linen carts are to be stored.

Similarly, regional storage rooms will have to be subject to specialized protection arrangements. If such areas are in close proximity to heavily trafficked corridors or, conceivably, through accessible windows or fire exits, protection by some form of electronic intrusion alarm equipment will have to be considered.

If the hospital maintains its own laundry within its complex special intrusion protection may have to be designed to protect the laundry during periods when there is no one in attendance.

STORAGE AREAS

Space availability and fire laws permitting it will be advantageous to design areas such as central surgical supply, general storage or maintenance supply and tool crib areas, in such a way that there is no direct exit through fire doors, nor any connection to the outside through windows. If this is not possible, consideration should be given to some form of electronic intrusion alarm protection.

Such arrangements should be taken into consideration when the grand master and sub master key setups are designed.

FOOD PRODUCTS

Failure to properly control the handling and storage of fresh meats and poultry can be very costly. It is vital, therefore, for the location of meat freezers and coolers, and storage areas for canned meats and poultry, to be carefully selected and that these areas be provided with suitable lockup devices during the planning phase.

Canned staple foods are second in priority from a security point of view. Reliable lockup hardware as well as possible intrusion protection by electronic means, depending upon the location of the food storage area, would have to be considered.

Lockup of dairy and produce freezers and coolers usually does not have to be quite as rigid as the system protecting the meat storage areas.

PHARMACY

Lockup requirements for narcotics and hypnotic drugs are clearly stipulated by Federal and State laws. As a general rule it is best to design the central pharmacy or any regional pharmacy which may serve the clinics in such a way as to limit access to pharmacists and their assistants only. This is often accomplished by equipping pharmacies with Dutch type doors or ledge equipped windows through which all negotiations between pharmacists and nursing personnel can take place.

EMERGENCY ROOM AND OUT-PATIENT CLINICS

The protection of individuals is of paramount importance in emergency rooms and out-patient clinics. Many clinics, for example, cannot safely function without guard coverage.

Nevertheless, a great deal can be done in the design and planning of these clinics to reduce opportunities for physical assault on the staff.

NURSES' RESIDENCE

Whether the nurses' residence is part of the complex, or a separate building connected by tunnel or bridge, entrance to the residence should be monitored. Monitoring can be achieved by guard coverage. Good advance planning, however, can sometimes achieve effective monitoring without the additional payroll expense for protection of the nurses' residence. Such devices as closed circuit TV, surveillance, public address systems, various types of door alarms and other mechanical or electronic devices can often be used instead.

PERIMETER SECURITY

Here a wide variety of problems and solutions are possible. There is little similarity between a rural or suburban hospital built on a large expanse and an urban hospital consisting of one massive building covering one or more city blocks. But the essential target for perimeter security remains the same regardless of the site. The complex is to be designed so as to inhibit an employee, visitor, or any person entering the hospital to emerge unobserved and unimpeded through a fire exit or any other door, window, air shaft, fire escape.

To attain this goal requires a comprehensive lockup system within existing fire regulations, supported by a practical monitor alarm system which deters and also exposes breaches of the perimeter.

THE GUARD FORCE

It is rare that a guard post, whether fixed or roving, can be justified on economic grounds unless the guard is required to perform multiple security duties. It is usually difficult to justify a guard's exclusive attention to the monitoring of employee traffic, or the surveillance of patients in the emergency room, or to the watching of activities on the receiving dock.

However, if guard duties, coverage and schedules are formulated during the blueprint stage, plans can incorporate physical and procedural measures permitting guard flexibility which makes their costs tolerable.

CONCLUSION

The presentation of these observations, of course, cannot be considered all-inclusive. This over-view of hospital security, it is hoped, will demonstrate that although the problems are complex, they are manageable through forethought and timing. Architects can make a contribution second to none in this grave and costly area by incorporating security considerations in their plans. Fortunately, some leading professionals are moving in this direction, but the response has been minor compared to the need.

66. Receiving Reports on Microfiche Saves Hospital Business Office Time, Money and Storage Space

Reprinted from the January 1977 issue of *Hospital Financial Management,* p. 30. Copyright 1977 Hospital Financial Management Association.

When in 1974 the Medical College of Virginia Hospitals, a 1,000 bed teaching hospital in Richmond, began receiving its computer reports on microfiche instead of paper, the price for the service went down.

Savings in paper cost and machine time needed to make extra copies allowed Shared Medical Systems to cut their price for the reports almost in half. In three months that price reduction paid for the ten readers the hospital purchased for $150 each.

Today, the hospital also receives copies of patient bills on microfiche, providing convenient storage for both archival purposes and daily use. All itemized and follow-up bills for the hospital's average 100 patients and 1,000 outpatients per day are contained on 6 to 8 microfiche.

Shared Medical Systems estimates that 90 percent of its clients use microfiche for one or more reports. The microfiche are made on two Kodak COM 80 machines (Computerized Output on Microfiche). Each prints 18,000 lines per minute, compared to the 2,000 lines per minute on the larger paper printers. Duplicates are sold to clients at only 75¢ per fiche—possible because they can be produced at the rate of 1,200 per hour.

"Every Monday morning we used to receive 15 or 16 cases of paper reports," says Forrest E. Perrin, Jr., data processing manager in the hospital's business office. "One report, the aged trial balance, regularly was 1,800 pages long. Reduced to microfiche, the report now is delivered on ten pieces of film."

The change to microfiche also encouraged the hospital to take advantage of more current reports. Daily reports now received by the office include: accounts receivable activity reports, revenue journal, listing of charges and credits posted, outpatient locator file, and a report of general ledger activity. These reports average about 4.5 microfiche a day.

Storage saving was important, but Perrin rates use of microfiche as a working tool equally high. The fifth and sixth carbon of a paper report were difficult to read and use, and the large books difficult to lift and handle.

Now eight readers are distributed around the business office in high-use locations. Five of these are in the collection department, each located adjacent to a group responsible for a portion of the alphabet.

In addition to following up on delinquent accounts, the collections clerks are constantly responding to telephone calls and correspondence from patients who request confirmation of the account balance, or who call to check that their last payment was credited.

"When you have a patient on the telephone," said one collections clerk, "you need to respond as quickly as you can. Using the paper statement book, it took us almost five minutes to walk back to the files and locate the data. Having our accounts on just two microfiche with the reader right here not only is convenient, but also saves the patient's nerves and our patience."

67. Checkless Payroll: Both Hospital and Employees Benefit

GEORGE N. PETRIE

Reprinted from the September 1978 issue of *Hospital Financial Management*, pp. 28–29. Copyright 1978 Hospital Financial Management Association.

For months, none of the employees of Waldo General Hospital has seen a paycheck. Instead, through automatic electronic banking, their wages are deposited directly into their bank accounts. This system, known as checkless payroll, is both an employee benefit and a method of reducing hospital expense.

In February 1975, the hospital's management began informal discussions of checkless payroll with a local branch of one of the major lending institutions in the state. The hospital's management wanted to know what benefits the bank could offer employees, if it received the total payroll deposit. The bank promised free personalized checks to all employees—a savings of $2 to $6 per employee per year. Next the hospital contacted a second adjacent major bank branch with whom it had no prior business dealings. Because the two banks were competing for the hospital's payroll account, it had the advantage of requesting and receiving service without charge for the hospital employees. The result—a free checking account in either of the two local branches of the two major banks for all hospital employees, with the first order of checks free.

The bank needed the following information to institute a checkless payroll system. (This information must be submitted for each payroll.)

1. employee's full name
2. ten-digit bank account number

3. pay by employee—net
4. total dollars of payroll—net
5. hospital name
6. pay date
7. Social Security number of each employee listed

In addition, the bank automatically credits the payroll checking account of the hospital for the net dollars distributed to the employee's account. Finally, no deposit receipt is issued by the bank to each employee. Rather, the pay stub prepared by the hospital serves as this receipt.

SELLING EMPLOYEES ON IT

Selling the employees on checkless payroll was a matter of communication. The most common questions—and their answers—were:

Q: What is the checkless payroll system?
A: Checkless payroll is a payroll system which electronically deposits an employee's net salary earned in a preceding time period to his/her bank account.

Q: Under a checkless system, do I receive a paycheck?
A: No. The employee receives an "employee earning record," which shows the gross amount of pay, the hourly rate, deductions and the net amount of pay. It is also the receipt of deposit.

Q: How do I open a checking account?
A: The hospital will provide the necessary forms to open a checking account.

Q: What if I do not want to bank at either of the two local banks? How will I get my money?
A: Either bank will provide free checks which will allow the transfer of the net amount of the paycheck to the bank of the employee's choice.

Q: If I bank at a branch other than those located close to the hospital, can I have my check deposited to the branch I am presently using?
A: Yes. Deposits can be made directly to any branch in either banking system, but not to banks outside those two systems. Free checking accounts are provided only at the two local branches.

Q: What advantages do I get from the checkless payroll system?
A: The hospital has negotiated with the banks for free checking accounts (no monthly service charge will be added by the bank no matter what your balance) for all employees willing to establish accounts. There is a potential savings of between $20 and $50 per year, depending upon how many checks you write. Also, it will no longer be necessary for employees to come in on

Friday at 3 p.m. to pick up their checks and deposit them in the bank, since the deposit to the bank is made automatically. Employee earning records may be picked up at the employee's convenience. This eliminates the possibility of an employee losing a paycheck. Finally, employees will be paid earlier.

Q: Do I have a choice of where I may bank?

A: Yes. By going to a checkless payroll system, the hospital does not dictate where the employee may bank. The only requirement is that the employee establish a checking account at either of the banks in order to facilitate the payment process.

After numerous small group meetings, the employees decided to go ahead with the checkless payroll system.

The savings to the hospital from a checkless payroll system came a number of ways. We were able to reduce our printing costs because the old system required a three-part check and the new one, a single face sheet. There was no longer a mass exodus from the hospital at 3 p.m. on Fridays to deposit payroll checks at local banks. Also the lines in front of department head offices and at the cashier's window of employees waiting to be paid have disappeared. Accounting also received benefits from the checkless payroll system: reduced time on payroll bank reconciliation; no lost checks; no outstanding checks, and less time spent on distributing payroll. Protecting checks from loss or theft was no longer a problem.

Finally, employees received an additional benefit. If an employee is on vacation, or ill, it is no longer necessary for a relative or friend to come in to pick up the check since it has already been deposited directly in the employee's account.

SOME DON'TS

1. Do not run two systems, check and checkless. If you are unable to institute a totally checkless system, do not double your headaches by creating two systems.
2. Do not sell employees on checkless payroll until you convince department heads and unions that it is advantageous to the employee.
3. Do not explain checkless payroll to large groups of employees. Instead, have several, smaller meetings over a short period of time.
4. Do not try to dictate checkless payroll; rather, negotiate it as an employee benefit.
5. Do not use more than two banks. More banks mean more paperwork and less bargaining power.

6. Do not switch to a checkless system without running both systems simultaneously (i.e., parallel) first. Be prepared for bank errors on the first run.
7. Do not try to negotiate free checking accounts with bank corporate headquarters. Instead, contact local branch managers. They have the authority to give you free checking.

In summary, we have found a checkless payroll system to be advantageous for the banks, the employees and the hospital. The banks got new accounts, teller lines are reduced and the potential number of individuals securing loans is greater. Employees have gained free checking accounts and free checks and spend less time in the banking process. The hospital has realized reduced cost and one additional benefit to offer all employees.

68. Disposables vs. Reusables: A Special Report

Reprinted with permission from *Hospital Purchasing Management,* February 1977, pp. 7–13.

American hospitals spend three to five times as much per bed on purchases in real terms (independent of price inflation) as they did fifteen years ago. A major cause of this explosion in spending is growing use of disposables. In some cases, the disposable has driven its reusable equivalent out of the market. In others, marketing battles between disposables and reusables are still raging.

To distributors of hospital supplies, disposables are almost an unmixed blessing. Instead of selling the hospital just once, they are sold over and over again. Consequently, the virtues behind the throwaway principle have not been undersold. In many institutions, in fact, the purchasing manager has allied himself with the supplier in persuading users to adopt disposables.

MIXED BAG

To their advocates, disposables are one of the few ways that a hospital can cope with soaring payroll costs. Almost all disposables are a convenient substitute for various cleaning and processing operations that are needed for reusables. The only question, in such cases, is whether or not the extra money paid out to the supplier is more than offset by saving in the hospital's internal costs.

In some cases, the disposable seems to win the cost battle hands down. In others, the disposable wins essentially because users like it and don't really care about the cost justification. Finally, some hospitals may think they are saving money with disposables but really aren't—either because the saving simply is not there or because they have been unwilling or unable to translate a reduction in labor hours into lower payroll costs.

QUALITY COMPARISON

There is also difference of opinion about quality characteristics of disposables. Obviously, this varies with product. The syringe that is used just once and thrown away is unquestionably sharper than its reusable equivalent. Other quality comparisons are somewhat fuzzier, however. The disposable usually, but not always, is the winner when the desired quality is sterility. On most other characteristics, the quality of the disposable is inherently sleazier. However, repeated sterilization of the reusable has an adverse effect on the quality of many products.

While the concept of the disposable is hardly "new," the substitution process is still going on. To gain more insight into what is happening, HPM [Hospital Purchasing Management] conducted a special survey of its readers and also interviewed several members of its editorial board.

CONTINUING GROWTH

HPM discovered that roughly one hospital in three is seriously contemplating at least one substitution of a disposable for a reusable. The smaller institutions of less than 200 beds are most likely to be happy with the status quo. Only about one in five is currently planning to substitute a disposable.

PURCHASING SAYS DISPOSABLE IS CHEAPER, BUT SOME USERS STILL SAY "NO THANK YOU"

About 10 per cent of HPM's respondents cited examples where users rejected disposables even though the purchasing manager thought they were not only cheaper but also met hospital quality standards. Rejects and rejecters are listed in order of popularity as follows:

Disposable Product	Rejecting User	Per Cent of Rejects
Wraps and Drapes	O.R. Nurses	17%
Wraps and Drapes	Surgeons	7
Suture Removal Sets	Medical Staff	13
Packs	Delivery Room	7
Thermometers	Nursing Staff	7

Both nursing and medical staffs received blanket indictments for rejection of a variety of disposables by a few readers. The medical staff was also cited specifically for rejecting instrument pads and lap sponges. Nurses, in various categories, rejected Scim's prep, various instruments including suture sets, lap sponges, linen, packs, and trays. Central supply resisted disposable bedpans and urinals while at least one lab refused to use disposable needles recommended by purchasing.

Smaller hospitals also probably use fewer disposables than larger ones, especially when they are located away from major urban centers. As Don Siegle, vice president of the Hospital Council of Western Pennsylvania, points out, the urban hospital is likely to "lose" far more reusables. They are simply stolen. Or careless employees may throw them out with the trash, and the reusable becomes a de facto disposable—but it costs more. Therefore, urban hospitals have a much stronger incentive to switch to disposables.

100% DISPOSABLE

In some cases, the switch to disposables has already taken place. No respondent, for example, said that his institution was planning to switch to disposable syringes. Continued growth seems guaranteed for other disposable products. Respondents in the aggregate cited about 50 different products for which there was at least one substitution of disposable for reusable being planned.

The trend toward disposables in textile products seems especially strong. Among respondents who mentioned specific products, almost one-fourth mentioned surgical packs, wrappers, and gowns. Sponges were also frequently mentioned as were washcloths, baby shirts, and baby blankets. Various respiratory therapy products seem to be among the leading candidates for substitution. Also, in a wide variety of products, disposable plastic items continue to replace reusable metals.

COST COMPARISON CRITICAL

Cost is the major factor influencing a switch to disposables according to 54 per cent of respondents (with little significant variation among hospitals of various sizes). Quality is cited as the major factor by 18 per cent and user preference by 15 per cent. Quality-related explanations account for most of the balance. For example, several hospitals mentioned longer shelf life as a major reason for switching to disposable surgical packs. In some cases, the substitution is only partial. For example, it is common practice to use disposable eating utensils, linens, etc., for patients who are isolated even though the hospital continues with reusables for "clean" patients.

LIFE OF REUSABLE

While the life cycle of the reusable is critical to any cost analysis which compares reusable and disposable, only one-third of the respondents said that their most recent decision to use disposables was influenced by a life cycle study within their own institution. As expected, a large hospital is much more likely to make such studies than a smaller institution. They were carried [out] by only 15 per cent of the hospitals with less than 200 beds but by 44 per cent of those with more than 500 beds.

In theory, a life cycle test would involve tracking a particular product through the system until it finally fails. This is not practical, however. Randall McDonnell, director of materials management, Massachusetts General Hospital, suggests annual purchases or disbursements of the reusable simply be related to existing inventory. If the hospital buys 100 per year and the inventory is 1,000, then the life cycle must be $1,000 \div 100 = 10$. Thus, the product is used 10 times on the average before it fails or simply disappears. If the product costs $5.00, then the effective depreciation cost for each application becomes 50¢.

ERRATIC DATA

Only about 20 respondents reported results of their own life cycle tests. When identical products were mentioned there was sometimes substantial variation in expected life. O.R. gowns can apparently be used as many as 30 or 40 times before they need to be replaced or their life cycle may be limited to 10 or 12. Some of this variation may reflect real differences among hospitals or particular products; HPM suspects that at least some of it lies in reporting and analysis techniques.

Accurate life cycle data becomes especially critical for products likely to be stolen. Based on comments by HPM readers, the thief is not necessarily a low-income employee or patient but may well display an MD on the plates of his Mercedes Benz. Items like scissors have life cycles of as few as four usages—a mere fraction of their technological life. In such cases, disposables look very attractive—although one reader points out that there is no saving from disposables if more of them are simply stolen in order to keep unauthorized users fully supplied.

PRODUCT DECISIONS

Information on which hospitals base their product decisions is usually (59 per cent of respondents) gathered in joint studies by purchasing and interested user groups. This is probably the most sensible way to do the job, particularly if the committee is careful to review all available alternatives, not just the product being pushed by a particular supplier.

In larger hospitals, in particular, the initiative (in roughly one-fifth of all cases) to use a disposable may come from the purchasing department. If he is convinced that the disposable is economic, the purchasing manager may simply ask the user to test the new product and if it is acceptable in terms of quality, the substitution is made.

SUPPLIER NOT OBJECTIVE

Only 10 per cent of respondents report that they base their decision to use a disposable on supplier cost studies—and this is probably just as well. The supplier is not the most objective judge of his own product. While the figures he presents may be literally correct, they are often either not relevant to the particular hospital or critical variables may simply be ignored.

For example, suppliers who are pushing disposables usually support their sales pitch with a "cost analysis" that "proves" that the hospital's saving in labor cost will more than offset higher aggregate purchase costs for the disposable item. The numbers presented to the hospital by the supplier are often not at all unreasonable and may be quite convincing.

ONLY CASH COUNTS

For example, a supplier promoting a disposable may show the hospital a cost estimate that cleaning and processing the reusable requires 15 minutes of labor at $3.00 per hour (or 5¢ per minute). Thus, labor cost for each re-use is 5¢ × 15 minutes = 75¢. The hospital reviews its own cleaning and processing operation and the supervisor agrees that about 15 minutes' time is indeed required and the $3.00 hourly rate is not too far out of line with the hospital's actual wage costs. Suppose that the disposable costs 50¢. Will the hospital then save 25¢ per application by changing over to the disposable?

Not necessarily, says Claude Trafas, director of purchases, Wilmington Medical Center. A labor saving often cannot be translated into a cash saving for the hospital, Trafas points out, simply because the organization structure of the hospital has been developed around reusables. As a result, the labor saving from the disposable simply translates into a longer coffee break for the employee who formerly handled the reusable. It is essentially for this reason that Wilmington Medical Center continues to use stainless steel bedpans. Time saved by switching to disposables would simply not translate into a big enough cash saving. Also, of course, hardly anyone steals the stainless steel bedpans and their quality and handling characteristics are good.

Unfortunately, only very large hospitals are likely to have industrial engineers who can make the detailed studies that are needed for rational decisionmaking on disposables vs. reusables. Only two respondents mentioned using such studies. However, 5 per cent did rely upon the experience of other hospitals, believing that a firsthand user report may be more reliable than supplier data.

Even under the best of circumstances, however, it is hard to get accurate cost data. It is difficult to estimate reprocessing costs and shrinkage or theft is even harder to estimate. However, these are usually the overriding reasons why hospitals switch from reusables to disposables on most products. About 60 per cent of respondents mentioned internal processing cost of the reusable as the major cost factor. Their comments suggested that "shrinkage" (usually a euphemism for theft) was often a major element of this cost. Unit product cost of the disposable itself was mentioned by 25 per cent while 15 per cent had other reasons for making the change.

FORCED DECISION

Several respondents said that they had been more-or-less forced to use disposables due to lack of autoclave capacity. New equipment requires a substantial cash outlay and is not immediately reimbursable by third parties. Also, several respondents believe that disposables may be a less risky alternative should poor product quality lead to a malpractice suit.* For ex-

---

*HPM intends to publish several articles on product warranty in 1977. Legal Editor Al Tabaka warns that the hospital does not necessarily come off scot-free when poor supplier quality is a direct cause of a malpractice suit. He plans to furnish readers with workable guidelines on this problem.

ample, the hospital is clearly liable if damages result because it simply forgets to sterilize something. On the other hand, the supplier would appear to be the guilty party if he sells the hospital a disposable that turns out not to be sterile.

LOST OPPORTUNITIES

Perhaps because they are more aware of such problems as malpractice suits and also less resistant to change, purchasing managers may be more "pro-disposable" than users. About 10 per cent of respondents believe that their hospital is actually foregoing opportunities to make substantial savings simply because of user resistance to change. The nursing staff is cited as being least likely to change its ways and the medical staff is a close second. As indicated in the table accompanying this article, disposables are most likely to meet user resistance in the textile area. Disposable suture removal sets and thermometers also often get a less-than-enthusiastic response from MDs and RNs, respectively.

Yet these and other disposables seem destined to expand their markets. If for no other reason, they get a better selling job than reusables, according to an overwhelming 74 per cent of respondents. Only 2 per cent, in contrast, believe that reusables get superior marketing while 21 per cent believe there is no difference in quality of selling. Purchasing managers in the smaller hospitals were markedly more impressed with the selling job on disposables than those in the very large hospitals.

RESISTANCE TO DISPOSABLES

About one-fifth of respondents expect to make additional substitutions of disposables for reusables in the near future. As indicated in [the survey] accompanying this article, reusable textiles appear especially vulnerable to disposables. At the moment, however, there are barriers to immediate application of these disposables. These include cost, user resistance, and possible supply problems. Also, as one purchasing manager commented, "there are only so many hours in a day and I simply cannot immediately investigate every cost reduction opportunity that is available and still get my day-to-day job done."

Cost is a much bigger barrier to adoption of disposables to the small hospital (38 per cent) than to the large one (26 per cent). This does not mean that small hospitals are more cost conscious. Disposables sometimes do not offer as great a saving to the smaller institution. Big institutions are almost always in big cities where expensive reusables are more likely to be stolen or thrown out by careless staff. In contrast, many hospitals with less than 100 beds are in small, rural communities where the rip-off is still frowned upon and also where non-professional employees may be more likely to take pride in their work.

User hostility to disposables, in contrast, is much greater (being cited by 32 per cent of respondents) in the very large hospital than in the small one (17 per cent). Potential supply problems with the disposable are not regarded as a major problem by either large or small hospitals. This was an inhibiting factor for only about 5 per cent of respondents even though the disposable, unlike the reusable, requires continuing flow of material from the vendor.

While almost all purchasing managers are confident they can keep their hospitals supplied with additional disposables, roughly one-fifth say they are not making additional substitutions right now simply because of lack of time. This is, of course, symptomatic of still another problem: the five-fold increase in physical volume of purchases per hospital that has occurred over the past 15 years has in some hospitals been accomplished with no increases whatever in purchasing personnel! In this case, the hospital may well be penny-wise on its personnel budget and pound-foolish in foregoing or postponing savings that could be made sooner.

Hospital storage space has also sometimes remained unchanged while physical volume of material handled—thanks largely to increasing application of disposals—has grown by leaps and bounds. As a result, some hospitals now find themselves saying "no" to additional applications simply because they do not have the extra space that is needed.

ANTI-DISPOSAL MOVEMENT

In fact, there is a counter-movement on disposables developing among purchasing managers as evidenced, in part, by Bob Cooper's guest editorial in this issue. The counter-movement is markedly more noticeable among very large hospitals than smaller ones. A third of the purchasing managers in hospitals with more than 500 beds are planning to switch at least one product back to reusable. This is reported by only 11 per cent of the respondents in hospitals with less than 200 beds. Some respondents simply do not like the sleazier quality of the disposable. Many complain about trash disposal and its cost.

The throwaway must indeed be thrown away—but where? The stuff used simply to be burned in the hospital's incinerator. In some areas, this is now impossible under any circumstances and in every area, trash disposal is a bigger and more costly problem than it used to be. This is bound to inhibit future growth of disposable products.

One purchasing manager arbitrarily boosts the cost of every disposable he buys by 5 per cent in order to allow for getting rid of the item after it is used. Another purchasing manager applies a 10 per cent allowance for trash disposal. No one probably really knows how much it costs to get rid of the disposables but the total expense is undoubtedly considerably greater than the cash charge made by the trucker who hauls it away.

Textile products are not only leading candidates among some hospitals for a switch from reusable to disposable, but they are also leaders in the reverse substitution movement. Some hospitals now using disposable linens, packs, pads, and garments are considering going back to reusables. In some cases, the original decision to use the disposable resulted from inadequate laundry or sterilizing capacity. New equipment has been purchased and the hospital is using reusables once again. In such cases, cost comparisons strongly favor the reusable. For example, one purchasing manager claims it costs his hospital just 18¢ to reprocess a garment while the price for the disposable is 44¢.

REUSABLE DISPOSALS?

Suture sets and IPPB circuits were frequently mentioned as candidates for a reverse switch. In the former case, two respondents reported that the users treated the disposable as if it were reusable so they finally decided to go back to the "real thing."

Other products mentioned as candidates for a switch back to reusables include suction units, "various respiratory therapy products," scrub trays, specimen trays, various utensils, and magnetic pads for holding OR instruments.

While it is widely believed that hospital and third party accounting practices have spurred adoption of disposables, 81 per cent of the respondents said these did not really influence any decisions on disposables vs. reusables. However, a number of respondents noted that particular disposables are often a direct, allowable charge while processing cost of the equivalent reusable is buried in the hospital's operating overhead.

Some Disposables Still Look Promising for Future Application

About one-fifth of HPM's respondents expect to make future substitutions of disposables for reusables. In order of popularity, these are as follows:

	Per Cent of Respondents Expecting to Substitute
Product	
Linens	17%
O.R. Wraps and Drapes	11
O.R. Packs	10
Thermometers	9
Instrument Trays	8
Urinals and Bedpans	6
Basins	5
Anesthetic Tubes	3
Diapers	3
Suture Sets	3

Other products cited as possible future substitutions by at least one respondent include scrub brushes, collection units, pumpers, and catheter kits.

INITIAL INVESTMENT

Of course, if a hospital is starting out from scratch, the reusable always requires a larger initial cash outlay and sometimes must be capitalized. For example, at current prices, even a small rural hospital might have several thousand dollars tied up in stainless steel bedpans. In contrast, the cash outlay need be little more than a few hundred dollars for an adequate inventory of plastic throwaways and, in some cases, this may be directly expensed. In addition, if the throwaway is incorporated into an admission kit that is an extra charge to the patient, so much the better from the narrow point of view of the hospital.

When third party rules distort hospital decisionmaking, no one really wins over the long term and, of course, the general public is an out-and-out loser. Purchasing managers are conscious of this and are working hard to make buying decisions that are not only in the best interest of their hospitals but also which work to cut the cost of care.

***

Disposable 8-Step Value Analysis Process

1. Make a careful life cycle analysis of the reusable. This is critical. If you do not know how long the reusable lasts, you cannot possibly make a rational decision. *Do not rely on supplier* *estimates.* Not only does the supplier have an ax to grind but the information he gets may not apply to your particular situation.

2. Compare your life cycle study with those of neighboring institutions. Be suspicious if your figures are markedly different from theirs. Either you or they may have made an error. Or conceivably your real problem is poor control of the reusable. In this case, you should do a better job of processing or administering the reusable and not necessarily switch to a disposable.

3. Divide the reusable's cost by its life. For example, if the reusable costs $10.00 and your life cycle study indicates it is good for 10 applications, then the effective cost per application is $1.00 plus processing.

4. Estimate both "cash" and "full" costs of handling and processing. In most cases, the "cash" cost will be much less than the "full" cost. Suppose, for example, that a particular reusable requires 15 minutes of labor to reprocess along with roughly 10¢ worth of steam. The 15-minute labor saving will not bring any cash saving at all until either the employee is laid off or she is given additional work that will result in additional revenue to the hospital. On the other hand, the 10¢ saving in steam is essentially a real cash saving since the hospital's utility bill is directly related to how intensively it uses its sterilizers.

5. Delay but do not necessarily reject substitutions that fail to yield a cash saving. It is not usually economic to substitute a particular disposable when the hospital is already stocked with the reusable. The labor saving in nursing or in central supply simply cannot be translated immediately into a cash saving because staff cannot be reduced. However, these savings can often be made when a group of disposables is substituted. For example, a series of substitutions may make it possible to reduce employment in central supply and the saving is then very real. Conversely, a hospital may not find it economic to substitute a particular reusable for a disposable if it is tight on sterilizer capacity. However, it may pay to buy the sterilizer if a sufficient number of economic substitutions can be identified.

6. Canvass the market before making a final decision. An imaginative sales representative will push a particular reusable or disposable against whatever the hospital is currently using. If the comparison looks favorable, the using department (but not the purchasing manager) sometimes wants to go ahead and give that supplier the order. The proper approach, of course, is to investigate all competitive brands; the purchasing manager may be able to make the substitution even more attractive.

7. Put a price on quality. In most cases, users will quite rightly make distinctions between competing products on the basis of quality. This is legitimate. But make sure that the hospital does not buy more quality than is needed to do the job. In addition, when the added quality is useful, the user should estimate how much this is worth to him. This estimate should then be incorporated into the cost analysis.

8. Last year's decision may not be valid this year. Continuing comparisons are essential if the hospital is to get maximum value. Relative prices and costs change and so do the products themselves.

Disposables vs. Reusables: Survey Shows the Battle Still Goes On

	—Per cent of respondents—		
	Small Hospitals	Large Hospitals	All Hospitals
1. Are you making or contemplating any additional substitutions of disposables for reusables this year?			
Yes	22%	35%	35%
No	78	65	65
2. What is the single, most important factor influencing your decision to substitute a disposable for a reusable?			
Cost	61	50	54
Quality	25	22	18
User Preference	14	17	15
Other Reasons	7	11	13
3. Were you able to make a study of the life cycle (i.e. the number of times it can be used before it disappears or wears out) of the reusable *in your own hospital* before making a decision to replace it with the disposable?			
Yes	15	44	33
No	85	56	67
4. What is the usual source of the information used to make decisions to substitute disposables for reusables in your hospital?			
Joint studies by purchasing and users	58	55	59
Comparative analysis by purchasing	16	25	20
Supplier cost estimates	16	15	10
Experience of other hospitals	8	0	5
Hospital engineering studies	0	3	2
Other	2	2	4
5. What is usually the most important cost factor when you decide to substitute a disposable for a reusable?			
Processing cost of reusable	56	60	59
Unit price of product	38	25	26
Other factors (usually investment in inventory or sterilizers)	6	15	15
6. Which products get the best selling job by vendors?			
Better selling on disposables	66	74	73
Better selling on reusables	2	5	2
No difference in selling	32	21	25
7. What is the major barrier preventing adoption immediately of disposables that you believe should be used?			
Cost not yet favorable	38	26	31
User indifference, hostility	17	32	26
Need time to investigate	29	26	21
Potential supply problems	1	5	7
Other reasons cited (including disagreement on product choice)	1	16	15
8. Are you presently using any disposables for which you are planning to substitute reusables?			
Yes	11	33	22
No	89	67	78

Note: For purposes of cross tabulation, a "large" hospital is one with 500 beds or more while a "small" one has less than 200 beds. Thus, a hospital with 200 to 500 beds would be included only in the tabulation of "all" hospitals since the median HPM reader is associated with a hospital of this size.

69. Telephone Equipment Analysis and Control System Can Reduce Costs

Reprinted, with permission, from *Hospitals, Journal of the American Hospital Association,* vol. 52, no. 3, February 1, 1978, p. 14.

The Bureau of Health Insurance ruling in January 1976 that "full" costs of items or services for the personal comfort of patients, such as telephones, be excluded from allowable costs made it advisable for hospitals to analyze and minimize these costs if they were not already doing so. Long before this ruling, Assistant Administrator John S. Zanghi recognized the lack of good internal control of telephone costs at Lakewood (OH) Hospital, a 378-bed, not-for-profit city hospital, and suspected that a possibility for cost reduction existed in this area. Zanghi therefore kept copies of old telephone equipment lists until sufficient manpower became available to conduct an analysis of the hospital telephone system.

In March 1975, Marcus L. McQueen, business office manager, began a study to identify all telephone and auxiliary telephone equipment in use and to further identify and remove unnecessary equipment. Each hospital room was inventoried, and the finds compared, item by item, with telephone company equipment lists. Differences were noted and traced back on old equipment lists. Questionable equipment also was reviewed with department heads, and all unnecessary telephones and auxiliary equipment were removed. The remaining telephones and equipment were cataloged and allocated to each hospital department by individual item and cost.

Subsequently, a letter containing an itemized list of differences between hospital and telephone company lists and requesting a refund for the overbilling was sent to the company. The company reviewed the hospital's request, sent a commercial record verifier to reinventory the hospital, and acknowledged the overbilling for nonexistent telephones and equipment.

An important result of the study has been the establishment of an effective system to control telephones and related costs, McQueen says. Prior to the study, departments submitted their requests to the central switchboard, which contacted the telephone company. As a result, unneeded and unused telephones and auxiliary equipment had accumulated throughout the hospital. In addition, no verification was made of telephone bills; they were simply accepted and paid.

McQueen established a procedure whereby each request for additional telephones or equipment is reviewed onsite with the requester. In this manner, an awareness of telephone costs is being instilled in hospital personnel. Telephone equipment lists and bills are reviewed monthly and reconciled with all changes posted to various departments. Disallowed patient telephone costs are readily identified and documented, thus maximizing reimbursement. In addition, the telephone study has enabled the hospital to identify and curb unauthorized long-distance calls by personnel. McQueen also keeps administration informed of telephone costs through a monthly cost report.

Lakewood Hospital received a one-time settlement of $7,664.57 from Ohio Bell Telephone Company for overbilling. Removal of excess equipment of $217.50 per month resulted in an annual savings of $2,610. These savings plus allowances for inflation and rate changes led to a projected cost savings of $70,000 over a 10-year period. However, this estimate was made prior to Ohio Bell's telephone rate increase in August 1976, which amounted to 28.9 percent for Lakewood Hospital and added another $12,600 to the 10-year projection. Another large rate increase in the 10-year period would add substantially to these savings. Not included in the projected figures are the savings earned by closely monitoring new telephone requests so that only essential and necessary telephones and equipment are installed.

Savings generated from this study, McQueen says, have freed monies currently budgeted and allowed funds to be diverted to other hospital areas for hiring additional personnel and/or purchasing essential supplies and equipment.

70. Special Report: Costs and Management at Tucson Medical Center, 1978 Update

DONALD G. SHROPSHIRE
Reprinted with permission from the author.

Many of us can remember, because it wasn't that long ago, when the hospital was a place of last resort. Staffed largely by volunteers and a few modestly paid nurses who got their training right there on the job, the hospital was little more than a dreary convalescent facility owing its existence to a handful of community benefactors. If you had to go to the hospital in those days, it meant that most everything else had been tried and your chances of survival were slim.

But all that changed after World War II. The Federal Government poured millions into medical research and financed thousands of hospitals throughout the country which could accommodate both the new breakthroughs in research and the new medical specialties that were developing around them. One after one, many of the diseases that had been dreaded for centuries were wiped away by the new knowledge, facilities and technology. Nowadays, the hospital is a place where productive living can be restored and hope can replace despair.

Along with these dramatic changes, though, have come high costs, enormous complexity, and an increasing interest on the part of the public to know more about what causes them. That is the purpose of this special report to our community. It is our attempt to show you how the largest hospital in this community, Tucson Medical Center, is managed, what some of its problems are and what it is trying to do about the cost of care. TMC is a 557 bed hospital with 2,189 employees and 627 physicians on its medical staff who took care of more than 98,000 patients last year; patients that came from all over the southwest—not just Tucson. At TMC a baby is born every two hours, a patient is admitted every 12 minutes, an operation is begun every 40 minutes, a patient is treated in the emergency room every 18 minutes and a laboratory test is run every 25 seconds. It's a busy place. That's because it offers a wide range of services including a coronary care unit, an intensive care unit, cardiac surgery, microsurgery, an intensive care nursery, a one-day surgery unit and a clinic that can detect your potential for having a stroke. These are services which have literally saved thousands of lives, but which you may be surprised to know didn't even exist here as recently as 15 years ago.

Often TMC's specialized resources make the difference between life and death, but saving a life may mean three months of round-the-clock supervision by a highly trained team and beyond normal use of expensive equipment or facilities. All regardless of whether the patient can pay the bills or not.

Similarly, if a particular unit doesn't pay for itself, and many do not, we can't close it down the way a business can shut down an unprofitable branch. For example, the nursery and the intensive care nursery lost $154,355 in 1977. One reason was that $149,471, or 96.8% of that total was the result of charity cases and just plain bad debts. But we can't close down the nursery or the intensive care nursery any more than we can close down the neurological unit that lost $102,788 or the pediatrics department that lost $379,392.

And it's not just charity or bad debts that cause losses to a hospital. Medicare, for example, only pays about 87% of charges and 40% of TMC's patients are on Medicare.

Because of these "facts of life," a hospital actually has very little control over how *much* money is spent or how *much* volume of service must be met. It does, however, have *considerable* control over *how* the money is spent and *how* the volume is accommodated. That is why management is so important.

MANAGEMENT

At TMC, management involves planning, organizing, directing and controlling the activities of 32 departments, 16 outpatient facilities and those 2,189 employees. Because we are so large and diverse, the key to our management system is information—beginning with budgets.

Each TMC department has a budget that is 'negotiated' with TMC administration at the beginning of the fiscal year. The budget is tied to departmental objectives which are also set then. Once a realistic budget is arrived at based on yearly revenue/expense projections and departmental objectives, each department is held responsible for staying within that framework. To help in this, TMC departments have a variety of facts available on a monthly, sometimes weekly, basis.

At any given time, for instance, department managers know instantly through a system of management information reports what their income and expense compared to budget is, what their percentage of overtime is compared to hours worked, how volume of services rendered compares to income and how their departments are progressing toward their objectives.

The value of this information is that it permits rapid decisions to be made by individual managers in a decentralized fashion to meet immediate problems without delay. Although major hospital-wide decisions or those dealing with capital expenditures are made centrally, almost all operational decisions are made by managers closest to the decision point, and TMC tries to make sure that they have the tools they need to do the job.

That job is insuring effectiveness at a reasonable, affordable cost to the patient and the hospital with respect to the main factors of production which, in a hospital, are people and facilities. Let's look first at people.

PEOPLE

The very nature of the hospital product, care of the ill and injured, requires a person-to-person relationship that no machine could ever duplicate. That relationship must exist 24 hours a day, which means that hospitals have to be staffed around the clock at specified levels. To do that costs a great deal because one out of every three TMC employees has special training.

Because of that, however, a little more than 60% of TMC's expense budget is spent on payroll and employee benefits—as opposed to about 25% in other industries. With more than 2,000 employees that came to $22,874,034 in 1977.

What has to be done then, is to make sure that these people perform in the most efficient way, consistent always with quality standards of care. Here are some of the things we have done to achieve that.

Productivity

In January, 1976, a task force of selected managers was appointed to identify productivity gains at TMC and to intensify efforts in areas where there could be improvements. Their first step was to work with department people to determine ways of measuring productivity. These included hours of work, dollars spent, quality factors, and formulas relating these things to each other. By April, 1977, the task force had accomplished the following:

1. It had improved the way individual departments used basic statistical reports, getting even more mileage out of the information system.
2. An analysis system for long-range planning had been started.
3. A measuring tool, called RMS (Resource Monitoring System) had been procured to help develop standards in 15 departments.
4. Five departments had already developed their own productivity systems.
5. A way of improving coordination between departments had been established.

Using these early tools, we were able to demonstrate areas of improvement amounting to approximately $450,000 during fiscal year 1976-77. For the next fiscal year projected cost savings as a result of productivity and wage measures was $346,546. The productivity measures were not achieved. A key reason is that while the hospital can control utilization of personnel, it cannot really control volume of service and during fiscal 1977-78, volume of service did not allow TMC to realize its projected gain. Predicting and scheduling to peaks and valleys in volume takes considerable skill and we are still developing our abilities in this regard. However, the net of dollars lost in productivity have been more than offset by dollar gains in wage variations and for the eight months of fiscal year 1977-78, TMC is $22,809 ahead of target projections, or a total savings for the period of $241,000.

We are working hard to develop a truly sophisticated system of measuring levels of productivity and part of doing that involves learning lessons along the way. On the basis of what we now know, 17 of our departments are anticipating productivity gains in fiscal year 1978-79 amounting to a dollar savings for TMC of $106,789; and we think we have a pretty good chance of achieving that.

Improved Personnel Utilization

One of the constants in the productivity equation is how effectively people use their time. Overtime is one of the factors involved. Overtime is a difficult situation in every organization, and particularly so in a hospital. The hospital runs 24 hours a day with three shifts, and often a technician is involved in something that simply cannot be dropped when the shift changes. Respiratory therapy is one of those areas, but efficient use of highly skilled respiratory therapists made it possible last year for that department to reduce overtime by 31% and save an additional $20,331 as well by not having to add extra staff. Overtime was also down 6% in Nursing Service, our biggest department; and our Environmental Services Department which takes care of all of the housekeeping chores in the hospital was able to reduce overtime 73% from last year. It was also able to save $55,000 in the Laundry just through better scheduling and utilization of personnel.

Turnover is another problem. Health workers tend to be a highly mobile group because their skills are in considerable demand. If they leave after a short time on the job, that means a loss to the hospital of not only their expertise, but also the time spent in training them. In Nursing, for example, it takes a month of orientation before an employee usually becomes really productive. Turnover can therefore be expensive, and it takes a concentrated, coordinated effort to create an environment in which people will want to stay and grow. In Nursing Service, turnover among registered nurses went from 44.2% in 1974 to 38.7% in 1977, and among nonprofessional personnel it went from 57.5% to 35% during that time period. Some of the reasons for slowing down the turnover rate there include improved hiring practices, a more effective new-employee orientation program, a suggestion program and improved communications among all the different kinds of nursing personnel.

Turnover is also down 10% from last year in our Central Services area—the people that provide all of the medical instruments and equipment for the doctors and nurses to use. Their turnover rate is down through improved management at the first line supervisory level.

These are some examples of why turnover among employees throughout the hospital was reduced by 3.4% last year, which the Personnel Department estimates has saved the institution approximately $51,600.

That's a direct savings but one place where low turnover has indirectly resulted in considerable savings is in the area of what we have to pay for unemployment benefits. As a not-for-profit organization, the state gives us two options. The first is to pay a tax on the first $6,000 of each employee's pay. If we had used that method, we would have had to pay out $409,291 last year. The other option, the one we selected, is to just simply reimburse the State of Arizona for the actual cost of unemployment benefits paid. Mostly because of low turnover among our employees, that amount came to only $68,099—a savings to the hospital of $341,192!

Education and Training

Education and training are absolutely vital to maintain effective performance in a field changing as fast as health care, so, in 1968 TMC established an Education Department with money from a foundation grant. Since that time the department has saved the hospital countless thousands of dollars by providing training at the hospital that would have to be purchased outside at much greater cost. It has also conducted programs on cost containment, showing TMC administrators how to be "cost effective" and conducts an eight-week supervisor course which aids TMC department managers in doing a better job.

In 1976 educational programs were begun for patients too. Every patient at TMC has televised health education programming available eight hours a day over the television set in the patient's room. The objective of these programs is to encourage patients to take responsibility for their health so that, perhaps, they can avoid coming back to the hospital.

The department sets up special need programs too. One such is a training program that has been established for maintenance engineers and mechanical maintenance men. The program is specially designed to familiarize these people with problems in maintenance unique to TMC's one-story horizontal physical plant. The result has been an increase in their ability to accomplish maintenance tasks in less time and with less supervision.

These are examples of the more than 30 educational programs conducted each month at TMC. Each can in one way or another be translated into cost savings for the community.

FACILITIES, EQUIPMENT AND SUPPLIES

Next to people, equipment, facilities and supplies are among the biggest expense areas in hospitals. For instance, guess what a wheelchair costs these days. Does $710.50 sound about right?

Actually, though, the really expensive sophisticated facilities we all read about are a fairly new phenomenon. Eleven years ago, for instance, TMC did not have a cardiac care unit—nor did many other hospitals in the United States. Because of that, three out of every 10 heart attack patients died. Today, thanks to facilities like TMC's cardiac care unit, almost 9 out of 10 such patients recover. 914 patients were treated there last year. The daily charge though is $230. That's because of the 16 specially trained people who work there and the $40,000 worth of defibrillators, heart monitors, and similar equipment that make up the unit.

The same story applies to other specialized facilities at Tucson Medical Center. The intensive care unit has only been open for 14 years and nuclear medicine, a powerful diagnostic tool, has just been open since 1969.

TMC's Intensive Care Nursery is another "new" service. It has been open for only ten years but its facilities have helped to reverse a grim trend toward death for high risk premature infants throughout all of southern Arizona. Before it opened, all babies who contracted hyaline-membrane disease—the major killer of newborns—died. Today, 80% are saved. But the average cost of treating a baby there is $326 a day; the room charge alone is $169.

Though less dramatic, equipment and supplies are part of the total cost containment package. Take forms for example. TMC uses about 1,000 different kinds of forms; all the way from those that record many different vital aspects of a patient's medical care down to routine routing slips. With 98,000 patients you can imagine the cost of just printing forms—around $100,000 last year. But, there are other large hospitals throughout the United States just like us, so we entered into a cooperative printing agreement with some of them which should save us about 10% next year. That's $10,000 at last year's rate.

Another example of shopping for the best price was in X-ray. One of their necessary pieces of equipment is an "image intensifier"—it illuminates X-ray images making them brighter. They needed two of them, but instead of paying $60,000 to one manufacturer our X-ray Department poked around and found an independent manufacturer who not only made a better product but sold it to us for $14,200 apiece—a savings of $31,600. There are lots of examples like that—the laboratory for instance managed to save $2,793 last year by simply switching brands of test tubes. Every little bit helps, because it all adds up; particularly in today's inflationary economy.

To help all of our departments do a good job of selecting materials and supplies, a Product Evaluation Committee exists at TMC. They help to establish criteria for many of the products we buy through careful research into the various alternatives available. And when it comes to highly technical (and usually very expensive) equipment, the physicians on our medical staff get into the act through their Special Equipment Committee; a group considered to be unique in the United States. Decisions are made only on the basis of an elaborate system of criteria and review panels, asking such questions as "How will costs affect patients," "How often will the item be used," "Will it affect patient care in a critical manner," "Will the item require additional kinds of ancillary personnel to run it and, if so, how expensive must their training be." The Special Equipment Committee prevents large amounts of money being spent through hastily conceived proposals and has saved the hospital thousands of dollars.

SAVINGS THROUGH TECHNOLOGY AND INNOVATION

There is no question that many of the advances in medical technology are very necessary and so also are many new concepts. By going in the right direction with these things, the hospital is often able to keep costs to the patient from skyrocketing. Take the Ambulatory Surgical Unit, for example. One-day surgery is still a new concept. The cost of building our one-day surgical facility back in 1974 was $714,000. Yet the charges for procedures done there are a fraction of what they would be if the patient had to come into the hospital. An adenoidectomy and myringotomy procedure would cost the patient $478 in the hospital. In Ambulatory Surgery the charge is $155—a saving of $323 for the patient. And hospitalization for an excision would normally run an average of $838 but the patient can save as much as $728 if it is done in Ambulatory Surgery, and last year 1,026 excisions were done there.

In just one year, TMC's Ambulatory Surgery Unit has saved people in southern Arizona $796,347 on *these two procedures alone.* The unit opened in February, 1974, and to date a total of 22,827 patients who have had one-day surgery there have saved considerable time which would have been lost from work or home, and they have saved hard-to-come-by dollars as well.

Another example, and an even more recent one, of savings in time and money to patients through appropriate extension of facilities is in the area of diagnosis of disease. More than 75% of the neurological services performed in southeastern Arizona are done at TMC. A key diagnostic procedure connected with neurology is brain scanning. In the past, a series of exhaustive, expensive and sometimes very painful tests had to be administered to a patient with a suspected neurological problem, but with the acquisition of a computerized scanner, many of these tests are eliminated. Here are a couple of typical cases in point:

Example A

Examinations that would have been required if the Brain Scanner had not been available:

	Charge
1. Two skull examinations	$ 60.00
2. PEG	225.00
3. Brain Scan	110.00
4. Arteriogram	333.00
5. EEG	35.00
6. Tomogram	42.00

Total charge $805.00

Examinations that were necessary with the availability of the Scanner:

1. Arteriogram	333.00
2. Standard Computerized Scan	120.00

Total charge $453.00

Saving to patient: $352.00

Example B

Examinations that would have been required if the Scanner had not been available:

	Charge
1. Two EEG's	$ 70.00
2. PEG	225.00
3. Two arteriograms	666.00
4. Skull examinations	30.00
5. Brain Scan	110.00

Total Charge $1,101.00

Examinations that were necessary with the availability of the Scanner:

1. Skull examination	$ 30.00
2. Standard Computerized Scan	120.00

Total Charge $150.00

Saving to patient: $951.00

The Brain Scanner cost TMC $382,500 but because it replaces some other diagnostic tests, such as pneumoencephalography and angiography, it saves the patient dollars, time and some pain. That's because a brain scan with this machine can often be done in 30 to 40 minutes on an outpatient basis. Without it, many people would have had to be admitted to the hospital for tests, some requiring up to three hours and almost all involving a recovery period because they involve injecting materials into the patient's body.

TMC acquired the Computerized Scanner in July, 1975. Since that time more than 11,823 patients have been provided brain scans. As a result of the heavy utilization, the hospital has been able to *reduce* the rates per scan.

With the reduction, patients now pay $120 for a "standard scan" as opposed to $175 when the scanner first went into operation, and for the more complicated "contrast scan," patients now pay $145 instead of $215.

The savings to patients are not only in dollars, but in time as well. Shortly after the scanner was made available a survey showed that 25% of the out-patient scans would normally have involved admission to the hospital for at least three days, and many of the inpatients receiving a brain scan went home two days earlier than they otherwise would have.

In addition to eliminating expensive stays in the hospital, TMC's Brain Scanner has also eliminated some expensive testing. Since 1974 the total number of cerebral angiograms, which costs $333 apiece, has decreased by 56.4% and pneumoencephalograms, at a cost to the patient of $225 apiece, have dropped off 96%.

Technology is also bringing savings in the laboratory with Uni-Lab II, which has been in operation for about a year. Selected after two years of researching many alternatives, Uni-Lab II is a complete computer system that automates many of the time consuming clerical and record keeping duties formerly done by laboratory technicians. The system frees them from hours of filling out reports, allowing them to concentrate on the technical work more in line with their training. Among other things, the Uni-Lab accepts test requests, tells the technician what tests are needed, organizes the laboratory workload with printed worklists, retrieves and displays patients' laboratory histories, prints specimen lists and labels and automatically bills the patient. Also, once a test or a patient is entered into the system, that record cannot be lost, offering fail-safe patient identification with each procedure.

TMC's laboratory processes more than 2,000,000 laboratory tests per year, and each one has to be precisely "what the doctor ordered." The new system enhances accuracy and monitors charges. It kept us from losing at least $231,379 worth of charges last year.

HOME GROWN SAVINGS

People who work in hospitals have a tradition of inventiveness, probably stemming from the days when there was precious little technology around to help with care. That tradition is alive at TMC and it helps us beat the high cost of equipment and facilities by literally resorting to our own devices.

For example:

- The Ambulatory Surgery Unit saved $2,000 by using light weight blankets that the laundry turned up instead of purchasing a blanket warmer.
- Instead of buying a commercial unit, our medical electronics technicians built their own power supply for the incubators that transport sick

babies. They also saved the Education Department $7,325 and the people in EKG $4,000 by modifying existing equipment rather than buying new. Actually, these folks save us a lot by just doing repairs of electronic equipment around the hospital—about 10 repairs a day.

- The Plant Services Department, the people who keep TMC's lights lit, the water running and generally keep the place humming, were able to reduce maintenance by 11% through a planned maintenance program. By also having their own people do things that might normally be contracted out, such as replacing steam lines, installing equipment and such, they saved approximately $33,000 last year.
- When our X-Ray Department needed a special radiation protection device for technicians doing work on coronary angiograms, they found that the commercial variety cost $450. The head of our carpenter shop caught wind of their need and built one that works just fine for $64.
- And our employees suggestion plan has worked very well, with cash awards as incentives for really effective cost saving ideas. Over the past two years we've awarded $550 to employees for good ideas that have resulted in savings to TMC of $24,400.

PURCHASING

The Purchasing Department has also saved significant dollars in the area of supplies and equipment through group purchasing via the Cooperative Purchasing Association of Arizona. Thirty-six hospitals in the state are members, and the way it works is this: All hospitals are surveyed on the products they use, then bids are let and the lowest bid consistent with established standards is accepted. The Product Evaluation Committee mentioned earlier helps with this process. A one-year contract is drawn up and if during that one year the price of the item changes, we don't have to pay the increased price. Total dollars saved by participating in the Cooperative Purchasing Association amounted to $395,247 in 1977.

There are some exceptions to using cooperative purchasing though; one is linen. We are one of about nine hospitals in the state with its own laundry. Because many hospitals do not have their own, they don't purchase linen so Cooperative Purchasing isn't involved in that item. We, therefore, use what we call the Prime Vendor concept for linen. We competitively select a linen vendor, and his contract with us requires that part of his price covers warehousing as well as supply, because it costs around 24¢ per $1.00 value to store linen. Using the Prime Vendor concept, we saved $19,240 in linen storage costs during the past two years.

UTILIZATION REVIEW

TMC has had a system for many years now helping to make sure that every patient admitted to the hospital really needs to be here. Within one day of being admitted, a special utilization review committee screens the patient's admission to determine its medical necessity and appropriateness. If the admission is deemed appropriate, an initial length of stay is assigned and if the patient has to stay longer than that, the reasons for the extension are reviewed. Meanwhile, the care rendered is compared with what the diagnosis indicates is necessary and the results of this comparison are measured against pre-set standards for that type of medical problem.

The hospital benefits from utilization review because its facilities are used more effectively. And the patient benefits too. Utilization review helps to keep the patient's stay down to what is necessary for the health and recovery of the individual. It also keeps his hospital bill pared to the minimum. While a patient will never be discharged until all of the people responsible for his care agree that he should be, utilization review aids in making that decision a realistic one and the patient is assured that he will be home just as soon as possible.

INTERNAL AUDIT

Internal auditing is an independent appraisal activity within the hospital by employees designated as internal auditors. They constitute a special committee which performs functions similar to those performed by external auditors, like the CPA firm that audits our records. But our Internal Audit Committee goes farther, checking into areas flagged as possible areas of concern by our outside auditing firm, our department heads and administration. As a result of six studies conducted during the past year by the Internal Audit Committee, $20,000 was saved. Examples of the studies include a review of equipment that departments either rent or lease, a review of accounts payable, distribution of invoices and analysis of the accounting for the capitalizing of building improvements and fixed equipment.

ENERGY MANAGEMENT

It's no news to anyone that energy is becoming an area of prime concern. For example, TMC is going to have to rely more and more on electricity because of the moratorium on gas, and electricity costs about four times as much as gas does. Last year our utility bill was over $1,000,000 so we're about to install a computerized energy management system that will give us precision control over how we use energy throughout the hospital. It will automatically "take our temperature" in all buildings and rooms and just as automatically turn all electrical systems on and off when they should be with an eye toward energy conservation. The boilers, chillers, thermostats and the volume of water in the water pipes and air in the air ducts will be stringently managed by the system to make sure that nothing is wasted. And just to make sure that we keep conservation uppermost in mind, the system will give us a computerized itemization of the money saved each day. This will help the Energy Management Committee, now being formed, in its task of overseeing our energy management program. The end result that we're aiming for is a 25% savings in the cost of energy at TMC.

SUMMARY

It would take many more pages to adequately describe the many, many ways that TMC tries to balance the fine line between quality and cost of care. This report has highlighted some of the primary ways that it is done and some of the things we intend to do.

We are a "labor intensive" organization that relies considerably on people and their skills, and because we must couple these skills with expensive technology in terms of both equipment and facilities and because we have little control over the volume of services required by our patients in any given year, we concentrate heavily on applied management expertise all down the line. Specifically, we consistently:

- Analyze our activities and act on the results of that analysis.
- Update and streamline procedures.
- Consult our people on newer and better ways of doing things.
- Take advantage of new technology when it will improve care and provide commensurate savings to patients and the hospital.
- Perpetually monitor the way patients and physicians use the hospital to make sure that the facilities are not occupied needlessly and that people are not charged for services they do not need.
- Engage in planning for the future; hence our working productivity measurement and our forthcoming energy management program.

It is our hope, certainly our goal, that by so doing the people who entrust TMC with their health and well being will have their expectations met as closely as possible.

71. Cost Containment at Jackson Memorial Hospital [Miami, Fla]

LEON ZUCKER

Reprinted with permission from the author.

The Cost Containment Committee was formed in January, 1977 composed of senior management, an attending physician and members of the house staff. Other specialized personnel participated in discussions as particular subjects were considered.

It was recognized at the outset that there are two broad areas of cost containment—the ordering of services to be provided to a patient, directly affecting volume of operations and charges, controllable by physicians, and the costs directly controllable by hospital management. Some of the savings are directly measurable, while others are measurable by broad statistical or "bottom-line" results.

On an overall basis, serving approximately the same number and types of patients, our charge per admission—the statistic reflecting what the patient is asked to pay—rose 7.2% for the fiscal year ended September 30, 1978 over the prior period. For the first six months of this fiscal year, the increase is 3.3% over the similar period of the last fiscal year. Costs per admission rose 7.9% and 5.8% respectively. Other pertinent statistics are shown on the attached table.

Specific efforts of the physicians centered about a formal program by the house staff of cost awareness, aimed at informing the doctors of the financial as well as the medical effects of their efforts. It is continually stressed that cost containment or cost effective medicine should not adversely affect, in any way, the quality of care. Results of this effort are shown in the

Public Health Trust
Jackson Memorial Hospital

Cost and revenue comparisons between periods

| | year ended September 30 | | | | | Six months ended March 31 | | |
| | 1976 | 1977 | | 1978 | | 1978 | 1979 | |
	Amount	Amount	Percentage of increase (Decrease)	Amount	Percentage of increase (Decrease)	Amount	Amount	Percentage of increase
Population statistics								
Total patient days	383,388	381,937	(0.4%)	380,868	(0.3%)	191,150	187,330	(2.0%)
Total admissions	43,813	45,056	2.8%	44,820	(0.5%)	22,174	22,703	2.4%
Total outpatient visits (including emergency room)	395,183	396,705	0.3%	431,497	8.8%	220,866	207,715	(6.0%)
Percentage of occupancy	87.3%	89.2%	2.2%	90.6%	1.6%	91.0%	91.4%	0.4%
Average length of stay								
Overall	8.9 days	8.6 days	(3.4%)	8.5 days	(1.2%)	8.6 days	8.3 days	(3.5%)
Excluding newborn	9.6 days	9.3 days	(3.1%)	9.4 days	1.1%	9.5 days	9.1 days	(4.2%)
Revenue[1]								
Gross inpatient charges	$99,500,205	$111,732,692	12.3%	$119,243,644	6.7%	$59,956,128	$63,409,006	5.8%
Charges per admission	2,271	2,480	9.2%	2,661	7.2%	2,704	2,793	3.3%
Gross outpatient charges	19,661,900	22,127,009	12.5%	23,604,620	6.7%	11,449,999	12,120,466	5.8%
Charges per visit	$49.75	$55.78	12.1%	$54.70	(1.9%)	$51.84	$58.35	12.6%
Cost[2]								
Total inpatient cost	$81,238,586	$92,439,509	13.8%	$99,192,418	7.3%	$48,707,603	$52,751,742	8.3%
Cost per admission	1,854	2,052	10.7%	2,213	7.9%	2,197	2,324	5.8%
Total outpatient cost	16,521,445	19,472,730	17.9%	22,218,130	14.1%	10,691,913	11,112,352	3.9%
Cost per visit	$41.81	$49.09	17.4%	$51.49	4.8%	$48.41	$53.30	10.5%

[1] Before adjustment for contractual allowances and provision for uncollectible accounts.
[2] Including House Staff and cost of faculty supervision of house staff and administrative function.

decrease in revenue from ancillary services and reflected in the lower charges per admission. Another area of physician involvement is participation in the hospital's Product Review and Analysis Committee [PRAC] which is charged with reviewing the specifications for supply and equipment purchases. The change in orientation and consequent results of this activity are discussed later.

Areas of more direct involvement and control by hospital management are in the costs of personnel and the services, supplies and other costs of operating the institution. First efforts were directed where measurable results could be achieved and would be on-going. Some major accomplishments are:

Energy: Recurrent annual savings of *$126,110* were generated the first year by time clock control of air handling equipment, improving condensation in boilers, solar sun control film on windows and other reductions in consumption.

Other Utilities: Recurrent savings of *$51,354* to date were created by telephone equipment reductions and replacements and *$8,024* by use of a well for boiler make-up water.

Purchasing: Methodologies of procurement have been reorganized to provide for the institutions's needs while considering quality and cost jointly in lieu of quality alone. Standardization and review of usage patterns by the PRAC Committee mentioned above, changes in contracting for maintenance of equipment, in food procurement, in vendors, all contributed to the documented savings the first year of *$339,630* and additional subsequent savings bring the total to approximately *$500,000* since the program started.

Services: A review of property insurance, coupled with changes in ratings and procurement methodology instigated savings of *$196,000* annually. An intensified safety program resulted in a decrease in employee injuries despite a rise in work-hours and a consequent reduction of *$185,000* in workmen's compensation premiums last year. Other savings by centralizing duplicating and copying functions and performing internally services formerly purchased from external sources and other efforts generated an additional *$128,000* in annual savings. Revising a microfiche contract, expanding its use in lieu of paper and other savings in computer operation generated an additional *$65,000* annual reduction in cost. A restructuring of the security function is anticipated to save *$123,500* annually.

Personnel: A program of reviewing each position as it became vacant was instituted late in 1978. In the first four months, 10 requisitions for replacement were cancelled and 9 requisitions were reclassified to lower classifications after discussions with supervisors for an annual savings of *$82,500*. In the last 18 months, quality of patient care was improved by the reprioritizing of personnel. 119 additions were made to patient care areas by the elimination of a similar number of positions in all other areas of the hospital. Also, hospital management positions are being reviewed as vacancies occur and a goal has been established to reduce the number of such positions by 10%.

At the start of the current fiscal year, it was determined that the opening of a new building would require 73 new positions. In addition, 69 new personnel were required for new programs that had previously been approved by the board of trustees. And for which building alterations, modifications or renovations were completed or due to be completed during the year. And for which equipment had been ordered or acquired. Forty-four nursing positions were also needed in various inpatient and outpatient areas to reach what had been deemed to be a desirable quality of care.

Finally other operational needs of 14 persons in various areas brought the total additional personnel required to 200 persons.

It was decided by the president, after a consultation with and recommendations by the executive staff, that 125 new positions would be created and the balance of the needed 75 positions provided by prioritizing the activities of the institution in all areas. The reductions were to be made by attrition. By the end of 8 months, 48 of the contemplated reductions had been accomplished and 27 are scheduled to be achieved by the end of the fiscal year.

Finance: Leasing was eliminated as a means of equipment acquisition. Improved collections have helped to narrow the gap between gross charges and net revenue, enabling the rise in charges to be below the rise in cost.

Much has been achieved and initial results are most dramatic. The process is continuing. Major areas under study for future savings include a telephone interconnect system, an incinerator to save the cost of garbage disposal while providing energy to heat water for the laundry as well as continued review of personnel requirements and deployment and use of contracted management and services. Measures of productivity and efficiency of operations have been developed in some areas and this program is being broadened to cover the major portion of hospital operations.

COST CONTAINMENT CAMPAIGN FOR HOUSE STAFF PHYSICIANS

Education

1. An orientation program has been designed for incoming House Staff

with topics for discussion to include Cost Containment, Risk Management and Medical Records. Proper usage of the Pharmacy, Blood Bank and Medical Examiner's services are also reviewed.

2. House Staff members are issued rate and charge manuals associated with those areas of his or her concern.
3. Patient's bills are randomly placed on medical charts for review by attending physicians and House Staff.
4. Costs of tests, diagnostic studies, equipment and drugs are placed on durable sheets on the patient's medical chart.
5. Third year medical students beginning clinical rotation receive a cost containment presentation by House Staff.
6. "The HPA SCOPE," a new House Staff newsletter, numerous memos, posters and a Cost Containment bulletin board promote cost effectiveness and awareness.
7. House Staff participate on all committees in the hospital that have an effect on patient care or cost effectiveness.
8. The House Staff Steering Committee and the Administration will enforce the policy of writing orders for discharge of patients 24-hours prior to their discharge.
9. Patient education and social service consultations in preparation for discharge should be started on the first day of admission.
10. Medical cases are presented at departmental "grand round" conferences. The format includes presentation of the actual cases, but with a discussion of the costs in addition to the results of the various tests and procedures.
11. Preventive medicine programs are emphasized to teach the patient about their own disease as well as cigarette and alcohol abuse. Education about nutrition is also focused to include information on the economics of the proper diet.
12. "What You Can Do To Hold Down Costs" is being prepared by the House Staff to be distributed to patients.
13. The House Staff Steering Committee is emphasizing to all physicians to critically review the need for specific lab tests before they are ordered.
14. Necessary admission and pre-operative laboratory test requirements are being reviewed.

Publicity

1. Campaign buttons and posters: "Let's Keep Costs Down"
2. Campaign stickers on charts.

3. Media coverage:
   a. House Staff, Hospital, University newsletter articles.
   b. Local and city newspaper, television and radio.
4. Promote program nationally; i.e. RPS, PNHA.

Research

1. Pilot studies focusing on accountability for medical supplies used and tests ordered were completed. Monitoring of supply room on each floor at peak hours was found to increase accountability significantly with the added potential for decreased waste.
2. Surveys of House Staff, Faculty, and Medical Students to assess attitudes and awareness of costs will be continued and expanded to also include nursing personnel and patients.
3. The House Staff will promote on-going surveys of physicians, nurses, technicians and aides directed at disclosing areas of wastefulness or potential improvements.
4. A computer audit will be designed in conjunction with hospital administrators to assess the results of the entire program.

BIBLIOGRAPHY OF PUBLICATIONS THAT CONTAIN MULTIPLE IDEAS ON COST CONTAINMENT PROJECTS

American Hospital Association. *Cost Containment: Digest of Hospital Projects,* 2d ed. Chicago: American Hospital Association, 1978.

American Hospital Association. *Cost Containment: Selected Bibliography,* 2d ed. Chicago: American Hospital Association, 1978.

Bennett, A.C. "Reducing Hospital Costs." *Hospital Topics,* February 1973 and March 1973 (Two parts).

"Case Histories of Hospitals Show They Were Able to Cut Costs." *Hospital Administration in Canada,* December 1971.

Cooper, R.J. "The Energy Crisis Challenge." *Hospital Progress,* May 1975.

Cost Containment Activities in Florida Hospitals. Jacksonville, Fla.: Blue Cross of Florida, 1977.

Cost Containment Programs. Jacksonville, Fla.: Blue Cross and Blue Shield, 1977.

Diaz, J. "Case Studies in Cost Containment." *Hospital Forum,* September 1976.

Foster, J.T. "Here Are 66 Ways Hospitals Cut Expenses." *Modern Hospital,* September 1965.

Foster, J.T. "93 Ways Hospitals Are Cutting Costs." *Modern Hospital,* April 1964.

Johannides, D.F. *Cost Containment Through Systems Engineering.* Germantown, Md.: Aspen Systems Corp., 1979.

Marsh, B., ed. "Cost Containment." *Southern Hospitals,* November-December 1977.

Michael, J.W. *Health Cost Containment: An Overview of Current Activities of the Medical Association.* San Francisco: California Medical Association, April-May 1978.

Optimizing Cost Containment in Medical and Health Care. Jacksonville, Fla.: Blue Cross and Blue Shield of Florida, 1976.

"There Are Ways Some Hospitals Cut Costs." *Modern Hospital,* September 1972.

The Workshop Program on Cost Containment in Health Care: Reducing Hospital Patient Days and Costs. Department of Health, Education and Welfare, U.S. Public Health Service, April 1977 (Region V, Chicago).

Thueson, J. "Hospital's Programs and Progress in Cost Containment Reported." *Hospitals, JAHA,* 16 September 1977.

Wesley, C. "How Hospitals Are Controlling Costs." *Hospitals, JAHA,* 16 May 1976.

INDEX

savings, 318, 319
See also No-Inventory
Investigations
incidents, 430
Investment
cost consciousness, 42, 43
disposables vs. reuseables, 576
inventory, 281, 282
Involvement. *See* Participation

J

Jackson Memorial Hospital, FL, 515, 591
cost comparisons, 598
energy management, 599
personnel, 599, 600
publicity, 601, 602
purchasing, 599
staff physicians, 600, 601
Jaspar, Norman, 514
Jefferies, John, 275
Joint Commission on Accreditation of
Hospitals, 48, 136
participatory management, 146
standards, 533
Johns Hopkins Hospital, MD, 62
Jones, Richard, J., 52
Judiciary Interpretations. *See*
Court Rulings

K

Kaiser-Permanente Health Plan, 66
Kast, William, 168
Kauffman, John, D., 168
Kellogg Foundation, 247, 267, 399
sharing services, 407
Kelly, Thomas F., 166
King, John G., 276
Kirchner, Merian, 2
Knapp, Sally, E., 402
Knowledge
health system engineers, 199-201
Kowalski, Jamie, 274
Kretschmar, Carl, G., 449

L

Labor
food service, 525
See also Personnel

Laboratories
cost control, 548-550
management, 514

Laundry
cost containment, 539
management, 288, 289
savings, 514
softened water, 545
supply vs. control, 544
wage incentive plans, 243
See also Services

Lakewood Hospital, FL, 515, 581, 582
Leasing
cost
analysis, 323, 324
measurement, 325, 326
tax rates, 326-329
vs.
conditional sale, 324, 325
purchasing, 275
See also Conditional Sale

Lesieur, Frederick, G., 242
Levine, E., 96
Lewis, Howard, L., 361
Liability
management, 506, 507
risk, 436

Liability Exposure. *See* Risk
Liability Management. *See* Management
Limitations
group purchasing, 339
Limits
inventory, 348
supply, 352
Lincoln, J. F., 241
Lindenmeyer, Carl, R., 168
Linen
reduction in changes, 348
savings, 514, 539
security, 558
softened water, 546
supply vs. control, 544
See also Services
Liswook, S., 2
Little Company of Mary Hospital, IL,
427
Losses
reduction, 427
Lovejoy, Robert, R., 402

DATE DUE

MAY 18 86		DEC 1 9 2002	
Feb 19 1986			
MAY 19 86			
NOV 07 86			
FEB 13 87			
APR 2 9 1988			
DEC 1 1989			
MAY 0 9 1991			

THE SYDNEY CIRCLE

A Novel by

Alice Ekert-Rotholz

Translated from the German by
Catherine Hutter

FROMM INTERNATIONAL PUBLISHING CORPORATION
NEW YORK, NEW YORK

Library of Congress Cataloging in Publication Data

Ekert-Rotholz, Alice Maria.
The Sydney circle.
I. Title
PT2609.K43P513 1983   833'.914   83-1448
ISBN 0-88064-009-X

For
Julia in Sydney
Robert in Melbourne
Margaret and Frances in Queensland
Patrick in Queensland

1

A Marriage in Sydney

I think often of what's wrong with my marriage. I'm a first-rate brooder. Father always said, "Don't worry. You have only one head." Mother would look at me thoughtfully and then say to Miss Jennings, "With a sour expression like that, Anne will never find a husband." Miss Jennings agreed.

Unlike me, Mother was lively, witty, and always busy. Understandably she wanted to get rid of me by marrying me off, but felt that I would turn out to be a dud in the London marriage market. She wrote thrillers that sold well, and Miss Jennings did the typing. After I was sixteen I didn't read Mother's thrillers any more. The hunt for the unknown perpetrator bored me and seemed somehow dated. Who on earth wants to know today who committed the murder in the hunting lodge? The only interesting thing is *why* anyone should prefer to shoot human beings rather than foxes or hares. But Mother went on working with her gaggle of suspects, and her bank account proved her right. Miss Jennings thought Mother was right too. Miss Jennings also had a bank account.

When Father wasn't practicing in Harley Street, he felt just as expendable as I did. We knew that Mother loved us in her way, but we would rather have been loved in our way. There's nothing new under the sun about that.

Our family home behind Avenue Road was old, rather dingy, and angular, but we liked it there. I crept daily into one or the other of its corners, and brooded to my heart's content. Father spent the little free time he had in the garden. He never pondered about our family life. He went to his club where everything was as it should be.

Mother enjoyed a happy marriage with her secretary. I couldn't stand Miss Jennings, and she reciprocated my feelings. When I was sixteen, I wrote my first poems. Mother wanted to know who on earth would want to publish anything like that. Poems were only another disgusting form of brooding. Of course she was right, but I had my pride and

1

went on writing poetry. Our cat watched me. The poor thing had to listen to it too. Miss Jennings shook her head, with its thin, dyed curls, as she held my lyrical productions at a safe distance and read them through her glasses. Then she laid my old notebook on a side table with her long, pointed fingers. It was as if she thought my outbursts of lyricism might be catching. "How about a nice little novel, Anne?" she asked, stressing a friendly tone, and poured our sixth cup of tea.

We were sitting in Mother's twilit studio with its view of the autumnal garden. All the windows and doors were drafty, and the approaching darkness painted grotesque shadows on the walls. A true London October day, ideal for planning family matters with a disastrous outcome. October to February was Mother's best time. Miss Jennings could barely keep up with Mother's arrangement of corpses, named or nameless. Even though she always used the same formula, she thought up a different variation every time. "What nonsense!" I said sullenly. "I can't write novels."

Miss Jennings didn't like to be told by a sixteen-year-old girl that her ideas were nonsense. At Mother's request, I had to apologize. Mother treated her secretary like fragile Chelsea porcelain; she wasn't a member of the family and could therefore give notice. I sat there brooding silently, but Mother brought me back to reality fast. "Of course you can write novels! There's nothing simpler. But you do have to keep your eyes open and observe people."

"You certainly do," Miss Jennings said, quite superfluously. "Where would we be if all of us spent our time daydreaming?" She closed the curtains and turned on the desk lamp. Our family life was over for the day.

I disappeared to my attic room with my poems. I loved every piece of furniture in it, from the creaky couch with its faded Turkish cover from Manchester, to the antique bureau and two wobbly armchairs. Later I was sad when Alexander labeled my old furniture junk, and only my great-grandmother's bureau was allowed to accompany us to Sydney. It stands in some corner or other of our house in Vaucluse and still brings back family memories. Alexander fixed up my bedroom according to his own ideas. He was right. The bright Australian sun would have exposed the tired wood and scratches mercilessly.

I tore up my poems. Mother was right again. All of them were right. My poems were lousy. Beautiful emotions were not enough. Form and style were everything. That was the only point on which Mother and Alexander agreed.

Since I had no chance of winning laurels with my poetry, Father got me a job in a travel bureau in Piccadilly. In the evenings I sometimes went to lectures on topical subjects in a club on Avenue Road, not far from us. They were fairly simple lectures. There were a lot of gray-haired members in the club, with scholarly backgrounds and acute arthritis. There was tea and a discussion period. Since I had nothing exceptional to say, I said nothing. Anyway, I was the youngest member. Here life began at seventy.

Mother had given up long ago trying to make an attractive young lady of me. Miss Jennings had always known what a futile effort it was. Father had got the job in the travel bureau for me shortly before he died, so now we three women were living alone in the old house on Avenue Road. What I liked to do best was lie on my couch and read general psychology for home use. If I had been a more active person I would probably have studied psychology. Mother could have taught me quite a lot in this respect, but she had no time for my hobbies. She had to concentrate on her plots. At meals she and Miss Jennings conversed mainly about murder by poison, hidden wills and bank robbery. On Sunday she clipped scandal articles from the paper. Miss Jennings had been keeping useful crimes on file for years, and could come up any time with scandalous, sensational material. If one took a look at this alphabetically listed raw material one got the impression that the London population was interested mainly in doing away with their nearest and dearest. My aversion to newspaper scandals and sensational crimes must date from that day.

Gradually I learned to hate the sight of all the newspapers lying around the house. The headlines wriggled like fat black worms on tables and chairs. I would have loved to leave home, but where was I to go? Since I didn't know, I stayed. Mother had resigned herself to my unavoidable presence at tea time long ago. She was even quite fond of me, although I had disappointed her in every conceivable way. Shortly before my engagement she sacrificed a little of her precious time and bought a small Chelsea vase for me at an auction. It brought tears to my eyes; my voice was choked when I thanked her. She asked sharply if I had a cold and sent hot milk and honey up to my room that night. Then she dictated to Miss Jennings for three more hours. She was never tired. Or perhaps she was just harder on herself than most people. Perhaps one has to be like that if one wants to be successful.

One day Alexander Rigby turned up at our travel bureau in Piccadilly: an architect from Sydney on a grand tour of Europe, very tall, very sympathetic, with an aura of Australian sea air about him. He was

3

forty years old, and his blond hair was attractively gray at the temples. He was planning a trip to the European continent. I was to arrange the itinerary for him. What he liked and wanted to see was rivers, or the ocean, and it was his intention to have a look at the architecture of various periods. He told me all this very casually in his Australian accent. It sounded as if his wishes weren't at all important, yet he expected them to be fulfilled. I could tell this by his nose, which was long and narrow, and was hooked imperiously. In his long, ascetic face, his lips were surprisingly sensual, but when he pressed them together he suddenly looked cautious and slightly cruel. Anyway, he gave me this impression once, but then it was quickly dispelled. Mr. Rigby was exceptionally pleasant and could laugh like a boy. He had been to Scotland to look up some relatives, but had found none left. His mother had married a man in New South Wales when she had been very young, and never left Australia again. The remark about his mother was the only biographical bit of information he gave me. Did he avoid speaking about himself out of modesty?

He wanted to discuss his trip over a good meal and for this purpose invited me, by phone, to come to his West End hotel. "This is Rigby again. I want to know more about Paris." He paused for a moment before he invited me. That I might turn him down evidently never entered his mind. Nor mine! I was very rarely invited out because I had so little to offer in the way of conversation. In spite of the fact that I was twenty-eight years old, I still reddened when I was asked to express an opinion in front of a lot of people.

Mr. Rigby was waiting for me in the lobby. He came up to me walking lithely and with a carefree air. He was taller than all the other people around us, and his nose jutted out of his face like the prow of a ship. The women looked at him surreptitiously and curiously; he didn't seem to notice it. Much later I found out that every glance cast at him by women registered with Alexander Rigby, and that he couldn't live without their admiration. But he hid this need just as carefully as he hid his whole private life. He was an amusing conversationalist, but not communicative. As long as I was in love with him, I appreciated the fact that he didn't confide any dissonances of his soul to me.

Besides Paris and Brussels, he wanted to see the old cities in Switzerland and South Germany, and the modern buildings in Stockholm. I had been to several of these places with my father, and answered his questions to the best of my ability, but I had an oppressive feeling in the pit of my stomach when Mr. Rigby said, "What a pity that you don't have a graphic memory."

4

I didn't know exactly what he meant by that, but I realized that Mother had had every reason to tell me I should be more alert. Mr. Rigby was looking at me out of the corner of his eyes—had he noticed how the wind had gone out of my sails for a moment? "Forget it," he said cheerfully. "I like you just the same."

He could afford to be generous. He had enough graphic memory for three architects. Form and color were realities for him. Of course he also had a mathematical memory which bordered on the miraculous, but about that he was tactfully silent. I could sense that architecture was a passion with him. I knew nothing about any of his other passions. Out of politeness I asked him about Sydney. He immediately took out some photographs and explained the views—radiant colors, deep blue water, a luminous sky, snow-white yachts in the sun, many green islands, a huge silver bridge in the background. "Port Jackson," he murmured. "Sydney's harbor."

I stared at the photographs. "Are the colors really like that?" I asked shyly.

"Of course! We have the most beautiful harbor in the world—San Francisco excepted." After a while he added, "And the best life."

It could have sounded boastful, but it was a simple statement of fact. I asked him what he thought Europe had to offer him. He laughed loudly. "Oh . . . a lot!" he said, and looked me suddenly in the eye. I reddened and swallowed my red wine the wrong way. He patted me on the back until I stopped coughing, then he looked calmly around the room again. "That woman should only wear gray-blue," he said unexpectedly. I hadn't even noticed her.

I found him extraordinary, and of course he lived on an exciting, sparsely populated continent. Sparsely populated? Mr. Rigby said that from Potts Point to King's Cross, Sydney was so densely populated, a kangaroo couldn't get through. Then he showed me a picture of his house in Vaucluse. It faced the water, in the background lay the bush, and it looked strangely uninhabited. "A beautiful house," I murmured. Mr. Rigby admitted that there were worse houses in Sydney. "We have a funny conglomeration of styles," he said. "All different, yet thrown together. And so much ornamentation."

I was silent as I thought that Alexander Rigby would probably fall flat on his face at the sight of our house with its gables, columns, and balconies, but fortunately he'd never get to see it. I would have liked to know if he was married, but didn't dare to ask. It was none of my business.

He spoke about hobbies, and raised his eyebrows in amusement

5

when I told him about my evenings at the club. He probably hated all indoor activities. When he wasn't setting houses with glass frontage into the rocky walls around Sydney, he was painting bush birds with strange names, or spending weekends in his summer home in Manly. He was apparently a bachelor. I found it unbelievable that he lived alone, but he apparently went in for a lot of activities suited to a loner: he fished and sailed, surfed in the Pacific when he was in Manly, and designed bold, stark buildings which evidently sprang out of his strong protest against Victorian, Spanish, and just plain ugly suburban villas. At least that's the impression I got after our sixth dinner in the West End. I still didn't know if he was married, but I didn't tell myself any more that it was none of my business. I had gathered from the discussions in the club that one should not drive the art of self-delusion too far. I did not like to think of Mr. Rigby's pending departure.

At our farewell dinner, the lobster didn't taste good to me, although I was seldom treated to such delicacies. Every bite stuck in my throat. Perhaps Alexander's radiant mood depressed me. He was looking forward too much to the trip. In three days he would be in Paris. He said you couldn't show your face in Sydney if you'd missed "gay Paree" on your European tour. Then he tried to lift my spirits by telling me a lot of Australian stories which at first didn't sound funny but afterwards made me laugh. Mr. Rigby's humor was discreet and dry. I always noticed a few seconds too late that the story had been meant as a joke; then, when I laughed, he winked and asked what was so funny.

Now and then his eyes dimmed, as if he had discovered unpleasant memories at the bottom of his wine glass. Then something seemed to be torturing him, but he kept whatever it was to himself. He did everything he could to play the dinkum, the honest-to-God Aussie, the Australian as he is supposed to be in Europe—a nice, simple fellow who knew the bush inside out. He really did know the bush in New South Wales and Queensland very well, but that wasn't what mattered most to him, which was to be an Australian like every other Australian. I couldn't pass any judgment on that. After all, Alexander Rigby was the first dinkum Aussie I had ever known.

He invited me to go to Paris with him.

I told them at home that I was going with a friend from the travel bureau. Mother was happy about it. After all, I was twenty-eight years old, and since Father's death had seen nothing more of the continent. Mother and Miss Jennings were busy right then with reports on the dealers in dope in Soho and Notting Hill, and as usual I was superfluous. My Aussie had only invited me because traveling in a foreign country left him little choice—that was perfectly clear to me—but I was happy just the same, and very grateful to him. He had no idea of how monotonous my life was, and I had taken good care not to let him know it. Mother did what she could for me. In spite of the royalties on her books, we never had enough money. We missed Father's income. The tax bureau seemed to be especially greedy to take a big bite out of the authors of thrillers. I looked in my closet and frowned. Oh well . . . Rigby knew my restaurant wardrobe, and my good black dress had even elicited a compliment. It was simple, but very well tailored, and the back was practically nonexistant. I sang as I pressed it, "Anne Carrington!" I called myself to order. "You must be crazy!" What I really wanted to do after finishing my ironing was write a poem, but then I had given up writing poetry. I stretched out on the couch and read Shakespeare's sonnets. Shakespeare had said everything much better.

Alexander and I became engaged in Paris . . .

He saved me from an uneventful life. I am not one of those people who can take the bull by the horns. I am shy, and was born with no initiative. Oddly enough, I hadn't even been unhappy in my little rut. I love the familiar things of life. Alexander tore me abruptly into a totally strange, new world where dreamlike beauty and the dross of a big city appear in a brazen light without transition. Contrasts have always startled me. How was I ever to get used to these surroundings? Instinctively I had avoided the extravagant thing, and from the photographs, Sydney had looked pretty extravagant to me. High-rise houses, their glass eyes trained on the Harbour Bridge, towered into the tropical sky like architectural exclamation marks over dark streets and Victorian business buildings. The pictures showed forlorn barracks, all the same shape, in the old quarters of the city, and the arrogant crystal facade of Alexander's villa in the eastern suburb. There was also a small replica of Hyde Park which had to appeal to any Londoner. After all that, Alexander showed me his pictures of the Taronga Zoo, a vast natural park in which animals of every period and zone lived in their own widespread preserves. "I spend every free minute I have in Taronga," Alexander said.

He may have been right, he probably was, but it irritated me that everything in Sydney had to be more grandiose than anywhere else. Even the filth and desolation in the old harbor area was a painterly achievement in his eyes. He was a local patriot and made no efforts to hide it. And he told all this so softly and casually that it didn't sound boastful. But I sensed that he would resent even the mildest criticism of Sydney in particular, and of Australia in general. Once he showed me an aquarelle sketch of an Australian bird. "You can paint too?" I asked, astonished. "Nonsense!" he said at once. "I just daub for my pleasure. But our birds are magnificent."

He was fifteen years older than I. This I found wonderful. I had a weakness for father figures because my own father had understood and respected me. I had missed him very much, and my psychology books provided no information as to how a girl was to get along without a father. The other fatherless girls I knew seemed to manage very well.

It was actually ridiculous that I looked upon Alexander Rigby as fatherly in those London weeks, but I saw in him what I wanted to see. I was probably very naive for my twenty-eight years. Anyway, Alexander called me "the innocent of Hampstead." And how should I have gotten any experience since I had accepted the meager portion fate had handed out to me without any resistance? I have undergone quite a change in Australia. Alexander doesn't like it. He married a grateful girl with no contrariness in her nature. To his dismay, I know now, after seven years of married life, exactly what I *don't* want! Like any Australian woman. Alexander Rigby's older sister, for instance, Miss Grace Rigby.

Naturally I didn't show Alexander that love was a foreign word in my vocabulary. In London I kissed him to the best of my ability. My awkwardness and reserve seemed to please him. He treated me with absurd caution. Mother said he came from a new country with old puritan morals. Although he could be lively enough, I considered him lacking in temperament, a dyed-in-the-wool bachelor who conversed with exotic birds in his free time. I am sure the whole Taronga Zoo couldn't have come up with such a prize sheep as myself!

I never gave a thought as to why Alexander Rigby transported such an insignificant creature as myself to his dream villa in Vaucluse to be his wife. Mother wondered about it right away. Surely this Aussie, with his appearance and position, had to have the choice of innumerable desirable girls in his hometown. Why did he choose a wallflower like Anne Carrington? Of course Mother didn't express what she was thinking; my happy face seemed to stop her. Miss Jennings evidently also wondered what possible snag there could be in my engagement to the Australian. Mother of course made all sorts of inquiries, but to Miss Jennings's disappointment, all Alexander's information turned out to be correct. He really was a famous architect in Sydney, partner in a prestigious firm, very wealthy, and the villa in Vaucluse belonged to him. Where was the snag? Both ladies considered unlikely the fact that he had fallen in love with me.

I told myself that Mother and Miss Jennings were suspicious for professional reasons. Alexander had fallen in love with me whether it suited Miss Jennings or not. After all, I wasn't bad-looking, especially when I wore my black dress. I had good posture, and could be alert when I wanted to. Even Mother had to admit, after some hesitation, that "this Mr. Rigby" was not going to provide any material for a new thriller, but that he was just what he professed to be: a true-blue Australian! Moreover he converted Miss Jennings effortlessly to the same conclusion simply by smiling at her pleasantly. From that moment on she looked upon him as an attractive, albeit somewhat primitive, nature man, an oceanic miracle from the fifth continent!

Mother asked Alexander what a dinkum Aussie really was. "Nothing exceptional, Lady Carrington. Just a fellow who won't take orders from anyone and is a good comrade." Mother found this touching but too good to be altogether true. But none of us really knew Rigby. How could we? We knew nothing of his uncontrollable and irrational devotion to his mob, as he called his friends and co-workers. I have meanwhile found out that the mob plays the main role in the life of the Australian male, whether he be a farmer in the bush, a veteran of both world wars, a member of the yacht club, harbor worker, cattle herder, wool shearer, ice dealer or a doctor on Sydney's famous Macquarie Street. The mob cements friendships with collective memories and seals the whole thing—with the rigorous exemption of the wives—with an enormous consumption of beer. The second thing he kept from me was his housekeeper, a gem, a jewel, who will never leave.

I still believe that Alexander really did fall in love with me in London. You can't quarrel about taste. He even found me beautiful. He is certainly not the man to say anything like that and not mean it. When he looked at me in London I grew more and more beautiful from minute to minute. My dull hair grew shiny, my too-light eyes gained depth, and the blood shot up to my pale face. In his presence I wasn't long and thin any more, but tall and slender. During the period of my engagement in London I was young for the first time in my life.

Mother looked upon Alexander naturally as the man who had saved me from a mundane life in an office and would be a splendid provider, but at the same time she felt an inexplicable dislike for him which she never lost. Miss Jennings suddenly respected me. I was of course the same person I had been before the great event, but I had, so-to-speak, in my sleep gained a certain aura. I am sure she felt that she would have been able to cope with the unknown duties awaiting me in Sydney much better than I would. Perhaps she asked herself for the first time in her life, faced with this triumph of indolence, whether indefatigable diligence and iron energy didn't perhaps frighten men off. They never knew what was good for them. She looked at Alexander's photographs with great interest. The idyllic beach at Balmoral evoked an outcry of delight. Alexander's father had spent his old age there, on the sun porch of a white house with a view of the harbor. Jonathan Rigby had lived and built in Parramatta, in New South Wales. Alexander had gone to school there. He told us that Parramatta was the oldest country town in New South Wales.

I asked him if he went there often. He drew an imaginary circle with his long, sinewy arms. "That's how big Parramatta is." After a pause he added, "There's a very nice old jail there, otherwise nothing but a lot of sheep, dairies, and a little industry."

We couldn't see enough of the beach pictures. "Australia! Land of the sun! How I would love to live there," Miss Jennings murmured. She wiped her glasses and ignored Mother's astonished look. Alex smiled at her enchantingly. He had discovered the unconscious worship in Miss Jennings' nearsighted eyes, and was very pleased. "You will have to visit us in Sydney, Miss Jennings," he said. Miss Jennings coughed happily, although she knew very well that nothing would ever come of the visit. She was no fool, and realized that her place was in the London fog, but for a moment the Australian sun had blinded her. "It must be wonderful," she said. "Such an exciting climate."

Why do people say that time heals all wounds? In seven years of married life, time has done little for me. Together with the Australian sun, it put wrinkles in my face. Wherever time may have distributed its healing medicines in Sydney and surroundings, it overlooked me. I am thirty-five years old and dead tired. Alex says that comes from brooding. Every day he reminds me more and more of Miss Jennings.

My husband finds my despondency repulsive, and I can't blame him. After all, I am living under the finest sun in Sydney. A spectacular waterfront and a dizzyingly high standard of living should satisfy anyone. Who do I think I am? I live with a background as depicted in the colorful travel bureau brochures in Martin Place. I must have remained a tourist. I have never penetrated the reality of this turbulent, young, enthusiastic city. They say there aren't any old people in Sydney. They're all young, wonderful—or dead!

Wherever I go everybody thinks Alexander is wonderful—I mean, as an architect. He grows higher into the sky daily, like the new skyscrapers in the city, with their constantly modernized facades. Alex is an exponent of cloud techniques.

The other day I overheard a conversation in the restaurant of the Chevron Hilton Hotel.

"Who built your house, Jim?"

"Rigby, of course. From Marchmont, Rigby & French. We chose him because he falls between two generations. Always the safest thing to do."

"Is he very expensive? We're expecting our fifth child."

"Well, yes. Rigby's best isn't cheap. He works with Bridgeford and Briggs in Hunter Street. If you'd like to talk to him . . . he's coming to dinner tomorrow. Lucy's crazy about him."

"How about his young wife?"

"She's a pommy import." Pommy . . . the Australian nickname for the English, with their cheeks as red as pomegranates.

"So?"

"Mrs. Rigby is a loner."

"She is? But then she can't be right for Alex. He didn't come down with the last shower. I saw him water-skiing in Manly the other day. I'm telling you—remarkable! Why, he could have had any girl he wanted in New South Wales."

"How long have you been living in Sydney, Buddy?"

"Let me see . . . four years. We were stuck in the bush."

"Then you can't talk about Rigby. There was something . . . it didn't go down very well. But that's water over the dam today. Only after that Alex couldn't find a suitable wife so easily, not in Sydney, not Rigby status. We're a great big democracy, to be sure, but you've still got to have the right wife."

"That's what I say, Jim. Cheers for your Lucy. She was born on a bed of sheep's wool, wasn't she?"

"The best you can find in the country. Cheers!"

"Which reminds me . . . I don't like the wool prices lately. They're not really bad yet, but where are we heading? The immigrants . . . thinking they can interfere with us old-timers on the wool exchange! Should be thankful that we let them in! What did they have in starvation Europe? Sure there are decent fellows among them who ought to be given a chance. But they should be thankful if we give them work in Darling Harbour. And they're perfectly happy at first, but then, on the wool exchange, at the races, on the beach, we could do without the Naussies. Cheers!" He was referring to the new Australians. "The beer isn't what it used to be either. What were we talking about? Oh yes, Rigby. The guy's unlucky. I think he paints, as a hobby. Portraits. Did you know that, Buddy?"

"No. But as long as he doesn't paint my daughter, I don't care. Girls go for that man, although he'll soon be out of the running. Must be pushing fifty. Then he must have been thirty-three or thereabouts when it took place. What really happened?"

"Strange that you didn't read about it in the papers. After all, Sydney doesn't come up with a scandal like that every day. And we're accustomed to a thing or two."

"I'm too tired to read in the evening. What did he do?"

"They never really found out. Nobody was in the Blue Mountains with him when it happened. But something always sticks, even when there's no conviction . . ."

And then whispers . . . whispers . . .

What I was eating stuck in my throat. I had invited my friend Shirley to have lunch with me. She lives with her family in a cheerful, old-fashioned house on the other side of Harbour Bridge. Shirley is my only friend in Sydney and New South Wales. I met her quite by chance—just as I met Alexander quite by chance—in a travel bureau. She was working with Qantas, Empire Airways, in Hunter Street. I wanted to go back to London at the time, but then I stayed after all. Mother was busy, and Miss Jennings would have known all along . . .

Shirley Cox drives twice daily over the bridge to the Qantas offices, a building Alex approves of. It shoves its bold swung-glass façade triumphantly into the narrow streets of the inner city. A small building, still in Victorian mothballs, is hunched beside the glass giant. It knows that its days are numbered. Shirley was sitting in the reception room of the glass palace: tall, blond, with thoughtful blue eyes and the most beautiful teeth in all five continents. She was a product of the Australian sun. In her too the simple friendliness and hospitality of the suburbs beyond the Pacific Highway sparkled.

Shirley listened to the conversation about Alex without batting an eyelash. I have no secrets from her, and she knew anyway what had happened in the Blue Mountains ten years before Alexander's jaunt to London. All water over the dam. Everybody knew about it except me. Everybody in Sydney knows all about the Rigbys. Alex's only sister is the publisher of a famous Australian women's magazine. Miss Rigby is a regular guest at the Chevron Hilton. But on that day, she wasn't there.

I rose abruptly. "Don't go, Anne!" Shirley said firmly. She is five years younger than I but much more experienced, and a delightful realist.

Of course Shirley never wrote poetry in her youth, but spent her free time in the fresh air on Bondi Beach. Bondi is more popular than Manly, where Alex and the yacht club swim. Shirley's mother broils wonderful steaks, and her brother, Douglas, is a police officer. They call him Curl because of his curly hair.

Once a week I drive to the Coxes in my little red sports car, and once a week Shirley has supper with me in Vaucluse. Alexander is hardly ever there, and his "jewel," in her black dress, sits on her own balcony with its view of the street. From our big terrace you see the ocean. The harbour lights are mirrored in the water and in the strangely fluctuating darkness. Two white hanging lamps burn in the unreal night, and the tropical air shivers with Alexander's secrets.

At nine Mrs. Andrews appears in her ridiculous black dress with a batiste apron, and serves iced pineapple or red melon. Our housekeeper has an unpronounceable Hungarian name, and Alexander engaged her shortly after "the tragedy." Like me, she knew no one in Sydney. She is thin, unbearable, and cooks marvelously. A jewel. A type that is constantly washed up on the Australian coast. I don't know to this day why Alexander preferred not to let me know of her existence, nor why Mrs. Andrews hates me. In seven years she has never once smiled at me. She worships Alexander, but isn't very much in evidence when he's around. Then she rolls out her paper-thin strudel in the kitchen and thinks her own dark thoughts. The two of us sit alone in paradise and never know when Alexander may bring twelve members of his mob to dinner, and when or if he's going to turn up at all. When he does, he of course wants dinner right away. Mrs. Andrews produces a meal as if by magic and serves the master. She is hungry for praise, and if Alex is in a good mood he says casually, "Very good, very tasty, Mary." Mary gives him a blissful look, medium-strength, and glides around with the goulash platter as if walking on air. Her evening is made. Ridiculous how this gray, gaunt person humbly scatters her incense around him, but Alexander accepts even incense with paprika.

I think he hates me because I see what he's like and not as he would like me to see him, as he was in London. He would prefer jealous scenes, stupid reproaches and cheap tears. Alexander can cope with anything like that with amiable brutality, but unfortunately I can't play along. I can't be jealous of women I don't know, and I am not interested in marital snooping. We have remained strangers. Alexander has no tenderness in his makeup. All he has is an uncontrollable thirst for beauty, and a peculiar avidity for admiration. If I could admire him, everything would be all right. He would forgive my so-called frigidity, my inability to enjoy the Aussies, or at least pretend to, and my slowness in conceiving children.

After I have brought Shirley home, late in the evening, I drive back in the moonlight, over the Pacific Highway to the Harbour Bridge, a gigantic silver span which prevents this strange, disorderly, magnificent city from falling apart. Shirley, amused by big figures, told me that the bridge was made of fifty-two thousand tons of steel, and that fifty million people crossed it every year.

For years now I have been one of those fifty million. I know about ten people in Sydney, counting Alexander, Miss Rigby, and Alex's jewel. Some of those fifty thousand tons of steel must have entered into me. One day Alexander appeared unexpectely for tea. A young girl got out of his big white sports car with him, a blond girl, about seventeen, I thought. I looked into her sly dark eyes. They reminded me of someone, but I'm slow. It didn't occur to me who it was.

"Daisy is going to live with us," said Alex.

The housekeeper, with a stony expression, served his favorite pastry and open sandwiches. I poured tea and saw to it that my hand didn't tremble.

"What are you talking about, Alex? You can't just pick up a young girl somewhere and . . ."

I stopped in the middle of the sentence. I could feel the housekeeper's hot eyes on my neck.

Alex asked, "What makes you think I pick up young girls somewhere? Really, Anne!" He was all hurt innocence, the great Rigby from Marchmont, Rigby & French. I said hesitantly that I had never seen this girl. I raised my voice, and Alexander's eyebrows went up. "My dear Anne, how are you ever going to get to know people if you sit at home all the time? Your friend Shirley Cox, and old John seem to be the only people in Sydney you approve of."

Professor John Darling was a friend of Alexander's student days. I liked him. I have never seen two such different people as Alexander Rigby and John Darling, a bachelor by inclination. But of course he knew Alexander's mob, and they knew him. There weren't many people who didn't know Professor Darling from the Sydney university. John came to see me sometimes. It was always a treat for me.

"I don't want any strange teenagers around, Alexander, and that's final!" I was behaving very badly. Mother would have shaken her head. Alexander looked at me with polite disgust. During every marital quarrel he was smooth as marble and just as hard.

14

"I know Daisy," he said finally, "and that's enough." He passed the cake plate to the girl. "Here, eat, little girl. You want to win at the swim meet, don't you? Are you training hard?"

"And how! Do you think I'll win a prize, Uncle Alex?"

I could feel a headache coming on.

"I think it would be best if Daisy moved into the room with the flowered drapes," Alexander said calmly. "She's in the flower stage."

The young girl giggled. Mrs. Andrews gave a good imitation of a forced smile. Daisy watched her Uncle Alex out of her sly, dark eyes. They were slightly slanted. At last it dawned on me—they were Mrs. Andrews's eyes, only narrower.

"The young girl will *not* move into that room!"

"Why not?" Alexander was still smiling amiably. He was the stronger in every one of our disputes, and he knew it. He was part of this alien, sunnily smiling continent, with the dark bush in the background.

"Why not?" I asked, too loudly. "Because I don't want it. And I hope you'll respect my wishes, Alexander." My voice sounded like a stranger's. When had I ever addressed anyone so sharply? Was this thin, tense person with the shrill voice still Anne Carrington?"

"I always respect your wishes," Alexander said, even more pleasantly. "Come along, Daisy. I'll take you back to your digs."

I didn't know where her digs were. Why hadn't Alexander told me about the girl?

A few weeks after this conversation, Daisy moved into the room with the flowered drapes. But she only stayed weekends. The big house stood empty. I couldn't prevent an indigent Australian like Mrs. Andrews from spending a weekend with her daughter. Sometimes I heard Daisy chattering and laughing with her mother. They sat on the little back veranda in front of Mrs. Andrews's bedroom. Often I could hear loud, male laughter: Alexander's.

I didn't know what to make of it. All I knew was that Alexander's housekeeper hated me. I don't know to this day what the young creature thought of me. I ignored her and she ignored me with the insouciance of youth. I couldn't blame her. I did nothing to make a good impression on the girl. Why should I have? She was an intruder. In the end I talked to John Darling about it.

John is of medium height, much too thin, has a long narrow face, and his hair is almost white. His eyes behind his rectangular glasses are keen. There is something of the pedigreed dog about him. He looks taller than he is, perhaps because he holds himself so straight, perhaps also because of his quiet air of authority. He moves slowly, thinks fast, and always has time for his friends. He comes from a family of famous old settlers near Camden. Once he took me with him to Darling Farm. One could believe one was in England there. In New South Wales a rural British idyll is the only tangible realization of the free English settler's dream. There were more oaks and elms than eucalyptus trees and Australian mimosa. I saw meadows like the ones in Surrey, rows of light trees. "John!" I cried. "You have poplars!" He smiled and led me into what he called the park. The main house, overgrown with ivy, stood in the middle. I had to swallow hard. I was in New South Wales, yet here I felt at home. In a corner of the park stood the little stone house of the first Darlings, built by convicts. But again, the church could have stood in England. John's brother supervises the farm with modern methods. Their cattle are famous. And the little stone house of John's ancestors watches . . .

The convicts came from England. Under the blue Australian sky they must have dreamt of the foggy moors and their pubs in London harbor streets, soggy with rain. I tasted the milk in the huge wainscotted hall of the main house. John's family were silent people, but they were friendly. Nobody asked about "the old lady"—England. They had never seen the land of their ancestors. They were dinkum Aussies.

I didn't open my mouth while John drove me back to Sydney. He didn't say anything either, but watched the road. Alexander was waiting for us in John's Spanish villa in Rose Bay. As far as he is concerned, John's house is a nightmare. Style, with no consideration for the landscape. The yellow stucco villa had thin, modest Baroque columns, arches, colonnaded walks and ornamental chimneys. Alexander would rather have drowned in the Pacific than live in John's Spanish villa. The fact that he never made a remark about the wrought-iron embellishments was testimony of his friendship for John. Alexander had recommended a Georgian-style house, but John liked the ambience of a Spanish mission. The influence of "depressing columns," as Alexander termed this pseudo-Baroque element, is evident in all Sydney suburbs. "John doesn't need to have good taste. John is first class." With which Alexander confirmed his loyalty to John and his columns once and for all.

So my husband could be a friend. Secretly he admired John, possibly because of John's kindness. And he loved John. Perhaps he didn't love me any more because, on a closer look, he had found nothing to admire in me. I suppose marriage is the cold shower after a feast of illusions. At any rate, this applies to our marriage in Sydney. In London,

Alexander had been quite different. He had only shown me his facade. That was his right. I had shown myself in my black dress and had tried to be entertaining.

I thought of the friendship between Alexander and John Darling. I noticed much too late that John—who liked to remain in the background—protected Alexander, as only the unpretentious person can protect the glamorous one. He saved Alexander from himself as long as he could. He was the only one who could contradict Alexander without creating an icy atmosphere in the blazing sun.

John is professor of anthropology at the University of Sydney, and works in an honorary capacity for the welfare bureau, for education, and for the integration of the native population of New South Wales. He sometimes brought me the magazine *Dawn*. I put it away in my antique bureau and never read it. I was so distracted by my backache that I hadn't let the black Australians enter my consciousness yet, although John said once, "The aborigines should have a place in your new experience, Anne."

One evening I was sitting with John on the terrace of our house. He had come because I needed him. He sensed it. I don't know how he was able to take the time to try and make an Australian of me. I must have seemed hopeless to him, more hopeless than the blackest of his black sheep. "What's the matter, Anne?"

I told him about Mrs. Andrews's daughter. "Alexander's interest in her is unnatural," I said, with unusual vehemence.

"Take it easy, Anne." John was looking at the red eucalyptus in our garden as if he had never seen it before. The red eucalyptus is a variation of the national original. "I find it quite natural that Alex wants to help. You surprise me, Anne."

I blushed, but then I told myself at once that John was one of those idealists produced by every country that is too practically oriented. As far as I could see, Alexander showed this friend of his only two of his many faces. Finally I said brusquely that I thought Daisy was Alexander's illegitimate daughter. Mother and daughter couldn't possibly be clinging to him like ivy otherwise.

John didn't laugh often, but now he laughed loud and long, and couldn't seem to stop. "Are you laughing at me, John?"

John shook his head. "You have read too many of your mother's thrillers, girl." And he was one of my mother's fans! "Let me reassure you—Mrs. Andrews brought Daisy with her from Hungary when she was a baby. Her husband didn't survive a dispute with a communist functionary. She left the child for a while with some people in Surry

Hills. It cost her the last piece of jewelry she had been able to smuggle out, but she was worried about getting the position Alex was offering if she applied for it with a screaming baby. And she was right. Alex is not patient."

"So why didn't he tell me anything about it? He's paying for the girl's education, you know. That's very decent of him."

"You're in a young country, Anne. Here people help each other without any musical accompaniment."

I said nothing. I realized how little I knew my husband.

"We are a nation of immigrants," said John. "Unfortunately not always with understanding for the newcomer. Yes, yes . . . Mrs. Andrews came here two centuries too late, and from the wrong country, I mean as far as language and tradition are concerned."

"It is always difficult to be in a strange country, John."

"Certainly. But our new Australians after the Second World War are having a harder time than our English ancestors. An historic abyss separates the immigrants from Italy, Hungary, Greece, Poland, from our satisfied settlers who take our high standard of living for granted. Oh dear heaven, all it is, really, is a conflict of manners and morals. We do much too little for these new arrivals, Anne. We're too easily satisfied with ourselves. That's the trouble."

"I admire you, John. You're so patient with me."

"I like you, you little idiot! You'll be all right. Just be a little more tolerant."

"Do you think I'm impossible?"

"I think you're young and—forgive me—inexperienced."

"I'm living on a dead-end street, John."

He smiled. "A funny expression for such a sprawling city. Tell me, Anne, is it really so difficult to get accustomed to living in Australia? It's the best country in the world."

"But it's all so strange! And the contrasts are so . . . so . . . harsh."

"It's a young country, Anne. You see too much civilization in Sydney. We find the city very Americanized. You should see the vast flatlands, experience the loneliness of the bush! Why don't you and Alex ever travel into the bush? Why don't you ever go with him to Taronga Park? Or to water-ski in Manly."

"He hasn't asked me to."

"The next thing you'll expect Alex and me to be introduced to you!" John said amiably. "Good heavens, girl! Alex didn't build that bleak glass house in Vaucluse for you to sit in for the rest of your life. Don't you swim?"

18

"I have a weak back. It hurts all the time. I'm always tired, John."

"Have a massage! Do something, Anne! Stand on your head! What are you interested in, anyway?"

What was I interested in? I had even put my lay psychology books away in the antique bureau. I said nothing. I felt as I had felt in school when I had been too shy to answer.

"I'll find out." John was smiling. "You'll see. Everything's going to be all right. After all, you didn't land yesterday!"

"If only Alex would help me! But he doesn't need me. He has the mob."

"He needs you, all right, but you don't make it easy for him. Alex wrote me such a happy letter from London."

"We were happy then."

"You'll get used to it, my dear. Alex ..." He hesitated. I didn't move. "Alex may not be very easy to understand, Anne. He doesn't have much use for the safe or intimate thing. He lives with his esthetic vision. And he can't show his feelings. In this country the monologue is the most popular form of conversation. With whom were the fellows to talk when they moved through the bush alone? Even when there were two of them, each one was lost in his own thoughts. They had told each other everything they had to say long ago."

"But that's all ages ago, John. I do find the bush legend sentimental."

"It is not a legend." John's voice was sharper than usual. "The bush plays a part in our lives ... as a eucalyptus forest, as an idea. Just as the old bush men talked to their waltzing Matildas, we in the city still like to talk to ourselves."

I knew that the waltzing Matilda was the lonely wanderer's knapsack. But we lived in Sydney, an Americanized island of happy materialism, with the bush and its monologues in the background. I had no idea what Alexander's conversations with himself were about. I saw the closed faces of John, Betty West, and Miss Rigby before me, and among them the pinched face of Alexander's housekeeper. What did they talk about when nobody else was listening? The floor seemed to be swaying under my feet. Mother and Miss Jennings had always expressed themselves clearly, especially over my and other people's deficiencies. I had known where I was at. But was John my friend? Had Alexander told him about his disappointment in his marriage? Or was everything a monologue?

"Alex doesn't care a thing about me," I said harshly.

"Nonsense! Then why did he marry you?"

"That's what I'd like to know. Perhaps he'll tell you."

"How about a nice cold glass of beer, Anne? It's very hot tonight, isn't it?

I was cold. I felt it in my bones that John Darling and old Marchmont of Marchmont, Rigby & French, knew every detail of the scandal. And I would be damned if they didn't know whether the rumors were founded or not. But I didn't ask John. Even if Alexander rejected the dialogue of marriage, even if he neglected me—he was my husband. He gave me a life for which I was envied. You could read in the Sydney *Morning Herald* about our parties and trips. I sat crouched on the top of the social ladder and could pick the big tropical stars. Naturally one falls harder when one sits on top, but there wasn't a shadow of scandal. I saw to that. I appeared with my husband whenever necessary. Sometimes he asked me to leave my martyr's face at home. I didn't know that I looked so dismal. I only noticed to my dismay that now I liked to nag almost as much as Mother or Miss Jennings. My housekeeper, who, after all, took all the everyday burdens off my shoulders, was my victim because, unlike Alexander, she was always there. I was unfriendly to young Daisy when I saw her in the garden during our weekends. I had nothing against the girl since I knew all about her, but after my conversation with John Darling, she was for a long time a symbol of my defeat. Alexander didn't respect my wishes in any way at all. I couldn't nag him. Either he laughed, or walked off silently to his shed in the garden. His distaste for dialogue left me high and dry and drove me slowly into the desert. For Alexander there was only the mob or the monologue. Gradually I got the hang of the monologue. It was my only distraction, and after all, I've always been a first-rate brooder. I knew exactly what I lacked. I didn't need analysis for that, as Miss Rigby advised. She was as friendly as ever, but she was about as comforting as the New South Wales Public Library. Alexander gave me everything, only not himself. But there was nothing new under the sun about that.

John looked up silently at the rising moon. The contrast between the beauty of my surroundings and the meagerness of my life was almost funny. I would have to be hellishly careful not to lose my respect for life. Vaucluse gradually became a void . . .

"Will you be at Miss Rigby's tomorrow night, too?"

John started. I had torn him out of his monologue. Then he said gently, "I am always at Miss Rigby's. I am part of the inventory."

"If you weren't going to be there, I'd stay home."

John looked at me, so astonished, that I reddened. The cold moonlight washed over us. Beautiful, merciless Australian night. "I was joking," I said apologetically.

"Then let's laugh," said John.

2

Among Us Old Australians

They say you haven't been in New South Wales if you haven't admired Harbour Bridge sufficiently, or the post office on Martin Place.
You also have to have seen Mrs. Macquarie's Chair, and of course the
Blue Mountains, where the scandal had taken place about which the
Rigby family preserved a deathly silence. There is so much you have to
see in this city. Sydney by night. The endless chain of lights that
stretches across hills, shines on bays and waterways, and how fifty-two
thousand tons of steel transform Harbour Bridge into a work of art.
And one has to see the "sheilas," the girls sauntering along King's
Cross, that little Soho of nostalgia. And no one should leave Australia
without having seen the sheep fair in Sydney. Then it's winter in this
hemisphere. At home it is June, and we wear summer dresses whether
it's raining, hailing, or snowing.

There is almost too much to see. I found the millions of sheep in
their dry, functional stalls remarkable, also the many people, wet from
the rain, standing in awe around this wealth of their land. One should
also visit hotels out in the country where, in white tiled bars, the men,
joking and singing, order countless rounds of beer for each other.
Alexander was never more of a stranger to me than when he came out
of a bar. Then he seemed taller, more brutish, and was in a state of excitement I never saw him in at home. Are we women different too
when we are among ourselves? Don't our men recognize us then
either? Anyway, my friends and I were not allowed to drink beer in the
men's sacred tap room, but in a stuffy ladies' salon. For me, however,
the most remarkable sight was Miss Rigby, Alexander's older sister,
publisher of a popular woman's magazine called *Insight*.

I shall never forget the party Miss Rigby gave in her house in Bellevue Hill. Miss Rigby isn't exactly enthusiastic about Alexander because
two incessant talkers have to be rivals. No sooner has Alexander collected a group of people around him, than he becomes a great talker.

Miss Rigby, seven years older than her brother, and, like him, someone you can't overlook, can be turned on any time, day or night. She is the Cicero of Sydney. Australian women, young and old, and from every walk of life, have been hanging on her lips for years, swallowing the nectar of her wisdom. *Insight*—an elegantly caparisoned parade horse of journalism, illuminates not only the reception rooms and verandas of the old colonial houses in the city, but also casts a sharp and universal eye on the farm women in the bush, and on the borderline bigwigs at the edge of the great desert. Nurses, models, students, masseuses, sales-girls, waitresses, and I—all of us read *Insight*, look at the glossy color illustrations and the fashions, modeled by a beautiful girl called Candy. Some of us skip Miss Rigby's stern but forthright editorials, but all of us read the unabridged novels of the Australian author, Elizabeth West. This lady has evidently tried out everything in the way of male love, of which the readers of *Insight*, especially the lonely creatures in no-man's-land, hadn't even dared to dream. Naturally Miss West takes the puritan morality of the continent into consideration, in spite of several pretty hot episodes. Sex is cautiously and subtly rationed.

Every inch an old Australian, Elizabeth West knows exactly how far she can go. Of course she was present at Miss Rigby's party. She is her bosom friend, insofar as one can speak of bosom where Miss Rigby is concerned. To be precise, Miss West inhabits several rooms in Miss Rigby's house in Bellevue Hill. Alexander can't stand her. Miss West has innumerable imaginary illnesses. In his eyes that is a deadly sin. When, a few years later, I began to need treatment for headaches and backache, he treated me like a criminal. He is disgustingly robust.

I had been in Sydney only four days when Miss Rigby's invitation made me panic. Actually it was a polite order. I sensed on the phone that Miss Rigby would never accept a refusal. Alexander had already prepared me in London for his only sister. He addressed her in the soft ironic tone she hates as "Miss Rigby." I found out from Alex that not only did his sister know everything, but that she could also ferret out every foible and weakness known to mankind! Later she told me that Alex unfortunately wrapped himself up in the cocoon of his sleeping bag in order not to have to face the truth about himself. What that truth was, she didn't say.

When Miss Rigby walked up to me in her huge reception room in Bellevue Hill, I felt like a student who was not going to get anywhere near the top of the class. And I was right. On that first evening Miss Rigby asked me if I wouldn't like to contribute something to the magazine on the subject of career women in London. All I could have offered her were my torn-up poems. I had never paid any attention to career women. Perhaps Mother and Miss Jennings had been enough. Of course we girls in the Piccadilly travel bureau had worked, but mostly we had been waiting for elevensies—tea with raisin bread. Instead of discussing social problems, most of the girls had talked about their beaux, and I can't deny that we found this topic quite interesting. Of course Miss Rigby would have approved highly of Mother, because she too preferred thrillers and detective stories to Miss West's romances.

I must admit that Miss Rigby was very nice to me, right from the start. She would never have wasted her time being unfriendly to an unimportant young woman. But she was really interested only in women with careers, if possible with university degrees, or in responsible positions. She was one of those amazons who were propagandizing for women in the Sydney war of social prestige. Naturally Miss Rigby also dealt in her magazine with the Australian housewife and mother's considerable problems, but these were relegated to the back of the magazine, and her editorials and the general tone of the paper was directed at the career woman, like Miss Rigby herself. A woman's magazine of course has to have recipes and fashion reports, and deal with questions of child behavior. But Miss Rigby dealt with such boring themes in her own way. The fashions were suited to women in the public limelight, and the recipes were for dishes that could be prepared in no time flat, with frozen and precooked foods, but they were so subtly described that you didn't notice it right away. The steaks served at the party resembled sacrificial lambs with vegetable garnish, all trembling under a layer of aspic. Alexander had eaten an honest-to-God steak at home. On the way back to Vaucluse, he compared his sister's garnished dishes with the contemporary architecture that ornamented honest walls with fake columns, treated fine wood to make it look like a different material, and offered practical items in grotesque packaging. After this party, contrary to his usual behavior, he talked his head off because he wanted to bridge an abyss. It was a deep abyss, and I fell into it in spite of his life belt. Namely, when Miss Rigby, Miss West, Alexander and I were drinking our last demitasse on the big veranda, Miss Rigby happened to mention the "tragedy" in the Blue Mountains. She had of course taken for granted that I knew all about it. But I didn't. On the way home I was still very upset, and Alexander's remarks about steak in aspic and fake columns fell on deaf ears. Finally I asked him how he had managed to keep such an important event from me. He replied that he had wanted a fresh start and the whole thing lay years back anyway.

That was all. I don't know how I got to my ultra-modern bedroom that night. I groped through the house like a blind man. I still remember sitting for half an hour beside my old bureau in the spare back room. It was ridiculous, of course, but I had to hang onto something familiar.

In all these years I never became really close to Miss Rigby. Her nonchalant yet superior attitude, her enormous intelligence, and amazing energy prevented any intimate relationship. Compared to her my mother was a warm hearth, even though thousands read Miss Rigby's books, and she was well known because of her many television appearances. But Mother was unobtrusive, whereas Miss Rigby was someone who couldn't be overlooked, if only for her size: endlessly tall, much too thin, and with an Australian eagle profile. Her short straight hair looked as if it had just been styled by a hairdresser; she was smartly dressed and immaculately groomed. She exhorted her readers to always dress as befitted the occasion and not to sit around on their verandas in old housedresses out of slovenliness, or in cowardly flight from the sun. That Miss West sat around just like that on all the verandas of Bellevue Hill was a well-kept secret. Miss West's heroines of course kept up appearances in city or bush.

Without having to do any research on it, I knew Miss Rigby's opinion of me. This was funny because usually I am a poor judge of the reactions of strange people. I had really believed that Alexander was in love with me. I don't know if the heat gave me a sixth sense, but I often heard in my mind what Miss Rigby was probably telling her friends about me.

"My dear . . . my brother has brought a young wife back with him from London. I like Anne, but the pommies are conservative and slow, no denying that. Anne will get used to things here. It isn't all that hard in Sydney. Of course she must try to acquire our habits and share our viewpoints; mechanical efforts to adjust don't suffice. I wonder often why Anne isn't more cheerful, but after all, she is married to my brother . . . On the other hand, she has nothing to worry about, and Vaucluse isn't the worst place in the world. In our set nearly all of us come from pioneer families. When I think what our ancestors had to put up with compared with Anne! Desert heat, loneliness, flies, mosquitos, drought, natives, bush fires, and whatever else. And of course with the hunger and sickness of our animals and children! But did our old Marchmonts and Darlings, or, pardon me, Rigbys, make sour faces like our immigrants today? No, my dear, they held their heads high and sang!

"Perhaps Alexander's young wife has it too good. Granted that she had a job before she married Alex. She ran a big travel bureau in London. But she's become as slipshod here as some of my problem children from the Outback. Naturally I answer every one of their letters. The poor things depend on me. I tell my readers in Queensland and West Australia: when do I get your articles about gold prospectors? Think of your forefathers! The heat is perfectly bearable when you live accordingly. Do your duty with a smile. The kookaburra in the bush laughs too. Girls, I say, tell your men what you think of their beer consumption. You women and mothers are more important than the mob with whom your man spends his Saturdays. Insist that he participate in your family life whether he wants to or not.

"Young Anne often has backache. I have recommended Molly Fleet, a very good masseuse. Unfortunately she has a disfiguring birthmark on her face, but I told Miss Fleet exterior beauty wasn't important. She wrote to the Mailbox, asking what she could do about her depression. I told her to throw away every mirror in her house. What I don't know doesn't hurt me. I invited her to tea at the office. We Rigbys come from Parramatta too. The Fleets are also real Australians. Molly's ancestors—female side—began life here in New South Wales as deportees. A very interesting criminal record from old Parramatta. Miss Fleet has bourgeois inhibitions because her ancestor was a convict, but I told her at once, 'Don't be silly, Molly! The largest and finest families in the country often started out like your matriarch. Mostly the poor souls hadn't done a thing, perhaps only looked at their masters the wrong way or drunk a gin or two too many. Just between us old Australians, you can be proud of your great-grandmother! Best British import!' Not to be compared with the odd people settling in New South Wales nowadays. They land here and expect us to learn Italian or Polish. They stick together and are interested only in their own families. Especially the new Australians from the unsettled countries in Europe. Always insulted when they're supposed to speak English! Yes, Alexander still has his Hungarian jewel.

"How about his marriage? My dear, you know my brother! The less said about it, the better. Just between us, he didn't tell Anne . . . oh, forget it. The tragedy's gathering dust, and Alex wanted a new start. A little naive, no? No, I don't know Anne's mother, but Lady Carrington must be considerably more energetic than her daughter. She writes excellent thrillers. But I can't tell Betty that. Our dear Miss West will tolerate no best sellers beside hers! Where is Betty from? From Adelaide. But she has only developed in Sydney under my influence. Nice young person. I've grown very accustomed to her. If only she weren't so untidy! She can make a total mess of any room in a matter of minutes. But then, all of us have our little weaknesses. Yes, my dear, I do too!

"I *would* like to do more for Alexander's wife. A very decent girl—clean, reliable, good background. But can you tell me where to find the time? No, Anne doesn't complain, but all of us know that Alexander is not a talented husband. Why does he keep on marrying? I thought he'd gone crazy when he cabled me from London that he was engaged. After his experience with Flora Pratt, I would have thought he'd had enough of marriage once and for all. But that's his problem. Young Anne will have to make the best of her life. I wonder what she would have thought of our Flora. The first thing I think I'll do is send Anne this masseuse from Parramatta. It is incomprehensible that such a young woman should have such a lot of ailments. I don't take them seriously because our dear Betty West has all sorts of imaginary illnesses too. We Rigbys are always well."

Alexander has told me nothing about his first marriage. His wife was a bar girl and considerably older than he. The scandal concerned her sudden death in the Blue Mountains. Miss Rigby calls the scandal a "tragedy." That sounds better.

It seems that the poor soul, the widow of a wealthy sheep farmer in New South Wales, fell off a precipice as she was looking over it. Alexander was unpacking the picnic basket when it happened. The poor old thing—bad luck! She had apparently been all dressed up in a ridiculous flowered hat and high-heeled shoes, as if going for a stroll in King's Cross. Miss West stared at Alexander unflinchingly while his sister tactlessly mentioned the first Mrs. Rigby. Miss West's fluttering eyelashes behind her fashionable glasses betrayed an earlier intimacy which Alexander chose to ignore. In Vaucluse, hours after the party, he explained impatiently that the first Mrs. Rigby had been just as nearsighted as she had been fun loving, but out of vanity she'd refused to take her glasses along on the outing. In her eagerness to see the grandiose view, she had walked too far across the rocky plateau and fallen into the abyss below. "Horrible mess," Alexander murmured, which I took was to cover the whole business. Because of her immense fortune, his friends had considered him an opportunist and a murderer, but Alexander shrugged and said, "One's friends always like to think the worst," Marchmont and John Darling excepted, of course. The two hadn't thought anything, while the damned cobbers had pestered the life out of poor Alex, until Mrs. Andrews had come to Vaucluse. Yes, her Hungarian cuisine had cheered him up considerably. *That* I could believe! He likes it when women spend hours thinking up what he is going to eat, and prepare his meals in this infernal heat. He lunches with Marchmont and French somewhere near his office.

In the end Alexander assured me that his friends had always meant well. He *could* of course have pushed the first Mrs. Rigby off the rocky prominence, but whatever I might be thinking, he had *not* done so. In short—he didn't hold it against his friends that they had chosen to question his morality. After all, all Sydney had been talking of nothing else. Yes, today he was again enjoying happy hours with the old devils at the yacht club. A nice mob . . .

Over lunch at her women's club in Elizabeth Street, Miss Rigby assured me that I should not brood over an embarrassing event that happened so long ago. With her psychological acumen she had noticed that brooding was my great talent. Alex had won out over the police at the time; as for the police—what did the fools know anyway? Miss Rigby shared the Australian disregard for authority in general and the police in particular. I looked at her long, fine face with its eagle-beak nose and her remarkable hairdo—every lock in place—and decided she must have suffered terribly over the scandal, but she betrayed as little emotion as every dinkum Aussie. In spite of which I got the feeling that she was not heartless. She had fine qualities, but she hid them carefully, according to the best Australian traditions. Like Alex in London, Miss Rigby wanted to demonstrate to the world that she was gloriously average. Suddenly I wished we could be friends, but I was too shy to make the overtures.

Grace Rigby also told me that the first Mrs. Rigby had fallen down the cellar stairs once. That was when she had been a bar girl, just before her marrige to a fabulously rich Merino farmer. "And now let's speak of more important things, Anne," with which Alexander's sister closed the book on the past. Controlled impatience made her voice sharper. Flora had simply been stupid. Glasses were there to be worn. For the rest of this intimate conversation, Miss Rigby discussed capital investments, television programming, her honorary activities in immigration centers, and John Darling's cultural efforts on behalf of the native Australian population.

"Have you and John Darling been friends for a long time, Miss Rigby?" I asked.

"Of course," she replied, with increasing impatience. "The old kangaroo is part of the inventory. Why aren't you eating anything?"

* * *

There isn't a picture of the first Mrs. Rigby in the whole house in Vaucluse. I have the feeling that Alexander didn't need the first Mrs. Rigby, and he doesn't need me either. He needs his friends, and occasionally the bees that make honey for him. But I can't be sure of anything. He is constantly being transformed in front of my very eyes into completely different men. It makes me feel queasy. Today I am sure of only one thing: all the gold and silver of Broken Hill can't bring back the man I knew in London.

In the evening I usually sit on the big terrace. The lanterns cast a ghostly light on the harbor. The moon is dreamy, a moon for beginners. It makes no impression on me any more. The wooded spits of land, speckled with houses that look like toys, stretch out into the water like giant crocodiles. Next week Alexander will be fifty. I think he dreads it. Just the same, or perhaps just because—he is giving a party for his mob.

My back aches all the time, but the girl from Parramatta is a good masseuse. Poor thing! In her case inner beauty has to do everything. Not easy when one is only twenty-two years old. By the way, in spite of the invigorating air up there, I haven't been alone with Alexander in the Blue Mountains in all these seven years. He might get ideas. . .

3

Elizabeth West, Author.
Sydney, N.S.W.

I was born in Adelaide some years ago. South Australia has an unfavorable climate for authors who write about romance. My home town has very straight streets; even the trees on our avenues look formal and severe. As a child I used to love the mountains behind our city; they were friendly and green. And then I loved my cat, Lake Torrens in the evening, and my friend Gretchen. Her parents had immigrated to Adelaide from Germany. Gretchen told me grim fairy tales. The names of the authors were Grimm too, and I found that hilarious. "What are you laughing at?" Gretchen asked, offended.

We quarreled only once. That was when she declared that German settlers had founded Adelaide. But I knew from my grandfather that Captain William Light had beaten Gretchen's ancestors to it. I heard my grandfather screaming the information across the garden fence to Mr. Breitschneider, his oldest German friend. My grandfather Withers was very old; he spat sometimes when he spoke and complained often about how many German names there were in the city. Of course Captain Light founded Adelaide. After a lot of back and forth Gretchen couldn't deny this historical fact any more, but then she insisted that it had been the Germans who had got Adelaide going economically. I had nothing to say against that. We did only what was necessary, and that was why we got some mileage out of our beaches and mountains and our weekends.

Later Gretchen and I lost track of each other. One can never say when childhood friendships end, but more often than not it happens from one day to the next. I cried because I missed her and because I didn't want to see her any more—very illogical of me, but I have never been able to break this behavior pattern with people I love. There was a time when I didn't want to see Alexander Rigby anymore; still I missed him wherever I went. I tried to tell myself that I could get along beautifully without him, but that only made things worse. Especially in the moonlight. When one is alone, the moon is an infamous invention.

When Gretchen disappeared from my circle of friends—we told our other friends that we were bored with each other—it was also the end of fairy tales for me. I didn't hear any more until I met architect Rigby in Sydney. He really is a good raconteur of fairy tales. The moonlight went so well with what he told, but unfortunately I nearly always closed my eyes. Today all I can say is that what I experienced with Alexander Rigby was just as grim as the tales of the Brothers Grimm. Only no blood was shed. And Alexander didn't do me in in a German fir forest but in the Hungarian Restaurant Szabo, in King's Cross.

That all happened over ten years ago. I have learned to live without Rigby. When I met him at Miss Rigby's with his second wife, I had to think of the times in George Street. It was about a hundred years ago, and the moon over Sydney was much brighter than it is today. I was still a stranger in the big city, and twenty years old. I knew nothing about men. In Adelaide the sexes didn't have their fun together, and little has changed in that respect. Even in cosmopolitan, worldly-wise Sydney an abyss yawns at every party between the men and the women. After conventional greetings, the men drink beer on "their" veranda, and we women gaze at the moon. Today I don't mind. Alexander Rigby has spoiled all personal romance for me. All I'd have to do is write down the opposite of what took place between us, and I'd have a nice love story, ready to go to press.

Perhaps I should have stayed in Adelaide. Then I would be sitting today in the botanical gardens with my children, and when the youngest boy would fall into the lake, my oldest would jump in after him. And we would go home happily to a white house with a garden. On the weekends my husband and the boys and I would drive to the mountains behind the city, away from the heat of the streets. Enormous red and white flowers bloom in our mountains. There, with wine and olives, I could have dreamt safely of men like Alexander Rigby, but no . . . I had to travel to relatives in Sydney to learn all about life.

When I think that in Sydney I was never able to get away from the Rigby family I have to laugh, as I did over the Brothers Grimm. And by the way—Alexander and Anne Carrington are about as suited to each other as a Tasmanian tiger and a koala bear. But that, thank God, isn't my problem. I only ask myself how long the whole thing will last. They've been married seven years, but strictly separate. You can sense that. Rigby doesn't know the meaning of love. Lucky man!

I began my famous career in Sydney as Alexander's secretary at Marchmont & Rigby in George Street. The first Mrs. Rigby had just died, and he had bought his way into the firm of the famous architect, Marchmont. French was probably still in diapers at the time, or playing with blocks. Marchmont & Rigby didn't have the ultramodern office then that they have today. They worked in smaller rooms in the shabbier section of George Street, where there were all sorts of junk shops, second-rate restaurants and sleazy apartments; in short, it was not the George Street of the Queen Victoria Building or Saint Andrew's Cathedral. That's the only section of Sydney's oldest street that's good enough for Alexander Rigby today. I fitted in with his beginnings in George Street.

Of course in those days I wasn't called Elizabeth. I was little Betty Withers, private secretary. Alexander has changed a lot in the course of the years, but at thirty-three he was just as ambitious and fanatical a worker, and in his spare time he had an eye for the ladies. Many visitors to Australia say that we don't have enough ambition, and that "Fair enough" is our slogan. That may be true in certain cases, but in what country isn't the average person satisfied with the average thing? And there are people like Rigby everywhere. Unfortunately, as a lover he spoiled me for the fair-enough boys. One can reject Rigby, but one can't forget him. His designs are just as remarkable as he is. He introduced the vertical line to Marchmont & Rigby. His houses reach high into the sky, like his dominant hooked nose. But it's no concern of mine any more.

When I gazed at the moon with Rigby ten years ago, I wasn't particularly attractive. My hair, instead of being shiny red, was dull brown and stringy. I had a round face—no powder—and wore dresses and lipstick in all the wrong colors. In order to do something to enhance my appearance, I was also wearing some pretty awful costume jewelry. Mother Nature hadn't treated me lavishly, and I didn't know yet how to improve on her. Young Mr. Rigby looked at me thoughtfully and hired me. He had noticed the servile admiration in my eyes behind my unbecoming glasses.

I was eager to learn and wanted to achieve something in Sydney. I at once decided to stay with Rigby until nothing short of death tore me away from my desk in the small anteroom. I was much too shy to look my young boss in the eye. I listened to his dictation, eyes lowered, had boundless respect for him, and stood in the doorway trembling when he was developing his plans for Marchmont & Rigby. Even then he scarcely raised his voice when he was excited but proposed new ideas casually, then waited with iron nerves to see how they turned out. I found him as beautiful as the Apollo on the Archibald Monument, and he had the advantage of not being bronze. Sometimes I dreamt about him, the way one dreams when one is barely twenty and has had a stern upbringing in Adelaide. Then I would wake up bathed in sweat in my furnished room in Paddington. Today I know that Rigby prefers stone, bold lines and glass to little girls. Perhaps one has to be like that if one wants to give the most powerful city in New South Wales the boldest silhouette in all Australia. Just the same, at thirty-three he still had a healthy appetite for moonlight, and he was still living in the poorer section of George Street.

He was very nice to me, which made me deliriously happy. When he smiled at me, I melted. "Do you never go out, Betty?" asked the grieving widower after six months of my chaste admiration.

"Where should I go? I don't know anybody in Sydney."

"Well, now—you know me."

I couldn't have heard right! *He* wanted to go out with *me*? I stammered that I had nothing to wear.

"Your dress is nice enough," he said, knowing better.

It was the only friendly thing he ever did for me. He came over and cleverly removed my fake coral necklace. "You must never wear red," he said. I was crushed. I had thought red was my best color. I asked him shyly what he thought I should wear. He said, quick as a flash, "Blue. Every shade of blue. That would be right for you. So tomorrow evening, when we're through here, we'll have dinner together. Where is the letter from Farrell & Sons? Please write: Dear Sirs . . . etc. etc."

I bought myself a blue dress with a month's salary. That was how it all began.

Of course my boss didn't take me to any of the elegant restaurants to which he invited Mrs. Trent. Mrs. Trent was a pretty, well-dressed client who rarely laughed. Rigby must have summed up her vapid solemnity as depth. His first wife, a bar girl, had been known in Sydney as kookaburra, the laughing bird. Evidently right now Rigby needed a serious redhead from Sydney's best and wealthiest circles. Patrick Trent was a well-known real estate agent, and Marchmont & Rigby was building him a house. Mrs. Trent appeared in George Street in elegant summer dresses and always wanted to speak to Mr. Rigby. Once I heard her sob, but when she left the private office of her architect, she ignored me just as arrogantly as ever. It always gave me a stab in the region of my heart that a wonderful man like my boss should have fallen into the clutches of a woman like Mrs. Trent. What wouldn't Rigby do in order to be able to build according to his ideas?

He took me to a restaurant in Pitt Street. There he could be sure that his friends from Vaucluse wouldn't see him with me. The place had a lot of colored marble and carved walnut furniture, and tried to demonstrate how the Italians had lived in the Renaissance. Rigby must have hated it. I thought the place was wonderful, especially the carved head of an angel over the bar. It reminded me of Gretchen. We had been such good friends. Sydney was so big and impersonal.

Alexander Rigby made no declarations of love. He wasn't that simple. He told me about a lady called Lola Montez who had appeared at the Royal Victoria Theatre in Pitt Street. The theatre and Lola were gone long ago. Pitt Street was very narrow, a gorge: women with market bags, girls with illusions, shops, a smell of gasoline, coffee shops, bars, whining radios, tooting horns, and anonymous sighs. When Rigby was already treating other secretaries to ice cream and kisses, I sometimes wandered down to Circular Quai where I could catch a whiff of seaweed, and crept around Pitt Street again. Perhaps Rigby would turn up suddenly where Lola Montez had delighted earlier Rigbys at the Victoria Theatre. But I imagined they liked to gamble just as much as Alexander, and met with bookies and the mob at the Hotel Tattersall, with the marble bar. After Gretchen and the Brothers Grimm, Rigby and Lola Montez were my murky stars. Once I lost my way and ended up at the Salvation Army by mistake, the folk place for teetotalers. It was during my meager time, two long years after Rigby had written me off.

My first manuscript was a historical romance, eight years after the Rigby episode. Lola Montez in Pitt Street. Of course not a soul was interested in it. It was naive and written without any elegance of style. One cliché after the other from beginning to end. I sent it to *Insight*, and Miss Rigby wrote me that the novel was so bad, things could only get better. By now I was twenty-eight.

Miss Rigby took me in hand. I was not to write any more novels, only short articles about Sydney today. Occasionally a short story in which people met on Harbour Bridge and told each other strange experiences that had taken place on Sydney's narrow streets or in the suburbs. That suited me better than an office desk, and Miss Rigby paid well. My first *Insight* novel was a sensation, and I was thirty. Grace Rigby had introduced me to her friends long ago, and I met her brother, Alexander, frequently at her villa in Bellevue Hill.

When I saw Rigby again in his sister's reception room he had been making a point of avoiding me for several years. I had gone back to Adelaide for a while. Gretchen was married and already had children. I worked in her husband's office and sometimes spent an evening with her when her husband was drinking beer with his friends. I saw how other people lived—not excitingly, not especially happily, but not especially unhappily either. Gretchen and her husband ate the bread of life in peaceful harmony—fair enough. She treated me with a note of condescension since I had come back from my excursion to fabulous Sydney somewhat the worse for wear, taciturn, and resigned. Defeats aren't easier to take in Adelaide than they are in Sydney. When I had had enough of my mother's complaints that I wasn't married yet, and when Gretchen's condescension suddenly became unbearable, I packed my suitcases and went back to Sydney. I made a mediocre impression in various offices and in the evening wrote in my diary in my new room in Bathurst, only to kill time. But it suited me that nobody knew me. I didn't know myself either.

Meeting Rigby again on Bellevue Hill was amusing. He's so smooth—love and hatred roll right off him. Miss Rigby was very proud of her "young talent." There was an illustrated article about my career and my best seller in the Sydney *Morning Herald* (Miss Rigby was related to the owner), and of course in the *Advertiser* and the *Adelaide News*. My friends at home could therefore read about me mornings and evenings. One of my finest moments was when I imagined Gretchen's face. We always want to prove to just one person that we're worth something. I was able to study Rigby's face after my triumph. I did so in Miss Rigby's reception room, and discovered only sincere pleasure at seeing me again. He was happy about my success, perhaps also about my red hair which went so well with my blue-green dress. *Who* was Rigby? I thought all night of the times he had once spent with me. Had he seen a second Lola Montez in Betty Withers? Years ago I had loved him naively and with exhausting passion. We lived together for six months. My provincial devotion must have bored him to death.

At the time Rigby let me go with two weeks notice because he sensed that I wanted to marry him. It's only fair to say that he had just recently been widowed and the scandal had to be lived down. Who would want to marry again when one's first wife had just died so tragically? I of course had the usual wish to get married. It had little to do with love but everything to do with the need for protection and security. I was in my third month. And the doctors in Macquarie Street don't make mistakes. I never tried to save money on doctors. Today Miss Rigby says I'm a hypochondriac and laughs herself silly over my various ailments. But at thirty things begin to go downhill.

After I had left the office with a sizable check, Rigby hired an older secretary with practical views and shoes. I sold costume jewelry, gloves, and cosmetics in a little shop on Pitt Street until shortly before the birth of the child. I didn't touch Rigby's check; the hospital was going to cost money. Once I saw Rigby's tall figure in front of the shop window of the little store. I was just selling a perfume for magical evenings and held up the small bottle like a fanfare as I found myself looking straight into Rigby's eyes. He stared back. Then he turned around and hurried away, and disappeared in one of the exotic little arcades. Was he afraid I'd run after him? In the whole episode, nothing seemed as unseemly to me as Rigby's hurry. He had been my hero; suddenly he was a man like any other. That this offended me beyond anything else was a result of my youthful innocence. Today, at cautious intervals, I pick up somebody on Bondi Beach, but my partners are temporary. After the first performance, they don't feel right. They want to be valued and praised for their favors. Fair enough, but still not good enough. Yet one can't live for *Insight* all the time. I wonder if Miss Rigby ever had a weak moment? Unthinkable!

Until his marriage to Anne Carrington, Rigby visited me twice a week in Bellevue Hill. He got his tea and his favorite pastries, and we talked. That's how I happen to know two or three of his faces. The wheel of time sometimes stood still in moments like those; sometimes it flew. I am writing my real novel, nothing saccharine. It will probably never be published. Rigby read the first ten chapters, then he got married in London. For *Insight* I write realistic stories with happy endings. The realism shows up only in the background material: Adelaide, Sydney, the bush in New South Wales and Queensland. Our subscribers want to feel firm Australian ground under their feet when they wander off into the land of beautiful dreams. I couldn't present them with a no-man's-land. They want to travel to where people are so much more attractive than on our sheep stations or in their shops or on their beaches. We are a rather monogamous and unromantic mob, but that doesn't mean that our girls and women don't dream just like their smarter and more skeptical sisters in other parts of the world. Yes, yes, I'll do the right thing by you! Hero and heroine get each other in the end, and the seducer or adventurer has to retire with his tail between his legs. The marriage is saved! Our readers can go on happily with their housework.

36

Miss Rigby doesn't know that years ago her brother and I conversed about Lola Montez in Pitt Street. And Alexander doesn't know that his child died soon after birth. He doesn't know anything at all about the brief existence of his son. I gave birth to his son without his knowledge, and buried the child without his assistance. If Miss Rigby knows anything about it, she doesn't say so. Apart from her unnerving love of order and superior knowledge, she is still the salt of the earth.

I never saw a brother and sister more unlike each other. She doesn't think much of Alexander, except for his talent. Of course we don't live in one of his houses; Miss Rigby would never spend that much money. We live in an old-fashioned villa with turrets and eaves, and a conventional reception room with many souvenirs from pioneer days. Our kitchen is American, and the bathrooms have a Roman luxury. The furnishings are up-to-date and lacquered. In our garden everything grows wildly, ivy climbs up the walls, and from the big veranda we have a view of the harbor. Rigby no doubt finds the house good enough, especially since the wide, shady verandas are in Colonial style, but he despises our esthetic indifference, and the stucco ornamentation on the roof and front door gives him cramps.

Do I hate Rigby? Why should I? He introduced me to pain, pushed me into deep waters and didn't throw me a life preserver. But through him I experienced the primeval night and the wild noon hour of nature. Sometimes he drew me gently into the magic circle of twilight in which homesteads and feelings dissolve and the Harbour Bridge is nothing but a gigantic steel ring, vibrant with music. I was with him on the wide, open plains, and under a deep blue sky looked at the faraway horizon, or we watched the moonlit flight of the bush birds in our lonely, violent woods.

Rigby prevented me from ever again living out of intellectual tin cans or looking through rose-colored spectacles. Without him my novels wouldn't have had a core of truth hidden under their obligatory icing. They would have ended in the wastepaper baskets of Adelaide and Alice Springs. Rigby forced me to see with my own eyes and to use my own words, not because he was particularly interested in me, but because he hated clichés. "Don't talk like a wooden parrot, Betty! Find your own damned words!" He was thirteen years older than I and had found his own lifestyle long ago. And his eyes weren't dimmed by love. Yet young, stupid and giddy as I was during that time in George Street, I could sense a silent conflict in Rigby. His taste and his need to be alone with mute material or with his birds conflicted with the Australian wish to simply be a good fellow among other good fellows. Not to be conspicuous. Not to be isolated from his cobbers by more talent or sensitivity. Today Rigby's dilemma is evident. He hurls himself with enthusiasm into the paradise of the average. Our Rigby is a rather difficult Australian . . .

It looks as if he still frequents the short-order kitchens of love. Things like that aren't important to him. He only needs a woman when he's completed a plan, and existence is suddenly as empty as the desert. And there always has to be a new woman. He mirrors himself in their eyes. He lives alone, a married bachelor, or spends his time with the mob. Australia was discovered for men. They feel best when they are among themselves. After we women have produced children, all we do is spoil the poor devils' fun. As soon as I had grasped that, I wouldn't have married Rigby, even if he'd given me a sack of black opals. To marry him meant to lose him, because he had all sorts of crazy ideas about freedom. He thinks that any marital consideration leads to slavery. In my opinion, with the right partner, it leads to freedom. But I didn't know that years ago when I gazed at the moon with Rigby. Beginners have such a hard time with love because they think it's so easy.

If I had married Rigby, I would have fallen into some sort of abyss, although not geographically as definable as, let's say, the Blue Mountains. I wonder if Alexander pushed the first Mrs. Rigby over the precipice because he needed her money, or was it because he couldn't stand her? Perhaps she stumbled and he only helped a little. I can easily imagine Alexander doing dark things when he just happens to have lost his moral balance. Rigby always was a gentle shocker.

Oddly enough, seven years ago, before he flew to London, he proposed to me. Evidently Betty Withers had changed to her advantage. But I wasn't a beginner any more. I knew a little something about the chasm between the sexes. I no longer expected love to be reciprocated. I knew better, whether the moon was shining or not. When Rigby proposed, I thought carefully of how I could turn him down and hurt him least. I didn't want to lose him as a friend. He meant too much to me. But I didn't want to jump in just because Rigby was suddenly sick of being alone. Otherwise why did he suddenly and so unexpectedly want to marry again? Was he getting old? But he was only forty-three at the time and even today is still much younger than I. Why did he suddenly, out of the blue, see happiness and rainbows over a hearth of one's own? I told him I had turned into an odd person and was afraid of marriage. He laughed. I asked him to forgive me for not appreciating the honor sufficiently. "Forget it," he mumbled sullenly. That was something I couldn't do on order. I can't forget good or bad things. His offer of marriage of course remained strictly between us two old Australians.

When Rigby brought his young English wife to Bellevue Hill for the first time, I had recovered from the surprise. His marriage had shocked me somewhat: again he had comforted himself with repulsive haste. I looked him straight in the eye for a second or two—he hadn't forgiven me. I don't know why he can't stand rejections of any kind; after all, nobody is spared them. In the next moment Rigby beamed at me and I beamed back, dutifully. Suddenly he seemed to me like someone seen in a dream. He stood before me, living, yet without substance. I knew that when I looked again, there'd be nothing but air. Anne Rigby was very pale, very beautiful, but she was frowning with tension, her eyes were lifeless, and her lips were closed tight. What was Rigby doing to her? Anne was a refined, unsuspecting girl from another world. Miss Rigby quite obviously intimidated her dreadfully, although she was very friendly to Rigby's new wife. You have to know Miss Rigby very well not to be intimidated by her. But she's a great old war horse!

Next week Alexander will be fifty! All the best . . .

I never met Flora Rigby, née Pratt. During those years I was witnessing Gretchen's marital happiness in Adelaide. When I came back to Sydney, Flora was already dust. Miss Rigby had lined a drawer with old newspaper that showed the first Mrs. Rigby before the accident. I looked at the picture for a long time. She was ridiculously over-dressed; she looked sly, vulgar, and somehow so tragic, it could make you weep. Somewhere under that flowered summer dress, which was much too youthful for her, a heart must have been beating. What had Alexander done to her?

A while ago Miss Rigby had a visitor, a girl from Parramatta. I don't like Molly Fleet. She is too busy minding other people's business. She is twenty-two, and in spite of her good figure and beautiful blond hair, she doesn't have a young man to invite her for ice cream or the movies. Unfortunately, with her birthmark, she doesn't exactly look appetizing. That is tragic in a city like Sydney where there are so many beautiful girls, the model Candy, for instance, who poses for fashions for city and bush in *Insight*. She is appetizing, all right.

Isn't it funny that Rigby has no idea that this girl from Parramatta knows him? I find it weird. She reminds me of a nightmare I had days ago in which I was being followed down Pitt Street by a lurking eye. When I turned around, the eye was gone.

Rigby doesn't know how often lately Molly Fleet has had her eyes on him. Miss Rigby doesn't like it. She told Molly Fleet that it couldn't possibly be her brother, it had to be someone who looked like him. Her brother had nothing to do in that section of Sydney. Miss Rigby also advised Molly to keep her mouth shut.

I don't know if I should warn Rigby. If the girl from Parramatta has mistaken him for someone else, how would Rigby take it? If there's anything he hates it's someone mixing in his affairs. And what concern is it of mine anyway? None at all.

4

Stanley F. Marchmont—Architect

"When Menelaus and his companions captured Proteus, he transformed himself in their hands into a lion, a leopard, a bear and a serpent. Then suddenly Proteus became a fountain, and after that a tree. Yet to those courageous men who held him captive throughout all his transformation, he finally had to confess the truth about himself."

CLASSIC TALES AND LEGENDS

After the Second World War, my old friend, Jonathan Rigby, brought his son Alexander to my office in George Street. Every word spoken by Jonathan was worth one Australian pound. He said, "There he is, Stan. Make something of him!" with which he shoved his bean pole of a son in my direction. It was the rainy season in New South Wales and the lights were on in our dark anteroom where later our famous Elizabeth West—at that time Betty Withers—worshiped Alex idiotically. He was very patient with her. He didn't fire her until she wept on the sketches and mixed up letters to contractors. We called little Betty "Sparrow." She must have gotten terribly on Alex's nerves. He was never a patient man, but he didn't fire her until none of us could stand her. Let's ring down the curtain on it. Alex is the best man in the world, a little difficult, perhaps, but only on holidays.

I looked at the young man. I liked what I saw. Young Rigby had graduated from the University of Sydney; his old man still lived in Parramatta.

Alex bowed almost imperceptibly. His eyes expressed a genial stubbornness, the Scottish dreams of his mother, and the burning wish to make a good impression on me. In this first hour he was determined to win my approval, come hell or high water. I pretended not to notice it, but somehow the young fellow touched me. He held his head, with its rebellious blond hair, lowered slightly, as if in this way he could better

41

hide his thoughts. "Will you take me on, Mr. Marchmont?" My appraisal was already taking too long to suit him.

He stood like a tree planted in my small office. When he stretched up full-length, his head touched the chandelier I had inherited. I nodded to Jonathan, he nodded back. Okay. Alex looked at the sketches and plans on the table with glowing eyes. We had a drink, and the matter was settled.

The first Rigby came to Australia as a stonemason, from some starvation area or other in Yorkshire. In Parramatta he built a little shack for his Scottish girl. Alex inherited his feeling for material from him. His long, strong fingers could sense the specific possibilities of glass, stone, iron, cement.

"What was it like at the university, young man?"

Alex threw back his head and laughed. "Boring! But you've got to go through with it. Now I know exactly what I *don't* want." He jumped up and stuck his long nose with the arrogant Rigby hook into my building plans.

"The young whippersnapper should be thankful that he could go to university," Jonathan growled. "*We* didn't have things that easy."

Alex pushed his tall old man aside, respectlessly but amiably. He had always loved his father, and later built the house in Balmoral for him. "I'm happy as a lark, Father." Suddenly he was silent. Then he stretched tall and said, "I will . . . I must . . ."

"Watch out for that chandelier, boy!" I cried, and both of us laughed. Alex found the electrified grapes very funny. The chandelier came from the old country. It had belonged to my grandmother. She had been very funny too.

I had all sorts of differences with young Rigby. In his wild soul the rascal nurtured the customary distaste for authority, and I happened to be the boss and pointed this out to him as gently as I could. I fired him four times. Four times he came back. I had no idea how he spent his time during his absence; probably in Taronga Park with the birds or in King's Cross with a sheila. That's what they called the young girls. Or he simply ran around studying the building styles in our city, the whole bit, from classic Colonial, past Victorian Gothic to modern.

When Alex turned up again several weeks later with a long face, and had his demon so far in control that he could at least show a respect he probably didn't feel, I didn't make things easy for him. No. I let him sweat blood. He had to apologize in one way or another, or he could look at the office from the outside. When he came back for a fourth time, a cool wind was blowing in the office in spite of the November heat. Before his last exodus, the young man had thrown my English porcelain teapot against the wall. I was attached to my teapot, and I hated broken china as a form of argument.

Alex put a silver teapot down on my desk. "This one can take a bounce or two, Boss," he said, grinning, embarrassed, and careful not to bump against the chandelier. I grimaced, but the hell with it, I was glad that the blond pup would be around again.

"I am waiting for an apology," I said stonily, ignoring the teapot for the moment. It happened to be just the sort of thing I liked.

Alex mumbled something—a lip reader might have been able to read an apology into it—then he laid down three sketches in front of me. I didn't look up so as not to have to look into his imploring eyes. So . . . I silently accepted his garbled apology. After all, you couldn't expect chicken meat from an ox!

The plans for a high-rise house in Potts Point and two villas for the bays were bold and precise. Even as a green lad, Alex was already a visionary. His designs reflected the two aspects of our city—the industrial landscape and the timeless, idyllic waterfront. I looked at the boy surreptitiously. No doubt about it, he had the secret of creativity. Like Proteus, he could change his shape. He became the tower he was building, the wide windows facing the sea, the stairs, the garden that was to frame the house. I pushed the teapot aside. "Why is the gate on this side?"

Alex reddened right up to the roots of his hair, but he swallowed my objection like a lamb. He stared at his sketch sullenly but intently. Finally he entered the change I had suggested with a red pencil. "Thank you, Boss. You're quite right." I didn't want any thanks. All we two wanted was good buildings for Sydney and New South Wales. We drank our reconciliatory beer. Alex beamed. Not a care in the world. He was back in his stable. I thanked him for the teapot.

Alex a woman chaser? Ridiculous! Where would he find the time for such amorous nonsense? Even during his brief marriage to Flora Pratt he spent most of his weekends and evenings with me. We sailed on his yacht around the sprawling harbor; we spent hours in Botany Bay where James Cook started the history of our land in the eighteenth century. I knew a lot about the first colony. The Marchmonts came to New South Wales with the Rigbys. Alex listened. They were happy hours for me. And during our excursions, Alex saw the architectural development of our city as if in a gigantic picture book. That was necessary for his development. He who wants to build the houses of the future must know the stones of the past.

On our trips we never mentioned Alex's marriage, but a young man who always has time for his friends can't be enjoying a fulfilled marital relationship. Alex strode through the streets—a race horse that had shaken off all reins, I thought sometimes. He looked at buildings and parks with mute, consuming participation. His love for the pure, unadorned line originated in these hours. He absorbed everything that bore the signature of Francis Greenway, our famous Colonial architect: churches, hospitals, the Hyde Park barracks. Alex loved the lyrical grace of Greenway's best buildings and the noble Georgian lines. But he was striving for a new classicism of the future. He admired Greenway as an example of his period. Ah yes, a convict like that, who had so quickly become government architect under Governor Macquarie, didn't land in Sydney Cove every day! Greenway was a Bristol man. Like the Rigbys, his ancestors had been English stonemasons and architects. It was a lucky day for Sydney when Francis Greenway had been caught forging promissory notes.

Alex wandered past Victorian buildings and statues. There was a house in Pitt Street overloaded with Victorian ornamentation. Alex called it "the wedding kitchen." Sometimes he would stop dead during our walks or travels through the suburbs, and take notes, stretched up tall in the sun, staring across the harbor and the bridge. He had a very personal relationship to the Harbour Bridge. He never spoke of his love for Sydney, but nodded contentedly, like a lover who can see his beloved over and over again without every tiring of her.

He wanted to transform the city, but he didn't know yet that Sydney was transforming him. All of us became a part of this centipede on the sea.

I lived through the scandal with Rigby. He continued to come to the office, but he wasn't really there. For the first time he laid his plans aside with indifference and stared down at George Street. "She is dead." That was all he said.

Evening after evening John Darling and I sat with him on the wide, empty terrace in Vaucluse. Sometimes Robbie French joined us. The Blue Mountains, where Flora had met her death, were all around us, a harsh memorial wall. We kept Alex company, not because he was so disconsolate but because the scandal had washed over him like a tidal wave. From one day to the next, the darling of the yacht club was isolated in a way that happens usually only among schoolboys. The press pounced on him and the police interrogations were no help. He was stubbornly silent, and we said only what was necessary. What was there to say?

Granted, I hadn't cared much for the aging bar girl with her tinny laugh. Alex never admitted to more than fifteen years difference in their age, but Miss Rigby told me that Flora Pratt was twenty-two years older than Alex. It was nobody's business. If Alex wanted a mama, why not? He wasn't the only one looking for a mother in marriage. But all the time the glowing fire of our continent was raging in him. In the open-air cage of Vaucluse, his eyes must have been following the flight of the bush birds . . . How had he been able to stand this marriage? Or . . . hadn't he been able to stand it? All my feelings, my knowledge of Rigby's creative powers, protested against this uncivilized suspicion. But hadn't Greenway, the forger, also created immortal monuments in this city?

I don't know if Alex knew what I was thinking. We were closer than most colleagues. I loved the fellow, goddammit! And I knew he was fond of me.

He stared out at the woods and the bays. His eyes were strangely empty. There had always been something of the restlessness of the wild black bush cockatoo in him. When the wilderness rose up in him, he always spoke softly. Then his voice crept like a tiger around the room. Once Alex appeared in George Street with a black eye. He had walked into something . . . Alex, who had the agility of the lifeguards on the beach? Then he had laughed suddenly, just as on the first day, when Jonathan Rigby had shoved him over to me. "I had a little difference of opinion with Flora." So *she* had given him the black eye. But what had he done to her? He didn't say and I didn't ask. Miss Rigby had already told me that the two were constantly having little "differences." Had they had a little difference in the Blue Mountains on the edge of a precipice? This in spite of the fact that I despised the virtuous mob in the yacht club because they thought it might have been murder, and talked about it in all the bars in the city. If he ever wanted to marry again, he wouldn't find a girl in Sydney. Not in all New South Wales! News travels fast in our gigantic nest.

I shall never forget those evenings in Vaucluse. We three could just as well have been traveling through the bush at night, a hundred years ago, with our blankets and our billy. Nothing but sky, eucalyptus trees, and three cobbers. We knew that one is born alone and dies alone, and we carried this stern wisdom together.

The harbor ferries plied slowly back and forth. The traces of their lights were swallowed up by the water. The Macquarie light tower cast its white beams from the foothills thirty miles into the night. Our young widower looked dark and stubborn. "Poor old thing," he murmured. "She did her best. Who wants some more beer?"

These few words in memory of the first Mrs. Rigby were sparse enough, but Alex had managed to get them out. After that he was silent again, until he gave me a sardonic look. "Do you think I'm glad she's dead? Go ahead. Think I'm a stinking murderer. I don't give a damn what you think, you old kangaroo."

Of course I ignored the look and what he said, as I always ignored Rigby's shamelessness. That brought him to his senses quicker than anything else. Right then he looked as if he'd like to smash something.

I never doubted that young Rigby had found Flora's money attractive. As long as I've known him, he's always been able to make wonderful use of any kind of capital. Not for his own needs—he has none—but for his plans and constructions. At the time his friends from the yacht club had been astonished when Alexander Rigby had married a shopworn bar girl with varicose veins, flowered hats, and a juicy vocabulary, since he was known for his esthetic commitment. But the mob didn't fuss about it for long and soon enjoyed playing cards with Mrs. Rigby now and then, exchanging dirty jokes and drinking beer with her. Alexander's presence wasn't necessary. Flora stood behind the counter, fat, rouged, and good-humored, as she was accustomed to. The villa in Vaucluse began to look like a tavern.

Miss Rigby was very decent to Flora, but these two Sydney exhibits were about as suited to each other as a falcon and a kookaburra. It was ridiculous, particularly because it was generally agreed that most old Australians got along well together. Without the aborigines and the immigrants of all colors and creeds, there would be no friction.

Miss Rigby knew her duty to the new family member and doggedly tried to think of it when plagued by dark thoughts. Too bad that the dialogue between Miss Rigby and Flora Pratt never made the stage.

Flora's visits to the *Insight* offices in Philip Street were a farce. *That* was a street she knew well. That was where the stupid, unfair police, who begrudged every dinkum Aussie his bit of beer and gambling, had their headquarters. Flora was a good poker player, and she could drink like a fish. But she held her fat fingers so tightly around her purse that Alex reddened whenever Flora mentioned money at any parties on the north shore. He also often had to pour her into the car in an inebriated condition, and take her home.

When Flora began to appear more and more often in the *Insight* offices, chattering with anyone waiting there for an interview—sometimes the waiting room rocked with laugher—Miss Rigby finally had to ask her to discontinue her visits. Miss Rigby would visit her once a week in Vaucluse, and she was as good as her word. She visited "Alexander's aunt," as the mob called the first Mrs. Rigby, every week, not without affection, and let the endless flow of Flora's words pass over her for exactly one hour, after which Grace Rigby drove to her club in Elizabeth Street, satisfied with her good deed. She never discussed Flora with anybody, not even with Alexander. But when the young man turned up at the office looking green, I'd ask Miss Rigby what in God's name was wrong in Vaucluse again. Then she'd tell me what a sobbing Flora had told her. Miss Rigby didn't feel sorry for Alex; the fool had paid no attention to her warnings. Miss Rigby hated it when her advice was ignored. Thousands of her readers obeyed her— why not Alex? If she felt sorry for him in spite of this, she probably stifled her feelings alone on her Bellevue Hill veranda.

Only once did she interfere. Alex had beaten Flora up so badly that she had been immobilized for days. She told Miss Rigby during her weekly visit that the "pig" had tried to kill her. And then he'd have her money! The poor woman was in a state of panic and seemed deathly afraid of her young husband. She disappeared from Vaucluse for several weeks and took up residence in her old quarters in Redfern. Alex went and brought her back. I implored him to treat his wife more gently, but he said a good beating was the only argument that made any impression on the old bitch. And laughed mirthlessly. If I hadn't been so horrified over his brutality, I would have felt sorry for him. He walked out of my office whistling and proceeded to make life hell for French. All with his mean, soft speech and his tiger eyes. French had had just about enough of Alex that day, although ordinarily he admired him with youthful enthusiasm. Alex liked the young man. A pity he couldn't beat him up too.

After Flora's death, Miss Rigby said compassionately, "She did so enjoy life. And what's left of it? A sackful of bones." The Rigby family expressed themselves emotionally about any tragedy. But Miss Rigby also told her younger brother not to give a damn about the scandal, and that was very decent of her, especially since no one knew what she was really thinking.

The old "aunt" had left Alexander, for better or for worse, such a fortune that, after a fitting lapse of time, we had to order a new sign: Marchmont & Rigby, and we moved to a better section of George

Street. Alex could spend money freely for the first time. He is lavish, and had already visualized the new office while he was beating up his old wife.

Robbie French is our new partner, an exceptionally nice young man, just as old as Alex was when Jonathan brought him to my office. Now Alex is making an architect of him. Robbie is the nephew of S. W. French, the General Motors–Holden people. So he has a golden background, round astonished eyes, and his own stubbornness. He likes statues for gardens and terraces.

He started out in life as a sculptor. Alex gave one of his statues the name *Weeping Susie*. She had two tiny heads, and unlike the statue of Queen Victoria in front of the post office, no clothes on at all. French wanted to send *Weeping Susie* off to a park in Rose Bay, where we had built a villa, but Alex went wild. Robbie hates to work for nothing, and besides, he needed the money. He still had quite a few homeless nudes from his sculpture period. Principally we had nothing against ladies with more than one head, and would have tolerated any gyrations in clay or stone if they had grown on Robbie's own stamping ground. But anyone could see that *Weeping Susie* and all the others were the result of the undigested life of an artist in Paris. Alex almost gave in as his favorite pupil wiped the sweat off his smooth, innocent forehead. The west wind was blowing, and it was infernally hot in the office without the struggle over *Weeping Susie*. "*You* ask your client if he wants your *Weeping Susie* whimpering here." Alex pointed to a secluded area on his sketch. "Of course we'll plant a lot of shrubs around her. And that's that, Robbie. I don't want to hear another word about *Susie!*" French swallowed happily. "And now may I get back to my work?"

Weeping Susie stands to this day in the park in Rose Bay, behind bushes and flower beds. The unsuspecting owners are even proud of her. And Alex said young French was going to be A-okay, and *Weeping Susie* could have been worse.

It has been a great joy to me to see Rigby training our new employees. These young men are to go on building when we have to leave our drawing boards. Alex has built a shed at home where he discusses ideas and ground plans with anyone who wants to, and he does it patiently and amiably. Today his dynamic ambition is a socially oriented power. Only the very best is good enough for the Sydney of the future he pounds into his young pupils. I consider it a privilege to have witnessed Alex's development. I did little for him. It is he who has the ability to make a vision technically useful.

Nowadays I mostly watch. The firm has grown, there are a lot of employees. The apprentices sweat on the third floor. I am seventy-four, an old bird perched contentedly on my terrance in Mosman Bay. One of my ancestors knew Archibald Mosman and told me about his whaling days. As a boy I would have liked above everything else to roam the South Pacific like Mosman and come home to our bay with oil and whalebone. Of course Mosman wasn't only an adventurer but also a very smart businessman. That he had from his Scottish ancestors, but doing business was easier in 1829 than it is today. Still, in 1840, everybody went broke because of the depression. We did too. My father had to start all over again. That's not unusual in our country. All water over the dam now. But I think of a lot of things when I look out at the bay and see the ferryboats plying toward Circular Quay.

Today I like nothing better than to watch my flowers. Wouldn't mind doing it until I'm ninety-five. I think Alex would too. We have done splendidly together. Alex still asks my advice when any important problems come up. Nobody would believe how much delicate feeling hides in that robust man. Once a week I go to the office. My doctor on Macquarie Street won't let me do more. Bertie grumbles—he wants to do something for his money. Splendid young man! We built a house in Avalon for James Dobson—he's Bertie's old man.

Miss Rigby likes young Anne. Of course she comes from quite another drawer than fat, funny Flora, but something's wrong in that marriage too. It can't be Alex's fault. To be sure he is restless, and the women always were after him. That's not his fault. No, no, I won't have anything said against Alex. And I said so to his dear sister the other day, just between us, at our weekly dinner together.

I'd like to know what she has against her brother. A good thing I swallowed my proposal that time in Windsor when Grace Rigby was showing me the historical houses there. Don't know what came over me. We would have quarreled constantly over Alex. I was too old for her anyway. Forget it! And *Insight* would have been a blight on our marriage. Not that Grace isn't a nice, reliable person even if she does know everything better than anyone else. When she keeps her mouth shut, she's still almost beautiful today. She always reminds me of French's *Diana* statue. I mean the figure, of course. French's *Diana* squints and her nose is crooked. But if he likes her, what do I care? Miss Rigby is fifty-seven now, and Alex will be fifty next week. Hard to believe when you see him surfing.

When I occasionally eat in Bellevue, Miss Rigby serves a good solid meal. No esoteric decorations for me! But I find the steep steps in her garden a bit difficult lately. Grace and young Betty West, née Withers, come running to meet me when Charles drives me there. Then we walk up the steps slowly. One gets the feeling that one's moving between walls of flowers. Nice girls, both of them. Very friendly to the old man.

I brought my chauffeur from Hobart with me when I was visiting friends. Charles Preston's real name is Carlo Pressolini, but he gets furious when you remind him of it. New Australians are more Australian than our kangaroos and emus. Charles drives well; one has to in today's traffic. His moods are no concern of mine. He can't dish them up to me. His people come from Genoa. He has relatives in Tasmania. The Italians are terribly family conscious, cling to each other like leeches. Not like us, thank God!

Miss Rigby told me something funny, and she knows what she's talking about. This girl from Parramatta is supposed to have told her something about Alex. She is Anne Rigby's masseuse. If she makes any trouble there, I'll have it out with this goddamned sheila personally. All of us have had more than enough of gossip about Alexander. What does this girl with the birthmark want in Sydney anyway? Of what concern is the birthmark to Miss Rigby? The girl should go back to Parramatta. Sydney is overpopulated as it is. It *must* be a mistake. What could Alex possibly want in *that* neighborhood? When he isn't with me, he's conversing with his birds in Taronga Park. He can sketch birds wonderfully—he has almost too many talents.

I must *not* listen to women's gossip. How right I was not to propose that time. Who can stand living with the same woman all his life? Alex seems to have had enough of married life again. At the time I thought he was crazy when he wired his engagement to Anne. But I will ask Alex if there's an element of truth in this bit of gossip. The boy was always rash. He'll probably laugh and I'll forget it. He's done a lot of crazy things over the years, but he's never lied to me. Alex wouldn't do anything like that to this old man.

5

Monologues of Some New Australians

Hungarian Rhapsody
Mary Andrews, née Margit Berzsenyi, housekeeper. Sydney.

In a few days Mr. Rigby will be fifty years old and we are giving a party. The new Mrs. Rigby is giving me a lot of superfluous advice in her pommy voice. Of course I don't obey a single one of her orders, or what would become of us?

She was a stenographer in London before she married my master. She knows neither our land nor her husband, and she ignores my daughter and me. For that God will punish her. My, Mr. Rigby does his best to cheer up this morose woman. What a wonderful man he is! But what was he thinking of when he married her? I almost fell flat on my face when he wrote from London that he had become engaged. At once I prayed to the Holy Mother to stand by my poor master. If he didn't have iron nerves—in spite of the fact that he is so gentle, and at least in my kitchen is a little cheerful—what would we do? My daughter Daisy—actually her name is Julika—worships Mr. Rigby. She is still only a child, but she knows when she's treated well. I would kiss the hand of our benefactor, but in this country that isn't done.

I have only been in Australia seventeen years and am therefore a very new Australian, but the second Mrs. Rigby is even newer. Yet she has my master, his house, his money, and his social position. She might also have his love if she tried harder. I suppose she thinks that would be beneath her—the fool! My poor master sometimes looks terribly worried. All of us suffer from her nagging. "Why didn't you put fresh flowers in my room, Mrs. Andrews?" or the fruit juice is too warm, or too cold, or too sweet, or too sour. If I didn't love my fellow man, I could gladly poison the second Mrs. Rigby. Then all of us would have peace, and eventually Mr. Rigby would marry my daughter. But perhaps heaven will have mercy and remove the second Mrs. Rigby in a natural way. Her backache and headaches must mean a weak constitution unless she's trying to attract my master's attention with them. But if she is, she's on the wrong track. Rigby hates invalids. I asked Molly Fleet today if Mrs. Rigby's back pains were worse. The girl from Parramatta said, with a very fresh glance at me, "Would you like that, Mrs. Andrews?" I turned my back on her. I hope she noticed that I consider it beneath me to react to such suspicions. But in this country they all think they can do whatever they like with us new Australians. Molly Fleet probably didn't even notice how insulted I was. The people here have no sensitivity. That fresh masseuse has already been punished by heaven with a birthmark. In Hungary people used to be very suspicious of anything like that. Good Christians don't have the fiery hand of Satan on their faces!

I wouldn't be surprised if the second Mrs. Rigby didn't end up in a wheelchair. She already walks quite stooped, a young woman of thirty-five! At that age I could uproot trees. Unfortunately I had to get out of Hungary just at that time. First we had the Nazis, then the Communists. That was a bit too much for my poor fatherland. It doesn't look as if Julika and I could ever go home again. So I've got to be satisfied with Vaucluse.

Once, before his English marriage, I asked Mr. Rigby if he wouldn't like to live in Europe, in Paris, for instance, where I once studied for two semesters. At that time my parents still had their estate, and every well-brought-up Hungarian learned French. Rigby laughed as if I'd made a huge joke. "Away from Australia? Are you crazy, Mary? This is the best land in the world!" I said nothing. He gave me a sharp look and said, "Aren't you happy here, old girl?" In the evening he brought me a box of chocolates. As the tears of gratitude welled up in my eyes he hurried out to the veranda. He can't abide tears. The box of chocolates was packaged in quilted silk. It's faded today, but it still stands on my beside table, beside my prayer book.

Why does such a wonderful man have such bad luck in marriage? I must admit, he's rather naive. How can one be happy in this country if one has lived in Hungary? Of course the Rigby's were born here and don't know any better, although Mr. Rigby was in Paris shortly before he became engaged to this Anne Carrington. That's where he must have gone off his head, the poor man. What would he do without me?

I noticed right after landing that Australia was too bright. I don't nag like Mrs. Rigby; I've always been known for my good-naturedness. "You are a too soft and generous soul," the father of my child said, shortly before the Russian occupation of Budapest. Of course it was sheer good-naturedness on my part that in the general rush I still let this doomed man give me a child. Yet I did not complain. The second Mrs. Rigby should take me as an example. But then she would have to pay more attention to me, and that would be too much trouble. She is the laziest woman I have ever known. In these seven years she hasn't even produced a son and heir for Marchmont, Rigby & French. I know that my benefactor is deeply disappointed in her. But he hasn't even complained about it to me, his old confidante. I can't understand it. The poor man needs someone to comfort him. But men never know what's good for them. There's nothing new about that. My student's name, by the way, was Ando. That's why I called myself Andrews when all Australia refused to pronounce my family name.

Without wanting to find fault, Australia is not only too bright, but the contours are too sharp. They stab like daggers. And I don't like Mr. Rigby's buildings. He may be a genius, but I prefer a real Hungarian castle with turrets and gables. The whole mishmash of Sydney is held together by Harbour Bridge, a not–very–pleasing sight. Sometimes I think if only the bridge would collapse and Mrs. Rigby would just be . . . But I must not think like that! I wish her all the best. She needs it.

To mention a very small objection I have to my new home: I miss all the talk in Budapest. Here I am reduced to holding monologues. Of course I could get together with my compatriots over here, but most of them are uneducated animals, and the few intellectuals are so critical of Sydney that their crass lack of gratitude vexes me. In the home where they settled us at first I cried every night over the miserable behavior of my compatriots. The home was of course wretched, but good enough for us. "Immigrants who make demands are ridiculous," I said to my grumbling fellow Hungarians, and Mr. Szabo threw a ripe tomato in my face. I sought and found solace in prayer, and in the botanical gardens, which are really beautiful. Mrs. Szabo and the others complained that they didn't have any money for shopping; their dear children would starve here. That was scandalous! We had enough to eat to keep us from starving, and I told my compatriots that immigrants couldn't expect chicken with wine sauce. And I prefer to draw the curtain of Christian love over what Mr. Szabo had to say to that. For weeks I couldn't bring myself to pray for the Szabo family, but then I told myself there had to be pigs in God's farmyard too, and I begged the Blessed Virgin to stand by these dreadful people. And my prayers were heard. Today Mr. Szabo has a big Hungarian restaurant in King's Cross and is loaded with money. Although everything he has, he has thanks to my prayers, I still have to pay for every meal when I feel like eating Hungarian food on my day off. Although the Szabos tell everybody what good Australians they are, they are just as inhospitable as they were in the immigration station. They had money at the time from relatives in America, who were quite right in wishing the Szabos at the other end of the world. Mrs. Szabo used to buy all sorts of goodies which the family ate with satisfaction in our presence. Not that I would ever have accepted anything from them, but they certainly should have offered us something. When I think how generously my parents treated even unwelcome guests! And the Szabos had come over with their passage paid in part by the Australian government! I had too, but I am grateful and satisfied with everything.

Unfortunately there is a great lack of intellectual activity in New South Wales. There are no animated conversations here as there were in Budapest, except about the price of wool and sports events, and no discussion at all about the eternal values of life. My daughter's father was studying philosophy in Budapest, and over our coffee we used to have discussions in which our intellects embraced. *That* you won't find here! The Aussies lack elegance when it comes to pairing in bed, and that's that. The men here have a primitive aversion to talking to their female partners. Their inherited collective ideal is the sheep in feminine form.

No wonder Miss Rigby and Miss West decided they could do without such partners. I admire both ladies, although with all due respect I have a few things to say against them. They pay too little attention to metaphysics. When I mentioned this to Miss Rigby, she said that first things came first, for instance the problem of the men finding work, and the women and children learning English. But Mrs. Laszlo and Miss Karasz came back to the home weeping from the English classes the government had arranged for them. They had been treated like ignoramuses! And Miss Karasz can write poems, and Mrs. Laszlo is clairvoyant and can do invisible mending! Why does Miss Rigby complain all the time about the lack of skilled workers among the Hungarians in Sydney? Aren't poems anything? Is a look into the obscure future worth nothing? Miss West gave the hopeless ones private lessons in English, but she didn't seem to be very patient, because the children often came running to me in tears. I taught them Hungarian, and all about Hungarian literature, so that they wouldn't forget our beautiful country. Poor children! After class the Misses Rigby and West often had tea with us, and once Miss Karasz recited a poem, in our language, of course. Whereupon the Misses Rigby and West left rather hurriedly. But they are really very kind to our little ones, and twice a week Miss

54

West goes swimming with them. I wonder when she writes her novels? This author swims too much!

In Sydney they simply have no neighborly feelings. Nobody asks anybody how they are, what their ideas are, or about their love life. Mr. Rigby never asked me with whom I lived in Hungary and what I had done there. What a paradise his married life could have been if he had conquered his specific needs and married me years ago! But he couldn't make up his mind to do so, and I was very careful not to bring up the subject.

At the time, seventeen years ago, his first wife had just died. He needed someone to look after him, and I needed someone to protect me against the unknown perils of Australia. Sometimes the good spirits of this youthful widower astounded me, but I noticed right away that he was conforming to the customary aversion to emotional demonstrations. But today I am again sometimes astonished over how cheerful my benefactor is, in spite of his dreadful marriage. When the mob meets in Vaucluse, they laugh and joke until late into the night. The second Mrs. Rigby goes to bed instead of looking after her guests. All that falls upon me. But what wouldn't I do for my Mr. Rigby! I would serve beer and make sandwiches until late into the night even if I was dead tired, which I usually am. After all, I'm over fifty now. But when the housewife sleeps, the housekeeper has to be up!

Actually Mr. Rigby must be feeling desperate. The second Mrs. Rigby makes life hell for him. She is always tired, something is always wrong, she sits on the veranda all the time with Miss Cox or Professor Darling. In Hungary there would have been something going on between those two long ago, but Professor Darling has ice water in his veins. With Mrs. Rigby I'm not so sure. The pale silent ones usually run deep. She's very young and would be very pretty if she didn't have such a sour expression. Mr. Rigby ignores it, just as he ignores the other tragic aspects of his marriage. Like all Australians, he doesn't want to suffer. I very soon noticed that in this country everybody flees from the pangs of the soul. It's a collective flight, and I consider it quite possible that one day a mass nervous breakdown will attack these cheerful people. But let's hope for the best.

My English is very good, still sometimes shopkeepers and uneducated people find it funny. English is a horrible, unmusical language. What would the Aussies do in Hungary? Or if Australia became an Asiatic colony? Nobody knows today where he'll have to emigrate to some day. Let's hope my master stays here, since he thinks this country is the best in the world.

When we immigrants came to Sydney seventeen years ago, we were received with friendliness. The Australians got on my nerves right way, but I must admit that my nerves weren't perhaps in the best shape any more. Anyway, I found the Australians too rough and unnaturally cheerful, but they did try to make us feel at home on the fifth continent. We were even served tea in some city hall or other, with perfectly terrible cookies. As I said, the Aussies did their best.

Later Miss Rigby spoke to us in a club for European immigrants, looking down on us a little perhaps, but that may have had something to do with her extraordinary height. She had brought along copies of *Insight*, a new magazine in those days, and like every native Australian, a sackful of good advice. We should try to change our way of thinking and former habits as quickly as possible. (Just try it! I thought.) In that way we would become real Australians all the more quickly, she said sternly. The inhabitants of this fifth continent, wanted to help us to do so. It sounded as if the Australians were the crowning achievement of creation. When compared with our poor, confused heap of humanity, they could feel that way. Miss Rigby then said at the tea table, where I had the honor of sitting next to her, something I shall never forget. Very cautiously she made it clear to us that we could not live in a new country under protest, and that we could only achieve the social recognition everybody needed if we grew to be part of the country. I said shyly, in my broken English, that this was easier said than done, and Miss Rigby agreed. I found this so wonderful of her, I could have kissed her hand.

Perhaps it is part of my nature that I always anticipate insults, but this trait of mine has taken on extraordinary proportions in Australia. Perhaps every immigrant is too thin-skinned but I must have lost six skins on my way over. I became suspicious. I had guilt feelings toward my hosts. Perhaps I hated accepting things from others; in my homeland I would have treated the Aussies royally.

Miss Rigby got me the job with her brother. At first I was so confused and exhausted by the heat that I broke Rigby's teacups, one after the other. He was very friendly and considerate. When I said, "Punish me, sir," he laughed and said, "I wouldn't dream of it, or you'll punish me with your cooking!" He never treated me like a slave. An intellectual housekeeper from Budapest with a fatherless child, or the wife of a minister from Canberra—they were all the same to him.

At the time Alexander Rigby was thirty-three. His youth probably helped him over the death of his first wife; anyway he seemed rather offensively genial to me. After all, the first Mrs. Rigby had fallen off a precipice before his very eyes. Miss Rigby had told me about it before introducing me to her brother. She brought me to Vaucluse herself. She didn't want me to spend the few shillings I had on a taxi. It was very friendly of her, but *when* did she work?

At first I couldn't find my way around this chaotic city. Harbour Bridge grinned at me from every direction. When I think of our Elizabeth Bridge! How intimate, how old, how noble! Well of course, Budapest wasn't built in a hurry.

Perhaps, deep down in his heart and in spite of his good humor, Mr. Rigby was grieving for his first wife. Perhaps people grieve differently in this sunny land. In the entire house in Vaucluse there wasn't a single picture of Flora Rigby. Probably my benefactor had loved his wife so much that a picture of her would have magnified his sorrow unbearably. After all, it was only years later that he married again. Poor man! He deserved a better wife.

Shortly after I had begun my employment in Vaucluse and Alexander Rigby began to eat my food with great enjoyment, a conversation took place between us. I was about to remove the empty platter of Szegediner goulash when, to my astonishment, he grabbed my arm. "Very nice, Mary."

"Thank you, sir. I do my best. I wasn't born a cook."

"I didn't mean the goulash; I meant you!"

My sense of refinement balks when I try to recapitulate what happened next, but without further ado, Mr. Rigby pinched my behind. I screamed and drew back, and the goulash platter fell at his feet. I stood up very straight. "Excuse me, sir, but you have no right to insult me just because I had to immigrate to this country!"

"What's the matter with you, woman? I was just paying you a compliment."

I was speechless. I wasn't accustomed yet to Australian jokes. Rigby leaned down and wanted to pick up the platter; I lunged forward and our heads collided. He thought this was very funny and laughed. I put the platter back on the table without saying a word.

"Why so funereal, Mary? What have I done this time?"

"I am in deep mourning, sir."

"So am I. And I need cheering up."

I had to think of my daughter's father, whom the communists had murdered. Granted, he had sometimes driven me crazy because he'd say his favorite sayings to me over and over again, but the dead are right because they are dead.

"Good night, sir."

"Where did you get your beautiful blond hair from anyway?"

"Good night, sir."

Mr. Rigby jumped up and took me roughly in his arms. In Hungary when one wants to seduce a woman one tells her first that one is interested only in her mind and soul. The rest then follows quite naturally. Nothing makes a woman so acquiescent to the physical side of love as a conversation about mind and soul. Naturally Rigby couldn't be interested in my mind since he didn't know that I did occasionally think. He believed only in what he saw. I didn't defend myself in his arms; I was much too run-down in spirits. He kissed me, not without passion, and unfortunately, after a proper moment of hesitation, I kissed him back.

"That's better, girl. Much better."

He let go of me abruptly. "Breakfast tomorrow morning at 7:00 on the dot. Good night."

He walked off into his studio. I stared at his broad back and his rebellious shock of hair. My knees were trembling. I crept off to my veranda and stared at the acacia tree. That night he came to me.

He was so experienced that even his routine seemed spontaneous. That a man and a woman sleep together and call it love is nothing new, but Alexander Rigby gave me an absolutely oceanic feeling, and this ocean carried me away from my mundane life. I don't know if he gives other women this feeling; anyway, that's none of my business. Perhaps ecstasy can be just as repetitious as cleaning vegetables.

Our affair lasted four months, three weeks, two days and one hour. This last hour, which he kept from me, seemed longer than the four months. The ocean is an infamous invention; when it spits us out, we're in no-man's-land again. I had been through difficult times before Alexander Rigby admired my hair, but now I learned what it meant to have absolutely nothing. Rigby once showed me some pictures of the Northern Territory—they call it the dead heart of Australia. Now I didn't have to travel to the Outback any more. No desert could be more deserted than my every day life. I lived from one day to the next in a shabby landscape where everybody looked alike. Yes, I lived in the Outback. That was my big Australian experience: endless monotony, dried up riverbeds, unslaked thirst and crippled trees under a merciless sky. I prayed like the early settlers in biblical territory, but the desert wind blew sand into my throat.

Of course women were embraced and deserted in Budapest, too. When we bored our men they sought other pastures. We didn't behave differently when we wanted another man or to be left in peace. But in the old Europe such ugly separations were accompanied by beautiful farewell speeches and a few final, tactful words. The men of course didn't mean a word they were saying, and we certainly didn't believe we were suddenly too good for the joys of the flesh. In love one believes only a yes or a no, yet this old-fashioned ceremony saves the self-respect of both parties. It is certainly just as important as pinching behinds and kissing.

Alexander didn't desire me any more. Perhaps I had been too intense. Perhaps not. Anyway, the fun was over. I waited for him night after night, idiot that I was! Once I even crept into his bedroom, but it was empty. Next day, in silent fury, I threw a bottle of his after-shave lotion on the kitchen floor. Rigby happened to come into the kitchen to tell me that he was going to dine at home, but I'd just taken his apple strudel out of the oven and he ate it like a little boy, straight from the wooden board. "What's stinking of musk here?" he asked. I was red with fury. He picked up the broken bottle and looked at it thoughtfully while I washed the dishes. Then he passed his hand across my hair and said, "Forgive me, but we couldn't go on like that." Then he got into his car and raced off to the city.

I wallowed rapturously in my wounds. I told myself a) Rigby hadn't deserved my love, b) he had a heart of stone, and c) he loved someone else. And then of course, d) he'd come back to me. The latter couldn't have been more foolish, but it gave me great pleasure to dream, in my kitchen, how Alexander Rigby would crawl on his knees before me and beg for my love. After a year had gone by I realized that this satisfactory scene would never come to pass. So gradually I became "Rigby's jewel." I needed money and a roof over my head. Miss Rigby would have considered me ungrateful if I had given notice, and where could I find refuge in this alien city? The real reason why I stayed, of course, was deeper: life with Alexander wasn't simple, but life without him was unthinkable! The daily sight of him was pleasant torture. Once, in a foul mood, I burnt his sacred dinner. He threw his napkin on the table, drove to King's Cross in a rage, and ate at the restaurant of my enemy, Szabo. He was crazy about Hungarian food, no doubt about it. The following week Mr. Szabo winked and asked me if the famous architect didn't like my cooking any more. That's my good compatriot for you!

When Rigby turned away from me, I tried going on a hunger strike. I arranged it so that I fainted in his presence. He stretched me out on a chaise lounge, shoved a pillow under my head, and poured so much water over my face that I preferred to wake up. "What's the matter?" he asked impatiently when he saw my tears. "Are you pregnant?" I shook my head. His sigh of relief didn't escape me. As a consolation prize he gave me a large opal. I never wear it.

Until his second marriage, Alexander talked a lot of things over with me. Since his brain was no longer befogged by passion, he noticed that I could think too. But since he has married again, he doesn't need me anymore. The second Mrs. Rigby can't stand me. That amuses me.

A while ago the masseuse from Parramatta looked at a photo of Rigby and began to laugh. Mrs. Rigby was on the phone in the next room. I watched Molly Fleet from behind the door, which was half-open. She picked up the photo and laughed again. How did she happen to know Rigby? He's always in George Street when his wife is getting her massage. I walked into the room on tiptoe. Miss Fleet turned around fast. She got so red, the birthmark on her cheek was as if on fire. In her fright, she dropped the picture and I picked it up without saying a word. That evening, when Rigby was sitting on the terrace alone, I asked him if he knew the masseuse. He looked surprised and asked, what about her? No, he didn't know her, had never seen her. I told him he hadn't missed anything, and he said he considered himself lucky to know one woman less. He laughed at my hurt expression.

Mrs. Laszlo has to give up her fortune-telling because her Australian clients already know everything. Miss Karasz helped her for a while. Then Mr. Laszlo made a lot of money with his tailoring and Mrs. Laszlo bought a delicatessen store. Since Miss Karasz couldn't live on her unpublished poems until she got married—nobody in this country takes the trouble to learn Hungarian—she helped Mrs. Laszlo in the store. Salami and cheese instead of lilies and larks. Then Miss Karasz got a job through Miss Rigby as a housekeeper for a Mr. Patrick Trent, a very rich real-estate agent for whom Mr. Rigby had built a house years before. Incidentally, the first Mrs. Trent had died a natural death, but I never mentioned it in Rigby's presence. In the house of a hanged man, one doesn't talk about rope. . . . Then something happened that the whole Hungarian colony hasn't gotten over to this day. . . . Miss Karasz, the hope of good Hungarian literature—caught this stinkingly rich Mr. Trent and actually married him five months ago! A female shark in the guise of a wallflower! All of us were horrified! Even Mr. and Mrs. Szabo admitted that they had never seen Miss Karasz as a siren."With that bosom!" said Mr. Szabo. He is just as vulgar in Sydney as he was in Budapest. If I had wanted to, I told him, I could have been Mrs. Rigby today, but I did my duty without grumbling and for thanks I was now being insulted constantly by Mr. and Mrs. Rigby.

Patrick Trent and Alexander drink together. For me Mrs. Trent is and remains Miss Karasz, no matter how expensive her bras are, and the fact that she pretends to have forgotten her mother tongue. She had the nerve to answer me, her former protector in the immigration station, in English, when she called on the Rigby's together with her fat, unsympathetic husband. I had prepared a cold buffet supper and then went to bed with a headache. The second Mrs. Rigby was furious, but I have no intention of ever waiting on Miss Karasz. Alexander didn't seem to care. He even brought me one of his wife's headache pills and seemed worried about me. Because of the dinner, of course. But I'd prepared everything and set it up in the dining room before I'd gone to lie down. "Don't do anything foolish, old thing," said Alexander, and slapped me so heartily on the shoulder, I nearly collapsed. I replied that I was the only person in the house blessed with common sense, whereupon he said he'd welcome it if it were a little more noticeable!

When the Trents had left and Mrs. Rigby was taking a shower, I tottered into the dining room to put the dishes away. Alexander was standing happily at the long table, eating leftovers. How he manages to stay so thin and eat so much is beyond me. Then he helped me wash up. He has his good sides. I tried not to ask what he thought of the second Mrs. Trent, but in the end I did. "I like her just about as much as the girl with the birthmark." When is this man ever serious? I said that I thought Miss Karasz was more Australian now than the Australians. Rigby said I should let it be an example to me. The tears welled up in my eyes and Rigby dried them with a paper towel. What's so wonderful about the Aussies that everybody's supposed to emulate them?

Yesterday, when I cleaned Mrs. Rigby's bedroom—I haven't been able to find a single love letter from Professor Darling—I couldn't find Alexander's picture which the girl with the birthmark had looked at so intently. *What* was going on in this house? Later I found out that Mrs. Rigby was getting a new frame for it. For his fiftieth birthday. Perhaps so that he can see what he looked like seven years ago when he was her fiancé. But I thought of course that the girl from Paramatta had stolen it for some dark reason or other. Why had she looked at it for such a long time? Why did she drop it when I came into the room quietly? And why had she laughed?

Ligurian Solo
Charles Preston, formerly Carlo Pressolini. Various professions, Sydney.

The first girl I met in Sydney was Molly Fleet. She came from Parramatta, wherever that it. After giving her a good looking-over, I crossed Parramatta off my map.

I met Miss Fleet in a coffeehouse in King's Cross. When the electric lights are turned on in the evening in this oasis of Sydney, one can imagine oneself back in Genoa. For a moment. The magic doesn't last. In Sydney I am a new Australian; at home I was a child of the land.

I studied law in Genoa. The university was housed in a palazzo, and that appealed to me. Beside my work at the university, I studied to be an opera singer, learned to chauffeur the automobile of the old signora through the streets at high speed, and had a few other professions. The usual intrigues at the Verdi Institute prevented my engagement at La Scala in Milan. In my country there are as many intrigues as fruit and tenors.

In Sydney I work as a waiter in the Restaurant Rosso in King's Cross. Nobody here appreciates my talents. The old Signora Pasolini in Genoa recognized the moment she laid eyes on me that there was something special about me. At home, unlike Australia, this is considered something desirable. I have been living in Australia for quite a few years now, but I still find it difficult to be like everybody else. By the way, my first job here was for old Marchmont, the architect, but he was rude to me, and we parted with mutual dislike. We Genoese are renowned for our difficult temperament and our pride. When we fly into a rage, the words stick in our throats. I often tried to explain the Genoese temperament to Mr. Marchmont, but he said he knew as much about it as he wanted to know. A furious devil deep down inside me, together with the grief over the arrogance of my new compatriots, forced me to leave. Marchmont and I gave each other notice at exactly the same time. It was the only moment of complete agreement between us. As I carried out my trunk I sang the grand aria from *Il Trovatore*. The old devil should have noticed what he had lost in me, but he went right on reading the Sunday *Morning Herald* without changing his expression for a moment. Still feeling very bitter about it, I applied for the position of waiter at the Restaurant Rosso in King's Cross. That was the best I could do because Mr. Marchmont had given me a useless recommendation. He hadn't even mentioned my extraordinary skill in maneuvering my way through the heaviest traffic in Sydney's business streets.

Raffaele Rosso also comes from Genoa, but his wife is a real Australian in every sense of the word. She calls him Raff, and all she can do is broil steaks. But she's okay. Raffaele embraced me with tears in his eyes when he heard that I came from his home town. He has never hired a Neapolitan. That gang lives five coffeehouses away from us, but as far as the Aussies are concerned, we all come out of the same pot.

Why did I stare at Molly Fleet's profile in the bar? Because she reminded me of Ginetta, my first girl friend. The same red-blond hair, the same long, narrow neck that stamps young girls as the victims of passion, the same full breasts and narrow waistline. Miss Fleet sat at the bar like a statue, with her profile to me. And how beautiful this profile was in the dimly lighted bar! It could have come from Liguria. In Genoa, as is well known, we have a surplus of beautiful profiles, the Campo Santo with angels and cypresses, the magnificent palaces and banks, Christopher Columbus, and the best artichoke torte in the world. Not to mention our famous pesto sauce. Shortly before I left Mr. Marchmont, I told him about this sauce, which is the very spice of life. I quoted with pride, "Once a foreigner has tasted our pesto sauce, he will never leave Genoa." And what did my Australian reply? Steak was good enough for him! I stuck my fists in my pockets and prayed to my guardian angel for help in this crisis. I would have liked to roast this steak eater on a grill!

Steak or no steak, at home we have girls with the most beautiful profiles, and since I was still homesick, I gazed at Miss Fleet's profile with nostalgia. Unfortunately she paid no attention to me. Her round forehead and the meekness of her neck would have inspired Fra Filippo Lippi to a Madonna portrait. No doubt about it, Miss Fleet was more beautiful even than Ginetta!

She was wearing a light-blue dress and gold sandals. Her legs, with their slim ankles, were remarkable. Poor Gina couldn't compete with them. I sat there for a while and dreamed. Ginetta and I had parted company years ago, but I still thought sometimes of our nights together. Molly Fleet's profile aroused memories in me. The grand passion, the feeling that flowers, earth, oceans and fire were alive in my blood, overwhelmed me for the first time in these surroundings.

At home I had had the possibilities for a brilliant future, but my turbulent inner life made an adjustment to the outside world difficult. It had to be conquered brutally, and I was a dreamer, yes, I'd like to say a poet, who produced too much to ever write it all down. My father was a civil servant of no consequence, with a sickly wife and eight children. During the Second World War, I celebrated my tenth birthday.

My father was a fascist like everybody else. Unfortunately this totalitarian deviation made life very difficult for us after the war, because my father, unlike most other men, could not deceive. And that was his misfortune. I couldn't go to university, which my father had planned for me because I was so brilliant; instead I started to work as a waiter in the Restaurant Pasolini in the old city. What a comedown! Signora Pasolini may not have been as old as she seemed to a young boy like me, but when I saw her I had a foretaste of what lay ahead. I can't deny that I was an extraordinarily handsome young man. The signora looked me over for a while with her glowing dark eyes under their heavy, bluish lids. She had black, smoothly parted hair, a bold, manly nose, thin lips, and very big ears. She always wore black, with a valuable cameo at her neckline. The help trembled before this big, heavy woman, and the scornful way she smiled when something didn't please her. I noticed after a while that her attitude toward me changed, but I couldn't say exactly how. I could only feel her glowing eyes looking at me strangely, but since she still spoke coldly and scornfully to me, I decided I'd just imagined it. I was even a little afraid of her. She was like a gigantic wave that could break my back. One evening she asked me what my plans for the future were, and from then on things began to look up. I had explained, modestly, that I wasn't born to be a waiter. She sent me to the university where I was to study law, to driving school, where I passed my test with honors, and she saw to it that I took singing lessons; she was a real mother to me. Anyway, that's the way I saw her for a long time. The frames of the mirrors in the restaurant were gilded, and sometimes I looked at myself in them pleased with what I saw, when the old signora and I ate a festive meal together in a corner reserved for us.

Around this time my father's youngest brother emigrated to Tasmania and asked me if I wanted to come along. But I laughed at him. I had so many brilliant careers ahead of me and would one day be Signora Pasolini's heir. My Uncle Fabio said I was a fool, and how much longer did I think the old witch was going to coddle me? He laughed suggestively, we punched each other around a bit, but then we embraced amid loud laughter, and Uncle Fabio went off to Tasmania. Yes, he said, when things in Genoa weren't going so well for me any more, there would always be a spare bed in Hobart for his favorite nephew. That was really nice of him because thanks to our little differences of opinion, he had a black eye and a broken rib. But I wouldn't hear a word against the old signora at that time. I called her "Mama" once, whereupon she slapped my face. She was forty-five years old and a young woman! She got out of her plush armchair laboriously, and that evening dined alone.

Uncle Fabio was right. She was a man-eater and devoured me skin and bone, but what could I do? I didn't go far at the university—unfortunately there were intrigues against me there too, but my voice was my treasure. Sometimes I drove the signora to a village near Genoa where she had spent her childhood. The village was built on a rocky hillside. Life must have been hard there. The signora was hard too, but when I sang for her, she softened. I had to sing a lot.

When Ginetta came to the Restaurant Pasolini as a waitress, everything ended fast. Ginetta was seventeen, gentle, intelligent, and beautiful. I was twenty-four. We went for outings together until the old signora found out that I was taking Ginetta to the seashore instead of studying. She rampaged like a grotesque goddess of vengeance in her black dress, which had two grease spots on the collar and was too tight across her bosom; then she threw us out.

I could write off my future and was miles away from riches and fame. The signora slandered me everywhere. I didn't mind giving up my law studies, which had bored me to death, but unfortunately nobody wanted my golden voice either. At first I tried to get a job as a chauffeur, but the owners of elegant cars who could afford a chauffeur wanted references. They did not hire anonymous vagabonds. Perhaps I did look a little wild in my misfortune; anyway the car owners behaved as if they thought I might cut their throats during an outing. The signora had done a good job on me. I finally did try to get a reference from her, but she laughed in my face like a Fury.

Gina couldn't get work anywhere as a waitress; the singora saw to that too. The poor girl hadn't learned anything practical. Her mother was a laundress and there was never any mention of a father. On my advice she tried to get a job as a nursemaid, since she didn't know how to cook, but all the married women in Genoa assured poor Gina that she was too young to look after children. She was of course only too beautiful for their husbands. I was desperate when my little Ginetta— so young, so devoted, so willing to work—had to provide the food we ate and the roof over our heads with the oldest profession in the world. I swore that I would repay her doubly and triply just as soon as I triumphed at La Scala. Unfortunately things turned out differently. First of all I couldn't vocalize because of the hot steam coming from the laundry, and then my music teacher refused to give me free lessons. The wretched man declared that the gold in my throat sounded tinny!

I hadn't been to see my parents for a long time because my brothers had made fun of my humiliation. They had always said I was a braggart, but that had been pure envy. To make a long story short, I had to make do with the proximity of the laundry. Out attic roof on the harbor was devoid of any of the comforts of home. When Gina came home, tired and teary, I didn't feel like any love play either. The steam from the laundry was slowly affecting my brain.

One day Gina came back from walking the streets of Genoa with a disease. That did it! I finished the braised squid which Gina's mother had prepared marvelously, and naturally withdrew from both women. I had to live with my parents—not easy—until I could emigrate. Under the circumstances I had to consider Australia.

When I met Gina in a café a few weeks later, she begged me to marry her and take her with me to the fifth continent. She would do any kind of work here until I became famous and wealthy. The poor thing must have gone out of her mind! The idea of marriage was ridiculous! How could I introduce a sick prostitute to my venerable mother as her daughter-in-law? Since Gina couldn't make any money right now, I sold my watch and gave her some of the money, also five percent from the sale of the gold bracelet Signora Pasolini had given me. Hard to believe, but Gina threw the money at my feet! With which she proved that she really had gone crazy. I picked up the money from the floor, enraged, and added another bill to it, but she tore it up and threw the pieces all over the kitchen. I was furious over having been parted so carelessly from my money, and decided to curb my generosity in the future. I left the kitchen without saying goodbye.

Until my Uncle Fabio sent me the travel money from Australia, I helped my mother at home. The past excitement had made me hoarse, and I had to give up my plans for the opera for a while. My Uncle Fabio had a gas station in Tasmania, and seemed to be doing very well. I couldn't get over it, because Uncle Fabio had never distinguished himself by any exceptional capabilities. At any rate, he seemed to be having better luck than I. He also wrote about the high standard of living in the workers' paradise of Australia. All of us had to laugh. With Uncle Fabio, every sparrow was a peacock. How could we in Genoa know that this time he was not exaggerating? I asked if there was an opera company in Hobart, but Uncle Fabio didn't reply to that. Did he still quarrel with his wife in Tasmania and celebrate tearful reconciliations? He had always been slightly secretive, but after all we were blood relations, and you can't choose your uncles.

When I was ready to leave for Australia, my youngest brother said he thought dry macaroni was better at home than roast chicken in a strange land. The little idiot was just envious, but I had no intention of having him follow me to Australia, and intended to advise Uncle Fabio not to send him money for the trip. We Italians have a family life that is perhaps too intense, and too many petitioners and intriguers on our own doorsteps. In Australia they say, "Mind your own business!" I never heard wiser words.

Uncle Fabio has been an Australian for a long time, but in a typical Italian way he sticks his nose into everything that doesn't concern him. When I told him later in Hobart that as Australians, we should stop this eternal spying on our neighbors, he laughed. Nothing seemed funnier to him than to conform to Australian customs. So why in the world hadn't he stayed in Genoa? Recently I have had to ask my compatriots to please stop addressing me as Carlo or Pressolini. My name is Charles Preston now, whether the people at home like it or not. When I told Uncle Fabio of my intention to change my name shortly before I moved to Sydney, he puffed himself up like a turkey and spat in my face. As far as he was concerned, I was still a Pressolini. We happened to be at his gas station, and I'd have liked to pour a can of gasoline over his head, but I'd have had to pay for it. I found breathing difficult, although actually the air in Tasmania feels quite European. I hated Uncle and Aunt Pressolini and their chattering daughter. The whole beautiful island was spoiled for me. I would have liked to throw myself into the Derwent River, but that would have given my brothers Guido, Felice, Roberto, Michele, Filippo, and my sister Angela, too much satisfaction.

In order to get my mind on other things, I sometimes went for an outing to the botanical gardens, or to Saint Mary's Cathedral in Patrick Street. Or I went down to the harbor where the Tasmanians throw colored ribbons to their friends from the shore. The natives paid no attention to me—that would have been unthinkable at home. In the shortest time everybody knows everybody in Genoa, but not even the Australian girls gave me a look. They don't know how to show a handsome young man their approval. Slowly I lost the ground under my feet. I betted like every native Australian. I tried everything I could to become an Australian, even if only a new one. In vain.

I would probably still be sitting staring at the ships in the harbor of Hobart, if Mr. Marchmont hadn't seen me in the garage and taken a fancy to me. Of course he never admitted it, everybody here is tongue-tied, but would he have taken me along to Sydney with him if he hadn't taken a liking to me? His old chauffeur had just died. That may have played a part. He needed a new one. We did a trial run around

Hobart—what a sleepy nest it is!—and I was hired. For the first time in his life, Uncle Fabio was speechless. Sydney! A metropolis! And an opera house was going to be built there soon! He paid my gambling debts—as a blood relative I had that coming to me—my aunt fried and baked Italian delicacies, insofar as she could get the necessary ingredients. My cousin, Claudia Pressolini, followed me everywhere. I imagine she hoped to get to faraway, exciting Sydney through me. All the time—calculations, intrigues, and secret ambitions! I smiled at Claudia. She was sixteen years old and pretty, with shiny black hair, but nobody in Hobart paid any attention to this pint-size Venus. And they didn't even know that Claudia was sly, brash, and insanely curious. She reminded me of Perugino's *Maria Magdelena* when she lowered her eyes and was silent. We embraced after the festive meal, I sang a long opera aria, Claudia coughed and stared at me enviously, and Uncle Fabio, with tears in his eyes, handed me a quite handsome sum of money.

We kissed on both cheeks. After all, I was his favorite nephew, and there would always be a bed for me in Hobart. I didn't say anything about how ridiculous his offer was; Uncle Fabio didn't know any better. Before I turned my back on Hobart and left with old Marchmont, I prayed in the cathedral for the soul of the unfortunate prostitute, Ginetta. She didn't deserve it, but one should forgive those who have treated one unjustly. Shortly before my emigration I had walked past Gina's house by chance. I wondered how she was doing, if she was cured of her illness, and had found a modest, honest job. I felt the pain of parting, and stared up at her dirty windows, lost in thought. Just then somebody opened the window. It was Ginetta, but how neglected she looked, her hair undone, her skin yellow. No sooner had she spotted me—unfortunately I stood rooted to the spot, I was so startled over her transformation as I stared up at her—then she grabbed a pail and poured the dismal contents over me and my new suit. At the same time she used such language to upbraid me—any jailbird could have learned a thing or two from her. How could such foul language pass beyond the lips of my gentle beloved? As soon as I came to, I of course screamed back at her, but in more civilized tones. After all, I had been to university, my father was a civil servant, and I had taken singing lessons from a professional. Our dispute might have ended peacefully if a crowd hadn't collected, as if my magic, around Gina's whorehouse, and encouraged my former sweetheart to give me hell. I had to beat up three men before I could get away. And for this creature I had prayed to heaven! I thought of the earlier Ginetta, who had worshiped me shyly and devotedly. Dreadful, how women change! I still see red today under Sydney's blazing sun when I think of her. In the time of our Ligurian moonlit nights, I had idealized her. That is always one of the errors of love.

And now, years later, a young and beautiful version of Ginetta was sitting beside me at the coffee bar. Somebody called out, "Hello, Molly Fleet!" But beautiful Molly didn't turn around, and I could go on looking at her profile. How reserved she was! I hadn't forgotten how readily Gina had embraced me. I had dreamt of intimacies, but the fulfillment came much too fast. It should never follow hard upon the dream.

The stranger in the coffeehouse seemed made of different stuff. Marble! Very pleasant in the heat. I imagined how mild, how refreshing such an Australian girl had to be: a crystal bird in the cool blue air. Molly Fleet. The name told me nothing. Lucia would have suited her better. She didn't turn to look at me, although she must have felt my burning eyes. After all, even an Australian was a woman. The full breasts, the narrow waistline, were made to be embraced. And her long, red-gold hair! Still I hesitated to accost her. In Genoa I wouldn't have wasted a second, but on this continent you never knew where you were at. Besides, who can seduce a woman with words when he's been drinking ice-cold beer for hours? Should I speak to Lucia?

Not long ago, on the beach, an Australian girl had been very rude when I had admired her bathing suit in my perfect English. The Aussies won't learn Italian, although it is the international language, daughter of Latin, the language of Dante! Should I address Lucia?

A year before I had got a punch in the jaw from a huge Australian with a red face and a bald head because I had smiled at his little lady in a Greek bar. Actually I had only been responding to *her* smile, but the idiot didn't know that because he was reading the paper all the time, and only looked up suddenly. I struck back, with pleasure, but who got thrown out by the manager? I did! The new Australian! The old Aussie, with his bald head and beefsteak neck was of course right. I'd like to meet *him* in Genoa! As I left he yelled something snide about my homeland, but I ignored it. He was too big and strong for me, a bush brigand who had somehow found his way to Sydney. His raucous, scornful laughter rang in my ears for days. He laughed as melodiously as a wombat! But it must be nice to always be right when pitted against a respectable immigrant.

It was high time to stop this monologue and to address Lucia Fleet. If only I hadn't done so! She got up indignantly and, head held high, left the bar. She even left her iced drink unfinished. She had to be an

Australian because they are born extravagant. I exchanged glasses surreptitiously and drank Molly's drink to the end. After all, it was paid for. Then I paid for my drink hurriedly and rushed after Miss Fleet.

The evening lighting effects in King's Cross confused me somewhat, and all around me people were talking in different languages. Miss Fleet was walking slowly down Sydney Boulevard. From whatever angle you looked at her, she had a gorgeous figure. That's what sports do for you. They finally did go in for sports at home, but the figures of the girls are not yet as Australian as they should be. In Genoa the girls remain more interested in men than in sports. You can't accuse Australian girls of that!

Molly-Lucia Fleet stopped under a street lamp and looked for something in her handbag. She still had her back turned to me, and I looked at her slim, naked legs with the narrow ankles. Her golden sandals were high-heeled. They made her as tall as I. I would have to look out that she didn't grow over my head.

At last I had caught up with her. Anyway, we were now standing side by side under the street light, in Genoa an explosive situation. Miss Fleet continued to turn her back on me and rummage around in her handbag. Was she looking for a handkerchief? I took a new lace handkerchief out of my pocket which I always carry with me for such occasions.

"Excuse me, miss. Did you leave this in the bar?"

Molly turned around abruptly and stared at me. The light fell full on her face. She seemed to have escaped hellfire, but she still bore the scars of the flames on her face. A birthmark covered her left cheek like a fiery hand—the eyelid, the earlobe—and ran down to her jaw. Nature had created a beautiful body and then, in a dark mood, had ruined it. The handkerchief fell out of my hand. I looked at the ruined beauty with fascination and horror. Molly Fleet stood motionless, only her lips trembled. Suddenly she pushed her long, red-gold hair across the disfigured half of her face like a curtain. I wanted to rush away, but couldn't move. I looked into her eyes and saw her despair. This girl was just as isolated as I was, in a world of naive self-satisfaction. Molly Fleet, too, had to be satisfied with the monologue.

I felt dizzy. Time passed. Was I experiencing an adventure that Odysseus had missed? But perhaps I was just suffering from too much sun, the result of shopping that morning in the market without a hat. Anyway, the European facade of King's Cross disintegrated into its individual parts before my eyes. The Restaurant Rosso whirled through the air, the pavement crumbled, a huge shark sailed up to me, its jaws wide-open. I teetered between attraction and disgust in the void of a nightmare.

A few seconds later, everything was in its rightful place again. As if in a trance, I raised my hand and pushed the curtain of hair aside and touched her cheek in a horrified caress. I had the curious feeling that I would never be the same again. I had taken a trip to Hades. Perhaps all this was nonsense. The hot wind in Sydney must have driven me crazy. What was so dreadful about a birthmark? I had touched it. The color hadn't come off. But my touch had awakened Miss Fleet out of her torpor, and she slapped my face. Not surprising. What right had I to stroke her face? She murmured something which, in my excitement, I didn't understand, but it didn't sound flattering. "Bloody foreigner," or something like that, suitable flattery for a new Australian.

Anyway, the veil that had isolated us for a few seconds from the rest of humanity had torn abruptly. The sweat was running down my forehead, although I was freezing. I probably had a fever. I wanted to run away from this person, but I stood as if paralyzed. The slap in the face burned like a fiery scar. I had wanted to console this unhappy Australian, that was the truth, but only I knew it.

Miss Fleet had walked away long ago. Why did I have the feeling that I would never sing again? Wasn't one punished for offering a sacrifice at the altar of horror? I shook my head. All over the world there was ugliness and despair, but Ligurian grief contains an element of poetry. Miss Fleet's sorrow was as dry as the Australian desert.

Mrs. Rosso came running up to me. She had on her apron, and her wispy, gray-blond hair waved around her thin, intelligent face with its long Australian nose. She looked like a tamed bird of prey. She had flown from the Northern Territory of Sydney one day and had captured my landsman, Rosso, forever and a day. Muriel Rosso was angry. I could see that. The first guests were arriving, and here was her waiter making an ass of himself. But when she took a closer look at me, she asked, "Are you all right, Charles? Come and lie down for a moment. I'll bring you a nice cold beer."

Beer is the universal remedy from Hobart to Sydney. Muriel Rosso meant well. I picked up the lace handkerchief for gallant introductions, carefully brushed the dust off it and handed it to Mrs. Rosso. She raised her sandy-colored eyebrows and thanked me, astonished. Muriel was very bright. For the first time I was glad that the Aussies preferred silence to talk. She led me back to the restaurant and gave me a beer without saying a word. She would have been a wonderful mother, but she was too old when she married Raffaele Rosso, restaurant owner in Sydney. "Take it easy, young man," she said, disappearing into the kitchen, and was at once in the midst of an endless dispute with Raffaele. They quarreled all the time and were very fond of each other. Rafaele obeyed Muriel in spite of all his noisy protest. He needed someone to tell him what to do. She protected him unobtrusively in his new fatherland. And me. She was a good old girl—faithful and solid, if lacking in imagination. Raffaele, the stupid fellow, could have done worse.

I hoped that I would never meet the girl with the birthmark again. I avoided the bar where I had admired her profile. I hid from her during the day and at night she poisoned my dreams. That was the thanks I got for compassion. She was taboo for any man. In my thoughts I laid a stone in front of her unknown door.

Three weeks later I saw her again. It was the hottest November I had ever experienced in Sydney. The sky was dusty and the grass in Hyde Park was dead. Molly Fleet was standing under a lamppost in Darlinghurst. She nodded as if we were old friends. And we were, in a sense. When one has seen pain in the eyes of a woman, one knows her intimately. The Italian is born with this knowledge and leaves the world with it.

Why didn't I run away from this fatal intimacy? Again I felt feverish and depressed. Nothing good could come of it. I stepped closer. Instead of running away, I asked, "Are you waiting for anyone?"

"No," said Miss Fleet. "Nobody waits for me."

6

Monologue of a Girl from Parramatta

Whenever I burst in on a group, there is a pause. People stop talking, stare at me, and a slimy silence rises in my gorge. Or those present suddenly start speaking so fast, I am sure they have been talking about me. But perhaps they've only been talking about the Anzac Monument, or about their experiences in the bush, or the latest newspaper scandal in Sydney. In any case, at times like this my birthmark is flaming red. Then somebody says, "Do sit down, Molly. You confuse me when you stand around like that."

It must be wonderful to have nobody staring at you. What I'd really like to do in Sydney is swim, underwater all day, because the sun sheds its bright light on everything. As a child I looked forward to the night because it erased all faces. Every morning I looked in the mirror to see if the night had erased my birthmark. My older sister, April, grinned. "There's no earthly reason for you to look in the mirror, little one," she'd say, and I'd go for her with my fists. She would have been pretty as a picture if her chronic meanness hadn't spoiled everything. April didn't have much imagination and not much love for her fellow man, but she was very pleased with herself. She hated anything ugly. She forbade me to wear her earrings. Evidently the idea that they might touch my face made her shudder.

When I had finished my training as a masseuse, I moved to Sydney. In Parramatta everybody knew everybody else, and I hoped that in Sydney I would pass unnoticed. In Parramatta, the streets crept up on me and threatened to crush me. Our city had been modernized, true, but it was still the oldest settlement in New South Wales. I looked forward to Sydney especially because my sister was staying home. April would never leave Parramatta, and why should she? She helped Father in the brewery he had inherited from his uncle, and then there was my grandparents' farm near Parramatta. My brother, Stephen, ran it since grandfather's death. That's where I felt at home. As a child I had been happy with my grandparents and the cows. The cows never stuck their heads together when I came to milk them. I loved them, and I think they loved me.

In Sydney I sometimes long for Parramatta. For instance when Mrs. Doody, my landlady in Darlinghurst, gets into one of her rages, or when her niece, Candy, doesn't choose to listen when I'm talking about myself. Then, from a distance, Parramatta seems damned friendly. Even if at home things were sometimes horrible, I was safe in the old city where I knew every street, and all the paths and obelisks in the park. And the people at home were used to the sight of me. I hadn't thought of that when I left. On the other hand, nobody would have spent a penny on massage in Parramatta. The farmers and merchants would have laughed in my face. In Sydney Miss Rigby got me top-drawer clients, for instance her sister-in-law, Anne. A while ago I saw a photograph of Alexander Rigby in his wife's room, but then the Hungarian housekeeper came in on tiptoe and startled me. If she knew why I laughed! Mama Doody says a married man is like the weather or a pimple on the nose—only stupid girls get excited over him. But the weather stays with us and our old men disappear. She should know. Nobody in Sydney has ever seen Mr. Doody. Did he remain stuck in Ireland? I haven't been able to find out. I find it great fun to snoop around in the secrets of the people here, otherwise I have very little distraction, and besides, I often find out while I'm about it that other people aren't as happy as they pretend to be. I thought Mrs. Rigby lived in paradise, but then I found out a lot of things about her husband. *Very* funny!

The Rigby's Hungarian housekeeper, who speaks such curious English, wanted to kill me the other day. Why are the new Australians constantly in such a state of excitement? For the least reason, the bush is burning. I think the Hungarian woman, whose name I can't pronounce, is madly in love with Mr. Rigby. How can she be? He's going to be fifty next week, and seems to be an unpleasant fellow. His nose is turned up all the time, even in the photo. I daren't think of it, or I laugh myself silly!

He *is* handsome, has a good figure, no stomach, although he's so old already. If I wasn't afraid of Miss Rigby, I could have some fun. But she's a tiger in a silk suit. I'm sure she has pots of money. She says I must have got her brother mixed up with somebody else; he was never in Darlinghurst. What does this arrogant old woman know about her brother? I said at once that, yes, I'd probably been mistaken.

My clients with the chronic backaches come from Miss Rigby. There they sit in their fine houses, and I don't like any of them. They think Sydney belongs to them, and they're probably right. My grandmother on the farm said you could never have a conversation with Sydney people because they always had twenty answers for the simplest question. Grandmother Fleet was in Sydney once, but never again! She thanked her heavenly maker when she got back to the Parramatta River, and the cows, and the cupboards with her preserves. She threw up her hands when I moved to Sydney. My brother was just milking the cows, automatic milking. All of us found milking by hand much more satisfactory, but Stephen runs with the times and wants to get the last drop of milk out of our cows. He mumbled that it was all the same to him if I wanted to move to Sydney or not, but on the farm there'd always be a place for me. That was the longest speech Stephen Fleet ever made. He was so startled about it himself, that he turned purple-red and teetered home from the tavern late that night. He's not a bad brother, only satisfied with everything. But perhaps I would be too, if I had the farm and a decent face, and the cows belonged to me. A short while ago Stephen bought some new, more efficient stanchion barns. For that Grandmother had the money, but when I needed new clothes for Sydney, they both said the machinery had cost too much. We have sixty cows. What Grandmother really meant was that with my face it didn't matter if I had a new dress or not. But for a goodbye present she gave me a sweet white dress that she'd sewn herself, and some of her best preserves. So she's a good soul, but grumpy. *Only* the cows do the right thing!

But where Lily II is concerned, I have to agree with her. She is the successor of Lily I, and just as sensitive. Sometimes I kiss her and she kisses me too, especially when I milk her by hand. Stephen won't admit that milking by machine has to confuse a sensitive cow. I heard a lecture about it not long ago in Sydney. Sometimes Lily looked at me quietly and sadly when I told her all sorts of things in her stall. If only I had her here in Sydney! But what would Mrs. Doody say to that? Yet her boardinghouse in Darlinghurst is a pigsty! The plaster is peeling off the walls, in the kitchen the tap drips, it stinks of rancid fat, and "Mama Doody," as her tenants call her, likes to run around in a slovenly housecoat with a towel over her shoulders and curlers in her hair. But I can save money here; she doesn't charge much rent. When I've earned enough with my massaging, we can enlarge the herd. Stephen and Grandmother Fleet have nothing against it, and the cows would belong to me, says Stephen. I can name them too. The farm lies in a sheltered area, and the pasturage is fine, a little limited if we enlarge the herd. But perhaps we could buy some more land from a neighbor. I'm reading a lot here about cattle disease, and hormones, and the chemical composition of milk, and so on. Grandmother Fleet advises me not to collect a lot of that sort of nonsense in my head: cows have always given milk without such knowledge. Grandmother has her own system and lives according to her own rules. She also has her own face. Her skin is stretched taut, sunburnt and sere over her massive cheekbones, and her blue eyes are still blue and keen. In the evenings she sits on the wooden veranda and watches the trees and the stars.

Sometimes she tells Stephen and me about the big droughts she experienced. The land looked like an endless strip of parchment and the riverbeds were dry. Grandmother Fleet belongs to South Australia. Once she showed me a picture of her family home, a medium-sized wooden shack standing lost between red eucalyptus trees. A few hens were visible on the fenced-in piece of land, and there were fruit trees, and Grandmother as a young girl with a basket of fruit on her arm. In the background were the Flinders Mountains, wild and forbidding. I have never seen anything as lonely as the three hens behind that fence. Grandmother said her parents were dissatisfied because the earth was unfruitful, but then the government or whoever put copper in the ground, and after that it was first-rate and everything began to bloom. Today the Tiger Moth planes spray the earth with fertilizers and chemicals, but Granny doesn't want to hear about that. She says the earth should nourish the earth. This in spite of the fact that as a young girl she had to drag every drop of water into the house in pails. On the other hand, she could already ride a horse before she knew her *ABC*'s.

Mostly she says nothing in the evenings. She's usually a little tired from preserving and cleaning, things like that, but of course she'd rather die than admit it. She is as rough and unapproachable as the Flinders Mountains, but just as in the mountains, there are gaps and narrow paths that at some time or other lead into an inhabited valley. I hope Grandmother Fleet will live forever. I don't mind how much she scolds me, I just want her to be there when I come to the farm. She will never understand why I moved to Sydney. Sometimes I think a swarm of mosquitoes must have bitten me. But I wanted to see the world. Until now all I've really seen is Darlinghurst. The villas of my clients are like the ones in the movies—everything so unbelievably beautiful and clean. I would like to see a toothbrush with worn-out bristles, like Stephen's, in one of the bathrooms. An old toothbrush like that is *real*, is used, and in my opinion, belongs to the household.

What I find funny and have still not been able to get used to is the noise in Sydney. Apart from the traffic, Mama Doody and her niece, Candy, talk all the time. My ears buzz. Or they sing, both of them, with raucous voices, that some idiot or other should stir the wallaby stew:

> So stir the wallaby stew,
> Make soup of the kangaroo tail,
> I tell you things is pretty tough
> Since Dad got put in jail!

In this way I found out that Mr. Doody is a jailbird. The whiskey tears run down Mrs. Doody's face when she sings the last two lines of the old bush song. Irish dreams are usually mixed with whiskey; that's why they burn so. Mrs. Doody is as Irish as if she had landed in Sydney yesterday. Her old man ended up in jail quite by chance, says she. She had tried her best to explain everything to the police, but had the dogs listened to her? Then she shrugged her fat shoulders and asked me who in Sydney ever listened to the Irish? No one! she yelled furiously, not one stinking soul from Darlinghurst to Vaucluse, where the money-bags were. Whoever has money may even come from Dublin!

Candy sometimes has a visitor, a huge Irish sugar daddy. He has a fat stomach and a villa somewhere in the finest district. He really may come from Dublin. Candy doesn't favor any of her admirers. Any of the bank accounts in New South Wales are all right with her. She is so beautiful, it could make you weep! Now she models in *Insight*, all through my influence. But the money slips through her fingers, and Mama Doody and Uncle Doody need a lot for their drinking. Candy gives Mama Doody much too much because the Irish are terribly family-conscious. Like the Italians. That waiter from Genoa bores me to death with dramas about his clan in Tasmania and Liguria. But I don't show him that I don't enjoy listening to it. He is the first and only man I have to go out with.

Why I really left Parramatta is my secret. I miss Lily terribly, and sometimes I'd like to be with Stephen again. If he were in a good mood, we'd talk about milk production and the vagaries of the cows. Hard to believe, but some animals have no social sense. They want to dominate the other cows, and always be first out on the field. Lily, of course, never pushes. When I tell Mama Doody or Candy about our Lily, they put their hands over their ears, or Mama Doody sings a dirty song in her rough voice. What good air there was in Parramatta! After all, it's a rural town; even if a lot of cars tear across Church Street today,

Parramatta doesn't smell *only* of gasoline, like Sydney. My city isn't called "Origin of the River" for nothing. The early natives called it that before the convicts from England landed. One of my ancestors on my mother's side was a convict and lived in the Women's Factory, as the jail was called, until she got married. She had to weave, and later was a maid on an estate in Parramatta. I was ashamed for years because of Great-Grandmother Cocker, but Miss Rigby says that our old Cocker was a good British import, not to be compared with the weird people landing in New South Wales today. When I think of Carlo Pressolini at the Restaurant Rosso, how he boasts and the act he puts on, I have to agree with her. But the Fleets are a clan of a different color. My mother and grandmother Cocker, née Bradley, always go around with their eyes lowered and have nothing to say. Father is a beast, of course, and weathered like an old eucalyptus tree. A grim man! But Mother had no choice. How big is Parramatta anyway? And after I turned up with a birthmark over half my face, Father looked at everything that was Cocker or Bradley with a scowl. But my birth was just as much his fault as my poor, shy mum's. But that I had to happen too, after she had turned out to be useless in the brewery because she was too weak physically, that was the last straw!

Stephen sometimes took me along to Parramatta Lake, but even if he didn't say a word to me, at least he brought me. We swam and sat under giant trees, and Stephen always had food and his billy with him. He is three years older than our sister, April. I'm the youngest, and what a sight! When Father saw me and drew his thick eyebrows together, I froze in the blazing sun. I couldn't help it; I was devastated about the flaming hand on my face. I tried even then to cover the thing with my hair, but once, when April and I were quarreling, she cut off my hair. Now I was naked, and hid in Parramatta Park. April laughed. After that I was sent to my grandparents on the farm for a while.

I tried to bite April on the cheek while she was sleeping, so that she would have something to suffer over too, but the bitch woke and beat me up. I screamed so loudly that Father came running. He thrashed us both and swore. But when April cried, he gave her beer. April was the only creature beside his dog that he loved. I couldn't sit down for three days, he'd beaten me that hard. Then Stephen took me to the farm, where I stayed for quite a while. I was five at the time, April was ten and Stephen thirteen. I was happy on the farm. I yelled bloody murder when I was supposed to go home again, but it didn't help. I learned at a very early age how ridiculous tears were, and in the future swallowed them.

My hair had grown again, but now I hated April. She had really done me in. Mother was never the least bit tender to me, and Grandmother Cocker kept to herself. She always said she was a burden in the house, and I think she was. She never contradicted anybody, which made Father and Stephen furious. She had a long, dolorous sheep's face with human eyes. Her mouth was thin, and drooped. Sometimes a drop that didn't want to fall hung from her long, sharp nose. Father hated the sight of it. Then Grandmother Cocker buried her face in a huge handkerchief and coughed humbly. Her hair hung down her forehead, thin, white, and stringy hair. Grandmother Cocker looked as if she had been born old, and begged everybody's pardon for being there. She was wonderful with flowers, and sometimes I heard her talking to them and the bushes in the garden. When Father came home from the brewery and caught Grandmother Cocker having her weird conversations, he started fearfully. If he had trampled on her flower beds, she wouldn't have objected. She was broken and finished and superfluous, and didn't even know how to die! She only died last year. Stephen said she had apologized constantly because she was bringing so much confusion into the house with her dying. Nobody had time for the funeral—I mean, not really. I would have been sad about her death if she had once dared to be nice to me. But she wanted to please Father, and pursued this hopeless undertaking for years. Grandmother Cocker would certainly have been happier in the Parramatta jail, but she never had the guts to do anything wrong. Father sometimes joked about her, but his jokes were grim, and only Grandmother Cocker laughed fearfully. She left no gap in our home. That is perhaps the saddest thing one can say about a good, honest creature. Grandmother Fleet on the farm would be missed terribly. All of us know that. But she is as indestructible as the bush. She loves life and life loves her. People like that have a lot of strength.

So why did I really leave Parramatta a few years ago? I wouldn't admit it to anybody, because it's pretty foolish. One day April didn't call me Molly anymore, but Mole. That means birthmark, as well as the little animal, and it was the worst thing that could have happened to me. The children in school also soon called me Mole, and one day I jumped into the Parramatta River and didn't want to come up again. But Stephen saw me and fished me out, cursing. He brewed tea and wrapped me in a blanket, and didn't tell anyone at home about it. He didn't know why I had wanted to drown myself, and I didn't tell him. But after that he kept an eye on me. April was a pretty girl. She was popular and often invited places. Father was proud of her nice little face and jolly talk. She wore mostly green because it went well with her red-gold hair and white skin. She had green glass earrings. Nothing seemed as wonderful to me as those earrings. Once I crept into her room and tried them on. I held my hair like a curtain over my left cheek. The green earrings sparkled. Just then April burst into the room and tore them off me with an expression of revulsion. Like Father, she hated anything ugly. That wasn't right, Grandmother Fleet told him. Although she sometimes gave me a good thrashing, Granny knew her way around the Bible very well, and sometimes I surprised her saying the rosary with a cross face and in a great hurry. But she sent me to confession and was furious when Stephen swore. She could swear pretty well too, but *she* was allowed to. For years I thought that Grandmother Fleet had a very special arrangement with heaven. I was too young to realize what Grandfather's sudden death had meant to her. But the next day she was already preserving fruit. I happened to walk by and could see her tears falling into the pot. She screamed for me to get out, and what did I want in the kitchen anyway? Then she went on cooking and weeping. I picked her a big bunch of mimosa. She loved mimosa. She put it in a clay bowl that had a crack and couldn't be used for cooking any more. She stroked my hair fleetingly, and pushed me out of the pantry. "Clean the shed, and make it fast!" she said. That evening my mimosa stood in front of Grandfather's picture.

April hardly ever came to the farm. Grandmother couldn't stand her, although she would rather have bitten her tongue off than admit it. She had created a cozy home for herself, Stephen and me, and that was that. She treated April with caution because she didn't like her. To Mother she was always compassionate and nice. This daughter-in-law naturally didn't suit her at all. Mother had the soul of a hen. She was so timid and parched and dry, like a piece of sunburnt Australian earth. She had been a milkmaid on the farm. Father had married her when she was expecting Stephen. I found a letter from Father in a drawer on the farm. There it was, in black and white . . . Mother sometimes opened her mouth when Father was angry with me, as if she wanted to say something. I always hoped she'd stand up for me, but not a single word passed her lips. I think I despised her, but a child isn't aware of anything like that. It is horrible when mothers won't say yes or no. Mother didn't even show her anger. She never punished me. I simply couldn't arouse her interest in anything I did. Sometimes I was dreadfully naughty and did silly things at the brewery, only to attract Father's attention. When he beat me black and blue I knew I was at least there for him. I tried in every possible way to please him, but all he did was look at me somberly. As if it were my fault that I had to run around with a fiery birthmark. And the children copied April, and called me Mole.

April grew up to be a beautiful, voluptuous cow and wanted to get married. In the evening she strolled along the river with young boys. I often followed her and knew that they necked, and how she squealed when the boys got fresh. She tried to catch the son of a rich sheep farmer near Parramatta, and she actually got him to the point where they became engaged. The two sat on the veranda, and Father treated to beer. I wrote April's fiancé an anonymous letter about what she was up to on the banks of the Parramatta River, and that was the end of that fine engagement. April is still at home, helping in the brewery. Nobody ever found out why the young farmer didn't come back. Soon after that he married another girl. His name was Robert Donahue. He was a big solid man and deserved something better than April anyway. As a small child I had loved and admired April. Why had she called me Mole? Why had she torn her earrings off my ears so that they bled? She had cooked her own goose.

When Mother died a year ago, April and I scarcely spoke to each other. After the funeral I drove to Grandmother Fleet at the farm. I noticed to my astonishment that Stephen must have loved our mother. His eyes were red, and he spoke even less than usual. In the evening he sat with his glasses on his nose near a hurricane lamp on the big wooden veranda. His beer and his dog, a very young dog, were waiting for him on the wooden table beside him. She was crouched there obediently. Stephen had a book on the control of disease in the cow barn in his hands, but he wasn't reading it, he was just staring straight ahead. He must have been thinking of Mother because he sighed twice and lunged furiously with the book against the flies. Then he drank his beer down in one gulp, and picked up his dog. He still had his glasses on. I followed him. He sat down on the shore. I asked if I could stay with him. He took off his glasses and said the shore was big enough for two. I cuddled up to him and he didn't seem to mind. He sat between the dog and me. It was very quiet. I asked him if he didn't know of any man for April; the brewery bored her, and after all she was a pretty, strong young girl. But Stephen said he didn't know anybody stupid enough for April. Suddenly I was terribly afraid of hell, although April had no idea who had spoiled things for her. But now I wanted her to get married and stop standing around like a bare eucalyptus tree after a bush fire. I hadn't confessed my sin yet. God knew all about it anyway, and I didn't think Father Kelly could do anything about it. Where could we get a man for April? Parramatta isn't a small town any more. There's a lot of industry along Parramatta Road all the way to Sydney, and good farm land around us, and the nice jail and shops and everything. But a country town like that can be monotonous when compared with Sydney. And people have very good memories. They didn't forget that April had been jilted, and the men in their pubs and the women over their tea still asked each other what could have been wrong with her. Where were we going to find a suitable man for her? The gossip was actually as old as the olive tree John MacArthur planted on the lawn of Elizabeth Farm in 1805. The story of the olive tree lives on in Parramatta too. And the olives are as hard and dry as April is today. One could throw stones at the crows—it's that dreary at home now.

On the farm too, things were different. My only girl friend wasn't there any more. She was a native aborigine and as brown-black as roasted coffee. Her name was Goonur. She had snow-white teeth and a sweet, friendly face, beautiful eyes, a flat nose, and full lips always ready to laugh. Goonur had been at a mission in New South Wales for four years, and helped on our farm with the cows. I saw her for the first time after I had tried to bite April on the cheek. I told Goonur what I had done, and she said she would pray for me. At the mission, religion had got into her system. She was very understanding where my Lily was concerned; she knew that Lily was my special cow and left me alone with her.

Goonur always wore brightly-checked cotton dresses and jewelry made of all sorts of little berries and dried fruit, and Grandmother Fleet let her be. She understood the animals and helped with the preserving of the fruit. She sang in a high, monotonous voice songs she had learned as a child with her tribe in the bush. They were always the same few songs about the stone frog or the two "wi-oombeen" brothers and the emu, about Eerin, the gray owl, or about the whirlwind and the rainbird. I wanted to teach Goonur our bush songs, but she shook her head with its black, wooly hair, and said her songs were good enough for her. She knew everything about trees and flowers, and spoke to them in a cooing voice. When anybody came, she giggled and ran away. Altogether, she often ran away, and then I would look for her, and weep when I couldn't find her. I'd stand at the lakeshore and cry, "Goonur, where are you?" and suddenly she would spring out of the bushes like a kangaroo and hop around me. I liked her a lot, and she never said anything about my face. She stroked my long red-gold hair and wove little wreaths for me out of wild flowers.

One day Goonur was gone. We looked for her everywhere, and Stephen even tried to find her in the bush. Grandmother Fleet made inquiries at the mission, but she hadn't turned up there. Her Bible lay on the kitchen table, wrapped in leaves. Either she was looking for her tribe or she had set out for Sydney. Grandmother was furious because I wept, and said nomads were nomads, and Goonur wasn't worth weeping over. But I could see Grandmother looking around surreptitiously for days, when she was with the cows or cooking or sewing a cotton dress for me. She had liked Goonur very much, but again didn't want to admit it.

Strange things happen in this world of ours. I would never have moved to Sydney if I hadn't seen a copy of Miss Rigby's magazine on a table at my teacher's house in Parramatta. I was still going to school, and Miss Conroy was sweet to me. I asked her if I could take the magazine back to the farm with me, and she said of course, but I was to please keep it clean; that would only be polite. Miss Conroy had a thing about politeness, but she was the best of the lot, Grandmother Fleet excepted. I read *Insight* from cover to cover in Lily's stall, and it did get a bit dirty. After the holidays I gave it back to Miss Conroy. I was somewhat upset, when she asked if the cows had read *Insight* too. It was true in a way. Grandmother was furious, but Miss Conroy remained calm. But she didn't give me a book or a magazine to take home again for a whole year. She let me read, though, on her veranda. This was a great honor, because Miss Conroy was something special, like Lily, and only she could teach me things.

She was incredibly patient and unbelievably good. On those afternoons, over tea, she told me that what counted was the inner beauty of a human being. I would have liked to believe her, but experience spoke against it. Possibly I haven't succeeded in achieving this inner beauty.

Miss Conroy was born an old maid and lived contentedly in a world without men. She came from a fine old family where I am sure nobody ever swore or yelled so that the eucalyptus trees shuddered. The Conroys owned a lot of property near Camden, and their family history was very interesting, dating back to the free settlers in New South Wales. She talked about it sometimes, and she sent the Conroy saga to Miss Rigby for *Insight*. I read it later in Sydney, and got a lump in my throat. Miss Conroy was a good egg. She was pretty as a picture, but untouchable. Ash-blond curls, pink-white skin, and a pleasant smile. She adorned her pleasant, well-meaning self with simple lace, and collars that she had inherited. It gave her a sexless and enchantingly old-fashioned charm. She was clever and polite and compassionate, and for years did what she could for me. But she came from such a silent, pleasant and secure world, that she no longer could console me when school and my childlhood were over. It was she who arranged that I study massage. Our pharmacist had had his daughter learn it in Sydney, and she taught it to me. Later, in Sydney, I took an examination. Miss Conroy gave me a letter of introduction to Miss Rigby. The Rigbys had lived in Parramatta once. My teacher was worried about me because I was having a hard time, and sometimes misbehaved. She loved poeple, she really was unbelievably good, but then nobody had ever caused her any trouble. And somehow she managed to drag politeness out of anybody or everybody with whom she came in contact. It bordered on magic!

Two years ago, when I went to say goodbye to her in Parramatta, she was already lying quietly and contentedly on her flower-laden veranda. We had our last tea together, with delicate pastries and the fine English bone china teacups from "the homeland." Every bite stuck in my throat. I spared her my confession to the trick I'd played on April. She was much too ill for any excitement. Her heart was tired, and I think Miss Conroy was tired too. She gave me her blessing in a toneless voice, and again whispered something about "inner beauty," which was all-important. And then she said that a button was missing on my blouse, and that I should always dress nicely in the city. As a memento she gave me an opal ring, a family heirloom.

I never saw her again. She died three weeks after I moved to Sydney. I went to Camden for the funeral and her family stared at me. Who was I, and what did I want with their clan? I was sad because I knew that my "inner beauty" wasn't anything to brag about. On the farm I wept until I couldn't weep any more, then I went back to Mama Doody and Candy in Darlinghurst. What would Miss Conroy have said to the Doodys' manners? And to the boardinghouse and Candy's men? But probably she would have imposed some sort of politeness even on Mama and Uncle Doody. Nothing was impossible for Miss Conroy. She was sorry for bad or coarse or ruined types, but who wants to be pitied? I would never have played a trick on her. She would have overlooked it, and that's no fun . . . She was perfect.

I had been living just about a week with Mrs. Doody in Darlinghurst, not far from the King's Cross places of amusement, when Candy arrived. She comes from a gold-prospecting family in Kalgoorlie, and what could she be but a gold digger? She is, moreover, the most beautiful girl I have ever seen, and it is hard to believe that she is Mama Doody's niece. Candy is a natural blond. Her broad smile is naive, yet calculating, and she thinks the life of a model and occasional call girl wonderful. The latter profession is supervised by Mama Doody.

If Candy were not so lethargic and totally lacking in ambition, with her looks she could be a film star in Hollywood. Or marry some minor prince in retirement. She laughed heartily when I told her that. "Forget it, Molly," she said. "Australia's good enough for me." She is perfectly satisfied with her rich clients. Funny, in a way, that such a beautiful person should not have been repelled by my face. But perhaps she liked to look at her reflection in a dark pond.

As a model much in demand, she could already have been living in style, on her own, but with her indolence and good nature, she stuck to her Aunt Doody. The venetian blinds were broken, the plaster was peeling off the kitchen walls, but it didn't bother anybody. Candy's room though had been redecorated and painted, her couch upholstered with pink material. I washed and ironed the slipcovers when they were soiled. Then Candy lay like a bonbon in a silk-covered box. When I looked at her I felt hot and cold. She was almost too beautiful.

Candy didn't like me very much. Who did? But since she was pleasant and lethargic by nature, she let me fuss over her. I did her shopping, washed her beautiful gold-blond hair, and massaged her, because she was afraid she might grow fat, like Mama Doody. Her fear was not entirely unjustified because she ate sweets all the time, and when it was hot, didn't like to move around. Soon she found me indispensable, even if I was nothing much more than a piece of furniture to her. I typed her letters for her too, and sometimes I wrote them for her, which Candy found terribly funny. I liked her because she wasn't cruel and never called me Mole. I had told her about it, without mentioning my crime and April's misfortune, and Candy's big baby-blue eyes had filled with tears. Later I found out that she cried easily. Her tears were meaningless.

She had the Irish temperament that flared up easily. She could rage or weep over the littlest things, but afterwards she always asked me to forgive her. From the start she treated me like an old factotum whom one would never fire. Once she cried when a chair collapsed, and in the movies she sobbed her heart out. But anybody could have dropped dead beside her, she'd never have noticed it. Miss Conroy had wept for me too, but she had only been thinking of what she could make of me. Had she had the feeling that the big city wouldn't be good for me?

For a few months I was hoping that Candy would be my friend. She was so pleasant, and thanked me for every little thing I did for her. I don't know from where she got her nice manners, certainly not from her Aunt Doody, but all my efforts to become her friend failed. Sometimes she reminded me of the Pacific Ocean in Manly: what you threw into it eddied around for a minute or two and then sank.

How startled the Italian in King's Cross was when he suddenly saw my face under the lamppost. I could have killed him, but of course all I did was slap his face when he touched my birthmark. I'm not a carnival puppet, and he should keep his dirty hands to himself.

Charles Preston's real name in Carlo Pressolini, and he works as a waiter in the Restaurant Rosso. I never wanted to see him again, but I did. And we went and had a drink in the bar where he had admired my profile. I sat down again exactly as I had sat before, and that made him feel better. Just the same I had the feeling that he would have preferred to run away, but I asked him questions about Genoa, and that kept him with me.

Today I told Candy about my first honest-to-goodness admirer, if one can call Carlo Pressolini that. Until now I'd had to dream my men up. Candy seemed to believe me, but she wasn't particularly interested. However, she did ask, "What does your Carlo look like?"

"You wouldn't like him," I said hastily. "He's a wop with oily hair."

"I'll have to take a look at him in the restaurant."

"No, you won't!" I said.

Candy's eyes opened wide. "What's the matter with you? Sunstroke?" I had gone too far. At once I was humble and willing, like Grandmother Cocker, God rest her soul.

Carlo was quite good-looking in his way, and he had a soft, gentle manner, whether he meant it or not. I think it must be quite nice in Italy. According to Carlo they drink wine there instead of beer. I think wine makes men gentle and hungry for love; with beer they growl like radios turned on too loud, and it makes them sleepy before things even get started. At least that's what I think. Carlo never kisses me, much less anything more than that. But I don't expect it. "There are always mavericks," Stephen would say, when one strayed from the herd and stood alone in the meadow. I am twenty-two years old. April lost her virginity and her fiancé long before that. I wonder what it would be like to be with a man. I would so like to have a baby, then he could disappear. A little one that depends on you—that must be beautiful! A baby like that must think, at least for a few years, that every mother has a thing like that on her cheek. My baby would have only me, and wouldn't turn its face away when I was feeding it. If Carlo would give me a baby—there'd be room on the farm. And it would be something new for Grandmother. That would be perfect. But I can't ask him . . .

no . . . I don't have that much courage. Father never comes to the farm. He doesn't get along very well with his mother, and if he tried to beat me because of the baby, now I'd hit back. I've grown big and strong. But it's nonsense to even think of Father being furious about my son. And April sits there with nothing. Why doesn't she find a man? She's still good looking at twenty-seven, and there's cash in the brewery. When she was seventeen she ran after everything in pants; what's the matter with her now? I shouldn't have done it . . .

I know so little about myself. I love Granny Fleet and Stephen; I'd do almost anything for them. And they deserve it. And then again, I have such dark thoughts and think up awful things and snoop around and hate people. Isn't that odd? If Carlo would love me and leave me like any other girl, then at least I'd have experienced something, and wouldn't be empty and sour, like an unripe lemon. I pray, of course, and sometimes I go to confession, but I don't carry anything through. If I looked like Candy, or like myself without the birthmark, I think I would be so grateful. I'd do a lot of good deeds. Then Father O'Brien wouldn't have to worry about me. He's got enough to worry about anyway, here in Darlinghurst.

If Carlo wasn't such a stranger, everything would be easier. But just sitting around in a coffee bar doesn't make for greater intimacy. He's just as much of a stranger to me as the second Mrs. Rigby and their Hungarian housekeeper. I think the new Australians laugh over different things than we do, and perhaps they cry over different things too. And then such a lot of them find something wrong in our country. Why don't they stay home when nothing here is good enough? This is the best country in the world; everybody knows that. But Grandmother says the Naussies know why they came here. Father is hiring a German in the brewery. But most of them want to live in the big cities, in Sydney, or Melbourne, or Brisbane. Carlo said the other day, "Sydney is a melting pot." He uses such fancy language because allegedly he went to the university in Genoa. I don't believe it, but in his free time he is always reading serious books, and I guess learns the stuff by heart. Why didn't he become a lawyer if his parents really sent him to university? And he says they live in a big villa and have a car in Genoa. So why is he a waiter at Rosso's? But if I were to ask him, that would be the end of it, I know.

Candy really does have rich clients. Mr. Trent is supposed to be great fun, but rich men like that can be damned nasty when something doesn't suit them. I see how arrogant they are in the city. The way they get out of their cars. But Mr. Trent, the Irish giant, handles Candy like gold. You can't say that about Mr. Rigby. In Darlinghurst we call him "Albert Ritter, traveling salesman." We believed him. Why not? I always watch him in the hall when he visits Candy on Wednesdays. Mr. Trent comes on Mondays. Ritter doesn't know me. I always stand half-behind the door.

When I saw the picture of her husband at Mrs. Rigby's the other day, I burst out laughing. So Albert Ritter is really Alexander Rigby! I haven't told Candy yet. Even in his picture, Rigby-Ritter looked arrogant. A hooked nose, a narrow mouth, but his eyes . . . no sheila should look too deeply into them. But Candy is stupid. I mean, emotionally she's a dope. But she takes good care of herself. She even got a few quite nice pieces of jewelry out of Rigby. Apparently she's a better gold digger than her ancestors in Kalgoorlie. None of them were able to make a go of it in western Australia, and Candy sits pretty right here. Models have it made these days. When Candy, with her long false eyelashes, strides along, hips swaying, and that scornful expression on her little doll face—the photographers have taught her that—then no queen or Hollywood star could look more disdainfully at us miserable creatures. Candy has the last word at *Insight* and other magazines. When she wants to go to a shop, she drives up in a limousine. There are no buses in the advertising world, says Carlo. Goonur told me that her tribe believes in the medicine man, and that's how the white Australians believe in Candy's soap, or the refrigerator, or the wrinkle cream which she is supposed to use, and which will restore any shattered marriage. You can read it in the letters Candy gets from *Insight*. The men want to know more about the perfume, "Blue Night," and suggest a dinner à deux. Rigby and Trent do the same thing, and both of them are married. The married men seem to be the craziest. Of course they pay double or triple. Mama Doody says they have to give their wives lots of presents because of their guilty consciences. Why do they get married when they'd rather be free? When the fine gentlemen come to see Candy—their cars always wait for them at a discreet distance—I have to think of the older men who sometimes came to the farm. They had big torn felt hats and weathered faces: cattle drovers with no herds in the dry season. Grandmother Fleet gave them tea in the dusty twilight, and damper, our flat Australian cake baked in ashes; then they moved on like long question marks on our endless country roads. Every now and then, when the wind whirled the dry earth in the air, the wanderers would disappear in a yellow cloud of dust. Funny how often I have to think of these vagabonds when Candy's johns come stalking up to Mama Doody's hovel. These gentlemen have left the herd too. Why do they take Candy's alms while their decent wives hold supper for them at home? Why are old married men as restless as bush runners?

It's none of my business. I don't have a husband and never will. But a young man would be well-off with me, in every way. Rigby has a nice, pretty wife, much more reliable than Candy . . .

Yes, I had to laugh when I saw Rigby's picture in Vaucluse. If he knew how intimately I know him! Candy tells me all about him, what he says, his jokes, and what he's like in bed. That may not exactly be decent, but it has to be. If I didn't know all about him, it wouldn't work. Because I write Candy's love letters to him for her.

7

It Is Hot in November

On the morning of his fiftieth birthday, Alexander Rigby felt at least a hundred years old. He wasn't a brooder, but on this hot November morning he was inexplicably depressed. "I must have caught it from Anne," he thought as he shaved. His wife beat every sulking record from England to New South Wales.

Unfortunately Rigby hadn't been aware of this seven years ago. He had found Anne a shy but jolly young girl who would give him straping sons and a little daughter for his leisure hours. A single daughter would have suited Rigby fine. Young women in numbers bored or frightened him.

He had proposed to Anne in Paris. She had been sweet there. "Paris—never again!" he thought as he lathered his face. Yes. And now there was still no hope for a successor to the architectural firm. And he was fifty. When was he going to begin to raise sons?

But the worst thing was that Anne had changed so much. It was as if in the course of time a cute little koala bear had been transformed into a porcupine that burrowed down into the earth whenever a human being showed up. Dammit! thought Rigby. Why was Anne so shy? And why did she complain constantly about backaches? She had a masseuse, didn't she? At fifty, he could still outdo all the greenhorns around. Last week—the spume had flown high—he had beaten French at water-skiing! Age just didn't count, he thought with satisfaction.

He hadn't changed in the last seven years. And if Anne would keep her eyes open, she'd soon find out that there were much worse and more boring husbands than he. But Anne didn't keep her eyes open. She was not all that interested in her husband.

Rigby shrugged. Marriage was a lottery, and you could pick a dud. Of course Anne wasn't exactly a dud. First of all, she was beautiful, and she was so well-mannered that she could fire the most unpleasant things at him quietly, almost amiably. When he thought of the uproar to which his first wife had treated him, differences with the second Mrs. Rigby were almost a pleasure.

Rigby stopped shaving, and out of the blue asked himself why Betty West, née Withers, had turned him down seven years ago. For years she hadn't looked at anybody but him. Her success must have gone to her head. He had been an idiot to teach her how to write, years ago, by kissing every cliché from her naive lips. Thanks to that, Withers now found him beneath her. But only figuratively speaking, because he was still taller than any woman around. He wasn't so old yet that he walked stooped and couldn't straighten up. The idea made Rigby laugh out loud.

Yesterday he had wanted to begin a new life with his wife. He tried every few years to overcome a dead point in his marriage and was hurt when his attempts were ignored. With that in mind he had taken the trip to the Blue Mountains with Flora. Was it his fault that this new beginning had been the end of the first Mrs. Rigby? All the world loves a newspaper murder, but no one had been able to prove anything. Maddening that on this festive day he had to think of his first wife! For years now he had banished Flora Pratt into one of the farthest corners of his mind. He had to think of something else at once.

The nicest thing that came to his mind in a hurry was the model, Candy. He had always had a weakness for anything lovely. It could be girls, or flowers, or a perfect line on a piece of paper. The girl, Candy, was, as her name implied, a sweetmeat. He didn't expect her to also be a Madame de Staël or even an Elizabeth West. Candy had a career in the illustrated world as a sight for sore eyes. She was the golden bird in a jungle of houses in the city. Besides, she wrote him darling letters, hardly to be expected from her, because her conversation was below average. Candy was probably shy, and he liked that. Anne, and her predecessor, Betty, had been shy at first too, but less expensive. Candy's letters went to a cover address. Rigby knew enough bachelors glad to do him the favor. One helped oneself as best one could. Nothing to worry about. The moment would come when he could repay. He was a good correspondent, and answered every letter Candy wrote. But, seen by the light of day, Rigby tore them up. Albert Ritter, traveling salesman, wasn't balmy enough to write the most intimate things, even under a false name, to a sleasy boardinghouse in Darlinghurst, where the police could find them some day. And since the police, in spite of their stupidity, still came across far too many things, they could eventually find out who Albert Ritter really was. And the scandal of the Blue Mountains had been quite enough for him.

If Rigby was perfectly honest with himself, he would have given up these excursions to Darlinghurst long ago—if Anne had paid more attention to him. But he couldn't just sit every evening on the terrace with this taciturn, aloof wife, and more often than not with John Darling there too. Rigby knew he could trust the old fellow completely, but he just couldn't stand the number three. Even worse was Anne's sudden conviviality as soon as John turned up in Vaucluse. And his housekeeper had noticed how his wife came to life in John's presence. Of course he didn't discuss his wife with Mrs. Andrews. He still had all his marbles! Actually, right now he would have preferred a pleasant married life to haring after models. That was really more French's style, but that young man was interested in nothing but sports, beer, and architecture. Today's youth was funny.

And he, with his new beginning? Anne should have realized that one could love him only on *his* conditions. A young person had to adapt herself. He was the older, unfortunately, and the wiser. Anne was slow, but surely one didn't need seven years to know one's way around with such a simple fellow as himself! Anne still didn't have the faintest idea how to handle him. Yesterday he had tried, as patiently as he could, to instruct her. Possibly he had been a little ironic in the course of the discussion. Anne hated irony. And metaphor. Perhaps she hated him, or had her love soured? In short, last night on the terrace, he had been at special pains to be nice to his wife, although it should have been the other way around. He had almost been tender. That hadn't happened for quite a while. The atmosphere had been right, too: soft lighting on the big terrace and the water shimmering like mother-of-pearl on the floodlights. Steamers and boats were painted in fluorescent colors, and the black woods stood watch in the background. There was nothing on earth to compare with Sydney at night; there was also nothing on earth to compare with Mrs. Rigby's icy inflexibility. After a pause, Anne had informed him that she didn't need charity. What on earth did she mean by such nonsense?

Rigby cut his chin as he though about it. God was his witness: he spent a fortune on his wife. Always the best of everything; he even paid for her massages. It was enough to drive one crazy! If there was anything he hated, it was ingratitude. He had brought Anne from a hideous suburban home to paradise, and he never once complained about what he spent on her.

Rigby wiped the last drop of blood off his chin and wiped the perspiration from his forehead. Although it was early, the sweat was already pouring down his naked torso. That was the west wind. When it blew through the city in the spring, Sydney was an oven. Tonight he would swim in the ocean with his guests in Manly. Anne didn't swim.

He combed his thick hair back from his forehead. It was graying at the temples. What did he demand from his marriage anyway? A nice friendly creature at the breakfast table, not too soft, not too loud, not too stupid, and not . . . oh, the devil take it!

Rigby stepped through the open French window onto his private veranda. The sun glittered on the water and gave the harbor panorama a sharp clarity. It was the finest panorama in the world, but today Rigby longed for a solid fog. He had experienced it three years ago in London. Without Anne. She hadn't felt any desire to see her mother and her nice old secretary again—what was her name? Jennings—right. Even he, who frankly could do without seeing his family for years, had been astonished by Anne's lack of feeling.

Rigby held his hand up to his eyes, the morning sun was so blinding. In London's pea-soup fog, all human beings and the towers of Westminster had suddenly become indefinable. You could give the city content and dreams according to your imagination. Lady Carrington had been in the midst of writing a thriller, and Rigby had been able to give her a few tips about accidents. Hmm . . . it was ridiculous, but even the London fog, which Flora had never experienced, reminded him of her. If things went on like this, he could hang himself at the end of his festive day!

"Am I really getting old?" he asked himself astonished. What was it like, anyway, to grow old? He fastened his belt absentmindedly. It was an old belt and still fitted perfectly. Not an ounce of fat. When he thought of Paddy Trent, how heavy he was, and his Hungarian wife who could also lose a few pounds, he could be satisfied. And Trent was younger. In the sea he looked like a walrus. But otherwise he was a very decent cobber. From Ireland. His ancestors had come to Queensland from Dublin. Trent and he had become fast friends right away. Too bad that Paddy's first wife, the serious redhead, had driven him, Rigby, crazy with her so-called love. Today, seventeen years later, he had no idea whether Trent had suspected anything. All he knew was that dear old Paddy would have been happy if his wife hadn't bawled him out whenever he wanted to have some fun with his mob. The young woman, whose reputation wasn't all that snowy either, had been so bold as to spy on poor Paddy, like a policeman. Anyway . . . the police . . .

Why did his friends also have such bad luck in their marriages? It couldn't be the fault of the men or the climate. Except for the west wind, Sydney had the best climate in the world.

Rigby picked up a sketch from his bedside table and looked at it. The new house for the Trents in Avalon. Trent made a small fortune in his real estate business. They were building like crazy in Sydney. Trent & Company and Marchmont, Rigby & French got along like turtledoves, and shoveled in the money. Paddy was an honest cobber, even if he didn't understand anything about architecture. He would get a flat roof, however much he wanted a gabled, red tile one. Of course the flat roof was more expensive; it would have to be carefully insulated against the heat. But that wasn't what mattered. Trent was old-fashioned and you couldn't give in to that. A flat roof with a cleverly concealed water tank fitted in with the times. Horribly romantic gables and things like that were prehistoric. The next thing somebody would be asking for was Tudor windows! Not from architect Rigby!

After Rigby had condemned his friend Paddy to modern functionalism, he put the sketch in his portfolio, satisfied. Trent always built a new house when he married, after an appropriate amount of time had elapsed; an amusing little thing this time around—Klari Trent, née Karasz. She was no Venus, but Rigby had seen considerably less prepossessing females in his time. Unfortunately one had to give Paddy, who knew more about beer than women, a few pointers. Well, that was what he was doing. He was a good fellow and loyal to his mob.

How was that again about growing old? Even if Rigby had felt a hundred early this morning, he already felt better as he thought of his breakfast with Anne. It was nice to have his young wife with him when he was eating. Anne looked just as fresh in the morning as she did in the evenings. The English complexion was indestructible. Rigby hoped that on his birthday his wife would be charitable and smile at him. One could have anything one wanted from him with a little good behavior and tenderness.

Did one change after fifty? Rigby frowned. Would nothing more exciting happen? Would erotic desires and naive delight with one's own existence diminish? Did the demanding extravagances of one's earthly realm lose their charm? Old Marchmont probably knew all the answers to these questions, but he was a churchgoer. Rigby had no use for anything like that. Anne called him a heathen, but she'd better forget about that. First she should remember her duties as a loving wife. She was too well-off with him, that was the trouble. He had always been proud of his ability to face reality. Why did he have such gro-

94

tesque thoughts today? Nobody really knew the truth about life after death. One had to be satisfied with letting it surprise one. There was time enough for that. When he looked back at the past years, he could in all modesty be satisfied. At any rate, insofar as his profession was concerned. But now a considerable portion of his life lay behind him. Beside the monotony of everyday life and little pleasures, would nothing be left eventually but work? Was aging mainly a physical experience or primarily one of the mind? Did it come as a treacherous shock or as a last roll call to one's conscience? Would he be the same Rigby ten years from now, or only a worshiper of the era of technology in a repulsively objective world?

Rigby looked at himself in his long built-in mirror, and what he saw didn't please him. If he went on brooding like this, the legendary girl with the birthmark would have to massage *his* back too. Until now he had fortunately not seen Miss Fleet face-to-face.

Where was Anne?

Was she going to oversleep on his birthday? "All the better," Rigby mumbled, but he didn't mean it. Birthdays, weddings and funerals were important events for the Rigbys. A birthday morning with nothing special going on was not his idea of a birthday. Before his marriage, the mob had arrived at dawn; they had all celebrated vociferously and breakfasted on the big terrace. And that was as it should be. But a breakfast with noise and song was unthinkable where the second Mrs. Rigby was concerned. My God, Flora had caroled like a lyre bird and a kookaburra in unions on his birthday. "Alexander's 'Aunt' wasn't the worst of wives," even Miss Rigby had admitted on several occasions. In the evening Miss Rigby and the *Insight* crowd had given him a rousing party. And during the brief period of his widowhood, Betty West had wished him luck, almost lovingly. Those were the days! But not good enough for idiot Rigby. He'd had to marry again!

And now, the hell with it—he wanted his breakfast! Had Andrews overslept too? She had never forgotten his birthday, but if it came down to it, he could celebrate solo! He didn't need a woman to sing his praises in the November heat. But Mrs. Andrews was standing on the terrace like a sentinel, and had already opened the parasol over the flower-bedecked table. There were worse women than Andrews, he had often said. "Devilishly hot this morning," he mumbled.

Mrs. Andrews coughed her agreement and held a bunch of flowers under Rigby's nose. Absolutely superfluous with everything blooming wildly in the garden. And what was this? Rigby was holding a small package in his hands. Andrews shouldn't spend money on him. He'd told her so often enough. He looked slightly bewildered at a volume of poems by Judith Wright. She wrote excellent postwar poetry, but he couldn't take poems on an empty stomach. Nor at other times. Arrangements in a glass, metal, and cement satisfied his poetic needs completely. Certainly the language of modern architecture was not as articulate yet as the lyricism of New South Wales, Victoria and Queensland, but it had also developed, with vision and experimentation, to an ever-bolder expressionism, especially in this wide-open water citadel that welcomed the architectural experience. Sydney's inhabitants were a visual lot. Mrs. Andrews couldn't grasp that, but he wasn't interested in her grasp of things. He had every reason to be cautious. His jewel had a built-in explosive device. Beside Miss Rigby he didn't know one practical woman. Oh, Andrews meant well. This evening she would be his guest. He was having the whole thing catered by a restaurant so that Andrews might enjoy herself too. Right now she looked as if she wanted to run away. Were all females in their early fifties so sour?

"Thanks for the book." Rigby laid the little volume down beside the flowers with a stony expression. What he needed was a new angel; Andrews knew it only too well. "I would like to be excused from tonight's party, please," she said formally.

"Why?"

"I don't fit in with the guests."

"Neither do I. We have fun on birthdays whether we like it or not. Is that clear?"

Rigby's jewel gave him a look of remembrance which he chose to ignore. Years ago, when he had let himself in for this foolish business with Andrews it had been a hot November too. The same west wind. Well, yes—only an arrant fool sought his fun in his own house. In the course of the years, Rigby had tried frequently to marry his jewel off to one of her former compatriots in Sydney. All of them had done very well. Restaurant-owner Szabo in King's Cross had tried very hard to find a husband for Andrews, if only to please his steady client Rigby, because personally he couldn't stand Mrs. Andrews, but she stuck to Rigby, and right now she was driving his wife quietly crazy. Were all jewels so complex? He must try to find out. Why the hell was Andrews constantly offended? After all, he hadn't robbed her of her virginity. She had arrived in Sydney with a baby. He had been wondering for quite some time whether he shouldn't adopt Daisy, since he had no children, but until now he had been afraid of Anne's reaction. Women were a problem. If only they would love him less, everybody would live happily ever after. When he recalled the scenes Andrews had made—

why did he have to think of them today?—he had to admit that he preferred her in her present, half-frozen condition.

"All the best to your half-century," said Andrews.

"Shut up!" Rigby looked irritably around his festively decorated table. "Where's my food?"

Andrews held up a letter. "For Mrs. Rigby." After a pause she said glumly, "A man's handwriting."

"It's none of my business," Rigby said loyally.

Mrs. Andrews left satisfied. The letter had vexed him, even if he had pretended that it didn't concern him.

Rigby leafed through the volume of Judith Wright's poems, frowning. Who was writing letters to his wife? *His* wife? Rigby turned the pages angrily. What was that supposed to be? Sculpture?

The shape that waited there was future, fate . . .

How did this sheila from Armidale know such things? Rigby came across the famous bird poems. Not bad. Rigby himself couldn't have done better than the one about the lyre bird. Once, in Queensland, he had had the patience and luck to listen to the arias of this rare Australian bird in the bush. The lyre bird's own specific melody blended with the mysterious imitation of all sorts of sounds, from the noise of a motorboat to the laughter of the kookaburra. The male could raise his magnificent tail in the shape of a Greek lyre. The female was nothing to look at, as it should be.

> I'll never see the lyre birds—
> The few, the shy, the fabulous,
> The dying poets . . .

Rigby closed the book abruptly just before Andrews appeared with the covered dishes that gave forth an aroma of eggs, bacon, grilled tomatoes, and steak. His jewel was not to catch him reading poetry in this infernal heat. But it would do no harm if he were to read what Judith Wright had written about the black cockatoos and currawangs when he got to his office. After the office he would take the ferry from Circular Quay and visit the birdhouse in the Taronga Zoo. The bird world calmed him. The thought made his face light up for a moment. But where was Anne? Did he have a birthday every day, and the fiftieth one at that? And what bastard was writing his wife long letters?

Anne Rigby knew that she should have set the alarm. She knew that Alexander was expecting her to appear for breakfast. She knew everything. But she lay in bed as if paralyzed, and the November heat crept slowly under her skin. The fuss Alex was making was ridiculous. The calendar meant nothing. Besides, they weren't two love birds any more, and a fiftieth birthday was no occasion for jubilation, not in her opinion. At that moment she couldn't remember when she had last laughed heartily. Perhaps with John Darling or Shirley Cox. Anne yawned and turned on her other side. She had a half hour or so, then she would have to get up. At any rate, she was going to try to, to please Alex, although she felt she was no means in duty bound to do anything to please him.

When Andrews knocked on the door three times, Anne sat up, startled. She didn't need the alarm any more. Andrews's expression was malicious. It didn't make Anne feel good.

"Mr. Rigby has almost finished his breakfast."

"But it's only six-thirty!"

Andrews looked at her wrist watch although she knew exactly what time it was. "Half-past seven, Mrs. Rigby."

"Thank you." Anne was so furious that she reddened.

Mary Andrews stood indecisively for a moment. Should she help Mrs. Rigby into her housecoat? Comb her hair? Impossible! Let Rigby see what he had married. But Andrews hadn't been able to stand the sight any more of Rigby waiting patiently for his wife to appear. Andrews closed the screen door quietly. Should she be an absolute angel and suggest to Rigby that he wait a little longer?

Anne got up laboriously. In spite of the massage her back ached. Badly. And Alex hated invalids. Anne was surprised herself at her constant physical complaints in Sydney. She had never been sick at home, except for an occasional cold. It had to be nerves. Apparently only a spiritual athlete could stand being married to Rigby. Anne wanted to be loved in her way, not in Alexander's domineering and unpredictable way. There were weeks when he paid no attention to her whatsoever, and then, suddenly, as last night, without any preparation, he had wanted to be tender. As if he were throwing alms to a beggar. But he hadn't counted on Anne's response. She was certainly not as talented, nor as popular, nor as charming as Alex, but you couldn't treat her like that! Drag her out of her corner because it happened to suit him, only to put her back in the corner again afterwards. For Anne, sympathy, to say nothing of love, was a thing of consistency.

She combed her beautiful long hair agitatedly as she thought of Alexander's mood yesterday. Perhaps she shouldn't have rejected him so brusquely. Perhaps marriage demanded constant forgiving and

98

never-failing tolerance. But all her honest efforts had aroused no love in Alex. It wasn't surprising that this condition of disappointment and isolation was making her ill. She was only thirty-five. And of course the fact that they had no children was the worst failure. Although Alex spent almost all his evenings away from home, he had wanted children. That was why he had married again. Naturally he couldn't have known that a healthy twenty-eight-year-old girl would let him down in this respect too. Besides that he accused her of being cold, indifferent, shy, and a spoilsport. What she held against Alex she preferred to keep to herself.

She appeared on the breakfast veranda, her present in her hand, just as Alexander's big white car was racing out of the garden gate. Anne's heart beat fast. The heat made her dizzy. Alex would never forgive her. Of course Mrs. Andrews had wakened her too late on purpose. She hadn't looked like the cat that swallowed the canary for nothing. Anne felt ill.

"Am I the one who is fifty today?" she asked her husband's empty wicker chair. There were lines on her forehead, like veins in marble. How could she give her life a new purpose? If only she could still write poetry. That had always relieved her, but she was too hollowed-out, and she felt she couldn't say anything that others hadn't said better before her.

If only John Darling had been there last night! But her only friend in Sydney was with his family in Camden for the reading of a will, just on Alexander's big day. Alex had accepted the fact grudgingly. John was part of the inventory. But Alex would have his whole mob assembled around him tonight, and Miss Rigby would see to it that all ran smoothy. She took everything off Anne's hands in spite of her legendary workload. She would be astonished to hear that Anne resented it. Miss Rigby had never felt superfluous in her life. She couldn't imagine that Anne had grown so shy because there was nothing for her to do in Vaucluse. Because the household had been run forever by the competent Mrs Andrews. And Anne was the last one to project herself or go in for power plays. She needed to be encouraged. Only her father had understood that.

Andrews brought Anne's breakfast on the silver tray that Elizabeth West had given her as a wedding present. Miss West would have been much better suited to Alex, Anne thought. She couldn't imagine why the two hadn't married. Both had been born and brought up in this country, and Miss West was resilient, even though she was of only medium height and not as slender or well-proportioned as Anne. But she was lively and self-assured, and Alex respected her for her achievements. Like the girl she had been in London, Anne saw perfectly clearly that everybody was right. What on earth was she doing here?

Mrs. Andrews put the breakfast platters and Anne's teapot down on the table and looked at the second Mrs. Rigby triumphantly before retiring. Anne drank the iced pineapple juice and sat there for a while, brooding. After a while she drank two cups of tea and with revulsion looked at the steak, which had grown cold, and the runny fried egg. Perhaps her great mistake had been to see a father figure in Alexander just because he was so much older, although she had always known that calendars lied. She felt a hundred and fifty years old, withered like a tree for which the centuries no longer counted. Dead eucalyptus trees were an ordinary sight in Australia.

And John Darling wasn't in Sydney. Anne was fully aware of the fact that it was ridiculous for her to need John so much, and how impossibly she was behaving when she occasionally told him so. He didn't want to hear it. He was Rigby's best friend. Anne often asked herself how Alex could deserve such a friend.

Mrs. Andrews appeared with a letter which she laid discreetly on the table. "Is there anything I can do for you, Mrs. Rigby?"

Anne thanked her. Andrews had done quite enough for her this morning.

Anne cut up the steak and fed it to her dog, then she opened the fat letter. It was from John Darling in Camden. He had never written her a letter before. Usually he addressed his letters to Mr. and Mrs. Rigby.

Anne had to read the letter three times before she had digested the contents. This was impossible! No, it *was* possible, and John had kept it to himself all these months.

Anne went back to bed as if in a trance. She was so tired that she fell asleep at once. The letter fell on the floor. Andrews came into the room on tiptoe to fetch Anne's blue evening gown that needed pressing. Rigby liked blue.

Mary Andrews saw the letter lying on the floor. Since hers was an orderly nature, she picked it up and laid it on the bedside table of the sleeping woman. Then she left the room on tiptoe again, the blue dress over her arm. Yes, of course, she had also read the letter. After all, she had to know what Professor Darling was writing to the wife of her Mr. Rigby. Six pages . . .

Anne slept for quite a few hours. The pills she had taken the night before finally worked. When she awoke, she read the letter again. Then she called her doctor. She felt feverish and wanted an injection. Alex would never forgive her if she was unable to attend his birthday party.

Mrs. Andrews knocked and brought fruit juice and the blue evening dress. On the hanger it looked like a blue corpse swinging on a gallows in the wind. "Thank you very much." Anne could hear her own voice as if from a great distance. Her bedroom was split up suddenly into white and blue-gray shapes that interlocked. The blue corpse was still swinging back and forth.

Mrs. Andrews put an ice compress on Anne's forehead. Alexander was there suddenly, asking, "What's the matter now?" Anne was coming to after a brief fainting spell, and seemed to be looking for something. Alexander, who was always one jump ahead of her, asked, "Are you looking for John Darling's letter?" Then he turned to Andrews, who was standing beside him, a half-full bowl of ice in her hands. He looked at her for a moment and knew at once by her expression that she had read the letter. "It's all right," he said calmly. "It's just the heat again. I'll help my wife to dress later."

He laid John Darling's letter back on Anne's bedside table and watched Andrews until she left the room. Then he opened the curtains, let the afternoon sun into the blue-white room through the corner window, and told his wife not to talk. "You must rest now, or you won't be fresh for this evening."

"Have you read John's letter?"

"Yes, of course. A big surprise, isn't it? Wouldn't have thought the old codger capable of it."

8

The Small Pleasures of Life

Rigby's birthday party outdid everything that had gone before. It was an open-air fête in the best of taste, arranged by a city elite with arcadian inclinations. After the reception in Vaucluse, in which official congratulators and members of the Architects Club participated, Rigby and his friends from the yacht club drove to his summer home in Manly. He had ordered a moonlit night. Except for Anne, everything was as it should be.

Rigby's white country house in Manly was surrounded by pines and looked down on the ocean from a wooded height. Whoever didn't want to enjoy the roof garden with its flowers, went swimming. Rigby's bathhouse in the garden offered everything conceivably necessary for improvised water games. Manly lay like a glittering jewel between harbor and ocean. Excursionists coming from Sydney could reach Manly by the ferry leaving Circular Quai every half-hour, and get off at the harbor bathing facility, or at the magnificent beach promenade, flanked by pines. If any of the swimmers found themselves in the neighborhood of sharks, in spite of all safety measures, they were invariably brought back to safety by the Volunteer Lifeguards, an Australian organization of men who practiced their dangerous, self-sacrificing duties year-in and year-out at the numerous bathing resorts and beaches. Rigby too had saved quite a few swimmers in the days of his youth.

Rigby was a radiant host. Whoever didn't know him well would never have guessed that on this day someone had thrown a monkey wrench into the proceedings. When he had read John Darling's letter to his wife, he had felt very simpleminded. Also he had felt dimly that Anne's indefinable relationship to his best friend was somehow the result of his own neglect. Actually he couldn't explain to himself why, in spite of his frequent absences from Vaucluse, he had to think so often of his wife. Her shadow darkened his small pleasures. Sometimes, during a conference at the office, he would see her suddenly, powdering herself after a bath, her face hard, or in an empty room, doing some little household chore rigidly and absentmindedly.

Rigby saw something almost funny in his marital problems. Hadn't he had to run away from women all his life? But there you were . . . the second Mrs. Rigby had fallen in love with his best friend. John Darling's letter left no doubt about that. Rigby couldn't think of anything more ridiculous.

While he was receiving his guests on the terrace at Vaucluse with Anne, he studied her unobtrusively. So she had more initiative then he had thought her capable of! And he had thought he knew women! Moreover, to his vexation, he found Anne looking especially pretty tonight. She was wearing the long pastel-blue dress he had picked out for her. So he was still good for *something!* And she was smiling her disinterested smile that always drove him crazy. Today she reminded him of the figurehead on a sinking ship, staring with indifference at the wild sea. During the reception he had to remind his figurehead from time to time that this was not a funeral. Once he grabbed her brutally by the arm and murmured, "Pull yourself together, for God's sake, or you'll be sorry! I've had just about enough!" Smiling at his wife as he said so, because of all the people around them.

At that moment Marchmont arrived. Rigby hurried to greet him. Anne was surprised to see with what warmth he greeted the old man with the eagle profile and his shock of white hair. No son could have been more loving. Alex helped his boss slowly and carefully up to the terrace. The senior partner of Marchmont, Rigby & French was not supposed to exert himself in any way right now, but of course Alexander's fiftieth birthday was a big exception. Stanley Marchmont sat on the terrace quietly and happily, in a comfortable chair, and all the important guests gathered around the founder of the famous architectural firm. But Marchmont had eyes only for Alex—God bless him! Since Rigby had constantly to greet new guests, Miss Rigby, Elizabeth West, and Robbie French looked after Marchmont. The old man shook his head impatiently: they were blocking his view. He wanted to enjoy his Alex.

The babel of voices was suddenly silent. The great moment had arrived. Speeches for Rigby. The first to speak was Robbie French, in the name of the firm and the generation to follow Rigby, to whom he had taught the tricks of their trade. Robbie French handed his senior partner a little statuette that he had sculpted himself, fortunately not a lady with two heads, but an emu in bronze. Rigby looked at the bird for a moment, silently and critically, until the pause became embarrassing for his audience. Then he slapped his junior partner on the shoulder so hard that it shook him. "Thank you, Robbie. The bird's not bad."

Coming from Rigby this was such high praise that French, confused, murmured that he had done his best, after which he took refuge behind old Marchmont, who nodded approvingly.

The "boys" from the government and city administration weren't going to be outdone. They expressed themselves with the customary brevity but with so much approbation that Marchmont had to cough twice. Rigby, according to them, lived for Sydney's architectural future, and the city wished to thank him today for past and future achievements. At that moment old Mr. Marchmont could see his cobber, Jonathan Rigby, and how he had shoved his beanpole of a son up to him like a piece of furniture and said, "Make something of him, Stan."

Parramatta was also represented. Their ambassador was much younger than Stanley Marchmont, but the green young man knew that Adam, Colin and Jonathan Rigby had planned and built Parramatta, and that Alexander's first architectural experience had been with the stone house the family had built. Marchmont looked sharply for a moment at his still youthful and now famous partner. His Alex was blushing like a schoolboy as he accepted a plaque with a painting on it of the first Rigby home in Parramatta, as a token from his native city. Miss Rigby looked pale, Elizabeth West was red as a beet, and Anne look stupefied. Architect Rigby, cobber Rigby, and husband Rigby were very different people. The mob didn't move; they were so proud of the old devil!

Old Marchmont stayed exactly an hour and twenty minutes; that was all Dr. Dobson, the young doctor on Macquarie Street, had allowed. Plenty of time for such an old heart. Anyway, after the ovations, Marchmont was glad to go back to his quiet terrace in Mosman Bay and think everything over quietly again. Dr. Dobson and Alex took him to his car, then went back silently to the guests.

And now Rigby was standing beside his wife again, on the terrace, greeting the latecomers, in the course of which he crossed silently and smoothly over the hill of his anger. His self-control was perfect. He looked radiant and invincible, and not even his wife knew what it was costing him. Anne found him even more of a stranger than during their happy London days. His metallic smile was threatening, like a mask in a nightmare.

Rigby handed his wife a full glass of wine and looked deep into her eyes in front of everybody. Anne shivered. Was she already standing on the brink of an abyss like the first Mrs. Rigby?

"Your health, Anne!"

The mob cheered. Wasn't she to be envied? And Alex? Some people had all the luck. Rigby was not only professionally successful, on top of everything else he had managed to snap up this pretty little doll! She sat at home like a good girl and waited for him. Try to find that again! Long live the old bush bandit! The drinks were first-rate.

Miss Rigby raised her glass. "Cheers, little brother!"

Rigby and his tall sister clinked glasses; he was still taller than she. He asked the old girl if she was satisfied. Miss Rigby thought it was a good show. "Father should have lived to see this," she said, her eyes on the dark trees around them. Then she clinked glasses with Alexander's young wife and told her she could be proud of her husband.

Dainty Elizabeth West's eyes were shining, her hair curled wildly. She whispered, "I'm so happy, Alex! It's a big day for you." Rigby replied, "You could have had your hair done for this big day. Look at my wife, for example."

At last it was Mrs. Andrews's turn. Until now she had kept modestly in the background. "My best wishes, Mr. Rigby."

"Why the funereal expression? This isn't a funeral, Mrs. Andrews. I keep having to tell the members of my household that."

"Is that a joke?"

"Maybe."

Andrews mumbled something to the effect that she would stand by her benefactor, come what may. Alex accepted the threat with a sour expression. If only Andrews would shut up! If only she would fade away! In her gray dress she reminded him of a room that wasn't lived in, with dust covers on the furniture. Yes, he'd have to let Andrews go; she read his wife's letters. No married man could permit such a breach of conduct. He would have to make quite a few changes in Vaucluse. Quite a few? Everything! But when he thought of firing Andrews, he got a queasy feeling in the pit of his stomach. She would make a scene. The thought of the possibilities inherent in the Hungarian temperament made him shudder. Naturally he couldn't fire her overnight, after so many years of faithful snooping. He'd have to talk with Bertie Dobson. Perhaps he could take on his Hungarian jewel. But at once dropped the idea. Old lady Dobson, who sat around in Bertie's bachelor apartment all the time, wouldn't put up with Andrews for ten minutes. Bertie's mother cooked very well and wouldn't let any cook spoil her broth! Meals at the Dobsons were remarkable. Bertie was very attached to his mother's cuisine. That was why he hadn't married yet, at thirty-eight. He'd never find anything to equal the life he was leading: peace and quiet and fabulous meals, a lucrative practice in Macquarie Street, and a little girl friend. All the boys were smarter than Rigby . . .

Meanwhile Andrews had moved off in the direction of the cold buffet. "Such junk, and for all that money!" she thought. Just to torture herself, she tasted one dish after the other. She had made up her mind not to enjoy the party for a single moment, and it satisfied her to see how successful she could be. When she looked at the former Miss Karasz, who had managed to catch rich Patrick Trent, she'd had it. This vain hope of Hungarian literature had ignored her guardian angel from the immigration station with unabashed impudence. But Andrews could remember how seven-year-old Klari Karasz had wept on her shoulder because she was so homesick. At the time she had been scared to death of the Aussies; and the friendlier they were, the more they frightened Klari. Tonight she was laughing loudly for all Australian ears to hear, and was strutting around in a dress that consisted for the most part of decolleté. Andrews was ashamed of her. Certainly it was hot in November, but that was no excuse for a Christian to run around three-quarters naked! Besides, Klari was flirting outrageously with Rigby. Disgusting! Andrews was sickened. Even on this day of honor, her Rigby was studying Mrs. Trent's voluptuous bosom whenever he had a chance. And this on the day that had shattered his marriage! Of course Andrews felt sorry for him, but at last, he would experience for himself how it hurt to be betrayed.

Although still waters ran proverbially deep, she had never thought it possible for the second Mrs. Rigby to have an affair. In Australia, one never knew where one was at with people. Even one's former compatriots weren't the same. Miss Karasz, for instance, had changed almost unrecognizably. Before her brilliant marriage she had been modest, unworldy, and dreamy. As Mrs. Patrick Trent she had developed a pathological and insatiable urge to shop, dress luxuriously, and make eyes at every man in New South Wales. The spectacle revolted Mrs. Andrews. Now she was laughing over one of her husband's jokes which no immigrant would ever understand. Who in Budapest had ever heard of *diggers* (war veterans) *graziers* (sheep station owners) or *sheilas* (girls)? But Miss Karasz was laughing hypocritically right along with the rest. She couldn't possibly find any of it funny. Andrews knew her too well.

Miss Rigby looked upon her husband's housekeeper as a hopeless case. She had observed, with irritation, that Mrs. Andrews's anger was directed at all those who had accepted the Australian experience positively, and they were in the majority. Why did Mary Andrews stick to her provisional attitude toward Australia? She would never go back to communist Hungary. She knew very well on what side her bread was buttered. Moreover, shortly after Alexander's second marriage, Miss Rigby had offered to find a new position for his housekeeper. With Mrs. Andrews's capabilities and the many bachelors in Sydney, this would not have been difficult, but here Miss Rigby had hit granite. As soon as the source of his food was endangered, there was no reasoning with Alex.

Meanwhile Andrews had arrived at a torte iced with baroque magnificence. Her recipe was better. Of course in the case of such huge cakes, butter, eggs, and sugar were used sparingly, but Rigby apparently wanted to throw his money into the Pacific. The icing, though, *was* remarkable. The Aussies could be effective on state occasions, when they took the trouble. She must remember the icing for Rigby's seventy-fifth. Not that he deserved it, but she loved even her enemies . . .

She saw Rigby whisper something to his wife. His smile couldn't deceive Andrews. Her boss was furious. She knew the wild look in his eyes by experience, whether it was aimed at a burnt omelet or adultery. Mrs. Rigby could consider herself fortunate if she met the dawn unharmed. There was something hunted in the expression of her eyes and the way she carried herself, because she couldn't put on nearly as good an act as Rigby. That was how the political prisoners in postwar Budapest had looked when the communists had interrogated them. Mrs. Andrews couldn't understand the second Mrs. Rigby. How could one run after a boring bookworm like John Darling when one had Rigby? Although he was a murderer of the spirit, Andrews still preferred Rigby to any of the rest of the mob. And how he still looked at fifty! Not easy to duplicate. Unfortunately Mrs. Rigby seemed to be in a state of panic. Andrews noticed how her long white hands moved restlessly over her hips. And for that she had pressed the blue dress? Andrews didn't envy Mrs. Rigby the discussion that would surely follow the party. Rigby would question her mercilessly: when, where, and how often? The tongue would stick to the mouth of this arrogant little fool. And in hell it was probably hotter than in Australia, and there were no iced drinks. The thought made Andrews smile for the first time that evening.

Anne looked from the roof garden across the illuminated scene below, and the dark blue ocean shore. Under the luminous moon the world looked calm and glowed in the pure colors of its spectrum. The miracle works of technology sank into the Pacific. Voices rose up to Anne. Daisy Andrews, the housekeeper's daughter, was laughing softly with Robbie French. A record was singing somewhere of love and the pain of separation. The ocean moved gently in an eternal rhythm. The sand shimmered like eggshell porcelain. Couples, their arms entwined, wandered along the beach, under the pines. Every now and then shining spots moved across the water along shore: ruby red, silver and green bathing caps. The world was unbearably still. Only the ocean waves rolled powerfully across the sand and were lost in it. Like love and hate, hope and disappointment. Everything was incomplete and fleeting. Why did she seek escape in cold symbolism? The others were enjoying the festive scene. Alexander too stepped out of the illuminated sphere into the dark of night. She was the only one stranded on the roof of the house.

Miss Rigby brought cold drinks and two plates of cold cuts. She couldn't possibly be enthusiastic about vegetating up here on the roof with Anne, because she had just been chatting animatedly in the garden about *Insight* and other lesser stars in the media heaven. But years ago Miss Rigby had also visited poor, giggly Flora Pratt in Vaucluse once a week. Really unfortunate that Alex kept getting married!

"Why don't you come down in the garden?" Miss Rigby asked. "Paddy Trent is telling jokes."

"I felt funny enough this afternoon," said Anne.

"I know, I know," Miss Rigby said impatiently. She pulled up a chair and put the food and drinks on a table. Anne was correct in her impression that Miss Rigby was making a big sacrifice on her behalf.

"Aren't you tired, Grace?" Miss Rigby had at last suggested to Anne earlier today that she call her sister-in-law by her first name.

"I am never tired."

Anne sighed. The tireless ones had no idea how tiring they could be. "Wouldn't you say it's a real Italian night?" she asked, just for something to say.

Miss Rigby answered promptly, "What do you have against an Australian night?" Her moon, here in Australia, was every bit as good as the one in Florence, if not better. Water was water wherever you were. And swinging lanterns were not a specialty only of Italy, even if the immigrants thought so. A stupid lot!

Grace Rigby hungrily ate her way through all sorts of different delicacies with no sense of order. She never had an upset stomach and nobody knew where she put all the food she ate. "Did John write?" She

108

was eating fruit cake with whipped cream and looked at Anne sideways.

"He sent Alex a telegram."

"That was to be expected," Miss Rigby said drily. "I mean, he must have told you about the big event. After all, one doesn't get married every day. I would never have thought it of the old codger."

"Of course he wrote to us about it." Anne's voice sounded flat. "In all the excitement I forgot it."

Miss Rigby swallowed her next remark. The whole thing was too stupid. Anne and old John Darling had been inseparable. Was that why Anne was so crushed? Had there been any real intimacy between her and John? Anything was possible in this lousy world, but she didn't think so. Old John was a man of principles, and had now married a woman with principles. Besides, Professor Darling hated complications which might rob him of the concentration he needed for his work. She knew the old codger like her own pocket.

"Do you know John's wife?" Anne asked. She hadn't intended to ask it, not at any price—it had just slipped out. John's letter had exhausted her. Delicately and anxiously, as was his nature, John had made clear to her that she was a young romantic. He had noticed, and it had worried him, that she had slipped into a certain dependency on him, quite unintentionally on his part. He was not as important as she thought. She shouldn't see anything special in him. He was a perfectly ordinary old codger; Miss Rigby had always said so. In short, Anne had to try to understand Alexander better, and knock all this nonsense about John out of her pretty little head. He remained her devoted friend and hoped sincerely that she and his wife would be good friends. That was the essence of his long and cautious letter. She had thrown herself at him, and John Darling had probably experienced moments of great embarrassment. He had none of Alexander's brutal nonchalance. John could feel his way effortlessly into a lonely young person's heart. She hadn't needed his company more and more for nothing. She had even toyed with the idea of marriage since Alexander seemed to be going his own way. But of course had never mentioned it. She had only envisioned this happy ending in her wishful dreams.

"Of course I know Ruth Eastman," said Miss Rigby. "A very efficient woman. Around forty. Ruth has worked for years for our natives, in missions and reservations. *Insight* once published an article on Eastman and her black sheep."

"Then she shares John's interests."

"Naturally," said Miss Rigby. "That's the basis of every sensible marriage." She wasn't looking anywhere in particular. She went on to say that the Eastmans were landowners in the Camden area, not as important as the Darlings, but good enough. Good fruit and excellent cattle. Miss Rigby found the marriage suitable. Yes, Ruth Eastman had worked for a year now on the Aboriginal Mission Board in Sydney, and over the weekends John had dictated his anthropological textbook for students to her. That was why John had never been able to come and see them on weekends, thought Anne. She had never visited him where he worked. For that she was too shy. She hadn't even read the paper, *Dawn*, that explained about the demands and integration of the aborigines. At first John had brought her several copies, but then he had stopped.

"I never visited John in his office," said Anne. "I was afraid of disturbing him."

"And you certainly would have. Anyway, during the last years the only way to John was over Ruth Eastman's dead body." Miss Rigby added that Miss Eastman—for a week now Mrs. John Darling—wouldn't put up with any nonsense from anybody.

"Have you known them both for a long time?"

"Since the creation of New South Wales," said Miss Rigby. "I haven't the faintest idea why it took John fifty years to propose to her. But there was something that prevented it. That's right—Ruth first had to nurse her mother and grandmother until they died, not both at the same time, of course."

Miss Rigby lit a cigarette, then offered her sister-in-law one. Anne thanked her—she already had enough smoke and fog in her head. Miss Rigby explained that on birthdays all the Rigbys turned up in a body at the Eastmans. "I have never seen such sob sisters as Mother and Grandmother Eastman," Miss Rigby went on. "Those two would have liked to tie Ruth to their bedposts until Judgment Day. Stupid people!"

"My mother wasn't so keen about my presence, either."

"Your mother has managed to make a marvelous career for herself, my dear Anne. You must ask her to visit us. We'd give her a dinkum reception at the club, get the press in on it, and all the rest. You see, my child, a career makes all the difference in the world. The ideas of the Eastman ladies on family life go back to the time of William the Conqueror. But you can't get away with anything with Ruth. She always knows what the score is."

Anne said nothing.

"Grandmother Eastman's funeral was really exceptionally nice," Miss

Rigby went on. "Much more enjoyable than Ruth's mother's. The mimosa was in bloom, a beautiful sight—the bushes blooming. You sit around in Vaucluse must too much, Anne . . . What else did I want to tell you? Oh yes—in the case of Ruth's mother, they couldn't get her under the ground fast enough. The Eastmans, of course, had all the time in the world. But the guests wanted to get it behind them. Here everybody's always tearing back to their animals. And they're right. All the chatter and the masses of food aren't going to bring the dead back."

"That's right," said Anne. Miss Rigby was always right. Somehow Anne couldn't imagine herself spending many evenings in the future with the Darlings. In order to contribute something to the conversation she asked what Miss Eastman's father had been like.

"Tom Eastman was great, absolutely great." Miss Rigby lit her fourth cigarette. She smoked as quickly and methodically as she did everything else. "Ruth's father was a loner. And when the weeping and wailing and shivering at home became too much for him, he went walkabout."

"What's that?"

"He wandered off. That's a word you should know by now, Anne. We took it over from the aborigines. Sometimes Tom Eastman turned up in Queensland, or in South Australia, where Betty comes from. And he spent a year in the Northern Territory. We've got plenty of room in this country if anybody finds his four walls too much for him. Every now and then he'd come home and attend to business. Ruth's brothers looked after things pretty well. When Mother Eastman died, the old man came back for good. Then he was alone with his two sons, and everything ran smoothly, the way he wanted it. Ruth went to the mission. We published Tom's report from Alice Springs in *Insight*. People like Tom die out slowly. The industry in New South Wales overpowers the old bush myths. I don't object. I'm always for the day after tomorrow."

Anne saw Miss Rigby as if through a veil. Where were they anyway? Still on the roof garden? She was exhausted, and fell suddenly into that light-headed condition in which, in the old ivy-overgrown house behind Avenue Road, she had once written poetry. She saw, heard, and understood with greater clarity than usual. Persons, things, landscapes, and dream pictures stepped forward, painfully lit, out of the dark zone of the consciousness into the light of conscience.

Perhaps this vast and mysterious continent bestowed a glowing vision on those very immigrants from more pallid regions. The first, second, and third periods of assimilation were hard because the land and people were so different from what they had been at home, in the old, tired, more skeptical lands. Not until the blazing sun on the country roads, the crippling summer heat, the indifferent looks, or the coarse jokes of the native population no longer tortured the new Australian, did the stoical, taciturn loneliness and courage of this virile continent begin to speak with a thousand tongues. Then Australia sang. After years of painful adjustment and absurd misunderstandings, the cities spoke with a new, buoyant voice, and this corner of the earth expressed itself through its last original inhabitants, who had strayed from the Stone Age into the twentieth century. Then the prehistoric mammals, the nightmare birds in the bush, the deep-sea wonders of the tropical north, came to life for the stranger. And the shower of blossoms on the monotonous garden houses gave the sprawling Australian suburbs a touch of poesy.

Anne had not yet reached the stage in which Australia would enrich her. Until now this sunny land had only robbed her of strength. But on Alexander's birthday, on the roof garden in Manly, she had an Australian vision for the first time. She saw the dance of the men and the sharks.

Young Australians, in the colorful uniforms of the Volunteer Lifeguards, passed across the beach like living bronze statues. Their light hair fluttered in the breeze. And at the head of the procession of the joy of life and the danger of death, marched Alexander. Anne recognized him. He walked like a boy and glowed without exertion. Anne had never known young Alexander . . .

The young demigods danced along the shores of the Pacific, rulers of Oceania, unfettered by the shackles of civilian existence. They dived into the sea, surfaced jubilantly, and celebrated their rebirth. Business and sheep stations, bank accounts, social status, electric toys, newspapers, tea kettles, blankets, razors, responsibilities—all were left behind on the shore somewhere, in stone palaces or bush huts, in hotels, boardinghouses and narrow marriage-barracks, where wives and tax officials waited.

They sang without words. Primeval, lusty sounds issued forth from their throats, an elementary shout for the nymph with no address, with no demands, and with no vocabulary. These swimmers were Neptune's bastard sons in Australia, and at last they knew it again. Never again would they crawl back into the homes or high-rise houses of the twentieth century! Never again would they lie to their loving women about where, how, and with whom they were spending the evening. From now on they would ride into infinity on the backs of the sharks. They would become one with the water, with the moonlight, and with the silence of the night.

The sharks heard their song and swam greedily toward the shore. They reared up high, as if they were greeting the audience in a theatre, and opened their predatory jaws as the intoxicated mob came dancing up and threw themselves, arms entwined, into the ocean. "Alex!" Anne screamed from the roof garden, but she screamed only deep inside her. Helplessly she watched how young Rigby moved fearlessly closer to the jaws of the tiger shark, while warning searchlights cut across the sky, and an invisible chorus of kookaburras, with their horrible humanlike voices, began a concert of laughter. Anne's outcry died away in the cosmic storm. Alexander hadn't shied away from danger at any age. It fascinated her, because he was forever in flight from familiar shores. Anne's voice hadn't even reached him when she had still loved and admired him.

She closed her eyes.

"What's the matter with you?" Miss Rigby tapped Anne gently on the arm.

Anne stared at the disappearing vision. Then she asked where Alexander was. On the beach, where else? said Miss Rigby. He was either running around with Paddy Trent or Betty. Alex and Elizabeth West were old beachcombers.

"I suppose they are," murmured Anne. Alexander could evidently not be separated from his dear Betty on land or in the water.

Miss Rigby rose. "Come, child. Off to bed with you. The whole thing's been too much for you."

"I hoped I'd make it."

"You made it," said Miss Rigby, but she didn't say what Anne had "made" on Alexander's birthday. She took the young woman to her bedroom, shaking her head. Anne swayed as if she had drunk several glasses of gin instead of fruit juice. Was she pregnant? That would make Alex very happy. But she said she was just exhausted.

Miss Rigby plumped up the cushions and exuded the horrible liveliness of a trained nurse. But she meant well, and Anne was grateful. She would have liked to please Miss Rigby with a nephew, but unfortunately there could be no thought of that.

Miss Rigby went back to the beach and looked around her. Where was Alex? It was high time that he paid some attention to his wife. Miss Rigby couldn't understand Anne, and her lifelessness made her impatient. But the young woman was actually quite brave. She had unfortunately remained an outsider in Sydney, but the pommies had a hard time acclimatizing, and besides, being married to Alex wasn't much fun. Granted, he knew a thing or two about buildings—the honors bestowed on him today had surprised her—but for all that he remained a lousy husband. He pursued his small pleasures and had no comprehension whatsoever for a sensitive creature like Anne. And she was too young for him. Grace Rigby had said so right away. She was thankful that dear Betty West hadn't fallen for Alex. For a while she had thought the two were seeing too much of each other. But she had kept her mouth shut, and so had Betty. Which had suited Grace Rigby fine. She found outpourings of the heart between women horrible. Anyway, Betty had had enough gumption in her little red head not to move from Bellevue Hill to Vaucluse. Anne, on the other hand, had walked from a nice, monotonous life straight into the jaws of the shark. Poor young creature! She had liked Anne at once. A decent girl with substance to her. She could sense anything like that from miles away. Much too refined for Alex, who took his marital duties too lightly. After a while he went his own way. Flora Pratt had also eaten alone until she had finally turned the house in Vaucluse into a men's bar. Miss Rigby hadn't liked it, but Flora had asserted herself in her own way. Anne never asserted herself. She treated Alex with cool rejection. Anne had just told her something that, even if one was used to taking a lot from Alex, was more than the traffic could or should bear.

Miss Rigby frowned as she looked across at the neighing mob. Alexander was not with Paddy Trent. So he was probably "on his way" with Betty West. Of course you could depend on Betty, but Miss Rigby felt it was high time that Alex gave up these amusing digressions. His little pleasures made him smaller than he was.

Miss Rigby had reached the promenade, and looked around for Dr. Dobson.

Although he was only in his early thirties, Bertram Dobson was automatically a member of Rigby's mob. His father had been their doctor. Then Bertie had taken over his practice on Macquarie Street. The elder Dobson meanwhile preferred to fish or listen to music or carry on friendly arguments with his wife. The mob was used to the Dobsons, and to the festive palm trees on Macquarie Street. And if Bertie sometimes couldn't get things straight, he could always consult his old man. Since Rigby's mob had known Dobson as a young rascal, and had frequently beaten him up, none of them had really noticed that Bertram had meanwhile become quite a famous internist. In short, whenever one of the cobbers had a bellyache, or his heart was acting up, or his gall bladder was behaving strangely, he'd toddle off to see Bertie, and that was that. While visiting him they could also run over to the wool exchange, or sit on Macquarie Plaza around the obelisk. This was where Australia's first orchard had stood. The plaza was still a peaceful patch of green in the centre of the metropolis. Or one walked over to the public library of New South Wales and did something for one's mind. A call on Dr. Dobson therefore included all sorts of other possibilities.

The young doctor was of medium height, reliable, and just as quick-witted as his father, and one could see that he was a hearty eater. Bertram was professionally successful because he evaluated his capabilities correctly. When in doubt, he called in a specialist. He was very modest, although he knew a lot more than the mob realized. His father was sure that Bertram was headed for a splendid career, but this was never mentioned. All the Dobsons were brilliant doctors. They were situated in Sydney, London, New Zealand, and some nephew or other was practicing in Brisbane. Besides medicine, they loved music and the classical philosophers. In his leisure time, Bertie read Virgil, and was terrified that the mob might find out. The mob liked sports, betting, and beer sessions. People with inclinations like the Dobsons had to watch their step. Except for the Virgil bit, they were of course dinkum through and through. On this continent everybody was equally good or equally mediocre. Bertie had learned this credo in his infancy, but newspaper reports about political catastrophes or the Australian labor unions, about cricket and gossip-column scandals, didn't satisfy him. As a student he had foraged around in old John Darling's books, and in Horace, Virgil and Seneca had discovered comrades of the spirit. On the day he had discovered the classics outside the schoolroom, his mother had been cooking some fowl or other in wine. Bertie could recall it exactly. When she was young, Mrs. Dobson had visited a friend in Queensland. The girl's family had owned French sugar plantations. Bertie's mother, an intelligent and enthusiastic woman, had learned to cook so well that even the toughest steak melted in your mouth.

In spite of being so much younger, Bertram was a close friend of the Rigbys, even though he never looked at *Insight* and didn't appreciate Alexander's way of life. Bertie had a residue of the puritanism of his English ancestors in his blood. He had fought with his conscience before he had finally acquired a girl friend. The thought of a lasting marital dialogue, such as his parents indulged in with obvious pleasure, frightened him. He started an affair with a nice, decent young girl who worked in an office on the next street, Bridge Street. Mavis had brought her mother to him as a patient. Her mother had heart trouble, and after that Bertie discovered that he was having trouble with his own heart . . . Now he and the young lady had been together for three years. That her office was nearby made things easier. Although a visit to a patient could never be too late or too far away, in the little free time he had, he liked his comforts. Once Rigby, with a wink, had asked him if he wouldn't like a change. After all, said wise Alexander Rigby, a man's wishes and needs changed every couple of years or so. Young Dr. Dobson had replied that one girl was pretty much the same as the other, since one always wanted the same thing from the sheilas. Why spend time looking and courting all the anxiety involved until one finally got to the point? He knew all the advantages and disadvantages of his Mavis, and the advantages were greater. He could still marry his girl friend from Bridge Street if worse came to worst, but there was plenty of time for that. Right now he preferred to watch soccer or listen to a concert—you could admit to hearing a concert to Rigby—than to waste time looking for a new girl. He didn't mention Virgil. Those were his strictly private friends. *Res severa est verum gaudium*—yes, serious things were a joy. Cobber Horace had already known that.

"It's sheer unbelievable, boy," Rigby had said. "You don't have a spark of erotic fantasy."

"Thank God!" young Dr. Dobson replied, very pleased with himself.

Rigby's fiftieth was dinkum. Bertie had swum for a long time, and was now strolling along the Pacific, alone. He was pleased with himself and the world because he knew all its tricks. One was never disappointed when one wished only for what was attainable. Perhaps, behind the wall of good sense, there were irrational pleasures, the kind Rigby was looking for, but Bertie stuck to the small, inconspicuous ones. What was wrong with his friend Mavis? She was no dazzling beauty, but she was pleasant to look at, played a good game of tennis, and kept her mouth shut when Bertie preferred to fish over the weekend. At first Mavis had of course tried to remodel Bertie and make a romantic lover of him, like the ones in Elizabeth West's novels. Naturally Mavis subscribed to *Insight*. But Bertie had come through this period unscathed. He had explained to the young lady that he was not a film star. Anyway, in private life film stars were either boring or alcoholics or neurotic sob sisters, or all three together. Mavis hadn't wanted to believe this, but Bertie had explained it all in detail until she'd got the picture. He was her first man. That worried him sometimes. He

116

would look for a nice young man for Mavis in case she suddenly began to talk marriage. Until now the subject hadn't come up.

Miss Rigby walked up to him. "Too bad that you don't have office hours on the beach, Bertie."

"What's the matter, Grace?"

"I wish you'd take a look at Anne."

"She was perfectly all right this afternoon after that little fainting spell, or I wouldn't have let her come tonight. I think it's nerves. Since when are you a mother hen, anyway?"

"Perhaps she needs a stronger sedative," Miss Rigby said hesitantly. "I was with her just now on the roof garden and got the impression that she wasn't exactly herself."

"Is she in a rage?" asked Dobson.

"Don't be silly!" Miss Rigby said indignantly. "Anne is never in a rage. She's not Alex."

"All right. I'll have a look at her again."

As they walked back to the house, Miss Rigby asked about Stanley Marchmont's heart. "He's got to be careful," said young Dobson. "An old heart like his needs rest."

"Nonsense!" said Miss Rigby. "My grandfather Colin ran around Parramatta like a weasel when he was eighty-five."

"Why do you ask if you know better?"

"I'm sorry, Bertie. I only meant that Stan Marchmont ..." She stopped, then finally mumbled, "He'll have to answer to me if he signs off."

"Fortunately he won't be alive to oblige."

Miss Rigby was silent for a moment, baffled. Then she said good-humoredly, "Bertie Dobson, you always were fresh!"

They had reached the house. "Anne's upstairs in the bedroom," said Miss Rigby. "Go on up, Bertie. Do something for your money."

Miss Rigby waited. Why did Bertie stay so long upstairs? When he finally appeared, she looked at him questioningly. "Nothing wrong," said Dobson, his eyes on a platter of ham that looked tasty. Miss Rigby shrugged, and fixed him several open-faced sandwiches. She knew Bertie!

"Thanks, dear. After swimming I'm always terribly hungry."

"You can always eat, Bertie. One can see where it goes."

At last Dr. Dobson had had enough. "I don't like the way Anne looks," he said slowly. "Everything's all right physically. As I said—it's nerves. I think I'll make an appointment for her with Morty." Dr. Gerald Mortimer was a nerve specialist on Macquarie Street and an old friend of Bertie's father.

"But she's not a mental case!"

"If she were, I'd send her to Frank Norfolk," Dr. Dobson said patiently. "But she is extremely nervous." He scratched his head, embarrassed. He couldn't possibly tell Miss Rigby that Anne was in a panic of fear of Rigby and believed that he intended to kill her. Such nonsense!

"Well anyway," he said calmly, "I want Morty to take a look at her. Perhaps she's unhappy."

"You're joking," said Miss Rigby. "Alexander is destroying her."

"It's not entirely impossible that she is also destroying him."

"You'd better go to a nerve specialist yourself, Bertie."

Dr. Dobson finished his beer. Beer was a great invention. Then he said amiably, "I don't know how you feel about it, but when there's something wrong between two people, every arrow comes back to the one who's shot it."

Miss Rigby said nothing. "Alex still has a lot to do," said Dobson. "He needs every ounce of strength he has."

"I've been worried for a long time," said Miss Rigby, "but about Anne. She's the weaker one."

'She has the resistance of the weak. I know that sounds funny," he said apologetically. "Perhaps all Anne needs after these seven years is a change of scenery. Couldn't you go somewhere with her?"

"Don't be foolish, Bertie. I'm in the office all day and every day."

"Couldn't Betty West take your place for a while?"

"Betty writes novels. And wherever she goes there's chaos within three minutes. Or she has another one of her imaginary illnesses. You know how fond I am of Betty, but at my desk? Over my dead body."

Bertie didn't want to hear another word about *Insight*. Mavis was always rebellious after she'd read the rag. "Maybe Morty will send your sister-in-law off to London for a while," he said.

"What an idea! She'd never come back!"

"Exactly," Dr. Dobson said quietly.

They walked back to the beach together. The sea glittered darkly. In the distance Rigby and Elizabeth West were walking arm-in-arm under the pines. "They were talking so animatedly a little while ago," said Dobson, "they didn't even notice me."

Miss Rigby was asking herself what could possibly be wrong with Alexander's marriage. She had the feeling that in spite of his misdemeanors, her brother was fond of Anne, and every now and then tried to do something to please her. But this evening he was different. "You're smart, Bertie," she said. "You have peace and quiet."

"One should never praise the day before the evening," he said. "But I'm going to do my best to preserve my peace and quiet." He looked at her from the side and thought she looked exceptionally pale. "Would you like me to prescribe something to pep you up, Grace? No extra charge."

Miss Rigby laughed. "Prescribe something for yourself!" She mustn't let Bertie see how worried she was. He was too smart. "Go back to your friends, Bertie. I'm no company for you."

"You can't order me around any more, Grace, however much you'd like to." He grinned. He had always had a soft spot in his heart for Grace, God only knew why. He had no intention of leaving her to her dismal thoughts.

"Should I speak to Alex about it?" she asked.

"For heaven's sake, no! Your talks always make everything worse. You know you're my only true love, Grace, but you don't know how to handle Alex!"

Miss Rigby looked at the ocean. "You know everything, Bertie. Can you tell me why Alex can't stick to one woman; why he changes them all the time?"

Miss Rigby could sense change in the air around Vaucluse. Before the tragedy of Flora Pratt she had felt it too. But this time there must not be a scandal. Stan Marchmont's heart couldn't stand it. Why was Alex so restless? Miss Rigby looked at the paradisial shore silently. Manly was being slowly hidden by the cloak of night. The houses, with their lights, lay in the mist of the moon, the living quarters of the well-to-do. Miss Rigby thought sometimes that only lucky people lived in these country houses, with washing machines and television sets and electric blenders. But actually she knew better. The bitter honey was locked away in the pantry.

"I don't really know Alexander very well, in spite of the fact that I'm his sister."

"Just because of that, Grace. And by the way, in the times that lie ahead, if you ever feel like talking, you know where to find me."

"If I'm not mistaken, you're in my address book. Listen, Bertie, I have a great idea."

"And that is . . ."

"Why don't you marry our Betty West?"

"Why should I marry your Betty West?"

"You'd be a very suitable couple. And your dear mother cooks so well. You can't expect that from Betty, of course."

"As far as I know, I've never asked her to cook for me."

Miss Rigby had been considering for some time how she should settle Betty favorably, just in case something should happen to her. Grace Rigby was only fifty-seven, and hoped to become just as old as her grandfather Colin, but you never knew. Betty had pots of money, but had no idea as to how to manage it. And when she wasn't writing, she needed somebody to look after her. She was a great big, precocious child.

"Don't be so stubborn, Bertie. You're in your mid-thirties now. It's high time, my son. Worse food would only do you good. Anyway, you should start eating less, considerably less."

"Why?" Dr. Dobson asked indignantly. "I hate meals thrown together, and Mother is happy when I enjoy my food."

Miss Rigby gave up. Old lady Dobson was happy above all that. Bertie was still attached to her apron strings. Both her daughters had gone off with absolute strangers.

"Come to your senses, boy!" said Miss Rigby. "Think of your big, empty house. What do you do in it all alone?"

"Enjoy my peace and quiet, just like you. Sorry, darling, but I never marry authors."

"You prefer illiterates?"

"There's a golden mean," Bertie said gently. His friend Mavis was solidly entrenched between the two.

"I'd like to know what you have against authors."

"They have too much imagination for everyday use. Let it be, Grace. Everybody is happy in his own way."

Young Dobson gave Miss Rigby a friendly dig in the ribs, since he couldn't pat her on the shoulder. He didn't reach that high.

Boys and girls paraded along the beach with torches. They belonged to some sports club or other, and were celebrating something. The red glow of their torches lit up Rigby and Betty West. For a moment it looked as if the two were walking through a provisional purgatory. Dr. Dobson reflected that Betty West was part of the inventory at the Rigbys'. On the other hand, a husband should be walking with his wife. Or what sense was there in marriage?

9

On the One Hand, On the Other Hand . . .

On the one hand Rigby enjoyed walking arm-in-arm with Betty West along the shore; on the other hand, right now she was nowhere near him. On the one hand Rigby was hungry to possess; on the other hand he found possession a burden. Was that why Elizabeth had turned him down seven years ago? All in all Rigby was astonished, and in a way insulted, that his relationship to the weaker sex didn't give anyone, not even himself, much joy.

His relationship to Elizabeth West, which had endured through so many storms, was basically too complicated. If she had married him, everything would have been all right. Would he have fled from little Betty four times a week? No. There would have been a togetherness between them. Probably children too. That would have made a hell of a lot of difference to him. Besides, Betty had a profession of her own which took up most of her time. In short, it would have been a dinkum marriage. The mob would have been astounded. Naturally Betty always had a heap of nonsensical ideas in her little red head, but he would have driven them out lovingly. Nothing had hurt him as much as Anne's reproach that he was brutal.

Elizabeth West had enjoyed Rigby's fiftieth birthday hugely. She was still thinking of all the honors he had received. "The mob was really surprised at all the speeches, Alex. Such praise!"

"That's the trouble. The boys always believe everything said about me."

"Too bad that John Darling couldn't be here."

"A terrible shame."

"You must be very happy today."

"I'm always happy."

When Rigby was in this kind of a mildly aggressive mood, Betty kept her mouth shut. He had seemed nervous all afternoon, but that could have been joyous excitement. One could talk to Rigby only about the weather, sports results, and occasionally about his work. Betty understood this because she too evaded questions about her private life. In interviews she gave information only about her professional life.

Rigby felt almost content as he walked beside the sea with Betty. The Pacific helped him to forget space and time, and the solemn pines moved in the evening wind. Rigby liked to wander with Betty because then the way was clear. They left all vagaries and concealments, and the tyrannies of convention, behind them. If he had paid more attention to the conventions now, he would have gone to his wife. At the thought of Anne his lips compressed into a thin line. Now, at last, he wanted to celebrate his birthday in peace.

On the one hand he would have liked to talk his marital difficulties off his chest; on the other hand one never spoke about one's wife. It was strange, but in Betty's silent sympathy he felt confirmed and secure. In spite of past misunderstandings—all Betty's fault—today they were good friends. Naturally one couldn't compare dainty, elegant Elizabeth West with a pair of old slippers, but she gave him that old-slipper feeling. No other sheila had ever been able to make him feel like that. Was it because he and Betty had known each other for so many years, and loved their country just the way it was? He didn't want to think any more about it. God bless the old slippers!

"You haven't grown all these years either. I was always able to spit on your head easily. Not that I ever did!"

Funny . . . the successful Elizabeth West still had an air of innocence about her, in spite of her Sydney polish, her style, and her wonderful sense of humor. "Withers from Adelaide" peered occasionally out of a corner of her consciousness and looked at the great Rigby with awe, as she had done years ago in the little office in George Street. And Rigby was usually tactful enough to ignore "Withers." As a matter of fact she surfaced rarely; usually West was in full charge.

Rigby wondered if Betty would have liked a closer relationship with him. On Sundays and holidays he sometimes thought along these lines, but he was never sure. Betty still had her puritan upbringing in Adelaide in her bones. Married men were taboo. And he was never able to rid himself of guilt feelings where Betty was concerned. He had really behaved badly, damn badly, during their springtime. But all that was over. There was much to be said for love cooled off. The soul took a lukewarm bath and passion was as unthinkable as black snow. The fire in the hearth of memory burned softly and pleasantly, no ecstasy, no neuroses, and no roses!

Betty too wanted things as they were now. When, after Rigby's disappearance, steak had tasted good to her for the first time, she had felt saved. It was a wonderful feeling and a healthier experience than Walpurgis nights in neon lighting.

"Don't regret anything, girl," said Rigby. He must have lived Betty's journey into the past with her. "I know you've had horrible experiences with me, but they're better than none, aren't they? Wear them like black pearls." Then Rigby asked how the big novel was going. Betty had started it before his marriage to Anne. Rigby had read the first chapters before he had flown to London. There had been something about it, even if it hadn't been right for the magazine.

"I couldn't do anything with it for a long time," said Betty. "It was as if the novels for *Insight* had taken the substance out of me. But a year ago I started all over again. It's going to be a quite different book. I've changed too."

"May I read some of it?" In the moonlight he could see Betty flush. How young she was! And how ambitious!

"You don't have any time, Alex. And it's probably no good."

"Probably. When do I get to see it?"

They walked on arm in arm. Betty was happy that Alex was so calm and content. Perhaps she had influence over him because for years now she had preserved the aloofness necessary for creative people. Sometimes she felt a vague pity for this brilliant and successful man, and this pity quite possibly neutralized the senses.

"How are you living nowadays, Betty? Do you have a new friend again?"

"I'm not a hundred years old yet," Betty West answered crisply. "When I have writer's cramp I occasionally need a man, but that has nothing to do with love."

"I have no idea what you're talking about."

Miss West cleared her throat. "Probably I've written about love so much, I can't participate in it any more. A professional disease, my dear."

"You're too young for that kind of withdrawal, pet. Does public acclaim at least pay you damages?" Rigby pulled her hair and Betty yelped. "Just don't drop dead," said Rigby. "Any new ailments in sight?"

"With your disgusting health you don't want to hear about anything like that."

"Correct!" Rigby heard about nothing but backaches, headaches, and exhaustion at home.

Betty sensed his sudden coldness and bitterness. "What's the matter at home?" she asked, quite against her principles.

"Nothing," Rigby said harshly. He tickled her neck. "So laugh, for God's sake, you little twerp!"

Rigby had taken his arm off Betty's shoulder. With every step she could feel him wandering away from her, but she pressed his hand impulsively. Was she the only one who knew about his virtues, which he liked to keep hidden? Actually she was showering Rigby with illusionary laurels. He had done her too much harm, but she knew his value. The fact alone that Rigby existed made her happy. The old love had grown away from the status of enchantment and torturous dependency long ago. Now she could present Alexander Rigby with a liberated heart. He probably had no idea of the value of such a gift.

Betty had to think of his son, to whom she had given birth alone and buried alone. Alexander had no children. Although Betty had sometimes been tempted, she had never told him the truth. In lonely hours, when her typewriter seemed to provide only destructive material, she thought sometimes of this decisive experience and felt that her life was proceeding without love and was bearing no fruit. She was in her mid-thirties now. Why had Rigby sent her away seven years ago? At the time she had told herself that she couldn't bear his faithlessness, and would lose him because of her reproaches. Today she was more mature, and Rigby was older. But his sister had told her that he still played around. Who really knew or understood Rigby?

He had embraced her, hurt her, and left her. On the other hand, he had driven the small-town out of her soul and pushed her onto a different path. And now they were strolling peacefully, hand-in-hand, along the seashore. Rigby had put his arm around her again.

"What would you have wanted to write about if I hadn't made you so angry?"

"About nothing," she said. "I would have been happy, just like other women."

"That's the simplest thing in the world!"

"We'd better go back, Alex. It's getting cool. I still have five installments to write for *Insight*, and can't afford pneumonia right now."

Rigby put his sweater on her and laughed because she was swallowed up by it. Betty said, "No, no! You'll catch cold."

"I'm not you!" Rigby buttoned up the sweater and kissed her on the nose. In spite of her protests, he took her to friends of his in Manly to spend the night.

A striking pair walked past them: a very beautiful young girl and a slim, dark-haired man who looked Italian. Rigby's sharp eyes recognized the model, Candy, and the necklace he had given her. His small pleasures cost money . . .

"Wasn't that Candy? The one who models for *Insight?*" Betty asked.

"No idea," said Rigby.

On the one hand Rigby had given his wife a lecture, and she had stared at him wide-eyed, as if he were about to wring her neck. On the other hand, he had by now got over his vexation and was ready to compromise. He was no model husband, and Anne was much too lacking in temperament to actually deceive him. He had been an idiot to even think so! If Anne would just make the least bit of a fuss of him, he'd stay home more. After all, he'd married her because he'd found her attractive. And one could really converse pleasantly with Anne, when she wanted to, whereas Candy had nothing but sawdust in her head. And Anne wasn't interested in his bank account. He'd always found that charming. In short, he was ready and willing to forgive her for this idiotic adoration of John Darling. He felt quite stimulated at the thought of a pleasant truce, which might eventually develop into a lasting marital peace. Anyway, there were a lot uglier girls around than Anne. She had looked absolutely adorable this evening.

He ran into her bedroom. It was empty. For a moment Rigby stood absolutely motionless. Was she still on the roof? It was much too cool up there. The night on the sea had its treacherous aspects. But Anne was nowhere to be found—not on the roof, not in the cellar, nor on any of the verandas or in any of the rooms, nor in the garden.

She had moved out. She had chosen to do so on the one day when he had been happy. A red hot rage welled up in him, to the roots of his hair. This was unforgivable. He had always considered Anne a decent human being in spite of her frigidity and chronic somnolence. After dinner Miss Rigby had given him John Darling's letter to Anne to read. It was quite evident that the old cobber had denied himself certain pleasures with Anne. And now she had deserted Rigby. But no divorce, please! He couldn't afford another scandal. She could go or stay wherever she damn pleased, but nothing was going to be made public this time!

Rigby was standing in Anne's bedroom. The curtains waved in the night wind like gigantic butterflies. He began to laugh loudly. He found his role as the abandoned husband funny. But he found the fact that he was a human being especially funny. Funny, and somehow eerie. Too many different Adams were alive in him. And something else . . . his bourgeois existence was beginning to fall apart, slowly and imperceptibly. Good fortune, or whatever one thought came under that heading, was dissolving like a chemical substance. On the one hand, private citizen Rigby was wandering on a jagged path, on the other hand he was looking for a code of law that brought order into the life process. Yet he was standing today, on his fiftieth birthday, in the impenetrable bush, and the seconds stretched to hours and eternities, and ran out between his fingers.

Rigby picked up the large Sèvres vase he had given Anne in Paris. His hair tumbled across his forehead and a murderous rage flamed in his narrowed eyes. One day he would wring that treacherous woman's neck! She didn't deserve anything better. He flung the priceless vase against the built-in cupboard of Queensland wood. He had designed the room with walls that had a transparent effect. Here he had wanted to sing the duets of a pleasant life with Anne, godammit!

Miss Rigby appeared in her dressing gown, buttoned up to her neck. From her room next door she had heard Rigby laugh and the noise of the vase breaking. Her long housecoat made her appear even taller than she was. Her clear-cut face with its narrow, scornful lips looked stern.

"What's the meaning of all this noise so late at night, Alex?"

Rigby stared at his sister. He had forgotten that she didn't drive back to Sydney when it got late. They had bought this house and the land it stood on together, with Patrick Trent's help. Alexander had renovated it and Grace looked after the garden when they spent weekends in Manly. Miss Rigby didn't seem to notice that Anne's bed was empty.

"What *are* you doing, Alex?"

"I'm smashing porcelain," Rigby said in a soft voice.

"Why don't you take the kitchen cups?" Miss Rigby asked. "But I suppose it's *your* porcelain. Don't you think you've smashed enough?"

"Stop talking," said Rigby.

"I've only just begun. Can't you speak a little louder? I'm not a lip reader."

Perhaps he couldn't speak louder. He was white now, as if the red anger had flowed out of him and drained him. He wiped the chest with his handkerchief. He hated scratches. Scratches spoiled the picture. Suddenly Miss Rigby had to think of their father who, on his deathbed, had asked her to look after Alex. But Alex had been a green boy then; now he was gray at the temples and was staring into dead-end streets.

"Sit down, Alex."

He fell into Anne's big, flowered chintz chair and stretched his long legs. Suddenly he was dead tired. "I'll make her pay for this," he mumbled. "These pommies with their goddamned refinement!"

"Don't be foolish. Anne is as she is."

Rigby jumped to his feet and kicked a blue brocade slipper under the bed. Anne had written him off, out of her life and he, Godforsaken ass, still wanted her in spite of her coldness. Her narrow little waist had enchanted him right from the start. And how grateful she had been to come to this wonderful country!

He might perhaps have learned to love her if she had let herself be loved. But she hadn't even played the game right on their honeymoon. For years now she had been putting him off like a beggar, with a smile or an excuse. For years she had neglected the simplest marital duties. Long before he had smiled at the little piece of Irish candy in Darlinghurst!

What else could he have done? At his wedding he had been forty-three and robust as a bull. When the hunger attacked him, he couldn't work. To this day he'd grow so restless, his pencil would go its own way. Damn it all, he hadn't married to receive charity! He hated martyrs in bed. And today he was only fifty and could tear up trees, clear a whole bush acre, roots and all if necessary. . . did Miss Rigby know anything?

"Why did she leave me?" he asked, his voice choked. "I didn't bother her much."

Miss Rigby said nothing. For the first time it dawned on her that perhaps Alex had also been denied a lot of what he had coming to him, but he had behaved abominably to his wife, and not only today.

"For a while now Anne has been receiving anonymous letters." Miss Rigby didn't look at her brother. She would have preferred it if Anne hadn't told her.

"What do you mean?"

"Can't you speak English?" Miss Rigby said sullenly. "The sort of thing you usually find written on toilet paper with no return address. That you spend your evenings with whores. And Anne should follow you some Wednesday to a certain boardinghouse in Darlinghurst . . ."

Rigby's face was red. Had Andrews followed him? Wednesday was her day off. Miss Rigby was thinking the same thing.

"I advised you after your marriage to get rid of that hysterical woman. She clings to you like a leech."

"At least there's one woman who clings to me."

"Anne is at Shirley Cox's in Lane Cove. Bertie Dobson took her with him because she insisted."

"She has a thing or two on her conscience as well," said Rigby. "But that's no longer interesting."

"Maybe she'll go to Queensland with Shirley."

"She has my blessing," said Rigby. "Desertion is grounds for divorce, but I'm not doing her the favor. If she sues me for adultery, then we're quits. I'll ask my lawyer. James Battleship is an old friend of mine and one of the best lawyers in Sydney."

"I know," said Miss Rigby. "You and your lawyer."

"It's all her fault!"

"That's what you think."

"Yes! That's what I think!" Rigby pounded his fist on the rosewood table he had found for Anne in Chelsea on his last trip to England. "I didn't have a marriage," he said, "whether you can grasp that or not." He wiped the sweat from his forehead and murmured, more to himself, "I couldn't stand it any more."

"You have no idea how much one can stand," said Miss Rigby, with a fleeting sense of compassion. "And just put all that nonsense about a lawyer right out of your head. Jimmy Battleship had quite enough of you last time round."

"You think so?" Rigby asked, menacingly, softly. "I was just going to propose a trip to the Blue Mountains to Anne."

"Don't, Alexander! So . . . what are you going to do?"

"I'll have to think it over," Rigby said harshly. "To a certain extent I'm grateful to have my peace and quiet. I wanted to change a few things in Vaucluse anyway." He frowned. If Andrews had written those anonymous notes, she'd have something coming to her. It could only have been his jewel. She hated Anne. She had been plotting these last seven years to get rid of the second Mrs. Rigby. She'd hear the angels in heaven singing tomorrow . . .

Miss Rigby was watching his face. "Please Alex—don't do anything stupid now."

"Goodnight." Rigby opened the door for his sister. "Terribly sorry, Miss Rigby, but I'm an old cobber now. My party has tired me a little."

"So—until tomorrow."

"Yes," said Rigby. "Until tomorrow."

128

10

Mama Doody's Boardinghouse

On the morning after Rigby's fiftieth birthday the papers featured illustrated accounts of the event, in which Miss Rigby played no small
part. She was somehow connected with all the newspaper people in
Sydney, and would return the favor when the opportunity arose.
Everybody read about Rigby's reception in Vaucluse and the party in
Manly. From top-ranking business executives to harbor workers, from
salesgirls to models, everybody knew who had been invited and how
graciously the enchanting young Mrs. Rigby had treated her guests.
From Balmoral to Darlinghurst, from Rose Bay to King's Cross, the
subscribers found out at breakfast that the famous author, Elizabeth
West, had been present too. Miss West was an old friend of the young
Mrs. Rigby. The pressmen stuck to the official reception at which
Marchmont, almost a legendary figure now, and the boys from Parramatta, had played a big part. The lady reporters described the women's
clothes, the cold buffet, and the radiant mood of the ridiculously
young-looking and charming fifty-year-old who had received his guests
at the side of his beautiful English wife. Architect Rigby was a great
man, no doubt about it, who practiced the Australian bush virtue of
hospitality as a matter of course in the big city of Sydney. The pictures
showed Rigby and his wife, arm-in-arm—it was touching.

In a boardinghouse in Darlinghurst, where the tired plaster dribbled
from the walls, Molly Fleet and Mama Doody were enjoying the Rigby
report over their morning tea. There you could see again how the rich
amused themselves. Mrs. Doody scolded in a fine rage, that is to say in
high spirits, about the bloodsuckers who could afford summer houses,
perfumed women and expensive food. Mama Doody herself liked to
celebrate and eat. She would have had nothing to say against Rigby's
house if it had belonged to her. She considered all rich people lazy and
herself a busy bee, because she had the enviable Irish gift of dressing up
the naked facts in fantasy until they became wish fulfillments of pure

silk. Now she sat in her sloppy housecoat, her hair in curlers, drinking her tea and talking without cease.

Candy yawned. She had been on the beach in Manly yesterday evening with Carlo Pressolini from the Restaurant Rosso. She had had eyes only for the handsome Italian and not even noticed Rigby's mob. Molly Fleet was not to know anything about this outing because Carlo was Molly's boy friend. But after all, Molly didn't own him, and he couldn't seriously be considering Molly as a girl friend. In her indolent way Candy had fallen in love for the first time. She had never met such a darling man, not in her West Australian home nor in Sydney.

"How was it yesterday with the new one?" asked Molly Fleet.

Candy started and looked sharply at Fleet's expression. She didn't seem aware of anything. It was simply the curious question of a girl who had never experienced anything.

"Quite nice," said Candy. "He says he's crazy about me." This was followed by a recital of what he said, what Candy had replied, what both of them had said, and what the new fellow had said on parting. Molly listened greedily, Mrs. Doody yawned. Men were dumb. "Does he have money?" she asked sharply. Candy said she didn't know yet.

Carlo of course didn't have a red cent. Candy had already loaned him money three times. He put every loan down in his notebook, although Candy would gladly have given him the money. She earned that much half-asleep! But Carlo was very strict with Candy. The thought of accepting money from a woman was unbearable. He didn't come from a background where men thought things like that were all right. After all, he had attended the university in Genoa. He came from a fine, wealthy family and had come to Australia straight from his father's villa with the marble columns. Candy wondered why he had given all this up. But then she found out: his father had disowned him because he had wanted to be an opera singer instead of going into his father's business. Candy had never heard of La Scala in Milan. Apparently they sang there. She had listened to Carlo, mouth agape. Even if he was only a waiter now in the Restaurant Rosso, his background was impressive. He looked like a film star, and in her eyes life was an exciting film.

Both of them laughed secretly over Molly Fleet. Candy had advised Carlo to go on taking Molly out on Monday evenings. That was the evening Candy always received her rich sugar daddy. Molly's suspicions must on no account be aroused. Candy didn't rightly know what it was about Molly that she didn't like. She was diligent and devoted and even wrote Candy's love letters. Of course Candy paid her for that. But

Candy had an undefinable fear of the girl, and was therefore exceptionally friendly. It was ridiculous, but the thought that Molly might find out about her love affair with Carlo Pressolini made Candy tremble.

Molly Fleet read the account of the Rigby festivities with an expressionless face, and looked at the picture of the happy couple. But the Sydney *Morning Herald* had a surprising final notice: Mrs. Anne Rigby had flown to London the following morning to visit her mother after an absence of seven years. She had only wanted to be there to celebrate her husband's birthday. Lady Carrington, Anne's mother, wrote popular thrillers which Molly Fleet devoured evenings in bed. She let the newspaper fall . . . Mrs. Rigby had not cancelled her massage, and she was always considerate about things like that. She must have decided to leave overnight . . .

Mrs. Doody went on expostulating about the rich men she and Candy lived on. Molly shrugged. As if money grew on trees! In a city like Sydney everybody ran hectically for a place in the sun. Molly sensed that yachts and dream villas cost money.

"You are perfectly right, Mrs. Doody," she said.

Nobody replied. Molly Fleet lit a cigarette and went on looking at Rigby's picture. Funny, but in Parramatta she had envisioned quite a different man. She hoped his wife would come back soon. Molly didn't feel right about the letters she was writing regularly for Candy. But Rigby would go his own way anyway, whether he got the letters or not. Since one could talk oneself into anything in the world, Molly had gradually convinced herself that with these letters she was doing Rigby's wife no harm. She also told herself that she wrote these letters because Candy paid her well for it, and she needed money for the farm. She hadn't yet admitted to herself that she felt more alive and happier when she was writing to this man, to whom she had never spoken and who never answered. But whether Molly Fleet admitted it to herself or not, she needed this one-sided correspondence. Her interest in Rigby had been theoretical for a long time. Now she *had* to find out what he told Candy, how he kissed, how he behaved when he came to see her . . . everything. Everything. Animosity toward this beautiful, carefree creature who couldn't tell the difference between a man like Rigby and her other lovers, welled up wildly in Molly Fleet with every letter she wrote. When Candy was amused by Rigby's changeable moods or spoke disparagingly of his portrait sketches, Molly Fleet shivered and felt a strange pain. She was furious with this golden goose. She was furious with Father O'Brien, who sometimes admonished her. She was furious with God! But above all she was furious with Rigby because he had fallen for a shop-window mannequin who unscrewed her head at night. Mrs. Doody was right: men were fools!

Molly was still staring at the photo of Rigby in the paper. In spite of her reserve, Mrs. Rigby had always been nice to her, and had mercifully chosen to overlook her birthmark. But a few weeks ago she had sent Molly at her own expense to a skin specialist on Macquarie Street. Although she had never mentioned the disfigurement, she must have sensed how unhappy Molly was about it. It wasn't Mrs. Rigby's fault that the specialist had advised against an operation. Miss Fleet's fiery birthmark—*naevus flammeus*—was too deep and too large for deep X-ray treatment or other radiological methods. The scars could result in an even worse disfigurement. The doctor had also advised against plastic surgery. In the case of such a large mark, there was the danger that with time, the scars could sink in and distort the features. Only small, port-wine spots could be operated.

Mrs. Rigby had told Molly the results. She had ordered tea and spoken quietly, yet so compassionately that Molly had drunk her tea together with the bitter tears of disappointment. Anne Rigby had murmured that there were worse things in life, and that Molly was so efficient and energetic, she would make a go of life in spite of the birthmark. After that Mrs. Rigby had closed her eyes for a moment. Molly had sat very still. Was Mrs. Rigby experiencing difficulties? Anyway, the girl from Parramatta had found out that afternoon that luxury and money were no guarantee of contentment. She'd wanted so much to do something for Mrs. Rigby. She wasn't used to having other people worry about her. But what could she do for Anne Rigby?

People had to fight and pray alone for the peace of their souls. As a child in the Parramatta church, Molly hadn't found this difficult because she had seen how Grandmother Fleet, with her wooden rosary attached to her belt, got through life very well. If Molly only knew why she stayed in Sydney! In this vast, soul-consuming city, life was dangerous, disappointing, and frightfully confusing. The people in their luxurious show places in Vaucluse weren't more content than Molly Fleet in Mama Doody's boardinghouse. The only truly satisfied person was Candy, but she was imperilled by her beauty. When she looked at Candy's enchanting, empty face, Molly Fleet sometimes pictured what Candy would look like with a birthmark on her face, or with horrible, badly healed scars. That was something Candy wouldn't be able to live with. The goose pimples ran down Molly's back. How could she think such dreadful things? Candy was always so nice to her.

And Candy couldn't get along without her any more. No wonder—Molly had gradually learned the art of making herself indispensable.

What was it like in the arms of a man, she wondered. Molly Fleet was twenty-two, and her wild, innocent dreams swung like storm lanterns in the dark. Was the love of a man a feast or a fire or a sin? Candy had given her the impression that sex was important to men only now and then. Sometimes Rigby only sketched her, Candy told Molly indignantly. But he paid just the same. Again Molly felt that strange pressure in the region of her heart. She even longed for a big disaster; if only she could experience something. She felt like the dry rocks and brushwood in the mountains.

Mama Doody snatched the paper from her and studied Rigby through the glasses that were slipping off her nose. "Candy!" she exclaimed. "This architect looks like our traveling salesman, Ritter!"

"You always find look-alikes, Auntie. To me all the men in Sydney are the same."

"And they are all the same," said Mrs. Doody, "Pigs, all of them! Is your sugar daddy coming today?"

"It's his Monday." Candy closed her eyes. She was bored with the whole thing. Molly Fleet was to be envied. Nobody bothered her.

"Come, Molly." Mrs. Doody pulled enviable Molly Fleet to the door.

"Molly!" cried Candy. "Do you see any resemblance between Ritter and Rigby?"

"Sure. They're both men." Molly grinned. "Have a nap, Candy. For your sugar daddy."

"He doesn't give a damn. He's crazy about me."

"Crazier than Mr. Ritter?" Molly asked hesitantly.

"Ritter is never crazy. That man doesn't have a spark of feeling. He gives me the creeps. But he pays."

"And that's all we want from him," murmured Molly. It was time for a love letter to Ritter. Molly blushed as she asked what he was most interested in. "In me, of course," said Candy. "What else?"

Mrs. Doody's boardinghouse in Darlinghurst was different from the houses next door only because of its inhabitants. These narrow, two-story tenements were waiting stoically to be demolished. The neglected, airless houses knew nothing about "Gracious Living"—a popular series in *Insight*—nothing about hygiene, nothing about the new status symbols. The houses had come to terms with their inhabitants and vice versa. Junk was hallowed by force of habit. The houses had high old-fashioned doors of dark wood, and narrow balconies with railings of rusty wrought-iron. This formerly attractive decoration in Colonial style couldn't banish the general air of neglect. The walls were tired and dirty; the sediment of earlier tenants stuck to them. Identical chimneys gave the crowded buildings a dreary uniformity. There were of course houses in Sydney's old section that were not dreary and ready to collapse. With their fenced-in front lawns and balconies, their attractiveness wasted here, these row houses bore witness to an earlier building period, like the old monuments in an ugly, crowded industrial city in England. And then there were the gloomy stone barracks down by the harbor which were built by the sweat of their brows and with their memories of a cozy, smoky pub in the fog at home, by the convicts imported from England under Governor Phillip. Whoever was freighted from the old country to the colony of New South Wales after 1788, found life in the settlement bitter as gall and unbearably sunny. The dusty confines of Mrs. Doody's boardinghouse still exuded the old nostalgia for a small, jolly, slovenly, pleasantly alcoholized world as the natives of Dublin or Manchester had known it.

At the time many residents of the old houses in Surry Hills and Darlinghurst had already moved out. These people moved with outspoken resentment into the clean, light apartments the city had built for its citizens. Mama Doody would pour a pail of dishwater on the head of any member of the building commission who dared to touch her house. In it she had things the way she wanted them: the heap of trash in front, the dirty wash in the kitchen, the dark, worn stairs, her neighbors, and the "living room" with its ancient, moth-eaten plush furniture, yellowed photographs of Dublin, and hideous plaster of paris figurines. The plaster Virgin Mary stood on the buffet and was astonished. The wallpaper with its faded flower pattern was peeling. A chronic faint odor of gas from the kitchen penetrated all the rooms. The living room was used only on holidays. Mrs. Doody lived in her chaotic kitchen, or she sat in Candy's room, scolding the girl whom she secretly loved. Candy's room lay to one side on the first floor, and Molly Fleet kept it clean. Candy's visitors got to her room through a narrow passageway. Nobody could understand why a model who earned such a lot of money didn't get herself a better apartment. But then nobody understood the strong family feeling of the Irish. Anyway, Candy had lived in even poorer surroundings in Kalgoorlie, as the great-granddaughter of an unsuccessful gold prospector.

On the attic floor lived the Umbrella Man, an old vagabond with the weathered face of an eagle, who had suspended a collection of umbrellas from his ceiling. Occasionally he sold one. He himself never used an umbrella. He had a gas hotplate in a corner under the sloping roof. He was either alone with his umbrellas or chatting with the old Viennese actor who lived on the first floor. Mama Doody took the Umbrella Man's meals up to him. He had appeared one day straight out of the limitless Australian loneliness, and looked as if he had years of wandering through deserts without an oasis behind him. His name was Doody too. Perhaps he was a relative. Anyway, he was Irish. He could do cabinet work when he felt like it. For the most part he drank gin and listened to Irish songs on the radio. He didn't know what he wanted, not in Sydney. Nobody knew. People just happened to come to the big city. Everybody in the house called him "Uncle," although he was pretty grumpy. Mrs. Doody loved him, and he seemed to be fond of her. When he was in a good mood he went to the tavern around the corner with the Viennese actor who had emigrated to Sydney shortly before the Second World War. The man from Vienna worked in a factory in Sydney, and came back to the boardinghouse in the evening. Then he sat in his narrow, hot room and conversed with his dead wife about performances at the Burgtheater or at the Josefstadt, performing-arts centers which none of Mrs Doody's guests had ever heard of.

On the attic floor, beside a small room filled with junk, lived an abo, short for aborigine, a black, wiry-haired Australian who had somehow drunk his way to Sydney from somewhere in New South Wales. When he felt like it, he worked in the harbor. His demands were so modest that he could afford to work part-time. He swept the house, carried heavy things up and down the stairs, repaired the gas stove, and sang when the clouds weren't depressing him. The clouds were mysterious moods that whirled around him like giant bush birds.

When Candy went out to eat or dance with her friends, the abo watched her go with glowing eyes in which the darkness of the Stone Age burned, and sang softly, "Lemon tree . . . very pretty." In his thoughts he called Candy "Lemon Blossom," and did what he could for her. Once he brought her some crushed mimosa. Candy smiled and said, "Thank you, Charlie Rainbow." He had received the first name, Charlie, and the family name, Rainbow, at a mission in New South Wales where his mother had abandoned him. He had been five when his mother's tribe had broken up camp and wandered farther into the bush. They hadn't been too pleased at the mission when they had found Charlie Rainbow. They had a lot of much nicer and diligent black children, and half-breeds who were cleaner and more grateful. Charlie didn't love anything or anybody except for flowers and Candy.

135

He had enjoyed gardening at the mission, but when the other children had washed their hands after work, he had run away. His hands stayed black, it didn't make any difference whether he washed them or not. He had tried once in vain to soap away the black color of his skin. Since then he looked upon soap as his personal enemy. He had made no friends among the other children. He lived for himself and couldn't think of any other way to live. Nothing attached him to his white teachers, although they did their best to win him. In the end he ran away. As a child he had been afraid of the whites; they reminded him of the dead white trunks of the eucalyptus trees, and the hair of one of his old teachers was gray bush grass.

Now Charlie Rainbow lived in the great wilderness of Sydney, but Candy reminded him of his beloved flowers that stood in boxes on Mama Doody's little balcony. Sometimes he looked in at a milk bar or, later, at beer halls, but he didn't dare to enter. He was not one of the abos to whom the government had issued a card for alcoholic beverages. In his case the powers that be were right, even if Charlie couldn't see it that way. The gin he got at Mama Doody's went straight to his head. Then he danced wildly all over the place and sang too loudly, or more accurately, howled like an Irish banshee. Mrs. Doody laughed. She had no nerves. Why shouldn't the blackfellow be merry too? Molly Fleet warned Mrs. Doody. Charlie Rainbow with gin inside him didn't know what he was doing. On the farm they had once had a good, nice abo and one day . . . Mama Doody laughed loudly and said nobody knew what they were doing when they had too much alcohol in them. She only had to think of her old man . . .

Charlie Rainbow had wandered a long way before finally arriving in Sydney. He had worked on a sheep station for a while, then he had moved on. When he finally arrived at Mama Doody's, all he had was a teapot, a bundle of dirty laundry, and his "garden" on his back. But he was so obliging! He hammered or carpentered or was busy with his plants. His garden was a box of seedlings, and now there were three. He had picked up the boxes at the harbor and filled them with earth. They had the necessary holes and cracks through which superfluous rainwater could run off. Charlie had lined the bottoms with stones, and shoveled the earth and sand over them. He put the boxes out in the sun in the morning and in the shade in the afternoon, and kept them carefully watered, just as he had learned from the bad white people in the mission. And when winter came—that is, when it was summer in Ireland and everywhere else in Europe—then Charlie covered his little garden with glass panes. He'd learned that too. He belonged to a union, and he worked in the harbor, but he only got paid when he worked and wasn't "crook" from gin. He had even made friends with a white colleague who got him gin on the sly. But suddenly it was all over. The white man avoided him. Perhaps the police had found out about the gin. So now Charlie hated his former friend. The whites could do what they liked with him. Sometimes they were friendly to the black man; sometimes they pushed him into a corner and walked off to a pub, arm-in-arm. They teetered all over the place, just like him, when they came out of the pub. A white drunk had stepped on Charlie's foot once as he, sober as a judge, was standing in front of the tavern, watching the people come out. Charlie had howled like a dingo, a wild Australian dog, and drawn his knife, whereupon the police had locked him up. He was booked for attempted murder, and all Charlie had intended was a warning to the drunken white buffalo. Charlie cried in prison, because of his flowers, but when he got back to Mama Doody's, his flowers had been watered and were blooming. Molly Fleet had looked after them. Charlie carved her a little arrow for thanks. It didn't have a poisoned head like some arrows in the bush; Charlie had painted it painstakingly with mysterious geometric lines and symbols. Miss Fleet had been very pleased. At first Charlie had been afraid of Miss Fleet. People were either black, which was the natural color, or they were pale as corpses. He had never seen a spotted face. Only tigers had spots . . .

A while ago Miss Candy had given him a mouth organ, and now he wasn't lonely any more. He blew the melodies of the forest, like the wind blew, or like the kookaburra laughed. It was great fun. Now Charlie Rainbow worshiped the beautiful white girl with the light hair.

Miss Candy should take care not to reject him when he asked what he could do for her. That was something Charlie Rainbow couldn't put up with. But Candy was a friendly creature and she felt a little sorry for the blackfellow. Not that it really hurt; just a whiff of compassion. She couldn't understand why he sometimes laughed aloud crazily, and danced up the narrow stairs. His flower boxes and the cheap harmonica were his entire delight. Sometimes he was as violent as a sandstorm.

In spite of his beautiful black eyes, Candy found him horribly ugly, but she instinctively hid her revulsion. As an additional slave, he was welcome. Sometimes he hid for weeks from Mrs. Doody's lodgers; sometimes he ran away. But when he came back and rushed to his flower boxes, fury raging inside him should his flowers be dead, he always found everything green and blooming. Once he stole a red watermelon from the market and laid it in front of Miss Fleet's door. She was

137

a benevolent tiger. He played something on his harmonica for her and she listened. Her hair was like the yellow poplars, and the right side of her face glowed like a red half-moon.

For some reason or other, Charlie Rainbow couldn't stand being in Sydney too long a time. Most of the poeple knew nothing about the forests. In Sydney the whites were innumerable and as much of a nuisance as sand flies. They were immodest in their hearts. Charlie Rainbow was as modest as the salt bush at the desert's edge.

On the day after Rigby's fiftieth birthday, the abo disappeared. Nobody seemed to notice it, but Molly Fleet went around with the watering can again. A whole world lay between her and Charlie, but both of them loved the Australian earth and everything that blossomed, bore fruit, or tried to. Just the same, neither of them could find their way anymore out of the city back to the country. Sydney held them with a thousand entrapping arms. However, they visited New South Wales. Molly Fleet went to the farm. She rarely went to see her father or her bitter sister in Parramatta. Charlie went walkabout, or he visited a blackfellow friend, who lived with his wife and children in a shack with a corrugated tin roof on the outskirts of the big city. The hovel stank of the sweat of many people; it was baking hot or dripping with rain, but it was cozy. Empty beer bottles, rusty pieces of iron, kitchen garbage, and trash lay in the narrow backyard. The dirtiest WC in New South Wales stood in one corner. It didn't bother anybody. Charlie's cobber was a good fellow. He liked his home.

The torn venetian blinds at the window let in the green, flickering light. One sat inside as in a pond. That was fun. They spent the evenings on the little wooden veranda that Charlie had built onto the shack. The big tropical stars and the cooler air calmed their confused and restless souls. The dark was comforting, a wide cloak from a dream world. All of them felt less helpless in the world of the whites after night had fallen. The stars belonged to everyone; they also looked down at the blackfellow amiably. But this magical union, which healed a torn ligament of nature, came and went with the night. Morning in the big city brought with it new misunderstandings, monotonous work, the unstilled thirst for *corroborees*—the native festivals—and for alcohol. The black and white world became a nightmare of sunshine and fear. Yes, all of them were afraid of their white brothers, even when they were friendly and helpful. They sent them, surely for their own good, to missions and reservations, but Charlie and his cobber were not packages. Wandering was in their blood. The whites also went walkabout. They even had a magazine with that name, which they had picked up from the native population. And why did the whites call themselves "old Australians"? All of them had come here recently. Charlie and his cobber were the *real* old Australians because their roots and soul pictures reached back into the time of dreams. In Sydney there was nothing but houses, humans, events, doubtful and incomprehensible projects of an alien spirit, which depressed the blackfellows. They experienced a quite different fulfillment and void, and stumbled—mute and crippled by not knowing—between the functional buildings and symbols of the whites.

Not far from the shack there were desolate little stores that sold cigarettes, soap, coffee, and sugar. The service was friendly, in the ice-cream parlor too, which the whites also frequented. Charlie's cobber worked in a little factory nearby.

Charlie Rainbow repaired the tin roof. There was enough bent metal and other junk lying around. His hands were quick and clever, as if they were additional live creatures attached to his thin arms, and independent of them. Charlie Rainbow knew that his know-how wasn't in his head; clever hands were more important. Charlie constructed a fence around the tiny plot for his friend, so that the neighbor's children couldn't trample over his "garden." The sweat poured down Charlie's body as he laid out a garden for his only cobber, which the latter didn't even want. But Charlie planted a few simple shrubs on the bare spot, with its tired, dried-up earth, and giggling all the time, even stuck some flower seeds into the loosened earth. They were to be a surprise for his friend and his *gin*, his native wife. The shrubs grew in this climate without any help, and a little fruit tree, which Charlie had stolen from a garden, already looked pretty and out of place in this miniature plot at the edge of the city. Charlie's friend was delighted with the fence. In the dark he passed his hands surreptitiously across the rough wood. The fence was a friend. It gave him a sense of security. It protected him from visitors and wild dogs.

Charlie Rainbow could have stayed with his cobber, and that would have been very good for him, but he didn't have an eye for what was good and useful. He saw the beautiful blond girl in Mama Doody's roominghouse. When the vision of Candy hurt very much, he crept back to Darlinghurst.

He often brought a present for Candy. Once he stood a cleverly carpentered and painted shelf in front of her door. He had never dared enter her room. Candy forgot to thank him, but Charlie didn't expect any thanks. After quite a time of brooding, he asked Miss Fleet if the shelf was a "bad shelf"? But Molly said it was a very fine shelf, and beautifully painted. Candy had all sorts of things standing on it, and had told Molly to thank him. Charlie let out a shrill cry of joy, then he ran up to his attic room. All he had wanted to know was if Miss Candy had thrown the shelf away.

Next morning, when Charlie was creeping past Candy's room, she came out of it. There she stood in her flowered dress and her shining hair. She murmured, "Thank you, Charlie Rainbow," and smiled at him. For a moment he was standing on the sunny side of life. Molly had reminded Candy to thank him.

Otherwise Candy never spoke to Charlie Rainbow. What could they have talked about? Charlie couldn't lay out a garden of words. In the daylight his mind was silent and fled to the dimly conscious memories of his tribe. Only his hands belonged in the twentieth century. They did good and bad things. They were immensely strong or immensely gentle, all according to whether he was furious or happy. Sometimes Charlie's hands were a bridge for Candy. She was night-blind. One night she was feeling her way home alone, and Charlie had been waiting for her, as usual. She couldn't see him. He was a twin of the dark. But he held out his hand to her, and his heart beating fast, helped her up the dark, wobbly stairs. That night he had sung for joy in his room and had danced until the Umbrella Man had knocked furiously on the wall.

Charlie Rainbow could have told the beautiful blond girl a lot of what he had seen with his eyes and smelled with his nose, but Candy never stayed long enough in one place for his heavy tongue to loosen up. Probably this girl didn't want to hear anything about sheep herds and hillsides, nothing about the luminous red-green rosella birds in the bush, nothing about horses bursting with strength and sunshine as they rushed to a waterhole. Charlie could also have told her about the mysterious twilight that tinted the blue sky of New South Wales, and hunted the cloud horses, and enfolded the rainbow snake, and summoned the spirits. The fractured light between day and night did all those things. Like all the members of his tribe, Charlie could smell the spirits of nature. He knew when they were approaching or remembered what his tribe knew. And then it didn't make any difference whether or not one had learned in a mission to sit still and how to dress, or whether one was naked and restless and destined to die out in the bush.

Miss Candy would never have listened to Charlie. He knew it in his heart, which was more agile and clever than his head. And he didn't have to tell the girl from Parramatta anything. Molly knew from childhood all about the desolate eucalyptus, the wide-fleeing horizon, the country road with burning dust, and the honey-sweet mimosa tree. She knew everything in New South Wales that greened, and its struggle against the wildness of nature; everything that bore fruit or withered stoically. Perhaps the girl also knew about some of the dark corners in Charlie Rainbow's soul. Molly had never forgotten her childhood friend, Goonur, who had stroked her golden-red hair and plaited wreaths of wild flowers for her. She had never told Charlie Rainbow about Goonur. The girl was hers alone, although she had not really known the child from the bush.

Until now Charlie Rainbow had always come back to Mama Doody's. It surprised Molly Fleet. Goonur had had a much better life with them on the farm. She had been allowed to help Grandmother Fleet to preserve fruit; still she had disappeared without saying good-bye. Who knew anybody anyway?

On the Monday after Rigby's fiftieth birthday, Molly Fleet was sitting alone in her room. Carlo was so busy at the restaurant that his day off had been changed. He was sorry, but he couldn't tell Molly when he would be free.

She sat in her narrow, hot room with nothing to do, and the emptiness and disappointment stuck like a knot in her throat. Why wasn't Carlo going out with her this Monday? Had he told her the truth? She had caught him telling all sorts of lies, and first-rate lying was requisite for anyone trying to test a memory like Molly Fleet's.

It never did her any good to sit alone and think. Although she didn't trust a living soul, it had never occurred to her that Candy, who had such rich friends, had taken her young man away from her. It was quiet in the house. The November heat had made Mrs. Doody drowsy. Now she was in her room, snoring. The abo was away, and Candy was waiting for her sugar daddy, who had no idea that right now he was paying Carlo Pressolini's debts.

The bell rang. Molly started. Candy's Monday visitor never came before seven. But it was he. She recognized him at once. A big, corpulent man with a full red face and dark Irish eyes. He was dressed impeccably and had curly black hair that was combed over the beginnings of a bald spot. A loose curl fell across his round forehead. His nose was fine and straight, his full lips drooped a little, as if with slight revulsion, or so it seemed to Miss Fleet. A hidden melancholy lay in his deep-set eyes with the dark rims around them. It didn't go with the laughter wrinkles in the corners. This gentleman was known in his circles as a prankster. He was a fleshy colossus, with a lot of thinking power behind his wrinkled brow.

Patrick Trent smiled at Miss Fleet, a little unsure. He saw her for the first time. "Excuse me, please," he said formally. "Could I speak to Miss Blyth?"

Molly said Candy was in her room. Perhaps she was still asleep. It had been such a hot day.

"Yes," said the stranger. "Very hot."

He could feel the girl's strange, flickering eyes examining him. Dammit! Candy had told him to come an hour too early. The girl had a memory like a sieve. Perhaps it wasn't a weak memory but only a lack of attention. To pay attention was important, and a rare thing between a man and a woman.

In spite of his smile, the visitor seemed to be apologizing for his presence in Mama Doody's boardinghouse. He seemed to feel even more uncomfortable than Albert Ritter. He looked around nervously, as if someone . . . his wife perhaps . . . was on his heels. At the same time he was surreptitiously looking at the girl with the birthmark. One of nature's bad jokes. He hated bad jokes. His were always funny . . .

He held his head a little to one side. Either it was too heavy for him or he wanted to excuse himself for his size. Nobody in this house knew that Candy's sugar daddy was an old member of Rigby's mob.

"Pardon me," The stranger laughed, suddenly and very naturally, and pushed his way past Molly Fleet with the odd agility of fat people. He had talked about the weather, as was proper, and that was enough. Molly Fleet would have liked to converse some more. There was something comforting about the visitor.

The old stairs creaked under his weight. Then Mr. Patrick Trent finally disappeared from Molly Fleet's hungry eyes.

142

11

A City Like Sydney

After Anne's departure, Rigby was as free as the kookaburra in the bush, but he didn't laugh as much. Never had a husband, who paid bills uncomplainingly and now and then even did a thing or two to please his wife, been deserted in such fashion! And on top of that, in a city like Sydney where life was so colorful and exciting. But in Vaucluse things were momentarily at a standstill. The big house was empty. Rigby's relief at the beginning not to hear any more complaints about backache, and to leave his cigarette case where it suited him, was gone. From the start, it hadn't been the relief he had felt after Flora's death. Perhaps he had only talked himself into thinking he would prefer to live alone. Anne must have become a treacherous habit. And he clung to his habits. That was why he still had Elizabeth West on his list. He hadn't heard from Withers in a long time, and he wasn't about to call her, not in his present situation! He thought friends looked after friends. Miss West had evidently never heard of such a thing. All Rigby would really have to do was ask his sister if Betty was dead or alive, in Sydney or away. He wondered if she was working on a new book or just loafing. Or swimming. Sydney was the right place for swimmers. Anne would never again find beaches like the ones here, five minutes from the heart of the city.

Rigby put out his cigarette furiously. He didn't know why, but right now he couldn't stand his house. Uncertainty and doubt had crept in at the gate. But perhaps security and permanence in private life were illusions for which every husband paid, sooner or later. Rigby didn't consider the fact this his frequent absences from home might have contributed decisively to the crisis in his marriage. He hadn't left his wife, and he had to have a little fun in the evenings. His visits to Candy Blyth didn't count. Besides, he had been on the verge of giving them up, whether Anne believed him or not. After all, marriage was the only satisfactory union: you had everything at home and didn't have to prowl around in strange, sleazy bedrooms. But Anne hadn't cooperated. It was all her fault.

Mrs. Andrews was no help either. She fluttered around like a tired swallow. She stuck her nose up in the air the same way too. Andrews got terribly on Rigby's nerves, but what could he do? He had to eat. Besides, Andrews was the only one who was fond of him. He'd always said so. And even his sister had to admit he was right. He hadn't seen her since his fiftieth birthday because right now he wasn't going to Manly on weekends. Miss Rigby was decent to the core, but he just couldn't stand women who had "always said so." Naturally he could never fire Andrews now. He wasn't totally crazy! Nobody could made Szegediner goulash like her.

As far as he could recall, he had finally decided to fire Andrews on his fiftieth birthday, and it was entirely Anne's fault that he now had to listen to her pearls of wisdom, just when his steak was tasting right again for the first time. Andrews always tried to ruin his steak for him; she considered steak unimaginative. But when he pounded on the table with his fist, Andrews and the proper steak appeared. Until now, what the master of the house wanted was still being carried out in Vaucluse. In seven years, Anne hadn't been able to grasp that.

When he thought of his many good resolutions which now couldn't be realized, Rigby felt lousy. Of course he now visited Candy in her old roominghouse. Since Miss West remained invisible and his wife had fled back to the pommies, he had to have something attractive to look at now and then. Candy at least didn't talk about metaphysics, and she never had a headache. She wasn't the worst girl around, if you overlooked her vocabulary. A ten-year-old was more articulate. But Candy was always in good spirits, not a nag like his wife. When he looked at it from every angle, Anne's absence was a blessing in disguise.

Rigby was absolutely furious when he thought how he had decided to make a fresh start on his fiftieth. He had wanted to sit on the terrace with Anne at least four evenings a week, in spite of her sour expression, and instead of his visits to Darlinghurst, he intended to visit Stan Marchmont more often. To be sure his boss needed a lot of rest now, but whenever Rigby went to see him, he was so pleased and didn't want to let him go. Marchmont couldn't sit with him on the terrace in Vaucluse as he had done after the disappearance of the first Mrs. Rigby. Why didn't he visit his old friend now? Marchmont said too little rather than too much, but to Marchmont, ridiculous as it might seem, Alexander Rigby was still "the young man." And he didn't want to see the disapproval in his boss's sharp blue eyes. He could sense it in every bone in his body: Marchmont was beside himself over the breakup of Rigby's second marriage. He worried about him. *That* wasn't necessary. He had always managed himself splendidly in the past. But tomorrow evening he would go to see Marchmont. No knowing how long he would still be able to do that.

A few evenings ago Rigby, in a feebleminded moment, had walked into Anne's room and in silent fury had tidied her drawers. She had left nearly all her dresses behind, but Rigby wasn't deceived by that. The full closet didn't necessarily mean that she was coming back soon. It might just as well mean that she didn't want to wear the dresses because he had bought them. As he tidied, Rigby came across an expensive, crushed chiffon dress. Anne's silver shoes with the high heels had torn a hole in it. It was scandalous, the way his wife had treated the things he had bought for her, *his* things! In that dress Anne had looked like an airy white egret about to fly away. Well, she had flown away.

Rigby was so disturbed that he pressed the dress to him. It was wrinkled anyway. And who should come into the room at that moment but Andrews! Rigby might have known it. With her mania for cleanliness, the woman could drive you crazy! Why the hell did she have to dust Anne's room? The second Mrs. Rigby would never see the dust. And even if she had stayed home, she wouldn't have noticed it. Rigby threw the white dress at Andrews to be mended. Andrews, accustomed to having things thrown at her, picked it up with dignity. She asked pointedly if the dress should be cleaned and sent to London.

Rigby's answer was unprintable, whereupon Andrews gave notice yet again, and Rigby had to talk her out of it. Again. How would she manage with strangers? In a city like Sydney, where nobody cared about anybody else? Andrews said she would get more appreciation anywhere than in this house. Rigby said he'd never heard anything so funny. Of course Andrews stayed. What would her Rigby do without her? One had to grant him some consideration. His wife was heartless. Andrews had always known it, but for once she kept her mouth shut. She didn't want to be strangled by Rigby just before going to the movies.

Rigby spent the evening alone on his big terrace, staring out to sea. Incredible how ill at ease he felt in his beautiful home! In spite of her nagging and constant ailments, Anne must have created an atmosphere that Rigby now missed. Anyway, Andrews had *not* written the anonymous letters to his wife. He knew when his jewel was lying. Andrews had been indignant that he had thought her capable of such a thing. Never would she have fallen so low! She loved her enemies and included them, grudgingly in her prayers. And of course she had given notice again, dumb creature!

So *who* had written those letters? It had to be someone who watched his little side steps. A damned uncomfortable feeling. As if someone were creeping up behind him and leaping out of a doorway when he turned around. Then he forgot about it. Whichever way you looked at it, Anne had flown away.

Rigby fell back on his work, because right now his fun was no fun. So why in heaven's name did he go to see Candy? Damn it all! He wasn't a hundred yet. Like every man, he needed distraction and a pretty female to look at. In a city like Sydney, you could find one on every street corner in King's Cross, on every beach, in every third villa . . . but Candy happened to be an exceptionally nice girl to look at.

Once he drove to the Blue Mountains, but it was not a success. Memories were too obtrusive. Either he had suddenly turned into an old woman or he was crazy: he could hear Flora Pratt giggling! He had jumped into his car and taken the Great Western Highway nonstop to Sydney. This was the road taken by settlers, soldiers, convicts and gold prospectors in the early colonial days. From the year 1793 people had tried to find a route across the stern, wild mountains. Rigby had spoken once at the Architects Club about the connection between Sydney and Bathurst, and had explained how in New South Wales nothing had been impossible, nor was it today. In 1850 Governor Macquarie, with his wife and an official commission, had driven across the new highway. Mrs. Macquarie had always taken part in anything her husband undertook, as was to be expected from a wife. That was why to this day the famous lookout spot was called "Mrs. Macquarie's Chair." Rigby had often stood there on his way back from the botanical gardens. Mr. Macquarie had never realized what a good thing he had had in his wife. He had probably taken for granted that Mrs. Macquarie lived and sweated with him. There were marriages like that too.

That evening Rigby got drunk with his mob.

As in his bachelor days, he now made frequent forays through the city. Sydney never disappointed nor tired him. Here he found unparalleled riches: beauty, new ideas, and old English traditions. The panorama of the sea and the uniform ugliness of many buildings and streets bore as many contrasts as Rigby's soul. The fragmentary and episodic character of this sprawling former settlement excited Rigby's fantasy, and his desire to shape things. A city like Sydney was rich, versatile, intoxicating. Sydney not only *was,* it *became* with every new year, with every new building. Every architectural dream was given form and life in the sober air under this blue sky. It was a delight to build here.

In the second half of the twentieth century, Sydney couldn't expect to be a showplace. 'Thank God!' thought Rigby. The city didn't shine with perfection. It had its memories and came up with honorable, anachronistic jokes. Because the Victorian houses and the fates of the wild convicts, the early settlers, and the English adventurers with sideburns, had put their stamp on the panorama of Sydney, just as much as the high-rise houses of glass and metal, and the sensual beauty of the luxury villas on the water. The Victorian houses with their columns and high, narrow windows and their ostentatious portals were legends in stone that made Sydney a gigantic bridge between the English past and the Australian future. The town hall or the post office or Martin Place were, for Rigby, touching, monumental monstrosities. You wandered around Sydney as in an architectural family album. He stood on York Street, in front of the ornamented cement facade of a palatial department store of the nineteenth century, or he let the hideous portal of the customs house on Circular Quai astonish him. He shook his head over the Witches House in Annandale, a naive Victorian freak that didn't fit into a climate where palms and tropical flowers grew amid spired towers and "romantic" narrow windows . . . all of it built for eternity. But in a city like Sydney, eternity only lasted decades. What place did a revival of Gothic architecture have in Australia? What room was there for Greek Classicism in this tropically tainted and hypermodern world? Time would tear more and more pages out of the old family album, and that was sad. It aroused in modern spectators a presentiment of loss, however ridiculous such Gothic jests may have been. Time raced on, nothing could stop it, and one day the buildings of Marchmont, Rigby & French would be just as anachronistic in an unknown Sydney as today's ornamental Huddart Parker House on Bridge Street. Or like Cochrane's Hotel, 1850, the consoling Colonial tavern that didn't try to be more modern than it was, and that, as the greatest concession to the present day, had only exchanged its wrought-iron fixtures for ones that used electricity. Rigby looked at the stylistic efforts of the past with affectionate eyes because he knew that never again would a wave of English civilization, with the historic pomposity and ornamentation intended for a foggy climate, flow over this city of the future. These high, solid, mercantile houses and public buildings would disappear with time, like the frock coats, the sideburns, and the piety of the English settlers.

Rigby stood on the quai of Darling Harbour where wool and other wares were being loaded for export. He looked across at the high-rise houses, but today he didn't feel his usual joy over the present Sydney. Who fitted into these high houses of glass and metal? Was architecture more progressive and less compromising than its creators? In the stern new palaces—Vaucluse had been built with the same idea—there were no shabby, cozy corners and alcoves as there had been in Anne's parental home behind Avenue Road, which had combined old-fashioned ornamentation with a certain naive dignity. No clean-cut lines, no feeling for material, no economy of design! But Anne, even after seven years of brooding and instruction on esthetics by Rigby, seemed to prefer this house to his model residence in Vaucluse. And of course she would prefer any pommy to old Rigby!

When finally, deep in thought, Rigby found himself standing in front of his former office on George Street, Elizabeth West suddenly appeared. He had just been wondering how many tears Withers must have shed for him in her little anteroom . . . oh yes, for him! Today Withers probably only wept within her own four walls in Bellevue Hill. Miss Rigby must have taught her to stop crying in public. Actually Withers had looked quite cute and rather touching with the tears running down her apple-fresh face. Rigby had often had to lend her a handkerchief. Withers had been born without a handkerchief.

Rigby turned his back determinedly on Miss West. She was with a man, and Rigby didn't want to intrude. She seemed to be enjoying an animated conversation with him. The man laughed like a neighing horse. Rigby was surprised. Betty had never been particularly witty. And he felt no desire to talk to her. She had behaved miserably. Or did she think Anne had withdrawn because of her? On his birthday, of course, it was she and not Anne who had spent hours with him.

"Alex!"

Rigby turned around. Miss West murmured introductions. The man with her was a journalist from Queensland. His name was Frank Grierson. He had taken a trip from Brisbane to New South Wales, and had naturally ended up in Sydney, like everybody else.

Rigby surveyed Betty's new man with shameless interest. The ash-blond gentleman could be forty. He wore glasses. Naturally. Glasses made one appear intelligent. He looked at Rigby amiably out of his light-blue eyes. To do this he had to raise his head. With his arrogantly hooked nose and wrinkled forehead, Rigby looked pretty formidable, but the gentleman from Brisbane seemed incurably friendly. He had a neutral, bookish face, but his movements were lithe and free. He was probably a good swimmer when he took off his owlish glasses, but then, every Queenslander swam like a fish. Rigby could find nothing exceptional about the fellow.

"Shall we have tea together?" asked Miss West. She sounded embarrassed. Rigby noticed it and wondered why. She could go out with whomever she pleased; fortunately, she was not married to him. Her question hovered in the air like a ball that didn't want to drop back on the pavement. When he found it fun, Rigby was a master of the embarrassed pause.

"Frank is thirsty," Miss West said, sharply now.

Rigby looked down his arrogant nose at his watch. "Sorry, my dear," he said amiably. "I have a pressing appointment."

Miss West reddened with vexation. Rigby had quite obviously been strolling along George Street. He had all the time in the world.

Mr. Grierson shifted from one foot to the other. Miss West had funny acquaintances. At this very moment Mr. Grierson took an instant dislike to this very tall, elegant man with the restless eyes and the cruel mouth. The man looked dangerous. Didn't Miss West notice it? To sum up people correctly was his business. Mr. Grierson would have liked to protect little Miss West from this man, but he didn't know how.

"Have you been in Sydney long?" Rigby asked the younger man.

Frank Grierson had been in this turbulent city for fourteen days. Rigby hadn't heard from Betty in fourteen days, nor had he seen anything of her. Not that he had missed her. Paddy Trent had been very good about seeing to it that he wasn't alone too much. John Darling was too intensively married now, and the former Miss Eastman got on Rigby's nerves. Trent always had time for a beer or fun of some kind, but right now Rigby didn't want to hear any of Trent's jokes, and had told him so. Paddy never took offense. He had only mumbled guiltily that all he'd wanted to do was cheer Rigby up a little. "Are you crazy?" Rigby exclaimed. "I'm in a terrific mood. Any camel could see that!"

Perhaps any camel would have seen it but it had escaped Paddy Trent.

"How do you like Sydney, Mr. Grierson?"

"Rather chaotic. Such disconcerting contrasts. And too much painterly dirt in the older sections for my taste."

"That's possible," Rigby sounded more aloof than ever. "For us it's good enough."

"Oh, Sydney is wonderful, of course!" the gentleman from Brisbane hastened to say. The people here were ridiculously sensitive. They couldn't take the slightest criticism of their imposing but disorderly city. "The new buildings are fantastic."

Rigby raised his eyebrows. Miss West would have liked to slap his face, but for that she'd have needed a footstool.

"The high-rise houses have nothing whatsoever to do with fantasy," Rigby said gently. "Every measurement is exact. Only people are fantastic, don't you think?"

"Hm," said Mr. Grierson. He sounded and looked uncomfortable.

"We must go," snapped Miss West. "We have a pressing appointment."

"Don't bite my head off!" Rigby gave Miss West an enigmatic look. "We're all friends here. So have a good time, Mr. Grierson. Are you going to write a book about Sydney?"

"I'm reporting for the radio."

"Then you're lucky," said Rigby. "A talk is not a piece of writing. I'll hope you'll do honorably by us on the air."

"I'll do my best."

"Very good, Mr. Grierson. I'd like to talk on the radio too. Small mistakes are never noticed."

"I collect my material as conscientiously as possible," Mr. Grierson said stiffly.

"That's rather difficult in a chaotic city like Sydney," Rigby said gently. He looked at his watch again, a present from Elizabeth West. "When do we meet again, little one?"

"Not right now. I'm going to Brisbane with Frank."

"How come I don't know anything about it?"

"Is this a police interrogation?" asked Betty West. Frank Grierson listened to the dialogue, his face expressionless.

"Miss West is part of our inventory," Rigby explained. "We look after her because she's still so little."

"Don't be foolish, Alexander!" Miss West was furious. What would her colleague think?

"What are you going to do in Brisbane?" asked Rigby.

"I'm going on the air."

"Reading your own works?"

"Naturally," said Miss West. "Just imagine, there are still people around who haven't read my books."

"I envy them," said Rigby. "I mean, I envy them the pleasure of getting to know your work. Bon voyage! Don't get stuck there."

Rigby nodded to both of them and walked off into the traffic. "Who

150

on earth was *that?*" asked Grierson. He hadn't caught the name when Betty had introduced him. "Tell me, Betty, when do I finally meet the famous architect, Rigby? They told me at home that an interview with him was an absolute must in Sydney."

"He just interviewed you," said Betty West.

Rigby drove straight to the Hungarian restaurant. He'd had enough of women for today and decided to leave his jewel in Vaucluse to her own resources. Somehow they had settled down to their own mode of conversation again since the second Mrs. Rigby had left the arena— that is, Andrews talked and Rigby pretended not to listen. When enjoyed at cautious intervals, Andrews's conversation wasn't as dumb as might have been expected. Just the same, Rigby was cautious.

Restaurant Szabo in King's Cross was pretty empty. It was early evening. Szabo's place was one of those small cellar restaurants which gave King's Cross an international ambient in the eyes of European immigrants. Besides the food, such places also offered the conversation and sometimes the music of the homeland. Rigby enjoyed the informal atmosphere. He liked to talk to Mr. and Mrs. Szabo, who with their harsh English and melting sentimentality, lived on the periphery of an alien Australian world. They had never penetrated outside this international zone of King's Cross. They served their own countrymen and the old Australians with the same zeal, and with the same interest in the personal affairs of their guests. They were burning to fathom the private lives of the Australians even more than those of their compatriots, but in this they were not successful. The Aussies were stubbornly silent when it came to their private sphere. They didn't even seem interested in their own business. If Andrews hadn't occasionally come out with some of the details of the Rigbys' married life, Mr. and Mrs. Szabo might just as well have been waiting on the Sphinx. Naturally they never mentioned the untimely demise of his wife in front of Rigby—for that they were too tactful, also too businesslike. In the many years they had spent in Sydney, they had had ample opportunity to study the reactions of the Aussies, who hated personal questions, whereas their Hungarian guests would have left the restaurant deeply hurt if Mr. Szabo hadn't questioned them about their ailments, business, mothers-in-law, vexations, amusements, and grandchildren.

There was usually little to tell about the grandchildren. The older generation rarely saw these young people. They had become Aussies. They were startled when their parents spoke Hungarian. They changed their names, frequently married Australians, and never came to the Restaurant Szabo. They weren't sure enough of themselves yet. They chatted among each other about racing, politics, newspaper articles, farming, films, about everything that contributed to their upbringing on this continent. Mr. Szabo nodded wisely when his old steady guests complained. Nothing to be done about it! After all, old Mrs. Varady could try to get accustomed to her Australian daughter-in-law. But Mrs. Varady shrugged in her inimitable way. She had nothing against dear Helen, but the paprika was missing. Mr. Szabo nodded again. The daughter of his friend, Ferenc Kuncz—Frances Connor for years now—had married the owner of a sheep station in Queensland. She had given up the violin, and visited her father in Sydney once in a blue moon. With the son-in-law the paprika was missing too. Nothing to be done about it! Curious people. The son-in-law didn't think much of his wife's father either. He told his best cobber confidentially that old Connor was a cranky old bastard, whereupon the two gentlemen drank a few more beers to which they treated each other with gales of laughter; then they spoke about more important things: sheep, and the price of wool. Mr. Connor had visited his disloyal daughter in Queensland once, but never again! Mr. Szabo had had to cook chicken in tokay sauce for him when he got back, he had returned so indignant. His son-in-law had treated him with a total lack of respect for his age, nor had he listened to Mr. Kuncz's opinion of Australia. Mr. Kuncz had tried in vain to start a really loud quarrel with his son-in-law, hoping for a touching reconciliation, but the Aussies would rather die than quarrel with him. Even his daughter had said, "Do be quiet, Father. I'm happy here. It's the best country in the world."

Mr. Szabo cooked, and calmed down old and new immigrants. It wasn't a bad country. Fair enough. Whoever wanted to work made headway here. That the Aussies didn't inquire about the health and the children of Mr. and Mrs. Szabo was something the couple had become accustomed to long ago. In a city like Sydney, you couldn't expect personal interest. And one should not try to be different from the rest. At home everybody wanted to be a genius, or at least for the children to have a better life than any other children, but that was frowned upon in Australia. Other countries, other customs. There was only one thing Mr. Szabo had never been able to grasp: the way the old Aussies insulted each other amicably, how they swore, and how rarely they turned around to look at a pretty girl. Was the paprika missing in their love life too? Mr. Szabo had bigger worries.

Rigby, however, liked to look at a pretty girl occasionally, despite the fact that he was a true-blue Australian. And his married life seemed almost as turbulent as in the best families in Mr. Szabo's homeland before the Communists had come. Rigby's jewel was not exactly discreet. And if she could make her stories a little more spicy, she dramatized shamelessly. The Szabos got the impression that Rigby beat his second wife regularly. No wonder the poor woman had fled back to England. Mr. Szabo found Mr. Rigby very nice, just a trifle brutal, and unapproachable like all the Aussies.

Rigby had his table in a far corner of the restaurant from which he could observe everything without being seen. Mr. Szabo always waited on him himself with special care. He had read in the paper what a famous regular he had in Rigby. And Rigby was generous. He gave terrific tips when something tasted especially good. A Magyar nobleman in old Hungary couldn't have been more generous. But Rigby didn't hurl his plate against the wall when he wasn't pleased with the food. Other countries, other customs!

Rigby was just discussing the menu with Mr. Szabo when he caught sight of Candy. It was his lucky day, apparently: all the women he knew were off with other men. Candy was accompanied by the man with whom she had been walking on the beach in Manly. He reminded Rigby of a greedy shark. Rigby missed the gold necklace he had given Candy. She always wore it. In all probability the shark had managed to get the necklace from Candy.

What Rigby was eating almost stuck in his throat when another well-known lady walked into the restaurant, accompanied by an Hungarian. This was the bloody end! Klari Trent, the Hungarian wife of his good cobber, was talking now in a dimly lit corner in her incomprehensible mother tongue! She couldn't see Rigby, so she didn't exercise any self-control. Her decolleté was just as low as it had been at Rigby's party. The sight of Klari Trent was nothing to complain about, but the devil take her! Naturally Rigby wouldn't tell his friend Trent anything about this meeting. The poor fellow was often away on business in the evenings, and here his wife was two-timing him right under Rigby's very nose. Paddy deserved better. That was the trouble with these foreigners; as if there weren't plenty of girls that were good to look at in a city like Sydney!

Rigby paid and left. Candy had eyes for no one but the young Italian. Klari Trent's eyes were closed. Probably all for the best.

Rigby drove back to Vaucluse in a foul mood. His house was deathly still. Life was being played out elsewhere, in the many small suburban villas Rigby had always felt were so boring. Where man and wife stuck to each other and brought up their children together and worked at their marriage. Where everyday life passed uneventfully, and the husband worked in the garden on weekends and washed the car. The wife had her midmorning coffee break with her friends, she cooked plain food, she loved her husband docilely, and before you knew it you were old and sat contentedly on your little veranda, while in the city the high-rise houses grew into the sky. But here, Rigby enjoyed the harbor panorama of Vaucluse in lonely glory, and Patrick Trent looked for his new wife in his new house. Anyway, that was how Rigby saw it. Why had Paddy married again? To sit alone in his big new glass palace?

Although he was no longer in the prime of life, Patrick Trent had married a second time for a very specific reason. But only he knew the reason . . .

12

A Man in His Second Prime

The first Trent had emigrated to Queensland from his starvation district in Ireland in 1867, eight years after the political separation from the mother state of New South Wales. In the new colony, Shawn Benedict Trent became a gold prospector, and experienced the whole adventurous gamut from the gold rush to the bitter awakening in the bush. He had two invaluable characteristics for a pioneer: he accepted conditions on the fifth continent as they were, and he could stand aside and see himself as he was and laugh at his misfortune. His disappointments in the new colony were bitter, but not important. Only one thing meant anything to him: the welfare of his soul. He had to live in harmony with God. Not that Shawn ever said so, or thought consciously along these lines, but he felt he would be insulting his Creator if, like most of the prospectors with no gold, he felt sorry for himself or cursed the new land. The first Trent had brought one treasure with him from his homeland: the energy of faith. In Queensland in those days, he needed every ounce of it. The country was not yet the "sunshine land of tourists" nor the "tropical wonderland" of today's travel brochures. All Trent experienced was the merciless miracle of the sun, and the perilous bush. The thousand miles of elegant beaches on the Pacific, the exploratory trips to the Great Barrier Reef arranged by the government, and the El Dorado of the rich were events that took place a hundred years after the first Trent's appearance in Queensland.

In 1867 they found gold in Gympie, on the shores of the Mary River, a hundred and twenty-three miles north of Brisbane. Shawn Trent became one of the thousands who looked for the mythical treasure in Queensland, New South Wales, and South Australia. Whenever Shawn thought he had reached his goal, a stubborn, unpretentious Chinese beat him to it. The Chinese took the search for gold more seriously than anything else life had to offer. They had identified happiness with riches for thousands of years. In this respect too they came from another part of the universe. Shawn had choked a Chinese man because the latter had tried to jump him when he had seen a gleam of the metal. Shawn was incredibly strong. The dainty little Chinese had looked like a pesky fly to him. But Mr. Li had not joined his ancestors. He had quickly played dead in order to remain alive. Next morning, when Mr. Li walked out of one of the Chinese tents, very much alive and smiling, Trent was so happy that he gave the little man the only lump of gold he ever found in Gympie. Of course Mr. Li despised the Irish giant for his naiveté, but he hastily pocketed the gold. Soon after that he opened a shop in Gympie, where he sold produce, tools for prospectors, and a Chinese miracle medicine at steep prices. In his own eyes, Mr. Li was the most successful gold prospector on the Mary River.

In the first year, Gympie produced eighty-five thousand ounces of gold, which saved the economy of the land after the big depression. Shawn's offspring in Queensland saw nothing more of the gold rush. When Patrick Trent was born in Brisbane, shortly before the First World War, there was already a modern dairy industry in Gympie, and the finest fruit in Queensland. Patrick Trent never visited the place where his ancestor had prospected in vain for gold. He had developed a distaste for the city that had made a fool of old Shawn. All the Trents were allergic to defeat, just as all of them loved music, and hid their love of God and humanity behind jokes. They had big hearts in which there was room for many things; for example, private disappointments which they tried to overcome silently and without anger. They felt compassion for every living creature, but hid this irritating Christian weakness behind ribaldry and anecdotes, roaring laughter, and the vain effort to be overlooked by everybody in general. The latter they might have spared themselves because they were a very striking family. To begin with, nobody could overlook their size and corpulence, and they betrayed their compassion with sidelong glances of their dark, Celtic eyes, a sudden lowering of the voice, and by a ceaseless running back and forth, which made whomever they were talking to nervous. The wives especially couldn't stand it. Moreover, the Trents had to be damned careful in the new land, because if there was one thing beside status differences and arrogance that the Aussies detested, it was the feeling that they were being pitied.

The first Trent had come to Australia in a sailing vessel, because in those early days the government of Queensland had offered each passenger two and a half pounds of bread or crackers, one pound of white flour, five pounds of oatmeal, two pounds of rice, and two ounces of tea, eight ounces of sugar, and eight ounces of syrup weekly. Shawn had never seen that much food on his isolated Irish farm. The food alone was worth a voyage to Queensland. It would have been worth a trip to the southern Australian desert! Every Trent could manage on what he found on the edge of an oasis, and what he didn't find, he invented.

The first Trent had been cook on the sailing ship for a short while because the hired cook had been unable to withstand the rigors of the trip. Trent's cooking was indifferent, but he spiced his improvised menus with jokes and words of encouragement. He had never cooked for so many people before. This pioneer in the ship's galley was a huge, childlike fellow who silently pitied the seasick boasters, who on their way over to the fifth continent were already planning to transform the new land into settlements of small Irish towns with churchs and taverns. On the ship the Irish were more or less on their own, as they were to remain in their first decade in Australia. During the many months they spent at sea, they were homesick, with choral singing and a prodigious thirst.

The first gold had already been found in Queensland in 1851. The Chinese had also been faster as immigrants than Shawn Benedict Trent. During the years to come, they peopled the continent so diligently that thirty years later the Australian government had to limit immigration. But even without the Chinese rivalry, Shawn wouldn't have found any more gold. It wasn't to be. At twenty-two he was too young to accept the judgment of fate without protest. He left the hovels of Gympie only to seek his fortune elsewhere. He had heard rumors of gold on the Walsh River, in the slimy sand of the Palmer Tributary.

Trent had only been in Gympie a few years, and left the place in good spirits, with a little money and his worn rosary in his pocket. He had taken on occasional jobs in Gympie, and now tried to get rid of his money as quickly as possible. Later he couldn't remember how long he had been on the road. Full of hope, he went the historical way of slow disillusionment in the northeastern section of the continent. But in these pioneer days, if a man wasn't stopped dead right away or, didn't get lost in the deadly bush, he could be considered a success story. Australia had not yet fulfilled the wishful dreams of the middle class.

At last Shawn reached the Palmer Valley, in a blue shirt and torn pants, a cone-shaped straw hat on his head. He had taken almost as much time in his wanderings as Odysseus, but unlike the hero of that epic, he had not spent his time with giants, sirens, and king's daughters. He had done every kind of work, as one had to do on a new continent. He didn't want to starve before he found his gold in Palmer.

Nobody sang the adventures of this Irish farmer in Australia; yet Trent, like thousands of immigrants, was an Odysseus who practically and heroically fought the monsters of thirst and hunger in the Australian wilderness.

The Palmer Valley brought thousands of Chinese and white prospectors their desired gold. In time it put the economy of Queensland on its feet. For a short while Cooktown was the paradise of adventurers, but for Shawn Benedict Trent it was a witches' cauldron. Everybody was suffering from incurable gold fever and fought with pickaxe, shovel, knives, and elbow grease for minute traces of gold in the sand of the damp, hot shore.

Two Irish friends had accompanied Trent from Gympie to the Palmer Valley. Like innumerable others, one of them was killed by an arrow of the wild blackfellows in the region. The other strayed too far away from the camp because he thought the big treasure would be in a lonelier spot. He got lost in the bush, and died of hunger and thirst. Shawn survived Palmer. Like all the others he shook his primitive sieve until the little gold kernels were washed clean, but his washed-out gold ran between his fingers in the dives and gambling dens of Cooktown. At first he swore all the Irish curses he could remember, then he prayed. He had sinned. He had sought earthly gold, although he knew that the true gold mines were not of this world. He had to shake his obdurate soul, not his sieve.

When, during sleepless nights, Shawn had finally recognized the truth, he was his old, jolly self again. He avoided the dives and gambling dens, and spent the rest of his money on a pair of cotton pants, food, and a horse. One morning, with his cobber, he left his Sodom of the fifth continent. His friend swore and cursed the murderous land; Shawn was silent. His friend from Dublin didn't know better. He had driven the saints out of his alcohol-besotted system. James Rowan was only forty-two, but he was as emaciated as a skeleton. The cruel sun had withered him. He reminded Shawn of a dying fig tree. Yes, Rowan had come to the end of the line. In Dublin he had been a prosperous businessman, but he had wanted to get rich quick and had forged checks. Queensland had promised him a new life and a new freedom, but the promises weren't worth any more than his forged checks. Palmer and rum had made a fool of him and sucked the marrow from his bones.

Sad and frightened, Shawn listened to the wild curses of his dying compatriot. He tried to conjure up the refreshing spring breezes of belief for his friend, but he was after all neither a preacher nor a prophet, and it was too hot to talk anyway. Even the shadows of evening glowed like a smoldering fire. The words of comfort remained stuck in Trent's dry throat. All he could do was start to sing an Irish hymn for the dying, but with his last strength, cobber Rowan shouted for him to shut his dirty mouth. He died as night fell over their provisional tent. Trent gave him a bush burial. He himself was at the beginning of his long Australian wanderings, and the beginning was in the bush.

Shawn Benedict Trent now rode on with two horses and his provisions in his knapsack. Then he sold the horses and worked on a cattle ranch which had sprung up on bush land. At night he slept happily on a cowhide spread across four flat, wooden blocks. His room on the ranch was wretched. The door hung loose on its hinges and the mosquitoes pursued him in his sleep. But there were wooden huts in the bush with bark roofs that were even less comfortable and hadn't even a chair or table. Shawn hadn't brought any pretentious demands with him from Queensland.

Later he worked as a woodchopper in the endless forest, and hummed cheerfully to himself when the overseer handed out flour and tea. One might have thought he had been given a sack of gold. The overseer decided that Trent was a naive fellow because he was content, but Shawn was completely indifferent to what people thought of him. He had the gift of being able to read their thoughts from their expressions, and his feelings were never hurt. He felt sorry for mean people.

For a while Shawn disappeared in the eucalyptus forests. He had preferred the rain forests. He hated the bare eucalyptus trunks with the raggedly hanging-down bark. He was no longer the same man who had sailed to Queensland with a fresh face and sensibilities. Sometimes he felt very tired. The sun had burnt his white skin brown long ago, and in spite of his gentle behavior, he looked like a real bush man with his wild dark hair and beard. But he wasn't one, at least not the kind of bush man later generations imagined. Life in the bush was not romantic; it was hard. In periods of drought even a hardy and religious man like Trent lost courage and hope. Then he felt he was living in a landscape of dust, and longed for the lakes surrounded by mountains and the still green meadows of his homeland. The gray-green scrub and the thickets of the bush depressed him. What a country! He couldn't seem to get accustomed to the screeching of the bush birds and the noise of the cockatoos, and the shrill laughter of the kookaburras startled him. Later, Patrick Trent would inherit his ancestor's sensitive ears. In the younger man's lonely, lean years, as well as in his salad days with Rigby's mob, he suffered from the shrill voices of women and birds.

159

On the other hand, all the Trents loved the kangaroos and the wallabies in the bush, and were highly amused by their leaps and the fur-lined pouches for their young. And when the Trents were very depressed their moods could hop back and forth, up and down, like a wallaby. Then they looked at the flowers and shrubs, and their beauty almost made them happy. The first Trent in Queensland had already found pleasure in the flowers. Whenever the rain forests in the north became a dreary, damp hell, somewhere the spring mimosa would shine, or the bluish-pink Cooktown orchid, the purple sarsaparilla blossom, and the vanilla lily would quench their thirst for beauty. Shawn Benedict Trent was probably the only gold prospector in Queensland for whom the golden miracle of the mimosa bush made up for a lost dream.

When Shawn had had enough of his nomadic existence, he worked on a small farm near Brisbane. There he met Rosaleen O'Grady, the sweet, robust farmer's daughter. The good-natured young giant from her homeland took to her at once, and with that Trent's wanderings came to an end at "the end of the world," as their Irish immigrants called the fifth continent.

Shawn Benedict Trent, who had become a roaming tree among trees, built fences to protect the sheep from the dingoes. Now he had a young wife in his bed and she gave birth to children. The farm was poor. From the start it had been nothing more than a piece of semi-dry grassland that had to be watered doggedly and laboriously. Trees had had to be burnt to make room for a house and grass. O'Grady and his son-in-law, Trent, had none of the machines or chemicals that help today in the fight with the tough, dry earth. They fought incessantly against drought and sickness of man and beast. When drought made life unbearable, O'Grady and the Trents, with their few sheep and household goods, wandered on, and in another area again built a primitive home and fenced it in against the wild dogs. Shawn Benedict had stopped singing songs long ago; his throat was as dry as the grass around him. But he never lost his good humor nor his appetite, and he never cursed the dry land or his hard life. Sometimes he thought of his search for gold in the days of his youth, and smiled indulgently. He had had six children. Four had died on their wanderings. Shawn grieved for them deeply, for a short while. God had taken the children to the eternal meadowlands, where they now sang and danced around evergreen fir trees. He lived contentedly and died contentedly. He left his progeny his wanderlust, his fine voice, his enormous appetite, and the vision of treasures in the Australian earth.

In spite of his poverty, he had possessed a lot because nothing had ever possessed him. Shawn Benedict Trent would have been astonished if he could have seen how Patrick lived in Sydney. He would have been deeply troubled about him because in his own gold-prospecting days he had seen the dangers and bitterness riches could bring. Shawn would have pitied Patrick. But the veil of time fell between the first Trent in his desolate grassland, watered only by the sources of mercy, and the last Trent. Patrick was a successful real-estate agent. He owned a luxurious villa in Barmoral, and he was a thirsty beggar in the aridity of a materialistic world.

Tyrone B. Trent, Patrick's father, was the first member of the family to move into the city. He worked for a short time in a rum factory in Brisbane. Before that, at the age of twenty, he had moved herds of cattle from Queensland to New South Wales. Then he suddenly gave up the life of a stockman. Like all the Trents, Tyrone liked change.

In Brisbane, the city of the many hills, Tyrone married young Mary Gallagher, a redheaded bar girl. She was half a laughing Eve, half a young mother. In the rum factory, Tyrone had acquired a taste for the liquor that set him on fire. He went to the cheap bar every evening and sang Irish songs for Mary Gallagher until she married him.

Both thought the marriage would be the beginning of a mutual hominess. Mary did stay at home in Brisbane with the children, but after the birth of the seventh, Tyrone went walkabout. Perhaps the tropical city made him restless, but in all probability he'd brought the restlessness to Brisbane with him. From then on he was seldom home. Patrick's mother worked in a jam factory to clothe and feed her children. Tyrone sometimes worked as a seasonal laborer in the bush land, and sent a pittance home. For two years he disappeared into the sugar cane fields of Queensland, and came back to Brisbane with a little money because he couldn't get along with the Italian workers. But the money was spent in beer halls and taverns.

The rich plantations on the Queensland coast fired Tyrone Trent's restless fantasies. Tropical Queensland was a state with exceptionally brilliant coloring. Trent thought in color and bequeathed this ability to his son, Patrick. Neither of them could paint on board or canvas; their pictures remained unfulfilled and unpainted in their souls.

Tyrone Trent returned again and again to his narrow, fetid home in

Brisbane, only to flee eventually to the plantations without a worry in the world. One day he would bring Mary and the children to such a plantation. He loved his wife in his way, but his wild Irish soul recognized all or nothing. And in the factories of Brisbane, nothing was waiting for him.

When Tyrone was at home he described to his silent wife how happily they would all live one day on a plantation, in a great airy house on the coast, surrounded by palms and fig trees. Who would ever have had anything like it in Ireland? Bananas, pineapples and earthnuts needed no particular care in this climate, Tyrone explained to his weary, worried wife, because that was what had become of the merry bar girl. Mary was an anxious mother now, working in a factory where the fruits of the plantation were canned. Tyrone fantasized with shining eyes about his future plantation. Somewhere far away the ocean would greet them day and night, and the mountains would nod to them like old friends.

"Aren't you happy?" he asked his silent wife. But Mary's dreams were modest. They grew on the hard ground of reality; a piece of land of her own would have meant bliss to her. Tyrone and the boys would build a wooden house, and she would plant vegetables and a few fruit trees. And herbs too, of course—watercress, and if the little piece of land was cool enough, she would grow cabbage, lettuce, and onions. She knew how to protect them from mildew with ash. Before she had served drinks and jokes in Sydney, she had grown up on a farm in Ireland. Her greatest wish was never to see a can of produce again. That was *her* idea of happiness.

Mary Trent made the mistake of indicating her idea of happiness. Tyrone reddened with fury and ran out of the house, wild with rage. Mary, deafened by his shouts, remained behind with her children in the stuffy room she had rented from some Irish people. In return Mary helped in the kitchen, and after her work in the factory, did her landlady's laundry. Patrick Trent saw how his mother lived, and swore that one day, should he ever marry, his wife would have a better life.

One evening his father got into a devilish fight in his favorite tavern in Brisbane. They brought him to his wife and children with a heart wound. Patrick Trent would never forget that his mother didn't shed a tear. He was still too young to recognize the dry pain that mercilessly tears the soul to pieces like the bush-saw rips the skin.

"I'll always stay with you!" Patrick promised wildly, and his mother nodded submissively. She'd heard that once before. Patrick was fifteen when his father died. Sometimes he was afraid of his own strength. It was a good thing for the family that in the end his father had managed to provide for his own Christian burial, because the man who wounded him in the tavern had fallen in the broken glass and pools of beer, and hadn't got up again.

Patrick's only amusement in the days of his youth were the droll koala bears in the Lone Pine Koala Sanctuary on the Brisbane River. He earned his money for such pleasures by helping out in a bakery and delivering orders by bicycle to the villas and bungalows of the elegant suburbs. The owner hired the fatherless boy out of friendliness, because actually his delivery truck brought his goods quicker and more reliably to the suburbs that rose, like an amphitheater, on the hills above the blue river. But Jimmy Hamilton had been one of Tyrone Trent's cobbers. After Tyrone's death, he employed Patrick's mother too, with light work in the bakery. Factory work had become too hard for her. The climate bothered her, and her husband's death had taken a great deal out of her. But like many of the Irish, she had indestructible vitality.

On his trips to the paradise of the successful, Patrick acquired his first knowledge of the value of real estate. In his thoughts he promptly chose a villa for his mother. It was like the castle-in-the-air his father had built for merry Mary Gallagher. The future Sydney financier explained excitedly to his mother that he intended to make enough money to set her up one day in a fine villa, where from the wooded heights, she could spit down into the Brisbane River.

Mary Trent said, "Don't shout! I'm not deaf!" But she passed her hand across the dark, tousled hair of her oldest son. His old man had fantasized just like that.

One morning Patrick was gone. He had left to seek the treasures of the land. Mary Trent's lips tightened. Then she went to work. The men went walkabout.

When, as an old woman, Mary lived in her white villa and looked down on the Brisbane River, she sometimes pinched herself to make sure she wasn't dreaming. With the help of God, Paddy had succeeded. The crazy little fellow!

Trent never forgot how he led his speechless mother into her house and asked fearfully: "What's the matter, Mother? Don't you like it?"

Mary Trent received her portion of luck in her old age. The Brisbane River washed away the tears of her youth. Now *she* could go walkabout. She traveled in Queensland, tirelessly and wide-eyed as a child, and at last got to know the tourist "Land of the Sun." With Patrick

163

she sailed in a white launch from Cairns to the Great Barrier Reef, and through the glass bottom of a boat was astonished by the coral gardens, the tropical fish, and the iridescent shells that Paddy had described to her as a young man. She had thought it was all nonsense, but she found the silent, undulating deep-sea life eerie, and longed to be back in her garden.

Shortly after this trip to the tropical north of Queensland, Patrick married a young girl from Sydney. His mother came once for a visit to get to know her daughter-in-law. When, years later, Patrick married his young Hungarian, his mother had gone to her eternal rest in the Blue Mountains. And that was all for the best . . .

Patrick Trent had given his mother the only joy in her life. This knowledge comforted him in his dreariness. In his search for the treasures of the earth, he had found opals, but he had never been able to unearth the treasures of married life. And that didn't change. Everything he was able to give his wives in the best years of his life, they could have done without, and what he was looking for in women at the age of fifty, he failed to find, just as Shawn Benedict Trent had failed to find gold in Queensland.

Like all the Trents, Patrick succeeded in the Australian way: he took the bull by the horns. After his disappearance from Brisbane, he became a cattle drover. An enterprising young man could find work like this everywhere. Patrick at twenty was still slim and lithe. He had the strength of an ox, and wasn't suffering yet from compassion for the frail human creature. He breathed free in the wide landscape. Naturally things were much easier for him than for Shawn. He wasn't a pioneer any more in cattle country. In his day there were already chemically fertilized fields, canalization against drought, and all sorts of remedies and preventatives for disease. The cattle provided the best export. There was still a struggle going on against the eucalyptus bushes beyond the canalized land, but the clearing of the forests proceeded more quickly and easily with the help of machines. The governments of the states also helped by permitting the cross-country migration of the cattle that were still endangered by poisonous plants and the lack of water. The cattle had changed too. The Australian cattle were first-rate now, and provided excellent meat for export.

Patrick and a second drover wore enormous felt hats, patched riding trousers, and worn, elastic-side boots. They drove the herds to market miles from the interior, and had to watch them day and night. They wandered off for months, all the way to the coast or to a railway station. They sang and whistled the herd ahead of them, because the human voice calmed the cattle.

After that Patrick Trent tried his luck for a while as a kangaroo hunter, but all the time he had the feeling that these were temporary jobs. Most of what he earned he sent to his mother and brothers and sisters in Brisbane. He felt guilty because he, the oldest, had abandoned them, but he had had to do so. He hunted kangaroos doggedly and boldly, because every stockman hated the characteristic Australian animal that ate everything away from the cattle and sheep in the interior. But Patrick remained restless, and felt that he had not yet achieved what he had set out to achieve—a life of ease for his mother.

Gold prospecting was a thing of the past, but there were opals. Patrick said farewell to the kangaroos. He asked his friend, an elderly hunter, if he wanted to come along on his search for opals. The cobber laughed at him. Only a fool dug for gems! That was just as dumb as digging for gold! He knew all the Australian stories about gold prospecting, and served them up to Patrick. But Patrick had heard that the earth in South Australia and New South Wales was rich in exceptionally pure opals. He registered officially as an opal miner, and trembling with excitement read the *Guide to Mining Laws* in New South Wales. He found out that he had to report his findings to the mine overseer within fourteen days.

He had never been in a mine before, and had imagined it would be cool. But he experienced the hardest apprenticeship of his life. He wrote to his mother that he couldn't send any money for a while because at this point he had nothing but debts, but the opals would eventually make him rich. Mary Trent wept dry tears as she read the letter, then she tore it into little pieces and went off wearily to the bakery.

One day Trent found black opals. He knew the find might be a fluke, but he stayed in Lightning Ridge. He found more opals, light and blue-green, but the black gems formed the basis of his fortune. He bought his mother the white villa on the Brisbane River, financed his brother's career, married off his oldest sister, and paid for the younger one's medical studies. Then he became a real-estate agent and learned all the tricks of his trade in an old, reputable firm in Sydney. Later he bought a partnership in the firm. The new sign read: Coleman, Trent & Company. Daniel Coleman, his senior partner, was a tough businessman and a soft father.

At the inaugural banquet in the house of his partner, Patrick Trent met two people who were to smile on his life: Celia Coleman, the beautiful red-haired daughter of his senior partner, and Alexander Rigby from Parramatta, who had learned the architect's profession under Stanley Marchmont in George Street. On this occasion he also met Flora Rigby, at first taking her to be the architect's mother. Then he happened to hear Alexander Rigby call the lady "Auntie." To his astonishment it turned out that the heavily rouged woman with the stiff little curls, wearing glasses and a flower-printed dress, and laughing all the time, was the wife of the young man. Trent didn't know whom to pity more—the witty, adroit and extremely pleasant Alexander Rigby, or "Auntie," who was making such desperate efforts to appear young. Flora's broad, barmaid humor was not particularly noticeable that evening.

Daniel Coleman was a puritan with thin, compressed lips and sharp eyes. He drank milk; stomach trouble prevented him from drinking anything stronger. He ate oatmeal while his guests fared considerably better, and he ignored Flora Rigby as much as was politely possible. His daughter Celia was obviously in love with Rigby. Coleman would have welcomed Rigby as a son-in-law in every respect, because he knew who the Rigbys were. He also knew who Flora Pratt was. He hadn't drunk milk all his life! He liked Patrick Trent, but would have preferred Rigby for his son-in-law.

Rigby and Trent quickly became friends, and Rigby showed Trent the consideration he evidently could express only to his cobbers. Trent suffered from his lack of general education and all his life felt a childish respect for those who had gone to a university. That was why he looked at Rigby's big library with awe. Rigby not only loaned his friend the right books, but recommended evening courses, and with astonishing patience discussed things with Trent. He could sense the spiritual strength in this highly talented, modest, and merry Irishman. You could steal horses with Trent! He soon became a member of Rigby's mob.

Shortly before Flora's tragic end, Trent asked his friend Rigby how he liked Celia Coleman. He wanted to marry her; her red hair reminded him of his mother. That was the only respect in which Celia Coleman was like Mary Trent. Rigby hesitated. Finally he said, "She looks like an angel."

But Trent wanted to know more. "Would you marry her, Alex?"

"No idea. I *am* married."

Trent was silent. After a while he said, "I think she's moody."

166

"All women are moody," said Rigby. "You should be married to my Flora!"

A few months after this conversation, Rigby suddenly began to sing Celia Coleman's praises. "She's really a nice prawn. You could do worse, Paddy."

"I don't think she cares a fig about me."

"Leave that to her. She likes you, you idiot! And what's more . . ." Rigby stopped abruptly. "Watch it! Here comes Auntie!"

After the wedding, Trent's father-in-law retired, and Patrick became top man in the firm. He had the real-estate business at his fingertips in no time. His friendship with Rigby helped too. But above all, Sydney was the right place for a man in the prime of life. There was still so much room for houses. There were thousands wanting to exchange a small house for a larger one, or one suburb for another. New department stores, supermarkets, movie houses, schools, hospitals, were being built constantly, pushing the bush of New South Wales farther back. Trent speculated cleverly and was lucky, because luck was just as much a part of success as was the manure in the earth of a flower garden. Every plan for a new center brought contracts for Trent's and Rigby's firms. Mr. Coleman congratulated himself on his son-in-law. He was a much more reliable fellow than Rigby, a solid fellow, as solid as the public library on Macquarie Street where Trent spent so much of his time. Coleman, ever the thoughtful father, was furious because his daughter, Celia, was evidently not as happy as Trent and Mr. Coleman.

When Celia had a miscarriage, Patrick Trent was in despair. It was one of those occasions when he had to test his faith and pray to God for mercy. It would have been a son, and, as was later ascertained, Celia could have no more children. She never shed a tear throughout the entire tragedy, but it left her moodier than ever. Trent couldn't do anything right anymore. If she ever *had* loved him, then her love was certainly not the kind that united two people. It only exposed their incompatibility. Trent didn't blame his wife for the wreckage of their marriage. Their estrangement was not a cause for guilt, and anyway, he always blamed himself for everything first. He felt sorry for this hectic, coquettish little woman who had married him so thoughtlessly.

Celia only became lively when Rigby appeared on the scene. Trent could understand this. Rigby was so attractive, while Trent, was putting on weight and finding his marital duties a burden. He simply didn't want intercourse with a woman who had remained a stranger.

He slept in a room of his own, and this seemed to suit his wife. Trent felt liberated . . . he was healthy and still in his best years, but he needed a deep, spiritual union in order to give or receive satisfaction. After the tragedy he became taciturn, and three years later, when he withdrew into a room of his own, he was a stranger in the beautiful new house that Rigby had designed.

The new house kept Celia busy, and she had all sort of plans which she often had to discuss with Rigby. It was just around this time that Flora Rigby died. Trent had never seen such a composed widower. One could almost have said he was cheerful, if the scandal hadn't fallen hard on the heels of Flora's death. Trent found the suspicion that Alex had murdered his wife outrageous and ridiculous. Why should he have done anything like that? True, Flora had transformed Rigby's house into a quasi-tavern, but Rigby had evidently had nothing to say against it. One had only seen him laughing and joking with Auntie. He wasn't even embarrassed when Flora was high and became tactless. She came from a world where one word led to the next, and nobody thought before they spoke, as she sometimes told her husband. She swam in her money like a fat, asthmatic fish. Trent didn't trust Flora Pratt; he didn't know why. And she hated him. Patrick was the only member of Rigby's mob whom she never invited to their festivities. The dislike was mutual, and was evident at their first meeting at old Mr. Coleman's. She sensed Trent's distrust, and it made her unsure. Shortly before her death, Patrick Trent paid the first Mrs. Rigby an unexpected visit. The visit ended in an hysterical fit of rage on Flora's part. She stood on the terrace and screamed unqualified obscenities after him as he left. He was speechless. How could Alex have married such a fury?

Rigby seemed never to have found out about Trent's visit. He was as friendly as ever when they met again, only perhaps a little too jovial. Now Trent forgave him for his nightly escapades. Who could stand being with such a woman? Still, in spite of everything, Trent was convinced even after Flora's death that Rigby had had nothing to do with it. After all, a man couldn't be cheerful, alert, and capable for years if his wife was slowly driving him crazy. Or could he?

After Flora's death, Rigby was suddenly isolated. When John Darling and Stanley Marchmont weren't sitting on his terrace with him, Rigby sat with Celia and Paddy on theirs. The new house was finished, and Celia and Rigby were as inseparable now as they had been when Trent, with his opals and the lonely aura of the bush, had turned up in Sydney.

Once Trent came home early from the office and found Celia in tears, her arms flung around Rigby's neck. "She got the house number mixed up, Paddy," he murmured, pushing Celia away gently. "She's weeping her eyes out because of me. Quite unnecessarily. I like being alone."

Celia ran out of the room. Trent watched her go, shaking his head. "Are you grieving at all for your wife?" he asked abruptly. Normally he would never have asked such a question, but the sight of his wife in tears had upset him. She never showed *him* any compassion.

Rigby was evidently thinking the question over carefully. Was he mourning his wife sufficiently? Then he said gently, "Any more questions?"

Trent stared at him. Rigby had always been a good friend, even if he had talked him into the marriage with Celia Coleman. Trent recognized the fact that Rigby had wanted to get rid of Celia because Flora was constantly making jealous scenes. Every married man wants peace and quiet. Trent realized this. But Rigby seemed to be composed of so many different personalities, Trent couldn't make him out. Then again, wasn't every person a prisoner of his past, his dreams, his impulses, and his spiritual unrest? Sometimes Trent got the impression that Alex was in a torturous state of uncertainty or stubborn despair.

"Of course I miss the old lady," Rigby murmured. "Do you think I'm a monster, Paddy? I mean . . . after all, I was used to her. I never thought that we were really suited to each other, but not because of her age. That's nonsense!"

"Cigarette, Alex?"

Rigby smoked hastily. "What do you think of the land in Kempsey? Were you there again?"

So they talked about the land in Kempsey. The fine view across the Macleay River. Trent wanted to have another look at it. It was pleasant to talk about houses and property. Then one had firm ground under one's feet.

At the time both of them had been in the prime of life. Afterwards, when he thought about it, Trent decided that those had been the most difficult years. They had taught him to endure a spiritual loneliness, and make it bear fruit. After Celia's death he wasn't lonelier, only more forlorn. His empty house filled up with books, pictures, visitors, music—with everything a man can cram into a big house. But it remained empty. For years . . .

When he began to suffer because of the emptiness, he married Klari Karasz. He was about fifty then. He felt sorry for Klari because she was homeless, but she filled the house with such unrest that he recalled the former emptiness with nostalgia. By now he had become very heavy, and there was fat around his heart. A deep crease had dug its way between his dark brows. He was an authority in his field, and his cobbers loved him. He laughed and joked with them as he had always done, only his eyes seemed to have grown darker and sunken, as if they were trying to look inward. Sometimes he was as absent-minded as an old man. Had his youthful wanderings made him so tired?

The opals had lost their sheen long ago, but he apparently still had a share in a prestigious jewelry shop on Castlereagh Street, and occasionally financed the search for opals in New South Wales. Personally he was not in the least interested in mining opals himself. And it would have been senseless, because he had more than he needed. Even more than a young wife needed, and that was saying something! But sometimes, for memory's sake, Trent visited a narrow little house in Darlinghurst, where an old opal expert cut the stones and prepared them for the jeweler. In his youth Jerry Stevens had also mined opals, but then he had learned the difficult art of cutting a fine opal without destroying it. Lately mass production operations had penetrated the processing of opals, but there were still a few opal cutters who had learned their trade from father or grandfather, and they loved the noble gem just as they received it. The high polish and the cold sheen of the ready-to-sell stone meant nothing to them. They clung to the lump that had come to them straight from the mine, and gave it shape. The opals brought their legend with them:

> October's child is born for woe,
> And life's vicissitudes must know.
> But lay an opal on her breast,
> And hope will lull those fears to rest.

Trent's first wife had been born in October. On their wedding night he had laid a black opal on her breast and murmured the verse like a spell. Celia Coleman had found this funny. There was nothing wrong with her. She had just won two prizes in water-skiing.

One day Trent found the black opal on the floor under Celia's vanity table. He picked it up and looked at it. A red sheen gave the valuable stone a gloomy fire. Trent locked the opal away. His wife hadn't even noticed that she had lost it. That had been years ago . . .

Once, when Trent was visiting the old opal cutter in Darlinghurst and was admiring an especially clear, transparent opal, a beautiful girl appeared in the workshop. "Hi, Gramp!" Candy said, in her coarse

Western Australian voice. Trent looked up. Where had he seen this girl before?

"Sit down and don't bother us," old Stevens said pleasantly. "If you want tea, you know where it is."

When Candy Blyth brought in the tea, Trent knew where he had seen her before—pictured in *Insight*. His second wife cut out the fashion photos, and had dyed her hair blond to look like Candy. Klari Trent didn't want to look like Klari Trent and certainly not like the former Miss Karasz. It was a sickness of the times. Film stars and models created the ideal images of the sixties ...

Candy Blyth was a neighbor of the opal cutter's. Like Candy and Trent, he was a compatriot of Mama Doody's. All their ancestors had emigrated to Australia from Ireland. And now here they were in Sydney.

That was how Trent got to know the idol of the magazines. By now he was an ascetic in a solid flesh shell, and had drawn the curtain on any such fun long ago. So he didn't write to Candy Blyth in order to enjoy her in bed for appropriate payment. He asked to visit her on Mondays for quite different reasons. In his prophetic compassion he could see the day coming when Candy's flesh would grow sere and her beauty fade. And what would she be then? A straw-haired old fool, boring the whole world with her withered blossoming. Then he would have to love her. It would be fatal and ridiculous and the end of him. Because Trent believed that even the emptiest marriage was a covenant binding a man and a woman irrevocably. He had never deceived Celia or Klari in the conventional sense. It was not their fault that they had remained strangers. He rarely performed his marital duties, but he had chosen to marry this young Hungarian, and that was that!

But Trent's vision of salvation left him no peace. He tried to arm the beautiful model against the ravages of time. Perhaps he wouldn't live much longer ... then who would look after this sweet little fool? He sat with her patiently in the small eateries in King's Cross and tried to prepare her for the second-best years of her life. But Candy was so young and so satisfied with her way of life that Trent might as well have been praying in the Australian desert. Anyway, he opened a bank account for her. In ten or fifteen years she'd need every penny of it, the poor thing. It was sad to know beauty only as a triumph of youth and cosmetics. And did all pretty girls talk such nonsense?

Rigby had no idea that Trent was giving Miss Blyth instruction every Monday. He would have laughed himself silly if he had. And it really was silly. Candy had no idea what her sugar daddy was talking about, but she was grateful to him. She knew the meaning of poverty from her childhood in Kalgoorlie. In her ignorance she was surprised that such an eccentric fellow could make so much money. Candy would have liked to do him the only favor she knew how to bestow on men. But Trent insisted on talking about incomprehensible things, was ever so nice and sometimes even jolly. But when Candy laughed loudly over one of his jokes, he put his big, workworn hand over her mouth. He couldn't stand loud laughter.

"Did he? Finally?" Mama Doody asked from time to time. But Candy always shook her head.

Mama Doody gave this some thought. "Maybe he's too fat." In her time she had once had a fat one, but he had been first-rate. Nobody could expect Mrs. Doody to have any ideas on the psychology of the sexes. Either it worked, or the fellow was impotent. That a client *could* but didn't want to was unimaginable. "What is he paying all that money for?" she asked, baffled.

"No idea!" Candy frowned. "I find him rather funny too. Actually I feel sorry for him."

"What's this country coming to when men in the prime of life . . . My steak!" she screamed. "Is he coming today?" she asked, as she ran into the kitchen.

Of course he was coming today. It was Monday. Candy found her aunt funny. Her benefactor was *not* in the prime of life. Besides, she respected him like a father.

When Mr. Trent turned up at Mama Doody's boardinghouse, Miss Blyth had gone out. This had never happened before. Silently he read the note Molly Fleet had handed to him without saying a word. She studied his face with consuming curiosity. Trent pretended not to notice. Silly young creature! She should be happy that men left her in peace.

Candy's handwriting hopped all over the paper like a wallaby. *What* had happened? Molly couldn't enlighten him. Her beautiful red-blond hair fell artfully across her face. Why didn't this friendly gentleman go out with *her?* It was, after all, his Monday? She would sit quietly beside him and let him talk. But Candy's friend left hastily. Molly always stayed behind, alone. She had no one to amuse her in the evenings but herself, and that wasn't enough. Or she watched the colorful lights in King's Cross, which never burned for her. They shone only for the big sharks and their dollars. Of course Molly Fleet knew why Candy had run away. She knew all about Candy, and hated her more every day.

172

13

Sharks and Dolls

Candy had always used her beauty as a tool: hammer, arrow, sword or hypodermic needle. Only with Charles Preston, whom in tender moments she called "Carlo," which annoyed him, did these weapons fail her. She was crazy about him. Despite her many affairs, her senses had slumbered until now. Perhaps that was why her effect on most men had been that of a picture. She was no more than a fabricated idol, cleverly manipulated, romantically photographed, and framed in artificial taboos. Yet only Charles remained unimpressed. He knew that this dream girl of the magazines brushed her teeth like everybody else, had to use deodorant, and had corns from wearing narrow shoes with too-high heels. For him the idol was a sheila like any other. His feelings for Candy were not deep. She had realized this long ago. What he really found wonderful was her money. But she didn't earn it quite as easily as he thought. It only looked that way.

She was not as naive as she pretended to be. She had no book wisdom, but life had taught her a thing or two: how one could get as much as possible out of a man with the least exertion. Or that a steak on one's plate was more important than a castle in the air. With Trent, Candy played the helpless child because she had noticed right away that this was the way to hold him. But one thing was clear to Trent: all Candy's thoughts were concentrated on her beauty. This was to be expected from a model, but in his wanderings in the bush, Trent had never come across such a specimen. She loved the life of ease. Her greatest fear was not God's anger, but any gain of weight. Candy made heroic efforts not to eat sweets. Trent's soliloquies were agony for her because for the life of her she couldn't grasp what he was talking about, and lately his voice sounded like the muted, dismal cry of the dugong. Candy had tasted and enjoyed this unique aquatic mammal with the pearl fishers in Broome. Prepared as they did it, dugong tasted like steak with bacon. In those days she hadn't been worrying about her weight. But when Candy told her benefactor about roast dugong, he had explained that the creature had nothing to do with food but was a singing mermaid, half-fish, half-girl. Odysseus had met her on his travels. Candy, irritated, asked, "And who is Odysseus?"

Lately she had rarely been able to make her corpulent guardian angel laugh. What was wrong with him? Candy looked surreptitiously at the deep groove between his brows. He wanted to send her, grown-up as she was, back to school. He declared that there were teachers in Sydney who could make her rough western Australian voice sound more pleasing. Apparently, like the dugong, she was expected to sing for her sugar daddy. She stared at Trent, her mouth open wide. What was wrong with her voice? Anyway, it didn't get photographed. Candy smoked sullenly. She felt insulted. Trent took the cigarette away from her. Smoking would make her voice even rougher. Candy shrugged. Why didn't he go to bed with her? Her voice wouldn't bother him then.

She asked the traveling salesman, Albert Ritter, if her voice bothered him. Rigby laughed uproariously. He didn't visit this beautiful call girl to hear her sing arias. But when he sensed Candy's feelings of insecurity, he said there were louder and rougher voices—the cockatoos in the bush, for instance. Ritter–Rigby was no consoler at a sickbed. Sometimes Candy envied the girl from Parramatta. Molly didn't have to be annoyed or bored by men. What was more, she was raising her price for writing Candy's love letters to Ritter. Which brought Candy's thoughts back to Molly Fleet again.

She was annoyed about having to leave Trent in the lurch today. Even more annoying was the fact that Molly knew why, because she had had to give her the note for Trent. Mama Doody was always visiting a neighbor when she was needed.

"Where are you going?" Molly Fleet had stared at Candy scornfully.

"To meet somebody."

"Don't be an idiot!" Molly Fleet said, her voice sharp. She had given up speaking to Candy in honeyed tones, and was no longer humble, nor was she so eager to be of service. "As if I didn't know whom you're meeting!" Molly's laugh was disagreeable. She had found out about Candy and Carlo Pressolini long ago. What did they think she was? A hollow nut? That Molly Fleet now didn't have a man to go out with anymore didn't improve her spirits. Carlo hadn't called again. Candy Blyth, who had a man for every finger on her hand, had taken the only man who had occasionally rescued Molly from the loneliness of her four walls. "Be careful!" she called out as her best friend walked off. It was said calmly, almost gently, but, although it was ridiculous, it caused a shiver to run down Candy's spine. She even looked around to see if Molly was following her; then she hurried off to the Taronga Zoo.

Charles Preston had sent her a hurried message; she was to meet him at the shark tank. Candy found this horrible; she hated the sight of the predatory fish. When she had visited the aquarium with Aunt Doody, shortly after her arrival in Sydney, she had looked a tiger shark straight in the jaw and had been scared stiff. She hadn't recovered until she rode the carousel and was squealing along with the rest of the children. And the penguins in the Taronga Zoo had delighted her. Mrs. Doody had shaken her head. This niece from western Australia, with her tall elegant figure, sometimes behaved like a schoolgirl. Candy loved animals, but when it came to beasts of prey, she drew the line. "We'll be safe, in the aquarium," Charles had written. Safe with the sharks?

Candy caught herself thinking that today she would rather have been with Trent. He was soothing. And he was good to her. Charles wasn't good to her. He didn't have to be. She loved him.

He had made a strong impression on her at once, the first time she had seen him at the Restaurant Rosso. It must have been love or she wouldn't have lost her appetite at the beginning. She had also lost a lot of her naive good humor. She wanted to marry Charles, even though he was a dog and a pimp. She didn't believe anymore that he had never accepted money from women. She didn't believe in his palatial home with the columns, nor in his opera career. He didn't write down what he owed her in his little notebook anymore, either. Why should he? He was sure of this doll. But just the same, he was cautious. Every now and then he acted out a little love scene for her benefit. Charles Preston really understood women; otherwise how could he have exploited them so thoroughly? He told himself that if he went too far, he might lose Candy. She was not Ginetta. You couldn't insult Candy. So, in spite of his violent temperament, he controlled himself. Instead of rage, he displayed irony. Fortunately, Candy didn't understand irony. When Charles smiled, he couldn't be angry, could he? Every time he was in trouble, he fed her sugar. He knew that he had to admire her constantly: it was what nourished her. Candy didn't know yet how miserable Charles would make her, but she was beginning to sense it.

Ever since Charles Preston had walked into her life, Candy was troubled. But she was trained to be a sex symbol, so she continued to show her public a radiant smile. She hadn't chosen this lover. Like a shark, Charles had circled around her and finally swallowed her. She couldn't bear life with or without him. He remained a cool stranger, with alien memories from his Italian homeland. Without ever having seen it, Candy hated Genoa. Everything was better there: sympathetic neighbors, serious conversations over a bottle of wine, passionate and obedient girls . . . "Why did you come to Sydney?" Candy wanted to know. Her patience was giving out. She hated complications. To avoid unpleasant or painful experiences cleverly was an Australian article of faith. Therefore, in more sober moments, Candy would have left this unpredictable and money-hungry lover. You lived with Charles about as cozily as in a railway junction!

There were also quite a few things about Candy Blyth that bothered Charles Preston. First and foremost was the error of birth—she was Australian. These inheritors of a young continent, born in freedom, were either companions of everyday life on equal terms, or they were the untouchable idols of the newspapers, films, concert halls, and television. Charles Preston not only came from a foreign country; he himself was a foreign country to Candy: impenetrable as the forests, more violent than a bush fire, and more changeable than the wind over Sydney. His erotic tradition—twilight experiences, vaguely mysterious dialogues—lay disagreeably between him and his Australian Eve. Or was she Lilith,, Adam's rebellious wife? Candy was as stubborn as a water buffalo. In his homeland Charles Preston had experienced either the gentle beloved or the stern matriarch. But Candy lacked the strength, the warmth, and the fertility to be a matriarch. This you could find only in the Australian Outback, in the lonely settlements beyond the cities. The civilization of the big city had changed Candace Blyth, a healthy Australian girl, into a baby doll with slightly neurotic tendencies. Sydney had robbed her of her naive sense of security.

Preston waited impatiently at the aquarium. Where was the girl? His Ginetta had always been a few minutes early. That had pleased him. In a foul mood, Charles stared at a tiger shark. The gigantic fish had been caught and brought to the tank in Taronga recently. Charles had read about it in the *Morning Herald*. The sharks didn't survive long in captivity. Perhaps the crowds watching them annoyed them. That was understandable. Charles Preston wouldn't have liked an audience to his captivity. After being robbed of their freedom, the sharks refused to eat for at least a week. They were really valuable only after they were dead. Their fins provided the Chinese restaurants in Sydney with their fine soup; their fat was used for margarine and soap, and their skin to make elegant handbags and shoes for the sheilas. Where was Candy with her sharkskin bag? In any case, dying captive sharks were worth more than a dying man in prison. Charles frowned. He had no intention of dying in an Australian prison. But there was a chance that he might . . .

Candy was twenty minutes late. She had rested a while in a Taronga rock garden. She wasn't used to hurrying, especially not in December, when it was much too hot. She hoped that Charles was planning a nice, tropical Christmas party with her, and would spare her the description of all the Christmas festivities and midnight masses in Genoa. Then Candy had visited her beloved black swans, an Australian specialty. Candy had seen them sometimes in coastal areas and rivers. In Taronga they were proud and serene, and their silver-gray young swam peacefully around them. The sight of them had calmed Candy. Charles didn't care for the animals in this unique natural park. He hated the Tasmanian devil, and had dreamt about this weird, coal-black, greedy mammal, living behind strong bars. It ate wallabies, birds, lizards, rats, and would certainly eat Charles Preston too. Nothing good had ever come to him from Tasmania. But his Uncle Fabio was getting wealthier there all the time, and right now Charles was flat broke.

Candy would have preferred to meet Charles on the upper floor of the aquarium, where the glittering tropical fish lived in illuminated tanks. But what could she do about it? Something must have happened. She sauntered with her studied, swaying walk down to the lower floor, and out of habit registered every admiring glance. She was troubled by a mute fear. Suddenly she felt unsure, as if she were stumbling at night, hand-in-hand with Charlie Rainbow. Only the abo and Mrs. Doody knew about Candy's night blindness. Molly Fleet had often wondered why Candy let her light burn all night.

Candy looked around the aquarium. There was Charles, in his new white linen suit, talking to the sharks. And what was that? There were two suitcases standing beside him. Was he going to run away?

Candy screamed, "Charles!" Some of the visitors turned to stare at her. One didn't scream in Sydney. A few stuck their heads together. Wasn't that beautiful girl in the white dress the model . . . Charles Preston looked around for a moment, furiously. Then he smiled and said, "Why not a little louder, baby doll?" Everybody smiled. The young man was apparently very much in love. What a pity that the beautiful girl had such an ugly voice!

"Where are you going, Charles?" Candy asked, her voice hoarse.

"Closer to the sharks," Preston whispered, and playfully drew Candy nearer to the edge of the tank. Candy drew back, afraid. Why didn't they sit down on one of the chairs or benches? Charles drew her right up to the edge to see the man-eaters better. But Candy was only imagining this. Preston just didn't want the people on the benches to hear him. Facing the sharks, nobody listened to the chatter of lovers. In the light, the steel-gray captive sea-robbers didn't look demonic. They aroused fear only because the Australians knew what they were capable of. Charles pointed out one of the slowly circling giants. "That tiger shark spat out a man's arm the other day. It was in the paper."

Candy ran out of the aquarium in a panic. Was that all Preston had wanted to tell her? He ran after her and grabbed her arm. "Not so fast! It was a joke!" His smile was distorted.

"Are you going away?" Candy caught her breath, looking around her. "Your suitcases. You've left them in the aquarium."

Preston went and got them. They were new, and real alligator leather. He despised synthetics. "Why so excited?" he asked irritably.

"They could have been stolen." Candy had been poor once; she knew what it was to feel the loss of an object as a personal anguish.

"Then they'd have been gone, and I'd have traveled without luggage."

Candy stared at him, wide-eyed. "No," she whispered.

"Yes. In an hour I'm leaving for Tasmania."

"Why?"

"I need a change of climate. Can you lend me some money?"

Next morning there was a quarrel at the Restaurant Rosso between Raffaele Rosso and his wife. "I'll report him," said Muriel Rosso from Darwin. "The bastard took my gold bracelet with him. My wedding present!"

"I'll give you another. Please, Muriel, don't bring the police in on this! Carlo is young and rash. He'll send us the money some day."

Muriel looked at her husband, her expression worried. "The little one," as she called the much younger Raffaele, had tears in his beautiful dark eyes and had turned yellow-gray.

"Don't get excited, Raff," she said sharply. "The doctor's forbidden it. A thief is a thief. Maybe a stay in jail will bring him to his senses."

"I won't let it happen! I'd rather go to jail myself!"

"Are you crook?" asked Mrs. Rosso. Her husband must have gone out of his mind! With her own sober little brain she always stood helpless in the face of such emotional explosions. "Why shouldn't I report him?" she asked gently.

"He comes from Genoa." Rosso's voice was choked. "His father is a civil servant. Fabio Pressolini in Tasmania is a respected businessman. His daughter married a wealthy man a month ago in Hobart!"

He was gasping. Mrs. Rosso, resigned, wondered how many more details of the family chronicle she would have to listen to. But Rosso had finished. Right now he wasn't in King's Cross. "I can't bear it when a Genoese is slandered," he murmured. He was trembling.

"All right, Raff. Take it easy. We'll drink a nice little beer now, all right? No, no, I won't tell a soul!"

"You do understand?"

"Of course not," Mrs. Rosso said energetically. "But that doesn't matter. What can I do about it?"

"I'll never forget what you've done for me." Rosso was as grateful as a child. He laid an arm around his colorless, overworked wife. "Muriel!"

"What now?"

"You are an angel!" He kissed her and whispered, "I'll buy you a much prettier bracelet, *carissima*."

"As soon as we've paid for the new refrigerator," Mrs. Rosso said quietly.

"When is Mr. Preston coming back?" Candy asked at the Restaurant Rosso. How should the new waiter know? Mrs. Rosso was not to be disturbed. She was keeping an eye on both waitresses. Raff was nowhere to be seen. A burning angle-light cast a dreamy reflection. Candy wasn't hungry, but she had to order something. Perhaps she'd catch a glimpse of Rosso later. She had the feeling she'd get nothing out of Mrs. Rosso. She ordered pizza and a shandy, a drink the Aussies often ordered—an ice-cooled mixture of beer and lemonade. The Italian guests, or the new Australians from Italy, of course drank wine with their meals.

Candy downed the shandy and asked for a second one. What had she done wrong? Why had Charles left her? She didn't believe for a moment that he had just gone to Hobart on a visit. He couldn't suddenly have felt a longing for Uncle, Aunt, or one of the Cousins Pressolini. Candy had never been able to make him out. He was full of contradictions. He was young, just the same, he was age-old. Sometimes his bed was a heaven, sometimes hell. And of course he drank wine. His disappearance had the advantage that Candy could at least drink her shandy in peace.

She had made a scene. In spite of her indolence, she had plenty of the explosive Irish temperament. After the outburst, she had begged him to forgive her. She had tried all evening not to interrupt him. In the end she had implored him to take her to Tasmania with him. She would work . . . He had laughed. Then he had made it clear to her how lazy and spoiled she was. Did she want to take her financial benefactors to Tasmania with her? Did she want to stand in a hot kitchen at Aunt Pressolini's instead of earning a lot of money as a model? Would she please come to the little senses she had! Charles had promised to write to her. Now five weeks had passed and not a word. She realized that she had miscalculated—she, who was so good at calculating. She had begged Preston to be kind. This she should not have done. In love one should never be modest. One should ask for all or nothing. Because nothing was more than a little . . .

Candy wouldn't have grasped the meaning of love with a clear head, but even the dull realization that she had made a mistake gave her a headache. In her misery she ordered a piece of cake with candied fruit, something she wasn't allowed to eat for professional reasons. Who had ever spread the idiotic idea that worry wasted you away?

Candy had just arrived at her fourth shandy, and wasn't seeing the world and King's cross all too clearly anymore. How small and narrow and ridiculous this little bit of Italy in Sydney was! Actually, it was rather touching. The menus were printed in Italian, but the Aussies were offered the food in the Queen's English. Chianti bottles—that in every trattoria in the old country were filled with wine—hung from the ceiling. Of course there was chianti in the Restaurant Rosso too, for homesick immigrants. A well intentioned oil painting of Genoa hung on the right wall; a faded picture of Rosso's parents, surrounded by a radiant group of children, hung over the bar; the grandparents kept a sharp watch over the cold buffet. Everybody was drinking red wine. Groggy with shandy, Candy could see an old wooden house in Western Australia through the walls of the restaurant. That was where she had seen the light of *her* world. Kalgoorlie, the city of the gold prospectors, had brought the Blythe family neither happiness nor wealth. Just the same, Candy had been content. She had felt firm ground under her feet until she had run away from Kalgoorlie. Every adventure of her life had begun with a drink: Kalgoorlie—Darwin—Broome—last stop, Sydney. Everywhere an absolute stranger had drunk a shandy with her.

14

Shandy with Candy

Candace Blyth had grown up in an Irish-Western Australian immigrant family whose only blessing had been children. At age twelve she had exhibited three traits that were later to bring her to Sydney: first, she couldn't listen; second, as a result of her exceptional beauty she developed a ruinous thirst for admiration at a very early age; and third, she couldn't see well in the dark. She never admitted to anyone that she was night-blind. She just couldn't see too well in the dark. She couldn't bear to have anything wrong with her, and never learned how.

Her need for admiration was energetically suppressed at home. Her mother removed the hazy mirror from her daughter's bedroom, and Candy's brothers beat her up just as if she were any other girl. But Candy knew better. Secretly she looked down on plain women like her mother and sisters, hiding her scorn behind an enchanting smile. That was easy because she mirrored herself in unattractive women as in a murky pond. Later, in Sydney, she was secretly delighted with Molly Fleet's birthmark. She enchanted strange men and women with her charm and brightness: it was her mother who discovered, early in Candy's life, her daughter's stony indifference to the sufferings of others. She fought this lack in her daughter with sharp words and secret prayers.

Candy's mother was faded before her time. She worked in a chocolate factory. Occasionally, when the girls fetched her, Candy waited eagerly for the admiration of her mother's co-workers. "Such a beautiful child, Mrs. Blyth!"

Caroline Blyth always answered, "Beauty isn't everything." She would have like to see the big, strong girl help more at home. But Candy left that to her brothers and sisters. "Lazy as sin," said Mrs. Blyth. She had very little to entertain her in Kalgoorlie. Finding fault with her husband and children was her main form of amusement.

Candy loved sweets, but there was chocolate in the house only at

Christmas. Mrs. Blyth brought it home with a sour face, a present from the factory administration. She wouldn't have brought the children sweets even if she had had the money. She was of the opinion that sweets ruined teeth and character. She had firm principles: enjoyment came from the devil.

Candy's father worked on the Western Australian Railroad. He was a sociable but naive man who lived either in the past or in the future, depending on how he happened to feel. With amiable indifference he overlooked the problems of the present—clothes for his seven children, the rent, the burden of work his wife carried. As a young man James Blyth had had the Irish charm which his wife, after years of marriage, saw as a disaster. After work he went off to a tavern where he could impress his cobbers. The pubs of Kalgoorlie, even in their early, primitive condition, had been an agreeable diversion for his gold prospecting ancestors. As time went by, Jimmy Blyth preferred his pub to his home, where his wife reproached him mercilessly for his failings. Her harsh voice didn't make her judgments easier to bear. Yet Caroline Blyth managed to keep the family together. Unfortunately Jimmy heard so often that she was the backbone of the family, that after Candy's birth he put in only the briefest appearances at home.

At twelve, Candy worshipped her father. Whenever she was able to get hold of him, he was so much more fun that her mother, and besides, he admired her. On Sunday, after mass, he would show off his youngest child to his colleagues from the railroad. His wife stood there with a sour face. "Come on, let's go home," she'd say irritably.

Later, when Candy left Kalgoorlie, her father envied her. As the years went by he turned more and more to the past. What else could he do? His future lay in the beer pools of the taverns. There everybody liked old Jimmy, but his health no longer permitted him to drink as much as he used to. Now he spent more time at home, but still didn't participate in the family's life. He studied the sketches of his ancestors who had worked the gold mines of Kalgoorlie in vain. Ignatius Blyth from Dublin had been the first member of the family to dig for the treasures of Australia. When Mrs. Blyth saw her husband poring over the yellowed pictures and chronicles he brought home from the library, she was furious. "There's no money in reading and lazing around," she yelled. "You're a failure, a drunkard, a fool!" (Later she used some of Ignatius Blyth's foolish sketches to start a fire.)

James Blyth went on reading as if he hadn't heard. He envied his ancestor because at the end of the nineteenth century, life in Perth had still been an adventure, however treacherous and godforsaken the gold fields may have lain in the blazing sun. In the year 1887, a young man had lifted a stone to throw at a crow. The stone had glittered strangely. Gold! For more than forty years, huge amounts of gold had been taken out of Kalgoorlie, but Ignatius Blyth had only been whipped by the desert wind and fooled by his illusions. Still he didn't leave. He cursed "the miserable hole" and "the death trap," but gold dust was in his brain. He stayed in the alien country of desert sands, oceans, mountains, swarms of insects, and heat waves, and was happy with his wife and children. When he watched the golden hills in the evening sun, he was content. Tomorrow was another day. They weren't starving. They were working for the conquerors of the gold fields. They had a few hens, their own hand-hewn hut, and the children laughed when a kangaroo hopped by.

Candy's father envied Ignatius Blyth because he had had a sweet, gentle wife. He mentioned her constantly in his diaries. Jimmy's wife, on the other hand, was like the spinifex, the inflammable Western Australian bush from which the abos made fish nets and baskets. Candy's mother was just as useful and thorny. James Blyth ignored his scolding, exhausted wife and read on. She was probably right a thousand times over, but he hated repetitions. His life in Kalgoorlie was not a tragedy; it was just sad, boring, and ugly, and that could have been termed a tragedy for a son of Ireland, but he had no intention of making one of it. His wife felt at home in Western Australia. Everyday life there suited her. The tragedy for her was that her husband didn't want to share it.

James Blyth knew without his wife's remarks that he was a failure and a beer drinker. But he was not a drunkard. He did see himself as a fool. Otherwise why would he have chosen this decent and self-righteous wife? Actually she had chosen him, but that had been so long ago, James had forgotten it. Who could succeed in anything if his wife thought nothing of him? Jimmy needed admiration just like his daughter Candy, and poor old Caroline couldn't possibly admire him. She was too disappointed and too tired from hard work and noisy children to put on a show of what might have made a different man of him. In thirty years of marriage she had served him vinegar instead of honey.

In Candy's childhood, Kalgoorlie, situated on the "Golden Mile" of Western Australia, was already a sober, modern city which still figured as the center for the eastern gold fields. Still, the region had become a part of Australia's past. Candy couldn't understand why they were poor. After all, the gold mines were so near. More than thirty million ounces of gold had already been taken out of the mines, but Candy couldn't buy herself a candy bar or a silk ribbon. As a teenager she was already thinking of how she could adorn herself as cheaply as possible. A good-natured friend sometimes invited her to the movies, where she learned how one got a man who could shower his girl with gold. Her mother didn't give her any money for the movies. Hollywood films came straight from the devil, too. Candy was such a good liar that even her mother didn't know what was going on. When there was no other way, Candy used her clever little head.

She was not unhappy at home. She laughed and chattered with her sisters, and interrupted them constantly. That was something else she didn't shake off later. But this rudeness wasn't a result of her vivacity; she simply wasn't interested in what other people had to say. She was also not interested in what happened to them. When her sister Brigid broke her arm, Candy wept buckets. But after that she never asked how her sister was getting along in the hospital. She visited Brigid not of her own volition, but because her mother ordered her to. She had watered the mishap with her tears for a few hours, then forgot it.

But Candy was always friendly, and became more beautiful every day. Although she was by now a big, well-developed girl, her father still called her "Sugar Baby." When she drank her first shandy with a young man from Darwin, she confessed her nickname to him. Mr. Kearney found it a little infantile, but Sugar Baby stuck to her like syrup to a dessert dish. She didn't really want to grow up.

She found her first experience with a young man romantic because she had seen something like it in the movies. Her soul was as dry as the earth of her home, although by now, with the help of artificial irrigation, there were flowering gardens in Kalgoorlie, and attractive parks where before there had been only hard, red earth, salt deserts, and thickets. But the aridity must have crept in and taken possession of the souls of some people. Candy was not the only one who was as hard and merciless under her beauty as the earth the first diggers had worked. Until Candy fell in love with Carlo Pressolini, she had never felt anything for her lovers. They gave her the cool poise and porcelain attraction that delighted her first man in Kalgoorlie, the journalist Rick Kearney, who mistook a lack of impulsiveness in this girl for strength of character.

At the age of sixteen, Candy was working as a packer in a small factory in Kalgoorlie, and turning the red head of the young foreman. She didn't stay long in the factory; her mother found a job for her as a domestic. She told Candy to work harder and be more modest. Beauty was a chance thing, nothing earned. But even Mrs. Blyth couldn't talk her daughter out of the belief that beauty wasn't the luckiest thing in the world. In the villa of her employer, Candy saw silk underwear, real jewelry and well-dressed men for the first time. When there were visitors, she served drinks and smiled radiantly at the men. For the ladies she had a different set of smiles. The only one who ever saw her with a sullen face was her mother. Candy couldn't stand criticism.

The master of the house followed Candy with his eyes, and when he secretly tried to kiss her, she laughed at him. Mr. Cook was very good-looking and an important figure in the railroad hierarchy, but Candy didn't start anything with married men. Not because it was a mortal sin, but because with a married man you always ended up with the short end of the stick. Candy knew this from her conversations with factory women. Mrs. Cook fired her because Candy had smiled at her husband. She didn't know that Candy smiled at most men. It didn't mean a thing.

But now Candy was out on the street. She didn't want to go home. She had her salary for the week in her pocket as she stumbled across the twilit garden. She wasn't afraid because she had no imagination as to what might be awaiting her in the dark. Three days later her father got her a job in a cafeteria.

Again she had to sleep in her family's dismal wooden house, and hated it. Her mother yelled at her not to interrupt her all the time. "Spinifex!" thought Candy, and smiled to herself. How could she get away? A few of her sisters were already married, or working hard and contentedly in shops or offices. Brigid was already fading. Candy looked scornfully at the tall, thin girl with the loving heart. A girl who refused to brush her hair for hours had to get by without men. But Brigid loved a man whom, to her sorrow, she couldn't marry. Candy despised her sister for her sentimentality. Brigid's eyes often betrayed the fact that she had been crying, whereas Candy looked blissful. Not a shadow of passion or renunciation darkened her enchanting face.

If she hadn't met Rick Kearney in the cafeteria, she would have run away with any other young man. All she wanted was to get away from the narrowness and the nonsense of her "Irish street."

Rick Kearney wrote articles about the "Golden Mile" of Kalgoorlie, those few miles of "the richest earth in the world." James Blyth could have told him a lot about it. There was the legendary Patrick Hannan, for instance, the redheaded Irishman who had found gold in the vicinity of Kalgoorlie, and the mine with the funny name, Hannan's Reward, which still reminds people today of the founder of Western Australian wealth. James Blyth would probably have shown the journalist the list of his ancestors, but Kearney only got to know his daughter.

He fired questions at Candy like pistol shots. Did she have a boy friend? How old was she? What did she do? Where was she living? Alone or with her family? Where could one find some harmless amusement in Kalgoorlie? Until how late could you drink in the bars? Every Australian asked this all-important question on arrival in any strange city. In this best of all worlds one couldn't drink whiskey at all hours.

Candy knew as much as a newborn koala bear. Funny creature! Where had she learned her affectations? From the magazines? The movies? Instinct? In spite of her young, blond charm, Candy gave the impression of being strangely tough. Mr. Kearney really preferred to devour his girls like soft-boiled eggs, but he was bored to death in this city with its faded gold brilliance. He was known in his circles for being able to enliven any party. He managed this with his hearty laugh, his anecdotes which were often cleverly concerned with himself, with his thirst and his vitality. Unfortunately, except for this half-frozen Sugar Baby, there weren't any people around to amuse.

Kearney's tactics weren't exactly subtle, but good enough for shandy with Candy. After giving it a little thought, the young man with the jolly eyes behind his glasses decided to take the girl with him to Darwin. She kept begging him to do so. Why shouldn't he invite her for a visit to this strange city on the edge of the desert? He was cautious enough to buy only one return ticket to Kalgoorlie.

Candy told her family that she had a job in Darwin, thanks to one of the guests at the cafeteria, as maid in a Darwin hotel, with good pay. She had to leave Kalgoorlie in a few days. Her father was beside himself, but Mrs. Blyth thought it was for the best since they weren't satisfied with Candy at the cafeteria anyway, and her days there were numbered. She was a dud, like her father, and she would soon find out when she got away how easy she'd had it at home, Mrs. Blyth said reproachfully. One lazy person less in the house! The girl would rather run around with holes in her stockings than darn them, she added after a pause. She stood there in her spotlessly clean kitchen, tall, gaunt, and gray-haired, like a vengeful goddess.

Understandably, Candy was dreaming of marriage. She expected Kearney's family in Darwin to receive her with open arms. You couldn't find such a pretty, pleasant daughter-in-law in ten golden miles. Candy let Rick kiss her, but wouldn't put up with any nonsense. There was time enough for that on the honeymoon.

186

Kearney was thirty years old, alert, intelligent. Marriage could wait. A long time. Besides, he would never marry a girl who constantly interrupted him. Kearney liked to hear himself talk, and he really did have a lot to say. He said it concisely, clearly, and with authority. Journalists are on the whole allergic to interruptions in the middle of their best sentences, but Kearney was positively rabid in this respect. He didn't show it, though, because this little Sugar Baby was absolutely delectable.

This experience taught Candy that one can't believe what a man says over shandy. In Darwin Rick declared that he wouldn't dream of marrying at this point. Candy couldn't possibly have taken him that seriously. Mr. Kearney had no family in Darwin, nor did he live there. He lived in Sydney, and at the moment was writing articles about Western Australia for the *Morning Herald*.

A week after their arrival in the Darwin Hotel, where they had separate rooms, Rick Kearney flew back to Sydney without any embarrassing farewells. He had wanted to seduce Candy, but after mature consideration had decided against it. When it came to virgins, he drew the line. Besides, the doll didn't care a damn about him. He'd found that out quite a while ago. A frigid young thing with a hideous voice! Why, for God's sake, did she always interrupt when he was telling his best stories, *and* with nothing to say? The only thing she was first-rate at was arithmatic. Mr. Kearney had found that out damned quickly too!

He left her a jolly farewell letter with a generous check. He left her unharmed and as gorgeous and dumb as on the day he'd met her. He regretted having spent so much money on her but he could write some of it off as business expenses.

A few days later Candy had forgotten him.

Of course Candy didn't go back to Kalgoorlie. She had never seen so much money at one time, but she knew how quickly it disappeared. She had to find work. She remembered the alleged job at the Darwin Hotel where until now she had been a guest. A Greek maid had just left, and Candy was hired, with a good salary.

In Kalgoorlie, Candy had had a support of sorts in her family life, even though so much hadn't suited her. When she left her home town, she walked out into a void on an empty continent. She didn't know how lonely one could be in her country. In the end she moved on to Sydney, where her Aunt Doody lived, not because she loved her but because she needed someone who admired her. And she was charming to Molly Flect until the young man from Genoa turned up. She could never get enough of seeing herself mirrored in men's eyes. She even beamed on abo Charlie Rainbow because his humble worship gave her a feeling of power.

But for the time being she was in Darwin, and Darwin was the capital and administration center for the vast Northern Territory and the revolving door to the Outback, the "dead heart" of Australia. Darwin was the civilized oasis for the transients and farmers of the Outback, and the focal point for various races. With its modern airport, the city crouched like a gigantic black and white bird on the northern edge of the huge continent. About two thousand white Australians lived in the territory, and six thousand blacks, and during her stay in Darwin, Candy got to know a lot of them. She was there for the wet season, and the rain and the many strange faces confused her. She bought chocolate for herself so as not to weep for homesickness, and for the first time in her life tried to hang onto a job. After all, she was only eighteen and a stray child. But she didn't want to go home. Did she sense that never again would she have the courage to go walkabout?

But the strange world of Darwin was empty and indifferent after Rick Kearney had left. The tropical flowers and colorful mix of people were no consolation. Nobody was admiring Candy, and she swallowed her tears as she made beds. The government officers in their snow-white uniforms, the abos in their shiny bush shirts, the Chinese women with their bright umbrellas, and the beautiful, aloof Greek girls all walked past her without paying any attention to her, as if she weren't the most beautiful girl in Kalgoorlie. The heavy scent of the frangipani blossoms gave her a headache. She had come from the Irish quarter of her home town to a city in Australia, that exotic continent tainted with practicality, where what was left over from the Stone Age and the numerous lonely white men from the no-man's-land of the bush, came together. An airport, a football field, and an air-force base stood like gigantic toys of the present, facing a vast emptiness.

Candy would have liked to run away, but where to? She sauntered all by herself through the Chinese quarter, and when it grew dark, crept back to her room which smelt of rain. She swam, lay on the beach under coconut palms, and gradually lost her roots. And after Rick Kearney had left her, she didn't trust any strangers. Moreover, all the young men seemed to have girls of their own. The color of their skin made no difference. Candy wafted in midair like the planes that landed in Darwin on their way from London and Malaya to Australia.

Candy spent the first bitter weeks of her life in Darwin. She found out that she couldn't stand her own company, and that was odd because until now she had been so very pleased with herself! She envied her sister Brigid who, safe in her mundane existence, was listening to their mother's harsh tongue. Candy would really have liked just once more to hear that beauty was a gift from the devil! If only to hear one familiar voice!

On Saturdays, Candy went to the movies. One day, in the lobby with its garish film advertisements, she ate some french fries which the Chinese cooks prepared on their little carts, and walked too late into the dark auditorium where government officers in their snow-white uniforms, graziers with their big felt hats, and half-breeds were buying themselves illusions. The usher, with her flashlight, was gone. Candy, in an ocean of darkness, panicked. Suddenly she saw a flickering white column and clung to it. But the white column was a man. In the semidarkness he clutched the girl. You never knew who was going to run into you in Darwin! Mr. Muir smiled. It might be worth while to take a look at this bit of clinging ivy in a decent light. Without any further ado he dragged Candy back into the lobby. Jeee-sus!

"Why are you afraid?" The sheila stammered that it was dark inside. "Of course it's dark inside," said Mr. Muir, "or you wouldn't see the picture. Why are you shivering, miss? Have you got rain fever?"

Candy shook her head.

Mr. Muir, a dealer in pearls from Broome, didn't ask any more questions about her health. It didn't interest him any more. Either this pretty sheila was drunk or she wasn't all there. But he was ready to buy her a drink. And he was looking for a young lady who did *not* come from Broome. What was this girl doing in Darwin? He had never seen her before. She looked lost. Mr. Muir recognized things like that. A single sharp lookout of his dark, shining eyes had sufficed. Had the little thing done something wrong? It wouldn't surprise him. In the bright light of the sun everybody had done something wrong, even if it never made the papers. "How about a drink, miss?"

Candy hesitated. She wasn't trembling any more, but she was bathed in the perspiration of fear. The stranger's eyes were dark and startling as the night, and the way they glowed gave them a lightning sharpness. Mr. Muir's lips were pressed tightly together as he looked Candy over mercilessly. His brutal lower lip dominated his bitter mouth. His big, prominent nose was very Australian. His powerful bald head looked naked, like a mask with glittering black eyes. They were not western eyes. They were almond-shaped, ancient, and could look into far-off worlds . . .

"Well?" the stranger asked, not very amiably. He wasn't accustomed to waiting for answers. Besides, Mr. Muir, who was a very rich man, didn't indulge in the complicated ceremony of politeness if he was going to pay. Finally Candy said she would like to drink a shandy.

Mr. Muir questioned Candy thoroughly over their shandy, but revealed nothing of his private life. At last she could chatter to her heart's content, but Mr. Muir only allowed her this pleasure over the first shandy. He had no intention of listening to any reprise of all this nonsense. He sat at the bar like a statue with glowing eyes, was silent, and didn't seem to hear the roaring, raucous laughter of the men who were celebrating their weekend in Darwin. When he spoke to Candy, he looked across her shoulder and saw Broome, city of the pearl fishers, a part of Candy's homeland, but a wall of mother-of-pearl separated this legendary place from the Irish quarters of Kalgoorlie. He hoped that his household staff weren't stealing any of his deep-sea treasures in his absence. Robert Muir knew how to treat thieves quickly and efficiently. They didn't steal his pearls or mother-of-pearl twice. Naturally every child in Broome knew that mother-of-pearl was much more valuable than pearls. That was why Mr. Muir's rage over its theft was feared more than the whirlwind or death by drowning.
Would Miss Blyth like to work at his house in Broome? Mr. Muir said, "We could do with a young girl." We? So he was married.
Candy hesitated, whereupon Mr. Muir quoted a fabulous salary. Candy grew increasingly suspicious. She hadn't learned anything. What would she be expected to do in his house? Mr. Muir said the first thing she would have to do was make up her mind. She would find out later what he expected of her. Then he was stonily silent. If Candy hadn't been so young and so forlorn, she would have let Mr. Muir fly back to Broome alone. While she was thinking it over, he took a costly mother-of-pearl brooch out of his pocket and laid it in her hand. At the same time he watched her eyes. A greedy doll. He had known right away that she could be bought. She reacted in a lively but superficial fashion to excitement, and wasted her emotions, like most women. Even those you couldn't buy with toys from Broome. Miss Blyth gave the impression of being soft and malleable. How could Mr. Muir have known that she was also stubborn and loved her freedom. At eighteen she was naiver than most girls and knew little about herself. At this point she had not yet grasped that she was white, of age, and sitting high and dry! She told Mr. Muir that the man she was engaged to had gone to Sydney, and she hadn't yet heard anything from

him. Her parents didn't like him very much, and that was why they had thrown her out.

"Too bad," murmured Mr. Muir, with an expressionless face.

Candy didn't know that such transparent lies lowered her value. Muir took a quick look at her well-groomed hands—she didn't do a thing at the hotel without rubber gloves—and eyed her beautiful body and the way she moved. This girl was made for love and indolence. Robert Muir wouldn't have kept a girl like this in his office for a moment. Whites, Malayans and Chinese worked there, outstanding for their diligence and speed. In the warehouses they also packed the priceless mother-of-pearl shells, as big as eggs, for export to Singapore, London, New York. A Chinese-Australian foreman, who could be trusted implicitly, never moved from his stand. But the abos in Broome didn't steal the big "eggs" anyway. When they found pearls on the beach, they gave them away for rum or cigarettes. There were still plenty of pearls in this city with its penetrating smell of oysters and its mother-of-pearl ornamentation on cars and cutlery. Besides, after the Second World War strict immigration laws had been enforced for the Japanese. After 1945, with patriotic zeal, European divers had been tried out, but no European had the strong heart, and skill, and the patience of the Japanese expert in deep-sea fishing. The fiasco of the dives from the West had elicited one of Mr. Muir's rare smiles. He could have told the government people ahead of time, if they had asked him.

Candy's voice reminded him of a creaky door. Muir was extremely musical, but he wasn't hiring the young girl as a lyre bird. Beside his hunger for power, his record collection was his only form of amusement in Broome. Not that he didn't have enough distraction. Jewel dealers from London, New York, Paris, Amsterdam, Singapore, and Sydney visited him regularly in the Muir villa. Framed by palms and illuminated poinciana trees, it looked down from a rocky promontory on Dampiers Bay, just as Mr. Muir looked down at the rest of the population. For a man born in Broome, this was not exactly a typical Australian attitude, but it was not Mr. Muir's ambition to be classified as a top-ranking dinkum Aussie.

His mother had been Japanese. From her he had inherited the inclination to treat all women despotically. That was all right with the lubras (the black natives), and the Chinese washerwomen in Broome. A Japanese cook came three times a week and reverently prepared the delicacies for the pearl fishers. On the other days there was steak, as there was everywhere. His gardeners were abos; his chauffeur was a Malayan.

The villa had several guest rooms which united the best of Eastern and Western decor. The beds were soft and comfortable, and there were chairs and desks for guests from the West. Japanese guests naturally slept on mats and used the traditional hard headrest. All the mirrors had costly mother-of-pearl frames. The toilet articles were of tortoiseshell and gold. The rooms were never locked, and no guest nor staff member had ever stolen anything. The walls, except for a few Japanese wall hangings, were bare. For Robert Muir the woodcuts by Japanese masters were a penetration of pure poetry into the Australian living space.

Only his Japanese servants had access to his private quarters. In these light, almost empty rooms, the pictures were changed constantly in order to freshen and renew the spirit during the hot season. The pictures in the Western guest rooms were never changed. Why? Because the Western visitor found beer more refreshing than cherry blossoms on a white piece of paper.

This was the house to which Candace Blyth of Kalgoorlie came.

Robert Muir had grown up in the family of his Japanese mother until his father, who had gone back to Scotland before the birth of the boy, had sent money to a bank in Broome for Robert's education. Young Muir had an Australian guardian with whom he spent his childhood in Dampiers Creek. He hated the friendly, cheerful lawyer, but there he was, like the sand hills, the abos, the red eucalyptus trees, the ruined hulls of old fishing boats on the beach, and the blazing tropical sun. Robert Muir's guardian gained the impression that this alert boy, with his father's build and his Far Eastern eyes, was very fond of him. As long as he was dependent on adults, Muir smiled and was exquisitely polite. His real life—a separate existence full of subterranean tensions and protests—was played out on the weekends, and sometimes, at the end of school vacations, in the Asiatic quarter of Broome. It was during these years that he learned all there was to learn about Japanese pearl fishers, Chinese dealers, Malayan travelers, and Indonesian boatsmen. Robert's Japanese uncles and his grandfather had hacked the shimmering shells out of the oyster beds at the bottom of the sea as long as the heart, lungs, and tenacity of the diver's life permitted. Robert hated his guardian's car that always brought him back to the Australian world. It was during this time that he developed the strong urge for spiritual and financial independence.

192

Robert Muir never forgave his country for deporting the Japanese to other parts of Australia, which took place because the government was afraid of spies. Muir forgot that during the Second World War the city of Darwin had been bombed by Japanese fliers, and there had been fear of a Japanese landing. He himself came back to Broome after the war as an officer of distinction.

During his school years in Perth, Robert Muir had been lonely. But he didn't want friends. He was a good student, even if his mind got results which could have been reached in much simpler ways, via very subtle deviations. But he was the unrivalled champion swimmer in the school. He hid his burning ambition behind his impassive face. Nobody really liked him, and he really didn't like anybody. You couldn't quarrel and laugh and joke with him. He was quiet, like a tiger stalking his prey. In Australia people step forward so that you can see somebody is coming; people help each other even when there's no advantage to it; people are younger, more naive, and heartier. In many respects Robert Muir had the advantage over his comrades, but advantage doesn't make friends on this young, self-conscious, democratic continent. Robert Muir had never been to Japan in his youth, and his family in Broome was not in a position to develop prejudices in him, nor to point out differences in status. He must have been born with both.

In postwar Broome, Muir built up an international pearl trade with Australian partners and his own fleet of divers. His Aussies were first-rate, quicker to grasp what was going on than he was, but not as smart. The firm flourished just because of this collaboration of diverse mentalities. At first his partners had offered Muir friendship and warmth but had been politely rejected. Mr. Muir found the arrangement pleasing as it was, and the lack of social contact didn't break his partners' hearts. They had their own friends and families.

After the war Muir traveled to the United States and Europe, alone or with his partners, also occasionally to Darwin where there was pearl fishing and gold too. Between business conferences and formal banquets, Muir had always found an opportunity to go to the art exhibits and museums of the West, and to the temples in Japan. His house could have stood just as well in New York, London, Paris or Tokyo, but the garden was luxuriously tropical. Muir loved Australia's flowers and Western music. He was a bachelor, and at forty-seven felt that he was too old for experiments. He lived exactly as it suited him. He had offered Candy a high salary for specific reasons, although he was just as frugal as his Scottish father. And what did he want from Candy? She was to entertain his friends from all over the world like a geisha. Of course she had no idea of his intentions. She lived in the Western-Eastern house in a state of stupefaction, and asked herself sometimes if she really was Candy Blyth from Kalgoorlie. She also asked herself sometimes if Mr. Muir had forgotten her.

No doubt about it: he was a master at the art of forgetting. The social climate of the fifth continent was foreign to the Japanese spirit in him. The idea of being "matey" horrified him. He did not share the Australian belief in equality. There were masters and convicts, wise men and fools, and there was Robert Muir and the cobbers. He had guilt feelings when he came upon a careless waste of food, feelings, or speech. He did not feel the strong, generous need for human contacts that created oases in the arid soul of this continent.

Candy looked at him with helpless astonishment, but she admired his wealth. Besides, she was afraid of him. If her congenital inertia and her thirst for a luxurious, indolent life hadn't paralyzed her, she would have run away again. She still had her money from Darwin.

Mr. Muir gave her priceless jewelry whenever he happened to remember her existence. Occasionally she was dusted off like an object to be exhibited, and displayed, namely when Mr. Muir was expecting guests, business friends from all over the world. Not that he cared in the least for their friendship. He had bought Candy beautiful dresses, and it was he who decided what she should wear and say on such occasions. But Candy was not a trained geisha; she was a naive but free Australian. When an American guest at a party in the Villa Muir found Candy bewitching, Mr. Muir politely offered him the girl for the night. This was why he had engaged her, and in spite of her meager talents as a conversationalist, was paying her very well. Candy screamed and tore out into the garden while the American tried to apologize. Since it was dark in the garden, she fell. The American picked her up and brought her back into the house. He apologized to Mr. Muir. He regretted infinitely not being able to spend the night in his house. He had forgotten that a friend from home was waiting for him at his hotel.

Next morning Mr. Muir dismissed the ignorant schoolgirl. He had never been so surprised in his life. It had never occurred to him that a girl, who after one shandy had been willing to fly to Broome with him, would suddenly put on the airs of a virgin! How could he know that Candy had never slept with a man?

"Where shall I go?" Candy's lower lip was trembling like a child's.

"I don't know, Miss Blyth." How could Mr. Muir know? Dreadful, the things girls asked! "Don't cry, Miss Blyth. It is undignified."

"Thank you very much for the jewelry and the dresses," Candy stam-

194

mered. Crying was unbecoming and bad for one's complexion, but what on earth did tears have to do with dignity? Candy swallowed her tears and asked if Mr. Muir wanted his presents back.

Mr. Muir, who in his life had met a lot of women who could be bought, stared at Candy, speechless. Had he become so old and stupid that he couldn't tell a decent girl from a whore any more?

"Why on earth don't you want to go back to your parents?" he asked brusquely. "You're still a child. You need a mother's care."

Candy was silent.

"I guess you weren't punished enough as a child, Miss Blyth." For the first time Mr. Muir smiled and looked almost human. "Of course you keep the presents. It is impolite to denigrate something beautiful so much that one prefers to offend the donor rather than keep them. Do you understand?"

"No," said Candy, with Australian candor.

Mr. Muir hadn't really expected her to because he didn't even get angry. He shrugged, resigned, and gave her a generous check which was in no way commensurate with her services. She had forgotten that Mr. Muir didn't want a whole flowering meadow on his table, only one beautiful branch. What *did* the whites learn in their schools? "Don't you have any other relatives?" he asked irritably.

"There's my Aunt Doody in Sydney."

"Who?"

"Aunt Doody. But she doesn't know me."

"Then she has that pleasure in store for her," Mr.Muir said drily. "Now listen to me and don't interrupt. *That's* something you've got to learn. I'm flying——"

"I never interrupt," Candy said, offended.

"I am flying to Sydney next week. I shall send your aunt a wire. If you don't like it in Sydney——"

"I'll love it in Sydney! Why shouldn't Sydney——"

"Shut up! If you don't like it at your aunt's, you have enough money to get back to Kalgoorlie." Mr. Muir cleared his throat. "If you like you may be my guest until you leave."

"You're terribly good to me!"

"Nonsense!"

Mr. Muir wanted to be rid of this little girl as quickly as possible. Her beauty and her affectations had deceived him. Hadn't she thrown her arms around his neck that night at the movies in Darwin? At the time he had thought she had mistaken him for a young man. Naturally he could still hold his own with any young man, and knew a lot better how to please a woman. But of what concern was Miss Blyth to him? His house wasn't a mission school, much less a home for infants. Very well, then—he'd made an ass of himself. He had hired a very beautiful girl as an entertainer and ended up with a stupid little fool. He would get hold of the real thing as soon as possible. There were plenty of pretty, adroit young girls in Broome, who didn't interrupt you and who knew how to behave with guests.

"Isn't your fiancé in Sydney?" Mr. Muir asked absentmindedly.

Candy grew fiery red.

"All right, all right." In his thoughts Mr. Muir was already with a jeweler on Martin Place. He would put Miss Blyth in a taxi at the airport in Sydney, and that was the last he wanted to see of her.

Candy had left the room. Mr. Muir watched her move slowly and attractively across the garden. She stopped at the oleander bushes to pick off a few twigs for good Mr. Muir. The sun shone on her gold-blond hair and gave her sweet little face a mother-of-pearl shimmer. If she had been born mute, Mr. Muir would have managed to resign himself to her inadequacies. He had never seen such a perfect white beauty. There had been a certain evening when he had felt the desire to see this young, perfectly formed body with nothing covering it. He would of course have paid for the pleasure. But the child would probably have screamed her head off as she had done last night. Fortunately he had fought this impulse stoically with well-organized artistic distractions. He had looked at several exquisite pictures and then listened to Mozart recordings. Since his youth he had suppressed desires which, as a bitter core, might conceal vexation or rejection.

In the garden Candy was wondering why Mr. Muir hadn't admired and loved her. He hadn't even gone swimming with her on the beach. And in her bikini she looked adorable. But Mr. Muir always swam alone before the sun rose and the moon had disappeared. It would have amused Candy to excite this cold man. That was really all she wanted. In Kalgoorlie, Rick Kearney had mussed up her hairdo, groaned ridiculously, and in the end had torn his own sparse hair. Candy wanted men to admire her, dream about her, and give her presents. But men were rough . . . Candy frowned. The best thing would be if, after a few years in Sydney, she married a man who was too old for love and too rich for a pretty girl. These frigid dreamers were fun. Sydney was a big city. There had to be a lot of men there.

Candy brought her flowers into the house. Mr. Muir permitted only one spray, or nondescript-looking grasses to be displayed. They didn't look in the least elegant on the table, with its cutlery with mother-of-pearl handles, and the hand-painted china. It was painted in such faint colors that at first Candy had thought the dishes were old and faded, and had thrown a few away. Mr. Muir had *not* been pleased.

At home Candy had seen a film about Sydney, but she had chattered with her friends and couldn't remember any of it and that's how Candy came to Sydney.

Her first lover was a taxicab driver. Michael Browne was an acquaintance of Mrs. Doody's, and was doing pretty well financially. He treated Candy to quite a lot of shandy until he lost patience with her. Since she sensed that he would soon leave her, like the journalist in Kalgoorlie, she did Mike Browne the small favor. After all, it would have to happen sometime! Her first night made little impression on her. *That* was all? That was what the movies and novels made such a fuss about? Mr. Browne, on the other hand, was not satisfied, although strangely sobered. Seen by the light of day, this gorgeous sheila had given him her all, yet nothing. But she was very young and inexperienced. Surely it would be possible to get her going. But not too stormily. Mr. Browne wanted to marry Candy. He was a jealous fellow and hoped she wouldn't start anything with his cobbers. Sex didn't seem to mean anything to her. Mike Browne couldn't have wished for anything better in marriage.

Candy would probably have married the nice but hotheaded young man if she hadn't experienced a form of luxury in the Villa Muir that had estranged her from reality. Mike Browne passed out of her life just as suddenly as he had turned up. With delight Candy had imagined his despair when she suddenly turned him down, but Mike had laughed at her. She wasn't the only pretty girl in Sydney, even if she thought she was. He tapped his forehead with his finger and laughed again. Candy screamed at him: get out! And he did, whistling as he walked to his car. Now would have been the time for repentance. This love was her great sorrow ... on the other hand she no longer had to listen to Mr. Browne babbling about football and racing. He had never taken her to the movies. He had never paid her a compliment nor given her any jewelry. She didn't shed a tear over him. It was a young press photographer who discovered Candy in the Restaurant Rosso. After a shandy, he brought her to the *Insight* office.

Until she became a model for *Insight*, and Alexander Rigby turned up, Candy drank shandy with several passersby who were much more attentive than Mike Browne, and who didn't want to marry her either.

On the contrary. Then she met Ritter, alias Alexander Rigby, and finally Patrick Trent turned up. And then, one evening, when she was dining with Trent in the Restaurant Rosso, Carlo waited on them. He avenged her for all her disappointing men because he aroused real feelings in her.

While Candy was smiling at all Australia in *Insight*, she had sent a few copies of the magazine to Mr. Muir with a dark wish for self-justification. Now at last he would realize that he had thrown out the most desirable model in Sydney. She wasn't childish enough to wait for weeks for a sign of recognition from him, which never came. Had she really been in Broome? The Asian quarter, Sheba Lane, the pearl fishers, the abo camp, and the Villa Muir, high up on the ocean? Had it all been as real once as Mama Doody's boardinghouse was now? Anyway, now she no longer felt any need for new horizons. In that part of the world where walkabout is a natural philosophy, Candy was satisfied with her explorations in King's Cross. She couldn't understand the restlessness that sometimes drove Rigby or Trent or even Charles Preston away from Sydney.

Candy sat all alone in the Restaurant Rosso, and the memories of Kalgoorlie, Darwin, and Broome did nothing to cheer her up. She was overcome by the old insecurity. Why had Charles left for Tasmania? To be alone was dreadful. One sat in the open air, whipped by heat waves and wind, and on the whole brown plain there wasn't an inn, not a man, not a sound. Loneliness was the wing-beat of the dully shining owl—soundless, soundless—and then, suddenly, a screech!

But Candy wasn't alone in the Restaurant Rosso. A young man had been watching her for some time. "Is that she?" he asked Mrs. Rosso. "She's even more beautiful than in the magazines. Do you suppose I could go over and sit with her, Muriel? I mean . . ."

"Since when are you so shy, Curl?"

The young man, who was called Curl because of his shock of curly hair, grinned. He tapped the evening paper he'd been reading lightly on Mrs. Rosso's shoulder, and whispered, "Does she know yet?"

"No idea," said Mrs. Rosso. "I don't think Miss Blyth is an avid newspaper reader."

"Good for her! Do you think she remembers the fellow? He doesn't give me the impression of a murderer, but mostly they don't. Or how would they wriggle out of it? See you later, Muriel."

"Excuse me, please. Is this chair free?"

Candy looked up at the lean, suntanned face with sharp, light blue eyes. The young man's blond hair tumbled over his forehead like a boy's. But he wasn't a boy. He was thirty-seven years old, and when you took a closer look at him you could see the lines of experience in his long, hard face. "May I order something for you?" he asked.

"I'd like a shandy," said Candy.

The stranger was a traveling salesman in sportswear and related items, but he didn't bore Candy with talk about football or tennis records. He let her talk. She brightened right away. No screeching owls were fluttering around in the restaurant now. Once, as a child, they had frightened Candy; the night was bad enough without the threat of birds. At the end of their amusing conversation, the traveling saleman in sportswear showed Candy the newspaper. He evidently found her so beautiful that he didn't take his eyes off her as she looked at the headline: CRIME OF PASSION. And the pictures that went with it. "The things that happen," said the stranger. "Did you know about it?"

"No. I haven't seen him in ages."

"So you knew him?"

"Of course. He wanted to marry me. But then one day he was gone."

"Then you were lucky, young lady. How about another shandy? Don't be angry, but you *are* the most beautiful girl I have come across in a long time."

"I'm a model," said Candy, with modest pride.

"You are?!" Boundless admiration. Candy gained confidence. The stranger found out that she had often gone dancing and swimming in Bondi with a traveling salesman. He wasn't all that young, but smart. Albert Ritter. Candy hadn't intended to mention the name; it had just slipped out. But she didn't mention Trent. Gratitude and respect stopped her. And anyway, Albert Ritter didn't live in Sydney but somewhere in New South Wales. Candy hadn't been listening attentively, but when the stranger had shown her the paper, she had felt dreadful. Murder! How horrible! But she didn't feel sorry for the accused. He had deserted her. Blood was disgusting . . .

Curl was called to the phone and got up, grinning. "My girl friend. Just a minute."

Candy waited, but the stranger didn't come back. He was probably a good dancer: tall and slim, with quick, lithe movements, like the panthers in the zoo. Perhaps his girl was mad at him over the phone. Candy thought sometimes how pleasant it would be if there weren't any other women in the world.

"I can't get anything sensible out of the girl," Curl told Muriel

Rosso. He had hung up the phone. "After all, Miss Blyth must have known the fellow pretty intimately if they were planning to marry. If she had, she'd be lying in the coffin today, under flowers."

"One can be with a man for quite a while without really knowing him," said Mrs. Rosso. The Aussies were silent even when they were in love. Her Raffaele was different. He expressed his fury, his joy, and his suffering to Muriel. Raff gave his all, body and soul; he didn't dish out alms to his Muriel.

"You're a smart woman, Muriel," said Curl. "If there's another call for me, tell them I'm on my way. Okay?"

"Okay. If you see Raff, don't tell him, please. He gets so excited about everything, even if it's none of his business."

"Okay," said Inspector Douglas Cox, and walked out of the back entrance of the restaurant into the hot Sydney night.

15

Love Letters

Elizabeth West, Brisbane to Alexander Rigby, Sydney

Mental draft:

Why haven't you answered my letters? Beast! This is my last private communication to you. We won't see much of each other in the future. I've had enough of borderline cases and the wretched years with you! You never knew the meaning of love, and you won't learn it now. How could you, since you avoid any true intimacy like the plague? Your wishes are satisfied shamelessly fast. For you an embrace is the beginning of the end. Shortly before I left Sydney I saw you with the model, Candy, on Bondi Beach. Are you teaching her how to write too? In case you think I'm jealous of the little idiot, go right on thinking. I was only surprised how modest a man *I* once loved could become with the passage of time. You'll end up with a seventeen-year-old illiterate! It always boils down to the same thing: you can't stand being with any woman for any length of time because you love only yourself and your work. Nobody admires your work more than I do, but you have made a habit of shutting out all emotion. That remains a deadly sin, however funny you may find it. You will gradually become a stone among stones, Alexander! That's why I didn't marry you. It wasn't easy to give you up. I had to carry my decision as high as a flag during the many empty years, and I'm not much good as a flag bearer. The damn things are too big and heavy. I was happy only when I could feel calm friendship for you, as on your fiftieth birthday, when we walked along the ocean, side by side. But after all, I'm only in my mid-thirties, and friendship alone doesn't suffice. Meanwhile life is tearing along, happily passing me by. If your son had lived, everything would have been different. Yes, Alexander, we had a child. I was often on the verge of telling you, but since your marriage with Anne produced no children, I didn't want to see your face. Anyway, your son only lived for a few hours. He wouldn't have wanted to wander around the world, fatherless. For me he would of course have meant a certain fulfillment. Forget it! Naturally I would have seen to it that our son didn't develop into a caveman. He might have learned to show a little consideration for the girl who happened to be sharing his bed. I guess even you will calm down eventually, with bedroom slippers instead of your seven-league boots, and with the melancholy comforts of your second-best years. It's none of my business. My present is moving with giant steps away from the past we shared.

During these last months you have become a piece of the past for me. You won't like that. I imagine you are still recalling the time when I was a mute songbird in your female zoo. To be sure you managed to squeeze a few songs out of me, and I'll always be grateful to you for that. But under what conditions did you teach me to sing? For days, weeks, months I saw and heard nothing from you after you fired me. I can understand that you found Betty Withers very funny. And what do you know about me today, Alex? For years now you've been seeing "Elizabeth West," the polished personality I've become. But I am still a woman just the same. The cage of ambivalence has become too narrow for me. Hate-love and love-hate can be quite amusing, and certainly better than nothing at all, but in the long run they're not enough. At last I realize that lions should never enter into a personal union with lambs. Naturally, at thirty-seven, I am not a lamb any more but a full grown sheep. Who knows that better than you?

I have often asked myself: why didn't I stay in Adelaide? Life in my home town is not as hectic as it is in Sydney. Compared with the traffic on Pitt Street, Rundle Street is idyllic. Shops and places of amusement are separate entities. The weekends are peaceful, with a glass of wine and soft-spoken conversation, and the golden autumn on Mount Lofry! Why did I come to Sydney? Why did you have to cross my path?

Now I am going to throw you out of my life, Alex! From now on I shall wear my glasses without embarrassment and eat whatever I feel like eating. You can't stand girls who wear glasses, and in the last ten years you never saw me with them on. At last I intend to live without waiting for you to call me. It is marvelous when one straightens up the household of one's feelings. I never want to be teased, kissed, punished, or rewarded by you again, you phony father-figure! I don't want to believe any more that there isn't another man in the world for me except you. There are a lot of nice men around, and I would like to belong to one of them before it is too late.

I am going to get married.

You met Frank Grierson briefly in Sydney, and treated him with embarrassing arrogance. You will understand when I tell you that he isn't exactly eager to see you again. We are going to be married very soon. I shall do my best to make Frank happy. He is a wonderful person—friendly, considerate, patient, faithful, and sensitive. To put it in a nutshell—the exact opposite of you. He has already managed to make me feel happy and content for the first time in years. I shall at last be leading a normal life, something you have successfully managed to prevent for fifteen years. And if in the future I don't have as much time to write as I used to, what does it matter? Too many novels are being written anyway.

I wish I were less bitter, considering the fact that you gave me so much. But you never gave yourself! Not even in the years you were free. That's why I'm grateful to you for everything and nothing. I can't help it, but actually I feel liberated. And only the free like to live, and live long . . .

The letter:

Dear Alex,

I haven't heard from you in weeks, and hope you and Anne are well. If your sister didn't write to me regularly, I could believe my life in Sydney had been nothing but a long dream!

You will be glad to know that I am about to settle down too. I am going to marry Frank Grierson. You met him once with me on George Street. He wishes to be remembered to you, and both of us hope that Anne and you will visit us one day. Through Frank I have already made some very nice friends in Queensland. Dr. Catherine Trent, for instance, a sister of your friend Patrick. She has a children's practice in Bundaberg, on the Burnett River. I've visited that attractive, peaceful city three times with Frank. Bundaberg is surrounded by sugar-cane fields, its streets are wide and shady, and I was especially attracted to the Burnett River. We celebrated our engagement at Catherine's summer place. She had already written to Patrick Trent about it. Right now I'm writing short stories because I don't want to let Grace down so suddenly. Would you please let me have my novel fragment back when you have a chance? I sent it to you after your fiftieth birthday. No hurry—I'm terribly busy.

I hope our friendship of so many years will endure even if we are not living in the same city any more. And I'd like to hear some time what the two of you are up to. We are going to live in the beautiful house Patrick Trent bought years ago for his mother. It's been standing empty for a long time, since right now Trent is living in Brisbane. The house has enough guest rooms for my many friends in Sydney.

Very best greetings and all good wishes for Anne and you,
Yours,
Betty

Alexander Rigby, Sydney to Elizabeth West, Brisbane

Mental draft:

You are an idiot! That boring ass in Brisbane will drive you up the wall with his sensitivity. You need excitement, my dear. You thrive on disappointments. You are prettiest when you are desperate. I'm laughing myself sick, Betty. But go ahead and marry this doormat. Frame the wedding certificate and hang it over your bed! That's all you seem capable of at the moment. But don't come weeping on my shoulder. You never did know what was good for you, or you would have taken *me* seven years ago. It was sheer stubbornness on your part.

Be bored to death with your Mr. Grierson as far as I'm concerned, you little dope! On George Street it looked to me as if, after an hour's animated conversation with him, a jump from Harbour Bridge would be imperative! But there's one good thing about this marriage—you won't have to take sleeping pills any more, and I won't have to worry about you. Why do you want to get married anyway? You had a lot of fun in Sydney. But above all, you're talented, girl. You have better things to do. Afraid old age is creeping up on you? That's nonsense! All you've got to do is look at yourself. You're terribly young and crisp, and truly sweet when you're het up. Of course, and much to your disgust, I know, you were never able to let your replusive moods and your *idées fixes* about illness out on me. I imagine that this is why you are marrying Mr. Grierson. But you have absolutely no talent for marriage. If a good idea occurs to you, you let the steak burn. I hope this happens so often that Mr. Grierson, who understandably is amiable and sensitive, smacks your little behind for you! Even marital patience has its limitations, my dear, especially at the kitchen range.

You write sometimes as if you'd swallowed the wisdom of Solomon, in spite of which you seem to believe seriously that marriage can solve emotional problems. My experiences should have warned you! Your imagination is running away with you again. You want to have a home, Betty, because that's a toy you've missed until now. Yet for years you managed to develop an exemplary routine without it. You have grown accustomed to the voluntary and bitter discipline of intellectual creativity. You're horrid on the phone if anyone so much as dares to call you while you're working. Mr. Grierson will call all the time. He'll call you from the office, he'll interrupt you in the middle of a sentence, he'll distract you and drive you crazy! You don't know yet that husbands are a disturbing element who don't want to be disturbed themselves. And what does this admirable Grierson know about you? How often has he seen you? He has no idea of the ghastly disorder you can create in five minutes wherever you go. And your thirty-five ailments per month are something else he doesn't know about, I am sure. The poor fellow will of course demand that from now on every one of your thoughts be directed toward him. I am sure he has no idea what it means to marry an author. You would have done better with me in this respect too. Because I can't stand it when a woman thinks of me all the time. That makes me as nervous as if ants were crawling all over me!

Naturally you will marry Mr. Grierson because that's what you've made up your mind to do in that pretty little red head of yours. You were always a hopeless case, Withers. By chance you know how to express yourself, but nasty old Rigby had to teach you that too.

I shall keep the fragment of your novel as a souvenir of Elizabeth West. *That* would have been a book! But you prefer to marry, so there's nothing we can do about it.

As a fatherly friend, may I give you a last piece of advice? Never look back at your life in Sydney. Remember that Lot's wife was turned into a pillar of salt. Go on having a good time. You always understood as much about men as my foot! But if . . . oh, forget it!

The letter:

Dear Betty,

Patrick Trent has already told me that you are going to get married. That was good news! My best wishes to you and Mr. Grierson. I had the pleasure of meeting your future husband on George Street.

I am very well. My wife is still with her ailing mother in London, but Lady Carrington's condition seems to be improving, and I imagine Anne will be able to come home soon. My house is pleasantly quiet since Daisy Andrews, my housekeeper's daughter, married a sports teacher last week. Lately everybody's marrying!

I swim a lot, and plan and build, and seem to be all over the place. Your marriage will make Sydney the poorer of one nice young woman. Fortunately there is no dearth in a charming new generation.

Of course we remain friends! Why not? By the way, I know your future home. Trent showed me the house when we were in Brisbane a year ago. It's gloriously situated, and the house itself isn't bad either, when you consider the time it was built. Of course you'll have to remove all that gingerbread in front, and if I were you I'd build a big glass veranda at the back. You'll need it. I take it you're buying the house from the Trents? Not a bad investment. I'd tear it down and build something new. The view of the Brisbane River seems to demand that. Of course I never told Trent what I thought of his big barn of a place. For him it was never a home, but a symbol. In such cases the professional keeps his mouth shut . . .

My very best to Cathy in Bundaberg. A great girl! When is she going to get married?

"Miss Rigby" is a brave woman, but I can tell how much she misses you. Of course Grace would rather die than admit to anything like that. We're worried about Marchmont. Bertie Dobson is silent about it.

Grace will buy a suitable present from both of us. You're to write and tell her what you would like.

All the very best, and much fun at the wedding! Warmest regards from Mrs. Andrews.

Yours,
Rigby

Alexander Rigby, Bowral, N.S.W. to Anne Rigby, London

Mental Draft:

What's the big idea of not writing for such a long time? I love Happy New Year wishes in March. Pull yourself together and come home. I have to lie to everybody that your mother's ill because not a soul here can imagine you'd rather be in London than in Sydney! I don't want another scandal—do you understand? I have no intention of giving you a divorce. It would be absolutely senseless because we could live very nicely together if you'd just throw your immature ideas into the Thames. I can't help it that you dreamed up a father-image that time in London, nor is it my fault that you're an icy virgin. Evidently you can't disassociate your image of what a man should be from the real thing! And that's foolish. After all, at thirty-five you're not exactly a teenager any more, and you're living in the same world and under the same natural laws as the rest of us.

I would be grateful if you would take a moment to think the matter over soberly, and I continue to wish your mother a speedy recovery. I shall try to drive the fear of love out of you. Do you need money? Anyway, here's another check.

Come home. I need you, you idiot!

The letter:

Dear Anne,

Thank you for your letter. I was glad to hear that you and your mother are well. I am spending a long weekend here in Bowral with Trent, who is temporarily a grass widower, because things at the office are hectic. Did you get my Christmas package? If not I must put in a claim at the post office.

206

Betty is getting married next month. Do write to her. You set such store by good manners.

It's pleasant and refreshing here between the mountains and the golf links. I make Paddy play golf every day. It's good for his stomach. The Hobart races were terrific. We celebrated for a long time afterwards with the mob.

I hope to hear from you soon. It must be near springtime in London. I'd like to walk in Regent's Park with you again, when everything starts to bloom so very gradually. Unfortunately I'm swamped with work and can't talk anything over with Stan Marchmont, because Bertie Dobson stands watch. Grace and I are only allowed to visit him for half an hour, once a week. We're hoping he'll make it after the last heart attack. He was always a man of iron.

An architect from California is coming to see us. That will keep us busy. That's why I'm spending a quiet weekend here with Trent. Bowral would do you good too, if you found it too hot in Sydney. There's always a fresh breeze from the mountains, and the air up here is crystal clear. I could visit you every weekend. Trent and I enjoy the farms all around. Maybe I'll build a country house here for us. It's quieter than Manly, and you'd be undisturbed. It's autumn here now, as I guess you recall. It's going to get cooler gradually, and if you came, let's say end of May, it would already be winter in Sydney. Of course there's no law against your coming sooner. You'd soon be rid of your headaches up here.

Very best greetings to your mother and Miss Jennings.

Alexander

Candy Blyth, Sydney to Charles Preston, Hobart, Tasmania

The letter:

Darling!

Why don't you write to me? I'm downright foolish with longing for you. Just a minute, my aunt wants me . . . The bulb in the hall is burnt out and she can't reach it, and our Umbrella Uncle up in the attic is drunk . . . There. All set. It's a little cooler in Sydney already. I've bought myself two new dresses, marked-down because I'm such a famous model. They show off my figure beautifully. One is white, the other is green, with a pleated skirt. I've dyed my hair red. The photo boys say I should be piquant for a change. I'm sending you three prints with my new hair. There are an awful lot of flies today. Do you have flies in Hobart? I'm doing without almost any sweets because of my career. Our neighbor, I mean her cat, had six kittens. They're adorable! I use silver nail polish now. Very sophisticated! I'm sending you money with the same mail, darling. I eat cake twice a week to cheer me up. Yesterday I drank quite a lot of sherry because I felt so blue. I won't be able to stick it out much longer without you. The other day they were selling black nylon lingerie in one of the department stores. I bought some for you! Do you remember our abo, Charlie Rainbow? He came back yesterday. Aunt Doody has a cold. That's because she runs around with just a towel over her head when she's washed her hair. The owner of the laundromat was operated on for appendicitis at St. Vincent's Hospital. I cried. Molly Fleet is terribly unfriendly to me. I don't know why. I'm so nice to her and gave her one of my cast-off dresses the other day. It was still fairly new and only had a little tear at the back. The zipper was broken, and there were two coffee stains. She threw it on the floor at my feet! What do you think of that? As if she could afford to buy herself such a good dress! Her figure is quite nice, but can't be compared with mine. I would even have paid her to have it cleaned. I mean the dress. Why did you send her a postcard from Hobart? Now I'm sure she thinks you'll want to go out with her again when you get back to Sydney. Which would be ridiculous! Fleet is very busy and makes a lot of money with her massaging. She wants to go back to the farm later. Then you can't go out with her any more anyway. She never gets any presents. Who would give Fleet anything anyway? I don't mean because of her birthmark. You don't see that in the night. I mean because of her character. She snoops and spies—things like that. I don't know why Aunt Doody doesn't throw her out. But she doesn't. She's too good-natured, that's why she has no money. I always cry when somebody's unlucky, but just the same, I know how to look after myself. That's my duty as a model.

The other day I was in Luna Park with my sugar daddy. It's great fun. We must go there right away when you get back. When are you coming back anyway? I don't know Hobart, but I'm sure it can't compare with Sydney. And I've been around in Australia. Our neighbor who cuts the opals is in the hospital too. He's very old. Fifty-eight. Aunt Doody visits him and says "hi" for me. I don't go to the hospital until things get really serious. I'm modeling fashions on television too. The other day I saw a neat movie about love and adultery in Rome. Cried my eyes out and had to borrow three tissues from my neighbor. The lover looked like you. The poor wife had to suffer a lot. In the end her husband threatened her with a carving knife. He wasn't particularly good-looking, but then he was the husband. Yesterday, in Martin Place, I saw three girls, laughing. They were wearing chic dresses. One of them was bowlegged. I wondered how she could be so cheerful with legs like that! Charlie Rainbow made me a frame for my mirror, and painted it. The poor fellow's black as the night, but so nice and helpful. And loyal! Of course he worships me. Just a minute, Aunt Doody's calling me. The food smells burnt. I love you so much, Charles! When are you going to write to your baby doll? I cry every night because of you, I mean every night I'm home. Sometimes I go dancing. What else can I do? Dancing distracts me. After all, I'm still young. The other day they arrested a fellow because he's suspected of murder. He wanted to marry me once. His name is Michael Browne, and he drives a taxi. I found him too vulgar, especially the way he spoke, and he didn't like to treat very much. That was when I'd just arrived in Sydney from Broome, and wasn't a famous model yet. When it was all over between Mike and me, I had to take the bus. Lucky me, or I might have been the one konked off! On the same evening that there was a picture of Mike Browne in the evening paper, because of the murder he'd committed. I met a nice, jolly young man at Rosso's. He treated me to a shandy. He showed me the paper with all about the murder in it, and I knew Mike intimately! It made me feel sick! He was a traveling salesman in sports gear, I mean the nice stranger at Rosso's. He had thick, curly blond hair. Mike Browne had a head of hair like that. I hope the strange young man isn't a murderer too! Haven't seem him again. He travels around too much with his sports stuff. Aunt Doody bought biscuits in the bakery around the corner. They were hard as nails, and she was furious. Nothing seems to turn out right for her these days. I laughed. The strange young man at Rosso's said I was the most beautiful girl he had seen in New South Wales in a long time. No, that he'd come across, that's what he said. That comforted me, since I'm so absolutely miserable because of you. The faucet in the kitchen is dripping again, and the plumber . . . oh, never mind. The other day I had ice cream for breakfast, from the Italian ice-cream parlor across the street. I had to cry because you're from Italy too. The ice cream was first-rate. You see, I like everything Italian! I hardly look at anybody else. Molly Fleet is moody and won't play along any more. She must have thought that you were going to go on going out with her. Such an idiot! Aunt Doody gave Charlie Rainbow gin the other day and he looked wild. She shouldn't give him any hard liquor. I don't know why she coddles him the way she does. After all, he's an abo and isn't used to it. The other day he was mad at her and put soap in the jam jar! But all she said was he could have jam for tea, and both of them laughed. The fence next door is broken. That's all the news from Sydney. I hope they build the opera house soon so that you can sing there.

How are you? How do you like living with the Pressolinis? Why don't they call themselves Preston too? Nobody can remember a long name like that. Yesterday we had cabbage and fruit jelly out of a package. Do you still love me? Is it really cool in Hobart? King's

Cross gets more and more crowded at night. Two new restaurants and a German coffee shop. The owner is a German woman. Her husband died in Adelaide. Car accident. Now she runs the coffee shop. Her name is Gretchen. I mean the widow. We sweated terribly here at Christmas time. The only place you could breathe in was in church. Molly Fleet helped Gretchen at Christmas. The shop's doing very well because the pastry is divine! Aunt Doody is going to visit her friend with the wooden leg in Surry Hills tomorrow. Aunt Doody helps her to take a bath. Afterwards they play cards. I have new bedroom slippers with feathers on top. Last night I sat on the balcony. Charlie Rainbow went out. Aunt Doody says he has a friend just outside the city. Her varicose veins are bothering her, but she won't go to a doctor. All her friends who went to a doctor died one after the other. But the population in Sydney is enormous just the same. You don't notice it when there's one or two less.

I can't think of anything more to write. Please come back soon, Carlo. I'll never interrupt you again. Word of honor! Lots and lots of kisses.

Candy

Molly Fleet, Sydney to Alexander Rigby, Sydney

Mental draft:

Dear Mr. Rigby,

I must tell you the truth at last. It is not right that a man like you should be exploited and deceived by Candy Blyth. She is a selfish, heartless little fool who gets money out of older men and gives it to her pimp. He is in Tasmania right now.

Quite by chance I found out from the newspaper that you are not the traveling salesman, Albert Ritter. You are Alexander Rigby, the architect. But I am keeping this strictly to myself. This is not a blackmail letter.

You are wasting your attentions on Miss Blyth. Please forgive me for interfering in your affairs, but Miss Blyth goes too far. She even lets me write her love letters! That surprises you, doesn't it? You don't know me and I don't want you to know me, but what I wrote in those letters is true. I think you are wonderful, Mr. Rigby. I would do anything for you. I hope you believe me.

Candy's friend is a foreigner, a wop. Why didn't he stay in Italy? It's a famous country, isn't it? I wouldn't mind seeing Rome myself, but who would invite me?

This is the first and last letter I shall ever write to you personally. My heart beats fast when I see your name in the paper. Your buildings are marvelous. I think Sydney is marvelous too. I come from Parramatta.

I am already twenty-two and I don't have a man. People think that doesn't matter, but I know better. I could tell them a lot of things that a decent girl doesn't tell. If only I could go out with you just once—nothing more, you understand—I would be the happiest girl in the world. I have a good figure, but that doesn't help. If you didn't have any money, I'd work for you. Unfortunately I am not the right girl for you. If you saw me, you'd know why. But you will never see me, Mr. Rigby.

Miss Blyth tore off to her fellow in Hobart a few days ago. That's what she's like! He didn't invite her to visit him. He's probably got another, richer pigeon. That's what he's like!

I massaged your wife. She is the best and sweetest person—Miss Conroy in Parramatta excepted. Unfortunately Miss Conroy is dead. I hope your wife comes back soon. I think sometimes it must be lonely for you in that big house with only that funny housekeeper. I think a lot about you, Mr. Rigby. Sometimes I have to laugh out loud because you don't know anything about it. I have already kissed you twice in my dreams, but not on the mouth. Just so ... And I pray for you every night. I don't know how to kiss a man so that he forgets everything. Miss Conroy, my teacher in Parramatta, always said it was inner beauty that counted, but that doesn't hold in Sydney, or Miss Blyth wouldn't have such rich friends.

Charles Preston went out with me first, then Miss Blyth took him away from me. I don't care. He's a stinker and a bastard. Miss Blyth made him believe she was only eighteen. She is twenty years, five months and three days old. She has a mole on her left hip. But you know that.

Her aunt is in a fine rage. I mean Miss Blyth's aunt. I asked Mrs. Doody what had she expected from Candy, who is after all a treacherous bitch. So now Mrs. Doody is angry with me! Nobody can say a word against Candy. What do you think of that?

When I see a really gorgeous built man in a film, I always think of you. You don't mind, do you? How do you like my love letters, Mr. Rigby? Parts of them I find in novels I borrow from the library, but most of what I write is out of my own poor head. Honestly! Sometimes I'm at the Taronga Zoo when you're sketching birds or just walking around. But I *never* follow you. I love to watch the birds in Taronga too. I love all animals, especially cows. And the emus with their soft feathers and helpless wings. But I imagine the emus are perfectly happy because none of them can fly. If every girl had my bad luck, I think I'd be content too.

The other day somebody from the police came to Darlinghurst. I recognized him from the newspaper. He was working on the Mike Browne murder case, Mike Browne the taxi driver. The man from the police was Inspector Cox. He is very friendly, and has a shock of curly hair, but his eyes are like knives. When he came to our boarding-house, Mrs. Doody had just gone out to see a friend. I'd just got home from work and ran straight into the entry of the house opposite. Curlyhead had wanted to ask our other roomers about Miss Blyth, but only Uncle Doody was there, and he was drunk. Good for him! We don't want anything to do with the police. The fellows snoop around until they find something. I think if one snoops around long enough anywhere, one finds something. The papers call Inspector Cox the toughest scoundrel between hell and New South Wales. Of course they don't write scoundrel, but that's what they mean. Perhaps Candy's fine friend has been up to something in Hobart. Or she has. She never has any money now because it all goes to her wop. Mrs. Doody is furious, and says Candy will come to a bad end. But Mrs. Doody always sees a bad end to everything. It's all the fun she has.

I followed Inspector Cox when he finally left. He went to the Restaurant Rosso. I asked Mrs. Rosso if she knew him. She said she didn't.

Please, Mr. Rigby, don't come here anymore.

This letter was never sent.

16

It Is Cold in Tasmania

Because of its cool climate and fruit plantations, Tasmania is a popular holiday paradise, but Candy Blyth was aware of none of this. Perhaps she shouldn't have followed Charles. But she was too young and too much in love to do anything else. In pretty, sunny Tasmania, which is known as "the Apple Island" or "the Diamond of the South Pacific," Candy was sitting on a milestone in a dark street. It was the street of sorrow, and you can find it anywhere—in Sydney, in Broome, in Darwin, and of course in Hobart. On this whole vast continent there isn't a single hiding place from sorrow. It finds its victims everywhere, and lurks especially in those vacation resorts that inspire travel bureaus to poetry. Like the octopus, sorrow has innumerable tentacles, and they are ice-cold. In Tasmania, Candy felt their frigid breath. This was especially unfortunate because it was cold anyway in Van Diemen's land, and it is just for this that visitors pay high prices, especially the people from Sydney, who this year, had had enough of the blazing-hot Christmas festivities. Although the height of the season was over by the time Candy arrived, it was still as cool as in Europe. If the invisible octopus hadn't stretched out its icy tentacles toward her, and if Charles Preston had been as faithful as the gold he had managed to squeeze out of her in the form of bank notes, everything would have been all right.

Some people have a sixth sense for invisible threats from behind. Like the funny little wombats in the bush, who sense danger even when the lyre bird is still trilling, and the old trees stand silently and unmoved by storms. The wombats burrow quickly into the earth, or hop away when the dangerous man approaches, while the giant trees don't notice that the sly lianas are choking them to death as they entwine around their trunks and tighten their grip gradually, until the eucalyptus or that legendary tree that still looked upon the black man in freedom, fall to the ground. The fat, nearsighted wombats save their lives, and the majestic tree giant is felled with a crash. In Australia nature is the great teacher.

The old bush runners can sense danger in time too, just like the wombats. They run away with their billies and waltzing Mathildas to where it is safe. But Candy Blyth came from Sydney. She was a city flower and a roaming fashion plate. Her face came to life thanks to the artistry of the photographers. She could smile and look dreamy only with their help, and assure readers that the new soap powder washed whiter than white, and would brighten their lives fundamentally. Although Charles Preston had lived in cities too, he instinctively recognized the trickery of the bush and the creepers' tactics. But Candy knew nothing of all this when she flew to Charles Preston in Hobart. She had got the address of his relatives at the Restaurant Rosso, and that's where she went. Where else could Carlo possibly be? Fabio Pressolini had meanwhile become a wealthy man. He had developed his one garage into a whole chain of garages, and had put Charles in charge of one of these little gold mines. The Italians are incurably family minded, and the Pressolinis in Hobart were no different from those in Genoa. They didn't think very much of Charles—he'd always been a show-off—but Uncle Fabio felt that blood was thicker than water, and that was that.

When Candy drove out to the Pressolini's pretty house in one of the suburbs, Charles Preston was conspicuous in his absence. "Where is he?" Candy asked, horrified. All the Pressolinis—father, mother, married daughter and Mr. Millington, the Australian son-in-law, nodded their heads. They looked like Chinese mandarins, sitting there and nodding. Uncle Fabio, intelligent and sympathetic, asked the pretty young girl from Sydney a lot of questions, then he nodded again. Why hadn't she written to them? Candy got the feeling that the family knew very well where Charles was, but they wouldn't tell, and talked about all sorts of other things, mostly about the neighbors—what they did, what they said, and where they traveled; who was going to get married, who had died, and who had bought a new car. Italian and Australian names whizzed past Candy's ears. She was stupefied. Of what concern were all these strange people to her? The Australian son-in-law was silent too. He looked Candy up and down, not in a friendly fashion: a flighty little chit! Suddenly father, mother and daughter were speaking Italian. Mr. Millington raised his sandy-colored brows, smiled pleasantly, and said, "Hey!" After which the Hobart saga was continued in the language of the land. Candy was stunned. Where was Charles? Why wasn't he living with his relatives any more?

214

"Angela has twins," Mrs. Pressolini was saying. "Sweet, God bless them. Angela's grandparents—they live in Spezia, no, in Filanesi—they had a fruit store and . . ."

"Nonsense, Mama!" said Mr. Pressolini. "They came from Ventimiglia, and they didn't have a fruit store. Shoes! They sold shoes! And Emilio drove a tourist bus to Genoa, and Angela's grandmother . . ." Mr. Pressolini continued in Italian. Mr. Millington cried, "Hey!"

"Where is Charles?" Candy asked harshly.

At last they told her. They were familiar with Australian doggedness. Mr. Millington looked at his compatriot from Kalgoorlie even more critically than the rest. What did this sheila want from his in-laws? She was only wasting their time. Millington still wanted to mow the lawn in his father-in-law's garden, and Claudia had to feed the baby. This city pigeon from Sydney in her low-cut dress, spoke in a voice that could rival a creaking door. He liked her less and less the more he heard and saw of her. He stood leaning against the door as if half asleep, his hands in his trouser pockets, his shirt open, a cigarette between his narrow, scornful lips. But he wasn't half asleep. He noticed everything. It was he who had thrown Charles Preston, formerly Pressolini, out of his in-laws' house. The elder Pressolini was the best cobber Millington could have wished for, but he was too guileless. A belief in "mateship" and all the rest was properly included in Mr. Millington's comprehensive system, but he looked people over carefully before he came closer. For "Presso," as he called his father-in-law in affectionate moments, it sufficed if a goddamned ne'er-do-well came from Genoa! Yet where business was concerned, Presso was a bloodhound, sly but absolutely honest. He was dinkum. Mr. Millington gave his father-in-law a sign, while Candy went on besieging the family with questions. Mr. Pressolini was helpless in the face of this flood of words until he caught his son-in-law's eye. The wink and surreptitious nod meant: Get her out of here!

Like every Aussie, Mr. Millington was a perfect mime. He offered Miss Blyth a cigarette. "Smoke-o?" And Mr. Pressolini wouldn't let the confused young thing go without a glass of beer. In his boundless benevolence he drove her back to her hotel. In spite of the wonderful big car, the trip was not pleasant because Mr. Millington sat like a watchdog beside Presso, and Claudia Millington, with the baby, sat in the back with Candy. The baby, with its apple-red cheeks finally upchucked its milk on Candy's suit. Candy shrank back with a cry of horror. Mr. Millington turned around and laughed for the first time "Give me the baby, love," he said, took his son and heir on his lap, and hummed some Aussie songs, while Candy and Claudia conversed across an abyss.

"It's cold in Tasmania," Candy muttered. "I think it's wonderful," said Claudia. For the life of her Candy couldn't understand how anyone could find it wonderful here if one had to share one's life with Mr. Millington.

When Mr. Pressolini deposited her at her hotel, and looked at her sympathetically out of his lively dark eyes, Candy thanked him for his kindness more warmly that was usual for her. There was a slight pause. Mr. Pressolini opened his mouth twice, but then seemed to think better of it. Like every good Aussie he simply said, "Orright," and drove off with his family to the Millington's fruit plantation.

After her introductory visit to the Pressolinis, Candy Blyth had to put up with her own company for a while. She wandered around the city with the European climate and the Dutch and English names in the telephone book, without a plan, and tried to think how she could tear Charles Preston out of the clutches of a certain Mrs. Pugh. It never occurred to her that he might not want to be torn out of Mrs. Pugh's clutches. She didn't know what to do with herself in this strange city. Slowly the old feeling of insecurity came back, and she had to force herself to think of her success in Sydney in order to still believe in it. In the evening she crept into her bed, dead-tired, and wept. She couldn't help it, even if tears made your skin blotchy. But she was only twenty, and her skin was smooth. The cooler air in Tasmania even painted a delicate natural rosiness on her face, as if by magic, but nobody admired it. She was too indolent to go back to Sydney, and surely *something* had to happen soon! Some day a nice man would put in an appearance, and inflate her self-confidence like a balloon, and take her *somewhere!*

But nobody came. The days passed. She was condemned to a monologue in her hotel room.

. . . Why did I fly to Hobart? I'm all through with the bastard! This hotel isn't worth the money. This morning my breakfast was cold. Everything's cold in Tasmania!

Nobody notices me. And I'm supposed to be known in the whole country as a model. A couple sits at the table next to mine in my hotel. The man has eyes only for his wife, in spite of the fact that she's wearing a dress you could have bought a year ago at a sale for a song. No sense of style! Has no idea what to wear! Her permanent is second-rate and her hair is cut too short at the back. I suppose she's never lived in Sydney, only in this dump of a city with its frumpy people. I wouldn't like to see her in a bathing suit! What on earth does the man see in this dud of a woman? She has no taste, and I'm sure no idea how to handle a man. She doesn't even use nail polish. Hasn't the man got eyes? She

216

reminds me of my sister Brigid. I haven't written home for a long time. The last time when my father died. He was the only one who was fond of me. I should have visited him sometimes. He kept writing: when was I coming at last? Or I should have sent him the money for the trip. I had such a lot of money in Sydney until Charles ran through my account. Funny how one always thinks of what one should have done when it's too late. I cried terribly when Father died. Why do I have to think of Kalgoorlie now? I really must send Mother something once I start making money again. I wanted to. Twice. Something always prevented me. But first I've got to get some new clothes and costume jewelry, things like that. Business expenses don't stop, even if right now . . . Anyway, Mother's got along without my help so far. She'll just have to wait a little longer. But I'm really going to do it this time.

Father called me Sugar Baby.

I've been sitting two weeks in this expensive hotel and had to sell a ring. I can't go on like this. Charles, the bastard, isn't doing a thing for me. It's very cold in Tasmania, but the apples are first-rate. I must speak to Mrs. Pressolini. I'm still so young and don't know what to do. Mrs. Presso is a very good, sweet person, but she interrupts all the time when I'm talking. I've got to tell her about it sometime, just between us. One doesn't interrupt in our country . . .

Spent the whole day at the Pressos. They're very glad when I come. I'm moving into their house this evening. Of course as a paying guest. But I don't think they'll take any money from me. They're stinking rich. Still, Mrs. Presso wears dresses I wouldn't touch with a ten-yard pole! Not because they're dirty. Mrs. Presso washes herself and her clothes like crazy! But they're so old-fashioned. Well, with her figure it would be a lost cause anyway. Flat and spread out like a pancake. But I like her a lot. Like a daughter likes her mama. She is gentle and has such beautiful eyes. I think she'd really be unhappy if I went away. Her daughter, Claudia, is busy with her husband and the baby, and Papa Presso has his garages to look after. She wouldn't have said I should come if she hadn't wanted me. I asked her twice if it was all right with her. And I said she was alone such a lot. She said she didn't mind, but I'm sure she only said that so as not to complain about her boring life. You can tell when somebody likes you. Tact tells you that. And when you're unwanted, people let you know soon enough. Mr. Millington certainly let me know! But perhaps he was so grouchy because he didn't want to make his wife jealous. I had on my white dress with the blue jacket, real sharp. My best outfit. Molly Fleet altered it for me before she went bonkers. I have lots of time to think but I still can't understand why Fleet got so nasty to me. Aunt Doody says she has a hard time, and so on. But that's ridiculous! Fleet is quite used to her birthmark. I'm looking forward to Mrs. Pressolini. At last I can talk sense with somebody! Aunt Doody is sweet and all that, but I can't talk to her.

She always starts talking about something else. She jumps from one subject to the other. No connection whatsoever. That's crook! But when I told her, she said people in glass houses . . . That's gratitude for you! When you think of all the things I did for her as long as I could. They're all good at taking from you. I learned that from dear Charles. A pimp and a liar. Mrs. Pugh should be ashamed to take on a low type like that!

If I babbled like Aunt Doody, I wouldn't have benefactors like Albert Ritter and Trent. They're spoiled. They hang on my every word, especially Ritter.

I've been with Carlo's relatives for two weeks now. I'm a little disappointed in Mrs. Presso. Either she was putting on an act, or she didn't want me here as much as she pretended to. Now that she has a nice jolly girl to talk to, she hardly says a word. Of course she's very busy in her big house, and always cooks everything herself for her husband, in spite of the fact that they have money to burn. They could eat in the finest restaurants, which I'd enjoy a lot more than eating at home. Or Mrs. Presso could buy canned and frozen foods instead of spending all her time cooking. "We don't like to eat out," she told me. I'm speechless! Italian men are the biggest tyrants in the home. Our men are satisfied with anything. They know very well that we're not going to spend all our time on their food. We live in a free country. I told Mrs. Pressolini so with the best intentions; one has to explain our customs to the new Australians. But she said, "Wait until you get married, Candy. If you want to keep your man, learn to cook from me. I'll be glad to show you." I thanked her politely. If one's got a figure like Mrs. Presso, I suppose one has to cook and bake for one's man. He's not bad-looking, actually quite interesting, and much *younger than she is.*

I help Mrs. Presso in the kitchen when I'm not too tired. She finds my rubber gloves funny. I find a lot of things funny in this house too, but I'm a guest. They won't take a penny from me. "It's only for the time being," said Mr. Presso. "Hang onto your money, Candy." Very decent *of him! Of course I'm only a temporary guest. What did he think? I rather like him. Not as fat as Trent and not as arrogant as Albert Ritter. I wonder what Ritter's doing without me? I'd love to see his long face when he comes to the house.*

This evening Mr. Pressolini said, "Go back to Sydney, child. My nephew isn't going to do a thing for you. You see, we threw him out, and that's something we don't do easily with a relative." When I didn't say anything, he went on. "I'm saying this for your own good." I asked him if he wanted to be rid of me. "Heavens, no!" he said, quite startled. "But you're still too young to be sitting around here. You have possibilities in Sydney."

I didn't want to tell him that I dreaded Molly Fleet's malicious satisfaction, and that Aunt Doody is used to seeing me at the top of the ladder. I can't bear to be pitied. Not by women! Mr. Presso and I went for a walk in the garden. He got one of his wife's woolen shawls for me because it's cold in Tasmania. "I'm so alone," I murmured. He didn't reply. And he talks a blue streak to his wife. I laid my head on his shoulder. "Fabio, help me," I whispered.

"What on earth are you talking about, Miss Blyth?" he said, and marched into the house without looking back at me once. Perhaps he's so much in love with me that he's playing it cool. His wife can't possibly satisfy a man like him. That same evening I heard voices in the bedroom. I was getting some coffee for myself in the kitchen. I don't listen at doors like Molly Fleet, but perhaps he was saying something about me to his wife. He said a lot, unfortunately in Italian. His wife seemed to be trying to calm him down. Suddenly he opened the door, but I turned my back on him and took my coffee to my room. He seems to think I'm running after him! Men are ridiculously conceited. If Fabio wants something, let him *come to* me.

Mrs. Presso makes marvelous coffee. She puts more in than Aunt Doody. I don't know why she's so silent. I was really quite mistaken about her. I discover new unpleasant sides to her every day. Fabio is still friendly, but at a distance of ten miles! I wonder if he dreams about me. Italians have so much imagination.

A week later:

At last I told Mrs. Presso that I've lost my work in Sydney. Insight *and the other magazines and television stations have dropped me. I couldn't fulfill my contracts because I had to fly to Hobart with my broken heart. After all, people should understand that. But nobody did. Not even the photo boys who made such a lot of money from me. Beasts! The only thing the whole beauty mob can do is make money with you. And I thought Australia was a free country! Only on paper.*

I must write to Aunt Doody that she must put more coffee in her coffee. And the food here is never burnt. If the Pressos were nicer I wouldn't mind staying here longer. Why aren't they nicer to me? Don't I bring life into their house?

I have advised Carlo once more to remember his true love. I wrote to him against my will, that I'm ready to forget and forgive. He must have a lot of money now from his old lady, but I didn't mention that I'd like to borrow some or I'll never see him again! The bastard only knows how to take. I am beside myself. Not that anyone would notice it. That would be the bloody end!

Miss Rigby's secretary wrote that they've found somebody to take my place. To take my place? I had to laugh. Bought a copy of Insight *to see what my replacement looked like. The dog comes from Mittagong. What can possibly come out of Mittagong? She is seventeen and has enormous ears. I am very relieved. The people at* Insight *will soon find out who made their subscription list shoot up sky-high! Especially in the Outback. Charlie Rainbow used to look at my photos, even though he's ill . . . illi . . . even though he doesn't like to read or write. I mean illiterate. I learned the word from Trent. He didn't mean me, of course. He compared me once to a mimosa blossom! I mean, I'm not a mimosa! Just because he won't touch me . . .*

Heard a story over the radio of a pickaninny brat that got lost in the bush. Very sad. Pressos were not impressed. She cried, "Cooh-eh!" I mean the mother of the pickaninny did. She followed the traces like a bloodhound. These lubras see in the dark just as well as in the light. Can't compete with them in that! It's thundering in on the radio, and a dingo is howling. He isn't in Tasmania. There are no more dingoes here. Except Charles Preston. I cried for the pickaninny child. Mrs. Presso asked her husband if he liked the fish with the new sauce. These people are heartless. And I always thought the wops were so emotional. Just an act. If I only knew where to go! At last Carlo is back from his trip. I read about it in the social column, where I always used to be featured, but this was only about Hobart: Mrs. Kenneth Pugh and her secretary, Mr. Charles Preston, have returned . . . so they call that a "secretary" now! I laughed myself sick!

Mrs. Pugh is the widow of a rich director of the electric works. Apples and electricity make up the wealth of this state. Now Charles Preston is spending his money. If I were the dear departed Mr. Pugh—accroding to Fabio he was decorated in the Second World War, and made great contributions to charity—I would be turning in my grave three times a day! The Pugh woman is gaunt and has a sour expression and red veins in her face. I could see that even on the photo, but she carries on like a young girl. I thought widows were supposed to grieve.

Saw Mrs. Pugh and her secretary drive off to the golf club today. I was waiting outside the villa. Charles had to come out some time! He drove. She looked a hundred and thirty-two years old! Charles was enthroned beside her. And to think that in Genoa he was a chauffeur, according to his uncle. In Genoa he was milking some old woman too. His parents were poor. All the things he told me in Sydney were stinking lies! That's him! I lie only when my self-respect demands it. I've written to Molly Fleet that I love it in Hobart, and that I'm a guest at the home of Charles's fine relatives. She'll bust! And I really am a guest. Mrs. Pugh and her secretary play golf at the Royal Hobart, I followed them in a taxi. When they stopped at the club house, I ran out and cried, "Hello, Charles!" I was wearing my pink dress, a dreamy creation. And a white coat and long gloves! "Hello, Charles!" I cried, louder. I was freezing, although the sun was shining.

Mrs. Helen Pugh, the famous hostess and widow of . . . anyway, Pugh's widow looked at me with piercing eyes and asked, "Who's that?" Charles was silent for a moment. He didn't look at me, although I was wearing my pink dress for him. "Somebody I knew in Sydney," he mumbled. "Come on, Helen." He wanted to get Mrs. Pugh into the club house fast. "I think I went dancing with her once," he added hurriedly.

I ran after them. They had to move slowly because of Mrs. Pugh's age. At least forty-three! I had to laugh and couldn't stop! Everything was going around and around in front of me.

"He thinks . . ." I screamed finally. "I want you to know, Mrs. Pugh! The dog lived for months . . . months . . . on my money! I want you to know . . ." I stopped. There was nothing but air around me. The two had disappeared into the club long ago. I wouldn't have thought the old bitch could run that fast! I stood in the sun and froze. A policeman came up to me. "Are you all right, miss?" It was then that I noticed I was still laughing and crying, "I want you to know . . ." Luckily a taxi stopped right in front of us. The policeman must have hailed it. "Go home, miss," he said, real friendly. "You're a little crook."

"There's nothing wrong with me!" I screamed. "I want you to know . . ."

My teeth were chattering. Mrs. Presso put me to bed and gave me aspirin with hot milk and honey. Oh yes, there was an egg yolk in it too. Aunt Doody would never have done that, I mean, beside everything else, add a whole egg! "Why are you shivering, Candy?" Mrs. Presso asked.

"It's cold in Tasmania," I replied hoarsely.

Next morning things went my way. Fabio had gone to the office, I had slept late because I'd had chills, Mrs. Presso was making fresh coffee. "I can do that," I said. She's quick as a race horse in spite of being so fat. Practice, I decided. I wouldn't like to be running back and forth all the time.

"You gave me a good scare, Candy." Mrs. Presso was pouring my coffee. Now she put an omelet down in front of me. It had not stuck to the pan. "What are you going to do now, girl?"

"How is it that your omelets never stick to the pan?" I asked. At last I wanted to learn something about cooking and she wouldn't explain it to me. She's not easy to live with. I don't know why I suddenly felt flat in my stomach in spite of the good breakfast: two pieces of toast with butter and orange marmalade, besides the omelet. Mrs. Presso was staring at me, her eyes wide. A strange look. As if she were sorry for me. With my figure? And as if she'd had enough of me. Who wants guests whose teeth chatter? It dawned on me at last—she wanted to be rid of me. Nicely. She is gentle and always friendly, but I don't know . . . It was weird. I left the room. I hadn't quite finished my toast,

but there was a lump in my throat. Not that Mrs. Presso had said anything nasty, but there was no warmth in her eyes any more. They were hard as gravel. I hadn't done anything. I asked her twice if my visit wouldn't disturb her, and I've only been here five weeks. Baked beans for lunch. I hate them.

In the evening Fabio, in a very friendly tone, told me that his daughter, Claudia, and the baby were coming to stay with them, and he was sorry but they were going to need my room. Mr. Millington was coming a week later. I asked when Claudia was coming, and could I stay three more days? Of course, both of them said. They would phone Claudia and tell her not to come until then. I felt so cold that Fabio had to turn on the electric fireplace. I'll sell the mother-of-pearl brooch and the gold necklace Mr. Muir gave me. Charles sold the necklace Ritter gave me in Sydney, but he forgot to give me the money. I can't write to Trent for money. I don't know his address, and if his wife opened the letter! I'd open every letter my husband got, if I had a husband, I mean, a man. I know the sheilas . . .

In this morning's paper I read that there was a burglary at the Villa Pugh. Charles Preston was arrested. A pearl necklace had been missing. She had found it in her secretary's room, skillfully hidden. He was having a bit of fun with the gardener's daughter while Mrs. Pugh was searching his room. So in her case love didn't seem to be blind. I wonder if Charles will go to jail now. You can't be too careful about the company you keep. The Pressos are very upset about it. I would be too if Carlo was my nephew.

The pearl necklace he had stashed away fortunately reminded me of the pearls in Broome. I had never thought of Robert Muir, but now I remembered how good-natured he had been. Money, presents, and a free airplane ticket to Sydney. Anyway, the Pressolinis paid for my ticket to Broome. Not because they wanted to be sure to get rid of me, but because I'm still young and can't look after myself. Anyway, not right now, with Insight *behaving so shabbily.*

It was an absolutely crackpot idea of mine to come to Hobart. Nobody in Sydney told me how cold it was in Tasmania. I wonder if that is why the Pressolinis were so frosty during the last weeks of my stay there. I'm glad I'm leaving. I tried very hard with them, but it's not *like being with our old Aussies.*

Mr. Muir may be a little surprised, but I'm sure he'll pay for my flight back to Sydney later. Perhaps the new prodigy at Insight *will get sick, or the girl from Mittagong will pick up a lousy lover. I wish her all the best, but in case anything should happen to her and* Insight *needed a new model, I could go back.*

If Muir lets me go!

I hope he's in Broome! But I don't like to ask. There's no time anyway. Mrs. Pressolini is making up the bed fresh for her daughter.

*　*　*

Candy landed at the airport in Broome toward evening. She was afraid of what the dark was hiding and what the morning would reveal. But the Villa Muir was brilliantly lit. Guests were walking up and down in the garden, which was festively illuminated by lanterns. Candy told the taxi driver to wait a minute. Then she drove to a hotel in the Chinese quarter. She had just remembered that Mr. Muir didn't receive uninvited guests.

She phoned from the hotel and was told that Mr. Muir was busy. "It's an emergency!" Candy sounded desperate.

"Who's speaking?" the secretary wanted to know. Candy recognized his voice.

"Candy," she said. "Candy Blyth."

"And what do you want?"

"I want to speak to Mr. Muir personally. Please ask him to come to the phone."

There was a click on the line. The secretary had hung up. He couldn't remember any lady called Candy Blyth, and Mr. Muir was busy.

Candy sat straight upright in her little hotel room. What would she do if Mr. Muir didn't remember her?

17

Cultured Pearls and Butterflies

Robert Muir took his Japanese guests to the airport next morning, and on his way home picked up Miss Blyth at her hotel. Despite his secretary, who watched over him jealously, Mr. Muir had not forgotten Candy. So the stupid girl was on the skids again. Mr. Muir had no illusions that she had flown to Broome because of his beautiful eyes, but why shouldn't he have a bit of fun with her? His Japanese guests had been with him for two weeks; he could do with a little relaxation. Candy was in luck, but she didn't know it.

When she had called Robert Muir, he had been discussing the price of pearls with his friends from Tatoku Island. He had only just returned to Broome after visiting the famous pearl culture station in Japan, on dreamlike Ago Bay. These pearls offered considerable competition to the pearl-fisher stations in Broome, but in Broome mother-of-pearl had always seemed more important than the pearls. And after the Second World War, even the high point had been surpassed.

Muir had never felt so content as on this visit to Japan, and he was thinking seriously of spending his remaining years in the land of his mother's ancestors. He wanted a town house in Tokyo and a country house on one of the many islands. In any case he had no intention of keeping up the villa in Broome for Miss Blyth's occasional visits. Candy hadn't grasped yet that everything in life changed faster than one realized, and that men could change too. Mr. Muir was so friendly this time that she wasn't the least bit afraid of him. He gave her some presents, but no cash. Candy was so speechless that she began to look more attractive to Mr. Muir.

She had now been living for fourteen days in his magnificent house and couldn't understand why Mr. Muir had turned into such a lamb! He wasn't *that* old! In his middle forties, at most. Candy believed that aging men were calmer and more generous because they no longer had the strength to be angry or passionate. Mr. Muir, age forty-seven, did not feel old, but it was the time of life when a man starts to meditate, leaves the business of the day to his partners, and thinks of a home in solitude. His metamorphosis from Australian businessman to a student of wisdom had begun in Japan. Since people and things gain in value in an aura of impending farewell, Robert Muir saw in Candy this time an Australian Venus, who would hardly cross his path in Japan.

On the evening after the farewell dinner for his Japanese guests, Robert Muir lay naked under his mosquito netting and did breathing exercises. Candy was in the garden, chattering with his secretary, a student from Perth, who was as faceless as required by Mr. Muir. He was nice to Miss Blyth now because Mr. Muir had taken her in. Mr. Muir yawned, and thought with satisfaction of the dinner. He had supervised his cook as the man had filled the beautifully lacquered platters and trays with exquisitely garnished delicacies: grilled lobster and crab, artfully fringed tentacles of roast octopus, consommé with seaweed (which was supposed to increase a man's potency), and naturally the Western Australian type of sashimi, a raw red fish served swimming in soy sauce between little heaps of horseradish. During the meal Robert Muir had been pleased to think that his steak days were nearly at an end.

He had also examined a collection of cultured pearls, and his Japanese guests had presented him with a few spectacular examples as a farewell gift. Mr. Mikimoto, the son of a poor pearl fisher, had produced the cultured pearl. Nothing had been able to hold this clever, fanatic Japanese back from his experiments—not the infinitely fine work of opening the shell and introducing the alien body; not the destruction of his shells by the *akashio,* the red tide, the microbes of which destroyed fish and shells; not the atomic war nor the American occupation troops—nothing had deterred Mr. Mikimoto from the development of his craft. "Patience," thought Robert Muir, lying on his bed in Broome. "Who has patience in Australia or America?"

With eyes half closed he watched his white tissue-paper butterflies that hung suspended from the ceiling by thin threads. It was unbreathably hot tonight, but whenever the faintest breath of air wafted through the open windows and door, these weightless Japanese toys danced up and down and gave the motionless man an illusion of coolness. The butterflies fulfilled their only function in the mechanized present with perfection, and Mr. Muir didn't expect anything more from them. He didn't expect these dainty paper dancers to make classical music or converse with him about the French theatre of the absurd. He had seen a few performances of Ionesco's short dramas during his last visit to Paris, and had been entranced by their existential nonsense. What was happening on the stage had been going on in Japan for thousands of years. But the mundane common sense of the West, all practically oriented, couldn't be expected to grasp the drama of existence.

Mr. Muir watched his dancing butterflies and in a roundabout way his thoughts reverted to Candy Blyth. As long as she fulfilled her function to his satisfaction, like these butterflies, she could go right on being charmingly inane as far as he was concerned. She provided the illusion of perfect beauty as long as she remained silent. On this pragmatic continent, Robert Muir needed certain illusions, and was prepared to pay for them.

Muir had noticed at once that the butterfly dust had fallen from the wings of his young Venus from Kalgoorlie. The girl lived in a consumer society and was the victim of frivolous and merciless male lust. She had told him that she had missed him. He had laughed aloud. Whom did she think he was?

Mr. Muir spent most of his evenings with his butterflies. Another week passed and he hadn't called Candy into his private rooms, which one entered only in stocking feet. She entertained his guests as best she could, and he didn't seem to notice her, although he was watching her all the time. After her arrival he had sent her to the hairdresser. Her red hair was impossible. The girl had all the guile of a butterfly; not even her alliance with the shark from Genoa had robbed her of her light-hearted optimism. This Mr. Preston had of course helped himself to her money and jewelry. Mr. Muir missed his presents too. He had his Scottish memory for things he had bought.

He put on his black silk robe and rang for Candy. He wanted to talk business with her. Candy smiled at him coyly. She could never tell whether Mr. Muir was in a private or official mood.

"I have bought an oyster bar, Miss Blyth," he said. "You will work there from five to seven. I take it you don't want to sit here forever, doing nothing."

"Of course not," said Candy, against her convictions.

"The manager will show you what to do. I'll take you there tomorrow morning, and I hope you'll like the work."

Mr. Muir hoped nothing of the sort—he was giving orders. Candy nodded. She knew that tone. "I hope it won't be too much for me," she said hesitantly.

"I hope not too, Miss Blyth. So what's new? Why so silent?"

Candy opened her eyes wide. Wasn't Mr. Muir always telling her to keep her mouth shut? "Something terrible has happened, Mr. Muir."

"Here in my house?"

"Nothing ever happens in your house. I mean in South Australia."

"I am not a mind reader, Miss Blyth. So . . . what happened?"

"I'll get the paper."

"Don't flutter around all the time. Try to think for a change."

His bright, dark eyes were fixed on her with a strange expression. They were boring holes into her. Suddenly she felt hot and cold. Was he trying to hypnotize her? After all, he was half a Jap, and the old people in Australia still told horror stories about the dirty deeds of the yellow man. Candy couldn't move. The butterflies on the ceiling weren't moving either.

Mr. Muir looked down again and asked if Candy had lost her tongue. She pulled herself together. She must have been mistaken because Mr. Muir was a hundred percent Scottish again. Candy reported that an immigrant family consisting of five people had lost their way in the northwest desert, miles from Birdsville. The poor creatures, tortured by unbearable thirst and hunger, had perished in the so-called "sand hills of the dead."

"Why do the fools come to Australia?" Mr. Muir lit a cigarette. "That wouldn't have happened to them in England."

"Don't you think it's terribly sad, Mr. Muir?"

Muir went on smoking, unmoved, and looked up at his lifeless butterflies. He asked languidly how the bodies had been found.

"By the blackfellows. Funny, but the blacks can follow any trail better than the dogs."

Mr. Muir said nothing; his face was a mask.

"The blacks led the boys from the police to the bodies."

"Did you think the police would have found them alone?" Mr. Muir asked gently.

"It must be terribly hot in the desert."

"It's colder in Siberia," said Mr. Muir.

"I know an abo in Sydney. His name is Charlie Rainbow, and he lives with us. He came one day with his box of flowers . . ."

"No biographies, please, Miss Blyth. I'm allergic to them. Besides it's too hot for them in the desert of Broome. Why are you crying again? Are you longing for the abo?"

"I'm sorry for those people." Candy's voice was trembling.

"The blackfellows or the English?" Mr. Muir asked in a strange voice. He closed his eyes. Lately he found talking to Miss Blyth enervating. For a moment he had to let his mind carry him away. This happened to him quite often when he dealt with certain types of Australians. Then, with the utmost concentration, he would manage to see waterfalls, rock formations, and clouds—the primeval stuff of the universe. They were an insurance against sensual attraction, because this foolish girl was becoming more and more threateningly attractive daily.

Candy's strident voice tore into his thoughts. He looked at her in silence. It was ridiculous, but for him this young creature had become a visual object of esthetic desire. Was it possible that he could conjure up a magnificent landscape of the spirit and in spite of it pine for this little fool? He knew that the struggle was lost. He had to touch those breasts and the narrow, swaying hips of this marble idiot! He had to shatter this sugar doll. After that he was willing to be poor, banished from the paradise of the senses, and would walk upright across the threshold of old age. Miss Blyth was not a child any more. She was sated with cheap and humiliating experiences. She couldn't express herself, but her body spoke. Her body was a hymn of immaculate beauty, the kind the white race produces only occasionally among thousands of misprints. Her body was a gift of God which this young creature was selling at marked-down prices between Kalgoorlie, Sydney, and Broome.

"Isn't it gruesome, to die so young?" Candy asked. "The youngest of that immigrant family was only ten."

"What's gruesome about it? Those people were spared a lot in Australia."

"It's the best country in the world!" Candy cried indignantly.

"And that's why. Too much preoccupation with body welfare leading to the typical sickness of spiritual deficiency."

"We're very progressive, Mr. Muir. We have a lot of universities and movies and television."

"Ah yes. Television." Mr. Muir was interested to see Candy's eyes fill with tears again. "And what's wrong now, Miss Blyth?"

"I can't stop thinking of those corpses in the desert. They can't ever go to the movies again. Or eat ice cream."

"Horrible!" said Mr. Muir. "You are enchanting when you cry, Miss Blyth. Unfortunately you were born without a sense of compassion. In five minutes you will have forgotten those unfortunate people in the desert."

"That isn't true!"

"Oh, but it is, Miss Blyth."

Unlike the casual Australians, Mr. Muir used the formal address. Candy had once called him "Bob" and he had given her a look that had

228

nipped any further attempts at informality in the bud. Mr. Muir decided who could be intimate with him, and when.

He moved closer to Candy. "Why do you feel so sorry for absolute strangers?" he said harshly. "If you want to weep, then weep for me!"

He had lit another cigarette and was smoking calmly. Candy was baffled. This man had everything—money, a luxurious villa, he traveled, gave parties, he had women! In Broome, gossip didn't stop at the Villa Muir. A while ago a French woman from Queensland had been a steady guest there.

"I should weep for *you?*" Candy asked. The bottom had fallen out of her world with a crash.

Muir was silent. He couldn't talk to this girl about the nature and the problems of this lonely continent. He couldn't possibly bare his soul to her. Should he tear open his wounds in front of this beautiful ignoramus? This country had given him nothing voluntarily. He had fought grimly and with very private difficulties for every success and all the respect he enjoyed today in Australian society. Not even in love had he been accepted without having to pay. Although he was in command of a whole repertoire of delights, no woman had ever left his house without a check. He was not simple or vain enough to give the appearances of love to the tyrannical demands of the flesh, but even the most unvarnished pleasure lost vitality and charm with the checkbook. That was why Mr. Muir had been living for months without the consolation of Venus.

"I think you are to be envied," said Candy.

"Let's stop this nonsense, Miss Blyth." Perhaps this blind chicken had found a kernel of corn? After all, he knew how to make his loneliness bear fruit, and was thus perhaps to be envied, even if the child had not meant it.

"Would you like tea?" asked Candy. Mr. Muir's silence was making her feel more and more unsure of herself.

"I don't want tea," he said brusquely. This girl, who was staring straight at him without a spark of understanding, was, perhaps for that very reason, becoming increasingly irresistible with every passing second.

He had to embrace her, wound her. Through Candy he would humiliate the white Australians. Then he would squash the butterfly in his fist and throw it away. The old dangerous hate-love, the basic motif of his divided existence on this continent, was concentrated at this moment on this unsuspecting girl. Robert Muir stood like a statue in his own twilight. He felt dizzy, with an avidity he was still trying to suppress. But it was too late. He had undressed Candy so many times in his mind. Why had she come back?

He closed his eyes again, but he was cruelly awake. This destructive lust, which in sober moments Mr. Muir found absurd and monotonous, had to be expiated! Sex was monotonous, but it brought deliverance from treacherous tensions and left him liberated, and with the reawakened desire for solitude and abstract thought . . .

Seconds had passed, but time seemed to be standing still. Candy tried to avoid Mr. Muir's eyes. They were black, hypnotic pools that grew increasingly eerie, a thunderstorm with lightning. Candy was trembling, but she couldn't move. She had never seen this man naked. This wasn't Mr. Muir who advised her kindly to shut up, and gave her dresses and jewelry. A strange, powerful figure, inexorable and terrifying, was moving toward her slowly, resolutely and mercilessly. The powerful shoulders, the bald head, the narrow hips and the long, sinewy legs were like marble, gleaming golden and barbarically in the dark. This was the night itself, which had always made Candy shiver. She stood naked and helpless under the spell of those eyes, their animal glow blinding her. With a childish motion she put her arms up in front of her face and screamed, "No!" But not a sound came out of her throat. The light and the everyday things as she knew them had fled.

"No! No!" In vain. Too late. The night was deaf and mute.

After that night Robert Muir found Candy's presence hard to bear. He was overwhelmed by a dark feeling of guilt right in his office, and it grew in his leisure hours. He had lured an ignorant young creature onto forbidden ground, and he didn't want to repeat the experiment. Candace Blyth lived in a different climate, on another emotional level—besides, she always remained the same. The rhythm of the seasons and feelings were foreign to her. The chain of absurdity that ran through her existence now weighed also upon him, and in a roundabout way conjured up guilt feelings. True, he had given her a valuable piece of jewelry, but he had the feeling that this time it had not roused the same enthusiasm. He had thoroughly confused the girl and now he was sorry. She crept around like a sick young animal. She worked at the oyster bar at the time assigned to her, dully and automatically. Dead inventory. He might have known. Politely and silently he began to hate her. He didn't desire her any more. She had given him all and nothing. An oyster without a pearl.

Mr. Muir lay all alone again in his immaculate room after work and the many business meetings. He looked at his butterflies. They were less impersonal than Candy Blyth. Why couldn't he get rid of this feeling of guilt? Finally he shrugged and told himself that the struggle between the sexes was waged with boomerangs that came back in deceptively playful detours to the ones who had thrown them.

Miss Blyth had to leave.

One morning Mr. Muir was gone. His secretary, who wasn't experiencing the end of an affair for the first time, brought Candy a letter. Mr. Muir suggested that she work in his oyster bar all day, because one waitress was out sick. But if she preferred to leave, his secretary would buy her a ticket to Sydney. Neither cash nor a check were enclosed this time.

On his return Mr. Muir found the young lady still at his house. His secretary, a young man with no attributes, experienced an uncomfortable half hour. Naturally he defended himself. He had tried his best but Miss Blyth was hard of hearing. Moreover, her listless behavior at the oyster bar had reduced the number of clients. Mr. Muir chose to overlook this observation. The oyster bar was none of his secretary's damn business!

That evening Mr. Muir spoke to Candy about her future. They were sitting on the big balcony facing the ocean. The moon shone dreamily in the tropical sky, but Mr. Muir was not feeling dreamy.

"I am going to write to my aunt in Sydney," Candy told him finally.

"Do that, child." This was followed by an uncomfortable silence. "Forgive me," Muir mumbled, "but everything has to end some time, doesn't it?"

Candy didn't notice the trace of impatience in his voice. "What did I do?" she asked stubbornly.

"Nothing," Mr. Muir replied truthfully. "What are you waiting for?" he asked irritably. Then he sank back into his basic and merciless introspection. He had a talent for creating a vacuum around himself.

He watched Candy as he had done at the end of her first visit, wondering that such an attractive body did not include an attractive spirit. He had tried at least to produce an artificial pearl—in vain. The girl's spirit was weighted down in a mundane life. Her soul was asleep. She was wandering along the edge of an abyss and didn't know it.

Muir frowned. At twenty Candy had seen and experienced more on this sprawling colorful continent than most young women in Europe or Japan, but no one and nothing made a lasting impression on her. And that was the true tragedy of any human being.

* * *

At last Candy wrote to Lydia Doody. They hadn't heard from her in months because she only remembered her relatives when she needed them. Mrs. Doody answered by return mail. Candy read the letter three times. Was this her Aunt Doody who had coddled her and waited on her? She didn't even call her "doll" once!

Dear Candy,

I'm glad you thought of your aunt at last. We've been racking our brains where you could possibly be. Your mother didn't know either. But I wrote her that you couldn't expect chicken meat from an ox.

That you want to come back to Sydney is the dumbest thing I've ever heard of. What do you expect to do here? You won't like it after Broome. You can't just throw over your elegant job in the oyster bar. You're twenty years old now, and still don't have any more gumption than a little brat. How do you think you can earn money here? I'm sending you—printed matter or it costs too much—a few issues of *Insight* with your successor in it. I cry often because you gave up your elegant job as a model where you earned so much money. Molly Fleet makes tea for me when I'm mad. She's a good egg.

Sydney has changed a lot. I'm broke because I miss the money you used to pay me. But I manage. I've had to raise the rents, though, so everybody's mad at you. But I always say—you can't count on anybody in this lousy world. Not even one's own flesh and blood. Charlie Rainbow laughs at me. I let him. A blackfellow doesn't often have anything to laugh about.

Our Albert Ritter, you know—the traveling salesman from New South Wales with the snotty face—never came back. Do you suppose he's dead? If only you didn't always forget to get his address, I'd have sent a wreath. Two of our neighbors died. I don't know what's come over Sydney. Everybody's dying! I hope I don't catch it.

Our dear Mr. Trent has been in Queensland now for quite some time. He came to see me a few times after you left, and helped me out with money and tried to comfort me because you were so disloyal. He said, Youth has little virtue, but that's nonsense. Even a young dog sticks to his master, doesn't he?

How can you ask if Molly Fleet is still with me? Of course she is! She's like a daughter to me. Don't know what I'd do without her. She comes home tired from work and scrubs the kitchen floor! I always say: it's heart that counts!

Mr. Trent is going to have a baby, I mean, his young wife is. Isn't that dinkum? I cried like anything when I heard the good news. Dear old Mr. Trent kept beating about the bush until he finally told me before he left. He gave me such a big check. I guess he was so happy, he didn't know what he was doing! I can do with it, I mean the check. Molly Fleet says Mr. Trent can't have been so unhappy with his wife as you always tried to tell us. A baby speaks its own language, says Molly. Mr. Trent sent you best greetings and all good wishes. He said, "I am truly happy that my young protegée is doing so well in Broome." By the way, I know Mr. Muir. I met him at a friend's house right here in Sydney! What do you say to that? Australia is a village. Trent and Muir never mentioned you. I made a point of asking because I wanted to know where you were. In the end Mr. Trent said he *thought* in Broome.

I would love to visit you at the Villa Muir. After all, you are my favorite niece and lived with me for a long time, didn't you? The fence is broken again. Charlie Rainbow has planted new flowers. But I guess all that doesn't interest you. You're an elegant young lady now in a luxurious house in Broome. Molly Fleet says there must be something fishy about it if you want to come back to us. But Molly sees something fishy in everything. Everybody has a little something wrong with them, like that. She also says she hopes you don't come to a bad end. I said if anybody has money to burn, like you do now, the bad end must be pretty far away. I know life and what I'm talking about. As soon as you send me the plane ticket, I'll come. I think it'll do you good to see an old piece of furniture out of your own family. I pray for you every day, and my friend with the wooden leg sends best greetings. Molly Fleet does too. We've all grown used to her birthmark. We don't see it any more. Charlie Rainbow and Uncle Doody send greetings too. Uncle wants to know if Mr. Muir would like to buy an umbrella. When shall I come?

But if you'd rather come back to us, you'll have to work. You can't count on your men any more, nor on the photoboys. Write right away what you decide. Molly Fleet is altering my best black dress. She says there are so many pearls in Broome. We'd love to have some! Molly says the pearls lie on the street in Broome. I hope I get to see them.

Your loving Aunt Doody

Candy tore up the letter. Did the friend with the wooden leg, Miss Fleet, Uncle Doody, and Charlie Rainbow perhaps want to settle down in the Villa Muir too? Why had she boasted so much? If she had written her aunt the truth, it would have been better. Mrs. Doody melted with pity for anyone unlucky, but she reacted sourly to lucky people. Candy felt panicky. She could only stay at the Villa Muir a few days longer, and the secretary wasn't the least bit helpful. Candy suspected him of being homosexual, but that wasn't the case at all. He was engaged, and spent all his free time with his fiancée.

Mr. Muir had given Candy her farewell present the night before. His meaning couldn't have been clearer. He was flying to Paris and bringing guests with him on his return. He gave Candy a butterfly of mother-of-pearl, set with pearls. The pearls were tears that wouldn't dry up, and the whole thing had to be worth a lot of money. Candy stared at the brooch, her lower lip trembling. Where was she to go? Nobody wanted to do anything for her. Nobody seemed eager for her company. But she was Candy! What was the matter with people?

She put the butterfly in her suitcase. She had to go walkabout again, and that was a nuisance and frightening. What had she done wrong in the Villa Muir? She didn't know and would never find out, even if she spent years thinking about it. She had only discovered one thing in Broome—there were tears behind everything . . .

"She's gone!" said Mrs. Doody. "Now I can't fly to Broome."

"It's all for the best," said Molly Fleet.

"But you said the pearls lie on the street there! And where is Candy? Maybe something's happened to her. I wrote her such a nice letter. I said she'd be welcome any time. After all, she's my own flesh and blood!"

"That's right," said Molly Fleet. "So where is she?"

"How should I know? You know, Molly, she goes walkabout, and that's that. She'll come to a bad end."

"She always lands on her feet," said Molly Fleet, unmoved.

"But you said yourself she'd come to a bad end."

"Possibly. I must have picked it up from you. Here's a tissue, Mrs. Doody. Don't cry. You won't get Candy's address that way."

Miss Fleet gave Mrs. Doody a sharp look. Except for the red veins in her fat face, she thought Mrs. Doody looked alarmingly pale. What on earth had the old woman written to Candy?

"If you wrote to her so nicely, and she still wants to run around all over the place, there's nothing you can do about it. I'll make you a quick cup of tea, Mrs. Doody. If you don't mind waiting a moment, I'll run over to Gretchen's and get us some pastry."

Mrs. Doody began to look in her bag for change. "My treat," said Molly. "We'll make it a little farewell celebration."

"Why? Are you going to take off too? I love you like my own daughter! And who'll scrub the kitchen floor?"

"Don't get upset, Mrs. Doody. I'm only going to Parramatta for a few days. My grandmother on the farm is ill."

"What's the matter with her?" Mrs. Doody asked animatedly.

"I don't know. My brother just wrote that she wanted to see me."

"And you'll surely come back?" Mrs. Doody sounded worried.

"I'm not your niece," Molly Fleet said with dignity.

18

How Big Is Parramatta?

After Grandmother Fleet's funeral, Molly sat with her brother, Stephen, on the big wooden veranda. The farm seemed empty. Molly didn't know what to say to her brother. She was like a bird dropped out of its nest. Stephen was silent. Molly looked at him shyly, sidelong. The protector of her childhood was now a strong, capable man who seemed to have forgotten how to speak. Molly looked around her. Everything was as she had always known and loved it—the house, Grandmother's kitchen and pantry, the living room with its worn furniture and an aroma of childhood, the stalls, the meadow, the evening stillness. Had it only been Grandmother Fleet, who with her sharp-tongued kindness and her faithfulness, made this place a home? That had to be it! Molly felt that with her grandmother's death, her youth had ended. But she was only twenty-two, and as people were always saying, her whole life still lay ahead of her. She pulled her grandmother's white shawl, that she'd been wearing for years now, tighter around her shoulders. Her grandmother had knitted it. Heaven only knew how she had found time with the work on the farm, to sew and knit for "the young one."

Molly had considered life on the farm as something indestructible. Every shilling she had set aside in Sydney she had thought of as something toward broadening and modernizing the place. And suddenly everything was different. Molly couldn't say what was separating her and Stephen. Evening had always been their most peaceful time. Stephen had taken his ledger—the little dog had sat beside him next to the wooden table—and had teased Molly every now and then. Grandmother had darned or rested after the strenuous work of preserving fruit and vegetables and all the business of the farm. Molly and the abo girl, Goonur, had sat around with her grandmother or played "farm" on the wooden veranda. Stephen had carved little animals and houses and a tiny fence for them. He had always been clever with his hands. And then there had been Lily, the good, clever cow. Molly hardly knew any of the cows now. She had only come to the farm for Easter and Christmas. Funny, there'd always been the three of them, as if her father and sister lived in another country. Yet the city of Parramatta wasn't far away. But the farm was the only place that had given Molly a feeling of belonging, and surely something like that had to remain, Molly thought, even when her grandmother wasn't sitting there any more. Milk and bread and the fields were ... eternal! The big word startled Molly, but that was the way things were when you looked at it all in the light.

Molly had come too late to see Grandmother Fleet alive. None of them had know how serious her illness really was. Two days before her death she had made breakfast for Stephen and the farm hands, and declared, heroically and stubbornly, that she was feeling dinkum and the doctor was an idiot! He had threatened Grandmother Fleet with the hospital when Stephen told him she was still getting breakfast and shooing the girls out of the kitchen. And when nothing came of the threat with the hospital, and Grandmother finally realized that old Dr. Hodge was not an idiot but knew what he was talking about, she had capitulated.

She had decided all by herself and all alone that she would die on the farm. That was where she had lived with and labored for her grandchildren, and prayed for "the young one." Then she had told Dr. Hodge he should tell his old friend, Reverend Campbell. Not until the Reverend drove up in his rattletrap wagon and brought everything requisite to saying farewell to the farm, did Stephen see the light. That was when he had written express to Molly, and his father and April. Nobody reproached Stephen. They had all thought Grandmother Fleet would never die, in spite of the fact that she had been rehearsing that ritual for quite a few months. Nobody was allowed to watch her because it was an act of love, totally private and only God knew about it. Yes, Grandmother Fleet had made her peace with the Lord in profound silence. She had been angry with Him for years because of "the young one." Such a little lamb shouldn't have had to bear a fiery mark on her face. It wasn't fair! Of course all people were subjected to trials, and they had to be borne, and they had to say to themselves over and over again that the Lord knew how much one could bear. But Grandmother Fleet had found this too heavy a burden for Molly. Grandmother Fleet had broad shoulders and would have liked to take this burden upon herself. The child wasn't a vain little brat, like April. Grandmother Fleet had never ceased bringing the matter to God's attention, as if He didn't know his creatures! And in the end she had spoken about it to Reverend Campbell, and after confession had felt much calmer. For the first time she believed that Molly would know how to cope with it. With God's help. And so, after a laying down of arms, had come the great peace.

Half a year ago, Grandmother Fleet had begun, beside her housework, to pack up her earthly existence. You had to start some time. Stephen, grumbling, had driven her to the notary in Parramatta. What did Grandmother want with the notary? There was plenty of time for a will. And she didn't have to make one anyway, Stephen said. Molly would always have a place on the farm, all of them knew that. What was there for the old pen-pusher to scribble? But Grandmother was not to be shaken. She had signed various "scribbles," and the papers had remained with the notary. Then she had driven home with Stephen, content. Yes, they had drunk a beer at Father Fleet's house, and Grandmother had even asked why April came to the farm so rarely. In spite of the fact that she couldn't stand April, that was how peaceful Grandmother Fleet had been after the visit to the notary.

After that she had sat on the veranda again every evening with Stephen and still enjoyed many healthy, contented days. She had sewn quite a few things for "the young one," and embroidered some dresses. She didn't trust the job they did at the factory in Sydney. Molly had such a beautiful, straight figure. Everything fitted her as if poured on her. Yes, Grandmother had still had time to embroider a white dress with mimosa blossoms for Sundays. That was during the last weeks, when sewing and embroidering were already torturous, and Stephen was right to make a scene about it. That was Stephen. When he wasn't silent, words poured from him like a raging waterfall. She would have to leave her sewing machine behind, Grandmother thought sadly, but then had called herself to order sharply. She had to start behaving like a proper candidate for death. And that was how she had stubbornly practiced for eternity.

In the end Grandmother had asked constantly, "Has the little one come?" By that time all of them were gathered around the bed: Father Fleet, the Reverend Campbell, and April, and the boys and girls who worked on the farm. But then there was nobody but the family and the Reverend. Suddenly Grandmother cried out, "Molly! Come closer, child!" She couldn't recognize the people standing around the bed properly any more. Stephen pushed his sister April forward. She stood there as usual, stiff as a ramrod, but finally she did kneel down, and Grandmother laid her old, work-worn hand on April's head. Then the prayers for the dead began. Grandmother Fleet looked damn peaceful,

Stephen thought. Younger, too, and smoother. He couldn't understand it.

Father Fleet and April went straight back to Parramatta after the funeral. The brewery had to go on functioning. Father Fleet had even asked Molly to stop and visit them for a while before she went back to Sydney. Molly wanted to pack up slowly in Sydney. Now was the time. She couldn't leave Stephen alone for good. She had saved quite a lot, and somebody had to do Grandmother's work. Mrs. Doody would understand. She would have to find one or two nice, decent girls to rent from her because there was no relying on Candace Blyth. She just bummed around.

Molly wanted to stay with her father for a week. He was lonely. He couldn't bark at his wife any more or scare Grandmother Cocker half to death. In the end, the two had escaped him. And April? His favorite daughter was as bitter as blackthorn. Molly knew that it was partly her fault. Why had she, stupid brat that she then was, got herself mixed up in April's affairs? But there was nothing to be done now about the broken engagement. She didn't hate her sister any more as she had done when April had called her Mole. April had become a stranger. Molly would spend a week in her father's house as an act of contrition. She found her father had aged considerably. "Is Father all right?" she asked Stephen.

"Sure. But he isn't getting any younger."

Finally Stephen told her that their grandmother had left her all sorts of things in her will. She had told him so during her last days. "The sewing machine too. And her only ring."

"There's time enough for that, Stephen."

"We're going to town tomorrow. They'll open the will."

Molly looked up at the violet night sky. The clouds were crowding together like strayed sheep. Molly said hesitantly, "Grandmother was first-rate. *She* was always there."

"She lived here."

"Father ran away from us all the time, Mother hid from us. Have you forgotten it all, Stephen? And Grandmother Cocker scurried away like a scared rabbit when I wanted to go up to her. She was a dud."

"Let's not bring old Cocker into this, Molly. The poor woman didn't know any better. Father wasn't nice to her."

"Anyway, Grandmother Fleet never ran away when we wanted her." Molly swallowed hard. "That's a wonderful thing. I mean—to be always there for your family. Grandmother Fleet . . ."

Stephen pounded on the table with his fist. "Stop it!" he yelled. "You don't have to explain her to me." He turned away brusquely. His dog licked his shoe, and Stephen mumbled, "Scram, you bastard!" But the dog wagged his tail, and Stephen forgot him. He stroked Molly's hair clumsily, as he used to do when she came running to him, weeping. How could he have yelled at Molly? She had only told the truth. Grandmother Fleet had been unique, and it was a good thing that the young one knew it. "Let it be, Molly. I'm not myself."

"I'll make tea for us, Stephen. Two sugars for you, and a lot of milk. Or has it changed?"

Of course Stephen drank his tea as he always had. Molly never forgot later that it had calmed her.

Shortly before she left for Parramatta, Stephen asked his sister what her plans for the future were. She had grown accustomed to being at home again. In these two weeks, Sydney had begun to fade. Mrs. Doody's roominghouse, Molly's clients in their fine villas, her lonely wanderings through King's Cross, her love letters to Rigby and her own last letter, which she had torn up—everything lay far behind her. She thought often these days that it might have been better if she had stayed on the farm. This was the place for her. Grandmother had left her her share. The farm now belonged to Stephen and her. But even without the will, it would have been the only home for her. Stephen and she had always held together. When he yelled at her it was only because he had to let off steam. He was the salt of the earth.

Molly had soon made friends with the new cows and helped wherever she could. She hoped this would please Stephen, but he didn't say anything. When one tried not to find one's home empty and worked as hard as the boys and girls on the farm, life was good and made sense. The only thing she and Stephen didn't touch were the preserves in the pantry. One day the wooden shelves were empty. Stephen had given Grandmother's preserves, in their glasses and stone jars, away. He had always experienced a slight shock when he had seen her clear script on the labels: content, date, how prepared, and how long the contents could be kept. Stephen had brooded. It wasn't right that things should outlive the person. Molly saw the empty shelves, but she said nothing. She had some of Granny's preserve jars in Sydney. She would remove the labels and keep them.

"What are you planning to do, Moll?"

Molly looked at her brother, surprised. If Stephen didn't know what she wanted to do, then who would? But she said quietly that she'd like to go on making money a while longer and then . . .

"Of course I'll come back to you, here on the farm. I may stay only a few more weeks in Sydney. I can't let Mrs. Doody down at a moment's notice."

Still Stephen said nothing.

"I've read a lot about dairy farming while I was in Sydney, and I've been to quite a few lectures. I think we should go right on modernizing. But I think I wrote you all that."

Stephen puffed on his pipe. The silence gradually grew oppressive. Why didn't he say anything? Molly sat up stiffly in her wicker chair with the faded cushions. Her hands were ice-cold. Didn't Stephen want her? When he still didn't say anything, she asked him, taking care that her voice shouldn't tremble.

"Don't ask such stupid questions," Stephen said gruffly. "This is and remains your home. Only . . . I want to . . . I intend to . . ."

"Do you want to sell the farm?"

"Don't shout! Granny hated it when you shouted."

"What's the matter, Stephen?"

"You don't have to whisper, either. Well, Moll . . . I'm going to get married at last."

He drew a deep breath. Praise be the Lord, he had spat it out! The young one sat there stiff as a statue. As if lightning had struck. Stephen began to feel uneasy.

"That doesn't mean you won't be welcome here, Molly. I've explained everything to Jennifer. Her folks have a farm near here. Not as many cattle and machines, but nice enough. Jenny grew up on the farm." Stephen couldn't remember ever having said so much in one go. He wiped the sweat off his brow.

"When do you intend to get married?" It cost Molly effort to ask.

"Pretty soon. Look, ducky, I can't run this place alone. I mean, there should be a woman here. And children."

"Of course." Molly Fleet got up. "I'm tired."

"Are you going to bed? Shall I bring you milk and honey?" He'd done that when the school children had called her Mole. Or when things had gone wrong with her.

"No thanks, Stephen. Goodnight."

"Goodnight."

Stephen Fleet sighed. What could he do? The girls in and around Parramatta were marrying all the time, only his sisters didn't. And

April was twenty-seven, Molly twenty-two, and Stephen had finally reached thirty. And he hadn't told Molly the most important thing, although he had promised Jennifer he would. Perhaps Molly would want it herself. "Moll!" he cried upstairs.

She came back slowly. She had on a flowered nylon robe, made in Sydney. You could see that ten miles away. Her golden hair fell over the side of her face. She looked thirteen, not a day older.

"What do you want, Steve?"

"Nothing. Go to bed, little one."

"But you wanted to say something."

The way she looked at him! Did she know anything? Stephen Fleet felt damned uncomfortable, but he had promised his fiancée . . . Jennifer was a decent girl, but she was an outsider. She didn't know Moll and she didn't know . . . Dammit! He couldn't let Jenny think he was a softy!

"There was something I wanted to discuss with you, Moll. Because you're going to Father's place from here."

Molly said nothing. Why the hell didn't she ask what he wanted to discuss with her?

"Grandmother left you a share of the farm."

"Yes."

"Now listen carefully, Moll. I thought . . . we thought, if you want to sell your share to me . . . you only have to say so." Stephen spoke fast. "It won't be to your disadvantage, chick. And . . . and your room will always be here for you. What do you think?"

When her silence became too pronounced, he looked at her. She was white as a sheet. He could see it even in the dim light. But she was standing up very straight, and somehow she reminded him of Grandmother Fleet. Godammit! Molly belonged here!

"I don't know what I'll do, Stephen. Not yet. I'll have to think it over." But she knew exactly—Stephen sensed it.

"As I just said, you . . ."

"Goodnight."

She was gone. Stephen whistled for his dog. Nothing good had ever come of a threesome. Jenny was right. But why was she in such a hurry? Why had she pestered him until he had promised to discuss the matter of Molly's share now? Life went on, and sometimes it passed over little girls and their wishes. It wasn't Stephen's fault. His fiancée had an uncle, a wealthy sheep farmer in New South Wales, who was willing to spend a large sum of money on their farm as soon as it belonged to Stephen and Jenny in equal parts. All perfectly legal. But Stephen knew that it was all wrong. He should have waited. Moll was stupefied by sorrow. Only yesterday she had packed Granny's things. Stephen had happened to see her with the old sewing machine—outmoded, dented, but crazily durable. She had been stroking it. When she had seen Stephen, she had run out of the room.

On the other hand, Stephen hadn't wanted a lawyer to talk to Molly about it. That would have been even more unsuitable. Only right now he should have kept his mouth shut. He stared at the river. "The young one" had always believed in him, like the *Amen* in church. Molly was a good egg. He'd look her up more often now in Sydney, when he spoke to the dairy cooperatives, and she'd spend all her vacations on the farm, as she always had done. And every damn weekend, if she wanted to. And Jenny's uncle could keep his stinking money! They'd gotten along very nicely until now without Jenny's goddamn uncle; Granny, Molly and he. And if Jenny didn't like it, if Moll decided to hang onto her share of the farm, then Jenny'd see another side of Stephen Fleet! Yes sir!

Stephen whistled quite cheerfully for his dog. He really believed he'd come to a decision, but the state of marriage had its own battle plan, and Stephen had already lost the first encounter. He didn't know it, but Molly did, although she was so much younger and less experienced than her big brother. Right then she was staring with burning eyes at the crucifix over her bed. She was taking leave of her home. As a little girl she had thought the Parramatta farm was vast. A whole world! But tonight the farm had grown so small and narrow that there was no room in it for Molly Fleet.

When Molly got back to the roominghouse, Mrs. Doody set the tea table with the good china Candy had bought for her. "What's the matter, Mrs. Doody? Is Candy back?"

"You know better than that!" A shadow crossed Mrs. Doody's full-moon face. "Damned little tramp! How was it in Parramatta?"

"Except for Grandmother's funeral, just the same."

"Nice or horrid?"

"Nice, of course," said Molly Fleet, her voice flat. "My brother's getting married."

"Everybody's getting married these days! I'll be the next one!" Mrs. Doody roared laughter. "I'm glad you're back, Fleet. Did you meet your sister-in-law?"

"Not yet. Stephen says she's very smart."

"When should he find that out if not now?" Mrs. Doody said slyly. "You stayed such a long time, I thought you weren't coming back."

"Who's coming? I don't want to disturb anyone."

"Are you crook, girl? Gretchen's coming. She's bringing German crumb cake, and some news!"

"Is she getting married too?"

"Of course! She can't manage the bakery alone anymore."

"That figures," said Molly.

"I don't know what it is, but right now everybody's dying or getting married. What do they do in between?"

"Act dumb."

"Did you eat a lot of lemons in Parramatta?"

Gretchen Curtis, née Breitschneider, had changed a lot since she had gone to school with Elizabeth West in Adelaide. She didn't tell anyone Grimm's Fairy Tales any more, and she shared the opinions of her deceased husband about Australia in general and in particular. The only German thing left was the diminutive of her name, Gretchen, to which she stuck stubbornly.

Gretchen thought often of Elizabeth West, née Withers. Life was a carousel. When Betty had turned up in Adelaide, tired and indifferent after her first stay in Sydney, Gretchen had been a happy wife, well-off, with children, and Betty had been a bored secretary in Mr. Curtis's office. And Betty's mother had begged Gretchen constantly to find a husband for her difficult daughter. Then Betty had gone back to Sydney, and everybody in Adelaide, Betty's mother and Gretchen in the lead, had thought that this would be the end of Betty Withers. Funny the way things turned around. Today Betty was a famous writer and Gretchen had turned into a shadow of her former youth.

Gretchen opened the latest copy of *Insight* and showed it to Mrs. Doody and Molly Fleet. "Doesn't Betty look elegant? Except for her messy hairdo."

The three ladies looked at the pictures of Elizabeth West and her fiancé from Brisbane. *Insight* had devoted a whole issue to its famous writer, with pictures of her in Adelaide, Sydney, and Queensland, with interviews and quotes. It had apparently been a whirlwind romance. "Some people have all the luck," said Mrs. Doody. "What was Miss West like when she wasn't famous?"

Gretchen thought hard. "Betty? Nothing special." She cut off a piece of cake for herself. "I know it must sound funny, but in school I wrote much better compositions. I don't know what got into Betty. You can believe me, but not a soul at home could understand how little Withers could suddenly write best sellers. My husband always used to say that successes like that in Sydney were fabricated." Gretchen drew a deep breath, and began to eat her excellent cake.

Molly Fleet said nothing. Mrs. Doody gobbled her cake as usual. "I'd like the recipe for that cake, Gretchen. Who fabricated Miss West's success? I don't think she's pretty. Her nose is too big. Can't be compared to my Candy."

Gretchen barely knew Candy, and Molly Fleet had written her off completely.

"Betty and I were always good friends," said Gretchen. "I wrote to her, care of *Insight*, and she answered. Now what do you think of that?"

"Why not?" said Miss Fleet. "I massaged her for a while. I congratulated her, and she answered."

"Have you been invited to the wedding?" Mrs. Doody asked Gretchen.

"I'm much too busy at the bakery. Miss Rigby's giving a big reception for Betty. I got an invitation, of course. Engraved."

"I did too," said Molly Fleet. "Miss West and I are good friends."

"We're going to have a real wedding with good eats and coffee," Gretchen said dreamily. "I don't like cocktail parties with a crowd of strangers."

Gretchen was marrying a restaurant owner of German extraction in King's Cross. Perhaps they would add on a coffee shop. She gave Mrs. Doody and Molly Fleet printed invitations to the wedding.

"I always thought Miss West was sort of married to Miss Rigby," said Molly. "Whenever I went to Bellevue Hill, the two seemed to be like two peas in a pod. It's not going to be easy for Miss Rigby."

Molly grew thoughtful. Her first piece of cake lay untouched on her plate. It was funny . . . you'd have two or three people from the big herd living peacefully together for years, and then one of them got married, and the herd scattered. The one left behind sat high and dry. As if a billabong in the desert had suddenly disappeared. The thirst, of course, remained.

"Don't you get married now, Fleet!" Mrs. Doody warned her. "Or who's to scrub my kitchen floor?"

19

A Wedding in Sydney

It wasn't easy for Miss Rigby, but she had wanted Betty to marry. At Alexander's fiftieth birthday party she had tried to hang her onto Bertie Dobson. Miss Rigby still didn't know why Bertie and Betty hadn't done her that small favor. It would have been a fine thing. Miss Rigby could reach Macquarie Street easily any time, and Alex would have built them a house, if Bertie had decided to move. In any case, Miss Rigby would have been able to keep her eye on them.

Why Bertie Dobson didn't want to marry Elizabeth West became evident to Miss Rigby at the big press and wedding reception for Betty. Bertie brought his bonny bride Mavis to Bellevue Hill. Miss Rigby couldn't find anything especially wrong with the girl. Betty was ten times as famous, ten times as witty, but of course ten years older than Mavis. But Bertie was beaming. It was simply ridiculous how Bertie, who had always clung to his mother's apron strings, showed his bride off. As if Mavis were a seven-day wonder! Men! thought Miss Rigby. She stood tall, distinguished, and charming beside Betty and Mr. Grierson, and greeted all who had come to congratulate. She also told her colleagues, the photo boys and reporters from Sydney, Adelaide, and Brisbane, how very suitable the marriage was. Frank Grierson was a well-known journalist and radio personality in Brisbane. When a young reporter suggested that perhaps Mr. Grierson could help his wife to write her novels, Miss Rigby thought it a brilliant idea.

She was being asked all the time: *Where* was Alexander? And she told everybody that her brother was going out to Manly, where there was to be a little extra celebration only for closest friends and relatives. It was absolutely disgraceful of Alex! But she was used to that sort of behavior from him. He thought it was funny! She didn't even know if he was in Sydney. The young couple would fly to Cairns right after the reception. They were honeymooning on the Great Barrier Reef. Everything as it should be. Miss Rigby looked across the battlefield: nothing was missing—i.e., her old friend Stanley Marchmont was not present. A reporter from Brisbane was sitting in his chair. Bertie Dobson had forbidden Marchmont to attend weddings and funerals.

Where was Alexander? thought Elizabeth West Grierson. She had been married for four hours and should really be thinking only of Frank, but four hours is a relatively short time. The years with Rigby would probably take time to erase. "I am happy," she told herself stubbornly. She pressed Frank's arm, feeling guilty, and he responded. "When can we get out of here, Betty?"

"Not yet. Grace would never forgive me."

"But that's ridiculous!" said Mr. Grierson, slightly irritated. He didn't know that Betty had already reserved one of the loveliest rooms in the big house in Brisbane for Miss Rigby. "Grace is sensible. Let's go, Betty," urged her very new husband.

At that moment Alexander walked into the flower-filled reception room. He was in great form, and greeted all his cobbers from far and wide, and the boys from the press. Marchmont, Rigby & French never turned down free publicity. Rigby didn't seem to see the young couple, but he chatted jovially and with flattering interest with some reporters from Adelaide. They were printing extra editions for the wedding of the famous novelist.

Patrick Trent, his young wife, and his sister, Catherine, followed Rigby around. For the first time in many years, Trent was the happiest man in this room. A heart-to-heart talk with his wife had cleared the stormy air, and now a baby was on the way. Grace Rigby watched Trent, more moved than she had ever been in his dismal days. At that time all those who knew him well were fully aware of the fact that his joviality was a mask. He had hidden behind it, resigned, for years. Now he looked years younger. It was almost ridiculous the way he danced attendance on his young wife. "Don't eat the fish salad!" he was just telling her, as he took the plate out of her hand.

Rigby and Catherine Trent watched the scene and smiled ironically. "Holy Moses!" cried Rigby. "Your wife isn't made of sugar!"

Trent told his wife to be sure to tell him when she felt tired. And she was pink as a peony! He was the one who felt weary. Did happiness make one tired, he wondered? Then he shook hands with Betty. "Do your best, little one," he said. "And God bess!"

Elizabeth didn't look at her old friend. Trent always saw too much. He seemed to know that it would have been easier for Betty to break with the past by writing . . .

"I'm so happy for you both," Betty told the Trents. "You must visit us soon in Brisbane."

Just then Rigby walked up to her, smiling radiantly. He looked bigger than ever, and was dressed to the nines. Had she really, seriously thought that her marriage would unhinge him?

He congratulated Betty as conventionally as if he were seeing her for the first time in his life. He chose to overlook the groom, but that may have been because Grierson barely reached his shoulder. "All the best, Grierson," he said finally, casually, and turned to leave.

"You're not leaving yet?" Betty cried, and reddened. Which did not escape Rigby. She was trying hard to control herself. She hadn't seen Alexander for a long time. He looked very much alive and as enigmatic as ever, like a giant python in the bush. His eyes glowed just like one.

"I'm terribly sorry, but I have visitors from California," he said gently.

"I thought they visited you a few weeks ago!" said Betty. It just slipped out.

Rigby was almost touched by her naiveté. "They postponed their visit, if you don't mind. All the best, girl. I've got to go."

"Stay!" Betty cried impetuously. Something was tying her up in knots. Fortunately Frank was talking to some friends from Brisbane. He had turned his back on Rigby. Frank was no fool, and everybody who knew him well knew it.

"You can't leave right away, just like that, Alex!" said Betty in a choked voice.

"Were you planning to take me on your honeymoon with you?"

He turned brusquely and left the big reception room in which, seven years ago, he had introduced Anne to his sister.

Grierson grew more and more impatient. The papers had everything they wanted, but he didn't have everything he wanted yet. He was happy to see that Betty was now ready to leave. She ran, eager as a little girl, over to Miss Rigby with whom she had worked and been friends for so long. Happy, rich years. Miss Rigby had protected her without mothering her. Suddenly Betty couldn't speak. Frank Grierson was standing beside her like a sentinel.

"Thanks so much for everything!" Betty finally managed to say.

"Don't forget Sydney, little one. And when you need your thirty-five medications, write to me."

"Believe it or not, Miss Rigby, we have pharmacists in Brisbane too," said Mr. Grierson.

Miss Rigby ignored the interruption. "When do I get the next manuscript, Betty?"

"As soon as I can, Grace. Promise!"

"First we're going on a honeymoon," said Mr. Grierson.

Miss Rigby also ignored this bit of information. "Be careful not to catch cold, little one. We'll send you anything you may have forgotten."

"Which will be just about everything," said Mr. Grierson. "But from now on I'll be looking after Betty's luggage."

"I've reserved the loveliest room in the house for you, Grace. You must visit me often."

"I have a small career on the side," Miss Rigby said drily. "But it's sweet of you."

She adjusted Betty's hopeless hairdo and held her protégée close for a moment. "Do your best, child. I don't want to hear any complaints, Frank."

"I never complain, Miss Rigby." Grierson's smile was ironical. He had had enough of the Rigbys, of Sydney, and of the circus on Bellevue Hill.

Miss Rigby had had enough of Betty's wedding too, but she still had to go through the traditional post-celebration in Manly. It would all look exactly like Alexander's fiftieth birthday, only she would feel the emptiness. Alex should have sacrificed this evening for his sister; it would have been the thing to do. She had sacrificed more than one evening for him when the scandal over Flora had hit him hard. Grace Rigby smiled stoically at a few latecomers, a famous lyricist from New South Wales, the gossip columnist from a rival magazine, and Mr. F.B. Lawson, one of the most important backers of *Insight*. "May we expect further contributions from Miss West?" he asked Grace Rigby in the course of their conversation.

"But of course! I'll see to that, if I have to go to Brisbane personally to get them!"

"I wouldn't put it past you." Mr. Lawson laughed, and Miss Rigby joined him. "You're unbearable, Grace! The pioneer spirit! What would we do without you?"

"That's what I'd like to know too," Miss Rigby said. She was satisfied.

Rigby drove straight to Vaucluse. The house was empty. Mrs. Andrews was on vacation. She was visiting her married daughter in Mittagong.

The brand new son-in-law would be delighted, Rigby thought, as he walked onto the terrace. There was nothing as empty in the world as an empty terrace.

He got a beautifully bound book from his library, a monograph on Edmund Blacket, who had designed the universities of Sydney and Melbourne, and several cathedrals, schools, hospitals, and department stores. Blacket was also one of those architects who had begun gradually to transform Sydney into a metropolis. Rigby studied his plans. You couldn't think of Sydney without thinking of Blacket.

Edmund Blacket had landed in Australia on October 3, 1842. He and his wife had come to the colony as free immigrants. Blacket's first impression in the harbor of Sydney had been the tower of the Church of Saint James, which Francis Greenway had built. A clear line ran between these early architects to Marchmont, Rigby & French. But those immigrants of the mid-nineteenth century had still been so closely tied to the motherland that Edmund Blacket's first lodgings had been close to the Methodist chapel in Sydney, because the landlady reminded him of someone he knew well in England. And for that reason alone, the man had settled down in Princes Street. Rigby frowned. Princes Street, and the chapel with the Doric-columned portal, had disappeared long ago. Anne was like Blacket. Since nothing in Sydney reminded her of Avenue Road, she had gone back to London. Pommies remained pommies!

Rigby looked at the plans for the country homes Blacket had designed for prominent members of the colony. Gothic arcades in the Australian landscape! Had Sir Thomas Mitchell, the Colonial official who had traveled around the world, wanted arcades for his Park Hall? Probably. These people had preserved their English outlook on the new continent. Marchmont, Rigby & French, on the other hand, aspired to an open-air synthesis in house and garden. Frank Lloyd Wright, the great American architect and city planner, had already tried to introduce this to the Midwest bourgeoisie in his country. The Japanese had been doing it for centuries. And here, in Australia, there was a new feeling for the endless spaces. The creators of a freed architecture smiled at the megalomania expressed in styles that were foreign to the land. Informal arrangements with wide, sliding glass windows and sundecks, had replaced the old-fashioned, unimaginative symmetry. Strange, thought Rigby. Architecture seemed to be far more advanced than the people who brought their dusty conventionality into these new buildings.

Rigby sat motionless, watching the darkening harbor scene. His own marital conflict could have taken place just as well in Victorian England, in festive rooms dimly lit by crystal chandeliers, with heavy drapes, clumsy furniture, hideous little ornaments, and a few really beautiful pieces of porcelain that were in everybody's way, just waiting to be knocked down. Formal, straitlaced sentimentality. Not a piece of furniture built in; everything on display as in a high-class junk shop, creating a static, stuffy atmosphere in which no Aussie could breathe! Of course buildings and furnishings had changed with time also in Europe, but more slowly, and soul and spirit came limping behind. Anne, with her narrow waistline and her long, slim neck would have fitted charmingly into one of those Victorian dresses, stiffened with whalebone, that contained the human body like valuables in a safe. In Rigby's model house in Vaucluse she had been as cold and reserved as her ancestors in their Victorian salons. For a moment Rigby had the impression that the technology of the twentieth century played rounders with its dull victims . . .

He closed the illustrated Blacket biography with a bang and began to smoke hastily as he crept out of the glassy light of ideas into the morass of emotions, and called himself to order. Did he want to end up in a labyrinth of unfulfilled wishes? Ridiculous! When you looked soberly at your losses, they could be transformed into winnings. Stanley Marchmont had always known how to do that. Grace managed it silently. Why couldn't he? Why, at his age, was he still unable to master the bookkeeping of his emotions? Why had Betty's wedding thrown him? She was neither his wife nor his lover. But for years she had been a source of joy and vitality for him, and he could not reconcile himself to the fact that this source had dried up.

He looked at his watch. He had spent nearly three hours studying Blacket's blueprints. Right now his house in Vaucluse resembled a ground plan; by chance a few pieces of furniture stood in it. Rigby stood stock-still on the terrace for a moment. Miss Rigby's guests would have left Manly by now so as to be back in Sydney before dark. How would it be if he kept Grace company tonight for a change?

So Rigby drove to Manly. He was in good spirits again and hummed his favorite song from the Outback:

> Get a bloody move on!
> Have some bloody sense!
> Learn the bloody art of
> Bloody self-defence!

"What do you want here?" asked Miss Rigby. "Everybody's gone."

"I want to eat. Did the mob leave anything?"

"Go and look. I've run around enough for one day."

"No more weddings?" Rigby grinned.

Later they grilled steaks, and fried potato sticks, just as they had done years ago after the death of their mother, when Grace had looked after her younger brother in Parramatta, before Rigby had burst into the lives of Anne Carrington, Flora Pratt, or Elizabeth West.

Grace ate heartily. She discovered to her astonishment that she had eaten practically nothing all day. Funny! She yawned, unabashed.

"Good night, old girl," said Rigby. "Get a bloody move on!"

Alex went walkabout for a while. Manly in the evening was refreshing. There were very few people on the ocean promenade. Somebody called out, "Hello, Alexander!"

Rigby turned around, annoyed. *That* was all he needed: Shirley Cox, his wife's bosom friend! Anne probably wrote a letter to her every week. The devil take all women!

"Hello, Shirley!" He smiled brightly. "What are you doing in Manly?"

"We were visiting friends." At that moment a blond, tough-looking man with sharp eyes and curly hair walked up to them. Shirley introduced her brother. Inspector Cox of course knew who Rigby was. Who didn't know Rigby in Sydney? Friends of the Coxes had had a crazy house designed for them in Manly. Cox had read the rest about the great Rigby in the daily papers. His fiftieth had really been a good show. Cox looked at the architect with interest, and expressed his pleasure at meeting him. Rigby, stony-faced, also remembered from the newspapers that Cox had recently solved a sensational murder case. Mike Browne, a chauffeur from Sydney, had been the murderer.

"Are you working on another murder, Inspector?" Rigby asked casually.

Cox laughed. "Are you building another house, Mr. Rigby?"

They drank beer at Rigby's place and talked about all sorts of things: the theatre, sports, and of course, new building. Anne wasn't mentioned. The Coxes left in fine spirits and Rigby accompanied them to the promenade. Then he walked off in the other direction. It was much too early to go to bed.

"How do you like the great Rigby?" Shirley asked her brother. Inspector Cox hesitated. Finally he said jerkily: "Not average. Hard to read. A little too amiable."

"Anne often complained about his unfriendliness. A lousy husband."

"That's often the case with impressive men," Inspector Cox said drily. "Nowadays most marriages are threatened. I'd like to know what Rigby has to complain about."

"Not a thing!" Shirley said angrily. "Anne is a saint. But in the end she lost patience."

"Just what is to be expected from a saint?" Inspector Cox lit his twelfth cigarette.

"Don't smoke so much," Shirley said irritably.

"Tell me, Shirley, some time in the Dark Ages, wasn't there a scandal about Rigby's first wife? I heard something to that effect."

"The first Mrs. Rigby met with an accident in the Blue Mountains."

"Was she drunk?"

Shirley laughed. "She's supposed to have been a bar girl. Much older than Rigby. Anne heard about it first from Miss Rigby. He hadn't told her a thing about it. What do you think of that?"

"Very sensible of him. There's much too much talk. What was the old girl's name?"

"Flora."

"And the rest?"

"I've forgotten. Why? Does it interest you?"

"Not especially. Rigby has a beautiful house here in Manly."

"He's a horror. But I'm sure he's not guilty in any way of his first wife's death," Shirley said quickly. She shouldn't have said anything. With her brother you never knew when it registered or when he'd choose to pick it up again. "I'm sure Anne will come back soon," she said. "How did you like her, Curl?"

The inspector had seen the second Mrs. Rigby frequently at Shirley's house. "I liked her. Why not? I'm not married to her!" He laughed, and Shirley laughed with him.

"Anne is sweet. When you think what a tough time she had with Rigby . . ."

"In what way?"

"He looks at every girl."

"He's got to look somewhere."

"I can't stand him," Shirley said angrily.

Her brother looked at her, astonished, and she blushed. "But don't think because of that, Rigby did away with his first wife!"

"I never think anything," Inspector Cox said calmly. "I believe only in facts. Besides, the Rigby scandal is water over the dam. I must have still been in school at the time."

A cool breeze wafted over the ocean. Shirley shivered slightly. Conversations with her brother sometimes had such curious endings. What had she said about Rigby? Why couldn't she stand him? He was very good-looking . . .

"Listen, Shirley . . . I've rarely enjoyed myself as much as tonight."

"Thanks for the compliment."

"Sorry, but for once I mean Rigby. He makes one want to be an architect," Inspector Cox said dreamily. "He knows what he's talking about."

Perhaps Rigby also knew what he was silent about. "Come on, Shirley!" Inspector Cox said, suddenly lively. "Get a bloody move on!"

20

My Forefather's Name Was Adam

Dear Alex,

I should have answered your letter long ago, but it is so difficult, and I tend to put off difficult things, hoping that time will help. But it only hurts ... The longer I carry this unwritten letter around with me, the more difficult it becomes to write. My reticence drove you crazy for seven years. I hope you get annoyed with me now for the last time.

I acknowledged your Christmas gifts and the checks long ago, by wire. It is truly scandalous to thank you for them with the right words at the end of May. They are all so wonderful—no wonder, with your exquisite taste—and much too valuable. I don't wear brocade dresses here, not even an evening dress. Why should I? And for whom? It's draughty here in summer and winter, so I've slipped back into my London uniform: jerseys and sweaters. I've packed away my beautiful robe from Sydney too. In the early morning the only people who see me are the milkman and Miss Jennings. Mother breakfasts in her room with her various corpses and the murderer of the chapter before the last. I mean, that's when he's revealed as the murderer for all to see. It doesn't interest me. Mother is unbelievably busy and writes so fast. Every thriller takes her about six months, and she works until late in the night. She still can't get over how I just sit around. But I don't just sit around. I go for walks in Primrose Hill Park, and brood. If you can recall, it's my only true talent.

I know how much you like to give me beautiful things, Alex, and I was very touched that you still remember my favorite color. I thought you'd forgotten everything. I really got that impression during the last years in Sydney. Forgive me for mentioning it. I know how you hate complaining women. You said once they were as attractive as vinegar in oatmeal.

Miss Jennings sends you her very best greetings. She goes crazy when I talk about Sydney. She would have fitted in better there. How you do love that city! Of course nobody can resist its influence, but for me Sydney has too much fireworks and too little substance. Forgive me for boring you again with my opinions. I simply don't fit into such dynamic, ambitious, and extravagant surroundings. You didn't choose Sydney as your home for nothing. You are wonderfully suited to each other. Perhaps you and I would have had a better life together if you had stayed in Parramatta. I was in your native city with you twice, and felt the calm every country town radiates, even today. But perhaps I would have been able to cope better with Sydney's incomparable atmosphere if you hadn't left me alone so much. Why didn't you help me? You knew how slow I am. No, that's nonsense! I realize today that with your stormy vitality you couldn't have had any understanding for my tempo.

Dear Alex, I shall try to explain the necessity of our separation to you. Believe me, I am sad about the failure of our marriage. A lot of it is my fault. I was always an unsatisfactory person. Mother and Miss Jennings would corroborate that. I am so ashamed of my withdrawal because it solved nothing. But I don't want to go on ruining your life. I know that some time, somewhere, you will find a suitable partner. You are so much younger than I am.

Your suppositions are all wrong, Alex. I don't have another man in London. I have nobody at all and feel just as superfluous as before my Australian adventure. Perhaps I was away from London too long. Most people have forgotten me. I can understand it, and am not offended. I try to live with myself. This is difficult but—forgive me— not quite as difficult as living with you! Perhaps the relationship between every man and woman is difficult, but nothing is left of our marriage after seven years but a catalogue of guilt feelings on both sides. What has become of our hopes? Perhaps one shouldn't build such a realistic institution as marriage on hope. Our illusions are of course our private possessions. That's why I'd rather bury them alone.

Perhaps I really am an "old maid" by nature, as you reproach me. You write, "My forefather's name was Adam." I know that, dear, but there are many ways of being close. I couldn't bear your sporadic love making any more because you became increasingly alien. For me love and marriage mean the efforts toward intimacy.

It is very difficult for me to write you all this, but I had to explain to you why I can't come back. Neither of us are going to, nor can we change.

The spatial distance between us has helped me to understand you better. I hope that you too know me better now and realize that my little store of initiative is exhausted.

You know how very honestly I thank you for everything you have done and are still doing, for Mother and me during these years. May I beg you, please, not to send me anything more because I have taken a job as a secretary.

If you really want to talk things over, then come to London, please. But don't think you can change my mind. Poor Alex—you were badly served with me!

You are and remain my best friend, and I would be sorry to lose you entirely.

Farewell. I shall always feel indebted to you.

Anne

Rigby sat in front of his cold breakfast. Anne's letter had robbed him of his appetite. That had happened to him only once before in his life: when the scandal over Flora Pratt broke out. He crushed Anne's letter in his fist and rammed it into his trouser pocket. Shouldn't he be congratulating himself that he was finally rid of this interminable brooder? But if Anne thought he would marry for a third time, she was on the wrong track. Way off! He was doubly annoyed because right now he could see her so clearly. What on God's earth did he see in this colorless, slow, discontented person? Anne was suffering from an inner life that had turned sour. She wanted a paradise without Adam. The devil take it!

Rigby decided not to give the nonsensical letter another thought. He had never understood Anne. A blessing that he was now free of a condition that was sapping his vitality. Rigby shook himself and was pleased.

He was still pleased when Mrs. Andrews appeared. She wanted to speak to him. He might have known it. She stood in front of him, motionless. What was wrong with her? Finally she came out with it. Rigby was stunned. She couldn't be serious! Mrs. Andrews wanted to leave! Impossible! She was as much a part of the inventory in Vaucluse as the harbor terrace, his workshop, and her goulash! But Rigby's jewel had made up her mind to move to her daughter in Mittagong. She had felt terribly forlorn lately in Vaucluse, and her daughter needed her. Daisy had married too young, and now she was expecting a baby. Her son-in-law too had begged Mrs. Andrews to come and live with them. The young man had taken a position in Blackheath, in the Blue Mountains. It was a well-known resort, seventy-five miles from Sydney, which could be reached easily by train. Mrs. Andrews wanted to spend the rest of her life there, recovering from Mr. Rigby. She could wander around in the Megalong Valley, and in the farming country all around, instead of being bawled out all the time . . . Naturally she didn't say any of this. All she said was that blood was thicker than water. Rigby shuddered at the cliché.

"Naturally I shall wait until Mrs. Rigby has come back from London," said Mrs. Andrews.

"I have no idea when she'll be back," said Rigby. "Her mother is seriously ill. Blood is thicker than water."

Mrs. Andrews reddened with anger. "Then I'll stay until I've found somebody suitable to take my place," she said stiffly.

"You don't have to do that, my dear. Miss Rigby can send me one of her retired photo models. Good morning." And he tore off to his car.

Mrs. Andrews watched him go. Unbelievable! She had lived for this man for years—on an excellent salary, granted—and now he didn't seem to give a damn whether she stayed or left!

Of course she *was* leaving. She had only half made up her mind. She hadn't expected Mr. Rigby to fall on his knees and beg her to stay, but *now* he'd gone too far! Nothing seemed to mean anything to him. A true Aussie! And if she had to spend a hundred years in Australia—her great-grandfather had died at the age of ninety-two and a half—she would never grow accustomed to the insufferable rudeness of the Australians! If an Aussie happened to have feelings, he hid them like gold dust in the sand.

Mrs. Andrews wasn't getting any younger—lately she'd had to admit it—but she still had feelings, and showed them, as had been customary where she came from. Rigby became more incomprehensible daily. He was full of contradictions, and sometimes she was afraid of him. Before his second marriage he had dragged her off into the bush once, at night. It had been gruesome! Mrs. Andrews had never seen flying mammals before. The gray-white animals with their fluttering eyes, gliding along the ground, had flown up suddenly between the eucalyptus trees and wound their long tails around the branches. She had screamed! Rigby of course had laughed. Then he had explained that in Australia nature showed imagination. Europe was a boring continent. The birds flew and the mammals stuck on the ground forever. Whom did it interest?

She had stared at him. Suddenly Rigby himself seemed like a gliding horror, who would crouch quietly on the ground and then, suddenly, with a giant leap, disappear into the dark. That was the time when Rigby wasn't sleeping with his pretty housekeeper any more because unfortunately she served only what was to be expected. But at the time she had still been desperately in love with him. Of course the night in the bush died away as if it had never happened. For months Rigby showed her his everyday face and roared his disapproval when the food wasn't to his liking. In the end Mrs. Andrews thought she had dreamt it all.

She decided to look in the Hungarian restaurant in King's Cross for somebody to take her place. Even if Rigby kicked her around, she loved her enemies. She would find a cook for him, not bad, but certainly not as good as herself. Rigby should know whom he had thrown out! By now she was convinced that *Rigby* had fired *her*. What a dirty thing to do! She took away the breakfast dishes, trembling with rage. Rigby's big teacup fell on the floor and broke. In Sydney, broken china was unlucky. In Australia everything was different . . .

Mrs. Andrews understood for the first time why the second Mrs. Rigby had moved out. Rigby would grow old and ill and die forsaken by everyone. The idea cheered her up. Although right now Rigby was enjoying the best of health and looked it, misfortune moved fast! The new Australians knew this from living in more thoughtful continents. Mrs. Andrews had often imagined how she would be the only one standing at his deathbed. *That* dream he had shattered!

She walked into the bedroom and told the maid, in Rigby's tone, to get a move on! Mrs. Andrews tore the bedding off the bed and threw it on the floor, where it collected some dust, and watched Bessie Towner make the bed. Then she rode off on her bicycle to do the shopping. Bessie, who had only been working in the empty house for a few weeks, sat down on the terrace, lighted one of Rigby's cigarettes, and made fresh tea for the gardener and herself.

A wonderful job! Bessie worked only in houses where there was no wife. Mrs. Andrews could rant as much as she wanted to, Bessie Towner knew how to handle new Australians in her sleep! First, Andrews should learn to speak English. She spoke too harshly, and the abos had made mashed potatoes of the language. The gardener suggested a picnic for the weekend. Bessie would see what Rigby's refrigerator could contribute, not too noticeably. "Okay, mate?" asked Miss Towner.

"A-okay," the young gardener answered, grinning. For Bessie Towner of Surry Hills, life in this house was one continuous picnic.

Rigby couldn't agree. His jewel had ruined his home for him as far as this weekend was concerned. By the time he had finished his business correspondence, it was eleven o'clock. Too late to arrange anything with his friends. They were all happily married now, and when things weren't going too well, they spent the weekends together anyway. Miss

Rigby was entertaining guests in Manly, and Rigby was not in the mood to meet people from *Insight*, or even worse, poets! Grace always warned him ahead of time. When Rigby and his cobbers used the country house, she stayed in Sydney. It was an excellent arrangement, but this time it left Rigby at loose ends. Involuntarily he recalled several very nice weekends he and Anne had spent together. Then he had belonged somewhere and hadn't had to arrange anything. He shuddered when he thought of the empty terrace in Vaucluse. Foolish of him, but Miss Rigby's *Insight* party made him think of the model, Candy. He hadn't thought of the pretty little thing for ages. During the last months he had spent most of his free time with Paddy Trent, but Paddy had become a regular stay-at-home. When he wasn't getting along with Klari, you could go horse-stealing with him!

Why shouldn't Rigby treat himself to a fun weekend with Candy Blyth? Why was he avoiding the sweet little thing like the plague? Suddenly there was no reason any more to start a new life. The old life had had its charms too. The wise, self-possessed Rigby of the last months was suddenly in a state of revolt again, which could spell danger for his steady, middle-class existence. His wife had evoked this mood automatically. That had been her second great talent. When he found the conditions under which he was living insupportable, he reacted like this, had done so even in Flora's time. Now, ten years later, it was being alone that he couldn't stand. "It's just lasting too long," he had told himself aloud sometimes during the last weeks. The repugnance he felt for his present way of life had driven him to the bars of Sydney. He had never drunk so much as in these past months. Although he could tolerate astounding amounts of whiskey or beer, still Dr. Dobson had told him to take it easy with the drinking, and for once in his life he had accepted advice. He had big building plans and needed a clear head. Anne must have left him her headaches. He had never had a headache in his life, not even while he was being suspected of having murdered Flora. Perhaps they came on because he couldn't stand rejection. Then nothing helped—neither alcohol, philosophy, nor hours in the surf. For his restoration he needed the uncritical admiration of a young woman. His forefather's name was Adam.

Rigby had arrived at William Street.

A neat young thing stood facing him at Mrs. Doody's boarding-house. Nothing to be said against the sheila except for a birthmark on her left cheek, but her beautiful hair almost covered it.

"May I speak to Miss Blyth?"

"She's away."

Why did the young girl stare at him so? What was the matter with her. "When is she coming back?"

"Please, won't you come in and sit down?"

Rigby was led into what was probably the "parlor," a room filled with dank air, ghastly furniture, and a plaster statue of the Virgin Mary. It turned out that Miss Blyth, like every good Aussie, had gone walkabout.

Miss Fleet had no idea where Candy might be right now. She was looking at "Mr. Ritter" as if hypnotized. Almost pleadingly. Rigby was surprised. What was there to look at? Was the girl bonkers? Oh no! The young thing was sunk in admiration. Exactly what Rigby had missed for such a long time. This sheila had enough gumption to differentiate between a boring buffalo and an amusing man.

Rigby's mood improved at once. He even smiled at the young sheila. She seemed to be the victim of an empty weekend too. Rigby's disappointment that Candy was away had disappeared. From far away she was ineffective. She was Eve and Lilith in one small package, granted, but she wanted to be admired all the time. Actually a rather boring noodle.

"What do you do on your weekends, miss?" he asked. Fatherly tone. "Are you going out with your boy friend tonight?"

Miss Fleet blushed. She was alone in the house. Mrs. Doody was visiting her friend with the wooden leg. Charlie Rainbow was holding forth with his cobber on the city limits about the old Australians who weren't really as old as the abos were. Gretchen had gone to Marouba with her fiancé. Every weekend the young couple forgot that Molly Fleet existed, but Molly didn't take offence because six days a week Gretchen was a nice, helpful person. Since her last experience in Parramatta, Molly knew that sooner or later a third person would always come and disrupt a beautiful friendship. She could of course have gone on an outing. Sydney was a wonderful starting point for outings. But foolish as it might be, Miss Fleet couldn't stand the sight of so many loving and married couples. She murmured something about having nothing planned, and that this was unusual. Rigby got the message.

Miss Fleet walked over to the window and with an abrupt motion tossed her hair forward over her cheek. She had an adorable profile. Rigby studied it as a connoisseur. Why shouldn't he give this lonely sheila a little pleasure? She didn't seem to have a soul who cared about her. And funnily enough, neither did Rigby!

"Who'd ever hang around Sydney on such a beautiful day?" he said. "Would you like to drive to the Blue Mountains with me?"

"I . . . with *you?*" Miss Fleet was blushing like a schoolgirl. She could barely breathe for joy. At first, because of her mature figure, Rigby had taken her for twenty, but she couldn't be more than eighteen, at the most. He wondered if she'd ever had a go with a man. He doubted it.

"Take a coat along, miss. It gets cool in the evenings in the mountains."

Miss Fleet tore upstairs and put on her best, light-blue dress. She couldn't grasp what was happening. Rigby—of course she would address him as Mr. Ritter—didn't seem to find anything wrong with her face. She poured half a bottle of perfume over herself, unfortunately also over the dress, and put on the opal ring Miss Conroy had given her. Then she powdered herself and arranged her mane of hair. Her big, floppy hat covered her left cheek almost completely. She presented herself to Rigby like a child thirsting for praise.

"You look very nice." Rigby ignored the radiant schoolgirl face.

During the drive to Katoomba, Rigby was enlightened about the character and habits of Miss Blyth. The explanation was longer than the Great Western Highway. He smiled indulgently. Women could not keep friendships. Miss Fleet didn't have to protect him from Candy Blyth. He had dealt successfully with more dangerous snakes. But he found out, to his astonishment, that his virtuous cobber, Patrick Trent, who prayed for him every Sunday, had visited Miss Blyth regularly for quite some time. That took the cake! "But Mr. Trent didn't have an affair with her. He's not her type," Miss Fleet went on hastily. Rigby couldn't imagine, however hard he tried, Paddy Trent visiting the young lady for her intellectual charms. Naturally he wouldn't say a word about Paddy's little indiscretion, especially since his wife, whom Rigby had witnessed two-timing Paddy a while ago in an Hungarian restaurant, was expecting a baby. It had saved Trent's marriage, and that was why Rigby was driving to the Blue Mountains now with this little girl. She must have been the one who had massaged his wife. There couldn't be two masseuses with a birthmark running around in Sydney!

Miss Fleet was a good hiker. She didn't take tiny steps like the first Mrs. Rigby on her high heels, nor did she complain, like the second Mrs. Rigby of headache and backache. Miss Fleet was a robust, solid creature. Rigby laughed aloud several times. The girl was really quite comical, and she worshiped him. She favored him with her exquisite profile as much as she could, the intelligent young thing! And then they were standing on a dizzifyingly high plateau, watching the sun set and looking across at the Three Sisters. These sandstone crags, swathed in gold by the setting sun, rose up high above the abyss of the Jamieson Valley. The plateau lay there in deepest silence. They were among the last visitors. Although Sydney was only thirty-five miles away, thousands of years separated the city from the primeval landscape. Here, in the old days, the blackfellows had wandered, designating the rocks, the streams, the valleys, and the sky as the homes of the spirits of nature. The vast forests, surrounded by stone, were already wrapping themselves in the veils of night.

"In the morning a blue mist covers it all," Rigby explained.

"Really?"

"Do you hang around Sydney all the time, Miss Fleet?"

"I used to hang around Parramatta. That's where I come from."

Rigby was silent. A twisted path had led him from Parramatta to the Three Sisters. They towered, monumental, over the abyss of time. Trees and fern grew around the crags, and some distance away, a few Australians had built their homes. They fought for bread and love, multiplied, had to adapt constantly to the shifting aspects of life, and innocently obeyed the laws of being born and dying. In his youth, Rigby had thought he stood like these craggy eminences: nothing could change or shake him.

From below came the gurgling sound of water cascading over precipitous rock. A call, a song, a cry . . . Rigby listened. "It must be like this in Switzerland," said Miss Fleet.

"It's like this in New South Wales. Good enough for me."

Molly looked at him shyly. Suddenly he was a total stranger, unfriendly, almost somber. She walked over to the edge of the plateau and looked down. Rigby yelled, "Careful!" and pulled her back brutally. "Are you crazy?"

Miss Fleet laughed. "I don't get dizzy."

She rubbed her arm, which hurt where he had grabbed her. Rigby apologized, but his mind wasn't on what he was saying. He was staring down at the abyss. This was where Flora had fallen into the depths below. Why in hell did he always come back to the Three Sisters? Only murderers with low IQ's did this sort of thing in the crime novels they sold in Katoomba.

"I'm hungry," he said brusquely.

Night was falling. Rigby led Molly back slowly to the City of the Blue Mountains. Suddenly she stopped dead.

"Are you tired, little girl?"

Rigby was standing close to her. The moonlight fell on his long, fine face, his nose with the arrogant hook, and his light, flickering eyes.

"I love you, Mr. Rigby!"

He was so astounded, he didn't even notice that she knew who he was. Before he could say anything, she had thrown her arms around his neck and was sobbing. Her hat had fallen off, and Rigby could smell the scent of her red-gold hair and her youth. He couldn't help it if youth sobbed and embraced him . . .

"I've loved you forever!"

"Nice of you."

"Not nice. Horrible!"

"Why?"

Miss Fleet said nothing. She covered her left cheek with her hand.

"There's nothing so bad about that, child." Rigby had understood. He looked at the young girl. He was ready to eat his hat if Miss Fleet had ever slept with a man. But no virgins for him. They clung like bees to acacia trees and one was never able to shake them off. He gave the girl a light kiss, and put his arm around her. Molly pressed close to him shyly. He had been right. The sheila didn't even know how to kiss.

"I'll bring you back to the lodge, Molly."

"And where are you going to sleep?"

"With friends." Friends, plural. That was a good idea. It should stop the lovesick little bird in her tracks.

"I . . . I want to stay with you."

"What would my friends say?"

The girl had intuition. She declared there weren't any "friends." Rigby laughed, but Molly Fleet didn't join him. With Candy he would have taken up quarters for the night in his friend's empty villa without giving it a thought. Miss Blyth was hard-boiled!

They drank a beer at the lodge. Rigby didn't entirely believe the young thing when she assured him that Mrs. Doody and Candy really thought he was Albert Ritter. He asked sharply if Molly was lying, but she assured him that she had seen a picture of him by chance when she came to massage his wife, and it sounded true. Then she said nothing more, just sat there innocently devouring him with her eyes.

Rigby thought it over. The girl was in love, beautifully built, and her disfigurement would dissolve in the dark. But he couldn't get Anne's letter out of his mind. If only the little thing wouldn't look at him so imploringly! He certainly had got himself into one hell of a mess!

"Molly," he said gently. "You're a sweet, clever little girl."

No reply.

"You're terribly young. Or are you an old nag?"

"No!"

"You see? And I think that someday you'll want to marry and have children."

"Nobody'll marry me."

"Nonsense!" This child should have seen Flora Pratt! Still, Rigby had married *her* . . .

"I don't even have a boy friend!"

"That's just it," said Rigby. "But you may. Any day. If I were to start something with you now . . ."

"You'd *never* start anything with me!"

"May I finish?" Rigby asked with a trace of impatience. "I'm a rolling stone, little girl. You would cry your pretty blue eyes out. You need someone steady."

"Will I ever see you again?"

"You'll see me tomorrow morning," said Rigby, a little more impatient now. "I want to show you the stalactite caves of Jenolan."

"Oh, that's wonderful!"

"Then we'll have lunch and drive back to Sydney."

Miss Fleet digested this information.

"Whenever I have time, Molly, I'll drive you out somewhere."

"Word of honor, Mr. Rigby?"

"Word of honor. If you like you can call me Alex."

"You're dinkum, Mr. Rigby." She threw her arms around him again and he felt her breasts.

"That's something I like to hear from charming young ladies," in spite of which honeyed words, he pushed her away. She should go before he asked her to stay . . .

Molly walked into her room, partially consoled. A young heart is modest. *He* had said she was charming. *He* had said she had beautiful eyes. *He* had . . .

Molly Fleet slept.

When Rigby got back to Vaucluse, the terrace was already lit up with the white angle lamps. From far off his sharp eyes could detect two men with drinks on the table in front of them. So Mrs. Andrews was still there! He raced like a schoolboy across the garden to the terrace: his cobbers hadn't forgotten him! He recognized Paddy Trent at once by his silhouette, but who was the other man? Rigby had never seen him before.

21

Ovid in Vaucluse

"This is Mr. Muir from Broome." Trent introduced the man. "He's staying with us, and he wanted to meet you, Alex."

Rigby had heard a lot about Muir's visits to Sydney, and looked at the tall man with the bald head and deep-set eyes with interest. Were they Asiatic eyes? The man stood as motionless as a statue.

"What are you doing in Sydney, Mr. Muir?"

"At the moment I am studying Mr. Trent's collection of opals, Mr. Rigby."

"There's nothing very much to it." Patrick never found anything much to his collection nor to himself.

"A very rare collection, my dear friend, or I wouldn't have wanted to see it again."

Rigby mixed cocktails. He had decided that he liked Mr. Muir.

"Would you be my guest tomorrow evening at the Chevron Hilton, Mr. Rigby? With Mr. Trent? I would consider it an honor." Mr. Muir was more formal than any Aussie Rigby and Trent had ever enjoyed drinks with.

"Thank you very much. I'll be glad to come."

There was a pause. Mr. Muir seemed to have no intention of starting a conversation. Rigby stared at him with undisguised pleasure. Funny guy! The man looked forty, then again more like a hundred and forty.

"I would like to discuss a certain business matter with you tomorrow evening, Mr. Rigby."

Rigby hid his astonishment. Why didn't the man say what he wanted right now? Had Trent sold him some real estate in New South Wales? Did he want to have a house built?

Mr. Muir was admiring the harbor scene. He liked the house in Vaucluse. Rigby, in his own way, built according to Japanese principles. Very impressive! Muir had seen residences, schools, and other

266

public buildings in Sydney that all bore the stamp of this architectural firm.

"You've built yourself a very beautiful home here, Mr. Rigby."

"Your house in Broome isn't bad either," said Trent.

"More like a cake with icing than an organism, my friend." Mr. Muir understood the art of understatement of which, generally speaking, only the Japanese and the English were in command. "Have you been to Japan often, Mr. Rigby?" Muir asked abruptly.

"Unfortunately never."

"I thought that perhaps you had gathered some inspiration in my mother's country," Muir said casually. "I would like to express my admiration for your work. You practice architecture as a poetic act on a mathematical basis, and that's the way it should be."

Mr. Muir looked at the indigo-blue water. It was glittering greenly, then gray, then violet. It changed color constantly, thus inspiring waves of meditation. During a walk through the garden, Muir had been struck by how brilliantly the architect had placed solid stone and shimmering glass to face the water, and achieved the effect of the houses seeming suspension in a great sea, participating in the metamorphoses of the elements.

Meanwhile, during the pause in the conversation, Muir had settled down comfortably. He didn't look up until Rigby offered him a cigarette. "Have you read Ovid, Mr. Rigby?"

"The *Ars Amatoria?*" Rigby grinned.

Muir shook his head. Ovid's love poems did not appeal to him. In Mr. Muir's opinion the elegant poet had never experienced grand passion. "I meant the *Metamorphoses.*"

"They're too highbrow for me," said Rigby. "I'm a little man."

Trent laughed loudly and Mr. Muir smiled. He liked Alexander Rigby.

"No, seriously, Mr. Rigby, I have the feeling that you would enjoy Ovid's *Metamorphoses.*

The stranger had hit the nail on the head. The *Metamorphoses* had delighted Rigby since his student days. The constant transformation of gods and humans into animals, plants, and stone; of nymphs into mute islands; the continuous interplay of conversion, change and renewal, of various viewpoints and moods—all of it was his element. Perhaps, in his poor efforts, he was just as much a virtuoso of the surface. Ovid was no mystic. And Rigby liked that. Mysticism came damn close to brooding.

Rigby asked Mr. Muir if he knew a lot of people in Sydney.

"Fortunately, no! Most people are two-legged streams of traffic."

"Or on wheels," said Trent. "Don't make yourselves out worse than you are, my friends!"

Only Trent knew how lonely Alex was. He had written to Anne about it but received no reply. He was very worried about Alex. Didn't the second Mrs. Rigby have eyes in her head? She'd never find a man like Alex again.

"A young lady from Sydney visited me in Broome," Mr. Muir said, communicative all of a sudden. "Trent knows her."

Rigby asked for her name. He was very interested in young ladies.

"Candace Blyth," said Trent. "Don't you know her, Alex?"

"I don't know *all* the young ladies in Sydney."

"She was a model. She used to work for *Insight*."

"Is she dead? Why the past tense?"

"She is more alive than is good for her," Mr. Muir interrupted. "I found her a short while ago in Perth. A few days ago I brought her back to her aunt in Sydney."

Mr. Muir had not yet recovered from Mrs. Doody's "parlor." Miss Blyth's pink room had been another nightmare. He wanted Rigby to build her a small house. The ignorant young thing could then perhaps learn a little something from her surroundings. If nothing else, her beauty would at least have a suitable frame. Of course Mr. Muir saw this house as an investment. Miss Blyth could live in it, and the furnishings would be a gift. But if she scattered her junk and her pink spreads all over the place, he was sorry, but he would have to give her a good beating.

Mr. Muir had picked Candy up in pretty bad shape in a bar in Perth. Until then she had lived on chance encounters. He had bought her clothes, listened to the shabby stories of her adventures, and as a precautionary measure had sent her to a doctor. He had slept with her again only after that. She was more beautiful than ever but got terribly on his nerves. He was sorry for her, of course, but his compassion was tinged with contempt. Well . . . then he had brought her to Sydney. He didn't know why he felt responsible for her, but she always seemed to force her way into his life. As long as he lived in Australia, she was a burden he couldn't shake off. The house would be his last contribution to her welfare because it was his intention to move, in due course, to Japan. In his opinion Miss Blyth suffered from several failings which would prove fatal: she wanted the triumphs of Venus without working for them, and she filled her mind with trivia.

268

"She has no sense and no upbringing," said Muir, to no one in particular.

Rigby said nothing. He was still digesting the news of Candy's return.

"Could I ask you to do me a favor, Mr. Rigby?"

"Certainly."

"Miss Blyth was once quite successful as a model. She sent me several copies of the magazine *Insight*. Could you perhaps do something for her there? Is your sister still editor-in-chief?"

"In full regalia!"

"Perhaps she could be persuaded to make an exception in this case? The little fool has to find work. She seems to be afraid of Miss Rigby."

"So am I!" Rigby said drily.

Mr. Muir smiled for the second time that evening. He gave Rigby a card on which he had scribbled a few words. "Just in case Miss Rigby would like a report on Broome. My secretary does that sort of thing with her eyes closed."

"I'm sure Grace will be very interested, Mr. Muir."

"An excellent magazine. Astonishing, when you think it's a women's paper."

Rigby and Trent looked at each other. A Japanese viewpoint, undoubtedly. Rigby invited Muir for dinner on the following Thursday, and called his sister. She accepted the invitation. She liked to meet interesting people.

Mr. Muir was delighted. At last he'd be rid of Candy Blyth. He wanted to talk about the house in the country with Trent and Rigby in his hotel, but first he had wanted to meet Rigby. He didn't buy a pig—or an architect—in a poke.

After dinner, which Mrs. Andrews had cooked to perfection, Trent left the room to phone his wife. He wanted to know how she felt and to beg her to rest as much as possible. Yesterday she had had stomach pains. Could this possibly harm the child?

"Send Trent to a good doctor," said Mr. Muir.

Rigby was surprised. 'Paddy is too fat, but he can uproot trees."

"I know," said Mr. Muir.

"Our Dr. Dobson is first rate. Internist in Macquarie Street. I mean . . . is anything wrong with Trent? Has he said anything to you?"

"Of course not. I'm afraid Mr. Trent eats and drinks too casually."

"I'll give him hell!"

"I wouldn't do that, Mr. Rigby. Please excuse me if I give you some advice. It would not be wise to alarm him."

"But what's wrong with him?" Rigby asked. "I'd like to know!"

Muir looked at Rigby for a moment silently. A splendid architect but a temperamental man. Impolite, like every dinkum Aussie.

"His breathing isn't right, Mr. Rigby. He is an unusually valuable human being. I want him to breathe for a long time to come."

"I suppose there's too much strain on his heart," said Rigby, feeling a sudden disquiet. He was very fond of his fat friend, very fond indeed. He'd better drag Paddy to Bertie Dobson. At once. Tomorrow. Whether he wanted it or not. Rigby coughed and said, "Excuse me, Mr. Muir. Ordinarily I'm no lamb, but I . . . I'm very fond of Trent." It all came out with great difficulty.

Muir was disarmed. "I understand," he said gently. "Mr. Trent may outlive all of us. There are so many people with dubious illnesses . . . isn't that so?"

"I don't know. Nothing's ever wrong with me."

"You are an exception, my friend. I heal my numerous ailments with regulated breathing and solitude. Trent is about fifty now. I think that is an age when one must face the fact that it is later than one thinks. A definite consolation in this miserable life, is it not?"

Just then Trent came back, beaming. "My wife feels wonderful!"

"And how do *you* feel, you old idiot?" Rigby asked angrily.

"Me?" Trent was surprised. "Don't have time to think about myself. I'm fine, as usual!"

Rigby drank several cups of strong black coffee. Trent sounded worried as he asked how could Rigby possibly sleep after that? "Look after yourself," Rigby said amiably. "I can always sleep."

"One can see that," said Mr. Muir. "I have a natural sleeping medicine for you, Trent." He didn't say what, and Trent didn't ask. It was so unimportant whether he slept or not.

Rigby was in a fine mood. He hadn't had such a nice evening in a long time. Contrary to all expectations, he'd even had a great weekend. He thought for a moment of Molly Fleet. So young and so much in love! Rigby thanked heaven that he had brought the little girl from Parramatta home untouched. He'd ask her out for dinner some time, or go for an outing with her again, since it seemed to mean so much to her. Really a nice, sweet girl. Much more serious, intelligent, and modest than Candy Blyth. According to Mr. Muir, Candy Blyth was considerably soiled around the edges but still looked like an orchid. But he had had enough of her. Odd! He was probably standing on the edge of

270

a metamorphosis again. Did Anne's farewell letter have something to do with it? What could he do about it? Nothing. One should never detain people who were traveling. Rigby smoked hastily. The thought of Anne darkened his bright vision of the future, like an ink spot spreading over white blotting paper. How grateful Molly Fleet had been! For absolutely nothing!

Muir talked about Broome and Japan, and Rigby listened with great interest. Then Muir invited him and Trent to Broome, and said they shouldn't put off the visit for too long because he didn't know how much longer he would be living there himself. Like Rigby he seemed to be thirsting for change.

Rigby had never been to Broome, and promised to come soon. The evening became increasingly congenial. Rigby had forgotten the outing in the Blue Mountains. In a few hours the young thing from Parramatta had faded and become a memory. Tomorrow she would be swallowed up by the daylight. But Molly Fleet had not forgotten Rigby.

22

Miss Rigby's Cold Coffee

From time to time Miss Rigby invited her friends for a cold meal and hot coffee. When she gave her farewell party for Mr. Muir, it was winter in Sydney, but Miss Rigby didn't dream of serving a hot meal in July. Her recipes for convivial professional hyenas were inspired by the refrigerator. Not until late in the night did the survivors grill sausages, bacon and tomatoes for themselves in the huge kitchen on Bellevue Hill.

Miss Rigby and Robert Muir had become friends. They appreciated the differences in their natures. Muir had found his stay in Sydney stimulating this time, thanks to Patrick Trent and the Rigbys. Now he would return to his chosen monotony interrupted only by his guests from abroad. Muir was in a meditative mood as he sat all alone in his room in the Chevron Hilton, furnished with all American comforts. Why had he been distrustful of his Australian compatriots for so many years? Had Sydney changed him? Or had Trent and the Rigbys done it? It seemed to him that the end of his long Australian day was to be enhanced by a glorious sunset. Muir had invited the Rigbys to visit him in Broome, and he hoped to be a host to them later in Japan.

Betty's marriage and Marchmont's illness may have made Miss Rigby more open to new friendships, but she had certainly taken to Robert Muir. Like Alexander, she recognized a free spirit and an individualist from miles away. Marchmont was a free spirit and Betty had imagination, but Muir had both in an elegantly unobtrusive balance which the Rigbys couldn't help but admire. Of course they treated him with perfectly natural friendliness, but that Miss Rigby, after their first meeting, spent some time every weekend with Muir in a restaurant in Sydney or in Manly, was most unusual. The Trents had also occasionally been present, but Mr. Muir could do very nicely without the presence of young Mrs. Trent. That was why he had moved into the Chevron Hilton. How Patrick could stand the young lady day after day was beyond his powers of comprehension. And Klari had once written poetry? Dear God in heaven! Poetry was an intimate dialogue, a delicate act of recognition between a soul and the primeval aspects of emotion. But Mrs. Trent spoke in her coarse and vulgar English solely about social events, the latest electronic gadgets, cars, the peptic ulcers of prominent people, and other status symbols. Sydney's *dolce vita,* the unsure, sleek, Americanized way of life of an urbane society, had not impressed Mrs. Trent. Patrick lived his own life, unperturbed. Muir asked himself if, perhaps before his departure from Australia, he hadn't met the true dinkum Aussies in Trent and in the Rigbys.

He spent most of his time with Patrick Trent. Actually he should have told Trent something he was going to find out sooner or later anyway, but he was silent. What one doesn't tell can hurt no one. He decided quite suddenly to ask Miss Rigby if he could come half an hour before the party, whereupon she had suggested that he breakfast with her on Bellevue Hill.

Miss Rigby, who was not easily surprised, could scarcely grasp what Robert Muir confided to her on this occasion. Her black coffee grew cold. Finally she promised that for the present she would say nothing. Muir asked if Alexander couldn't speak to Trent, and Miss Rigby said she knew her brother was very fond of Patrick, but he had as much tact as an elephant.

"What are you going to do?" asked Muir.

"Something will come to me. Trent left for Queensland yesterday, on business."

"Is he going to stay there long?"

"At least four weeks." Miss Rigby drank her coffee absentmindedly. She felt queasy. Patrick was looking forward so much to the child . . .

Muir looked at her fine, energetic face with its sharp eyes and the narrow, ironic lips. He felt that a human being was hidden behind the façade of this elegant, successful editor, a human being with whom perhaps very few people were familiar. Miss Rigby's persona was of exceptional perfection. Not a crack in the wall of her self-control. But behind this wall Muir realized suddenly, there was a woman who knew that there were tears in things . . .

Grace Rigby took Muir's coffee cup from him. He drank his coffee black, sweet, and boiling-hot. "I'll make us fresh coffee, or you'll hate me."

"Not necessarily. *You* may even serve me cold coffee."

"Since when do you pay compliments?" Miss Rigby asked, laughing.

"I never pay compliments. May I call you Grace?"

Miss Rigby, who lived in an unconventional milieu, had no idea what this request cost a man like Muir, especially since Miss Rigby's bluntness and dynamic energy would be incomprehensible, almost repulsive, to a Japanese. But Grace and he understood each other across the abyss. She had a profound and discreet understanding for Australian mixed races. In this sense she inspired and published a magazine that was read throughout Australia because of its varied points of view and reports. Muir had grasped that the fashion and cookery items were a necessary concession to the women on this male continent. Miss Rigby would have admitted it, smiling, and begged him to keep it to himself.

Muir had described his childhood and youth in Broome. After that they had become friends. Finally Grace had said, "You've had a hard time. But you have imagination, and that gives one power over circumstances. I am only a realist."

And then she spoke to this strange man who had become such a friend, about little Betty West, how she had brought color and joy into her sober working life. Muir sensed how much Grace Rigby was suffering because of the changed circumstances, and to his astonishment it touched him. Although he was considerably younger than she, he was emotionally just as secure and lacking in sentimentality. This wonderful woman needed a friend now to fill the gap Betty West had left. And here was Robert Muir, with his Scottish practicality, reliable and proud and humble as his Japanese ancestors. He was at her disposal. Of course they would only be able to see each other between long intervals, but his future island home in Japan was waiting for her.

His question still hung in the air. Why did Muir want to call her by her first name? Wasn't he a fanatic representative of aloofness, not spontaneous and warm like the Aussies? And of course he despised superficial contacts. In spite of which he was offering her, who did nothing but listen to him quietly, a pearl.

Miss Rigby's reaction was un-Australian. She said she was honored.

Robert Muir's farewell party was a huge success. Important people from the press and writers from New South Wales came, bringing healthy appetites with them. To say nothing of thirst. Robert Muir was introduced to a great many prestigious people and, ridiculous as it may seem, was treated as a guest of honor and interviewed constantly. Very few journalists had visited Broome, but Muir's name and his reputation as an international businessman, along with the stories of his regular visits to New York and Paris, had preceded him. His surroundings did the rest. Miss Rigby indicated that *Insight* was going to publish a series of articles on Broome. "Dammit!" thought her rivals. "She's beaten us to it again!" The Rigby nose was really long.

Miss Rigby's cobbers from the Sydney *Morning Herald* naturally turned up also, and everything proceeded according to plan, just as it had done at Betty's wedding. But today Miss Rigby was in high spirits. She actually looked beautiful, a Diana in a silk suit. She had obviously left her dragon's teeth at the office. She answered all questions about Elizabeth West with the patience of a saint, and what she didn't tell, Alexander Rigby made up for. The journalists were doubled over with laughter. For years there had been rumors in Sydney that Rigby had had an affair with young Elizabeth West. If so, the fellow had latched onto someone else long ago. Nobody asked about Rigby's wife, and it wouldn't have been good for anybody if he'd done so.

Bertie Dobson was present, naturally. He beamed at his young wife and introduced her to the intelligentsia of Sydney. Mavis behaved charmingly and modestly in this new world, and Bertie was bursting with pride. Miss Rigby winked at him. Both of them were thinking of Alexander's fiftieth, when she had tried to talk Bertie into taking on Betty. Miss Rigby was perfectly satisfied with Mavis: a nice, practical girl.

In the middle of all the fun, young Dr. Dobson was called to the phone, after which he told his wife and Miss Rigby unobtrusively that he was leaving, and made his way through the crowd. The conversations continued; Miss Rigby didn't seem to be quite as cheerful.

In a corner some journalists were talking about the daily papers in Sydney, Melbourne, Adelaide, and—in honor of Robert Muir—the press in Broome. Mr. Muir said there was nothing to say about it, it spoke for itself. But nobody could get out of him *what* it said. The guest from Broome was almost as secretive as "our Rigby." After persistent questioning he finally told them that the Australian dailies were easy for teenagers to understand, and gave the impression that they were published mainly for that age group. That might be true for Broome, said a guest from the *Melbourne Herald*. Mr. Muir didn't contradict him. For that he was too polite and too indifferent. He hated any kind of sensationalism, and the Australian ranked the sensational item even above the sports news. How many people read the serious editorials and contributions in the papers and magazines? Pictures, crimes, society scandal, and again pictures. In the larger Australian cities a society bewitched by television and films was in the making which chose only the cheapest, most sensational items, some from the

American press and certain London papers. But Muir said nothing of all this. The men from the press were far too intelligent not to know about it themselves. They wrote mainly for the subscriber—an old story in a young civilization.

Around Miss Rigby there was talk about the problem of power. The men were declaring that women were using their power professionally and privately, to gain ever more prestige. The men on the other hand used the ideas and technology of power for purely impersonal purposes . . .

"Robert," whispered Miss Rigby. "I've just had bad news. Please tell Alexander when our guests have gone. We can't both disappear at the same time."

Muir brought her a brandy. She looked pale but she went right on smiling at her guests who were gradually dispersing. The fun was over again for a while.

"Can I do anything for you?" asked Muir.

"Please stay with my brother. He should come as soon as he can get away." She gave Muir an address. Dr. Dobson had asked Miss Rigby to come first, alone.

Stanley Marchmont was waiting on the harbor bridge to eternity because before the big crossing he wanted to beg Grace Rigby to look after Alex. Marchmont lay quietly and completely conscious in his sunny study on Mosman Bay, and was ready for the trip. It was very quiet all around him. The sounds of this world, to which he had listened tirelessly throughout his entire life, had turned into the drumming of raindrops on a corrugated tin roof in the Outback. It was strange, but even his beloved Sydney, with its high-rise houses and colossal Harbour Bridge, was barely different right now from the Outback. Even if Sydney were to grow farther up into heaven, the city would always remain of this world.

Marchmont had never had much talent for being ill, and he had had quite enough of being bedridden. All he still had to do was tell dear Grace to look after Alex. Who would bring the rascal to his senses when he wasn't there any more to give him hell? Why had Anne run away? He wanted to see Alex once more, but not to tell him off. Grace laid her ear against his blue lips. How weak his metallic voice had become! But she understood every word and nodded.

Alex stormed into the room. His features were distorted, but he forced himself to be calm when his boss gave him a sharp look. "Don't excite him," Miss Rigby whispered.

"Leave us alone." Rigby's voice was hoarse, but Grace had already left the room and was sitting in the breakfast room with Bertie Dobson.

"Alex mustn't stay too long," Bertie mumbled.

"Let him be, Bertie," said Miss Rigby. "It's the way Stan wants it."

Five minutes later Dobson left. Miss Rigby watched him go, but he looked strangely misty. She sat alone in the darkening room and bade Stanley Marchmont farewell. In her youth she had loved him and wanted to marry him, but he hadn't seemed to be aware of her deep attachment. Marchmont had had nothing on his mind but Alex. Like her own father . . . And no wonder. Alex had always been so much more brilliant and charming than she.

Just then Rigby appeared. He looked at his sister as if he had never seen her before and murmured, "He's gone and done it."

He drove straight back to Vaucluse. He wouldn't speak to anybody, he didn't want to see anybody. How fortunate that he was living in an empty house! Grace would understand. She had to understand! He felt torn inside. The spiritual umbilical cord that had bound him to Marchmont since his youth had been cut. How often had Marchmont thrown him out of the old office in George Street, and he had always come back! The silver teapot he had given his boss as a peace-offering . . . in the gray past . . . they had used it to the end. Rigby had seen it on a table in the room of the dying man. That was the moment when this wild, dark pain that was still tearing him apart had overpowered him like a Tasmanian tiger.

Rigby drove slowly up the hill to Vaucluse. The moon was up and was transforming the city that he had discovered as a greenhorn, with Marchmont's help, into a crater landscape—ashen, cold, desolate, a wasteland of stone and dead grass. And still this wasteland radiated merciless beauty, and was chastened by a lively wind. How much ecstasy, how many storms, how many dead had this city seen?

Marchmont had walked in these streets, and now they were empty and filled with dangers. Rigby would grow old, his senses dulled. He would succumb to illness and in the end have to retire. He would experience everything Marchmont had had to experience, but he didn't have Marchmont's dignity, his patience, and his resignation to God's will. He would be just as unable to resign himself to his exit from the stage of life as he had been unable to cope with the loss of Anne. He couldn't resign himself to anything! Marchmont had always said so. Why had everything run so treacherously smoothly for him for so many years? He couldn't shake the thought that at the firm, slowly,

slowly, he was becoming "the old man." Just as Marchmont had. French sometimes jokingly called him just that: the old man. In time it would be meant seriously. Especially when an even younger partner would join them. Which of course would have to take place. Building, the shaping of the future—nothing else mattered. Marchmont had pounded it into him as a young man. And it still held good.

At home Rigby flung himself into a big easy chair and stretched his long legs. The telephone rang. He let it ring until it stopped, discouraged. Rigby had closed his eyes and was going walkabout once more, with his boss.

"Alex doesn't answer." Miss Rigby put down the receiver after her second try.

"Don't let it worry you." Muir had waited for her patiently in the empty reception room and ignored the astonished looks of the housekeeper Miss Rigby had had for years. In the end Mrs. Parker had brought coffee. Miss Rigby had told her what had happened and urged the good soul to go to bed. She could not stand tears. After her vain efforts to reach Alex, she sat in front of her coffee, speechless. Strange, but life kept getting emptier. She took a sip of the coffee and put down her cup. If there was one thing she couldn't stand, it was cold coffee. But life was gradually becoming just that. When one was young, one got all excited over ideas and feelings, then came the lukewarm period, and finally life tasted like ...

Where was Muir? She hadn't noticed his leaving. At that moment he brought in some piping hot coffee.

"What do you think you're doing?" she said gruffly. But the hot coffee renewed her. At last she could talk about Marchmont. Then she got up and walked over to the window. The indifferent night lay outside.

Muir brought a second cup of coffee. She wanted to thank him but didn't trust her voice. Too much had happened in just one day.

"I have to go now, Grace. My plane leaves tomorrow."

"I'll come to the airport."

"Please don't. This is not farewell. When may I expect you and Alexander in Broome?"

"As soon as we can. And ... yes ... thanks for everything, Robert."

Muir looked at Grace Rigby, an intense, melancholy look. He felt that she would not bury herself in her sorrow. Later she took her new friend back to the Chevron Hilton in spite of his protests, and drove to

Vaucluse under the big stars. She saw light in Alexander's study, and hesitated for a moment. Then she drove home. She was very calm now.

She lay awake for a long time that night and thought of her years with Marchmont. His friendship had been a steadying pole in her life. He hadn't had any extraordinary command of words, but it had been a rich poverty. When it counted he could talk, thunder, and convince. He had wielded the whip of perfection over Alexander's head. He alone had made of his young colleague what he was today. But even Marchmont had been unable to prevent the crises in Alexander's private life. Today Rigby was chasing after two or three birds and therefore caught none. Grace sighed. The hours passed by like scornful kangaroos and disappeared in the thicket of time.

Miss Rigby thought of Robert Muir again. He was chasing nothing and no one. Perhaps that was why Australia gave him everything he wanted of the continent. She knew nothing about his life or his relationship to women. Why had he suddenly saddled her again with the model, Candy? Either he wanted to sleep alone for a change, or play Adam with another Eve. That was his business . . .

Miss Rigby could see Candy Blyth: beautiful, young, and hungry for life. A little kitten like that had an easier time with men. She herself had always been too energetic, too cool, too critical. And sometimes she had added more acid to the lemons of disappointment. Of course she had never possessed the sensual beauty that electrified or moved a man, and bound him against his will to create a career for a fool. For years she had run up against closed editorial doors and finally pushed them open with great exertion. But sometimes these doors had closed again, and she had been left standing outside. Alex had always had an easier time of it. Already in his youth, so much had come his way—success, women . . .

Grace Rigby asked herself if she had tried too hard and too often. Would Marchmont have learned to love her if she had been a little more stupid? Or softer? Or more in need of help? No. She could never have brought it off. And so she had had to look on, outwardly unmoved, at how the door to Marchmont's heart had opened hesitantly years ago on an outing to Windsor, only to fall shut again soundlessly. She had never been able to resign herself to it and tried again and again to push the door open. Marchmont was seventeen years older, and had once advised her to find someone her own age. She hadn't had to run after men. Several colleagues had wanted to marry her, but stubbornly she had compared them to Marchmont. That had been foolish. But she had stuck to her conviction that she and Marchmont would have been a good married couple, and she had simply never been able to resign herself to the fact that he thought differently. In the end she had had to realize that a steady drop of water did not always hollow out a stone.

She had also tried to force other things with her will. Today, in her fifties, she knew that it had been wrong. Robert Muir had become her friend without her having to move a finger. Wasn't one supposed to fight for the possession of a heart?

She didn't know. She lay on her couch, sleepless, and groped for solutions. Was she trying too hard again?

It only seemed so. She was on the track of a recognition and was fortunately too weary to pursue it with her razor-sharp logic. Just because of that she sensed suddenly the presence of a providence that unpredictably makes life bearable, even precious, and refreshes the thirsting spirit in a wonderful fashion: when one door falls shut, another opens.

23

Visions in Darlinghurst

There were no visible signs in Mrs. Doody's boardinghouse that Candy had returned. Molly Fleet, Charlie Rainbow, the Umbrella Uncle, Mrs. Doody and Candy spent their days as they always had done, but they kept inconspicuously out of each other's way. There was a tear in the weave of their everyday life which Mrs. Doody mended as best she could every now and then. She hated any unpleasantnesss. *She* was the one who might scold, and she scolded enough for all the rest. And she was especially sensitive about Candy. Nobody was allowed to criticize her. Mrs. Doody had forgotten completely that some time ago she had written her niece a rather unfriendly letter. It had bothered her only for a few days.

Sydney had given Mrs. Doody a hard time. She had had to defend herself for years to the best of her ability. But like every good Aussie, she had mastered instinctively the art of self-defense. She had always been sly; now she had also grown hard. Candy, however, was the painful toe that she hid in her shabby slippers. The logics of feelings are scandalously illogical. So Mrs. Doody was insulted when Molly Fleet quite openly disliked her niece. The two girls spoke to each other only when absolutely necessary. Not that Mrs. Doody noticed it, because she did most of the talking. Molly Fleet continued to write love letters for Candy, but the crazy traveling salesman, who had been so avid for them, seemed to have disappeared into thin air. Candy missed neither him nor Trent. She didn't miss any man; she found them all interchangeable.

Aunt Doody, on the other hand, was not only a member of the clan; she was her mother surrogate. Candy's mother would have criticized her mercilessly and condemned her. *Insight* had not been a success in Kalgoorlie. Mrs. Blyth had looked at her daughter's pictures with horror. The shameless hussy was showing herself to all Australia in a bathing suit! Mrs. Blyth could see Satan behind her daughter's profession.

After her husband's death she had grown even more bitter. She wrote to her sister in Sydney that Candace would come to a bad end, and that *she* was not to blame.

After this letter Mrs. Doody scolded Molly Fleet and Charlie Rainbow, who threw a sofa cushion at her head and "accidentally" broke the old teapot. That evening Mrs. Doody and Charlie were laughing uproariously in the kitchen. Molly, in her room, heard it and ran out into the street. Candy had gone out with a new admirer. Charlie was so full of gin that Uncle Doody, who could drink gin by the quart, shoved him into his room in a rage. Charlie, who secretly loved the old man, brought him another umbrella. Mr. Doody growled: that was the last thing he needed. His room was full of the damn things! He threw the umbrella on the floor and Charlie saw it roll under the bed. He slunk off sadly, but that evening Uncle Doody hung Charlie's present on a hook with all the other umbrellas. Then Charlie was proud. The threadbare umbrella with the split handle had cost quite a bit. You didn't get anything for nothing in Sydney. Charlie also called the old Irishman "Uncle" and made a table for him, which Mr. Doody accepted graciously. He even went so far as to tell Mrs. Doody that the abo was the best lodger in the whole damn house. The old man couldn't stand Candy, but since he was paying no rent, he said nothing. He wanted to thrash the little whore with Charlie's big umbrella, because Candy ignored him whenever they met, so he didn't greet her either.

And then, one day, he "forgot" one of his umbrellas on the staircase. If Charlie hadn't helped Candy to stumble upstairs—the old man had turned out the light too—she might have broken her neck. Mrs. Doody hurled the umbrella into the old man's room and gave him notice for the hundred and eighty-fifth time. Later they were singing Irish songs to the accompaniment of the radio. Uncle Doody and his umbrellas were part of the inventory.

Sometimes, before an earthquake, a tremor runs through the house. The furniture wobbles, the tea cups clatter, family photographs drop off the wall, and a cold shiver passes through the bodies of the inmates. After that, all is still and everyday life comes into its own again. The archangel's trumpet is silenced by the chatter of the morning hour. People talk about the price of eggs again . . . so soothing . . . and tell each other who got married, is traveling, or has kicked the bucket. The heavy silence of the night is temporarily dispelled and waits for the next opportunity to outwit the day. But the day, with its wonderful immobility, is limited.

The night appears punctually and plagues the day-worshipers with nightmares, visions, wild, suppressed desires, and a lust for revenge which no decent person would let cross the threshold of consciousness. The visions are worst of all. They pour like tidal waves across the sleeper, and when he is drowning, he screams for the lifeboat of day. With the day, routine begins, heaven be praised! With the first cup of coffee the specters of our dreams sink powerlessly into the ocean of forgetfulness.

"Do you know who came to see Candy yesterday, Molly?" asked Mrs. Doody.

"No idea."

"Charles Preston! What nerve!"

"Why?"

"Why? The bastard stole from his Mrs. Moneybags in Hobart and he's been sitting in jail ever since. A fine fellow! And now the stinker wanted to get money out of my Candy again. But this time he's come to the wrong address!"

"I thought she was crazy about him. She ran off to Hobart after him, didn't she?"

"Rubbish! He begged her to come. Candy told me so herself. I threw him out. We don't want anything to do with pimps. Besides we need our dó-ré-mi ourselves."

Mrs. Doody drank her fourth cup of coffee. Candy was still asleep. She had had bad dreams in the night and screamed aloud. It had been dreadful. She hadn't really been dreaming, she had *seen* it all. She was walking back and forth in front of a big mirror, a silk shawl across her shoulders. She was practicing a pose for the photoboys. The sun shone through the green venetian blinds and suffused her room with a pallid light. It wasn't the room in Darlinghurst at all. She was standing in the ocean in Manly, mirroring herself in the water. Then she could feel somebody coming up behind her. Suddenly it was darkest night, and she couldn't see who it was. She turned around abruptly, and found herself staring into a huge, fathomless eye. It was not an eye. It was the night, which had always been her enemy. No. It was a man. She could sense it. She wanted to run away, but she couldn't. She turned to face the ocean again because then the eye of night would be behind her. She didn't have the shawl around her shoulders any more, only a rope, and the emissary of the night—it was Charles Preston—pulled at the rope until she couldn't breathe. Then she screamed.

"The bastard was going to choke me!" she sobbed, as Mrs. Doody ran into her room.

"Who, my sugar doll?"

"Charles! You shouldn't have thrown him out. I . . . I'm afraid!"

"You must try to go back to sleep, darling."

"I can't. He'll come back!"

"Rubbish! The bastard knows that I'd get the cops." She gave Candy a sleeping pill, and talked the whole thing over with Uncle the next morning. Uncle said he was willing to wallop the wop over the head with one of his umbrellas.

"Do that! You're an angel, Uncle. My doll is so frightened. I could hear her screaming with Charles."

"Have a gin, Lydia."

"Not in the morning," Mrs. Doody said virtuously. "But thanks just the same." She waddled off into the kitchen and drank strong black coffee with Molly Fleet. Candy's hoarse cries had gone right through Mrs. Doody. Such a beautiful young creature shouldn't have to be afraid.

Candy was right back where she had left off. The photoboys and the *Insight* subscribers were all for her again. Candy had always known that there wasn't another model like her in Sydney, but she wished it would never be night. Others wished that the sun might never set, but what good were wishes when you were faced with the dictatorship of the night?

So they lived as they always had. Nobody in the boardinghouse sensed the fact that the ground was beginning to tremble under their feet. They couldn't sense it because Mrs. Doody's kitchen table wobbled without any geological assistance. One of these days the building commission would come and test the foundation of the house. That's what they were doing everywhere. But no building commission would find out why Mrs. Doody's boardinghouse was trembling, because it was being undermined by hatred.

Molly Fleet from Parramatta hated Candy Blyth.

Candy had always taken everything away from Molly Fleet. First Charles Preston and now Mrs. Doody. They still sat together in the kitchen, and Molly still scrubbed the floor, but it wasn't the same. Mrs. Doody saw and heard no one but Candy. She was too good-natured to give Molly the cold shoulder, but she didn't need her any more. Since Candy's return, Mrs. Doody was as indifferent to Molly as she had been before Candy left. Molly didn't show that she was hurt, but she was. After her departure from the farm, the boardinghouse had become her only home. She had felt safe there. Molly was too young to know that her misfortune was a very general occurrence. Every day people lose something—house keys or money or—people. If everybody were to sing mournful songs or shed tears about it, the world would be a funereal chorus or a drowning planet. Perhaps it would have been preferable for Candy to have hated Molly too. Anything would have been better than the indifference of the Doodys.

Molly could of course have moved, or gone back to her father in Parramatta, but she waited with the stubbornness of youth for Rigby's visit. He had promised her in the Blue Mountains that he would come again to take her for an outing. Molly always kept her promises, and it didn't occur to her that Rigby had simply forgotten her. Perhaps not forgotten, but was just not in a hurry to keep his promise. He was grieving for Marchmont, and there was a lot of work at the office. He spent most of his weekends with his sister in Manly because his empty house seemed emptier all the time. Besides, he and Grace intended to visit Robert Muir in Broome in a few weeks, if French didn't swallow too much water surfing. The junior partner often came to Manly now, with Rigby, when Grace happened to have guests in Sydney. Rigby lived as in a men's club. Molly couldn't know any of this, but even if she had, she would have been on the lookout for Rigby's visit.

Gretchen had married and had little time for Molly. Just the same, she was the only one who hadn't forgotten her, and occasionally invited her to come over. She had attached her bakery to the restaurant, and Gretchen's crumb cake was actually the only thing that hadn't changed in Molly's narrow world.

Gretchen found Molly unusually pale, and urged her to go to a doctor. But Molly wouldn't hear of it. No doctor could help her. She had to accept life as it was. Gretchen meant well as far as Molly was concerned, but she could do very little for her. Why didn't she go back to her family in Parramatta? If she couldn't earn as much there as she did in Sydney, she could work in the brewery, or on the farm. Everything Gretchen suggested during these coffee klatches was very sensible— Molly realized that—but she stayed on at Mrs. Doody's. She dreamt often of the farm, but always with Grandmother Fleet there, and Stephen doing his accounts on the veranda, and his dog sitting beside him at the wooden table.

Molly Fleet didn't scream in her dreams, not did she cry when she woke up. She had met Stephen's wife at their wedding. Jennifer was a good egg. She had asked Molly repeatedly to spend all her free time on the farm, just as before. Molly's room had been fixed up as a nursery, and she was to sleep in her grandmother's room. But the big, old-fashioned room belonged to Grandmother Fleet. Jennifer's lips had tightened when Molly had protested. What nonsense! Old Mrs. Fleet was dead and nothing on the farm belonged to her any more. Jenny's uncle hadn't given them the money because Molly hadn't sold her share of the farm to them. Such stubbornness! Stephen agreed. He had told Molly so. Since then Molly hadn't been to the farm. She only went there in her sleep. There was no end to Grandmother's preserves. Molly ate them every night. The fields had never been so verdant, the hides of the cow so shiny!

Molly helped Charlie Rainbow with his flower boxes. She had to feel something blooming between her fingers and to smell earth even during the day. Charlie Rainbow didn't mind. He respected Miss Fleet and grew miraculous flowers for Candy.

Since Candy had come back to Darlinghurst, Charlie Rainbow hadn't gone walkabout anymore. He waited for her in the evenings as he used to do, and in the morning he tried to catch a glimpse of her when she went out. Unfortunately Miss Blyth often slept so late that Charlie didn't get to work on time, and the harbor boss didn't like that.

Candy found the abo droll. Besides, he was so willing, and everything she asked him to do made him crazily happy. On the day after Charles Preston's visit, Charlie waited for a long time in front of her door. He was bringing her the most beautiful flowers he had ever grown. But what was wrong? When Miss Blyth came out of her room, she looked at him so angrily that he stepped back.

"Get out of my way!" she shrieked.

Wordlessly he held his flowers out to her. "For you, miss!" he wanted to say, but his lips were trembling so, he couldn't get his disobedient tongue to utter a word, and his black eyes clouded over like the night in the bush. Because Miss Blyth, in a fit of rage, tore the flowers out of their box, murdered them by trampling on them, and threw the box down the stairs. "Leave me alone, for God's sake!" she screamed, hoarse with fury. Then she rushed back into her room and slammed the door.

Charlie Rainbow stared after her. Rage sat like a caged animal within the four walls of his soul. Nothing but a muted singsong issued from his throat as he looked at the destruction. He held his kinky head to one side, as if thus he could see the crime in its entirety. His head burned as if the sun had fallen on it.

He didn't go to work but picked up the box with the broken glass cover, the good earth and the crushed flowers in his arms. Uncle Doody had heard the noise and stuck his foxy old head out of his door. "What's the matter, Charlie-boy?" But the abo just stared at him, his lips moving.

"Lydia!" cried Uncle Doody. "Bring Charlie some coffee! The fellow's crook!" Uncle Doody even came down the stairs and took Charlie by the arm gently. "Come, come, young man." He wanted to take the flower box because the abo was swaying like a young tree in a storm. But Charlie howled, tore what was left of his loving gift out of Uncle Doody's hands and ran out of the house.

"He's gone," growled Uncle Doody as Mrs. Doody appeared with the coffee.

"What happened?"

"Ask your dear niece." Uncle Doody's hands were fists in his trouser pockets, and he stumbled, cursing, back to his umbrellas.

Candy listened, yawning, to her aunt's halfhearted lecture. But she was a little sorry that she had been so mean to the poor blackfellow. She had had bad dreams and was scared to death of Charles Preston, and she had to let it out on *someone,* she explained. She would have liked to apologize to Charlie Rainbow, she really would. She even cried a few fat tears. But two days later she had forgotten all about it. After all, she couldn't pour ashes on her head because she'd broken a few flowers.

Three days later Mrs. Doody was standing on her balcony. Wasn't that Charlie Rainbow, sauntering along slowly? "Molly!" she yelled. "Run downstairs! Charlie's standing in front of the door and doesn't want to come in!"

But Charlie wanted to come in. He was only taking a good look at the boardinghouse. As if he didn't know the old decrepit building! Funny fellow.

Candy smiled at him radiantly, and he smiled back. He waited for her in the dark again too. Everything was dinkum again. Mrs. Doody had got excited for nothing, as usual, but she just couldn't stand it when Charlie got hurt in her house! It was his first and only home.

On the following day, a Saturday, Molly Fleet wanted to take a walk through the coffee bars of King's Cross, when suddenly Rigby appeared. *"You!"* Molly stammered. "Is it really you, Mr. Rigby?"

"In the flesh! And the name is Ritter. How are you, young lady? And why so pale? Lovesick?"

At that moment Candy appeared at the top of the stairs, in full regalia. She saw Mr. Ritter and remained standing, rooted to the spot. The fellow looked so much handsomer than she remembered him! "Hey!" she cried cheerily.

"Hey!" cried Rigby, even more cheerily.

He had no idea that Candy was modeling for the magazines again. He never read the stuff. But he hadn't looked at a beautiful girl in weeks, or was it months? Much less taken a bite . . . and now here she was! In his eyes something sparkled that had been snuffed out for a long time, the spark of sex and the arousing of illusions that either die down quickly or start a raging fire.

Molly stood there in her pretty light-blue dress and knew that Mr. Rigby had forgotten her. He was already halfway up the stairs. "Listen to me!" Molly cried out in her despair. "I was the one who wrote the love letters. I . . . I was . . ."

Rigby turned around, surprised. Had the little Fleet girl gone crazy? What letters was she talking about? Of course! Candy's charming letters. Candy laughed shrilly and Rigby had to laugh too. He came down the stairs again and patted Miss Fleet on the shoulder. "Take it easy! You little girls certainly do the craziest things!" Then he ran up the stairs again and disappeared into Candy's room. Later, from behind the curtains, Molly saw them leaving the house, arm-in-arm. It wasn't fair!

Mrs. Doody came home from visiting her friend with the wooden leg and looked for Candy. Then she asked Molly where her sugar doll had gone.

"She's gone out." Molly poured tea and turned her back on Mrs. Doody. She still had on her light-blue dress.

"How's Gretchen?" Mrs. Doody asked, settling down comfortably. "Are they expecting a little one yet?"

"No idea."

"You don't seem to have an idea about anything. Sit down, for heaven's sake! You make me dizzy, running around. Would you like a gin?" Then she gave Molly a sharp look. "What's the matter, child?" she asked, almost gently, but Molly only shook her head like a dummy in the Tunnel of Love at Luna Park.

Night fell over Darlinghurst. Molly Fleet was lying in bed, unable to sleep. Candy had pushed her out of the Tunnel of Love, laughing all the time. It wasn't fair. It would perhaps have been better if Molly had never spent that day with Rigby up in the clouds, weeks ago.

She sighed and took a sleeping pill, which she did rarely, but she had to forget Rigby and Candy. She had always loved the night and wasn't afraid of nightmares. Anything was better than the merciless day.

288

Charlie Rainbow couldn't sleep either. It looked as if Miss Blyth wasn't coming home at all. That wouldn't do. She had to come back. Charlie wanted her to come back.

He stared into the dark and caught sight of a trail. It led from the boardinghouse in Darlinghurst across the city limits into the bush. Charlie had to follow this trail. Every blackfellow knew how to, just as he understood the language of trees and stones.

What did Charlie want any more in the big city anyway? He couldn't part from the beautiful white bird yet, but one day he would be free. No Candy. No more waiting. He just had to be patient.

He walked up to the little window that had been set into his attic room like a dim eye. He saw lightning shoot through the clouds. In the dream age, when this continent had still belonged to the black man, the spirit of lightning had chased all sinners on land and in the water. They could hide wherever they wanted to: in the ocean, in the bush, in the dust of the plains, behind rocks. The lightning had always struck, burnt, riven, and left them to rot under the blazing sun until nothing was lying around any more but bones. Then the lightning had shot back up into the sky. He who sang the praises of lightning stood in the light of justice.

Charile Rainbow sang the praises of lightning. He smiled in his sleep. Was he already seeing the new day? He knew that there were three kinds of days: the dead day of yesterday, the everydayness of today, and the unborn day that dispensed the light of justice. Charlie Rainbow waited in ecstatic expectation.

24

Schlesisches Himmelreich in Parramatta

Molly Fleet, faced again with a lonely weekend, decided without any further ado to visit her father in Parramatta. She couldn't stand it anymore, seeing Candy leave the house smiling blissfully. Of course she was meeting Rigby! Molly was positive of it. Actually the only person Candy saw during these weeks was Charles Preston. On his return to Sydney there had been a tearful reconciliation in the Restaurant Rosso. Dear old Raffaele had overflowed with compassion for the prodigal son. Poor Carlo had been an innocent man in jail. Exactly what one could expect from the police. Mr. Rosso's opinion of the police coincided with that of his Australian compatriots. He had received Carlo with open arms—grand opera in King's Cross! Muriel let "Ha, so you're back in Sydney," suffice. She took things and her waiters as they came. She found Charles Preston more sensible than she had ever known him to be. His experiences in Hobart had evidently had a sobering effect on him. And he brought Muriel's bracelet back to her. He had redeemed it from the pawnshop with his uncle's money. Candy, of course, had melted, as Charles had expected. Both of them were sensualists and lived for the moment. That was Italian, and oddly enough, also Australian. Charles's Ligurian imagination had caught the girl from sober Western Australia. His descriptions were palpable; anyone could have grasped them. He painted pictures of his home for Candy. With a gesture he could describe a landscape, light, colors, flowers, fruit, smiling girls with their hair parted like madonnas, hymns in their voices, a café on a piazza, the outlines of a palace ruin in the background. When Candy asked how he could stand it in Australia after that, he replied that his memories sufficed. Australia was the land of the future. Candy asked him how he thought he was going to manage. Charles shrugged, as if he didn't have a care in the world. Something would turn up. He mumbled, *"Da tempo al tempo."* Leave time a little time. He had inherited the motto. At times like these he was a stranger to Candy, just as he had been when they had first met. Now she had the oppressive feeling that Charles Preston's splendid future would take off without her. What she wanted was for him to stay a waiter and marry her! But she didn't dare express such old-fashioned ideas.

Right now, though, the future wasn't raining any Australian pounds. Charles hated to do it but he had to borrow from Candy. It was more practical to have an egg today than a hen tomorrow. Or a shandy with Candy here rather than a case of wine in the clouds.

Charles Preston didn't put in an appearance at the boardinghouse in Darlinghurst again. That vulgar Irish bitch had hurt his feelings. "The first one to leave an argument is the one with breeding," Charles had finally bellowed at her. Then he had slammed the door behind him.

So Molly never found out about the big reconciliation. Candy had apologized to Charles. She didn't know why she had been so horrid to him when she loved him so much! Yes, in her misery over what had taken place in the boardinghouse, she had thrown Charlie Rainbow's flowers downstairs. Charles listened, unmoved. He couldn't be expected to be interested in the abo too!

Only Molly Fleet looked after Charlie Rainbow. He was just as alone as she was. Molly still stood on the veranda, looking for Rigby, but he never came. She didn't know that Rigby didn't want to see Candy again. She didn't know that being with Candy left him feeling flat. She didn't know anything.

Actually Rigby felt uncomfortable about Molly Fleet. She had looked at him as if he were a ghost when he had come to invite Candy for an outing. Poor young thing! Molly had worshiped him so naively; he really could have been nicer to her. He was always nice to girls when they were nice to him. To make a long story short, he wanted to do something to make Molly happy this weekend. Her youth had done damn little for her. But when he called on Saturday morning to take her for an outing, she wasn't there. Uncle Doody looked at him with ill-concealed disgust. The fellow was too elegant for him. Uncle Doody said he didn't know when Miss Fleet would be back.

Rigby drove to Patrick Trent's house. Klari needed rest in the mountains in Bowral. It seemed to Rigby that lately the Trents weren't as happy as they had been, but he could be mistaken. Anyway, Paddy had time again for his cobber Alex. Everything was a-okay.

At the boardinghouse Rigby had left his regards to Molly Fleet, but Uncle Doody didn't pass them on to her when she came back from Parramatta. He proceeded to hit rock bottom in a miasma of gin and had forgotten his visitor.

Molly expected to find the usual humdrum life at the brewery. Her father had always been grumpy and monosyllabic, and April, with her sour face, used to pore over the accounts like a broody hen on her eggs. For years she had been brooding over nothing but figures. In the evenings Molly and her sister would sit in front of the television while their father, in his room, wondered why his daughters didn't marry. There should be a man in the brewery. He felt his age more all the time, in his legs, at the back of his neck. He hoped Stephen and Jennifer would produce a son who would later remind people that there had been Fleets in Parramatta. He didn't know why the youngest one didn't go out to the farm any more. Mr. Fleet didn't understand his daughters, but he told himself, with some justification, that it wouldn't change anything if he did understand them. It wouldn't bring a son-in-law into the brewery. Lately he had been more friendly to his youngest daughter, since it was evident that April's good looks hadn't done a damn thing for her. She was twenty-seven and souring fast before his very eyes. Nothing he could do about it.

Years ago he had been bitterly disappointed when April's first-rate engagement had been broken off. To this day he didn't know that his youngest daughter, in her childish rage, had written April's fiancé an anonymous letter about April's behavior with the boys. Molly always felt guilty in the brewery. If only she could find a husband somewhere for her sister!

But when Molly arrived at the brewery this time, she noticed a change. April was wearing a green dress and she'd had a permanent. Her red-gold hair was done up high, making her look taller and more elegant. But Mr. Fleet was the greatest surprise of all!

He was in fine spirits, didn't bawl his daughters out, and—wonder of wonders—sat with them for a while in the evening in front of the television set. And on the evening of her arrival, Molly knew why. A European man in the prime of life had been recently employed in the brewery. He appeared for dinner in a neatly pressed sports shirt. His hair was parted with mathematical precision and his tie hung down straight as a dye. He was tall, broad-shouldered, and serious. His slim, well-shaped hands looked as if they were familiar with musical instruments. He smiled in a friendly fashion, a little unsure, and spoke English correctly with a north-European accent. In short: a new Australian. His name was Kurt Hildebrand, and he came from the Polish city of Wroclaw, which before the war had been the German city of Breslau.

"How do you do?" asked Molly Fleet.

To her astonishment he gave a fairly lengthy account of how he did. He took the conventional greeting at its face value. Where he came from, people really wanted to know how one "did"; otherwise they didn't ask.

The new Aussie didn't seem to notice Molly's birthmark. This was not surprising, because he had eyes for no one but April. She was enthroned on her wicker chair as in her best days, smiling and with artificial poise. She felt attractive because a man's eyes were resting on her. Just the same, the effect was cold and indifferent. She had evidently fled from life for too long.

Did Mr. Hildebrand think this was Australian? He stared at April and kept his thoughts to himself.

Kurt Hildebrand was the first German the Fleets had got to know well. This time Molly stayed a week in Parramatta, and found out in what sinister ways many new Australians had reached this sunny continent. It was as if Mr. Hildebrand had kept his experiences stored up inside him for years. Nobody had asked him how he had happened to come storming into the brewery. Mr. Fleet and April never asked questions. As good Australians they minded their own business. That had been the most difficult hurdle for Kurt Hildebrand. In Breslau, the city where he had spent his early childhood, everybody knew what everybody else did. The capital of Silesia was a big, friendly, small town. But Molly asked questions. She knew how hard it was to live without communicating. And so it all came pouring out. In his excitement, Kurt Hildebrand occasionally lapsed into German.

When Kurt Hildebrand was born in Breslau, Germany in 1935, he was no longer able to grow up among poets and philosophers. The Nazis determined what was to be written and thought. The Hildebrands were well-to-do brewers, and their beer was more important to them than politics. That was why they interrupted with "Hush . . . the little one!" when one of them spoke disparagingly about Adolf Hitler in front of six-year-old Kurt. They had voted Social Democrat until one could no longer do so, and they opposed the new regime, but that didn't prevent the downfall of their world. Anyway, the brewery kept them too busy.

Kurt understood nothing his parents were talking about, nor the grumbling of his grandfather, who came from Upper Silesia. He played with his friends in Park Poludnia, at the time still called Südpark. In the winter the boys went sledding in the nearby Riesengebirge, or

Giant Mountains, and in the summer they sailed on the small Oder River boats to friendly restaurants where Hildebrand beer was served together with *Breslauer Korn,* or schnapps.

When Kurt wasn't allowed to join the Hitler Youth movement—this was in 1943, and he was eight years old and a big strong boy—he retired to his room, ashamed, and wept. He lost his school friends, his rollicking self-assurance, and the fun of being a schoolboy. All his older cousins "belonged." Only Kurt was left out because his father was so dumb! He didn't even go to the *Frühschoppen,* his early morning ale at Kempinski's any more. At about this time, Kurt's grandfather died, and Kurt's father said it was the best thing that could have happened to the old man. Then, in his general feeling of world-malaise, he bawled out his son, who was standing there staring at him open-mouthed. His mother said hastily, "Leave the boy alone, Friedrich," and then they all ate *Schlesisches Himmelreich,* an undigestible dish consisting of pickled meat and stewed fruit, served with dumplings, which required a Silesian stomach and enthusiasm. "Go on, child. Eat!" said his mother. Nobody could cook Silesian "heavenly pudding" like Mrs. Hildebrand.

Kurt found it weird that his father had gone for him like that. He had been a peaceful, even timid man, who when he was with his family joked and laughed, but now world events had him by the throat. Kurt couldn't realize yet that in the Hitler era, no one would stay the same. Not even the Hildebrands who lived quietly and minded their own business. When Kurt was sad and silent, he and his mother would play music. Kurt was going to study music, "later." He sang and played the violin, and his mother accompanied him on their fairly decent piano. Mrs. Hildebrand prayed regularly in church for Breslau and for her enemies. As the years went by, Kurt's mother had more and more enemies even though she was an established citizen of Breslau. But his mother's enemies were Nazis, and in her innocence she prayed to God to forgive her for not praying for Gauleiter Hanke, the führer of their district. Gauleiter Hanke had everyone worried to death because he had bellowed at his constituents in January, 1945 that Breslau would never surrender to the Russian pigs. Kurt's father was listening to him over the radio and asked nobody in particular how Gauleiter Hanke could talk such absolute nonsense? The entire structure was crumbling daily and in his opinion the Thousand-Year Reich had been German beer gone flat for quite some time. His fearful wife held her hand in front of his mouth when he uttered such blasphemies. Hadn't Gauleiter Hanke hanged the mayor in public because the latter no longer believed in victory, and in his straightforward, Silesian way hadn't hesitated to say so? What would she and Kurt do if Mr. Hildebrand was hanged? Fortunately Gauleiter Hanke had more important things to do than listen in on what his dissatisfied constituents were saying. He was transforming the old Oder city into a fortress, with the result that the Russians arrived in Breslau a little later and the entire south and west end of the city was destroyed. Gauleiter Hanke didn't wait to witness this. Shortly before the capitulation, he fled.

Before the arrival of the Russians, Mr. Hildebrand drank one strong schnapps after the other because his fear of the future made him feel sick to his stomach, but the wheat of certainty can be just as indigestible as the chaff of doubt. Of course nobody gave a damn anymore whether Kurt had sung the Horst Wessel Song in the Hitler Youth movement, or Schubert or Mahler; whether he fiddled a march or bumbled his way through a Brahms violin concerto. That was life.

The Hildebrands were very much alone, and sat like mice in a trap. Except for the few who felt as they did, they had lost all their former friends, and for their Jewish friends, life had either ended involuntarily and abruptly, or they had saved their skins by emigrating to "wild" countries, where no one read the *Schlesische Zeitung*, or knew anything about the magnificent Breslau Jahrhunderthalle, to say nothing of Kant, Schopenhauer, and *Schlesisches Himmelreich*. In the end even Kurt Hildebrand emigrated to such a country and landed by chance in Australia. His life had always been ruled by chance.

There had been no stability in Germany when he was born. Before the Hitler era, in 1930, the unemployed had fought each other on the streets of Breslau—communists against Nazis and vice versa, Catholics, Protestants, pacifists, and all of them united against the Social Democrats. The Hildebrand family stuck it out for a comparatively long time in postwar Breslau. They opted for Poland because they didn't know where to go, and the occupation troops would probably drink Hildebrand beer. But as Breslau became more and more clearly Wroclaw, father and son no longer knew their way around in their own city. The Jahrhunderthalle was called Hala Ludowa, the honorable department store Wertheim had a name they couldn't pronounce, and what had become of the Café Fahrig, which had had the Breslau intelligentsia, students, artists, to thank for its existence? Ashes to ashes and dust to dust . . .

The Poles began to move in en masse. The schoolchildren learned that Wroclaw had always been Polish, just as Kurt had learned that Breslau had always been German, even though in Upper Silesia, where his grandfather had come from, there had been a lot of Polish names in the registries before 1914. But what were names?

In 1949, Friedrich and Kurt Hildebrand were on the verge of emigrating. Mrs. Hildebrand was dead. She had been hit by a stray bomb shortly before the capitulation. Friedrich Hildebrand said it was a good thing. But Kurt Hildebrand had to bury his father in his homeland too, before he emigrated. Friedrich Hildebrand hadn't felt like going along with things for a long time, and the good Lord, who knew his Silesians, took him before he had to go to a foreign country. Because Friedrich Hildebrand had already looked upon Berliners as foreigners . . .

Kurt Hildebrand now joined these "foreigners." The old saying that every third Berliner came from Breslau finally became true in the postwar era. Kurt took any kind of job he could get in West Berlin. He lived with distant relatives and thought of Silesia as the aborigines think of their dream era. In 1955 he was working in a Berlin brewery. He was twenty, Berlin was grimly divided and not *"gemütlich"* any more. A big wall was rising up all around him, but it wasn't the actual wall of a later day. West Berlin was still feverishly striving for freedom, but Kurt saw the city in the diminishing glass of the homeless. He counted his savings and moved on to Hamburg because it was a port city. This might be the gateway for him to the outside world. He wanted nothing, nothing to remind him of Breslau! In this respect New South Wales was to fulfill his highest expectations.

He was taken on by a German freighter and landed in Sydney. His mates had taught him as much English as he'd need for a start. All of them had done the trip to Melbourne and Sydney several times. A beer brewer couldn't go thirsty in Australia, his new friends told him. Beer was the nectar of the fifth continent.

Many years later, after wandering around taking odd jobs, Kurt read an ad. A Mr. Fleet in Parramatta was looking for an experienced assistant for his brewery. By now Kurt was almost thirty, and he was finding Sydney too restless, too noisy, too grand. When he heard that Parramatta was an old country town, he applied for the job. He was an Australian citizen now, and his immigrant's agony had subsided as the years had gone by. Hildebrand, like his grandfather and father, was a thorough and fanatically dedicated worker. He was a perfectionist in a modest sphere of action, and suffered the tortures of the damned in a country where "fair enough" was dogma. Kurt also liked to give advice. Nothing was less desired on this continent. But by the time he came to Mr. Fleet's brewery, he had left all the malaise of immigration

296

behind him. He never gave advice anymore, and minded his own business with a heavy heart. He sometimes played the violin, but mostly it was too hot to practice. And somehow or other he missed his mother, the Breslau living room, and *Schlesisches Himmelreich.* He was a lonely man in the prime of life. Occasionally he slept with a girl, but that wasn't what he wanted. In his thick Silesian head he could see a quiet young woman who was there only for him and would give him children. And this young woman could be April Fleet, if she was prepared to meet him halfway.

Whenever Molly Fleet sat on the veranda with Kurt Hildebrand or went for a walk with him beside Parramatta Lake, she brought up the subject of her sister.

"April. What a strange name!" said Kurt. "Where I come from it's the most unpredictable month of the year."

"But my sister isn't unpredictable," said Molly, although she knew better.

"Of course not!" Mr. Hildebrand was shocked. "Miss April is wonderful!" Whereupon Molly took the bull by the horns and took Mr. Hildebrand at his word. She asked why didn't he marry April, since he found her so wonderful?

"Aber Kindl," Mr. Hildebrand lapsed into German. *"Sie nimmt mich doch im Leben nicht! Sie kann doch jeden bekommen!"* He blushed as he translated. "But she'd never take me! She could have anyone she wants!" Molly tried not to laugh. She knew a little more about April's chances.

"Ask April," she said, with Australian straightforwardness.

"What would your father say?" Kurt was on the best of terms with Mr. Fleet, but surely he hadn't been in Parramatta long enough to be a son-in-law.

Molly Fleet could very well imagine her father's satisfaction if at last April made the grade. And with an expert who could later run the brewery when Mr. Fleet, whether he liked it or not, joined his wife and Grandmother Cocker. In short, Molly made it quite clear to Mr. Hildebrand that he would not be unwelcome.

Kurt took a deep breath. April was pretty as a picture, and she didn't chatter all day. And she knew a lot about bookkeeping. She would give him children. And he'd give her the recipe for *Schlesisches Himmelreich!* Now he would really start to save seriously for a good violin and piano. For Kurt Hildebrand, April was the Australia of his dreams. She was the only one who could give him the new home he craved but couldn't build with his two hands. Four hands and two hearts built a home wherever it was to be built . . .

"Does April play the piano?" he asked dreamily.

"Here she comes!" said the youngest one, and disappeared.

Molly Fleet said goodbye to a radiant, engaged couple. April was smiling like a young girl capable of making a solid, warm-hearted, good-looking young man happy. They intended to marry soon, and Molly would come to the wedding. Mr. Fleet had asked, not exactly tactfully, how long April, at twenty-seven, intended to wait before producing a grandson for him. April had laughed out loud; then Mr. Fleet had joined in hesitantly.

When Molly got back to the boardinghouse in Darlinghurst, she felt inexplicably depressed. Naturally she had expected no paradise, but the house looked so dark and empty by the light of the street lamp. Charlie Rainbow's boxes of flowers stood on the narrow balcony with its attractive wrought-iron railing, but the flowers were drooping.

Molly Fleet didn't suffer from premonitions. She stood with her two feet planted firmly in harsh reality. But she started even before she heard the wild cry. It came from the entry of the dark house. Was it a cry of triumph or agony? The bulb in the hallway had burnt out. Molly felt her way cautiously up to her room. Then she almost cried out. In front of her door stood a stone figure, black, mute, the arm raised as if to hurl a boomerang. How in God's name had the statue of the black-fellow from the Parramatta town hall got here?

But of course it was Charlie Rainbow, and he wasn't about to hurl any boomerang. He was lighting up the stairway with his flashlight. Molly began to laugh. She must have been seeing things because she was so tired.

"Welcome, Miss Molly. Nobody home."

A strip of light shone down from the attic floor. So Uncle Doody was home. "Uncle is always home," said Charlie Rainbow. "Uncle not go-out man. Uncle like Charlie."

He laughed again, very high and shrill, and—it seemed to Molly—crazily. But that was the way the abos laughed, if they laughed at all.

"Good night, Charlie. I'm tired."

"Me too," Charlie Rainbow said softly, and suddenly seemed to shrink before her eyes. His arms dangled like broken pine branches, his muscular body went limp, and he rolled his eyes very slowly. They looked like circling black opals.

"Charlie, are you crook?"

298

The abo took Molly's hand and shook it wildly, then he lowered his kinky-haired head and doubled up like an opossum in a hollow tree, a trapped animal. Molly had never seen him behave like that, and it frightened her. On the other hand, she felt sorry for him.

"Go to bed, Charlie. Tomorrow everything will be better."

"Tomorrow everything more bad."

How did he know? Molly asked him if he'd like some tea.

"Tea is good," Charlie Rainbow said dreamily. He looked ecstatic, as if he were already gulping down the hot, golden-brown drink. "But my friend fire gone out, Miss Molly. No fire, no tea. Only lemons." Charlie Rainbow laughed shrilly and leapt up to the attic. Molly could hear him singing.

Only Charlie wasn't really singing; rather, it was more as if he were weeping, and every sound seemed to catch in his throat. Then Molly heard him laugh again. She walked into her room and closed the door. It had a lock, but the lock was rusty and the key was lost.

Molly didn't drink any tea either. She lay in bed and couldn't sleep, and tried to figure out how many miles the Silesian heaven in Parramatta was from Mrs. Doody's boardinghouse: exactly fifteen miles.

25

The Smoke Signal

Charlie Rainbow listened. The night had caught his scream in its black cover. He had dreamt of a girl in a bottle tree. She looked like beautiful Candy, held flowers in her hands, and sat naked among the branches. She laughed scornfully and waved to Charlie to climb up to her. The bottle tree got bigger and bigger. It grew up into the clouds, and Candy became more inaccessible all the time. Now she was laughing to rival the cockatoos, was tearing the heads off the flowers and throwing them at Charlie Rainbow's feet. Then Gheeger-Gheeger, the evil storm wind, penetrated Charlie's heart, shook it like a rotten tree until it split and the lotus bird flew out. In his dream Charlie knew it was the lotus bird. It flew around the bottle tree, rumpled Candy's hair, stuck its bill into her face, and beat its wings at her. Candy screamed and fell down. At that moment the lotus bird became Charlie Rainbow again. He climbed down from the bottle tree and twisted the white neck of the girl who had torn the heads off the flowers, and strangled her. And now the storm wind was a prisoner in Charlie's soul. It couldn't howl or rage any more, or shatter the eucalyptus tree or destroy the crows' nests.

Was that a car? Charlie looked cautiously out onto the street. The car raced by. The time hadn't yet come . . .

There were voices coming from Uncle Doody's room. He was talking to a customer who was just as old and weathered as Uncle Doody. Uncle Doody's cobber wanted a used umbrella for his wife, his sister, and his daughter in the Outback. They could take turns using it. The cobber was trying to get the price down. Uncle Doody shook his long, narrow fox-head. The women could mend the holes, couldn't they? "Get a bloody move on, mate!" Charlie Rainbow heard the old men laughing. They were probably drinking gin. Tonight Charlie didn't want any gin. He wanted nothing to make his eyes bleary. He had to see what happened on the street clearly, and what was passing by in the heavens. Gin was a no-good drink. The liquid fire made the abos merry or furious. But sometimes they needed the liquid fire, just like the white man. When somebody humbled them, for instance, or despised their gifts.

That time when Candy had killed his flowers and thrown his box down the stairs, that was when Charlie had needed the no-good drink. He had never grown any more flowers for Candy, but she didn't seem to miss them. Charlie looked at his watch. Eleven o'clock. He crept down the creaky staircase. She had to come home soon. Lately she had been coming home alone because she didn't want Molly Fleet to see whom she'd been out with. Charlie didn't know with whom she went out in the evening. Candy's men were not like emus who moved together. Charlie only helped Candy humbly up the stairs because the bulb burned so dimly.

Charlie stood in front of the boardinghouse and looked up at the night sky. He laid his kinky head on his right shoulder. He looked as if he were conversing with the stars. The street was empty. At this hour things were lively only in King's Cross. The big stars burned like white fire. Charlie nodded to them. He recognized and understood the ways of the stars, the wallabies, the snakes, lizards, opossums, and the birds in the bush. The only things he didn't understand, although he lived in Sydney, were the habits and the fancies of the white Australians. The hectic city unnerved him and was gradually using up the emotional reserves he had accumulated in childhood. The visual attractions—shop windows, neon lights, white flesh shining through flowered dresses—were all destroying his inherited vision. The technology of everyday life in the city—food in tin cans or in the deep freezer, the shopping for practical things without having to seek them out or fight for them, the baskets and nylon bags made by machine, the electric lighting and the metal birds in the air, the distorted pictures of reality on Mrs. Doody's television screen—all of it frightened and confused him. He was increasingly horrified in the stony lap of a big city that ceaselessly spat out all these surrogates. In the mission, the wonders of a civilization that could be bought with money had already aroused hostile feelings in Charlie Rainbow, isolated him, and made him difficult to handle. In Sydney he experienced the growing social integration of the aborigines and half-breeds with helpless astonishment. He had nothing in common with these young boys and girls who were fighting against the extinction of their race, and were trying, with the help of their white brothers and teachers, to understand the new Australia. For Charlie Rainbow the nature of the bush was and remained the element that

301

gave life. It was fiery warmth and creative darkness. Trees, animals, and plants were his brothers and sisters. His early curiosity to get to know the white world had died within him. Sydney was a sack full of riddles and misunderstandings, and he had to shake off the burden. An evil spirit had found shelter in Miss Candy. He wanted to cast this bundle of vexation into the dust in the street.

When a dingo vexed a blackfellow, he threw his spear at the animal, but you couldn't do that to the city people. You had to strike them in different ways. The thoughts in one's brain had to be as sharp as the stone axe that lifted honey slices out of the hives of wild bees. Charlie had been sharpening his thoughts for many days and nights now. He made various signs with his fingers, and the stars nodded. They understood him.

And the time had come. A veil broke loose from the stars and wafted like a gigantic smokescreen across the night sky. Only Charlie saw it and knew what it meant. The magical knowledge rested in him like the pit in a fleshy fruit. You didn't learn it in the mission and you couldn't read it in a book. The magic of nature was as old as the memory of the black man and as enduring as the stone of antiquity that he wore on his chest, under his checked sport shirt. But the intimacy with living nature was a burden in the age of the machines, and you couldn't shake it off or talk it away or dilute it. Charlie saw the smoke signal and wanted to laugh or cry or scream. But all he did was throw his head far back as if offering his throat to a knife. His wide-open eyes saw pictures in the star smoke. He could see what was happening right now miles away from the boardinghouse. He saw an accident on the street, and a little later he saw a stone frog. Then the smoke signal dissolved in the clouds. The pictures disappeared and the stars gleamed without any magical fire.

Charlie Rainbow was shaking as if he had chills, but he didn't cry out any more. He had seen it all.

Press bulletin, Sydney:

A tragic accident took place last night at eleven o'clock on a side street in Darlinghurst. Miss Candace Blyth, the well-known model, ran straight into a passing car and was seriously injured. She was trying to cross the street where there was no traffic light.

St. Vincent Hospital reports that Miss Blyth is off the critical list, but the doctors can't say anything definite yet about her condition.

The beautiful young victim of our traffic, which becomes more hectic all the time, explained today how it happened. Miss Blyth declares that somebody pushed her from behind just as the car was rushing by.

Mr. Billy Hall, a well-known Sydney industrialist and owner of Holden Cars, described the accident. He was obviously shaken. Police Officer E.F. Lewis, who was on duty in the area, questioned everybody standing in the vicinity. Nobody saw anyone who could possibly have pushed Miss Blyth. But everyone saw her rush straight into the car before the driver had a chance to stop. Mr. Hall is not being held responsible. Under the circumstances he will not have to pay damages.

Police Officer E.F. Lewis found Miss Blyth's address in her handbag, and saw to it that she was taken straight to the hospital. Mrs. Lydia Doody, who runs a boardinghouse in Darlinghurst and is Candace Blyth's aunt, told us, in tears, that her niece was night blind. This was corroborated by Miss Molly Fleet, Mr. Edward E. Doody—no relative of Mrs. Doody's—and Mr. Charlie Rainbow, all lodgers. Mr. Rainbow also explained that he often helped Miss Blyth up the stairs, and on this tragic evening had been waiting in front of the house for her to return.

The two pictures show the famous model from Kalgoorlie, Western Australia. Like so many young people, Candy Blyth came to Sydney to seek her fortune. *Insight* and the *Australian Teenager's Weekly* were good enough to let us release the pictures which show Candy in all her fresh, blond beauty. We wish the beautiful young model a speedy recovery so that she may continue to enchant her innumerable admirers in magazines and on television.

Before Candy was allowed to leave the hospital, Charlie Rainbow went walkabout again. Everybody was accustomed to his periodic disappearances, and nobody in Mrs. Doody's boardinghouse knew that this time he had gone for good.

There was no more fun for Charlie in Darlinghurst. Mrs. Doody wept and wailed all day, and even Miss Fleet, who had so often been annoyed with Candy, went around looking glum. Umbrella Uncle sat in the kitchen all the time, cursing and scolding, as he tried to cheer up his old friend. Naturally everybody was wondering what Candy would do now. The wounds on her face would heal, but the neurologist had told Mrs. Doody, cautiously, that her niece's spine was badly injured. When Mrs. Doody, in her blackest moments, envisioned Candy ending her days in a wheelchair, Uncle Doody got mad as hell with her. In his own Irish fantasy, he saw the same picture. Both the old people pestered Molly Fleet with questions: Did she think massage might help? She had worked miracles, hadn't she? Anyway, right now Molly was the most important person in the boardinghouse, and she liked that. Mrs. Doody kept urging her to go to the hospital and massage Candy.

303

All she herself could do was pray for the poor thing. But since Mrs. Doody was out of practice in this respect, she doubted that her prayers would be effective. That was why she went to Father O'Brien to get an expert in on it who had better connections "up there."

Charlie Rainbow first visited his friend on the outskirts of the city. He wanted to stay a day with him and then wander off into the bush. Perhaps working with lumber, and as a friend of the plants and the birds, he would one day find his nomadic tribe. Charlie had a good nose for that sort of thing and followed every footprint with instinctive assurance. The melting pot of Sydney had not been able to dilute his visionary core.

Charlie and his cobber laughed and tore around like children. Since there were only two of them, they couldn't perform a *corroboree*, the ceremonial campfire dance, and they no longer knew the ritual songs of their tribe. They had become fence watchers in their big tribe, and could remember only from their earliest childhood that the dancers were painted with white clay, charcoal, red and yellow ocher, and had worn ornaments and feathers on their naked bodies. The echo of hunting songs, war songs, animal, wind, water, and tree songs lived in their souls. In the mission Charlie had learned songs about a foreign savior which had remained incomprehensible. He continued to believe in the spirits of nature.

The life in Mrs. Doody's boardinghouse was already seeping out of his memory. Even his mute inner revolt against policemen, machines, and white wisdom quickly became part of the past. Charlie didn't even thank his cobber for following Candy patiently for so many evenings until at last, with a precisely calculated blow, he had propelled her into the car. There is a certain spot in the back of a human being that hurts so intensely when struck that the person thus hit rushes forward like someone possessed. Charlie's cobber had acted swiftly, and in the general excitement had been able to get away unnoticed. He had the neccessary striking power and presence of mind when in danger, and was a master at disappearing unobtrusively and with lightning speed, just like the humans and animals in the bush. It had not been Charlie's intent to avenge himself personally on Miss Blyth, but she had broken the backs of his flowers, and for him they were living creatures.

Charlie and his cobber laughed and danced in the sunshine. Before Charlie left the shack on the city limits, he planted the flowers of the season and two more fruit trees. The young men threw their painted boomerangs into the sunlit air until the woman called them in to eat.

That was life.

At last Charlie's cobber went back to work in the harbor, but Charlie didn't go with him. He had seen a smoke signal in the heavens the night before, and packed his bundle. The bundle was important. It was almost a part of himself. In the old days the bush wanderers, the gold prospectors, and the adventurers from Europe had called their bundle "Matilda." During the months of loneliness they had wanted something to hold in their arms, and Matilda circled around with them, was soft and warm, and kept her mouth shut. Charlie's bundle didn't have a name, but contained the obligatory blanket that comforted the body.

Thus in his fatalistic humility he followed the smoke signal. He had been born approximately twenty years earlier under a eucalyptus tree, and under a eucalyptus tree he would one day die. He knew all the colors of light and darkness, and that was good enough for him. He had already forgotten the neon lights in the big city, just as he had forgotten what he and his friend had done to Miss Blyth. For him the reality of Sydney had sunk into the abyss of time passed.

Charlie's sinewy body disappeared soundlessly from the big city. He had been a transient in Sydney, astray in a bush of cement and glass. His cobber watched him go. At first Charlie was still a man with a kinky head of hair and thin arms and legs. Then slowly he became a dancing shadow. When the people in the shack finally sat down to eat, Charlie Rainbow had become a dot in the story of the Australian creation.

26

Waltzing Matilda

Charlie Rainbow was not the only one leaving Sydney at about this time. Two months later Patrick Trent said farewell to the big city that had witnessed his triumphs and defeats for so many years. Trent had put the new villa Rigby had built for him and his second wife up for sale the day before. Like the bushman with his bundle, all Trent wanted to shoulder was his sack of memories. Turning his back on Sydney was not easy. Every city that has held us prisoner for any length of time holds onto some part of us. One goes forth poorer, but one goes forth free!

Trent had always been on good terms with pain; that was why he had hidden it under a barrage of jokes. Pain was part of the natural order of things, and Trent could bear it better when he wasn't holding a living woman in his arms, but only "Matilda." In Sydney millions of people were together but alone. As in his youth, Trent wanted to go walkabout.

And now he was sitting with Rigby on the big terrace in Vaucluse for the last time, having to break the news to his friend. He was hesitant, but not from weakness. The truth in his soul made him feel strong. He had lived too long with lies. After a bitter struggle, he had found his way to the core of his soul, to the discreet place where the truth rests in all its strength and glory. "I must talk to you, Alex. My time in Sydney has come to an end."

"I don't believe it, Paddy!"

Rigby had known for years that Paddy was a little crazy. A brooder in his way, like Anne. Wasn't it funny how Rigby always ended up with the brooders? Even funnier how he seemed to like them? "You're joking!" he said, but he knew that Trent was serious. He sat there so quietly. Patrick Trent never bored his cobbers with endless, excited talk, but Rigby felt that there was something special about Trent's silence now. It was stony. What in God's name had happened? Why did his friend want to leave Sydney?

Trent wanted to go back to Queensland, and not even his beloved friend Rigby could do anything to change his mind. Trent drank his beer and assured Alex that nothing would ever change between them. Trent had been moving a lot of his real-estate business to Queensland for years now, and had been in Brisbane noticeably often lately. His partner in Sydney could run the office without him. The business wasn't important anyway, he declared. He had more money and opals than he needed. He had bought a house in Bundaberg on the Burnett River, near his sister, Catherine.

The peaceful city between the sugar cane fields had also appealed to Elizabeth West. Dr. Catherine Trent was a gynecologist there, Rigby suddenly remembered. What the devil was the meaning of it all? Why did Trent want to vegetate in a small city like that? And what did Klari have to say about it? The baby was expected in a few months. Did Trent want to bring up his son in Queensland? Rigby stared at his friend, speechless. But by now Trent had come trundling out of his stony silence and with a hearty appetite was tackling an enormous steak which Rigby's housekeeper had grilled to perfection. (Andrews was giving a final performance. She had found and "trained" a new house-keeper, and Rigby was going to have to make the best of it.)

Trent helped himself to a second serving of fried potatoes, which infuriated Rigby. "Don't eat so many potatoes! You're a regular walrus already!"

Trent laughed. Rigby finished his beer hastily. If Paddy was suffering brain damage because he was about to be a father, his appetite had certainly not been affected. Rigby looked at the deep furrow between Trent's brows, the trace of gray at his temples, and his calm, full face with the shiny dark eyes. He found Paddy unusually pale.

"What does Klari have to say about all this idiocy?" Even Rigby knew that expectant mothers needed restful surroundings. Was she still in Bowral?

"I have sent Klari away," Trent said calmly. "It's all for the best."

Rigby jumped to his feet and knocked over a beer bottle, and scraped the shards together, cursing. "Now I know you've gone crazy!" he mumbled, not looking at Trent. "What do you mean? Is Klari already in Queensland?"

"No," Trent said. "She is in Melbourne, and that's where she's going to stay."

"Patrick! You don't mean it!"

Trent sat quietly, his steak growing cold in front of him. He looked at Rigby with deepest sympathy. Throughout the years Alex had been a true friend, loyal, even patient, and still he had to leave him to his own resources now. He couldn't live in a grave. He saw Candy Blyth once. He had gone to the hospital every day, but she hadn't wanted to see anyone. Poor child! Candy had lived in an artificial world: photographers, the press, television, cosmetics . . . a world with no corner for comfort and no roof for a rainy day. Sensations had been her daily bread. What would she do now? Trent was going to ask Rigby to keep an eye on the unfortunate girl. But Alex had damn little talent as a good samaritan. Trent intended to go to the boardinghouse once more tomorrow morning, and see if he couldn't talk some sense into Candy.

Rigby tore him out of his reflections. He shook Trent's arm brutally. "Wake up, man!" he cried angrily. "You can't send your wife off to Melbourne now. Just between us—it stinks! Say something, Paddy, for God's sake!"

Rigby mopped his brow. Trent began to walk restlessly up and down. "Sit down!" Alex yelled. "You're making me nervous!"

"I'm sorry, Alex."

"What's the meaning of all this nonsense? Did you two have a falling out?"

Trent sat down obediently in "his" chair. It was a very wide wicker armchair that fitted his huge proportions. Even Rigby looked lost in it. "I wonder who'll sit in my chair now," Trent said dreamily.

Rigby poured another beer for Paddy, and moved the cheese nearer. Trent noticed nothing. His dark eyes had grown even darker. He cleared his throat, then he explained the "situation" to Rigby. Even a tragedy became a "situation" in Trent's restraint. An Aussie remained an Aussie.

Trent had come to the end of his explanation, throughout which he had barely raised his voice or changed his expression. The case of Klari Trent was already a thing of the past. Anyway there was no possibility of a future together.

"I'll be damned!" mumbled Rigby. He didn't look at his friend but was watching a harbor ferry. But when Trent referred to his wife as "a poor little thing," Rigby exploded in righteous fury. The woman deserved a good beating, and if Trent wouldn't do it, Alex would be delighted to. Besides . . .

"Please, Alex. Not so loud."

Trent couldn't stand loud voices, whether he was in a "situation" or not. Alex stopped thundering and tried to dissuade him. If Klari wanted to stay with him, in spite of everything, he didn't have to send her away. He had been looking forward to the child, hadn't he?

"You mean well, Alex," Trent said gently, but he was going to abide by his decision. He had recognized it as the right thing to do. He had sent his wife away to where she belonged—to the father of her child.

Rigby never forgot how simply and calmly Trent explained the situation to him. But just that was what had been so eerie. Paddy should have been raging, breaking beer bottles, swearing, and then dreaming up a revenge that would be worth something! In short, he should be doing what Rigby would have done. But Trent had his own methods. Yes . . . he had tried first and foremost to bring some sort of order and decency into his and Klari's life. Were she and the unborn child to live with lies? The child's father was an engineer from Hungary who had a good job in Melbourne. Although Rigby, according to his sister, was as tactful as an elephant, this time he kept his mouth shut and behaved like a gentleman. He had seen Klari Trent several times with a compatriot in the Hungarian restaurant, talking intimately, but he had thought it was just a little paprika flirtation, the kind he himself had sometimes indulged in when Anne was waiting for him in Vaucluse. Nothing serious. And now the compatriot had made Mrs. Trent pregnant, and Paddy had found out. How, when, where?

Rigby never found out. He really didn't want to know. The little kernel of virtue that he was so careful to hide from everyone, stopped him. But if ever Rigby had admired anyone silently, then it was Patrick Trent in his "situation." He was firm, dignified and—goddamn the woman!—compassionate.

But Trent did not want to remain in Sydney.

"I'll visit you often in Queensland," Rigby said gruffly. "If it gets to be too much for you, you can throw me out!"

Before he moved to Queensland, Trent went once more to the boardinghouse in Darlinghurst. But this time too he did not get to see Candy. Finally the Umbrella Uncle appeared.

"What's going to happen now?" Trent asked the old man.

Edward Doody shrugged. Candy's spine was damaged. She sat in the wheelchair Trent had bought for her, and made life difficult for her aunt. "She's never going to get over it," said the old man. Of course he meant his friend, Lydia Doody.

"Please don't send any more money, mister. Mrs. Doody has to spend it all on liquor for the sick sheila." He said it disapprovingly, as if he had never drunk anything stronger than milk in his life. "Do you hear, mister?"

Hoarse, drunken sounds came from Candy's room. Trent recognized her harsh voice. "Waltzing Matilda ... Waltzing Matilda ..." and then silence.

Trent walked slowly up the stairs. As he opened the door to Candy's room cautiously, an empty bottle of gin hit him on the temple. "Out!" screamed the girl in the wheel chair.

"You bitch!" cried Uncle Doody. "I'll give you one on your head!"

He slammed the door and swore every Irish curse in his rich repertoire.

Trent held his handkerchief over his bleeding forehead, and Uncle Doody bandaged it for him. "Here it hails glass," he growled. "The sheila is possessed of the devil. How about an umbrella for the trip, mister?"

But the old Irishman only asked out of habit. He had raised his fox head and was listening. Again maudlin singing, and then a whimpering that died down.

"Waltzing Matilda," the old man murmured grimly. "That's life, mister."

27

A Murder in Sydney

"Please have another piece, Mrs. Doody. You know you love my apple cake."

Gretchen pushed the cake plate across the table, ignoring Mrs. Doody's red-rimmed eyes. Candy had tried to commit suicide and failed. She sat in her wheelchair, her hands tied, and threatened to do it again.

"I'm finished, Gretchen." Like Caesar, Mrs. Doody could do two things at a time: eat cake and cry.

"You mustn't get so excited, Mrs. Doody. Not after your heart attack. Candy will adjust to her condition, you'll see." But Gretchen spoke without conviction. She asked what Molly Fleet was doing.

"She's gone to Parramatta, to her sister's wedding."

"How nice that April got married. It's the only right thing to do." Gretchen was very happy in her second marriage. Mr. Lange was an excellent restaurateur, and so nice to her children from her first marriage, who needed a father. And that's just what Mr. Lange was. He had always liked young people, and after years of bachelorhood had taken over the duties of a father happily.

"How are Molly and Candy getting along?" Gretchen asked. She knew how difficult Candy was to handle now. Gretchen felt for the girl although she had never liked her, but she wasn't one of the people who were really taking Candy's accident to heart. The kookaburras in King's Cross were sorry for Candy with a shade of malice. Candy hadn't played the game. She had set herself up on a throne between the professional call girls and the more modest prostitutes.

Mrs. Doody took the last piece of apple cake and said that at first Molly had behaved wonderfully to Candy. But now things had changed. "Just think, the other day when Candy called her 'Mole,' Molly went berserk! I don't know why. It was just a joke."

"But it wasn't very nice of Candy."

"Candy was always so good-natured. In the movies she'd cry over people she didn't even know. She has a warm heart. I don't know what got into her. Molly should be more considerate."

Gretchen said nothing. She would have been furious too if someone had reminded her so cruelly of a physical flaw. Mrs. Doody was a good old woman, but she was so crazy about Candy that she was entirely unjust to others.

"Since then they don't speak to each other. I think Molly hates my poor little love." Mrs. Doody began to cry again. "How many eggs did you put in this cake, Gretchen? It really is first-rate. Nice of you to be so good to me. Apple cake always comforts me. But I have to go, child. It's been a real rest. I mean, to talk to a normal person, now that Molly's away. What's going to become of us?"

"Candy should be moved to Kalgoorlie. It's really too much for you, Mrs. Doody, and the doctor said you should avoid excitement."

"What do the doctors know?"

"Why don't you write to Candy's mother? After all, a mother is a mother, especially when things go badly."

"Not my sister! All she does is preach. And she never did love Candy. She was too beautiful. No, no, Gretchen, Candy stays with me, even if it's the death of me!" said Mrs. Doody, proud of her martyrdom. But she truly loved the girl, and nobody else did that. Without her Candy would be utterly abandoned.

"What's Charles Preston doing?" Gretchen asked. "You can trust me to keep my mouth shut, Mrs. Doody."

"I know, Gretchen. You're loyal. The Germans are known for that."

"I was born in Australia," Gretchen said stiffly. "My great-grandfather came from South Germany."

"That's what I mean. If you didn't wage war all the time, you'd be a very nice mob. Hardworking and clean. What was I going to say? Oh yes—Charles Preston, the bastard! Just imagine—he doesn't want to marry Candy now! And after getting all that money out of her! And he was in jail, too. Just like my old man," Mrs. Doody added generously. "I tell Candy all the time: You'll get somebody else when your back's okay. Do you think Candy will ever be able to dance again, I mean, after a while?"

"Let's hope." Gretchen was fighting tears.

"Now don't you cry too." Mrs. Doody blew her nose vigorously. "Oh Gretchen, I can't go on!"

"I'll drive you home, Mrs. Doody."

"But your husband's coming any minute."

"I'll leave a note for him on the kitchen table. My Friedrich will understand."

"Is a little one on the way?"

Gretchen blushed, and Mrs. Doody patted her on the shoulder. "I'm so happy for you! I always hoped Candy and Charles Preston would give me a little one. But now he's through with her, the dog! Those two shout at each other so that the walls shake when he does happen to turn up. Unfortunately she gave him everything that dear, good Mr. Trent put in the bank for her. We have nothing!"

"Everything may still turn out all right, Mrs. Doody. Of course Preston must marry her now. You can't take that much money from a girl and then ..."

"You don't know life, Gretchen, even if you are in your middle thirties. I can say that, can't I? You look so much younger. Yes, yes, happiness keeps us young. But we're in a hell of a mess, and nobody helps us out. But I love my Candy, even if I don't get any more money from her." Mrs. Doody wept again, partly for Candy but also because all the money was gone.

"Don't cry, Mrs. Doody. Couldn't you get some money from Albert Ritter?"

"If I only knew where he was! I'd ask him to help us, all right. Candy wrote several times to his cover address, but the letters came back. He docsn't seem to be in New South Wales any more. He's a mean dog too!"

"Can't Molly find out where he is? She went for an outing with him once to the Blue Mountains, if I'm not mistaken."

"Uncle Doody remembered the other day that he came and wanted to take Molly out. But that was long ago. Molly was in Parramatta. Now he's probably over the hills and far away. How are we ever going to get hold of some money?"

"May I lend you a little, Mrs. Doody?"

"I don't take money from my friends. At the most, five pounds, if you can spare it. God bless you! You'll get it back with interest!"

"I don't want any interest, Mrs. Doody." Gretchen blushed as she handed Mrs. Doody a ten-pound note.

"God bless you!" Mrs. Doody said again, pocketing the money hastily. "When you're in trouble you know who your friends are. Mr. Trent was first-rate, but he's in Queensland now. How am I going to get gin for Candy? Uncle Doody gets so mad ..."

"He's right. You shouldn't give her any hard liquor. It only excites her."

"But that's all she has!"

Mrs. Doody cried all the way to Darlinghurst and Gretchen watched the traffic. "Do come in just for a minute," Mrs. Doody begged. She dreaded being alone with Candy.

"All right. But just for a minute." Gretchen couldn't leave the miserable, helpless old woman to go into the house alone. It was eerily quiet as the two went upstairs.

"Let me take a look first," murmured Mrs. Doody, sounding almost frightened. "If Candy's going to rage, I won't let you in. Not in your condition."

Gretchen stopped halfway up the stairs. Huffing and puffing, Mrs. Doody reached Candy's door. Gretchen waited. She didn't know why, but she felt uneasy. The old house had such a deserted feeling. Uncle Doody's room was dark. It was six o'clock. That was Mr. Doody's time for a beer in the pub. Gretchen thought of the child she was expecting, and wished she was at home. But Mrs. Doody had looked at her so imploringly. If only Molly were here!

A scream from Candy's room. Gretchen trembled. Who had screamed? Candy or Mrs. Doody? Gretchen walked up to Candy's room. She felt dizzy, and her heart was beating fast. If only Fritz were here! He'd always disapproved of Gretchen's friends at the boardinghouse, but he let her go. Gretchen knocked on the door. No answer. What should she do? She called, "Mrs. Doody! *Mrs. Doody!*" When there was still no answer, she pushed open the door. With all her powers of self-control, she suppressed a scream. Oh God, oh God, oh God! Mrs. Doody lay motionless on the floor. And Candy? Candy, in her wheelchair, had her back turned to Gretchen. All Gretchen saw was her blond hair hanging over the back of the chair. But what was *that?* The end of a nylon stocking hung over the back too. Gretchen walked up to the chair, shivering. Then she screamed.

Candy had been strangled with a nylon stocking.

For one crazy moment, Gretchen wondered if Mrs. Doody had done it in her despair. No, no! She could never have done anything like that. With every ounce of strength, Gretchen forced herself to calm down. She knelt beside her unconscious friend and sprayed some of Candy's cologne on her face. At last Mrs. Doody opened her eyes, and as soon as she returned fully to consciousness, she crossed herself. "Please don't look," she said.

With Gretchen's help, Lydia Doody walked to her room. "Cover her, please," she said hoarsely, tearless. The big, corpulent Irish woman

314

was in such a state of shock, that the tears which usually came so easily, wouldn't flow.

Gretchen touched nothing in Candy's room. She knew from the crime novels she'd read that this was something one shouldn't do. Still trembling she went out into the hall and called the police.

The eerie stillness in the boardinghouse was soon transformed into an atmosphere of palpable activity. Inspector Cox, Sergeant Cunningham, the coroner, and a photographer appeared and filled every corner of the house with their presence. The police car in front of the door had such magical attraction that the neighbors stood around it as if in front of a popular movie. A young policeman pushed back the sensation-hungry crowd. "Nobody is allowed in!" he cried every now and then. "Go home, mates!"

"What happened?" everyone wanted to know.

The policeman didn't answer. Now the curious were standing a small distance away, talking to each other, pleasantly excited. It was homicide, of course! *Who* had been murdered?

"You can tell me, young man," said a fat, jolly woman. "I deliver Mrs. Doody's groceries."

The young policeman suppressed a smile. He'd rather be playing soccer than disappointing these people. Besides, he didn't know who had been murdered, but he would never have admitted that.

Inspector Cox went through the whole house with his sharp eyes. Nobody was allowed to leave. He wanted to know who lived here. Gretchen, terribly agitated, answered. She was so frightened that she looked guilty, and blushed fiery red at every question. But inspector Cox, "the best bloodhound between hell and New South Wales" as the press called him, knew faces. After taking Gretchen's name, address, occupation and relationship to Mrs. Doody and Miss Blyth, she was allowed to go home. She was to remain at their disposal, but Inspector Cox could see no reason for her presence now. Sergeant Cunningham accompanied Gretchen to her car, pushing the people in front of the boardinghouse aside with his long arm. "That's the inspector," somebody whispered, and Cunningham didn't object to being taken for Inspector Cox. One had to be satisfied with small honors too.

In the house the inspector was in the parlor which was never used, with its moth-eaten, plush-upholstered furniture. He was looking at the yellowed photographs of Dublin, Candy's best pictures, which were stuck on the wall with thumbtacks, and the tasteless holy figures. The plaster-of-paris Mother of God looked down on Inspector Cox with sympathy. It was going to be a tough job, Cox was thinking. Had Mrs. Doody got rid of the girl like a superfluous piece of furniture? The house stank of decay. But the dead girl must have made a lot of money at her modeling. What had happened to it? With puritanical repugnance, Inspector Cox took in the pink room where Miss Blyth had received her admirers in happier days. He'd find out who had visited the girl.

Mrs. Doody's deposition corroborated what Gretchen had said: Candy had phoned while the two had been drinking tea. Lately Candy had been calling Mrs. Doody all the time. She had evidently found solitude unendurable. Mrs. Doody declared that she couldn't possibly have been eating cake with Gretchen and strangling Candy at the same time! Until now nobody had ever managed to be in two places at the same time, had they? But this shameless policeman seemed to think it was possible! Mrs. Doody's face was red, and she screamed something that wasn't in the book at Inspector Cox, who remained friendly.

"It is not my intention to be insulting, Mrs. Doody. A murder has been committed here. I am only trying to get some useful information from you."

"All of us here, every one of us, is absolutely decent," Mrs. Doody said, a little more subdued now. "We're not going to let the police accuse us of murder. I just want you to know that, sir!"

"Who lives here?"

Mrs. Doody gasped; she saw an insult in even the simplest question.

"Well—who lives here?" Inspector Cox asked, a little sharper now.

"Right now, Miss Fleet and Mr. Edward Doody."

"A relative of yours?"

"I don't know. There are loads of Doodys at home. Possibly he's a relative. What's that got to do with Candy?"

"You have another empty room in the house. Who lived there?"

"You mean the junk room?"

"I mean the room next to Mr. Doody's. There's a bed in it."

"That's where I put my mending, and all my Candy's magazines and bottles of gin, full and empty."

"Who slept in the bed?"

"I'll have to think. Everything's turning around and around in my head!" Mrs. Doody burst into tears and Inspector Cox waited patiently for her to calm down. Finally she said grumpily that a Mr. Heller, an unemployed actor, had slept there. A new Aussie, but not young any more.

"Does Mr. Heller still come here?"

316

"Why not?" Mrs. Doody was indignant again. "We don't have fleas!"

"When was he here the last time?"

"Yesterday. Around this time he usually has a beer with Mr. Doody at MacQuarie's Chair, the pub around the corner."

"Where does Charlie Rainbow live?"

Mrs. Doody's eyes opened wide. "How do you know that our Charlie ... have you been snooping around here?"

"Does Mr. Rainbow still live here?"

"Not right now. Charlie always stays a while, then he goes walkabout."

Inspector Cox didn't like people who came and went. He asked where Charlie Rainbow was now.

"No idea! The things you want to know! Our Charlie wouldn't hurt a fly! All he did once was put soap in my jam jar. A dumb young fellow, like a lot of others."

"When is Mr. Doody coming home?"

"Uncle ... I mean, Edward should be back any minute. He was going to buy me a new fly swatter."

"What does he do for a living?"

"He's old and there's not a lot he can do. Sometimes he sells an old umbrella. He'll be punctual today. We're having goulash for supper. Just a minute, inspector. I have to put the meat on. Uncle gets mad when it's tough. An old man like that shouldn't get excited."

"We won't be able to spare him a certain amount of excitement today," the inspector said drily. "He can't be that frail. Just a minute, Mrs. Doody. I haven't finished. Sorry about the goulash."

"Then we'll just have to eat later. I can't eat anything anyway."

"Where is Miss Fleet?"

"You mean our Molly? She's gone to a wedding in Parramatta."

"Her wedding?"

"No. She's gone to see her sister get married."

At that moment Uncle Doody and his cobber came marching up to the house, singing happily. They were so drunk they didn't even notice the people in front of the house. But they did notice the policeman, and Uncle Doody asked, not exactly politely, what the hell he was doing there.

"Get in and don't ask stupid questions," said the young policeman, and shoved the two drunks through the door, which he locked immediately.

Uncle Doody's drunken friend was questioned first. He was the old

Viennese actor who had emigrated to Sydney shortly before the Second World War, and had lived in Mrs. Doody's boardinghouse for a while. He lived nearby now, and after work in a paper factory, he still conversed with his wife about performances in the Burgtheater and the Josefstadt. He had been at the pub with Mr. Doody. They had forgotten to buy the fly swatter. Mr. Franz Heller told Inspector Cox in his Austrian English that the business about Candy was horrible.

"Why?" asked the Inspector.

"*Why?*" The old doctor threw back his white-haired head, the head of a character actor, and got all set for a big scene. "You ask why, Inspector? You don't have a heart? Everybody wants to live. The poor little thing did too. She went through enough with that fellow, a lying bastard, if you ask me!"

"Whom are you talking about?"

"Whom am I talking about?" Mr. Heller liked rhetorical questions. "About the wop, of course. Who else?"

"If you mean an Italian, please say so. And which Italian are you talking about?"

"About Carlo Pressolini, of course. He works in the Restaurant Rosso in King's Cross and calls himself Charles Preston. A *very* new Australian, if you ask me. My friend Doody tells me that Charles threatened Candy a while ago. I'm not surprised. He's a good cross between Rigoletto and a pimp!"

"In what respect did Mr. Preston threaten the girl?"

"I wasn't there," Mr. Heller said cautiously. "But from what I heard, handsome Carlo wanted to wring the girl's neck. My friend Doody said Mr. Preston was a violent man, like every wop—sorry, Italian—but he couldn't stand her nagging him much longer."

"Why?"

"Candy wanted him to marry her! The good Lord knows he got enough money out of her, the good-for-nothing lout! You know something, Inspector Cox? Carlo reminds me of Liliom."

"Who is Liliom and where does he live?"

"Where does he live? In heaven, that's where he lives! When I played Liliom in the Burgtheater, everybody cried, even the archduchess and the whole audience! Do you know Charles Preston, Inspector?"

Inspector Cox wasn't sitting in Mrs. Doody's parlor to answer questions. A long time ago he had read a file from Hobart on Charles Preston, and at the time had wanted to ask Candy, here in the boardinghouse, if she was missing anything of value. But nobody had been home. Inspector Cox knew a lot more about the boardinghouse than Mr. Heller did. He also intended to investigate Charlie Rainbow's whereabouts. Perhaps the abo had wanted to take revenge on Miss Blyth for some reason or other.

"Did you know Charlie Rainbow, Mr. Heller?"

"The blackfellow? Of course."

"Do you know where he is?"

"*He* didn't do it, Inspector. Charlie used to strew the ground with flowers for Miss Candy to walk on. He worshiped her, like Othello his Desdemona, if you know what I mean."

Inspector Cox wanted to ask another question, but he hadn't counted on a former actor.

"You should have seen me as Othello, Inspector! There wasn't an Othello to equal me. Not even in Vienna. I can show you the reviews. They're a little yellowed from the heat here, but you'd be surprised! When I emigrated to Sydney thirty years ago, because of my Mitzi, I was *the* Othello! People stood in line to see me, Inspector!"

"Do you know where . . ."

"Not a single Aussie knew about my Othello!" Mr. Heller sounded indignant. "And they have blackfellows right here in their own country! It's fantastic! I told my Mitzi. She was with the Vienna opera, and she'd have sung Elsa, and *Die Frau ohne Schatten* for them just like that, if that idiot Hitler hadn't objected to my Mitzi's Jewish grandfather. And her grandfather had the finest, but really the finest fur shop in the Kärntnerstrasse. Do you know what the Kärntnerstrasse in Vienna means?"

"I would like to know what . . ."

"I don't want to seem argumentative, Inspector, but compared to the Kärntnerstrasse, George Street is . . ." The Burgtheater actor sounded condescending. "I'd like to give you some idea, but I simply can't describe it!"

Thank God! thought Inspector Cox. But before he could ask another question, Mr. Heller informed him that Mitzi's mother, a blond just like Hitler had wanted but never got—the damned vegetarian—that Mitzi's mother, who had been a natural blond like Miss Candy . . .

"You can tell me all about that another time. A murder has been committed here."

"I know," Mr. Heller said with indifference. "When you think how many talented actors Adolf Hitler . . ."

"When and where did you see Candy Blyth last?" the Inspector asked patiently. With the new Australians, if one didn't accept their entire private history together with all the rest, one didn't find out anything.

"I saw Candy months ago with Charlie, the blackfellow, at the front door. He used to help her upstairs because she couldn't see in the dark. Strange, the way Charlie Rainbow reminds me of Othello."

"My time is limited, Mr. Heller. I would like to know exactly . . ."

"Wait just a minute, Inspector. What's the hurry? Try to understand us new Aussies. We find our way into our graves soon enough. You can see that with Candy. I always said to my Mitzi: I don't like the Nazis! I can't stand the sight of those brown shirts any more, and all because of your grandfather. But even the Nazis knew my Othello. You have to grant them that!"

"Thank you, Mr. Heller. That's all I want from you right now. You may go home."

"But I'd like to stay to tea. I'd like to give Madame Doody something else to think about. Mine is a very sociable nature, Inspector. You see, I grew up with the wine. What do you people here in Sydney know about the *Heurigen?* Nothing! Absolutely nothing! *Servus,* Inspector Cox."

Inspector Cox took a deep breath and lit a cigarette. At least he had found out that Charles Preston and the dead girl had been quarreling lately. The blackfellow would be more difficult to find than the waiter in King's Cross, but they would send out another blackfellow after Charlie Rainbow, an abo who worked for the Criminal Investigation Bureau. You never knew . . .

Sergeant Cunningham brought in Mr. Edward Doody, without his umbrella. Uncle Doody looked as sly and secretive as only an honest man can look when faced with the police. His gin inebriation was almost gone because of the shock, and he was his usual pleasant self. He was holding his cat in his arms and spoke sometimes to it, sometimes to the police fellow. Sergeant Cunningham sat in the back with his notebook. He had taken down Mr. Heller's testimony, Othello included. One never knew if a kernel of important information might not be hidden in the wild underbrush of a witness's garrulousness.

"How long have you known Miss Blyth, Mr. Doody?"

"Be quiet," said Uncle Doody, meaning the cat, which seemed to think it was being interrogated too. "Excuse me please, Inspector. I was speaking to the little beast here. I knew Candy since she came to Sydney."

"Was she a pleasant lodger?"

320

Uncle Doody looked at the fellow, speechless. *"That* fresh sheila? . . . Get out of here, you pest!" He threw the cat like a sack in the direction of Sergeant Cunningham, who let the animal out. Now one would at least know to *whom* Mr. Doody was speaking.

"So you didn't like Miss Blyth?"

"Not my type, if you know what I mean."

"I'd like to know what you mean."

"The fellow who did her in did a good deed. She was too dumb to do it herself. Since her accident, as God is my witness, she was a punishment from heaven! She pestered everybody!"

"Whom, for instance?"

"Me, of course. And poor old Lydia, who clung to the little bitch like an ivy vine. Molly Fleet can tell you a thing or two too."

"Weren't the two young girls friends? I mean, two young girls living in the same house. Usually there's a lot of whispering and giggling." Inspector Cox sounded downright jovial, and offered Mr. Doody a cigarette.

"They whispered, all right. But I think Molly hated Candy because of that fellow Ritter."

Inspector Cox listened carefully. There had been no mention of a man called Ritter until now. "When is Miss Fleet coming back?"

"No idea. I'm not waiting around for her. But Molly is a decent girl, not a whore, if you know what I mean."

This time the inspector knew what was meant, and he asked who had visited Candy.

"Well, Albert Ritter, of course, an arrogant fellow with a long nose, if you know what I mean."

"Do you know where Mr. Ritter happens to be now?"

"I imagine the police can find out things like that."

"We're grateful for any help we can get," Inspector Cox said. "Listen, Mr. Doody . . . you seem to be the only intelligent person in this place. You keep your eyes open, don't you?" Uncle Doody nodded, flattered. "Did Mr. Ritter show his face here often after Candy's accident?"

"You don't believe that yourself, Inspector! That client made himself scarce, all right. Of course he's a traveling salesman. They're on the go all the time. Just between us, these slick fellows only want to have a good time with the sheilas. When something goes wrong, they're gone. Am I right?"

"Like the amen in church," said Inspector Cox.

"Ritter was a pretty crazy fellow. He used to sketch Candy, can you imagine? In my day I'd have known something better to do with the sheilas. Candy was pretty, sure, but not my type. I like something round and soft in my arms. But that's quite a while ago."

Uncle Doody smiled at the inspector and the inspector smiled back as he gave Cunningham a sign. The sergeant left, and in a short time found Mr. Ritter's portrait sketches of Candy between some papers and unpaid bills. Tomorrow they would go through the house again with a fine-tooth comb. On the stairs Mrs. Doody asked the sergeant if the police would ever leave them in peace. She didn't feel like eating anything, but it would soon be suppertime. Cunningham grinned and went back to the parlor with Rigby's sketches in his leather briefcase. Uncle Doody hadn't noticed his disappearance and was conversing animatedly with Inspector Cox about Charles Preston, whom he couldn't abide. Apparently Mrs. Doody and Charlie Rainbow were the only two people in the house he liked.

"Was Mr. Preston jealous of Candy's admirers?"

"How should I know? Lately they were fighting like cats and dogs. Charles is a very excitable man, a *very* new Australian. He's been here quite a few years but never seems to learn."

"What did Miss Blyth and Mr. Preston quarrel about?"

"Because suddenly she wanted to marry him. Before that he wasn't good enough for her, but now that she'd been put out of action, she didn't want to let him off the hook. I'm telling you, that fellow can shout! And in tune, like a wop opera."

"Do you think Mr. Preston could be violent?"

"You mean, did he strangle Candy? Out of the question. He hasn't got the guts."

"And Mr. Rainbow?"

Uncle Doody laughed out loud. "Our Charlie is the last one on the track, absolutely! A regular long shot! He was much too good to Candy. If you ask me, then I'd rather bet on Preston." Uncle Doody seemed to be off to the races. "I don't know, though, Inspector . . . no, Preston can't win either. I'd say Ritter was the favorite. Or . . . maybe not."

"Somebody murdered Miss Blyth, didn't they?"

"Sure. But who?"

"We'll find out. And if you should happen to notice anything here, or if Mr. Ritter perhaps comes to pay his respects, please let me know. I know a bright old fellow when I see one, Mr. Doody."

"I do too!" Uncle Doody had chosen not to say a word about Trent.

"You can always get in touch with me at the Criminal Investigation

322

Bureau, or leave a message there for me. And please see to it that everybody in the house is available. That goes for Miss Fleet too, when she gets back."

"She was supposed to come back today." Flattery made Mr. Doody very communicative. Today, the day of the murder, Miss Fleet was supposed to have been back? Interesting . . .

"Does Miss Fleet have a proper profession, or is she a call girl too?"

"In my day, Inspector, there were only bitches or decent girls. I suppose you could call Molly Fleet a decent girl. She's a masseuse, nice, fine figure. I'm telling you, Inspector, that sheila could hold her own with the strongest man!"

Inspector Cox listened silently to the story of Miss Fleet's accomplishments. This young lady would have to be watched; she rated a thorough investigation too. Apparently Albert Ritter had driven both sheilas crazy, and they had probably quarreled over him. And he wondered why one had only to "suppose" that Molly Fleet was a decent girl.

"I guess you'll be questioning the neighbors now?" said Uncle Doody.

"Now I'm going home to Mother's to eat!"

"We're having goulash," said Uncle Doody. "After all, one's got to eat, right, Inspector? I hope it's tender. All in all I'm a lamb, but when it comes to meat like leather, I'm dangerous!"

"I can't imagine that, Mr. Doody."

"Ask Lydia! There've been times when I've thrown my plate at the wall." Uncle Doody laughed and the inspector laughed with him.

"I don't want to hear any complaints, Mr. Doody. By the way, one of my men will be keeping an eye on this house for a while."

"Why? Are we in danger?" The old man looked frightened.

"Just routine. So's you won't be molested by curious people. You can sleep in peace."

Cox nodded amiably and got ready to leave. Sergeant Cunningham was to stay until the body had been removed. The photographer and fingerprint expert had already left. The silence of death sank over the scene of the crime. In the kitchen Mrs. Doody, sobbing, was stirring the goulash and drinking a double gin for support.

The coroner was waiting for Cox in the police car. Cox gave his report through the radio, then he sat back and took a deep breath. "Where to?" asked the driver.

"To the Restaurant Rosso in King's Cross." Cox would have liked to go straight home to his mother—it had not been a joke—but he wanted to take Charles Preston by surprise before the news of the murder reached the restaurant.

"A horrible case," said the pathologist. "My wife often cut pictures of Candy Blyth out of the magazines. The girl had terribly bad luck, wouldn't you say?"

Cox nodded. The coroner said that such a very pretty young girl like Candy probably would have enemies. Men . . .

"Or women," Cox said drily. He had to think of Molly Fleet again. How strangely the members of the household had spoken about her. They "supposed" she was a decent girl? What did that mean? Hadn't Miss Fleet found a boyfriend after Ritter? *Who* was Ritter? And *where* was he?

"Do you have a suspect?" asked the doctor.

"*A* suspect?" Inspector Cox raised his eyebrows. "You're joking, doctor! Right now I suspect everybody except Mr. Doody's cat!"

28

The Kookaburras of King's Cross

The kookaburra is a bold, sociable bird which from time to time
bursts into shrill laughter that sounds very human.

Inspector Cox spent a long evening among the kookaburras in King's
Cross. First he went to the Restaurant Rosso to question Charles Preston. Could he be a serious suspect in Candy's murder? Cox watched the
young man sharply and felt that the horror on Charles's face when he
was told the news was sincere. The usual hubbub of King's Cross was
all around them, but for seconds Charles seemed petrified. The shrill
laughter of the sheilas didn't register. Either he was innocent, or he was
a superb actor. Then he shrugged his shoulders fatalistically and without any transition whatsoever was again the right hand of Raffaele
Rosso.

Cox went on watching him, then called him into the Rossos' private
room. His alibi was unassailable. Both Rossos corroborated his statement that he had spent that whole afternoon and evening taking inventory of their stock of wines. He hadn't even gone out to the market.
Cox asked if Mr. Rosso had seen Charles all the time. Raffaele said that
he had *not* accompanied Charles to a certain place, and asked the inspector, his eyes flashing, if "Carlo" was under suspicion because he had
emigrated to Australia from Italy. Mr. Rosso went on to say that he
loved Charles like his own son, and if the young man was a murderer,
so was he! And were immigrants from Genoa especially suspect?

"Stop talking nonsense, Rosso!" said Cox, more sharply than he had
intended. The fat, excitable restaurateur was as deeply insulted over
every question as Mrs. Doody. It could drive you frantic! However, Inspector Cox preserved his cool and continued to question Mr. Preston
amiably. He was curious: the young man had accepted money from the
dead girl for months, and admitted it at once. He had of course given

her valuable presents from her own money because this went along with having an affair.

Charles also told the inspector that Candy had loved him madly. Women were happiest when they were making sacrifices for their lovers. After this bit of instruction, Charles, again without any transition, recommended the daily special, and Mr. Rosso brought a fine red wine to the table. "On the house," he declared with dignity.

Of course Charles Preston wasn't exactly at ease. Because of his success with the most beautiful model in Sydney, he now found himself trapped. He managed to look indifferent, but he was upset. Cox came to the conclusion that the two had quarreled constantly, then made up only to become mutually abusive again. Preston declared that after his return from Hobart, Candy had forced money on him. The first thing he had done was look her up, but he had been thrown out. Shortly after that though she had appeared at the Restaurant Rosso and begged him to forgive her. Fair enough.

"And did you forgive her?" asked the inspector, with such casual irony that Preston never noticed it.

"Yes sir!" And he had kept Mrs. Rosso informed regularly about the affair.

"Why?" Cox wanted to know.

"But that's perfectly natural, Inspector. Mrs. Rosso is like a mother to me."

"Isn't she a bit young for that?"

Preston explained that this did not depend on the chronological age but on understanding, and he valued understanding highly. He had saved money and offered to show the inspector his bank book.

"Not necessary." Cox was gradually beginning to see through the façade of this melodramatic passion. Mr. Preston was no paragon of virtue, but by now Cox was almost sure that even when provoked, Charles would not commit murder; he would simply get the hell out of wherever. He was much more sensible and realistic than he pretended to be. His operatic affectations, his excitement over Candy's murder, his despair over the tragic death of youth and beauty, would have prompted a less experienced detective to arrest him. But Cox had more subtle methods. He waited until Preston had finished his solo, then he moved on to the business of the day: Preston's alibi and his plans for the future.

"Did you intend to marry Miss Blyth?" he asked suddenly.

"Certainly not!" Preston replied.

"Why not?"

"I would never have married a model, Inspector. Too spoiled and too unreliable."

"But that didn't prevent you from accepting considerable sums of money from Miss Blyth."

"I came to this country as a penniless immigrant. All the old Australians have too much money, if you ask me. What do you know about what we go through here?"

"Let's stay with the subject, Mr. Preston. Why did you accept money from Miss Blyth? You're a healthy young man who can work."

"She gave it to me. What was I to do? I couldn't possibly have taken Miss Blyth out and given her presents in the style to which she was accustomed. She rode on a high horse. But since then a dozen moons have sunk into the ocean."

"You could have persuaded Miss Blyth to a more modest lifestyle. After all, you were older and more sensible." The latter was added with little conviction.

"*Only* the most expensive things were good enough for her!" said Preston, with an unfeigned bitterness. "The little fool was a public idol! She would order a meal that an Italian family could have lived on for a week! Ask her! Oh . . . In my pain I don't know what I'm saying!"

"Why did you ask the young lady to come to Hobart?"

"I *am* going mad!" Preston ran his fingers wildly through his dark hair. "Believe it or not, Inspector, Miss Blyth followed *me* to Hobart, *not* at my invitation! I'd already had enough of her. Monotonous beauties make me nervous, if you know what I mean."

"I know."

"She wrote to me all the time, rambling nonsensical stuff, if you know what I mean."

"I know."

"I had other interests in Hobart. I had no time for Candy. Ask my relatives in Hobart. The Pressolini garages are famous all over Tasmania. Miss Blyth had the nerve to settle herself down with my relatives, and pursued me! No pride! No dignity! I was Mrs. Pugh's secretary in Hobart."

"I know," said Inspector Cox for the third time. Mr. Preston blushed and mumbled something to the effect that anybody could be unlucky.

"Why did you come back to Sydney, Mr. Preston? Did you want to live at Miss Blyth's expense again after all?"

"The hell I did! Do you think Miss Blyth was the only girl in Sydney? Besides, I wanted to be on my own."

"That's nothing to get excited about, Mr. Preston. I hoped to get some useful information from you that would throw light on Miss Blyth's character and her background. After all, a horrible crime has been committed. I beg you therefore to understand my questions in light of this."

"I know I'm the number one suspect," said Preston, with a trace of vanity. "The lover is always the guilty one. We know that from the movies. I have atoned for my bad luck, sir. Do you think Mr. and Mrs. Rosso would have taken me back if they hadn't known I wanted to start a new life? *Without* Candy! But after her accident, I wanted to comfort her. May I be struck dead if this isn't true!"

"One corpse a day is enough for me."

"Now I'm supposed to be an idiot!" Preston said angrily. "Candy's lover in Broome threw her out."

"And who was that?"

"How do I know? Ask Mrs. Doody."

Later Charles waited on the inspector, excellently, once he wiped the tears from his face. Cox looked at Preston's smooth forehead under his shiny dark hair, his fiery eyes, his soft, sensual mouth, and flat ears, almost too delicate for a man. The outer rim was bent like a question mark. The whole man was an emotional question mark, but he was not a murderer.

Meanwhile the restaurant had filled up. More and more laughing birds appeared. Some sat down at the bar, others at small tables with colored lamps. For the most part the ladies were much younger than their partners.

Charles Preston drew the inspector's attention to several girls who had known Candy. Cox took down their names and addresses because he wanted to question them next day. "Do you know Miss Fleet?" he asked, so suddenly that Preston started.

"Who doesn't know Molly Fleet? You can't mistake her for any other girl. Not my type, if you want to know. Rough. No soul. But a gorgeous figure. Too energetic for my taste, though. I prefer the clinging vine."

"Where did you meet Miss Fleet?"

"In a small bar. She was all alone. I went out with her once or twice, but I found her creepy, if you know what I mean."

"No, I don't," said Cox.

"And by the way—she hated Candy. It was mutual."

"Why?"

"Well, because of me, of course."

"Of course," said Inspector Cox. "You're damn lucky, my boy, with your alibi."

"A little more Parmesan cheese, Inspector?"

"Yes, please."

"I loved Candy in my way," Preston said dreamily, and poured the inspector a glass of wine. "But I would never have married her."

"Not even after the accident?"

"I want a respectable wife, and children. Candy would never have accepted that. Where do you suppose a woman's understanding is located?"

"No idea."

"In her womb," Charles said dispassionately. "Where I come from we don't strangle young women because we don't want to marry them. Practically speaking, sir, that would make no sense. You either pass the girl on to your best friend or you marry the right girl. Discreetly. I got married last week. Discreetly."

"Why discreetly?"

"I didn't want to break Candy's heart. My young wife is an old Australian, naturally. Fourth generation of innkeepers. In Mittagong. Lovely scenery. Later I'll take over the inn."

"Well, congratulations." Inspector Cox looked at Preston thoughtfully, and Preston must have noticed something in the look because he said hastily that he had told his wife all about his "difficulties" in Hobart. Of course that would remain strictly between them. It was none of his in-laws' business. Moreover, their ancestors had immigrated as convicts, who naturally had been guilty of nothing.

"Here comes my wife!" he cried, his eyes shining. "Excuse me for a moment, please, Inspector. I'll be right back. I can recommend the pineapple salad highly. Would you like it on ice?"

"That would be fine."

Charles's young wife looked so much like Candy that for a moment Cox was shocked. He had never seen the beautiful model alive, but he imagined that this was what she must have looked like. But Preston's choice was an obviously respectable girl: natural, no makeup, but with very promising hips.

While he ate his pineapple salad—Preston, on his best behavior, had added a shot of maraschine—Cox, in his mind, closed the file on that young man. Mr. Preston must have always known what he really wanted, and that took real talent. The *commedia* with the tragic ending was now part of the gray past.

The wedding breakfast had taken place at the Restaurant Rosso. Good old Raffaele had shed tears of joy and given the young couple a check, and Mrs. Rosso had presented the bride with a dozen Irish linen dishtowels. Yesterday, on the advice of his wife, Charles had quietly broken the news of his marriage to Candy. That was the cause of all the hellish noise Uncle Doody had heard.

Inspector Cox finished his excellent dinner thoughtfully. In answer to his question as to who had visited Candy regularly, Preston had repeatedly mentioned a Mr. Ripper, or Ritter. The same name had come up during the questioning of Mr. Edward Doody. Perhaps a trail led from Miss Fleet to this mysterious traveling salesman? The sketches of Candy showed artistic talent. Why did Preston find Miss Fleet "creepy"? Was she strong enough to have tightened the noose around Candy's throat? Perhaps she had been in Sydney on the afternoon of the murder without anyone in the boardinghouse knowing it? But Cox didn't want to draw any hasty conclusions. Had Miss Blyth been a regular prostitute, or had she chosen the somewhat higher-prestige position of call girl? This seemed more likely in the case of a well-salaried model. But perhaps the beautiful girl had only joined the race as an outsider. The kookaburras of King's Cross ought to know. Nor had anyone mentioned Trent, Candy's former benefactor.

"Candy Blyth *was* an outsider!" Beatrice Fright said contemptuously. There were very few guests in the Greek Bar in King's Cross, and Miss Fright and her friend, Antigone, were drinking the drinks to which Inspector Cox was treating them. They downed them astonishingly fast. "I mean, we girls are friendly and help each other when it's necessary, but Candy Blyth only helped herself." In spite of her name, Miss Fright was a call girl with first-rate addresses in her book. She nudged her friend. "Right, Gonnie?"

Antigone had come to Sydney a few years ago. She was a waitress in a Greek restaurant, and for a small percentage Miss Fright gave her telephone numbers she wasn't using any more. Miss Fright was tall and statuesque, twenty-eight years old, and street-smart. Antigone from Athens, was shy. She had left her home with her family as a child. Called "Gonnie" in Australia, she was trying to make a living at the oldest profession in the world. Miss Fright's laughter scared her. She towered over the poor little girl from Greece who had to solicit her clients on the street and was often arrested for it. Miss Fright stared at Inspector Cox, her face expressionless. She knew how to handle cops. She had her own apartment in King's Cross and only accepted johns who had been recommended to her. She was born in Sydney, the daughter of a tailor, but needle and thread had proved too boring.

"Candy Blyth was unfriendly," she said contemptuously. Inspector Cox knew Miss Fright, and it was not to her disadvantage that she occasionally helped the police. She knew all the kookaburras in King's Cross, and most of them were afraid of her.

"Do you know a Mr. Ritter?" Cox asked, after the third espresso.

Miss Fright thought hard. "Ritter?" Then she shook her neatly curled head regretfully.

"He was a friend of Miss Blyth's," said the inspector. "Try to remember." But no, Miss Fright had never heard of a man called Ritter.

"I know him," Antigone said shyly.

"*You?*" Miss Fright was furious, and her pride was hurt. This girl, Antigone, just over with the last boat, with no assurance, only fear, and clumsy at that, knew someone whom she . . .

"Just a minute, Miss Fright." There was a hunter's gleam in Cox's sharp eyes. "Where did you see Mr. Ritter, miss?"

"In King's Cross," the frail little girl stammered. "He treated me to coffee in my restaurant."

"Where does he live?"

"In Moss Vale. He doesn't come to Sydney often. He's a traveling salesman. He doesn't want anything, just to talk."

"With you?" Miss Fright roared with laughter.

"Please, Miss Fright," Cox said sternly.

"Tell the truth," Miss Fright said, on their way home. "You never saw Ritter in your life!"

"I just wanted to say something too," the little Greek girl said softly. "Nobody in Sydney pays any attention to me."

"Or *is* there a man called Ritter?" Miss Fright sounded threatening.

"I'm sure there is," Gonnie said dreamily. "But I don't know him."

On Preston's advice, Cox questioned one more kookaburra from King's Cross, a streetwalker whom the Three Graces had created in anger. Miss Fletcher had had enough of love, and it showed. Her hair hung like a ragged straw fringe across her forehead—not a windblown hairdo: Miss Fletcher had been shaken by a real storm. "Why should I still go to the hairdresser, Inspector?" she asked aggressively. "What I need for my business is a new face!" And she really laughed like a kookaburra in the bush. She needed a new body too, and certainly a new brassiere. But of what concern was that to the police?

Miss Fletcher had never known such an unpleasant fellow as this Fox or Cox. She was furious over being questioned about Candy Blyth. Of course she knew the model. She would have liked to throw acid at that pretty face because Candy Blyth had looked scornfully right past her in the bars in King's Cross. She had hated Candy, not for professional reasons, but because of the girl's arrogance.

"Can you tell me with whom Miss Blyth went out? We'll be glad to pay for any useful information, Miss Fletcher."

"I don't mind earning an honest penny," said Miss Fletcher. "But I'm not an informer. I haven't sunk that low."

"Come, come, Miss Fletcher. All you'd be doing is your duty as a citizen. This is a case of murder."

"The bitch died none too soon, if you ask me."

"I've been asking you all this time. Cigarette?"

Miss Fletcher looked at the inspector out of her clever, colorless eyes. In her youth they had been blue. "Thanks, I don't smoke." She smoked like a chimney, but she didn't accept cigarettes from cops.

"Do you know a man called Albert Ritter, Miss Fletcher? He's supposed to have been a friend of Miss Blyth's. Also of Miss Fleet's."

Miss Fletcher laughed loudly again. Just like a jackal, thought Cox. "Miss Fleet has no boy friends," she said. "Whoever sold you that story? I'm sorry, Inspector, but I don't know any Mr. Ritter."

Miss Fletcher was speaking the truth; traveling salesman Albert Ritter didn't exist, but she had seen Candy Blyth quite frequently with Alexander Rigby, whose picture had been in all the papers on his fiftieth birthday. Ritter? Rigby? The husband from the elegant eastern suburbs probably called himself Ritter when he went out on the town.

Miss Fletcher could have given the inspector a valuable tip. The more she thought about it the surer she was that Ritter *was* Rigby. But she said nothing. Although Candy had chosen to snub her, the miserable streetwalker behaved according to her professional ethic. Besides, Miss Fletcher came from a family where it was a matter of principle not to speak badly of the dead. And since Miss Fletcher had nothing good to say about Candy Blyth, she was silent.

After having questioned the kookaburras of King's Cross, Cox looked up a painter who lived near Mrs. Doody's boardinghouse. He had been told that Mr. Bolter was a curious loner.

Cox found Bolter in his favorite pub. The painter explained proudly that he had been born in Sydney's Central Station, then he reverted to his favorite topic—the arts. "I practice the art of the impossible," he said. "I would like to give Australia an old soul."

Mr. Cox dealt with the situation with his usual patience, but decided that if Bolter ever had to take the witness stand, the judge would have a heart attack. So he interrupted a lecture on art theory with the question: had Mr. Bolter known Candy Blyth?

"Who didn't know her? But if you think I murdered the sheila, then you're on the wrong track, Inspector. I don't think very highly of the female sex—too little brains and too many dangerous curves."

"Interesting," said Inspector Cox. If Mr. Bolter wasn't interested in women, it didn't mean by a long shot that he wouldn't wring one of their necks in an emergency. Bolter seemed to read the inspector's thoughts because he flung back the hair hanging over his forehead and said gently, "I don't strangle girls, Inspector. Why should I? I wish them all the best. Do you know Plato?"

"Do you know Ritter?"

"Certainly," said the painter. "A splendidly-built example. Not very young any more, but in excellent shape. In his case every muscle is where it should be."

"That sounds good."

"If I am not being inappropriate, I could do with another beer. Thank you very much, Inspector. I saw Ritter often with Candy, in Bondi. His first name is Albert."

Cox asked casually for his present address. "I can't tell you that," said Bolter, slightly piqued. He was always sensitive when a cop asked him for the address of a man. If the Greeks of antiquity had been fascinated by male beauty, why not Mr. Bolter?

The inspector hurriedly changed the subject and asked the painter about his work. He had formulated a plan that could be realized only via the arts. Mr. Bolter painted portraits. That was what Cox had hoped. At last he got the painter to the point where he drew a pencil sketch of Ritter on the back of a menu. Cox stared intently at the portrait, so quickly sketched with a few sure strokes. Where in the world had he seen this sharp profile before? Right now he couldn't place it, damn it! He asked the painter to sign the sketch.

"You're going to keep it?" asked Mr. Bolter, astonished and flattered.

Cox put the sketch in his portfolio and said, smiling, "My first original." Then he ordered another beer and asked the painter if he knew Molly Fleet.

"Indeed I do!" Mr. Bolter said admiringly. "The girl's strong as a horse. She cured my back with her massage. A very efficient young woman. Unfortunately she has no luck with men."

"Too strong?" Inspector Cox smiled. "When did you see her last?"

"Wait a minute . . . My memory's failing me, and I'm only thirty-five! Funny, I could recite Plato's entire *Symposium* for you . . ."

"Another time, Mr. Bolter. *When* did you see Miss Fleet?"

"If I'm not mistaken—yesterday. That's right, Inspector. I was at the movies and she sat in front of me. You can't mistake her."

"In what movie house?"

"I think it was the Plaza, on George Street."

"Are you sure?"

"I don't keep a record of my amusements, Inspector. The films are mostly for children or minors. Did you see the last film at the Variety, in Pitt Street? What did you think of—"

"Perhaps you saw Miss Fleet at the Variety."

"Of course, Inspector. At the Variety. How did you know? That's quite uncanny."

Inspector Cox did not betray in any way how valuable this bit of information was to him. He talked for a few minutes more about films, Plato, a new fried-fish place and the Elizabethan theatre. Then he was called to the phone. The report came from Mrs. Doody's boarding-house. Miss Fleet had just arrived from Parramatta.

"I'll be right there," said Inspector Cox. "She's not to leave the house!" He said a hurried goodbye to Mr. Bolter, who was a little surprised at the abrupt ending of their conversation. You could never trust a cop.

Inspector Cox had been given so many divergent opinions of Molly Fleet that his curiosity was aroused, but she didn't make any extraordinary impression. A strong girl who had not entirely shed the country town she came from. A small waistline, long red-gold hair worn flopping over the left half of her face, and the muscular arms of a masseuse. Had she or hadn't she? Whatever Miss Fleet might be, she was certainly not "creepy." Cox couldn't understand why, except for the mysterious Mr. Ritter, she hadn't found a boy friend. The girl looked decent, neat, and the birthmark on her left cheek might help the woman at the movie box-office to identify her. There were no fingerprints; the murderer had apparently worn gloves. No gloves had been found at the boardinghouse.

Miss Fleet didn't seem to be frightened, nor did she make a sly or false impression. But that didn't have to mean anything. If the painter in Darlinghurst hadn't been mistaken, it would be difficult for Miss Fleet to explain why she had been incognito in Sydney on the afternoon of the murder. Cox was still looking her over. Except for the birthmark, she was pretty. Somehow or other he was touched by the way this lively girl arranged her red-gold hair like a curtain over the left half of her face. After all, she was only twenty-two and wanted to be attractive to men. All her character was in her chin. Miss Fleet could probably be tough, but her lips were shy and inexperienced. In her eyes, however, there was a gleam of rebellion. "I didn't do it!" she said, louder than was necessary.

"Nobody says you did, Miss Fleet."

They were seated opposite each other in Mrs. Doody's parlor.

"Then why are you following me?"

"You go to the movies too often," Cox said gently.

"I hardly ever go! I hate those sloppy love films!"

"What was the last time you went to the movies, Miss Fleet?"

"I don't know. Why?" Miss Fleet sounded hostile.

"I am the one who asks the questions, young lady." Cox's voice was a little sharper, and Molly Fleet noticed it. "You are a qualified masseuse?"

"Yes."

"How long have you been working in Sydney?"

"A little over two years."

Cox leafed through his file. "Why didn't you stay in Parramatta?"

"Nobody there needs me."

A shadow fell across her young face. Miss Fleet's moods changed with baffling speed. A sensitive girl. Cox decided to "gently" force her to tell all she knew.

"Well, naturally, Sydney is more amusing for a young lady. King's Cross, dancing, movies. Oh, I forgot, you don't go to the movies."

"I don't go out very much." Miss Fleet blushed.

"I like it when girls are well-behaved."

Molly looked at Cox almost gratefully. The young thing was evidently not spoiled. "I guess Miss Blyth was always on the go."

"Before the accident, every evening. That's the way models live."

"Did you like her?"

"She was a lot of fun," Miss Fleet said cautiously. "I mean, before the accident."

"And after that?"

"She wasn't funny anymore." Miss Fleet's tone made it quite clear that she had never heard such foolish questions. "You can figure that out for yourself."

"There are supposed to be people who become pleasanter through misfortune."

"Well, Candy wasn't one of them. May I go now?"

"What's your hurry?"

"I've got a lot of things to attend to. I'm going back to Parramatta tomorrow."

"Have you a certain reason?"

"My father doesn't want me to go on living in this house."

"You're of age, aren't you?"

"I don't want to either."

"Why?"

"Well, you can imagine why."

"I have no intention of thinking for you, Miss Fleet. I want to know why you intend to leave again so soon."

"I want to. That's all."

"That is not all by any means, young lady. Nobody leaves this house without police permission."

"I have to treat my patients. To do that I have to leave the house."

"Wasn't it your intention to leave tomorrow? How many patients do you think you can massage between midnight and dawn?"

"If you won't let me go back to Parramatta, I would like to spend my time usefully. What's wrong with that?"

"Nothing. Can't you make yourself useful here?"

"I could help Mrs. Doody, of course," Molly said sullenly. "She does nothing but cry."

"Which is understandable, since her niece was so violently murdered."

"I imagine with a stocking it doesn't hurt," said Molly.

"How do you know that, Miss Fleet?" The inspector was looking at Molly strangely. A shiver ran down her spine.

"I didn't say I knew it. I said I imagined it."

"Why do you think so?"

"I saw something like it in a movie. The girl was killed immediately. She didn't even scream."

"Didn't you just say you don't go to the movies?"

"On that day I did."

"Aha! On that day you did." There was a hideous pause—at least it seemed hideous to Molly. Cox suddenly stepped up so close to her that she shrank from him. His eyes were boring holes in her face. She closed her eyes.

"Why are you afraid to look at me?"

"I am *not* afraid." Molly opened her eyes. "I'm tired. That's why I closed my eyes."

"Tired of lying? Let me tell you something, Miss Fleet: if you go on like this, you'll lie your head and neck off. I'm just warning you because I'm good-natured."

Sergeant Cunningham, who was taking it all down, looked up. Things were looking up.

"I don't lie. Lying is a sin."

"Do you consider murder commendable when it doesn't hurt?"

"I have no experience in that respect."

"Perhaps you massaged Miss Blyth a little too vigorously. Nobody was home yesterday between five and seven."

"How do you know that?"

"Here *I* am the one who asks questions. And if I don't get some sensible answers out of you soon, you'll be sorry. You are far too stubborn, Miss Fleet." Cox pounded on the table with his fist so that the holy figures wobbled.

"Why are you so furious with me? *I* didn't do it!"

"Then who did?"

"I don't know." There were tears in Molly's voice, but she controlled them. "I've only just arrived in Sydney."

"Are you sure?"

"Of course I'm sure!"

"Well, you seem to be asking for it, Miss Fleet. You arrived in Sydney yesterday, the day of the murder."

Molly stared at him, horrified. Something was very wrong here. She was trembling from head to toe.

"Why did you come back to Sydney yesterday? Put your cards on the table, you stupid little thing. At least assure yourself of mitigating circumstances."

"I didn't do it! Please, please believe me!"

"Why did you come back secretly?"

"That's my private business, Inspector. Really it is."

"If you want to go on living your private life, I advise you to tell me the truth. It's your only chance."

Molly was silent. Then she said haltingly that her presence in Sydney had nothing to do with the murder. Inspector Cox ignored this as utter nonsense.

"Were you at the Variety movie house yesterday afternoon?"

"For a little while."

"Why did you leave earlier? To visit Miss Blyth?"

"No!" Molly screamed.

"Please keep your voice down. You could wake the dead." Cox

cleared his throat. It hadn't been a very good way to put it. Sergeant Cunningham suppressed a grin.

"For the last time—where were you yesterday between five and seven?"

"If I tell you, I'll involve somebody else . . ."

"You'd better worry about involving yourself! In a murder case, it's every man for himself. Don't you know that? So—where were you?"

Molly closed her lips firmly.

"I'll wait exactly two minutes because you're so young and silly." Suddenly Inspector Cox sounded quite friendly. He looked at Mrs. Doody's wall clock. "One more minute, Miss Fleet. After which I shall arrest you for suspicion of murder."

Miss Fleet let out a shrill cry and made for the door. The inspector caught her in his arms. "And attempt to escape." He nodded to the sergeant, who wrote it down. "You're making life very hard for yourself, Miss Fleet."

Cox pushed the trembling girl down onto the plush sofa. Molly looked as if she were about to faint. The sergeant got water from the kitchen and splashed some in Molly's face.

Mrs. Doody was playing patience and heard Molly's scream. She stuck her head in the door. "What are you doing to our Molly?" she asked harshly.

"Nobody is to come in here! Miss Fleet and I are talking." Cox closed the door in Mrs. Doody's face. Since the key was missing, Sergeant Cunningham planted himself against it. More effective than a key. Nothing less than an earthquake could have shaken him.

Inspector Cox's success lay in lightninglike changes of method. Like the winds of Sydney, he was sometimes gentle, sometimes rough. Instead of arresting Molly Fleet, he asked some more questions, quietly. The young girl was scared to death. He intended to calm her before playing his trump card. He asked Molly about her home in Parramatta, and offered her a cigarette. His favorite aunt lived in Parramatta too. As Molly, with the optimism of youth, gradually began to forget the danger of her situation, Inspector Cox asked suddenly why she had spent the night in a hotel.

"I wanted to make saying goodbye to Mrs. Doody as short as possible. She would have spent the whole night begging me to stay, and I'd have given in."

"Do you have such a soft heart?"

"When people are good to me—yes."

338

The inspector was silent. For a moment he looked at Molly Fleet with true human interest. He even found himself wishing that this nice young girl were innocent. She was so different from the kookaburras of King's Cross, damn it! She looked so *clean*. She was living in the wrong surroundings. She should marry, have children, and be happy. That was what she was cut out for.

"So where were you late yesterday afternoon?"

It turned out that Miss Fleet had been with Albert Ritter after massaging Miss Rigby. Of course Cox knew the editor-in-chief of *Insight*. He would have the time checked.

"Do you massage Miss Rigby regularly?"

"From time to time. She's very busy."

"What did you do after the massage?"

"I visited Albert Ritter."

"Did you massage him?"

Molly blushed. "Of course not!" she said stiffly. "He's in great shape."

"How do you know that?"

"You can see that he is," said Miss Fleet, and suppressed a smile.

"What did you want from Mr. Ritter?"

At last Cox could see the light at the end of the tunnel, but he didn't betray it. Miss Fleet was calmer now and had revealed her secret quite easily.

"I wanted money from him."

The inspector's sympathy was quickly dispelled. This young woman was quite evidently pulling his leg by seeming so innocent. So she indulged in a little blackmail too. Things were getting better and better.

"Do you blackmail Mr. Ritter often?"

Molly blushed purple with indignation. "I never blackmailed him!" she said vehemently. "What do you take me for?"

"Nothing bad."

"I wanted the money for Candy." Now there were tears in her eyes. "We weren't speaking to each other any more, and Candy was so horrid to me after the accident, but I did feel sorry for her. Such a stupid girl! What was she going to do? We didn't have any money."

"But you earn quite a bit, Miss Fleet. If you felt so strongly for your friend that you were ready to blackmail strange men for her sake, why didn't you contribute something yourself?"

"I have to save. I'm all alone in the world. Besides . . ." Molly hesitated.

"What were you going to say?"

"Mr. Ritter is not a stranger. I know him very well."

"You like him?"

"That's *my* business." Again Molly blushed.

"Not any more, Miss Fleet. I am interested in Mr. Ritter. I am interested in everybody who ever came to this house. So—do you like this man?"

"Not at all!" Molly said harshly. "Once I thought he was wonderful, but he is sly and disloyal, and only sees things superficially."

"Most men do. Is that all you have to say against your Ritter?"

"He is *not* my Ritter! He was Candy's man. He had plenty of fun with the poor thing. I felt he should help her now. I told him not to be such a pig!"

"Are you always so polite when you want something from a man? Did Mr. Ritter give you the money?"

"He did not!" Miss Fleet said scornfully. "He just lead us by the nose!"

"Who do you mean by 'us?'"

"Candy and me. Once he took me for an outing in his car, and then it was all over. And he had promised . . ." Now Molly was sobbing.

"Why didn't he give you the money? Doesn't he have any?"

"He's stinking rich!" Miss Fleet's outburst left nothing to the imagination. "But he said he had enough of being blackmailed, and there was the door!"

"Enough of being blackmailed? Had Mrs. Doody asked him for money?"

"She doesn't know his address. He's no dope!"

"How do you happen to know his address?"

"I massaged his wife for a while, and saw his picture in her room. The bastard looked so elegant!"

"Is that so?" said Cox. In spite of her abusive language, Miss Fleet quite obviously was infatuated with this mysterious Mr. Ritter. But he wouldn't be mysterious much longer.

"Then what blackmailing was Mr. Ritter referring to?"

"Candy's. All the time after the accident."

"Did she have his address?" Cox had heard from all sides that Ritter was constantly on the road, and nobody knew where he lived.

"I gave Candy his address after the accident. The letters she wrote to his cover address kept coming back."

"So you betrayed Mr. Ritter to the Doodys. Do you think that was a very noble thing to do, Miss Fleet?"

"I meant well. The dog could have done something for us, once," Molly said stubbornly.

There was an uncomfortable pause. Then the inspector asked for Mr. Ritter's address.

Molly paled. She said she couldn't give the police his address because it would have dreadful consequences.

"Now don't get brazen!" Cox thundered suddenly. He jumped up and stared piercingly at the petrified girl. Then he said with frightening calm, "The case is fairly clear, Miss Fleet. You planned the murder together with Mr. Ritter, and you crept into this house yesterday afternoon. You are completely under the influence of this man. You should be ashamed of yourself, a girl from a respectable family!"

Molly stared at Cox, so flabbergasted that he began to wonder if his theory was right. "I didn't do it!" she sobbed, and wiped her tears away like a child. "I am not . . . under the influence of this man. I *have* no man."

"And I am supposed to believe that?"

The young girl looked at him in despair from behind the curtain of her hair. Cox understood. She had a complex about her birthmark. But that didn't concern him now. All cats were gray in the dark.

"Ritter is *not* a murderer!" The words burst from Molly Fleet.

"Do you want to teach me my business? How do you know that?"

"He was at home at the time of the murder, and I was with him."

"How long?"

"I don't know. Until he said, 'There's the door!' "

Molly found the inspector's silence more frightening than his questioning. "May I go now?" she asked shyly.

"I'm afraid you must give me a few more minutes of your time. Now listen to me carefully, Miss Fleet. If you lie to me *now*, it will cost you your head! *"Where does Mr. Ritter live?"*

Molly was so horrified that all the color drained from her face. Only her left cheek burned a fiery red. "No . . ." she whispered.

"His address!"

Molly looked at Cox like a trapped animal, but her mind began to work feverishly. She could not saddle herself with a murder rap for Rigby's sake. He had to understand that. "Albert Ritter is not his real name."

"So who is he? This man here?"

Inspector Cox held out Bolter's sketch. It was his trump card. Rigby was so clearly recognizable on the sketch that Molly felt dizzy. She grasped her head with her slim, strong hands.

"Headache?" asked the inspector. "That's what I'd have in your place. That is he, isn't it?"

Molly nodded, stupefied. The police in the house were more terrible than in a film. They knew everything and then some . . .

"Who is this man?" asked Cox.

"You know who he is."

"I want to hear it from you!"

"Alexander Rigby from Vaucluse," Miss Fleet said tonelessly.

This time Cox knew that Molly Fleet wasn't lying. Of course! The long narrow nose with its arrogant hook, the cool, scornful expression—that was Alexander Rigby as he and his sister Shirley had seen him on his fiftieth birthday in Manly. How could he have missed it?

He pushed a few loose papers across the table and told the young girl, "Sign your statement, please. But first read everything through carefully. It's in your interest, Miss Fleet."

Molly began to read, Cox watching her all the time. "I made one mistake," she murmured, sounding thoroughly intimidated.

"In what connection?"

"I didn't go to see Mr. Ritter until eight o'clock. He didn't have time before that."

"What did you do after you massaged Miss Rigby?"

"I . . . I ate dinner in a restaurant."

"Where?"

Molly mentioned a place in Pitt Street and Sergeant Cox entered it on the report. Cox asked what Molly had done after eating.

"I told you. I went to see Mr. Rigby at eight o'clock. Then I went back to my hotel and cried."

"Why?"

"I just cried," said Miss Fleet. "Because it's all so terrible."

"You're young. If you've been telling the truth, and I'll soon find out if you have, you have your whole life ahead of you."

"It's always the same."

"Nonsense! Come along, Miss Fleet."

"Where to?" Molly asked, startled.

"Come on, come on! Get a bloody move on!"

He grabbed Molly by the shoulders and shoved her through the door. As they drove through King's Cross in his police car, it seemed to Molly as if all the kookaburras were laughing at her . . .

29

The First Mrs. Rigby

Inspector Cox took Molly Fleet to the restaurant and the Variety movie house for identification purposes, and had inquiries made as to whether the girl had visited Miss Rigby at the time stated. Molly seemed to have a perfect alibi. What Inspector Cox had to do now was find out what Alexander Rigby had been doing on the day of the murder between five and seven. And the inspector would try to cast more light on the relationship between Molly Fleet and the architect. The whole thing gave him a funny feeling. Had the two hired a third person to commit the crime? In spite of her reticence on the subject, there was no doubt in the inspector's mind that Miss Fleet hated Candy.

Rigby's jewel ushered him onto the terrace. One might as well have a beautiful view if one was to be molested by the police. Mrs. Andrews had said farewell to her family a few days before, and returned to Vaucluse. She had come to the conclusion that she would rather be vexed by Rigby than by her son-in-law. With Rigby she at least knew where she was at. Naturally he hadn't asked her why she had come crawling back, and in this case the indifference of the Aussies was a boon. Rigby sent the housekeeper Mrs. Andrews had "trained" to Elizabeth West Grierson in Brisbane. That lady could write novels, but as a cook her husband found her too inexperienced.

Rigby had not rolled out the red carpet for Mrs. Andrews's return, but he usually ate at home, and that came perilously close to a declaration of love. Moreover, the second Mrs. Rigby was apparently gone for good. No more letters from London. On one occasion, when Mrs. Andrews mentioned it, Rigby slammed the door in her face, polite as ever. But he seemed pleased that she had come back because he slammed doors a little more gently. And yesterday he had put a box of chocolates in her room. That was after she had cooked chicken in wine. The way to Rigby's heart had always been through his stomach. She was evidently the only woman who had ever grasped this simple truth. She wondered if the first Mrs. Rigby had cooked, but Mrs. Andrews was careful never to ask the boss any questions about his wives.

Inspector Cox was told that Mr. Rigby would not be coming home today. It was his intention to spend the weekend in Manly, and he would proceed straight there from the office. "We are not murderers," Mrs. Andrews declared.

She reacted to every question as if it were a personal insult. She sat in her big chair on the terrace and drank coffee. She did offer her arch-enemy a cup; she knew how to behave. "There's no poison in it today," she said, and was surprised when Cox laughed. He was wondering if Mrs. Andrews would be the third Mrs. Rigby. She looked so pleased with herself.

"Were you employed in this house while the second Mrs. Rigby was living here?"

Mrs. Andrews laughed long and dramatically. "I came to this house quite a bit earlier than the second Mrs. Rigby," she said with poorly disguised scorn. "One might say that the second Mrs. Rigby was a transient, passing through Sydney. I became Mr. Rigby's housekeeper just after he lost his first wife under very tragic circumstances."

"Was that a long time ago?"

The inspector knew exactly when it had happened, but he had the feeling that Mrs. Andrews knew a lot that hadn't been entered in the files.

"Poor Mr. Rigby was thirty-five years old at the time and inconsolable, naturally."

"Naturally," said Inspector Cox.

"I did my best to distract him."

"Did you succeed, Mrs. Andrews?"

"Sometimes I made him laugh, and that was something, considering how unhappy he was. Of course he inherited an enormous fortune, and that *can* be a comfort. Unfortunately I wasn't in very good spirits myself, since I had had to leave my beautiful homeland, penniless, and had only been in Sydney a short time."

"Did you come from Poland or from Greece?"

"From *Hungary!*" Mrs. Andrews said sternly. "Budapest. One of the great cultural centers of the world. Perhaps you have heard about it?"

"Plenty!" Cox said drily. "Today you can stretch culture like a rubber band. Why did you leave Hungary?"

"For political reasons. And what do you know about that over here?"

"We hear enough from our new Australians. You're not exactly reticent."

"I have lived in Sydney for fifteen years and remained a stranger," Mrs. Andrews said grimly, and poured her third cup of coffee. "I came to this young country as a pilgrim. I wanted to kiss the very earth. I wanted to worship, Inspector. But I soon gave up."

"Why do you suppose that was, Mrs. Andrews?" Cox was amused.

"It was not my fault. I soon noticed that the primitive materialism that rules this country was murdering my soul."

"I wouldn't come to a murderous conclusion so fast." The inspector was smiling. "Your coffee is first-rate, Mrs. Andrews."

Rigby's jewel relaxed and offered the inspector a second cup. "What do you want from Mr. Rigby?" she asked suspiciously.

"Some routine questions. I've just come from his sister."

This bit of information seemed to calm Mrs. Andrews. "Miss Rigby is a real lady," she said. "But she can give you a hard time. Too little heart. She was here for dinner yesterday and she spoke about the tragic murder so icily. *I* didn't close my eyes for two nights!"

"Were you a friend of Miss Blyth's?"

"*I?* A friend of *hers?* You must be joking, sir! I don't associate with whores. I am accustomed to quite different social contacts at home."

"So why couldn't you sleep?"

"Because of Alex—I mean, Mr. Rigby." Mrs. Andrews coughed. "The news upset him terribly."

"How did he find out?"

"From the paper. Like all of us. We don't have any courier service between Vaucluse and the boardinghouse in Darlinghurst, if that's what you mean."

"I don't mean anything, Mrs. Andrews. I'm just asking if you can give me any useful information about Miss Blyth."

"Mr. Rigby knew her," Mrs. Andrews said, mollified. "Not that I spy on him, but I had the opportunity of seeing my boss with her in Bondi. I swim there occasionally. The beach is for everybody, no?"

"This is a free country. I swim there too, when I have the time."

"Molly Fleet does too," Mrs. Andrews said thoughtfully. "She sometimes massaged the second Mrs. Rigby. What nerve that girl has! Just imagine—she came here to see Mr. Rigby on the day of the murder. I wasn't listening, but I happened to overhear their conversation as I was about to serve some refreshments. Mr. Rigby was so enraged that I stopped with the drinks in front of the door, I was trembling so."

"It isn't easy to work for a choleric man." The inspector sounded sympathetic.

"He wouldn't behave like that with *me*. But I must say, I read his every wish."

"That is remarkable. But Miss Fleet apparently doesn't know how to handle Mr. Rigby."

"He threw her out! He yelled something about not letting himself be bled white, and that he'd wring anybody's neck who tried it again. He didn't mean it literally, Inspector."

"Let's hope not, for his sake." The inspector laughed, and even Mrs. Andrews managed a bitter-sweet smile.

"I watch over Mr. Rigby, Inspector. Barking dogs don't bite. But right now he's so nervous that I speak to him as little as possible."

"Is he working very hard?"

"Yes. That on top of everything else. Since this murder he has been beside himself. Unfortunately when Mr. Rigby is upset it is very hard on those around him. He raves! When the first Mrs. Rigby came to such a tragic end, they say he actually flogged himself."

"You're joking, Mrs. Andrews!"

"I'm not. All Sydney knows it. It only goes to show that the first Mrs. Rigby was just as unable to get along with him as the second one."

"I thought you didn't know the first Mrs. Rigby?"

"I knew her like my own pocket. All Sydney said at the time that my boss pushed her over the cliff. She was always overdressed and drunk. He couldn't get a housekeeper after that, although the police couldn't pin anything on him. Of course he would never have done such a thing!"

"Did Mr. Rigby tell you all this himself?"

"Of course not! The subject is taboo in this house. Miss Rigby prepared me for the gossip before I took on the job. The first Mrs. Rigby must have driven him crazy. Miss West, the writer, said so once."

"To you?"

"To Miss Rigby, of course. The ladies were waiting here for Alex—I mean, Mr. Rigby, and I was serving tea. I heard excited voices, so I waited discreetly until Miss West had calmed down. Authors are always ridiculously excited. Of course Miss West was madly in love with my boss, but it didn't get her anywhere."

"You have such interesting things to tell, Mrs. Andrews. I could listen to you for hours, but I'm taking up too much of your time."

"I am hungry for conversation, Inspector! Right now Mr. Rigby is a regular Trappist. Do help yourself to the apple strudel."

"Did you bake it? . . . It's wonderful!"

"A recipe from home. Forgive me if I say that we new Aussies understand a little more about the art of cooking than you natives. Steak—morning, noon, and night. No true culinary culture! But the beer in Sydney is really good."

"It doesn't have to be baked," said Cox. "I would be very grateful for the recipe for that apple strudel when I come the next time. I'll try to explain to my mother how it should taste."

"I'm honored, Inspector! It would make me very happy. If I may say so, you aren't like a policeman at all!"

"Policemen like to eat well too. So don't forget, next time. . . ."

Mrs. Andrews beamed. But then it occurred to her that the inspector, albeit most pleasantly, had announced a second visit. She said Mr. Rigby couldn't tell the inspector anything more than she had already told him. Frankly, Cox was afraid that Rigby would have much less to say. He calmed Mrs. Andrews, assuring her it would be an absolutely routine visit. He simply had to question everyone who had known Miss Blyth.

"But I have strict instructions not to let anyone see Mr. Rigby," said Mrs. Andrews. "As I just tried to explain . . . it's his nerves. Unfortunately he's a pretty wild fellow by nature, and when he speaks softly, he's dangerous. The second Mrs. Rigby used to tremble before him. On the other hand, Mr. Rigby can be a darling, as trusting as a little boy. Especially when he has enjoyed his food."

Cox digested this bit of information. He offered Mrs. Andrews a cigarette. "Things can't have been easy for you after the death of the first Mrs. Rigby."

"I didn't come to Sydney to lead an easy life, Inspector. By coming to this innocent continent I saved myself and my daughter. Believe me, from the very first day I had the patience of a saint where Mr. Rigby was concerned, although he hurt my feelings daily. I told myself he didn't know any better."

"But he makes a highly intelligent impression. Or am I wrong?"

"Too intelligent sometimes, Inspector. There are times when I find him downright eerie!"

"Why?"

"He can hear the grass growing. But the murder in Darlinghurst he did *not* anticipate. Nor could he sense the fact that the first Mrs. Rigby was going to fall over the cliff. The poor old thing was nearsighted, but she wouldn't wear glasses, out of pure vanity, because she wanted to look young."

"Who told you that?"

"Miss Rigby. It was a terrible tragedy. When his wife fell into the abyss, Mr. Rigby was just unpacking the picnic basket."

"So I suppose that was the end of the picnic."

"Oh, *he* can always eat!" Mrs. Andrews said good-naturedly. She must have been nurturing a morbid jealousy of the first Mrs. Rigby throughout all these years, thought Cox. "If I were to be quite frank with you, Inspector . . . but no. No. I've already said too much."

"Not at all," said Inspector Cox cheerily, and he meant it. "As I just said, I could listen to you for hours. I have seldom come across such perspicacity combined with tact. So—what were you going to say?"

"Well . . . that it was a blessing for Mr. Rigby that the old woman bowed out. Life with her must have been hell."

"Did Miss Rigby tell you that too?"

"Not she! She's too much of a hypocrite to speak that frankly. Quite by chance I found a letter from Mr. Rigby's first wife in his desk. The stupid woman was threatening to sue him for assault!"

"How could Mr. Rigby leave a letter like that lying around?"

"He leaves everything lying around! In this respect he's a real Aussie. I'm sorry, Inspector! At home we hid threatening letters like that in a metal box and wore the key around our necks."

"A very good safety measure."

"That was before the communist regime. After that no one wrote letters any more."

"Did the first Mrs. Rigby write anything else?"

"She wrote that she had no intention of letting him wring her neck. Have you ever heard anything like that?"

"No."

"And she wasn't going to throw her money at him anymore, either!"

"Did she have money to throw?"

"Did she ever! She was the widow of a very wealthy sheep farmer in New South Wales. If I may draw a comparison with antiquity—I studied literature and philosophy in Paris—the first Mrs. Rigby owned the Golden Fleece!"

"Nice for Mr. Rigby."

"Later, Inspector. Later. Alex—I mean, Mr. Rigby at once offered me a generous salary. After the death of the first Mrs. Rigby he could afford to. The second Mrs. Rigby owned no more than the dress she had on!"

"Did the second Mrs. Rigby want a lot of money too?"

"That woman?" Mrs. Andrews said scornfully. "That sleepyhead was even too lazy to spend money! We're happy to be rid of her at last, after seven years."

"I can imagine that."

"To be honest, I have never seen such blackmail letters as Miss Candy wrote after her accident."

"Did Mr. Rigby let you read the letters?"

"I found them on the floor, all crumpled up and torn. I mean the first letters. Suddenly, two weeks before the murder, Mr. Rigby locked them up. I don't know why."

"We can ask him," the inspector suggested.

"Not I! I don't want him to wring my neck. Figuratively speaking, of course."

"Of course, Mrs. Andrews."

"I did happen to read the last letter before the murder. Quite by chance. Believe me, I only did so because I was so terribly worried about Alex ... I mean, Mr. Rigby. He left the letter lying on the breakfast table because he was called to the phone. I was just bringing in his ham and eggs and there ..."

"Very understandable, Mrs. Andrews. You were worried. . . ."

"My blood turned to ice in my veins. How much longer was my boss going to be blackmailed like this? The young woman—I mean Candy—couldn't make any more money. . . ."

"But why did Mr. Rigby pay up? It's not exactly like him, is it?"

"Not exactly," said Mrs. Andrews hesitantly. "Listen to me, Inspector. My Mr. Rigby wouldn't have given that little gold digger another penny if she hadn't threatened that she ..." Mrs. Andrews looked out into the garden and stopped, petrified. "Excuse me, Inspector. I have to go to my kitchen."

"But I thought Mr. Rigby had gone to Manly!"

"Here he comes!" Mrs. Andrews stood poised for flight. "He is *so* unpredictable. He's just putting the car in the garage."

Inspector Cox had already noticed Rigby's arrival out of the corner of his eyes. What had Candy Blyth threatened? And what lay behind that threat?

"If you want to see a picture of the first Mrs. Rigby, Inspector, I put the painting of her in the flowered hat in our spare room, beside the bureau of the second Mrs. Rigby." After which words, she disappeared.

Rigby took the terrace steps three at a time. He looked at Cox, his eyes narrowed. "Good evening, Inspector. I was expecting you. What would you like to know?"

30

Rigby's Monologue

When I saw Inspector Cox sitting on the terrace with Andrews, I knew at once what game he was playing. The fellow's a regular fox! Andrews was red as a beet and took herself to the kitchen on the double. The cop stayed for supper, naturally. That's one of our customs when we have agreeable visitors.

"I just want to ask some routine questions, Mr. Rigby."

I'm sure that's all you want to do, I thought. Funny, but my various wives always reproached me for a lack of tact, when actually I am plentifully endowed with it. For instance, I sensed for years that the thing with Flora would come to a bad end. She just giggled too much. I also could feel how Anne and I were slowly slipping into a fallow season: she became more silent all the time. And I feel—godammit—that Andrews, with the best intentions, had just dug my grave; why else would Cox be grinning at me with such satisfaction? The only sure thing in life is that one day we're going to lose it. While Cox asked me his routine questions, smiling amiably, I knew that I was being grilled alive. But I'm tough, and decided not to make it easy for him. He has a nice curly head of hair and I am sure he is a model son and brother. Yes, there sat Cox, smiling apologetically because he had to bother me with this nuisance of a murder case. He merely wanted to find out if I'd wrung Candy's neck or only provided the nylon stocking! Idiot that I am, I gave her a dozen pairs after the accident. Of course I admitted it at once. I even added that girls can never have enough stockings.

"But it was one stocking too many," Cox replied, and I didn't contradict him. Still, I hadn't given Miss Blyth the stockings to strangle her, and I made that point quite clear. Cox was waiting for my confession and I was waiting for my steak.

The inspector gradually turned the conversation to the time of the murder, and "for routine reasons," asked where I had spent the hours between five and seven. I had gone for a walk. That's always the worst possible alibi, but that was his problem.

Had anyone seen me on my walk? Yes—at least three hundred drivers. Not all at once, naturally! Cox reddened, either with pleasure over my innocence or fury over my sass. Who can tell? I used to wander through Sydney regularly with Marchmont, frequently between five and seven. We saw the city as it had been and as it was going to be. I saw skyscrapers in the sky and Stan explained the Victorians to me. In short, I went for a walk this time too.

French had accompanied me for a while, but I didn't want to drag Robbie into this interview with the inspector, and get him into trouble with the police just as innocently as Andrews had managed to. The young man is shaping up splendidly, and is thoroughly decent. Interested in nothing but sports and architecture. So . . . I said I had gone out by my soul-searching self, and shall inform French to this effect tomorrow.

"What did Miss Fleet want from you?"

Cox had already questioned Molly Fleet. I had that from Grace. Grace doesn't like the whole business. She keeps thinking of the scandal over Flora. Who can blame her? Over the cheese I became aware of the fact that Andrews must have told some wild tales about my first wife. I had to admire the way Cox led the conversation to the subject of kookaburras, and tried to get out of me what role I had played in Flora's death in the Blue Mountains. This was where my appetite came in again. I can't deny that I ate three-quarters of the contents of the picnic basket at the scene of the disaster. The shock hit me in the stomach. Already at the time the police had seen my appetite as a symptom of hard-boiled criminality, whereas I couldn't see what cold pork could possibly have to do with murder! And now I noticed that Inspector Cox would also have found it more sympathetic if the picnic basket had arrived at headquarters untouched. Naturally Cox had already been through all the files on *that* case. I was certain that he had not enjoyed reading that even the chief of police hadn't been able to pin anything on me. To this day I am sure that it was my sister who scared the living daylights out of them.

Cox asked if I had visited Candy frequently after the accident. To his disappointment, I had to say no. I had had enough of that sheila's sparkling conversation long ago. I had felt sorry for her, but it wasn't my fault that she'd run into a car. One thing though I couldn't know was that after the accident, this little gold digger from Kalgoorlie intended to live off me for the rest of her life. Of course the inspector had harried Molly Fleet until she had admitted her visit to me. Ethical motives had prompted Molly to mobilize the blackmail effort. She had suddenly and unexpectedly developed such compassion for Candy that she had given the girl my address. Noble as I am, I might have gone on paying for a while if Candy hadn't behaved so shamelessly. I don't let dolls like that touch upon my marriage.

I showed Inspector Cox the last letter. I prefer to put my cards on the table as long as it doesn't cost me my neck. Cox read it with rather flattering interest and remarked that under these circumstances, Candy's death must have been very convenient. I wasn't dumb enough to deny it. Then Inspector Cox thanked me for a delightful evening, and left.

I watched him go and didn't feel good about it. Andrews removed the dishes without saying a word. I asked her what she had told the inspector, and she said, "Nothing." Just what I thought. The people who mean as well by me as Mary Andrews are of necessity my ruination.

"I hope the inspector doesn't come back," she said.

"If we didn't have that to hope for, I'd be a goner," I told her. "Don't rattle the dishes so, Mary. I have a splitting headache."

Later she came over to the couch I was lying on and sobbed. She said that she had committed the murder so that the blackmailing bitch would finally leave me in peace. I asked her where she'd got hold of this information, although I knew she'd been going through my correspondence for years. Then I told the poor thing to go to bed.

The fallow season began for me after the death of my first wife, with a vast emptiness. Socially they had buried me. Only Marchmont, John Darling, and of course Paddy Trent had stuck to me although they must have had their own doubts about my innocence.

This time things are different. The *saison morte* comes at a wildly busy time. We are planning extensive projects at the office and the inspector and I are going steady in Vaucluse. He usually arrives before me. Instinct or coincidence? Cox is a most genial, patient man and I'm sure it often pays off. And he argues elegantly, I have to grant him that. A new generation I suppose, with a new technique. They are big on psychology and don't stumble around like our grandfathers. But psychiatric tact is lost on me, and Cox is much too cunning not to become gradually more pointed. I don't have much patience, but I've got to be patient this time or he'll nab me. I imagine Andrews has told him that I can be very unpleasant, and reports of my beating up Flora are in the file. Cox will soon know the story of my past by heart. Now he only asks questions in an effort to somehow, sometime, trip me up. I have to be damned careful not to lose track of my surroundings and let Cox catch me in his web.

Grace has written to Robert Muir. I wish he'd invite me to Japan now. But Cox would justifiably see my departure as a flight attempt. His reply to any request of this kind would be to remain at his disposal until the murder is solved. I hate superfluous questions just as I hate questions that are asked just to lure me out of my lair. Flora used to drive me crazy like that. She would constantly ask me if I still loved her, when she knew all the time that I'd never gone that far astray. At the beginning, giggling behind the bar in Pitt Street, she had been very sympathetic. I called her "Kookaburra," and the name stuck.

During these last days I get the feeling that somebody is trying to throttle me from behind with a nylon stocking. I may not be as emotional or sensitive as some of the ladies I know, but I don't have to ask Cox whether I am now seriously a suspect. Like everyone else in Sydney, I read the papers, and what they print daily is as repugnant to me as it must be to the inspector. The voice of the scandal sheets gets louder and louder: Are the police asleep? How much longer are the honest citizens of Sydney to be exposed without protection to the "nylon murderer"? And is a certain inspector, known as the sharpest bloodhound between hell and New South Wales, now herding sheep in the meadows? I can imagine how delighted Cox and his chief must be when they read these daily questions. I can hear the chief mumbling, "Get a bloody move on, Cox!"

Cox simply has to come up with an arrest soon, if only for the sake of his reputation. I told him everything I know. It may not be much, but everything depends on how you approach the material. To be blackmailed for life is not a pleasant prospect, and the inspector had read black on white that this was just what Miss Blyth intended to do. Why hadn't I torn up the letter? he asked, almost compassionately. I told him I hadn't come down with the last shower. When Miss Blyth suddenly and unexpectedly departed this life, it had been my intention to sue her. After that Cox didn't appear for days. By then he had recovered from the blow, and the day before yesterday he had everything he needed.

A Mrs. Evans, who delivers Mrs. Doody's groceries, had reported something, not for the express purpose of breaking my neck, but because all the women in Darlinghurst, and all the kookaburras in King's Cross, were in a state of panic thanks to the nonsense printed in the papers. They feared the unknown murderer. Mrs. Evans had rummaged around in her memory. At the time of the murder she had seen "a very tall man" enter Mrs. Doody's boardinghouse. She had just delivered flour, sugar, and tea, and had brought something extra for Candy to enjoy. The door to the boardinghouse was always ajar so that the neighbors could look in on the girl when nobody else was there. That was on the day of the murder. Mrs. Evans had found only Candy at home. When she was back in her shop, she happened to look out the door and saw this "very tall man" coming out of the boardinghouse. Cox must have shown her my picture and the dumb creature had nodded.

The stupid thing is that I actually was at the boardinghouse on the afternoon of the murder, since in that morning's mail I had received Candy's most despicable letter. I spent a few minutes with her, long enough to tell her off and to warn her that I would sue if she didn't stop. Whether the inspector wants to believe it or not, at 5:05 Candy was still very much alive. She hurled abuses at me, and I wondered where the little angel-face could have picked up such obscene language. Flora's insults were bouquets in comparison.

After my visit to Candy, I was so furious that I went back to the office and tried to calm myself with work. Robbie French was still there, and that's when we went for a walk together. He noticed that I was enraged about something, and after a while let me go on alone. I had told Molly Fleet to come and see me after supper because she insisted she had to speak to me.

Since I had not done Miss Blyth in, I didn't see why I should attract more suspicion by admitting that I had been at the boardinghouse that afternoon. My common sense told me that Cox would never have let that sort of an incident pass. How could he? I wouldn't have believed it myself. Nobody in the world believes coincidences like that. That's why mystery writers have such a hard time with the reviewers. Yet things like that happen more frequently than we realize, and break a lot of people's necks.

And how had Candy known my wife's London address? Molly told me without batting an eyelash. In her natural friendliness, Anne had sent Molly Fleet a card from London. Candy had seen the address while Molly was out working. It would therefore have been quite simple for Candy to inform my wife that I was still fooling around with little girls. And I'd only been out once with the little bitch after her return from Broome. But Anne would never have believed it. In short—I felt that I had gradually shelled out enough for that bit of fun. But Mrs. Evans remembered . . . damn her!

Inspector Cox appeared secretly, silently, and softly as I—assisted by Robbie French—was instructing our second generation of would-be architects in Vaucluse, in the art of modern architecture. We had just tacked a plan on the wall when Cox appeared with Sergeant Cunningham. I saw at once that Cox had found out everything, and was perfectly calm. We can only live one life and die only one death. I don't know who strangled the girl, but I know whoever it is is going to laugh himself silly.

Cox proceeded according to regulations. He called me out of the room and told me he had a warrant for my arrest, and that I was accused of murdering Miss Blyth. He said, "I must warn you that anything you may say from now on will be put on record and can be used as proof against you."

I asked the young man to be less formal, and with as much respect as he had coming to him, told him he had come to the wrong address. But the inspector was there officially, and this time there was no cozy supper on the terrace. Fortunately it was Andrews's day off, so I was spared a Hungarian rhapsody.

"Get a bloody move on, Inspector!" I said amiably. "Unfortunately I don't have much time this evening. We're working in here with our young ones."

In the meantime French had appeared and was staring at the two cops, speechless. "Go on working, Robbie," I told him. "You're going to laugh but I'm being accused of murder."

French turned pale. Now he'll have to find the partner I've been painting on the office wall since Marchmont's death. Good thing our senior partner is sleeping where no one can waken him.

Meanwhile Robbie had found his voice again and was asking the inspector if he had gone mad.

"I would advise you to express yourself more cautiously, young man," said Inspector Cox.

"Alex!" Robbie yelled. *"Say something!"*

"Draw up plans for a new jail," I told him. "The one we have now has no style, and oh yes, one more thing, Robbie. Call Jimmy."

James Battleship was my lawyer. Robbie nodded. His eyes were rounder than ever with astonishment. I patted him on the shoulder. "Do a good job, partner."

Robbie's face trembled and he looked away. "Let's go," said Cox, at just the right moment.

I've been locked up now for four days, and it seems like four years. I'm tough by nature, but right now I can't see how I'm possibly going to stick this out for a lifetime. I'm trained to be free. Even marriage seemed a robbery of freedom.

My lawyer is persuasive. He really knows his business. He got me out of the mess that time with Flora; he didn't waste any time today either. First he brought regards from Grace and Robert Muir, who is keeping Grace company right now. Good for Grace!

Jimmy said, "You have a lot of things going for you. The girl tried to commit suicide once. And she certainly was blackmailing you. Thank God you saved the letters. I've told Howard everything."

Howard Clifford is Sydney's top defense counsel, and always works with Jimmy. The fact that Jimmy was already mentioning Clifford now, at the beginning, didn't sound promising. But Jimmy said at once that we'd swing it. No doubt about that. Naturally he would like to know . . .

"I didn't do it, Jimmy. I just tried to bring the stupid girl to her senses on the wrong day. And that's my funeral, mate. Who's going to believe me?"

"I am," said Jimmy Battleship.

"Good of you."

My headache was coming back. There wasn't a trace of the murderer, and Jimmy found this a handicap too. Both of us knew that Cox was a decent human being and had to be totally convinced of my guilt or he wouldn't have arrested me. Everything spoke against me, just as in the first scandal. But the thing with Flora had been much more compli- cated. I had not been as innocent as I was this time. It's quite possible that old guilt feelings can take one by the throat. Anything is possible in this lousy world. I thought of some cases where people had sat under lock and key for years before the murderer, shocked out of his compla- cency for God-knows-what reasons, confessed his guilt. But until then . . .

Jimmy got up. "Cox is still searching."

"Glad to hear that." I sounded hoarse.

"Chin up, Alex!"

"Tell Grace she's not to write to my wife about any of this nonsense. Anne hates scandal. How is Grace taking it?"

"Very well, to all appearances. Robert Muir is a great help."

Jimmy had to go. He could simply walk out into freedom. I had never given a thought to what a great thing that was. I mean, you open the door, nobody stops you . . . Jimmy waved, as if we were at Central Station, but my train was on a dead-end track. My old cobber looked tired.

"Don't take it to heart," I said. "I'm not worth it."

"Rubbish!" said Jimmy.

I asked him what he was going to do over the weekend. I wanted things to go on as normally as possible. Jimmy was going out to Manly, to see Grace.

"Why don't you go dancing?"

Jimmy said I should let him do what he wanted with his weekend. Then he told me that Bertie Dobson had been to see Grace and prescribed sleeping pills.

"Is she taking them?"

"You know your sister."

I could see Grace tossing the sleeping pills into the Pacific. Too bad. It wouldn't do her any harm to have a good sleep before the big show in court. I hoped that my case would not be tried too soon. It would be better if all of them had a chance to forget me a little, so that I would be little more than a vague abstraction. With negative signs, naturally. Would they take down the plaque on our house in Parramatta? The one they'd put up for my fiftieth birthday? It only went to show how embarrassingly premature honors can be. On my fiftieth birthday everybody thought I'd march into eternity crowned with laurels. Perhaps I was the only one who knew at the time that I'd only be playing for a few more seasons. I asked Jimmy how Andrews was taking it.

"She's very silent these days. Too silent. Robbie French looks in on her sometimes after office hours. So do Grace and Bertie Dobson." And John Darling had flown back to Sydney from a research trip. Together with Muir, they had descended upon Cox. John is busily married now and spends his free time working for the benefit of our primitive Australians, but he's always there when you need him.

"Any other guests at the Rigbys'?"

"Paddy Trent, of course. He arrived from Brisbane yesterday. He's in Betty West's room."

It was all properly set up as for a funeral, but my cobbers were first-rate. As private detectives, however, they'd hardly manage to compete with Inspector Cox. A dead race.

"Be careful what you say at the hearing," Jimmy warned. "It's your turn in three days."

"I'll tell them where to get off, you can depend on that!"

"And that's just what you're not going to do," said Jimmy, in his stiffest manner. "Whatever you keep to yourself can't be held against you, my boy."

I asked him if I should fall on my knees and thank them for pinning a murder rap on me. I could feel the blood rush to my head. My heart was pounding, and there was the taste of ashes in my mouth.

"I'm telling you one thing, Jimmy—nothing in the world can stop me from . . ." I was trying to swallow.

"Take it easy, Alex. I'll think up something. And don't forget our Clifford. He's not exactly a beginner."

I was holding my head in my hands. Jimmy asked if I wanted something to drink. I said there was time for that after the verdict. Then I apologized, and he mumbled that it was okay. After that I asked him to leave me alone. He cleaned his owlish glasses and injected one of his famous, carefully measured pauses, which gave his clients a chance to calm down. Finally he said that I must not give up now. It would all be cleared up in the end.

"I hope I live to see it," I said. "Hmm . . . thanks a lot for everything."

Jimmy didn't like to hear anything like that, so I hastily asked him to pass on my best regards to the mob. "You're unlucky with your friends, Jimmy. But this is the last time you'll have to worry about me. I can imagine how they're all slandering me again."

"All Sydney is in an uproar, Alex. The Architects Club is going to get in touch with someone in the upper echelons tomorrow."

"Murder is murder, Jimmy. You should know that. I suppose the yacht-club flag is flying at half mast."

"I'll come again soon." Jimmy nodded encouragingly, and was gone.

Perhaps it wouldn't be such a bad idea to try prayer. But I'm so out of practice that whatever I have to offer is not going to impress anyone in heaven.

I don't know when I first wished Flora dead. A death wish develops slowly, like a cancer. Then suddenly death is unavoidable and there is no cure any more. The desire to be free gnaws, eats you up, and you become morally emaciated. As I lie here listening to the limping footsteps of justice, the past, with flowered hats and shrill laughter, rises up to meet me. I never knew whether Flora was laughing at me when she giggled like a kookaburra, but one day I knew, and began planning her death. Now she is avenged. Her shrill laughter fills my cell day and night. You can't take any pills for that.

I was thirty at the time; Flora was forty-five. Of course I married her for her money. I needed it. I wanted a brilliant career, and I was honest and stupid enough to tell Flora. She couldn't possibly think—or so I believed in my innocence—that a young man of thirty, healthy and virile, would love a shopworn bar girl with a double chin and red veins in her face. I don't know what goes on in the minds of these over-the-hill women, but Flora certainly overestimated her charms. She really believed in true love, right on up—or down, rather—to the grave. I don't know where she picked up this romantic nonsense. Before she married her rich sheep farmer and nursed him to his death, she was a jolly bar girl who knew her way around Sydney. Perhaps the romantic side of her arrived with menopause. She was in sexual purgatory when I turned up. She was, as I already mentioned, forty-five, a dangerous age. It cast a shadow on our marriage. My situation became increasingly precarious. Maybe I *am* a bastard. I probably am. But gradually it became too much for me when Flora told my friends she was keeping her money under lock and key because I was too extravagant.

In a very short time she had turned my house in Vaucluse, which I had built with her money, into a jolly men's bar. What could I do about it? I was a bad-tempered guest in my own house, and sat around with John Darling or Marchmont. Trent hadn't arrived in Sydney yet, and because I was bored I had a little affair with Celia Coleman, his future wife. Flora was idiotically jealous. When we met good old Paddy Trent at the Colemans for the first time, I decided to hand Celia over to him because she wasn't worth Flora's outbursts of jealousy. Paddy fell in love with Celia right away. I wouldn't have advised him to marry an old bat. The first time I met Trent at the Coleman house I found him extraordinary. Flora hated him. Once she told him never to come to the house again. I'm sure that had never happened to him before. But he had come to see Flora and advise her to be a little more cautious with me.

That was the time I used to beat her up when she was fresh, but one thing must be said for her—she could be pretty abusive herself. Once I came to the office with a black eye, and had to tell Stan Marchmont I'd run into an open door . . . not that Marchmont believed me. When he narrowed his eyes and said nothing, I knew he knew.

Once when Flora was left an invalid on the battlefield—she had hurled obscenities at me which no gentleman would repeat—she ran away. Grace brought her back. Grace behaved wonderfully, although she didn't approve of my behavior. Flora told her at the office that I had tried to strangle her that night. All I did was press a little harder than usual—that was all.

After she came back, things were better for a while. Then she boiled over again, and all Sydney was beginning to laugh at me. Since I wasn't sleeping with her any more—I'm much too normal to love and beat up the same person—Flora told my cobbers I couldn't get it up anymore. She didn't express herself in that civilized a fashion, and the mob at the yacht club must have laughed themselves sick when "Auntie" served them the details of her past and present from behind the bar in Vaucluse.

So that's the way we lived.

When strangers thought she was my mother, I was to blame. Once I took a kitchen towel and wiped the bright red rouge off her face and made a mess of her stiff curls. I resented the fact that she awoke sadistic instincts in me. It was a monstrous relationship. When I saw her motionless bird-eyes staring at me, when she wanted me to embrace her, the very idea made me shudder . . . I asked myself sometimes how she could imagine that even a bastard like me could function under such conditions.

I suggested a divorce. She could get the hell out of my life with her money, her profanity, and her varicose veins. All she did was laugh shrilly. Kookaburra! I was ashamed. Not only was she a dead weight, not only was she devouring my virility, but she was making the name of Rigby a joke in Sydney. She slept with anyone who had the stomach for it, and handed out gifts—gold cuff links or checks. Dr. Dobson gave her tranquilizers. She threw them away. One day I found on my place at the breakfast table some quck nostrum intended to restore male potency. She stared at me, hard and sly, and laughed. I laughed too, but I saw red. That was the morning I decided on the outing to the Blue Mountains. I only had to wait for the appropriate time.

One day I stopped up my ears with plugs because Flora was making so much noise. That night she came to my room. "Be good to Auntie, and good things will come your way," she gurgled. I threw her out, and she screamed that I'd regret it.

Jimmy Battleship had spoken to her several times and explained that I was willing to take all the blame, but Flora told him everything was all right. I was just overworked. She was older and felt responsible for me. Why on earth should we get a divorce? Flora suggested I should go live somewhere else if I wanted to. She was sure I'd soon come back to the fleshpots of Vaucluse. I went to see Jimmy again. "Try a little harder," was his advice. "Perhaps if you're friendly, things will get better."

"Perhaps," I said, not meaning it. Jimmy gave me a sharp look, but he didn't say anything.

That night I went to Flora. It was the shabbiest thing I've ever done in my life. But I had to make up with her or she wouldn't come to the Blue Mountains with me. She was horribly grateful, and I felt . . . Forget it, Alex!

"Now everything's going to be all right," she sobbed. For the first time in years I felt sorry for her. The old thing was starved for affection. I had embraced her, so I loved her. All that was needed was for her to take out her checkbook . . .

Things became worse. I could never repeat the performance; I could feel that in my bones. All I could do was ski out into the Pacific as far as I could and let the ocean wash over me. But I wanted to build, and Marchmont said I was getting better all the time.

She didn't let me work. She came between me and my vision with her aging doll's face, her unbridled temper, her insatiable need for a quarrel, a beating, a drink. I hardly ever spoke to her. She didn't seem to care. I slept with her, so nothing was wrong. A fat old lady in the hay. And I was a searcher for beauty, and a bastard.

We drove off, and Flora told dirty jokes. She was wearing high-heeled shoes, one of her flowered hats, and no glasses. She giggled, and I felt feeble. Godammit! I felt sorry for the old fool. But I had to keep my cool. In those five years she had finished me off, I mean as a man. I never looked at a girl any more. I was afraid. Once I'd spoken to old Dr. Dobson. I told him about a "friend," but Bertie's old man knew whom I was talking about. So there was something like psychic impotence! Damn, damn . . . In our office in George Street I locked myself in the john and wept. The last time I had wept was when Mother had died and Grace told me. I was still in short pants at the time. I wished Mother were still in Parramatta and not in heaven . . .

We had taken a picnic basket with us to the Blue Mountains, and wanted to have our lunch on the plateau facing the Three Sisters. How it happened, I don't know, but before I had finished unpacking the basket we were engaged in the most violent quarrel of the season. Flora shouted her usual obscenities and I reacted for a while with silence.

Only when she screamed that I had come to her one night only to "milk" her financially afterwards, I walked up to her slowly. She must have seen something in my eyes—Flora was no fool—because she cried out. We were all alone. It was still too early for tourists. I came closer, slowly, slowly, and she shrank back, farther and farther, in her high-heeled shoes and deadly fear, and with her nearsightedness. She stepped back until she was standing at the edge of the cliff.

When I saw it, I stretched out my arm to pull her back. You can imagine pushing someone down into an abyss as much as you want, until the moment for such a gesture arrives. Then things look quite different.

Flora misunderstood my gesture. She had always misunderstood me. "Don't touch me, you pig! Help! Help!" she screamed, and tripped backwards, over the edge.

It all happened in seconds. Words are lame, just like justice.

So here I am, a sitting duck because for five long years I murdered Flora Pratt in my mind. That is the truth, even if Inspector Cox won't accept it. It's a true black comedy. Perhaps Candy Blyth's murderer will one day also atone for a murder he didn't commit. I wonder if Cox will interrogate him . . .

31

A Good Crime

Inspector Cox was waiting for a telephone call that didn't come. In spite of his patience, he was nervous. Rigby's hearing was scheduled for the day after tomorrow. Cox was still brooding about the murder in Darlinghurst, although with Mrs. Evans's testimony Rigby's guilt seemed established. He had admitted everything except the murder.

Cox had done everything his experience and conscience demanded. The Evans witness had been confronted with six men, Rigby among them, and with the assurance of a sleepwalker, she had walked straight up to Rigby and declared this was the man who had entered the boardinghouse shortly after five. Rigby must have done it. All the other suspects had watertight alibis. The inspector had also carefully gone through the file on Flora Rigby (Accidental Death) once more because he was looking for character information, and had gained the impression that Rigby certainly was capable of a violent act if sufficiently provoked.

Why couldn't the inspector reconcile himself to the facts? Certainly not because Alexander Rigby was well-placed socially, with a whole collection of status symbols and a villa in Vaucluse. Where murderers were concerned, Cox was democratic. For him a blackfellow who hurled a boomerang was just as important as Alexander Rigby, who had done so much for Sydney and could afford the best lawyers. Naturally Charlie Rainbow, if they ever found him, would have a good lawyer allocated to him by the court, but Rigby, Battleship, and Clifford were a formidable trio. Not that this was worrying Cox. All he cared about was seeing justice done.

Rigby couldn't be freed on bail because he was accused of murder. Why did Inspector Cox stay in his office after hours, waiting for a phone call? He was looking for some material that would possibly provide some psychological proof of Rigby's guilt. Only once in his career had Cox felt like this after an arrest, and then too he had silently, secretly taken all possible measures to find the murderer. And in the end had found him. That had been years ago, and now . . .

He had asked the Evans woman three times if she had noticed any other persons on the day of the murder. After the witness had assured him for the third time that the only person she had seen coming out of the house was Rigby, instinct and experience gave the inspector an idea.

He turned this idea around and around in his mind like something priceless, then he detailed Inspector Carmody—one of his most conscientious men—to watch the boardinghouse. Carmody was wearing civilian clothes and looked like any other fellow lounging around between the boardinghouse and the pub. The instinct that gave Cox the reputation of being the sharpest bloodhound between hell and New South Wales, now told him what instructions to give to Inspector Carmody. The inhabitants of Mrs. Doody's boardinghouse were to enjoy a feeling of security. It was now a house like any other in Darlinghurst. Mrs. Doody, Molly Fleet, Umbrella Uncle, Candy's mother, Catherine Blyth, who was staying there temporarily, were to live as they always had. Gretchen came to see them, Mrs. Doody wept every now and then, Uncle Doody drank his beer and bitters with old Heller from next door—the actor was a steady guest at the house again. Mrs. Evans delivered flour, crackers, and salt, and Candy's tragic end wasn't mentioned. Molly Fleet came home tired from work at night, and Mrs. Blyth preached morality to her as she had done years ago—without success—to her own daughter, Candace. The murderer, Cox decided, had to be one of these people—with the exception of Mrs. Blyth who had come from Kalgoorlie—if Rigby, all the evidence against him notwithstanding, had not committed the crime.

Cox got up and locked the file on the first Mrs. Rigby in his desk. He looked at his watch: six-thirty. He turned to go. Another day . . . nothing. Just then the phone rang. Inspector Carmody reported what Cox had been waiting for day and night. Carmody had quite possibly found nothing but a clue; however, it had to be followed up at once with great caution.

One of Mrs. Doody's lodgers had brought a trunk into the house and removed Charlie Rainbow's flower boxes from the balcony. Who was leaving? And why had the boxes been taken away? Molly Fleet had continued to care for them; there seemed to be no reason to remove them unless . . . they held evidence of some kind.

364

"Shall I detain the person?" asked Inspector Carmody. Names were never mentioned over the phone.

"No. Just keep an eye on whoever it is. I'll be right over. Well done, young man!"

Mrs. Blyth opened the door to the inspector. A trunk stood in the hall, and turned out to be hers, and had journeyed from Kalgoorlie to Sydney with her. But Cox wasn't disappointed. There had to be a second trunk in the house—but where?

Cox looked at the hard, sharp face of Candy's mother, her sparse gray hair, and bitter mouth. The tall, thin woman was dressed in black and looked like a threatening exclamation mark. Of course she was unfriendly; she hated the police, just like every old Aussie did. "I am Mrs. Blyth," she told Inspector Cox. They were seated in the parlor. "I came to my daughter's funeral. I hope I won't be strangled before I leave here."

Mrs. Blyth seemed to be under the impression that her family was going to be exterminated. The inspector murmured a few words to reassure her. The police were keeping an eye on——

"They should have kept an eye on the house earlier! What are we paying taxes for when we don't get any protection? I was always against my daughter living in Sydney. Sodom and Gomorrah! A snake pit, if you ask me!"

"Why didn't you use your authority earlier?"

Mrs. Blyth's expression hardened. "I was through with Candace when she went off with some stranger or other. She had nothing but fun in her head. People like that are doomed." Inspector Cox found Mrs. Blyth deplorably heartless. "Our bread at home was too dry for my daughter," she mumbled. The inspector was silent. For the first time he could imagine why the beautiful young girl had yearned for love, luxury, and recognition.

It was very quiet in Mrs. Doody's parlor. There was an odor of hell, self-justification, and mothballs—the latter from Mrs. Blyth's dress. She had worn it last at her husband's funeral. "Candace was like her father," she said, disparagingly. "No sense of duty. No sense of decency. No faith."

The madonna above Mrs. Blyth's head frowned, or so it seemed to the inspector. "So I have to reconcile myself to *this* blow too," Mrs. Blyth said grimly. "The potter forms the clay and breaks it according to his will."

"How long are you going to stay in Sydney, Mrs. Blyth?"

"Until my sister has packed her few belongings. Lydia Doody is terribly slow." Mrs. Blyth sounded as if she were talking about someone she had only just met.

Mrs. Doody appeared with tea and greeted Inspector Cox like an old friend. Mrs. Blyth didn't approve, that much was obvious. Lydia was simpleminded. She ought to be careful that this fox with the curly hair didn't arrest all of them for some reason or other. Mrs. Blyth, who not only had a sharp tongue but also a keen mind, was telling herself correctly that the inspector had come for a purpose.

"I hear you are leaving Sydney, Mrs. Doody," Cox said in a friendly tone.

"Is there anything wrong with that, Inspector?" Candy's aunt asked tearfully. She had lost a lot of weight, and her love of chatter had run out of her like sawdust out of a broken doll.

"I have nothing to say against it, Mrs. Doody. Why should I?"

"You never know with the police," Mrs. Doody said. "Will they hang Candy's murderer? Or don't they hang people any more in this country? Another cup of tea, Inspector?"

"Thank you, Mrs. Doody. You look exhausted. You should see a doctor."

"My sister will recover in Kalgoorlie. The police visits have taken it out of her." Mrs. Blyth stood up. She didn't like the sharp way the inspector was looking at her. "Now don't talk nonsense," she told her younger sister, and left the room without so much as a nod to the inspector.

"My sister is so upset about Candy's death," Mrs. Doody murmured apologetically. "She loved her above everything else. Catherine has a fine character, even if she doesn't show it."

"Do you really want to leave Sydney, Mrs. Doody?"

"I don't know." She had grown very red and was trembling. "My sister says I should keep my mouth shut when the police question me. Excuse me, please."

"But we're old friends, Mrs. Doody. This is just a little private visit. I wanted to ask how Miss Fleet was feeling. All of you have hard days behind you."

Mrs. Doody nodded and wiped the tears from her eyes. "I always fussed so over the poor child. Perhaps that's not the right love. My sister says I spoiled her. She knows better. And then . . . I really don't like to talk about it . . ."

"You can tell *me*, Mrs. Doody."

"My sister will be angry if she finds out."

"She won't find out. What's troubling you?"

"You won't tell anyone?"

"Not a soul."

"I mean, I can't stop reproaching myself. I let Candy give me so much of her hard-earned money, and bought gin for Uncle with it."

"You mean Edward Doody?"

"That's what I said. Uncle. He's such a wreck, and the gin is all he has."

"What's wrong with Mr. Doody?"

"It's his heart. The doctor's been here twice. Since the dreadful thing happened to Candy, it's terrible. He shouts out loud in the night."

"Does Mr. Doody want to go to Kalgoorlie with you?"

"I don't know. But my sister won't have him."

"Why not?"

"She says she'll let no drunkard into her house. She's probably right, but we're all so fond of Uncle Doody. I can't imagine life without him."

"Where is he planning to go?"

"I don't know. He came here from the bush. He always says this is his only home. But my sister says that's no concern of mine. She's praying for Uncle Doody, and that's good enough. She's very religious, even if she doesn't express it very nicely. But Uncle Doody says the Bible words stink in her mouth. The two just don't like each other. Uncle is funny too. He's only all right with me and Charlie Rainbow."

"Is Mr. Doody home?"

"Don't go up to see him, Inspector. He's . . . he's a bit tipsy right now. The pain . . ."

"If I remember correctly, Mr. Doody was not one of Miss Blyth's admirers."

"You mustn't pay any attention to him. Our Molly says nobody can talk as much nonsense as Uncle Doody."

"When is Miss Fleet coming home?"

"Not at all today."

"Where is she?"

"At Gretchen's. Gretchen Lange from the bakery. Oh heavenly day! We must go! We were supposed to go over there, my sister and I."

"Don't let me stop you, Mrs. Doody."

Cox waited until both ladies were gone. This suited him fine. Carmody was waiting downstairs.

Cox knocked on Mr. Doody's door. When he got no answer, he

pushed it open. Uncle was lying on his bed, a half-empty bottle on the floor beside him. "What do *you* want here?" he growled.

"Just saying hello." The inspector walked slowly into the room. He could see nothing unusual. The umbrellas were hanging from the ceiling as always. Uncle's eyes fluttered as he watched the inspector. "What are you looking for?" he asked.

"Nothing. Or do you have something stashed away?"

"Only a corpse in the closet."

The inspector laughed and walked over to the closet. Mr. Doody jumped up and planted himself, swaying a little, in front of the piece of furniture. "Hands off!" he cried. "I'll teach you a thing or two, Inspector. You're trespassing!"

The inspector pushed the old man aside. "I want to see your corpse in the closet."

He lugged a heavy trunk out of the closet. In the far corner stood two flower boxes. "Are you planting flowers in your closet?" he asked.

"I cut the flowers for Mrs. Doody. She's a good egg."

"But the boxes are going to dirty your things."

"I've packed them."

"Where are you going?"

"Somewhere."

"When?"

"Don't know."

"But you've packed everything."

"Just in case."

"And what do you mean by that?"

"Don't you speak English? Leave me alone! You have your murderer, and we can do what we like. This is a free country."

"How do you know I have my murderer?"

"From the papers. How's he doing?"

"I don't know. Do you?"

The old man stared at the cop. A wild light flickered in his gin-dimmed eyes. "Don't joke with a sick old man," he mumbled.

"When did you buy this trunk?"

"Yesterday."

"Not today?"

"Not today!" shouted Mr. Doody. "And now you'd bloody well better leave me alone!"

"As soon as you tell me where this trunk was until this afternoon."

Edward Doody had turned pale. So the cops had been watching him. He explained that he'd taken the trunk to be repaired. He named a shop in Surry Hills. Later it turned out that no such shop existed.

"I can't buy myself stinking elegant luggage like that murderer, Rigby."

The inspector lifted the trunk with one hand, shook it, and put it down again. "Unpack it, Mr. Doody," he said.

"I'm an old man! I just packed the bloody thing! I can't stoop that much. Leave me alone. My train leaves in an hour."

The inspector ignored this surprising information. "I can wait," he said, his voice dangerously quiet. "Get going, Doody! Or do you want me to help?"

The atmosphere in the narrow room had changed considerably. Cox could sense danger. The old man drew a knife out of one of his umbrellas and threw it, uncertainly, in the direction of the inspector. Cox ducked. "What's the meaning of this?" he asked casually, and laid the bush knife on the table.

"You're to leave us alone!" Mr. Doody drank the rest of the gin and hurled the bottle against the wall. Then he teetered to the trunk and unlocked it. He threw the contents at Cox's feet, with the exception of the newspaper at the bottom. Cox picked up the dented old trunk and shook it.

"If you damage my trunk, I'll sue!"

"You won't need your trunk any more," the inspector said, almost regretfully. He had removed the newspaper and was holding up a pair of gloves, dirty with earth. The gloves seemed to have a life of their own as he dangled them in front of the eyes of the old man. They looked like the hands of a man who had slung a nylon stocking around a girl's neck. "Why did you keep them?" asked the inspector.

"I don't know."

But Uncle knew very well. The gloves reminded him of what he had done for Lydia Doody. He hadn't been able to watch her any longer fluttering around the moody, sick girl, and the end of all jollity and comfort that was a part of Mrs. Doody, like the creaky doors in her house, the visits of the neighbors, her greed for money, but above all—her warmth. For Uncle Doody, Lydia was daughter, friend, his host in this small piece of homeland. By all the saints she had deserved something better than to be tortured by Candy! Finally Uncle Doody had had enough. With his scant contact with reality he had formulated his plan in his gin-besotted brain.

"It was a good crime!" he said loudly and rebelliously.

Cox was looking out the window. He didn't even turn around to see if Doody was going to throw something at him again. He knew he was safe. He said quietly that there were no good crimes, and murder was a mortal sin. Had Uncle Doody forgotten?

Uncle rubbed his dim eyes. Then he laid a dirty hand over his heart. He didn't have much more time; he knew that just as well as the jackass doctors in Macquarie Street. His heart was acting so strangely lately, ever since he had planned the murder. It hadn't been easy. The cop at the window was not to think it had. Uncle Doody had grown up with a thorough knowledge of the register of sins, and at home he had knelt like a lamb to take the sacraments. He thanked God for the gift of his life, and now he owed him his death.

So he had crept around Candy for days like a bushman hunting a bird. He had waited and waited and listened patiently to what Candy had to say. He couldn't bring it off right away. That was to be expected. He'd stood several times behind Candy's chair. At first he'd been overwhelmed by a sort of horror, although his life had always been rough. Three years once for just a minor theft. But when Mrs. Doody had had her heart attack because Candy was driving her crazy . . . that was when Uncle Doody had bought the gloves, or rather exchanged them for an umbrella. Then he had crossed himself and sworn a little and prayed a little because one couldn't be sure what the saints would think of a good crime. Uncle Doody knew of course that God's mills ground slowly, but for him it had all been too slowly. And when things had been very bad at the boardinghouse, he'd looked at the gloves—God forgive him—and was really happy that Mrs. Doody would soon be relieved. He hadn't wished Candy any bad luck. No, her accident had upset him terribly. The poor thing hadn't been equal to it. But when she had giggled and said that now Aunt Doody would never be rid of her, not in her whole life, that was when Uncle Doody had put on the gloves. The sheila was so drunk, she was half asleep, half awake, and it had all happened fast. A clean ending and a good crime.

But it couldn't have been all that good because when it was over he didn't feel calm and happy as he had thought he would. Even so, he had put the gloves away in a safe place. Without the owner noticing it, he had hidden them in an old chest in the pub. Uncle Doody had seen Rigby leave, then he had gone to Candy's room. Yes, yes, that's how it had been. Then out of the house and to the pub! And Mrs. Evans paid no attention to him because she knew that Uncle Doody went to the pub late every afternoon. The person you see all the time becomes invisible! And that was why Inspector Cox had continued to have the house watched.

Uncle Doody had been terribly shocked when Rigby was arrested, but in his simple mind he had manufactured a wonderful theory: the cops couldn't do anything to Rigby because he *wasn't* the murderer. After all, Uncle knew who the murderer was! So he kept his mouth shut. Rigby was safe. They'd have to let him go soon, obviously! Uncle had been waiting daily for it to happen. After Rigby's arrest—and what a noise the press made about it!—Uncle had got the gloves from the pub, and at night had buried them in Charlie Rainbow's flower boxes. He remembered it exactly. There was no moon, and he had found it difficult to part with them. And that the glvoes would get dirty had bothered him too. They'd been as good as new. He didn't know why, but somehow they fascinated him. And that was why he had put the flower boxes in his wardrobe. The gloves had to go with him on his wanderings. In his tipsy mind he decided that one day, when his lousy life on earth was over, he would show them when he got "up there." The gloves had freed Lydia Doody, and he was ready to take the blame. He was quite happy that the cop—a nice fellow, but not very smart— had tracked him down. Now he had come to the end of the line. And when, behind the cop's broad back, he took a secret look at his life— what had there been to it? A lot of violence, cursing, ugliness, a while in the slammer, wandering through the bush, and a few hearty Irish songs. Fair enough . . .

Inspector Cox looked down at the dreary street. And behind him was the old fellow with his "good crime," and Cox had to arrest him as the law demanded. And he would never have nabbed the old man if the sight of the gloves hadn't thrown him. Sometimes the inspector found his job damn difficult—good and evil got so mixed up. They weren't as cleanly separated as in the law books, and they sometimes made the people Cox had to arrest ridiculously lovable . . .

Edward Doody ran his fingers through his rumpled hair and coughed discreetly. The cop was standing in front of the window as if rooted to the spot. What was the matter with him? Uncle was feeling fine now. All he needed was a small room, only a corner, really, of this vast land, and a cell was a small room. Much better for Lydia to move to Kalgoorlie. She'd have peace and quiet now. In a short while she'd be laughing and chattering again, and would grow fat and be content. Mr. Muir had sent Mrs. Doody a nice sum of money after Candy's death. Decent of him. But the most important thing was that Mr. Doody would be sitting in the right compartment when the saints came marching in.

He walked up to the window and tapped the cop gently on the shoulder. "Hey, Inspector! Get a bloody move on!"

* * *

When Rigby was called to the warden's office, he had just made out his will. In spite of her orneriness, Anne was to get most of what he had because he didn't want her to spend the rest of her life working in a stuffy London office. Grace and his cobbers should get their share too. Paddy Trent had turned his new house in Queensland into a children's home for aboriginal children, but white orphans were accepted happily too. Perhaps Paddy and John Darling could use the house in Vaucluse for the same purpose. As for himself, he'd rot here, since Cox had decided he was guilty.

Tomorrow was the interrogation. He'd been in jail a week now. What did the warden want from him? A new house? Marchmont, Rigby & French had built him one five years ago, in Mosman Bay.

The warden explained that Inspector Cox had something to tell him. Aha! The fellow was there again too! Rigby stood and waited expectantly undaunted. But he was pale and he was frowning. He had lowered his head like a bull about to charge, his eyes were wild and half closed.

"We are dropping charges against you," Inspector Cox said formally. Rigby asked why the sudden change of mind. Then he pressed his lips together tightly again.

"As a result of new information and events, we are withdrawing all charges."

"If you'd listened to me in the first place, things would have been easier for you, Inspector."

Cox didn't move. The warden drummed on his desk with his fingers. Rigby hated it. Flora had sometimes drummed with her fingers . . . For a second Rigby looked the warden in the eye and had the strange feeling that Cox had personally saved his life, even if he chose to hide behind all this official nonsense. But he might be wrong . . .

"Shall I get you a taxi, Alexander?" asked the warden. They were both members of the yacht club and knew each other well.

"Not a bad idea, Gerald," Rigby replied casually. "And thanks for everything."

The warden had already picked up the receiver. Cox mumbled, "Are we friends again?"

Rigby was silent. It was none of the cop's business that he had spent the week in this stable working on the case of Flora Pratt. He looked past Cox and murmured, "I'll see what I can do, Inspector."

* * *

372

Rigby drove straight to Vaucluse. He didn't want to speak to his sister or his good friends now. Tomorrow. Or the day after tomorrow. First he had to give the Harbour Bridge a nod and smell the evening meadows. He had to look at the illuminated shoreline and the moon over Sydney, New South Wales.

Tomorrow, after sunrise, he would drive to Parramatta and stand firmly in front of the Rigby house. He had to tell Adam, Colin and Jonathan Rigby that he was in the running again. He had to sweat the five days of solitary confinement out of his system, the vision of the trial with himself in the dock between the protectors of the law. He didn't want to see the court wigs any more, hear Clifford's defense, which he had constantly corrected in his mind while waiting, or remember the faces of the jury and all the enemies who could at last do him in. One doesn't go unpunished for living for years in circles where embarrassing situations were handled with kid gloves . . .

Rigby knew that he would never have been dragged into this mess if Anne hadn't sent him that friendly farewell letter, and what was more—if Anne hadn't received that anonymous letter on his fiftieth birthday, which had precipitated her flight. Who the hell had hated him so much as to want to destroy his marriage? *Who?* He would never know. Candy Blyth had not been as naive as everyone had thought. No one can be a professional gold digger without cunning. She had been smart enough to play the beautiful dumb blond. After his fiftieth birthday she had recognized his picture in the paper and had followed him one day to Vaucluse. It hadn't been necessary for Molly Fleet to reveal who Ritter was. The only thing Candy had found out from Molly during the last weeks of her life was Anne's London address. From Molly's mail.

Perhaps it was a good thing that Candy had taken her wretched secret into eternity. It was certainly good for Mrs. Doody, and Rigby could do without enlightenment. He had been too inconsiderate of Anne. If one was too thick-skinned, did one get a good beating at the apex of one's life? Rigby realized that he was brooding. But first he wanted to celebrate his return to life in profound stillness. In old Parramatta, where his ancestors had lived and built.

32

Meeting in Parramatta

Molly Fleet went back to Parramatta. The dissolution in Darling-hurst, the police interrogations, Rigby's release from prison—a real press feast, that one—and Uncle Doody's silent departure had all been too much for her. Now she was the fifth wheel on the wagon again. In family relationships nothing changed. Wars came and went, a murder in Sydney became a media event, buildings rose into the sky—in Parra-matta none of it meant anything. Molly had only a few clients, and they demanded cheaper prices because they'd always known young Molly Fleet. One day she'd go back to Sydney. There was nothing for her here in Parramatta. The young married couples were self-sufficient and satisfied with their futures. Molly saw her father only in the eve-nings, and he hadn't grown any pleasanter. Nobody could get out of him whether he was happy to have his youngest daughter back. For Molly, life stood still.

After the recent happenings in Sydney, this was at first quite pleas-ant, but gradually she became restless. She tried to find some warmth and recognition with her family, but they treated her with amiable in-difference. So she helped in the brewery and with the bookkeeping. But in the long run that wasn't the right work for a young girl. Not even the cows on the farm were her faithful companions any more. She de-cided she had been in the city too long. Or had the cow, Lily, belonged to her childhood? Stephen was living happily on the farm with his wife, and soon his children would be running around.

Molly was sitting on the shore of Parramatta Lake one Sunday, star-ing into the water, when somebody cried, "Hello!" It was Inspector Cox with his curly hair and sharp eyes. "Do you want to arrest me again?" Molly asked harshly.

"Have you done anything wrong?"

"What are you doing in Parramatta?"

"I'm visiting my aunt. How are you, Miss Fleet?"

374

"What do you care?"

Molly covered her left cheek with her glossy hair, and the gesture touched Cox, as it had done before. He sat down beside Molly and offered her a cigarette. "It's nice and quiet here," he said, and sighed.

Molly stared at him, astounded. He didn't look at all dangerous, but younger, and *different*. If he hadn't once frightened Molly almost to death, she would even have found him nice. He *was* nice, but she wouldn't admit that to herself.

"What are you doing here, Miss Fleet?"

"Helping in the brewery. I had more to do in Sydney."

"And more going for you, of course. Why don't you go back? A smart girl like you who has learned a trade shouldn't be stagnating here."

"My father wants me to stay."

"That isn't true." But it sounded friendly. "You can't put anything like that over on me, Molly Fleet." He laughed, and patted her on the shoulder.

"Don't touch me!"

Her hostility surprised him. But he had treated her roughly while she was under suspicion. What a damned business it had been! How could he make it clear to the girl that he meant well? She needed a friend, and here he was. He simply hadn't been able to forget her. And now she was refractory and unapproachable. He looked at her profile. Her lips were trembling like a child's.

"You're not happy here, are you?"

He said it so gently, that Molly looked up. "I'm very happy here," she said stubbornly.

"Nonsense! Tell me, would you come back to Sydney if you had somewhere to stay?"

"I have nowhere to stay."

"That's where you're wrong." The inspector sounded quite cheerful. "There's a very nice room free in our house. My sister got married last week. Right now everybody's marrying."

"Here too," Miss Fleet said thoughtfully. "You should see April."

"Who is April?"

"My sister. She married Kurt."

"And who is Kurt?"

"Kurt Hildebrand, and he has her eating out of his hand."

"That's the way it should be." Cox winked at her, and suddenly Molly had to laugh.

"April used to be a beast, but now she's fine."

"That's what marriage does. Don't you want to get married?" Molly's face darkened. "Can't you take a bit of fun?"

"Not about marriage," Molly said gruffly. "I know I'll never find a husband."

"Why don't you get a second opinion on that?"

Molly laughed bitterly, the way a young creature shouldn't have to laugh. Cox gently stroked her hair from her left cheek. She pushed him away angrily, tears in her eyes. "Get out of here!" she screamed.

"There, there," Cox murmured soothingly. The stupid little thing thought that because of her birthmark, she couldn't please a man!

"Listen to me, Miss Fleet. You had a devilishly hard time in Sydney these last weeks. And I . . . I mean . . ." Inspector Cox had never been at a loss for words before.

"Do you mean that you were perfectly horrid to me?"

"Something like that," Cox said stiffly. Damn it! All he'd done was his duty. After explaining that to Molly, he asked her if she'd like to stay with his mother. Mrs. Cox could do with some massage; she often had a backache. Or Molly could stay with friends of his, if his presence disturbed her.

"You're away most of the time," she said with her usual candor.

"That's right." Cox tried not to smile. "And by the way, I've made inquiries at two hospitals. You can get steady work there. A young woman like you is always needed in a big city like Sydney."

Molly was watching the horrid cop, mouth agape. She was speechless. Cox was the first man who had ever given her a thought and wanted to help her. "Whatever makes you . . ." She couldn't go on.

"Makes me what?"

"Want to help me?" she asked, her voice hoarse. "What concern is it of yours how I live?"

Cox didn't reply. When he had first seen Molly in Mrs. Doody's boardinghouse—young, alert, strong—he had known that the girl from Parramatta didn't belong in these surroundings. Dust, flies, moth-eaten plush, moral lethargy, and obvious neglect everywhere. And the room of the dead model! Cox could still see the hideous pink lampshades and silk coverlets, and smell the stagnant atmosphere of perfume, sugar daddies, and pathetic Hollywood fantasies. He had felt somehow responsible for Molly Fleet then, even though he hadn't realized it at the time, and had wished he could shepherd this stray lamb from New South Wales to a good herd. Molly knew hardly anything about everyday life in Sydney.

376

His mother was perfectly agreeable to taking in the young lodger. "Do you intend to marry her?" she had asked, smiling, but her son laughed, and shook his head. Who would marry a cop? He was rarely home, and when he did come home, he was too tired for talk or love. All he wanted to do then was eat and sleep, and what young woman would like that? But he wanted Molly Fleet to be treated well for a change, and his mother would soon talk her out of this *idée fixe* she had about her birthmark. Or he would, if Molly learned to trust him. "Think it over," he told her. "We'd like to have you with us."

"And I'd love it!" she cried impulsively. "It's damn good of you, Inspector. But what if your mother can't stand the sight of me?"

"Don't be foolish, Molly!"

"What do *you* know about things like that?" Molly cried passionately. "You're a handsome man. Plenty of girls must be running after you. Here they used to call me 'Mole'!" Now she was sobbing.

Cox cleared his throat. He realized suddenly what this girl must have suffered. He spoke soothingly to her, but she shook off his arm. "You're only saying that to be nice."

"I'm not famous for being the nicest fellow around," said Cox. "But a pretty, smart girl like you shouldn't be so vain."

"You think I'm *pretty?*"

"You heard me," Cox said drily.

"And you're not saying all this because you feel sorry for me?"

"Any more foolish questions?"

He smiled. Molly smiled back shyly. "What are you doing tonight?" she asked.

"Nothing."

"Will you come to us for a beer? But it's hopelessly boring at our house."

"Thank you, Miss Fleet. I'd like to meet your family."

"As I said, only Kurt is nice."

"I can hardly wait to meet this miracle of manhood. But right now I prefer you."

He looked at her and she blushed. Dear heaven, how innocent the girl had remained despite Mrs. Doody's gin house!

"Why are you staring at me like that?" Molly stammered. "What do you want to know now?"

"Nothing, pet," said Inspector Cox. As happened so often—one look and he knew what he wanted to know.

"We're having steak tonight," Molly Fleet said after a pause.

"Great. By the way, can you cook?"

"Of course I can cook! Grandmother Fleet taught me on the farm. But I'm not very experienced."

"Maybe it'll be good enough for me. If you like you can call me Curl."

"Come on!" cried Molly, jumping to her feet. "Let's run all the way to the brewery. Whoever gets there first wins!"

"You've won already. I'm an old man of thirty-seven."

Molly laughed and started off, but Cox was used to a chase. He was waiting for her, calm and relaxed, in front of the brewery, which he had taken a look at earlier.

"Phew!" gasped Molly. "I can't keep up with you. For an old man you run first-rate. Nobody's ever beat me."

"High time somebody did."

Just then Mr. Fleet came out of the brewery and looked over the young man who was joking with his youngest. He didn't seem pleased about it.

"This is my father," Molly murmured apologetically.

"And who is *he?*" asked Mr. Fleet.

"A friend of mine from Sydney."

A friend of *yours?*" Mr. Fleet's eyebrows went up.

Cox gave his name. Fortunately Mr. Fleet understood it. He read the papers too, and would rather not have trouble with a cop. "How about a beer?" he asked the tall man with the sharp, light eyes. "And it doesn't have to be just one, mister."

"Thank you very much," said Inspector Cox. "When it comes to beer, I can take a lot."

"In other respects too," Molly said sassily. "You're a tough guy!"

"Who says so, Miss Fleet?"

"I do!"

"Well, then it must be true," the inspector said thoughtfully. "Mr. Fleet, your daughter can hear the grass growing."

That night Molly tried to recall her life in Sydney. Had she really lived at Mrs. Doody's or had it all been a bad dream? In her childhood on the farm she had taken reality like a bull by the horns. She'd learned that from Grandmother Fleet and Stephen. Did a lot of people in Sydney live like Candy and the Doodys? The inspector was different.

Molly couldn't make up her mind to accept his offer. She didn't want to say thank you, and that was odd. Her father had always said that in

378

the end nobody got along with his youngest daughter. After all, he knew her; when she was at home she was sullen. She was sure that secretly Cox didn't think she was exactly something to show off. He probably had a lot of pretty sheilas on tap. When he laughed he looked extraordinarily young, and he could run like a weasel. Why had he offered her a room in his house?

That evening they had taken a walk by the sea, and he had said she had landed in a wrong corner of Sydney. Then he had pushed the hair away from her face again, and had stroked her red cheek gently. She had wanted to run away, but Cox had assured her that a real man saw beneath the facade. The main thing was for the heart to be in the right place. And besides, Molly was a very good-looking young lady. But . . . he hadn't kissed her. When things got serious he was just like other men.

Molly stared into the dark. Cox felt sorry for her because she didn't have a boy friend, and because he was a good human being. But she had to stay and rot in Parramatta because she had no intention of being a burden to anyone. And anyway, there was no real difference. At home her days were just as uneventful as they had been in Sydney. They came and went like the clouds in the sky of New South Wales.

After three horrid months, Molly couldn't stand it any longer. She wrote to Cox and asked him if he still knew who she was, and whether she could still come.

She took the Vynyard bus and drove over the Harbour Bridge to Lane Cove. The inspector was waiting outside the garden gate. He had come home from headquarters a little earlier. It was a beautiful, roomy house and the garden was gorgeous.

"Why didn't you come sooner, Miss Fleet?"

"I thought you might have regretted it."

"We've been expecting you for quite a while. But I couldn't exactly come crawling to you on my knees, could I?"

The very idea was so funny that Molly burst out laughing. "I'm so happy," was all she could say. "The garden is enchanting."

"Just like the residents. We hope you will feel at home with us. Next week I shall introduce you at the hospitals. Until then you can work on Mother's back if you like."

"What's wrong with her?"

"My mother was a member of the police force in New South Wales for years. She was on duty in all kinds of weather. She gave it up when Shirley and I were born."

Inspector Cox smiled as he thought how Police Sergeant Edith Roberts had developed into a very contented Mrs. Cox. Lillian Armfield, the first woman police officer in New South Wales in the year 1915, who had hunted down criminals fearlessly with her male colleagues, had inspired young Edith Roberts. A few weeks ago Miss Rigby had asked the inspector's mother for an autobiographical sketch for *Insight*. When Inspector Cox had interviewed Miss Rigby for the first time, in spite of the embarrassing situation, Miss Rigby had found out that he was the son of Edith Roberts-Cox, who today was helping to train the new female recruits. Cox had admired Miss Rigby at the time. She had guts. Rigby, too, had behaved damn well.

"Was your father a cop too?" Molly asked shyly.

"Naturally. It's hereditary."

"Is your mother very strict?"

"What makes you think so?"

"I mean . . . because . . . after all, she had to arrest girls."

"That was a long time ago. Besides, at home we don't bite."

He led Molly through the garden. "If I get to be too much for you," she said fearfully, "you must throw me out. Father always said nobody could put up with me for long."

"Mother says that about me too. Parents always think like that."

"I won't be home much anyway," Molly said consolingly.

"Neither will I. You see, we were made for each other. Mother isn't around much either."

Molly swallowed hard. At last she managed to say, "There's something I must make clear, Mr. Cox."

"Now what?"

They had remained standing under a blossoming magnolia tree, and Molly's excitement was written all over her face. "Don't look at me like that!" she said.

"I've got to look somewhere, don't I? So . . . what is it?"

"I'll go for a walk or stay in my room when . . . when your girlfriend comes to see you."

"My *what?*"

"Surely you have a pretty sheila you go out with. I mean when you have time."

"When I have time I swim or sleep. I warned you in Parramatta: hands off the cops. They're a crashing bore."

"I find you terribly interesting, Mr. Cox."

"Well that's fine. And you can call me Curl."

"Thank you, Mr. Cox. I don't know why you're so nice to me."

"I don't know either."

"I really have nothing to offer, I mean as far as conversation is concerned."

"I enjoy talking to you very much when you're not being foolish."

"The men I knew in Sydney were quite different."

"How many were there?"

"I didn't have a boy friend, you know that. I only knew Candy's men." Molly hesitated. "I'm really not a very nice girl, Mr. Cox. I used to write Candy's love letters to Mr. Rigby for her."

"What do you know about love?"

"I go to the movies."

"Oh yes, I forgot—the movies." Miss Fleet's visit to the movies on the day of the murder had been a sticky wicket in the interrogation. "If you don't want to get out of practice, why don't you write me a love letter?"

"You?"

"Why not? I like to read that sort of thing. After all, I'm a man."

"Well, sure. But you're so experienced. You'd laugh yourself silly over my nonsense."

"Or weep. You're not nearly as naive as you pretend to be, Molly Fleet. Well, if you don't want to write me a love letter, you could whisper something nice in my ear."

"I'm not that sort of person," Molly replied stiffly. "Besides, I respect you much too much."

"That's what an old man likes to hear."

"But you're not *that* old, Mr. Cox. You can run like a fox. I mean, you're a little old only compared with me, right? But that's no reason . . ." Molly hesitated, embarrassed. The inspector was looking at her so strangely again.

"What were you going to say?"

"Nothing," Molly stammered.

"Don't worry. I'll find out. But it would be nice if you could trust me a little more. Every now and then you're going to need some good advice, child. You're too green for a city like Sydney."

"I have *loads* of experience." Molly sounded hurt.

"I found you in one hell of a mess, young lady. How did you ever get into Mrs. Doody's gin house?"

"I saw the sign: Room to Let. I didn't know anybody in Sydney, and I didn't want to sit around at home all the time." Cox said nothing. "My friend Gretchen even told me—that was before Candy was . . . was murdered—that I could have a room in her house."

"So why didn't you go there? Mrs. Lange is a very respectable woman."

"Gretchen's husband wouldn't have liked it, I'm sure. Now they have an adorable baby."

"Do you like children?"

"I love them!" Molly cried ecstatically. "I'd like to work with sick children. Gretchen said I could give their little son a bath occasionally. Isn't that wonderful?"

"If you like children so much, you're going to have to put up with a husband." Inspector Cox was amused.

"I wouldn't mind marrying." Molly was silent suddenly. When one got married, one knew where one belonged. Then she said aloud, "But most men are false."

"I shall examine your future husband with a magnifying glass," said the inspector, "or you'll get into a mess again. You know nothing about men, Molly Fleet."

"What I know is quite enough."

"It will do you no harm to learn a little more. And if you get into a jam again, just call on me."

"You . . . you're too good to me. I'm not used to it."

Cox was silent again. This young sheila was very different from the chattering, fast-moving kookaburras of King's Cross, whom she probably admired and envied. But in spite of her misadventures in Darlinghurst, she had remained true to herself. She had probably thought everybody in Sydney lived like the Doodys. How could she know that this city had room for thousands of individual ways of life, and offered a wealth of human experience. Molly had grown up in a country town and on a farm, and had been transplanted in foreign soil. But she had great reserves of strength, and a stubborn innocence. She brought with her to the big city an aura of the quietude in Parramatta, wild bush flowers, and the old Australian sense of moderation.

"May I plant some more flowers?" she asked hesitantly. "I always had a flower garden on the farm."

"Of course you may," said Inspector Cox. "But not right now. Mother is expecting us for tea." He gave Molly Fleet a friendly shove. "Hey, young lady! Get a bloody move on!"

33

On Harbour Bridge

Rigby drove back to Vaucluse in the late afternoon. He had attended a conference outside the city, and was looking forward to his dinner. Bertie Dobson had insisted that after her heart attack, Rigby's jewel should enjoy some peace and quiet with her family. Rigby thought that with Andrew's move there would be an end to the family's peace and quiet, but he had agreed. Andrews was a good egg, but she had participated far too much in his life. Once in a while he had even gotten the impression that she would have liked to be the third Mrs. Rigby, and was just biding her time. If so, she had backed the wrong horse. To begin with, he was still married to Anne, which Andrews liked to ignore, and he had had enough of marriage. Andrews had trained a young woman before she left. She wasn't much of a cook, but in his fallow season he had learned a thing or two: if necessary he could eat simply.

He stopped with a swarm of other cars before Harbour Bridge and looked at the lively world on the water and greeted the harbor. He had jumped from the ocean of error onto land. The triumphant arch of the bridge swung across the just and the unjust. He had managed to come through once more. Now all he had to do was free himself from the jail within him, and that was not easy. For that he would have needed Anne, but that chapter was over. All he knew was that he had been an idiot. He had thought love lasted forever. The truth of the matter was, one experienced it only for a short time. He watched the ferries and boats. They came and went, as Anne had come and gone. If he had known then what he knew now, he would have held onto her with both hands. Too late! Anne had written him a letter. She was sorry that he was in trouble again and hoped things would turn out all right. He had torn it to pieces after they had let him out. When he recalled how Miss Rigby and his cobbers had practically devoured him with their joy, he could climb the walls over Anne's cool reaction to the mess.

But he forgot his anger because he had big plans and was a man, not a self-pitying infant.

He was still waiting before the bridge. The afternoon sun illuminated the magnificent shoreline and the high-rise houses. The light, the breadth, the mute experience of the stone . . . Rigby's life had remained fragmented, with no solid foundation. Why was he such a bungler in love? He could plan and build, he knew the laws of measurement and the balance between material and motion. Probably the building of emotion needed a solid foundation too. In his fallow season, Rigby had balanced his books, and had found out why he had still gone running after little girls in his mature years. After his experience with Flora Pratt he had had to prove his virility over and over again. His humiliation had provoked his need for female admiration. Did this happen to other men too?

He sat behind the wheel, motionless. The still poetry of the Harbour Bridge melted away in the harshness of his thoughts. Damn it all! There came a time when a man simply had to stop behaving like a fool! He had to strive for bold thinking, clear action, and loyalty in his feelings. In short, the dignity of age had to conquer the enchanting foolishness of youth. And that was that!

The Harbour Bridge opened up and Rigby drove back to Vaucluse.

He had put the car in the garage and was standing in the garden. Everything was blooming and greening innocently, and with brilliant superfluity. This earth did not produce a lean harvest.

A blond young woman in a white dress came down the terrace steps and walked up to Rigby. He stood rooted to the spot. "I don't believe it!" His heart was beating fast and the blood rushed to his head. Then Anne was in his arms. He kissed her and she responded to his kisses. At last Rigby pushed her away and looked at her. She was unbelievably beautiful, and more alive than he had ever seen her. For a moment he stood absolutely still, then a strange sound issued from his throat and he stretched his powerful arms high. He looked as if he were trying to grasp the evening sun with both hands. He was victorious. He had not crept down into the misty underworld, like Orpheus, to retrieve his wife. Eurydice had come back to this Australian earth of her own free will. But would she stay? Would she never look back?

Rigby's arms sank to his sides. The ecstatic moment was over. If Anne was only passing through, she could take the next plane back to London. He didn't want to look for only one day at what he had lost. If Anne left him again now he would live like a half-dead fish in a

384

dried-up ocean, waiting under a merciless sun for the flood that never came—a dumb, shrinking, wriggling fish. That he would have to hate what he loved, and in spite of his unfaithfulness, had always loved—that would be the sickness of his old age and finally his death. Still, the only thing that could be of any use to him now was the truth. The moment of perception on Harbour Bridge could only be a new beginning if there was to be clarity between him and Anne.

He looked silently at her fine features, her soft blond hair, her pastel beauty. But she had turned pale suddenly, like a dying woman, who still felt his kisses but was inexorably bidding him farewell. He smiled coldly.

"Don't you want me?" she asked.

"Only under certain conditions."

"And what do you mean by that?"

"I mean that I'm not going to let you make a fool of me!" Rigby cried in very unphilosophical fury. There was no resemblance any more between him and the serene man on Harbour Bridge. But Anne had balanced her books in her fallow season too, and learned a thing or two about marriage. After much soul-searching she had recognized that her frigidity could only make a man like Rigby more difficult. She had had too little patience with him and had wanted to transform him into a tamed domestic animal. She sensed now that Rigby could even be domestic if one didn't force him. He had loved her at first, perhaps he loved her still. His kisses had spoken their own language. What was more—after family life on Avenue Road Anne found it most agreeable for someone to be excited over her.

"I don't know what you're talking about, Alex," she said casually.

"There's nothing new about that! I mean—if you're only passing through, you can swim right off again!"

"On my first visit to Sydney I stayed seven years."

"Why did you come? Have you quarreled with your dear mother?"

"Nobody can quarrel with my dear mother. She didn't even notice that I was back."

"If you've come to console me over my second scandal, you've come a day late, as usual. I'm feeling fine. Every goddamned day!"

"Stop swearing," the second Mrs. Rigby said sternly. "I've come back and that's all."

"Why?"

Anne stood on tiptoe so that she could look into his eyes. "Can't you imagine why?"

"I never imagine anything," Rigby growled, but he felt appeased.

"Seriously, Alex," said the second Mrs. Rigby, "without you it was even worse."

After thinking it over for a moment, Rigby found this was fair enough. He laid his arm across Anne's shoulder, and they went into the house.